A TEXTBOOK
OF
PHYSICAL CHEMISTRY

A TEXTBOOK
OF
PHYSICAL CHEMISTRY

ARTHUR W. ADAMSON
UNIVERSITY OF SOUTHERN CALIFORNIA

ACADEMIC PRESS   New York San Francisco London
A Subsidiary of Harcourt Brace Jovanovich, Publishers

COPYRIGHT © 1973, BY ACADEMIC PRESS, INC.
ALL RIGHTS RESERVED.
NO PART OF THIS PUBLICATION MAY BE REPRODUCED OR
TRANSMITTED IN ANY FORM OR BY ANY MEANS, ELECTRONIC
OR MECHANICAL, INCLUDING PHOTOCOPY, RECORDING, OR ANY
INFORMATION STORAGE AND RETRIEVAL SYSTEM, WITHOUT
PERMISSION IN WRITING FROM THE PUBLISHER.

ACADEMIC PRESS, INC.
111 Fifth Avenue, New York, New York 10003

United Kingdom Edition published by
ACADEMIC PRESS, INC. (LONDON) LTD.
24/28 Oval Road, London NW1

LIBRARY OF CONGRESS CATALOG CARD NUMBER: 72-88328

PRINTED IN THE UNITED STATES OF AMERICA

Illustrations by Ana Hernandez

He thought he saw a Royal Beast
    Cavorting with a Mate:
He looked again, and found it was
    A P. Chem. Text sedate.
"The choice is clear," he said, "to whom
    The book to dedicate!"

                      with apologies

CONTENTS

Contents

Contents

Contents

7 CHEMICAL EQUILIBRIUM

8 LIQUIDS AND THEIR SIMPLE PHASE EQUILIBRIA

Contents

Contents

Contents

14 KINETICS OF GAS-PHASE REACTIONS

15 KINETICS OF REACTIONS IN SOLUTION

Contents

Contents

18   MOLECULAR SPECTROSCOPY AND PHOTOCHEMISTRY

19   THE SOLID STATE

Contents

PREFACE

It might seem that there are only a limited number of ways in which the contents of the first course in physical chemistry can be presented to the student, and that all have already been tried. The pedagogical problem is a complex one, however; it is also one that shifts with time. We have seen the appearance of a great deal of traditional first year physical chemistry in beginning general chemistry texts, usually in curtailed form. At the same time, material which in the past was more commonly found in graduate courses is now appropriate for the undergraduate. The problem is that it is very easy to add new material to a course, and very difficult to avoid making it just an addition.

The older physical chemistry texts gradually evolved a coherent, integrated presentation in which the student progressed steadily through an accepted sequence of material, with each subject building on the previous one. The attempt here has been to achieve something comparable in the contemporary vein.

The traditional physical chemistry course performed a second function—one with which I think we dare not dispense. This was the function of indoctrinating the student, by practice as well as by precept, in scientific thinking. The student was asked to develop at least the beginnings of a critical understanding of the principle and of the approximations that go into each physical chemical relationship. He could be expected to know something about the limitations of a treatment and thus to have a real appreciation of its scope. The better student would acquire the ability to vary the principle or the assumptions to produce modified derivations. I have felt it to be essential that the newer material that is added be presented in reasonable depth so that the same demands can be made on the student as with the traditional topics. The effort has been to avoid letting physical chemistry become a descriptive course in which the student is asked to accept the results of advanced treatments but is not afforded the basis for being critical of them.

The order as well as the philosophy of presentation of material in this text deserves some explanation. An immediate problem is that which arises from the presence of two aspects of modern physical chemistry. One aspect is macroscopic and phenomenological in nature; it is exemplified by the topics of thermodynamics, phase equilibria, and electrochemistry. This is the classical aspect; the traditional textbook devoted itself almost exclusively to it. The second aspect is molecular and theoretical, exemplified by statistical thermodynamics and wave mechanics. The contemporary course gives about equal emphasis to these two main streams of physical chemistry, but there are differences of opinion as to their best order of presentation and the various existing texts differ noticeably in this respect. To be blunt, the choice has seemed to be whether to cover wave mechanics in the first or in the second half of the book. On the one hand, the theoretical approach provides great insight and it may therefore seem proper that it precede the classical material. On the other hand, phenomenology comprises that which we know as scientific, that is, experimental truth. It seems logical, for example, that the great concepts of thermodynamics precede theories about molecular details. An important practical point is that the macroscopic approach provides an entrée to physical chemistry which is easier on the student than is an initial burst of wave mechanics. The scientific maturity of students increases noticeably during the year course in physical chemistry and wave mechanics *is* a difficult subject.

I have adopted an order of presentation which attempts to be responsive to each of the above considerations. The first half of the book follows the general macroscopic stream, but with a great deal of the molecular approach presented at the same time. Thus Chapter 2 on kinetic molecular theory follows the opening one on gases; and Chapter 2 introduces the Boltzmann principle. Chapter 3 continues the emphasis of the molecular level with a discussion of polarizability, and of dipole and magnetic moments; it applies the Boltzmann principle to the treatment of molar polarization. (Chapter 3 includes the phenomonology of light absorption since this topic is too useful as a tool to be deferred to the much later chapter on molecular spectroscopy; the chapter also provides an early opportunity to discuss systems of units.)

The next group of chapters takes up thermodynamics. Classical and statistical thermodynamics are given almost equal emphasis—the two aspects *should* be together. The pedagogical problem of an early introduction of statistical thermodynamics is met as follows. First, the repeated use of the Boltzmann principle in the preceding chapters prepares the student for the formal development of partition functions. It is assumed that the modern student enters his physical chemistry course well aware that molecules have translational, rotational, and vibrational energy states, and it is straightforward to then derive the detailed statistical expressions for the various thermodynamic properties of ideal gases. The wave mechanical equations for the spacings of energy states must, of course, be used; however, their derivation (which comes later in the text) is not essential to the understanding of the thermodynamic concepts.

Chapters 7–13 complete the traditional sequence of chemical and phase equilibria, and electro-chemistry. The early introduction of statistical thermodynamics allows a good deal of reference to the molecular point of view.

Chapters 14 and 15 are innovative in that they divide chemical kinetics between gas phase and solution phase aspects. It seems to me that quite different emphases are involved and that such division is overdue. In gas kinetics, theory is concerned with the kinetic molecular treatment of collisions or, alternatively, with the statistical thermodynamics of the transition state (treated as an ideal gas). Solution kinetics seem better understood in terms of diffusional encounters, with the encounter complex generally requiring activation energy if reaction is to occur. The role of the solvent cannot be ignored. Also, of course, the mechanisms proposed for gas phase and for solution phase reactions often draw on rather different chemistries.

Surface chemistry is too often relegated to a dispensable chapter in the physical chemistry text. It seems better to spread surface chemical topics among various chapters, according to where their inclusion is most appropriate. For the same reason, the methods of colloid chemistry for molecular weight determination have been included in the chapter on colligative properties.

Chapters 16–18 carry the student through wave mechanics and its applications. The subject presents the problem that all but the very simplest results require so extensive a mathematical approach that their presentation could easily transform the course into one on mathematical methods. Fortunately, these simpler results do in fact provide the basis for the great majority of applications outside of serious chemical physics. Thus the solutions for the hydrogen atom supply the language of chemical bonding as well as the basis functions for many first order calculations. Hydrogen-like wave functions are, accordingly, discussed in considerable quantitative detail. Further, the treatment of chemical bonding rests to a high degree on the use of the symmetry properties of molecules. The central role that group theory plays in this respect makes it an appropriate and again overdue subject in the physical chemistry course. I have found that group theory used in conjunction with hydrogen-like wave functions provides students with a better appreciation of chemical bonding than does the usual approach. Knowledge of some formal group theory is also necessary to the treatment of electronic and vibrational excited states. Finally, much time is lost in certain senior courses if the student is not reasonably well acquainted with group theoretical methods. For these various reasons, the topic receives the attention of a full chapter.

The chapter on molecular spectroscopy and photochemistry takes a somewhat broader view than is usual. The excited state is presented as a chemical species which differs from the ground state in structure as well as in energy, and which can undergo various chemical and physical processes. Vibrational spectra can be discussed in terms of normal modes because of the group theoretical background supplied by the preceding chapter.

Crystal structure, colloid and polymer chemistry, and radio and nuclear chemistry are placed at the end. The material is not terminal with respect to any pedagogical scheme, of course. The situation is simply that these three subjects are not prerequisite to any others in the text and therefore have no unique logical positioning.

An explanation should also be given of the manner in which the text is structured. As usual, there is more material than can be covered in the normal year course in physical chemistry. I have felt that some distinction is needed between that which is essential, that which is important, and that which is interesting but merely descriptive. To assist both the instructor and the student in making such distinction, each chapter is divided into three parts.

The first portion of every chapter is deemed essential to the topic; collectively, these portions comprise a coherent core. The second part of each chapter is called Commentary and Notes. In this section we look back over the chapter in terms of commentaries on one aspect or another; also, additional material may be presented, but generally without detailed derivation. The Commentary and Notes sections are intended to be descriptive in nature and to be helpful, rather than a burden to the student. With a few exceptions, no problems are written on these sections.

The last part of each chapter is called Special Topics. As the name suggests, various specific topics are presented; these are given in the same detail as is material in the core. Certain topics are placed in this section because, although they are standard, they are judged to be of lower priority than core material, and not to be prerequisite to it. Examples are: magnetochemistry, the Joule–Thomson effect, the Hittorf method in transference measurements, heterogeneous catalysis, and blackbody radiation. Other special topics cover advanced material whose study should be valuable, time permitting. Examples are: use of the Lennard–Jones potential function in the treatment of nonideal gases, the statistical thermodynamic treatment of equilibrium constants, first order perturbation theory, ligand field theory, the Hückel method. The core does not draw appreciably on any special topic; assignment of a special topic is therefore entirely optional (occasionally a special topic will refer to a preceding one).

The problems at the end of each chapter consist of Exercises (with answers given), Problems, and Special Topics Problems. Some are in the style of those in my study-aid book, "Understanding Physical Chemistry," Benjamin, 1969; others are of the longer, calculational type. Especially long ones are marked as requiring the use of a calculator or desk type computer. I do feel that many aspects of physical chemistry cannot properly be appreciated unless the relevant calculations are actually made in detail.

Some acknowledgments are in order. Much of this book was written while the author was a guest at the University of Western Australia. I am greatly indebted to the hospitality extended by Professor N. Bayliss as Chairman of the Department of Chemistry, and by all members of the department individually. My thanks go to D. W. Watts both as a friendly critic and for his many special efforts on our behalf. I sincerely appreciate the assistance of E. Leffler, whose proofreading included reworking many problems, and the efforts of colleagues at the University of Southern California and elsewhere, who helped greatly in their reviewing of various chapters. I should mention J. Aklonis, R. Bau, T. Dunn, and G. Segal, among others. The physical chemistry class of 1970–1971 was unmerciful in its discovery of errors (at 50¢ a piece), as were my graduate students; their contribution was a major one. My daughter Jean spent an Australian summer typing much of the manuscript; M. Beverly and S. Cutri, secretaries, and the late M. Reinecke, draftswoman, were indispensable. C. Bruce proofread the entire book, as did Vida Slawson, whose overall contributions I deeply appreciate. Last and not least the many hours spent by Virginia my wife, from reading galleys to indexing, has made the book (if not the subject) partly hers. Finally, I wish to acknowledge my appreciation of a "can do" publisher and of the competence and efficiency of its editorial staff.

I know from experience that errors and maladroit passages inevitably remain in spite of all efforts. I sincerely hope that readers will freely call such to my attention.

A Note to the Reader

Many of the topics are sufficiently involved that I have used a spiral approach to them. By this I mean that the initial presentations sometimes are made on the most direct basis, with certain sidelights or elegancies deferred until later in the chapter. I suggest that the core portion of each chapter be read in its entirety before detailed study is undertaken. Because of this aspect and also because of the structuring of the chapters into divisions, I have tried to make the Index unusually complete. It is intended to be used routinely.

1 IDEAL AND NONIDEAL GASES

1-1 Introduction

Physical chemistry may be defined as the quantitative and theoretical study of the properties of the elements in their various states of combination. The definition is a sweeping one—it includes the behavior and the structure of individual molecules as well as all the various kinds of intermolecular interactions. At one time physical chemistry was considered to be a part of physics; and physics, yet earlier, lay within the formal discipline of natural philosophy. This historical relationship is reflected in the name "doctor of philosophy" for the highest degree in science. The name should not be considered as a purely archaic one, however; the chemist and other scientists *are* philosophers in that they inquire into the underlying causes of natural behavior.

Science, or the second philosophy as it is sometimes called, has progressed far indeed; moreover, its development shows no signs of slackening. For example, we need not go back very far in time—say thirty years—to observe that many topics in this book were once either unknown or at the research frontier. During this thirty year period an avalanche of facts has been compressed by the physical chemist into tables of standard data and into far-reaching empirical relationships, and the great theories of physics and chemistry have been made more precise and more capable of treating complex situations. New phenomena—the natural world is still full of surprises—have been discovered, measured, and then fitted within a theoretical framework. The same processes are going on today—the student thirty years from now will no doubt be confronted with much material not to be found in present texts.

1

The textbook of physical chemistry has never been easy to assimilate (or to write!) —there is so much to cover and there are so many important things to emphasize. The major empirical laws must be described and the great theories of molecular dynamics, statistical thermodynamics, and wave mechanics must be treated in sufficient detail to provide both a real appreciation and a foundation for more advanced work. Furthermore, throughout the book the tone of the writing should be quantitative, not descriptive; the student should experience the scientific method at work.

The material that follows has been written in as plain and direct a way as this writer knows. Much attention has been given to its organization. The student should read the preface carefully; it describes the philosophy of the book, its structure, and various practical aspects of its use. One point should be mentioned here. It is assumed that the student has taken a modern course in introductory college chemistry and that he is reasonably familiar with the gas laws, simple thermodynamics and the concept of chemical equilibrium, and the elements of chemical kinetics. Such background material is generally reviewed briefly early in each chapter. The student is also assumed to be comfortable with the qualitative language of wave mechanics and chemical bonding, although no detailed background in these subjects is required.

We proceed now to the topic of this chapter. In keeping with the above assumptions, we will not belabor the ideal gas law or its simple applications. We do show, in Section 1-3, how the law is obtained, but with the purpose of demonstrating how it is used to define a temperature scale. The procedure provides a beautiful illustration of the scientific method; a quantity such as temperature is a very subtle one in its ultimate "meaning," yet we are able to define it exactly and unambiguously.

The barometric equation receives a good deal of attention in this chapter. This is partly because of its own usefulness and partly because the equation serves to introduce a principle of far-reaching importance—the Boltzmann principle. The rest of the chapter deals with the behavior of nonideal gases and with critical phenomena. Some previous experience with this subject is assumed and the material is therefore covered rather briefly. The main emphasis is on the van der Waals equation because it is so widely used for the qualitative treatment of real gases. A glimpse of the more rigorous, modern approach is given in the Special Topics section.

1-2   Equations of State

A system at equilibrium may be described by the macroscopic properties of volume v, pressure P, and temperature t. (Temperature is defined for the moment by means of some arbitrarily chosen thermometer, and we neglect the need to specify what magnetic, electric, or gravitational fields are present.) That is, all other properties of the system are determined if these variables are specified. The *equation of state* of a system is just the functional relationship

$$v = mf(P, t), \tag{1-1}$$

where m is the mass present and $f(P, t)$ is some function of pressure and temperature. If V denotes the molar volume, an alternative form of Eq. (1-1) is

$$V = f(P, t). \tag{1-2}$$

As a matter of convenience, an equation of state usually is written for a pure chemical substance; if a mixture is involved, then composition is added as a variable.

Note that P, t, V, and density $\rho = m/v$ are *intensive* quantities. That is, their value does not depend on the amount of material present. Total volume v and mass m are *extensive* quantities. The latter gives the amount of the system and the former is proportional to m as indicated by Eq. (1-1). It is customarily assumed that an equation of state can always be written in a form involving only intensive quantitives as in Eq. (1-2). This expectation is more a result of experience than a fundamental requirement of nature. We know, for example, that if a sufficiently small portion of matter is sampled, then its intensive properties *will* depend on its mass. In fact, one way of taking this aspect into account is by adding a term for the surface energy of the system. Such a term is ordinarily negligible and will not be considered specifically until Chapter 8.

To resume the original line of discussion, an equation of state describes a range of equilibrium conditions for a substance. That is, we require Eq. (1-2) to be obeyed over an appreciable range of the variables and that its validity be independent of past history. Suppose, for example, that some initial set of values (P, t) determines a molar volume V_1, and that P and t are then varied arbitrarily. It should be true that if they are returned to the original values, then V returns to V_1.

An equation such as Eq. (1-2) is a *phenomenological* one; it summarizes empirical observation and involves only variables that are themselves experimentally defined. Such relationships are often called *laws* or *rules*. In contrast, *theories* or *hypotheses* draw on some postulated model or set of assumptions and may not be and in fact usually are not entirely correct. A phenomenological relationship, however, merely reflects some aspect of the behavior of nature, and *must* therefore be correct (within the limits of the experimental error of the measurement).

1-3 Development of the Concept of an Ideal Gas; the Absolute Temperature Scale

The first reported reasonably quantitative data on the behavior of gases are those of Robert Boyle (1662). Some of his results on "the spring of air" are given in Table 1-1; they show that for a given temperature, the PV product is essentially

Table 1-1. *"The Spring of Air" (Boyle, 1662)*

v	P (in. Hg)	Pv
48	$29\frac{2}{16}$	1400
44	$31\frac{5}{16}$	1405
40	$35\frac{5}{16}$	1412
28	$50\frac{5}{16}$	1409
16	$87\frac{14}{16}$	1406
12	$117\frac{9}{16}$	1411

constant. Much later, in 1787, Charles added the observation that this constant was a function of temperature. At this point the equation of state for all gases was observed to be

$$PV = f(t). \tag{1-3}$$

Very accurate contemporary measurements add some important refinements. A selection of such results is given in Table 1-2, and we now see that not only does the PV product depend on pressure at constant temperature, but it does so in different ways for different gases. The data can be fitted to the equation

$$PV = A + BP + CP^2 + \cdots . \tag{1-4}$$

Table 1-2. *Isothermal P–V Data for Various Gases at 0°C*

V (liter mole^{-1})	P (atm)	PV (liter atm mole^{-1})	
O₂			
22.3939	1.00000	22.3939	
29.8649	0.75000	22.3987	
44.8090	0.50000	22.4045	
89.6384	0.25000	22.4096	
Ne			
22.4280	1.00000	22.4280	
33.6360	0.66667	22.4241	
67.6567	0.33333	22.4189	
CO₂			
22.2643	1.00000	22.2642	
33.4722	0.66667	22.3148	
44.6794	0.50000	22.3397	
67.0962	0.33333	22.3654	
89.5100	0.25000	22.3897	

The important observation is that while B, C, and so forth depend also on the nature of the gas, the constant A does not. As $P \rightarrow 0$, Eq. (1-4) becomes

$$PV = A(t), \tag{1-5}$$

where, at 0°C, $A(t) = 22.4140$ for V in liter mole^{-1} and P in atmospheres. Note that Eq. (1-5) is a *limiting law*, that is, it gives the behavior of real gases in the limit of zero pressure.

If now the value of $A(t)$ is studied as a function of temperature, one finds the approximate behavior to be (as did Gay-Lussac around 1805)

$$A = j + kt. \tag{1-6}$$

The values of j and k depend on the thermometer used; moreover, the temperature dependence of A is not exactly linear. Specifically, the results obtained using a mercury thermometer are not quite the same as those obtained using an alcohol thermometer. It is both arbitrary and inconvenient to have a temperature scale tied to the way some specific substance, such as mercury or alcohol, expands with temperature. The constant A, however, is a universal one, valid for all gases and we therefore use Eq. (1-6) as the defining equation for temperature.

The limiting gas law thermometer, or, as it is usually called, the *ideal gas thermometer* is commonly based on a centigrade scale; the specific defining statements are as follows:

(1) $t = 0$ at the melting point of ice, at which temperature $A = 22.4140$;
(2) $t = 100$ at the normal (1 atm) boiling point of water, at which temperature $A = 30.6194$;
(3)   intervening t values are defined by $A = j + kt$.

On combining these conditions, we have

$$j = 22.4140, \qquad k = 0.082057$$

(using liter mole^{-1} and atmosphere units). Equation (1-6) then becomes

$$A = 22.4140 + 0.082057t = 0.082057(273.16 + t), \tag{1-7}$$

where t is now the familiar temperature in degrees Centigrade (or Celsius).

The next step is obvious. Clearly Eq. (1-7) takes on a yet simpler and more rational form if a new temperature scale is adapted such that $T = 273.16 + t°C$. We then have

$$A = 0.082057T, \tag{1-8}$$

or, inserting the definition of A into Eq. (1-5), we obtain

$$\lim_{P \to 0} PV = RT. \tag{1-9}$$

5

Table 1-3

Units	R
liter atmosphere mole^{-1} degree^{-1}	0.082057
cubic centimeter atmosphere mole^{-1} degree^{-1}	82.057
joule mole^{-1} degree^{-1}	8.3143
erg mole^{-1} degree^{-1}	8.3143×10^7
calorie mole^{-1} degree^{-1}	1.987

T is called the absolute temperature and R is the gas constant, whose numerical value depends on the choice of units. Some useful sets of units and consequent R values are given in Table 1-3.

The procedure for obtaining Eq. (1-9) has been described in some detail not only because of the importance of the equation, but also because the procedure itself provides a good example of the scientific method. We have taken the phenomenological observation of Eq. (1-5), noticed the approximate validity of Eq. (1-6), and then defined our temperature scale so as to make Eq. (1-9) exact. In effect, the procedure provides an operational, that is, an unambiguous experimental, definition of temperature. At no point has it been in the least necessary to understand or to explain why gases should behave this way or what the fundamental meaning of temperature is.

To summarize, Eq. (1-9) is an equation obeyed (we assume) by all gases in the limit of zero pressure. As Boyle and Charles observed, it is also an equation of state which is approximately obeyed by many gases over a considerable range of temperature and pressure.

At this point it is convenient to introduce the concept of a hypothetical gas which obeys the equation

$$PV = RT \tag{1-10}$$

under all conditions. Such a gas we call an *ideal gas*. It is important to keep in mind the distinction between Eq. (1-9) as an exact limiting law for all gases and Eq. (1-10) as the equation for an ideal gas or as an approximate equation for gases generally. This type of distinction occurs fairly often in physical chemistry, such as, for example, in the treatment of solutions.

1-4 The Ideal Gas Law and Related Equations

Equation (1-10) can be put in various alternative forms, such as

$$Pv = nRT \qquad (n = \text{number of moles}); \tag{1-11}$$

$$Pv = \frac{m}{M} RT \qquad (M = \text{molecular weight}); \tag{1-12}$$

$$PM = \rho RT \qquad (\rho = \text{density}). \tag{1-13}$$

Equation (1-13) tells us, for example, that the molecular weight of any gas can be obtained approximately if its pressure and density are known at a given temperature. Furthermore, since the ideal gas law is a limiting law, the limiting value of P/ρ as pressure approaches zero must give the exact molecular weight of the gas. In effect, by writing Eq. (1-4) in the form

$$\frac{Pv}{m} = \frac{RT}{M} + \frac{BP}{M} + \frac{CP^2}{M} + \cdots,\qquad(1\text{-}14)$$

one notes that the intercept of Pv/m (or P/ρ) plotted against P must give RT/M for any gas. Such a plot is illustrated schematically in Fig. 1-1.

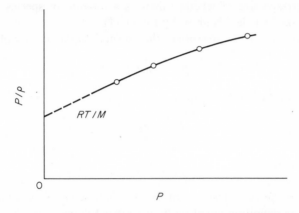

Fig. 1-1. *Variation of P/ρ with P for a hypothetical nonideal gas.*

It is generally useful to have an accepted standard condition of state for a substance. Often this is 25°C and 1 atm pressure. In the case of gases, an additional, frequently used condition is that of 0°C and 1 atm pressure. This state will be referred to as the *STP* state (standard temperature and pressure).

1-5   Mixtures of Ideal Gases; Partial Pressures

So long as the discussion about gases deals with a single chemical species it is immaterial whether volume is put on a per mole or a per unit mass basis. If the amount of gas, expressed in either way, is doubled at constant temperature and pressure, the volume must also double. Suppose, however, that a container holds 1 g of hydrogen at STP, and 1 g of oxygen is added. The STP volume of the mixture will not be doubled; it would be, however, if 16 g of oxygen were added. (This last statement is strictly true only if the condition is the limiting one of zero pressure rather than 1 atm.)

We are involved at this point with another observation, embodied in the statement known as *Avogadro's hypothesis*, which says that equal volumes of gases at the same pressure and temperature contain equal numbers of moles. Again this is really a limiting law statement, exact only in the limit of zero pressure, but approximately correct for real gases. In effect, the constant A of Eq. (1-4) is a universal constant only if V is volume per mole, and not, for example, per gram of gas. A more general form is thus

$$Pv = nA + nBP + nCP^2 + \cdots . \tag{1-15}$$

Since A is independent of the nature of the gas, n is simply the total number of moles of gas, irrespective of whether there is a mixture of species present. The corresponding ideal gas law is given by Eq. (1-11).

We now define the partial pressure of the ith species in a mixture of gases by the equation

$$P_i v = n_i RT. \tag{1-16}$$

Dividing Eq. (1-16) by Eq. (1-11) then gives

$$\frac{P_i}{P} = \frac{n_i}{n}$$

or

$$P_i = x_i P, \tag{1-17}$$

where x_i denotes the mole fraction of the ith species. Since the sum of all mole fractions must by definition equal unity, it further follows that

$$\sum P_i = P, \tag{1-18}$$

that is, the total pressure of a mixture of ideal gases is given by the sum of the partial pressures of the various species present. This is a statement of *Dalton's law*.

A useful quantity which can now be defined is the average molecular weight of a gas, given by

$$M_{\text{av}} = \frac{m}{n}, \tag{1-19}$$

where m and n are respectively the total mass and number of moles present. Further, we have

$$M_{\text{av}} = \frac{\sum m_i}{n} = \frac{\sum n_i M_i}{n} = \sum x_i M_i . \tag{1-20}$$

It also follows, on combining Eqs. (1-13) and (1-18), that

$$PM_{\text{av}} = \rho RT. \tag{1-21}$$

Thus the procedure illustrated by Fig. 1-1 will, for a mixture of gases, give the average molecular weight.

A complication may now arise. In order to determine the exact average molecular weight of a gas mixture, it is necessary to extrapolate P/ρ to the limit of zero pressure, yet it can happen that the composition of the mixture is itself dependent on the pressure. Thus, gaseous N_2O_4 will actually consist of a mixture of NO_2 and N_2O_4 in amounts given by the equilibrium constant for the process $N_2O_4 = 2NO_2$:

$$K_P = \frac{P^2_{NO_2}}{P_{N_2O_4}}. \tag{1-22}$$

The proportion of NO_2 present will increase as the total pressure decreases, so that M_{av} now varies with pressure. In effect, one now knows the species and hence their molecular weight and K_p is the unknown. Equation (1-22) for K_p is exact only for ideal gases, however, and the following procedure is necessary. One first determines M_{av} for a series of total pressures using Eq. (1-21). Each determination provides a value for K_p, assuming ideal gas behavior, and these values are then plotted against pressure. The true K_p is given by the intercept at zero pressure.

An example at this point will illustrate a number of the details of using the ideal gas law. Some data for the N_2O_4–NO_2 equilibrium at 25°C are given in Table 1–4, where a denotes the initial number of moles of N_2O_4 present per liter, that is, the total number of grams of gas divided by 92.0, the molecular weight of N_2O_4. Thus for $a = 6.28 \times 10^{-3}$, P is 0.2118. For this temperature and pressure, we have, from Eq. (1–21),

$$M_{av} = \frac{\rho RT}{P} = \frac{mRT}{PV} = \frac{(6.28 \times 10^{-3})(92.0)(0.08206)(298.2)}{0.2118} = 66.75 \quad g \; mole^{-1}.$$

Since by Eq. (1–20)

$$M_{av} = 66.75 = 46x_{NO_2} + 92x_{N_2O_4}$$

$$= 46(1 + x_{N_2O_4})$$

$(x_{NO_2} = 1 - x_{N_2O_4})$, it follows that $x_{N_2O_4} = 0.451$. Application of Eq. (1-17) then gives

$$P_{N_2O_4} = (0.451)(0.2118) = 0.0955 \quad atm$$

and

$$P_{NO_2} = 0.1163 \quad atm.$$

The value of K_P is then $(0.1163)^2/(0.0955) = 0.142$ atm.

The values of K_P so computed are given in Table 1-4; clearly they are not constant, but increase with decreasing pressure. When plotted against pressure, the extrapolated value at zero pressure is 0.1426, the true equilibrium constant for 25°C.

Although the preceding complication is serious if accurate K_P values are desired, often what is needed is merely a determination of whether a given substance has the gas molecular weight corresponding to its formula or whether it may exist as a dimer or higher polymer. Thus aluminum chloride vapor is found to be largely dimerized, as are also the vapors of formic and acetic acids. On a yet simpler level, one may know only the elemental analysis of a substance, which gives just

Table 1-4. *The* N_2O_4–NO_2 *Equilibrium at 25°C[a]*

$a \times 10^3$ (mole liter^{-1})	P (atm)	K_P (atm)
6.28	0.2118	0.1419
12.59	0.3942	0.1340
19.84	0.5996	0.1412
29.68	0.8623	0.1261

[a] From F. H. Verhoek and F. Daniels, *J. Amer. Chem. Soc.* **53**, 1250 (1931).

the empirical formula or ratios of atoms. Thus for example, an analysis would establish that hydrogen peroxide has the formula H_xO_x, that is, that hydrogen and oxygen were present in a 1:1 ratio. The vapor molecular weight measurement would give a molecular weight of 34, which would give the molecular formula as H_2O_2. In such cases, a somewhat approximate molecular weight is all that is needed, and one therefore assumes ideal gas behavior for the vapor.

1-6   Partial Volumes; Amagat's Law

The partial volume v_i of a component of a gaseous mixture is defined as the volume that component would occupy were it by itself at the pressure and temperature of the mixture:

$$v_i = \frac{n_i RT}{P}.$$ (1-23)

Since $\sum n_i = n$, it follows that

$$\sum v_i = v$$ (1-24)

and, further, that

$$v_i = x_i v.$$ (1-25)

Equation (1-24) is a statement of *Amagat's law of partial volumes*, and although its derivation assumes ideal gas behavior, the equation is often more closely obeyed by real gases than is its counterpart involving partial pressures, Eq. (1-17).

1-7   The Barometric Equation

It was mentioned in Section 1-2 in discussing equations of state that initially we were neglecting to include as variables any magnetic, electric, or gravitational fields present. Ordinarily all three are present in any laboratory, but the first two are so small that they occasion only a negligible variation in intensive properties from one part of the system to another. The earth's gravitational field is large enough, however, that it cannot always safely be neglected. In the case of liquids the variation of hydrostatic pressure with depth can be quite significant. The same is true for gases if a long column of gas is involved, as in dealing with the atmosphere. Not only is the gravitational field occasionally important, but the derivation of its effect that follows leads to an important new type of equation.

Consider a column of fluid of unit cross section as illustrated in Fig. 1-2. The

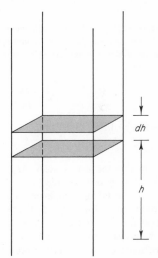

Fig. 1-2. *The barometric effect.*

pressure, or force per unit area, at level h must be just the total weight of the column above that level. The change in pressure dP between h and $h + dh$ is then just the weight of fluid contained in the unit cross section in the column between the two levels:

$$dP = -\rho g \, dh, \tag{1-26}$$

where g is acceleration due to gravity. Equation (1-26) is general. If the fluid is a liquid which is assumed to be incompressible, then ρ is independent of h and integration gives

$$P_2 - P_1 = -\rho g \, \Delta h, \tag{1-27}$$

which is just a statement of the variation of hydrostatic pressure with height.

If, however, the fluid is taken to be an ideal gas, then use of Eq. (1-13) or (1-21) gives

$$dP = -\frac{PM}{RT} g \, dh$$

or

$$\frac{dP}{P} = d(\ln P) = -\frac{Mg}{RT} \, dh. \tag{1-28}$$

[It is common to write $d(\ln x)$ for dx/x or $-d(1/x)$ for dx/x^2, and so on, as an anticipation of integration.]

Equation (1-28) cannot be integrated unless something is known about how M, g, and T vary with h; one simple case is that in which these quantities are taken to be constant. The result, known as the *barometric equation*, is then

$$\ln \frac{P_h}{P_0} = - \frac{Mgh}{RT} \tag{1-29}$$

or

$$P_h = P_0 e^{-Mgh/RT}. \tag{1-30}$$

As an example of the application of Eq. (1-29) consider a column of atmosphere of $M_{av} = 29$ g mole^{-1}, $T = 298°$K, $g = 980$ cm sec^{-2}, and $P_0 = 1$ atm at $h = 0$. The exponential term must be dimensionless, so R must now be in ergs degree^{-1} mole^{-1} and h in centimeters. One then finds

$$P_h = \frac{\exp[-(29)(980)h]}{(8.31 \times 10^7)(298)} = \exp(1.148 \times 10^{-6}h).$$

Thus if $h = 1$ km, or 10^5 cm,

$$P_h = e^{-0.1148} = 0.892.$$

Note that in the mks system, $M_{av} = 29$ g mole^{-1}, $g = 9.8$ m sec^{-2}, and if h is in meters, then R should be in joules degree^{-1} mole^{-1}.

It is worth taking a moment to discuss some of the mathematical aspects of an exponential equation such as Eq. (1-30). In the example here a plot of P versus h appears as shown in Fig. 1-3. Note that at $h = 6.04$ km, $P_h/P_0 = 1/2$ or $P = 0.5$ atm. The "half-height" or $h_{1/2}$ (the height for the pressure to decrease by a factor of one-half) is independent of the actual value of P_0. Thus, starting at 6.04 km, the pressure will decrease by half again in another 6.04 km, and so will be 0.25 at $h = 12.1$ km, and so on, as illustrated in the figure.

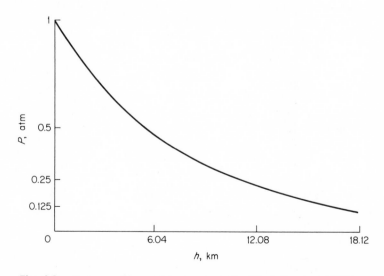

Fig. 1-3. *Decrease of barometric pressure with altitude for air at 298°K.*

Equation (1-30) is of the general form

$$y = y_0 e^{-kx} \qquad (1\text{-}31)$$

and the value of x for $y/y_0 = 1/2$, or the "half value" of x, $x_{1/2}$, is related to k as follows:

$$\text{if } \frac{y}{y_0} = \frac{1}{2}, \qquad \text{then } \ln \frac{1}{2} = -kx_{1/2}$$

or

$$(1\text{-}32)$$

$$kx_{1/2} = -\ln \frac{1}{2} = 0.6932.$$

Thus, in the example just given $h_{1/2} = 0.6932/0.1148 = 6.04$ km.

A further point is as follows. In view of the previously discussed laws for mixtures of ideal gases, Eq. (1-30) applies separately to each component of a mixture. Thus each component of the earth's atmosphere has its own barometric distribution, with the consequence that the pressures and hence concentrations of the lighter gases decrease less rapidly with altitude than do those of the heavier ones. As a result the proportion of, for example, helium in the atmosphere increases with altitude. Various distribution curves illustrating the effects of molecular weight and temperature are shown in Fig. 1-4. (Actual atmospheric concentrations reflect temperature variations, mixing by wind currents, and so forth.)

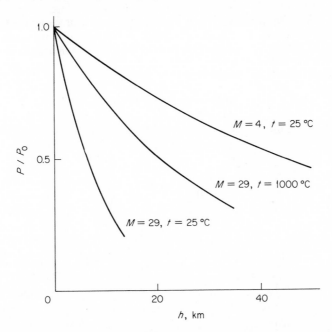

Fig. 1-4. *Effect of molecular weight M and temperature t on the barometric falloff of pressure with altitude.*

Equation (1-30) may be expressed in yet a different way, and one which is very instructive. Under the assumed condition of constant temperature it follows from the ideal gas law that concentration C is proportional to pressure:

$$C = \frac{n}{v} = \frac{P}{RT}.$$ (1-33)

Hence

$$C_h = C_0 e^{-Mgh/RT} = C_0 e^{-mgh/kT},$$ (1-34)

where m is now the mass per molecule and k is the gas constant per molecule, known as the *Boltzmann constant*. The quantity mgh is just the potential energy of a molecule at height h in the gravitational field, and Eq. (1-34) is a special case of the more general equation

$$p = (\text{constant}) e^{-\epsilon/kT},$$ (1-35)

where p is the probability, here measured in terms of the concentration or pressure, of a molecule having an energy ϵ. Equation (1-35) is a statement of the *Boltzmann principle* and is of central importance in dealing with probability distributions, as in gas kinetic theory and in statistical thermodynamics.

1-8 Deviations from Ideality—Critical Behavior

The equation of state of an actual gas is given in one form by Eq. (1-4),

$$PV = A(T) + B(T)P + C(T)P^2 + \cdots,$$

where $B(T)$, $C(T)$, and so on are not only functions of temperature, but also are characteristic of each particular gas. A form that is more useful for theoretical purposes is the following:

$$PV = A(T)\left[1 + \frac{B(T)}{V} + \frac{C(T)}{V^2} + \cdots\right]$$ (1-36)

or

$$\frac{PV}{RT} = 1 + \frac{B(T)}{V} + \frac{C(T)}{V^2} + \cdots.$$ (1-37)

This type of equation is known as a *virial equation*, and $B(T)$ and $C(T)$ are called the second and third virial coefficients, respectively. This form is more useful than Eq. (1-4) because molar volume is a measure of the average distance between molecules and an expansion in terms of V is thus an expansion in terms of intermolecular distance. The virial coefficients can then in turn be estimated by means of various theories for intermolecular forces of attraction and repulsion.

The left-hand term of Eq. (1-37), PV/RT, is called the compressibility factor Z and its deviation from unity is a measure of the deviation of gas from ideal behavior. Such deviations are small at room temperature for cryoscopic gases, that is, low-boiling gases such as argon and nitrogen, until quite high pressures are reached, as illustrated in Fig. 1-5, but can become quite large for relatively higher-boiling ones, such as carbon dioxide. Figure 1-6 shows that for nitrogen at $t_3 = 50°C$

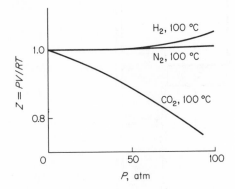

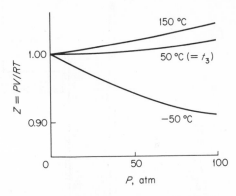

Fig. 1-5. *Variation of compressibility factor with pressure.*

Fig. 1-6. *Variation of compressibility factor with temperature and pressure for nitrogen.*

(curve 2), the plot of the compressibility factor Z against P increases steadily with increasing pressure, but at a lower temperature, it first decreases. At one particular temperature, the plot of Z versus P approaches the $Z = 1$ line asymptotically as P approaches zero. This is known as the *Boyle temperature*. The analytical condition is

$$\left(\frac{\partial Z}{\partial P}\right)_T \to 0 \qquad \text{as} \qquad P \to 0, \tag{1-38}$$

where it will be recognized that the partial differentiation sign ∂ means that the derivative of Z is taken with respect to P with the temperature kept constant. A gas at its Boyle temperature behaves ideally over an exceptionally large range of pressure essentially because of a compensation of intermolecular forces of attraction and repulsion.

The gas of a substance which can exist in both the gas and liquid states at a given temperature is often distinguished from gases generally by being called a vapor. Clearly, as a vapor is compressed at constant temperature, condensation will begin to occur when the pressure of the vapor has reached the vapor pressure of the liquid. The experiment might be visualized as involving a piston and cylinder immersed in a thermostat bath; the enclosed space contains a certain amount of the substance, initially as vapor, and the piston is steadily pushed into the cylinder. The arrangement is illustrated in Fig. 1-7. At the point of condensation, reduction in volume ceases to be accompanied by a rise in pressure; more and more vapor simply condenses to liquid at constant pressure P^0. Eventually all the vapor is

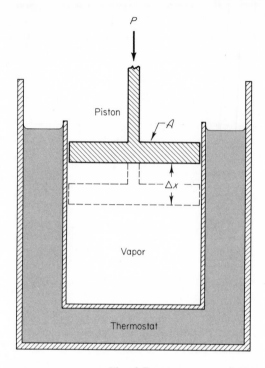

Fig. 1-7.

condensed, and the piston now rests against liquid phase; liquids are generally not very compressible, and now great pressure is needed to reduce the volume further. The plot of P versus V corresponding to this experiment is shown in Fig. 1-8, where P^0 denotes the vapor pressure of the liquid and V_l its molar volume. The plots are for constant temperature, or isothermal, processes and are therefore called *isotherms*.

As further illustrated in Fig. 1-8, at some higher temperature the isotherm will lie above the previous one, and the horizontal portion representing condensation will be shorter. This is because, on the one hand, $P^{0\prime}$ is larger than P^0, so the molar volume of the vapor at the condensation point is smaller, and on the other hand, the liquid expands somewhat with temperature, so $V_l\prime$ is greater than V_l. One can thus expect, and in fact does observe, that at some sufficiently high temperature the horizontal portion just vanishes. This temperature is called the *critical temperature* T_c, and the isotherm for T_c is also shown schematically in Fig. 1-8. The broken line in the figure gives the locus of the end points of the condensation lines, and hence encloses the region in which liquid and vapor phases coexist.

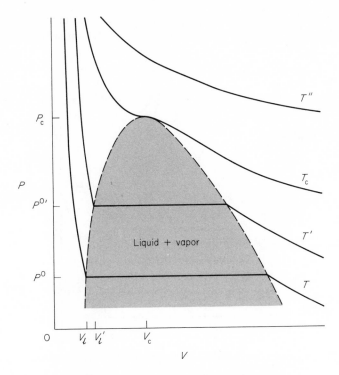

Fig. 1-8. *P–V isotherms for a real vapor.*

There is not only a critical temperature, but also a *critical point*, which is the vestigial point left by the condensation line as it just vanishes; alternatively, the critical point is the maximum of the broken line of the figure. This point then defines a *critical pressure* P_c and a *critical volume* V_c as well as T_c. The critical temperature can also be considered as the temperature above which we speak of a gas rather than of a vapor. Compression of a gas (that is, in this context, a gaseous substance above its critical temperature) results not in condensation, but only in a steady increase in pressure, as illustrated by the curve labeled T'' in Fig. 1-8.

Figure 1-8 also illustrates the difficulty of displaying a function of three variables on a two-dimensional plot. A true graph of $V = f(P, T)$ requires a three-dimensional plot, such as is represented in Fig. 1-9. On the other hand, while such a three-dimensional plot can thus be visualized, it is difficult to work with; hence the use of isothermal cross sections. It should be recognized, however, that cross sections can be taken in other ways. Thus the lighter lines in Fig. 1-9 correspond to the profiles of cross sections at constant temperature, or *isotherms,* and the broken lines to cross sections at constant volume, or *isosteres* (*isometrics*). A schematic set of *isobars* (constant-pressure plots) and isosteres is shown in Fig. 1-10. In general at sufficiently high temperatures and especially at sufficiently large

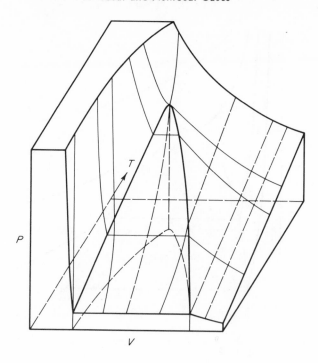

Fig. 1-9. *Perspective view of the P–V–T surface for a vapor showing condensation and critical behavior.*

volumes the curves for any substance will approach those for an ideal gas. In this limiting case one then has

isotherms given by $\quad P = \left(\dfrac{RT}{V}\right) \quad$ or hyperbolas,

isobars given by $\quad V = \left(\dfrac{R}{P}\right) T \quad$ or straight lines,

isosteres given by $\quad P = \left(\dfrac{R}{V}\right) T \quad$ or straight lines.

At the other extreme, that of low temperatures and especially of small volumes, one has the liquid phase. The isotherms are then given by the coefficient of compressibility of the liquid, β, defined as

$$\beta = - \frac{1}{V} \left(\frac{\partial V}{\partial P}\right)_T \tag{1-39}$$

Values of β for liquids are small, about 10^{-5} atm^{-1}. Thus for small changes in volume the slope of the P–V isotherm for a liquid will be approximately $-(1/V\beta)$; for water at 20°C it is about 1.2×10^6 atm liter^{-1}. Thus the curves in this region

18

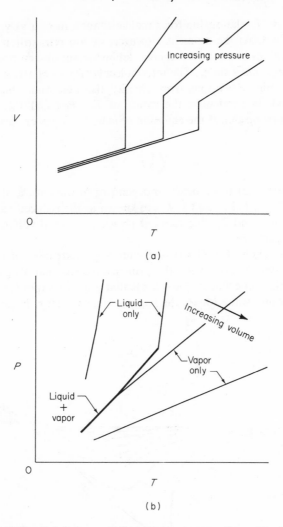

Fig. 1-10. *(a) Isobars and (b) isosteres corresponding to Fig. 1-9.*

of Fig. 1-8 are nearly vertical lines. The isobars are given by the coefficient of thermal expansion α defined as

$$\alpha = \frac{1}{V}\left(\frac{\partial V}{\partial T}\right)_P \tag{1-40}$$

Values of α are likewise small, about $10^{-4}\ ^{\circ}K^{-1}$ and the slope of the V–T isobar for a liquid will thus be $V\alpha$ for small changes in V. For water $V\alpha$ is about 8.0×10^{-6} liter $^{\circ}K^{-1}$. Consequently the region of Fig. 1-10(a) corresponding to the liquid appears as nearly horizontal lines.

The preceding digression was intended to help fix characteristic general features of the typical P–V–T relationship for a real substance, insofar as vapor and liquid phases are involved. At the moment, however, we are primarily interested in the vapor and gas regions and for these there is an important observation known as the *principle of corresponding states.* The intermolecular forces of attraction and repulsion which determine deviations from ideality also determine the conditions for condensation and, in particular, the values of T_c, P_c, and V_c. It is therefore perhaps not surprising that if the equation of state for a gas or vapor is written in the form

$$\frac{V}{V_c} = f\left(\frac{P}{P_c}, \frac{T}{T_c}\right), \tag{1-41}$$

the function f turns out to be nearly independent of the nature of the substance. The quantities P/P_c, V/V_c, and T/T_c are known as the reduced variables and are denoted by P_r, V_r, and T_r, the reduced pressure, reduced volume, and reduced temperature, respectively.

This statement about Eq. (1-41) is essentially a statement of the *principle of corresponding states.* Alternatively, the principle affirms that all gases at a given P_r and T_r have the same V_r. A corollary is that gases or vapors in corresponding states have the same value for Z, the compressibility factor. Figure 1-11 may be

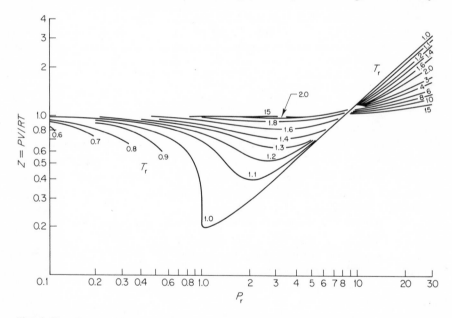

Fig. 1-11. *Hougen–Watson chart for the calculation of pressure, volume, and temperature relations at high pressure. (From O. A. Hougen and K. M. Watson, "Chemical Process Principles," Part II. Copyright 1959, Wiley, New York. Used with permission of John Wiley & Sons, Inc.)*

used to obtain a fairly good value for the compressibility factor and hence for V if P and T are known, for any substance whose critical constants are also known.

Table 1-5. *Critical Constants and Related Physical Properties*[a]

Substance	Melting point (°K)	Boiling point (°K)	T_c (°K)	P_c (atm)	V_c (cm³ mole⁻¹)
He	<1	4.6	5.2	2.25	61.55
Ne	24.5	27.3	44.75	26.86	44.30
H_2	14.1	20.7	33.2	12.8	69.68
O_2	54.8	90.2	154.28	49.713	74.42
N_2	63.3	77.4	125.97	33.49	90.03
Cl_2	172.2	238.6	417.1	76.1	123.4
CO	74	81.7	134.4	34.6	90.03
NO	109.6	121.4	177.1	64	57.25
CO_2	216.6[b]	194.7	304.16	72.83	94.23
H_2O	273.2	373.2	647.3	218.5	55.44
NH_3	195.5	239.8	405.5	112.2	72.02
CCl_4	250.2	349.7	556.25	44.98	275.8
CH_4	90.7	109.2	190.25	45.6	98.77
C_2H_2	191.4	189.2	308.6	61.65	112.9
C_2H_4	104.1	169.5	282.8	50.55	126.1
CH_3OH	175.3	338.2	513.1	78.50	117.7
C_2H_5OH	155.9	351.7	516.2	62.96	167.2
CH_3COOH	289.8	391.1	594.7	57.11	171.2
C_6H_6	278.7	353.3	561.6	47.89	256.4

[a] Critical constants from E. A. Moelwyn-Hughes, "Physical Chemistry." Pergamon, Oxford, 1961; melting and boiling points from "Handbook of Chemistry and Physics," 51st ed. Chemical Rubber Publ., Cleveland, Ohio, 1970.

[b] At 5.2 atm.

The critical constants for a selection of substances are given in Table 1-5. As an example of the use of this table with Fig. 1-11 let us suppose that we wish to find the molar volume of ammonia gas at 212°C and 224 atm pressure. Then P_r and T_r are $224/112 = 2.0$ and $485/405 = 1.2$. From Fig. 1-11 the value of Z for $P_r = 2$ and $T_r = 1.2$ is 0.57. The molar volume of the ammonia is then $V = 0.57RT/P = (0.57)(0.0821)(485)/(224)$ or $V = 0.112$ liter.

1-9 Semiempirical Equations of State. The van der Waals Equation

The relative success of the principle of corresponding states, as illustrated in the use of the chart of Fig. 1-11, suggests that it should be possible to find a not too complicated analytical expression for the function $f(P_r, T_r)$ of Eq. (1-41). In fact quite a number of such functions have been proposed, some of which are given in the Commentary and Notes section at the end of the chapter. Such functions, being analytical, are in many ways more convenient than a graph such as Fig. (1-11); they permit more precise (although not necessarily more accurate) calculations. If the function is so constructed that its form and the constants it contains have at least an approximate physical meaning, then it also provides a basis for seeing physically why different gases differ in their critical and nonideal behavior.

A semiempirical equation that meets the preceding criteria fairly well is the *van der Waals equation*, which may be assembled as follows.

First, one recognizes that molecules take up space, so that the volume occupied by a gas is only partly free space. It thus seems reasonable to replace V in the ideal gas law by the free-space volume $V - b$, where b is the effective volume occupied by a mole of molecules. This volume b is not the actual molar volume, but is the so-called *excluded volume*. The point involved is illustrated in Fig. 1-12. In the case

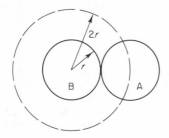

Fig. 1-12.   *Illustration of excluded volume.*

of two identical spherical molecules the center of an approaching molecule A cannot come closer than a distance $2r$ (r being the radius) to the center of another like molecule B. Thus the excluded volume is $(4\pi/3)(2r)^3$. The effect is a mutual one, however, and further thought indicates that, per molecule, the excluded volume should be four rather than eight times the volume per molecule. One thus expects b to be something like four times the molar volume, but clearly this expectation is approximate since molecules are not impenetrable and in general are not spherical. At any rate, the corrected equation is now

$$P(V - b) = RT. \tag{1-42}$$

Next the pressure exerted by a gas must originate, on the molecular scale, as a result of a bombardment of the walls of the container by the molecules of the gas. There must be some mutual attractive force between the molecules, however; the fact that a vapor will condense to a liquid is clear enough evidence of this. As a consequence one expects that the actual pressure observed should be less than that for an ideal gas, where such attractive forces are not present. In the van der Waals equation this correction takes the form of a correction a/V^2 applied to the observed pressure. The complete equation is then

$$\left(P + \frac{a}{V^2}\right)(V - b) = RT. \tag{1-43}$$

The exact form of this last correction can only be defended approximately. V is a measure of the average volume per molecule and hence of the cube of the average distance apart of molecules. V^2 is then proportional to r^6, where r is this average distance. There are a number of indications that the potential energy of attraction between molecules does vary as the inverse sixth power of their distance of separation (see Chapter 8, Section 8-ST-1). We can thus see that the correction term to the pressure should somehow depend inversely on V and that the actual $1/V^2$ dependence used is not unreasonable.

The van der Waals equation may be put in the form of a virial equation. On solving Eq. (1-43) for P and then multiplying both sides by V/RT one obtains

$$Z = \frac{PV}{RT} = \frac{1}{1 - (b/V)} - \frac{a}{RTV}.$$
(1-44)

The first term on the right can be expanded in a power series in b/V, and on collecting terms we have

$$Z = 1 + \left(b - \frac{a}{RT}\right)\frac{1}{V} + \left(\frac{b}{V}\right)^2 + \cdots.$$
(1-45)

The second and third virial coefficients are thus

$$B(T) = b - \frac{a}{RT}, \qquad C(T) = b^2.$$

Since b/V is usually a small number in the case of a gas, the cubic and higher terms of Eq. (1-45) can be neglected. An approximate form of Eq. (1-45) valid for small pressures and hence large V is obtained when only the first two terms on the right are kept and V is replaced by RT/P:

$$Z = 1 + \frac{P}{RT}\left(b - \frac{a}{RT}\right) + \left(\frac{b}{RT}\right)^2 P^2.$$
(1-46)

As P approaches zero, this coefficient approaches the value

$$\lim_{P\to 0}\left(\frac{\partial Z}{\partial P}\right)_T = \frac{1}{RT}\left(b - \frac{a}{RT}\right).$$
(1-47)

According to the van der Waals equation, then, the slope of a Z versus P plot should be positive at small pressures if $b > a/RT$ and negative if $b < a/RT$. It should be zero if $b = a/RT$. Recalling the discussion in Section 1-7 on the Boyle temperature [see Eq. (1-38)], we conclude that

$$T_B = \frac{a}{bR}.$$
(1-48)

The physical meaning assigned to the a and b coefficients confirms the earlier analysis that at the Boyle temperature there is a balance between intermolecular attraction, measured by a, and intermolecular repulsion, measured by the excluded volume b.

The van der Waals equation allows calculation of isotherms such as those shown schematically in Fig. 1-8. This is best done by solving Eq. (1-43) for P,

$$P = \frac{RT}{V - b} - \frac{a}{V^2}.$$ (1-49)

Then, for a given choice of a and b a value of P can easily be found for each of a series of values of V. The isotherms of Fig. 1-13 were computed by this procedure for water with $a = 5.72$ liter^2 atm mole^{-2} and $b = 0.0319$ liter mole^{-1}. (See the next section for a discussion of the problem of choosing van der Waals constants.)

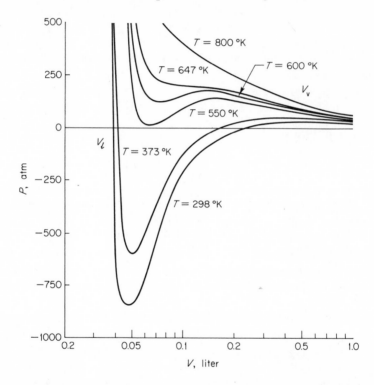

Fig. 1-13.   *Isotherms calculated from the van der Waals equation ($a = 5.72$ liter^2 atm mole^{-2}, $b = 0.0319$ liter mole^{-1}).*

The most obvious aspect of Fig. 1-13 is that many of the isotherms show a maximum and a minimum; this is to be expected since Eq. (1-43) [or (1-49)] is a cubic equation in volume:

$$PV^3 - (Pb + RT) V^2 + aV - ab = 0.$$ (1-50)

For a given P there should in general be three roots or values of V. However, for any given choice of a and b there will be a particular value of T for which these three roots become equal. Above this value of T two roots become imaginary, leaving one real root. At high temperatures, then, the isotherms of Fig. 1-13 look much like Fig. 1-8 for a real substance. The problem is to rationalize the region showing a maximum and a minimum in Fig. 1-13 with the region showing a horizontal line in Fig. 1-8. This is done as follows.

For a real substance isothermal compression across the flat portion of an isotherm corresponds to conversion of vapor to liquid at constant pressure. The amount of mechanical work done, as in the piston and cylinder arrangement of Fig. 1-7, is given by

$$w = \text{work} = \int_{V_v}^{V_l} P \, dV. \tag{1-51}$$

Notice that if a piston under pressure P sweeps a volume dV, then, as shown in the figure, the total force acting on the piston is $f = P\mathscr{A}$ and this force acts through a distance dx, where $dV = \mathscr{A} \, dx$. Thus the integral of Eq. (1-51) corresponds to $\int_{x_1}^{x_2} f \, dx$ and indeed gives the work done. The limits of integration for Eq. (1-51) are from the molar volume of the vapor when condensation just starts, V_v, to the molar volume of the liquid when condensation is just completed, V_l. Since $P°$ is constant, the work is just

$$w = P°(V_v - V_l). \tag{1-52}$$

We turn now to the van der Waals equation; referring to Fig. 1-13, it seems clear that the section labeled V_v must represent the molar volume of the gaseous state of the substance, while that labeled V_l should correspond to the liquid state. The van der Waals equation connects these two branches with the section showing a maximum and a minimum, but a real substance takes the short cut of direct condensation when P reaches $P°$ as illustrated in Fig. 1-14. We would like to know how to locate the horizontal line of this short cut, and hence the liquid vapor pressure $P°$.

We can regard the route taken by the van der Waals equation and that given by the short-cut as alternate paths requiring the *same amount of work*. That is, we require the integral $\int_{V_v}^{V_l} P \, dV$ to be the same along the curved path *abcd* in Fig. 1-14 and along the straight-line path *ad*,

$$w = P°(V_v - V_l) = \int_{V_v}^{V_l} P \, dV \quad \text{(curve)}. \tag{1-53}$$

Graphically, this amounts to equating the two differently shaded areas in the figure; it also amounts to requiring that the net area between the line *ad* and the curve *abcd* be zero. Figure 1-15 repeats Fig 1-13, but with horizontal lines added, as located by the preceding criterion. It is thus possible to interpret the van der Waals equation so as to obtain liquid vapor pressures or $P°$ values.

There are some further interesting aspects to the above considerations. The section *abcd* of the van der Waals isotherm of Fig. 1-14 represents an unstable situation. Thus along the portion *ab* the pressure of the vapor is greater than the

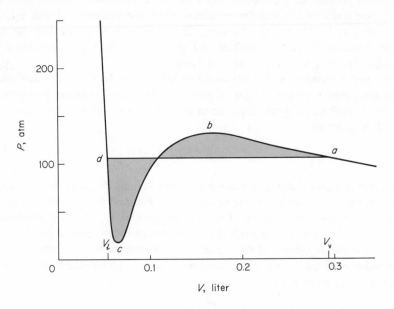

Fig. 1-14. *Condensation and the van der Waals equation.*

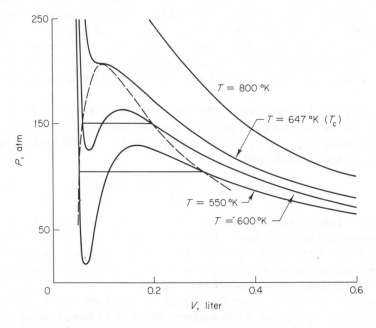

Fig. 1-15. *Figure 1-13 with condensation lines added.*

condensation pressure for the liquid state. It is actually possible to compress vapors beyond the condensation pressure; the system is unstable toward condensation, but, if the vapor is free of dust, the first appearance of liquid droplets may be delayed. The effect is known as *supersaturation* and occurs because a small liquid drop has a higher vapor pressure than does the bulk liquid, by virtue of having a large surface-to-volume ratio and consequently an appreciable added energy due to the surface energy. Similarly, the section *dc* is metastable; here liquid is under less pressure than its vapor pressure and should spontaneously form vapor bubbles. Liquid surrounding a small cavity exerts a lower vapor pressure than normal, however, again because of a surface tension effect. This relationship connecting size of droplet or bubble, surface tension, and vapor pressure is given by the Kelvin equation, discussed in Section 8-9.

As a further point note that in Fig. 1-13 the lowest van der Waals isotherm reaches negative pressures. The implication is that a liquid can exist under tension, as a metastable condition. This, too, has been verified, and for water a tensile strength of as much as 100 atm has been found (see Commentary and Notes section). Finally, the section *bc* must represent a totally unstable region as opposed to a metastable one, since it calls for volume to increase with increasing pressure.

The van der Waals equation, although fairly simple algebraically, thus describes not only nonideal gas behavior, but also condensation and regions of vapor and liquid metastability; and, of course, it can be used for calculation of the coefficients of compressibility and thermal expansion for both liquids and gases. As discussed in the following section it also predicts critical phenomena and is consistent with the principle of corresponding states. The simplicity of the equation, the wide range of properties which can be treated, and the rather straightforward physical meaning assigned to the *a* and *b* constants have combined to make the van der Waals equation by far the one most commonly used in approximate applications.

1-10   The van der Waals Equation, Critical Phenomena, and the Principle of Corresponding States

As noted in the preceding section, for a given set of *a* and *b* values there will be one single temperature at which the van der Waals equation will have three equal roots. At this temperature the equivalent straight-line section will have diminished to a point; this is the critical temperature for a van der Waals substance. The van der Waals critical point may be related to the *a* and *b* constants. Perhaps the most convenient way is as follows. At the point of three equal roots the maxima and minima must have just merged. This means that at this point the isotherm for T_c must be horizontal and, moreover, have an inflection point (as illustrated in Fig. 1-13).

The mathematical statements of these conditions are that $(\partial P/\partial V)_T = 0$ and $(\partial^2 P/\partial V^2)_T = 0$. On applying the indicated differentiations to Eq. (1-49), we have

$$\left(\frac{\partial P}{\partial V}\right)_T = 0 = \frac{-RT_c}{(V_c - b)^2} + \frac{2a}{V_c^3}, \tag{1-54}$$

$$\left(\frac{\partial^2 P}{\partial V^2}\right)_T = 0 = \frac{2RT_c}{(V_c - b)^3} - \frac{6a}{V_c^4}. \tag{1-55}$$

On solving Eqs. (1-49), (1-54), and (1-55) simultaneously we find

$$T_c = \frac{8a}{27bR}, \qquad V_c = 3b, \qquad P_c = \frac{a}{27b^2}. \tag{1-56}$$

Alternatively, we have

$$b = \frac{RT_c}{8P_c}, \qquad a = \frac{27(RT_c)^2}{64P_c}. \tag{1-57}$$

Finally, the expressions for V_c, P_c, and T_c may be combined to give

$$P_c V_c = \tfrac{3}{8} RT_c. \tag{1-58}$$

The van der Waals equation also conforms to the principle of corresponding states. From Eqs. (1-56), $P = (a/27b^2) P_r$, $V = 3bV_r$, and $T = (8a/27bR) T_r$, and substitution into the van der Waals equation (1-43) then yields

$$\left(P_r + \frac{3}{V_r^2}\right)\left(V_r - \frac{1}{3}\right) = \frac{8}{3} T_r. \tag{1-59}$$

As required by Eq. (1-41), we now have a relationship connecting V_r, P_r, and T_r which contains no constants specific to the particular substance.

Table 1-6 gives pairs of van der Waals constants for a number of substances. Different sources give somewhat different values for these constants, however. They may be obtained in various ways. One is from the critical constants, with Eqs. (1-56). Another is by a best fitting of the van der Waals equation to the gas (as opposed to the vapor) portion of the compressibility chart of Fig. 1-11. The constants can also be obtained from the coefficients of compressibility and thermal expansion for a liquid, and so on. Since the van der Waals equation is still only an approximate equation, each method will yield somewhat different a and b values. Any one set will then be best suited for calculations around that region of conditions for which the set was obtained and will be apt to give poor results when used in calculations for some quite different pressure and temperature region.

As an example, the a and b values for water used in calculating Fig. 1-13 give a good fit to P–V–T data for water well above its critical temperature and pressure. They are appreciably different from the ones calculated from the critical point for water (since V_c is 55 cm^3 mole^{-1}, this would give $b = 18.5$ cm^3 as compared to

Table 1-6. *Van der Waals Constants for Gases*[a]

Substance	a (liter² atm mole⁻²)	b (liter mole⁻¹)
He	0.03412	0.02370
Ne	0.2107	0.01709
H_2	0.2444	0.02661
O_2	1.360	0.03183
N_2	1.390	0.03913
Cl_2	6.493	0.05622
CO	1.485	0.03985
NO	1.340	0.02789
CO_2	3.592	0.04267
H_2O	5.464	0.03049
NH_3	4.170	0.03707
CH_4	2.253	0.04278
C_2H_2	4.390	0.05136
C_2H_4	4.471	0.05714
C_2H_6	5.489	0.06380
CH_3OH	9.523	0.06702
C_2H_5OH	12.02	0.08407
CH_3COOH	17.59	0.1068
C_6H_6	18.00	0.1154

[a] Landolt–Bornstein, "Physical Chemistry Tables." Springer, Berlin, 1923.

31.9 cm³ used for Fig. 1-13). One result is that while one would expect the 25°C curve of Fig. 1-13 to cross the $P = 0$ line at about 18 cm³ mole⁻¹, the molar volume of liquid water, the calculated curve does so at 31.9 cm³ mole⁻¹. Clearly, a different set of a and b values would better represent this region of the $P-V-T$ plot for water. It is as a consequence of such quantitative deficencies of the van der Waals equation that various more elaborate analytical equations of state have been proposed. Some of these are mentioned in the Commentary and Notes section.

COMMENTARY AND NOTES

A section of this type occurs at the end of the main portion of most chapters. The purposes are, first, to provide some qualitative commentary on interesting but less central aspects of the chapter material and, second, to supply, for reference purposes, additional quantitative results. The latter will ordinarily be presented without derivation or much discussion.

There are, for example, a number of other semiempirical equations of state that have found use. Some of these are

Clausius equation:

$$\left[P + \frac{a}{T(V + c)^2}\right](V - b) = RT. \tag{1-60}$$

Berthelot equation:

$$\left(P + \frac{a}{TV^2}\right)(V - b) = RT. \tag{1-61}$$

Dieterici equation:

$$P(V - b) = RTe^{-a/RTV}. \tag{1-62}$$

Beattie–Bridgman equation:

$$P = \frac{RT(1 - \epsilon)}{V^2}(V + B) - \frac{A}{V^2}, \tag{1-63}$$

where $A = A_0[1 + (a/V)]$, $B = B_0[1 - (b/V)]$, and $\epsilon = c/VT^3$, and A_0 and B_0 are constants.

Benson–Golding equation:

$$\left(P + \frac{a}{V^{5/3}T^{2/3}}\right)(V - bV^{-1/2}) = RT. \tag{1-64}$$

(See Glasstone, 1946; Weston, 1950; Benson and Golding, 1951.)

These equations tend to be of the form of the van der Waals equation, but with improvements designed to allow for a temperature dependence of a and b. The Beattie–Bridgman equation was designed for gases at high pressures.

Some of the various properties that an equation of state should in principle be able to predict were mentioned in the discussion of the van der Waals equation. A brief elaboration is worthwhile. For example, the idea of a tensile strength for a liquid may seem unexpected. The experimental problem, of course, is that one cannot simply pull on a column of liquid as one might on a rod of solid material. What one actually does is to fill a capillary tube with liquid at some elevated temperature and then seal the tube. On cooling, the liquid should contract, but to do so a bubble of vapor would have to form, and if the liquid is free of dust or if the cooling is rapid enough, the column of liquid remains intact and therefore under tension. One calculates this tension from the coefficient of compressibility, knowing how much the liquid has been forced to expand in order to keep filling the capillary at the lower temperature. Negative pressure may be applied mechanically, but less easily. This situation does occur, however, with a boat propeller; liquid behind the rotating blades is momentarily under tension. An important practical problem is to avoid *cavitation*, or the formation of vapor bubbles; the sudden collapse of such bubbles not only hampers the propeller but can pluck out metal grains to roughen and eventually destroy the surface.

Another property which can be calculated from an equation of state is the surface tension of a liquid. We ordinarily think of pressure as a scalar or non-directional quantity, but in the case of a crystalline, nonisotropic solid, application of a uniform pressure will distort the crystal. To avoid this, we would have to exert different pressures on each crystal face. In general, then, pressure can be treated as a set of stresses or directional vectors.

Since a liquid does not support stress, the pressure around any portion of a liquid must be isotropic. This is not true, however, in the surface region. The pressure normal to the surface must indeed be the same as the general pressure throughout the system. However, the pressure parallel to the surface varies through the interface. Analysis shows that the surface tension γ can be calculated if the difference between the pressure normal to the surface and that parallel to the surface is known as a function of distance through the interface. The equation is

$$\gamma = \int_{\text{vapor phase}}^{\text{liquid phase}} (P - p)\, dx, \tag{1-65}$$

where P is the general, isotropic pressure, p is the local pressure component parallel to the surface and x is distance normal to the surface. If we can, by some analysis, calculate how the density or molar volume varies across a liquid–vapor interface, then use of an equation of state such as the van der Waals equation allows a calculation of p as a function of x, and hence of the surface tension (see Tolman, 1949).

A final brief consideration concerns the determination of the critical point of a substance. The reality of a critical point can be seen by means of the following type of experiment. A capillary tube is evacuated and then partly filled with liquid, the remaining space containing no foreign gases but only vapor of the substance in question; the tube is then sealed. On heating, opposing changes take place. The liquid phase increases its vapor pressure, and the vapor density increases as vaporization occurs; this acts to diminish the volume of liquid phase. On the other hand, the liquid itself expands on heating. If just the proper degree of filling of the capillary was achieved, these two effects will approximately balance, and the liquid–vapor meniscus will remain virtually fixed in position as the capillary is heated. A temperature will then be reached at which the meniscus begins to become diffuse and then no longer visible as a dividing surface. At this temperature the system often shows opalescence; the vapor and liquid densities are so nearly the same and their energy difference is so small that fluctuations can produce transient large liquidlike aggregates in the vapor and *vice versa* in the liquid. There is still an average density gradient. However, at a slightly higher temperature, perhaps 5–10°K more, the system becomes essentially uniform. This last is the critical temperature; knowing the amount of substance and the volume of the capillary, one also knows the critical molar volume.

This type of visual experiment, although quite interesting, does not allow a very precise determination of the critical point. An alternative procedure makes use of a series of isotherms such as are shown in Fig. 1-8. However, while the broken line joining the end points of the condensation lines can be fairly well established, its exact maximum point is hard to fix exactly. This locus may alternatively be plotted as temperature versus the equilibrium vapor and liquid densities ρ_v and ρ_l as illustrated in Fig. 1-16. A useful observation, known as the *law of the rectilinear*

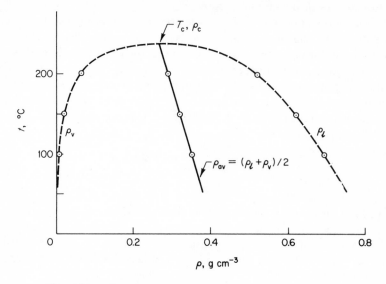

Fig. 1-16. *Illustration of the law of the rectilinear diameter.*

diameter, states that the average density $\rho_{av} = (\rho_l + \rho_v)/2$ is a linear function of temperature, as also illustrated in the figure. The essentially straight and nearly vertical line of ρ_{av} versus T makes an easily defined intersection with the curved line of densities. This intersection then gives the critical temperature and density.

SPECIAL TOPICS

The Special Topics section at the end of each chapter takes up either more specialized or more advanced aspects of the chapter material. The intention is to provide a section, separated from the main body of material, which can be considered if time in the course permits, or as self-study on the part of the interested student. Although the material in the main body of suceeding chapters will not draw on previous Special Topics sections, subsequent Special Topics sections may make use of the results of preceding ones.

The van der Waals and other equations of state cited in this chapter are illustra-tions of a semiempirical approach in which the goal is to obtain a definite functional form for the equation of state. Contemporary theoretical chemists now pursue the line of using a detailed expression for the intermolecular potential between two molecules to obtain values for the virial coefficients of Eq. (1-37). The potential function will be somewhat approximate or semiempirical, but the ensuing and generally quite elaborate theoretical development may be rigorous.

If the mutual potential energy between two molecules as a function of the sepa-ration r is denoted by $\phi(r)$, then a statistical mechanical derivation, which is beyond the scope of this text, gives the following equation for the second virial coefficient (see Hirschfelder *et al.*, 1954):

$$B(T) = 2\pi N_0 \int_0^\infty (1 - e^{-\phi(r)/kT}) \, r^2 \, dr, \tag{1-66}$$

where N_0 is Avogadro's number.

A very qualitative rationale of the treatment is as follows. It was noted in Section 1-5 that the barometric equation could be regarded as a particular appli-cation of the Boltzmann principle Eq. (1-35). The principle stated that the probab-ility of a molecule having an energy ϵ is proportional to $e^{-\epsilon/kT}$. In the case of an ideal gas, ϵ is just the kinetic energy and application of the Boltzmann principle gives the relative probabilities of finding molecules of various kinetic energies. This aspect is developed in Chapter 2.

If now molecules experience mutual attractive and repulsive forces, $\phi(r)$ can be expected to have a form of the type illustrated in Fig. 1-17. That is, as two mole-cules approach each other they will at first be attracted and then, at small separa-tions, repelled. Correspondingly, their mutual potential energy is zero at infinite separation and diminishes to a maximum negative value at some separation r_0 At $r = \sigma$, the potential energy is just zero again; and for $r < \sigma$, it is positive and very rapidly increasing.

The average total energy of the pair of molecules can be written

$$\epsilon_{tot} = \epsilon_{r \to \infty} + \phi(r). \tag{1-67}$$

Thus ϵ_{tot} diminishes to a minimum at r_0 and then rises rapidly as r is decreased. In terms of the Boltzmann principle, the effect is to make separation distances around $r = r_0$ relatively more probable and separation distances of $r < \sigma$ rela-tively less probable than for an ideal gas.

A second effect of $\phi(r)$ is on the ability of molecules to exert a pressure. Perhaps a

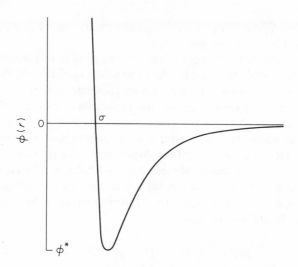

Fig. 1-17. *Variation of potential energy as two molecules approach each other.*

helpful although very crude physical explanation is as follows. Two molecules at a distance r_0 apart have less energy than the average, and were they to dissociate without any energy being supplied, they would end up as separate molecules making less than the average contribution to the pressure. Conversely, a pair of molecules at $r < \sigma$ should make a greater than average contribution to the pressure. Thus the presence of intermolecular forces affects both the distribution of intermolecular distances and the expected pressure of the now nonideal gas.

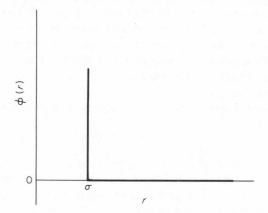

Fig. 1-18. *Square-well potential plot.*

The way in which Eq. (1-66) works can be illustrated by the following example. Consider the gas molecules to be hard spheres so that the potential energy plot is as shown in Fig. 1-18. That is, there are no attractive forces, and $\phi(r)$ jumps to infinity at $r = \sigma$. The integral of Eq. (1-67) can then be written in two parts:

(a) at $r > \sigma$, $\phi(r) = 0$, $e^{-\phi(r)/kT} = 1$,

$$\int_{\sigma}^{\infty} (1 - e^{-\phi(r)/kT})\, r^2\, dr = 0,$$

(b) at $r < \sigma$, $\phi(r) = \infty$, $e^{-\phi(r)/kT} = 0$,

$$\int_{0}^{\sigma} (1 - e^{-\phi(r)/kT})\, r^2\, dr = \tfrac{1}{3}\sigma^3;$$

and

$$B(T) = \tfrac{2}{3}\pi N_0 \sigma^3. \tag{1-68}$$

Since σ corresponds to a molecular diameter, $B(T)$ is just four times the volume of a mole of molecules, or has essentially the same meaning as the van der Waals constant b. Considering only the second virial coefficient, we see that the equation of state of the hard-sphere gas is then

$$\frac{PV}{RT} = 1 + \frac{B(T)}{V} = 1 + \frac{b}{V}. \tag{1-69}$$

If the approximation is made that $1/V = P/RT$, then Eq. (1-69) reduces to Eq. (1-42), $P(V - b) = RT$.

The hard-sphere model provides only a poor approximation to real gases, just as Fig. 1-18 is a most crude approximation to Fig. 1-17. Theoreticians make use of more realistic potential functions than the hard-sphere one. However, the determination of really accurate functions is a wave mechanical problem that has not been fully solved as yet. What one usually does is to take a semiempirical form chosen both for its probable approximate correctness and for mathematical convenience. A commonly used such form is the *Lennard–Jones potential*

$$\phi(r) = -\frac{\alpha}{r^6} + \frac{\beta}{r^{12}}. \tag{1-70}$$

As mentioned in Section 1-7, the attractive potential between molecules is expected to vary as $1/r^6$ at least for large separations; the first term on the right of Eq. (1-70) assumes this attractive potential to apply at all distances. The second term on the right is undoubtedly incorrect theoretically but constitutes a mathematically convenient way of providing a steeply rising repulsive potential.

The effect of introducing both attractive and repulsive potentials is to make $B(T)$ a complicated quantity as far as physical significance is concerned. It is now temperature-dependent and moreover, may be positive or negative. A calculated curve for $B(T)$ as a function of temperature using the Lennard–Jones potential is given in Fig. 1-19. Here B is given in terms of b_0, where b_0 is the hard-sphere value

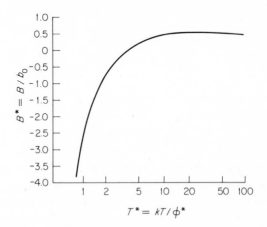

Fig. 1-19. *Reduced plot for the calculation of B(T) of Eq. (1-69) assuming a Lennard–Jones potential. (Adapted from J. O. Hirschfelder, C. F. Curtiss, and R. B. Bird, "Molecular Theory of Gases and Liquids," corrected ed. Copyright 1964, Wiley, New York. Used with permission of John Wiley & Sons, Inc.)*

of $2\pi N_0\sigma^3/3$; T^* is the reduced temperature, defined as kT/ϕ^*. As shown in Fig. 1-17, ϕ^* is the minimum in the potential curve. The quantities σ and ϕ^* are natural ones to use in connection with the Lennard–Jones potential, since this function takes on a rather simple form in terms of them:

$$\phi(r) = 4\phi^* \left[\left(\frac{\sigma}{r}\right)^{12} - \left(\frac{\sigma}{r}\right)^6 \right] \tag{1-71}$$

One may use Fig. 1-19 to calculate $B(T)$ for various gases if their parameters σ and ϕ^* are known, and some of these values are given in Table 1-7. Notice that the existence of a single curve for $B(T)$ is an illustration of the principle of corresponding states. Here B/b_0 and kT/ϕ^* are the reduced variables. The Lennard–Jones potential becomes a rather poor approximation, however, as one goes to diatomic and polyatomic molecules, especially those which are polar and nonspherical and the treatment as outlined is much too simple to give a good representation of the P–V–T behavior of such gases over more than a narrow range of

Table 1-7. *Lennard–Jones Parameters from Second Virial Coefficients[a]*

Gas	ϕ^*/k (°K)	σ (Å)	b_0 (cm³ mole⁻¹)
Ne	34.9	2.78	27.10
Ar	119.8	3.40	49.80
Kr	171	3.60	58.86
Xe	221	4.10	86.94
N_2	95.1	3.70	63.78
O_2	118	3.46	52.26
CH_4	148.2	3.82	70.16
CO_2	189	4.49	113.9

[a] From J. O. Hirschfelder, C. F. Curtiss, and R. B. Bird, "Molecular Theory of Gases and Liquids," corrected ed., p. 165. Wiley, New York, 1964.

conditions. A more accurate potential function would, for example, include the dependence on the relative angular orientation of two approaching molecules.

The second virial coefficient, as indicated by the form of Eq. (1-66), is determined by the form of the potential energy of interaction between two molecules. The third virial coefficient involves the mutual interaction potential for molecules taken three at a time. Although many such calculations have been made, they are obviously quite complicated and the reader is referred to advanced texts at this point.

GENERAL REFERENCES

The references at the end of each chapter are generally to specialized monographs from which more detailed information can be obtained on the subject or subjects of the chapter. See the Preface for some additional comments.

GLASSTONE, S. (1946). "A Textbook of Physical Chemistry," 2nd ed. Van Nostrand–Reinhold, Princeton, New Jersey. A good although partially outdated general reference.

HIRSCHFELDER, J. O., CURTISS, C. F., AND BIRD, R. B. (1964). "Molecular Theory of Gases and Liquids," corrected ed. Wiley, New York. An excellent advanced treatise on the statistical mechanical approach to the properties of gases.

MOELWYN-HUGHES, E. A. (1961). "Physical Chemistry," 2nd ed. Pergamon, Oxford. A useful intermediate-level general text.

PARTINGTON, J. R. (1949). "An Advanced Treatise on Physical Chemistry," Vol. 1. Longmans, Green, Boston, Massachusetts. A very detailed reference.

In addition, a collection of worked-out examination questions is available: ADAMSON, A. W. (1969). "Understanding Physical Chemistry," 2nd ed. Benjamin, New York.

CITED REFERENCES

BENSON, S. W., AND GOLDING, R. A. (1951). *J. Chem. Phys.* **19**, 1413.

GLASSTONE, S. (1946). "Textbook of Physical Chemistry." Van Nostrand–Reinhold, Princeton, New Jersey.

HIRSCHFELDER, J. O., CURTISS, C. F., AND BIRD, R. B. (1964). "Molecular Theory of Gases and Liquids," corrected ed. Wiley, New York.

MACDOUGALL, F. H. (1936). *J. Amer. Chem. Soc.* **58**, 2585.

WESTON, F. (1950). "An Introduction to Thermodynamics. The Kinetic Theory of Gases, and Statistical Mechanics." Addison-Wesley, Reading, Massachusetts.

Exercises and Problems

As noted in the Preface, each section of this type is divided into three parts. The first consists of *Exercises*, or very straightforward illustrations of the textual material. The *Problems* section contains more demanding and often longer applications of the same material; and, as the name indicates, *Special Topics Problems* draw on the Special Topics section of the chapter.

Exercises

1-1 Calculate the molar volume V and the density of methane gas at STP assuming ideal behavior.

Ans. $V = 22.414$ liters. $\rho = 7.138 \times 10^{-4}$ g cm^{-3}.

1-2 Repeat Exercise 1 but for 25°C and 1.5 atm pressure.

Ans. 9.809×10^{-4} g cm^{-3}.

1-3 In the Dumas method one determines the molecular weight of a gas by a direct measurement of its density. A glass bulb weighs 25.0000 g when evacuated, 125.0000 g when filled with water at 25°C, and 25.01613 g when filled with a hydrocarbon gas at 25°C and 100 Torr pressure. Calculate the molecular weight of the gas, assuming ideal behavior.

Ans. 30.0 g mole^{-1}.

1-4 Calculate V and ρ for dry air at STP. Repeat the calculation for air saturated with water vapor at 25°C and at 1 atm total pressure. Assume ideal behavior.

Ans. (a) $V = 22.414$ liter, $\rho = 0.001285$ g cm^{-3}; (b) $V = 24.460$ liter, $\rho = 0.001163$ g cm^{-3}.

1-5 Calculate M_{av} under the conditions of the fourth line of Table 1-4 and verify the value of K_P given.

Ans. $M_{av} = 77.47$ g mole^{-1}.

Problems

1-6 Calculate the partial volumes of H_2O, O_2, and N_2 in air saturated with water vapor at 50°C and at 1 atm total pressure. Assume ideal behavior and one mole of total gas.

Ans. $V_{H_2O} = 3.228$ liter, $V_{O_2} = 4.657$ liter, $V_{N_2} = 18.63$ liter.

1-7 What is $h_{1/2}$ for argon—that is, the elevation at which the pressure of argon in the atmosphere is half of its sea level value? Assume 20°C.

Ans. 4.31 km.

1-8 A good vacuum for many purposes has a pressure of 10^{-10} atm. Treating air as a single gas of molecular weight 29, at what elevation will this pressure be found? Assume −70°C.

Ans. 1.369×10^2 km (assuming g to remain constant).

1-9 Derive the van der Waals equation for n moles of gas.

Ans. $[P + (an^2/v^2)](v - nb) = nRT$.

1-10 Calculate the second and third virial coefficients for CO_2 assuming it to be a van der Waals gas.

Ans. $B(T) = 0.04267 - (43.77/T)$ liter; $C(T) = 1.82 \times 10^{-3}$ liter^2.

1-11 What is the Boyle temperature of CO_2 assuming it to be a van der Waals gas?

Ans. 1026°K.

1-12 Tables 1-5 and 1-6 come from different sources and are not necessarily consistent. Calculate the van der Waals constants for H_2O from its critical point.

Ans. $a = 5.447$ liter^2 atm mole^{-2}, $b = 0.0304$ liter mole^{-1} [Eq. (1-57)], 0.0185 liter mole^{-1} [Eq. (1-56)].

1-13 Fifty moles of NH_3 is introduced into a two-liter cylinder at 25°C. Calculate the pressure if (a) the gas is ideal and (b) it obeys the van der Waals equation.

Ans. (a) 611 atm, (b) 5820 atm.

1-14 Using Fig. 1-11, calculate the molar volume of NH_3 at 100°C and 50 atm pressure. Compare this with the ideal gas volume.

Ans. Figure 1-11: 0.45 liter; ideal gas: 0.612 liter.

1-15 What is the critical temperature of a van der Waals gas for which P_c is 100 atm and b is 50 cm^3 mole^{-1}?

Ans. 487.5°K.

Problems

1-1 A tank of compressed nitrogen gas has a volume of 100 liters; the pressure is 2000 atm initially (at 25°C). Owing to a faulty valve, gas is leaking out at a rate proportional to the difference between the pressure inside the tank and the pressure outside (1 atm). The initial rate of leakage is 1.0 g of gas per second. If we assume that the process continues iso-thermally at 25°C, how long will it take for half the gas initially present in the tank to leak out?

1-2 The McLeod gauge (see accompanying figure) is a device enabling one to make a manometric measurement of very low pressures (down to 10^{-7} Torr). The device is operated as follows. Initially the mercury level is below point a so that the entire apparatus is at the uniform low pressure P_1 which is to be measured. By raising

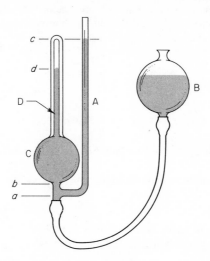

the reservoir B, the mercury level is raised past point b and then further until the meniscus in tube A is at the level c. Once the mercury passes b, the gas in the bulb C is trapped and as the mercury level is raised further, this gas is com-pressed into the capillary tube D and the meniscus in the capillary reaches level d when the level in tube A reaches c. The distance between c and d is now related to the value of P_1. If V denotes the volume (in cubic centimeters) of bulb C and if the capillary tube is of total length d and of uniform radius r (in millimeters), then if x denotes the distance between c and point d, derive the relationship between x and P_1. In the case of a particular McLeod gauge, V is 250 cm³, d is 10 cm, and r is 0.5 mm; calculate x for P_1 equal to 10^{-5}, 10^{-4}, 10^{-3} Torr, respectively.

1-3 Bulb A, of 500 ml volume, initially contains N_2 at 0.7 atm pressure and 25°C; bulb B, of 800 ml volume, initially contains O_2 at 0.5 atm pressure and at 0°C. The two bulbs are then connected so that there is free passage of gas back and forth between them and the assembly is then brought to a uniform temperature of 20°C. Calculate the final pressure.

1-4 The vapor of acetic acid contains single and double molecules in equilibrium as shown by the reaction $(CH_3COOH)_2 = 2CH_3COOH$. At 25°C and 0.020 atm pressure, the Pv product for 60 g of acetic acid vapor is $0.541RT$, and at 40°C and 0.020 atm, it is $0.593RT$. Calculate the fraction of the vapor forming single molecules at each temperature and the value for the equilibrium constant at each temperature, $K_P = P^2_{CH_3COOH}/P_{(CH_3COOH)_2}$ [see MacDougall (1936)].

Problems

1-5 One problem in using tanks of compressed gas is that the pressure drops as gas is taken out, so that toward the end of its life, the gas in a tank may not be usable because of being at too low a pressure. The head of a chemical storeroom gets the idea that expensive gas could be saved if the gas in a partly used large cylinder could be compressed into a smaller tank so as to build up the pressure. His thought is to avoid having to use high-pressure pumps and to accomplish the pressure build up by connecting a small cylinder to the partly exhausted large one, then cooling the small cylinder to some low temperature. After the gas has equilibrated between the two cylinders, the connection is shut off, and the small cylinder allowed to warm up. To take a specific example, suppose that the large cylinder contains He gas at a pressure of 1000 atm at 27°C. The small cylinder has one-third the volume of the large one, and it is desired by this procedure to fill it with enough He so that at 27°C the pressure in the small cylinder will be 2000 atm. Calculate the temperature to which the small cylinder must be cooled in order to achieve this result.

1-6 Derive the value of T_r such that

$$\frac{d(P_r V_r)}{dP_r} = 0 \quad \text{as} \quad P_r \rightarrow 0,$$

that is, the value of T_r at the Boyle temperature of a van der Waals gas.

1-7 Derive an expression for the coefficient of thermal expansion α,

$$\alpha = \frac{1}{V}\left(\frac{\partial V}{\partial T}\right)_P,$$

for a gas that follows (a) the ideal gas law and (b) the van der Waals equation.

1-8 Calculate the pressure versus volume isotherm for C_6H_6 at 360°K using the van der Waals equation ($a = 18$ liter² atm, $b = 0.1154$ liter mole⁻¹). Plot the resulting curve (up to 30 liter mole⁻¹). (a) Indicate on the graph how you would estimate the vapor pressure of benzene at this temperature. (b) Obtain the slope dV/dP (at constant T) for $P = 1$ atm, and calculate the coefficient of compressibility of the liquid at this pressure:

$$\beta = -\frac{1}{V}\left(\frac{\partial V}{\partial P}\right)_T$$

Compare the result with an experimental value. (c) Estimate the tensile strength of benzene (liquid) at this temperature.

1-9 At sea level, the composition of air is 80 mole % nitrogen and 20 mole % oxygen. Estimate the altitude (in miles) at which, according to the barometric formula, the air should contain only 15 mole % oxygen. Assume t is 0°C.

1-10 Using the Hougen–Watson chart (Fig. 1-11) and the critical constants (Table 1-5) for CO, obtain the value for the second virial coefficient for CO at 25°C. It is suggested that a graphical method be used.

1-11 A certain gas obeys the van der Waals equation with $a = 10^7$ atm cm⁶ mole⁻² and $b = 100$ cm³ mole⁻¹. Calculate the volume of four moles of the gas when the pressure is 5 atm and the temperature is 300°C.

1-12   Derive from the van der Waals equation an expression for the Boyle temperature in terms of the constants a, b, and R. Remember that at the Boyle temperature

$$\left(\frac{\partial(PV)}{\partial P}\right)_T = 0 \quad \text{as} \quad P \to 0.$$

1-13   The curve for $T/T_c = 0.8$ in the Hougen–Watson chart (Fig. 1-11) ends abruptly. Reproduce this curve in a sketch, and show by means of a dotted line what a continuation of it should look like. Also sketch in for reference the complete curve shown for $T/T_c = 1$.

1-14   Derive a modified version of the barometric formula for the case where air temperature is t on the ground and decreases linearly with altitude. By means of this formula, calculate the barometric pressure at an elevation of 1 km, assuming 1 atm at sea level and that the temperature drops $0.01°C$ per meter. Use $25°C$.

1-15   The following data are obtained for a certain gas at $0°C$:

P (atm)	0.4000	0.6000	0.8000
ρ/P (g liter^{-1} atm^{-1})	0.7643	0.7666	0.7689

Calculate the molecular weight of the gas by the extrapolation method.

1-16   Make a plot of V versus P at $25°C$ for a substance which obeys the van der Waals equation and whose critical temperature and pressure values are those for water. The plot should extend over the range from liquid to gaseous state so as to show the minimum and maximum in pressure that the equation predicts. Estimate from the plot (making your procedures clear) (a) the tensile strength of liquid water, (b) the compressibility of liquid water at $25°C$ (compare with the experimental value), and (c) the vapor pressure of water at $25°C$ (compare with the experimental value).

1-17   A column of ideal gas experiences conditions such that $\ln P = (\text{const})\, x^2$, where x denotes distance from a reference point. Describe two possible experimental situations for which this equation applies.

1-18   (Calculator problem)   Calculate P versus V for NH_3 using the van der Waals equation. Do this for $40°C$ intervals between $0°C$ and $200°C$ and plot the results. Recast the data in terms of compressibility factor Z in terms of P_r for various T_r and plot these curves.

Special Topics Problems

1-1   Calculate $B(T)$ for NH_3 at $25°C$ (a) using its van der Waals constants and (b) assuming the hard-sphere model and using only the density of liquid ammonia.

1-2   Verify Eq. (1-71). That is, show that ϕ^* is the minimum potential energy and that σ is the value of r when ϕ is zero.

1-3 Using Table 1-5 and Fig. 1-19, calculate the compressibility factor for CO_2 at 5 atm and 25°C and at 5 atm and 200°C.

1-4 The value of $B(T)$ for Xe gas is -130.2 cm³ mole⁻¹ at 298.2°K and -81.2 cm³ mole⁻¹ at 373.2°K. Find the value of $\phi*/k$ which, using Fig. 1-19, will reproduce this ratio of $B(T)$ values, and from this $\phi*$ and b_0 .

2 KINETIC MOLECULAR THEORY OF GASES

2-1 Introduction

The treatment of ideal and nonideal gases in Chapter 1 was carried out largely from a phenomenological point of view. Behavior was described in terms of the macroscopic variables P, V, and T, although some molecular interpretation was included in the discussion of the a and b parameters of the van der Waals equation (Section 1-7) and in the Special Topics section. We take up here the detailed model of a gas, that is, the kinetic molecular theory of gases. In this model, a gas is considered to be made up of individual molecules, each having kinetic energy in the form of a random motion. The pressure and the temperature of a gas are treated as manifestations of this kinetic energy. In its simplest form, kinetic theory assumes that the molecules experience no mutual attractions.

The elementary picture is the familiar one of a molecule having an average velocity u and bouncing back and forth between opposite walls of a cubical container. With each wall collision a change in momentum $2mu$ occurs, where m is the mass of a molecule. If the side of the container is l, the frequency of such collisions is $2l/u$, and the momentum change per second imparted to the wall, that is, the force on it, is mu^2/l. The pressure, or force per unit area, becomes mu^2/l^3 or $mu^2/\mathbf{v}$. The quantity u refers to the velocity component in some one direction, and the total velocity squared, c^2, is $c^2 = u^2 + v^2 + w^2$, where v and w are the components in the other two directions; on the average these components should be equal, and so we conclude that $u^2 = c^2/3$, and obtain the final equation

$$P\mathbf{v} = \tfrac{1}{3}mc^2,\tag{2-1}$$

where $\mathbf{v}$ denotes the volume per molecule. Per mole, this becomes

$$PV = \tfrac{1}{3}Mc^2, \tag{2-2}$$

where M is the molecular weight of the gas.

One now takes note that the simple picture corresponds, for real gases, to the limiting condition of zero pressure, for which the phenomenological law is the ideal gas equation

$$PV = RT \tag{2-3}$$

and the relationship which is intuitively expected to exist between kinetic energy and temperature is simply

$$RT = \tfrac{1}{3}Mc^2 = \tfrac{2}{3}(\text{kinetic energy}), \tag{2-4}$$

the molar kinetic energy being $\tfrac{1}{2}Mc^2$. Alternatively, one writes

$$c^2 = \frac{3RT}{M} \tag{2-5}$$

or

$$c^2 = \frac{3kT}{m}, \tag{2-6}$$

where k is the gas constant per molecule, called the Boltzmann constant, as noted in Section 1-7.

This treatment is unsatisfactory at some points. Clearly, it is unrealistic to take all molecules as having the same velocity. Even occasional intermolecular collisions must eventually bring about a distribution of velocities, and since we are describing a theory for time-invariant or equilibrium properties of a gas, we should be dealing with velocity distributions. The quantity c^2 must then really be some kind of average quantity. The argument that one should use $\tfrac{1}{3}c^2$ for the velocity component squared in some one direction is plausible but is not a proof. The sections that follow take up a more elaborate but more satisfying way of obtaining not only the above results, but much additional information as well.

There remain a number of important properties of a gas which cannot be explained unless a finite molecular size is specifically assumed. The model at this point becomes one of molecules that act as hard spheres. By "hard" we mean that they behave like spheres of definite radius r and that their collisions are elastic so that kinetic energy as well as momentum is conserved. Beyond this lie more advanced treatments which allow for the presence of attractive as well as of repulsive forces between molecules. Some aspects of these will be taken up in the Special Topics section.

The immediate task, however, is the treatment of velocity distributions. Here the central assumption will be that of the Boltzmann principle. As was stated in Section

1-7, according to the Boltzmann principle the probability of a molecule having an energy ϵ is given by

$$p(\epsilon) = (\text{constant}) \, e^{-\epsilon/kT}. \qquad (2\text{-}7)$$

This principle was adduced as a generalization of the barometric equation; it can, however, be reached in other ways, one of which is given in the next section.

2-2 The Boltzmann Distribution Law

The Maxwell–Boltzmann principle (often referred to as the Boltzmann principle) is so central to all of the statistical aspects of physical chemistry that it merits a more general derivation than that of Section 1-7. We want to consider a system that is isolated, so that its total molar energy E is constant and the total number of molecules N is constant. The molecules making up this system can have various quantized energy states; let them be called ϵ_1, ϵ_2, ϵ_3, and so on.

There will be many ways in which the N molecules could be assigned specific energies so as to give the same total molar energy E. For example, let E be 20 units of energy and N be ten molecules, and suppose that there are three possible states of one, three, and five units of energy. Possible distributions are given in Table 2-1. In this case there are three different ways of satisfying the two requirements of fixed N and fixed E.

If the molecules were labeled, there would be 5! ways in which those occupying the ϵ_1 "box" could be permuted in the case of system 1, and an additional 5! ways in which those in the ϵ_2 box could be permuted. The total number of combined permutations would then be 5!5!. For system 2 the total permutations would be 6!3!1!, and for system 3, 7!1!2!. This means that the different systems have different statistical weights or intrinsic probabilities.

The statistical weight that we actually want is obtained as follows. If we were just putting N molecules in as many boxes, their permutations would be $N!$.

Table 2-1. *Ways of Distributing Molecules between States[a]*

System	Number in given state[b]		
	$\epsilon_1 = 1$	$\epsilon_2 = 3$	$\epsilon_3 = 5$
1	5	5	0
2	6	3	1
3	7	1	2

[a] Assuming ten molecules and total system energy of 20 units.

[b] Energy in arbitrary units.

However, we consider only molecules in different energy states as distinguishable. That is, the N_1 molecules in the ϵ_1 box are taken to be indistinguishable, as are the N_2 molecules in the ϵ_2 box, and so on. We must then divide out the permutations that should not be present.

The general statements of the preceding conditions are then

$$N = \sum N_i = \text{constant}, \tag{2-8}$$

$$E = \sum N_i \epsilon_i = \text{constant}, \tag{2-9}$$

$$W = \frac{N!}{N_1!\, N_2!\, N_3! \cdots} = \frac{N!}{\prod_i N_i!}, \tag{2-10}$$

where N_i denotes the number of molecules in the ith state of energy ϵ_i and W is the statistical weight or probability of the particular distribution. To repeat, the denominator of Eq. (2-10) serves to take out those permutations that do not count because of the indistinguishability of molecules in the same energy state.

One further point completes the basic picture. If N is a very large number, for example, Avogadro's number, it turns out that W will peak very sharply at some one distribution. That is, there will be some set of N_1, N_2, and so on values giving the largest W, and relatively small departures from this proportion will cause W to drop sharply. This largest W is called W_{max}. Thus the set of requirements of Eqs. (2-8)–(2-10) acts to define a most probable distribution and one which is assumed, in the case of a large number of molecules, to be *the* distribution.

The preceding conditions and assumptions are in fact sufficient to give the immediate precursor to the Boltzmann distribution law, namely the conclusion that

$$p(\epsilon) = (\text{constant})\, e^{-\beta \epsilon}, \tag{2-11}$$

where $p(\epsilon)$ is the probability that the molecule has energy ϵ. The constant β will be identified with $1/kT$ in Section 2-4, when a consequence of Eq. (2-11) is compared with the ideal gas law.

First, we can obtain Eq. (2-11) as follows. Since we are considering a system at equilibrium, the distribution will be one for which W is at a maximum—that is, we expect the equilibrium distribution to be the one that is the most probable. We now imagine that a small redistribution δ of molecules takes place, subject to the restriction that neither N nor the total energy of the system changes,

$$\sum_i \delta N_i = 0 \tag{2-12}$$

$$\sum_i \epsilon_i \, \delta N_i = 0. \tag{2-13}$$

Since W is at a maximum, it also follows that δW must be zero. It is convenient at this point to take the logarithm of Eq. (2-10):

$$\ln W = \ln N! - \sum_i \ln N_i!$$

and write as the condition

$$\delta(\ln W) = 0 = \sum_i \delta(\ln N_i!) \tag{2-14}$$

since $\delta(\ln N!) = 0$. We are dealing with very large numbers and it is permissible to replace factorials by Stirling's approximation,

$$\ln x! = x \ln x - x. \tag{2-15}$$

Equation (2-14) becomes

$$0 = \sum_i \delta(N_i \ln N_i - N_i)$$

$$= \sum_i \left[N_i \frac{\delta N_i}{N_i} + (\ln N_i)\, \delta N_i - \delta N_i \right],$$

$$\sum_i (\ln N_i)\, \delta N_i = 0. \tag{2-16}$$

Equations (2-12)–(2-14) impose three different conditions on the δN's and are to be obeyed even though the system makes small, arbitrary fluctuations. A way of handling such a situation is Lagrange's method of undetermined multipliers [see, for example, Blinder (1969)]. We add the three conditions, but in some ratio which is to be determined; that is, we write

$$\sum_i (\alpha + \beta \epsilon_i + \ln N_i)\, \delta N_i = 0, \tag{2-17}$$

where Eqs. (2-12) and (2-13) have been multiplied by the undetermined coefficients α and β, respectively.

Equation (2-17) can be written out in detail as a sum of terms in δN_1, δN_2, δN_3, and so on:

$$(\alpha + \beta \epsilon_1 + \ln N_1)\, \delta N_1 + (\alpha + \beta \epsilon_2 + \ln N_2)\, \delta N_2$$
$$+ (\alpha + \beta \epsilon_3 + \ln N_3)\, \delta N_3 + \cdots = 0. \tag{2-18}$$

Now, if there were only two states, say ϵ_1 and ϵ_2, Eqs. (1-8) and (1-9) would absolutely fix the distribution (for example, system 1 of Table 2-1). With three states the most probable population of ϵ_3 could be varied, but given δN_3, this would then determine δN_1 and δN_2. With a larger number of states, δN_3, δN_4, and so on could be chosen arbitrarily, and this would then fix δN_1 and δN_2. If we elect to choose values for α and β such that the terms of Eq. (2-18) in δN_1 and δN_2 are zero, which can be done since α and β are adjustable constants, then the equation reduces to the requirement that the sum of all the terms in δN_3, δN_4, and so on must be zero. Since the variations δN_3, δN_4, and so on are arbitrary, the only way for this requirement to be generally true is for each term separately to be zero. The general condition is therefore

$$\alpha + \beta \epsilon_i + \ln N_i = 0 \tag{2-19}$$

or

$$N_i = e^{-\alpha}e^{-\beta\epsilon_i} = (\text{constant})\, e^{-\beta\epsilon_i}, \qquad (2\text{-}20)$$

which is Eq. (2-11).

This result, namely that the most probable number of molecules in a state of energy ϵ_i is proportional to $e^{-\beta\epsilon_i}$, may seem startling in that it is obtained on so general a basis. To repeat, it is a consequence of the restrictions of Eqs. (2-12)–(2-14) plus the assumption that molecules will find that energy distribution having the greatest statistical weight as given by the permutation formula of Eq. (2-10).

2-3   The Distribution of Molecular Velocities

We start by applying the Maxwell–Boltzmann distribution equation (2-7) to the case of a one-dimensional gas, that is, to a system of molecules having only kinetic energy due to motion along one direction in space, say the x direction. The Boltzmann equation then gives

$$p(u) = (\text{constant})\, \exp\!\left(-\frac{mu^2}{2kT}\right), \qquad (2\text{-}21)$$

where u is the velocity in the x direction (and could be either positive or negative), and $\epsilon = \frac{1}{2} mu^2$. The more quantitative way of stating Eq. (2-21) is to say that it gives the fraction of molecules $dN(u)/N_0$ (where N_0 is the total number of molecules, taken here to be Avogadro's number) having velocities between u and $u + du$,

$$\frac{dN(u)}{N_0} = A\!\left[\exp\!\left(-\frac{mu^2}{2kT}\right)\right] du. \qquad (2\text{-}22)$$

The proportionality constant A can be evaluated by the requirement that the sum of probabilities for all possible velocities must be unity:

$$\int \frac{dN(u)}{N_0} = 1 = A \int_{-\infty}^{\infty} \left[\exp\!\left(-\frac{mu^2}{2kT}\right)\right] du. \qquad (2\text{-}23)$$

The integral of Eq. (2-23) can be put in a standard form, that is,

$$\int_0^{\infty} \left[\exp(-a^2 x^2)\right] dx = \frac{\sqrt{\pi}}{2a}, \qquad (2\text{-}24)$$

where in the present case $a = (m/2kT)^{1/2}$. Because the distribution must be symmetric with respect to plus and minus directions, we have

$$\int_{-\infty}^{\infty} \left[\exp\!\left(-\frac{mu^2}{2kT}\right)\right] du = 2 \int_0^{\infty} \left[\exp\!\left(-\frac{mu^2}{2kT}\right)\right] du = \left(\frac{2\pi kT}{m}\right)^{1/2}$$

The constant A, called the normalization constant, is thus $(m/2\pi kT)^{1/2}$ and Eq. (2-22) becomes

$$\frac{dN(u)}{N_0} = \left(\frac{m}{2\pi kT}\right)^{1/2} \left[\exp\left(-\frac{mu^2}{2kT}\right)\right] du. \tag{2-25}$$

The plot of Eq. (2-25), that is, of $(1/N_0) \, dN(u)/du$ versus u, is shown in Fig. 2-1 for the case of a gas of molecular weight 28, such as nitrogen, at 25°C and 1025°C.

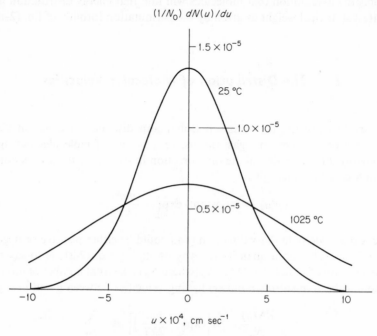

$(1/N_0) \, dN(u)/du$

$u \times 10^4$, cm sec^{-1}

Fig 2-1. *Molecular velocity distribution in one dimension for* N_2.

The coefficient of u^2 can be written $M/2RT$ and is thus equal to $28/(2)(8.314 \times 10^7)$ $(298.1) = 5.649 \times 10^{-10}$ at 25°C and 1.297×10^{-10} at 1025°C, with u in centimeters per second. The coefficient A can likewise be written $(M/2\pi RT)^{1/2}$ and has the values 1.34×10^{-5} and 0.644×10^{-5} sec cm^{-1} at the two temperatures, respectively. Note that the distribution is symmetric and that the most probable velocity is zero. This latter statement is true because there are equal chances for a molecule to gain a velocity increment in either the positive or in the negative direction. Finally, the spread of the distribution, as measured, for example, by the width at half-maximum, increases with increasing temperature.

The case of a two-dimensional gas follows in a straight forward manner. We now allow velocities along the x and y directions, given by u and v. The net velocity c of a molecule having components u and v is

$$c^2 = u^2 + v^2 \tag{2-26}$$

and the Boltzmann equation is

$$\frac{dN(u, v)}{N_0} = A\left\{\exp\left[-\frac{m(u^2 + v^2)}{2kT}\right]\right\} \, du \, dv, \qquad (2\text{-}27)$$

where $dN(u, v)/N_0$ is now the fraction of molecules having velocity components between u and $u + du$ and v and $v + dv$. Equation (2-27) factors into two integrals, each analogous to that of Eq. (2-23), with the result that on carrying out the normalization procedure, one finds that $A = m/2\pi kT$, and the complete distribution equation becomes

$$\frac{dN(u, v)}{N_0} = \frac{m}{2\pi kT}\left\{\exp\left[-\frac{m(u^2 + v^2)}{2kT}\right]\right\} \, du \, dv. \qquad (2\text{-}28)$$

The distribution function of Eq. (2-28) now requires a three-dimensional plot for its display, as illustrated in Fig. 2-2. Again the maximum is at u and v equal to zero, and, of course, it is symmetric with respect to positive and negative velocities.

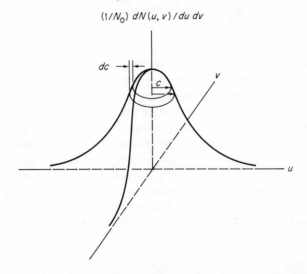

$(1/N_0) \, dN(u, v) \, / \, du \, dv$

Fig. 2-2.   *Molecular velocity distribution for a gas in two dimensions.*

It is ordinarily of more interest to deal with the net velocity c than with the separate components. That is, although the u and v velocity components represent independent ways in which the molecule can have kinetic energy, it is the net velocity of the molecule and its total kinetic energy $mc^2/2$ that are needed for most applications. Now the sum of all the possible ways in which the net velocity can increase from c to $c + dc$, that is, by adding increments du and dv to various combinations of u and v, is given by the area of the annulus shown in Fig. 2-2.

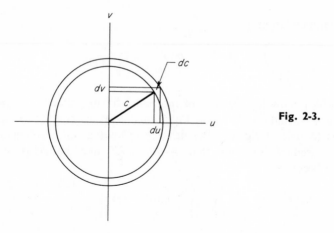

Fig. 2-3.

This argument is illustrated in more detail in Fig. 2-3. The effect is that $du\,dv$ can be replaced by $2\pi c\,dc$, so that the distribution law becomes

$$\frac{dN(c)}{N_0} = \frac{m}{kT}\left[\exp\left(-\frac{mc^2}{2kT}\right)\right]c\,dc. \tag{2-29}$$

The two-dimensional distribution law for c, Eq. (2-29), can now be plotted on an ordinary graph, since only the net velocity is involved; also we have lost the information as to whether c is positive or negative and plot only its magnitude. Some sample graphs, again for a gas of molecular weight 28, are shown in Fig. 2-4. Notice that there is now a nonzero most probable velocity, in contrast to the situation in Fig. 2-2. The reason is that, while the probability of individual velocity components u and v decreases with their increasing values, the number of ways in which a given velocity magnitude c can be made up of the u and v components increases in proportion to c. For a while the latter effect overrides the former. Notice also that the most probable c value increases with increasing temperature and that the half-width increases with increasing temperature.

The extension to three dimensions follows the same series of steps. The basic distribution law is

$$\frac{dN(u, v, w)}{N_0} = A\left\{\exp\left[-\frac{m(u^2 + v^2 + w^2)}{2kT}\right]\right\}du\,dv\,dw, \tag{2-30}$$

where w is the added velocity component in the z direction. This again can be factored into three integrals, so that the normalization constant becomes the cube of that for the one-dimensional gas, to give

$$\frac{dN(u, v, w)}{N_0} = \left(\frac{m}{2\pi kT}\right)^{3/2}\left\{\exp\left[-\frac{m(u^2 + v^2 + w^2)}{2kT}\right]\right\}du\,dv\,dw. \tag{2-31}$$

Again the chief interest is in the net velocity, now given by $c^2 = u^2 + v^2 + w^2$,

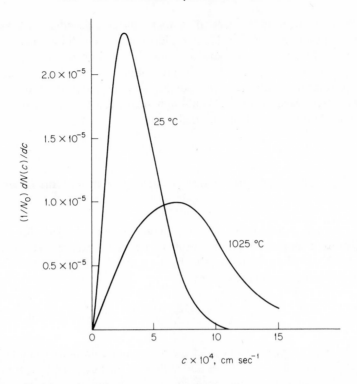

Fig. 2-4.   *Molecular velocity distribution for* N_2 *in two dimensions.*

and the number of ways in which a velocity increment dc can be obtained is related to the separate increments by

$$4\pi c^2 \, dc = du \, dv \, dw.$$

The distribution law in net velocity c is then

$$p(c) = \frac{dN(c)}{N_0 \, dc} = 4\pi \left(\frac{m}{2\pi kT}\right)^{3/2} \left[\exp\left(-\frac{mc^2}{2kT}\right)\right] c^2. \qquad (2\text{-}32)$$

This distribution is plotted in Fig. 2-5 and looks much like the one for a two-dimensional gas. The maximum or position of most probable velocity has moved outward, however. This most probable velocity c_p may be evaluated analytically if $dp(c)/dc$ is set equal to zero. On doing this, one obtains from Eq. (2-32) the condition

$$-\frac{m}{2kT}\left[\exp\left(-\frac{mc_p^2}{2kT}\right)\right](2c_p)(c_p^2) + \left[\exp\left(-\frac{mc_p^2}{2kT}\right)\right](2c_p) = 0$$

or

$$c_p^2 = \frac{2kT}{m}. \qquad (2\text{-}33)$$

53

As a final comment on the general character of these distribution laws, we note that the probability of a given velocity rapidly decreases with increasing c owing to the exponential term. There is, however, always a finite probability for any given velocity, no matter how large. For example, the fraction of molecules per unit velocity increment having a velocity of $5c_p$ is only about 10^{-10} of that having velocity c_p itself. Such a number, although small, can be quite significant when chemical reaction rates are being treated.

2-4 Average Quantities from the Distribution Laws

It is a common experience to take the average of some property for a collection of objects. For example, the average value of a coin in a bag of mixed coins would be obtained by dividing the total value by the number of coins. In more detail, the operation is one of dividing two sums:

$$\bar{s} = \frac{\sum s_i N_i}{\sum N_i}.$$

(2-34)

That is, the product of the value s_i of the ith type of coin times the number N_i of such coins is summed over all types and is then divided by $\sum N_i$, the total number of coins. The average of any property could be obtained in this way; if s denotes the mass of a given type of coin, then $\bar{s}$ would now be the average mass of a coin, and so on.

If there are a very large number of objects with many gradations of the property s, then these summations can be approximated by an integration procedure. The principal change is that N_i is now replaced by a probability or distribution function $p(s)$, where $dp(s)$ gives the chance of finding objects with s lying between s and $s + ds$:

$$\bar{s} = \frac{\int_0^\infty s \, dp(s)}{\int_0^\infty dp(s)} = \frac{1}{N_0} \int_0^\infty s \, dp(s).$$

(2-35)

The integral $\int_0^\infty dp(s)$ simply represents the sum of all objects and must therefore equal N_0, their total number.

We can apply Eq. (2-35) to obtain two important types of average velocity for the three-dimensional case. The first is simply the average velocity $\bar{c}$ given by

$$\bar{c} = \frac{1}{N_0} \int_0^\infty c \, dN(c)$$

or

$$\bar{c} = 4\pi \left(\frac{m}{2\pi kT}\right)^{3/2} \int_0^\infty \left[\exp\left(-\frac{mc^2}{2kT}\right)\right] c^3 \, dc.$$

(2-36)

The integral may be evaluated as follows. We let $x = mc^2/2kT$, and so obtain

$$\bar{c} = 4\pi\left(\frac{m}{2\pi kT}\right)^{3/2} 2\left(\frac{kT}{m}\right)^2 \int_0^\infty xe^{-x}\,dx. \tag{2-37}$$

The integral is now a standard one known as a gamma function[†] and its value is just unity. The resulting expression for $\bar{c}$ is thus

$$\bar{c} = \left(\frac{8kT}{\pi m}\right)^{1/2} \tag{2-38}$$

The second average is that of c^2; this is given by

$$\overline{c^2} = 4\pi\left(\frac{m}{2\pi kT}\right)^{3/2} \int_0^\infty \left[\exp\left(-\frac{mc^2}{2kT}\right)\right]c^4\,dc. \tag{2-39}$$

When we let $x = mc^2/2kT$ the integral reduces to one of the form $\int_0^\infty x^{3/2}e^{-x}\,dx$, again a gamma function, and one whose value is $\frac{3}{4}\sqrt{\pi}$ [see the footnote following Eq. (2-37)]. On working through the algebra, we find

$$\overline{c^2} = \frac{3kT}{m}, \tag{2-40}$$

or, alternatively, the average molar kinetic energy E is then

$$E = \tfrac{3}{2}RT. \tag{2-41}$$

Note that the right-hand sides of Eqs. (2-6) and (2-41) are identical. Thus the average velocity referred to in the introductory section is really the square root of the average of velocities squared, $(\overline{c^2})^{1/2}$, or the root mean square velocity. Another important point is as follows. The derivation of the Boltzmann equation in Section 2-2 led to Eq. (2-11) in which the exponent could only be said to involve a constant, β, times ϵ. The entire development of the preceding and present sections could have been carried out with this indeterminate form of the Boltzmann distribution equation. Equation (2-40) would then have come out in the form

$$\overline{c^2} = \frac{3}{\beta m}. \tag{2-42}$$

At this point, a comparison of Eqs. (2-6) and (2-42) would have identified β as equal to $1/kT$ and completed the derivation of the Boltzmann equation (2-7). A formal treatment would have proceeded in such a manner, but the approach used here seemed easier to follow.

[†] Integrals of the type $\int_0^\infty x^{n-1}e^{-x}\,dx$ occur frequently in physical chemistry; this integral is called the gamma function $\Gamma(n)$. Standard tables of $\Gamma(n)$ are available for $0 < n < 1$ and $1 < n < 2$; some important values are $\Gamma(1/2) = \sqrt{\pi}$ and $\Gamma(1) = 1$. Also, a very useful relationship is $\Gamma(n+1) = n\Gamma(n)$ for n a positive integer.

In conclusion to this section, the three characteristic velocities for a gas in three dimensions are

most probable $\quad c_{\mathrm{p}} \quad = \left(\dfrac{2kT}{m}\right)^{1/2}$ [Eq. (2-33)],

average $\qquad \bar{c} \quad = \left(\dfrac{8kT}{\pi m}\right)^{1/2} = 1.13c_{\mathrm{p}}$ [Eq. (2-38)],

root mean square $\quad (\overline{c^2})^{1/2} = \left(\dfrac{3kT}{m}\right)^{1/2} = 1.22c_{\mathrm{p}}$ [Eq. (2-40)].

These three velocities are located on one of the distributions of Fig. 2-5 so as to show their relative positions.

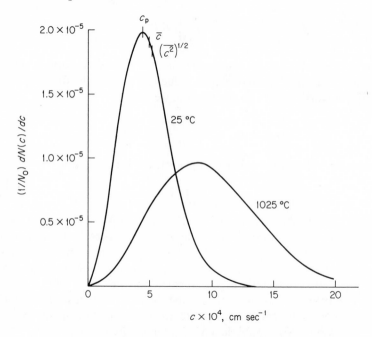

Fig. 2-5. *Three-dimensional velocity distribution for* N_2.

2-5   Some Applications of Simple Kinetic Molecular Theory. Collision Frequency on a Plane Surface and Graham's Law

An important quantity given by simple kinetic molecular theory is the frequency with which molecules hit a plane surface. This frequency is, for example, central to the kinetic treatment of adsorption–desorption processes or, more generally, to those of evaporation and condensation.

The relationship can be derived fairly simply as follows. Since all directions in space should be equivalent, the result should be independent of direction; we can therefore assume that the molecules impinging on a plane surface are doing so from the x direction, so that only their velocity components in that direction need be considered. The distribution law for such x components is given by Eq. (2-25):

$$\frac{d\mathbf{n}(u)}{\mathbf{n}_0} = \left(\frac{m}{2\pi kT}\right)^{1/2}\left[\exp\left(-\frac{mu^2}{2kT}\right)\right] du,$$

where $\mathbf{n}$ and $\mathbf{n}_0$ denote numbers of molecules per unit volume, $\mathbf{n}_0$ being the total concentration; $d\mathbf{n}(u)/\mathbf{n}_0$ is again the fraction of molecules having velocity between u and $u + du$.

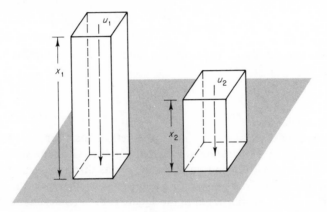

Fig. 2-6.   *Volumes swept out in unit time by molecular velocity groups u_1 and u_2 .*

As illustrated in Fig. 2-6, if we consider a particular group of molecules of velocity component u_1 , the ones that will reach the surface in the next second will be those within the distance x_1 , where $x_1 = u_1$. Per unit area of surface, the total number of molecules of this velocity group reaching the surface per second will then be $\mathbf{n}(u_1)u_1$ (since u_1 times the unit area gives the volume containing the successful molecules of that velocity group). For some other group of, say, lower velocity u_2 the number of that group reaching the surface per second will be $\mathbf{n}(u_2)u_2$. In effect, then, we need to weight the distribution equation by u to get $dZ(u)$, the number of molecules per unit volume reaching the wall whose velocity component lies between u and $u + du$:

$$dZ(u) = \mathbf{n}_0\left(\frac{m}{2\pi kT}\right)^{1/2}\left[\exp\left(-\frac{mu^2}{2kT}\right)\right]u\, du. \qquad (2\text{-}43)$$

We obtain Z, the total surface collision frequency per unit area, by integrating over all acceptable values of u, namely from zero to plus infinity, where a plus velocity is one toward the surface. On carrying out this integration, we obtain

$$Z = \mathbf{n}\left(\frac{kT}{2\pi m}\right)^{1/2} \tag{2-44}$$

(the subscript to the concentration $\mathbf{n}$ is no longer needed).

Equation (2-44) can be phrased in some alternative ways. On referring to Eq. (2-38) for the average velocity $\bar{c}$, we see that

$$Z = \tfrac{1}{4}\mathbf{n}\bar{c}. \tag{2-45}$$

Alternatively, the kinetic molecular theory at this level of sophistication implies ideal gas behavior, and since the concentration $\mathbf{n}$ is then equal to P/kT, we have

$$Z = P\left(\frac{1}{2\pi mkT}\right)^{1/2} = PN_0\left(\frac{1}{2\pi MRT}\right)^{1/2}. \tag{2-46}$$

Finally, the mass collision frequency Z_m follows if Z is multiplied by the mass per molecule:

$$Z_m = \rho\left(\frac{kT}{2\pi m}\right)^{1/2}, \tag{2-47}$$

where ρ is the density.

The preceding discussion provides a theoretical basis for understanding a conclusion reached in 1829, known as *Graham's law*. Graham studied the rate of *effusion* of gases, that is, the rate of escape of gas through a small hole or orifice. He found that for a given temperature and pressure difference, the rate of effusion of a gas is inversely proportional to the square root of its density. For two different gases, then, we have

$$\frac{n_1}{n_2} = \left(\frac{\rho_2}{\rho_1}\right)^{1/2}, \tag{2-48}$$

where n denotes the number of moles escaping per unit time. Since the comparison is at a given pressure and temperature, an alternative form of Graham's law is

$$\frac{n_1}{n_2} = \left(\frac{M_2}{M_1}\right)^{1/2}, \tag{2-49}$$

where M is molecular weight.

Graham's law follows directly from Eq. (2-46) if it is assumed that in an effusion experiment the rate of passage of molecules through the hole is proportional to the rate at which they would be hitting the area of surface corresponding to the area of the hole. Effusion rates are thus often assumed to be given directly by Z. There is a problem in that, unless the hole is very small, there may be both a pressure and a temperature drop in its vicinity, which introduces a correction term dependent on the effusion rate and hence on the molecular weight of the gas.

It is also important in effusion that the flow be molecular, that is, the molecules should escape directly through the hole without collisions with the sides of the hole or with each other. Should such collisions occur, then some molecules will be reflected back into the vessel whence they came. The limiting case in which many molecular collisions occur as the gas flows through a channel is one of *diffusion*, a much slower process than effusion; and the limiting case in which molecules make many collisions with the sides of the hole, but not with each other, is called *Knudsen flow*, again a slower process than effusion.

A sample calculation is appropriate to illustrate the use of units and to give an order-of-magnitude appreciation of Z. Consider the case of a water surface at 25°C and in equilibrium with its vapor. At equilibrium the rates of evaporation and of condensation must be equal, and we can calculate the latter with the assumption that every vapor molecule hitting the surface sticks to become part of the liquid phase. The vapor pressure of water at 25°C is 23.76 Torr or 0.0313 atm or 3.17×10^4 dyn cm^{-2} or 3.17×10^3 N m^{-2}. The moles of collisions per square centimeter per second Z_n is then given by Eq. (2-46) as

$$Z_n = 3.17 \times 10^4 \left[\frac{1}{(2)(3.141)(18)(8.314 \times 10^7)(298.1)} \right]^{1/2}$$

$$= 0.0189 \quad \text{mole cm}^{-2} \text{ sec}^{-1}.$$

The frequency Z is then 1.14×10^{22} molecules cm^{-2} sec^{-1}. In the mks system (see Section 3-CN-2), P becomes 3.17×10^3 N m^{-2}, R is 8.314 J mole^{-1}, and N_0 is 6.023×10^{23} molecules mole^{-1}, so

$$Z_n = 3.17 \times 10^3 \left[\frac{1}{(2)(3.141)(0.018)(8.314)(298.1)} \right]^{1/2}$$

$$= 189 \quad \text{mole m}^{-2} \text{ sec}^{-1} = 1.14 \times 10^{26} \quad \text{molecule m}^{-2} \text{ sec}^{-1}.$$

This result carries the implication that the evaporation rate is also 1.14×10^{22} molecule cm^{-2} sec^{-1}. Now, an individual water molecule occupies about 10 Å^2 area or 10^{-15} cm^2 and the evaporation rate from this area is then 1.14×10^7 molecules sec^{-1}. Thus the lifetime of a surface water molecule must be about 10^{-7} sec, so that the water surface is far from quiescent on a molecular scale.

2-6 Bimolecular Collision Frequency and Mean Free Path

There are a number of important properties of a gas which we cannot explain without specifically invoking a molecular size. Clearly, the frequency of intermolecular collisions is one of these properties, as is the related quantity, the mean free path between collisions. It is less obvious perhaps, but equally true, that the explanations of properties such as viscosity, thermal conductivity, and diffusion rates also require the assumption of some finite molecular diameter.

The model that will be assumed at this point is that of a spherical molecule that can be treated as having a definite radius r and which undergoes elastic collisions. Using this "hard-sphere" model one neglects the fact that molecules are actually "soft," in that colliding molecules approach closer in a violent collision than in a mild one, and one also neglects intermolecular forces of attraction. Treatments not involving these approximations properly belong in advanced treatises. The derivations, even with these assumptions, will not be given here in full detail [see, for example, Moelwyn-Hughes (1961)]. Rigorous treatments will generally modify the derivations given here by only a small numerical factor, however.

A. Bimolecular Collision Frequency

The frequency of collisions between like molecules, Z_{11}, may be derived on a very simple basis. As illustrated in Fig. 2-7 we imagine a molecule of radius r_1 moving with an average velocity c_1. As it moves it will contact, that is, collide with, any second molecule lying within a cylinder of radius $2r_1$ (see also Fig. 1-12).

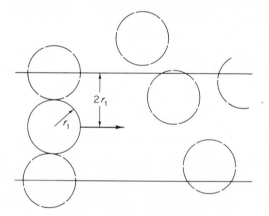

Fig. 2-7. *Molecular collision diameter.*

The volume swept out in each second is thus $\pi(2r_1)^2\bar{c}_1$ or $\pi\sigma_1^2\bar{c}_1$, where $\sigma_1 = 2r_1$ and is the collision diameter of the molecule, which is assumed to be spherical. If $\mathbf{n}_1$ is the concentration of molecules, then the average number of collisions per second is $\pi\sigma_1^2\bar{c}_1\mathbf{n}_1$. This gives Z_1, the frequency with which a given molecule collides with others. For all molecules in a unit volume we multiply Z_1 by $\mathbf{n}_1$ to get $\pi\sigma_1^2\bar{c}_1\mathbf{n}_1^2$, or Z_{11}.

This relationship for Z_{11} is correct except for a numerical constant. First, the argument counts collisions twice, and so a factor of one-half comes in. Second, the fact that the molecules are moving relative to each other introduces a correction factor of $2^{1/2}$ for both Z_1 and Z_{11}, so that the correct results are

$$Z_1 = 2^{1/2}\pi\sigma_1^2\bar{c}_1\mathbf{n}_1 = 4\sigma_1^2\left(\frac{\pi kT}{m}\right)^{1/2}\mathbf{n}_1 \qquad (2\text{-}50)$$

and

$$Z_{11} = \pi \left(\frac{1}{2}\right)^{1/2} \sigma_1{}^2 \bar{c}_1 n_1{}^2 = 2\sigma_1{}^2 \left(\frac{\pi kT}{m}\right)^{1/2} n_1{}^2. \qquad (2\text{-}51)$$

Z_{11} gives the collisions per unit volume per second and $\bar{c}$ is given by Eq. (2-38).

Although the derivation for collisions between like molecules gives a result which is correct except for the small correction factor, a somewhat more elaborate approach is needed to obtain the correct form for Z_{12}, the collision frequency between unlike molecules.

We now have two kinds of molecule, 1 and 2, and the frequency with which a single molecule of type 1 will collide with molecules of type 2 is

$$Z_{1(12)} = 2\sqrt{2}\, \sigma_{12}^2 \left(\frac{\pi kT}{\mu_{12}}\right)^{1/2} n_2. \qquad (2\text{-}52)$$

Here n_2 is the concentration of species 2 in molecules per unit volume, σ_{12} is the average collision diameter, $(\sigma_1 + \sigma_2)/2$, and μ_{12} is the reduced mass,

$$\mu_{12} = \frac{m_1 m_2}{m_1 + m_2}. \qquad (2\text{-}53)$$

The frequency of all collisions between the two types of molecule is then

$$Z_{12} = 2\sqrt{2}\, \sigma_{12}^2 \left(\frac{\pi kT}{\mu_{12}}\right)^{1/2} n_1 n_2. \qquad (2\text{-}54)$$

As an example of calculations using the collision frequency equations let us consider hydrogen and oxygen gases at 25°C. The respective σ values have been found to be 2.74 and 3.61 Å. First, if we have the separate gases each at 1 atm, then, assuming the ideal gas law, we find the concentration of each to be given by P/RT or $1/(82.06)(298.1)$, or 4.089×10^{-5} mole cm^{-3}, and the quantity $(\pi kT/m)^{1/2}$ is $[(3.141)(8.314 \times 10^7)(298.1)/(2)]^{1/2}$, or 1.973×10^5 cm sec^{-1} for hydrogen, and $[(3.141)(8.314 \times 10^7)(298.1)/32]^{1/2}$, or 4.934×10^4 cm sec^{-1}, for oxygen. [As a matter of convenience the equivalent expression $(\pi RT/M)^{1/2}$ was actually calculated.] We then have, from Eq. (2-50),

hydrogen: $Z_{H_2} = 4(2.74 \times 10^{-8})^2(1.97 \times 10^5)(4.09 \times 10^{-5})$
              $= 2.396 \times 10^{-14}$ mole sec^{-1}
              $= 1.440 \times 10^{10}$ collisions sec^{-1}.

oxygen: $Z_{O_2} = 4(3.61 \times 10^{-8})^2(4.934 \times 10^4)(4.09 \times 10^{-5})$
              $= 1.051 \times 10^{-14}$ mole sec^{-1}
              $= 6.336 \times 10^9$ collisions sec^{-1}.

Note that by using moles per cubic centimeter, c, we obtain Z_1 in moles of collisions per cubic centimeter per second. The bimolecular collision frequencies given by Eq. (2-51) are

hydrogen: $Z_{H_2-H_2} = \frac{1}{2}Z_{H_2}c_{H_2} = (1.457 \times 10^{10})(4.089 \times 10^{-5})(\frac{1}{2})$
              $= 2.979 \times 10^5$ mole cm^{-3} sec^{-1}.

oxygen: $Z_{O_2-O_2} = \frac{1}{2}Z_{O_2}c_{O_2} = (6.336 \times 10^9)(4.08 \times 10^{-5})(\frac{1}{2})$
              $= 1.295 \times 10^5$ mole cm^{-3} sec^{-1}.

To get Z_{11} in terms of moles of bimolecular collisions we include Avogadro's number N_0 as a factor. Thus if if $\mathbf{c}$ denotes number of moles per cubic centimeter, so that $\mathbf{c}_1 = \mathbf{n}_1/N_0$, then Eq. (2-51) becomes

$$Z_{11} = 2\sigma_1^2 \left(\frac{\pi k T}{m} \right)^{1/2} N_0 \mathbf{c}_1^2, \tag{2-55}$$

where Z_{11} is in moles of collisions per cubic centimeter.

Let us next consider a mixture of hydrogen and oxygen at 25°C and 2 atm total pressure, so each gas remains at 1 atm partial pressure. The value of σ_{12} is now the average value of (2.74 + 3.61)/2, or 3.175 Å, and μ_{12} is given by (2)(32)/(2 + 32), or 1.882 g mole^{-1}. The quantity $(\pi kT/\mu_{12})^{1/2}$ is thus close to that for hydrogen, 2.003×10^5 cm sec^{-1}, and $\mathbf{c}_{H_2} = \mathbf{c}_{O_2} = 4.089 \times 10^{-5}$ mole cm^{-3}. For this case of an equimolar mixture $Z_{H_2(H_2-O_2)}$ is the same as $Z_{O_2(H_2-O_2)}$ as given by Eq. (2-52):

$$Z_{H_2(H_2-O_2)} = Z_{O_2(H_2-O_2)} = (2)(2)^{1/2}(3.175 \times 10^{-8})^2 (2.003 \times 10^5)(4.089 \times 10^{-5})$$

$$= 2.335 \times 10^{-14} \quad \text{mole sec}^{-1} = 1.407 \times 10^{10} \text{ collisions sec}^{-1};$$

then, for $Z_{H_2-O_2}$, Eq. (2-54) gives

$$Z_{H_2-O_2} = (1.407 \times 10^{10})(4.089 \times 10^{-5}) = 5.75 \times 10^5 \quad \text{mole cm}^{-3} \text{ sec}^{-1}.$$

Two comments are necessary concerning this example. First, using the ideal gas law to calculate the $\mathbf{n}$ values while the equations for the Z quantities are based on the assumption of a finite molecular diameter is inconsistent. However, using an equation having an excluded volume term such as Eq. (1-42) to calculate the $\mathbf{n}$'s would have added length and no particular illumination to the discussion.

Second, there is a seeming chemical paradox. We know that the mixture of hydrogen and oxygen will explode if sparked. On the other hand, we also know from experience that in the absence of a spark or a catalyst the mixture would be indefinitely stable at 25°C. However, the mixture is inherently unstable; how is it then that no reaction occurs, in view of the very large frequency of hydrogen–oxygen collisions? The answer lies in the concept of chemical activation energy and is treated in Section 14-6.

B. Mean Free Path

As the name implies, the mean free path λ of a molecule is the average distance traveled between collisions. As a slightly intuitive definition, λ is just the mean velocity divided by the collision frequency, and so it follows from Eq. (2-50) that

$$\lambda = \frac{\bar{c}}{Z_1}$$

or

$$\lambda = \frac{1}{\sqrt{2}\,\pi\sigma^2 \mathbf{n}}. \tag{2-56}$$

Equation (2-56) applies to a gas consisting of a single molecular species, and, as they are not needed, the subscripts of Eq. (2-50) have been dropped. For an ideal gas the concentration in molecules per unit volume, **n**, is equal to P/kT, and an alternate form of Eq. (2-56) is

$$\lambda = \frac{kT}{\sqrt{2}\,\pi\sigma^2 P}.$$ (2-57)

The mean free path may also be calculated for, say, molecules of type 1 in a mixture of species 1 and 2. To obtain $\lambda_{1(12)}$, for example, we now divide $\bar{c}_1$ by the sum of Z_1 and $Z_{1(12)}$ as given by Eqs. (2-50) and (2-52):

$$\lambda_{1(12)} = \frac{\bar{c}_1}{Z_1 + Z_{1(12)}}.$$ (2-58)

We can continue the example of the preceding section by calculating the mean free paths of hydrogen and of oxygen at 1 atm pressure and 25°C. For each gas **n** is $(4.089 \times 10^{-5})(6.02 \times 10^{23})$ or 2.462×10^{19} molecules cm^{-3}, so we have

hydrogen: $\lambda_{H_2} = 1/\sqrt{2}\,(3.141)(2.74 \times 10^{-8})^2(2.462 \times 10^{19})$

$\qquad\qquad = 1.217 \times 10^{-5}$ cm.

oxygen: $\lambda_{O_2} = 1/\sqrt{2}(3.141)(3.61 \times 10^{-8})^2(2.462 \times 10^{19})$

$\qquad\qquad = 7.015 \times 10^{-6}$ cm.

2-7 Transport Phenomena; Viscosity, Diffusion, and Thermal Conductivity

Transport phenomena, as the name implies, refer to the transport or spatial motion of some quantity. In the case of *viscosity* the quantity transported is momentum: in *diffusion* one deals with molecular transport or the drift of molecules from one place to another; in *thermal conductivity* one deals with the flow or transport of heat down a temperature gradient. The three quantities have much in common and the kinetic molecular theory treatment of them leads to somewhat similar equations.

A. Viscosity

The *coefficient of viscosity* η of a fluid is defined as a measure of the friction that is present when adjacent layers of the fluid are moving at different speeds. For example, if a fluid is flowing between parallel plates, as illustrated in Fig. 2-8(a), we ordinarily assume that the material immediately adjacent to the walls is stationary; the material farther away then moves increasingly rapidly. The arrows in the figure give this velocity profile. Alternatively, if the fluid is stationary but the walls are moving with equal and opposite velocities, the velocities of various

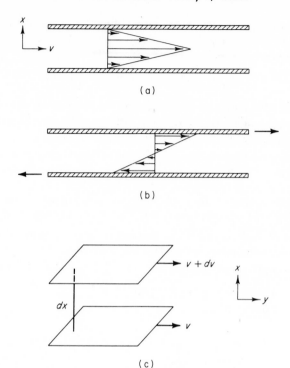

Fig. 2-8.   *Velocity profiles and defining model for viscosity.*

layers of the fluid are as shown in Fig. 2-8(b). If we now consider two layers of fluid parallel to the walls and separated by distance dx, then, as indicated in Fig. 2-8(c), their velocities will differ by dv or alternatively by $(dv/dx)\,dx$. If the area of each layer is $\mathscr{A}$, then the frictional drag or force f between the layers is given by η and

$$f = \eta \mathscr{A} \frac{dv}{dx}. \tag{2-59}$$

Equation (2-59) is in fact the defining equation for the coefficient of viscosity and is known as *Newton's law of viscosity*. In the cgs system the unit of viscosity is the *poise* (abbreviated P, and equivalent to grams per centimeter per second). The unit is a relatively large one; ordinary gases have viscosities of 10^{-3}–10^{-4} P and liquids of around 10^{-2} P. The reciprocal of viscosity is called the *fluidity*.

The experiment corresponding directly to the defining equation (2-59), namely that of measuring the drag between oppositely moving plates, is not a convenient one. More often one determines instead the pressure drop required to produce a given fluid flow rate down a cylindrical tube. The appropriate equation, derived in Section 8-ST-2, is

$$\eta = \frac{\pi(P_1 - P_2)r^4 t}{8Vl}, \tag{2-60}$$

where $P_2 - P_1$ is the pressure drop down the tube, usually a capillary, of radius r and length l; and V is the volume of fluid flowing in time t. In the case of gases V is a strong function of pressure, and in application of the equation V should be evaluated at the average pressure $(P_1 + P_2)/2$. Equation (2-60) is known as the *Poiseuille equation.*

The coefficient of viscosity of a gas may be derived theoretically, and the derivation that follows represents one of the triumphs of early kinetic molecular theory. The experimental observation was that the viscosity of a gas does not vary appreciably with pressure; this was very hard to understand on an intuitive basis, since it seemed that the denser a gas, the greater should be its viscosity. Kinetic molecular theory provided the explanation.

In simple theory molecules of a gas do not interact except by means of collisions, and these occur on the average only after a free flight distance given by the mean free path λ. The theoretical picture is then one of molecules moving in free flight back and forth between adjacent layers of gas, the layers being separated on the average by the distance λ. As illustrated in Fig. 2-9, a molecule of layer 1 will have a

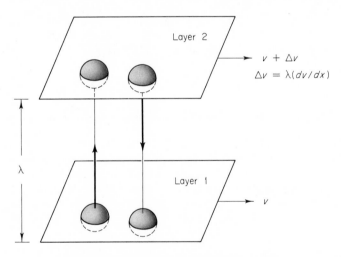

Fig. 2-9. *Model for calculation of gas viscosity.*

velocity component v corresponding to the average flow velocity of the gas in that layer. On arriving at layer 2 the molecule then experiences a collision which delivers the directional momentum mv to the molecules of that layer. Since these have on the average a net velocity component of $v + \Delta v$, corresponding to the layer velocity of layer 2, the net momentum loss realized in layer 2 is $m\,\Delta v$. The same momentum transfer occurs with opposite sign when a counterpart molecule of layer 2 arrives at layer 1.

If we consider each layer to be of area $\mathscr{A}$, then by the surface collision formula (2-46), the number of molecules arriving each second at layer 2 from layer 1 will be $\frac{1}{4}n\bar{c}\mathscr{A}$, and likewise the number of counterpart molecules arriving at layer 1 from layer 2. The total momentum transport per second is then

$$\frac{d(mv)}{dt} = \frac{\mathscr{A}(2)}{4} \mathbf{n}\bar{c}m \, \varDelta v. \tag{2-61}$$

By Newton's law a portion of matter, in this case a layer, acted on by a force shows a momentum change with time, and $d(mv)/dt$ due to the interchange of momentum by the gas molecules will appear as an equivalent force f acting between the layers. Also, since $\varDelta v$ is given by $\lambda(dv/dx)$, we can write

$$f = \mathscr{A}\left(\frac{\mathbf{n}\bar{c}m\lambda}{2}\right)\frac{dv}{dx}. \tag{2-62}$$

Equation (2-62) has the same form as the defining equation for viscosity, Eq. (2-59), and on comparing the two equations, we conclude that

$$\eta = \tfrac{1}{2}\mathbf{n}\bar{c}\lambda m. \tag{2-63}$$

Further, since $\mathbf{n}m$ gives the density of the gas, we have

$$\eta = \tfrac{1}{2}\rho\bar{c}\lambda. \tag{2-64}$$

A yet more instructive form is obtained on elimination of λ between Eqs. (2-64) and (2-56):

$$\eta = \frac{m\bar{c}}{2\sqrt{2}\,\pi\sigma^2}, \tag{2-65}$$

or, using Eq. (2-38) for $\bar{c}$,

$$\eta = \frac{1}{\pi\sigma^2}\left(\frac{kTm}{\pi}\right)^{1/2}. \tag{2-66}$$

This last form shows explicitly that although gas viscosity depends on $T^{1/2}$, it is independent of any change in pressure or density at constant temperature. The physical rationale of this result is that, whereas the frequency of molecules moving back and forth between layers increases in proportion to the pressure, the mean free path, or effective distance between layers, decreases in proportion to the pressure and the two effects just cancel with respect to the momentum transport per unit distance.

Referring to the example in Section 2-6B, we see that the value of λ for a gas around 1 atm and 25°C is about 10^{-5} cm, while $\bar{c}$ at 25°C is about 10^5 cm sec^{-1}. The molar volume of a gas under these conditions is about 30 liters, so for a gas such as oxygen, the density would be about 10^{-3} g cm^{-3}. Thus, from Eq. (2-64), the viscosity would be around 10^{-3} P.

B. Diffusion

Diffusion is a process of spatial drift of molecules due to their kinetic motion; the physical picture is one of successive small, random movements. The process is often referred to as a random walk, the analogy being to a person taking successive steps but with each step unrelated in direction to the preceding one (the alternative scientific colloquialism is the "drunkard's walk"). A given molecule will then drift away from its original position in the course of time, and purely as a statistical effect there will be a net average drift rate from a more concentrated to a more dilute region. The matter is discussed in more detail in Section 10-7, but the defining phenomenological equation, known as Fick's law, is

$$J = -\mathscr{D}\,\frac{d\mathbf{n}}{dx},\qquad(2\text{-}67)$$

where J is this net drift expressed in molecules crossing unit area per second, and $d\mathbf{n}/dx$ is the concentration gradient in the drift direction. The coefficient $\mathscr{D}$ is known as the *diffusion coefficient*; in the cgs system its units are square centimeters per second. Diffusion coefficients for gases are around unity and for liquids are about 10^{-5} cm^2 sec^{-1} or less.

There is an alternative way of defining $\mathscr{D}$, suggested by Einstein. As illustrated in Fig. 2-10 a molecule will, as a result of its random walk, find itself some distance x from its starting point after an elapse of time t. Because we are not dealing with a direct velocity but with a molecular drift, x increases only as $t^{1/2}$.

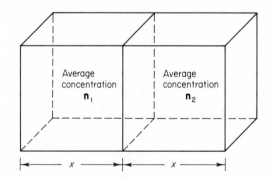

Average concentration $\mathbf{n}_1$

Average concentration $\mathbf{n}_2$

Fig. 2-10. *Random walk.*   Fig. 2-11. *Here $\mathbf{n}_1$ and $\mathbf{n}_2$ are average concentrations.*

This conclusion can be demonstrated as follows. We consider a situation in which there is a concentration gradient in one direction only, as in the case of diffusion along the length of a long tube or cell. There will be some average distance x which a molecule will diffuse along the tube in time t. If we take a reference cross section, then, as illustrated in Fig. 2-11, half of the molecules within a distance x on either side will cross the reference plane in time t. The diffusional flow from left to right is therefore $\frac{1}{2}\mathbf{n}_1 x$, while that from right to left is $\frac{1}{2}\mathbf{n}_2 x$. In the cgs system both are in moles per square centimeter per second.

Since $\mathbf{n}_2 = \mathbf{n}_1 + x(d\mathbf{n}/dx)$, where $d\mathbf{n}/dx$ is the concentration gradient, the *net* flux across the reference plane is

$$ J = \frac{1}{t}\left[\frac{1}{2}\,\mathbf{n}_1 x - \frac{x}{2}\left(\mathbf{n}_1 + x\,\frac{d\mathbf{n}}{dx}\right)\right] = -\frac{x^2}{2t}\frac{d\mathbf{n}}{dx}. \tag{2-68} $$

Comparison with Eq. (2-67) gives

$$ \mathscr{D} = \frac{x^2}{2t}. \tag{2-69} $$

Equation (2-69) allows a very simple derivation of $\mathscr{D}$ from kinetic molecular theory. Although the displacement x can be the net result of many random steps, it can also be put equal to the smallest step which is random with respect to suceeding ones. This smallest step is the mean free path distance λ. During such a step the molecule is moving with velocity $\bar{c}$, so the average time between steps is just $\lambda/\bar{c}$. On substituting $x = \lambda$ and $t = \lambda/\bar{c}$ into Eq. (2-69) we get

$$ \mathscr{D} = \frac{1}{2}\lambda\bar{c}. \tag{2-70} $$

For a gas at 1 atm and 25°C, λ was found in Section 2-6B to be about 10^{-5} cm, and since molecular velocities at 25°C are about 10^5 cm sec^{-1}, typical values of $\mathscr{D}$ are around 1 cm² sec^{-1}.

Equation (2-70) applies to the interdiffusion of molecules of a single kind. Such a diffusion is called *self-diffusion*, and can be measured experimentally by the use of isotopic labeling. That is, in the experiment corresponding to Fig. 2-11, there can be no overall pressure gradient since otherwise there would be a wind or viscous flow of gas. However, labeling the molecules on, say, the left of the reference plane, makes possible the measurement of their net diffusion migration across it even though the total concentration of all molecules is uniform.

The case of interdiffusion of molecules in a mixture of gases will not be treated here, because of its complexity. The general situation is that now each type of molecule has its own mean free path and intrinsic diffusional drift. Because of the differing drift rates, a pressure gradient does develop until balanced by an opposite bulk flow or wind. The observed interdiffusion or mutual diffusion coefficient is determined by the intrinsic diffusion rate as modified by the bulk flow.

C.   Thermal Conductivity

The phenomenological equation for thermal conductivity, or the equation analogous to Newton's law for viscous flow, Eq. (2-59), and to Fick's law for diffusional flow, Eq. (2-67), is attributed to Fourier and is

$$ J = -\kappa\,\frac{dT}{dx}, \tag{2-71} $$

where J is now the flow of heat per second across unit area perpendicular to a temperature gradient dT/dx. The quantity κ is the *coefficient of thermal conductivity*.

The kinetic molecular theory analysis is quite similar to that for viscosity. Again the picture is one of molecules moving back and forth between planes a distance λ apart, but now planes 1 and 2 of Fig. 2-9 are at different temperatures. Molecules from plane 1 carry energy ϵ_1 and those from plane 2 carry energy ϵ_2 and if the collision at the end of a mean free path results in complete energy exchange, the energy transported is then $\lambda \, d\epsilon/dx$. Following the same arguments as for Eqs. (2-61) and (2-62), we write

$$-J = \frac{d\epsilon}{dt} = \frac{2\mathbf{n}\bar{c}\lambda}{4} \frac{d\epsilon}{dx}$$

or

$$J = -\frac{\mathbf{n}\bar{c}\lambda}{2} \frac{d\epsilon}{dT} \frac{dT}{dx}. \tag{2-72}$$

The thermal conductivity coefficient is, on comparison with Eq. (2-71),

$$\kappa = \frac{\mathbf{n}\bar{c}\lambda}{2} \frac{d\epsilon}{dT}. \tag{2-73}$$

The quantity $d\epsilon/dT$ is simply the molar heat capacity of the gas (at constant volume) C_V, or mc_V, where c_V is the heat capacity per unit mass. Equation (2-73) then becomes

$$\kappa = \tfrac{1}{2}\mathbf{n}\bar{c}\lambda mc_V, \tag{2-74}$$

or, invoking the equation for viscosity, Eq. (2-63),

$$\kappa = \tfrac{1}{2}\rho\bar{c}\lambda c_V = \eta c_V. \tag{2-75}$$

Molar heat capacities for gases are about 5 cal deg^{-1} mole^{-1}, and for a gas such as oxygen c_V would then be about 0.17 cal deg^{-1} g^{-1}. Since in this case η is about 10^{-3} P, κ is about 1.7×10^{-4} in cgs units.

2-8 *Summary of Kinetic Molecular Theory Quantities*

A variety, perhaps a bewildering variety, of quantities have been derived from the kinetic molecular model for gases. The following discussion is intended to summarize these in an organized way so that a general picture can emerge. First are the fundamental Boltzmann distribution functions and the various average velocities derived from them. Immediate applications are the identification of the average kinetic energy with $\tfrac{3}{2}kT$ and the derivation of the surface or wall collision frequency and its application to effusion.

Table 2-2. *Summary of Kinetic Molecular Theory Quantities*[a]

Symbol	Quantity	Formula	Equation number	Approximate value[b]
$p(c)$	Three-dimensional distribution law	$4\pi(m/2\pi kT)^{3/2}[\exp(-mc^2/2kT)]c^2$	(2-32)	—
c_p	Most probable velocity	$(2kT/m)^{1/2}$	(2-33)	1.24×10^5 cm sec^{-1}
$\bar{c}$	Average velocity	$(8kT/\pi m)^{1/2}$	(2-38)	1.40×10^5 cm sec^{-1}
$(\overline{c^2})^{1/2}$	Root mean square velocity	$(3kT/m)^{1/2}$	(2-40)	1.52×10^5 cm sec^{-1}
Z	Surface collision frequency	$\frac{1}{4}n\bar{c}$	(2-45)	1.43 moles cm^{-2} sec^{-1}
Z_1	Collision frequency for a molecule	$4\sigma_1^2(\pi kT/m)^{1/2}\mathbf{n}_1$	(2-50)	2.00×10^{10} collisions sec^{-1}
λ	Mean free path	$1/\sqrt{2}\,\pi\sigma^2\mathbf{n}$	(2-56)	7.02×10^{-6} cm
Z_{11}	Bimolecular collision frequency, like molecules	$2\sigma_1^2(\pi kT/m)^{1/2}\mathbf{n}_1^2$	(2-51)	4.09×10^5 moles cm^{-3} sec^{-1}
Z_{12}	Bimolecular collision frequency, unlike molecules	$2\sqrt{2}\,\sigma_{12}^2(\pi kT/\mu_{12})^{1/2}\mathbf{n}_1\mathbf{n}_2$	(2-54)	—
η	Viscosity coefficient	$\frac{1}{2}\rho\bar{c}\lambda$	(2-64)	6.44×10^{-4} P
$\mathscr{D}$	Self-diffusion coefficient	$\frac{1}{2}\bar{c}\lambda$	(2-70)	0.49 cm^2 sec^{-1}
κ	Thermal conductivity coefficient	$\frac{1}{2}\rho\bar{c}\lambda c_V$	(2-75)	1.01×10^{-4} cal cm^{-1} sec^{-1}

[a] Definition of symbols: m, mass per molecule; $\mathbf{n}$, molecules per unit volume; μ_{12}, reduced mass; ρ, density; c_V, heat capacity per unit mass; σ, collision diameter or $2r$.

[b] Calculated for a gas at 25°C and 1 atm, of molecular weight 32, and collision radius 3.61 Å.

Up to this point the finite size of molecules has been accepted, but has played no direct role in the treatments. That is, bimolecular collisions act to redistribute momenta and energies but do not change the overall statistical situation. Next, however, molecules are specifically considered to be hard spheres of definite radius r or collision diameter σ, which now permits the calculation of the various types of collision frequencies and mean free paths.

The three transport phenomena discussed involve the presence of a gradient in pressure, in concentration, or in temperature. The systems are no longer in equilibrium but it is assumed that the gradients are not such as to perturb the general distribution equations significantly. It is then possible to calculate the rate of mass flow, of concentration change, and of heat flow due to these gradients. The effect of intermolecular attractive forces is disregarded in all of these derivations.

The principal relationships are assembled in Table 2-2, together with the approximate values for the various quantities for a typical gas. The table can then be used, for example, to estimate the numerical value of a quantity for some other type of gas or condition.

Finally, in Table 2-3 are collected the experimentally measured values for the viscosity, self-diffusion, and thermal conductivity coefficients of some actual gases. These provide a means for testing the accuracy of the hard-sphere model.

Table 2-3. *Transport Coefficients for Various Gases at 1 atm[a]*

Gas	Collision diameter σ (Å)	Temperature (°K)	Self-diffusion coefficient $\mathscr{D}$ (cm² sec⁻¹)	Viscosity $10^4 \eta$ (P)	Coefficient of thermal conductivity $10^4 \kappa$ (cal cm⁻¹ sec⁻¹ deg⁻¹)
He	2.18	100	0.270[b]	0.951	1.744
		300	1.669[b]	1.981	3.583
Ar	3.64	100	0.023	0.815	0.154
		300	0.186	2.271	0.422
N_2	3.75	100	0.027	0.698	0.232[b]
		300	0.205	1.663	0.602[b]
		500	0.495[b]	2.657	0.876[b]
O_2	—	273.2	0.18	—	0.58
		280	—	1.959	—
CH_4	—	273.2	0.206	—	0.73
		280	—	1.052	—
		353.2	0.318	—	—
CO_2	—	273.2	0.0970	—	0.35
		280	—	1.402	—
HCl	—	295	0.1246	—	—

[a] From J. O. Hirschfelder, C. F. Curtiss, and R. B. Bird, "Molecular Theory of Gases and Liquids," corrected ed. Wiley, New York, 1964.
[b] Estimated values.

COMMENTARY AND NOTES

2-CN-1 *Some Further Comments on the Various Distribution Laws*

The distribution law in one dimension, Eq. (2-25),

$$\frac{dN(u)}{N_0} = \left(\frac{m}{2\pi kT}\right)^{1/2} \left[\exp\left(-\frac{mu^2}{2kT}\right)\right] du,$$

has the same functional form as an equation that is obtained in quite a different connection:

$$p(x) = \frac{1}{\sigma(2\pi)^{1/2}} \exp\left(-\frac{x^2}{2\sigma^2}\right). \tag{2-76}$$

Equation (2-76) follows from Eq. (2-25) if x is set equal to u and σ^2 to kT/m; it is known as the *normal error function*. The quantity σ is called the *standard deviation* (from the mean) and $p(x)$ is the probability of observing an error or departure x from the mean.

The normal error function is usually derived from consideration of the case of a measurement that is subject to cumulative error arising from the random effect of a large number of small errors, each of which may be positive or negative. For a large number of such measurements σ^2 has the alternative meaning of being the average of the squares of the deviations from the mean.

Equation (2-25) is thus an "error" curve for velocities in that it gives the chance of finding some given velocity or deviation from the most probable velocity. That is, if repeated samplings of a gas are made, the error curve gives the frequency with which different specific velocities are be observed. If a large number of such samplings are made, then σ^2 gives the average of the squares of the observed velocities, that is, the mean square velocity. Thus

$$\sigma^2 = \overline{u^2} = \frac{kT}{m}. \tag{2-77}$$

Equation (2-25) gives the velocity distribution for a one-dimensional gas, a rather fictitious substance. However, it also gives the distribution of the x-velocity components of a real gas. This is now a perfectly meaningful quantity; Eq. (2-25) was used, for example, in obtaining the surface collision frequency.

The distribution function for a two-dimensional gas, Eq. (2-28), corresponds to the product of two normal curves, and from a similar analysis we conclude that

$$\overline{u^2} + \overline{v^2} = \frac{2kT}{m}. \tag{2-78}$$

An important corollary is that the kinetic energy can be regarded as being made up of additive contributions from each velocity component:

x component:
$$\epsilon_{\substack{\text{kin.}\\1-\text{dim}}} = \tfrac{1}{2}m\overline{u^2}.$$

x and y components:
$$\epsilon_{\substack{\text{kin.}\\2-\text{dim}}} = \tfrac{1}{2}m\overline{u^2} + \tfrac{1}{2}m\overline{v^2}. \qquad (2\text{-}79)$$

x, y, and z components:
$$\epsilon_{\substack{\text{kin.}\\3-\text{dim}}} = \tfrac{1}{2}m\overline{u^2} + \tfrac{1}{2}m\overline{v^2} + \tfrac{1}{2}m\overline{w^2} = \tfrac{1}{2}m\overline{c^2}.$$

The total kinetic energy is equal to $\tfrac{3}{2}kT$ [by Eq. (2-41)]; the three components should be equal, so each must then contribute $\tfrac{1}{2}kT$.

As a final point, there is a situation in which one *can* think of a two-dimensional gas. This is the case of molecules absorbed at a solid or liquid surface; in effect, the interface provides a two-dimensional space in which the molecules move freely. Their average kinetic energy is then kT rather than $\tfrac{3}{2}kT$.

2-CN-2   *Verification of the Distribution Laws*

The Boltzmann distribution laws are, of course, verified indirectly by the agreement of experiment with various derived quantities, such as effusion rates or transport coefficients. A direct verification requires sampling a gas to obtain the actual frequency of occurrence of various molecular velocities.

Such experiments are quite difficult, but have been carried out (see Herzfeld and Smallwood, 1951). The usual experimental approach is to select molecules of a given velocity by requiring that they have a certain time of flight between two points.

A schematic arrangement for doing this is illustrated in Fig. 2-12. Molecules effusing from a small hole in a reservoir are first required to travel in a certain

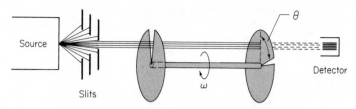

Fig. 2-12.   *Schematic velocity selector apparatus.*

direction by means of a succession of slits. The collimated beam now encounters a pair of disks mounted coaxially and rotating. Each disk has a slit in it and one sets the relative position of the slits and the speed of rotation. If the disks rotate at ω revolutions per second and the slits are θ degrees apart, then the second slit comes into position $\theta/\omega 360$ sec after the first one. Only those molecules in the beam that take $\theta/\omega 360$ sec to travel the distance between the disks will get through the slits.

One then varies this time-of-flight requirement and, by means of a detector, determines the relative numbers of molecules of various velocities. Accuracy is not high, but reasonable agreement with the expected distribution law has been found.

2-CN-3 Molecular Diameters; Avogadro's Number

The simple kinetic molecular theory treatment of transport phenomena leads to expressions for the viscosity coefficient η, self-diffusion coefficient $\mathcal{D}$, and thermal conductivity coefficient κ in which the only unknown is the collision diameter σ. The equations are summarized in Table 2-2.

The experimentally measured coefficients may then be used in calculations of molecular diameters. Some such results are given in Table 2-4 along with values calculated from the van der Waals constant b. The agreement is not bad, and this speaks well for the merits of the hard-sphere model as a first approximation. We find that the greatest discrepancy occurs with σ values from thermal conductivity; part of the difficulty is that with polyatomic molecules the heat capacity reflects both internal energy and kinetic energy, although it is largely the latter that is transferred in a collision. As a result c_V in Eq. (2-74) becomes a semiempirical quantity itself, along with σ.

In order to calculate σ from the kinetic molecular theory one must use the theoretical expression for λ, which requires knowing the value of **n**, the concentration expressed as molecules per unit volume. This in turn implies a knowledge

Table 2-4. *Molecular Diameters $(\mathring{A})^a$*

Gas	From gas viscosity	From self-diffusion	From van der Waals b constant[b]
Ar	3.64	3.47	5.7
N_2	3.75	3.48	5.0
O_2	3.61	3.35	2.6
CH_4	4.14	3.79	5.1
CO_2	4.63	4.28	5.1

[a] The experimental transport coefficients are from measurements at 0°C and 1 atm. The values from viscosity and self-diffusion are as given by J. O. Hirschfelder, C. F. Curtiss, and R. B. Bird, "Molecular Theory of Gases and Liquids," corrected ed., p. 545. Wiley, New York, 1964.
[b] The van der Waals b constant is taken to be $V_c/3$.

of Avogadro's number. Alternatively, one may use the van der Waals constant b, or some other independent measurement of molar volume, and, with some algebraic manipulation, combine this information with a measured viscosity or self-diffusion coefficient to obtain a value for Avogadro's number. Approximately correct answers result.

2-CN-4   *Transport Phenomena; Phenomenological Equations*

There are some aspects to the transport phenomena which provide an important illustration of the workings of the scientific method.

We start with an empirical observation, or law, which in this case is of the form

$$
\begin{aligned}
\text{rate of transport} &= (\text{constant})(\text{driving force}), \\
\text{rate of momentum transport} &= (\eta)(\text{velocity gradient}), \\
\text{rate of mass transport} &= (\mathscr{D})(\text{concentration gradient}), \\
\text{rate of heat transport} &= (\kappa)(\text{temperature gradient}).
\end{aligned}
\tag{2-80}
$$

The driving force in each instance is given by a gradient of an intensive property: velocity, concentration, or temperature. The quantity transported is an extensive property closely related to the intensive one: momentum, mass, or heat. Rate processes generally obey this form, particularly in systems not too far from equilibrium; the detailed elaboration of this observation by Lars Onsager won him a Nobel prize.

Second, having observed empirically that a relationship of the type of Eq. (2-80) is approximately obeyed by systems generally, and appears to be exactly obeyed under some limiting condition, one then uses the equation as a defining equation for the proportionality constant η, $\mathscr{D}$, or κ. The equations involve only macroscopic properties of the system and are thus phenomenological in nature. The definitions are unambiguously phrased in terms of experiment and are thus operational definitions (see Bridgman, 1946). The scientific method provides this procedure for defining quantities exactly without having to first supply any kind of theoretical explanation.

We have a similar situation with the ideal gas law. As a limiting law, we have the phenomenological statement that $PV = \text{constant}$ for any gas at a given temperature and in fact used this to define an absolute temperature scale.

Now the statement $PV/T = R$ is not exactly correct for a real gas. One could proceed by tabulating "R" values for real gases under various conditions. It is, of course, more convenient to use instead the deviation from unity of the compressibility factor PV/RT, or to use a virial expansion. A similar situation applies to transport phenomena. The defining equations (2-80) are not ordinarily obeyed exactly. Thus diffusion rates generally depend not just on the concentration gradient, but also on the actual level of concentration. As with the compressibility factor, we must report values of η, $\mathscr{D}$, or κ for a specified state of the gas.

The task of theory is then not only to explain the limiting laws but also to predict how the coefficients which they define should vary with the state of the system.

2-CN-5 Verification of the Kinetic Molecular Theory

The kinetic molecular theory is so well established that it may seem unnecessary to even raise the matter of its validity. However, the question of what is meant by the "validity" of a theory has subtleties which are worth illustrating in the present context.

A theory will always start with some sort of model. The model may be a physical picture; it may be a set of mathematical premises (as in wave mechanics). The first question to ask about a theory is whether there is evidence that the model is qualitatively correct. In the case of the kinetic molecular theory, we do have much evidence that matter comes in small units or molecules and, from the time-of-flight experiments mentioned earlier, that the molecules of a gas do have a velocity distribution.

The second question is whether the theory leads to the correct form or parametric dependence of the quantity treated. That is, does it give the phenomenological limiting law and does it give the observed approximate dependence of the coefficient in question on the state variables of the system? Again, kinetic molecular theory meets the test. It leads to relationships matching the defining equations for the various transport processes and correctly predicts the approximate dependence of η, $\mathscr{D}$, and κ on the state of the gas. It has been mentioned, for example, that one of the early triumphs of kinetic molecular theory was its prediction that viscosity should be independent of pressure.

The third, and in this discussion, final question to be asked of a theory is whether it predicts precisely how the theoretically derived quantity or coefficient varies with conditions. It is here that theories generally fail—even the best ones—presumably because the model is not adequate in detail.

Kinetic molecular theory, as developed in terms of the hard-sphere model, is no exception. Thus, as illustrated by the data of Table 2-4, the values of σ from viscosity and from diffusion measurements are not exactly the same. The theoretical parametric dependence is not exactly obeyed either. Equation (2-66) requires that viscosity be independent of pressure and although this is true of dilute gases, it ceases to be so for dense ones. The equation further predicts that viscosity should be proportional to $T^{1/2}$ and this is not quite correct, even for dilute gases. Thus the viscosity of oxygen at 200°K is 1.48×10^{-3} P and at 800°K is 4.12×10^{-3} P, considerably more than twice as much.

Such defects may be handled by recognizing that molecules do experience mutual attraction. By adding a suitable attractive potential, but still assuming hard spheres, Sutherland obtained the equation

$$\eta = \frac{\eta^0}{1 + (S/T)},$$ (2-81)

where S is an empirical constant. Equation (2-81) is quite successful in fitting viscosity data.

The yet more sophisticated modern approach is to use a detailed potential function for both attractive and repulsive forces, including, for diatomic and polyatomic molecules, a dependence on the relative orientation of approaching molecules. By now, the mathematical problems have become formidable and approximate computational methods have to be used.

In effect, one says at this point that the theory is exactly correct and that any quantitative defects can in principle be corrected by a suitably elaborate potential function. This is the terminal stage of development of a major theory. Its validity is taken for granted, and effort is concentrated on refinements of the model and on ways of avoiding mathematical approximations. What, then, is meant by the "validity" of a theory? Let the reader answer!

SPECIAL TOPICS

2-ST-1   Use of a Lennard–Jones Potential Function

It was mentioned in the preceding Commentary and Notes section that more elaborate treatments of transport phenomena make use of a potential function that allows for attractive forces, such as the widely used Lennard–Jones function described in the Special Topics section of Chapter 1. The function is [Eq. (1-70)]

$$\phi(r) = -\frac{\alpha}{r^6} + \frac{\beta}{r^{12}},$$

where the first term represents the attractive part of the potential and the second that of the repulsive part. Thus molecules are considered also to be somewhat "soft" in that the repulsion rises rapidly but not infinitely rapidly as two molecules come to within their collision diameter σ. Equation (1-70) is plotted in Fig. 1-17, in which are given the two characteristic quantities σ and ϕ^*. As a reminder, σ is now the internuclear separation at which ϕ is just zero and ϕ^* is the value of ϕ at the potential energy minimum.

In the more advanced treatment [see, for example, Hirschfelder *et al.* (1964)], it is necessary to consider in detail the trajectories of approaching molecules for various impact parameters **b**. As illustrated in Fig. 2-13, the *impact parameter* is

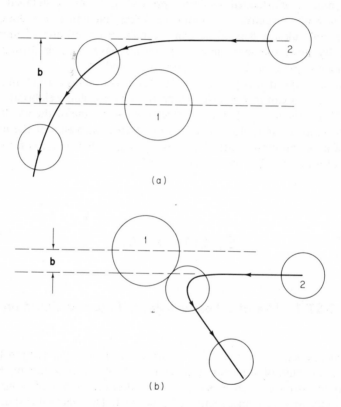

Fig. 2-13.   *Molecular trajectories in the presence of an attractive–repulsive potential.*

the minimum internuclear distance that a pair of approaching molecules would reach were there no interaction between them. The figure also illustrates the point that as a result of the attractive potential, molecule 2 may swing behind molecule 1 (taken as stationary) and thus be deflected. In the treatment of viscosity, for example, we need detailed calculations to obtain the average momentum exchange for all possible impact parameters, using the Lennard–Jones potential function. This averaging integration has been carried out, and the result can be expressed as a correction to Eq. (2-66):

$$\eta = \left[\frac{k^{1/2}}{\pi^{3/2} N_0^{1/2}} \right] \frac{(MT)^{1/2}}{\sigma^2 A(T)}, \tag{2-82}$$

where $A(T)$ is this integral, which is temperature-dependent, and the collection of constants has the value 2.72×10^{-5} for η in poise and σ in angstroms.

The function $A(T)$ obeys the principle of corresponding states in that it may be tabulated in terms of the reduced temperature $T^* = kT/\phi^*$. A plot of $A(T)$ versus T^* is given in Fig. 2-14. Actual viscosity data are now used in the calculation of the values of ϕ^*/k and σ which give the best fit for a given gas, and some of these values are collected in Table 2-5.

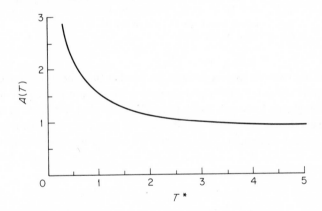

Fig. 2-14. *Viscosity parameter A(T) [Eq. (2-82)] as a function of T*. (Data from J. O. Hirschfelder, C. F. Curtiss, and R. B. Bird, "Molecular Theory of Gases and Liquids," corrected ed. Wiley, New York, 1964.)*

For example, the viscosity for CO_2 at 800°K would be calculated as follows. Since, from Table 2-5, ϕ^*/k is 190, it follows that $T^* = 800/190 = 4.21$; from Fig. 2-14, $A(T)$ is then 0.960. Also, from Table 2-5 we find $\sigma = 4.00$ Å. Substitution into Eq. (2-82) gives

$$\eta = \frac{2.72 \times 10^{-5}(44.0)^{1/2}(800)^{1/2}}{(4.00)^2(0.960)} = 3.32 \times 10^{-4} \quad \text{P.}$$

The experimental value is 3.29×10^{-4} P.

Note that $A(T)$ is not a function of pressure or of gas density. This is because the gas has been assumed to be sufficiently dilute that it is only during actual bimolecular collisions that the potential function exerts an influence. Alternatively,

Table 2-5. *Parameters for the Lennard–Jones Potential from Viscosity Coefficients*[a]

Gas	ϕ^*/k (°K)	σ (Å)
Ar	124	3.42
Kr	190	3.61
N_2	91.5	3.68
O_2	113	3.43
CH_4	137	3.82
CO_2	190	4.00

[a] From J. O. Hirschfelder, C. F. Curtiss, and R. B. Bird, "Molecular Theory of Gases and Liquids," corrected ed. Wiley, New York, 1964.

one is neglecting trimolecular collisions. Note also that the σ parameters of Table 2-5 are not quite the same as the corresponding ones given in Table 1-6. The latter were obtained when a Lennard–Jones potential treatment was fitted to the observed second virial coefficients of the gases. This discrepancy illustrates the point that even the more advanced treatments are approximate and retain a semiempirical aspect.

GENERAL REFERENCES

HIRSCHFELDER, J. O., CURTISS, C. F., AND BIRD, R. B. (1964). "Molecular Theory of Gases and Liquids," corrected ed. Wiley, New York.

KAUZMANN, W. (1966). "Kinetic Theory of Gases." Benjamin, New York.

TAYLOR, H. S. (1931). "A Treatise on Physical Chemistry," 2nd ed. Van Nostrand–Reinhold, Princeton, New Jersey.

CITED REFERENCES

BLINDER, S. M. (1969). "Advanced Physical Chemistry." Macmillan, New York.

BRIDGMAN, P. (1946). "The Nature of Modern Physics." Macmillan, New York.

HERZFELD, K. F., AND SMALLWOOD, H. (1951). "A Treatise on Physical Chemistry" (H. S. Taylor and S. Glasstone, eds.), 3rd ed., Vol. 2. Van Nostrand–Reinhold, Princeton, New Jersey.

MOELWYN-HUGHES, E. A. (1961). "Physical Chemistry." Pergamon, Oxford.

Exercises

The student is reminded to make a consistent choice of units in carrying out the following calculations.

2-1 Calculate the fraction of O_2 molecules per unit velocity interval, $(1/N_0) \, dN(u)/du$, having velocity u such that their kinetic energy in one dimension is equal to kT at 25°C. Repeat the calculation in two and in three dimensions where, in each case, the velocity c is such that the corresponding kinetic energy is kT at 25°C.

Ans. 0.527×10^{-5}, 1.87×10^{-5}, 2.11×10^{-5}.

2-2 Repeat the calculations in Exercise 2-1, but taking the one-, two-, and three-dimensional velocities to be 10^5 cm sec^{-1}.

Ans. 2.25×10^{-8}, 2.03×10^{-7}, 5.81×10^{-7}.

2-3 Calculate the values of c_p, $\bar{c}$, and the root mean square velocity for argon gas at (a) 25°C and (b) 200°C.

Ans. (a) 3.52×10^4, 3.98×10^4, 4.32×10^4
and (b) 4.44×10^4, 5.01×10^4, and 5.44×10^4 (all in cm sec^{-1}).

2-4 Consider N_2 gas at 77°K and 0.1 atm pressure. Calculate (a) $\bar{c}$, (b) **n**, (c) Z in moles per square centimeter per second hitting a surface, and (d) Z_m in grams per square centimeter per second hitting a surface.

Ans. (a) 2.41×10^4 cm sec^{-1}, (b) 9.53×10^{18} molecules cm^{-3},
(c) 0.0953 mole cm^{-2} sec^{-1}, (d) 2.67 g cm^{-2} sec^{-1}.

2-5 From Exercise 2-4, if every N_2 molecule that strikes the surface sticks and each N_2 molecule occupies 16 Å^2, how long should it take for an initially clean surface to be 1% covered with nitrogen?

Ans. 1.10×10^{-10} sec.

2-6 An evacuated bulb has a pinhole of 1×10^{-4} cm^2 area. How many moles of air ($M_{av} = 29$ g mole^{-1}) should leak into the bulb per minute at 25°C?

Ans. 0.00282 mole min^{-1}.

2-7 An astronaut's spacesuit has a pinhole leak. If the suit contains air of normal composition, what should be the composition of the gas escaping into space from the pinhole, according to Graham's law?

Ans. 18.95% oxygen.

2-8 What is the collision frequency in air at 25°C (a) between oxygen molecules, (b) between N_2 molecules? Take the collision diameters to be 3.61 Å for O_2 and 3.75 Å for N_2.

Ans. $Z_{O_2-O_2} = 5.18 \times 10^3$ mole cm^{-3} sec^{-1}, $Z_{N_2-N_2} = 9.55 \times 10^4$ mole cm^{-3} sec^{-1}.

2   Kinetic Molecular Theory of Gases

2-9   Calculate the frequency of O_2–N_2 collisions under the conditions of Exercise 2-8.

Ans. 4.45×10^4 mole cm^{-3} sec^{-1}.

2-10   For good insulation the pressure in the evacuated space of a Dewar or thermos flask should be reduced to the point that the mean free path is greater than the distance between the walls. What should the pressure of air be at 25°C if the mean free path is to equal 0.5cm?

Ans. 1.336×10^{-5} atm. (We estimate from Exercise 2-8 that σ_{av} is 3.70 Å.)

2-11   Calculate the mean free path of argon gas at 10^{-11} atm (an obtainable pressure under modern ultrahigh-vacuum conditions) and 0°C, taking σ to be 3.64 Å.

Ans. 6.32×10^5 cm.

2-12   The viscosity of air at 0°C is 1.71×10^{-4} P. What should the volume flow rate of air be, in liter sec^{-1} through a capillary tube 10 m long and 0.1 mm in radius if the pressure drop is 15 atm?

Ans. 3.44×10^{-4} liter sec^{-1}.

2-13   Calculate σ_{av} for air using information supplied in Exercise 12.

Ans.   3.76 Å. (We use 1.71×10^{-4} P as the viscosity of air at 0°C.)

2-14   Calculate the self-diffusion coefficient for helium at STP taking σ to be 2.18 Å. Also calculate the viscosity and the thermal conductivity coefficient taking C_V to be 3.00 cal °K^{-1} mole^{-1}.

Ans. $\mathcal{D} = 1.060$ cm^2 sec^{-1}, $\eta = 1.891 \times 10^{-4}$ P, $\kappa = 1.418 \times 10^{-4}$ cal °K^{-1} cm^{-1} sec^{-1}.

2-15   Referring to Exercise 2-14 for data, how far should a helium atom at STP diffuse in 1 sec? How long should it take to diffuse 1 cm?

Ans.   1.46 cm,   0.472 sec.

Problems

2-1   (Calculator problem—see Preface) Calculate enough values of $(1/N_0)\, dN(c)/dc$ for methane at 100°C to make a reasonably accurate plot of probability versus velocity. Verify by a graphical or an analytical method that the plot is normalized. Locate c_p, $\bar{c}$, and $(\overline{c^2})^{1/2}$ on the plot.

2-2   Make the change of variable $E = \frac{1}{2}mc^2$ to derive from Eq. (2-29) the expression for the fraction dN/N_0 of molecules having energy in two dimensions between E and $E + dE$, as a function of E. Calculate the fraction of molecules of a gas which have an energy equal to or greater than ten times their average kinetic energy (which is $3kT/2$).

2-3   The collision diameter for argon is 3.64 Å. Calculate Z_{Ar-Ar} at STP. The average concentration of molecules which are in the act of colliding may be estimated as given by their collision frequency times the collision lifetime of about 10^{-13} sec. Calculate the frequency, in moles of events per liter per second, with which such a collision pair will undergo collision with an argon atom—that is, the frequency of triple collisions.

2-4 A quantity of liquid nitrogen (nbp $-195°C$) is placed in a Dewar flask as illustrated in the accompanying figure. The space between the walls has been evacuated and contains air at a pressure of 0.001 Torr and the wall area is 300 cm². If the inner wall remains at $-195°C$

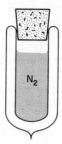

and the outer wall is at 25°C, calculate the rate of evaporation of the liquid nitrogen, in grams per hour, assuming that evaporation is entirely due to heat conduction through the walls (heat of vaporization of N_2 is 45 cal g⁻¹). [*Note*: The pressure is low enough so that it may be assumed that air molecules travel from wall to wall without hitting each other on the way. It is further to be assumed that gas molecules hit the cold wall, remain there long enough to come to its temperature, then fly off, hit the warm wall, and again remain long enough to come to temperature equilibrium. For steady-state conditions, the rate or traffic in each direction is the same.]

2-5 Calculate the mass per second of CO_2 striking each square centimeter of a leaf in air containing CO_2 at a partial pressure of 0.0010 atm at 25°C.

2-6 What quantity of heat in calories per centimeter length per second will be lost through conduction by gas molecules by a filament 0.2 mm in diameter heated electrically to 200°C in a light bulb containing argon at 0.01 mm pressure, the wall temperature of the bulb being 25°C? [*Note*: This pressure may be assumed to be low enough so that gas molecules travel from filament to wall and back again without hitting each other on the way. Therefore argon atoms hit the filament, then leave it with a kinetic energy corresponding to 200°C, and fly to the wall to be "cooled down" to 25°C. For steady-state conditions, the rate of leaving the filament should be the same as the rate of hitting it.]

2-7 The coefficient for the interdiffusion of two chemical species is given by

$$\mathscr{D}_{12} = 2.6280 \times 10^{-3} \frac{[\, T^3(M_1 + M_2)/2M_1M_2 \,]^{1/2}}{P\sigma_{12}^2} \quad (cm^2\ sec^{-1}),$$

where M denotes molecular weight. Deduce what the units of P and σ_{12} must be and calculate $\mathscr{D}_{12}$ for the interdiffusion of oxygen and nitrogen in air at STP.

2-8 Three of the *experimentally measurable* quantities listed in Table 2-2 may be combined as a dimensionless product (or quotient). Find one such combination, calculate its theoretical value, and compare with experiment.

2-9 Derive the expressions for $\bar{c}$ and $\overline{c^2}$ for a two-dimensional gas.

2-10 Work Exercise 2-3 doing the entire calculation in mks units.

2-11 Argon gas is present in a flask at 25°C and pressure P. The flask has a pinhole which may be regarded as a cylindrical hole of 2×10^{-4} cm² area and 0.20 cm length. Calculate the rate of escape of the argon assuming that the process is one of (a) effusion and (b) diffusion, and for $P = 1$ atm and $P = 10^{-7}$ atm. Express your answer in moles of gas per second.

2-12 Suppose we have an equimolar mixture of $^{13}CH_4$ and $^{12}CH_3D$ (species A and B, respectively) at STP. Calculate Z_A and $Z_{A(A-B)}$. Explain if the answers are different. (The collision diameter which is needed is implicit in the data of Table 2-3.)

2-13 Show that the average volume occupied by a molecule can be regarded as a cylinder of area πr^2 (r being the actual molecular radius) and length $4\sqrt{2}\,\lambda$.

2-14 Calculate $\lambda_{1(12)}$ for an equimolar mixture of H_2 and O_2 at 25°C, each at 1 atm pressure.

2-15 Calculate C_V for methane at STP from the data of Table 2-3.

2-16 (Calculator problem) (a) Calculate W for each system of Table 2-1. (b) As a means of exploring a slightly more realistic case, consider 20 molecules which may be distributed between states of energy one, two, three, four, or five units. List the possible systems and calculate W for each. Assume the average energy to be the same as in (a).

2-17 (Calculator problem) Calculate and plot the one-, two-, and three-dimensional velocity distributions for He gas at 100°C.

Special Topics Problems

2-1 Calculate the viscosity of CH_4 at 280°K using Eq. (2-82) and compare your result with the experimental value.

2-2 The viscosity of Xe is 2.235×10^{-4} P at 290°K and 3.954×10^{-4} P at 550°K. Devise a trial and error method so as to calculate reasonably matching values of ϕ^*/k and σ.

3 SOME ADDITIVE PHYSICAL PROPERTIES OF MATTER

3-1 Introduction

In this chapter we take up a number of physical properties of matter, especially of liquids and gases, which are useful and important to know about but whose detailed theory is somewhat specialized for a text at this level. In contrast to Chapter 2, then, the present chapter will be in a somewhat descriptive vein.

The properties to be discussed have an aspect in common. They arise from the interaction of an electric or magnetic field with molecules and, to the first approximation, are determined by the separate behavior of atoms or small groups of atoms within a molecule. As a consequence the properties are approximately additive. By this is meant that the molar value of the property, which is what is measured experimentally, can be formulated as a sum of contributions from various parts of the molecules present. The presence of additivity on a molecular scale means also that the value of the property for a mixture of species will be additive.

To be more specific, if $\mathscr{P}$ denotes the molar property, then if the molecular formula is $A_a B_b C_c \ldots$, additivity means that

$$\mathscr{P} = a\mathscr{P}_A + b\mathscr{P}_B + c\mathscr{P}_C + \cdots, \tag{3-1}$$

where $\mathscr{P}_A$ and so on denote the atomic properties. For a mixture of species the average molar property is

$$\mathscr{P}_m = x_1\mathscr{P}_1 + x_2\mathscr{P}_2 + \cdots = \sum_i x_i\mathscr{P}_i, \tag{3-2}$$

where $\mathscr{P}_i$ is the molar property of the ith species and x denotes mole fraction. This last attribute becomes very useful in that, by means of the physical measurement, one may determine the composition of a mixture or, as in chemical kinetics, follow changes in composition with time.

We have already encountered some additive properties. Mass is strictly additive (neglecting relativity), so molar mass or molecular weight obeys Eqs. (3-1) and (3-2) exactly. Volume at constant pressure and temperature is additive, but usually only very approximately so in the case of liquids. The properties to be taken up here will similarly be at least approximately additive.

3-2 Absorption of Light

The term "light" will be used in the present context to mean electromagnetic radiation generally. That is, the radiation need not be of wavelength corresponding to the visible region: It could be ultraviolet, infrared, or microwave radiation. Such radiation can interact with matter to show various effects such as refraction, scattering, and absorption. It is only the last that we discuss at the moment. The phenomenon of optical activity is taken up in Section 18-ST-2.

When light is absorbed its energy is converted into some other form, and we accept that this conversion can only occur in the discrete amount given by the quantum of energy of the light. It is part of the quantum theory of light that this quantum of energy is given by $h\nu$, where h is Planck's constant and ν is the frequency of the light. The usual consequence of absorption of a light quantum is that some particular molecule gains energy $h\nu$ and is thereby put in some higher energy state, that is, in some excited state.

A point of importance here is that although light can only transfer energy in units of quanta, it otherwise behaves as a wave. One consequence is that the train of waves passing through a region of matter may or may not interact with any of the molecules present. There is only a certain probability that interaction will occur. The derivation of the absorption law is then based on a probability analysis.

Let k_x be the probability that light of a given wavelength will be absorbed per unit length of matter; $k_x x$ is then the probability of absorption in some small distance x. The probability that the light is not absorbed is $1 - k_x x$. Further, the probability that light will not be absorbed in a second increment of distance x is $(1 - k_x x)^2$ and the probability of its not being absorbed in n such distances becomes $(1 - k_x x)^n$.

Now let l be the total distance, $l = nx$. We want to keep the same path length l, but to take the limit of $n \to \infty$, that is, the limit of an infinite number of infinitesimal lengths x:

$$\lim_{n\to\infty}\left(1 - \frac{k_x l}{n}\right)^n = e^{-k_x l}. \tag{3-3}$$

{It should be recognized that $\lim_{n\to\infty}[1 + (1/n)^n] = e$.} The probability that light will not be absorbed in distance l is then $e^{-k_x l}$. If light of intensity I_0 is incident on a portion of matter, then the probable intensity after a distance l is

$$I = I_0 e^{-k_x l}. \tag{3-4}$$

I/I_0 is the fraction of light transmitted through, that is, not absorbed by, a sample of thickness l.

Equation (3-4) is a statement of Lambert's law, where k_x is the *linear absorption coefficient* (also called the Napierian extinction coefficient b). However, since the absorption process is a molecular one, it is somewhat more rational to recognize that, per unit area of target, a depth l will contain $l\rho/m$ molecules, and to write Eq. (3-4) as

$$\frac{I}{I_0} = e^{-k_N N}, \qquad k_N = \frac{k_x m}{\rho}, \tag{3-5}$$

where ρ and m are respectively the density and the mass per molecule of the material, N is the number of molecules traversed per square centimeter, and k_N is now the *molecular absorption coefficient*.

An important special case is that in which the absorbing species is present in solution. If we can assume that k_N is not affected by concentration, then, since $N = N_0 C l/1000$, where C is in moles per liter, that is, in units of molarity M,

$$\frac{I}{I_0} = e^{-\alpha C l}, \qquad \alpha = \frac{k_N N_0}{1000}. \tag{3-6}$$

The constant α is called the *molar absorption coefficient*, and Eq. (3-6) is a statement of the combined Beer–Lambert law for light absorption.

Finally, a common modification of Eq. (3-6) is

$$\frac{I}{I_0} = 10^{-\epsilon C l}, \qquad \epsilon = \frac{\alpha}{2.303}. \tag{3-7}$$

If we now define the *optical density* D as equal to $\log(I_0/I)$, we have

$$D = \epsilon C l. \tag{3-8}$$

The quantity D is alternatively called the *absorbance* and is denoted by the symbol A. Also, the *extinction coefficient* ϵ is alternatively called the *molar absorptivity*.

Returning to the derivation that led to Eq. (3-3), if more than one type of interacting species is present, then the probability k_x of absorption per unit distance will now be given by a sum over all species, $k_{x,\text{tot}} = \sum k_{x,i}$. The same applies to the other absorption coefficients. In particular, for a solution of more than one species, we get

$$D = l \sum \epsilon_i C_i. \tag{3-9}$$

Often the product $\epsilon l C$ for the solvent is abstracted from the sum to give

$$D = D_s + l \sum \epsilon_i C_i \, . \tag{3-10}$$

Optical density or absorbance is thus an additive property of mixtures, to the extent that changing concentration does not change the character of the species present. It may also be additive with respect to chromophoric groups within a molecule; this is especially common in the case of infrared spectra where vibrational excitations of the various types of bonds contribute somewhat independently to the overall absorption. It should perhaps be emphasized that ϵ is very much a function of wavelength so that any statement of an ϵ value must be accompanied by the wavelength to which it pertains.

The following example is designed to illustrate most of the common operations involving light absorption. A 0.01 M solution of $Cr(NH_3)_5(NCS)^{2+}$ (as the perchlorate salt) absorbs 88.79% of incident light of 500 nm wavelength when placed in a 1-cm spectrophotometer cell. The solvent medium absorbs somewhat at this wavelength; a 10-cm cell filled with solvent transmits 31.6% of incident light at 500 nm.

On standing, the reaction

$$Cr(NH_3)_5(NCS)^{2+} + H_2O = Cr(NH_3)_5(H_2O)^{3+} + NCS^-$$
$$\quad\quad\text{A} \quad\quad\quad\quad\quad\quad\quad\quad\quad\quad\quad\quad \text{B}$$

occurs and the reaction goes to completion in several weeks at 45°C. The per cent transmission of this final solution through a 1-cm cell is 44.64. How far had the reaction proceeded after 75 hr at 45°C if, after this time, the optical density of the solution in the 1-cm cell was 0.650? Also calculate the extinction coefficients of the complex ions A and B.

First, the various statements should be reduced to optical densities for a 1-cm path length. For the original solution, $D_0 = \log(I_0/I) = -\log(0.1121) = \log(8.92) = 0.950$. For the solvent, $D_s = -\log(0.316) = \log(3.16) = 0.500$, or, for a 1-cm path length, $D_s = 0.050$. The net optical density due to the starting complex is then $0.950 - 0.050 = 0.900$, and the extinction coefficient is therefore $\epsilon_A = 0.900/0.01 = 90.0$ liter mole^{-1} cm^{-1}. After complete reaction, $D_\infty = -\log(0.4464) = \log(2.24) = 0.350$. The net optical density due to the product is then $0.350 - 0.050 = 0.300$ and the extinction coefficient of the product is $\epsilon_B = 0.300/(1 \times 0.01) = 30.0$ liter mole^{-1} cm^{-1}.

The net optical density after 75 hr is $0.650 - 0.050 = 0.600$. Then, by Eq. (3-10)

$$0.600 = (1)(90.0C_A + 30.0C_B) = 60.0C_A + 0.300$$

(since $C_B = 0.01 - C_A$), or $C_A = 0.300/60.0 = 0.0050$ M. The reaction had thus proceeded to 50%, or by one half-life.

3-3   Molar Refraction

A second type of interaction of light with a medium is refraction, measured by the index of refraction n, which gives the ratio of the velocity of light in vacuum to that in the substance. The actual experimental measurement is based on the bending of a light ray as it passes from air into the medium.

The theory involves the interaction of the oscillating electric field of electromagnetic radiation with the various characteristic frequencies for electrons in an atom or collection of atoms, and leads, in first order, to the equation

$$n = 1 + \sum \frac{a}{\nu_0{}^2 - \nu^2},$$ (3-11)

where the sum is over the various characteristic frequencies ν_0 for a given frequency of radiation ν. Ordinarily, ν is small compared to any ν_0, so the index of refraction does not vary much with the wavelength of light used, although for n to be purely characteristic of the atom, ν should be zero. Often, however, a standard wavelength, such as that of the yellow emission from a sodium lamp, is used. There is an important exception to this situation. If the compound absorbs light this means that there is some transition between states of differing energy. This energy corresponds to a frequency $h\nu_0$ and, as a consequence, the index of refraction will vary rapidly as the frequency of the light used, ν, is varied through the value of ν_0, that is, through a region of strong light absorption. For most small molecules, however, ν_0 is rather large; in fact, $h\nu_0$ often corresponds approximately to the ionization energy of the molecule.

An early treatment by H. A. Lorentz and L. V. Lorentz in 1880, as well as more modern ones, considers that the index of refraction should vary with the density of a medium of given atomic composition according to the relationship

$$\mathbf{R} = \frac{n^2 - 1}{n^2 + 2} \frac{M}{\rho}.$$ (3-12)

Here M/ρ is the molar volume and $\mathbf{R}$ is a quantity called the *molar refraction*. If molecules are treated as perfectly conducting spheres and light of infinite wavelength is used in measuring n, then $\mathbf{R}$ is the actual molar volume of the molecule.

There is an alternate way of treating this limiting situation. An imposed electric field $\mathbf{F}$ will in general displace the electrons in an atom somewhat to produce a dipole moment as illustrated in Fig. 3-1. A charge separation occurs in the initially

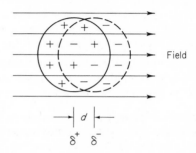

Fig. 3-1. *Molecular dipole moment induced by an electric field.*

electrically symmetric atom, equivalent to having small equal and opposite charges $\delta^+ e$ and $\delta^- e$ separated by distance d. The dipole moment μ is defined as

$$\mu = \delta e d, \tag{3-13}$$

where e is the charge on the electron. The traditional unit for dipole moment is the debye (D), defined as 10^{-18} esu cm. Since d is of the order of 1 Å and e has the value 4.803×10^{-10} esu, dipole moment quantities generally come out as some small number of debye units. (In the mks and SI systems, dipole moment is given in coulomb-meter units.)

The induced dipole moment is proportional to the electric field,

$$\mu_{\text{ind}} = \mathbf{m}_\alpha = \alpha \mathbf{F}, \tag{3-14}$$

where the proportionality constant α is called the polarizability and the symbol $\mathbf{m}$ is used for moments induced by various individual effects. Only one such effect is present in Eq. (3-14), so that here μ_{ind} and $\mathbf{m}_\alpha$ are the same. The symbol μ is reserved for the experimentally observed dipole moment; if it is induced, the subscript "ind" may be used. In general, μ_{ind} may be the sum of more than one term [as in Eq. (3-18)]. In the cgs system, the field is in esu per square centimeter, the dipole moment in esu-centimeter, and α is then in cubic centimeters. Usual values of α are about 10^{-24} cm³ or about actual atomic volumes. (In the mks system and SI systems, because of the dimensions assigned to dielectric constant or permittivity, polarizability has the dimensions of coulomb square meter per volt and $\mathbf{F}$ of volts per meter; see Commentary and Notes.)

The conducting sphere model provides a connection between index of refraction at infinite wavelength, n_∞ [$\nu = 0$ in Eq. (3-11)] and the polarizability of the sphere, again given by Lorentz and Lorentz. This relationship is

$$\mathbf{R}_0 = \frac{n^2 - 1}{n^2 + 2} \frac{M}{\rho} = \frac{4}{3} \pi N_0 \alpha, \tag{3-15}$$

where N_0 is Avogadro's number. Thus α corresponds to the cube of the radius of the sphere.

As suggested by the summation of Eq. (3-11), molar refraction is, ideally, an additive property; empirically, it is very nearly one. Thus values of $\mathbf{R}$ can be assigned to individual atoms in an organic molecule, and some, as determined using the sodium D line, are given in Table 3-1.

Somewhat better results are obtained if molar polarizations are assigned to types of bonds rather than to individual atoms, and some bond refractions and corresponding polarizabilities are included in the table.

By way of illustration let us calculate the molar refractions for two isomeric liquids at 20°C, acetic acid and methyl formate. The respective molar volumes M/ρ are $60.05/1.0491 = 57.24$ cm³ mole⁻¹ and $60.05/0.9742 = 61.64$ cm³ mole⁻¹; and the refractive indices with the sodium D line are 1.3721 and 1.3433, respectively. Substitution into Eq. (3-12) gives molar refractions

Table 3-1. *Some Atomic and Bond Refractions*

Atom	Molar refraction[a] (cm^3 mole^{-1})	Bond	Molar refraction,[b] R_0 (cm^3 mole^{-1})	$\alpha_0 \times 10^{25}$ (cm^3)
C	2.418	C—C	1.204	4.75
H	1.100	C—O	1.411	5.95
O (in CO group)	2.211	C—H	1.654	6.51
O (in ethers)	1.643	O—H	1.849	7.28
O (in OH group)	1.525	C=O	3.344	12.71
Cl	5.967	C=N	4.692	18.48
Br	5.865	C=C	2.789	10.98
I	13.900	C≡C	4.785	18.85
C=C bond	1.7333			
C≡C bond	2.398			

[a] For sodium D line. (From S. Glasstone, "Textbook of Physical Chemistry." Van Nostrand–Reinhold, Princeton, New Jersey, 1946.)

[b] For infinite wavelength. (From E. A. Moelwyn-Hughes, "Physical Chemistry." Pergamon, Oxford, 1961.) The values of R_0 and α_0 are for zero-frequency light.

of 13.013 cm^3 mole^{-1} for acetic acid and 13.033 cm^3 mole^{-1} for methyl formate. The respective values from the atomic refractions are 12.972 and 13.090 cm^3 mole^{-1} (and those from the bond refractions, 12.770 and 12.782 cm^3 mole^{-1}, but now for infinite wavelength).

The preceding example shows that it is in principle possible, but in practice sometimes difficult, to decide between isomeric structures by means of molar refractions. One can, however, use the molar refraction table in combination with a measured density and index of refraction to obtain an empirical formula for an unknown substance.

3-4 Molar Polarization; Dipole Moments

It was stressed in the preceding section that, on theoretical grounds, the index of refraction should be for zero-frequency light in the calculation of molar refraction. As an alternative, one may directly impose an external low- or zero-frequency electric field on the medium by having it between the plates of a capacitor. The capacity of a parallel plate capacitor is

$$C = \frac{q}{\mathbf{E}} = \frac{qD}{\mathbf{E}_0} = C_0 D, \qquad (3\text{-}16)$$

where q and $\mathbf{E}$ denote the charge on each plate and the effective field between them, respectively. (In this section we use $\mathbf{E}$ to denote an applied field and $\mathbf{F}$ to denote the actual local field experienced by a molecule; both are expressed in volts per centimeter.) In the presence of a medium other than vacuum, the effective field, instead of being equal to $\mathbf{E}_0$, the applied potential difference, is reduced to $\mathbf{E}_0/D$, where D is the dielectric constant. The effect is to increase C over the value for vacuum C_0. The value of C_0 is related to the dimensions of the capacitor,

$$C_0 = \frac{\mathscr{A}}{4\pi d}, \tag{3-17}$$

where $\mathscr{A}$ is the area of the plates and d their separation.

From a molecular point of view, the presence of the field induces a proportional dipole moment in the molecules as in Eq. (3-14). At the low frequencies which characterize dielectric constant measurements there are now two (main) contributions to μ_{ind}. As before there is the dipole moment arising from the polarizability of the molecule, $\mathbf{m}_\alpha$, and there is also the effective moment $\mathbf{m}_\mu$ resulting from the partial net alignment by the field of any permanent molecular dipoles that are present. This second type of induced dipole moment is again proportional to the field acting on the molecules (as discussed later) and the proportionality constant is called the orientation polarizability α_μ. Equation (3-14) becomes

$$\mu_{\mathrm{ind(tot)}} = \mathbf{m}_\alpha + \mathbf{m}_\mu = (\alpha + \alpha_\mu)\mathbf{F} \tag{3-18}$$

or

$$\mathbf{m}_{\mathrm{tot}} = \alpha_{\mathrm{tot}}\mathbf{F}. \tag{3-19}$$

If the molecules are far apart, as in a dilute gas, the total induced polarization simply acts to reduce the apparent field $\mathbf{E}_0$; from an analysis of the situation using Eq. (3-17) one finds

$$\mathbf{E} = \mathbf{E}_0 - 4\pi\mathbf{I}, \tag{3-20}$$

where $\mathbf{I}$ is the total polarization per unit volume, $\mathbf{I} = \mathbf{m}_{\mathrm{tot}}\mathbf{n}$ and $\mathbf{n}$ denotes concentration in molecules per cubic centimeter.

More generally, however, the degree of polarization of each molecule is affected by the field of the induced polarization of the other molecules, and it is necessary to take this into account. This corrected, or net effective local field $\mathbf{F}$ is now given by

$$\mathbf{F} = \mathbf{E} + \tfrac{4}{3}\pi\mathbf{I}, \tag{3-21}$$

or, from Eq. (3-20), remembering that $\mathbf{E}_0 = D\mathbf{E}$,

$$\mathbf{F} = \tfrac{1}{3}(D + 2)\mathbf{E}. \tag{3-22}$$

On eliminating $\mathbf{E}$, we obtain

$$\mathbf{F}\left(1 - \frac{3}{D+2}\right) = \frac{4}{3}\pi\mathbf{I} = \frac{4}{3}\pi\mathbf{m}_{\mathrm{tot}}\mathbf{n},$$

and, on eliminating $\mathbf{F}$ by means of Eq. (3-18), we obtain

$$\frac{D-1}{D+2} = \frac{4}{3}\pi\mathbf{n}\alpha_{\text{tot}}. \tag{3-23}$$

Since $\mathbf{n} = N_0\rho/M$, the final form is

$$\mathbf{P} = \frac{D-1}{D+2}\left(\frac{M}{\rho}\right) = \frac{4}{3}\pi N_0\alpha_{\text{tot}}. \tag{3-24}$$

$\mathbf{P}$ is called the *molar polarization* and the contribution to $\mathbf{P}$ from the polarizability α of the molecules is denoted $\mathbf{P}_\alpha$. Theoretical analysis shows that $\mathbf{P}_\alpha$ should be equal to $\mathbf{R}$, the molar refraction, provided the latter is the limiting value from indices of refraction at infinite wavelength, $\mathbf{R}_0$.

The contribution of α_μ [Eq. (3-18)] to the total polarizability is quite important if the molecules have a nonzero dipole moment μ. This will be the case if bonds between unlike atoms are present, as in NO or HCl, provided there is no internal cancellation of such bond dipoles, as happens in CH_4 or CO_2 owing to molecular symmetry. The relationship between α_μ and the permanent molecular dipole moment μ is as follows.

If a molecule has a permanent dipole moment, it will tend to be oriented along the direction of the local electric field $\mathbf{F}$. That is, the energy ϵ of the dipole in the field would be zero if it were oriented perpendicular to the field and it would be $\mu\mathbf{F}$ if it were oriented in line with the field. For some intermediate orientation

$$\epsilon = \mathbf{F}\mu\cos\theta, \tag{3-25}$$

where, as shown in Fig. 3-2(a), θ is the orientation angle defined such that $\mu\cos\theta$

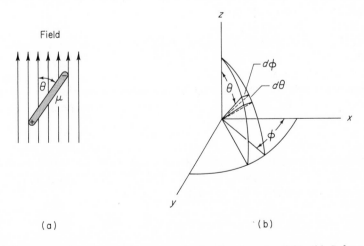

(a) (b)

Fig. 3-2. *(a) Component of dipole moment in the direction of a field. (b) Polar coordinate system.*

gives the component of μ in the field direction. At 0°K all dipoles should orient completely, but at any higher temperature thermal agitation will prevent this and the probability of a given orientation is proportional to the Boltzmann factor $e^{-\epsilon/kT}$. At infinite temperature the effect of the field becomes negligible; all orientations are then equally probable and the average net dipole moment of a collection of molecules is zero.

What is now needed is the average orientation or, more precisely, the average of $\mu \cos \theta$ which gives the average net dipole moment $\mathbf{m}_\mu$. The procedure followed is that discussed in Section 2-4; that is, one writes the averaging equation

$$\mathbf{m}_\mu = \frac{N \int_0^\pi (\mu \cos \theta)\, e^{-(\mathbf{F}\mu\cos\theta)/kT}(2\pi \sin \theta\, d\theta)}{N \int_0^\pi e^{-(\mathbf{F}\mu\cos\theta)/kT}(2\pi \sin \theta\, d\theta)}\,, \qquad (3\text{-}26)$$

where N is the number of molecules and $(2\pi \sin \theta\, d\theta)$ gives $d\omega$, the element of solid angle.

In the polar coordinate system used (shown in Fig. 3-2b) an element of solid angle is given by

$$d\omega = \sin \theta\, d\theta\, d\phi.$$

Integration over all directions gives

$$d\omega = \int_0^{2\pi} \int_0^\pi \sin \theta\, d\theta\, d\phi = |-\cos \theta\,|_0^\pi \,|\,\phi\,|_0^{2\pi} = 4\,\pi. \qquad (3\text{-}27)$$

In the present case the energy is not affected by the ϕ angle, so this is integrated out in Eq. (3-26) to give the factor 2π.

The integrals of Eq. (3-26) may be evaluated as follows. Let $a = \mu\mathbf{F}/kT$ and $x = \cos \theta$, so $dx = \sin \theta\, d\theta$; then

$$\frac{\mathbf{m}_\mu}{\mu} = \frac{\int_1^{-1} e^{ax} x\, dx}{\int_1^{-1} e^{ax}\, dx}\,.$$

The integrals are now in a standard form, and algebraic manipulation gives[†]

$$\frac{\mathbf{m}_\mu}{\mu} = \frac{e^a + e^{-a}}{e^a - e^{-a}} - \frac{1}{a} = \coth a - \frac{1}{a}\,. \qquad (3\text{-}28)$$

Under ordinary experimental conditions $\mu\mathbf{F}/kT$ is small compared to unity, and on expansion of the expression ($\coth a - 1/a$), the first term is $a/3$. To a first approximation we have

$$\mathbf{m}_\mu = \left(\frac{\mu^2}{3kT}\right)\mathbf{F}. \qquad (3\text{-}29)$$

[†] $\cosh x = \frac{1}{2}(e^x + e^{-x})$ and $\sinh x = \frac{1}{2}(e^x - e^{-x})$; $\coth x = (\cosh x)/\sinh x$.

Comparison with Eq. (3-18) gives

$$\alpha_\mu = \frac{\mu^2}{3kT}. \tag{3-30}$$

The expression for **P** [Eq. (3-24)] may now be written explicitly as

$$\mathbf{P} = \frac{4}{3}\pi N_0 \alpha + \frac{4}{3}\pi N_0 \frac{\mu^2}{3kT}. \tag{3-31}$$

Thus the molar polarization **P** as obtained from dielectric constant measurements should vary with temperature according to the equation

$$\mathbf{P} = a + \frac{b}{T}, \quad \text{where} \quad a = \mathbf{P}_\alpha = \mathbf{R}_0 = \frac{4}{3}\pi N_0\alpha, \quad b = \frac{4}{3}\pi N_0 \frac{\mu^2}{3k}. \tag{3-32}$$

Equation (3-32) is known as the Debye equation, and typical plots of **P** versus $1/T$ are shown in Fig. (3-3). Equation (3-32) is valid for gases. In liquids, especially

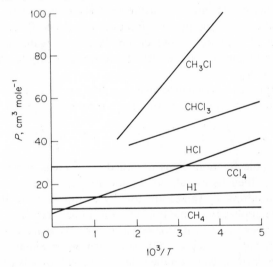

Fig. 3-3. *Variation of molar polarization with temperature.*

associated ones, the molecular dipoles may not be able to respond freely to the applied field.

Some sample calculations are now in order. First, the statement that $\mathbf{F}\mu/kT$ is ordinarily a small quantity can be verified. A capacitor might be charged to as much as 6000 V cm^{-1}, or to 6000/300 V esu cm^{-1}. Taking this as the approximate local field **F**, and taking μ to be in the usual range of about 10^{-18} esu cm, we have

$$\epsilon = 10^{-18}\frac{6000}{300}2 \times 10^{-17} \quad \text{erg.}$$

If T is about 300°K, then kT is $(1.38 \times 10^{-16})(300)$ or about 4×10^{-14} erg. Then ϵ/kT is about 5×10^{-4}, and is indeed a small number.

This calculation may also be made in the mks-SI system (see Commentary and Notes). Now

F is 6000 V per 0.01 m or 6×10^5 V m^{-1}. A dipole moment of 10^{-18} esu cm now has the value $10^{-18}/10c$ C meter, where c is the velocity of light, used here as 3×10^{10} cm sec^{-1}; μ is thus $\frac{1}{3} \times 10^{-29}$ C meter. The energy of the dipole in the field is still μF, and has the value (6×10^5) $(\frac{1}{3}) \times 10^{-29}$ or 2×10^{-24} J (joule); the Boltzmann constant is now 1.38×10^{-23} J $^\circ$K^{-1}, so kT becomes 4×10^{-21} J. The ratio ϵ/kT is then 5×10^{-4}, as before.

Turning next to an application of the Debye equation, we find that the dielectric constant of gaseous HCl at 1 atm pressure is reported (International Critical Tables) to be 1.0026 at 100°C and 1.0046 at 0°C. The molar volume RT/P is then 30.62 and 22.41 liter mole^{-1} at the two temperatures, respectively. The corresponding **P** values are, from Eq. (3-24), 26.52×10^3 and 34.31×10^3 cm^3 mole^{-1}. The straight line through these two points on a plot of **P** versus $1/T$ gives an intercept $a = 5.27$ and slope $b = 7.93 \times 10^3$.

From Eq. (3-32), $\alpha = (3)(5.27)/(4)(3.141)(6.023 \times 10^{23})$ or $\alpha = 2.09 \times 10^{-24}$ cm^3 (a better value is 2.56×10^{-24}). We also have $\mu^2 = (9)(1.38 \times 10^{-16})(7.93 \times 10^3)/(4)(3.141)(6.023 \times 10^{23})$ or $\mu^2 = 1.30 \times 10^{-36}$ and $\mu = 1.14$ D (debye). This calculation, while illustrating the use of the Debye equation, gives somewhat approximate values for α and μ because of the inaccurate evaluation of a and b from just two points (a better value is 1.05 D).

Dipole moments may also be determined from measurements at a single temperature if a dielectric constant measurement is combined with one of index of refraction. The latter gives the molar refraction and hence $\mathbf{P}_\alpha$ directly, for use in Eq. (3-32). Indices of refraction, however, are usually measured with visible light, as with the sodium D line, and some corrections are necessary to convert the value of **R** so obtained to $\mathbf{R}_0$.

This general approach may be extended to solutions. The molar polarization of a solution is an additive property, so that for a solution

$$\mathbf{P} = \frac{D-1}{D+2} \frac{x_1 M_1 + x_2 M_2}{\rho} = x_1 \mathbf{P}_1 + x_2 \mathbf{P}_2 , \tag{3-33}$$

where x denotes mole fraction. $\mathbf{P}_1$ is obtained from measurements on the pure solvent and $\mathbf{P}_2$ can then be calculated for the solute. To discount solute–solute interactions, the resulting $\mathbf{P}_2$ values are usually extrapolated to infinite dilution. To obtain $\mathbf{R}_2$, one applies the same procedure to molar refractions from index of refraction measurements and then proceeds as before to calculate a dipole moment for the solute. Not only is this procedure somewhat approximate, but the solvent will often have a polarizing effect on the solute as a result of solvation interactions. Consequently $\mathbf{P}_2$ and corresponding μ values will not in general be exactly the same as those obtained from the temperature dependence of the dielectric constant of the pure solute vapor. In the case of nonvolatile, solid substances, however, the solution procedure may be the best one available for estimating molecular dipole moments.

3-5 Dipole Moments and Molecular Properties

It is conventional and very useful to regard a molecular dipole moment as an additive property. One assigns individual dipole moments to each bond and the addition, of course, is now a vectorial one.

In the case of diatomic molecules the bond moment is just the measured dipole moment of the molecule. One can proceed a step further. If the internuclear distance is known from crystallographic or spectroscopic measurements, then from the definition of dipole moment $\mu = \delta e d$ [Eq. (3-13)], the fractional charge δe on each atom can be calculated. This is, in effect, the degree of ionic character of the bond.

Some dipole moment values are given in Table 3-2 and the calculation may be illustrated as follows. The bond length for HCl is 1.275 Å and the dipole moment is 1.05 D (debye). The fraction of ionic character δ is then $1.05 \times 10^{-18}/(1.275 \times 10^{-8})(4.80 \times 10^{-10}) = 0.17$. The H—Cl bond is thus said to have 17% ionic character. The similarly obtained values for HF, HBr, and HI are 45%, 11%, and 4%, respectively. This set of values has been used to relate the electronegativity difference between atoms and the degree of ionic character of the bond [see, for example, Douglas and McDaniel (1965)].

Turning to triatomic molecules, Table 3-2 shows a zero dipole moment for CO_2. This is not because the individual C=O bonds are nonpolar, but because the two bond dipoles cancel, as illustrated in Fig. 3-4(a). This arrangement of two dipoles end-to-end corresponds to a quadrupole (see Special Topics) and the experimental quadrupole moment of -4.3×10^{-26} esu cm² for CO_2, when combined with the known C=O distance, indicates that each oxygen atom carries a charge of about $0.3e$.

Water, on the other hand, shows a net dipole moment because the bond angle is not 180° and the two H—O dipoles fail to cancel. As illustrated in Fig. 3-4(b), the

Table 3-2. *Dipole Moments and Polarizabilities*[a]

Substance	Polarizability (Å³)	Dipole moment (D)
He	0.204	—
Ar	1.62	—
H_2	0.802	—
N_2	1.73	—
Cl_2	4.50	—
HCl	2.56	1.05
HBr	3.49	0.807
HI	5.12	0.39
CO_2	2.59	0.00
H_2O	1.44	1.82
NH_3	2.15	1.47
CH_3Cl	—	1.87
C_6H_6	25.1	0.00
C_6H_5Cl	—	1.70
p-$C_6H_4Cl_2$	—	0.00
o-$C_6H_4Cl_2$	—	2.2
m-$C_6H_4Cl_2$	—	1.4

[a] From R_0 values.

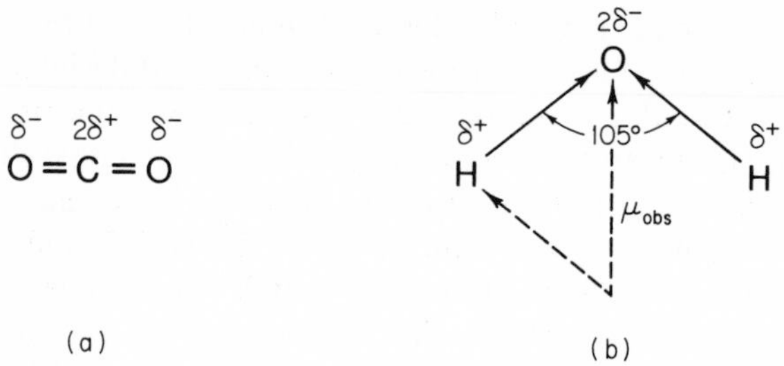

$$
\overset{2\delta^-}{O}
$$

$$
\overset{\delta^-}{O} = \overset{2\delta^+}{C} = \overset{\delta^-}{O}
$$

(a)   (b)

Fig. 3-4. *(a) A molecule with zero dipole moment (but nonzero quadrupole moment). (b) Vector addition of bond dipole moments for water.*

actual angle is 105° and the observed moment is the vector sum of the two bond moments.

The situation becomes increasingly complicated with polyatomic molecules. The net dipole moment of ammonia is now the vector sum of three $N-H$ bond moments, while for the planar BF_3 molecule the three bond moments cancel to give zero molecular dipole moment. The same cancellation occurs for CH_4, which is unfortunate, since one thus gets no information about the $C-H$ bond moment. An indirect estimate (Partington, 1954) gives -0.4 for μ_{C-H} (carbon is negative), and this now permits the calculation of other bond moments involving carbon. Thus μ_{C-Cl} can now be obtained from the dipole moment of CH_3Cl and a knowledge of the bond angles.

A few such bond moments are collected in Table 3-3. It must be remembered, however, that the resolution of a molecular moment into bond moments is somewhat arbitrary. Thus one could assign a moment to the lone electron pairs in water or ammonia as well as to the bonds. Also the dipole moment of a molecule is merely the first term in an expansion of the function which describes the complete radial and angular distribution of electron density in a molecule (see Special Topics). This function, however, is in general not known or can only be estimated theoretically, and the bond moment procedure just given is adequate for many purposes.

Finally, molecular dipole moments can provide useful qualitative information. Thus the zero moment for p-$C_6H_4Cl_2$ must mean that the $C-Cl$ bonds lie on the molecular axis, while the nonzero moment for p-$C_6H_4(OH)_2$ (of 1.64 D) indicates

Table 3-3. *Some Bond Dipole Moments[a]*

Bond	Moment (D)	Bond	Moment (D)
$O-H$	-1.53	$C-Cl$	1.56
$N-H$	-1.31	$C-O$	0.86
$C-H$	$(-0.40)^b$	$C=O$	2.4
$C-F$	1.51	$C=N$	3.6

[a] The sign of the dipole moment indicates that of the first-named atom.
[b] Assumed value.

that the O—H bonds lie out of the plane of the ring. The series of p-, m-, and o-isomers of $C_6H_4Cl_2$ can be identified since the order given should be that of increasing dipole moment. As an example from inorganic chemistry, the isomers of square planar PtA_2B_2 complexes can be distinguished on the basis of their dipole moments. That of the *trans* isomer should be small or zero, whereas that of the *cis* isomer should be fairly large. As a specific example, the isomers of $Pt[P(C_2H_5)_3]_2Br_2$ have dipole moments of zero and 11.2 D.

COMMENTARY AND NOTES

3-CN-1 Additive Properties

An additive property that has had some historical importance, but which is not in much current use, is that known as the *Parachor*. The general idea is that the molar volume of a liquid should be an additive property, that is, we should be able to arrive at a molar volume by summing atomic or functional group volumes. Volume additivity is not actually very well obeyed, and Sugden (1924) suggested that one should correct for the effect of intermolecular forces on molar volumes. One indication of such forces is the surface tension of the liquid, and the specific proposal was that the following corrected molar volume should now be an additive quantity:

$$[P] = \frac{\gamma^{1/4} M}{\rho},$$
(3-34)

where $[P]$ was called the Parachor and γ denotes surface tension. Values of $[P]$ are largely temperature independent and are in fact approximately additive. Tables of atomic and group Parachors may be found in more detailed texts [see Glasstone (1946), p. 526] and are used in much the same way as the **R** values of Table 3-1.

As a general comment, the observation that some property is additive with respect to the atoms or functional groups of a molecule has served several purposes. First, it may be possible to distinguish between structural isomers of the same empirical formula. However, as the example in Section 3-3 illustrated, this is not always easy with organic molecules. The advent of various modern tools in spectroscopy, such as infrared absorption and nuclear magnetic resonance, has provided more certain means of determining structural formulas. In addition, of course, the computerization of x-ray crystallographic studies has made actual structure determinations a much more routine matter than formerly.

The second application of an additivity principle is in predicting a physical property of some particular substance. Thus use of Table 3-1 would allow a prediction of the index of refraction and of the constant *a* of Eq. (3-32). One can use Parachor tables to arrive at a prediction of the surface tension of a liquid. The Pascal constants of Table 3-6 (Section 3-ST-2) allow a prediction of the diamagnetic susceptibility of a substance, and so on. This second type of use continues to be important and makes the material of this chapter of contemporary relevance.

Finally, as mentioned in Section 3-1, properties that fail to be closely additive in terms of the atomic constituents of a molecule will often be accurately additive for mixtures. Optical density is an example of an additive property that often cannot be resolved into atomic or group components, but usually can be treated as the sum of contributions from the different constituents of a mixture. A very general and important use of additive properties, then, is in chemical analysis.

3-CN-2   Systems of Units

It is appropriate at this point to comment on the contemporary usage of systems of units. The standard metric or cgs system leads to the erg and the dyne as the units of energy and of force, and, through the mechanical equivalent of heat, to the calorie as an alternative unit of energy. Force is defined by means of Newton's first law,

$$f = ma, \tag{3-35}$$

where *a* denotes acceleration, and the dyne is that force required to accelerate 1 g by 1 cm sec^{-2}. The units of dyne and erg are g cm sec^{-2} and g cm^2 sec^{-2}, respectively. The volume unit is the cubic centimeter, with the liter or 1000 cm^3 as a secondary unit.

Electrical units derive from two experimental laws. In the esu set of units, charge *q* is defined in terms of Coulomb's law,

$$f = \frac{q^2}{r^2}, \tag{3-36}$$

which states that in vacuum, unit charges will repel with a force of 1 dyn if at a distance *r* of 1 cm. The more general form

$$f = \frac{q_1 q_2}{Dr^2} \tag{3-37}$$

states that this force is reduced in a medium other than vacuum according to the dielectric constant *D*. The emu system derives from similar defining laws. Unit magnetic poles repel with a force of 1 dyn if separated by 1 cm; magnetic field intensity **H** is 1 Oe (oersted) if a unit magnetic pole placed in it experiences a force of 1 dyn. Both definitions are for vacuum. The field in a medium is reduced from that in vacuum by the magnetic permeability μ.

The current i in both the esu and emu systems is defined as the number of unit charges per second, but in the emu system it is defined operationally as that current which in a single-turn circular loop of wire of 1 cm radius produces a magnetic field intensity of 2π Oe. The names of the units are the statampere (esu) and the abampere (emu).

Potential is defined in terms of the work required to transport unit charge. Unit potential difference exists between two points if 1 dyn is required to transport unit charge between the points. The definition leads to the statvolt (esu) and the abvolt (emu).

The corresponding esu and emu units differ by the factor c, the velocity of light. Thus

$$1 \text{ esu of charge} \sim 1/c \times \text{emu of charge} \tag{3-38}$$
$$\text{(or statcoulomb)} \qquad \text{(or abcoulomb)}$$

and the electronic charge is then 4.802×10^{-10} esu or 1.60×10^{-19} emu. Similarly,

$$1 \text{ esu of current or statampere} \sim 1/c \times \text{emu of current or abampere.} \tag{3-39}$$

As a result of the difference in the unit of quantity of electricity, we have

$$1 \text{ esu potential difference} \sim c \times \text{emu potential difference.} \tag{3-40}$$
$$\text{(or statvolt)} \qquad \text{(or abvolt)}$$

A third, practical system of units developed along with the esu and emu quantities. In this system the ampere and coulomb are one-tenth of the respective abquantities. The volt is defined to require 1 J for the transport of 1 coulomb and is thus 10^8 abvolt or $1/300$ statvolt.

The mks system makes several major changes. The unit of force is still given by Eq. (3-35), but in terms of kilogram meter per squared second and is now called the newton. One newton (N) is then 10^5 dyn. The unit of energy is now in kg m² sec⁻², or the joule (J); 1 J is 10^7 erg. In a subsequent development the separate emu and esu systems were eliminated in favor of a single system of electrical and magnetic units, the fundamental one of which was the ampere (A), the same as the previous practical ampere. The system of units became at this point the mksa system.

In order to use the fundamental laws, such as Coulomb's law, in the mksa system, it is necessary to assign a nonunity value to the dielectric constant and the permeability of vacuum. Further, since certain equations of electricity and magnetism contain factors of 2π or 4π [Eq. (3-20) is an example] the redefinition is made so that such factors do not appear in situations where geometric intuition does not seem to call for them. Coulomb's law is now written

$$f = \frac{q_1 q_2}{4\pi D_0 r^2}, \tag{3-41}$$

where D_0, the dielectric constant of vacuum, has become $10^7/4\pi c^2$ or $8.854 \times 10^{-12}\,\mathrm{kg^{-1}\,m^{-3}\,sec^4\,A^2}$. If now q is given in coulombs and r in meters, f will be in newtons. A similar redefinition of magnetic interaction requires μ_0, the permeability of vacuum, to be $4\pi \times 10^{-7}\,\mathrm{kg\,m\,sec^{-2}\,A^{-2}}$. Notice that $D_0\mu_0$ is $1/c^2$.

The mksa system has been further codified by a set of international commissions into what is called the Système International d'Unités, or the SI system (McGlashan, 1968). In addition to making a critical evaluation of the numerical values of fundamental constants, the SI commissions have recommended standard nomenclatures for the various physical quantities. They also recommended avoiding special names for subunits, such as the liter, micron (10^{-6} m), and angstrom (10^{-8} cm), and suggested that fractions and multiples be designated as listed in Table 3-4. The calorie is declared obsolete, in favor of the joule for all energy quantities. Finally, although the unit of mass is the kilogram, molecular weights are still to be in g mole^{-1}.

As of the time of this writing the situation appears to be as follows. The mksa/SI system is widely used in physics, and, in chemistry, has received official sanction on the part of major chemical societies in Great Britain. It is in use in some high school chemistry courses in the United States, but not generally in college level chemistry texts or in American chemical journals. It is always dangerous to predict a future course of events, but in the judgment of this writer the present mixed situation will continue for some years. The liter will remain a convenient unit for chemists, as will the cubic centimeter (the latter partly because various physical properties of water have values around unity in the cgs system). Again, because of its convenience, the calorie will remain in use, but alongside the joule. The esu system is again a natural one because of the fundamental role of Coulomb's law in much of wave mechanics and electrochemistry.

Accordingly, the principal system used in this book is the cgs-esu-emu-practical set of units. Numerical calculations will frequently be worked in both this and the mks/SI systems. In addition, much of the recommended SI nomenclature is followed.

Table 3-4. *SI Naming of Multiples and Decimals*

Multiple	Prefix	Symbol	Decimal	Prefix	Symbol
10	deka	da	10^{-1}	deci	d
10^2	hecto	h	10^{-2}	centi	c
10^3	kilo	k	10^{-3}	milli	m
10^6	mega	M	10^{-6}	micro	μ
10^9	giga	G	10^{-9}	nano	n
10^{12}	teta	T	10^{-12}	pico	p
			10^{-15}	femto	f
			10^{-18}	atto	a

SPECIAL TOPICS

3-ST-1   *The Charge Distribution of a Molecule*

The wave mechanical picture of a molecule is that of an electron density distribution; the charge density at each volume element (or the probability of an electron in that element) is given by the square of the psi function ψ for that molecule. Recalling the coordinate system of Fig. 3-2, we see that this charge density is in general some complicated function of r, θ, and ϕ, $\rho(r, \theta, \phi)$. Now, just as a wavy line can be approximated by a series of terms in cosines and sines, that is, by a Fourier expansion, so can a function in three dimensions be approximated by an expansion in spherical harmonics. In fact, it turns out that the wave mechanical solutions for the hydrogen atom consist of one or another spherical harmonic (Section 16-7). These are just the s, p_x, p_y, p_z, d_{z^2}, $d_{x^2-y^2}$, d_{xy}, d_{xz}, d_{yz}, and so on, functions.

An s function is spherically symmetric and is everywhere positive (or, alternatively, everywhere negative). The sum or integral over a charge distribution given by the s function,

$$q_e = \sum_i q_i = \int \rho(r, \theta, \phi) \, d\tau, \tag{3-42}$$

where $d\tau$ is the element of volume, simply gives a charge q_e due to the electron cloud behaving as though it were centered at the nucleus (Fig. 3-5a). The algebraic sum of q_e and the nuclear charge gives the net charge q. An atom or molecule whose charge distribution is given by an s function behaves like a point charge q. The energy of interaction with a unit charge q_0 is

$$\epsilon = \frac{q_0 q}{r} = qV. \tag{3-43}$$

Here V is the potential of the test charge,

$$V = \frac{q_0}{r}. \tag{3-44}$$

A p function has positive and negative lobes, as illustrated in Fig. 3-5(b). The

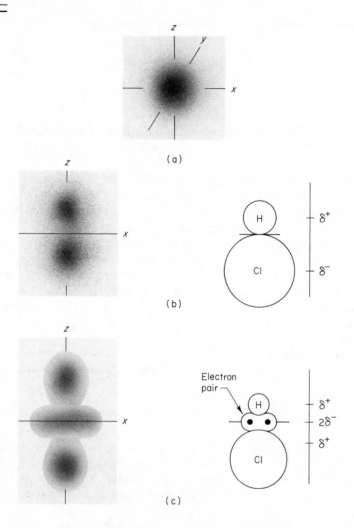

Fig. 3-5. *(a) Charge distribution according to an s function. A monopole. (b) Charge distribution according to a p function. A dipole. (c) Charge distribution according to a d_{z^2} function. A quadrupole.*

sum over such a charge distribution is zero according to Eq. (3-42). However, the sum or integral

$$\mu = \sum_i q_i r_i = \int r\rho(r, \theta, \phi) \, d\tau \qquad (3\text{-}45)$$

is not zero. This now corresponds to a dipole moment. Next, an electron distribution as given by the d_{z^2} function looks as in Fig. 3-5(c). There is now no dipole moment, but Q is nonzero as given by

$$Q = \sum q_i r_i^2 = \int r^2 \rho(r, \theta, \phi) \, d\tau, \tag{3-46}$$

where Q is called the quadrupole moment.

Thus for a molecule such as HCl, the first approximation, or s contribution, says the molecule is neutral. The second term in the expansion, or the p_z contribution, gives the dipole moment. In this approximation the atoms can be regarded as having net charges δ^+ and δ^- separated by the bond distance d. The third term in the series expansion, giving the complete charge distribution, would be the contribution of the d_{z^2} term. This recognizes that the electrons are not spherically disposed around each atom, but concentrate to some extent between the atoms, that is, form a bond. In terms of point charges, a quadrupole consists of two equal, opposing dipoles.

In the case of a neutral diatomic molecule like HCl, the complete charge distribution is given by the sum of the dipole and quadrupole contributions. With more complicated molecules yet higher moments would be needed. Not many quadrupole moments are known; the ones that are have been obtained from analysis of spectroscopic data. A few values are given in Table 3-5.

Equation (3-44) gives the potential V due to a point charge. The potential energy of a molecule having a charge, a dipole moment, and a quadrupole moment can be expressed in terms of the electric potential at that point and its derivatives:

$$\epsilon = Vq + \mu \frac{dV}{dx} + \frac{Q}{2} \frac{d^2V}{dx^2} \tag{3-47}$$

Table 3-5. *Some Quadrupole Moments[a]*

Substance	Quadrupole moment $\times 10^{26}$ (esu cm^2)
H_2	0.65
O_2	−0.4
N_2	−1.4
CO_2	−4.3
C_2H_6	−0.8
C_2H_4	2.0

[a] From A. D. Buckingham, R. L. Disch, and D. A. Dunmur, *J. Amer. Chem. Soc.* **90**, 3104 (1968).

or

$$\epsilon = Vq + \mu\mathbf{F} + \frac{Q}{2}\frac{d\mathbf{F}}{dx}.$$

It is assumed that the dipole and quadrupole are aligned in the x direction, and dV/dx gives the field $\mathbf{F}$ in this direction. The verification of Eq. (3-47) is left as an exercise.

3-ST-2 Magnetic Properties of Matter

The magnetic properties of matter are of less general interest to the chemist than are the electrical properties. In some cases, however, important information about the electronic structure of a molecule can be obtained.

We measure a quantity called the molar magnetic susceptibility χ_M, which is rather analogous to molar polarization in the electrical situation. A convenient way of making this measurement is by means of a Gouy magnetic balance, illustrated in Fig. 3-6. An electromagnet establishes a field $\mathbf{H}_0$ and one measures

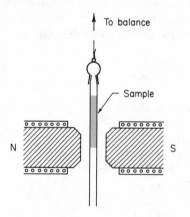

Fig. 3-6. *The Gouy balance.*

the resulting change in weight of a sample. The sample is contained in a tube which is suspended between the pole pieces of the magnet, with the bottom of the sample at the centerline. The hollow lower portion of the tube compensates for the action of the field on the tube itself. The suspension is attached to a sensitive balance, and one measures the change in pull that occurs when the magnetic field is turned on.

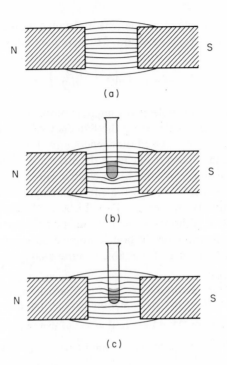

Fig. 3-7. *Lines of magnetic force in (a) vacuum, (b) a diamagnetic substance, and (c) a paramagnetic substance.*

As illustrated in Fig. 3-7(b) the sample may be diamagnetic, in which case the magnetic field within it is less than H_0 and magnetic lines of force deflect away from the sample. Alternatively, as in Fig. 3-7(c), the sample may be paramagnetic and show the reverse effects. In the first case the pull decreases when the field is applied; and in the second case it increases. A straightforward derivation shows that the change in force f on the sample, is given by

$$f = \frac{1}{2} \mathscr{A} \chi_M \frac{\rho}{M} H_0^2, \tag{3-48}$$

where $\mathscr{A}$ is the area of the tube, ρ is the sample density, and M is the molecular weight.

From the molecular point of view, χ_M is made up of two contributions: that due to the inherent magnetic polarizability α and that due to the alignment in the field of any permanent magnetic moments present. Just as with dipolar molecules in an electric field, the alignment of permanent molecular moments is opposed by the randomizing effect of thermal agitation. The actual equation is

$$\chi_M = N_0\!\left(\alpha + \frac{\mu_M^2}{3kT}\right), \tag{3-49}$$

where μ_M is the permanent molecular magnetic moment.

As in the electrical case α describes the tendency of the applied field to induce an opposing field in an otherwise homogeneous medium. A physical description of the effect is that the applied field causes the electrons of the atoms to undergo a precession; this precession gives rise to an electric current which in turn generates an opposing magnetic field. We call the effect diamagnetism, and report a molar diamagnetic susceptibility $N_0\alpha$ or χ_α. Pascal observed around 1910 that χ_α's are approximately additive, although as with molar polarization or refraction, corrections are needed for special types of bonds. Some atomic and bond susceptibilities are given in Table 3-6; the use of the table is quite analogous to that of Table 3-1.

As a numerical illustration, suppose the magnet to provide a field H_0 of 10,000 Oe, $\mathscr{A}$ to be 0.1 cm², and the sample to consist of water at 25°C. The value of χ_α for water is -13×10^{-6} and $\chi_\alpha(\rho/M)$ is then -0.722×10^{-6} cm⁻³. Substitution into Eq. (3-48) gives

$$f = -\tfrac{1}{2}(0.1)(0.722 \times 10^{-6})(10^4)^2 = -3.61 \text{ dyn} \quad \text{or} \quad -3.7 \text{ mg}.$$

The force is negative, meaning that the sample will be 3.7 mg lighter when the field is on.

Permanent magnetic moments arise first of all from the orbital motion of electrons. For a single electron this moment is related to its angular momentum

Table 3-6. *Some Molar Diamagnetic Susceptibilities[a]*

Atom or bond	Molar susceptibility $\times 10^6$	Ion	Molar susceptibility $\times 10^6$
H	−2.93	Na⁺	−5
C	−6.00	NH₄⁺	−11.5
N (open chain)	−5.55	Fe²⁺	−13
N (ring)	−4.61	Cr³⁺	−11
O (alcohol,		Co³⁺	−10
ether)	−4.61	Cl⁻	−26
O (carbonyl)	−1.72	NO₃⁻	−20
Cl	−20.1	SO₄²⁻	−40
C=C	5.5		

[a] From P. F. Selwood, "Magnetochemistry," 2nd ed. Wiley (Interscience), New York, 1956.

and therefore to the orbital quantum number l, where $l = 0$ for an s electron, $l = 1$ for a p electron, and so forth. Analysis gives

$$\mu = \frac{eh}{4\pi mc} [l(l + 1)]^{1/2}, \tag{3-50}$$

where the quantity $(eh/4\pi mc)$ is known as the Bohr magneton μ_B. Substitution of the numerical values for Planck's constant h, the mass of the electron m, and the velocity of light c gives $\mu_B = 9.273 \times 10^{-21}$ erg Oe^{-1} (and 9.273×10^{-24} A m^{-2} in the mks/SI system).

The second contribution to the permanent magnetic moment is that from the spin of the electron itself. Orbital motion is quantized in units of angular momentum $h/2\pi$ and spin angular momentum is quantized in units of $\frac{1}{2}h/2\pi$. Since the quantity $h/2\pi$ appears in both cases, it is not surprising that the spin magnetic moment is related to μ_B:

$$\mu_s = 2\mu_B[s(s + 1)]^{1/2}, \tag{3-51}$$

where s is the spin quantum number.

The orbital contribution, Eq. (3-50), is often small; this is because orbital motions of electrons may be so tied into the nuclear configuration of the atom that they are unable to line up with an applied field. As a fortunate consequence only the spin contribution is then important. If more than one unpaired electron is present, the individual spins combine vectorially,

$$\mu_s = 2\mu_B[S(S + 1)]^{1/2}, \tag{3-52}$$

where S is just one-half times the number of unpaired electrons. The molar susceptibility is then

$$\chi_M = \frac{4\mu_B^2 N_0}{3kT} [S(S + 1)]^{1/2}. \tag{3-53}$$

The total observed χ_M is the sum of the negative diamagnetic contribution $N_0\alpha$ and the positive contribution from Eq. (3-53).

Equation (3-53) often applies adequately to elements through the first long row of the periodic table, and therefore allows a determination of the number of unpaired electrons present per molecule. Thus a ferrous compound should have four unpaired electrons on the iron and therefore a moment of $[2(2 + 1)]^{1/2}\mu_B$ or $4.90\mu_B$. The observed value is $5.25\mu_B$.

GENERAL REFERENCES

HALLIDAY, D., AND RESNICK, R. (1962). "Physics." Wiley, New York.
SELWOOD, P. (1956). "Magnetochemistry," 2nd ed. Wiley (Interscience), New York.

CITED REFERENCES

DOUGLAS, B. E., AND MCDANIEL, D. H. (1965). "Concepts and Models of Inorganic Chemistry," p. 84. Blaisdell, Waltham, Massachusetts.

GLASSTONE, S. (1946). "Textbook of Physical Chemistry." Van Nostrand–Reinhold, Princeton, New Jersey.

HANTZSCH, A., AND DÜRIGEN, F. (1928). Z. Phys. Chem. 136, 1.

International Critical Tables. National Research Council, McGraw–Hill, N. Y., 1926–1933.

MCGLASHAN, M. L. (1968). Physico–Chemical Quantities and Units. Royal Inst. of Chem. Publ. No. 15, London.

PARTINGTON, J. R. (1954). "An Advanced Treatise on Physical Chemistry," Vol. 5, p. 476. Longmans, Green, New York.

RINGBOM, Z. (1938). Anal. Chem. 115, 332.

SUGDEN, S. (1924). See GARNER, F. B., AND SUGDEN, S. S. (1929). J. Chem. Soc. 1929, 1298.

Exercises

3-1 Gaseous bromine has an extinction coefficient of 120 liter mole^{-1} cm^{-1} at 400 nm. Calculate (a) α, (b) k_N, (c) k_x, and (d) the per cent of incident light of this wavelength which would pass through a 1.5-cm cell filled with Br_2 at 100 Torr pressure and 25°C.

$\quad$ *Ans.* (a) 276.4, (b) 4.588 × 10^{-19}, (c) 1.486 cm^{-1}, (d) 10.76 %.

3-2 The extinction coefficient for benzophenone is 500 liter mole^{-1} cm^{-1} at 300 nm. Calculate the optical density of a 1.5 × 10^{-3} M solution for a 2-cm cell and assuming that the solvent, ethanol, has an optical density of 0.05 cm^{-1} at this wavelength.

$\quad$ *Ans.* 1.60.

3-3 The optical density of a 0.02 M solution of $Cr(NH_3)_6^{3+}$ is 0.589 at 462.5 nm with a 0.5-cm cell; that of the aqueous solvent alone is 0.200. Calculate the extinction coefficient for this complex ion and the percentage of incident light absorbed by the solution.

$\quad$ *Ans.* 38.9 liter mole^{-1} cm^{-1}, 74.2%.

3-4 The extinction coefficients of benzophenone and of naphthalene are the same at 300 nm, namely 500 liter mole^{-1} cm^{-1}. Naphthalene does not absorb at 350 nm, but benzophenone does, with an extinction coefficient of 110 liter mole^{-1} cm^{-1}. Neglecting solvent·absorption, calculate the composition of a mixed solution of these two species if the optical density in a 1-cm cell is 0.500 at 300 nm and 0.030 at 350 nm.

$\quad$ *Ans.* 2.73 × 10^{-4} M benzophenone and 7.27 × 10^{-4} M naphthalene.

3-5 Calculate the molar refraction of ammonia if the index of refraction of the gas at STP is 1.000373.

$\quad$ *Ans.* 5.57 cm^3 mole^{-1}.

Problems

3-6 The molar refraction of HI is $13.74 \text{ cm}^3 \text{ mole}^{-1}$. Calculate the index of refraction of HI at 25°C and 0.1 atm pressure and the polarizability of the HI molecule.

$$\textit{Ans.} \quad n = 1.0000842, \alpha = 5.45 \times 10^{-24} \text{ cm}^3.$$

3-7 The index of refraction of liquid water is 1.333. Calculate the molar refraction and the polarizability of water.

$$\textit{Ans.} \quad \mathbf{R} = 4.00 \text{ cm}^3 \text{ mole}^{-1}, \alpha = 1.58 \times 10^{-24} \text{ cm}^3.$$

3-8 The dielectric constant of liquid water is 78.54 at 25°C. Calculate the molar polarization of water, and in conjunction with Exercise 3-7, the dipole moment of water. Explain why your value for μ is incorrect.

$$\textit{Ans.} \quad \mathbf{P} = 17.4 \text{ cm}^3 \text{ mole}^{-1}, \mu = 0.807 \text{ D}.$$

3-9 As an alternative calculation to Exercise 3-8, the dielectric constant of water vapor at 1 atm varies from 1.005471 at 384.3°K to 1.004124 at 444.7°K. Calculate the dipole moment of water from this information.

$$\textit{Ans.} \quad 1.84 \text{ D}.$$

3-10 The dielectric constant of chloroform gas at 120°C and 1 atm pressure is 1.0042. Given that the dipole moment is 1.02 D, calculate the polarizability of chloroform and the dielectric constant of liquid chloroform.

$$\textit{Ans.} \quad \alpha = 11.5 \times 10^{-24} \text{ cm}^3, D(\text{liq}) = 4.859.$$

3-11 Calculate the bond length in HBr.

$$\textit{Ans.} \quad 1.53 \text{ Å}.$$

3-12 Calculate the dipole moment for the $H-O$ bond in H_2O from information in Section 3-5.

$$\textit{Ans.} \quad 1.49 \text{ D}.$$

Problems

3-1 The accompanying table gives the extinction coefficients for ferrocyanide ion and for ferricyanide ion at various wavelengths.

(a) Make a semilogarithmic plot (on semilog graph paper) of extinction coefficient versus wavelength for these two species. (b) Calculate the percentage of light of 350 nm absorbed by a $0.0005 \, M$ solution of each species in a 2-cm cell. (c) The reaction

$$2Fe(CN)_6^{3-} + H_2O + CN^- = 2Fe(CN)_6^{4-} + CNO^- + 2H^+$$

is being followed spectrophotometrically; CN^- and CNO^- do not absorb in region of wavelengths covered in the accompanying table. The solution initially is 0.001 M in ferricyanide; after 10 min the optical density of the solution (in a 1-cm cell) is 0.906 at 320 nm. Calculate the percentage of the ferricyanide that has reacted.

Wavelength (nm)	Ferrocyanide ϵ	Ferricyanide ϵ
280	970	1100
290	550	1350
300	300	1550
310	285	1350
320	315	1100
330	320	800
340	260	520
350	165	300
360	130	320
370	70	430
380	40	590
390	15	750
400	7	890
410	0	1000
420	0	1010
430	0	870
440	0	650
460	0	250

3-2 At a wavelength of 500 nm the optical density of a 0.0100 M solution of the complex ion $[Co(NH_3)_5H_2O]^{3+}$ is 0.470, while that of a 0.00200 M solution of the ion $[Co(NH_3)_5(SCN)]^{2+}$ is 0.356. At 345 nm, the two optical densities are 0.530 and 1.33, respectively. The optical densities at 500 and 345 nm are then determined for a solution containing a mixture of the two complex ions and found to be 0.319 and 0.611, respectively. Calculate the concentrations of the complex ions in this solution.

3-3 At a wavelength of 300 nm the optical density of 0.001 M potassium ferricyanide solution is 1.55, while that of a 0.002 M potassium ferrocyanide solution is 0.600. These densities are for a 1-cm cell, and are corrected for any absorption due to the solvent (water). At 360 nm the optical densities, determined in the same way, for the same two solutions are 0.320 and 0.260. It is desired to analyze a solution containing unknown concentrations of ferricyanide and ferrocyanide, but no other absorbing species. Using a 10-cm cell, it is found that the optical density of the solution (corrected for solvent absorption) is 4.00 at 300 nm and 1.03 at 360 nm. Calculate the concentrations of ferricyanide and of ferrocyanide in this solution.

3-4 The amount of a certain substance A is to be estimated by measuring with a spectrophotometer the extinction E $(E = \epsilon l C)$ for a solution of A. The intensity of the transmitted light I can be measured within an error of 1.0 % of the initial intensity I_0 (i.e., $\delta I/I_0 = 0.01$). At what value for E will the relative error in the amount of A be minimized, and what is that error? (Ringbom, 1938.) [Note: The extinction E is an alternative term for the optical density D: $E = D = \epsilon l C = \log(I_0/I)$. It is necessary to obtain an expression for $\delta E/E$ and then to set $d(\delta E/E)/dE$ equal to zero, thus getting the minimum value of $\delta E/E$. In this way the solution of A can be diluted so that the error in E and hence C is a minimum.]

3-5 The molar refraction R is 1.643 for oxygen in an ether group $(R-O-R)$. It is 6.818 for methane and 13.279 for dimethyl ether. Calculate the value for diethyl ether.

3-6 Given that the molar refractions for methane, ethane, *n*-propionic acid, and methyl propionate are 6.818, 11.436, 17.590, and 22.326, respectively, calculate the atomic refractions for H, C, carbonyl oxygen (C=O), hydroxyl oxygen (—OH), and ether oxygen (—O—R). Use only the above information plus the fact that the molar refraction for *β*-hydroxy propionic acid is 19.115.

3-7 The molar polarization of a certain vapor is found to obey the equation $P = 60 + (20.500/T)$ (in cubic centimeters). Assuming ideal gas behavior, calculate the index of refraction and the dielectric constant of the vapor at STP. What molecular properties can be obtained? Calculate their values.

3-8 The accompanying data are reported for solutions of ethyl ether in cyclohexane at 20°C [from Glasstone (1946)].

Mole fraction ether	Dielectric constant	Density (g cm⁻³)
0.04720	2.109	0.7751
0.08854	2.178	0.7720
0.12325	2.246	0.7691
0.17310	2.317	0.7664

The molar refraction for the ether is 22.48 cm³. Using the extrapolation method, calculate the molar polarization of the solvent and of the ether and the dipole moment of the latter.

3-9 The accompanying data have been obtained for aqueous LiCl solutions at 19°C (Hantzsch and Dürigen, 1928).

Grams of salt per 100 g solution	Density (g cm⁻³)	Index of refraction
0	0.9984	1.3334
3.44	1.0180	1.3397
6.77	1.0357	1.3462
9.99	1.0524	1.3523
16.12	1.0862	1.3644

Calculate the molar refraction of water at 19°C and, by the extrapolation method, that of LiCl(*aq*).

3-10 The polarizability of CH_4 is 2.58 Å³. Calculate the index of refraction and the dielectric constant for the gas at STP and for liquid methane.

3-11 The angle of inclination of the N—H bonds to the molecular axis is 111° in the case of NH_3. The molecular dipole moment is 1.48 D; calculate the dipole moment for a N—H bond.

3-12 The dipole moment of SO_2 is 1.61 D, the length of each S—O bond is 1.45 Å, and the bonds have approximately 25% ionic character. Calculate the bond angle, that is, the angle between the two S—O bonds.

3 Some Additive Physical Properties of Matter

3-13 The dipole moment of water is 1.82 D and the two H—O bonds are at 105° to each other and each have 25% ionic character. Calculate the H—O bond length in angstroms.

3-14 The dipole moment of HCl is 1.03 D and the bond length is 1.30 Å. Calculate the fractional ionic character to the HCl bond, that is, the charge on each atom expressed as a fraction of the electronic charge.

3-15 Repeat the calculations of Problem 3-10 using the mksa system of units.

3-16 Repeat the calculations of Problem 3-7 using the mksa system of units.

Special Topics Problems

3-1 Carbon monoxide has a dipole moment of 0.10 D and a quadrupole moment of -1.3×10^{-26} esu cm². Calculate the potential energy of interaction of CO with a Na^+ ion 15 Å away. Assume that C is negative in CO and that the molecular axis points toward the ion, that is, $Na^+ \cdots C$—O. Express your result as ϵ/kT for 25°C.

3-2 Derive Eq. (3-47).

3-3 The energy of adsorption of polar molecules on ionic solids is attributed in part to ion–dipole interaction. Suppose a silica–alumina catalyst to have sites of charge -1 widely enough separated that each adsorbed H_2O interacts with only one site. Taking the dipole moment of H_2O to be 1.83 D, calculate the ion–dipole interaction energy as a function of distance from the surface from 3 to 15 Å assuming that the water molecule is oriented so that its dipole is (a) parallel to the surface and (b) perpendicular to the surface. Express your results as ϵ/kT at 25°C.

3-4 The magnetic field in a Gouy apparatus is calibrated by measurement of the pull for a sample of Mohr's salt. The tube is 3 mm in diameter and the packing of the solid is such that its density in the tube is 3.5 g cm⁻³. Calculate H_0 if the pull is 40 mg. Assume 25°C.

3-5 The molar susceptibility of benzene is -54.8×10^{-6} in cgs units. What force should be observed in a Gouy balance if a 0.5-cm-diameter tube is used with a field of 8000 Oe? Assume 25°C.

3-6 Calculate χ_M for the Cr^{3+} ion and for the complex ion $Cr(NH_3)_6^{3+}$, allowing for the diamagnetic corrections. What increase in weight should be observed if a 0.01 M solution of $Cr(NH_3)_6Cl_3$ in water is placed in a 1-cm-diameter tube and weighed in a Gouy balance for which H_0 is 9500 Oe (allow for solvent). Assume 25°C.

3-7 The following results are obtained for a 0.5 M solution of a nickel coordination compound. With a field of 10,000 Oe and a tube of 0.1 cm² area, the net pull (after allowing for solvent) is 12.3 mg. The diamagnetic correction for the nickel compound itself is -2.0×10^{-4} in cgs units. Calculate the number of unpaired electrons per nickel atom. Assume 25°C.

4 CHEMICAL THERMODYNAMICS. THE FIRST LAW OF THERMODYNAMICS

4-1 Introduction

Modern chemical thermodynamics has two interpenetrating structures. The first structure is that of classical thermodynamics, which is based on a set of far-reaching phenomenological laws. The detailed logical elaboration of these laws permits their precise application to very complicated chemical and physical situations and leads to relationships and conclusions that are otherwise far from obvious. However, all these relationships and conclusions are themselves phenomenological; that is, they deal with macroscopic, operationally defined quantities. They contain nothing that is not already implicit in the laws of thermodynamics themselves.

This aspect of thermodynamics has a strength and a weakness. The strength lies in the fact that since the laws rest entirely on experimental observation, they are correct to the extent of the accuracy and generality of such observations. The weight of evidence is by now so massive that we have no doubt that the laws are valid within our present scientific ken. Should some totally new reach be achieved, the laws might be expanded, but their present application would not be altered.

There is a not too old example of just such a situation. The first law of thermodynamics affirms the conservation of energy. In the absence of external fields (electrical, magnetic, or gravitational) this amounts to saying that chemical energy, heat energy, and work or mechanical energy may be interconverted but that their sum is constant for an isolated system. The discovery of radioactivity and, later, of nuclear fission showed that vast amounts of energy could be released by matter–energy conversion. The first law now has to include nuclear energy, or, alternatively, to affirm that the mass of an isolated system remains constant, recognizing that total mass includes energy mass. The point, however, is that the discovery of the whole new domain of nuclear energy in no way altered the laws of thermodynamics with respect to phenomena not involving nuclear changes. No new discovery, however enormous, is expected to do otherwise.

The weakness of classical thermodynamics stems from the fact that, being phenomenological, it deals only with the average behavior of many molecules. It provides no detail about individual molecular behavior. Also, while it can relate macroscopic properties, it cannot predict them separately. Thus thermodynamics provides a relationship between the heat capacity of a gas and its coefficients of compressibility and thermal expansion, but it cannot predict the actual heat capacity of any particular gas. It relates vapor pressure and heat of vaporization, but is unable to say what the actual vapor pressure of a given liquid will be.

The second structure is that of statistical thermodynamics. Here one applies the Boltzmann principle to formulate the distribution of molecules among all of their possible energy states, much as is done in gas kinetic theory, and the various average quantities so computed can be identified with classical thermodynamic ones. It is now necessary to provide a great deal of detailed information about energy states, and in simple cases it is possible to do this through the use of wave mechanics. For example, statistical mechanics can give the actual heat capacity of a particular dilute gas with some precision.

In principle, then, statistical thermodynamics not only leads to the relationships of classical thermodynamics but also provides values for all the thermodynamic properties of individual substances. The practice is not so easy. Wave mechanics does not provide accurate energy states for any but the simplest of molecules, let alone for the multitudinous interactions among molecules in a condensed state. Even for gases the intermolecular potential functions that determine nonideality are as yet semiempirical. The full statistical mechanical treatment of liquids is barely within reach for a monatomic one such as argon but otherwise seems hopelessly complex.

A consequence of the complexity of rigorous treatments is that various simplifying assumptions are introduced. These may take the form of neglecting certain categories of energy states, of making some structural assumptions that simplify the listing of such states, or of various mathematical approximations to make the computations feasible. In other words, statistical mechanics as practiced is very often based on simplified models and is essentially semiempirical. Herein lies a danger. Because the results appear in classical thermodynamic language, there is a tendency to imbue them with the full status of classical, phenomenological thermodynamics. This is at times quite easy to do if the simplifying assumptions are not stated explicitly but are implicit in some detail of mathematics or in the manner of counting of energy states.

However, because the two types of thermodynamics are so interpenetrating, the practice in this text will be to present the statistical treatments along with or closely following the classical ones. Use will be made of wave mechanical results, some of which are derived only later. For the present such results are introduced simply as accepted statements about the spacings of different kinds of energy levels.

4-2   The Story of a Man

It is not possible in a text of this type to delve into the historical background of each subject. Such background is often fascinating, however, and it seems worthwhile to offer an occasional account in sufficient depth to illuminate the human side of science.

The origins of the first law of thermodynamics, or the conservation of energy, lie in the 18th and early 19th centuries, with the developing realization that heat and work were interconvertible in fixed ratio. The first clear, although qualitative, realization of this interconvertibility is attributed to Count Rumford, who at one stage in his career was able to observe the great amount of heat liberated in the operation of boring cannon. His observations convinced him that the heat resulted from the dissipation of mechanical work and was not some substance released by the iron chips. For example, he noted that a dull tool produced no chips, yet about the same amount of heat. That is, he thus attacked the then prevalent idea that heat was a substance (called caloric).

It remained for James Joule to make the conclusion quantitative in the 1840's. One of Joule's experiments consisted in churning up water in a container by means of a paddle driven by a falling weight. He observed a temperature rise and from this calculated the mechanical equivalent of heat.

In modern terms the relation is

$$1 \quad \text{cal} = 4.184 \quad \text{J}, \tag{4-1}$$

where the calorie was originally that amount of heat required to raise the temperature of 1 g of water by 1°C. In modern practice it is defined in terms of the joule using Eq. (4-1). The joule is the amount of work corresponding to the action of unit force, the newton, over unit distance, the meter; the newton, in turn, is defined as that force that gives 1 kg an acceleration of 1 m sec^{-2}. In the cgs system gram and centimeter are substituted for kilogram and meter, respectively; the unit of work is the erg; $1 \text{ J} = 10^7 \text{ erg}$; and the unit of force is the dyne, $1 \text{ N} = 10^5 \text{ dyn}$. In Joule's experiment the work done by the falling weight would be given by the product of the force acting on it (mass times acceleration due to gravity) and the distance it fell.

To return to the title of this section, the story of a man is that of Count Rumford. The following account is reproduced by permission of the Los Angeles Times. Let the reader contribute his own reaction!

SCIENTIST AND SCOUNDREL, AND GOOD IN BOTH LINES[†]

E. C. Krauss

A bit of little-known history about the U.S. Military Academy has recently come to light after being buried in old records for generations. The story is that West Point had a narrow escape: it was almost established under the care of a man who had been both one of the world's most brilliant scientists and a scoundrel without a shred of character.

This curious individual, who might be called attractive in a revolting sort of way, was Benjamin Thompson; born at Woburn, Mass.; Sir Benjamin by action of His Majesty, King George III, and Count Rumford, a noble of the Holy Roman Empire.

When he was at the British court in the late 1790's, he proposed to Rufus King, our Minister, that he start an American military academy similar to one he had established for the Grand Duke of Bavaria. King knew him only as a man of apparently brilliant attainments and recommended him to President John Adams, who was on the point of naming him—would have named him but for a dispute over rank, Thompson asking to be made a full general, equal to Washington.

At this point, British officials who knew about the seamy side of Thompson's career gave King an earful about him that made the appointment impossible. Minister King gave Thompson a choice: he would tell the world why Thompson was not acceptable, and thus bring all the scandal to light; or Thompson would be publicly offered the appointment but must refuse it. The latter course, which saved face both for the United States and for Thompson, was agreed upon. And West Point started (in 1801) under somebody else.

What was the scandal? This being a family newspaper, not all of it can be told. However, Thompson started early: in Portsmouth, N. H., where he was teaching school, he won the heart of a rich widow of 32 and set up, at 19, as the local squire and a major in the militia. This was 1774 and Thompson was run out of town after being accused of being a spy for Gen. Gage, British commander in Boston. He was, but the patriots couldn't prove it at the time.

In Boston, he tried for a year to get a commission in the Colonial Army, but the New Hampshire patriots stopped that; so he went over openly to the British side. Finally Gen. Gage sent him to London as a member of a committee to explain to Lord George Germain, Colonial Secretary, the evacuation of Boston. He became a favorite of Lord George at once and was made undersecretary for Carolina and Georgia. In 1779 he took a cruise with the British Navy and in 1781 made a deal with a man named Lutterloh and a Frenchman named LaMotte to sell British naval secrets to the French.

The plot was detected; Lutterloh confessed and turned King's evidence; but Lord George would not permit the prosecution, or even the exposure of Thompson. LaMotte was convicted, hanged, drawn and quartered, and Thompson was sent to America as a lieutenant colonel of Dragoons. But the war was about over.

Thompson—he was Sir Benjamin by this time—then went to Bavaria where his great talents won him quick favor. He became Minister of War, Minister of the Interior and Royal Scientist; and he was also a spy for the British. However, at the Bavarian court he carried on further scientific experiments. At London, he had devised apparatus for measuring the force of gunpowder, and practically invented the science of ballistics. In Bavaria he disproved the "caloric theory" of heat, devised a new method of boring cannon, invented the cookstove (all cooking had been done on open fires) and reinvented the central heating system which the ancient Cretans had invented millenniums before. He invented the drip coffeepot and was the inventor of baking powder.

One of his achievements in the realm of statesmanship was to arrest the 2600 beggars of Munich and put them to work making clothing for the army.

[†] Copyright, 1955, Los Angeles Times. Reprinted by permission.

Meanwhile he was grafting and stealing with both hands, as he had been in London; it was estimated that he stole the equivalent of much more than $1,000,000 during his public career—an incredible fortune for that day.

Thompson broke with the British spy system in 1785 and in 1791 was made a count. He went back to London in 1795 in the guise of a distinguished scientist, to read papers before the Royal Society and remained a year. On his return to Munich he was made Prime Minister; but he made so many enemies that he had to flee to London two years later, pausing only to appoint himself Bavarian Minister to the Court of St. James's.

The British court refused to accept him as such, giving the excuse that the King could not well receive as a foreign envoy one of his own subjects.

When the West Point deal fell through, Thompson, or Count Rumford, drifted to Paris where he became very chummy with Napoleon, who admired his artillery studies. And if the Americans did not want him as a military instructor, Napoleon did and the count established the famous school of St. Cyr, the French West Point.

At 60, he married the widow of the great French chemist Antoine Lavoisier—he who was guillotined when the court ruled that "the republic has no need of scientists." Mme. Lavoisier had a handsome fortune. But she cared for society and Count Rumford didn't; at their divorce he took half her inheritance.

His science kept equal pace with his scoundrelism; he invented the photometer for measuring light, first used the term "candle power" as a standard, and also invented the steam radiator.

The count lived in easy circumstances till 1814 and remembered his birthplace by endowing a professorship at Harvard—which is still in force.

Here was surely one of the strangest mixtures of good and evil the world ever saw.

4-3 Energy and the First Law of Thermodynamics

The interconvertibility of heat and work makes it possible to define energy as the ability to produce heat or to do work. With this definition we appear to restrict ourselves to measuring only those energy changes which produce one or the other effect. To be more precise, we state that

$$\Delta E = q - w, \tag{4-2}$$

where ΔE is the internal energy change and

$$q = \text{heat absorbed by the system,} \tag{4-3}$$

$$w = \text{work done by the system.} \tag{4-4}$$

The sign convention is such that ΔE for the system is negative if it furnishes either overall heat or work to its surroundings. Also, q and w will be treated as algebraic quantities. That is, if heat is produced by the system, q will be negative, and likewise w, if work is done on the system.

We know, of course, that energy appears to reside in a system in different ways. We think of *thermal energy*—a system that releases heat or does work usually becomes cooler; the energy content of a system must then be a function of its temperature. However, if ice absorbs heat at 0°C or if two blocks of ice are rubbed together (as was done in 1799 by Humphry Davy), melting, but not necessarily any change in temperature, occurs. There is thus a difference in the energy content of ice and of water. We call this a latent energy or *latent heat*. Further, an electro-chemical cell can produce work, as in the starting of a car by means of a lead storage battery. There is no particular temperature or phase change, but now a chemical reaction has occurred. Evidently the products contain a different amount of energy than do the reactants. We thus also have *chemical energy*.

In view of these various forms of energy and our lack of complete understanding of them, might it not be possible for a system to change its energy even though $q - w$ were zero? We can examine the implications of such a happening as follows. Suppose that state A, of energy E_A, could convert to state B, of lower energy E_B, but with $q_{AB} - w_{AB} = 0$. There must in general be some state C such that C can be converted to A with some values of q and w, $q_{CA} - w_{CA}$, and that B can be converted to C with some other values, $q_{BC} - w_{BC}$. We now carry out the process in which state C is first converted to state A, then state A is converted to state B, and state B is in turn converted back to state C. The situation is illustrated in Fig. 4-1.

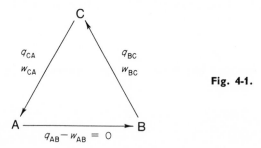

Fig. 4-1.

The result of this cycle is to return the system to its original condition. That is, we define the state of a system by its macroscopic properties. If these are all the same for the initial and final state C, then the system has been returned identically to its original condition; the cycle, for example, should be repeatable indefinitely. Now the consequence of the cycle is that some total (algebraic) heat has been absorbed, $q_{CA} + q_{AB} + q_{BC} = q_{tot}$ and work has been done, $w_{CA} + w_{AB} + w_{BC} = w_{tot}$. There are two extreme cases. First q_{tot} might be zero, but not w_{tot}. This would mean that work has been done on or by a system with no change in the system. Alternatively, if w_{tot} is zero, heat has been absorbed or released by the system, but again with no change. This is contrary to experience. More generally, it is entirely contrary to experience that net heat or work can be put into or withdrawn from a system without some change in that system. The particular possibility of net work or heat being supplied by a system was for a while intensively tested by attempts to contruct a perpetual motion machine, that is, by attempts to find some cyclic process that produced overall work or heat. The reverse of being able endlessly to insert work or heat into a system without changing it, while less appealing to the inventor, has never been observed either.

We generalize our inability to find a perpetual motion machine by saying that $q_{tot} = w_{tot}$ for any cyclic process. ΔE must also always be zero for any such process since the cycle returns the system to the identical state variables of the initial condition; we cannot imagine identical states as having different energies. We thus conclude that ΔE is completely defined by Eq. (4-2) and, further, that ΔE must be zero for any process for which $q = w$. In terms of the example here, this means that ΔE_{AB} must be zero (since $q_{AB} = w_{AB}$). We also conclude that $\Delta E_{CA} = -\Delta E_{BC}$, irrespective of the nature of state C. Alternatively put, our experience requires that energy changes as defined by Eq. (4-2) be entirely specified when the initial and final states of the process, cyclic or otherwise, are specified. Thus the defining equation (4-2) is not really restricting; it affirms a law of nature of great generality.

The defining equation gives only an energy difference, however; it provides no absolute scale of energy. Ordinarily we pick some standard or reference state as having an assumed energy, usually zero, and then obtain the energy of all other states through Eq. (4-2). In this sense, then, we speak of energy as a state function; we mean that changes in it are defined if the change of state is defined.

The various preceding statements are ways of affirming the First Law of Thermodynamics. To summarize, the alternative statements are:

$\Delta E = q - w$.
The internal energy of an isolated system is constant.
The internal energy change in a cyclic process is zero.
Internal energy is a state function.

$$(4\text{-}5)$$

The expression "internal energy" is the correct one for E; it emphasizes that we are referring to the energy content of a definite portion of matter. When indicated by a capital E internal energy will be on a molar basis. The expression "molar thermodynamic energy" has been recommended by international commissions; we will often abbreviate both to call E just energy or energy per mole, where no confusion is likely to result.

Returning to the example of Fig. 4-1, we see that the requirement to satisfy our experience with respect to perpetual motion machines is that $q_{tot} = w_{tot}$. Thus, per cycle, it would be allowable for work to be done on the system and an equivalent amount of heat evolved. It would also be allowable for heat to be absorbed and an equivalent amount of work to be done. The first situation encounters no objections, but the second turns out to have a restriction, again as a result of experience. The restriction is stated by the Second Law of Thermodynamics, taken up in Chapter 6.

As a final comment, the first law has so far been justified in terms of negative arguments, that is, in terms of the lack of observations of certain behavior. There is a similar aspect to the second law. However, both lead to relationships that have abundantly been verified. There is thus a great amount of direct evidence for the validity of the laws of thermodynamics.

4-4   *Mathematical Properties of State Functions. Exact and Path-Dependent Differentials*

The conclusion that the internal energy change is zero for a cyclic process or that E is a state function carries a further implication. Referring once again to Fig. 4-1, we see that the change in energy on going from A directly to B, ΔE_{AB}, must be the same as that on going from A to C and then from C to B, ΔE_{ACB}. Otherwise, the first law of thermodynamics would be violated. We conclude therefore that ΔE cannot depend on the path taken or that, for some small change, dE is independent of path.

We know, however, that q and w do depend on path. This is a matter of common experience, examples of which are illustrated in Fig. 4-2 and as follows.

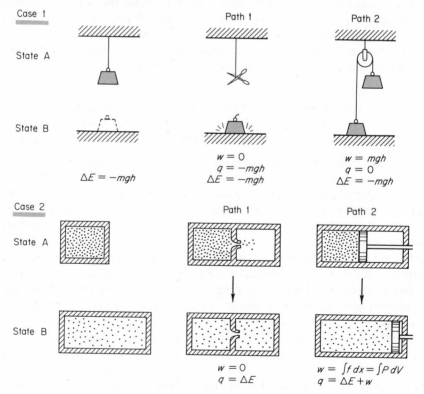

Fig. 4-2. *Reversible and irreversible processes.*

CASE 1   *State A*:   mass m at height h.
  State B: mass m at $h = 0$.

Path 1: The object is dropped in free fall and gains kinetic energy mgh, which is dissipated as heat when it strikes the stop at $h = 0$. No work is done, and so $w = 0$, but $q = -mgh$. Thus $\Delta E = q - w = -mgh$.

Path 2: The object is counterbalanced by a very slightly lesser mass, which is then raised from $h = 0$ to h. The work done is now $w = mgh$, and $q = 0$, as no significant kinetic energy is developed. $\Delta E = q - w = -mgh$.

CASE 2 *State A*: Gas at T_1, P_1, and V_1.

State B: Gas at T_1, P_2, and V_2.

Path 1: The expansion is allowed to occur by rupture of a diaphragm, temperature being kept constant by means of a thermostat bath. No work is done, $w = 0$, $q = \Delta E$.

Path 2: The expansion occurs against a piston. The work done is (force on piston) × (displacement) or $w = \int f \, dx = \int P \mathscr{A} \, dx$, where $\mathscr{A}$ is the area of the piston. Hence $w > 0$, $q = \Delta E + w$.

Thus one of the very important corollaries of the first law is that while ΔE depends only on the initial and final states, it is given experimentally by the difference between two quantities q and w which separately do depend on the path taken in going from the initial to the final state. As will be seen in the ensuing material we take advantage of this situation by choosing paths of convenience between two states to facilitate calculation of q and w, knowing that the resulting ΔE will be independent of our choice of path. In differential form Eq. (4-2) becomes

$$dE = \delta q - \delta w, \tag{4-6}$$

where the deltas are used to emphasize that the path must be specified for q and w.

There is a mathematical parallel which can be developed as follows. First, the state of a system is defined by any two of the state variables V, P, and T. That is, if we know two of these, the equation of state (for example, the ideal gas law) gives the third. Since E depends only on the state, it follows that E is some function of any two of the state variables, and as a matter both of convention and of convenience we pick V and T and write $E = f(V, T)$. (For the present it is assumed that no chemical changes can occur; otherwise chemical composition would also have to be specified.) The general mathematical situation is that of a dependent variable y which is some function of variables u and v, $y = f(u, v)$.

A schematic representation of the surface given by $y = f(u, v)$ is shown in Fig. 4-3. We can define two slopes: $(\partial y/\partial u)_v$ and $(\partial y/\partial v)_u$, where the partial differential sign ∂ signifies that the subscript variable is held constant. As shown in the figure, these slopes are those of lines of constant v and constant u, respectively. Now suppose we wish to go from a point y_1 to a point y_2. Two possible paths would be that marked ab and that marked cd. Accordingly, Δy can be expressed in two ways:

$$\Delta y = \underset{(a)}{\left(\frac{\Delta y}{\Delta u}\right)_{v_1}} \Delta u + \underset{(b)}{\left(\frac{\Delta y}{\Delta v}\right)_{u_2 = u_1 + \Delta u}} \Delta v,$$

$$\Delta y = \underset{(c)}{\left(\frac{\Delta y}{\Delta v}\right)_{u_1}} \Delta v + \underset{(d)}{\left(\frac{\Delta y}{\Delta u}\right)_{v_2 = v_1 + \Delta v}} \Delta u.$$

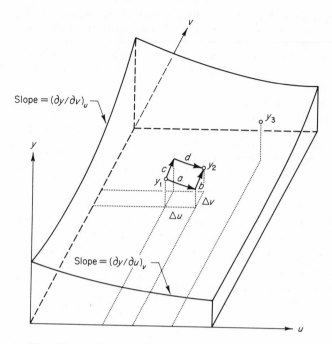

Fig. 4-3.   *Surface illustrating total and partial differentials.*

In the limit of very small differences, $\Delta y = dy$, and $(\Delta y/\Delta u)_{v_1} = (\Delta y/\Delta u)_{v_1+\Delta v} = (\partial y/\partial u)_v$. A similar relation exists for the other slope. The resulting mathematical statement is

$$dy = \left(\frac{\partial y}{\partial u}\right)_v du + \left(\frac{\partial y}{\partial v}\right)_u dv \qquad (4\text{-}7)$$

and the corresponding one for E is

$$dE = \left(\frac{\partial E}{\partial V}\right)_T dV + \left(\frac{\partial E}{\partial T}\right)_V dT. \qquad (4\text{-}8)$$

If dy is integrated between y_1 and some value y_3, the integral is simply $y_3 - y_1$, and, of course, is independent of the path. However the integrals $\int_{u_1}^{u_3} (\partial y/\partial u)_v \, dv$ and $\int_{v_1}^{v_3} (\partial y/\partial v)_u \, du$ are path-dependent. By way of illustration, let $y = uv^2$, so that

$$dy = v^2 \, du + 2uv \, dv. \qquad (4\text{-}9)$$

Let us integrate between the points $(u = 2, v = 1)$ and $(u = 4, v = 3)$, as indicated in Fig. 4-4. First,

$$dy = y_2 - y_1 = 36 - 2 = 34,$$

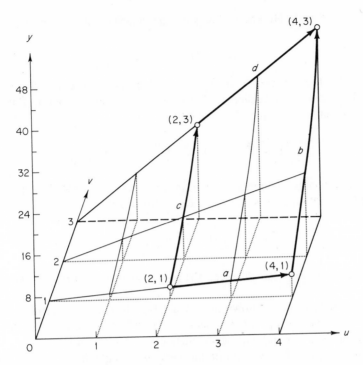

Fig 4-4. *The function* $y = uv^2$.

and this result must be independent of the integration path. Two possible paths are as follows.

Path 1:

    (*a*) (2, 1) to (4, 1): $v^2 \int du = (1)^2 (4 - 2) = 2$;

    (*b*) (4, 1) to (4, 3): $2u \int v \, dv = 8[(3^2/2) - (1^2/2)] = 32$;

    Sum : 2 + 32 = 34.

Path 2:

    (*c*) (2, 1) to (2, 3): $2u \int v \, dv = 4[(3^2/2) - (1^2/2)] = 16$;

    (*d*) (2, 3) to (4, 3): $v^2 \int du = 9(4 - 2) = 18$;

    Sum: 16 + 18 = 34.

Thus although the two integrals $v^2 \int du$ and $2u \int v \, dv$ depend on path, their sum does not.

    The differential dy in Eq. (4-7) is known as an *exact differential*; its integral is independent of path. However, this is not necessarily true of every expression of the form

$$dy = M \, du + N \, dv. \tag{4-10}$$

For example, the expression $(v \, du + 2uv \, dv)$ is not an exact differential. It is possible to test an expression such as Eq. (4-10) on this point. Referring to Eq. (4-7), for an exact differential, we have

$$\left(\frac{\partial M}{\partial v}\right)_u = \left(\frac{\partial^2 y}{\partial u \, \partial v}\right), \qquad \left(\frac{\partial N}{\partial u}\right)_v = \left(\frac{\partial^2 y}{\partial v \, \partial u}\right).$$

Most thermodynamic functions are continuous and single-valued, so the order of partial differentiation makes no difference. It follows that

$$\left(\frac{\partial M}{\partial v}\right)_u = \left(\frac{\partial N}{\partial u}\right)_v. \tag{4-11}$$

The expression $(v^2 \, du + 2uv \, dv)$ meets the test of Eq. (4-11) whereas $(v \, du + 2uv \, dv)$ does not.

Where the differential is known to be exact Eq. (4-11) is very useful in providing an additional relationship. Such a relationship is known as an *Euler* or a *cross-differentiation equation* and will occur fairly often in Chapter 6.

Mathematics provides two additional very useful equations. Since u and v are independent variables du and dv may be chosen independently. In particular they may be chosen so that $dy = 0$. Equation (4-7) then becomes

$$0 = \left(\frac{\partial y}{\partial u}\right)_v du + \left(\frac{\partial y}{\partial v}\right)_u dv,$$

or expressing the constancy of y in the equation,

$$\left(\frac{\partial u}{\partial v}\right)_y = -\frac{(\partial y/\partial v)_u}{(\partial y/\partial u)_v}. \tag{4-12}$$

Thus

$$\left(\frac{\partial V}{\partial T}\right)_E = -\frac{(\partial E/\partial T)_V}{(\partial E/\partial V)_T}. \tag{4-13}$$

A specific example may help at this point. Let $V = f(P, T)$. Then

$$dV = \left(\frac{\partial V}{\partial P}\right)_T dP + \left(\frac{\partial V}{\partial T}\right)_P dT. \tag{4-14}$$

If the gas is ideal $(\partial V/\partial P)_T = -RT/P^2$ and $(\partial V/\partial T)_P = R/P$; by Eq. (4-12), $(\partial P/\partial T)_V$ is given by

$$\left(\frac{\partial P}{\partial T}\right)_V = -\frac{(\partial V/\partial T)_P}{(\partial V/\partial P)_T} = -\frac{R/P}{-RT/P^2} = \frac{P}{T}.$$

The derivative $(\partial P/\partial T)_V$ may be found directly. Thus $P = RT/V$, so $(\partial P/\partial T)_V = R/V = P/T$. The result is the same as by the indirect method.

Second, if there is some quantity z which is a function of u and v, then one can impose the condition on du and dv that z be constant:

$$dy_z = \left(\frac{\partial y}{\partial u}\right)_v du_z + \left(\frac{\partial y}{\partial v}\right)_u dv_z .$$

This constancy is usually indicated in partial differential form by dividing through by du_z or by dy_z ; thus

$$\left(\frac{\partial y}{\partial v}\right)_z = \left(\frac{\partial y}{\partial u}\right)_v \left(\frac{\partial u}{\partial v}\right)_z + \left(\frac{\partial y}{\partial v}\right)_u . \tag{4-15}$$

For example, since $P = f(V, T)$, on applying the condition of P constant to Eq. (4-8), we obtain

$$\left(\frac{\partial E}{\partial T}\right)_P = \left(\frac{\partial E}{\partial V}\right)_T \left(\frac{\partial V}{\partial T}\right)_P + \left(\frac{\partial E}{\partial T}\right)_V . \tag{4-16}$$

4-5 Heat and Work for Various Processes

A. Evaluation of q; Heat Capacity

As emphasized earlier, the value of q for a change of state depends on the path, so the path must always be specified. There is, of course, an infinite number of possible types of paths that a system might follow in going from one state to another, but we find it very convenient, both experimentally and theoretically, to emphasize a few special ones. We thus make much use of the following types of process.

(1) *Adiabatic.* $q = 0$. The system is insulated so that no heat can enter or leave.

(2) *Isochoric.* The system is constrained to a definite volume. We introduce the coefficient $(\partial q/\partial T)_V$ or, as a convenient nomenclature, specify the path by writing q_V , and hence dq_V/dT. This type of coefficient is called a heat capacity (the term *specific heat* refers to heat capacity relative to that of the same mass of water) C. For a constant-volume path C becomes C_V :

$$C_V = \frac{dq_V}{dT} .$$

Further, under constant-volume conditions no mechanical work w can be done. (For example, in Fig. 4-2, path 2 of case 2, $w = P\,dV$, so $w = 0$ if $dV = 0$.)

As a consequence $\Delta E = q_V$, or $dE_V/dT = C_V$. Alternatively, by Eq. (4-8) we can write

$$\left(\frac{\partial E}{\partial T}\right)_V = C_V = \frac{dq_V}{dT}.$$

(4-17)

(3) *Isobaric.* The system is maintained at a particular pressure during the process. Following the preceding formalism we have

$$C_P = \frac{dq_P}{dT}.$$

(4-18)

B. Evaluation of w; Reversible Work

We will not ordinarily consider situations such as case 1 of Fig. 4-2, involving work in a gravitational field, nor, for the present, situations involving chemical work. However, a number of very useful results in chemical thermodynamics follow from treatments of mechanical or pressure–volume work. As noted in Section 4-4, mechanical work occurs if a system is compressed or is allowed to expand. Although it is helpful to visualize a gas, the following discussion applies to any type of substance. As illustrated in Fig. 4-5, we imagine the substance to be contained in

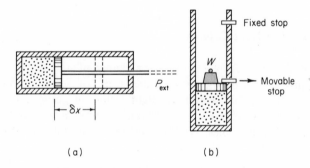

(a)   (b)

Fig. 4-5.   *Reversible and irreversible expansions.*

a piston and cylinder arrangement. There is an external pressure P_{ext} on the piston and the force on the piston is then $P_{ext}\mathscr{A}$, where $\mathscr{A}$ is its area. Since work is given by $f\,dx$, we can write

$$w = \int f\,dx = \int P_{ext}\,\mathscr{A}\,dx.$$

However, $\mathscr{A}\,dx$ is just the volume change, so a more useful form is

$$w = \int P_{ext}\,dV.$$

(4-19)

At this point an important practical consideration enters. We want w as defined in connection with Eq. (4-2), that is, the work done by the system on its surroundings, or by the surroundings on the system. Thus the pressure in Eq. (4-19) must be the pressure felt by the piston, that is, the external pressure P_{ext}. However, while the value of P_{ext} would be important in obtaining the work output of a machine, it is not directly significant to the thermodynamics of the fluid. For example, the cylinder might contain a gas at 1 atm pressure confined by a piston held in place by means of a stop as shown in Fig. 4-5(b). The pressure P_{ext} is defined by some weight W placed on the piston. The weight W might be such as to make $P_{ext} = 0.1$ atm. The stop is pulled out and the piston flies back to the second stop, thereby doubling the volume. The work done is then $0.1V$, in liter atmosphere. Were W such as to make $P_{ext} = 0.2$ atm, then w would have been $0.2V$, and so on. Thus w could have any value from zero ($W = 0$) up to maximum value. What we are interested in is this maximum value.

Clearly, the maximum possible value of w would be obtained if P_{ext} (or W in the figure) were steadily adjusted so as always to be only slightly, or, in the limit, infinitesimally less than the pressure of the gas, which is the pressure P. Not only do we now have the maximum work, but since $P_{ext} = P$, we now know how P_{ext} must vary with the volume. That is, the equation of state of the substance gives us P as a function of T and V, $P = f(T, V)$, so Eq. (4-19) becomes

$$w_{max} = \int P \, dV = \int f(T, V) \, dV. \tag{4-20}$$

We speak of the condition of $P_{ext} = P$ as giving the *reversible work*. Thus from Fig. 4-5(a) if P_{ext} is slightly less than P, expansion occurs, while if P_{ext} is made slightly more than P, compression occurs. Thus the direction of the process can be reversed by an infinitesimal change in P_{ext}. Reversible processes will be of central importance in the development of chemical thermodynamics, since by means of them we can calculate w if we know the equation of state of the substance and since they give the limiting or maximum value of w.

We may next consider w in terms of the various standard processes.

(1) *Adiabatic* $q = 0$. We do not know w directly, but, by the first law, it follows that

$$dE = -\delta w = -P \, dV. \tag{4-21}$$

(2) *Isochoric* $w = 0$. This follows since $dV = 0$, as noted previously. Then

$$dE = C_V \, dT. \tag{4-22}$$

(3) *Isobaric* $w = P \, \Delta V$. Since pressure is constant, it may be put in front of the integral of Eq. (4-20). Also,

$$dE = C_P \, dT - P \, dV. \tag{4-23}$$

Where only reversible mechanical work is involved, the first law evidently can be written in the form

$$dE = \delta q - P \, dV. \tag{4-24}$$

The various special cases then follow from Eq. (4-24). It should be emphasized that whenever P rather than P_{ext} is used, the process must be a reversible one.

4-6 Enthalpy. An Alternative Form of the First Law

The first law takes on a particularly simple form for an isochoric process, in that dE is simply $C_V \, dT$. Actual experiments are more often done under constant-pressure conditions, and the following alternative statement of the first law is very useful. We define a new molar quantity H called the *enthalpy*:

$$H = E + PV. \tag{4-25}$$

Since the volume and pressure of a system are determined solely by its state, as is E, H must also be a state function. The differential form of Eq. (4-25) is

$$dH = dE + P \, dV + V \, dP \tag{4-26}$$

and, using Eq. (4-24), we have

$$dH = \delta q + V \, dP. \tag{4-27}$$

We then have the following special cases, corresponding to the standard processes.

(1) *Adiabatic* Since $q = 0$, it follows that

$$dH = V \, dP. \tag{4-28}$$

(2) *Isochoric*

$$dH = C_V \, dT + V \, dP. \tag{4-29}$$

(3) *Isobaric* Since dP is zero,

$$dH = C_P \, dT \qquad \left[\text{or} \quad \left(\frac{\partial H}{\partial T} \right)_P = C_P \right]. \tag{4-30}$$

Since H is a state function, its value depends on those of the state variables, P, V, and T, any one of which can be eliminated by means of the equation of state of the system. In the case of E, it is natural to pick V and T as the independent variables; in the case of H, the natural choices are P and T. Since dH is an exact differential, we have

$$dH = \left(\frac{\partial H}{\partial P} \right)_T dP + \left(\frac{\partial H}{\partial T} \right)_P dT \tag{4-31}$$

and

$$\left(\frac{\partial P}{\partial T}\right)_H = -\frac{(\partial H/\partial T)_P}{(\partial H/\partial P)_T}. \tag{4-32}$$

The introduction of the enthalpy function allows the following derivation of an important relationship for the difference between C_P and C_V:

$$C_P - C_V = \left(\frac{\partial H}{\partial T}\right)_P - \left(\frac{\partial E}{\partial T}\right)_V,$$

or, from the definition of H, Eq. (4-25),

$$C_P - C_V = \left(\frac{\partial E}{\partial T}\right)_P + P\left(\frac{\partial V}{\partial T}\right)_D - \left(\frac{\partial E}{\partial T}\right)_V. \tag{4-33}$$

On eliminating $(\partial E/\partial T)_P$ by means of Eq. (4-16), we obtain as the final result

$$C_P - C_V = \left[P + \left(\frac{\partial E}{\partial V}\right)_T\right]\left(\frac{\partial V}{\partial T}\right)_P. \tag{4-34}$$

This equation is discussed further in the Commentary and Notes section.

4-7 Applications of the First Law to Ideal Gases

A. Internal Energy Change for an Ideal Gas

The application of the first law to the case of an ideal gas not only provides simple illustrations of its use but turns out to be of considerable importance generally. To anticipate a little, the reason for this last statement is that ideal gas behavior is the limiting behavior of all real gases, so that the results are not hypothetical but provide the reference condition for treating nonideal behavior. Further, any solid or liquid is in principle in equilibrium with its vapor; knowledge of the thermodynamic properties of the vapor may therefore be used as an indirect path to treatment of the solid or liquid state. Finally, most gases are approximately ideal, so the thermodynamics of the ideal gas is often used directly to give approximate results, usually of acceptable accuracy, for real gases and vapors at ordinary pressures.

We owe again to Joule a fundamental piece of information—this time about an ideal gas. His experiment, described in 1843 and illustrated in Fig. 4-6, consisted of allowing air under pressure (up to 10 or 20 atm) to expand from one vessel into another. There was no change in the temperature of the gas. Alternatively, the two bulbs were immersed in a water bath; no change in the temperature of the bath

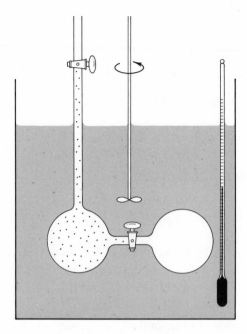

Fig. 4-6. *Joule's experiment.*

could be observed when the expansion occurred. The significance of this result is that since no work was done, $w = 0$, and since no temperature change occurred, $q = 0$; therefore ΔE was zero.

More accurate later experiments have shown that Joule's experiment does in fact lead to small temperature changes (see Special Topics) but that in the limit of ideal gas behavior, his conclusion was correct. The conclusion, in partial differential form, is

$$\left(\frac{\partial T}{\partial V}\right)_E = 0 \qquad \text{(ideal gas).} \tag{4-35}$$

(Equations valid specifically for an ideal gas will be so labeled.) It then follows from Eq. (4-13) that

$$\left(\frac{\partial E}{\partial V}\right)_T = 0 \qquad \text{(ideal gas)} \tag{4-36}$$

and, from Eq. (4-8), that

$$dE = \left(\frac{\partial E}{\partial T}\right)_V dT \qquad \text{(ideal gas)}$$

or

$$\frac{dE}{dT} = \left(\frac{\partial E}{\partial T}\right)_V = C_V \qquad \text{(ideal gas).} \tag{4-37}$$

This last, very important result says that for an ideal gas the change in energy with temperature is always given by $C_V\, dT$, *regardless of the actual path*; that is, regardless of whether V is constant or not.

A similar situation holds for enthalpy. It follows from the defining equation for H that

$$\left(\frac{\partial H}{\partial P}\right)_T = \left(\frac{\partial E}{\partial P}\right)_T + \left(\frac{\partial (PV)}{\partial P}\right)_T .$$

The last term is zero for an ideal gas; also

$$\left(\frac{\partial E}{\partial P}\right)_T = \left(\frac{\partial E}{\partial V}\right)_T \left(\frac{\partial V}{\partial P}\right)_T$$

(a partial derivative may be expanded in this manner if the same quantity is held constant in all terms), and since $(\partial E/\partial V)_T$ is zero, it follows that

$$\left(\frac{\partial E}{\partial P}\right)_T = 0 \qquad \text{(ideal gas)}. \tag{4-38}$$

The result is therefore that

$$\left(\frac{\partial H}{\partial P}\right)_T = 0 \qquad \text{(ideal gas)}. \tag{4-39}$$

Then, from Eqs. (4-31) and (4-30),

$$\frac{dH}{dT} = \left(\frac{\partial H}{\partial T}\right)_P = C_P \qquad \text{(ideal gas)}. \tag{4-40}$$

Thus for an ideal gas the change in enthalpy with temperature is always given by $C_P \, dT$, *regardless of the actual path.*

We can also relate C_P and C_V. By Eq. (4-34),

$$C_P - C_V = (P + 0)\frac{R}{P}$$

or

$$C_P - C_V = R \qquad \text{(ideal gas)}. \tag{4-41}$$

B. Various Processes for an Ideal Gas

The various quantities are as follows for the indicated type of reversible process.

Isochoric

$$w = 0,$$
$$dE = C_V \, dT = dq_V \qquad \text{[Eq. (4-22)]},$$
$$dH = C_P \, dT \qquad \text{[ideal gas, Eq. (4-40)]}.$$

Isobaric

$$dw = P \, dV = R \, dT, \qquad w = R \, \Delta T \qquad \text{(ideal gas),} \tag{4-42}$$
$$dE = C_V \, dT \qquad \qquad \qquad \text{[ideal gas, Eq. (4-37)]},$$
$$dH = C_P \, dT = dq_P \qquad \qquad \text{[Eq. (4-30)]}.$$

The isothermal or constant-temperature process was not considered in Section 4-5 since it leads to no specialized forms in the general case. However, for an ideal gas if dT is zero, then $dE = 0$ and $dH = 0$. It follows that $q = w$, and $w = P\,dV = (RT/V)\,dV = RT\,d(\ln V)$. Since at constant temperature

$$\ln V + \ln P = \text{constant}, \quad d(\ln V) = -d(\ln P) \quad \text{and} \quad w = -RT\,d(\ln P).$$

In summary we have the following results.

Isothermal

$$q = w,$$
$$dw = RT\,d(\ln V) = -RT\,d(\ln P) \qquad \text{(ideal gas)}, \tag{4-43}$$

or

$$w = RT\ln\frac{V_2}{V_1} = RT\ln\frac{P_1}{P_2} \qquad \text{(ideal gas)}, \tag{4-44}$$
$$dE = 0, \qquad dH = 0.$$

Finally, for an adiabatic process, q is zero and since, for an ideal gas, dE is always $C_V\,dT$, Eq. (4-21) can be written

$$C_V\,dT = -P\,dV = -RT\,d(\ln V)$$

or

$$C_V\,d(\ln T) = -R\,d(\ln V) \qquad \text{(ideal gas)}. \tag{4-45}$$

Alternatively, $d(\ln P) + d(\ln V) = d(\ln T)$ for an ideal gas, so, on eliminating $d(\ln V)$ and remembering that $C_P = C_V + R$, we get

$$C_P\,d(\ln T) = R\,d(\ln P) \qquad \text{(ideal gas)}. \tag{4-46}$$

If the heat capacities are independent of temperatures (as discussed later) then the equations may be integrated directly. In summary we have the following results.

Adiabatic

$$dq = 0, \qquad dw = -dE,$$

$dE = C_V\,dT$	[ideal gas, Eq. (4-37)],
$dH = C_P\,dT$	[ideal gas, Eq. (4-40)],
$C_V\,d(\ln T) = -R\,d(\ln V)$	[ideal gas, Eq. (4-45)],
$C_P\,d(\ln T) = R\,d(\ln P)$	[ideal gas, Eq. (4-46)],

and, if C_V and hence also C_P are constant,

$$C_V\ln\frac{T_2}{T_1} = R\ln\frac{V_1}{V_2} \qquad \text{(ideal gas)}, \tag{4-47}$$

$$C_P\ln\frac{T_2}{T_1} = R\ln\frac{P_2}{P_1} \qquad \text{(ideal gas)}, \tag{4-48}$$

$$PV^\gamma = \text{constant}, \qquad \gamma = \frac{C_P}{C_V} \qquad \text{(ideal gas)}. \tag{4-49}$$

The last form is obtained as follows. Equation (4-47) may be written as $(T_2/T_1) = (V_1/V_2)^{R/C_V} = (V_1/V_2)^{\gamma-1}$. Since $(T_2/T_1) = (P_2V_2/P_1V_1)$, elimination gives $(P_2/P_1) = (V_1/V_2)^{\gamma}$ or $P_1V_1^{\gamma} = P_2V_2^{\gamma}$. Equation (4-49) is a generalization of this last conclusion.

C. Heat Capacity of an Ideal Gas

This subject is treated in more detail in Section 4-8. For the present, it is useful to consider qualitatively a special case of the general heat capacity behavior for an ideal gas. The special case is that of an ideal, monatomic gas. Such a gas can have only kinetic energy; its molar internal energy is then, from Eq. (2-4),

$$E = \tfrac{3}{2}RT.$$

The heat capacity of the gas is therefore

$$C_V = \tfrac{3}{2}R \qquad \text{(ideal monatomic gas)} \qquad (4\text{-}50)$$

and C_P, of course, is $(C_V + R)$, or

$$C_P = \tfrac{5}{2}R \qquad \text{(ideal monatomic gas).} \qquad (4\text{-}51)$$

Gases, even though ideal, will in general have a higher heat capacity than that given here. If the molecule has more than one atom, then as the temperature is raised energy goes into vibration and rotation as well as into increased kinetic energy. The degree to which this happens increases with increasing temperature; some typical heat capacity curves are given in Fig. 4-7. It is convenient for many

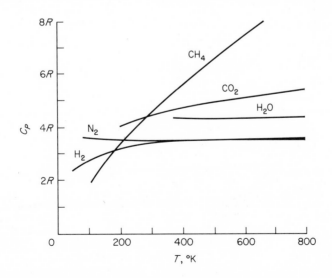

Fig. 4-7. *Heat capacity C_P as a function of temperature for various gases.*

calculational purposes to represent this temperature variation by means of a polynomial in temperature:

$$C_P = a + bT + cT^{-2} + \cdots \qquad (4\text{-}52)$$

and some values for such coefficients are given in Section 5-6.

D. Some Calculations for an Ideal, Monatomic Gas

A number of equations have been introduced in this section for processes involving an ideal gas. The following example is intended to illustrate their application in a way that will also bring out important features of the first law of thermodynamics. We will use one mole of an ideal, monatomic gas as the working fluid—we can then use the constant values of C_V and C_P of $\frac{3}{2}R$ and $\frac{5}{2}R$, respectively, and thus simplify the calculations.

The gas initially is in state 1 at 0°C and 10 atm pressure, and hence at 2.241 liter volume. It is put through the following reversible cycle, cycle A in Fig. 4-8.

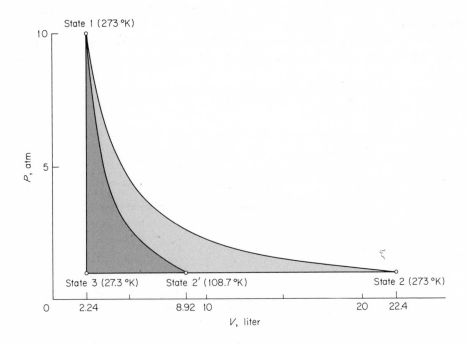

Fig. 4-8.   *Two reversible ideal gas cycles (see text).*

State 1 *to state* 2: Isothermal expansion to 1 atm. Then

$$V_2 = 22.41 \text{ liter}, \qquad T_2 = 273.1°\text{K},$$

$$w = RT \ln \frac{P_1}{P_2} = R(273.1)(2.303)(1) = 628.9R,$$

$$q = w = 628.9R, \qquad \Delta E = \Delta H = 0.$$

The results can all be expressed in units of $(R)(°\text{K})$; we can obtain the actual values in calories by putting $R = 1.987$ cal $°\text{K}^{-1}$ mole^{-1}, or in joules by using $R = 8.314$ J $°\text{K}^{-1}$ mole^{-1}.

State 2 *to state* 3: Isobaric cooling to 2.24 liter. Then

$$T_3 = \frac{V_3}{V_2} T_2 = 27.31°\text{K}, \qquad P_3 = 1 \text{ atm},$$

$$w = R \,\Delta T = R(27.31 - 273.1) = -245.8R,$$

$$q = C_P \,\Delta T = \tfrac{5}{2}R(-245.8) = -614.5R,$$

$$\Delta E = C_V \,\Delta T = \tfrac{3}{2}R(-254.8) = -368.7R,$$

$$\Delta H = C_P \,\Delta T = q = -614.5R.$$

State 3 *back to State* 1: Isochoric heating to 273.1°K, 10 atm, and 2.241 liter. Then

$$w = 0, \qquad q = C_V \,\Delta T = \tfrac{3}{2}R(273.1 - 27.3) = 368.7R,$$

$$\Delta E = q = 368.7R, \qquad \Delta H = C_P \,\Delta T = 614.5R.$$

The results for cycle A are summarized in the top part of Table 4-1. Notice that for the cycle $q = w$ and ΔE and ΔH are zero. A further point is that

Table 4-1. *Calculations for the Two Cycles of Fig. 4-8*[a]

Change of state	Process	q	w	ΔE	ΔH
Cycle A					
1 to 2	Isothermal	628.9	628.9	0	0
2 to 3	Isobaric	−614.5	−245.8	−368.7	−614.5
3 to 1	Isochoric	368.7	0	368.7	614.5
Cycle		383.1	383.1	0	0
Cycle B					
1 to 2′	Adiabatic	0	246.6	−246.6	−411.0
2′ to 3	Isobaric	−203.5	−81.4	−122.1	−203.5
3 to 1	Isochoric	368.7	0	368.7	614.5
cycle		165.2	165.2	0	0

[a] All values in terms of $R(°\text{K})$.

since $w = \int P \, dV$, if a path is plotted as P versus V, then w is given by the area under that path. The area is positive for a left-to-right direction of progress along the path and negative for a right-to-left one. As a result the total work associated with a closed path or cycle is just the area enclosed by the cycle.

Next consider a second reversible cycle B using the same starting point; this is also shown in Fig. 4-8. The steps are now as follows.

State 1 to state 2′: Adiabatic expansion to 1 atm. Then $\log(T_{2'}/T_1) = (2/5)\log(P_{2'}/P_1) = -0.400$ or $T_{2'} = 0.3981\,T_1 = 108.7°K$. Then

$$V_{2'} = (108.7/273.1)(10/1)(22.41) = 8.92 \quad \text{liter.}$$

Then

$$q = 0,$$
$$\Delta E = C_V \, \Delta T = \tfrac{3}{2}R(108.7 - 273.1) = -246.6R,$$
$$w = -\Delta E = 246.6R,$$
$$\Delta H = C_P \, \Delta T = \tfrac{5}{2}R(108.7 - 273.1) = -411.0R.$$

State 2′ to state 3: Isobaric cooling to 2.24 liter; $T_3 = 27.31°K$ and $P_3 = 1$ atm, as before. Then

$$w = R \, \Delta T = R(27.3 - 108.7) = -81.4R,$$
$$q = C_P \, \Delta T = \tfrac{5}{2}R(-81.4) = -203.5R,$$
$$\Delta E = C_V \, \Delta T = \tfrac{3}{2}R(-81.4) = -122.1R,$$
$$\Delta H = q = -203.5R.$$

State 3 back to state 1: Same as for cycle A.

This second set of results is assembled in the bottom part of Table 4-1. Again ΔE and ΔH are zero for the cycle, but notice in Fig. 4-8 that the P–V plot of the adiabatic expansion $1 \rightarrow 2'$ is steeper than that of the isothermal one $1 \rightarrow 2$. The physical reason for this is that in the adiabatic expansion the energy for the work done is supplied by a cooling of the gas. The temperature thus drops steadily during the expansion and the volume at each stage is less than at the corresponding pressure during the isothermal expansion. As a result the area under the P–V plot for the adiabatic process is smaller than that under the one for the isothermal process, and this is in conformity with the lesser amount of work done. The further consequence is that less work is done by cycle B than by cycle A, and a correspondingly smaller amount of heat is absorbed.

Notice also that while q and w are different for the sequences $1 \rightarrow 2 \rightarrow 3$ and $1 \rightarrow 2' \rightarrow 3$, the values of ΔE and ΔH are the same. We thus have a further illustration of the point that q and w are dependent on the path taken between two states, but ΔE and ΔH are not.

4-8 Molecular Basis for Heat Capacities. The Equipartition Principle

It was pointed out in the preceding section that since the internal energy for an ideal monatomic gas consists only of its kinetic energy, C_V is therefore $\frac{3}{2}R$. Also, in Section 2-CN-1, it was noted that the heat capacity for a one- and a two-dimensional gas is $C_V = \frac{1}{2}R$ and R, respectively. Thus each independent velocity component has associated with it a molar kinetic energy of $\frac{1}{2}RT$ and corresponding heat capacity of $C_V = \frac{1}{2}R$. These three independent modes of translation in three dimensions reflect the fact that three coordinates are needed to specify the position of a particle in space and, by means of their time derivatives, the velocity of a particle in space.

We speak of the number of degrees of freedom f of a system as the number of variables that must be specified to fix the position of each particle or the velocity of each particle. For one mole of particles there are $3N_0$ degrees of freedom. Consider next the case of an ideal gas composed of diatomic molecules. There are now two moles of atoms and so, per mole of molecules, $f = 6N_0$. To generalize, a gas consisting of n atoms per molecule will have $3nN_0$ degrees of freedom per mole, or $f = 3n$ per molecule.

Returning to the case of the gas consisting of diatomic molecules, although one could specify the positions of all atoms by means of $6N_0$ coordinates per mole, there is a more rational and very useful alternative scheme. One recognizes that the gas in fact consists of molecular units of two atoms each. Of the six degrees of freedom required to locate two atoms, one first uses three to locate the center of mass of the molecule. One now needs to specify the positions of the two atoms relative to their center of mass. As illustrated in Fig. 4-9 two angles will be needed

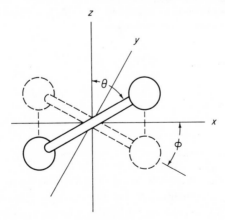

Fig. 4-9.

or, alternatively, the degrees of rotation around the x axis and around the y axis. Rotation about the molecular or z axis does not change the nuclear positions and hence contributes no information. (In the case of a nonlinear molecule, however, all three rotations would be needed.) If now we also specify the distance between the atoms, the description of their position in space is completely fixed. Thus six coordinates are also needed in the alternative scheme. In general, the number of coordinates sufficient to describe the positions of a set of n atoms cannot depend on the scheme used but is always equal to the $3n$ degrees of freedom.

As just noted each degree of translational freedom implies an energy of $\frac{1}{2}RT$ per mole and a heat capacity contribution of $\frac{1}{2}R$ per mole. In the alternative scheme of describing the positions and velocities of atoms the rotational degrees of freedom must likewise contribute $\frac{1}{2}R$ each to C_V. It might be supposed that the same should be true for those degrees of freedom describing interatomic distances. Here, however, a new factor enters. The atoms of a molecule are held together by the attractive forces of chemical binding. They execute vibrations, rather than simple motions, and their interatomic distances are therefore some periodic function of time. Thus in the case of the diatomic molecule of Fig. 4-9, dr/dt is also a function of time. It is zero at the end of a vibrational stretch or compression and a maximum in between; consequently dr/dt is insufficient to specify the total energy of the vibration, and one needs to state the potential energy as well as the kinetic energy for each value of r.

The conclusion from this analysis is that each vibrational degree of freedom should contribute twice the usual amount to the heat capacity, or that the total heat capacity associated with vibrations should be Rf_{vib}, where f_{vib} denotes the number of vibrational degrees of freedom. This same conclusion is obtained in Section 4-12 as a result of a quantum statistical mechanical treatment.

In summary, we have the following results.

Atoms per molecule	n
Total number of degrees of freedom per molecule	$f = 3n$
Translational degrees of freedom per molecule	$f_{trans} = 3$
Rotational degrees of freedom per molecule	f_{rot}
Linear molecule	$f_{rot} = 2$
Nonlinear molecule	$f_{rot} = 3$
Vibrational degrees of freedom per molecule	f_{vib}
Linear molecule	$f_{vib} = 3n - (3 + 2)$
	$= 3n - 5$
Nonlinear molecule	$f_{vib} = 3n - (3 + 3)$
	$= 3n - 6$
Heat capacity per mole	$(f_{trans} + f_{rot})(\frac{1}{2}R) + f_{vib}R$

Some representative applications are given in Table 4-2.

This treatment of heat capacity is based on two principal assumptions. The first is that potential energy contributions are present only for vibrations within the molecules and not for those between molecules. The gas is therefore assumed to be ideal. The second assumption is that each degree of freedom has associated with it

Table 4-2. *Applications of the Equipartition Principle*

Molecule	f	f_{trans}	f_{rot}	f_{vib}	Equipartition heat capacity per mole in units of R	
					C_V	C_P
Ar	3	3	0	0	3/2	5/2
N_2	6	3	2	1	7/2	9/2
CO_2 (linear)	9	3	2	4	13/2	15/2
H_2O (nonlinear)	9	3	3	3	12/2	14/2
CH_4	15	3	3	9	24/2	26/2
Monatomic crystalline solid	3	0	0	3	6/2	~6/2
MX type of crystalline solid	6	0	0	6	12/2	~12/2

a heat capacity contribution of $\frac{1}{2}R$ (or R, if a vibration). The principle which states this assumption is known as the *principle of the equipartition of energy*. It is a principle based on classical mechanics and, as will be seen in Sections 4-11 and 4-12, it can be in serious error. A glance at Fig. 4-7 shows that, at best, the equipartition values of heat capacities are only approached at high temperatures. A closer look suggests that for molecules around room temperature the equipartition contributions from translation and rotation have been reached and that the main discrepancy lies with the vibrational contribution. An important function of the statistical mechanical treatments that follow is the providing of a detailed explanation of how and why heat capacities vary as they do with temperature.

4-9 Statistical Mechanical Treatment of First Law Quantities

A. The Partition Function. The Average Energy per Molecule

It is sufficient for the present to regard a system as being made up of non-interacting molecules each of which has various translational, rotational, and vibrational energy states. According to the Boltzmann principle (Section 2-2), the probability of a molecule being in some energy state ϵ_i is proportional to $e^{-\epsilon_i/kT}$. It is now very useful to write the sum over all such energy states and to give this sum the special name of *partition function* $\mathbf{Q}$:

$$\mathbf{Q} = \sum_i g_i e^{-\epsilon_i/kT}. \tag{4-53}$$

The factor g_i is a weighting factor allowing for the possibility that certain independent configurations have identical energies. Such a situation is called a *degeneracy*; that is, if a molecule can have an energy ϵ_i in more than one way, that energy state is said to be *degenerate*.

We can now write an expression for the average energy of a molecule, following the usual averaging procedure, given by Eq. (2-34):

$$\bar{\epsilon} = \frac{\sum \epsilon_i g_i e^{-\epsilon_i/kT}}{\sum g_i e^{-\epsilon_i/kT}} . \qquad (4\text{-}54)$$

It is an assumption in statistical mechanics, the rigorous defense of which will not be given here, that the average energy $\bar{\epsilon}$ which a particular molecule should have is also the average energy per molecule in a large collection of molecules, E. (Small capitals will be used to denote quantities on a per molecule basis.) Now, from Eq. (4-53), $dQ/dT = \sum_i (\epsilon_i/kT^2) g_i e^{-\epsilon_i/kT}$; consequently Eq. (4-54) can be written in the form

$$\text{E} = kT^2 \frac{dQ/dT}{Q} = kT^2 \frac{d(\ln Q)}{dT} \qquad (4\text{-}55)$$

or, per mole,

$$E = RT^2 \frac{d(\ln Q)}{dT} . \qquad (4\text{-}56)$$

Equation (4-56) may be written in the form

$$E = -R \left[\frac{\partial(\ln Q)}{\partial(1/T)} \right]_V \qquad (4\text{-}57)$$

since $(-1/T^2)\, dT = d(1/T)$ (as noted in Section 1-7). The expression for $\bar{\epsilon}$ [Eq. (4-54)] is for the average molecular energy, and its temperature dependence does not include any pressure–volume work, so that constancy of volume, implicit in the equation, is now stated explicitly.

Since $C_V = (\partial E/\partial T)_V = -T^2[\partial E/\partial(1/T)]_V$, we obtain from Eq. (4-57)

$$C_V = \frac{R}{T^2} \left[\frac{\partial^2(\ln Q)}{\partial(1/T)^2} \right]_V . \qquad (4\text{-}58)$$

Enthalpy may also be expressed in terms of the partition function,

$$\text{H} = \text{E} + P\text{v} = kT^2 \left[\frac{\partial(\ln Q)}{\partial T} \right]_V + kT\text{v} \left[\frac{\partial(\ln Q)}{\partial \text{v}} \right]_T ; \qquad H = N_0\text{H}; \quad (4\text{-}59)$$

the small capitals denoting quantities per molecule. The derivation is best made using the second law of thermodynamics, however, and is therefore postponed until Section 6-9.

B. Separation of the Partition Function into Translational, Rotational, and Vibrational Parts

The energy ϵ_i of the ith state of a molecule will in general consist of the sum of the translational, rotational, and vibrational energies. In addition, if the state is one of electronic excitation, then this is added, too. As is discussed in the material immediately following, each type of energy is quantized. A molecule thus might be in the nth translational energy level, in the tenth rotational level, and in the second vibrational level, as a specific example. To a good first approximation, however, the energy of, say, the tenth rotational state is independent of what translational or vibrational state the molecule is in. If this approximation is made, then a very convenient factoring of the partition function becomes possible.

Suppose that just two kinds of energy states are possible, denoted by ϵ_i and ϵ_i'; these might, for example, be translational and rotational states. The molecule may then be in state ϵ_1, ϵ_2, ϵ_3, ... with respect to the first kind of energy and at the same time in state ϵ_1', ϵ_2', ϵ_3', ... with respect to the second kind of energy. Possible total energy states would then be $(\epsilon_1 + \epsilon_1')$, $(\epsilon_1 + \epsilon_2')$, $(\epsilon_1 + \epsilon_3')$, ..., $(\epsilon_2 + \epsilon_1')$, $(\epsilon_2 + \epsilon_2')$, $(\epsilon_2 + \epsilon_3')$, ..., $(\epsilon_3 + \epsilon_1')$,.... . The corresponding partition function would then be

$$\mathbf{Q} = e^{-(\epsilon_1 + \epsilon_1')/kT} + e^{-(\epsilon_1 + \epsilon_2')/kT} + \cdots + e^{-(\epsilon_2 + \epsilon_1')/kT} + \cdots .$$

(We may avoid using the weighting factors g_i simply by listing each state as many times as it is degenerate.) This equation can be written as

$$\mathbf{Q} = (e^{-\epsilon_1/kT} e^{-\epsilon_1'/kT}) + (e^{-\epsilon_1/kT} e^{-\epsilon_2'/kT}) + \cdots + (e^{-\epsilon_2/kT} e^{-\epsilon_1'/kT}) + \cdots .$$

It is then possible to group terms:

$$\mathbf{Q} = e^{-\epsilon_1/kT}(e^{-\epsilon_1'/kT} + e^{-\epsilon_2'/kT} + \cdots) + e^{-\epsilon_2/kT}(e^{-\epsilon_1'/kT} + e^{-\epsilon_2'/kT} + \cdots)$$
$$+ e^{-\epsilon_3/kT}(e^{-\epsilon_1'/kT} + e^{-\epsilon_2'/kT} + \cdots) + \cdots .$$

If we make the stated assumption, namely that a given ϵ' state has an energy value that is independent of which ϵ state is involved and vice versa, then the sums in parentheses are identical, and the whole expression reduces to the product of two sums. Thus

$$\mathbf{Q} = \left(\sum_i e^{-\epsilon_i/kT}\right)\left(\sum_i e^{-\epsilon_i'/kT}\right)$$

or, returning to the use of g_i weighting factors,

$$\mathbf{Q} = \left(\sum_i g_i e^{-\epsilon_i/kT}\right)\left(\sum_i g_i' e^{-\epsilon_i'/kT}\right)$$

or

$$\mathbf{Q} = \mathbf{Q}\mathbf{Q}' .$$

The assumption of the mutual independence of energy states therefore allows the partition function to be expressed as a product of the separate partition functions for each kind of state. We can write

$$\mathbf{Q} = \mathbf{Q}_{\text{trans}}\mathbf{Q}_{\text{rot}}\mathbf{Q}_{\text{vib}}\mathbf{Q}_{\text{elec}} . \tag{4-60}$$

It then follows from Eq. (4-56) that

$$E = E_{trans} + E_{rot} + E_{vib} + E_{elec} . \tag{4-61}$$

The approximation then leads to the reasonable conclusion that the total average energy can be regarded as a sum of the separate average energies of translation, rotation, etc. It further follows from Eq. (4-58) that C_V may also be written as a sum of corresponding contributions:

$$C_V = C_{V(trans)} + C_{V(rot)} + C_{V(vib)} + C_{V(elec)} . \tag{4-62}$$

The same is true for H.

We will neglect partition functions due to a sum over electronic excited states because the energy of such states is usually so large that they are not populated at ordinary temperatures. We do this by setting $\mathbf{Q}_{elec}$ equal to unity, on the following basis. If the first and higher electronic excited states are large in energy compared to kT, then all but the first term in $\mathbf{Q}_{elec}$ will be negligible, and

$$\mathbf{Q}_{elec} = e^{-\epsilon_1/kT},$$

where ϵ_1 is the energy of the first electronic state. In general, we do not know absolute energy values, only relative ones, and we can set $\epsilon_1 = 0$ as our reference point. However, even if ϵ_1 were assigned some nonzero value, the consequence would simply be to add this value to E. Thus, referring to Eq. (4-55), we obtain

$$\mathbf{E}_{elec} = (kT^2) \frac{\epsilon_1}{kT^2} = \epsilon_1 .$$

Our neglecting of $\mathbf{Q}_{elec}$ then amounts, at the most, to regarding the absolute energy of the first electronic state as making a constant contribution to E. We ordinarily do set $\epsilon_1 = 0$ for electronic energy, but in the case of vibrational energy, we will use a nonzero value for energy of the first state (see Section 4-12).

4-10   *Translational Partition Function for an Ideal Gas*

A result from the wave mechanical treatment of a particle in a box, which will not be derived until Section 16-5B, gives the sequence of energy states that corresponds to a particle which is free of any interaction with other particles. In this respect, the picture is analogous to that used in Section 2-1 for the simple kinetic theory derivation for an ideal gas. The wave mechanical result is

$$\epsilon_n = \frac{n^2 h^2}{8a^2 m} , \tag{4-63}$$

where n is a quantum number taking on all integral values, h is Planck's constant, m is the mass of the particle, and a is the length of the box. Equation (4-63) is actually for a one-dimensional box, that is, translation along only one direction in space is considered. It allows us to obtain the partition function for translation in one dimension, but, in view of the preceding analysis, it is evident that

$$Q_{trans(3-dim)} = Q_{trans(x)}Q_{trans(y)}Q_{trans(z)} = Q_{trans(1-dim)}^3 . \qquad (4-64)$$

The desired partition function for three-dimensional translation will therefore be just the cube of that for the one-dimensional case.

We obtain the one-dimensional Q from the summation

$$Q_{trans(1-dim)} = \sum_{n=0}^{n=\infty} \exp\left(-\frac{n^2h^2}{8a^2mkT}\right). \qquad (4-65)$$

In this case, an excellent approximation results if integration is substituted for the summation. The reason is that the quantity $h^2/8a^2m$ is a very small one. For example, if the dimension a is 1 cm, then the quantity is $(6.62 \times 10^{-27})^2/(8)(1)^2(30/6.02 \times 10^{23})$ for an atom of atomic weight 30. This value is about 1×10^{-31} erg molecule^{-1}, as compared to the value of kT at 25°C of $(1.38 \times 10^{-16})(298)$ or about 4×10^{-14} erg molecule^{-1}. Thus the exponential in Eq. (4-65) will not begin to diminish from unity until extremely large n values, and we are dealing almost with a continuum of energy states. In integral form, Eq. (4-65) becomes

$$Q_{trans(1-dim)} = \int_0^\infty \exp\left(-\frac{n^2h^2}{8a^2mkT}\right) dn, \qquad (4-66)$$

which is of the standard form $\int_0^\infty \exp(-b^2x^2)\, dx$. The result is

$$Q_{trans(1-dim)} = \frac{(2\pi mkT)^{1/2}}{h}\, a. \qquad (4-67)$$

Finally, we have

$$Q_{trans(3-dim)} = \frac{(2\pi mkT)^{3/2}}{h^3}\, v, \qquad (4-68)$$

where the volume v replaces a^3.

Equation (4-68) gives the translational partition function per molecule, and for the present purposes it may be abbreviated as

$$Q_{trans} = \alpha T^{3/2}. \qquad (4-69)$$

Insertion of this result into Eq. (4-55) gives

$$E_{trans} = kT^2\left\{\frac{\partial[\ln(\alpha T^{3/2})]}{\partial T}\right\}_v$$

145

or

$$E_{trans} = \tfrac{3}{2}kT$$

and

$$E_{trans} = \tfrac{3}{2}RT. \tag{4-70}$$

This is the same result as obtained from the kinetic molecular theory of an ideal gas. Moreover, $C_{V(trans)}$ is then $\tfrac{3}{2}R$, as given by the equipartition principle.

Further, $[\partial(\ln Q_{trans})/\partial v]_T$ is just $1/v$, so by Eq. (4-59)

$$H_{trans} = E_{trans} + (kTv)\frac{1}{v} = E + kT$$

or

$$H_{trans} = E_{trans} + RT.$$

This is the result expected for an ideal gas, from Eq. (4-25) and the ideal gas law.

An important point is that Q_{trans} depends on the volume v per molecule and thus on the macroscopic condition of the gas. As will be seen in the following sections, the rotational and vibrational partition functions do not have this dependence. They are computed purely on the basis of the spacing of energy states of the individual molecule and do not involve v. Often, then, Q_{rot} and Q_{vib} are grouped separately as giving the internal or intramolecular partition function, $Q_{int} = Q_{rot}Q_{vib}$, so that $Q = Q_{trans}Q_{int}$.

4-11   The Rotational Partition Function

The rotational energy states for a diatomic molecule are given by wave mechanics as

$$\epsilon_{rot} = J(J+1)\frac{h^2}{8\pi^2 I}, \tag{4-71}$$

where J is the rotational quantum number, which may have the integral values 0, 1, 2, ..., and I is the moment of inertia, given by

$$I = \mu d^2, \qquad \mu = \frac{m_1 m_2}{m_1 + m_2}, \tag{4-72}$$

where μ is the reduced mass [Eq. (2-53)] and d is the interatomic distance (Section 16-ST-2). The partition function for rotation is then

$$Q_{rot} = \sum_{J=0}^{\infty} (2J+1)\exp\left[-J(J+1)\frac{h^2}{8\pi^2 IkT}\right], \tag{4-73}$$

where the factor $(2J+1)$ is the degeneracy g_J of each J state. This degeneracy factor gives the number of ways in which J rotational quanta can be assigned to the two independent axes of rotation. For $J = 0$, $g_J = 1$, since the rotational quantum number can only be zero for each axis. The degeneracy for larger J values arises from the number of ways the total angular momentum of a molecule can be quantized with respect to spatial orientation.

The summation called for by Eq. (4-73) cannot be made in closed form, and, as with translational energy level spacings, one makes the approximation of replacing the summation by an integration.

Rotational energy level spacings are generally small compared to kT. For example, μ for HCl is $35.5/36.5 = 0.973$ g mole^{-1} and the bond length is 1.28 Å. The moment of inertia is then $(0.973/6.02 \times 10^{23})(1.28 \times 10^{-8})^2 = 2.60 \times 10^{-40}$ g cm^2, and $h^2/8\pi^2 I = (6.63 \times 10^{-27})^2/(8)$ $(3.14)^2(2.60 \times 10^{-40}) = 2.14 \times 10^{-15}$ erg. Recalling the similar calculation in the preceding section, we see that the value of kT at 25°C is 4.12×10^{-14} erg, so at 25°C the quantity $h^2/8\pi^2 IkT =$ 0.052. That is, rotational energy levels are spaced about $kT/20$ apart at room temperature. The summation of Eq. (4-73) will thus begin to converge only after many terms, and its replacement by an integral does not introduce serious error. At low temperatures, however, rotational spacings do become comparable to or greater than kT, and the summation procedure must be used. A detailed example of the analogous situation for vibrational energy states is given in the next section.

Equation (4-73) becomes

$$\mathbf{Q}_{\rot} = \int_0^\infty (2J + 1)\ \exp\left[-J(J + 1)\frac{h^2}{8\pi^2 IkT}\right] dJ. \qquad (4\text{-}74)$$

The quantity $h^2/8\pi^2 Ik$ has the dimension of temperature and is called the characteristic rotation temperature $\theta_{\rot}$. If we let $y = J(J + 1)$, the integral reduces to a standard one, and the result is simply

$$\mathbf{Q}_{\rot} = \frac{T}{\theta_{\rot}}. \qquad (4\text{-}75)$$

An expression for the general case of a polyatomic molecule is given in the Commentary and Notes section, but it should be mentioned here that for A–A-type molecules $\mathbf{Q}_{\rot}$ is reduced by a symmetry factor of one-half from the value for A–B-type molecules given by Eq. (4-75).

We can now calculate some thermodynamic quantities. Since $d(\ln \mathbf{Q})/dT$ is just $1/T$, we obtain from Eq. (4-55) that

$$\mathrm{E}_{\rot} = kT \qquad \text{or} \qquad E_{\rot} = RT. \qquad (4\text{-}76)$$

The heat capacity $C_{V(\rot)}$ is then R. Thus as in the case of translational motion, the result is the same as that obtained from the equipartition principle. There is no dependence of $\mathbf{Q}_{\rot}$ on volume, and therefore no such contribution to H.

That the equipartition values are obtained for E and for C_V is evidently a consequence of using the integration approximation, that is, the limiting case in which $\theta_{\rot}$ is much smaller than T. At the other extreme, where $\theta_{\rot} \gg T$, only the first rotation state will be populated and the situation will be similar to that considered

147

for electronic excited states. Then ϵ_{rot} becomes just the absolute energy of this first rotational state, taken to be zero; in any event, being constant, $E_{0,rot}$ now makes no contribution to the heat capacity. Thus the quantum mechanical treatment predicts that at a sufficiently low temperature the rotational contribution to the heat capacity will disappear. This effect is indeed observed and is illustrated in Fig. 4-7 in the case of H_2. Below about 200°K the heat capacity begins to drop increasingly rapidly from $\frac{7}{2}R$ for C_P to $\frac{5}{2}R$, the value for translation only. By about 50°K this limit is essentially reached. The quantum treatment thus shows that the equipartition value for rotational heat capacity is a maximum, limiting one and that the actual value may be significantly lower. In the case of translation, however, the energy level spacings are so very close together that deviation from the equipartition value for translational heat capacity is never observed for dilute or ideally behaving gases.

4-12   The Vibrational Partition Function

As in the preceding two sections, the wave mechanical formulation of the spacing between states is merely presented for use at this point. In the case of vibration the first-order treatment for a diatomic molecule is based on the assumption of a harmonic oscillator. The result is

$$\epsilon_{vib} = (v + \tfrac{1}{2})\, hv_0 , \tag{4-77}$$

where v is the vibrational quantum number, having values 0, 1, 2, ..., and v_0 is the characteristic frequency, related to the reduced mass μ and the force constant ℓ by

$$v_0 = \frac{1}{2\pi} \left(\frac{\ell}{\mu}\right)^{1/2}. \tag{4-78}$$

In the harmonic oscillator, the restoring force is simply ℓx, where x is the displacement from the minimum potential energy position. Although more elaborate treatments are available (see Commentary and Notes), the one given here is adequate for the first few vibrational energy states.

The vibrational partition function is then

$$Q_{vib} = \sum_v e^{-\epsilon_{vib}/kT} = e^{-hv_0/2kT} + e^{-3hv_0/2kT} + \cdots . \tag{4-79}$$

This particular series can be summed as follows. Let $x = \exp(-hv_0/2kT)$; Eq. (4-79) reduces to a series whose sum is given by the binomial theorem:

$$Q_{vib} = x(1 + x^2 + x^4 + \cdots) = \frac{x}{(1 - x^2)}$$

or

$$Q_{vib} = \frac{\exp(-h\nu_0/2kT)}{1 - \exp(-h\nu_0/kT)} = \frac{\exp(-\theta_{vib}/2T)}{1 - \exp(-\theta_{vib}/T)}, \qquad (4\text{-}80)$$

where, as with rotational states, we define a vibrational characteristic temperature as $\theta_{vib} = h\nu_0/k$. Differentiation gives

$$\frac{d(\ln Q)}{dT} = \frac{\theta_{vib}}{2T^2} + \frac{\theta_{vib}}{T^2} \frac{\exp(-\theta_{vib}/T)}{1 - \exp(-\theta_{vib}/T)}$$

and, by Eq. (4-55),

$$E = \frac{1}{2} h\nu_0 + kT \frac{\theta_{vib}/T}{\exp(\theta_{vib}/T) - 1} \qquad (4\text{-}81)$$

and

$$E = \frac{1}{2} N_0 h\nu_0 + RT \frac{\theta_{vib}/T}{\exp(\theta_{vib}/T) - 1}. \qquad (4\text{-}82)$$

In the limit of very low T the second term of Eq. (4-82) drops out and $E = \frac{1}{2}N_0 h\nu_0$. This energy of the lowest vibrational state is called the zero-point energy. At the other extreme, where $\theta_{vib} \ll T$, Eq. (4-82) reduces to

$$E = \frac{1}{2}N_0 h\nu_0 + RT. \qquad (4\text{-}83)$$

In this limit the heat capacity contribution is thus

$$C_{V(vib)} = R, \qquad (4\text{-}84)$$

which is the equipartition value for one degree of vibrational freedom. As with Q_{rot} there is no dependence of Q_{vib} on volume, so $H_{vib} = E_{vib}$. Thus the equipartition contribution of R per degree of freedom to vibrational heat capacity arises naturally from the mathematical treatment.

The general expression for C_V is obtained by differentiation of Eq. (4-82). This gives

$$C_{V(vib)} = R \left(\frac{\theta_{vib}}{T}\right)^2 \frac{\exp(\theta_{vib}/T)}{[\exp(\theta_{vib}/T) - 1]^2}. \qquad (4\text{-}85)$$

The expression reduces to zero for $\theta_{vib} \gg T$ and to R for $\theta_{vib} \ll T$. It is fortunate that it is possible to sum Eq. (4-79) explicitly since the usual situation is one lying between these extremes.

Force constants [k in Eq. (4-78)] are about 10^5 dyn cm^{-1}, and for a molecule like HCl, μ is about unity per mole, so ν_0 is about 10^{14} sec^{-1} and $h\nu_0/k$ is about 5×10^3 °K. Thus θ_{vib} may correspond to several thousand degrees Kelvin. For HCl, $\nu_0 = 8.98 \times 10^{13}$ sec^{-1} so that $\theta_{vib} = 4.308 \times 10^3$ °K. The energy of the first vibrational transition, from $v = 0$ to $v = 1$, which is just $h\nu_0$, is thus 4308/298 or $14.5kT$ at 25°C. Thus the relative probability of even the first excited vibrational state being populated is only $e^{-14.5}$, or about 10^{-6}, at 25°C. Very little energy is present in the form of vibrational excitation, and the contribution to heat capacity is therefore quite small. Equation (4-85) is plotted in Fig. 4-10 as $C_{V(vib)}$ versus

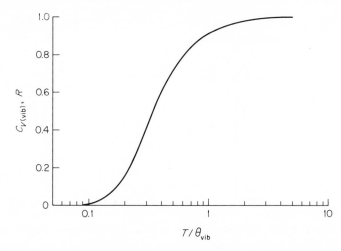

Fig. 4-10.   *Variation of $C_{V(vib)}$ with temperature according to Eq. (4-85).*

T/θ_{vib}, and the result confirms that vibrations contribute very little to the heat capacity of HCl around room temperature. On the other hand, for a more weakly bonded, heavy-atom molecule such as I_2, $\nu_0 = 214 \text{ cm}^{-1}$, or less than one-tenth that of HCl. Now $\theta_{vib} = 306°K$ and from Fig. 4-10 the vibrational heat capacity contribution for I_2 is nearly at the equipartition value at room temperature.

The varying extent to which vibrations contribute to heat capacity is also illustrated in Fig. 4-7. Although there is only one vibrational degree of freedom for a diatomic molecule, the number increases rapidly with molecular complexity. The total vibrational partition function will then be factorable, in the manner of Eq. (4-60), into a product of the separate ones for all of the independent vibrational modes:

$$\mathbf{Q}_{tot(vib)} = \prod_i \mathbf{Q}_{vib} . \tag{4-86}$$

Such independent modes are called normal modes (see Section 18-5). The quantitative result is that a simple function such as plotted in Fig. 4-10 is no longer applicable, but, qualitatively, the result is much the same as for diatomic molecules. A reasonable rule of thumb for polyatomic molecules is that about 20 % of the equipartition vibrational heat capacity will be developed at room temperature (and all of the equipartition translational and rotational contributions). For example, propane, C_3H_8, has a molar heat capacity $C_P = 19.7 \text{ cal mole}^{-1}$ at 25°C. On the basis of the rule just given, we would estimate

$$R + \tfrac{3}{2}R + \tfrac{3}{2}R + 0.2(27)R = 9.6R \quad \text{or} \quad 19 \quad \text{cal °K}^{-1} \text{ mole}^{-1}.$$

COMMENTARY AND NOTES

4-CN-1   Internal Pressure

There are some interesting aspects of Eq. (4-34),

$$C_P - C_V = \left[P + \left(\frac{\partial E}{\partial V} \right)_T \right] \left(\frac{\partial V}{\partial T} \right)_P \qquad [\text{Eq. (4-34)}].$$

For an ideal gas $(\partial E/\partial V)_T = 0$ and $(\partial V/\partial T)_P = R/P$, with the result that $C_P - C_V = R$. More generally, the heat capacity difference can be thought of as made up of two types of contributions. The first is the work against the external pressure P due to the change in volume on heating given by $P(\partial V/\partial T)_P$. The second is the work against the attractive forces between the molecules of the substance, given by $(\partial E/\partial V)_T (\partial V/\partial T)_P$. The quantity $(\partial E/\partial V)_T$ has the dimensions of pressure, and since it gives the measure of these attractive forces, it is called the internal pressure P_{int}.

The internal pressure is zero for an ideal gas and for most real gases it is small compared to P. An alternative thermodynamic relationship, derived in Section 6-ST-1, gives

$$\left(\frac{\partial E}{\partial V} \right)_T = T \left(\frac{\partial P}{\partial T} \right)_V - P. \qquad (4\text{-}87)$$

By means of this expression, we find that for a van der Waals gas,

$$\left(\frac{\partial E}{\partial V} \right)_T = \frac{a}{V^2}. \qquad (4\text{-}88)$$

As an example, $a = 3.59$ liter^2 atm mole^{-2} for CO_2, so at STP the internal pressure is only 0.0071 atm, which is quite small. Equation (4-88) provides a means of obtaining E for a van der Waals gas; on integrating, we find

$$E(V, T) = -\frac{a}{V} + f(T). \qquad (4\text{-}89)$$

The first term represents the contribution of attractive forces, and the second turns out to be the same as for an ideal gas, $\frac{3}{2}RT$.

In the case of liquids (or solids) the internal pressure is usually much greater than the external pressure. For water at 25°C, $P_{int} = 16,000$ atm, whereas for liquid hydrocarbons P_{int} is about 3000 atm. These data are obtained from the experimental coefficients of thermal expansion and compressibility, but again P_{int} values may be estimated by means of the van der Waals equation. Thus for water, $a = 5.46$ liter² atm mole⁻² and when $V = 18$ cm³ mole⁻¹, the calculated P_{int} is 16,850 atm. The coefficient $(\partial V/\partial T)_P$ is small for liquids and partly compensates for the high P_{int} values but $C_P - C_V$ may be quite appreciable (note Table 8-5).

4-CN-2   Additional Aspects of Statistical Mechanical Treatments

It is correctly suggested by the statistical mechanical treatment that it is the partition function for translation that determines ideal gas behavior. It gives the same value of E as from simple kinetic molecular theory, the same relationship between H and E, and leads to the ideal gas law. A gas, however, may be ideal and yet exhibit complex heat capacity behavior owing to the quantization of rotational and vibrational energy levels. Thus, by neglecting intermolecular forces, we make the gas ideal but are still free to consider in detail the structure of individual molecules and the intramolecular forces present. Alternatively put, in advanced kinetic molecular theory the emphasis is on treating intermolecular forces, including suitable modifications to $\mathbf{Q}_{trans}$, while in this chapter we have been more interested in $\mathbf{Q}_{int}$.

The treatment presented of $\mathbf{Q}_{int}$ was introductory, and a few of the complications might be mentioned here. First, $\mathbf{Q}_{rot}$ was derived only for the case of an A–B-type molecule. The general formula is

$$\mathbf{Q}_{rot} = \frac{1}{\pi\sigma} \left(\frac{8\pi^3 IkT}{h^2}\right)^{n/2}, \tag{4-90}$$

where n denotes the number of independent rotation axes (two for a linear molecule and three otherwise) and σ is a symmetry number. This last is the number of indistinguishable positions into which the molecule can be turned by rotations. For an A–A molecule, $\sigma = 2$, for example, while for NH_3, $\sigma = 3$, and for CH_4, $\sigma = 12$. A nonlinear molecule will in general have three independent moments of inertia, and in such a case, I is their geometric mean, $I = (I_A I_B I_C)^{1/3}$. Equation (4-72) gives the definition of I for the diatomic molecule; in the general case $I = \sum m_i d_i^2$, where d is the perpendicular distance from the rotation axis. The three mutually perpendicular axes pass through the center of mass and usually are oriented to conform with the molecular symmetry.

With vibrations two types of complications enter immediately. An experimental one is that in the case of polyatomic molecules there are a number of vibrational modes, and the observed absorption spectrum will show transitions between various combinations of the different vibrational excited states. Therefore it can be difficult to analyze such a spectrum in order to obtain the separate fundamental frequencies.

The second complication is that the assumption of harmonic oscillator behavior is not strictly correct. As illustrated in Fig. 4-11(a) the assumption leads to a

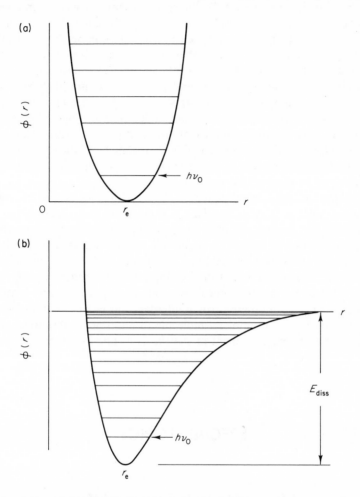

Fig. 4-11. *Potential wells for (a) a harmonic and (b) an anharmonic oscillator.*

parabolic potential energy function with equally spaced vibrational energy states. The actual situation is that shown in Fig. 4-11(b), where for a diatomic molecule the interatomic potential resembles somewhat the Lennard–Jones form used for intermolecular potentials (Fig. 1-17), although the theoretical basis for the attractive part is now one of chemical bonding rather than van der Waals forces. At any rate, the effect is to make the potential well asymmetric, or to introduce anharmonicity in the vibrational behavior. The successive states become closer and closer in energy until a definite final state is reached beyond which dissociation occurs. In the case of H_2, there are 15 such bound states before dissociation. Fortunately, at the temperatures of most heat capacity calculations only the first few vibrational levels are important, so that the anharmonicity effect is usually of little consequence.

However, with the development of the space program it has become necessary to deal in practice with energies and heat capacities of small molecules at very high temperatures. These quantities are important in determining the practical thrust developed by a given fuel. Here, anharmonicity may seriously complicate a theoretical calculation of the vibrational contributions. (In addition, Q_{elec} may have to be considered.) We can also understand why gases are not likely ever to reach vibrational equipartition. For them to do so the temperature must be large compared to θ_{vib}, which means that the average molecule is in a high vibrational state. Since there are only a limited number of states before the dissociation limit, an appreciable fraction of the molecules will be dissociated and the experimental heat capacity will no longer be that of the original molecule only, but rather that of a mixture of it and its dissociation products.

An important exception to this situation occurs with some liquids and especially with atomic crystals such as metals. This is discussed in more detail in the Special Topics section, but, briefly, one may find heat capacities closely approaching the vibrational equipartition limit. The qualitative explanation is that the vibrations are now between atoms that are held in a lattice and thus cannot dissociate.

A final point to mention is that the assumption of the independence of energy states which led to Eq. (4-60) is not fully valid. The approximation is very good with respect to Q_{trans}, but there is some interdependence of vibrational and rotational energy levels. For example, a molecule in an excited vibrational state will have a somewhat different moment of inertia from one in the ground or $v = 0$ state.

SPECIAL TOPICS

4-ST-1   The Joule–Thomson Effect

It was mentioned in Section 4-7A that Joule's experiment of allowing free expansion of a gas does in fact lead to small temperature changes. While no mechanical work is done by the gas on the surroundings, for any real gas there is work done against the intermolecular forces of attraction. This is another manifestation of the internal pressure of a gas discussed in Section 4-CN-1. The expansion, moreover, is essentially adiabatic, so q is zero, and the process is therefore one in which E does not change. The work against the internal pressure thus is balanced by a temperature change in the gas, and we define the *Joule coefficient* as

$$J = \left(\frac{\partial T}{\partial V}\right)_E. \tag{4-91}$$

Since by Eq. (4-12)

$$\left(\frac{\partial T}{\partial V}\right)_E = -\frac{(\partial E/\partial V)_T}{(\partial E/\partial T)_V} = -\frac{1}{C_V}\left(\frac{\partial E}{\partial V}\right)_T \tag{4-92}$$

we can write, using Eq. (4-87),

$$J = -\frac{1}{C_V}\left[T\left(\frac{\partial P}{\partial T}\right)_V - P\right] = -\frac{P_{\text{int}}}{C_V}. \tag{4-93}$$

The Joule coefficient thus provides a direct measure of the internal pressure P_{int}.

For CO_2 at STP, P_{int} is found to be 0.0071 atm using the van der Waals equation [and Eq. (4-88)]. For CO_2, $C_V = 6.6$ cal $°K^{-1}$ mole^{-1} at STP, or 270 cm^3 atm $°K^{-1}$ mole^{-1}. $J = -2.6 \times 10^{-5}$ $°K$ mole cm^{-3}, or rather small.

The measurement of the Joule coefficient is a difficult one, and alternative experimental arrangements have been devised to obtain closely related quantities. An important such arrangement is the Joule–Thomson (Kelvin) experiment illustrated in Fig. 4-12. One allows a gas to expand through a porous plug so that

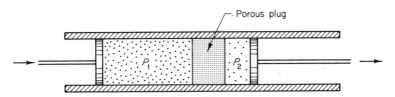

Fig. 4-12. *The Joule–Thomson experiment.*

entering gas may be kept at pressure P_1 and exiting gas at pressure P_2. This is shown schematically in the figure as a double piston and cylinder arrangement. The porous plug is made of thermally insulating material so that q is zero. The gas is initially at P_1 and V_1 and the final state is at P_2 and V_2. Since $q = 0$, $E = -w = P_1V_1 - P_2V_2$, so

$$E_2 - E_1 = P_1V_1 - P_2V_2, \quad \text{or} \quad H_2 = H_1.$$

The experiment is therefore at constant H. The change in temperature of the gas is measured and the *Joule–Thomson coefficient* is defined as

$$\mu = \left(\frac{\partial T}{\partial P}\right)_H .$$

(4-94)

By the nature of the experiment ΔP is always negative, so a positive μ corresponds to cooling on expansion. Around room temperature, all gases except hydrogen, helium, and neon exhibit such cooling. At a sufficiently low temperature all gases do. The Joule–Thomson coefficient also depends on pressure, and the point at which $\mu = 0$, known as the *Joule–Thomson inversion point*, is then a function of pressure and temperature.

The Joule–Thomson coefficient may also be calculated from the equation of state of the gas. Since by Eq. (4-12)

$$\left(\frac{\partial T}{\partial P}\right)_H = -\frac{(\partial H/\partial P)_T}{(\partial H/\partial T)_P} = -\frac{1}{C_P}\left(\frac{\partial H}{\partial P}\right)_T ,$$

(4-95)

an equation analogous to Eq. (4-87), but again derived later (Section 6-ST-1), gives

$$\left(\frac{\partial H}{\partial P}\right)_T = -T\left(\frac{\partial V}{\partial T}\right)_P + V$$

(4-96)

and combination of this with Eq. (4-95) yields

$$\mu = \frac{1}{C_P}\left[T\left(\frac{\partial V}{\partial T}\right)_P - V\right].$$

(4-97)

The van der Waals equation may be used for the calculation of μ and it gives moderately good agreement with experiment.

The Joule–Thomson effect is generally larger than the Joule effect. For CO_2 at STP, $\mu = 1.30°K \ atm^{-1}$ (as compared to $0.73°K \ atm^{-1}$ calculated from the van der Waals equation), and for O_2, $\mu = 0.31°K \ atm^{-1}$. The Joule–Thomson effect may be produced in a cyclic operation, and machines that do this are widely used in the liquefaction of gases. In practice, the expansion may be through a throttle rather than a porous plug.

As a final comment, the accuracy of measured μ values suffers because of the difficulty in preventing heat exchange with the porous plug. An alternative measurement is of the quantity of heat that must be supplied when the expansion occurs at constant temperature. This gives the isothermal Joule–Thomson coefficient $\phi = (\partial H/\partial P)_T$ or $-\mu C_P$.

4-ST-2   The Heat Capacity of a Solid

This subject might have been assigned to the chapter on the crystal structure of solids but is treated here instead since it ties in very closely with the discussion of heat capacities. Before taking up the quantum mechanical aspect we first consider an extension of the equipartition principle.

In the case of a crystalline solid in which each lattice position is occupied by a single atom, there can be no translation (other than of the crystal as a whole!) and no rotation. The $3N_0$ degrees of freedom per mole are thus entirely vibrational, and one predicts an equipartition molar heat capacity of $3R$ as noted in Table 4-2. This prediction explains an old observation, known as the *law of Dulong and Petit*, to the effect that the molar heat capacity of a monatomic crystalline solid is about 6.2 cal °K^{-1} mole^{-1}. This law is obeyed by a number of metals; for example, the heat capacities for Ca, Fe, and Ag are 6.0, 6.2, and 6.0 cal °K^{-1} mole^{-1}, respectively, around room temperature. These are C_V values; Eq. (4-34) may be used to obtain C_P.

The Dulong–Petit law finds useful application in metallurgy. The composition of a binary alloy can be estimated just from its heat capacity per gram, since division into 6.2 gives the average molecular weight. Table 4-2 includes an entry for an MX-type crystal, such as NaCl. The point here is that the equipartition value per mole is now doubled since there are two moles of atoms per formula weight.

While it is not appropriate here to cover the statistical mechanical treatment of solids in much detail, there is a simple and useful extension of the material of Section 4-12 to the case of a crystalline solid in which the lattice sites are occupied by atoms (or monatomic ions). If the $3N_0$ vibrations can be viewed as independent oscillators, then the total partition function is just the product of $3N_0$ individual ones, as in Eq. (4-86), or $\mathbf{Q}_{\text{vib}}^{3N_0}$, where $\mathbf{Q}_{\text{vib}}$ is given by Eq. (4-80). The effect is simply to multiply the expression for E [Eq. (4-81)] by $3N_0$, with the result that the molar heat capacity is just three times that given by Eq. (4-85):

$$C_{V\text{(crystal)}} = 3R \left(\frac{\theta_{\text{vib}}}{T} \right)^2 \frac{\exp(\theta_{\text{vib}}/T)}{[\exp(\theta_{\text{vib}}/T) - 1]^2}. \tag{4-98}$$

This treatment, due to Einstein, leads to a predicted variation of $C_{V\text{(crystal)}}$ with T/θ_{vib}, which is the same as that shown in Fig. 4-10 except that the heat capacity scale is now from zero to $3R$. The high-temperature limit is $3R$, or the equipartition

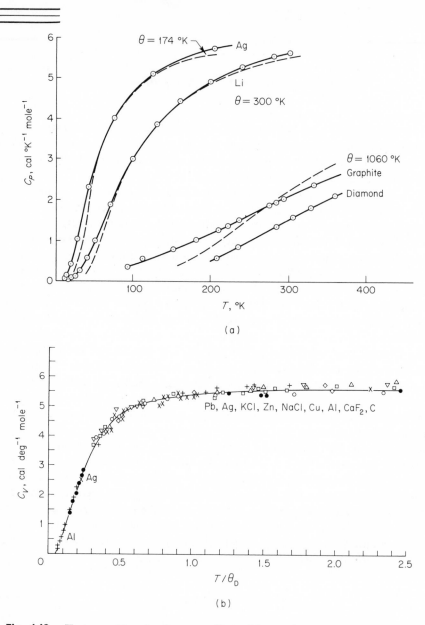

Fig. 4-13. *Heat capacities of various crystalline solids as a function of temperature. (a) The best-fitting curves according to the Einstein equation (4-98), dashed lines. (b) Scaled by the best choice of θ_D to give a fit to the theoretical Debye curve (solid line). [Adapted from S. M. Blinder, "Advanced Physical Chemistry." Copyright 1969, Macmillan, New York.]*

value (and that given by the Dulong–Petit law). Experimental results agree fairly well with the *Einstein equation*, as shown by the broken lines in Fig. 4-13(a). In each case θ_{vib} is empirically determined so as to give the best fit. Significant deviation sets in at low temperatures, however, and the theory was considerably improved by Debye. He assumed a range of possible ν_0 values up to a maximum ν_{max}, using the same distribution function as for blackbody radiation (Section 16-ST-1). This ν_{max} is simply a cutoff at the point where a total of $3N_0$ frequencies is reached and is an empirical parameter of the theory. The characteristic temperature is now defined as $h\nu_{\text{max}}/kT$ and is thus also an empirical quantity.

The actual Debye equation is sufficiently complicated that it does not seem worthwhile to derive it here. Moreover, in view of the artifical nature of the cutoff at ν_{max}, the equation is theoretically sound only at temperatures sufficiently low that the most populated vibrational states lie well below this level. For the low-temperature region the Debye treatment predicts that the heat capacity should be proportional to T^3, and this provides a valuable limiting law. It is used, for example, in extrapolating experimental heat capacity values toward $0°K$ when calculating thermodynamic quantities.

The preceding treatments, of course, run into difficulty in the case of a molecular solid, that is, with crystals the lattice points of which are occupied by molecules or molecular ions. Some of the degrees of freedom will now be associated with intra-molecular vibrations, and possibly rotations, and the observed heat capacity will derive from these plus the lattice vibrations. The case of liquids is yet more complex since now molecules may be in a rather broad potential well; the same is true for dense gases. The various statistical mechanical approaches to the problem are both difficult and approximate, and beyond the scope of this text. One interesting situation might be mentioned, however. Liquid water has a molar heat capacity of $18 \text{ cal} °K^{-1} \text{ mole}^{-1}$, which is the equipartition value assuming only vibrational degrees of freedom. This suggests that, on the average, the molecules in water are so interwoven by hydrogen bonding that neither translation nor free rotation is important. The $9N_0$ degrees of freedom per mole are thus entirely vibrational. Moreover, the effect of hydrogen bonding must be to make the vibrational states lie much closer together than in the free molecule, so that the equipartition value of the heat capacity can be reached even at room temperature.

GENERAL REFERENCES

BLINDER, S. M. (1969). "Advanced Physical Chemistry." Macmillan, New York.
HIRSCHFELDER, J. O., CURTISS, C. F., AND BIRD, R. B. (1954). "Molecular Theory of Gases and Liquids." Wiley, New York.

Exercises

4-1   Given the function $y = u(u + v)$, evaluate (a) $(\partial y/\partial u)_v$ and (b) $(\partial y/\partial v)_u$. Calculate Δy, $\int (\partial y/\partial u)_v \, du$, and $\int (\partial y/\partial v)_u \, dv$ for (c) path $(u_1, v_1) \to (u_2, v_1)$ followed by $(u_2, v_1) \to (u_2, v_2)$ and (d) path $(u_1, v_1) \to (u_1, v_2)$ followed by $(u_1, v_2) \to (u_2, v_2)$, where $u_1 = 2$, $u_2 = 5$, $v_1 = 3$, and $v_2 = 6$.

> *Ans.*   (a) $2u + v$, (b) u,
> (c) $\Delta y = 45$, $\int (\partial y/\partial u)_v \, du = 30$, $\int (\partial y/\partial v)_u \, dv = 15$,
> (d) $\Delta y = 45$, $\int (\partial y/\partial v)_u \, dv = 6$, $\int (\partial y/\partial u)_v \, du = 39$.

4-2   For a right circular cylinder of radius r and length l, the area is $\mathscr{A} = 2\pi rl$ and the volume is $V = \pi r^2 l$. (a) Evaluate the coefficients $(\partial \mathscr{A}/\partial r)_l$, $(\partial \mathscr{A}/\partial l)_r$, $(\partial r/\partial l)_{\mathscr{A}}$, $(\partial V/\partial r)_l$, $(\partial V/\partial l)_r$. (b) Evaluate $(\partial \mathscr{A}/\partial V)_l$ by expressing $\mathscr{A}$ as a function of l and V only and then carry out the indicated partial differentiation. (c) Using Eqs. (4-13) and (4-15), express $(\partial \mathscr{A}/\partial V)_l$ in terms involving only partial derivatives listed in (a) and thus evaluate $(\partial \mathscr{A}/\partial V)_l$ indirectly.

> *Ans.* $2\pi l$, $2\pi r$, $-\mathscr{A}/2\pi l^2$, $2\pi rl$, πr^2. (b) and (c) $1/r$.

4-3   Express $(\partial E/\partial T)_P$ in terms of derivatives which you can evaluate from the ideal gas law.

> *Ans.* $(\partial E/\partial T)_P = C_P - P(\partial V/\partial T)_P = C_P - R$.

4-4   A certain gas obeys the equation $P(V - b) = RT$. (a) Evaluate $(\partial V/\partial T)_P$ and $(\partial V/\partial P)_T$. Obtain $(\partial P/\partial T)_V$ by (b) use of Eq. (4-12) and (c) direct differentiation.

> *Ans.*   (a) R/P, $-RT/P^2$, (b) and (c) $R/(V-b)$.

4-5   The coefficient of thermal expansion for Al is $(1/V)(\partial V/\partial T)_P = 2.4 \times 10^{-5} \,°\mathrm{C}^{-1}$, and $(\partial E/\partial V)_T$ is estimated at 1.0×10^5 atm. Calculate $C_P - C_V$ for Al at $25°\mathrm{C}$ and atmospheric pressure.

> *Ans.* 0.59 cal mole^{-1}.

4-6   One mole of an ideal, monatomic gas at STP undergoes an isochoric heating to $25°\mathrm{C}$. Calculate (a) P, (b) q, (c) w, (d) ΔE, and (e) ΔH.

> *Ans.*   (a) 1.09 atm, (b) 74.3 cal, (c) 0, (d) 74.3 cal, (e) 124 cal.

4-7   The same gas as in Exercise 4-6 undergoes an isobaric heating to $25°\mathrm{C}$. Calculate the same quantities as before, plus (f) the final volume.

> *Ans.*   (a) 1 atm, (b) 124 cal, (c) 49.5 cal,
> (d) 74.3 cal, (e) 124 cal, (f) 24.5 liter.

4-8   The same gas as in Exercises 4-6 and 4-7 undergoes a reversible adiabatic compression such that the final temperature is $25°\mathrm{C}$. Calculate quantities (a)–(f).

> *Ans.*   (a) 1.24 atm, (b) 0, (c) -74.3 cal,
> (d) 74.3 cal, (e) 124 cal, (f) 19.6 liter.

Problems

4-9 Ten moles of an ideal gas of $C_V = 3.5$ cal $°K^{-1}$ mole^{-1} undergoes a reversible isothermal compression from 0.2 to 5 atm at 100°C. Calculate (a) the initial and final volumes, (b) q, (c) w, (d) ΔE, and (e) ΔH.

> *Ans.* (a) 1530 and 61.2 liter, (b) −23,900 cal, (c) −23,900 cal, (d) 0, (e) 0.

4-10 Calculate the equipartition heat capacity C_e for (a) O_3, (b) Xe, (c) HCl, and (d) C_2H_4, assuming ideal gas behavior, and C_V for (e) diamond and (f) NaCl (solid).

> *Ans.* (a) $7\frac{1}{2}R$, (b) $2\frac{1}{2}R$, (c) $4\frac{1}{2}R$, (d) $16R$, (e) $3R$, (f) $6R$.

4-11 A foam plastic has cells of 0.1 mm dimension. Calculate (a) the quantum number n for the one-dimensional translational state whose energy would be equal to kT at 25°C in the case of argon gas and (b) $Q_{trans(3-dim)}$ at 25°C assuming the cells to be spheres of radius 0.1 mm.

> *Ans.* (a) 7.1×10^6, (b) 1.02×10^{21} cm^3.

4-12 The rotational constant B_e of a linear molecule is defined as $B_e = h/8\pi^2 cI$, where c is the velocity of light; $B_e = 1.93$ cm^{-1} for CO. Calculate (a) the moment of inertia I for CO, (b) the quantum number J for the rotational state whose energy is equal to kT at 25°C, (c) the characteristic rotational temperature, and (d) Q_{rot} at 25°C.

> *Ans.* (a) 1.45×10^{-39} g cm^2, (b) about 10, (c) 2.78°K, (d) 107.

4-13 The vibrational characteristic temperature is 3084°K for CO. Calculate (a) $h\nu_0$, (b) the force constant ℓ,(c) the energy of the $\nu = 2$ state, (d) $C_{V(vib)}$ at 25°C, (e) Q_{vib} at 25°C, and (f) E_{vib} at 25°C.

> *Ans.* (a) 4.26×10^{-13} erg, (b) 1.86×10^6 dyn cm^{-1}, (c) 1.07×10^{-12} erg (or $25.8kT$ at 25°C), (d) $3.6 \times 10^{-3}\,R$, (e) 5.68×10^{-3}, (f) 2.13×10^{-13} erg (or $5.2kT$).

Problems

4-1 Derive the equation $C_P - C_V = -(\partial P/\partial T)_V[(\partial H/\partial P)_T - V]$.

4-2 Suppose that for a certain gas $(\partial E/\partial V)_T = 0$, but $P(V - b) = RT$. Calculate $(\partial H/\partial V)_T$ and $C_P - C_V$.

4-3 The area $\mathscr{A}$ of a right cone is given by $\pi r(r^2 + h^2)^{1/2}$, where r is the radius of the base and h is the altitude, and the volume is $(\pi/3)r^2 h$. Evaluate $(\partial \mathscr{A}/\partial r)_h$, $(\partial \mathscr{A}/\partial h)_r$, $(\partial r/\partial h)_{\mathscr{A}}$, $(\partial V/\partial r)_h$, $(\partial V/\partial h)_r$, and $(\partial r/\partial h)_V$. Evaluate $(\partial \mathscr{A}/\partial V)_h$ by expressing $\mathscr{A}$ as a function of h and V only and then carrying out the indicated partial differentiation. Finally, evaluate $(\partial \mathscr{A}/\partial V)_h$ in terms of the differentials given here only, using the various partial differential relationships given in the chapter.

4-4 One mole of an ideal monatomic gas undergoes the following processes: 1. Adiabatic expansion from P_1, V_1, T_1 to P_2, V_2, T_2. 2. Return to initial state by the straight line path shown in the accompanying diagram (p. 162). Calculate ΔE, ΔH, q, and w for each step and for the cycle if $P_1 = 2$ atm, $T_1 = 0°C$, and $V_2 = 2V_1$.

161

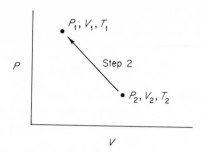

4-5 One mole of an ideal monatomic gas may be taken from the initial condition $P_1 = 3$ atm, $V_1 = 10$ liter to the final condition $P_2 = 0.5$ atm, $V_2 = 2$ liter by either one of the following paths: Path 1. (a) decrease in volume at constant pressure followed by (b) decrease in pressure at constant volume. Path 2. (a) decrease in pressure at constant volume followed by (b) decrease in volume at constant pressure.

For each path calculate ΔE, q, and w. If the gas is taken from P_1, V_1 to P_2, V_2 by path 1 and returned to the initial state by path 2, what are the values of ΔE, q, and w for the cycle?

4-6 Calculate ΔE, ΔH, q, and w when 1 mole of an ideal monatomic gas initially at 0°C and 2 atm is taken to a final pressure of 15 atm by the reversible path defined by the equation $PV^2 = $ constant. Calculate (by means of a derivation) the heat capacity along this path, that is dq/dT for the path.

4-7 One mole of an ideal monatomic gas may be taken from the initial condition $P_1 = 2$ atm, $V_1 = 15$ liter to the final condition $P_2 = 4$ atm, $V_2 = 40$ liter by either of the following paths: Path 1: (a) increase in volume at constant pressure followed by (b) an increase in pressure at constant volume. Path 2: (a) increase in pressure at constant volume followed by (b) an increase in volume at constant pressure.

For each path calculate ΔE, q, and w. If the gas is taken from P_1, V_1 to P_2, V_2 by path 1 and returned to the initial state by path 2, what are the values of ΔE, q, and w for the cycle?

4-8 One hundred grams of nitrogen at 25°C are held by a piston under 30 atm pressure. The pressure is suddenly released to 10 atm and the gas expands adiabatically. If C_V for nitrogen is 4.95 cal °C^{-1} mole^{-1}, calculate the final temperature of the gas. What are ΔE and ΔH for the process? Assume the gas is ideal.

4-9 Carbon dioxide gas is compressed isothermally at 334.6°K from volume V_1 to volume V_2, the pressure rising from 10 atm to 100 atm. Plot P versus V (P as ordinate) assuming (a) ideal gas behavior and (b) nonideal gas behavior, according to the Hougen–Watson chart, Fig. 1-11. Calculate the minimum work done per mole on the gas for cases (a) and (b). If the gas were compressed from the ideal gas law volume at 10 atm to the ideal gas law volume at 100 atm, would the minimum work done according to case (b) be more or less than that according to case (a)?

4-10 In each of the following cases show how to estimate the number of atoms per molecule. (a) A gas obeys the ideal gas law and has a ratio C_P/C_V of 1.40 at 25°C; assume no vibrational contribution to the heat capacity. (b) An ideal gas has an equipartition value of C_P/C_V of 1.083.

4-11 One mole of CO_2 at 100°C at 80 atm is compressed isothermally to 100 atm. The pressure is then reduced to 80 atm by cooling at constant volume. Finally, the original state is regained by warming at constant pressure. Assuming that CO_2 obeys the van der Waals equation with constants as given in Table 1-6, calculate q and w for each step and for the cycle.

4-12 Referring to Exercise 4-13, calculate the heat capacity C_V for CO for various temperatures between 25°C and 1000°C and plot the results as C_V versus t.

4-13 Calculate the heat capacity C_V for O_2 at 1500°C given that θ_{vib} is 2239°K. At what temperature would I_2 have the same heat capacity if its θ_{vib} is 307°K?

4-14 Calculate the vibrational heat capacity $C_{V(vib)}$ for CH_3I at 25°C given that the fundamental vibration frequencies ν_0 are $\bar{\nu}_1 = 2970$ cm^{-1}, $\bar{\nu}_2 = 1252$ cm^{-1}, $\bar{\nu}_3 = 533$ cm^{-1}, $\bar{\nu}_4 = 3060$ (2) cm^{-1}, $\bar{\nu}_5 = 1440$ (2) cm^{-1}, and $\bar{\nu}_6 = 880$ (2) cm^{-1}. Frequency is given in terms of wave number $\bar{\nu}$, or the reciprocal of the wavelength corresponding to the ν_0 ; here (2) indicates that two vibrations have the same frequency. Each frequency may be assumed to make its independent contribution to the heat capacity.

4-15 The rotational temperature is 66°K for HD. Calculate the average rotational energy at 30°K and at 40°K and estimate the rotational contribution to the heat capacity of HD at 35°K.

Special Topics Problems

4-1 Derive the equation

$$C_V = C_P \left[1 - \mu \left(\frac{\partial P}{\partial T}\right)_V\right] - V \left(\frac{\partial P}{\partial T}\right)_V.$$

4-2 Gases such as H_2, O_2, or N_2 are termed "noncondensable" because they cannot be liquefied at ordinary temperatures, although, of course, liquefaction does occur if they are cooled at the proper pressure to a temperature below the critical temperature. If the Joule–Thomson coefficient is positive, the cooling may be accomplished by allowing the compressed gas at room temperature to expand to 1 atm pressure, part of the gas liquefying if the conditions are right. In the commercial process based on these facts the liquefied gas is collected (at its boiling point at 1 atm pressure), and the residual unliquefied gas is made to exchange heat with the incoming compressed gas so as to precool it. With a good heat exchanger the emerging residual gas (at 1 atm) is essentially at room temperature. As an example, the process per mole may be written

$$O_2(\text{gas, 200 atm, 298°K}) = xO_2(\text{liq., 1 atm, 90°K})$$
$$+(1 - x)O_2(\text{gas, 1 atm, 298°K}).$$

Since the process is adiabatic, the Joule–Thomson condition holds, tnat is, $\Delta H = 0$. Calculate x, the mole fraction of the oxygen liquefied, given the following information: 1. The Joule–Thomson coefficient for oxygen is such that on free expansion from 200 atm to 1 atm, the drop in temperature is 50°C (thus H for O_2 at 200 atm, 298°K equals H for O_2 at 1 atm, 248°K). 2. C_P is 6.7 cal °K^{-1} mole^{-1} (assume to be independent of temperature). 3. The heat of vaporization of liquid oxygen is 1600 cal mole^{-1}.

4-3 Calculate the Joule coefficient J and the Joule–Thomson coefficient μ for CH_4 assuming it to be a van der Waals gas. Assume STP.

4-4 The Debye characteristic temperature $\theta_D = 86°K$ for Pb. Estimate the heat capacity of Pb at $-100°C$ and at $25°C$. Calculate θ_{vib} for Pb for the best-fitting Einstein equation.

4-5 The heat capacity of Pt is (in calories per gram) 0.00123 at $-255°C$, 0.0261 at $-152°C$, 0.0324 at $20°C$, and 0.0365 at $750°C$. Estimate the Debye characteristic temperature θ_D and θ_{vib} for the best-fitting Einstein equation. Plot the data as heat capacity versus temperature along with the two theoretical curves.

5 THERMOCHEMISTRY

5-1 Introduction

The preceding chapters have dealt with the physical properties and changes of state of pure substances or fixed mixtures of substances. We now consider the application of the first law of thermodynamics to chemical changes—a subject called *thermochemistry*. The subject is of great practical importance since it deals with the organization of the large amount of data concerning energies of chemical reactions. It also provides the foundation for obtaining chemical bond energies and hence for some aspects of theoretical chemistry.

This chapter also serves to introduce the general notation used in the application of thermodynamics to chemical change. The balanced equation for a chemical reaction is in the strict sense merely a particular affirmation that atoms are conserved in chemistry. Thus the equation

$$a\mathrm{A} + b\mathrm{B} + \cdots = m\mathrm{M} + n\mathrm{N} + \cdots, \tag{5-1}$$

is no more than a statement that substances A, B,..., if taken in the molar amounts a, b, ..., will collectively contain the same number of each kind of atom as will substances M, N, ..., taken in the amounts m, n, ... The equation does not predict that the chemical change will in fact occur, or that if it does occur, that other types of reactions may not also be present. It is part of the practice of chemistry to devise experimental situations such that the measurements made can be analyzed into contributions from one (or more) specific chemical processes.

From the point of view of the first law, each substance has an internal energy and an enthalpy which are functions of the state of that substance. Thus

$E_A = f_A(V_A, T_A)$, $E_B = f_B(V_B, T_B)$, and so on, and similarly $H_A = f_A'(P_A, T_A)$, $H_B = f_B'(P_B, T_B)$, and so on. To be complete, therefore, Eq. (5-1) should specify the state of each substance:

$$aA(V_A \text{ or } P_A, T_A) + bB(V_B \text{ or } P_B, T_B) + \cdots = nN(V_N \text{ or } P_N, T_N)$$
$$+ mM(V_M \text{ or } P_M, T_M) + \cdots. \qquad (5\text{-}2)$$

(It is sufficient to give T and either P or V since the three are related by the equation of state for the substance.) The substances are not necessarily at the same temperature and pressure or at the same temperature and molar volume. We then use the symbol Δ as an operator which may be applied to any characteristic extensive property $\mathscr{P}$ such as E, H, or V to signify the following operation:

$$\Delta\mathscr{P} \quad \text{means} \quad (m\mathscr{P}_M + n\mathscr{P}_N + \cdots) - (a\mathscr{P}_A + b\mathscr{P}_B + \cdots) \qquad (5\text{-}3)$$

or

$$\Delta\mathscr{P} = \sum_{\text{products}} n_p\mathscr{P}_i - \sum_{\text{reactants}} n_r\mathscr{P}_i,$$

where n_p and n_r are the stoichiometric coefficients in the balanced equation. The property $\mathscr{P}$ is for the indicated substance in that state specified by the chemical equation. Thus the value of $\Delta\mathscr{P}$ must always refer to a definite, completely described equation. In the case of reactions involving solutions chemical composition must be specified; the detailed thermochemistry of solutions is deferred until Chapter 9.

As an illustration, the reaction by which water is formed from hydrogen and oxygen might be written

$$H_2 \text{ (gas, 25°C, 1 atm)} + \tfrac{1}{2}O_2 \text{ (gas, 25°C, 1 atm)} = H_2O \text{ (liq, 25°C, 1 atm)}. \qquad (5\text{-}4)$$

For this reaction ΔH is

$$\Delta H = H(H_2O) - H(H_2) - \tfrac{1}{2}H(O_2), \qquad (5\text{-}5)$$

where the individual enthalpies are per mole of the substance in the indicated state. Note that the phase (gas, liquid, solid) of the substance must be specified if there is any possible ambiguity.

Unlike the situation with some extensive quantities, such as volume or mass, we have no absolute values for the internal energy or enthalpy of a substance. Although the first law permits us to calculate changes in E or H, its application never produces absolute values. The same is true in thermochemistry; ΔE and ΔH give the changes in internal energy and enthalpy that accompany a chemical reaction, and while either may be expressed in the form of Eq. (5-3), we do not know the separate E or H values. It is partly a consequence of this situation that much use is made of standard or reference states. Two systems of standard states are in use. The first is one of convenience, 1 atm pressure and, if so specified, 25°C. In the case of a reaction for which the reactants and products are all in a standard state, such as Eq. (5-4), one writes $\varDelta E_{298}^0$ or $\varDelta H_{298}^0$, where the superscript zero means that the pressure is one atm and the subscript gives the temperature chosen. As will be seen, a large body of thermochemical data is reported on this basis.

The second system takes as the standard state the substance devoid of any thermal energy, that is, at $0°K$. This is a more rational as well as a very useful approach and is developed in the Special Topics section. Its implementation does require either extensive knowledge of heat capacity data or sufficient spectroscopic information to allow evaluation of the various partition functions.

5-2   Measurement of Heats of Reaction: Relationship between ΔE and ΔH

The practice of thermochemistry involves the measurement of the heat absorbed or evolved when a chemical reaction occurs. That is, the determination is one of q in the first law statements:

$$dE = \delta q - \delta w, \tag{5-6}$$

$$dH = \delta q + V\,dP. \tag{5-7}$$

For simplicity, one attempts to choose conditions such that either volume is constant, so that no work is done, in which case $\varDelta E = q_V$, or such that pressure is constant, in which case $\varDelta H = q_P$. In either event, if heat is evolved, the reaction is said to be *exothermic*; q is negative and likewise the corresponding $\varDelta E$ or $\varDelta H$. If heat is absorbed, the reaction is said to be *endothermic*, and q and $\varDelta E$ or $\varDelta H$ are positive. One generally measures q by carrying out the reaction under adiabatic conditions. That is $q = 0$, and one finds $\varDelta E$ or $\varDelta H$ by means of the temperature change that occurs.

The equipment for such measurements is the *calorimeter*; it may be either of the constant-volume or the constant-pressure type. In the first type, the reactants are placed in a closed vessel and the reaction is initiated either by some mechanical means of bringing the reactants into contact as in Fig. 5-1(a), or, in the case of a combustion reaction, by means of a hot filament or spark as illustrated in Fig. 5-1(b). The heat of reaction is calculated directly from the temperature of the products, or, very often, the calorimeter is immersed in a water bath and the rise in temperature of the bath is then determined. This last arrangement has the advantage that the temperature of the products remains close to the initial temperature, which facilitates making the necessary corrections for reporting the results as a standard energy of reaction, that is, as $\varDelta E_{298}^0$. The amount of energy corresponding to the measured temperature change of the calorimeter plus bath is usually found by determining how much electrical heating is needed to produce the same effect. Modern calorimetric measurements are therefore often recorded

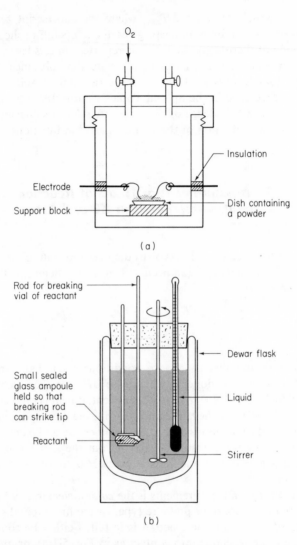

Fig. 5-1. *(a) Simple calorimeter such as might be used for measuring a heat of solution or of mixing. (b) Constant-volume combustion calorimeter.*

directly in joules rather than in calories. In an alternative approach, the calorimeter is packed in ice and the heat of reaction is calculated from the amount of ice melted. The ice calorimeter, used as early as 1780 by Lavoisier and Laplace, provides a strictly isothermal as well as adiabatic measurement [see Hock and Johnston (1961)].

Constant-volume calorimeters are generally used when a reactant or product is gaseous, as in combustion reactions. Since the measured heat is a q_V, one obtains a ΔE of reaction, and it is usually desirable to convert the result to a ΔH of reaction. It follows from the definition of H that for a reaction

$$\Delta H = \Delta E + \Delta(PV), \tag{5-8}$$

and further

$$\Delta H^0_{298} = \Delta E^0_{298} + P\,\Delta V, \qquad P = 1 \quad \text{atm}, \tag{5-9}$$

where ΔV is given by Eq. (5-3). Molar volumes of liquids and solids are not large and their contribution to the ΔV of a reaction is usually of the order of a few cubic centimeters; the $P\,\Delta V$ term of Eq. (5-9) would then amount to only about 1 cal. If gases are involved, however, the correction can be quite appreciable. If we let Δn_g denote the number of moles of gaseous products minus the moles of gaseous reactants, then the $P\,\Delta V$ term becomes $(\Delta n_g)PV$. If the gases are nearly ideal, then an approximate form of Eq. (5-8) is

$$\Delta H \simeq \Delta E + (\Delta n_g)RT. \tag{5-10}$$

Thus in the case of Eq. (5-4)

$$\Delta H^0_{298} = \Delta E^0_{298} - \tfrac{3}{2}(1.987)(298.1) = \Delta E^0_{298} - 888 \quad \text{cal}.$$

The $P\,\Delta V$ term for $H_2O(l)$ amounts to only 18 cm^3 atm or about 0.4 cal, so neglecting it introduces only a small error.

Constant-pressure calorimeters are especially convenient for reactions involving solutions. The process may be one of the dissolving of a substance in a solvent, in which case a *heat of solution* is obtained. Or a solution may be diluted by the addition of more solvent, so that a *heat of dilution* is obtained. Heats of chemical reactions may be studied by mixing two reacting solutions in the calorimeter. Since the calorimeter is open to the atmosphere or is at some constant pressure, the result gives ΔH directly.

The equipment is often very simple. It may be sufficient to use an adiabatic calorimeter consisting of a well-insulated container, such as a Dewar flask, in which the solvent or one of the solutions is placed, as shown in Fig. 5-1(b). The solid or the other solution is placed in a glass or metal vial which is immersed in the first liquid. The temperature of the system is determined, the vial is broken or opened, and after the reaction is complete, the final temperature is measured. The heat of the process is calculated from the temperature change and the heat capacity of the system (which may again be determined by an electrical heating experiment).

In very accurate work, a correction is needed for the heat loss that will occur even with good insulation. Such loss may be greatly reduced by the following experimental modification. The reaction vessel is now placed in a water bath which can be heated electrically. On causing the reaction to occur, one supplies just that amount of electrical heat to the bath so that its temperature and that of the reaction mixture are always the same. Since the two are kept at the same temperature, no heat flows between them and the reaction condition is accurately adiabatic.

The principal chemical requirement in calorimetry is that the measured q must be assignable to a definite process. This means that the products must be well defined and preferably should result from a single, clean chemical reaction. Correction for incomplete reaction can be made, but it is very desirable that the reaction go to completion. In addition, the reaction should be fairly rapid; otherwise maintenance of the adiabatic condition of the calorimeter becomes very difficult. Most of the reactions of organic chemistry fail to meet one or another of these criteria, and for this reason organic thermochemistry deals mainly with combustion and hydrogenation; these processes generally can be made to go rapidly and cleanly. Heats of solution and dilution offer no great difficulty, and many inorganic reactions are easy to study. A good example of the latter would be a heat of neutralization of an acid by a base. On the other hand, coordination compounds often react too slowly for good calorimetry and are not easy to burn to well-defined products.

5-3 *Some Enthalpies of Combustion, Hydrogenation, and Solution*

The general type of calorimeter used for measuring heats of combustion was described in the preceding section. With excess pure oxygen present, most organic compounds will burn cleanly to carbon dioxide and water. Halogens or nitrogen present in a compound may appear as a mixture of the element and its oxides, and the exact proportions of such products may have to be determined for each experiment. In working problems in this text, however, it will be sufficient for the reader to assume that only the free element is formed, that is, Cl_2, Br_2, I_2, or N_2.

Some typical enthalpies of combustion are collected in Table 5-1. They are generally quite large, and since it is the difference among various enthalpies of combustion that usually is wanted (see next section), a very high degree of precision is desirable. This has indeed been achieved; most of the results in the table are accurate to a few tens of calories or better. Notice that compounds containing oxygen, such as ethanol and acetic acid, have lower enthalpies of combustion than the corresponding hydrocarbons. In a sense such compounds are already partly "burned."

The hydrogenation of unsaturated hydrocarbons is another reaction that has been used. One procedure is to pass a mixture of hydrogen and the hydrocarbon through an adiabatic calorimeter which contains some platinum catalyst. The rate of heating of the calorimeter is then determined for a known flow rate of the gases and, if necessary, the effluent gas is analyzed so that the degree of reaction may be found. As illustrated by the values in Table 5-1 enthalpies of hydrogenation are generally much smaller than those of combustion. It is now possible to obtain fairly accurate differences in enthalpies of hydrogenation of isomeric compounds.

Table 5-1. *Some Enthalpies of Reaction*[a]

Substance	Reaction	ΔH^0_{298}	
		kcal	kJ
Combustion[b]			
$H_2(g)$	$H_2 + \frac{1}{2}O_2 = H_2O$	−68.317	−285.84
C(graphite)	$C + O_2 = CO_2$	−94.052	−393.51
C(diamond)	$C + O_2 = CO_2$	−94.502	−395.40
$CO(g)$	$CO + \frac{1}{2}O_2 = CO_2$	−67.636	−282.99
$CH_4(g)$	$CH_4 + 2O_2 = CO_2 + 2H_2O$	−212.86	−890.36
$C_2H_2(g)$	$C_2H_2 + 2\frac{1}{2}O_2 = 2CO_2 + H_2O$	−310.62	−1299.63
$C_2H_4(g)$	$C_2H_4 + 3O_2 = 2CO_2 + 2H_2O$	−337.23	−1410.97
$C_2H_6(g)$	$C_2H_6 + 3\frac{1}{2}O_2 = 2CO_2 + 3H_2O$	−372.82	−1559.88
$C_3H_8(g)$	$C_3H_8 + 5O_2 = 3CO_2 + 4H_2O$	−530.61	−2220.07
$C_6H_6(g)$	$C_6H_6 + 7\frac{1}{2}O_2 = 6CO_2 + 3H_2O$	−789.08	−3301.51
$C_2H_5OH(l)$	$C_2H_5OH + 3O_2 = 2CO_2 + 3H_2O$	−326.71	−1366.95
$CH_3COOH(l)$	$CH_3COOH + 2O_2 = 2CO_2 + 2H_2O$	−208.5	−872.36
Hydrogenation			
$C_2H_4(g)$	$C_2H_4 + H_2 = C_2H_6(g)$	−32.747	−137.01
cis-$CH_3CH{=}CHCH_3(g)$	$C_4H_8 + H_2 = C_4H_{10}(g)$	−28.570[c]	−119.54
trans-$CH_3CH{=}CHCH_3(g)$	$C_4H_8 + H_2 = C_4H_{10}(g)$	−27.621[c]	−115.57
Solution			
$H_2SO_4(l)$	$H_2SO_4 + \infty H_2O = $ solution	−22.99	−96.19
$H_2SO_4(l)$	$H_2SO_4 + 50H_2O = $ solution	−17.53	−73.34
$HCl(g)$	$HCl + \infty H_2O = $ solution	−17.96	−75.14
$NaOH(s)$	$NaOH + \infty H_2O = $ solution	−10.246	−42.87
$NaCl(s)$	$NaCl + \infty H_2O = $ solution	0.930	3.89
$NaC_2H_3O_2(s)$	$NaC_2H_3O_2 + \infty H_2O = $ solution	−4.3	−18.0

[a] Values from F. A. Rossini *et al.*, eds. (1952). Tables of Selected Values of Chemical Thermodynamic Properties. Nat. Bur. Std. Circ. No. 500. U. S. Gov't. Printing Office, Washington, D. C.
[b] Combustion products are $CO_2(g)$ and $H_2O(l)$.
[c] For 355°K, from A. B. Kistiakowsky and co-workers, *J. Amer. Chem. Soc.* **57**, 65, 876 (1935).

The third type of experimental heat of reaction which is listed in the table is that of solution. These are known as *integral* enthalpies of solution (see Section 9-ST-1) and the reaction consists in mixing the pure substance with the indicated amount of water so that a solution is formed. Notice that a heat of solution may be large, as in the case of sulfuric acid, or small, as with sodium propionate. It may be positive, as with sodium chloride. Generally when heat is absorbed on dissolving, the value is small in magnitude. The heat of solution also depends on the final concentration obtained. As might be expected, the value (disregarding sign) tends to be larger for the limiting case in which an infinitely dilute solution is formed than for that involving some higher concentration. This last point is illustrated by the data for sulfuric acid and further in Table 5-3.

5-4 Combining ΔH or ΔE Quantities

Table 5-1 provides a very small sample of the many individual reactions and types of reactions that have been studied experimentally. A complete tabulation of such individual results would be both clumsy and difficult to use. The first step toward systematization, taken in Table 5-1, is to reduce all values to a standard pressure and temperature, the latter usually being 25°C (see the next section for the manner of doing this). The second and very important step is to report results as standard heats of formation (also discussed in the next section). The basis for doing this is that, according to the first law, E and H are state functions, so that ΔE and ΔH for a given overall process are independent of the path taken. The principle was formulated independently by Hess in about 1840 and is sometimes known as *Hess's law of constant heat summation*.

The principle may be illustrated as follows. Consider the following two reactions:

$$C_2H_6(g) + 1\tfrac{1}{2}O_2(g) = CH_3COOH(l) + H_2O(l), \quad \Delta H^0_{298} = -164.5 \quad \text{kcal}, \quad (5\text{-}11)$$

$$CH_3COOH(l) + 2O_2(g) = 2CO_2(g) + 2H_2O(l), \quad \Delta H^0_{298} = -208.3 \quad \text{kcal}. \quad (5\text{-}12)$$

These correspond to first oxidization of ethane to acetic acid and then burning of the acetic acid to carbon dioxide and water. The net result of the two steps is simply the combustion of ethane:

$$C_2H_6(g) + 3\tfrac{1}{2}O_2(g) = 2CO_2(g) + 3H_2O(l), \quad \Delta H^0_{298} = -372.8 \quad \text{kcal}. \quad (5\text{-}13)$$

It is a common procedure in chemistry to obtain the net result of a series of chemical steps by the algebraic summation of the corresponding equations. Thus Eq. (5-13) results from the addition of Eqs. (5-11) and (5-12) and the cancellation of $CH_3COOH(l)$ since it appears once on each side of the equality sign. This procedure is always possible with balanced chemical equations, and the result must also be a balanced equation. The further conclusion of importance here is that the ΔH^0_{298} quantities combine similarly. If we write each according to its detailed meaning as given by Eq. (5-3) we have

$$\Delta H^0_{298}[\text{Eq. (5-11)}] + \Delta H^0_{298}[\text{Eq. (5-12)}]$$

$$= \left[\underset{(l,\,25°C,\,1\,\text{atm})}{H_{CH_3COOH}} + \underset{(l,\,25°C,\,1\,\text{atm})}{H_{H_2O}} - \underset{(g,\,25°C,\,1\,\text{atm})}{H_{C_2H_6}} - \underset{(g,\,25°C,\,1\,\text{atm})}{1\tfrac{1}{2}H_{O_2}} \right]$$

$$+ \left[\underset{(g,\,25°C,\,1\,\text{atm})}{2H_{CO_2}} + \underset{(g,\,25°C,\,1\,\text{atm})}{2H_{H_2O}} - \underset{(l,\,25°C,\,1\,\text{atm})}{H_{CH_3COOH}} - \underset{(g,\,25°C,\,1\,\text{atm})}{2H_{O_2}} \right]$$

$$= \left[\underset{(g,\,25°C,\,1\,\text{atm})}{2H_{CO_2}} + \underset{(g,\,25°C,\,1\,\text{atm})}{3H_{H_2O}} - \underset{(g,\,25°C,\,1\,\text{atm})}{H_{C_2H_6}} + \underset{(g,\,25°C,\,1\,\text{atm})}{3\tfrac{1}{2}H_{O_2}} \right].$$

The quantities H_{CH_3COOH} cancel since each is for the same substance in the same state, and the result is just ΔH^0_{298} for the net equation (5-13). The sum of -164.5 kcal and -208.3 kcal is indeed -372.8 kcal.

The general conclusion is that ΔH (or ΔE) quantities add (or subtract) as do the corresponding equations provided that the substances that are cancelled are in the same state. This last requirement will necessarily be met if standard ΔH's are used.

The lack of dependence of ΔH and ΔE on path is useful in the following ways. It allows the calculation of a ΔH or ΔE for a process that is difficult or impossible to carry out directly or which simply has not yet been measured. As an example, one can determine experimentally the heats of combustion of graphite and of diamond:

$$C(graphite) + O_2(g) = CO_2(g), \quad \Delta H^0_{298} = -94.052 \quad kcal, \quad (5-14)$$

$$C(diamond) + O_2(g) = CO_2(g), \quad \Delta H^0_{298} = -94.502 \quad kcal. \quad (5-15)$$

We may subtract Eq. (5-15) from Eq. (5-14) to get

$$C(graphite) = C(diamond), \quad \Delta H^0_{298} = (-94,052) - (-94,502) = 450 \quad cal. \quad (5-16)$$

The conversion of graphite to diamond (or *vice versa*) is not a feasible laboratory reaction, but by combining the two enthalpies of combustion one obtains the desired ΔH^0_{298}.

Enthalpies of combustion may, in fact, be used quite generally to obtain enthalpies of other reactions. Thus the reaction

$$C_2H_4(g) + H_2(g) = C_2H_6(g) \quad (5-17)$$

may be written as

$$C_2H_4(g) + 3O_2(g) = 2CO_2(g) + 2H_2O(l), \quad \Delta H^0_{298} = -337.23 \quad kcal, \quad (5-18)$$

$$H_2(g) + \tfrac{1}{2}O_2(g) = H_2O(l), \quad \Delta H^0_{298} = -68.317 \quad kcal, \quad (5-19)$$

minus

$$C_2H_6(g) + 3\tfrac{1}{2}O_2(g) = 2CO_2(g) + 3H_2O(l), \quad \Delta H^0_{298} = -372.82 \quad kcal. \quad (5-20)$$

Then ΔH^0_{298} for Eq. (5-17) must be $(-337.23) + (-68.32) - (-373.82) = -32.73$ kcal. Notice that the result is not exactly the same as the directly determined value of -32.747 kcal. As mentioned earlier, the problem is that in using enthalpies of combustion we are combining very large numbers to give a small net result. Even small percentage errors in the former propagate to give a large percentage error in the result.

The example may be generalized. We may obtain ΔH^0_{298} for any reaction by adding the standard enthalpies of combustion of the reactants and subtracting the sum of those of the products:

$$\Delta H^0_{298} = \sum_{\text{reactants}} n_r \, \Delta H^0_{c,298} - \sum_{\text{products}} n_p \, \Delta H^0_{c,298}, \quad (5-21)$$

where $\Delta H_{c,298}^0$ denotes a standard enthalpy of combustion. As an illustration, ΔH_{298}^0 for the (unlikely) reaction

$$2CH_4(g) + CH_3COOH(l) = C_3H_8(g) + CO_2(g) + 2H_2(g)$$

is given by

$$2\,\Delta H_{c,298}^0\,(CH_4) + \Delta H_{c,298}^0\,(CH_3COOH) - \Delta H_{c,298}^0\,(C_3H_8) - 2\,\Delta H_{c,298}^0\,(H_2).$$

There is no term for CO_2 since by definition its enthalpy of combustion is zero. A table of standard enthalpies of combustion thus implies a knowledge of ΔH_{298}^0 values for all reactions that can be formulated as a combination of combustion reactions.

5-5 Enthalpies of Formation

A. Standard Enthalpy of Formation for Compounds

A particularly useful way of summarizing thermochemical data is in terms of the standard enthalpy of formation. The reaction is that of formation of the compound from the elements, each element being in its stable chemical state and phase at 25°C and 1 atm pressure. For example, the reaction giving the standard enthalpy of formation of $H_2O(l)$, $\Delta H_{f,298}^0$ (H_2O, l), is

$$H_2(g, 298°K, 1\ atm) + \tfrac{1}{2}O_2(g, 298°K, 1\ atm) = H_2O(l, 298°K, 1\ atm).$$

(This particular enthalpy change is also that of the combustion of hydrogen.) That for methane is

$$C(graphite, 298°K, 1\ atm) + 2H_2(g, 298°K, 1\ atm) = CH_4(g, 298°K, 1\ atm),\quad (5\text{-}22)$$

and so on.

It is not always possible to determine a heat of formation directly, as in the case of water, and the values are usually calculated by the indirect precedure. Thus $\Delta H_{f,298}^0(CH_4)$ could be obtained by application of Eq. (5-21) to the heats of combustion of graphite, hydrogen, and methane. Extensive tables of standard enthalpies of formation have been built up, and a sampling is given in Table 5-2. The table includes values for unstable forms of some elements, such as O_3, and C (diamond) and in some cases also gives values for both gaseous and liquid states, as for water. The difference between two such values is simply the enthalpy of vaporization.

One may calculate the standard enthalpy change for any chemical reaction involving substances whose standard enthalpies of formation are known. The

Table 5-2. *Standard Enthalpies of Formation*[a]

Substance	$\Delta H^0_{f,298}$		Substance	$\Delta H^0_{f,298}$	
	kcal mole^{-1}	kJ mole^{-1}		kcal mole^{-1}	kJ mole^{-1}
$AgCl(s)$	−30.36	−127.03	$H_2O(l)$	−68.317	−285.84
$Br_2(g)$	7.34	30.71	$H_2O(g)$	−57.789	−241.79
C(graphite)	(0.000)	(0.000)	$HCl(g)$	−22.063	−92.31
C(diamond)	0.4532	1.896	$HBr(g)$	−8.66	−36.23
$CaCO_3(s)$	−228.45	−1206.87	$HI(g)$	6.20	25.94
$CaO(s)$	−151.9	−635.5	$KCl(s)$	−104.175	−435.87
$CO(g)$	−26.416	−110.52	$NaCl(s)$	−98.232	−411.03
$CO_2(g)$	−94.052	−393.51	$NH_3(g)$	−11.04	−46.19
$CH_4(g)$	−17.89	−74.85	$NO(g)$	21.600	90.37
$C_2H_2(g)$	54.19	226.73	$NO_2(g)$	8.091	33.85
$C_2H_4(g)$	12.50	52.30	$N_2O_4(g)$	2.58	10.8
$C_2H_6(g)$	−20.24	−84.68	$O_3(g)$	34.0	142.3
$C_3H_8(g)$	−24.82	−103.85	$P(g)$	75.18	314.6
$C_6H_6(l)$	11.718	49.028	$PCl_3(g)$	−73.22	−306.4
$C_6H_6(g)$	19.820	82.93	$PCl_5(g)$	−95.35	−398.94
$C_2H_5OH(l)$	−66.356	−277.63	S(rhombic)	(0.000)	(0.000)
$CH_3COOH(l)$	−116.4	−487.0	S(monoclinic)	0.071	0.30
$CCl_4(l)$	−33.3	−139.3	$SO_2(g)$	−70.96	−296.9
$Fe_2O_3(s)$	−196.5	−822.2	$SO_3(g)$	−94.45	−395.2
Glycine					
$H_2NCH_2COOH(s)$	−126.33	−528.56			

[a] Data from F. A. Rossini *et al.*, eds. (1952). Tables of Selected Values of Chemical Thermodynamic Quantities. Nat. Bur. Std. Circ. No. 500. U.S. Gov't. Printing Office, Washington, D.C.

combining rule is similar to Eq. (5-21) for heats of combustion, but reversed in sign (why?):

$$\Delta H^0_{298} = \sum_{\text{products}} n_{\text{p}}\, \Delta H^0_{f,298} - \sum_{\text{reactants}} n_{\text{r}}\, \Delta H^0_{f,298}. \qquad (5\text{-}23)$$

As an example, we may calculate the heat of hydrogenation of ethylene [Eq. (5-17)] using heats of formation:

$$\Delta H^0_{298} = \Delta H^0_{f,298}\,(C_2H_6\,,\,g) - \Delta H^0_{f,298}\,(C_2H_4\,,\,g)$$
$$= -20.24 - 12.50 = -32.74 \quad \text{kcal mole}^{-1}.$$

There is no term for hydrogen because its heat of formation is zero by convention.

B. Standard Enthalpies of Aqueous Solutes and of Ions

Some values of enthalpies of solution were included in Table 5-1. Such data may be incorporated into the standard enthalpy of formation scheme by assigning the entire heat of solution to the solute. For example, the heat of dissolving of HCl (*g*) in water to give an infinitely dilute solution is, per mole of HCl, -17.96 kcal (Table 5-1). We use the notation aq to denote the condition of infinite dilution, and may now write

$$\tfrac{1}{2}H_2(g) + \tfrac{1}{2}Cl_2(g) = HCl(g), \quad \Delta H^0_{f,298} = -22.06 \quad \text{kcal},$$

$$HCl(g) + aq = HCl(aq), \quad \Delta H^0_{298} = -17.96 \quad \text{kcal}.$$

Then we have

$$\tfrac{1}{2}H_2(g) + \tfrac{1}{2}Cl_2(g) + aq = HCl(aq), \quad \Delta H^0_{f,298} (HCl, aq) = -40.02 \quad \text{kcal}.$$

The same convention may be applied to solutions of any concentration. Thus the standard enthalpy for the following reaction is -17.65 kcal:

$$HCl(g) + 100H_2O = \begin{cases} \text{solution of concentration} \\ m = 0.55 \text{ mole per 1000 g } H_2O \end{cases}, \quad \Delta H^0_{298} = -17.65 \quad \text{kcal}.$$

The standard enthalpy of formation of HCl in 0.55 molal solution is then $(-17.65) + (-22.06) = -39.71$ kcal mole^{-1}.

In the case of infinitely dilute solutions of electrolytes it is convenient to proceed a step further. For such solutions the ions have no mutual interaction and the state of any given ion is entirely independent of the nature of its counter ion. It is therefore possible to combine equations as in the following example:

(a) $\quad \tfrac{1}{2}H_2(g) + \tfrac{1}{2}Cl_2(g) = H^+(aq) + Cl^-(aq), \qquad \Delta H^0_{298} = -40.02 \quad \text{kcal},$

(b) $\quad Na(s) + \tfrac{1}{2}Cl_2(g) = Na^+(aq) + Cl^-(aq), \qquad \Delta H^0_{298} = -97.30 \quad \text{kcal},$

(c) $\quad Na(s) + \tfrac{1}{2}Br_2(l) = Na^+(aq) + Br^-(aq), \qquad \Delta H^0_{298} = -86.18 \quad \text{kcal},$

(d) $= (a) + (c) - (b)$:

$\quad \tfrac{1}{2}H_2(g) + \tfrac{1}{2}Br_2(l) = H^+(aq) + Br^-(aq), \qquad \Delta H^0_{298} = -28.90 \quad \text{kcal}.$

HCl(aq) has been written as $H^+(aq) + Cl^-(aq)$, and similarly for NaCl(aq) and NaBr(aq) not only because it is more nearly correct but also because it emphasizes that the $Cl^-(aq)$ of the HCl solution cancels the $Cl^-(aq)$ of the NaCl solution.

This procedure is unnecessarily clumsy. If the enthalpy of formation of some one ion were known, it would then be possible to calculate those of all other ions. Such a value is not known, since ionic chemical reactions always involve combinations of ions such that the equation is balanced electrically (see Section 13-CN-3 for a further comment). By the same token, however, one may arbitrarily assign a value to the standard enthalpy of formation of some one ion, and the values then calculated for the other ions must always occur in any thermochemical equation in such a way that the assumption cancels out. The convention is that $\Delta H^0_{f,298}(H^+, aq)$ is zero.

Some representative standard enthalpies of formation of solutes and of individual aqueous ions are given in Table 5-3. We may now obtain the values of ΔH^0_{298} for reactions (a), (b), (c), and (d) simply by adding the appropriate individual ion values.

Table 5-3. *Standard Enthalpies of Formation of Aqueous Species[a]*

Solute	$\Delta H^0_{f,298}$ kcal mole^{-1}	kJ mole^{-1}	Ion	$\Delta H^0_{f,298}$ kcal mole^{-1}	kJ mole^{-1}
HCl			H^+	(0.000)	(0.000)
in ∞H_2O	−40.023	−168.32	Li^+	−66.554	−278.46
in $100 H_2O$	−39.713	−166.16	Na^+	−57.279	−329.66
H_2SO_4			K^+	−60.04	−251.21
in ∞H_2O	−216.90	−907.51	Ag^+	−25.31	−105.90
in $100 H_2O$	−211.59	−885.29	OH^-	−54.957	−229.94
NaOH			F^-	−78.66	−329.11
in ∞H_2O	−112.236	−469.60	Cl^-	−40.023	−167.46
in $100 H_2O$	−112.108	−469.06	Br^-	−28.90	−120.92
NaCl			I^-	−13.37	−55.94
in ∞H_2O	−97.302	−407.11	ClO_4^-	−31.41	−131.42
in $100 H_2O$	−97.250	−406.89	SO_4^{2-}	−216.90	−907.51
NH$_4$Cl			CO_3^{2-}	−161.63	−676.26
in ∞H_2O	−71.76	−300.24			
in $100 H_2O$	−71.63	−299.70			

[a] Data from F. A. Rossini *et al.*, eds. (1952). Tables of Selected Values of Chemical Thermodynamic Quantities. Nat. Bur. Std. Circ. No. 500. U. S. Gov't. Printing Office, Washington, D.C.

5-6 Dependence of ΔH and ΔE on Temperature

The temperature dependence of individual H and E values is given by the equations

$$dE = C_V \, dT \qquad \text{[Eq. (4-22)]},$$
$$dH = C_P \, dT \qquad \text{[Eq. (4-30)]},$$

or, in integral form,

$$E_2 = E_1 + \int_{T_1}^{T_2} C_V \, dT, \tag{5-24}$$

$$H_2 = H_1 + \int_{T_1}^{T_2} C_P \, dT. \tag{5-25}$$

As discussed in Section 4-7C, heat capacities are in general temperature-dependent and the experimental values are usually summarized in the form of a power series in temperature. Three terms suffice to represent data over a considerable range of temperature. Thus we write[†]

$$C_P = a + bT + cT^{-2}. \tag{5-26}$$

[†] A widely used alternative power series is of the form $C_P = a + bT + cT^2$.

The power series formulation is convenient in allowing easy integration of Eq. (5-25). Values of a, b, and c are given in Table 5-4 for a number of gases, liquids, and solids.

The procedure for calculating the change in a heat of reaction with temperature is quite analogous to the preceding. Let ΔH_2 be the enthalpy of reaction at T_2 and ΔH_1 that at T_1. The general reaction equation (5-2) may then be written

$$\Delta H_2 = [aH_2(A) + bH_2(B) + \cdots] - [mH_2(M) + nH_2(N) + \cdots]$$

$$= \left\{ a\left[H_1(A) + \int C_P(A)\,dT\right] + b\left[H_1(B) + \int C_P(B)\,dT\right] + \cdots \right\}$$

$$- \left\{ m\left[H_1(M) + \int C_P(M)\,dT\right] + n\left[H_1(N) + \int C_P(N)\,dT\right] + \cdots \right\}.$$

On collecting terms, we obtain

$$\Delta H_2 = \Delta H_1 + \int_{T_1}^{T_2} \Delta C_P\,dT, \tag{5-27}$$

where the operator Δ in ΔC_P has its usual meaning. The coefficients a, b, and c in the series expression for each individual heat capacity may be combined according to Eq. (5-27) so that ΔC_P may be written

$$\Delta C_P = \Delta a + (\Delta b)T + (\Delta c)T^{-2}. \tag{5-28}$$

A formal integration of Eq. (5-27) gives

$$\Delta H_2 = \Delta H_1 + (\Delta a)(T_2 - T_1) + \left(\frac{\Delta b}{2}\right)(T_2{}^2 - T_1{}^2) - (\Delta c)\left(\frac{1}{T_2} - \frac{1}{T_1}\right).$$

$$\tag{5-29}$$

The procedure is most commonly applied to ΔH^0 values, that is, to ΔH quantities for 1 atm pressure, and the C_P values of Table 5-4 are for this standard pressure. Analogous equations involving C_V apply to the calculation of a ΔE_2 from a ΔE_1.

Equations (5-24) and (5-25) are applicable to a change of temperature which is not accompanied by any phase change. As illustrated in Fig. 5-2, a substance may exist in some phase α below a certain temperature and in some phase β above that temperature. The most common situations are those in which α is a solid phase and β the liquid phase, or in which α is the liquid phase and β the gaseous one. If we take H_1 and T_1 as the reference points, then Eq. (5-25) is obeyed up to the temperature of the phase transition $T_{\alpha\beta}$. At this temperature additional heat is needed to bring about the transition and H increases by the enthalpy of the transition $\Delta H_{\alpha\beta}$. Above $T_{\alpha\beta}$, ΔH again rises in accord with Eq. (5-25), although now the heat capacity is $C_P(\beta)$ rather than $C_P(\alpha)$. An entirely analogous analysis applies to the behavior of E.

Table 5-4. *Variation of C_P^0 with Temperature[a] $C_P^0 = a + bT + cT^{-2}$*

Substance	a	$10^3 b$	$10^{-5} c$
Gases (from 298 to 2000°K)			
Monatomic	4.97	—	—
gases	(20.78)		
H_2	6.52	0.78	0.12
	(27.28)	(3.26)	(0.50)
O_2	7.16	1.00	−0.40
	(29.96)	(4.18)	(−1.67)
N_2	6.83	0.90	−0.12
	(28.58)	(3.77)	(−0.50)
CO	6.79	0.98	−0.11
	(28.41)	(4.10)	(−0.46)
Cl_2	8.85	0.16	−0.68
	(37.03)	(0.67)	(−2.85)
CO_2	10.57	2.10	−2.06
	(44.23)	(8.79)	(−8.62)
H_2O	7.30	2.46	—
	(30.54)	(10.29)	
NH_3	7.11	6.00	−0.37
	(29.75)	(25.10)	(−1.55)
CH_4	5.65	11.44	−0.46
	(23.64)	(47.86)	(−1.92)
Liquids (from melting point to boiling point)			
H_2O	18.04	—	—
	(75.48)		
I_2	19.20	—	—
	(80.33)		
NaCl	16.0	—	—
	(66.9)		
Solids (from 298°K to melting point or 2000°K)			
C(graphite)	4.03	1.14	−2.04
	(16.86)	(4.77)	(−8.54)
Al	4.94	2.96	—
	(20.67)	(12.38)	
Cu	5.41	1.50	—
	(22.64)	(6.28)	
Pb	5.29	2.80	0.23
	(22.13)	(11.72)	(0.96)
I_2	9.59	11.90	—
	(40.12)	(49.79)	
NaCl	10.98	3.90	—
	(45.94)	(16.32)	

[a] G. N. Lewis and M. Randall, "Thermodynamics," 2nd ed., (revised by K. S. Pitzer and L. Brewer). McGraw-Hill, New York, 1961. Values in cal °K⁻¹ mole⁻¹; values in parentheses in J °K⁻¹ mole⁻¹.

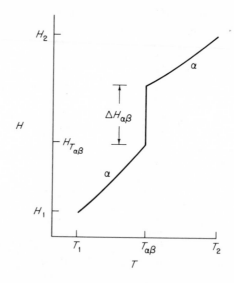

Fig. 5-2. *Variation of enthalpy with temperature for a substance undergoing a phase change.*

The presence of phase transitions introduces a corresponding complication in the calculation of a ΔH_2 from a ΔH_1. In such a case Eq. (5-27) may still be used but with a $\Delta' C_P$ which is computed only for those reactants and products not involved in phase changes. We then have

$$\Delta H_2 = \Delta H_1 + \int_{T_1}^{T_2} \Delta' C_P \, dT + \sum_{\text{products}} n_{\text{p}}(H_2 - H_1) - \sum_{\text{reactants}} n_{\text{r}}(H_2 - H_1),$$

$$(5\text{-}30)$$

where the last two terms represent the separately calculated changes in enthalpy for those reactants and products that undergo phase changes.

Equation (5-30) is best clarified by means of a specific example. We have the enthalpy of combustion of benzene (liquid) to give water (liquid) at 25°C and want to calculate the heat of combustion of benzene (gaseous) to give water (gaseous) at 90°C. To simplify matters we will use the approximate heat capacities in Table 5-5, assumed to be independent of temperature. Also, the

Table 5-5. *Approximate Heat Capacities*

	C_P^0 (J mole^{-1})
Benzene(l)	130
Benzene(g)	100
$O_2(g)$	30
$CO_2(g)$	47
Water (l)	75
Water (g)	34

enthalpies of vaporization are 34,000 and 44,000 J mole^{-1} for benzene and for water, respectively, at their normal boiling points of 80 and 100°C. The standard enthalpy of combustion of benzene (liquid) is -3268 kJ mole^{-1} at 25°C.

We may organize the calculation by means of the following scheme:

$$
\begin{array}{ccc}
C_6H_6(g,\,90°C) + 7\tfrac{1}{2}O_2\,(g,90°C) & \xRightarrow{\Delta H^0_{90°C}} & 6\,CO_2(g,\,90°C) + 3H_2O(g,\,90°C) \\
\uparrow q_3 & & \uparrow q_6 \\
C_6H_6(g,\,80°C) & \int \Delta' C_P\,dT & 3H_2O(g,\,100°C) \\
\uparrow q_2 & & \uparrow q_5 \\
C_6H_6(l,\,80°C) & & 3H_2O(l,\,100°C) \\
\uparrow q_1 & & \uparrow q_4 \\
C_6H_6(l,\,25°C) + 7\tfrac{1}{2}O_2(g,\,25°C) & \xRightarrow{\Delta H^0_{25°C}} & 6CO_2(g,\,25°C) + 3H_2O(l,\,25°C)
\end{array}
\tag{5-31}
$$

The $\Delta' C_P$ term is $(6)(47) - (7\tfrac{1}{2})(30) = 57$ J and $\int_{25°C}^{90°C} \Delta' C_P\, dT$ is then $(57)(65) = 3700$ J. We next calculate ΔH^0 for taking liquid benzene at 25°C to gaseous benzene at 90°C. This is given by $q_1 + q_2 + q_3$. These are: $q_1 = (130)(55) = 7150$ J; $q_2 = 34,000$ J; and $q_3 = (100)(10) = 1000$ J; their sum is 42,150 J. Similarly, ΔH^0 for taking liquid water at 25°C to gaseous water at 90°C is given by $q_4 + q_5 + q_6$. Note that we must vaporize the water at 100°C since it is for this temperature that the enthalpy of vaporization is given. We have: $q_4 = (3)(75)(75) = 16,870$ J; $q_5 = (3)(44,000) = 132,000$ J; and $q_6 = (3)(34)(-10) = -1020$ J; the sum is 149,900 J.

We can now assemble the various contributions:

$$
\begin{aligned}
\Delta H^0_{90°C} &= -3268 \quad kJ + (3700 + 149,900 - 42,150) \quad J = -3268 \quad kJ + 111.5 \quad kJ \\
&= -3156 \quad kJ.
\end{aligned}
$$

The calculation has been made in joules in recognition of the common use of this energy unit in thermochemistry.

COMMENTARY AND NOTES

5-CN-1 Explosions, Flames, and Rockets

The emphasis of this chapter has so far been on ΔE and ΔH quantities for reactions under standard conditions, and, in the preceding section, on the calculation of ΔE or ΔH at some temperature T_2 given the value at T_1. There is an interesting and important special case in which the chemical reaction occurs under essentially adiabatic conditions so that the heat of the reaction is confined to the system and therefore heats it as the reaction proceeds. This situation occurs in an explosion which takes place in an isolated system such as is approximated by an open flame and in the combustion of rocket fuel.

The confined explosion is the simplest case for us to treat more quantitatively.

We can do so in terms of a generalized combustion reaction of a hydrocarbon using a scheme similar to that of the example of the preceding section:

$$C_nH_{2n+2}(g, T_{max}) + \frac{3n+1}{2}O_2(g, T_{max}) \overset{\Delta E_{T_{max}}}{=} nCO_2(g, T_{max}) + (n+1)H_2O(g, T_{max})$$

$$q_1 \qquad\qquad \Delta E = q_v = 0 \qquad\qquad q_2 \qquad\qquad (5\text{-}32)$$

$$C_nH_{2n+2}(g, 298°K) + \frac{3n+1}{2}O_2(g, 298°K) \overset{\Delta E_{298}}{=} nCO_2(g, 298°K) + (n+1)H_2O(g, 298°K)$$

To simplify matters, we avoid phase changes by specifying all species to be gaseous. Also, since the system is to be at constant volume, we must deal with E's and C_V's. We are interested in the value of T_{max}, the maximum temperature attained under adiabatic conditions. This means that the overall process is the one indicated by the arrow labeled $\Delta E = q_V = 0$. The desired T_{max} may be calculated as follows. We allow the reaction to proceed at 298°K and apply the heat of reaction to warming the products, which means the q_2 must just equal ΔE_{298}:

$$0 = \Delta E_{298} + \int_{298°K}^{T_{max}} [nC_V(CO_2) + (n+1)C_V(H_2O)]\, dT$$

or, in general,

$$0 = \Delta E_{T_1} + \int_{T_1}^{T_{max}} \sum_{products} n_p C_V\, dT. \qquad (5\text{-}33)$$

The heat capacities should be known as a function of temperature, and on carrying out the integration, one obtains an equation which is then to be solved for T_{max}.

The maximum temperature calculated for situations such as this may be quite high. Using the example of the preceding section, the enthalpy of combustion of gaseous benzene was found to be -3156 kJ at 90°C. Since $\Delta n_g = \frac{1}{2}$, we find by means of Eq. (5-10) that $\Delta E_{90°C} = -3156$ kJ $- \frac{1}{2}(8.31)(363)$ J $= -3158$ kJ. The total heat capacity $\sum C_V$ of the products is $(6)(39) + (3)(26) = 312$ J °K^{-1}. If these are assumed not to change with temperature, it follows that

$$3.158 \times 10^6 \quad J = (312\ J\ °K^{-1})(T_{max} - 363)$$

or

$$T_{max} = 11,000°C\ (!).$$

The actual maximum temperature of such a combustion will be much less than that calculated, for several reasons. First, the heat capacities of the water and carbon dioxide will increase with temperature, and the average values will be considerably greater than the ones used in the problem. A more accurate result in this respect would be obtained if we used the heat capacity expressions of Table 5-4 in carrying out the integration called for in Eq. (5-33). The result would be a cubic equation in T, the solution of which would give T_{max}. The result would still not be accurate, since the heat capacity expressions are not valid above 2000°K, and also would not be correct for the high pressures developed. Likewise, because of gas nonidealities, the difference between C_P and C_V will not be exactly R.

Second, from a practical point of view, some excess oxygen should be present. The excess then remains and the summation of Eq. (5-33) should include the heat capacity of this excess. Were air used rather than pure oxygen, the added heat capacity of the nitrogen would be included as well. For example, were air used in sufficient amount to provide a 100 % excess of oxygen, after combustion, 60 moles of nitrogen and 7.5 moles of oxygen would remain, and on repeating the calculation, we would obtain a T_{max} of only about 1850°C.

More fundamental hazards to calculations of this type are the following. Since ΔE is negative, we expect from Le Châtelier's principle that the equilibrium will shift progressively to the left with increasing temperature. This means that combustion reactions which go to completion at 25°C may fail to do so at some very high temperature. An even more serious difficulty is that other equilibria begin to be important at very high temperatures. Water may be partly dissociated into H, HO, and O radicals; carbon dioxide begins to dissociate into CO and O_2 and further into C and O. Gases inert at room temperature, such as nitrogen, begin to enter into the reaction, and so on. All of these effects act either to reduce the amount of reaction or to expend some of the heat of the reaction in dissociating the products into fragments. The result is to reduce T_{max} below its simple theoretical value, and often considerably so.

The problem becomes a very acute one in the field of aerospace engineering. A rocket exhaust is essentially a flame which has reached some high temperature by virtue of the heat of reaction of the propellants, and it is essential to know both the actual T_{max} and the chemical composition of the exhaust if the thrust of the rocket is to be computed. The various dissociative equilibria mentioned here themselves depend on temperature, and the temperature reached depends on the extent of such dissociation. The consequence is that one must make a very involved series of successive approximations in order to arrive at a result.

SPECIAL TOPICS

5-ST-1   Chemical Bond Strengths

One of the important contributions of thermochemistry to physical chemistry and chemical physics is that it provides chemical bond energies. The definition of bond energy is simple in the case of a diatomic molecule; it is just the dissociation energy. Thus

$$H_2(g) = 2H(g), \qquad \Delta H^0_{298} = 104.2 \quad \text{kcal}, \qquad (5\text{-}34)$$

$$HI(g) = H(g) + I(g), \qquad \Delta H^0_{298} = 71.4 \quad \text{kcal}. \qquad (5\text{-}35)$$

The H—H and H—I bond energies are then 104.2 and 71.4 kcal, respectively.

It would seem reasonable to use ΔE values for bond energies in order that the meaning be precisely the same as in the quantum mechanical picture of Fig. 4-11. There the dissociation energy was defined as the potential energy difference between the lowest vibrational state and the beginning of the continuum. In fact, many bond energies for diatomic molecules come from spectroscopic rather than from calorimetric or other thermodynamic measurements. The spectroscopic value actually gives ΔE_0, the value at $0°K$, or for the dissociating molecule devoid of rotational and vibrational excitation. There is undoubtedly some confusion in that spectroscopic ΔE_0 values and thermochemical ΔH^0_{298} values have been used somewhat interchangeably. The two values are not greatly different, however. For example, ΔE_0 for the atomization of hydrogen is 103.2 kcal, as compared to the ΔH^0_{298} of 104.2 kcal. The practice here will be use the standard enthalpies.

Bond energies may also be obtained for polyatomic molecules. The enthalpy of atomization of methane is taken to be four times the average C—H bond energy:

$$CH_4(g) = C(g) + 4H(g), \qquad \Delta H^0_{298} = 397.2 \quad \text{kcal}. \qquad (5\text{-}36)$$

The average C—H bond energy is then 99.5 kcal. The ΔH^0_{298} value is obtained by summing the following steps:

$$
\begin{array}{lll}
CH_4(g) = C(\text{graphite}) + 2H_2(g), & \Delta H^0_{298} = & 17.9 \quad \text{kcal}, \\
2H_2(g) = 4H(g), & \Delta H^0_{298} = & 208.4 \quad \text{kcal}, \\
C(\text{graphite}) = C(g), & \Delta H^0_{298} = & 170.9 \quad \text{kcal}, \\
\hline
CH_4(g) = C(g) + 4H(g), & \Delta H^0_{298} = & 397.2 \quad \text{kcal}.
\end{array}
\qquad (5\text{-}37)
$$

Among these values the heat of sublimation of graphite has been the most uncertain because of the great experimental difficulties involved; as a result, several values appear in the chemical literature. For this reason, different references may report somewhat different C—H bond energies. It should also be stressed that the value given here is the *average* C—H bond energy. The process of dissociating one hydrogen atom at a time to give CH_3, CH_2, CH, and then C will require somewhat different energies for each step; that for the first step is estimated to be 102 kcal, for example. The H—O bond energy may be obtained from the sum of reactions

$$
\begin{array}{lll}
H_2O(g) = H_2(g) + \tfrac{1}{2}O_2(g), & \Delta H^0_{298} = & 57.8 \quad \text{kcal,} \\
H_2(g) = 2H(g), & \Delta H^0_{298} = & 104.2 \quad \text{kcal,} \\
\tfrac{1}{2}O_2(g) = O(g), & \Delta H^0_{298} = & 59.2 \quad \text{kcal,} \\
\hline
H_2O(g) = 2H(g) + O(g), & \Delta H^0_{298} = & 221.2 \quad \text{kcal.}
\end{array}
\tag{5-38}
$$

There are two H—O bonds in water, and so the average H—O bond energy is 111 kcal. The N—H bond energy follows from an analogous calculation involving ammonia.

We next assume that bond energies are additive, that is, that the strength of a given type of bond is independent of its chemical environment. For example, the enthalpy of dissociation of ethane into atoms can be calculated from its enthalpy of formation and the enthalpies of sublimation of graphite and of dissociation of hydrogen. We get

$$
C_2H_6(g) = 2C(g) + 6H(g), \quad \Delta H^0_{298} = 674.6 \quad \text{kcal.}
$$

Ethane consists of six C—H bonds and one C—C bond, and the assumption is that the sum of these bond dissociation energies should equal the overall enthalpy of atomization. The C—H bond is taken to be the same as the average value in methane, so that the C—C bond energy should be $674.6 - 597 = 77.6$ kcal. Repetition of the same type of calculation for propane leads to a C—C bond energy of 78 kcal, so the assumption is at least approximately correct. Application of the above procedure to methanol yields a C—O bond energy, and so on.

A number of such bond strengths are given in Table 5-6 along with some useful heats of sublimation of elements. Note that the value given there for the C—C bond energy, 83 kcal, is higher than the one just calculated; the figure of 83 kcal is offered as a better average value for general use.

In some cases the discrepancy between an observed enthalpy and that calculated from bond energies appears to be real—that is, due to a specific, neglected factor. For example, one obtains from the enthalpies of formation of benzene and of atomization of graphite and hydrogen

$$
C_6H_6(g) = 6C(g) + 6H(g), \quad \Delta H^0_{298} = 1318 \quad \text{kcal.}
\tag{5-39}
$$

Table 5-6. *Bond Strengths and Enthalpies of Formation of Atoms[a]*

Atom	$\Delta H^0_{f,298}$		Bond	ΔH^0_{298}	
	kcal mole⁻¹	kJ mole⁻¹		kcal mole⁻¹	kJ mole⁻¹
H	52.1	218.0	C—H	99.5	416.3
O	59.2	247.7	C—C	83	347
N	112.9	472.4	C=C	146	611
S	53.2	223.8	C≡C	198	828
P	75.2	314.6	C—N	72	301
C	170.9	715.0	C=N	147	615
F	18.3	76.6	C—O	85	356
Cl	29.0	121.3	C=O	175	732
Br	26.7	111.7	C—Cl	78	326
I	25.5	106.7	O—H	111	464
Na	26.0	108.8	O—O	33	138
K	21.5	90.0	N—H	93	389
Ca	46.0	192.4	N—N	39	163
Al	75.0	313.8	N=N	100	418
Ni	102	426.8	—	—	—
Fe	96.7	404.6	—	—	—
Ag	69.1	289.1	—	—	—

[a] The values are adapted from various sources. See NBS Circular 500 (Table 5-3); K. S. Pitzer, "Quantum Chemistry," Prentice-Hall, Englewood Cliffs, N.J., 1953; T. L. Cottrell, "The Strength of Chemical Bonds," Butterworth, London and Washington, D.C., 1958.

Benzene, if written in the Kekulé structure

would be assigned six C—H bonds, three C—C bonds, and three C=C bonds, which total 1284 kcal. The discrepancy of 34 kcal suggests that benzene is more stable than expected in terms of this structure. The modern explanation is that there are no fixed C=C bonds and that the electrons which might go into such bonds interact instead in a diffuse or delocalized way and are spread over the whole molecule. This difference between the estimated energy of a fixed bond structure and the actual energy of a delocalized bonding structure is called the *resonance energy*.

Although the assumption of additivity of bond strengths can lead to appreciable error, it does provide a means of estimating enthalpies of formation of compounds not yet studied or difficult to study. In the case of flames, for example, one may need an estimate of the enthalpies of formation of various radicals. A similar situation occurs in chemical kinetics, where it is desirable to estimate the energy required to produce possible reaction intermediates [see Benson (1965)].

5-ST-2   Internal Energy and Enthalpy Functions

The fact that we do not know absolute values for internal energies and enthalpies is reflected in our procedures in thermochemistry. Thus we tabulate standard enthalpies of formation of substances and not their absolute enthalpies. That is, we take the elements in their standard state as a point of reference. Since we are interested in ΔH or ΔE for a chemical reaction, only the differences between enthalpies or energies of formation are involved, and the choice of reference state cancels out. Were the absolute H and E values known for the elements, we could then convert all of the standard heats of formation to absolute values. However, such a set of values would lead to exactly the same ΔH or ΔE for a chemical process as before. (The proof of this statement is left as an exercise.)

The choice of reference state is therefore mainly a matter of convenience. Although the usual choice is well suited for the compilation of thermochemical data, there is an alternative, a more natural one from the point of view of statistical thermodynamics. This alternative may be introduced as follows. By Eq. (4-22),

$$\left(\frac{\partial \mathrm{E}}{\partial T}\right)_V = \mathrm{c}_V,$$

where, it will be recalled, E is the average energy per molecule. Integration then gives

$$\mathrm{E} = \mathrm{E}_0 + \int_0^T \mathrm{c}_V \, dT. \tag{5-40}$$

The energy E_0 is the energy per molecule at $0°K$ and hence the energy in the lowest translational, rotational, vibrational, and electronic energy state. The first two we regard as zero, the third is the zero-point energy, $\frac{1}{2}h\nu_0$, and the fourth is unknown. In fact, $\mathrm{E}_{0,\mathrm{elec}}$ is essentially unknowable, since our experience, as embodied in the first law, is that we can only determine changes in energy and not absolute values. If we now define a quantity $\mathrm{E} - \mathrm{E_0}$, the internal energy function, we have

$$\mathrm{E} - \mathrm{E_0} = \int_0^T \mathrm{c}_V \, dT \tag{5-41}$$

and the quantity on the right is in principle experimentally determinable. It is, for example, actually $\mathrm{E} - \mathrm{E_0}$ that is given by Eq. (4-56),

$$\mathrm{E} - \mathrm{E_0} = kT^2 \left[\frac{\partial(\ln \mathbf{Q})}{\partial T} \right]_V, \tag{5-42}$$

or, per mole,

$$E - E_0 = RT^2 \left[\frac{\partial(\ln \mathbf{Q})}{\partial T} \right]_V. \tag{5-43}$$

The statistical thermodynamic treatment in Chapter 4 showed that it is usually possible to factor a partition function into the separate translational, rotational, and vibrational contributions. Thus

$$E - E_0 = E_{\text{trans}} + E_{\text{rot}} + E_{\text{vib}}. \tag{5-44}$$

Also, from the definition of H,

$$H - E_0 = (E - E_0) + PV \tag{5-45}$$

and

$$H^0 - E_0 = (E - E_0) + PV, \tag{5-46}$$

where the zero superscript denotes that H is for the standard pressure of 1 atm; $H^0 - E_0$ is the standard enthalpy function.[†] For an ideal gas,

$$H^0 - E_0 = (E - E_0) + RT \quad \text{(ideal gas)}. \tag{5-47}$$

The standard enthalpy function may be related to experiment as follows. For the general reaction

$$a\mathrm{A} + b\mathrm{B} + \cdots = m\mathrm{M} + n\mathrm{N} + \cdots,$$

we can write ΔH^0 for some temperature T as

$$\Delta H_T{}^0 = \Delta(H^0 - E_0)_T + \Delta E_0. \tag{5-48}$$

[†] More often, this term is applied to $(H^0 - H_0{}^0)/T$ as discussed in Section 6-ST-3.

If we know $\Delta(H^0 - E_0)_T$, ΔE_0 can be calculated from the experimental heat of reaction. Since ΔE_0 is the internal energy change when the reaction occurs with each species in its lowest energy state, it is a fundamental quantity for the reaction. Thus ΔH_T^0 has been written as the sum of ΔE_0, about which nothing can be calculated, and a term $\Delta(H^0 - E_0)_T$, which can be calculated. It is a way of concentrating the full capabilities of thermodynamics into a single term.

We can now proceed to examine the calculation of $(H^0 - E_0)_T$ for a substance. There are two independent ways of doing this. First, we can obtain $(E - E_0)_T$ and hence $(H^0 - E_0)_T$ by means of Eq. (5-41). This requires a complete knowledge of the heat capacity of the substance from $0°K$ up to the desired temperature. If phase changes occur in the process of heating the substance from $0°K$, then the energies of these changes must be included, essentially in the manner indicated in Fig. 5-2. Alternatively, $(H^0 - E_0)_T$ could be obtained from a similar heating at constant pressure and from the variation of C_P with temperature and the enthalpies of any phase changes. This approach is discussed further in Section 6-ST-3.

The heat capacity approach does not really add anything over the discussion in Section 5-6 on the temperature dependence of ΔH and ΔE. It is of more importance that $(H^0 - E_0)_T$ can be calculated by the methods of statistical thermodynamics. Thus if the various energy states are known, $(H^0 - E_0)_T$ can be obtained directly through Eq. (5-44). By repeating the calculation for each substance involved in a chemical reaction, one then obtains $\Delta(H^0 - E_0)_T$ and, by means of Eq. (5-48), ΔE_0. Having ΔE_0, one can now calculate ΔH_T^0 for any temperature. There are some considerable further advantages to the use of enthalpy functions in dealing with applications of the second law of thermodynamics; these are discussed in the Special Topics section of the next chapter.

To illustrate the application of statistical thermodynamics to thermochemistry, consider the reaction

$$3H_2 + N_2 = 2NH_3, \qquad \Delta H_{298}^0 = -22.08 \quad \text{kcal.} \qquad (5\text{-}49)$$

We assume that each gas is ideal and can apply the methods of Chapter 4 to the calculation of $E - E_0$ for each species. It is safe to assume that at $25°C$ the equipartition values will be reached with respect to the translational and rotational contributions. The calculations then center on obtaining E_{vib}; we use Eq. (4-81) and need the fundamental frequency or characteristic vibrational temperature θ_{vib} for each mode of vibration. The latter is given by $\theta_{\text{vib}} = h\nu_0/k$ or, if ν_0 is in cm^{-1}, $\theta_{\text{vib}} = hc\nu_0/k = 1.439\nu_0$. Then E_{vib} is [Eq. (4-62)]

$$E_{\text{vib}} = RT \frac{x}{e^x - 1} = RTf(x),$$

where $x = \theta_{\text{vib}}/T$ and $f(x) = x/(e^x - 1)$.

The calculation for each species may be assembled as follows.

Hydrogen

translation:	$E_{\text{trans}} = \frac{3}{2}RT =$		888 cal
rotation:	$E_{\text{rot}} = RT =$		592 cal
vibration:	$\nu_0 = 4160.2$ cm^{-1}, $\theta_{\text{vib}} = 5987°$K, $x = 20.08$, $f(x) = 0.0000$:		
	$E_{\text{vib}} = RTf(x) =$		0 cal

1480 cal

Nitrogen

translation: same as for H_2		888 cal
rotation: same as for H_2		592 cal
vibration: $\nu_0 = 2230.7$ cm^{-1}, $\theta_{\text{vib}} = 3210°$K, $x = 10.77$, $f(x) = 0.0003$:		
$E_{\text{vib}} = 0.0003RT =$		0 cal

1480 cal

Ammonia

translation: same as for H_2 and N_2 — 888 cal

rotation: $E_{\text{vib}} = \frac{3}{2}RT =$ — 888 cal

vibration: there are six vibrational degrees of freedom, but only four frequencies since two are doubly degenerate; thus

$\nu_1 = 3337$ cm^{-1}, from which $f(x) = 0.0000$:	$E_1 =$	0 cal
$\nu_2 = 950$ cm^{-1}, $f(x) = 0.047$:	$E_2 = 0.047RT =$	28 cal
$\nu_3 = 3414$ cm^{-1} (twice); $f(x) = 0.0000$:	$E_3 =$	0 cal
$\nu_4 = 1627.5$ cm^{-1} (twice); $f(x) = 0.003$:	$E_4 = (0.003)2RT =$	4 cal

1808 cal

The value of $\Delta(E^0 - E_0)$ is then

$$\Delta(E^0 - E_0) = 2(1808) - 1480 - 3(1480) = -2304 \quad \text{cal}$$

and

$$\Delta(H^0 - E_0) = -2304 - 2RT = -3489 \quad \text{cal}.$$

Finally, from Eq. (5-48),

$$\Delta E_0 = -22.08 - (-3.49) = -18.59 \quad \text{kcal}.$$

Knowing ΔE_0, we could repeat the entire calculation for any other temperature to obtain a ΔH^0 for that temperature. The temperature could, for example, be one not easily accessible for direct experimental measurements.

The preceding discussion illustrates several points. First we see again that the energy of an ideal gas is a function of temperature only; the calculations of $E - E_0$ did not require a value for the pressure. Second, the major contributions to $E - E_0$ were from translation and rotation. This will generally be true for small, strongly bonded molecules around 25°C (the discussion of Section 4-12 on the molecular interpretation of heat capacities is relevant at this point). Considerations such as this last one are often helpful in estimations of the vibrational contribution when quantitative information is not available. Thus the use of the enthalpy function allows an intermixing of phenomenological or classical thermodynamics and statistical thermodynamics.

GENERAL REFERENCES

COTTRELL, T. L. (1958). "The Strengths of Chemical Bonds." Butterworth, London and Washington, D. C. (Bond dissociation energies.)

ROSSINI, F. A., *et al.*, eds. (1952). Tables of Selected Values of Chemical Thermodynamic Properties. Nat. Bur. Std. Circular No. 500. U. S. Gov't. Printing Office, Washington, D. C. (A source for thermochemical quantities.)

STURTEVANT, J. M. (1959). "Physical Methods of Organic Chemistry" (A. Weissberger, ed.), 3rd ed., Vol. 1. Wiley (Interscience), New York. (Experimental calorimetry.)

CITED REFERENCES

BENSON, S. W. (1965). *J. Chem. Ed.* **42**, 502.

BROSEN, E. J., AND ROSSINI, F. D. (1946). *J. Res. Nat. Bur. Std. A* **36**, 274.

HOCK, M., AND JOHNSTON, H. L. (1961). *J. Phys. Chem.* **65**, 856.

KNOWLTON, J. W., AND ROSSINI, F. D. (1949). *J. Res. Nat. Bur. Std. A* **43**, 113.

WAGMAN, D. D., KILPATRICK, W. J., TAYLOR, W. J., PITZER, K. S., AND ROSSINI, F. D. (1945). *J. Res. Nat. Bur. Std. A* **34**, 155.

Exercises

5-1 Calculate ΔH^0_{298} and ΔE_{298} for the reaction

$$C_2H_6(g) + CH_3COOH(l) + NH_3(g) = 2CH_4(g) + H_2NCH_2COOH(s).$$

Give the answers in kilocalories and in kilojoules.

Ans. $\Delta H^0_{298} = -14.43$ kcal or -60.38 kJ; $\Delta n_g = 0$ so $\Delta E = \Delta H$.

5-2 Calculate ΔH^0_{298} and ΔE_{298} for the incomplete combustion reaction

$$C_6H_6(g) + 1\tfrac{1}{2} O_2(g) = 6C(s) + 3 H_2O(l).$$

The heat of vaporization of benzene is 94.3 cal g^{-1}.

Ans. $\Delta H^0_{298} = -224.77$ kcal or -940.4 kJ; $\Delta E = -223.29$ kcal or -934.2 kJ.

5   Thermochemistry

5-3   Calculate ΔH^0_{298} per mole for the conversion of graphite into diamond.

> *Ans.*   0.450 kcal or 1.882 kJ.

5-4   Calculate ΔH^0_{298} per mole for the *cis* to *trans* isomerization of $CH_3CH=CHCH_3$.

> *Ans.* -949 cal or -3.97 kJ.

5-5   A small catalytic hydrogenation unit has a heat capacity of 300 cal $°K^{-1}$. What should its rate of heating be if an equimolar mixture of ethylene and hydrogen gases is passed through it at the rate of 2 millimoles of mixture per minute? Assume complete reaction.

> *Ans.*   0.109 $°C\ min^{-1}$.

5-6   A sample consisting of 0.200 g of $CH_3COOH(l)$ is ignited in a bomb calorimeter containing pure oxygen. The heat capacity of the calorimeter is 12,000 J $°C^{-1}$. What temperature increase should occur?

> *Ans.*   0.243 °C.

5-7   Calculate ΔH^0_{298} for the process

$$Ag + HCl(aq) = AgCl(s) + \tfrac{1}{2}H_2(g).$$

The heat of formation of $AgCl(s)$ is -127.0 kJ.

> *Ans.*   41.3 kJ or 9.87 kcal.

5-8   Obtain ΔH^0_{298} for the formation of $NH_4OH(aq)$.

> *Ans.* -86.70 kcal or 363 kJ.

5-9   What is ΔH^0_{298} for the dilution process NaOH (in 100 moles H_2O) $=$ NaOH(aq)?

> *Ans.* -128 cal   or -535 J.

5-10   Calculate ΔH_f^0 of NH_3 at 500°C.

> *Ans.* -12.92 kcal or -54.0 kJ.

5-11   Calculate ΔH_f^0 of $CH_3COOH(g)$ at 100 °C given that ΔH_v is 405 J g^{-1} at the normal boiling point or 118°C and that the values of C_P are 2.30 J $°C^{-1}\ g^{-1}$ and 6.27 J $°C^{-1}\ g^{-1}$ for liquid and gaseous acetic acid, respectively.

> *Ans.* -107.2 kcal mole^{-1} or -448.4 kJ mole^{-1}.

Problems

5-1   Calculate ΔH^0_{298} and ΔE_{298} in kilocalories and in kilojoules for the reaction

$$C_2H_4(g) + H_2(g) + \tfrac{1}{2}O_2(g) = C_2H_5OH(l).$$

Problems

5-2 Calculate ΔH^0_{298} and ΔE_{298} in kilocalories and in kilojoules for the reaction

$$2H_2O(l) + CCl_4 + 3SO_2 = S(\text{monoclinic}) + CO_2 + 4HCl(g) + 2SO_3(g).$$

5-3 The heat of sublimation of graphite to carbon atoms has been estimated as 170 kcal mole^{-1}. The dissociation of molecular hydrogen into atoms, $H_2 = 2H$, has $\Delta H^0 = 103.2$ kcal mole^{-1}. From these data and the value for the heat of formation of methane, calculate ΔH^0 for

$$C(g) + 4H(g) = CH_4(g).$$

One-fourth of this value is a measure of the C$-$H bond energy in methane.

5-4 At 25°C and constant pressure, the heat of formation of CO_2 from graphite is -94.272 kcal mole^{-1} and the heat of combustion of CO is -67.263 kcal mole^{-1}. Calculate ΔH for the formation of one mole of CO from C and CO_2 (at 1000°K) if the following equations are valid for the molar heat capacities:

for C (graphite) $C_P = 1.20 + 0.0050T - 1.2 \times 10^{-6}T^2$;
for $CO_2(g)$ $C_P = 7.40 + 0.006T - 1.50 \times 10^{-6}T^2$;
for $CO(g)$ and $O_2(g)$ $C_P = 6.5 + 0.0010T$.

5-5 For the following reaction at 25°C, $\Delta H = -56$ kcal:

$$2HI(g, 1\text{ atm}) + Cl_2(g, 1\text{ atm}) = 2HCl(g, 1\text{ atm}) + I_2(s).$$

Given that the heat of sublimation of $I_2(s)$ is 6.1 kcal mole^{-1} at 185°C; the heat capacities C_P for the gases HI, HCl, Cl_2, and I_2 may be taken to be 6.5 cal °C^{-1} mole^{-1} and independent of temperature; the heat capacity C_P for $I_2(s)$ is 12.6 cal °C^{-1} mole^{-1} (independent of T); calculate ΔH for the following reaction at 125°C:

$$2HI(g, 1\text{ atm}) + Cl_2(g, 1\text{ atm}) = 2HCl(g, 1\text{ atm}) + I_2(g, 1\text{ atm}).$$

5-6 Calculate the maximum temperature achieved by the mixture when 0.100 g of methane gas is exploded in a constant-volume adiabatic (that is, insulated) calorimeter containing 10 g of air. The initial temperature is 25°C. Assume ideal gas behavior.

5-7 One-half mole of methane at 25°C is exploded in a large excess, ten moles, of oxygen, burning completely to carbon dioxide and water. Calculate the final temperature under adiabatic conditions (a) assuming the explosion to be at constant pressure, (b) assuming it to be at constant volume.

5-8 Given the following data: heat of combustion of liquid benzene to CO_2 and liquid water is 781.4 kcal at 25°C (that is, for reactants and products all at 25°C); heat of fusion of benzene at 5°C is 30 cal g^{-1}; heat of vaporization of water at 100°C is 540 cal g^{-1}; heat capacities at constant pressure:

liquid benzene: 0.40 cal °C^{-1} g^{-1}
liquid water: 1.00 cal °C^{-1} g^{-1}
solid benzene: 0.30 cal °C^{-1} g^{-1}
water vapor: $7.00 + 2.77 \times 10^{-3}T$
carbon dioxide: $7.70 + 5.3 \times 10^{-3}T$
oxygen: $6.76 + 0.61 \times 10^{-3}T$;

calculate the *difference* between the given heat of combustion and ΔH for the reaction

$$C_6H_6(s, 0°C) + 7\tfrac{1}{2}O_2(g, 0°C) = 6CO_2(g, 0°C) + 3H_2O(g, 0°C).$$

5-9   The heats of combustion at 25°C and 1 atm of cyclopropane, $[(CH_2)_3(g)]$, graphite, and hydrogen are -499.85 kcal mole^{-1}, -94.051 kcal mole^{-1}, and -68.317 kcal mole^{-1}, respectively [values for graphite and hydrogen are from Wagman *et al.* (1945)]. At 25°C, ΔH for the formation of propene, $CH_3CH=CH_2(g)$, from the elements is 4.879 kcal (Brosen and Rossini, 1946). Find ΔH for (a) the formation of one mole of cyclopropane from the elements, (b) the isomerization of one mole of cyclopropane at 25°C and 1 atm (Knowlton and Rossini, 1949).

5-10   Calculate ΔH^0_{298} for the process

$$HCl(aq) + NaOH(aq) = NaCl(aq) + H_2O .$$

Estimate the value for the same reaction if the solutions are about 0.5 molal.

5-11   The temperature of a hydrogen–oxygen flame is found to be 2000°K. Assuming constant-pressure conditions and that oxygen is initially present in a threefold molar excess over hydrogen (that is, 3:1 mole ratio), calculate the degree of combustion of the hydrogen to water.

5-12   (Calculator problem) Find the best (least-squares) fit of C_P^0 for CO_2 between 298°K and 2000°K to an equation of the form $C_P^0 = a + bT + cT^2$. (Heat capacity data are often reported in this form rather than in the one used in Table 5-4.)

Special Topics Problems

5-1   Calculate ΔH^0_{298} for formation of isobutene, using bond energies.

5-2   The standard heat of combustion of naphthalene (solid) is -1231 kcal mole^{-1} at 25°C (to CO_2 and liquid water) and the heat of sublimation is about 9 kcal mole^{-1}. Estimate the resonance energy for naphthalene.

5-3   Calculate E_0 for the reaction $CO(g) + \frac{1}{2}O_2(g) = CO_2(g)$ from the known ΔH^0 at 25°C and the spectroscopic constants as given in Table 6-1. Then calculate ΔH^0 for the reaction at 1000°C. Compare your result with the value obtained using the heat capacity expressions of Table 5-4 and the value of ΔH^0 at 25°C. B_e is 0.3906 cm^{-1} for CO_2 , a linear molecule, and the fundamental vibration frequencies are $\nu_1 = 1388.3$ cm^{-1}, $\nu_2 = 667.3$ cm^{-1} (twice), and $\nu_3 = 2349.3$ cm^{-1}.

6 THE SECOND AND THIRD LAWS OF THERMODYNAMICS

6-1 Introduction

The second law of thermodynamics stems from general conclusions drawn from experience about the difference in nature between heat energy and work energy. The qualitative observation is that work energy can always be converted completely into heat energy but that the reverse is not possible in the absence of other change. Examples of the first part of the statement are common. The experiments of Count Rumford on the boring of cannon and Joule's experiments of heating water by means of a weight-driven paddle wheel were cited in connection with the first law. The braking of any motor reduces its work output to heat, the impact of a falling object converts its kinetic energy to heat, and so forth. In general any change or process capable of doing work may be arranged to produce instead the equivalent amount of heat, if only by providing sufficient friction.

As a further example, imagine an ideal gas contained in a cylinder with a piston, the whole in thermal contact with the surroundings, that is, at constant temperature. As illustrated in Fig. 6-1(a), the expansion might be reversible; the piston turns a wheel which drives a cam so designed that at each stage of the expansion the opposing force of the weight being lifted is only infinitesimally less than the force of the gas on the piston. The process is isothermal and since the gas is ideal, $\Delta E = 0$ and $q = w$. Thus work w has been done at the expense of heat energy q from the surroundings, but with a change in state of the gas. The gas could be returned to its original state if the weight were made infinitesimally heavier. The work would now be $-w$ and the heat $-q$. The net for the cycle would be $w = 0$ and $q = 0$. Now consider the experiment depicted in Fig. 6-1(b). A valve in the piston is opened,

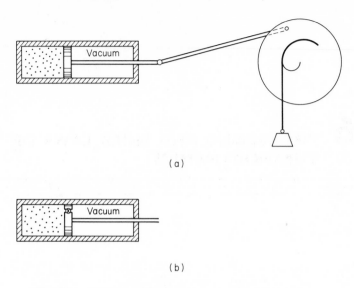

Fig. 6-1. *(a) Reversible and (b) irreversible expansions.*

allowing the gas to expand freely. ΔE is still zero and now $w = 0$, so that $q = 0$. However, to return the gas to its original state with the least possible work, the valve would have to be closed, and the minimum possible weight hung from the cam. Work would be $-w$ and heat $-q$; the net effect of this cycle would be that the surroundings have supplied work w, which has been entirely converted to heat. In the isothermal irreversible cycle, work has been converted to heat; in the isothermal reversible cycle there is no net conversion either way. This last represents the best we can do; we cannot find an isothermal cycle for our gas the net effect of which would be to convert heat into work.

One statement of the second law is simply a generalization of the above conclusion: *It is not possible to convert heat into work by means of an isothermal cyclic process*. This is a negative statement but one that summarizes much experience. Were the statement incorrect, it should be possible to devise a cycle, or essentially an engine, that operates isothermally and which supplies work energy at the expense of the heat energy of the surroundings. Such an engine could, for example, drive a ship at sea by drawing on the heat energy of the ocean. Engines of this type are known as *perpetual motion machines of the second kind* and the above statement of the second law admits our inability to discover such an engine.

A second facet of observations such as those just referred to is that a process which will take place spontaneously can be made to do work. A gas expands spontaneously into a vacuum; and the arrangement of Fig. 6-1(a) illustrates a means of obtaining work out of the same change in state of the gas. If the process were carried out reversibly, the arrangement would give the maximum possible work. Another type of spontaneous process is the flow of heat from a higher to a lower temperature. As illustrated schematically in Fig. 6-2(a), a bar heated at one

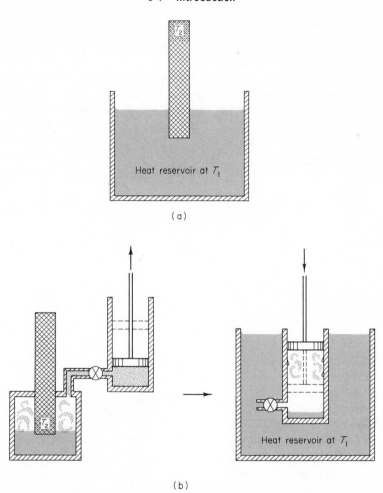

Fig. 6-2. *(a) Irreversible and (b) partially reversible use of heat at T_2.*

end has the other end in contact with a lower-temperature heat reservoir. The spontaneous change will be for heat to flow into the reservoir until the entire bar is at the reservoir temperature T_1. Alternatively, however, work could be obtained. As sketched in Fig. 6-2(b), the hot end of the bar might be used to convert some water into steam, which could then be introduced into a piston and cylinder setup. If the unit should be immersed in the cooler heat reservoir, the steam would condense, pulling down the piston and thus providing work. The end result would be that the same amount of energy would be lost by the bar as before, but now with some of it appearing as work rather than as heat at T_1.

A third type of spontaneous process is the chemical process. A battery contains chemicals that will react spontaneously if allowed to. The spontaneous reaction will occur if the chemicals are directly mixed or simply if the battery is short-circuited. The chemical energy that is released appears as heat. Alternatively, the battery may be made to run a motor and thus do work. The same chemical energy now appears partly as work.

The quantitative aspects of the second law have to do with specifying the maximum work that a spontaneous process can provide. This is not necessarily given by the internal energy change. For example, the isothermal expansion of an ideal gas provides work, but without an internal energy change of the gas. Next, in the case of heat flow from a hotter to a colder system we can see that the relative temperatures must play a role in determining how much work can be obtained. To pursue the point further, consider the coiled spring shown in Fig. 6-3(a). It can

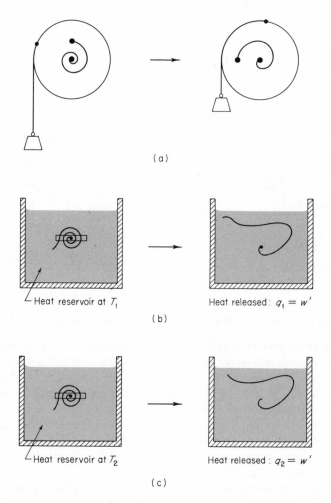

(a)

Heat reservoir at T_1 Heat released: $q_1 = w'$

(b)

Heat reservoir at T_2 Heat released: $q_2 = w'$

(c)

Fig. 6-3. *Conversion of work into heat. (a) A coiled spring does work w' directly. (b) The work is converted into heat at T_1, or (c) at T_2.*

do a certain amount of work w' on uncoiling (as by lifting a weight). If, instead, the spring is placed in a heat reservoir at T_1 and then allowed to uncoil, it does no work, but an equivalent amount of heat energy q_1 is added to the reservoir. Suppose, instead, that the spring had uncoiled in a reservoir at a higher temperature T_2 as illustrated in Fig. 6-3(c); it would then produce the same amount of heat as before, but at temperature T_2. Clearly the heat at T_2 could be used in the same way as the hot bar, namely, to do some work w by means of a heat engine operating between T_2 and T_1. The situation is now that $w = q_1 + q_2$, where q_2, a positive number from the definition of q, is the heat absorbed from the reservoir at T_2, and q_1, a negative number, is the heat evolved to the reservoir at T_1.

We can expect that if the operations are reversible the work done will be the maximum possible and thus be at a unique value. Also, in a qualitative way we would expect that the greater the difference between T_2 and T_1, the greater should be the fraction of q_2 that can appear as work. A more detailed analysis, as in the next two sections, leads to the conclusion that the measure of *unavailability* of heat energy for work is given by q_{rev}/T. In fact the increment q_{rev}/T turns out to have the properties of a state function; the integral from one state to another is independent of path. This is the central mathematical statement of the second law of thermodynamics and, accordingly, a new state function, *entropy*, is introduced, where

$$dS = \delta q_{rev}/T. \tag{6-1}$$

Again in a qualitative way, the example of the hot bar losing its heat to the lower-temperature heat reservoir involves an increase in entropy—successive "elements" of heat are being transferred from a higher to a lower temperature so that T in Eq. (6-1) decreases. The process is also a spontaneous one, and another way of generalizing the second law is to say that in a closed system (such as bar plus reservoir) the entropy increases in a spontaneous process.

The various introductory statements of the second law are then as follows:

It is not possible to convert heat into work by means of an isothermal cyclic process.

q_{rev}/T is a state function.

The entropy of an isolated system will increase if spontaneous processes can occur.

The basis for the second law is a negative observation—our inability to construct a perpetual motion machine of the second kind. Similarly, the first law rests on our inability to construct a perpetual motion machine of the first kind—one that creates energy. As with the first law, there is also a positive side. The various implications of the second law lead to phenomenological relationships that have been abundantly verified. Both laws of thermodynamics are thus most solidly a part of our understanding of the behavior of nature.

6-2   The Carnot Cycle—Heat Machines

Some of the major advances in the early understanding of thermodynamics were made around 1824 by S. Carnot. Carnot was very interested in the efficiency of steam and other heat engines, and one of his most useful contributions was in showing how the essence of a heat engine could be represented by a reversible four-step cycle using an ideal gas. A heat engine has an operating fluid, such as steam or, in this case, an ideal gas. The fluid is heated to a temperature T_2 by means of a heat source or heat reservoir at T_2 and then expands, doing work. Depending on the design, the expansion might be approximately but not exactly adiabatic. The path might be of the general type $PV^a = \alpha$ with an exponent a between unity and γ, the heat capacity ratio. We will represent this expansion by an isothermal step followed by an adiabatic one, rather than as a single intermediate kind of path. As a result of following the adiabatic component of the path, the fluid is cooled to T_1. At this point it is in an expanded state and at T_1; it must now be returned to the original state in order to complete a cycle. It will not do for us to return it by the same path, since we want some net work to be done. The simplest thing is to reverse the order, that is, to have an isothermal compression at T_1 followed by an adiabatic compression back to the initial state. The advantage of this cycle is that heat exchange occurs only at the initial temperature T_2 and at T_1 and not over a range of temperatures, thus greatly facilitating the analysis.

The preceding description is intended to emphasize that the Carnot cycle does correspond to a real, although idealized heat engine. The actual cycle is shown in Fig. 6-4. We want to relate the heat absorbed during the isothermal expansion at T_2 and that evolved during the compression at T_1 to the net work done. To do this, we analyze each step, assuming one mole of gas.

Step ab   Isothermal expansion at T_2 from V_a to V_b :

$$w_{ab} = RT_2 \ln \frac{V_b}{V_a}, \qquad \Delta E_{ab} = 0, \qquad q_{ab} = q_2 = w_{ab}$$

Step bc   Adiabatic expansion from T_2 to T_1 and from V_b to V_c :

$$q_{bc} = 0, \qquad -w_{bc} = \Delta E_{bc} = C_V \Delta T = C_V (T_1 - T_2),$$

(we assume a constant heat capacity)

$$C_V \ln \frac{T_1}{T_2} = -R \ln \frac{V_c}{V_b} \qquad \text{[ideal gas, Eq. (4-47)].}$$

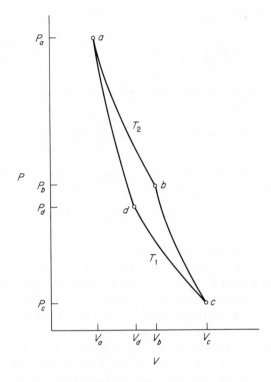

Fig. 6-4.   *The Carnot cycle.*

Step cd   Isothermal compression at T_1 from V_c to V_d :

$$w_{cd} = RT_1 \ln \frac{V_d}{V_c}, \qquad \Delta E_{cd} = 0, \qquad q_{cd} = q_1 = w_{cd} \, .$$

Step da   Adiabatic compression from T_1 to T_2 and from V_d to V_a :

$$q_{da} = 0, \qquad -w_{da} = \Delta E_{da} = C_V \, \Delta T = C_V(T_2 - T_1),$$

$$C_V \ln \frac{T_2}{T_1} = -R \ln \frac{V_a}{V_d} \qquad \text{[ideal gas, Eq. (4-47)].}$$

The two equations based on Eq. (4-47) provide a relationship between the four volumes:

$$C_V \ln \frac{T_1}{T_2} = -R \ln \frac{V_c}{V_b} = R \ln \frac{V_a}{V_d} \, ,$$

so that

$$\frac{V_b}{V_c} = \frac{V_a}{V_d} \qquad \text{or} \qquad \frac{V_b}{V_a} = \frac{V_c}{V_d} \, . \tag{6-2}$$

201

We now assemble the terms for w_{tot} :

$$w_{tot} = RT_2\left(\ln \frac{V_b}{V_a}\right) + C_V(T_1 - T_2) + RT_1\left(\ln \frac{V_d}{V_c}\right) + C_V(T_2 - T_1).$$

The terms involving C_V cancel, and using Eq. (6-2), we get

$$w = w_{tot} = R\left(\ln \frac{V_b}{V_a}\right)(T_2 - T_1) \tag{6-3}$$

(the subscript is no longer needed for clarity). Since $q_2 = RT_2 \ln(V_b/V_a)$, this further reduces to

$$w = \left(\frac{q_2}{T_2}\right)(T_2 - T_1) = q_2 \frac{T_2 - T_1}{T_2}. \tag{6-4}$$

The efficiency of the heat engine is just w/q_2 ; this gives the work done per unit amount of heat energy supplied at T_2. The result is in accord with the qualitative statements of the preceding section. Thus the greater the difference between T_2 and T_1, the greater is the fraction of q_2 that can be converted to work. An additional point is that the ultimate in efficiency is reached if $T_1 = 0°K$ (or $T_2 = \infty°K$); w is now equal to q_2. This result is restricted for the moment to the reversible Carnot cycle for an ideal gas but is otherwise quite general. Thus Eq. (6-4) is, of course, independent of the scale of the cycle, that is, of the number of moles of gas used, and of the number of cycles carried out. It is also independent of the value of C_V (or of the heat capacity ratio γ) and of the expansion ratio V_c/V_b, which determines the temperature ratio T_2/T_1. Yet, as illustrated in Fig. 6-5, cycles that appear to be quite different result as these variables are changed.

There is an important corollary equation to Eq. (6-4). Since $\Delta E = 0$ for the cycle, it follows that

$$w = q_1 + q_2. \tag{6-5}$$

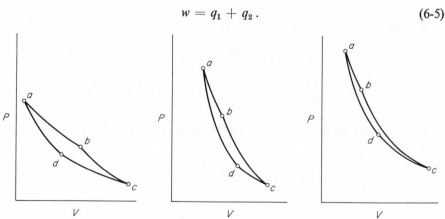

Fig. 6-5.   *Ideal gas Carnot cycles come in various shapes!*

Combination of Eqs. (6-4) and (6-5) leads to a relation between q_1 and q_2:

$$\frac{q_1}{T_1} = -\frac{q_2}{T_2}. \tag{6-6}$$

We emphasize that Eq. (6-6) is derived for a reversible cycle, so that q_1 and q_2 are reversible heats.

Consider now the specific case of a Carnot heat engine operating between 100°C and 0°C. If 1000 kcal is absorbed at 100°C, the work done by the engine is (1000)(100)/(373) = 268 kcal; the efficiency is thus 26.8 %. The remainder of the 1000 kcal, or 732 kcal, appears as heat delivered to the reservoir at 0°C. The analysis is shown schematically in Fig. 6-6(a).

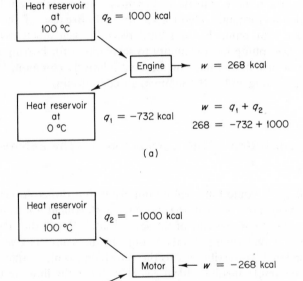

(a)

(b)

Fig. 6-6. *(a) The heat engine. (b) The heat pump.*

The Carnot cycle is based on reversible steps and can therefore be operated in either direction with no change in the fundamental equations governing it. We could, for example, follow the cycle in a counterclockwise direction. It is now necessary to do work on the system. The net result is that by doing 268 kcal of work, 732 kcal have been taken from the reservoir at 0°C and this heat, plus the work energy, appears as 1000 kcal at 100°C. In this mode of operation, the Carnot cycle functions as a *refrigerator*. The 732 kcal abstracted at 0°C would, for example, correspond to the freezing of about 90 kg of ice. The relevant performance factor is now the ratio $| q_1 |/| w |$, or 2.73.

The cycle, in this reverse mode of operation, is acting as a *heat pump*, transferring heat from a lower to a higher temperature. It could thus be used as a heating unit. If installed in a house with 0°C weather outside, the expenditure of 268 kcal of work would deliver 1000 kcal of heat at 100°C. The performance factor is, from this point of view, $| q_2 |/| w |$, or 3.73. An advantage of using heat pumps now becomes apparent. The same 268 kcal of work could be converted directly into heat at 100°C (by means of an electric heater, for example), but now only 268 kcal of heat would result. Thus the performance factor of 3.73 is in fact the theoretical advantage factor of the heat pump over a direct heating system. In the case of the heating of a house, a more realistic set of temperatures might be 0°C and 25°C, in which case the performance factor rises to 14.9. Because of its greater initial capital cost the heat pump has not until recently been much used for heating. However, the heat pump has the ability to serve either for heating or for cooling, and this type of installation has now become relatively common. In the winter it provides space heating and in the summer, air conditioning.

6-3 *Generalization of the Carnot Cycle—The Entropy Function*

The Carnot cycle would represent an important but rather specialized situation except that we can now bring in the second law statement about our inability to find a perpetual motion machine of the second kind. Recall that the Carnot cycle could represent a real engine, idealized only in the sense that we have reduced friction and related irreversibilities to the vanishing point, so that $w = w_{\mathrm{rev}}$ and hence is the maximum possible. Ideal gas behavior is the limiting behavior of all real gases, so the use of an ideal gas is not completely unrealistic.

Let us suppose, then, that some other heat engine is to be matched against a Carnot engine. This second engine operates between the same two temperatures T_2 and T_1 and the scale of the Carnot engine is adjusted so that q_2 for it is equal to $-q_2'$ for the second or test engine. The situation is summarized as follows.

Test engine Absorbs heat q_1' at T_2, evolves heat q_1' at T_1, and produces work w'.

Carnot engine Evolves heat q_2 at T_2, $-q_2 = q_2'$; absorbs heat q_1 at T_1; and requires work w to be done on the cycle.

Since the heat absorption and evolution are balanced at T_2, q_2(net) = 0. Suppose that w' is greater than w, so that there is a net production of work by the combined machines. By the first law, $w_{\mathrm{net}} = q_1 + q_1'$ (the q_2's cancel); since w_{net} is a positive number, more heat must have been absorbed at T_1 by the Carnot engine than evolved at T_1 by the test engine. That is, there must be a net absorption of heat at T_1. The overall result is therefore that heat energy at T_1 is converted into work, and we have a perpetual motion machine of the second kind. This is affirmed to be impossible by the second law, and we conclude that w' cannot be greater than w. The most efficient possible performance of the test engine, according to the second law, would be that $w' = w$, so that the combined engines would produce no net work and absorb no net heat at T_1.

The inescapable conclusion is that the Carnot efficiency is the maximum possible for any heat engine operating between the two temperatures. Equation (6-6) can thus be upgraded to the status of a general law of nature.

Now that we have established the generality of the conclusions from the Carnot cycle, it is very useful to put the cycle itself on a more abstract and general basis. Fig. 6-7 depicts a reversible cycle between two states A and B. The paths A → B

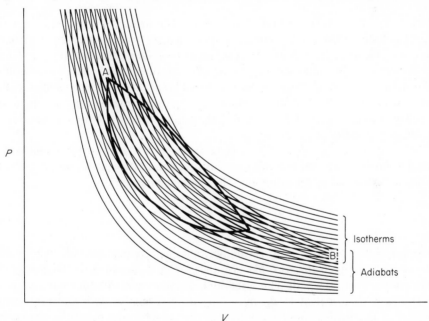

P

Isotherms

Adiabats

V

Fig. 6-7. *Approximating a general ideal gas cycle by means of a series of Carnot cycles.*

and B → A are arbitrary but can be approximated by a set of Carnot cycles. The interior portions cancel, and so the net result is to give the stepped path traced in heavy lines. Since Eq. (6-6) applies to each cycle, it must be true for the set of cycles that

$$\sum \frac{q_i}{T_i} = 0. \qquad (6\text{-}7)$$

This sum can be divided into two parts, that for the terms that are made up by the contour from A to B and that for the terms made up by the contour of the path from B to A:

$$\sum_{A \to B} \frac{q_i}{T_i} + \sum_{B \to A} \frac{q_i}{T_i} = 0. \tag{6-8}$$

Recalling Fig. 6-5, we see that each Carnot cycle may be made as thin as desired, so in the limit we may reproduce the arbitrary path as closely as we please. For an infinite number of small steps, Eq. (6-8) takes an integral form:

$$\int_A^B \frac{dq_{rev}}{T} + \int_B^A \frac{dq_{rev}}{dT} = 0, \tag{6-9}$$

or

$$\oint \frac{dq_{rev}}{T} = 0, \tag{6-10}$$

where $\oint$ denotes a cyclic integral, that is, one taken around a path, and the subscript has been added to q to emphasize again that the process must be reversible.

It is possible to go from A to B by some other reversible path, and to return from B to A always by the same path. Equation (6-9) does not depend on the specification of the path, and it must therefore be true that $\int_A^B dq_{rev}/dT$ is independent of path. This conclusion, as well as the statement of Eq. (6-10), means that the quantity dq_{rev}/T is a total or perfect differential. Referring to Section 4-4, we see that this is the defining property of a state function.

The recognition that dq_{rev}/T is a state function is the principal quantitative contribution of the second law. We give this function its own name, *entropy* (Greek for change), denoted by the symbol S. The defining equation is

$$dS = \frac{dq_{rev}}{T}. \tag{6-11}$$

To repeat, S, like E and H, is a thermodynamic quantity that depends only on the state of the system, so that ΔS, like ΔE and ΔH, is determined by the change of state, irrespective of the path. This last is an important point. The defining equation (6-11) allows us to calculate ΔS by setting up a reversible path and evaluating $\int dq_{rev}/T$. The resulting value of ΔS must be the same for that particular change in state regardless of the path used.

We can now write some combined first and second law equations. Thus Eq. (4-24) becomes

$$dE = T \, dS - P \, dV \tag{6-12}$$

and Eq. (4-27) becomes

$$dH = T \, dS + V \, dP. \tag{6-13}$$

As with E and H, the practice will be to use S to denote the entropy per mole and s that per molecule. Entropy has the same units as the gas constant and heat capacity and ordinarily is expressed as calories per degree Kelvin per mole. The same alternative sets of units that are used for R may, of course, also be used for entropy. Some have considered that it is undignified for so important a thermo-dynamic quantity to have a composite dimension and have used the term EU, meaning entropy unit. The equivalent but preferred designation in this text will be calories per degree Kelvin.

6-4   Calculations of ΔS for Various Reversible Processes

A.   Changes of Temperature

Phase changes will be considered in Section 6-4C. In their absence q_{rev} for a change in temperature is given by

$$q_{rev} = \int C \, dT,$$

where C is the heat capacity for the path, which may be some arbitrary one. The general expression for ΔS is therefore

$$\Delta S = \int \frac{C}{T} \, dT = \int C \, d(\ln T). \tag{6-14}$$

Usually, however, we consider only isochoric and isobaric paths, for which ΔS is then given by

$$\Delta S = \int C_V \, d(\ln T), \tag{6-15}$$

$$\Delta S = \int C_P \, d(\ln T). \tag{6-16}$$

B.   Processes Involving an Ideal Gas

We now extend the considerations of Section 4-7 to include calculations of ΔS for the various standard processes. Previously, the process was required to be reversible in order that P_{ext} might be replaced by P, the pressure of the gas. We again require each process to be reversible, now both for that reason and because the defining equation for entropy, Eq. (6-11), requires the use of q_{rev}.

Equation (6-12) takes a special form in the case of an ideal gas. We replace dE by $C_V \, dT$ [Eq. (4-37)] and P by RT/V:

$$C_V \, dT = T \, dS - \frac{RT}{V} \, dV.$$

This rearranges to

$$dS = C_V \, d(\ln T) + R \, d(\ln V) \qquad \text{(ideal gas)}, \qquad (6\text{-}17)$$

or, since $d(\ln V) = d(\ln T) - d(\ln P)$,

$$dS = C_P \, d(\ln T) - R \, d(\ln P) \qquad \text{(ideal gas)}. \qquad (6\text{-}18)$$

Equations (6-17) and (6-18) may be applied as follows (the results of Section 4-7B are included for completeness).

Isochoric process:

$$w = 0, \qquad dE = C_V \, dT = \delta q_V, \qquad dH = C_P \, dT,$$

$$dS = \frac{\delta q_V}{T} = C_V \, d(\ln T), \qquad \varDelta S = C_V \ln \frac{T_2}{T_1} \qquad \text{(ideal gas)}. \qquad (6\text{-}19)$$

Isobaric process:

$$\delta w = P \, dV = R \, dT, \qquad w = R \, \varDelta T,$$

$$dE = C_V \, dT, \qquad dH = C_P \, dT = \delta q_P,$$

$$dS = \frac{\delta q_P}{T} = C_P \, d(\ln T), \qquad \varDelta S = C_P \ln \frac{T_2}{T_1} \qquad \text{(ideal gas)}. \qquad (6\text{-}20)$$

Isothermal process:

$$\delta q = \delta w = RT \, d(\ln V) = -RT \, d(\ln P),$$

$$q = w = RT \ln \frac{V_2}{V_1} = RT \ln \frac{P_1}{P_2},$$

$$dE = 0, \qquad dH = 0,$$

$$dS = R \, d(\ln V), \qquad \varDelta S = R \ln \frac{V_2}{V_1}, \qquad \varDelta S = R \ln \frac{P_1}{P_2} \qquad \text{(ideal gas)}. \qquad (6\text{-}21)$$

Adiabatic process:

$$\delta q = 0, \qquad \delta w = -dE; \qquad dE = C_V \, dT; \qquad dH = C_P \, dT;$$

$$dS = \frac{dq}{T} = 0 \qquad \text{(ideal gas)}.$$

$$C_V \, d(\ln T) = -R \, d(\ln V) \qquad \text{[ideal gas, Eq. (4-45)]},$$

$$C_P \, d(\ln T) = R \, d(\ln P) \qquad \text{[ideal gas, Eq. (4-46)]}. \qquad (6\text{-}22)$$

Note that Eqs. (4-45) and (4-46) follow from Eqs. (6-17) and (6-18) on setting $dS = 0$ for the adiabatic process.

An interesting and important result is obtained if we consider the overall entropy change for the gas plus its surroundings. By surroundings, we mean the rest of the system or apparatus that is involved. In the isochoric process, the surroundings gain (algebraically) $-q_V$, and therefore suffer an entropy change of $-\int dq_V/T$ or $-C_V \ln(T_2/T_1)$. The total entropy change for the gas plus surroundings is thus zero. The same result is obtained for the isobaric process, in which the surroundings gain $-dq_P/dT$ or $-C_P \ln(T_2/T_1)$ in entropy, and this just balances the entropy change of the gas. The overall entropy change is again zero for the isothermal process, and, of course, for the adiabatic one since here both q and ΔS are zero.

The conclusion is that in a reversible process the *total* entropy change is zero for the *entire* system. Since the entire system contains all the changes that occur, and therefore does not exchange heat with anything outside of itself, we speak of it as a *thermally isolated* system. Although the examples cited are for an ideal gas, the result can be shown to be quite general (Section 6-6):

$$\Delta S = 0 \qquad \text{for any reversible process in a thermally isolated system.} \qquad (6\text{-}23)$$

The Carnot cycle may be presented as an entropy versus temperature plot. Thus, referring to Section 6-2, $S_{ab} = R \ln(V_b/V_a)$; $S_{bc} = 0$; $S_{cd} = R \ln(V_d/V_c)$; and hence, from Eq. (6-2), $S_{cd} = -S_{ab}$; $S_{da} = 0$. The corresponding plot for the cycle is shown in Fig. 6-8. Here, too, ΔS for the cycle plus its surroundings is zero.

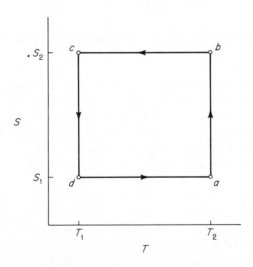

Fig. 6-8. *The Carnot cycle as an S versus T plot.*

The entropy change for the ideal gas at T_2 is q_2/T_2, and is just balanced by the equal and opposite entropy change in the heat reservoir at T_2. Similarly, the entropy change at T_1, q_1/T_1, is again balanced by the equal and opposite entropy change in the reservoir at T_1.

C. Phase Changes

In the case of a pure substance, that is, in the absence of chemical equilibria, a change of phase occurs sharply at a definite temperature for a given pressure. This means that at the particular T and P the two phases are in equilibrium; the process of converting one phase into the other is thus a reversible one. As noted in Section 5-6, there is a latent heat for a phase change, usually determined at constant pressure; this is a q_P and is equal to ΔH for the change. We have

$$\Delta S = \int \frac{dq_{\text{rev}}}{T} = \frac{1}{T} \int dq_{\text{rev}} = \frac{\Delta H}{T}. \qquad (6\text{-}24)$$

As an example, consider the process

$$H_2O(l, 100°C, 1 \text{ atm}) = H_2O(g, 100°C, 1 \text{ atm}), \qquad \Delta H^0_{373} = 9.720 \quad \text{kcal.} \qquad (6\text{-}25)$$

The process is reversible; since liquid and vapor are in equilibrium, an infinitesimal temperature change one way or the other will cause either evaporation or condensation. To carry out the process as written, we suppose that a heat reservoir infinitesimally above 100°C supplies the necessary heat. The entropy change is then $\Delta S = 9720/373 = 26.1$ cal °K^{-1} mole^{-1}. The heat reservoir, naturally, loses this amount of heat at 100°C, and shows an entropy change of -26.1 cal °K^{-1}; as with the ideal gas processes, the entropy change for the entire system is zero.

6-5   Calculation of ∆S for Various Irreversible Processes

Irreversible processes are important because of their bearing on the question of equilibrium. In an irreversible process there is some imbalance—P_{ext} may be different from P or T_{ext} from T, or a chemical driving force may be present. In all cases the irreversible process is one that can occur spontaneously. By contrast, a system at equilibrium cannot be subject to spontaneous change. Thus the reversible process is associated with equilibrium and the irreversible one with a lack of equilibrium.

It is entirely possible to calculate ΔS for an irreversible process provided the initial and final states are given. It is only necessary to devise a reversible path for accomplishing the same change of state. As an example, suppose that one mole of an ideal gas initially at STP is allowed to expand into an evacuated space and thereby double its volume. Since the gas is ideal, there is no change in temperature, and the final state is 0.5 atm pressure and 44.8 liters. As illustrated in Fig. 6-9, the equivalent reversible process is an isothermal expansion against a piston. As given in the preceding section, $\Delta S = R \ln(V_2/V_1) = R \ln 2 = 0.693R$, and this same value applies to the irreversible process. Note that in this particular irreversible process the gas is in effect its own thermally isolated system, and that now the system entropy change is $0.693R$, or positive.

(a)

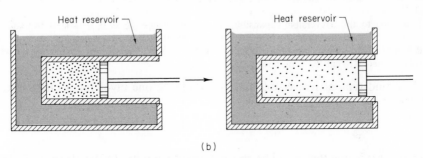

(b)

Fig. 6-9. *(a) Irreversible and (b) reversible expansion of a gas.*

A somewhat more elaborate example may be useful. Suppose that the situation is now that shown in Fig. 6-10. The gas is contained by a piston and cylinder and the unit is immersed in a heat reservoir at 0°C. The piston is free moving and has a weight on it corresponding to a pressure $P_{ext} = 0.1$ atm; it is initially held in place by a stop. The stop is removed and the piston flies back to a final position corresponding to a doubling of the original volume. This is again an irreversible process, but one in which some work is done. The work is simply the constant pressure of 0.1 atm times the volume change:

$$w = 0.1(44.8 - 22.4) = 2.24 \quad \text{liter atm} = 54.6 \quad \text{cal.}$$

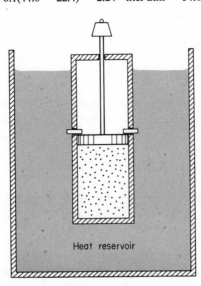

Heat reservoir

Fig. 6-10. *Irreversible expansion in which some work is done.*

This is less than the reversible work of an isothermal expansion, which is given by

$$w_{\text{rev}} = RT \ln \frac{V_2}{V_1}$$

$$= (1.987)(273.1)(2.303)(0.301) = 376.1 \quad \text{cal.}$$

The entropy change for the reversible expansion is just w_{rev}/T (since $\Delta E = 0$), or 1.38 cal $^\circ\text{K}^{-1}$ mole^{-1}.

Returning to the irreversible expansion, we see that since $\Delta E = 0$, $q = w = 54.6$ cal. The heat reservoir loses this amount of heat, which is, for it, a reversible loss. The reservoir then suffers an entropy change of $-54.6/273.1$ or -0.20 cal $^\circ\text{K}^{-1}$. The entropy change for the whole system is then 1.18 cal $^\circ\text{K}^{-1}$, or positive.

A second type of irreversible process would be one involving a phase change. Consider the process

$$H_2O(l, -10^\circ C) = H_2O(s, -10^\circ C). \tag{6-26}$$

The process is one that *could* be realized experimentally. In the absence of dust, a liquid may be supercooled below its freezing point. Water is, in fact, particularly prone to this, and in careful experiments it has been possible to supercool water to -40°C. Such supercooled water is unstable of course, and will eventually freeze. Since the process (6-26) is written as an isothermal one, we suppose that the water is in contact with a heat reservoir at -10°C; otherwise the latent heat released on freezing would warm the system.

In order to calculate ΔS for Eq. (6-26), we must produce the same change of state by means of reversible steps. This may be done as follows:

(a) $H_2O(l, -10^\circ C) = H_2O(l, 0^\circ C)$,

(b) $H_2O(l, 0^\circ C) = H_2O(s, 0^\circ C)$,

(c) $H_2O(s, 0^\circ C) = H_2O(s, -10^\circ C)$.

Step (a) is reversible even though the liquid water is unstable toward freezing. That is, a system may be *metastable*—unstable toward some particular process but otherwise in equilibrium with its surroundings. A chemical example is a mixture of hydrogen and oxygen which is unstable toward chemical reaction but which, in the absence of a catalyst, will still behave as a nearly ideal gas toward reversible temperature and pressure changes.

The entropy and heat changes for the three steps are as follows. (The heat capacities of solid and liquid water are 9.1 and 18 cal $^\circ\text{K}^{-1}$ mole^{-1}, respectively, and the heat of fusion of water at 0°C is 1435 cal mole^{-1}.)

Step (a): $\Delta H = q_p = \int C_P \, dT = 18(273.1 - 263.1) = 180$ cal.
$\Delta S = C_P \, d(\ln T) = 18 \ln(273.1/263.1) = 0.67$ cal $^\circ\text{K}^{-1}$
[by Eq. (6-16)].

Step (b): $q_P = \Delta H = -1435$ cal.
$\Delta S = q_P/T = -1435/273.1 = -5.25$ cal °K^{-1}.

Step (c): $\Delta H = q_P = 9(263.1 - 273.1) = -90$ cal.
$\Delta S = 9 \ln(263.1/273.1) = -0.33$ cal.

The overall entropy change for the water is then $(0.67 - 5.25 - 0.33) = -4.91$ cal °K^{-1}. The overall $\Delta H = (180 - 1435 - 90) = -1345$ cal; this is also q_P for the actual irreversible reaction, Eq. (6-26), and gives the heat absorbed by the heat reservoir at $-10°$C. The entropy change of the reservoir is therefore $1345/263.1 = 5.11$ cal °K^{-1}. The overall entropy change is then $-4.91 + 5.11 = 0.20$ cal °K^{-1}, or again positive.

These results suggest that we can expect ΔS to be positive for a system and its surroundings, that is, for a thermally isolated system, in which a spontaneous process occurs. The conclusion is correct and may be proved by reference to the Carnot cycle. An ideal gas may still be carried through the succession of states of the Carnot cycle even though one or more of the steps may now be irreversible. For example, the opposing pressure on the piston during the first isothermal expansion, P_{ext}, might be less than P. The expansion is then irreversible and spontaneous—it would not be reversed by an infinitesimal increase in P_{ext}. The process is still isothermal and still goes to the same final volume V_b in Fig. 6-4, so ΔS for the gas is the same as before. The heat reservoir at T_2 has supplied less heat than in the reversible process, however, and its entropy change, a negative number, will now be less than $| q_{2(rev)}/T |$. There will thus be an overall increase in entropy for the cycle plus its surroundings. Any irreversibility in the cycle must have the effect that either less heat is absorbed by the gas at T_2 or more heat is evolved at T_1. In either case, we find $\Delta S > 0$ for the gas plus the heat reservoirs.

It was shown in Section 6-3 that no actual cycle can do better than a Carnot cycle without violating the second law. Therefore, we can write the general statement that for any process in a thermally isolated system

$$dS \geqslant 0, \qquad (6\text{-}27)$$

where the equal sign holds for a reversible process and the inequality sign for an irreversible or spontaneous process. The thermally isolated system is a special one, and Eq. (6-27) may be made yet more general. In each case examined the effect of irreversibility has been to decrease w (algebraically) and hence to decrease q (algebraically) relative to the reversible value. Since the entropy change is determined by q_{rev}, the general statement is

$$dS \geqslant \frac{\delta q}{T}, \qquad (6\text{-}28)$$

where the equal sign holds for q_{rev} and the inequality sign holds otherwise. In the thermally isolated system, δq is zero and we return to Eq. (6-27).

6-6   Free Energy. Criteria for Equilibrium

A.   The Gibbs Free Energy G

Our preoccupation so far has been with entropy and heat quantities. In chemistry, we are also interested in the work that a process can perform, especially the chemical work. With the discovery that $\delta q_{rev}/T$ is a state function, we have a powerful tool for evaluating w_{rev}, or the maximum work permitted by certain important types of change in state. First, we have to recognize that chemical as well as mechanical work is possible. A good example of the former is the work that a battery can provide. We therefore write that in general

$$\delta w_{rev} = P\, dV + \delta w'_{rev}, \tag{6-29}$$

where $\delta w'_{rev}$ denotes all work other than pressure–volume work, or, for us, chemical work. The more general combined first and second law statement is then

$$dE = T\, dS - P\, dV - \delta w'_{rev}. \tag{6-30}$$

It is now convenient to introduce a new thermodynamic quantity G defined as

$$G = H - TS. \tag{6-31}$$

Differentiation gives

$$dG = dH - T\, dS - S\, dT = dE + P\, dV + V\, dP - T\, dS - S\, dT. \tag{6-32}$$

Elimination of dE between Eqs. (6-30) and (6-32) gives

$$dG = -S\, dT + V\, dP - \delta w'_{rev}. \tag{6-33}$$

For a process at constant temperature and pressure Eq. (6-33) reduces to

$$dG = -\delta w'_{rev}. \tag{6-34}$$

and the usefulness of the G function is now apparent. The negative of dG gives the reversible and hence the maximum chemical work for a reaction at constant temperature and pressure. It is the free or available work energy, and G accordingly is called the *Gibbs free energy*, after an illustrious American scientist (see Commentary and Notes section).

An alternative type of free energy function, the *Helmholtz free energy A*, is defined as

$$A = E - TS. \tag{6-35}$$

Differentiation gives

$$dA = dE - T \, dS - S \, dT, \tag{6-36}$$

and, in combination with Eq. (6-30), this gives

$$dA = -S \, dT - P \, dV - \delta w'_{\text{rev}}. \tag{6-37}$$

For a process at constant temperature $-dA$ gives the maximum total work, mechanical plus chemical.

B. Criteria for Equilibrium

We can now derive two criteria for equilibrium, including chemical equilibrium. If Eq. (6-28), $dS \geqslant \delta q/T$, is considered in terms of the first law, we obtain

$$dE \leqslant T \, dS - \delta w \quad \text{or} \quad dE \leqslant T \, dS - P \, dV - \delta w', \tag{6-38}$$

where the equal sign applies for a reversible process and the inequality sign for an irreversible or spontaneous one. Equation (6-38) may be rearranged to yield

$$dS - \frac{dE + \delta w}{T} \geqslant 0. \tag{6-39}$$

If the system is isolated, δq, and hence $dE + \delta w$, is zero. We thus regain Eq. (6-27):

$$dS \geqslant 0 \quad \text{(for an isolated system)}.$$

The significance of this last statement with respect to equilibrium is that the entropy of an isolated system will increase until no further spontaneous processes are possible. As illustrated in Fig. 6-11(a), the entropy must then reach a maximum. At this point any change is a reversible one, and the system is in equilibrium.

Insertion of relationship (6-38) into Eq. (6-32) gives

$$-dG - S \, dT + V \, dP - \delta w' \geqslant 0. \tag{6-40}$$

If the processes are restricted to constant temperature and pressure, then

$$-dG \geqslant \delta w' \quad \text{or} \quad dG \leqslant \delta w'. \tag{6-41}$$

If there is no provision for the system to do chemical work, $\delta w' = 0$, and

$$dG \leqslant 0 \quad \text{(constant } T \text{ and } P, \text{ no chemical work)}. \tag{6-42}$$

The significance of this statement is that the free energy of a system at constant temperature and pressure (and which may contain various reacting chemical species) will decrease until no further spontaneous processes are possible. As

215

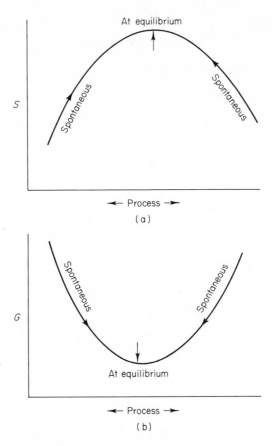

Fig. 6-11. *(a) For an isolated system S is a maximum at equilibrium. (b) For a system at constant T and P, G is a minimum at equilibrium.*

illustrated in Fig. 6-11(b), the free energy is then at a minimum. Any changes around this minimum are reversible, and the system is at equilibrium. The restriction of constant temperature and pressure may seem severe. It is not, however. Should some spontaneous fluctuation produce a local change in pressure or temperature, the reestablishment of uniform pressure and temperature equilibrium between the system and its surroundings would occur spontaneously. Thus no spontaneous irreversible changes at all can occur when G is at a minimum.

The condition of $\delta w' = 0$ is the usual one in chemical equilibrium. That is, we do not ordinarily arrange to extract chemical work. The usual form of Eq. (6-33) is therefore

$$dG = -S\,dT + V\,dP. \tag{6-43}$$

This applies to reversible changes in temperature and pressure under conditions such that $\delta w' = 0$. (Just as $dE = T\,dS$ applies under constant-volume conditions where $\delta w = 0$.) Also, G is defined in terms of state functions [Eq. (6-31)] and hence is itself a state function; ΔG is independent of path and is determined only by the initial and final states. ΔG has a *direct physical* significance, however, only when the two states are at the same temperature and pressure. It then gives the maximum chemical work that is obtainable by the process at constant pressure and temperature that takes the system from the initial to the final state.

Like G, the Helmoltz free energy A is a state function by definition. The usual form of Eq. (6-37) is

$$dA = -S\,dT - P\,dV. \tag{6-44}$$

As in the case of Eq. (6-43), Eq. (6-44) applies to reversible changes in temperature and pressure under conditions such that $\delta w' = 0$.

C.   Calculations of Free Energy Changes

The Gibbs free energy will be used throughout the rest of this text and its various applications will be illustrated as they come up. However, two very useful results may be written down immediately from Eq. (6-43). First, for a constant-pressure process, the change in G with temperature is $dG = -S\,dT$, that is,

$$\left(\frac{\partial G}{\partial T}\right)_P = -S \tag{6-45}$$

or

$$\Delta G = -\left(\int S\,dT\right)_P \tag{6-46}$$

For a constant-temperature process, the change of G with pressure is $dG = V\,dP$, or

$$\left(\frac{\partial G}{\partial P}\right)_T = V \tag{6-47}$$

and

$$\Delta G = \left(\int V\,dP\right)_T \tag{6-48}$$

In the case of an ideal gas, $V = RT/P$ and Eq. (6-48) becomes

$$dG = \frac{RT}{P}\,dP = RT\,d(\ln P) \qquad \text{(ideal gas)} \tag{6-49}$$

or

$$\Delta G = RT \ln \frac{P_2}{P_1} \qquad \text{(ideal gas).} \tag{6-50}$$

Thus, from the example of Fig. 6-10, ΔG for the expansion is given by $\Delta G = (1.987)(273.1)(2.303) \log(0.5/1) = -376.1$ cal. Alternatively, ΔG could be found from Eq. (6-31) as $\Delta H - T \Delta S$; ΔH is zero, and again $-T \Delta S = -376.1$ cal. We emphasize that while Eq. (6-49) or (6-50) will be extremely useful, dG or ΔG does not have a simple meaning since the process is not one at constant temperature and pressure.

It similarly follows from Eq. (6-44) that

$$\left(\frac{\partial A}{\partial V}\right)_T = -P \qquad (6\text{-}51)$$

and

$$\left(\frac{\partial A}{\partial T}\right)_V = -S. \qquad (6\text{-}52)$$

These expressions are not suited to the usual applications of free energy in physical chemistry, but are very useful in theoretical treatments because of the relation of A to internal energy and entropy.

Free energy changes may be obtained for chemical reactions and are then used in much the same way as are enthalpies in thermochemistry. One may use either free energies of formation, as discussed in Chapter 7 (on chemical equilibrium), or the so-called free energy functions, described in the Special Topics section of this chapter.

6-7 Second Law Relationships

It is worthwhile to assemble the various basic equations before deriving a few relationships. These basic equations are as follows.

Statements of definition:

$$H = E + PV \qquad [\text{Eq. (4-25)}],$$
$$A = E - TS \qquad [\text{Eq. (6-35)}],$$
$$G = H - TS \qquad [\text{Eq. (6-31)}].$$

Alternate forms of the combined first and second laws:

$$dE = T \, dS - P \, dV \qquad [\text{Eq. (6-12)}],$$
$$dH = T \, dS + V \, dP \qquad [\text{Eq. (6-13)}],$$
$$dA = -S \, dT - P \, dV \qquad [\text{Eq. (6-44)}],$$
$$dG = -S \, dT + V \, dP \qquad [\text{Eq. (6-43)}].$$

Immediate consequences of the definitions of entropy:

$$\Delta S = \frac{\Delta E}{T} \qquad (V \text{ and } T \text{ constant}), \qquad (6\text{-}53)$$

$$\Delta S = \frac{\Delta H}{T} \qquad (P \text{ and } T \text{ constant}), \qquad (6\text{-}54)$$

$$C_V = T\left(\frac{\partial S}{\partial T}\right)_V \qquad [\text{Eq. (6-15)}],$$

$$C_P = T\left(\frac{\partial S}{\partial T}\right)_P \qquad [\text{Eq. (6-16)}].$$

Criteria for equilibrium:

$$dS \geqslant 0 \qquad \text{(isolated system)} \qquad [\text{Eq. (6-27)}],$$
$$dG \leqslant 0 \qquad \text{(constant } T \text{ and } P) \qquad [\text{Eq. (6-41)}].$$

These relationships provide a number of secondary ones. For example, the alternative forms of the combined first and second laws are all exact differentials. This means that each generates an Euler or cross-differentiation relationship [Eq. (4-11)]. Two important cross-differentials come from the statements for dA and dG:

$$\left(\frac{\partial S}{\partial V}\right)_T = \left(\frac{\partial P}{\partial T}\right)_V, \qquad (6\text{-}55)$$

$$\left(\frac{\partial S}{\partial P}\right)_T = -\left(\frac{\partial V}{\partial T}\right)_P. \qquad (6\text{-}56)$$

A more general and complete picture is given in the Special Topics section along with some derivations of useful special equations.

6-8 The Third Law of Thermodynamics

A. Entropy and Probability

We now take another look at entropy—in a way that will lead to the third law of thermodynamics as well as introduce the statistical mechanical approach.

Consider the situation shown in Fig. 6-12. We have a flask of volume V_1 connected to a second flask of equal volume, so that the combined volume V_2 is twice V_1. The flasks are kept at some uniform temperature. Suppose that a single molecule of an ideal gas is present in the system. Clearly, the chance of the molecule being in V_1 is $\frac{1}{2}$. If two molecules are present, the chance of both being in V_1 is

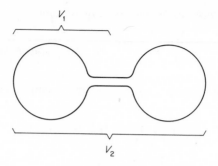

Fig. 6-12.

$(\frac{1}{2})^2$; being molecules of an ideal gas, their behavior is independent of one another. If N_0 molecules are present, the chance that all of them will accidentally collect in V_1 must be $(\frac{1}{2})^{N_0}$.

The probability calculation may be generalized to the case of an arbitrary ratio of V_1 to V_2. The probability of all of the molecules being in V_1 is now $(V_1/V_2)^{N_0}$. As a further generalization, we can assign an individual probability weight p to a molecule being in a given volume. That is, p_1 for a molecule being in volume V_1 is proportional to V_1, and, similarly, p_2 is proportional to V_2. The ratio of p values will then give the relative probability of any two volume conditions for a molecule. Thus for the general process

State 1 (molecule in V_1) → State 2 (molecule in V_2),

the relative probability is V_2/V_1. For N_0 molecules, the relative probability is then $(V_2/V_1)^{N_0}$. We can make the dependence on the number of molecules additive rather than exponential by introducing a new variable r, defined as $r = k \ln p$ (the reason for introducing the Boltzmann constant will be apparent shortly). Then for the process

state 1 (N_0 molecules in V_1) → state 2 (N_0 molecules in V_2),   (6-57)

we have

$$N_0 \, \Delta r = k \ln\left(\frac{p_2}{p_1}\right)^{N_0} = k \ln\left(\frac{V_2}{V_1}\right)^{N_0}$$

or

$$N_0 \, \Delta r = k N_0 \ln \frac{V_2}{V_1} = R \ln \frac{V_2}{V_1}.$$ (6-58)

The right-hand side of Eq. (6-58) is the same as that of Eq. (6-21), so for isothermal volume changes of an ideal gas we can identify $N_0 \, \Delta r$ with ΔS, or Δr with the entropy change per molecule. Alternatively, we see that the entropy of a state can be written

$$s = \alpha + k \ln p,$$ (6-59)

where s is the entropy per molecule, p is the probability weight of the state, and α is a constant. The relation between entropy and probability was proposed by Boltzmann in 1896 [see also Eq. (6-66)].

Although Eq. (6-59) was obtained by consideration of volume changes for an ideal gas, the analysis can be made in quite general terms, where p would be the probability weight of a given state. In quantum theory, molecules are limited to definite energy states; p is now interpreted as the number of ways in which a molecule could, over a period of time, have a given average energy $\bar{\varepsilon}$. Alternatively, for N equivalent molecules, p^N is proportional to the number of ways for their average total energy to be $N\bar{\varepsilon}$.

There is one condition such that p should be unity. That is the situation in which only one arrangement of molecules in energy states is possible. For this to be true, there can be only one energy state and all molecules must be equivalent. The physical picture meeting this requirement is that of a perfect crystalline solid at 0°K. At 0°K all molecules must, by the Boltzmann principle, be in their lowest possible energy state, and if the solid is perfectly crystalline, all lattice positions are equivalent. The entropy per molecule should then be just the constant of Eq. (6-59).

B. The Third Law of Thermodynamics

The third law of thermodynamics has evolved out of considerations such as those just given. It adds one additional statement, namely, that the constant α is intrinsic to each element (α could, for example, include some nuclear probability weight). If we now consider a general chemical reaction

$$a\mathrm{A} + b\mathrm{B} + \cdots = m\mathrm{M} + n\mathrm{N} + \cdots,$$

then ΔS for the reaction must be zero at 0°K. That is, no chemical reaction can change the number of each kind of atom, and therefore the constants for each atom must cancel out. Since we do not know the α's and since they must always cancel out, we simply proceed on the basis that they are zero. Acceptance of this assumption or reference point allows the third law to be stated in the following useful way:

Third law of thermodynamics: The entropy of all perfect pure crystalline substances is zero at 0°K.

C. Application of the Third Law of Thermodynamics

Since the third law affirms that $S_{0°K} = 0$ for any perfect pure crystalline substance, we can calculate its entropy at some higher temperature, using the methods of thermochemistry. Suppose we want S_{298} for some gaseous substance. We start with the crystalline solid as close to $0°K$ as possible and determine the entropy change on warming it to its melting point:

$$\varDelta S_1 = \int_{0°K}^{T_f} C_P(s)\, d(\ln T).$$

There is next an entropy contribution for the melting of the solid:

$$\varDelta S_2 = \frac{\varDelta H_f}{T},$$

where $\varDelta H_f$ is the enthalpy of fusion. The liquid is then further warmed to its normal boiling point:

$$\varDelta S_3 = \int_{T_f}^{T_b} C_P(l)\, d(\ln T).$$

We now add the entropy of vaporization:

$$\varDelta S_4 = \frac{\varDelta H_v}{T_b}.$$

Finally, the gas is warmed to $298°K$:

$$\varDelta S_5 = \int_{T_b}^{298} C_P(g)\, d(\ln T).$$

The sequence is illustrated in Fig. 6-13; the sum of all the terms then gives the entropy at $298°K$:

$$S_{298}^0 = S_0 + \varDelta S_1 + \varDelta S_2 + \varDelta S_3 + \varDelta S_4 + \varDelta S_5,$$

where S_0 is the entropy at $0°K$ and is affirmed to be independent of the chemical state of the substance or, in practice, zero. In the analogous calculation of the enthalpy changes on heating, shown in Fig. 5-2, the enthalpy at $0°K$ became equal to the internal energy E_0, but this latter depends on the chemical state. That is, $\varDelta E_0$, unlike $\varDelta S_0$, is definitely *not* zero for a chemical process at $0°K$.

The detailed experimental basis of calculations such as the preceding can be quite difficult to achieve. It is not possible actually to reach $0°K$ (see Commentary and Notes section), and one generally has heat capacity data only down to some low temperature close to $0°K$; an extrapolation to $0°K$ must be made, usually by means of the Debye theory (Section 4-ST-2). Many substances fail to crystallize properly or perfectly, in which case S_0 will not be zero. Often there will be a succession of stable crystalline forms. Thus low-temperature ice has a crystal structure of tetrahedral symmetry; this transforms to ordinary hexagonal ice at about $-80°C$, and the entropy of this transition must be included in the summation of the entropy changes. These problems have limited the number of experimentally

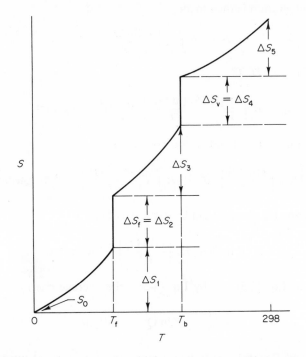

Fig. 6-13.   *Sequence of steps involved in obtaining a third law entropy.*

determined S_{298}^0 values to perhaps a few dozen. As examples, that for Ag is 10.20 cal $°K^{-1}$ mole^{-1} and that for a nearly ideal gas such as N_2, is 45.77 cal $°K^{-1}$ mole^{-1}. As will be seen in the next section, statistical thermodynamics provides an alternative means for calculating S_{298}^0 values for ideal gases. The matter is also discussed further in the Commentary and Notes section.

6-9   Statistical Mechanical Treatment of Second Law Quantities

A.   Entropy

Entropy may be expressed in terms of the partition function $\mathbf{Q}$, using Eq. (4-58), which gives the statistical thermodynamic formulation for C_V,

$$C_V = \frac{R}{T^2}\left[\frac{\partial^2(\ln \mathbf{Q})}{\partial(1/T)^2}\right]_V .$$

The required integration is then made:

$$\int dS = R \int \frac{1}{T^3}\left[\frac{\partial^2(\ln \mathbf{Q})}{\partial(1/T)^2}\right]_V dT$$

or, since $d(1/T) = -dT/T^2$,

$$S = R \int \frac{1}{T}\left\{\frac{\partial[T^2\,\partial(\ln \mathbf{Q})/\partial T]}{\partial T}\right\}_V dT + \text{constant}. \qquad (6\text{-}60)$$

Equation (6-60) may be expanded into two terms,

$$S = 2R \int \left[\frac{\partial(\ln \mathbf{Q})}{\partial T}\right]_V dT + R \int T\left[\frac{\partial^2(\ln \mathbf{Q})}{\partial T^2}\right]_V dT + \text{constant}$$

and, on integrating the second term by parts, we obtain

$$S = R \ln \mathbf{Q} + RT\left[\frac{\partial(\ln \mathbf{Q})}{\partial T}\right]_V + \text{constant}. \qquad (6\text{-}61)$$

The last term in Eq. (6-61) is, by Eq. (4-56), the average energy divided by T:

$$S = \frac{E}{T} + R \ln \mathbf{Q} + \text{constant}. \qquad (6\text{-}62)$$

The constant of Eq. (6-61) may be set equal to zero for most purposes, on the following grounds. As $0°K$ is approached only the first term of the partition function is important, and so $\mathbf{Q}$ reduces to $g_0 e^{-\epsilon_0/kT}$, where ϵ_0 is the energy of the lowest state and g_0 is its degeneracy. Then $\ln \mathbf{Q}$ becomes $-(\epsilon_0/kT) + \ln g_0$. The average energy E becomes $N_0\epsilon_0$ and we have

$$S_0 = \frac{N_0\epsilon_0}{T} - \frac{N_0 k\epsilon_0}{kT} + N_0 k \ln g_0 + \text{constant},$$

or

$$S_0 = N_0 k \ln g_0 + \text{constant}. \qquad (6\text{-}63)$$

Equation (6-63) corresponds to Eq. (6-59) for $0°K$ and per mole. Thus the constant corresponds to α and $N_0 k \ln g_0$ corresponds to the probability weight of the ground state. As already discussed, α will always cancel out in any process, and is conventionally set equal to zero. Although the ground state of a molecule may often be described as degenerate, at the limit of $0°K$ even the most minor perturbation would remove such degeneracy, so we can expect g_0 to be unity. It is thus essentially as an aspect of the third law of thermodynamics that we take S_0 to be zero. An interesting exception to this is mentioned in the Commentary and Notes section.

The resulting equation for S,

$$S = \frac{E}{T} + R \ln \mathbf{Q} \qquad \text{(distinguishable molecules)}, \qquad (6\text{-}64)$$

applies, as indicated, to the case where molecules in different energy states are distinguishable. This is true for the case of an ideal crystal and also for the internal energy states (rotation and vibration) of the molecules of an ideal gas.

As one way of seeing this reservation, we can now return to discuss the quantity p in Eq. (6-59) in more detail. It is usually called the *thermodynamic probability* and is the number of distinguishable ways in which molecules can be permuted among their most probable energy states. That is, p is the same as the quantity W_{max} that was described by Eq. (2-10). As a reminder, the number of ways of permuting N_0 molecules is just $N_0!$, but these molecules populate energy states such that N_1 are in state ϵ_1, N_2 are in state ϵ_2, and so on, and we regard the molecules of a given energy state as indistinguishable. We must then divide out the numbers of ways of permuting N_1 molecules within state ϵ_1, of N_2 molecules within state ϵ_2, and so on. The net number of distinguishable permutations is then

$$W = \frac{N_0!}{N_1!\,N_2!\,\cdots\,N_i!} = \frac{N_0!}{\prod_i N_i!}, \tag{6-65}$$

where the populations of the various states are the most probable ones; for this case W is usually called W_{max}.

Equation (6-59) now becomes

$$S = \alpha + k \ln W_{max}. \tag{6-66}$$

It is essentially this form of Eq. (6-59) that was proposed by Boltzmann. We proceed to evaluate W_{max} using Stirling's approximation; we also set α equal to zero. Then we have

$$S = k[N_0 \ln(N_0) - N_0] - k \sum_i [N_i \ln(N_i) - N_i]$$

or

$$S = kN_0 \ln N_0 - k \sum_i N_i \ln N_i \tag{6-67}$$

since $\sum N_i = N_0$. The second term of Eq. (6-67) can be written as follows. We can write

$$N_i = N_0 \frac{e^{-\epsilon_i/kT}}{\sum e^{-\epsilon_i/kT}} = \frac{N_0 e^{-\epsilon_i/kT}}{Q}.$$

We substitute this into Eq. (6-15),

$$T\left(\frac{\partial S}{\partial T}\right)_V = C_V.$$

The summation term of Eq. (6-67) becomes

$$k \sum N_i \ln N_i = k \sum \left(N_i \ln N_0 - \frac{N_i \epsilon_i}{kT} - N_i \ln Q\right)$$

$$= kN_0 \ln N_0 - \frac{E}{T} - kN_0 \ln Q$$

and after the substitution, the terms $kN_0 \ln N_0$ cancel to give

$$S = \frac{E}{T} + R \ln \mathbf{Q},$$

which is the same as Eq. (6-64).

The thermodynamic probability W_{max} is proportional to the probability of a state of the system but obviously is usually a very large number. It is not the same as the probability itself—this last is a number which does not exceed unity and might be given by W divided by some normalizing factor.

It is the assumption of distinguishable molecules, on which Eq. (6-64) is based, that allows us to write the entropy for a mole of particles as just N_0 times the entropy per particle. The situation is somewhat similar to that discussed in Section 4-9B except that we are now talking about the total partition function for a set of N_0 molecules. If the energy states for each molecule are distinct, then the total partition function $\mathbf{Q}_{tot}$ can be written

$$\mathbf{Q}_{tot} = \mathbf{Q}_1 \mathbf{Q}_2 \mathbf{Q}_3 \cdots \mathbf{Q}_{N_0} = \mathbf{Q}^{N_0}.$$

$\mathbf{Q}$ enters in the various expressions for thermodynamic quantities as $\ln \mathbf{Q}$, and since $\ln \mathbf{Q}_{tot} = N_0 \ln \mathbf{Q}$, the effect is that the quantity per mole is always N_0 times that per molecule.

This element of distinguishability is not present, however, in the case of translational energy states. Thus the translational energy of a molecule of an ideal gas is determined wave mechanically as that of a standing wave occupying the whole space. The translational energy states for a set of molecules are, in other words, not localized; the molecules are in this respect indistinguishable. The result is that when we take the product of the partition functions for each molecule, $\mathbf{Q}_{tot}$ has too high a multiplicity. We have overcounted the number of distinguishable energy states by the number of ways of permuting N_0 molecules among themselves, or by the factor $N_0!$. For the ideal gas, then, we have

$$\mathbf{Q}_{tot} = \frac{1}{N_0!} \mathbf{Q}^{N_0}. \tag{6-68}$$

The factor $1/N_0!$ does not affect the average energy, since E involves only the derivative $\partial(\ln \mathbf{Q}_{tot})/\partial T = N_0 \, \partial(\ln \mathbf{Q})/\partial T$. This complication could therefore be ignored until now. The entropy, however, depends on $\ln \mathbf{Q}_{tot}$ and not just on its derivative.

Equation (6-64) should now be written

$$s = \frac{E}{T} + k \ln \mathbf{Q}_{tot} \tag{6-69}$$

or

$$S = \frac{E}{T} + R \ln \mathbf{Q} - k \ln N_0!. \tag{6-70}$$

The last term is evaluated by means of Stirling's approximation, $\ln x! = x \ln x - x$, and Eq. (6-70) becomes

$$S = \frac{E}{T} + R \ln Q - R \ln N_0 + R \qquad \text{(indistinguishable molecules).}$$
$$(6\text{-}71)$$

This result is the one that must be used for an ideal gas. We ordinarily consider the partition function as a product $Q_{trans}Q_{rot}Q_{vib}$ and, if this is done, we use Eq. (6-71) to obtain S_{trans} and use Eq. (6-64) to obtain S_{rot} and S_{vib} . Otherwise we would be applying the correction more than once.

We thus have two limiting situations. Equation (6-64) applies to rotational and vibrational contributions, and hence to perfect crystals and to the internal degrees of freedom of ideal gas molecules, while Eq. (6-71) applies to the translational contribution of the ideal gas molecules. Liquids present a very awkward intermediate case—one in which the energy states are largely but not entirely localized. Various statistical thermodynamic models have been suggested as a means of counting the number of distinguishable energy states for liquids, but the subject is clearly a difficult one.

B. Free Energy and Related Quantities

Once we have obtained the expressions for S in terms of the partition function, those for the free energy quantities A and G follow fairly directly. Thus, by Eq. (6-35), $A = E - TS$, we have from Eq. (6-64)

$$A = -RT \ln Q \qquad \text{(distinguishable molecules)}, \qquad (6\text{-}72)$$

and from Eq. (6-71),

$$A = -RT \ln Q + RT \ln N_0 - RT \qquad \text{(indistinguishable molecules).} \quad (6\text{-}73)$$

In order to evaluate G and H we need a statistical thermodynamic expression for pressure and can now use Eq. (6-51) in combination with Eq. (6-72):

$$P = -\left(\frac{\partial A}{\partial V}\right)_T = RT\left[\frac{\partial(\ln Q)}{\partial V}\right]_T. \qquad (6\text{-}74)$$

Then, by Eq. (6-31) we have

$$G = H - TS = A + PV = -RT \ln Q + RTV\left[\frac{\partial(\ln Q)}{\partial V}\right]_T$$

$$\text{(distinguishable molecules)} \qquad (6\text{-}75)$$

and

$$G = -RT \ln Q + RTV\left[\frac{\partial(\ln Q)}{\partial V}\right]_T + RT \ln N_0 - RT$$

$$\text{(indistinguishable molecules).} \qquad (6\text{-}76)$$

Enthalpy is now also obtainable. From its definition, with Eq. (4-56), we get

$$H = E + PV = RT^2 \left[\frac{\partial(\ln Q)}{\partial T} \right]_V + RTV \left[\frac{\partial(\ln Q)}{\partial V} \right]_T \qquad (6\text{-}77)$$

If the absolute energy at 0°K is $H_0 = E_0$, this term must be added to Eq. (6-77).

C.   Statistical Thermodynamic Quantities for an Ideal Gas

The usual approximation of writing the partition function as a product, $Q = Q_{trans}Q_{rot}Q_{vib}$, was discussed in Section 4-9. Since all of the statistical thermodynamic expressions involve $\ln Q$ or its derivatives, the effect is that the contribution from each set of energy states is additive and can be taken up separately; that for translation is perhaps the most interesting. Using Eq. (4-68),

$$Q_{trans} = \frac{(2\pi m k T)^{3/2}}{h^3} \, v,$$

and Eq. (4-70),

$$E_{trans} = \tfrac{3}{2}RT,$$

and substituting into Eq. (6-71) gives

$$S_{trans} = \frac{3}{2} R + R + R\left[\ln\left(\frac{2\pi m k T}{h^2} \right)^{3/2} \frac{V}{N_0} \right]. \qquad (6\text{-}78)$$

Note that the entropy expression for indistinguishable molecules has been used as appropriate for an ideal gas, and that we use V, the volume per mole, in Eq. (4-68), instead of v, the volume of a general system.

Equation (6-78) is known as the *Sackur–Tetrode equation*; it is one of the more valuable relations of statistical thermodynamics since it gives the absolute translational entropy of an ideal gas. Further manipulation puts the equation in the form

$$S_{trans} = \frac{5}{2} R + R \ln\left[\left(\frac{2\pi}{h^2} \right)^{3/2} \frac{1}{N_0^{\,4}} R^{5/2} \right] + R \ln\left(\frac{T^{5/2} M^{3/2}}{P} \right) \qquad (6\text{-}79)$$

(V has been replaced by RT/P). On evaluating the collections of constants, we see that Eq. (6-79) reduces to

$$S_{trans} \text{ (cal °K}^{-1}\text{ mole}^{-1}) = R \ln(T^{5/2} M^{3/2}) - 2.31 \qquad (6\text{-}80)$$

for an ideal gas at 1 atm pressure. [The units of R as used in various parts of Eq. (6-79) must be chosen with care!] As an example, the entropy of argon at 298.1°K may be calculated as follows:

$$S_{298} = 1.987 \ln[(298.1)^{5/2}(39.95)^{3/2}] - 2.31 = 36.98 \quad \text{cal °K}^{-1}\text{ mole}^{-1}.$$

A variation of the Sackur–Tetrode equation, important in surface chemistry, is the version for a two-dimensional gas. The physical situation is that of molecules adsorbed at an interface but able to move freely about on it. They thus behave as a two-dimensional gas, for which Q_{trans} can be found by interpolation between Eqs. (4-67) and (4-68):

$$Q_{trans(2\text{-dim})} = \frac{2\pi m k T}{h^2}\, \mathscr{A}, \tag{6-81}$$

where $\mathscr{A}$ is the area of the surface. Insertion of this into Eq. (6-69) (remembering that E is now just RT) gives

$$S_{trans(2\text{-dim})} = 2R + R \ln\left(\frac{2\pi m k T}{h^2}\,\frac{\mathscr{A}}{N_0}\right). \tag{6-82}$$

On substituting numerical values for the various constants, we obtain

$$S_{trans(2\text{-dim})} = R \ln(MT\sigma) + 65.8 \quad \text{(cal °K}^{-1}\text{ mole}^{-1}), \tag{6-83}$$

where σ denotes the area per molecule. As an example, argon at 25°C and 1 atm pressure has a concentration such that the molecules are, on the average, about 34 Å apart. A corresponding state for argon as a two-dimensional gas would then be one with $\sigma = (34)^2$ Å^2 per molecule. Substitution of this value into Eq. (6-83) gives

$$S_{Ar(2\text{-dim})} = 1.987 \ln[(39.95)(298.1)(1.16 \times 10^{-13})] + 65.8$$

$$= 23 \quad \text{cal °K}^{-1}\text{ mole}^{-1}.$$

Notice that this value is about two-thirds of that for the three-dimensional gas at 1 atm and 25°C. Why?

Now that both E_{trans} and S_{trans} have been evaluated through statistical thermodynamics, the remaining thermodynamic functions follow directly. One simply uses the defining equations as assembled, for example, in Section 6-7.

The contributions from rotation and vibration are obtained by substitution of the appropriate partition function expressions into Eq. (6-64). We use this equation since the internal energy states do not mix between molecules, that is, are distinguishable between molecules. Then

$$S_{rot} = R + R \ln \frac{T}{\theta_{rot}} \tag{6-84}$$

for an A–B type molecule [from Eq. (4-75) and remembering that $E_{rot} = RT$]. A_{rot} and G_{rot} are the same since Q_{rot} does not depend on volume:

$$A_{rot} = G_{rot} = -RT \ln \frac{T}{\theta_{rot}}. \tag{6-85}$$

The vibrational partition function is given by Eq. (4-80): using it and E_{vib} from Eq. (4-82), we get

$$S_{vib} = R\left[\frac{\theta_{vib}/T}{e^{\theta_{vib}/T} - 1} - \ln(1 - e^{-\theta_{vib}/T})\right]. \qquad (6\text{-}86)$$

Notice that the $\frac{1}{2}h\nu_0$ term in the expression for E cancels out. Again, $A_{vib} = G_{vib}$, so

$$A_{vib} = G_{vib} = N_0\left(\frac{h\nu_0}{2}\right) + RT\ln(1 - e^{-\theta_{vib}/T}). \qquad (6\text{-}87)$$

As with E and H, the zero-point energy term $\frac{1}{2}h\nu_0$ is now present.

The preceding equations, plus those of Sections 4-11 and 4-12, allow the calculation of the rotational and vibrational contributions to the various thermodynamic quantities provided θ_{rot} and θ_{vib} are known. These are generally obtained spectroscopically from an analysis of the spacings of rotational and vibrational energy states. These, in turn, are given by the absorption spectrum of the molecule, infrared for vibration and rotation and microwave for rotation only. The discussion of molecular spectroscopy as such is deferred until Chapter 18 but it is useful at this point to supply some of the results. These are given in Table 6-1 for some gaseous diatomic molecules. In the case of polyatomic molecules there is more than one degree of vibrational freedom and hence more than one θ_{vib}. Additional data for such molecules are given in the reference cited with the table.

We can illustrate the use of the preceding equations by calculating the thermodynamic quantities for $N_2(g)$ at 25°C and 1 atm pressure, assumed to be an ideal gas. For translation, we have

$$E_{trans} = \tfrac{3}{2}RT = 888 \quad \text{cal mole}^{-1},$$

$$S_{trans} = 1.987 \ln[(298.1)^{5/2}(28)^{3/2}] - 2.31$$

$$= (1.987)(2.303)(8.3563) - 2.31 = 35.94 \quad \text{cal °K}^{-1}\text{ mole}^{-1}.$$

Table 6-1. *Spectroscopic Constants for Some Diatomic Molecules[a]*

Molecule	ν_0 (cm^{-1})	θ_{vib} (°K)	θ_{rot} (°K)
H_2	4160.2	5986	87.5
N_2	2330.7	3353	2.89
O_2	1556.4	2239	2.08
CO	2143.2	3084	2.78
$H^{35}Cl$	2885.9	4152	15.2
HBr	2559.3	3682	12.2
$^{35}Cl_2$	556.9	801.3	0.351
I_2	212.3	306.8	0.0538
HI	2230.1	3209	9.43

[a] Adapted from S. M. Blinder, "Advanced Physical Chemistry," p. 450. Macmillan, New York, 1969.

Then

$$H^0_{\text{trans}} = E_{\text{trans}} + RT = 1480 \quad \text{cal mole}^{-1},$$

$$G^0_{\text{trans}} = H^0_{\text{trans}} - TS_{\text{trans}} = -9220 \quad \text{cal mole}^{-1}.$$

(The superscripts merely confirm that the pressure is 1 atm.)
    For rotation, $\theta_{\text{rot}} = 2.89\ °\text{K}$; E_{rot} is then given by the equipartition value,

$$E_{\text{rot}} = RT = 592 \quad \text{cal mole}^{-1}.$$

By Eq. (6-84),

$$S_{\text{rot}} = 1.987 + (1.987)(2.303) \log \frac{298.1}{2(2.89)}$$

$$= 9.82 \quad \text{cal } °\text{K}^{-1} \text{mole}^{-1}$$

(the factor of two enters because the symmetry number for N_2 is two). Then

$$H_{\text{rot}} = E_{\text{rot}} = 592 \quad \text{cal mole}^{-1},$$

$$G_{\text{rot}} = A_{\text{rot}} = E_{\text{rot}} - TS_{\text{rot}} = -2340 \quad \text{cal mole}^{-1}.$$

Finally, for vibration, $\theta_{\text{vib}} = 3353°\text{K}$, so $\theta_{\text{vib}}/T = 11.2$. The consequence is that the vibrational contribution is negligible in all cases.
    The total values are as follows:

$$E_{\text{tot}} = E_0 + 888 + 592 = E_0 + 1480 \quad \text{cal mole}^{-1}$$

(where E_0 represents the unknown absolute energy at $0°\text{K}$),

$$H^0_{\text{tot}} = E_0 + 1480 + 592 = E_0 + 2070 \quad \text{cal mole}^{-1},$$

$$S^0_{\text{tot}} = 35.9 + 9.82 = 45.7 \quad \text{cal } °\text{K}^{-1} \text{mole}^{-1},$$

$$G^0_{\text{tot}} = E_0 - 9220 - 2340 = E_0 - 11,560 \quad \text{cal mole}^{-1}.$$

    Certain points of interest are brought out by the preceding calculation. First, the calculated S^0_{tot} is in quite good agreement with that obtained from heat capacity data using the third law. As cited in Section 6-8C, the third law value is 45.77 cal $°\text{K}^{-1}$ mole^{-1}. It seems amazing that the calculated value, resting entirely on the partition functions for N_2 as an ideal gas, agrees with the thermal value obtained by considering the warming of crystalline nitrogen through its melting point and boiling point. The basic reason is that the entropy is zero for the perfect crystalline solid at $0°\text{K}$ and is also zero for the hypothetical ideal gas at $0°\text{K}$. For that transition, ΔS is thus zero, and what we are observing is that entropy is a state function whose value is independent of path. The situation may be shown as follows:

$$
\begin{array}{l}
\text{N}_2(\text{ideal gas, } 0°\text{K, 1 atm}) \searrow \\
\uparrow \Delta S = 0 \qquad\qquad \text{N}_2(g, 298°\text{K, 1 atm}). \\
\text{N}_2(\text{crystal, } 0°\text{K}) \rightarrow \text{liquid} \nearrow
\end{array}
$$

A second point has to do with the large negative values for $(G^0 - E_0)$. These arise from the contribution of the $-TS^0$ term. Had the calculation been made at some lower temperature, the contribution of this term would have been smaller, not only absolutely, but relative to E and H^0. In effect, at low temperatures H^0 makes the principal contribution to G^0, while at high temperatures the $-TS^0$ term dominates.

COMMENTARY AND NOTES

6-CN-1 Summary of the Statements of the Laws of Thermodynamics

The remainder of this text will make much use of the results of thermodynamics, but in terms of specific applications. This seems an appropriate place to collect the various alternative general statements of the laws of thermodynamics.

First Law of Thermodynamics [Eq. (4-5)]:
   $dE = \delta q - \delta w$.
   The internal energy of an isolated system is constant.
   The internal energy change of a cyclic process is zero.
   Internal energy is a state function.

Second Law of Thermodynamics:
   $dS = \delta q_{\text{rev}}/T$; $dS > q_{\text{irrev}}/T$.
   Entropy is a state function.

Corollaries are:
   It is not possible to convert heat into work by means of an isothermal, cyclic process.
   The entropy of an isolated system tends to a maximum.

Third Law of Thermodynamics:

If the entropy of each element in some perfect crystalline state is taken as zero at 0°K, then the entropy of any perfect crystalline substance is also zero at 0°K.

ΔS for any isothermal process is zero at 0°K.

This last statement is sometimes known as the *Nernst heat theorem*. The various standard thermodynamic equations have been summarized in Section 6-7 and need not be repeated. A more general approach to obtaining such relationships is referred to in the Special Topics section.

6-CN-2   Statistical Thermodynamics—Ensembles— and J. Willard Gibbs

An account was given in Section 4-2 of a brilliant scientist, Benjamin Thompson or Count Rumford. Another brilliant scientist, also American by birth, was Josiah Willard Gibbs. The two men differed in all other respects, however, in about the most complete way imaginable. Gibbs was born in New Haven, Connecticut, on February 11, 1839 and died there in April 1903. He was of English descent, the fourth son of Sir Henry Gibbs of Warwickshire, who came to Boston about 1658. One of the descendants of Sir Henry was Professor of Sacred Literature in the Yale Divinity school from 1824 to 1861, and it is his son, of the same name, whose life we are describing.

The young Gibbs entered Yale College in 1854 and graduated in 1858, receiving several prizes in Latin and mathematics; he received his doctorate in 1863 and was for a while appointed a tutor. He then spent several years abroad, in Paris, Berlin, and Heidelberg, with exposure to such eminent scientists as Magnus, Kirchhoff, and Helmholtz. In 1871 he was appointed Professor of Mathematical Physics at Yale College, which position he retained until his death. He never married, and lived with his sister and her family. As a person, he was modest and of a retiring disposition; his constitution was weak as a result of a childhood bout with scarlet fever. As a scientist he was thorough and meticulous, never publishing until he had worked and reworked even the most minor aspects of a paper. The one perhaps unfortunate consequence of this extreme care is that each word in his writings conveys a precise meaning and that no words are wasted; therefore, Gibbs' papers must be studied word by word—they cannot be speed-read!

Gibbs was one of the most brilliant scientists of the last century. He had the insight and power to perceive the most far-reaching logical consequences of fundamental postulates and had great inventive powers in mathematics. He made major contributions in vector analysis, as in the development of the theory of dyadics, and in the electromagnetic theory of light. He enjoyed geometry and graphical

233

approaches. For physical chemists, Gibbs is almost the father of thermodynamics, both classical and statistical. He began publishing a series of lengthy articles in the *Transactions of the Connecticut Academy* in 1873. He developed in great depth the thermodynamic structure for dealing with heterogeneous equilibrium; he discovered the phase rule (Chapter 11) which bears his name and largely developed the thermodynamics of systems having an interface. We speak of the Gibbs adsorption equation in surface chemistry. He built much of the structure of statistical mechanics. Although his work was before the development of wave mechanics, statistical thermodynamic results do not require the use of quantum ideas—they are derivable and were derived by Gibbs on the basis of classical mechanics.

There were some delays in the general appreciation of Gibbs—perhaps because he chose to publish in a relatively obscure journal. Later, private copies of his papers were in circulation throughout the European scientific world and were avidly studied by his peers. Today the "Collected Works of J. Willard Gibbs" (Gibbs, 1931) remains virtually a bible for serious students of physical chemistry. By the late 1870's Gibbs had become an honored man, and he received a great variety of awards and honorary degrees during the following two decades. A major award of the American Chemical Society today is the J. Willard Gibbs medal.

Gibb's made much use of what are called *"ensembles."* This is a rather elegant word whose simple paraphrasing would be "collections" or "assemblies." An ensemble is simply the set of molecules, states, or other entities which is being examined. In statistical thermodynamics, it is the set which is being considered and over which summations are to be made. We have used, for example, a set called the *microcanonical* ensemble. This is the set of molecules, usually N_0 in number, which occupies a specified volume and is at a specified total energy. As discussed in Section 2-2, if the energy is specified, there will be only certain ways in which the molecules can be distributed among the energy states. For most purposes the results obtained from the microcanonical set are the same as those from a *canonical* ensemble. This last corresponds to a collection of molecules occupying a specified volume and at a specified temperature. The system is in thermal contact with a heat reservoir and is not isolated as is the microcanonical set. The effect is to allow variations in average energy. However, if the number of molecules is large, this variation will be minute; the distribution will peak so sharply at the same place as that for the microcanonical ensemble of the same average energy that the difference is neglected unless the fluctuations themselves are being examined. The general derivations of thermodynamic quantities have so far been based on a canonical ensemble.

The third type of ensemble, known as the *grand canonical* ensemble, is a set of sets of molecules, each in thermal contact with the surroundings. The different sets of molecules may vary, however, in the number of molecules they contain. We speak of the grand canonical ensemble as an open system, meaning that molecules are allowed to enter or leave. This type of ensemble is used in statistical thermodynamics in calculations of a change in a thermodynamic property per mole of substance primarily in dealing with mixtures or solutions. While the elaborate formality of the grand canonical ensemble will not be used here, it does constitute the statistical thermodynamic basis for treating partial molal quantities as discussed in Chapter 9.

6-CN-3 Additional Comments on the Third Law of Thermodynamics and on the Attainment of 0°K

A corollary of the Nernst heat theorem (Section 6-CN-1) is the statement: It is impossible to reduce the temperature of any system to absolute zero in a finite number of steps. To understand this statement, we need to consider how, in general, one can try to reach absolute zero. There is no lower-temperature heat reservoir now, and the only way to have a system cool itself is by a spontaneous adiabatic process. Suppose that the system consists of a hypothetical ideal gas; then since $dS \geqslant 0$, by Eq. (6-17),

$$C_V \ln \frac{T_2}{T_1} + R \ln \frac{V_2}{V_1} \geqslant 0.$$

Let T_1 and V_1 be the starting condition, and now let the gas expand adiabatically to V_2; we want T_2 to be exactly 0°K. The term $C_V \ln(T_2/T_1)$ has now become minus infinity, and so the term $R \ln(V_2/V_1)$ must exceed plus infinity—clearly an impossibility!

The same type of analysis can be made in a more general way, but the added elaboration seems unnecessary. The conclusion remains the same: One can approach closer and closer to 0°K by some series of adiabatic processes but one cannot attain it in any finite number of steps.

The adiabatic expansion of an ideal gas is unrealistic as a practical procedure; all substances are solid near 0°K. A very imaginative method, developed by W. F. Giauque is the one generally used. It is known as *adiabatic demagnetization* and the procedure is to cool a paramagnetic material to as low a temperature as possible (liquid helium temperature) while in as strong a magnetic field as possible. The field is then turned off and the temperature drops. A temperature of 2×10^{-5} °K has been reported (de Klerk *et al.*, 1950). The physical reason that the temperature drops on demagnetization is roughly as follows. The magnetic field tends to align the molecular magnetic poles (discussed in Section 3-ST-2), reducing the entropy of the system because of the greater order or lower thermodynamic probability of the system. It is, in effect, a restriction on the thermal motion of the molecules. On removal of the magnetic field, new energy states become available and more randomness or greater thermodynamic probability is sought. Since the system is adiabatic, the increase in entropy must be accompanied by a decrease in temperature. The formal analysis is not actually very different from that for the adiabatic expansion of a gas into a larger volume.

Although 0°K has not been reached exactly, nor is ever expected to be reached, it has been approached closely enough to suggest that heat capacity data can be extrapolated accurately from a few degrees Kelvin to 0°K by means of the Debye theory (Section 4-ST-2). The thermochemical procedure outlined in Section 6-8C has been carried out for a number of substances, with representative results as given in Table 6-2. As a specific example, the entropy of nitrogen at 25°C was obtained from the series of increments given in Table 6-3.

The third law of thermodynamics may be checked in two types of way. A most satisfying one is through statistical thermodynamics. If the final state is that of an

Table 6-2. *Thermochemical and Statistical Thermodynamic Entropies at 298.1°K*[a]

Substance	Thermochemical (cal °K^{-1} mole^{-1})	Calculated (cal °K^{-1} mole^{-1})
Solid		
Ag	10.20	—
AgCl	23.00	—
Al	6.77	—
C(graphite)	1.37	—
Ca	9.95	—
CaO	9.5	—
Cd	12.37	—
Cu	7.97	—
Liquid		
Br$_2$	36.4	—
H$_2$O	16.73	—
Hg	18.17	—
Gas		
CH$_4$	44.47	—
CO	46.20	47.3
CO$_2$	51.08	—
Cl$_2$	53.29	53.31
H$_2$	31.21	31.23
HCl	44.64	44.64
HBr	47.6	47.53
N$_2$	45.90	45.79
NO	50.34	50.43
O$_2$	49.01	49.03

[a] From G. N. Lewis and M. Randall, "Thermodynamics," 2nd. ed. (revised by K. S. Pitzer and L. Brewer). McGraw-Hill, New York, 1961; and E. A. Moelwyn-Hughes, "Physical Chemistry," 2nd ed. Pergamon, Oxford, 1961.

Table 6-3. *The Entropy of* N_2 [a]

Step	Entropy increment (cal °K⁻¹ mole⁻¹)
0–10°K (by extrapolation)	0.458
10–35.61°K (integration of heat capacity data)	6.034
Crystal structure transition at 35.61°K	1.536
35.61–63.14°K (integration of heat capacity data)	5.589
Melting at 63.14°K	2.729
63.14–77.32°K (integration of heat capacity data)	2.728
Vaporization at 77.32°K	17.239
77.32–298.2°K (integration of heat capacity data)	9.37
Correction for gas nonideality	0.22
Total	45.9

[a] W. F. Giauque and J. O. Clayton, *J. Amer. Chem. Soc.* **55**, 4875 (1933).

ideal gas, then the equations of Section 6-9C may be used. The sample calculation given there led to S^0_{298} for nitrogen of 45.76 cal °K⁻¹ mole⁻¹ using the Sackur–Tetrode equation for an ideal gas and spectroscopic data giving the rotational and vibrational temperatures. The thermochemical value is 45.90 cal °K⁻¹ mole⁻¹. The agreement in this and several other cases is remarkably good, as shown in Table 6-2.

The second way of checking the third law is by means of a net chemical reaction. For example, combination of the separate thermochemical values for S^0_{298} gives $\Delta S^0_{298} = -19.32$ cal °K⁻¹ for the reaction

$$C(graphite) + 2H_2(g) = CH_4(g).$$

If now q_{rev} can be determined for the reaction, then ΔS is also given, by the second law, as q_{rev}/T. Several verifications of this type have been made, again with good agreement. Parenthetically, the usual procedure actually is to determine the equilibrium constant for the reaction and its temperature dependence (Section 7-4), but this amounts to the same thing.

In the process of checking thermochemical and statistical thermodynamic entropies, occasional discrepancies have been found, of the order of a few calories per degree Kelvin per mole, always with the thermochemical entropy too low. Instances where freezing produces a glass rather than a crystalline solid can be explained immediately on the basis of a residual entropy of disorder of the glassy structure. However, in cases such as CO, N_2O, and H_2O the crystals appear perfect, and the problem has been traced to a disorder on a molecular scale. Thus with CO the two atoms are so nearly the same that when the solid first crystallizes the end-to-end orientation of the CO is essentially random; that is, a crystal layer might appear thus:

$$\text{CO} \quad \text{OC} \quad \text{OC} \quad \text{CO} \quad \text{CO} \quad \text{OC} \quad \text{CO}$$
$$\text{CO} \quad \text{OC} \quad \text{CO} \quad \text{CO} \quad \text{OC} \quad \text{OC} \quad \text{CO}.$$

The effect is that each CO has two possible positions, so for N_0 molecules the thermodynamic probability is 2^{N_0} and a contribution of $R \ln 2$ is predicted by Eq. (6-59). As $0°K$ is approached, all the CO's should orient one way or the other but apparently they are prevented by an energy barrier from doing so in a finite time. Thus the thermochemical summations start with $R \ln 2$ or 1.4 cal $°K^{-1}$ mole^{-1} rather than with zero entropy and come out too low. The actual results are: spectroscopic entropy, 47.30; thermochemical entropy, 46.2. Adding 1.4 brings the thermochemical value to 47.6, or a little too high. Evidently the disorder is not complete.

Ice constitutes another type of example. Here one has a three-dimensional network of hydrogen bonds, and since hydrogen atoms could not be located by x-ray crystallography, for a long time it was uncertain whether they were positioned midway between oxygens or whether each hydrogen was closer to one oxygen than to another. A calculation on the latter supposition, assuming that each oxygen has two close and two distant hydrogens, but randomly chosen, leads to a thermodynamic probability of $(\frac{3}{2})^{N_0}$. This corresponds to an entropy contribution of $R \ln \frac{3}{2}$ or 0.806 cal $°K^{-1}$ mole^{-1}, which matches closely the discrepancy between the spectroscopic and thermochemical values. The two-position picture for hydrogen bonding in ice has since been confirmed by neutron diffraction measurements, which show (statistically) half a hydrogen atom at each of two positions between oxygens: $O-\frac{1}{2}H-\frac{1}{2}H-O$. The result is interpreted to mean that each oxygen has two close and two distant hydrogens but that the pattern throughout the crystal is random.

SPECIAL TOPICS

6-ST-1 *Thermodynamic Relationships*

The various defining equations and statements of the combined first and second laws were summarized in Section 6-7. There are a number of thermodynamic relationships that stem from these and that can be produced in a fairly organized manner. We summarize such procedures here and use them to obtain a few of the more useful additional thermodynamic equations.

The various forms of the combined laws are repeated for convenience:

$$dE = T\,dS - P\,dV \qquad \text{[Eq. (6-12)]},$$
$$dH = T\,dS + V\,dP \qquad \text{[Eq. (6-13)]},$$
$$dA = -S\,dT - P\,dV \qquad \text{[Eq. (6-44)]},$$
$$dG = -S\,dT + V\,dP \qquad \text{[Eq. (6-43)]}.$$

First, the equations lead directly to several simple coefficients. Thus

$$\left(\frac{\partial E}{\partial V}\right)_S = -P, \qquad \left(\frac{\partial E}{\partial S}\right)_V = T,$$

$$\left(\frac{\partial G}{\partial P}\right)_T = V, \qquad \left(\frac{\partial G}{\partial T}\right)_P = -S,$$

represent four out of the total of eight; the complete listing seems unnecessary.

Second, the equations are all exact differentials. This means that each generates an Euler or cross-differentiation relationship [Eq. (4-11)]. We then have four new equations

$$\left(\frac{\partial T}{\partial V}\right)_S = -\left(\frac{\partial P}{\partial S}\right)_V, \tag{6-88}$$

$$\left(\frac{\partial T}{\partial P}\right)_S = \left(\frac{\partial V}{\partial S}\right)_P, \tag{6-89}$$

$$\left(\frac{\partial S}{\partial V}\right)_T = \left(\frac{\partial P}{\partial T}\right)_V \qquad \text{[Eq. (6-55)]},$$

$$\left(\frac{\partial S}{\partial P}\right)_T = -\left(\frac{\partial V}{\partial T}\right)_P \qquad \text{[Eq. (6-56)]}.$$

These equations find a great deal of use in thermodynamic derivations.

Third, the four original statements of the combined laws generate a set of four equations based on the general procedure of Eq. (4-12). Thus

$$\left(\frac{\partial S}{\partial V}\right)_E = -\frac{(\partial E/\partial V)_S}{(\partial E/\partial S)_V} = \frac{P}{T}, \tag{6-90}$$

$$\left(\frac{\partial S}{\partial P}\right)_H = -\frac{(\partial H/\partial P)_S}{(\partial H/\partial S)_P} = -\frac{V}{T}, \tag{6-91}$$

$$\left(\frac{\partial T}{\partial V}\right)_A = -\frac{(\partial A/\partial V)_T}{(\partial A/\partial T)_V} = -\frac{P}{S}, \tag{6-92}$$

$$\left(\frac{\partial T}{\partial P}\right)_G = -\frac{(\partial G/\partial P)_T}{(\partial G/\partial T)_P} = \frac{V}{S}. \tag{6-93}$$

In addition, one may hold a dependent variable constant to give, for example,

$$\left(\frac{\partial G}{\partial P}\right)_V = -S\left(\frac{\partial T}{\partial P}\right)_V + V. \tag{6-94}$$

Finally, one can in a general way express $E = f(V, T)$, $H = f(P, T)$, $A = f(V, T)$, and $G = f(P, T)$ and obtain relationships such as Eq. (4-14). Rules for obtaining any desired partial differential coefficient have been worked out (Lewis and Randall, 1961).

Some brief applications of these secondary relationships are as follows. If we differentiate Eq. (6-12) with respect to volume at constant temperature, we get

$$\left(\frac{\partial E}{\partial V}\right)_T = T\left(\frac{\partial S}{\partial V}\right)_T - P. \tag{6-95}$$

Use of Eq. (6-55) then gives

$$\left(\frac{\partial E}{\partial V}\right)_T = T\left(\frac{\partial P}{\partial T}\right)_V - P. \tag{6-96}$$

Equation (6-96) is called a *thermodynamic equation of state*. It provides a relationship among E and the state variables P, V, and T, which is valid for all substances. Its application to the calculation of internal pressures was discussed in Section 4-CN-1. A completely parallel derivation beginning with the differentiation of Eq. (6-13) with respect to pressure at constant temperature and using Eq. (6-56) leads to a similar thermodynamic equation of state:

$$\left(\frac{\partial H}{\partial P}\right)_T = -T\left(\frac{\partial V}{\partial T}\right)_P + V. \tag{6-97}$$

As discussed in Section 4-ST-1, Eq. (6-97) allows an evaluation of the Joule–Thomson coefficient from an equation of state such as the van der Waals equation.

We can now develop Eq. (4-34) further. The equation is

$$C_P - C_V = \left[P + \left(\frac{\partial E}{\partial V}\right)_T\right]\left(\frac{\partial V}{\partial T}\right)_P.$$

On replacing $(\partial E/\partial V)_T$ by means of Eq. (6-96), we get

$$C_P - C_V = T\left(\frac{\partial P}{\partial T}\right)_V\left(\frac{\partial V}{\partial T}\right)_P. \tag{6-98}$$

or, since

$$\left(\frac{\partial P}{\partial T}\right)_V = -\frac{(\partial V/\partial T)_P}{(\partial V/\partial P)_T} = \frac{\alpha}{\beta} \qquad \text{[Eq. (4-14)]},$$

where α is the coefficient of thermal expansion and β the coefficient of compressibility,

$$\alpha = \frac{1}{V}\left(\frac{\partial V}{\partial T}\right)_P, \qquad \beta = -\frac{1}{V}\left(\frac{\partial V}{\partial P}\right)_T, \qquad (6\text{-}99)$$

the final form of Eq. (6-98) becomes

$$C_P - C_V = \frac{\alpha^2 V T}{\beta}. \qquad (6\text{-}100)$$

6-ST-2 Thermodynamic Treatment of a Nonideal Gas—Fugacity

This topic is included for two reasons. First, gases are generally assumed to be ideal in this text, and it seems desirable to indicate in at least one place how to proceed if the assumption is to be avoided. Second, the procedure is a fairly typical one in chemical thermodynamics and will be used again in connection with nonideal solutions. In the case of an ideal gas, various thermodynamic relationships, such as Eq. (6-50), contain pressure as a variable by virtue of the ideal gas law. One now seeks to find an effective or thermodynamic pressure for a nonideal gas, defined so that it can be used in thermodynamic equations in the same way as actual pressure is in the case of an ideal gas. This thermodynamic pressure is called the *fugacity* of a gas and is arrived at as follows.

For an ideal gas, Eq. (6-50) can be written in the form

$$RT \ln P_2 = G_2 + (RT \ln P_1 - G_1). \qquad (6\text{-}101)$$

We want the *same form* to apply for a nonideal gas, that is,

$$RT \ln f_2 = G_2 + (RT \ln f_1 - G_1), \qquad (6\text{-}102)$$

where f denotes fugacity. We now use the fact that all real gases approach ideal behavior in the limit of zero pressure and define fugacity by the equation

$$RT \ln f_2 = G_2 + \lim_{P_1 \to 0}(RT \ln P_1 - G_1). \qquad (6\text{-}103)$$

In the limit, $RT\,d(\ln P_1)$ must equal dG_1, and so the actual values can only differ by a constant at a given temperature. It therefore follows that

$$RT\,d(\ln f) = dG + \text{constant}$$

or

$$\left(\frac{\partial(\ln f)}{\partial G}\right)_T = \frac{1}{RT}. \tag{6-104}$$

Also, using Eq. (6-47), we find

$$\left(\frac{\partial(\ln f)}{\partial P}\right)_T = \frac{V}{RT}. \tag{6-105}$$

The fugacity of a nonideal gas may be obtained conveniently by the following procedure. We define α as $V_{\text{ideal}} - V_{\text{actual}}$, or

$$\alpha = \frac{RT}{P} - V. \tag{6-106}$$

We replace V in Eq. (6-105) and write the equation as a constant-temperature integration,

$$\int_0^P d(\ln f) = \int_0^P d(\ln P) - \frac{1}{RT}\int_0^P \alpha\,dP.$$

Since f and P become identical in the limit of zero pressure, the equation reduces to

$$\ln f = \ln P - \frac{1}{RT}\int_0^P \alpha\,dP. \tag{6-107}$$

The integral may, for example, be obtained graphically from a plot of α versus P. Where the nonideality is not large, a useful rule is that the observed pressure of a gas will be the geometric mean of the fugacity and the ideal gas law pressure given by RT/V:

$$P_{\text{actual}} = \left(\frac{RTf}{V}\right)^{1/2}. \tag{6-108}$$

The procedure for determining the fugacity of a gas in a mixture is similar, although more complicated.

A final point is that neither the definition of fugacity nor the preceding derivations require that the substance be gaseous. We can obtain the fugacity of a solid or a liquid by integrating Eq. (6-105). The molecular weight used must be that of the gas at $P \to 0$, however, since this is the condition on which the definition of f is based.

6-ST-3 The Free Energy Function

We continue here the approach initiated in Section 5-ST-2. In that section the internal energy function $E - E_0$ was introduced, obtainable through either Eq. (5-40) or Eq. (5-43):

$$E - E_0 = \int_0^T C_V \, dt \quad \text{or} \quad E - E_0 = RT^2 \left(\frac{\partial (\ln \mathbf{Q})}{\partial T} \right)_V.$$

It could thus be determined either thermochemically or spectroscopically. Similarly, the enthalpy function $H^0 - E_0$ is defined by Eq. (5-46). It is now convenient to introduce a more symmetric function, $H^0 - H_0^0$, given by

$$H^0 - H_0^0 = \int_0^T C_P \, dT, \tag{6-109}$$

or, from Eqs. (5-43) and (6-74)

$$H^0 - H_0^0 = RT^2 \left[\frac{\partial (\ln \mathbf{Q})}{\partial T} \right]_V + RTV \left[\frac{\partial (\ln \mathbf{Q})}{\partial V} \right]_T. \tag{6-110}$$

The *enthalpy function* may therefore also be determined either thermochemically if the substance is an ideal gas or from spectroscopically obtained values of θ_{vib} and θ_{rot} and the various partition functions given in Section 6-9. Recall that the superscript zero denotes 1 atm pressure and the subscript zero the value at 0°K.

Since by definition $G = H - TS$, we can write

$$\frac{G^0 - H_0^0}{T} = \frac{H^0 - H_0^0}{T} - S^0 \tag{6-111}$$

(H_0^0 has merely been substracted from both sides). The quantity $(G^0 - H_0^0)/T$ is called the *free energy function* and $(H^0 - H_0^0)/T$ the *enthalpy function*. As with the other functions, $(G^0 - H_0^0)/T$ may be obtained purely from thermochemical data, including now a third law determination of S^0, or, in the case of an ideal gas, from the various partition function expressions including now Eq. (6-71) for S.

We now consider data for some chemical reaction. For the general reaction

$$a\text{A} + b\text{B} + \cdots = m\text{M} + n\text{N} + \cdots$$

we can write ΔG^0 for some temperature T as

$$\frac{\Delta G^0}{T} = \frac{\Delta(G^0 - H_0^0)}{T} + \frac{\Delta H_0^0}{T}. \tag{6-112}$$

Similarly,

$$\Delta H^0 = \Delta(H^0 - H_0^0) + \Delta H_0^0. \tag{6-113}$$

If $\Delta G^0/T$ can be evaluated for the reaction and $\Delta(G^0 - H_0^0)/T$ obtained either thermochemically or spectroscopically, then ΔH_0^0 can be determined. For this reaction ΔH_0^0 is a constant and Eq. (6-112) can be used for the calculation of ΔG^0 at any other temperature. As in thermochemistry the practice is to compile values of ΔH_0^0 for reactions in which a given substance is formed from the elements. One can then calculate ΔH_0^0 for any other reaction in the same way as with enthalpies of formation [Eq. (5-23)].

It is well at this point to summarize the reasons for using the above functions. First, they provide a natural arrangement that facilitates the use of statistical thermodynamics. Once ΔH_0^0 has been determined for a reaction we can often calculate $\Delta(G^0 - H_0^0)/T$ for any desired temperature without recourse to further experimental data. In this way we can find ΔG^0 for a reaction at a temperature not experimentally accessible. Second, the free energy function $(G^0 - H_0^0)/T$ changes much more slowly with temperature than does G^0 itself. Tabulations of this function may then be for rather widely spaced temperature intervals. Tables 6-4 and 6-5 give some illustrative data of this type.

Table 6-4. *Free Energies for the Elements[a]*

Element	$-(G^0 - H_0^0)/T$ (cal $°K^{-1}$ mole^{-1})					$H_{298}^0 - H_0^0$ (kcal mole^{-1})	ΔH_0^0 [b] (kcal mole^{-1})
	298.15°K	500°K	1000°K	1500°K	2000°K		
$Br_2(g)$	50.85	54.99	60.80	64.31	66.83	2.325	8.37
$Br_2(l)$	25.5	—	—	—	—	3.240	0
C(graphite)	0.53	1.16	2.78	4.19	5.38	0.251	0
$Cl_2(g)$	45.93	49.85	55.43	58.85	61.34	2.194	0
$F_2(g)$	41.37	45.10	50.44	53.74	56.17	2.110	0
$H_2(g)$	24.42	27.95	32.74	35.59	37.67	2.024	0
$I_2(g)$	54.18	58.46	64.40	67.96	70.52	2.148	15.66
$I_2(s)$	17.18	—	—	—	—	3.154	0
$N_2(g)$	38.82	42.42	47.31	50.28	52.48	2.072	0
$O_2(g)$	42.06	45.68	50.70	53.81	56.10	2.07	0

[a] From G. N. Lewis and M. Randall, "Thermodynamics," 2nd ed. (revised by K. S. Pitzer and L. Brewer), p. 680. McGraw-Hill, New York, 1961 (where additional values are given).

[b] Of formation from the element in its standard phase; H_0^0 includes the $\frac{1}{2}h\nu_0 N_0$ contribution from the zero-point vibrational energy.

Table 6-5. *Free Energies for Various Gaseous Compounds[a]*

Compound	$-(G^0 - H_0^0)/T$ (cal $°K^{-1}$ $mole^{-1}$)					$H_{298}^0 - H_0^0$ (kcal $mole^{-1}$)	ΔH_0^0 [b] (kcal $mole^{-1}$)
	298°K	500°K	1000°K	1500°K	2000°K		
CH_4	36.46	40.75	47.65	52.84	57.1	2.397	−15.99
C_2H_2	39.98	44.51	52.01	57.23	61.33	2.392	54.33
C_2H_4	43.98	48.74	57.29	63.94	69.46	2.525	14.52
C_2H_6	45.27	50.77	61.11	69.46	—	2.856	−16.52
C_3H_8	52.73	59.81	74.10	85.86	—	3.512	−19.48
C_6H_6	52.93	60.24	76.57	90.45	—	3.401	24.00
C_2H_5OH	56.20	62.82	75.28	85.15	—	3.39	−52.41
CO	40.25	43.86	48.77	51.78	53.99	2.073	−27.202
CO_2	43.56	47.67	54.11	58.48	61.85	2.238	−93.969
HBr	40.53	44.12	48.99	51.95	54.13	2.067	−8.1
HCl	37.72	41.31	46.16	49.08	51.23	2.065	−22.019
H_2O	37.17	41.29	47.01	50.60	53.32	2.368	−57.107
NH_3	37.99	42.28	48.63	53.03	56.56	2.37	−9.37
NO	42.98	46.76	51.86	54.96	57.24	2.194	21.48
SO_2	50.82	55.38	62.28	66.82	70.2	2.519	−70.36

[a] From G. N. Lewis and M. Randall, "Thermodynamics," 2nd ed. (revised by K. S. Pitzer and L. Brewer), p. 682. McGraw-Hill, New York, 1961.
[b] Of formation from the elements.

It will be seen later (Section 7-2) that ΔG^0 determines the equilibrium constant for a reaction, the equation being

$$\Delta G^0 = -RT \ln K, \tag{6-114}$$

where K is the equilibrium constant. Equation (6-112) may then be written in the form

$$\ln K = -\frac{1}{R}\left[\frac{\Delta(G^0 - H_0^0)}{T} + \frac{\Delta H_0^0}{T}\right]. \tag{6-115}$$

The ability to calculate a ΔG^0 for a reaction is equivalent to the ability to determine its equilibrium constant; hence the great importance of ΔG^0.

The following calculation will demonstrate the use of the tables. Consider the reaction

$$3H_2 + N_2 = 2NH_3. \tag{6-116}$$

We used this in Section 5-ST-2 to illustrate the calculation of $H^0 - E_0$ from partition functions. We now want to obtain ΔG^0 (and hence the equilibrium constant) at 1000°K. First, ΔH_{298}^0 is just the standard enthalpy of formation of 2 moles of ammonia. From Table 5-2 we get $\Delta H^0_{298} =$ $-2(11.04) = -22.08$ kcal, and from Tables 6-4 and 6-5 we have

$$\Delta(H^0_{298} - H^0_0) = 2(2.37) - 3(2.024) - 2.072 = -3.40 \quad \text{kcal.}$$

Then from Eq. (6-113) we have

$$\Delta H^0_0 = -22.08 - (-3.40) = -18.68 \quad \text{kcal.}$$

We next calculate $\Delta(G^0 - H^0_0)/T$ for $1000°$K using the tables:

$$\frac{\Delta(G^0 - H^0_0)}{T} = -2(48.63) - [-3(32.74) - 47.31] = 48.27 \quad \text{cal }°K^{-1}$$

or, multiplying by $T = 1000°$K, we get

$$\Delta(G^0 - H^0_0) = 48.27 \quad \text{kcal.}$$

Finally, we have

$$\Delta G^0 = 48.27 - 18.68 = 29.59 \quad \text{kcal.}$$

We can complete the calculation by obtaining the equilibrium constant. From Eq. (6-115) we have

$$\ln K = -\frac{29,590}{(1.987)(1000)} = -14.89 ,$$

$$K = 3.41 \times 10^{-7}.$$

This example could have been made yet more complete if we had carried out the evaluation of $G^0 - H^0_0$ for each substance at $1000°$K using the appropriate partition functions. Essentially the same calculation was made in Section 6-9C for N_2 at $25°$C.

GENERAL REFERENCES

BLINDER, S. M. (1969). "Advanced Physical Chemistry." Macmillan, New York.
LEWIS, G. N., AND RANDALL, M. (1961). "Thermodynamics," 2nd ed. (revised by K. S. Pitzer and L. Brewer). McGraw-Hill, New York.

CITED REFERENCES

DE KLERK, D., STEENLAND, M. J., AND GORTER, C. J. (1950). *Physica* **16**, 571.
GIAUQUE, W. F., AND BLUE, R. W. (1936). *J. Amer. Chem. Soc.* **58**, 831.
GIBBS, J. W. (1931). "Collected Works of J. Willard Gibbs." Longmans, Green, New York.
LEWIS, G. N., AND RANDALL, M. (1961). "Thermodynamics," 2nd ed. (revised by K. S. Pitzer and L. Brewer), p. 667. McGraw-Hill, New York.

Exercises

6-1 An ideal heat engine operates between $-40°C$ and $40°C$. How many joules of work does it deliver per joule of heat energy absorbed at the upper temperature?

Ans. 0.256 J.

6-2 The same machine as in Exercise 6-1 is operated as a refrigerator. How much power (in watts) must be supplied to the machine so that its low-temperature coils can maintain a cryostat bath at $-40°C$? The bath gains 100 cal sec^{-1} from its surroundings.

Ans. 144 W.

6-3 The same machine as in Exercise 6-1 is used as a heat pump. How much power must be supplied to it if its hot coils are to replace a 40,000 Btu hr^{-1} house furnace. (This is a Canadian winter with $-40°C$ outside, and the $40°C$ inside temperature will make the house rather warm!)

Ans. 3000 W.

6-4 The available cooling water for an ideal heat engine is $10°C$. What must be the upper operating temperature if the efficiency is to be 35 % (and the lower temperature $10°C$)?

Ans. 162°C.

6-5 One mole of an ideal monatomic gas is initially at STP and is put through the following alternative reversible processes. For each process, calculate w, q, ΔE, ΔH, and ΔS. (a) Isochoric cooling to $-100°C$. (b) Isothermal compression to 100 atm. (c) Isobaric heating to $100°C$. (d) Adiabatic expansion to 0.1 atm.

Ans. (a) $w = 0$, $q = -298$ cal, $\Delta E = q$, $\Delta H = -497$ cal, $\Delta S = -1.36$ cal °K^{-1} mole^{-1}.
(b) $w = q = -2500$ cal, $\Delta E = \Delta H = 0$, $\Delta S = -9.15$ cal °K^{-1} mole^{-1}.
(c) $w = 199$ cal, $q = \Delta H = 497$ cal, $\Delta E = 298$ cal, $\Delta S = 1.55$ cal °K^{-1} mole^{-1}.
(d) $w = -\Delta E = 490$ cal, $q = \Delta S = 0$, $\Delta H = -817$ cal.

6-6 Five moles of an ideal gas of $C_V = 7.50$ cal °K^{-1} mole^{-1} and initially at STP are compressed adiabatically and reversibly until the temperature rises to $500°C$. Calculate the final pressure.

Ans. 145 atm.

6-7 Two moles of an ideal monatomic gas initially at 1 atm and $25°C$ undergo an irreversible adiabatic expansion in which 200 cal of work is done. Calculate, if possible, the final state of the gas and q, ΔE, ΔH, and ΔS for the change.

Ans. $q = 0$, $T_f = 265°K$, $\Delta E = -200$ cal, $\Delta H = -330$ cal (the final volume or pressure and ΔS cannot be obtained without more knowledge of the details of the expansion).

6-8   What is the change in entropy when one mole of water freezes at 0°C?

Ans. -5.25 cal °K^{-1} mole^{-1}.

6-9   What are the changes in energy, enthalpy, and entropy when one mole of water condenses at 100°C from vapor at 1 atm to liquid water?

Ans. $\Delta H = -9.717$ kcal mole^{-1}, $\Delta E = -8.976$ kcal mole^{-1},
$\Delta S = -26.04$ cal °K^{-1} mole^{-1}.

6-10   Calculate from the data of Tables 5-4 and 6-2 the molar entropy of liquid water at 100°C and 1 atm pressure and of water vapor at 200°C and 1 atm pressure.

Ans. S^0(H$_2$O liq, 100°C) = 20.78 cal °K^{-1} mole^{-1},
S^0(H$_2$O gas, 200°C) = 48.81 cal °K^{-1} mole^{-1}.

6-11   Calculate ΔG for the isothermal expansion of one mole of water vapor at 25°C from 20 to 0.5 Torr.

Ans. -2185 cal.

6-12   Calculate the value of ΔG when one mole of water is taken from liquid at 1 atm and 100°C to vapor at 1 atm and 100°C and thence to vapor at 0.5 atm and 200°C. (Assume ideal gas behavior for the vapor.)

Ans.   (a) $\Delta G = 0$, (b) $\Delta G = -5440$ cal mole^{-1} (the process is not isothermal and so the negative sign does not imply spontaneity).

6-13   Show from Eq. (6-98) that $C_P - C_V = R$ for an ideal gas.

6-14   Calculate the coefficients of compressibility and of thermal expansion for an ideal gas.

Ans. $\beta = 1/P$, $\alpha = 1/T$.

6-15   Verify the constant -2.31 in Eq. (6-80).

6-16   Verify the constant 65.8 in Eq. (6-83).

6-17   Calculate the translation entropy and Helmholtz free energy of H$_2$O gas at 1 atm and 100°C.

Ans. $S^0 = 35.73$ cal °K^{-1} mole^{-1}, $A^0 = -12,220$ cal mole^{-1}.

6-18   Calculate the vibrational contribution to the entropy and free energy of ^{35}Cl$_2$ at 100°C; neglect the zero-point energy contribution.

Ans. $S_{vib} = 0.811$ cal °K^{-1} mole^{-1}, $A = G = -92.1$ cal.

6-19   Calculate the rotational contribution to the entropy and free energy of ^{35}Cl$_2$ at 100°C.

Ans. $S_{rot} = 15.84$ cal °K^{-1} mole^{-1}, $A = G = -5168$ cal.

Problems

6-1 A reversible heat engine operates between 20°C and an upper temperature T_2 with 25% efficiency; it produces 10,000 J per cycle. Calculate T_2, q_1, and q_2. Make a plot of S versus T for the Carnot cycle corresponding to this engine. Also calculate the performance factors for the engine operating as a refrigerator and as a heat pump.

6-2 A heat engine operates between 0°C and 1000°C and is ideal except that 20% of the work produced is dissipated by friction at 0°C. How much heat must be supplied at 1000°C if 1000 J of useful work is to be done by the machine?

6-3 A system experiences the following reversible constant-pressure process:

$$(P_1 = 1 \text{ atm}, V_1 = 3 \text{ liter}, T_1 = 400°\text{K}) \rightarrow (P_2 = 1 \text{ atm}, V_2 = 4 \text{ liter}, T_2 = 700°\text{K}).$$

The heat capacity of the system for this process is 20 cal °K^{-1}; the entropy of the system is initially 30 cal °K^{-1}. Calculate ΔE, ΔH, ΔS, ΔG, q, and w for the process.

6-4 Show that $(\partial E/\partial V)_T = 0$, for an ideal gas, using the first and second laws and related definitions.

6-5 Calculate ΔS and ΔG for the process

$$\text{one mole } H_2O \ (10°C) + \text{two moles } H_2O \ (40°C) = \text{three moles } H_2O \ (t \ °C),$$

that is, the two portions of water are mixed in an insulated vessel to give a mixture at some final temperature t determined by the temperature and amount of each of the two portions. The specific heat of water is 1.00 cal °K^{-1} g^{-1} and the molar entropy of water at 25°C is 16.75 cal °K^{-1} mole^{-1} (this is the absolute entropy).

6-6 The heat of fusion of mercury is 2.82 cal g^{-1} at its melting point of $-39°$C and the heat capacities of solid and liquid mercury are both 6.76 cal °K^{-1} mole^{-1}. Calculate ΔS and ΔG for the irreversible process

$$\text{Hg}(l, -50°C) \rightarrow \text{Hg}(s, -50°C).$$

The negative ΔS found does not mean that supercooled liquid mercury will not spontaneously freeze, because the process to which the ΔS refers is not one that could occur in an isolated system. Show that this last statement is correct and write down the process that would occur if the same supercooled liquid mercury were isolated from its surroundings and then the spontaneous process took place. Calculate ΔS for this second process (neglect mechanical work due to volume changes, assume $C_V = C_P$ and $\Delta H = \Delta E$).

6-7 Given the process

$$H_2O(s, -10°C, 1 \text{ atm}) \rightarrow H_2O(l, -10°C, 1 \text{ atm})$$

and the necessary thermal data from handbooks, (a) calculate ΔS. Note that ΔS is positive; explain whether this means that the process is spontaneous. If not, set up and calculate ΔS for the process [starting with $H_2O(s, -10°C)$] that would be spontaneous. (b) Calculate ΔG and ΔH for the first process.

6-8 Calculate ΔS, ΔH, and ΔG for the process

$$18 \text{ g ice } (0°C) + 200 \text{ g } H_2O \ (50°C) = \text{ equilibrium system at } t \ °C.$$

The process is carried out by placing the water in a Dewar flask and then dropping the ice in; it may be assumed that the flask is perfectly insulated.

6-9 Calculate ΔG for the following changes of state for one mole of an ideal monatomic gas initially at $0°C$ and 1 atm pressure: (a) volume doubled at constant pressure; (b) pressure doubled at constant volume; (c) pressure doubled at constant temperature. Assume S_{273} at 1 atm to be 26 cal $°K^{-1}$ $mole^{-1}$.

6-10 Derive the equation

$$C_V = C_P\left[1 - \mu\left(\frac{\partial P}{\partial T}\right)_V\right] - V\left(\frac{\partial P}{\partial T}\right)_V$$

from the first and second laws and related definitions (μ is the Joule–Thomson coefficient).

6-11 Derive the equation

$$\left(\frac{\partial H}{\partial T}\right)_P = \left(\frac{\partial E}{\partial T}\right)_V + \left[P + \left(\frac{\partial E}{\partial V}\right)_T\right]\left(\frac{\partial V}{\partial T}\right)_P$$

from the first and second laws and related definitions.

6-12 Suppose that for a certain gas $(\partial E/\partial V)_T = 0$ but $P(V - b) = RT$, where b is a constant. Calculate $(\partial H/\partial V)_T$ and $C_P - C_V$.

6-13 Calculate ΔG and ΔA for three moles of an ideal gas that expands irreversibly from 2 atm at 25°C to 0.1 atm at 25°. Repeat the calculation for ammonia assuming it to obey the van der Waals equation.

6-14 The principal vibrational frequencies for CO_2 are $\nu_1 = 1388.3$ cm^{-1}, $\nu_2 = 667.3$ (twice), and $\nu_3 = 2349.3$ cm^{-1}. Calculate the vibrational partition functions for CO_2 at 25°C and at 50°C and make an approximate calculation of the vibrational contribution to the heat capacity at 37°C. Compare this with the experimental value. Also calculate the percentage of the equipartitional heat capacity that is present at 37°C. Finally, calculate the vibrational contribution to the entropy of CO_2 at 25°C.

6-15 The vibrational frequency for I_2 is 214 cm^{-1}. Calculate (a) the separation of the first vibrational level from the ground state in calories per mole; (b) the vibrational contribution to the energy at 100°C; and (c) the vibrational contribution to the entropy at 100°C.

6-16 An adsorbed molecule is often thought to be confined or localized to a relatively small area around a particular active site of the adsorbent. Calculate the spacing between the $n = 1$ and $n = 2$ levels of translational energy for the case of argon molecules each confined to a two-dimensional box of 25 Å² area, assuming 0°C. Explain whether the approximation made in obtaining Eq. (4-66) should still apply.

6-17 Calculate the total entropy of HCl gas at STP assuming it to be an ideal gas and taking the fundamental vibration frequency to be 2886 cm^{-1} and the moment of inertia to be 2.72×10^{-40} g cm². That is, calculate and sum the translational, vibrational, and rotational contributions to the entropy.

Problems

6-18 Calculate the molar entropy of Kr gas at STP assuming it to be ideal and using the Sackur–Tetrode equation. Also calculate the entropy per mole of Ar adsorbed on a surface assuming that it behaves as an ideal two-dimensional gas and that its state is 0°C and a surface concentration such that the average distance apart of molecules is the same as in the three-dimensional gas at STP.

6-19 Giauque and Blue (1936) obtained the following data for hydrogen sulfide:

T (°K)	C_P (cal °K^{-1} mole^{-1})	T (°K)	C_P (cal °K^{-1} mole^{-1})
20	1.25	110	11.79
30	2.48	120	13.27
40	3.56	126.2	(^{b})
50	4.56	130	13.25
60	5.51	140	13.33
70	6.43	150	13.45
80	7.31	170	13.92
90	8.26	187.6	(^{c})
100	9.36	190	16.21
103.5	(^{a})	210	16.31
105	11.25	212.8	(^{d})

^{a} Solid-state transition with $\Delta H = 368$ cal mole^{-1}.
^{b} Solid-state transition with $\Delta H = 121$ cal mole^{-1}.
^{c} Melting point, $\Delta H = 568$ cal mole^{-1}.
^{d} Normal boiling point, $\Delta H = 4463$ cal mole^{-1}.

Below 20°K the heat capacity obeys the law $C_P = aT^3$. Calculate the absolute entropy of hydrogen sulfide at 1 atm and 212.8°K.

6-20 One mole of an ideal monatomic gas expands adiabatically and reversibly from 500°C and 10 atm to 25°C. Calculate ΔS, ΔH, ΔE, q, and w.

6-21 The same gas as in Problem 6-20 expands adiabatically and irreversibly to 1 atm doing 100 cal of work. Calculate ΔS, ΔH, ΔE, q, and w.

6-22 One mole of an ideal monatomic gas at STP expands into an evacuated flask so that its volume triples. Calculate ΔS, ΔE, ΔH, ΔG, q, and w.

6-23 A cylinder which is closed at both ends has within it a frictionless piston head. Both the piston and the walls of the cylinder are of insulating material so that no heat can pass through

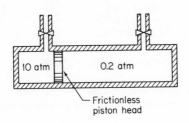

Frictionless
piston head

them. Initially the left side of the cylinder contains one mole of gas at 10 atm while the right side contains one mole of gas at 0.2 atm, as illustrated in the accompanying diagram. Both sides are initially at the same temperature, 25°C, and the gas is ideal and monatomic. The catch holding the piston in place is released and the piston moves to its equilibrium position. Calculate the final temperature and pressure on each side and ΔE, ΔH, and ΔS for the overall process.

Special Topics Problems

6-1 The general equation for $C_P - C_V$ is given by Eq. (6-100). (a) Show that the dimensions are the same on both sides of the equation. (b) Calculate $C_P - C_V$ for liquid water at 20°C. (c) Show that the equation reduces to $C_P - C_V = R$ for an ideal gas. (d) Show that $C_P - C_V = R + (2aP/RT^2) + (a^2P^2/R^3T^4)$ for a van der Waals gas. [*Note*: This equation is obtained by making certain approximations. Start with the van der Waals equation in the form $PV = RT - (a/V) + bP + (ab/V^2)$, then neglect the term ab/V^2 and approximate a/V by aP/RT.] (e) Using the van der Waals constants, calculate $C_P - C_V$ for CO_2 at 35°C and 10 atm.

6-2 Assume that a gas obeys the equation $P(V - b) = RT$. Derive an expression for the fugacity of such a gas as a function of pressure and temperature.

6-3 (Computer problem)   Assuming that water vapor obeys the van der Waals equation, calculate the activity coefficient of water vapor at 200°C from zero pressure up to the saturation vapor pressure. Activity coefficient is the ratio of fugacity to ideal gas law pressure.

6-4 (Computer problem)   Find the appropriate data in a handbook and calculate the fugacity of CO_2 as a function of pressure at 25°C up to 20 atm pressure.

6-5 Calculate ΔG^0 and the corresponding equilibrium constants at 298°K and at 1000°K for the reactions

$$3C_2H_2 = C_6H_6(g) \quad \text{and} \quad H_2 + Cl_2 = 2HCl(g).$$

6-6 Verify the value of $(G^0 - H_0^0)/T$ at 298°K for $O_2(g)$ given in Table 6-4 by evaluating the appropriate partition functions.

6-7 Calculate the degree of dissociation of $I_2(g)$ at 1000°C using data from Table 6-4 and the appropriate statistical mechanical calculation for the I atom.

6-8 (Computer problem)   Calculate S^0, $E - E_0$, and $G - E_0$ for H_2 from 80°K to 25°C at close enough intervals to allow accurate plots to be made of these two quantities against temperature. Do the same for N_2. Both gases are in their standard states of 1 atm pressure.

6-9 Calculate $\Delta S^0_{298°K}$ for the reaction $H_2 + Br_2 = 2\,HBr$.

6-10 Consider the following hypothetical attempt to approach 0°K by successive adiabatic expansions of an ideal monatomic gas. We start with 1000 moles of gas at 10^4 atm and 0°C and let it expand adiabatically to 1 atm. We then take one-third of the expanded, cold gas and compress it adiabatically to 10^4 atm; the compressed gas is then allowed to come to thermal equilibrium with the remaining two-thirds that is still cold. The 1000/3 moles of compressed, cooled gas is allowed to expand adiabatically to 1 atm. Calculate the final temperature.

6-11   Calculate K_P for reaction (6-116) at 2000°K.

6-12   Calculate K_P for $C + 2H_2 = CH_4(g)$ at 298°K, 1000°K, and 2000°K.

7 CHEMICAL EQUILIBRIUM

7-1 Introduction

Early chemists considered that different substances exhibited either empathies or antipathies towards each other. Those that reacted were thought to possess some kind of mutual affinity, and alchemical language was rich in phrases implying almost emotional attitudes on the part of various chemicals. Chemistry was then largely preparative in nature; reactions either occurred or did not occur. The concept of equilibrium gradually developed, however, with one of the first advances being made by C. L. Berthollet in 1801. Berthollet served as an advisor to Napoleon in an expedition to Egypt in 1799 and had observed that there were deposits of sodium carbonate in various salt lakes. He concluded that the usual reaction

$$Na_2CO_3 + CaCl_2 \rightarrow CaCO_3 + 2NaCl$$

could be reversed in the presence of a sufficiently high salt concentration, so that chemical affinity was more than an inherent attribute of a substance but also depended on its concentration.

Later, in the period 1850–1860, L. Wilhelmy and M. Berthelot added the important conclusion that chemical equilibrium resulted from a balance between forward and reverse reaction rates, rather than being a static condition. Their particular studies dealt with the hydrolysis of sugars and of esters, but the general conclusion was that for a reaction such as

$$A + B = M + N \tag{7-1}$$

the forward and reverse reaction rates must be equal at equilibrium. These rates were taken to be proportional to the concentrations, in what is known as the law of mass action. Thus for the preceding reaction

$$\text{forward rate} \quad = R_f = k_f(A)(B), \qquad (7\text{-}2)$$

$$\text{backward rate} = R_b = k_b(M)(N), \qquad (7\text{-}3)$$

where the parentheses denote concentrations. At equilibrium $R_f = R_b$, and on equating the respective expressions, we find

$$K = \frac{k_f}{k_b} = \frac{(M)(N)}{(A)(B)}. \qquad (7\text{-}4)$$

A more general formulation for a chemical reaction is

$$aA + bB + \cdots = mM + nN + \cdots \qquad (7\text{-}5)$$

and the corresponding equilibrium constant becomes

$$K = \frac{(M)^m(N)^n \cdots}{(A)^a(B)^b \cdots}. \qquad (7\text{-}6)$$

The constant K is known, in this context, as the *mass action equilibrium constant*.

In more modern language, the contribution of the mass action approach was in establishing that, experimentally, an equilibrium system is one in dynamic balance. The important consequence is that a small change in condition, such as that caused by the addition or removal of one of the reactants or products, shifts the position of equilibrium accordingly. The same is true for a small change in temperature or pressure. Such changes are therefore reversible ones. Since they do not occur spontaneously, by the criterion for equilibrium of Section 6-6B, the free energy of the system is at a minimum.

One of the initial difficulties was in distinguishing between amount as such and concentration. Berthollet's reaction was between a concentrated NaCl solution and the $CaCO_3$ present in limestone or as a solid. The problem was in recognizing that the equilibrium depends on the amount of sodium chloride present, since this does affect its concentration, but does not depend on the amount of limestone, since this does *not* affect the concentration of $CaCO_3$. After a period of some confusion, it was realized that the mass action formulation had to be phrased in terms of "active masses" or concentrations. Another early problem lay in understanding the role of catalysts. If a catalyst can change the rate of a reaction, might it not also change the position of equilibrium? One of the important contributions of thermodynamics to chemical equilibrium studies is the conclusion that the free energy change for a chemical reaction is determined by the states of the reactants and products and is therefore independent of path. As a consequence, the position of equilibrium cannot be affected by a catalyst; some further analysis of this point is given in the Commentary and Notes section.

Another difficulty with the mass action approach is that rates will not necessarily be given by the simple mass action law based on the overall reaction, such as Eqs. (7-2) and (7-3). As will be seen in Chapter 14, the actual rate law depends on the detailed reaction path or mechanism. Thus, the equilibrium constant written in terms of concentrations, or the mass action equilibrium constant, is not in general simply related to the separate expressions for the experimental forward and reverse reaction rates. The thermodynamic approach, however, deals only with initial and final states, so that this treatment of chemical equilibrium by-passes questions of reaction mechanism. In effect, the application of thermodynamics to chemical equilibrium separates the subject from that of chemical kinetics.

The treatment of chemical equilibrium is restricted in this chapter to reactions involving gases only, or gases and pure solid phases. The thermodynamics is quite general, however, and is applied to solution equilibria in Chapter 12 with only minor modifications in terminology.

7-2 The Thermodynamic Equilibrium Constant

The formal statement of the free energy change accompanying a chemical reaction such as that of Eq. (7-5) is

$$\Delta G = (mG_M + nG_N + \cdots) - (aG_A + bG_B + \cdots). \tag{7-7}$$

In the case of a gaseous species the molar free energy is given by Eq. (6-49), which is, in integrated form,

$$G = G^0 + RT \ln P. \tag{7-8}$$

G^0 is the molar free energy of the gas in its standard or reference state of unit pressure, ordinarily taken to be 1 atm. Equation (7-8) applies to an ideal gas; in general the fugacity f replaces P, as discussed in the Special Topics section. Equation (7-7) becomes

$$\Delta G = (mG_M{}^0 + nG_N{}^0 + \cdots) - (aG_A{}^0 + bG_B{}^0 + \cdots)$$
$$+ RT[(m \ln P_M + n \ln P_N + \cdots) - (a \ln P_A + b \ln P_B + \cdots)] \tag{7-9}$$

if we assume that only ideal gases are involved and that the process is written for some constant temperature T. Equation (7-9) reduces to

$$\Delta G = \Delta G^0 + RT \ln \frac{P_M{}^m P_N{}^n \cdots}{P_A{}^a P_B{}^b \cdots} = \Delta G^0 + RT \ln Q, \tag{7-10}$$

where ΔG^0 is the free energy change when the reaction occurs with the reactants and products in their standard states of 1 atm. The equation is a general one, in the sense that it gives the free energy change when the process occurs with pressures $\dot{P}_M$, P_N, P_A, P_B, and so on, defining some arbitrary value of Q.

The general case will not be one of chemical equilibrium, and reaction in one direction or the other will occur spontaneously so as to reduce the free energy of the system to a minimum. At this point ΔG will be zero for any small degree of reaction in either direction and the system will be in equilibrium. Equation (7-10) becomes

$$\Delta G^0 = -RT \ln K_P, \qquad (7\text{-}11)$$

where K_P is the equilibrium value of Q, and is the thermodynamic equilibrium constant for the reaction.

It should be appreciated that any set of individual pressures which combine to give the value of K_P will represent an equilibrium system. Alternatively, K_P is determined by ΔG^0, which depends only on the standard-state free energies of the reactants and products and is a constant for the system. However, ΔG^0 and hence K_P will vary with temperature, as discussed in Section 7-4. The value of ΔG^0 is a measure of the tendency of the reaction to occur. If it is large and negative, K_P is a large number, and at equilibrium the concentrations of products will be large compared to those of the reactants. Conversely, if ΔG^0 is a large positive number, K_P will be small, and the degree of reaction will be small at equilibrium. Finally, Eq. (7-11) relates equilibrium constants to the general body of thermodynamic data. Free energies for individual substances may be obtained from spectroscopic information through the methods of statistical thermodynamics so that equilibrium constants can be calculated indirectly (Section 7-8) or measured equilibrium constants can be given a thermodynamic interpretation.

The equilibrium constant for a reaction involving ideal gases may be expressed in several alternative forms. Since $P_i = (n_i/N)P$, where N and P are, respectively, the total moles present and the total pressure at equilibrium, it follows that

$$K_P = \frac{n_M{}^m n_N{}^n \cdots}{n_A{}^a n_B{}^b \cdots} \left(\frac{P}{N}\right)^{\Delta n} = K_n \left(\frac{P}{N}\right)^{\Delta n}, \qquad (7\text{-}12)$$

where Δn denotes the number of moles of products minus those of reactants. Since K_P is independent of pressure, it is evident that K_n must be a function of pressure. Therefore K_n is not a true equilibrium constant; it is useful, however, as an intermediate quantity in equilibrium constant calculations. Similarly, we have

$$K_P = \frac{x_M{}^m x_N{}^n \cdots}{x_A{}^a x_B{}^b \cdots} P^{\Delta n} = K_x P^{\Delta n}, \qquad (7\text{-}13)$$

where x denotes mole fraction; K_x, like K_n, is a function of pressure.

We may also express K_P in terms of concentration since $C = n/v = P/RT$. We obtain

$$K_P = \frac{C_M{}^m C_N{}^n \cdots}{C_A{}^a C_B{}^b \cdots} (RT)^{\Delta n} = K_C (RT)^{\Delta n}, \qquad (7\text{-}14)$$

where K_C, like K_P, is independent of pressure and is a true equilibrium constant. It is customary to specify units. Thus the units of K_P will usually be (atmosphere)$^{\Delta n}$ and those of K_C, (moles per liter)$^{\Delta n}$ (see Commentary and Notes).

It is important to remember that an equilibrium constant is written for a specific reaction. Thus we have

$$2H_2 + O_2 = 2H_2O, \qquad K_P = \frac{P_{H_2O}^2}{P_{H_2}^2 P_{O_2}} \quad (atm)^{-1}$$

$$H_2 + \tfrac{1}{2}O_2 = H_2O, \qquad K_{P'} = \frac{P_{H_2O}}{P_{H_2} P_{O_2}^{1/2}} \quad (atm)^{-1/2}.$$

Halving the scale of a reaction halves the value of ΔG^0 and makes the new equilibrium constant the square root of the original one. A related aspect is that of adding or subtracting equations. One adds or subtracts ΔG^0 values, as with other Δ quantities, but multiplies or divides the corresponding K_P's. For example,

$$(a) \qquad H_2O(g) + C(s) = CO(g) + H_2(g)$$

$$(b) \qquad H_2(g) + \tfrac{1}{2}O_2(g) = H_2O(g)$$

$$\overline{\phantom{(c) = (a) + (b) \qquad C(s) + \tfrac{1}{2}O_2(g) = CO(g)}}$$

$$(c) = (a) + (b) \qquad C(s) + \tfrac{1}{2}O_2(g) = CO(g)$$

It follows that $\Delta G_{(a)}^0 + \Delta G_{(b)}^0 = \Delta G_{(c)}^0$ and $K_{P(a)} K_{P(b)} = K_{P(c)}$.

7-3 The Determination of Experimental Equilibrium Constants

A. Experimental Procedures

Equations (7-12)–(7-14) provide alternative specifications for the quantities that must be determined for an equilibrium system. Since K_P varies with temperature, we assume that the temperature has a known, specified value. Several types of experimental approaches are used. A direct one is simply to analyze an equilibrium mixture for its constituents. It is necessary, of course, that the equilibrium not shift during the process of analysis, which means that the reaction must be slow. This will be the case if the equilibrium is being studied at some high temperature and samples of the equilibrium mixture are cooled suddenly, or "quenched." The effect is to freeze the system at its equilibrium composition, so that analyses may be made at leisure. Alternatively, if a catalyst is used to hasten equilibration, then removal of the catalyst makes chemical analysis possible. As an example, the reaction

$$H_2 + I_2 = 2HI \qquad (7\text{-}15)$$

is rapid at high temperatures or in the presence of a catalyst such as platinum metal. A sample of the mixed gases, cooled rapidly to room temperature and away from the catalyst, is now just a mixture of nonreacting species. The I_2 and HI can be absorbed in aqueous alkali and analyzed and the hydrogen gas determined by gas analysis methods.

The overall composition of an equilibrium mixture is usually known from the amounts of material mixed. In the example here if the initial mixture consists of certain definite amounts of hydrogen and iodine, then analysis of the hydrogen in the equilibrium mixture suffices. The amount of hydrogen lost indicates the number of moles of HI produced and the amount of I_2 reacted and hence the number of moles of I_2 remaining. Equation (7-12) then gives K_P if the total pressure of the equilibrium mixture is known.

It is often possible to determine the equilibrium composition without disturbing the system. For example, the concentration of the various species may be found from some characteristic physical property. Thus I_2 vapor has a distinctive absorption spectrum and measurement of the optical density of an equilibrium mixture at a suitable wave length gives the I_2 concentration directly. Such a measurement, in combination with the initial composition, allows calculation of the concentrations of H_2 and of HI, and hence of K_C. The equilibrium

$$N_2O_4 = 2NO_2 \tag{7-16}$$

can be followed by magnetic susceptibility measurements. Nitrogen dioxide is paramagnetic, while N_2O_4 is diamagnetic.

Methods such as the preceding are specifically tailored to the individual system; they have in common that the amounts or concentrations of specific species are determined. The degree of reaction may also be found from the P–v–T properties of the equilibrium mixture provided that Δn is not zero. Thus the density of an equilibrium mixture gives its average molecular weight:

$$M_{\mathrm{av}} = \frac{\rho RT}{P}. \tag{7-17}$$

In the case of Eq. (7-16), we have

$$M_{\mathrm{av}} = 46x_{NO_2} + 92x_{N_2O_4} = 92 - 46x_{NO_2} \tag{7-18}$$

and so a determination of M_{av} gives x_{NO_2} and $x_{N_2O_4}$. Substitution into Eq. (7-13) gives K_P. This approach would not work for reaction (7-15); since $\Delta n = 0$ the average molecular weight does not change during the course of the reaction.

B. Effect of an Inert Gas on Equilibrium

It might be supposed that, by definition, an inert gas should have no effect on an equilibrium. This is true in the sense that the presence of the inert gas does not affect K_P. Further, if one has an equilibrium mixture contained in a vessel at a given P and T, then introduction of an inert gas in no way affects the equilibrium composition (assuming ideal gas behavior). This is the intuitive expectation and it may also be shown to follow from Eq. (7-12). Addition of the inert gas increases both P and N but their ratio remains constant, and hence *so does* K_n. The numbers of moles of reactants and products remain the same.

If, however, inert gas is added, keeping the pressure constant, then N increases but not P. Therefore K_n must increase if Δn is positive and decrease if Δn is negative. In other words, if the number of moles increases with the degree of reaction, then the equilibrium must be shifted toward more reaction on dilution with the inert gas. Thus the degree of a reaction such as (7-16) should increase on dilution with an inert gas at constant pressure. Conversely, the degree of a reaction such as the following should decrease on such dilution:

$$3H_2 + N_2 = 2NH_3 . \tag{7-19}$$

The effect of adding an inert gas at constant pressure is to increase the volume of the system and the results are just the same as if the equilibrium mixture were expanded into the larger volume. With no inert gas now present the total pressure decreases, and by Eq. (7-13), the mole fractions of products must increase if Δn is positive and decrease if Δn is negative.

C. Some Sample Calculations

The algebraic techniques for obtaining an equilibrium constant from experimental data generally require use of the stoichiometry of the reaction. In the experience of this writer, a good approach is to set up statements for the various mole numbers and first to evaluate K_n. Where intensive quantities such as density are given it may be useful to assume a certain amount of equilibrium mixture; the assumption should later cancel out. Also, a convention that is very helpful is to express by $n°$ the amount of a species that would be present were the mixture entirely unreacted.

As one series of illustrations based on reaction (7-16) suppose that 9.2 g of NO_2 is introduced into a 36-liter flask at 25°C. The total equilibrium number of moles is found to be 0.147. Thus $n°_{NO_2} = 9.2/46 = 0.2$ and $N = 0.147$. The equilibrium pressure must then be $P = (0.147)(0.082)(298)/(36) = 0.1$ atm. We have the material and mole balance statements

$$0.2 = n_{NO_2} + 2n_{N_2O_4} , \qquad 0.147 = n_{NO_2} + n_{N_2O_4} ,$$

from which $n_{N_2O_4} = 0.053$ and $n_{NO_2} = 0.094$. Then we have

$$K_P = K_n \frac{P}{N} = \frac{(0.094)^2}{0.053} \frac{0.1}{0.147} = 0.113 \quad \text{atm.} \tag{7-20}$$

The same equilibrium mixture might alternatively be described as one consisting of 9.2 g of NO_2 introduced into a 36-liter flask at 25°C and giving an equilibrium pressure of 0.1 atm. One then calculates that $N = 0.147$ and proceeds as before. Yet another description would be that the equilibrium mixture at 25°C is found to have a density of 0.255 g liter^{-1} and an equilibrium pressure of 0.1 atm. In this case the average molecular weight is calculated from Eq. (7-17): $M_{av} = (0.255)(0.082)(298)/(0.1) = 62.3$. We *assume* that there is a total of one mole in the equilibrium mixture, so that

$$62.3 = 46n_{NO_2} + 92n_{N_2O_4} \quad \text{or} \quad 1.35 = n_{NO_2} + 2n_{N_2O_4}$$

and

$$1 = n_{NO_2} + n_{N_2O_4}.$$

On solving these equations simultaneously, we obtain $n_{N_2O_4} = 0.35$ and $n_{NO_2} = 0.65$; then

$$K_P = \frac{(0.65)^2}{0.35}\frac{0.1}{1} = 0.11 \quad \text{atm.}$$

The total number of moles N could have been left as an unknown and would have canceled out in the calculation of K_P.

Reactions such as Eq. (7-16), in which a single species dissociates into products, are often characterized by a degree of dissociation α. We write

$$n_{N_2O_4} = n^\circ_{N_2O_4}(1 - \alpha), \quad n_{NO_2} = n^\circ_{N_2O_4}(2\alpha), \quad N = n^\circ_{N_2O_4}(1 + \alpha).$$

The equilibrium-constant expression is

$$K_P = \frac{4n^\circ_{N_2O_4}\alpha^2}{n^\circ_{N_2O_4}(1 - \alpha)}\frac{P}{n^\circ_{N_2O_4}(1 + \alpha)} = \frac{4\alpha^2}{1 - \alpha^2}P = 0.11 \quad \text{atm.} \qquad (7\text{-}21)$$

For this example, since $P = 0.1$ atm, $\alpha = 0.46$. If the equilibrium pressure were 1 atm, then α would be 0.165. As expected from the preceding discussion, an increase in pressure shifts the equilibrium to the left.

Suppose, finally, that we take the original equilibrium mixture, with $P = 0.1$ atm, and add inert gas at contant pressure until the volume is 50 liters instead of the original 36 liters. The various statements of mole numbers become

$$n_{NO_2} = n_{NO_2}, \quad n_{N_2O_4} = n^\circ_{N_2O_4} - \tfrac{1}{2}n_{NO_2} = 0.1 - \tfrac{1}{2}n_{NO_2},$$

$$n_g = n_g(\text{inert gas}), \quad N = n_g + 0.1 + \tfrac{1}{2}n_{NO_2}.$$

The total number of moles N is also given by the ideal gas law, $N = (0.1)(50)/(0.082)(298) = 0.205$. Substitution into Eq. (7-12) gives

$$K_P = 0.11 = \frac{n^2_{NO_2}}{0.1 - \tfrac{1}{2}n_{NO_2}}\frac{0.1}{0.205}.$$

On solving for n_{NO_2}, we obtain 0.104, or $\alpha = (0.104)/(2)(0.1) = 0.52$. Thus the degree of dissociation has increased from 0.46 to 0.52 on dilution with the inert gas.

A second illustration can be based on reaction (7-19). A mixture of hydrogen and nitrogen in a 3:1 mole ratio is passed over a catalyst at 400°C. $K_P = 0.00164 \text{ atm}^{-2}$. What should the total pressure be if the mole fraction of ammonia in the equilibrium mixture is to be 10%? Again it is convenient to set up a table of mole quantities, letting y denote the number of moles of ammonia present in a sample of equilibrium mixture which consists initially of three moles of hydrogen and one of nitrogen:

$$n_{NH_3} = y, \qquad n_{H_2} = 3 - \tfrac{3}{2}y, \qquad n_{N_2} = 1 - \tfrac{1}{2}y, \qquad N = 4 - y,$$

where n_{H_2} and n_{N_2} are given by the stoichiometry of the reaction. We want y/N to be 0.1, or $y/(4 - y) = 0.1$, whence $y = 4/11$ and $N = 40/11$ moles; n_{H_2} is then 27/11 and $n_{N_2} = 9/11$. Inserting these values into Eq. (7-12) gives

$$0.00164 = \frac{(4/11)^2}{(27/11)^3(9/11)} \frac{(40/11)^2}{P^2}.$$

Recall that $\Delta n = -2$ in this case; note also that the denominators for the various mole numbers cancel out. The result obtained when we solve for P is thus independent of the original choice of amount of reaction mixture.

As a final example, consider the reaction

$$PCl_5(g) = PCl_3(g) + Cl_2(g). \tag{7-22}$$

An equilibrium mixture consists of 1 mole of each species, in volume V and at temperature T. Three and one-third moles of Cl_2 are now added, keeping P and T constant. Calculate the number of moles of Cl_2 present when equilibrium is reestablished and the ratio of the new to the original total volume. For the original mixture

$$K_P = \frac{(1)(1)}{1}\frac{P}{3} = \frac{P}{3}.$$

We let y equal the number of moles of PCl_3 in the new equilibrium mixture, so that $1 - y$ gives the PCl_3 lost as a result of the shift in equilibrium to the left. The table of mole quantities is

$$n_{PCl_3} = y, \qquad n_{PCl_5} = 1 + (1 - y) = 2 - y,$$

$$n_{Cl_2} = 1 + 3\tfrac{1}{3} - (1 - y) = 3\tfrac{1}{3} + y, \qquad N = 5\tfrac{1}{3} + y.$$

We then have

$$K_P = \frac{P}{3} = \frac{y(3\tfrac{1}{3} + y)}{2 - y}\frac{P}{5\tfrac{1}{3} + y}.$$

The pressure cancels out, and on solving for y we obtain $y = \frac{2}{3}$. The total number of moles present is then $5\frac{1}{3} + \frac{2}{3} = 6$, as compared to the original three moles. Since the pressure has remained constant, the volume must have doubled. Had no reaction occurred, the added Cl_2 would have increased the total number of moles to $3 + 3\frac{1}{3} = 6\frac{1}{3}$.

7-4   The Variation of K_P with Temperature

One of the valuable features of Eq. (7-11) is that it permits a thermodynamic treatment of the variation of K_P with temperature. According to Eq. (6-45),

$$\left(\frac{\partial G}{\partial T}\right)_P = -S.$$

If this result is applied to each term in Eq. (7-7), we get

$$\left[\frac{\partial(\Delta G)}{\partial T}\right]_P = -\Delta S. \tag{7-23}$$

Equation (7-23) holds for ΔG^0 as well, so we have

$$\left[\frac{\partial(\Delta G^0)}{\partial T}\right]_P = -\Delta S^0. \tag{7-24}$$

We can thus obtain the standard entropy change for a reaction from the temperature coefficient of ΔG^0.

Alternatively, we have

$$\left[\frac{\partial(G/T)}{\partial T}\right]_P = -\frac{1}{T^2}G + \frac{1}{T}\left(\frac{\partial G}{\partial T}\right)_P = -\frac{1}{T^2}(G + TS). \tag{7-25}$$

By definition, $G = H - TS$, so Eq. (7-25) becomes

$$\left[\frac{\partial(G/T)}{\partial T}\right]_P = -\frac{H}{T^2}. \tag{7-26}$$

Since a chemical reaction is written with each substance at the same temperature, Eq. (7-26) can be applied to Eq. (7-7) term by term to give

$$\left[\frac{\partial(\Delta G/T)}{\partial T}\right]_P = -\frac{\Delta H}{T^2} \tag{7-27}$$

and also

$$\left[\frac{\partial(\Delta G^0/T)}{\partial T}\right]_P = -\frac{\Delta H^0}{T^2}. \tag{7-28}$$

263

Substituting the expression for ΔG^0 from Eq. (7-11) gives

$$\frac{d(\ln K_P)}{dT} = \frac{\Delta H^0}{RT^2}. \tag{7-29}$$

The restriction of constant pressure is not required for ideal gases. Equation (7-28) is usually called the *van't Hoff equation*, after a famous Dutch physical chemist. Since $dT/T^2 = -d(1/T)$, an alternative form is

$$\frac{d(\ln K_P)}{d(1/T)} = -\frac{\Delta H^0}{R}. \tag{7-30}$$

Equation (7-29) provides some immediate qualitative information. If ΔH^0 is negative, so that the reaction is exothermic, then K_P decreases with increasing temperature. Conversely, a positive ΔH^0 means that K_P increases with increasing temperature. More quantitatively, Eq. (7-30) indicates that a plot of $\ln K_P$ versus $1/T$ should be a straight line of slope equal to $-\Delta H^0/R$. Integration of Eq. (7-30) gives

$$\ln K_P = I - \frac{\Delta H^0}{RT}, \tag{7-31}$$

where I is an integration constant, or if carried out between limits,

$$\ln \frac{K_{P,T_2}}{K_{P,T_1}} = \frac{\Delta H^0}{R} \left(\frac{1}{T_1} - \frac{1}{T_2} \right). \tag{7-32}$$

By way of illustration, some data from Holland (1913) on the equilibrium for the dissociation of PCl_5, Eq. (7-22), are summarized in Table 7-1 and plotted according to Eq. (7-31) in Fig. 7-1. From the plot, $K_P = 10$ atm at $1/T = 1.73 \times 10^{-3}$ and

Table 7-1. *The $PCl_5 = PCl_3 + Cl_2$ Equilibrium[a]*

T (°K)	α	K_P (atm)
439	0.124	0.0269
443	0.196	0.0329
462	0.244	0.0633
485	0.431	0.245
534	0.745	1.99
556	0.857	4.96
574	0.916	9.35
613	0.975	40.4

[a] Adapted from E. A. Moelwyn-Hughes, "Physical Chemistry," 2nd revised ed., p. 998. Pergamon, Oxford, 1961.

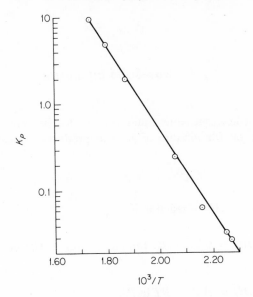

Fig. 7-1. *Variation with temperature of K_P for the equilibrium $PCl_5 = PCl_3 + Cl_2$ (data from Table 7-1).*

0.1 atm at $1/T = 2.15 \times 10^{-3}$ and the slope is therefore $(\log 10 - \log 0.1)/(2.15 - 1.73)(10^{-3}) = 4.76 \times 10^3$. Then

$$\Delta H^0 = (2.303)(1.987)(4.76 \times 10^3) = 21,800 \quad \text{cal.}$$

The foregoing integration assumed that ΔH^0 was itself independent of temperature. As discussed in Section 5-6, this is not strictly correct, since $\Delta C_P{}^0$ will not in general be zero. Equation (5-29) may be written in the form

$$\Delta H_T{}^0 = B + aT + bT^2 - \frac{c}{T}, \tag{7-33}$$

where B is a constant of integration. The constant B is not accurately equal to $\Delta H_0{}^0$, however, since the expression used for $\Delta C_P{}^0$ is not valid at very low temperatures. The formal integration of Eq. (7-30) then gives

$$\ln K_P = -\frac{B}{RT} + \frac{\Delta a}{R} \ln T + \frac{\Delta b}{R} T + \frac{\Delta c}{2R} \frac{1}{T^2} + I. \tag{7-34}$$

In order to use Eq. (7-34), we must know ΔH^0 at some one temperature so as to determine B, and K_P at some one temperature so as to evaluate the integration constant I. In addition, of course, the coefficients Δa, Δb, and Δc for the temperature dependence of the heat capacity of reaction are needed. The application is tedious, although straightforward. A more elaborate but ultimately more convenient approach was described in Section 6-ST-3.

7-5 Gas–Solid Equilibria

A special case of heterogeneous equilibrium is that between a pure solid phase (or phases) and a gas (or mixture of gaseous products). Consider, for example, the reaction

$$CaCO_3(s) = CaO(s) + CO_2(g). \qquad (7\text{-}35)$$

The expression for the ΔG of reaction is

$$\Delta G = G^0_{CO_2} + RT \ln P_{CO_2} + G^0_{CaO} - G^0_{CaCO_3} \qquad (7\text{-}36)$$

or

$$\Delta G = \Delta G^0 + RT \ln P_{CO_2}. \qquad (7\text{-}37)$$

At equilibrium $\Delta G = 0$ and

$$\Delta G^0 = -RT \ln P_{CO_2}. \qquad (7\text{-}38)$$

The equilibrium constant for the reaction is simply $K_P = P_{CO_2}$. However $-RT \ln K_P = \Delta G^0$, which involves the standard free energies of all three substances. The point is that unless CO_2 is in equilibrium with both $CaCO_3(s)$ and $CaO(s)$, its pressure will not correspond to K_P. With only one gaseous species present there is an all-or-nothing aspect to the equilibrium. If $CaO(s)$ is exposed to a pressure of CO_2 less than the K_P value, no $CaCO_3(s)$ forms at all. If the pressure is increased to the equilibrium value, then further addition of CO_2 results in conversion of $CaO(s)$ to $CaCO_3(s)$, the pressure remaining constant. Once the conversion is complete, the CO_2 pressure may increase again. The situation is illustrated graphically in Fig. 7-2(a), which shows the phases present for systems of various overall compositions and pressures. The system might, for example, be contained in a piston and cylinder arrangement at constant temperature. For system compositions lying between CaO and $CaCO_3$ if P is greater than K_P, then no gas phase is present at all but just a mixture of the two solids.

The corresponding temperature–composition diagram is shown schematically in Fig. 7-2(b), for a system under 1 atm pressure. The equilibrium pressure K_P is 1 atm at T_0. Below this temperature a system of overall composition x_1 consists of just CO_2 and $CaCO_3$. When heated to T_0, the $CaCO_3$ decomposes to give more CO_2, plus CaO, and above T_0 only the last two phases are present. A system of overall composition x_2 initially consists of $CaCO_3$ and CaO; again the former dissociates at T_0, and above T_0 only CO_2 and CaO are present. Diagrams of this

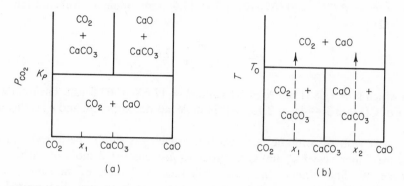

Fig. 7-2. *The system CO_2–CaO. (a) Pressure versus composition. (b) Temperature versus composition.*

type thus have the aspect of a phase map. They are discussed further in Chapter 8 (on liquids) and in a more formal way, in Chapter 11 (on the phase rule).

As another example of solid–gas equilibrium, K_P for the reaction

$$NH_4HS(s) = NH_3(g) + H_2S(g) \tag{7-39}$$

is

$$K_P = P_{NH_3}P_{H_2S} . \tag{7-40}$$

As in the preceding case, solid NH_4HS must be present in order for the ammonia and hydrogen sulfide pressures to be equilibrium pressures. One may also phrase K_P in terms of the total dissociation pressure above $NH_4HS(s)$. Since NH_3 and H_2S are formed in equal amounts, the pressure of each is half of the total pressure, so we have

$$K_P = \tfrac{1}{4}P^2. \tag{7-41}$$

A third example will serve to illustrate an important point in stoichiometry. For the decomposition of methane $K_P = 23$ atm at 800°C:

$$CH_4(g) = C(s) + 2H_2(g), \qquad K_P = \frac{P_{H_2}^2}{P_{CH_4}} = 23. \tag{7-42}$$

Suppose that we initially have 3 mole of CH_4 in a 5-liter vessel at 800°C and wish to calculate the number of moles of each species at equilibrium. Let y be the number of moles of H_2 present. Then we have

$$n_{H_2} = y, \qquad n_{CH_4} = 3 - \tfrac{1}{2}y, \qquad N = 3 + \tfrac{1}{2}y.$$

Also $P/N = RT/V = (0.082)(1073)/5 = 17.6$ atm   mole^{-1}. Substitution into Eq. (7-12) gives

$$23 = \frac{y^2}{3 - \frac{1}{2}y}\, 17.6,$$

from which $y = 1.68$. Then $N = 3.84$ and $P = 17.6N = 67.5$ atm. The number of moles of CH_4 are $3 - \frac{1}{2}y$ or 2.16, so 0.84 mole has decomposed, and n_C is therefore 0.84.

We next wish to compute how much hydrogen gas should be introduced into the same 5-liter vessel at 800°C in order to *just* convert 3 mole of carbon into methane. We first observe that there will then be 3 mole of methane, so that $P_{CH_4} = 3(17.6) = 52.8$ atm. Since the carbon is to have just disappeared, the hydrogen pressure will be the equilibrium pressure, or $P_{H_2}^2 = K_P P_{CH_4} = (23)(52.8)$, $P_{H_2} = 34.8$ atm, and $n_{H_2} = 35/17.6 = 1.98$ mole. The total number of moles of hydrogen required is then 1.98 plus the number of moles required to convert the carbon to methane, or plus an additional 6 mole, or a total of 7.98 mole. Thus the stoichiometry of the reaction must be considered as well as the equilibrium pressure.

7-6   Le Châtelier's Principle

A principle put forth by H. Le Châtelier about 1890 reads as follows: *A change in a variable that determines the state of an equilibrium system will cause a shift in the position of the equilibrium in a direction tending to counteract the effect of the change in the variable.* We can see qualitatively that this principle must hold quite generally. Were the opposite to hold, namely, that a small change in a variable would cause a shift which magnified the effect of the change, then equilibrium systems would never be stable. A small fluctuation in condition would lead to a large change, which is contrary to observation.

Specific applications of Le Châtelier's principle to gas equilibria follow. First, it was observed in Section 7-3B that if an equilibrium system is diluted or expanded, then a shift occurs such as to increase the number of moles of gas present and therefore such as to oppose the effect of the expansion. That is, owing to the shift, the change in pressure on expansion is less than it would be otherwise. The examples of Sections 7-3C and 7-5 illustrated the point that addition of a product causes a shift in the equilibrium to the left, or such as to consume some of the added species. Thus addition of Cl_2 to the PCl_5–PCl_3–Cl_2 equilibrium causes more PCl_5 to form, and the addition of hydrogen to carbon causes the formation of methane.

The effect of temperature also obeys Le Châtelier's principle. As noted in Section 7-4, if heat is evolved by the reaction, then an increase in temperature shifts the equilibrium to the left, or in the direction such as to absorb heat and thus reduce the change in temperature that a given amount of heating would otherwise produce. Conversely, if the reaction absorbs heat, addition of heat to the system shifts the equilibrium to the right.

7-7 Free Energy and Entropy of Formation

Free energies of formation are defined in the same way as were enthalpies of formation in Section 5-5, and a number of values are given in Table 7-2. The combined Tables 5-2 and 7-2 then allow a calculation of entropies of formation from the relationship

$$\Delta G_f^0 = \Delta H_f^0 - T \, \Delta S_f^0. \tag{7-43}$$

The use of ΔG_f^0 values is similar to the use of ΔH_f^0 values.

Table 7-2. *Standard Free Energies of Formation[a]*

Substance	$\Delta G^0_{f,298}$ (kcal mole^{-1})	Substance	$\Delta G^0_{f,298}$ (kcal mole^{-1})
$AgCl(s)$	-26.224	$H_2O(l)$	-56.6902
$Br_2(g)$	0.751	$H_2O(g)$	-57.6357
$C(diamond)$	0.6850	$HCl(g)$	-22.769
$C(graphite)$	(0.000)		
$CaCO_3(s)$	-269.78	$HBr(g)$	-12.72
$CaO(s)$	-144.36		
$CO(g)$	-32.8079	$HI(g)$	0.31
$CO_2(g)$	-94.2598	$KCl(s)$	-97.592
$CH_4(g)$	-12.140	$NaCl(s)$	-91.785
$C_2H_2(g)$	50.000	$NH_3(g)$	-3.976
$C_2H_4(g)$	16.282	$NO(g)$	20.719
$C_2H_6(g)$	-7.860	$NO_2(g)$	12.390
$C_3H_8(g)$	17.217	$O_3(g)$	39.06
$C_6H_6(l)$	29.756	$P(g)$	66.77
$C_2H_6(g)$	-7.860	$PCl_3(g)$	-68.42
$C_2H_5OH(l)$	-41.77	$PCl_5(g)$	-77.59
$CH_3COOH(l)$	-93.8	$S(rhombic)$	(0.000)
$CCl_4(l)$	-16.4	$S(monoclinic)$	0.023
$Fe_2O_3(s)$	-177.1	$SO_2(g)$	-71.79
Glycine, $H_2NCH_2COOH(s)$	-88.61	$SO_3(g)$	-88.52

[a] Data from F. A. Rossini *et al.*, Selected Values of Chemical Thermodynamic Quantities, Nat. Bur. Std. Circ. No. 500. U. S. Govt. Printing Office, Washington, D.C., 1959.

As an illustration, the example used in Section 5-5A on the calculation of the enthalpy of hydrogenation of ethylene may be repeated using free energies of formation. The reaction is

$$C_2H_4(g) + H_2(g) = C_2H_6(g). \tag{7-44}$$

$\Delta G^0_{298} = -7.860 - 16.282 = -24.142$ kcal. The corresponding ΔH^0_{298} was previously found to be -32.74 kcal, and by Eq. (7-43), $\Delta S^0_{298} = [(-32,740) - (-24,142)]/298.2 = -28.8$ cal $^{\circ}K^{-1}$. Also, from Eq. (7-11), log $K_P = 24,142/(2.303)(1.987)(298.2) = 17.6$, whence $K_P = 4.9 \times 10^{17}$ atm^{-1}. (See Commentary and Notes regarding the use of units at this point.)

If we ignore the complication of the $\Delta C_P{}^0$ for the reaction and assume that ΔH^0 is constant, then we may use Eq. (7-32) to obtain K_P at some other temperature, say 200°C. We have

$$\log \frac{K_{P,200°C}}{K_{P,25°C}} = -\frac{32,740}{(2.303)(1.987)} \left(\frac{1}{298.2} - \frac{1}{473.2} \right)$$

$$= -8.873$$

or $K_{P,200°C} = (4.9 \times 10^{17})(1.34 \times 10^{-9}) = 6.6 \times 10^8$ atm. As expected from Le Châtelier's principle, K_P decreases with increasing temperature.

It was noted in Section 6-CN-3 that we may obtain absolute standard entropies thermochemically, using heat capacity data close to 0°K and assuming the third law of thermodynamics. A number of values so determined were given in Table 6-2. The study of chemical equilibria interacts with such results in two ways. First, the temperature dependence of measured equilibrium constants gives experimental values for ΔS^0 of reaction. These may then be compared with the values calculated from third law entropies, and one of the major evidences of the validity of the third law is the excellent agreement that has resulted. (The other is the agreement between thermochemical and spectroscopic absolute entropies.)

The second interaction is that if ΔS^0 is found experimentally for a reaction for which absolute entropies are known for all but one species, then the absolute entropy for this additional species can be calculated. A large number of the entries in the tables of absolute entropies have been obtained in this way. Just as an illustration, the absolute entropies for $H_2(g)$ and $C_2H_4(g)$ are 31.21 and 52.45 cal $^{\circ}K^{-1}$ mole^{-1}, respectively, at 298°K. The experimental ΔS^0_{298} was found to be -28.8 cal $^{\circ}K^{-1}$ mole^{-1} for reaction (7-44); hence

$$S^0_{298}[C_2H_6(g)] = -28.6 + 31.21 + 52.45 = 54.86 \quad \text{cal } ^{\circ}K^{-1} \text{ mole}^{-1}.$$

7-8   Application of Statistical Thermodynamics to Chemical Equilibrium

The various expressions for obtaining the translational, rotational, and vibrational contributions to the enthalpy, free energy, and entropy of an ideal gas were developed in Section 6-9. Their application to the case of $N_2(g)$ at 25°C was illustrated in Section 6-9C and the statistical thermodynamic calculation of the enthalpy change for the reaction $3H_2 + N_2 = 2NH_3$ was carried out in detail in Section 5-ST-2.

An important point is that statistical thermodynamics can give the absolute entropy of a substance if the translational, rotational, and vibrational partition functions are known but cannot give the absolute energy, enthalpy, or free energy. The reason is that while the third law allows us to set the entropy equal to zero at $0°K$, we do not know the energy at $0°K$. As a result, the statistical thermodynamic calculations yield, for some temperature T, S^0, $(H^0 - E_0)$ or $(H^0 - H_0^0)$, and $(G^0 - E_0)$ or $(G^0 - H_0^0)$. The subscript zero denotes values at $0°K$, and enthalpies and free energies can only be obtained relative to E_0 or to H_0^0. The differences $H^0 - H_0^0$ and $(G^0 - H_0^0)/T$ are known as the enthalpy and free energy functions, respectively.

The consequence is that if all the partition functions are available, statistical thermodynamics can give ΔS^0 for a reaction and quantities such as $\Delta H^0 - \Delta H_0^0$ and $\Delta G^0 - \Delta H_0^0$. It is therefore necessary to have an experimental value of ΔH^0 for some one temperature; this allows ΔH_0^0 to be calculated, and hence ΔH^0 and ΔG^0, at any other temperature.

Because of their natural relationship to the statistical approach, the enthalpy and free energy functions are now often tabulated instead of free energies of formation, as in Tables 6-4 and 6-5. A further advantage is that the quantity $(G^0 - H_0^0)/T$ varies only slowly with temperature. It is therefore possible to tabulate it for rather widely spaced temperature intervals, and tables of such values allow a calculation of a ΔG^0 of reaction over a wide range of temperature without the awkwardness of Eq. (7-34). The approach using free energy functions, although valuable, is somewhat specialized, and is not emphasized here. The procedure is detailed in Section 6-ST-3. Yet another way of applying statistical thermodynamics to the formulation of equilibrium constants is given in Section 14-ST-2.

An alternative and often useful approach is as follows. We can write the standard free energy of a substance as

$$G^0 = E_0 + G_T^0, \tag{7-45}$$

that is, as the sum of its energy at absolute zero and of the free energy developed on raising the temperature to T. The free energy G_T^0 may be calculated, for example, from Eq. (6-75) or (6-76); alternatively, it may be written as a sum of contributions for translation, rotation, and vibration as given by the explicit statistical thermodynamic expressions.

We next define a quantity $\mathbf{q}$ as

$$\mathbf{q} = \exp\left(-\frac{G_T^0}{RT}\right). \tag{7-46}$$

Equation (7-11) may be written as

$$K = \exp\left(-\frac{\Delta G^0}{RT}\right) \tag{7-47}$$

and on using Eqs. (7-45) and (7-46), we obtain

$$K = K_{\mathbf{q}} \exp\left(-\frac{\Delta E_0}{RT}\right), \tag{7-48}$$

where K_q is the product and quotient of the **q**'s for the reaction products and reactants; thus for a reaction $A + B = C$, $K_q = q_C/q_A q_B$. We can think of **q** as a statistical thermodynamic concentration (sometimes called the rational activity—see Section 9-CN-3).

If the species are all ideal gases, then the expression for **q** becomes rather simple. Thus combination of Eqs. (4-68) and (6-76) gives

$$q_{trans} = \left(\frac{2\pi m k T}{h^2}\right)^{3/2} \frac{1}{N_0}, \qquad (7\text{-}49)$$

provided the standard state is taken to be 1 molecule cm^{-3}. Equation (6-85) yields

$$q_{rot} = \frac{8\pi^2 I k T}{h^2} = \frac{T}{\sigma \theta_{rot}} \qquad (7\text{-}50)$$

for a linear molecule and

$$q_{rot} = \frac{\pi^{1/2}}{\sigma} \left[\frac{8\pi^2 (I_x I_y I_z)^{1/3} kT}{h^2}\right]^{3/2} \qquad (7\text{-}51)$$

for a nonlinear molecule, where I_x, I_y, and I_z are the three principal moments of inertia and σ is a degeneracy factor defined as the number of equivalent ways of orienting the molecule in space. Thus $\sigma_{H_2} = 2$, $\sigma_{HI} = 1$, $\sigma_{H_2O} = 2$, $\sigma_{NH_3} = 3$, and $\sigma_{benzene} = 12$.

Finally, Eq. (6-87) gives

$$q_{vib} = \prod \left[1 - \exp\left(-\frac{\theta_{vib}}{T}\right)\right]^{-1}, \qquad (7\text{-}52)$$

where the product is over all vibrational modes. The total **q** is then the product $q_{trans} q_{rot} q_{vib}$.

If K is known for a gaseous equilibrium at some one temperature, a calculation of ΔE_0 is in principle possible from spectroscopic values of θ_{rot} and θ_{vib}. One may then calculate K for any other temperature.

COMMENTARY AND NOTES

7-CN-1   Chemical Equilibrium and the Second Law of Thermodynamics

Equations (7-29) and (7-30) constitute one of the major triumphs of the second law of thermodynamics. The connection between the temperature dependence of an equilibrium constant and the enthalpy change of a reaction is not otherwise deducible and provides a means for obtaining a calorimetric quantity, ΔH^0, from equilibrium constant data, that involves only measurements of equilibrium con-

Table 7-3. *Comparison of Calculated and Calorimetric Heats of Reaction*[a]

		ΔE^0 (kcal)	
Reaction	$K_{P,298}$	Calculated	Calorimetric
$2HCl = H_2 + Cl_2$	5.50×10^{-34}	43.96	44.0
$2HBr = H_2 + Br_2$	1.05×10^{-19}	24.38	24.2
$2HI = H_2 + I_2$	5.01×10^{-4}	2.95	2.94

[a] Adapted from E. A. Moelwyn-Hughes, "Physical Chemistry," 2nd revised ed., p. 994. Pergamon, Oxford, 1961.

centrations. The equations provide a means for verifying the second law, since the ΔH^0 of a reaction obtained using them should be the same as the directly determined calorimetric value. A number of such checks have been made, and three examples are given in Table 7-3. Since $\Delta n = 0$ for the reactions in question, $\Delta H^0 = \Delta E^0$. It is quite likely that the calculated ΔE^0 values are more accurate than the directly measured ones, but the two agree within experimental error.

Another application of the second law yields the conclusion that a catalyst cannot affect the equilibrium constant for a reaction. Consider the situation illustrated in Fig. 7-3. A reaction A + B to give products M + N ordinarily

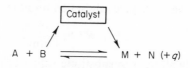

Fig. 7-3.

proceeds by some direct path. Alternatively, it may occur with the aid of a catalyst. Thus the reaction $H_2 + I_2 = 2HI$ is a direct reaction, but it may also be catalyzed by platinum metal. Suppose that, as indicated in the figure, the catalyst affects only the forward reaction. In its presence, the sum of the forward rates would clearly be larger than otherwise, while the backward rate would be unchanged. The position of equilibrium would therefore shift to the right, by the law of mass action. If we suppose further that the reaction produces heat q when it occurs, then a violation of the second law would be possible. We first allow equilibrium to be reached without the catalyst (Pt, in the case of the formation of HI), and then add the catalyst, and heat δq is produced as the equilibrium is shifted. This heat is used to run a machine, and thus do work, cooling the system back to its original temperature in the process. We then remove the catalyst and the equilibrium shifts back. Heat δq is now extracted from the surroundings, which must warm the system back to the ambient temperature. A cycle has therefore been completed for which the net effect has been the isothermal conversion of heat energy into work, and a perpetual motion machine of the second kind has been found.

We conclude that the supposed situation is impossible and that the catalyst must accelerate the forward and backward reactions equally. A catalyst is simply a chemical intermediate that is regenerated and hence not consumed in the reaction; it is in this respect no different from any reaction intermediate through which the reaction can proceed. We also conclude that for any reaction path the forward and backward rates must be the same at equilibrium. Further, if a reaction can occur by two or more different paths, catalyzed or not, at equilibrium the molecular traffic must be balanced for each path separately. This general conclusion is known as the *principle of microscopic reversibility*. It will be of use in Chapter 14 (on chemical kinetics).

A minor point has to do with the use of unit designations for equilibrium constants. It was mentioned in Section 7-2 that K_P is usually given in atmosphere units and K_C in moles per liter units. Equation (7-11) relates $\ln K_P$ to ΔG^0, and there appears to be a difficulty since it is mathematical nonsense to take the logarithm of a quantity having dimensions. One is, in effect, taking the base e to a power expressed in atmospheres, which is meaningless; all exponents must be dimensionless numbers. The problem traces back to Eq. (7-8), which, in turn, was obtained by integration of Eq. (6-48):

$$dG = \frac{RT}{P}\,dP.$$

The limits of integration used in obtaining Eq. (7-8) were from $P = 1$ atm and $G = G^0$ to P and G, so the more precisely stated result is

$$G_i = G_i{}^0 + RT \ln \frac{P_i}{1\ \text{atm}}.$$

Thus, while it is perfectly all right to substitute values of pressures in atmospheres in equations such as this, the values are really relative to 1 atm, and hence dimensionless. The statement of units in writing a K_P or a K_C supplies the necessary information as to the unit of pressure or of concentration to which inserted values are relative.

7-CN-2   Some Important Gas Equilibria

Every subject has its horror stories. One that deals with chemical equilibrium is that of the engineer who designed and supervised the construction of a chemical plant for the fixation of nitrogen based on the use of high temperatures to speed up the reaction. Only after unsuccessful trials was it discovered that he had neglected to calculate the equilibrium constant for his operating temperature and that the maximum thermodynamic yield was negligibly small.

As the story suggests, there are a number of important reactions where a balance must be found between rate and equilibrium considerations. The equilibrium constant for the formation of ammonia from nitrogen and hydrogen decreases with increasing temperature, while the rate of approach to equilibrium increases. Great effort has been spent in finding catalysts (usually mixtures of iron and other oxides) to increase the rate without requiring such temperatures that the equilibrium is unfavorable. There is a similar problem with the reaction $2SO_2 + O_2 = SO_3$, for which K_P is about 10^{24} at $25°C$, but only about 0.1 at $1000°C$. Again catalyts such as platinum or oxides of nitrogen are necessary.

The water gas reaction, $CO_2 + H_2 = H_2O + CO$, is better in this respect; K_P is not very temperature-dependent, being 2.0 at $1120°C$ and 3.5 at $1550°C$. The lack of dependance in this case might have been anticipated in terms of statistical mechanics. The reaction is a symmetric one since a diatomic molecule and a triatomic molecule are present as reactants and as products; the translational and rotational partition functions should be virtually the same, and the vibrational ones nearly so. As a consequence ΔS^0 for the reaction should be small, and hence also the temperature variation of K_P, by Eq. (7-24).

Another reaction of commercial importance is one of the type

$$nCO + (2n + 1)H_2 = nH_2O + C_nH_{2n+2},$$

known as the Fischer–Tropsch synthesis. This is a reaction whereby hydrocarbons may be produced from carbon monoxide and water and it is usually catalyzed by Co–ThO_2–MgO mixtures supported on finely divided clay. The reforming of hydrocarbons, whereby methane, for example, is made to react with a high-molecular-weight hydrocarbon to give one of intermediate size,

$$5CH_4 + 4C_{12}H_{26} = C_5H_{12} + 8C_6H_{14},$$

plays a major role in the petroleum industry. Catalysts may be mixtures of alumina and silica gels. Finally, hydrogenation reactions with platinum or nickel catalyst are common, both industrially and in preparative chemistry.

In all these cases it is essential to be able to compute the equilibrium constant for various conditions of pressure and temperature. The material of this chapter provides the foundation for such calculations.

SPECIAL TOPICS

7-ST-1 Effect of Pressure on Chemical Equilibria Involving Gases

There are two quite different ways in which the total pressure of a mixture of gases affects the equilibrium. The first was discussed in Section 7-3B and involves the Le Châtelier principle. The second, the subject here, involves nonideal behavior.

The material so far has been developed on the basis that gases are ideal; the assumption is a good one for low-boiling gases and pressures around 1 atm. Otherwise rather serious errors can develop.

It was shown in Section 6-ST-2 that a quantity known as the fugacity f functions as a thermodynamic pressure. By this is meant that all thermodynamic equations calling for the partial pressure P_i of an ideal gas remain exact for nonideal gases if f_i is used instead. Equation (7-8) then reads

$$G_i = G_i^0 + RT \ln f_i \tag{7-53}$$

and on carrying through the subsequent derivation, Eq. (7-11) becomes

$$\Delta G^0 = -RT \ln K_f, \tag{7-54}$$

where K_f has the same form as K_P, but with fugacities instead of partial pressures.

The fugacity is so defined that $f_i \to P_i$ as $P_i \to 0$. In the limit of low pressures, then, the exact equations using fugacities all reduce to the usual ones using pressures. The numerical evaluation of the fugacity of a gas is by means of Eq. (6-107):

$$\ln f = \ln P - \frac{1}{RT} \int_0^P \alpha \, dP,$$

where α is the difference between the ideal and the actual molar volume,

$$\alpha = \frac{RT}{P} - V.$$

The extensive tables of P–V–T data that exist for gases have also been expressed as fugacities as a function of pressure and temperature.

Recall that the law of corresponding states amounts to the observation that a plot of the compressibility factor Z against reduced pressure P/P_c for various reduced temperatures T/T_c gives a set of plots which are well-obeyed by all gases. This was illustrated in Fig. 1-11. It should not be surprising that fugacities obey the law of corresponding states fairly well. Actually, it is more convenient to introduce a further quantity, the activity coefficient γ defined by $f_i = \gamma_i P_i$. The activity coefficient is the factor by which the fugacity differs from the actual pressure of the gas. Activity coefficients also obey the law of corresponding states and Fig. 7-4 shows a chart of γ versus P_r for various T_r. It is used in much the same way as is Fig. 1-11.

The activity coefficient data of Fig. 7-4 may be used to calculate a thermodynamic

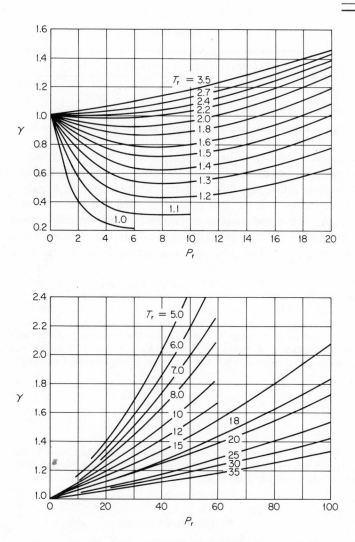

Fig. 7-4. *Activity coefficients for gases as a function of reduced pressure P_r for various reduced temperatures T_r. [From R. H. Newton, Ind. Eng. Chem., **27**, 302 (1935). Copyright 1935 by the American Chemical Society. Used by permission of the copyright owner.]*

equilibrium constant from an experimental K_P. The expression for K_f may be put in the form

$$K_f = \frac{f_M{}^m f_N{}^n \cdots}{f_A{}^a f_B{}^b \cdots} = \frac{P_M{}^m P_N{}^n \cdots}{P_A{}^a P_B{}^b \cdots} \frac{\gamma_M{}^m \gamma_N{}^n \cdots}{\gamma_A{}^a \gamma_B{}^b \cdots} = K_P K_\gamma. \qquad (7\text{-}55)$$

Table 7-4.

	P_c (atm)	P_r	T_c (°K)	T_r	γ
NH_3	112.2	5.33	405.5	1.91	0.90
N_2	33.5	18.0	126.1	6.12	1.35
H_2	12.8	46.8	33.3	23.3	1.22

The procedure is to evaluate γ for each species, calculate K_γ, and then calculate K_f. Certain approximations are tolerated at this point. First, the law of corresponding states will begin to fail at very high pressures, as the individual shapes of molecules begin to be important. Second, it is usually assumed that in a mixture of gases the fugacity of any one component is determined by the reduced pressure of that component, based on the total gas pressure. Again at high pressures this assumption will lead to some error. The procedure is adequate, however, for most purposes.

As an illustration, the observed K_P for the reaction $3H_2 + N_2 = 2NH_3$ is 0.424 at 500°C and 600 atm pressure. The various values of P_r, T_r, and γ are summarized in Table 7-4. Then $K_\gamma = (0.90)^2/(1.22)^3(1.35) = 0.404$ and therefore $K_f = (0.424)(0.404) = 0.171$. The K_f is the thermodynamic equilibrium constant and its value should be independent of pressure. Specifically, it should be about the same as K_P when K_P is evaluated at low pressure. This test succeeds approximately. For the equilibrium at 10 atm total pressure $K_P = 0.145$, or not far different from 0.171. The activity coefficient correction, while not exact, has greatly improved matters.

GENERAL REFERENCES

BLINDER, S. M. (1969). "Advanced Physical Chemistry." Macmillan, New York.
LEWIS, G. N., AND RANDALL, M. (1961). "Thermodynamics," 2nd ed. (revised by K. S. Pitzer and L. Brewer). McGraw-Hill, New York.

CITED REFERENCES

FENTON, T. M., AND GARNER, W. E. (1930). *J. Chem. Soc.* **1930**, 694.
HOLLAND, C. (1913). *Z. Elektrochem.*, **18**, 234.

Exercises

7-1   Calculate ΔG^0 and K_P at 298°K for the reaction C(graphite) $+ 2H_2 = CH_4$.

Ans. $\Delta G^0 = -12,140$ cal, $K_P = 7.78 \times 10^8$ atm^{-1}.

Exercises

7-2 Calculate ΔG^0 and K_P at 298°K for the reaction $SO_2 + \frac{1}{2}O_2 = SO_3$.

Ans. $\Delta G^0 = -16.73$ kcal, $K_P = 1.78 \times 10^{12}$ atm$^{-1/2}$.

7-3 The value of ΔG^0 is -29.82 kcal for the reaction $2CH_4 + C_2H_2 = n\text{-}C_4H_{10}$ at 25°C. Calculate the free energy of formation of n-butane at this temperature.

Ans. -4.10 kcal mole^{-1}.

7-4 Given the reaction $CO_2(g) + H_2(g) = CO(g) + H_2O(g)$, calculate K_P, K_n, and K_C if after the mixing of 1 mole of CO_2 and 1 mole of H_2, the equilibrium mixture at 0.1 atm and 25°C contains 0.16% by volume of CO.

Ans. $K_P = K_C = K_n = 1.03 \times 10^{-5}$.

7-5 A flask initially contains 1 mole of HI and then equilibrates according to the reaction $2HI = H_2 + I_2$. The equilibrium degree of this dissociation is 0.220 at 45°C and 1 atm total pressure. Calculate K_P. Calculate also the degree of dissociation if the equilibrium mixture is allowed to expand until the pressure falls to 0.1 atm.

Ans. $K_P = 0.0200$; $\alpha = 0.220$ (unchanged).

7-6 The value of K_C is 3.20×10^{-4} liter mole^{-1} at 900°C for the reaction $2SO_2 + O_2 = 2SO_3$. Calculate the value of K_P and the equilibrium composition and pressure if 2 moles of SO_3 are introduced into a 50-liter flask at 900°C.

Ans. $K_P = 3.32 \times 10^{-6}$ atm^{-1}, $n_{SO_3} = 5.00 \times 10^{-3}$, $n_{SO_2} = 2.00$, $n_{O_2} = 0.9985$; $P = 5.77$ atm.

7-7 The reaction $4HCl + O_2 = 2Cl_2 + 2H_2O$ comes to equilibrium in the presence of a suitable catalyst. A mixture initially contains 50 mole % of HCl and of O_2 and at 480°C, 75% of the HCl is converted to Cl_2 at equilibrium if the total pressure is 720 Torr. Calculate K_P.

Ans. 11.92 atm^{-1}.

7-8 K_P changes by 0.200% deg^{-1} (around 100°C) for a certain reaction. Calculate ΔH^0.

Ans. 553 cal.

7-9 For the reaction $2SO_2 + O_2 = 2SO_3$, $K_P = 1.45 \times 10^{-3}$ atm^{-1} at 800°K and 0.038 atm^{-1} at 900°K. Calculate ΔH^0.

Ans. 46.73 kcal.

7-10 Calculate K_P at 298°K and at 398°K for the reaction $SO_3 + CO = SO_2 + CO_2$. Use data from Tables 5-2 and 7-2.

Ans. 5.01×10^{32}, 4.27×10^{24}.

7-11 Verify the plot in Fig. 7-1 of the data in Table 7-1 and the calculated value of ΔH^0.

7-12 In a study of the equilibrium $3Fe(s) + 4H_2O = Fe_3O_4(s) + 4H_2$ it was found that if the partial pressure of water vapor is 10.0 Torr, then at 900°C the total pressure of the equilibrium gases is 24.2 Torr. Calculate K_P and the percentage of steam converted at 1 atm to H_2 when it is passed over iron at 900°C.

Ans. 4.066, 58.7%.

7-13 Calculate K_P at 25°C for the reaction $2C(s) + 3H_2(g) = C_2H_6(g)$. How many moles of hydrogen must be added to a 5-liter flask containing 12 mg of carbon at 25°C in order to just convert all of the carbon to C_2H_6?

Ans. $K_P = 5.78 \times 10^5$ atm^{-2}; 1.83×10^{-3} mole.

Problems

7-1 Let ρ_r be the density of an equilibrium mixture of N_2O_4 and NO_2 divided by the density that would be observed at the same temperature and pressure if the N_2O_4 were not dissociated. Derive an expression for K_P involving only ρ_r and the equilibrium total pressure P. Find the degree of dissociation α and K_P for an equilibrium mixture if P is 500 Torr at 50°C (use Table 5-2).

7-2 When 0.1 mole of Cl_2 and an excess of solid I_2 are placed in a 5-liter vessel at 300°K, the total equilibrium pressure is 0.767 atm. The vapor pressure of solid I_2 is 0.030 atm at this temperature. After this first equilibrium is established 0.1 mole of Br_2 is introduced into the vessel. It is found that the weight of the excess solid iodine present diminishes by an amount corresponding to 0.03 mole (calculated as I_2) when the new equilibrium is established. From a spectrophotometric study it is also determined that the partial pressure of Br_2 in this new equilibrium mixture is 0.2 atm. Calculate the equilibrium constants at 300°K for the three processes

$$
\begin{aligned}
Cl_2 + I_2 &= 2ICl & (K_1), \\
Cl_2 + Br_2 &= 2BrCl & (K_2), \\
Br_2 + I_2 &= 2IBr & (K_3).
\end{aligned}
$$

7-3 Determine the ratio of initial partial pressures of SO_2 and O_2 that will give the maximum yield of SO_3 in the reaction $2SO_2 + O_2 = 2SO_3$, assuming a flask of constant volume and temperature.

7-4 Solid $NaHSO_4$ is transformed on heating to $Na_2S_2O_7$. The equilibrium pressure over the salts is 2.15 Torr at 140°C and 17.84 Torr at 180°C. What amount of heat must be added to 1 mole of $NaHSO_4$ to convert it all to $Na_2S_2O_7$ at constant temperature?

7-5 Ammonium carbamate dissociates completely in the vapor phase as shown by the equation $NH_4CO_2NH_2(s) = 2NH_3(g) + CO_2(g)$, and at 25°C the dissociation pressure at equilibrium is 0.117 atm. The dissociation pressure at 25°C for the equilibrium $LiCl \cdot 3NH_3(s) = LiCl \cdot NH_3(s) + 2NH_3(g)$ is 0.168 atm.

(a) Neglecting the volume of the solid phases in comparison with the volume of the vapor phase, calculate the final total pressure when equilibrium is reached in a 24.4-liter vessel at 25°C when it initially contains 0.050 mole of $CO_2(g)$ and 0.20 mole of $LiCl \cdot 3NH_3(s)$.

(b) Calculate the number of moles of each solid phase present at equilibrium.

(c) Calculate the equilibrium total pressure at 25°C in a 24.4-liter vessel containing initially 0.050 mole $CO_2(g)$ and 0.10 mole of $LiCl \cdot 3NH_3(s)$.

7-6 At high temperatures iron and platinum are catalysts for the dissociation of gaseous ammonia to the elements. (a) Pure ammonia gas was led over an incandescent platinum wire, the remaining ammonia was removed by washing with concentrated sulfuric acid, and the gaseous mixture was then passed over an iron catalyst at 901°C and 30 atm. The outflowing gas was bubbled through 20 cm³ of hydrochloric acid. By means of a gasometer, the remaining gas was found to correspond to 2020 cm³ of dry gas (STP). (b) Pure ammonia gas was led over the same iron catalyst at 30 atm and 901°C. The outflowing gas was similarly bubbled through 20 cm³ of hydrochloric acid; the rest was 1820 cm³ of dry gas (STP). On titrating 20 cm³ of the original hydrochloric acid to pH 5.5–6.0, 18.72 cm³ of 52.3 mM KOH was consumed. After the gas had been bubbled through, the hydrochloric acid in (a) consumed 15.17 cm³ of KOH and that in (b) 15.42 cm³ of the KOH. What values do experiments (a) and (b) give for K_P?

7-7 For the reactions (a) $H_2 = 2H$, (b) $Cl_2 = 2Cl$, (c) $2HCl = H_2 + Cl_2$, the values of log K_P at 2000°K are (a) -5.509, (b) -0.245, and (c) -5.560 (pressures in atm). By successive approximations find the equilibrium pressures accurate to one or two places (that is, to about 10 %) for HCl, H_2, Cl_2, H, and Cl on heating HCl(g) to 2000°K at the total pressure of 1 atm.

7-8 A glass bulb initially contains a mixture of N_2 and NO at a total pressure of 1 atm. Some Br_2 is added such that the total pressure would have been 2.25 atm (T constant) had not the equilibrium $2NO + Br_2 = 2NOBr$ been established; as a result of the equilibrium the actual pressure after adding the bromine was 2.12 atm. A second addition of bromine was made such that the total pressure would have been 22.75 atm had no reaction at all occurred, while the actual equilibrium total pressure was 22.50 atm. Calculate K_P for the equilibrium. Nitrogen is inert.

7-9 Ammonium iodide (solid) dissociates into NH_3 and HI; in a particular experiment excess $NH_4I(s)$ is introduced into an evacuated flask and at 400°C the equilibrium pressure of the gases is 705 Torr. Eventually the HI dissociates into H_2 and I_2, its degree of dissociation being 21 % at this temperature. Calculate the final equilibrium pressure above the solid ammonium iodide.

7-10 A mixture of SO_2 and O_2 at a certain P and T is passed over a catalyst so that the equilibrium amount of SO_3 is formed. Assuming constant P and T throughout, derive mathematically the ratio of SO_2 to O_2 in the entering gas that will give the highest number of moles of SO_3 per mole of SO_2 in the effluent gas. Derive the corresponding equation for the case where a mixture of SO_2 and air (1 mole of O_2 to 4 mole of N_2) is used and show that the optimum ratio of initial number of moles of SO_2 to number of moles of air is now less than the ratio of SO_2 to O_2 in the first part of this problem.

7-11 The density of acetic acid vapor at 453.66 Torr and 110.1°C corresponds to an apparent molecular weight which is 1.520 times the simple mole weight (formula weight). The corresponding figure is 1.190 at 458.37 Torr and 155.73°C. Find ΔH^0 for the reaction $2HAc(g) = (HAc)_2(g)$ assuming the gas to contain only single and double molecules (Fenton and Garner, 1930).

7 Chemical Equilibrium

7-12 The following mechanism is proposed for the formation of ammonia (that is, for the process $3H_2 + N_2 = 2NH_3$):

1. $H_2 \rightleftharpoons H + H$;	4. $N + H_2 \rightleftharpoons NH_2$;
2. $N_2 + H \rightleftharpoons NH + N$;	5. $NH_2 + H \rightleftharpoons NH_3$.
3. $NH + H \rightleftharpoons NH_2$;	

These are all gas-phase processes. Show that the equilibrium constant derived from the mass action principle is the same as the thermodynamic one.

7-13 Given the following C_P^0 values (cal $°C^{-1}$ mole^{-1}):

$$H_2(g): \quad 6.85 + 0.00028T + 0.00000022T^2,$$
$$CH_4(g): \quad 4.38 + 0.01417T,$$
$$C(\text{graphite}): \quad 1.22 + 0.00489T - 0.00000111T^2.$$

For the reaction

$$C(\text{graphite}) + 2H_2(g) = CH_4(g)$$

($\Delta H_{298}^0 = -18{,}062$ cal, $\Delta G_{298}^0 = -11{,}994$ cal), calculate (a) ΔC_P^0, (b) the equation giving ΔH^0 as a function of temperature, (c) ΔH^0 at $873°K$, (d) the equation giving ΔG^0 as a function of temperature, and (e) ΔG^0 and K_P for the reaction at $873°K$.

7-14 For the gaseous reaction $C_2H_2 + D_2O = C_2D_2 + H_2O$, $\Delta H = 520$ cal and $K_P = 0.80$ at 25°C. How many moles of C_2D_2 are formed when 2 mole of C_2H_2 and 1 mole of D_2O are mixed at 100°C and at a total pressure of 1 atm? Assume that C_P for C_2H_2 is the same as for C_2D_2 and that the C_P values for D_2O and H_2O are the same.

7-15 For the equilibrium $2HI = H_2 + I_2$ with $K_P = 0.020$ at 184°C and $\Delta H = 3000$ cal, the following calculations are to be made on the basis of one mole of total gases. Assume that ΔH does not vary with temperature and that the heat capacities per mole are the same for the three gases. On heating of an equilibrium mixture, there would be no change in the heat capacity except for the fact that an increasing dissociation occurs with an attendant absorption of heat. The heat capacity of the mixture will therefore be, per mole, $C_P = C_P^0 + C_P'$, where C_P^0 is the constant heat capacity per mole of HI, H_2, or I_2 and C_P' is the added effect due to the increasing dissociation.
  (a) Calculate the change in equilibrium constant ΔK_P for the temperature ranges 0–1°C and 100–101°C.
  (b) Calculate the change in number of moles of H_2 or I_2 over the two temperature ranges.
  (c) What is the heat absorbed by the dissociation that occurs over the two temperature ranges, that is, C_P'?
  (d) On the basis of the results, sketch the expected variation of C_P with temperature between 0°C and 300°C.

7-16 (Computer problem) Calculate ΔG_{298}^0 for the reaction $CO_2(g) + H_2(g) = CO(g) + H_2O(g)$. Use Table 5-4 to express the temperature dependence of ΔG^0 as a polynomial in temperature and plot ΔG^0 versus T from 25°C to 1500°C. Calculate and similarly plot ΔH^0 and ΔS^0 for the reaction.

7-17 (Computer problem) The following data are reported for the reaction $SO_2 + \frac{1}{2}O_2 = SO_3$.

t (°C)	K_P (atm$^{-1/2}$)	t (°C)	K_P (atm$^{-1/2}$)
528	31.3	727	1.86
579	13.8	789	0.96
627	6.55	832	0.63
680	3.24	897	0.36

Obtain the best least squares slope for the plot of $\ln K_P$ versus $1/T$ and calculate ΔH^0 for the reaction and its standard deviation.

7-18 Calculate K_P for $CO + \frac{1}{2}O_2 = CO_2$ at 25°C from free energies of formation and find the K_q [Eq. (7-48)] from the spectroscopic constants for the molecules. Evaluate ΔE_0 for the reaction and calculate K_P at 1000°C. The rotational constant B_e is 0.3906 cm^{-1} for CO_2, where $B_e = k\theta_{rot}/hc$, and the fundamental vibrational wave numbers are $\nu_1 = 1388.3$ cm^{-1}, $\nu_2 = 667.3$ cm^{-1} (twice), and $\nu_3 = 2349.3$ cm^{-1}.

7-19 Calculate K_P for $H_2 + I_2 = 2HI$ from free energies of formation and K_q [Eq. (7-48)] from the spectroscopic constants for the molecules. Evaluate ΔE_0 and calculate K_P at 2000°C.

7-20 Calculate the statistical mechanical value of K_P for the reaction $H_2 = 2H$ at 2000°C. Assume ΔE_0 is 103.2 kcal mole^{-1}.

7-21 Derive Eq. (7-49); calculate q_{trans} for I_2 at STP.

Special Topics Problems

7-1 Calculate the fugacity of methane at 25°C and 500 atm pressure.

7-2 Calculate K_P for the reaction $3H_2 + N_2 = 2NH_3$ at 1000°C, assuming a low total pressure, then evaluate K_y if the pressure is 800 atm, and obtain the K_f for this condition.

7-3 Calculate K_f for the equilibrium $C_2H_2 + H_2 = C_2H_4$ at 300 atm total pressure at 400°C. (Obtain K_P from the appropriate tables of free energies and enthalpies of formation at 25°C, applying the necessary heat capacity corrections, or use Table 6-4.)

8 LIQUIDS AND THEIR SIMPLE PHASE EQUILIBRIA

8-1 Introduction

The study of the liquid state may be approached from several points of view. On the macroscopic level there is a body of phenomenological data dealing with the thermodynamic properties of a liquid, including surface energy and free energy, and with the equilibrium between a liquid and either its vapor or its solid. This aspect will make up the bulk of the present chapter. Still at the macroscopic level are dynamic coefficients such as those of viscosity and diffusion; some features of viscosity that are special for liquids will be mentioned, but the subject of diffusion is deferred until Chapter 10.

The molecular or microscopic treatment of liquids constitutes a rather difficult field. Some qualitative material on the structure of liquids is given in the Commentary and Notes section. The problem here is that liquids are neither so dilute that intermolecular forces can be neglected in a first approximation, as with gases, nor so highly regular in molecular structure that they can be treated in terms of a repeating lattice, as with solids. The time scale over which a measurement applies makes a difference. The vibrational frequencies of molecules are around 10^{13} sec^{-1} and properties that depend on the average behavior over intervals long compared to 10^{-13} sec tend to equate a liquid to a rather dense gas. For example, the various equations of state for nonideal gases predict the thermodynamic properties of liquids fairly well. The picture is one of molecules in random motion, although strongly experiencing each other's potential fields.

On the other hand, x-ray diffraction studies suggest a different emphasis. Although the diffraction patterns are very diffuse, they are not as diffuse as they would be if intermolecular distances were entirely random. The x-ray findings may be reported as the density, relative to the average density, of molecules at a given distance from some particular molecule. Two such results are illustrated in Fig. 8-1.

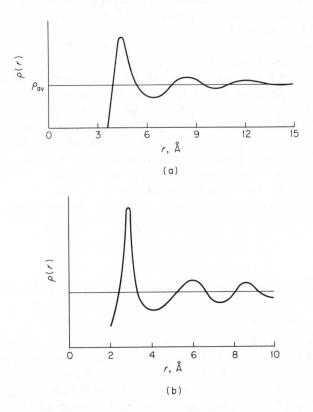

Fig. 8-1. *Radial distribution functions. (a) Liquid potassium. [From C. D. Thomas and N. S. Gingrich, J. Chem. Phys.* **6**, *412 (1938).] (b) Liquid mercury. [See C. N. J. Wagner, H. Ocken and M. L. Jashi, Z. Naturforsch.* **20a**, *325 (1965).]*

In the case of liquid potassium it is probable that a potassium atom will have a neighbor at a distance of about 4.5 Å; the probability of finding one at twice this distance is larger than for a random distribution, but beyond this the liquid appears isotropic. The result for mercury is similar, the nearest-neighbor spacing being about 3 Å. In the case of liquid water the nearest neighbors are at about 2.9 Å. The general picture of a liquid is thus one of a semicrystalline local order, with each molecule tending to have a certain number and geometry of nearest neighbors. The structure fluctuates with time, however, and is not perfectly regular. The consequence is that any regularity around a given molecule has essentially vanished by the third or fourth molecular diameter distance away.

This local crystallinity or organization is often called the liquid or *solvent cage.*

Individual molecules are regarded as vibrating within their nearest-neighbor confines somewhat as though they were in a crystal, but only for a relatively few vibrational periods. Fluctuations break the cage and establish a new one. This structural picture of a liquid becomes very important in dealings with dynamic processes—viscous flow, diffusion, and rates of chemical reaction. It will be invoked in Chapter 15 (on chemical kinetics).

The central problem of the statistical mechanics of liquids should now be evident. On the one hand, the properties to be determined are thermodynamic quantities whose values depend on average rather than transient structures. On the other hand, specific, detailed assumptions as to structure are necessary if energy states or thermodynamic probability functions are to be formulated, and any accurate picture will lead to extremely complex mathematics. The natural result is that various model structures are tried which are designed not to be too unrealistic but also with an eye on mathematical tractability. It is consequently difficult to assert that more than semiempirical agreement with experiment has resulted.

This discussion has been intended to explain why the central part of this chapter is mainly phenomenological. Much of the formal thermodynamic material is, incidentally, as applicable to solids as to liquids.

8-2 The Vapor Pressure of Liquids (and Solids)

Perhaps the most important thermodynamic leverage on the properties of either a liquid or a solid substance is that obtained through its vapor pressure. The reason is that at equilibrium the molar free energy of the condensed phase must be the same as that of the vapor phase—otherwise, by the free energy criterion for equilibrium, Eq. (6-42), spontaneous evaporation or condensation should occur. The vapor phase will generally be nearly ideal as a gas, and will be treated so here; this means that the thermodynamics of an ideal gas can be related to that of a solid or a liquid.

We can write Eq. (6-43) for each phase separately. Thus, for the gas phase we have

$$dG_g = -S_g \, dT + V_g \, dP \tag{8-1}$$

for any small change in temperature and pressure. Similarly, for the condensed phase, solid or liquid, but for the moment designated as liquid we have

$$dG_l = -S_l \, dT + V_l \, dP, \tag{8-2}$$

where P must be the vapor pressure since no other gas is present in the vapor phase. If the two phases are in equilibrium, G_g must equal G_l, and if they are to remain in equilibrium after a small change in temperature, then for this change dG_g must equal dG_l. This means that dP must so change that

$$-S_g\, dT + V_g\, dP = -S_l\, dT + V_l\, dP \qquad (8\text{-}3)$$

or

$$\frac{dP}{dT} = \frac{S_g - S_l}{V_g - V_l} = \frac{\Delta S}{\Delta V}, \qquad (8\text{-}4)$$

where ΔS and ΔV refer to the process

$$\text{liquid}(P, T) = \text{vapor}(P, T). \qquad (8\text{-}5)$$

This is a constant-temperature process and is reversible, so that $\Delta S = q/T$; it is also at constant pressure, so that $q = q_P = \Delta H$. Equation (8-4) can therefore be written

$$\frac{dP}{dT} = \frac{\Delta H}{T\,\Delta V}. \qquad (8\text{-}6)$$

Equation (8-6) is known as the *Clapeyron equation*. On looking back over the derivation, we see that it applies to any phase transition. This includes not only a solid–vapor equilibrium, but also that between two condensed phases. Equation (8-6) is thus valid for the general process:

$$\text{substance in phase } \alpha(P, T) = \text{substance in phase } \beta(P, T), \qquad (8\text{-}7)$$

where α and β may be any two coexisting phases. Of course, if α and β are both condensed phases, then no vapor is present, and the pressure is whatever mechanical pressure is established. The most important example of this situation is that of the equilibrium between a solid and a liquid discussed in Section 8-4.

Where β is a vapor phase we customarily make two approximations. The first is to neglect V_l as compared to V_g—for vapor pressures around 1 atm, the molar volume of the vapor will be a thousand times or more that of the liquid. We then further assume the vapor to be ideal and replace V_g by RT/P.[†] Equation (8-6) then becomes

$$\frac{dP^\circ}{dT} = \frac{\Delta H_v}{T(RT/P^\circ)}$$

or

$$\frac{d(\ln P^\circ)}{dT} = \frac{\Delta H_v}{RT^2}. \qquad (8\text{-}8)$$

The superscript to P is introduced to make it clear that the pressure is the equilibrium vapor pressure, and ΔH is now specifically designated as an enthalpy of

---

[†] The approximation may alternatively be thought of as writing $P(V_g - V_l) = RT$, which amounts to neglecting a/V^2 in the van der Waals equation.

vaporization. Equation (8-8) is known as the *Clausius–Clapeyron equation*. It is of sufficient importance that its behavior should be examined in detail.

Integration, assuming that ΔH_v does not vary with temperature, gives

$$\ln P^\circ = A - \frac{\Delta H_v}{RT},\tag{8-9}$$

or, if performed between the limits of T_1 and T_2,

$$\ln \frac{P_2^\circ}{P_1^\circ} = \frac{\Delta H_v}{R}\left(\frac{1}{T_1} - \frac{1}{T_2}\right).\tag{8-10}$$

Equation (8-9) leads us to expect that a plot of $\ln P^\circ$ versus $1/T$ should be a straight line. Moreover, the slope of the line should give $-\Delta H_v/R$. This expectation is fairly accurately met, provided that the equilibrium vapor density is not too high. This means that liquids should be well below the critical temperature; there is usually no problem with solids.

Liquid or solid vapor pressure is just that—the equilibrium pressure of vapor in the presence of the condensed phase. In the experimental procedure, however, one must make sure that the measured pressure does not include that of air or any other foreign gas. A simple way of doing this is by means of the *isotensiscope*, illustrated in Fig. 8-2. A sample of the liquid is vaporized to form, by condensation, a manometer of liquid in the adjacent U-tube and, in the process, to sweep out any foreign gases. One then adjusts the level of the mercury manometer outside so that the levels of the inside manometer are the same and reads the vapor pressure on the mercury manometer. One may, alternatively, bubble a known amount of inert gas through a known weight of liquid and determine the weight loss of the liquid. The exiting gas is saturated with respect to the liquid vapor, whose partial pressure is therefore P°. By Dalton's law, the ratio P°/P, where P is the atmospheric pressure, must equal the mole fraction of vapor present:

$$\frac{n_v}{n_A + n_v} = \frac{P^\circ}{P}.\tag{8-11}$$

The number of moles of inert gas n_A is known and the number of moles of liquid vaporized n_v is given by the weight loss. Thus P° can be calculated from Eq. (8-11).

Some experimental vapor pressures are plotted in Fig. 8-3(a) as a function of temperature and again in Fig. 8-3(b) in the form of a semilogarithmic graph of P° versus $1/T$. Note that Eq. (8-9) is rather well obeyed, not only for the liquids but also for the solids. The normal boiling point may be read off the graphs as well since it is, by definition, the temperature at which the vapor pressure is 1 atm.

As an illustration of the use of Eqs. (8-9) and (8-10), let us use the data for water. The normal boiling point of water is, of course, 100°C. Its vapor pressure at 80°C is 0.4672 atm. On rearrangement of Eq. (8-10), we have

$$\Delta H_v = \frac{(2.303)\,RT_2T_1\,\log(P_2^\circ/P_1^\circ)}{\Delta T},\tag{8-12}$$

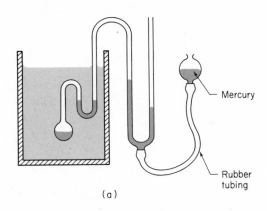

(a)

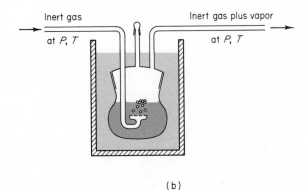

(b)

Fig. 8-2. *Vapor pressure determination. (a) The isotensiscope. (b) The evaporation method.*

where $\Delta T = T_2 - T_1$. Then, since $\log(P_2°/P_1°) = \log 2.140 = 0.3304$, we have

$$\Delta H_v = \frac{(2.303)(1.987)(373.16)(353.16)(0.3304)}{20}$$

$$= 9960 \quad \text{cal mole}^{-1}.$$

Alternatively, the plot for water in Fig. 8-3(b) is, around 100°C, a straight line for which $1/T = 2.200 \times 10^{-3}$ at $P° = 10$ atm and 3.140×10^{-3} at $P° = 0.1$ atm. The slope of the line is then

$$\text{slope} = \frac{2.303(\log 10 - \log 0.1)}{(2.200 - 3.140) 10^{-3}} = -4.900 \times 10^3.$$

By Eq. (8-9), ΔH_v is

$$\Delta H_v = -(R)(\text{slope}) = -(1.987)(-4.900 \times 10^3) = 9730 \quad \text{cal.}$$

The first result is the less precise of the two, being based on just two datum points. Even the second result suffers in precision because it involves the reading of intercepts from a graph; it is,

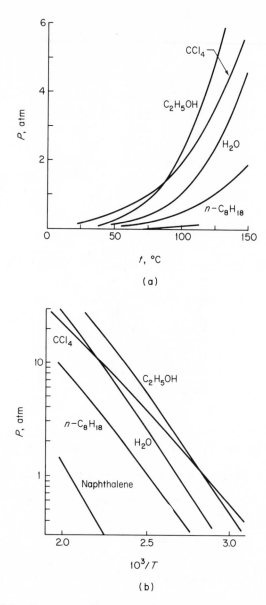

Fig. 8-3. *Temperature dependence of some liquid vapor pressures.*

however, fairly close to the value quoted in Table 8-1. The tabulated value is probably based on a least squares analysis of data around the boiling point. The example thus illustrates not only the use of the equations but also the care needed if precise results are to be obtained. For this reason good calorimetric enthalpies, being directly determined, are usually more precise and more accurate than enthalpies based on equally precise vapor pressure data.

One of the assumptions that we made in obtaining the integrated forms, Eqs. (8-9) and (8-10), was that ΔH_v does not vary with temperature. Figure 8-3(b) shows that this is a fairly good assumption but that curvature does set in at the higher pressures. Some curvature is expected at all temperatures; we know from Eq. (5-27) that $[\partial(\Delta H_v)/\partial T]_P = \Delta C_P$. For water ΔC_P is about -10 cal $°K^{-1}$ $mole^{-1}$, so at low pressures, where constancy of pressure is not an important restriction, ΔH_v for water should decrease by about 10 cal $°K^{-1}$—not a very large effect. The situation at high pressures is more serious. At the critical temperature the two phases have become the same and ΔH_v must approach zero. This decrease toward zero is not strong, however, until the vapor density is several per cent of that of the liquid or until perhaps eight-tenths of the critical temperature has been reached. This is illustrated in Fig. 8-4 for CO_2, which shows the liquid and vapor

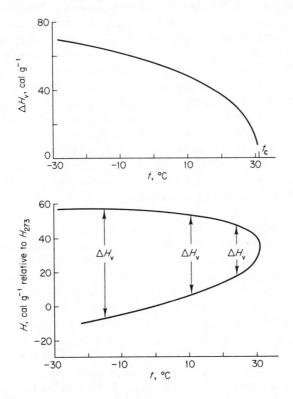

Fig. 8-4. *Liquid and vapor enthalpies for CO_2, and the heat of vaporization of CO_2 as functions of temperature.*

enthalpies (relative to that of the liquid at 0°C) as functions of temperature. The difference between the two enthalpies gives the heat of vaporization at each temperature. ΔH_v is dropping fairly rapidly even at -30°C, which is about 0.8 T_c; the vapor density at this point is about 4 % of that of liquid CO_2. For this region, then, one must go back to Eq. (8-6) in treating the data; in fact the fugacity or thermodynamic pressure of the gas should be used in place of P (see Section 6-ST-2) since gaseous CO_2 has become appreciably nonideal.

8-3 Enthalpy and Entropy of Vaporization; Trouton's Rule

The Clapeyron equation, the Clausius–Clapeyron equation, and the van't Hoff equation, which applies to chemical equilibrium (Section 7-4), belong to a family which marks one of the major achievements of thermodynamics. They all rest on the combined first and second laws of thermodynamics and have in common that the temperature dependence of an intensive quantity, vapor pressure in the present case, gives a thermochemical property, ΔH_v. That is, from vapor pressure measurements alone one is able to calculate the calorimetric heat of vaporization. In the case of the van't Hoff equation the temperature dependence of the equilibrium constant gives the ΔH^0 of reaction. The relationships are phenomenological—no model or other picture of molecular properties is needed. Except for deliberately introduced approximations, as in the Clausius–Clapeyron equation, they are as exact and as valid as the laws of thermodynamics themselves; and they can be verified by doing the calorimetry. These equations have become commonplace in physical chemistry, but we should not therefore become inured to their remarkable power. One practical consequence is that much laborious calorimetric work is made unnecessary; many thermochemical quantities are determined indirectly through these relationships.

With this preamble, let us look at some actual enthalpies of vaporization, assembled in Table 8-1, and mostly calculated from vapor pressure data. Enthalpies of vaporization are usually reported at the normal boiling point of the liquid, as in the table. This is partly a matter of convenience and of convention. Also, however, the normal boiling temperatures represent approximately corresponding states (Section 1-10); the normal boiling temperature of a liquid is often about two-thirds its critical temperature. In a related series of compounds, such as the *n*-alkanes, ΔH_v increases regularly with increasing molecular weight; otherwise, however, there is little consistency in this respect. Thus oxygen although it has a higher molecular weight than water, has a much lower enthalpy of vaporization. Iodine is heavier than most metals and yet the latter have far higher ΔH_v values. This matter is important because it bears directly on the size and nature of intermolecular forces. We have many indications that these forces are short-range. One is that the ordering in a liquid does not extend much beyond immediate neighbors, as mentioned in Section 8-1. Other indications come from surface chemistry. Figure 8-5 shows how the heat of adsorption of butane on glass falls off rapidly with increasing thickness of the adsorbed film. The strong forces that hold butane tightly to glass have nearly disappeared by the time the average thickness of the

Table 8-1.   *Enthalpies and Entropies of Vaporization and Fusion*[a]

Substance		Liquid $\leftrightharpoons$ Vapor			Solid $\leftrightharpoons$ Liquid	
	t_{nbp} (°C)	ΔH_v^0 (kcal mole⁻¹)	ΔS_v^0 (cal°K⁻¹mole⁻¹)	t_f(°C)	ΔH_f^0 (kcal mole⁻¹)	ΔS_f^0 (cal °K⁻¹ mole⁻¹)
He	−268.944	0.020	4.7	−269.7	0.005	1.5
H₂	−252.77	0.216	10.6	−259.20	0.028	2.0
N₂	−195.82	1.333	17.24	−210.01	0.172	2.72
O₂	−182.97	1.630	18.07	−218.76	0.106	1.95
CH₄	−161.49	1.955	17.51	−82.48	0.225	2.48
C₂H₆	−88.63	3.517	19.06	−183.27	0.683	7.60
HCl	−85.05	3.86	20.5	−114.2	0.476	2.99
Cl₂	−34.06	4.878	20.40	−101.0	1.531	8.89
NH₃	−33.43	5.581	23.28	−77.76	1.351	6.914
SO₂	−10.02	5.955	22.63	−75.48	1.769	8.95
n-C₄H₁₀	−0.50	5.353	19.63	−138.350	1.114	8.263
CH₃OH	64.7	8.43	24.95	−97.90	0.757	4.32
CCl₄	76.7	7.17	20.5	−22.9	0.60	2.4
C₂H₅OH	78.5	9.22	26.22	−114.6	1.200	7.57
C₆H₆	80.10	7.353	20.81	5.533	2.531	8.436
H₂O	100.00	9.7171	26.040	0.000	1.4363	5.2581
Fe(CO)₅	105	8.9	23.5	−21	3.25	12.9
CH₃COOH	118.3	5.82	14.8	16.61	2.80	9.66
Hg	356.57	13.89	22.06	−38.87	0.557	2.37
Cs	690	16.32	16.95	28.7	0.50	1.6
Zn	907	27.43	23.24	419.5	1.595	2.303
NaCl	1465	40.8	23.8	808	6.5	6.3
Pb	1750	43.0	21.3	327.4	1.22	2.03
Ag	2193	60.72	24.62	960.8	2.70	2.19
Graphite[b]	4347	170.9	—	—	—	—

[a] From F. A. Rossini *et al.*, Tables of Selected Values of Chemical Thermodynamic Quantities. Nat. Bur. Std. Circ. No. 500. U. S. Govt. Printing Office, Washington, D.C., 1959.
[b] Sublimes.

film is about one and a half molecular layers. Thus butane adsorbing on itself shows virtually no influence of the glass phase which is a few angstroms away.

The conclusion that intermolecular forces are short-range means that, to a first approximation, the vaporization process can be viewed as shown in Fig. 8-6. Figure 8-6(a) illustrates schematically an attractive potential between two molecules eventually overridden by a short-range repulsion. The maximum attractive potential ϕ_0 occurs at the equilibrium separation r_0. If in the liquid a molecule has n nearest neighbors, then, to a first approximation, its total interaction with them is $n\phi$. As illustrated in Fig. 8-6(b), the energy of vaporization should then be $n\phi/2$, the factor of two entering because ϕ is a shared energy between two molecules.

The wide variation in enthalpies and hence in energies of vaporization then implies a wide variation in ϕ between different kinds of atoms and molecules.

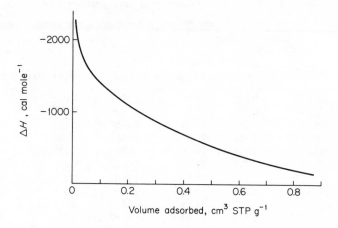

Fig. 8-5. *Heat of adsorption of butane on glass spheres as a function of fraction of a mono-layer θ. [From R. T. Davis and T. W. Dewitt, J. Amer. Chem. Soc.* **70**, *1135 (1948). Copyright 1948 by the American Chemical Society. Used by permission of the copyright owner.]*

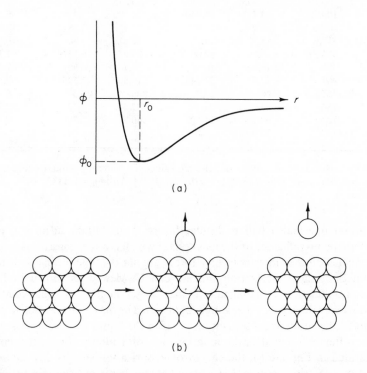

Fig. 8-6. *(a) Qualitative potential function for the interaction between two molecules having a van der Waals type of mutual attraction. (b) Schematic process for estimating energies of vaporization.*

Intermolecular forces in fact, fall into several main categories. The potential ϕ may arise from direct chemical bonding, as in diamond or graphite; it may reflect the metallic bond, as in metals; or it may result largely from direct Coulomb's law interactions, as in the alkali halide crystals. In many cases none of these types of interaction can be present, and we observe a weaker but very general attraction between molecules. These secondary forces are responsible for condensation to molecular liquids and crystals, as in the case of the rare gases, nitrogen, and the hydrocarbons. Such interactions have come to be known as *van der Waals forces* because of their representation in the *a* constant of that equation. Finally, molecules having a somewhat acidic proton, such as water and alcohols, can hydrogen-bond. Thus in ice each oxygen has four hydrogens around it, two closer and two farther away; if stretched out, a single chain of oxygens would look like this:

$$
\begin{array}{ccccc}
\text{H} & & \text{H} & & \text{H} \\
| & & | & & | \\
-\text{O}-\text{H} & -\!\!-\!\!- & \text{O}-\text{H} & - & \text{O}-\text{H}- \ . \\
| & & | & & | \\
\text{H} & & \text{H} & & \text{H}
\end{array}
$$

The actual crystal of ice has a three-dimensional network of such hydrogen bonds as shown in Fig. 8-7, and liquid water is confidently thought to have local regions of hydrogen-bonded clusters. The structure of water is discussed further in the

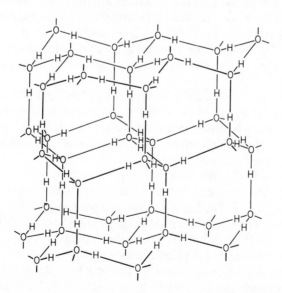

Fig. 8-7. *Hydrogen-bonded clusters in liquid water.* [*From A. Nemethy and H. A. Scheraga, J. Chem. Phys.* **36**, *3382 (1962)*.]

Commentary and Notes section and the subject of van der Waals forces is taken up in the Special Topics section. It is sufficient for the present to have emphasized the molecular significance of enthalpies of vaporization.

Returning to Table 8-1, we observe one very great regularity, namely that enthalpies of vaporization increase almost linearly with T_{nbp}. The result is that the entropy of vaporization is nearly constant. With the principal exceptions of He and H_2, the values lie between 17 and 26 cal $°K^{-1}$ mole^{-1} over a range of boiling points from $-195°C$ to over $2000°C$. A good average value for most ordinary liquids is about 21; this consistency of behavior was noted as early as 1884, in what is known as *Trouton's rule*:

$$\frac{\Delta H_v}{T_{nbp}} = 21 \quad \text{cal } °K^{-1} \text{ mole}^{-1}. \tag{8-13}$$

Trouton's rule may be rationalized on a very simple basis and one which has suggested a useful model for liquids. Most liquids are somewhat expanded in comparison to their solid phase, usually by about 10% (the exception, water, is explained as due to the partial collapse of the very open ice crystal structure on melting). This expansion provides an extra or free volume V_{free} for the molecules to move around in; it amounts to perhaps 3 cm^3 mole^{-1} for an ordinary liquid. If we assume that the liquid is merely a highly compressed gas whose effective volume, or $V - b$ term in the van der Waals equation, is about 3 cm^3 mole^{-1} and further assume that Q_{int} is the same for both vapor and liquid (that is, that the rotational and vibrational partition functions are the same), then ΔS_v is assigned entirely to the difference in translational entropy between liquid and vapor. By the Sackur–Tetrode equation, Eq. (6-78), $S_{trans} = \text{constant} + R \ln V$, so $\Delta S_{v(trans)} = R \ln(V_g/V_{free})$. The molar vapor volume for a liquid boiling around 80°C is about 30,000 cm^3 mole^{-1} and so we compute $\Delta S_{v(trans)}$ to be about $R \ln(10^4)$ or about 18 cal $°K^{-1}$ mole^{-1}.

This is too simple to be more than suggestive of an approach to the statistical thermodynamics of liquids. One of the more serious treatments assumes each molecule to be in a cell formed by its near neighbors, that is, a cage. Its potential function along a cross section might look as in Fig. 8-8(b), as compared to that for an atom in a crystalline solid, illustrated in Fig. 8-8(c). The model allows estimations of energy levels and hence of the partition function. An alternative has been to view the free volume as present in the form of actual pockets or holes, each of about molecular size. The liquid can then be treated as an intimate mixture of condensed, even crystalline, phase and rapidly moving holes. In fact, the law of the rectilinear diameter (Section 1-CN) suggests that if molecular size holes are present, the concentration of holes in the liquid is always about equal to the concentration of molecules in the equilibrium vapor. In this way the average density of the two phases remains nearly independent of temperature. The "hole" model has been useful in the treatment of rate processes, such as viscous flow and diffusion (see Special Topics section).

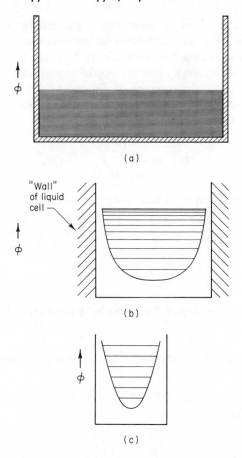

Fig. 8-8. *Potential function and corresponding energy levels for (a) a gas, with extremely closely spaced translational energy levels, (b) a liquid with each molecule in a liquid cell or cage, with closely spaced energy levels corresponding to vibrations in a relatively flat potential well, and (c) a solid with each molecule in a crystalline lattice with rather widely spaced vibrational levels corresponding to harmonic oscillation.*

To return to the data of Table 8-1, we see that water is unusual in having both a larger heat of vaporization and a larger entropy of vaporization than other liquids of similar molecular weight. We regard these differences as reflections of a relatively high degree of structure in liquid water as a result of hydrogen bonding. Hydrogen bonds have a bond energy of 5–7 kcal mole^{-1} and the breaking of such bonds on vaporization gives water a much higher heat of vaporization than would be expected were only ordinary van der Waals interactions present. (Compare, for example, water with methane.) The entropy of vaporization is high because of structure in the liquid. Structure reduces the number of ways in which a system can have energy, and hence reduces its thermodynamic probability and therefore its entropy. The entropy of liquid water is thus abnormally low, so ΔS_v is high.

Other molecules capable of hydrogen bonding generally show the same type of behavior; the Trouton constants are large for methanol and ethanol, for example. Liquid ammonia also is classified as hydrogen-bonded, as is acetic acid. In this last case, however, an unusually low entropy of vaporization is observed because the vapor contains a high percentage of dimers. In fact, it is the study of the dissociation of dimeric acetic acid vapor that provides one estimate of hydrogen bond energies. The dimer is believed to have the structure

$$H_3C-C \underset{\displaystyle O\text{---}H-O}{\overset{\displaystyle O-H\text{---}O}{<}} >C-CH_3$$

and its heat of dissociation of 14 kcal mole^{-1} gives the value of 7 kcal mole^{-1} per hydrogen bond quoted earlier. A better average value for an $O-H--O$ type of hydrogen bond would be about 5 kcal mole^{-1}, as estimated for water and various alcohols.

8-4 Liquid–Solid and Solid–Solid Equilibria. Phase Maps

It was noted that Eq. (8-6) applies to any phase equilibrium. We now apply it to the process

$$\text{solid}(\mathbf{P}, T) = \text{liquid}(\mathbf{P}, T). \tag{8-14}$$

The equation then reads

$$\frac{d\mathbf{P}}{dT} = \frac{\Delta H_f}{T_f \Delta V_f}, \tag{8-15}$$

where, in the absence of an equilibrium vapor phase, $\mathbf{P}$ is the pressure applied, either mechanically or by means of an inert gas, ΔV_f is the molar volume difference $V_l - V_s$; and ΔH_f is the enthalpy of fusion. Equation (8-15) is not amenable to much simplification, although for a small range of pressure ΔV_f will be approximately constant. The equation then represents a straight-line plot of $\mathbf{P}$ versus T_f. This is illustrated in Fig. 8-9 for the important case of the ice–water equilibrium. Here ΔV_f is negative; the molar volume of water is 18.02 cm^3 mole^{-1} and that of ice is 19.63 cm^3 mole^{-1} at 0°C. From Table 8-1 $\Delta H_f = 1436$ cal mole^{-1}, so we have

$$\frac{d\mathbf{P}}{dT} = \frac{(1436)(82.06/1.987)}{(273.2)(18.02 - 19.63)} = -135 \quad \text{atm } °K^{-1}.$$

Thus around 0°C the freezing point of ice decreases by 0.74°C per 100 atm pressure. To obtain a more exact result, we would have to know ΔH_f and ΔV_f as functions of temperature and of pressure. We will not concern ourselves with this level of complication.

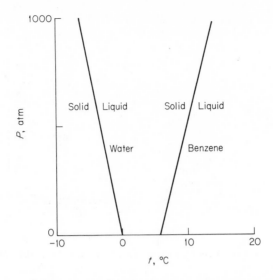

Fig. 8-9. *Variation of melting point with pressure for water and benzene.*

As further illustrated in the figure, ΔV_f is positive for most liquids, so the slope of the **P** versus T_f plot is usually positive, with the melting point increasing with pressure.

A number of enthalpies and entropies of fusion are also given in Table 8-1. No particular regularities are present—there is no equivalent to Trouton's rule in the case of entropy of fusion. This quantity is now very dependent on the degree of structural loosening that occurs on melting. As indicated in Fig. 8-8, the potential function for the vibration of a molecule in a liquid is weaker than that in a solid; the energy level spacings are closer, the partition function is larger, and hence so is the entropy. The effect is too sensitive to details of structure to allow much generalization, although a simple monatomic liquid and its solid, such as argon, can be treated fairly well, and so can small, nonhydrogen-bonded molecules.

Returning to Fig. 8-9, we see that a rather large pressure is needed to produce a significant change in a melting point. The field of high-pressure chemistry is an interesting one and much of the work in this area has been done by Bridgman and his co-workers [see Bridgman (1949)]. Values as high as 400,000 atm have been reached using special construction materials, hydraulic presses, and other devices. Parenthetically, the very measurement of such large pressures becomes difficult.

High-pressure chemistry leads to more than just simple extensions of diagrams such as Fig. 8-9. Reactions become feasible that do not occur ordinarily, such as the conversion of graphite into diamonds (small ones) and the formation of new types of crystal phases. The water system now looks as shown in Fig. 8-10. At around 2000 atm, the ordinary hexagonal structure of ice rearranges, that is, undergoes a phase transition, to a different and denser crystal structure known as ice III. The freezing point curve now slopes to the right. Further phase transitions

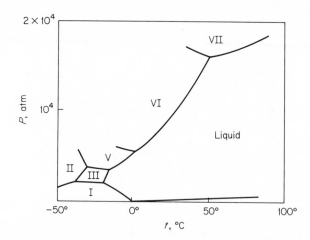

Fig. 8-10. *Phase map or phase diagram for water, including the various high-pressure forms.*

take place at successively higher pressures to give ice V, ice VI and, finally, ice VII. Equation (8-6) applies also to transitions between two solid phases and governs the lines showing the effect of pressure on the transition temperature between any two of the solid forms of ice. The figure has taken on the appearance of a phase map. At a temperature below a two-phase equilibrium line only the lower-temperature phase is present; conversely, at a temperature to the right of the line only the higher-temperature phase exists. The various marked regions thus each consist of a single phase only and the boundaries are lines of two-phase equilibrium.

We return to the low-pressure region to include the liquid–vapor equilibrium line in the phase map for water, shown schematically in Fig. 8-11. Included as well is the ice–vapor equilibrium line, or the plot of the sublimation pressure of ice versus temperature to which the Clausius–Clapeyron equation (8-8) applies. The pressure scale of a diagram of this sort has a dual significance. In the case of the solid–vapor and liquid–vapor lines, pressure is the vapor pressure of the phase in question. For the solid–liquid line, however, no vapor phase is present, and pressure is now mechanically applied pressure.

Note that the solid–vapor line is steeper than the liquid–vapor line; this is because the enthalpy of sublimation is greater than that of vaporization of the liquid. This must always be so:

$$
\begin{array}{llll}
\text{(a)} & \text{solid} = \text{liquid,} & \Delta H_f, & \\
\text{(b)} & \text{liquid} = \text{vapor,} & \Delta H_v, & \text{(8-16)} \\
\hline
\text{(c)} = \text{(a)} + \text{(b)} & \text{solid} = \text{vapor,} & \Delta H_s = \Delta H_f + \Delta H_v. &
\end{array}
$$

ΔH_s must be the sum of ΔH_f and ΔH_v, and since both are positive, the conclusion follows that $\Delta H_s > \Delta H_v$. One consequence is that the solid–vapor and liquid–vapor lines must cross in the manner shown. In the case of water, they do so at

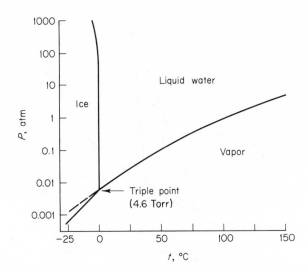

Fig. 8-11.   *Phase diagram for water in the low-pressure region, showing the ice I–liquid–vapor triple point at 4.6 Torr.*

0.0099°C and at the common vapor pressure of 4.579 Torr. This crossing is known as the *triple point* since three phases are in equilibrium: solid, liquid, and vapor. A further consequence is that the solid–liquid equilibrium line must also cross the other two at the triple point. The general rule is that any triple point marks the intersection of the lines representing the three ways of taking two phases at a time. Figure 8-10, for example, shows several triple points.

The subject of phase equilibria and phase maps, commonly called *phase diagrams*, is taken up in Chapter 11. However, one other often encountered phase diagram is that for sulfur, shown in Fig. 8-12. The pressure scale is somewhat schematic, so as to make the diagram more easily displayed. Below 95°C rhombic sulfur is the stable crystal modification and line *ab* gives the sublimation pressure for this form. Transformation to monoclinic sulfur occurs at 95°C and line *bc* gives its sublimation pressure: point *b* is then the rhombic–monoclinic–vapor triple point. Monoclinic sulfur melts at about 125°C and the vapor pressure of liquid sulfur is given by segment *cd*. A second triple point, at *c*, marks the monoclinic–liquid–vapor point. Rhombic sulfur is denser than monoclinic sulfur so the two-phase equilibrium line be, slopes to the right; and monoclinic sulfur is denser than the liquid, and so line *be* also slopes to the right. The relative slopes are such, however, that the two lines intersect at point *e*, a third triple point, at which one has a rhombic–monoclinic–liquid equilibrium.

An additional aspect shown Figs. 8-11 and 8-12 is *metastable* phase equilibrium. Thus liquid water may be cooled below its freezing point (to as low as −40°C); the liquid–vapor line in this region represents a *metastable equilibrium* since the liquid is unstable toward freezing. Such lines are shown in the figures as dashed

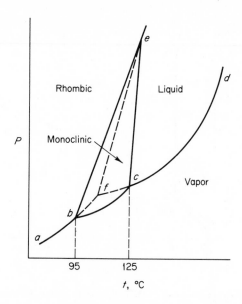

Fig. 8-12. *Phase diagram for sulfur. Dashed lines represent metastable equilibria.*

lines. In the water diagram the extension of the liquid–vapor line is possible; a solid cannot be metastable toward melting, however, nor can a liquid or a solid be metastable toward establishing an equilibrium vapor pressure. However, one crystal modification can be metastable with respect to another. Thus rhombic sulfur can be heated above 95°C without immediately converting to the more stable monoclinic form; its metastable vapor pressure curve is given by line *bf* in Fig. 8-12. Liquid sulfur can be supercooled along line *cf*. The diagram therefore shows a fourth, metastable triple point for the rhombic–liquid–vapor equilibrium. This completes the possibilities; that is, four phases can show a maximum of six two-phase equilibrium lines and four triple points. A triple point may be entirely hypothetical, however, and not just metastable. For example, if rhombic sulfur happened to be less dense than monoclinic sulfur, line *be* of Fig. 8-12 would then slope to the left, and the rhombic–monoclinic–liquid triple point would be a hypothetical or totally unstable one lying somewhere in the vapor phase region.

8-5 The Free Energy of a Liquid and Its Vapor

Equation (8-1) gives G_g as a function of T and P; values of $(G_g - E_0)$ (E_0 being the internal energy at 0°K) can be obtained, for example, from the spectroscopic constants for the gas, using the appropriate partition functions, as discussed in the preceding chapter. The graphical display of G_g would look approximately as shown in Fig. 8-13; G_g decreases with increasing temperature and increases with increasing pressure. The function G_l for the liquid is not easily evaluated theoretically but should have the qualitative appearance shown in the figure; the pressure dependence should be much less than for G_g, for example, and at low temperatures the surface must lie below that for G_g since the liquid is then the stable phase. We also know that the line of intersection of the two surfaces must correspond to the $P–T$ line of liquid–vapor equilibrium. A third surface for G_s also exists; its intersection with the other two would give the solid–liquid and solid–vapor equilibrium lines.

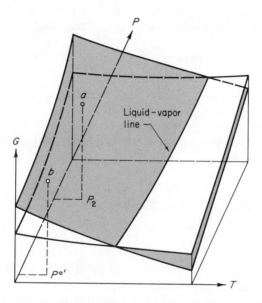

Fig. 8-13.   *Plot of G as a function of P and T for a liquid and its vapor. The crossing of the two surfaces marks the line of liquid–vapor equilibrium and hence gives vapor pressure versus temperature for the liquid.*

Along the liquid–vapor line, then, $G_g = G_l$, and a convenient way of describing G_l is in terms of the free energy of the vapor. We ordinarily deal with vapor pressures not much over 1 atm and will therefore make the assumption that the vapor behaves ideally. The free energy of a gas is given by Eq. (6-49), which becomes, in the present context,

$$dG_g = RT \, d(\ln P) \qquad \text{(ideal gas)} \qquad (8\text{-}17)$$

or

$$G_g = G_g^0 + RT \ln P \qquad \text{(ideal gas)} \qquad (8\text{-}18)$$

for a change in pressure at constant temperature. Here G_g^0 is the free energy of the vapor or gas phase at the temperature in question and 1 atm pressure, and is thus the standard-state free energy. It follows that

$$G_l^0 = G_g^0 + RT \ln P^\circ, \tag{8-19}$$

where G_l^0 is the free energy of the liquid in its standard state and P° is the liquid vapor pressure. Strictly speaking, G_l^0 refers to the liquid under its own vapor pressure, but the small difference between this value and that for the usual standard state of 1 atm pressure can be neglected here.

Equation (8-19) will be very useful in dealing with solutions. An immediate application is as follows. Returning to Eq. (8-2), we see that the free energy of a liquid increases with pressure at constant temperature; integration gives

$$G_{l,2} = G^0 + \int_{P^\circ}^{\mathbf{P}} V_l \, dP \simeq G^0 + V_l \, \Delta\mathbf{P}, \tag{8-20}$$

where P° is the vapor pressure of the liquid and $\mathbf{P}$ is some imposed mechanical pressure. If this higher pressure is established by using an inert gas to compress the liquid, there will still be a gas phase and the liquid will still have an equilibrium vapor pressure $P^{\circ\prime}$. This vapor pressure $P^{\circ\prime}$ corresponds to a vapor free energy of $G_g^0 + RT \ln P^{\circ\prime}$, so we have

$$G_{l,2} = G_g^0 + RT \ln P^{\circ\prime}. \tag{8-21}$$

On combining Eqs. (8-19)–(8-21), we obtain

$$RT \ln \frac{P^{\circ\prime}}{P^\circ} = \int_{P^\circ}^{\mathbf{P}} V_l \, \Delta(dP) \simeq V_l \, \Delta P. \tag{8-22}$$

Returning to Fig. 8-13, $G_{l,2}$ corresponds to point a located on the free energy surface for the liquid at temperature T and mechanical pressure P_2. The vapor having the same free energy at T is in the state given by point b, or at vapor or gas pressure $P^{\circ\prime}$.

A numerical illustration is as follows. Water has a molar volume of 18 cm³ mole⁻¹ and if we neglect its compressibility, then for 100 atm pressure, the integral of Eq. (8-22) is just (18)(100) = 1800 cm³ atm. At 25°C, $RT = (82.06)(298.2) = 24,470$ cm³ atm and log($P^{\circ\prime}/P^\circ$) becomes (1800)/ (24,470)(2.303) = 0.0319 and $P^{\circ\prime}/P^\circ = 1.076$. The vapor pressure is thus increased 7.6% by the application of 100 atm pressure.

8-6 The Surface Tension of Liquids. Surface Tension as a Thermodynamic Quantity

We have so far considered only bulk properties, that is, properties of a portion of matter which, if extensive, are proportional to the amount of substance or which, if intensive, apply to the interior of the phase. We now recognize that energy resides in the interface between two phases and, more specifically, that work is required to form or to extend an interface. For the present, the discussion is limited to the liquid–vapor interface of pure liquids. The treatment of solutions is deferred to Section 9-ST-2.

The requirement of work to increase a liquid–vapor surface is most easily demonstrated experimentally by means of soap films, since these persist long enough to be handled. As illustrated in Fig. 8-14(a), if a soap film is formed in a

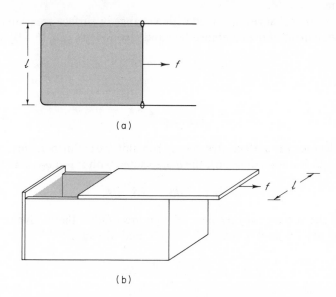

(a)

(b)

Fig. 8-14. *Work of extending a surface: (a) Extending a soap film held in a wire frame by moving a side. (b) Extending the surface of a liquid by sliding back a cover of inert material.*

frame one side of which can move freely, one finds that the film will spontaneously contract, and that to prevent contraction, a force f must be applied. If f is decreased slightly, contraction occurs, and if f is increased, the film extends. The process is then a reversible one, and the work involved is reversible, constant-temperature and constant-pressure work. It therefore corresponds to a free energy quantity.

For a small displacement dx of the movable side of the frame the work done by the film is

$$w = -f\,dx = -\gamma l\,dx, \tag{8-23}$$

where γ is the force per unit length exerted by the film and is called the *surface tension*. The units of surface tension are evidently force per unit length, or, in the cgs system, dynes per centimeter. Since $l\,dx$ is the change in area of the film $d\mathscr{A}$, a less geometrically specific form of Eq. (8-23) is

$$w = -\gamma\,d\mathscr{A}. \tag{8-24}$$

Evidently, γ can also be expressed in units of energy per unit area, or as ergs per square centimeter. The two sets of units are equivalent, and surface tension may be stated in either way. The experiment with a pure liquid, rather than a soap solution, is the hypothetical one shown in Fig. 8-14(b). We imagine a container filled with the liquid and at a given T and P. There is a movable lid that can be slid back and forth to change the amount of liquid surface. (We stipulate that there is no inter-action between the liquid and the material of the lid.) The force on the lid is then γl as before.

The free energy change associated with a change in surface area can be added to the usual statement of the combined first and second laws [Eq. (6-43)] to give

$$dG = -S\,dT + V\,dP + \gamma\,d\mathscr{A}. \tag{8-25}$$

Thus

$$\gamma = \left(\frac{\partial G}{\partial \mathscr{A}}\right)_{T,P} = G^{\mathrm{s}}, \tag{8-26}$$

where G^{s} denotes the surface free energy per unit area. Further, since the process of Fig. 8-14(b) is a reversible one, the q associated with it is a q_{rev}, and we have

$$dq = T\,dS = TS^{\mathrm{s}}\,d\mathscr{A}, \tag{8-27}$$

where S^{s} is the surface entropy, also per unit area. Other thermodynamic relation-ships apply. By Eq. (6-45), $(\partial G/\partial T)_P = -S$, and likewise,

$$\left(\frac{\partial G^{\mathrm{s}}}{\partial T}\right)_P = -S^{\mathrm{s}} \tag{8-28}$$

or

$$\left(\frac{\partial \gamma}{\partial T}\right)_P = -S^{\mathrm{s}}.$$

Also

$$H^{\mathrm{s}} = G^{\mathrm{s}} + TS^{\mathrm{s}}. \tag{8-29}$$

Often, and as a good approximation, H^{s} and the surface energy E^{s} are not distin-guished, so Eq. (8-29) is usually given in the form

$$E^{\mathrm{s}} = G^{\mathrm{s}} + TS^{\mathrm{s}} \tag{8-30}$$

or

$$E^{\mathrm{s}} = \gamma - T\frac{d\gamma}{dT} \tag{8-31}$$

(constancy of pressure being assumed for $d\gamma/dT$).

The thermodynamics of curved interfaces constitutes a very important topic, one aspect of which is developed here. This is known as the *Laplace equation* and relates the mechanical pressure across an interface and its curvature. To illustrate the physical reality of the effect, we again use a soap film, now in the form of a soap bubble. As shown in Fig. 8-15, a manometer is attached to the soap bubble pipe, and after the bubble has been blown, the stem of the pipe is closed off. The manometer will now show a pressure difference. For an actual soap bubble this is about 1mm H_2O for a bubble of 2 mm radius. The physical explanation for the higher pressure inside the bubble is that the film tends spontaneously to decrease its area and hence its total surface free energy but, in doing so, shrinks the bubble to the point that the increased pressure prevents further change.

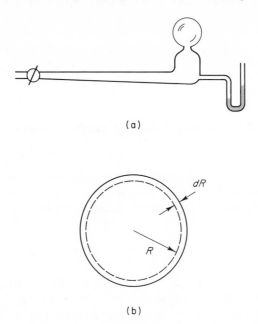

(a)

(b)

Fig. 8-15. *(a) The pressure inside a soap bubble is larger than that outside. (b) Derivation of the Laplace equation for a spherical surface.*

The relevant equation may be derived as follows. Consider a bubble of radius R as shown in Fig. 8-15(b). Its total surface free energy is $4\pi R^2\gamma$ and if the radius were to decrease by dR, then the change in surface free energy would be $8\pi R\gamma\, dR$. Since shrinking decreases the total surface free energy, at equilibrium the tendency to shrink must be balanced by a pressure difference across the film ΔP such that the work against this pressure difference $(\Delta P)4\pi R^2\, dR$ is just equal to the decrease in surface free energy. Thus we have

$$(\Delta P)4\pi R^2\, dR = 8\pi R\gamma\, dR$$

or

$$\Delta P = \frac{2\gamma}{R}. \tag{8-32}$$

Equation (8-32) is the Laplace equation for a spherical interface. An important conclusion is that the smaller the bubble, that is, the smaller the value of R, the larger is $\Delta\mathbf{P}$. Conversely, $\Delta\mathbf{P}$ goes to zero in the limit of $R \to \infty$, which corresponds to the case of a plane interface.

Parenthetically, common usage defines γ as the surface tension for one interface. Because of this it would be better to use 2γ instead of γ in relationships such as Eq. (8-32) when they are applied to soap or other films.

In summary, the two most important relationships developed so far are Eq. (8-31) for surface energy, $E^s = \gamma - T(d\gamma/dT)$, and the Laplace equation (8-32), $\Delta\mathbf{P} = 2\gamma/R$. The latter is one of the four principal special equations of surface chemistry, the other three being the Kelvin equation (Section 8-9), the Gibbs equation (Section 9-ST-2), and the equation of Young and Dupré [see Adamson (1967)].

8-7 Measurement of Surface Tension

We do not usually devote much space to experimental procedures, but the various ways of measuring surface tension are so closely related to basic surface phenomena that discussion of the former illustrates the latter.

A. Capillary Rise

If a small-bore tube is partially immersed in a liquid as shown in Fig. 8-16(a), one usually observes that the liquid rises to some height h above the level of the general liquid surface. This phenomenon may be treated by means of the Laplace equation. If, as shown in more detail in Fig. 8-16(b), the liquid wets the wall of the capillary tube, then if the radius of the tube r is small, the meniscus will be hemispherical in shape. Its radius of curvature is then equal to r, that is, $R = r$, and Eq. (8-32) becomes

$$\Delta\mathbf{P} = \frac{2\gamma}{r}. \tag{8-33}$$

If, as further illustrated in the figure, $\mathbf{P}_1$ is the general atmospheric pressure, then the pressure just under the meniscus must be $\mathbf{P}_1 - (2\gamma/r)$. The $\Delta\mathbf{P}$ in the Laplace equation is always such that the higher pressure is on the convex side of the curved surface. The pressure $\mathbf{P}_1$ is also the pressure on the flat portion of the liquid surface outside the capillary tube, and hence the pressure at that liquid level inside the capillary. Then $\mathbf{P}_1 - \mathbf{P}_2$ must correspond to the change in hydrostatic pressure of the liquid, $\rho g h$. We can thus write

$$\rho g h = \frac{2\gamma}{r} \tag{8-34}$$

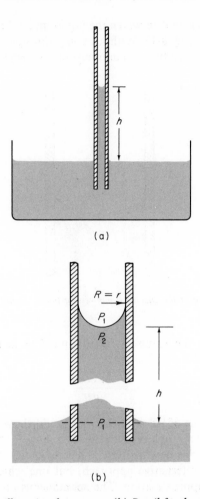

Fig. 8-16. *(a) The capillary rise phenomenon. (b) Detail for the case of a spherical meniscus.*

or

$$h = \frac{2\gamma}{\rho g r}. \tag{8-35}$$

(Strictly speaking, one should use $\Delta\rho$, the difference in density between the liquid and vapor phases.) The quantity $2\gamma/\rho g$ is a property of the liquid alone and is called the *capillary constant* a^2. Equation (8-35) may then be put in the form

$$a^2 = rh, \tag{8-36}$$

which tells us that the plot of capillary rise h versus r is a hyperbola. Equation (8-36) is exact only in the limit of small r; otherwise corrections are needed.

A more general case is that in which the liquid meets the capillary wall at some angle θ as illustrated in Fig. 8-17. Without going through the details of the geometry, we can say that the radius of curvature of the meniscus R is now given by

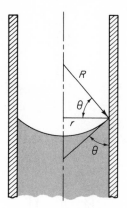

Fig. 8-17. *Capillary rise in the case of a nonwetting liquid. Detail shows the meniscus profile assuming a spherical shape.*

$R = r/\cos\theta$ (assuming the meniscus is still spherical in shape) and Eq. (8-35) becomes

$$h = \frac{2\gamma \cos\theta}{\rho g r}. \tag{8-37}$$

A liquid making an angle of 90° with the wall would show no capillary rise at all. Mercury, whose contact angle against glass is about 140°, shows a capillary *depression*. That is, $\cos\theta$ is now negative and so is h.

The following is an alternative approach, but one which is equivalent to the preceding in the first approximation. The spontaneous contractile tendency of a liquid surface acts as though there were a surface force γ per unit length. In the capillary rise situation, the total such force is $2\pi r\gamma$ (or, more generally, the vertical component would be $2\pi r\gamma \cos\theta$). This force is balanced by the force exerted by gravity on the column of liquid which is supported, or $(\pi r^2)(\rho g h)$. On equating these two forces, we have Eq. (8-34) [or (8-37)].

The capillary rise phenomenon is not only the basis for an absolute and accurate means of measuring surface tension but is also one of its major manifestations. The phenomenon accounts for the general tendency of wetting liquids to enter pores and fine cracks. The absorption of vapors by porous solids to fill their capillary channels and the displacement of oil by gas or water in petroleum formations constitute specific examples of capillarity effects. The waterproofing of fabrics involves a direct application of Eq. (8-37). Fabrics are porous materials, the spaces between fibers amounting to small capillary tubes. As shown in Fig. 8-18(a), coating the fibers with material on which water has a contact angle of

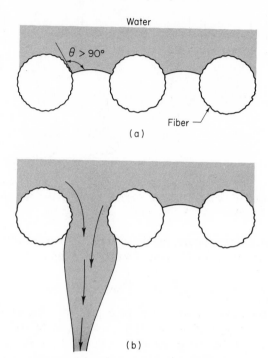

Water

$\theta > 90°$

Fiber

(a)

(b)

Fig. 8-18. *Mechanism of water repellancy.*

greater than 90° provides a Laplace pressure which opposes the entry or "rise" of water into the fabric. The material is *not* waterproof; once the Laplace pressure is exceeded (as, for example, by directing a jet of water onto the fabric or merely by rubbing of the wet fabric), then penetration occurs, and water will seep freely through the filled channels as illustrated in Fig. 8-18(b).

B. Drop Weight Method

It was pointed out earlier that one can assign a force γ per unit length of a liquid surface as giving the maximum pull the surface can support. In the case of a drop of liquid which is formed at the tip of a tube and allowed to grow by delivering liquid slowly through the tube, a size is reached such that surface tension can no longer support the weight of the drop, and it falls. The approximate sequence of shapes is shown in Fig. 8-19. To a first approximation, we write

$$W_{\text{ideal}} = 2\pi r \gamma, \tag{8-38}$$

where W_{ideal} denotes the weight of the drop that should fall and r is the radius of the tube (outside radius if the liquid wets the tube). Equation (8-38) is known as *Tate's law*.

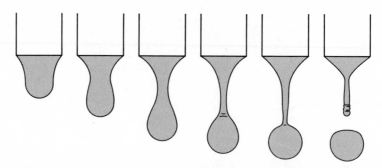

Fig. 8-19. *Sequence of shapes for a drop that detaches from a tip. [From A. W. Adamson, "The Physical Chemistry of Surfaces," 2nd ed. Copyright 1967, Wiley (Interscience), New York. Used with permission of John Wiley & Sons, Inc.]*

As also illustrated in the figure, the detached drop leaves behind a considerable residue of liquid, and the actual weight of a drop is given by

$$W_{\text{act}} = W_{\text{ideal}}f, \tag{8-39}$$

where f is a correction factor which can be expressed either as a function of r/a, where a is the square root of the capillary constant, or of $r/V^{1/3}$, where V is the volume of the drop. Table 8-2 gives some values of f; a more complete table is given in the reference cited therein. Note that the correction is considerable. The method, using the correction table, is accurate and convenient, however. In practice, one forms the drops within a closed space to avoid evaporation and in sufficient number that the weight per drop can be determined accurately. It is only necessary to form each drop slowly during the final stages of its growth.

C. Detachment Methods

A set of methods that are somewhat related in treatment to the drop weight method have in common that one determines the maximum pull to detach an

Table 8-2. *Correction Factors for the Drop Weight Method[a]*

$r/V^{1/3}$	f	$r/V^{1/3}$	f
0.30	0.7256	0.80	0.6000
0.40	0.6828	0.90	0.5998
0.50	0.6515	1.00	0.6098
0.60	0.6250	1.10	0.6280
0.70	0.6093	1.20	0.6535

[a] See A. W. Adamson, "Physical Chemistry of Surfaces," 2nd ed. Wiley (Interscience), New York, 1967.

object from the surface. If the perimeter of the object is p, then the maximum weight of meniscus that the surface tension can support is just

$$W_{\text{ideal}} = p\gamma. \tag{8-40}$$

The so-called *du Nouy tensiometer* uses a wire ring, usually made of platinum, and p is then $4\pi R$, where R is the radius of the ring, and one is allowing for both the inside and the outside meniscus. As with the drop weight method, rather large correction factors are involved, and these have been tabulated [see Adamson (1967)].

If, instead of a ring, one uses a thin slide, either an actual microscope slide or a metal one of similar size, then it turns out that Eq. (8-40) is quite accurate and may be applied directly. The method is now known as the *Wilhelmy slide* method and is shown schematically in Fig. 8-20. Alternatively, the slide need not be detached but

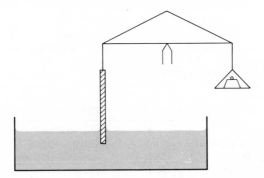

Fig. 8-20.   *The Wilhelmy slide method. A thin plate is suspended from a balance.*

need merely be brought into contact with the liquid and then raised until the end is just slightly above the liquid surface. The extra weight is again the meniscus weight and is given by Eq. (8-40). The Wilhelmy method is one of those most widely used today. It is especially valuable in studying the surface tension of solutions and of films of insoluble substances.

8-8   Results of Surface Tension Measurements

Some representative surface tension values are assembled in Table 8-3. Notice the very wide range in values, from 0.308 dyn cm^{-1} for liquid helium to 1880 dyn cm^{-1} for molten iron. An important datum is the value for water, 72.75 dyn cm^{-1} at 20°C; other common solvents have surface tensions around

Table 8-3. *Surface Tension of Liquids*

Liquid	Temperature (°C)	γ (dyn cm^{-1})	$d\gamma/dT$
He	−270.7	0.308	−0.07
N_2	−198	9.71	−0.23
Perfluoroheptane	20	10.98	—
n-Heptane	20	19.7	—
n-Octane	20	21.80	−0.10
Ethanol	20	22.75	−0.086
CCl$_4$	20	26.77	—
Benzene	20	28.88	−0.13
Water	20	72.75	−0.16
KClO$_3$	368	81	—
NaNO$_3$	308	116.6	—
Ba(NO$_3$)$_2$	595	134.8	—
Sodium	97	202	−0.10
Mercury	20	476	−0.20
Silver	1100	879	−0.184
Iron	1535	1880	−0.43

Liquid–Liquid Interfaces, 20°C

Liquids	γ (dyn cm^{-1})	Liquids	γ (dyn cm^{-1})
n-Butanol–water	1.8	Water–mercury	415
n-Heptanoic acid–water	7.0	Ethanol–mercury	389
Benzene–water	35.0	*n*-Heptane–mercury	378
n-Heptane–water	50.2	Benzene–mercury	357

20–30 dyn cm^{-1}. Some values for the interfacial tension between two liquids are included.

One may use the table to illustrate characteristic values in the various methods for determining surface tension. The capillary constant a^2 is about 0.14 cm^2 for water, about 0.05 cm^2 for a typical organic liquid, and around unity for a molten metal. Equation (8-36) then allows an easy estimate of the capillary rise. Thus, for water in a 0.1-cm-diameter capillary, $h = 0.14/0.05 = 2.8$ cm and for a 0.01-cm-diameter capillary, $h = 28$ cm.

Turning next to the drop weight method, if the outside radius of the tube were 0.3 cm, the ideal drop weight for water would be $(2\pi)(0.3)(72.35) = 136.4$ dyn or 0.1392 g. The actual drop weight would be about 0.084 g. That is, $V^{1/3}$ would be approximately 0.44 and $r/V^{1/3}$ about 0.68, so that f from Table 8-2 would come out close to 0.61. To reverse the order of the calculation, if a drop weight of 0.084 g were observed, f would be 0.61 and the calculated surface tension would be

$$\gamma = \frac{(0.084)(980)}{(2\pi)(0.3)(0.61)} = 72 \quad \text{dyn cm}^{-1}.$$

Finally, for a Wilhelmy slide having a typical width of 3 cm, the meniscus weight for water at 20°C would be

$$W = (2)(3)(72.75) = 436.5 \quad \text{dyn} \quad \text{or} \quad 0.445 \quad \text{g}.$$

We assume the slide to be thin enough that the edges do not contribute appreciably to the perimeter. An edge effect does exist and usually is allowed for by using slides of varying widths.

The table lists values for $d\gamma/dT$ for several liquids. Surface tension decreases with temperature, often almost linearly, and a relationship due to Eötvös gives

$$\gamma V^{2/3} = k(T_c - T). \tag{8-41}$$

Another, due to Guggenheim, is of the form

$$\gamma = \gamma^\circ \left(1 - \frac{T}{T_c}\right)^n, \tag{8-42}$$

where $n = 11/9$ for organic liquids. Both equations correctly predict that the surface tension should go to zero at the critical temperature T_c and the former, in combination with Eq. (8-31), requires that the surface energy E^s should be independent of temperature if V is constant. E^s does remain nearly constant until fairly close to the critical temperature, and then drops rapidly toward zero. The situation in this respect is similar to that for enthalpies of vaporization.

8-9 The Kelvin Equation. Nucleation

According to the Laplace equation (8-32) a small drop of liquid should be under an excess mechanical pressure $\Delta P = 2\gamma/R$. We can combine this result with Eq. (8-22), which gave the effect of mechanical pressure on the vapor pressure of a liquid. If V_l is assumed to be constant, we get

$$RT \ln \frac{P^{o\prime}}{P^\circ} = V_l \Delta P = \frac{2\gamma V_l}{R}$$

or

$$RT \ln \frac{P^{o\prime}}{P^\circ} = \frac{2\gamma V_l}{r}, \tag{8-43}$$

where r is the radius of the drop. Equation (8-43) is known as the *Kelvin equation* and, as mentioned earlier, is one of the four principal equations of surface chemistry.

The effect predicted by Eq. (8-43) is not very large until quite small values of r are reached. Thus for water at 25°C, $P^{o\prime}/P^\circ$ is about 1.001 if $r = 10^{-4}$ cm and 1.114 if $r = 10^{-6}$ cm. The equation has been verified experimentally for water, dibutyl phthalate, mercury, and other liquids, down to radii of about 10^{-5} cm (by using aerosols). For the inverse case of a vapor or gas bubble in a liquid, $P^{o\prime}$ is less than P°

The increase in vapor pressure called for by the Kelvin equation is not large enough to be of any concern in the case of macroscopic systems. The phenomenon is central, however, to the mechanism of vapor condensation. If a vapor is cooled or compressed to a pressure equal to the vapor pressure of the bulk liquid, then condensation should occur. The difficulty is that the first few molecules condensing can only form a minute drop and the vapor pressure of such a drop will be much higher than the regular vapor pressure. In practice, condensation may occur on the walls of the container or on dust particles, but in clean systems, large degrees of supersaturation are possible. In the case of water, for example, the vapor at around $0°C$ may be compressed to about five times the equilibrium vapor pressure before spontaneous homogeneous condensation sets in. Similar results have been found for many other vapors.

The crucial step in the condensation process is the formation of droplets big enough that their further growth by condensation of vapor onto them is rapid. Such droplets are called *nuclei* and their formation is called *nucleation*. The theory of homogeneous nucleation calculates the excess surface free energy of a drop as a function of its size. The free energy necessary to form a given drop is then determined by size and by the ratio of the actual pressure of the vapor P to $P°$. For each value of P there is a certain critical drop size; drops larger than this decrease in free energy with increase in size and should grow spontaneously. One next obtains the concentration of drops of this critical size, using the Boltzmann equation, and their rate of growth, using the surface collision frequency equation (2-46). The final conclusion is that only when P has reached a certain critical ratio with respect to $P°$ will the rate of condensation suddenly become rapid. Nucleation theory has been fairly successful; predicted and observed values of $P/P°$ agree well.

The same analysis and, with modifications, the same equations apply to the supercooling of a liquid, where the critical nuclei are now incipient crystals, and to the precipitation of a solute from solution. As an example of this last, aqueous $S_2O_3^{2-}$ slowly decomposes in acid solution to give elemental sulfur. At first the sulfur produced simply builds up in solution, but at a very sharp critical concentration nucleation begins, and thereafter all further sulfur produced adds to the existing nuclei. The result is a dispersion of sulfur which consists of spherical particles of virtually uniform size. Such monodisperse sulfur sols now show beautiful light scattering effects—incident white light is scattered as a rainbow of color. The same effect occurs, incidentally, with natural opals. These consist of close-packed spheres of silica, originally slowly deposited from solution which are monodisperse. The flashes of color seen in an opal are again due to interferences among light rays scattered from the arrays of spheres.

8-10 Viscosity of Liquids

The viscosity of liquids is considered briefly here as an example of an important nonthermodynamic property. The subject of viscosity was treated in an introductory way in Section 2-7 with special emphasis on the kinetic molecular theory of gas viscosities. Perhaps the most common manifestation of viscosity in the laboratory and in engineering is in the flow of a fluid through a pipe or tube. The basic observation is that the volume rate of flow is proportional to the pressure drop, provided the flow is streamline, as illustrated in Fig. 2-8. The actual equation, known as the *Poiseuille equation*, was also given earlier [Eq. (2-60)],

$$\eta = \frac{\pi(\mathbf{P}_1 - \mathbf{P}_2)\, r^4 t}{8 V l},$$

where η is the viscosity (in poise, abbreviated P), $\mathbf{P}_1 - \mathbf{P}_2$ is the pressure drop (in dynes per square centimeter), r is the radius of the tube (in centimeters), V is the volume flowing (in cubic centimeters), l is the length of the tube (in centimeters), and t is time (in seconds). Equation (2-60) is derived in the Special Topics section and only its application is considered here.

Viscosities may be measured experimentally by the direct application of Eq. (2-60). Some liquids have viscosities that vary greatly with the rate of shear, and measurements on them should be made with a carefully controlled flow rate. Often a coiled capillary tube is used. For example, if a capillary of 0.1 mm radius and 1 m long is used, then a rather viscous liquid of 30 P would have a flow rate under 10 atm (10^7 dyn cm^{-2}) pressure drop of

$$\frac{V}{t} = \frac{(\pi)(10^7)(0.01)^4}{(8)(100)(30)} = 1.32 \times 10^{-5} \quad \text{cm}^3 \text{ sec}^{-1} \quad \text{or} \quad 0.048 \quad \text{cm}^3 \text{ hr}^{-1}.$$

In the case of the usual, well-behaved liquid it is much more convenient to use an *Ostwald viscometer*, illustrated in Fig. 8-21. A definite volume of liquid is intro-

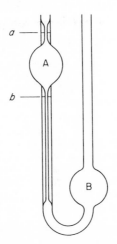

Fig. 8-21. *An Ostwald viscometer.*

duced into bulb B and the liquid is sucked up into bulb A and past the mark a; the volume is such that bulb B is not quite emptied. The liquid is then allowed to flow back and the time for the meniscus to pass from a to b determined. The theory of the viscometer is essentially that of Eq. (2-60), except that the pressure drop changes with time, as the liquid level drops, and hence so does the flow rate. The average pressure drop is proportional to the density ρ of the liquid, however, and the other terms of Eq. (2-60) are constant. We then write

$$\eta = \mathbf{k}\rho t, \qquad (8\text{-}44)$$

where $\mathbf{k}$ is a constant for a given viscometer and is determined by measurement of the time of flow for a liquid of known viscosity.

A selection of viscosity data is given in Table 8-4. Ordinary solvent liquids have viscosities of a few centipoise. Oils, such as heavy lubricating oils, lie in the range of a few poise; glycerin has a viscosity of about 10 P at 25°C. Viscosities are generally very temperature-dependent, as also illustrated by the data of the table. The fluidity ϕ, or reciprocal of the viscosity, usually varies nearly exponentially with temperature:

$$\phi = A \exp\left(-\frac{E^*}{RT}\right). \qquad (8\text{-}45)$$

As the form of Eq. (8-45) suggests, the temperature dependence is attributed to the presence of a characteristic energy for flow to occur, and values for E^* are included in the table. These are around 2 kcal mole^{-1}, except for water, whose value is unusually high, presumably because of the structure-breaking that must occur in flow (see both Commentary and Notes and Special Topics sections).

Table 8-4. *Viscosity of Liquids^a*

	Viscosity (cP)			E^*
Liquid	0°C	20°C	40°C	(cal mole^{-1})
H_2O	1.792	1.005	0.656	4300
n-Octane	0.7060	0.5419	0.4328	3000
Ethanol	1.773	1.200	0.834	3200
Benzene	0.912	0.652	0.503	2540
CCl_4	1.329	0.969	0.739	2600
Mercury	1.684	1.547	1.483	600

^{a} From International Critical Tables, Vol. 7. McGraw-Hill, New York, 1930.

COMMENTARY AND NOTES

8-CN-1 Additional Thermodynamic Properties of Liquids

There are, of course, fairly extensive tabulations of the free energies, enthalpies, and entropies of various liquids. A selection of these may be found in the tables of Chapter 5 and Table 7-2. More complete listings are given by the National Bureau of Standards, Circular No. 500 (Rossini *et al.*, 1959). The remaining thermodynamic properties of interest consist of coefficients such as those of thermal expansion and compressibility and of heat capacities. A sampling of these quantities is given in Table 8-5.

Coefficients of compressibility and of thermal expansion are small for liquids, of the order of 0.01–0.1 % volume change per atmosphere or per degree. The two coefficients are related to the heat capacity difference $C_P - C_V$ as discussed in Section 6-ST-1 and given by Eq. (6-100):

$$C_P - C_V = \frac{\alpha^2 V T}{\beta}.$$

The difference can be surprisingly large. The explanation is, clearly, not in terms of the work of expansion against atmospheric pressure, as with gases, but rather in terms of expansion against the internal pressure, P_{int} (see Section 4-CN-1).

Table 8-5. *Some Thermodynamic Coefficients for Liquids at 25°C[a]*

Liquid	$10^3\alpha$ (°K^{-1})	$10^5\beta$ (atm^{-1})	V (cm^3 mole^{-1})	P_{int} (atm)	Heat capacity (cal °K^{-1} mole^{-1})		
					$C_P(l)$	$C_V(l)$	$C_V(g)$
H_2O	0.48	4.6	18	3,110	18	17.3	6.0
CCl_4	1.24	10.6	97	3,486	31.5	21.4	18.7
CS_2	1.22	9.5	60	3,829	18.1	11.3	10
C_6H_6	1.24	9.7	89	3,811	32.1	22	22
$Hg(l)$	0.18	0.34	14.8	15,800	6.65	5.6	3.0
$Zn(s)$	0.0893	0.15	7.1	—	6	5.7	—

[a] $\alpha = (1/V)(\partial V/\partial T)_P$. $\beta = -(1/V)(\partial V/\partial P)_T$.

From the definition of P_{int} it follows that

$$C_P - C_V = \alpha V(P + P_{int}) \tag{8-46}$$

or

$$P + P_{int} = \frac{\alpha T}{\beta}. \tag{8-47}$$

The table includes values for P_{int} and these are indeed far larger than P (which is 1 atm). Notice, however, that $C_P - C_V$ is relatively small for a solid, as illustrated by the listing for zinc metal.

One ordinarily measures C_P directly; this gets around the experimental task of confining a liquid to a fixed volume while measuring its heat capacity. Water, as usual, is unusual. The density of water goes through a maximum at 4°C, and α is therefore zero at this temperature, and is still unusually small at 25°C. The immediate consequence is that the difference $C_P - C_V$ is small, and P_{int} likewise is smaller than one would expect. All this is yet another reflection of the structural changes that are occurring in liquid water as it is warmed from 0°C (and as discussed later).

It is instructive to compare the values of $C_V(l)$ and $C_V(g)$. The increase from 3.0 to 5.6 cal °K^{-1} mole^{-1} on going from Hg(g) to Hg(l) strongly suggests that the $3N_0$ degrees of freedom per mole of mercury atoms are present in the liquid as vibrations rather than as translations. That is, the heat capacity of the liquid is close to $3R$ in value, rather than to $\frac{3}{2}R$ (see Section 4-8). The same is true for water; the value of $C_V(l)$ of about 17 cal °K^{-1} mole^{-1} is close to that for $9N_0$ degrees of vibrational freedom per mole, or $9R$ in heat capacity. Again, it appears that water molecules have exchanged translational motion for vibrations in going from the gas to the liquid phase. Moreover, the fact that the heat capacity is close to the equipartition value must mean that the vibrational energy states are close together. That is, θ_{vib} (Section 4-12) must be small. Now, for gaseous water the internal vibrations of the molecule have values of $\theta_{vib}/T \geqslant 8$ at 25°C. This means that there is very little vibrational contribution to the heat capacity of the gas (as is also reflected in the low value of 6.0 cal °K^{-1} mole^{-1} for C_V, which amounts to little more than translation plus rotation). Yet in liquid water, not only have translation and rotation been converted to weak vibrations, but the internal vibrations have weakened to some low θ_{vib} value. We again interpret the effect as due to hydrogen bonding in water.

The other three liquids are of the "normal" van der Waals type, and here it is interesting that the C_V values for the liquid and the gas are not much different. We conclude that rotations and internal vibrations have remained about the same in the liquid state as in the gaseous state, and, further, that the intermolecular potential function is something like that of Fig. 8-8(b), or such that translational-type motions of the molecule have only a weak vibrational character.

320

8-CN-2   The Structure of Water

Water has been described rather frequently in this chapter as "unusual." It does not obey Trouton's rule well, having too high an enthalpy and entropy of vaporization. The liquid is denser than the solid and shows a maximum density at 4°C, so that between 0°C and 4°C the density increases with temperature. Its heat capacity is abnormally large and suggests that all $9N_0$ degrees of freedom per mole are involved as weak vibrations. The surface tension of water is unusually high for so small a molecular species. The x-ray scattering data give radial distributions (as in Fig. 8-1) suggesting about 4.5 nearest neighbors, as compared to 4.0 in the ice structure.

Water is, after all, the most important chemical in our lives, both biologically and geologically. The problem of the structure of water has thus presented a scientific challenge not only of great intrinsic interest but also of great general significance. Ice has a very open structure, and the increase in density on melting was at first explained as just due to the breakdown of the ice into individual water molecules, with perhaps small hydrogen-bonded units present. This picture could not account for many of the properties, including the high critical temperature of water.

Next, a number of models were proposed which involved extensive structuring different from that of ice. L. Pauling, for example, suggested cages of hydrogen-bonded water molecules with an additional molecule in the center. Structures of this type have seemed too crystalline and rigid. Current theory is along the following lines. H. S. Frank and co-workers suggested that hydrogen bonding might be somewhat cooperative, that is, the formation of a second and a third hydrogen bond should be easier, based on dipole moment considerations, than that of the first bond. The effect would be that once a few molecules had hydrogen-bonded, a rather large cluster would grow easily. A later fluctuation would cause the cluster break up. The idea is one of "*flickering clusters.*" Dielectric studies on water show that molecules are able to respond to an alternating electric field up to very high frequencies, about 10^{10} sec^{-1}. This means that any structured region must be very short-lived—about 10^{-10} sec, or about 10^3 vibrations; hence the term "flickering clusters." Judging from the characteristic energy for the change in fluidity with temperature and similar energy values obtained from dielectric relaxation and from sound absorption, it would appear that a cluster lasts until fluctuation in the local energy density gives it 4–5 kcal of extra energy per molecule; it then breaks up while, on the average, another cluster is forming elsewhere in the liquid. A schematic illustration of this model is given in Fig. 8-22.

The cluster model was further developed by Nemethy and Scheraga (1962) in terms of a statistical thermodynamic calculation. Energies were assigned according to the average number of hydrogen bonds per oxygen, which ranged from zero for

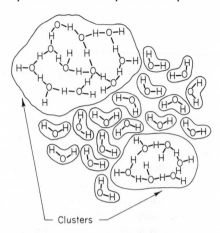

Clusters

Fig. 8-22. *The "flickering cluster" model for liquid water. The structured and unstructured regions come and go quickly. [From A. Nemethy and H. A. Scheraga, J. Chem. Phys.* **36**, *3382 (1962).]*

uncoordinated molecules to a maximum of four. A product of partition functions was then set up, with appropriate expressions for vibration, rotation, and translation of each type of cluster. The result led to moderately good agreement with a number of properties of water, and this type of picture is generally accepted as correct in principle if not in detail. It leads to rather large clusters—ones with 50–100 water molecules are fairly probable.

The thermodynamic and other properties of water are thus those of a highly structured medium. A related consequence is that water as a solvent behaves unusually. It appears, for example, that small ions order their immediately neighboring water molecules into a local structure which is not compatible with the general liquid structure, so that there is a nonstructured transition zone between the hydrated ion and the solvent. Nonpolar solutes such as hydrocarbons show a peculiar behavior. There is a small, negative ΔH of solution, strongly counterbalanced by a very large negative entropy change. An early idea, from H. S. Frank and M. J. Evans, was that such solutes induced a local structuring of the water—the picture was, in 1945, known as the *"iceberg"* model. A more recent, although similar interpretation, is that nonpolar molecules prefer the interstices between clusters and in this way promote structure and hence decrease the entropy of water.

SPECIAL TOPICS

SPECIAL TOPICS

8-ST-1   Intermolecular Forces

It was noted in Section 8-3 that several distinct types of intermolecular and interatomic forces are known. Here we take up those that are loosely described as *van der Waals forces*, that is, interactions that are not due to actual chemical bond formation nor to simple electrostatic forces as in an ionic crystal. The hydrogen bond is also excluded. What remains are the attractive forces that neutral, chemically saturated molecules experience.

These may be divided into the following categories: (a) dipole–dipole, (b) dipole–induced dipole and ion–induced dipole, and (c) induced dipole–induced dipole (dispersion).

It is best to start with Coulomb's law, according to which the force between two point charges is given by

$$f = \frac{q_1 q_2}{r^2}.$$
(8-48)

We assume a dielectric constant for vacuum, that is, unity in the cgs system (see Section 3-CN-2); r is the distance of separation. The potential energy of interaction, $\phi = \int f \, dx$, is given by

$$\phi = \frac{q_1 q_2}{r}.$$
(8-49)

The potential V of a charge q is defined as

$$V = \frac{q}{r},$$
(8-50)

with the meaning that unit opposite charge q_0 will experience a potential energy $-q q_0 / r$ at a separation r. The sign of V is negative if that of q is negative.

We next consider a molecule having a dipole moment μ (see Section 3-4), that is, one in which charges q^+ and q^- are separated by a distance l, giving a dipole moment $\mu = ql$. A dipole experiences no net interaction with a uniform potential since the two charges are affected equally and oppositely. If there is a gradient of the potential, or a field, defined as $\mathbf{F} = dV/dr$, then there is a net effect. As illustrated in Fig. 8-23(a), the potential energy of a dipole in a field is

$$\phi(\mu) = -Vq + \left(V - \frac{dV}{dr}\, l\right)q = -\mu\mathbf{F}. \tag{8-51}$$

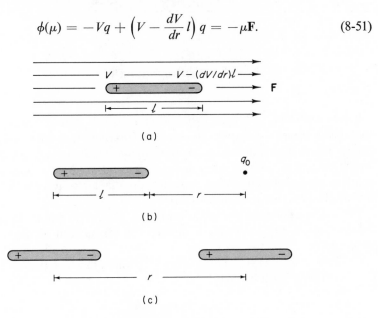

(a)

(b)

(c)

Fig. 8-23.

Conversely, a dipole produces a potential. Thus a test charge q_0 experiences the potential energy (Fig. 8-23b)

$$\phi(q_0) = -\frac{qq_0}{r} + \frac{qq_0}{r + l}\, ;$$

if l is small compared to r, then

$$\phi(q_0) = -\frac{qq_0}{r} + \frac{qq_0}{r}\left(1 - \frac{l}{r}\right)$$

$$= -\left(\frac{\mu}{r^2}\right)q_0\, , \tag{8-52}$$

or the potential of a dipole is

$$V(\mu) = \frac{\mu}{r^2} \tag{8-53}$$

and its field is

$$F(\mu) = \frac{2\mu}{r^3} .$$

(8-54)

(Potentials and fields are reported with a positive sign; the interaction energy of a charge or a dipole is minus if attractive and positive if repulsive.)

Two dipoles then interact each with the field of the other to give

$$\phi(\mu, \mu) = -\mu \frac{2\mu}{r^3} = -\frac{2\mu^2}{r^3} .$$

(8-55)

This is the interaction for dipoles end-on, as shown in Fig. 8-23(c). In a liquid, thermal agitation tends to make the relative orientations random, while the interaction energy acts to favor alignment. The analysis is similar to that of Eq. (3-31) and leads to the result [due to W. H. Keesom in 1912]:

$$\phi(\mu, \mu)_{av} = -\frac{2\mu^4}{3kTr^6} .$$

(8-56)

This *orientation* attraction thus varies inversely as the sixth power of the distance between the dipoles. Remember, however, that the derivation has assumed separations large compared to l.

A further type of interaction is that in which a field induces a dipole moment in a polarizable atom or molecule. We have from Eq. (3-19) that the induced moment is proportional to F:

$$\mu_{ind} = \alpha F,$$

or, by Eq. (8-51),

$$\phi(\alpha, F) = -(\mu_{ind})(F) = -\tfrac{1}{2}\alpha F^2$$

(8-57)

(the factor $\frac{1}{2}$ enters because, strictly speaking, we must integrate $\int_0^F \mu_{ind}\, dF$). The induced dipole is instantaneous (as compared to molecular motions) and the potential energy between a dipole and a polarizable species is therefore independent of temperature:

$$\phi(\mu, \alpha) = -\frac{1}{2}\alpha \left(\frac{2\mu}{r^3}\right)^2 = -\frac{2\alpha\mu^2}{r^6} .$$

(8-58)

The interaction must be averaged over all orientations of the dipole; one then obtains

$$\phi(\mu, \alpha) = -\frac{\alpha\mu^2}{r^6} .$$

(8-59)

This is known as the *induced* attraction, worked out by P. Debye in 1920.

Both types of attraction show an inverse-sixth-power dependence on distance, as is found experimentally, for example, in the a/V^3 term of the van der Waals equation. However, van der Waals interactions are not as sensitive to temperature as the orientation attraction calls for and also exist between molecules having no dipole moments, such as N_2 and other homopolar diatomic molecules, symmetric ones such as methane, and of course, rare-gas atoms. Yet another type of attraction must be present, and its source was discovered by F. London in 1930. The London effect is known as the dispersion attraction, and the derivation, while basically a quantum mechanical one, can be explained as follows.

The energy of an atom 1 in a field is, by Eq. (8-57),

$$\phi(\alpha_1, \mathbf{F}) = -\tfrac{1}{2}\alpha_1 \mathbf{F}^2.$$

The source of the field is attributed to the average dipole moment (root mean square average) for the oscillating electron–nucleus system of the second atom, or

$$\mathbf{F}_2 = \frac{2\bar{\mu}_2}{r^3}.$$

Now the polarizability of an atom can be expressed as a sum over all excited states of the transition moment, *ex* (charge times displacement) squared, divided by the energy. If approximated by the largest term, then for atom 2 we have

$$\alpha_2 = \frac{\overline{(ex)^2}}{h\nu_0}, \tag{8-60}$$

where $h\nu_0$ is the ionization energy. The quantity $\overline{(ex)^2}$ is now identified with $\bar{\mu}_2^{\,2}$, so we have

$$\phi(\alpha, \alpha) = -\frac{1}{2}\alpha_1\left(\frac{2\bar{\mu}_2}{r^3}\right)^2 = -\frac{2\alpha_1\alpha_2 h\nu_0}{r^6} = -\frac{2\alpha^2 h\nu_0}{r^6}.$$

A more accurate derivation gives for the *dispersion* (or induced dipole–induced dipole) attraction

$$\phi(\alpha, \alpha) = -\frac{3\alpha^2 h\nu_0}{4r^6}. \tag{8-61}$$

The situation to this point is summarized in Tables 8-6 and 8-7; in Table 8-7 expressions in boxes are for the three types of net attractive interactions between neutral molecules. They all vary with the inverse sixth power of the distance between molecules and all are approximate, particularly in assuming that the distance between molecules is large compared to the molecular size. Nonetheless,

Table 8-6. *Electrical Interactions*

A molecule with:	Produces:		Has an energy of interaction with:	
	Potential V	Field $\mathbf{F}$	A potential V	A field $\mathbf{F}$
Charge q	$\lvert q/r \rvert$	$\lvert q/r^2 \rvert$	$\phi = qV$	—
Dipole μ	$\lvert \mu/r^2 \rvert$	$\lvert 2\mu/r^3 \rvert$	—	$\phi = -\mu \mathbf{F}$
Polarizability α	—	—	—	$\phi = -\frac{1}{2}\alpha \mathbf{F}^2$

Table 8-7. *Interaction Energies ϕ*

	Ion q	Dipole μ	Polarizable molecule α
Ion q	$\lvert q^2/r \rvert$	$\lvert q\mu/r^2 \rvert$	$-\frac{1}{2}\alpha q^2/r^4$
Dipole μ	—	$\lvert 2\mu^2/r^3 \rvert$	$-2\alpha\mu^2/r^6$
		$\boxed{\phi_{\text{av}} = -2\mu^4/3kTr^6}$	$\boxed{\phi_{\text{av}} = -\alpha\mu^2/r^6}$
Polarizable molecule α	—	—	$\boxed{-\frac{3}{4}\alpha^2 h\nu_0/r^6}$

it is instructive to compare their relative magnitudes. The calculated energies will be in ergs if dipole moments are given in units of esu centimeter, polarizabilities in cubic centimeter and ionization energy $h\nu_0$ in ergs. Table 8-8 summarizes some

Table 8-8. *Contributions to the Interaction Energies between Neutral Molecules[a]*

Molecule	$10^{18}\mu$ (esu cm)	$10^{24}\alpha$ (cm^3)	$h\nu_0$ (eV)[b]	$10^{60}\phi r^6$ (erg cm^6)		
				μ–μ [c]	μ–α	α–α
He	0	0.2	24.7	0	0	1.2
Ar	0	1.6	15.8	0	0	48
CO	0.12	1.99	14.3	0.0034	0.057	67.5
HCl	1.03	2.63	13.7	18.6	5.4	105
NH$_3$	1.5	2.21	16	84	10	93
H$_2$O	1.84	1.48	18	190	10	47

[a] Adapted from J. O. Hirschfelder, C. F. Curtiss, and R. B. Bird, "Molecular Theory of Gases and Liquids," corrected ed., p. 988. Wiley, New York, 1964.

[b] One electron-volt (eV) corresponds to 1.602×10^{-12} erg (or 23 kcal mole^{-1}).

[c] Calculated for 20°C.

calculations. The dispersion attraction is large for all types of molecules, the induced attraction is relatively small for all types, and the orientation attraction can be dominant for very polar molecules. The numbers in the table are for ϕr^6 and actual energies can be obtained on insertion of a value for the intermolecular distance. For example, if we set $r = 4$ Å, then ϕ for argon becomes $48 \times 10^{-60}/$ 4.1×10^{-45} or 1.17×10^{-14} erg molecule^{-1} or 170 cal mole^{-1}. If the liquid is close-packed, each atom has 12 nearest neighbors and the energy of vaporization should be $12\phi/2$, or about 1000 cal mole^{-1}. The actual value is 1600 cal mole^{-1}. The calculation for water leads to about 5 kcal mole^{-1} for ΔE_v, and the much higher observed value of 10 kcal mole^{-1} is explained in terms of hydrogen bonding.

8-ST-2   The Viscosity of Liquids

Before we take up some further aspects of the viscosity of liquids, the derivation of the Poiseuille equation (2-60) is in order. The situation is illustrated in Fig. 8-24(a), which shows the flow lines for a liquid undergoing streamline flow down a circular tube. An inner cylinder of radius r has an area of $2\pi r$ per unit length of tube, or a total area of $2\pi r l$. It therefore experiences a frictional

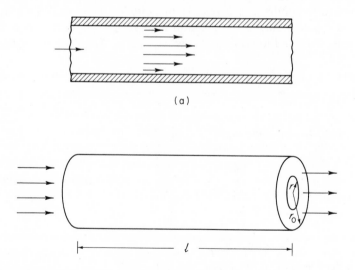

(a)

Fig. 8-24. *Streamline flow down a cylindrical tube: (a) velocity profile, (b) derivation of Eqs. (8-64) and (2-60).*

drag or force, according to the defining equation for viscosity, Eq. (2-59):

$$f = \eta(2\pi r l)\frac{dv}{dr}.\tag{8-62}$$

This force is balanced by the pressure drop acting on the area πr^2, so we have

$$(\mathbf{P_1} - \mathbf{P_2})(\pi r^2) = \eta(2\pi r l)\frac{dv}{dr}$$

or

$$dv = \frac{\mathbf{P_1} - \mathbf{P_2}}{2\eta l}\,r\,dr.\tag{8-63}$$

Integration now gives the velocity profile. We take v to be zero at the wall, and so obtain

$$v_r = \tfrac{1}{4}(\mathbf{P_1} - \mathbf{P_2})(r_0{}^2 - r^2),\tag{8-64}$$

where v_r is the velocity at radius r, and r_0 is the radius of the tube. The volume flow of an annulus of thickness dr is $v_r(2\pi r)\,dr$ and the total volume flow through the pipe is obtained by integration [Eq. (2-60)]

$$\frac{V}{t} = \frac{\pi(\mathbf{P_1} - \mathbf{P_2})r_0{}^4}{8\eta l},$$

which is the desired equation.

We turn now to a different aspect. An important theory of liquid viscosity is due to H. Eyring. The liquid is viewed as being somewhat structured, as shown in Fig. 8-25, so that in order for a molecule to pass into a nearby hole, it must get through a bottleneck or energy barrier. It must, in other words, escape from the solvent cage spoken of earlier. Were it not for this barrier, the rate of jumping through would be about that corresponding to a vibration frequency—for a vibration of energy $h\nu_0$ equal to kT, the frequency ν_0 is kT/h, and we take this to be the natural jump frequency. The presence of the barrier reduces the probability of the jump by the Boltzmann factor $e^{-\epsilon^*/kT}$, where ϵ^* is the energy required. We now have

$$\text{rate of jumping} = \frac{kT}{h}\,e^{-\epsilon^*/kT}.\tag{8-65}$$

In the absence of any stress, jumps occur equally frequently in either direction, but if a shear force is applied, then the effect is to make jumps easier one way than

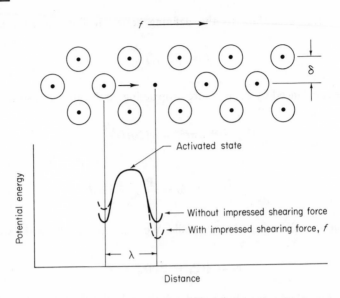

$f \longrightarrow$

δ

Activated state

Without impressed shearing force

With impressed shearing force, f

Potential energy

λ

Distance

Fig. 8-25. *Theoretical model for viscous flow. (From J. O. Hirschfelder, C. F. Curtiss, and R. B. Bird, "Molecular Theory of Gases and Liquids," corrected ed. Copyright 1964, Wiley, New York. Used by permission of John Wiley & Sons, Inc.)*

the other. If the force is f per unit area and the effective area of a molecule is σ, then the theory assumes that the energy barrier gains or loses an increment of energy equal to $f\sigma$ times the distance over which the force acts. This last is taken to be $\frac{1}{2}\lambda$, where λ is the jump distance. Thus we have

rate of forward jumps: $\dfrac{kT}{h} e^{-(\epsilon^* - \frac{1}{2}f\sigma\lambda)/kT}$

rate of backward jumps: $\dfrac{kT}{h} e^{-(\epsilon^* + \frac{1}{2}f\sigma\lambda)/kT}$.

The net rate of jumping is the difference between the forward and backward rates:

net jump rate: $\dfrac{kT}{h} e^{-\epsilon^*/kT} [e^{f\sigma\lambda/2kT} - e^{-f\sigma\lambda/2kT}]$.

The quantity $f\sigma\lambda/2kT$ is usually small compared to unity, and so the exponentials are customarily expanded and only the first terms taken:

net jump rate: $\dfrac{kT}{h} e^{-\epsilon^*/kT} \dfrac{f\sigma\lambda}{kT}$.

The net flow velocity in the layer is the jump rate times λ, so we have

$$v = \frac{kT}{h} e^{-\epsilon^*/kT} \frac{f\sigma\lambda}{kT} \lambda.$$

Since f is the relative force between adjacent layers, v is therefore the relative layer velocity. It follows that the velocity gradient dv/dx is just v/δ. From the definition of viscosity, Eq. (2-59), we have

$$\eta = \frac{\text{force/unit area}}{dv/dx},$$

so

$$\eta = \frac{f/\sigma}{v/\delta} = \frac{\delta}{\sigma^2\lambda^2} h e^{\epsilon^*/kT} \tag{8-66}$$

or

$$\eta \simeq \mathbf{n} h e^{\epsilon^*/kT}, \tag{8-67}$$

where $\mathbf{n}$ denotes the concentration in molecules per cubic centimeter.

Equation (8-67) is now in the same form as Eq. (8-45), where A of the latter equation is equal to $1/\mathbf{n}h$ according to the Eyring theory. The preceding discussion is not complete in that the theory adds, in effect, that the jump frequency may be $(kT/h)A'e^{-(\epsilon^*/kT)}$, where A' is an added factor. Equation (8-67) does not fare too badly, however. As an example, $\epsilon^* = 2600$ cal mole^{-1} for CCl_4 (from Table 8-4) and $\mathbf{n} = 6.02 \times 10^{23}/97$. Insertion of these numbers into the equation gives $\eta = 0.51$ (centipoise) at 0°C, as compared to the observed value of 1.329.

An interesting point is that the energy for the jump process looks rather similar to that required for vaporization. One finds, in fact that the characteristic energy for viscosity tends to be about one-third the energy of vaporization. The values are also not very different from the surface energies per mole. There are a number of interrelations among the various properties of liquids whose general explanation can be given now but whose rigorous treatment is yet to come.

GENERAL REFERENCES

ADAMSON, A. W. (1967). "The Physical Chemistry of Surfaces," 2nd ed. Wiley (Interscience), New York.

HILDEBRAND, J. H., AND SCOTT, R. L. (1950). "The Solubility of Non-Electrolytes," 3rd ed. Van Nostrand-Reinhold, Princeton, New Jersey.

CITED REFERENCES

ADAMSON, A. W. (1967). "Physical Chemistry of Surfaces," 2nd ed. Wiley (Interscience), New York.

BRIDGMAN, P. W. (1949). "The Physics of High Pressures." Bell, London.

NEMETHY, G., AND SCHERAGA, H. A. (1962). *J. Chem. Phys.* **36**, 3382.

ROSSINI, F. A., *et al.* (1959). Tables of Selected Values of Chemical Thermodynamic Quantities. Nat. Bur. Std. Circ. No. 500. U. S. Govt. Printing Office, Washington, D.C.

Exercises

8-1 The normal boiling point of acetone is 56°C and its heat of vaporization is 124.5 cal g⁻¹. Calculate its vapor pressure at 25°C.

Ans. 0.317 atm.

8-2 Calculate the boiling point of CCl_4 under 2 atm pressure; its normal boiling point is 76.8°C and its heat of vaporization is 46.4 cal g⁻¹.

Ans. 102.1°C.

8-3 The vapor pressure of liquid nitrogen is 1 Torr at -226.1°C and 40 Torr at -214.0°C. Calculate the heat of vaporization of nitrogen and its normal boiling point.

Ans. 1683 cal mole⁻¹, 74.4°K (the actual boiling point is 77.3°K; why is the calculated answer so far off?).

8-4 Calculate the weight loss due to evaporation that should occur if five liters of dry air is bubbled through liquid benzene at 26°C. The vapor pressure of benzene is 100 Torr at this temperature. The air volume is measured at 1 atm at 26°C, and atmospheric pressure is 755 Torr.

Ans. 2.43 g.

8-5 Estimate the vapor pressure at 25°C of a liquid which obeys Trouton's rule and whose normal boiling point is 100°C.

Ans. 0.0700 atm.

8-6 Calculate the vapor pressure at infinite temperature of a liquid which obeys Trouton's rule and whose heat of vaporization does not change with temperature.

Ans. 3.89×10^4 atm.

8-7 Using data from Table 8-1, calculate the change in the freezing point of benzene under 1000 atm pressure. The densities of liquid and solid benzene near the melting point are 0.8787 and 0.9000 g cm⁻³, respectively.

Ans. 5.5°C.

8-8 The melting point of a substance increases 0.100°K per 1500 atm applied pressure; the respective liquid and solid densities are 2.300 and 2.350 g cm⁻³. Calculate the entropy of fusion.

Ans. 3.38 cal °K⁻¹ g⁻¹.

Problems

8-9 Calculate ΔG for the process

$$\text{Hg}(l, 357°\text{C}, 1 \text{ atm}) = \text{Hg}(g, 357°\text{C}, 0.1 \text{ atm})$$

(the normal boiling point of Hg is 357°C).

Ans. -2880 cal mole^{-1}.

8-10 Calculate the free energy change and the increase in vapor pressure if liquid benzene at 26°C is subjected to 500 atm mechanical pressure. The ordinary vapor pressure is 100 Torr at 26°C and the density of liquid benzene is 0.879 g cm^{-3}.

Ans. ΔG increases by 1075 cal mole^{-1}, the vapor pressure increases by 510 Torr.

8-11 The surface tension of water around 25°C decreases by 0.14 dyn cm^{-1} °K^{-1}. Calculate the surface energy of water at 25°C.

Ans. 115 erg cm^{-2}.

8-12 The surface tension of a soap solution is 6 dyn cm^{-1}. What is the value of ΔP for a soap bubble blown with this solution and of radius 2 cm?

Ans. 9.1×10^{-3} Torr.

8-13 Obtain the value for the square root of the capillary constant a for benzene at 20°C and the height of capillary rise for benzene in a 0.1-mm diameter capillary.

Ans. $a = 0.258$ cm, $h = 13.3$ cm.

8-14 Find the ideal and the actually observed drop weight in the case of benzene at 20°C and a dropping tip of 3 mm diameter. The density of benzene is 0.879 g cm^{-3}.

Ans. 27.9 mg, 17.7 mg.

8-15 What pull should be required to detach a 3-cm wide Wilhelmy slide from the surface of benzene?

Ans. 174 dyn or 177 mg.

8-16 Calculate the percentage increase over the normal value of the vapor pressure exerted by a mist of 1 μ (1 micron, 10^{-6} m) radius droplets of benzene at 25°C.

Ans. 0.21%.

8-17 How many liters per second of n-octane should flow through a 0.1-mm-diameter, 200-cm-long tube at 40°C? The pressure drop is 2 atm.

Ans. 5.67×10^{-7} liter sec^{-1}.

Problems

8-1 Calculate the vapor pressure of water at 25°C if the water is present in a tank of compressed nitrogen gas at 2000 lb in.$^{-2}$ pressure (state your assumptions).

333

8-2 Show that, according to Trouton's rule, all liquids should have the same hypothetical vapor pressure at infinite temperature. Assume that heats of vaporization do not vary with T.

8-3 Eighteen grams of water supercooled to $-10°C$ are placed in a bomb, completely filling it. The bomb is placed in a thermostat at $-10°C$. Eventually ice forms and the pressure increases until equilibrium is established. Calculate the number of moles of ice present at equilibrium and the final pressure if the heat of fusion of water is 80 cal g^{-1} (independent of T) and the compressibility of liquid water is $\beta = -(1/V)(\partial V/\partial P)_T = 5 \times 10^{-5}$ atm^{-1} (independent of T). Assume ice to be incompressible; molar volumes are water, 18 cm^3 and ice, 20 cm^3 (independent of T).

8-4 A sealed vessel contains 1 mole of liquid water in equilibrium with 1 mole of water vapor and is at 100°C. Calculate the heat capacity of this system at 25°C, 100°C, 110°C, and 125°C, and make a sketch of C versus T, that is, calculate the heat capacity dq/dT at these temperatures, ignoring the heat to warm up the vessel itself. [*Note*: Assume that ΔH of vaporization is 9.7 kcal mole^{-1} at 373°K and that C_P for water liquid and vapor is 18 and 8 cal °K^{-1} mole^{-1}, respectively. Assume also that the volume of vapor is constant (that is, ignore the relatively small changes in vapor volume due to evaporation or condensation to give more or less liquid water), and assume the vapor to be an ideal gas and water to be incompressible.]

8-5 A closed system contains only water and its vapor but is subject to the normal gravitational field. As shown in the accompanying diagram, there is a flat surface of water with a capillary at one side, up which the water level has risen to the height h. According to the formula for effect of surface radius on vapor pressure, the vapor pressure of water immediately above the meniscus must be less than the vapor pressure above the flat water surface. It is proposed that this arrangement constitutes a perpetual motion

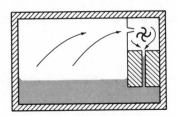

machine, the gradient in water vapor pressure causing a flow of vapor from the flat surface to the meniscus. Such a flow could be made to do work, as shown schematically by the paddle wheel. Since no heat or other form of energy enters the system, this would be a perpetual motion machine.

(a) Demonstrate (mathematically) the fallacy in the preceding statement.
(b) If the statement were true, would the machine be a violation of the first or of the second law of thermodynamics?

8-6 Derive the equation for the height of capillary rise between two parallel glass plates d centimeters apart. Assume the liquid wets the glass and that end effects may be neglected, that is, the plates are very long, and only the rise in the middle is being considered. (See accompanying diagram.)

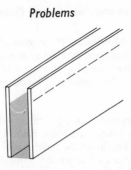

8-7 The surface tension of an organic liquid is determined by the drop weight method. With a tip whose outside diameter is 0.5 cm and whose inside diameter is 0.01 cm, it is found that the weight of 15 drops is 0.60 g. The density of the liquid is 0.85 g cm⁻³; the liquid wets the glass tip. Calculate the surface tension of this liquid using Table 8-2.

8-8 For the case of zero contact angle, a more accurate capillary rise equation than that given is one which takes into account the weight of the meniscus: $\gamma = \frac{1}{2}\rho g r (h + \frac{1}{3}r)$. Derive this equation.

8-9 The surface tension of a liquid of density 0.80 g cm⁻³ is measured by the differential capillary rise method as shown in the accompanying diagram. One capillary has a radius of 0.05 cm and the other a radius of 0.20 cm. The difference in height of the two menisci is 2.50 cm. Calculate the surface tension of the liquid.

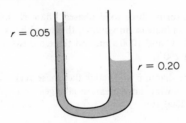

$r = 0.05$

$r = 0.20$

8-10 A method of determining surface tension by means of a weighing operation makes use of the U-tube shown in the accompanying diagram. One leg of the U-tube consists of a capillary of radius r_1 having a reference mark on it and the other leg consists of a somewhat larger tube of radius r_2. The U-tube is filled with water until the meniscus in the capillary reaches the reference mark, and the assembly is then weighed. It is then filled with ethanol, again so that the meniscus in the capillary is at the reference mark, and again weighed. Similarly,

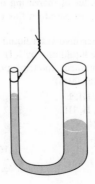

the procedure is repeated with benzene. If the mass of the contents when filled with water is 1.560 g, when filled with ethanol is 1.685 g, and when filled with benzene is 1.620 g, then, knowing that the surface tensions of water and of ethanol are 72 and 22 erg cm^{-2}, respectively, calculate the surface tension of benzene. Densities may be obtained from a handbook; assume 25°C.

8-11 The surface tension of an organic liquid is determined by the drop weight method. Using a tip with outside diameter 0.4 cm and inside diameter 0.1 cm, it is found that the weight of 20 drops is 0.964 g. The density of the liquid is 0.88 g cm^{-3}; the liquid wets the glass tip. Using Table 8-2, calculate the surface tension of this liquid. What error would have been made had Tate's law been used?

8-12 The contact angle of water against Teflon (polytetrafluoroethylene) is 108° at 20°C. Calculate the value of h in the capillary rise equation for the case of a Teflon capillary dipped into water at 20°C. The capillary has 0.3 cm outside diameter and 0.1 mm inside diameter.

8-13 From the following information make a rough sketch of the phase diagram for acetic acid, and explain what phases are in equilibrium under the conditions represented by the various areas and curves in the diagram: (a) Its melting point is 16.6°C under its own vapor pressure of 9.1 mm; (b) solid CH_3COOH exists in two modifications, I and II, both of which are denser than the liquid, and I is the stable modification at low pressure; (c) phases I, II, and liquid are in equilibrium at 55.2°C under a pressure of 2000 atm; (d) the transition temperature from I to II decreases as the pressure is decreased; (e) the normal boiling point of the liquid is 118°C.

8-14 Carbon tetrabromide forms three solid phases. Phase II changes to I at 50°C and 1 atm; I melts at 92°C with an increase in volume; the liquid boils at 190°C. The triple point for I, II, and III is at 115°C and 1000 atm, and there are two phases at 2000 atm and 135°C and at 2000 atm and 200°C.

(a) Draw the phase diagram and letter the phase regions.
(b) Draw a curve showing how pressure changes with volume at 120°C for a pressure increase from 1 to 2000 atm.

8-15 Several solid forms of ammonium nitrate are known, all capable of existing in stable equilibrium with the vapor. These forms are designated as S_1, S_2, ..., and the following triple-point temperatures are known:

S_1, S_2, V	18°C		S_4, S_5, V	125°C
S_2, S_3, V	32°C		S_5, L, V	169°C
S_3, S_4, V	83°C		S_2, S_3, S_4	50°C.

Also, it is known that the order of increasing density is $L < S_3 < S_4 < S_5 < S_2 < S_1$. Sketch a reasonable P–T diagram based on this information.

8-16 The phase equilibrium for water involves a liquid and six solid phases for pressures up to 45,000 atm. Denoting by L the liquid and by I, II, III, V, VI, and VII, the solids (no phase designated by IV has been obtained), the triple points in the system are at the following temperatures (°C) and pressures (atm):

I, III, L	−22	2045
I, II, III	−34.7	2100
III, V, L	−17	3420
II, III, V	−24.3	3400
V, VI, L	0.16	6176
VI, VII, L	81.7	22,400

Problems

The pressures and temperatures of some two-phase equilibria in this system are as follows:

I, II	−75	1800
II, V	−32	4000
V, VI	−20	6360
VI, VII	−80	20,000
VII, L	149	32,000

(a) Draw a phase diagram for this system in the range −80 to 160°C and 1–45,000 atm and letter the phase regions.

(b) Which of the crystalline forms will float in the liquid?

8-17 The accompanying P–T diagram is for phosphorus; dashed lines denote that the two-phase equilibrium in question is unstable with respect to some other phase change. S_1 and S_2 denote white and red phosphorus, respectively.

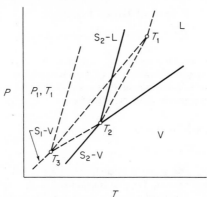

(a) Write along each line the two phases which are supposed to be in equilibrium.

(b) State the phases supposed to be in equilibrium at each triple point. Are all four triple points realizable as a stable or metastable equilibrium? Explain.

(c) Under what conditions (if any) is white phosphorus stable with respect to red phosphorus. How might it be possible to prepare white phosphorus from red phosphorus?

(d) What would you expect to happen on heating at constant pressure some white phosphorus initially at point P_1, T_1 ?

8-18 The vapor pressure of antimony is given here for various temperatures. Make a semilogarithmic plot of P versus T and calculate the heat of vaporization, the normal boiling point, and the value for the Trouton constant.

P (Torr)	50	100	200	300	400	500	600
t (°C)	1070	1137	1190	1225	1252	1280	1300

8-19 (Computer problem) Determine the best least squares straight line for the plot of Problem 8-18 and the standard deviation in the calculated heat of vaporization.

8-20 Equation (8-9) was obtained with the assumption that the heat of vaporization does not change with temperature. Derive the corresponding equation assuming that there is a constant ΔC_P for the vaporization process. Would a plot of $\ln P$ versus $1/T$ still be linear? If not, would the slope at any point give the correct ΔH_v for that temperature?

8-21 Using data from a handbook, make a semilogarithmic plot of the vapor pressure of water against $1/T$ from 25°C up to the critical temperature. Evaluate ΔH_v for various temperatures from this graph, and plot ΔH_v against T.

8-22 The coefficient of compressibility of liquid acetic acid is 9.08×10^{-11} cm^2 dyn^{-1} and its coefficient of thermal expansion is 1.06×10^{-3} °K^{-1}, both at 20°C. Calculate the internal pressure of acetic acid, and the difference $C_P - C_V$. Compare your value of P_{int} with that obtained from the van der Waals constant a for acetic acid.

8-23 The value of P_{int} for water in Table 8-5 is rather different from that given in Section 4-CN-1. Comment on the discrepancy.

Special Topics Problems

8-1 Using the data of Table 3-2, calculate (a) the interaction energy between a nitrogen molecule and a point electronic charge 4 Å away and (b) the interaction energy between two nitrogen molecules separated by 4 Å. Explain in each case whether the interaction is attractive or repulsive. The ionization potential of N_2 is 15.5 eV.

8-2 Make the calculations needed to add a line to Table 8-8 for HI. The ionization potential for HI is 12.8 eV.

8-3 (Calculator problem) Consider two identical dipoles regarded as consisting of point charges q^+ and q^- separated by distance l. The first is held fixed at the origin and directed along the x axis, while the second is a distance x away, also with its center on the x axis, but is allowed to rotate as shown in the accompanying figure. Suppose first that $x = 100l$ and calculate the mutual interaction energy between the two dipoles as a function of θ and also the field

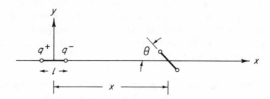

of the rotating dipole at the origin, defined as $\phi = -\mu F$. Plot F as a function of θ. Do the same for the case where the center of the rotating dipole is a distance $x = 1.2l$, $1.5l$, $4l$, $10l$, and $30l$ from the origin and plot F as a function of θ in each case. Finally, plot F as a function of x for various θ; compare the behavior of these plots with the inverse-third-power law given by Eq. (8-54).

8-4 Derive the equation corresponding to Eq. (8-64) but for the case of flow between parallel plates separated by distance r and of length l. The flow V, is now per centimeter width.

8-5 Look up the necessary data and calculate ϵ^* for water and for glycerin. Test how closely Eq. (8-67) gives the actual viscosities, using your values for ϵ^*.

9 SOLUTIONS OF NONELECTROLYTES

9-1 Introduction

We introduce, with this chapter, the physical chemistry of systems for which composition is a state variable. A solution is a mixture at the molecular level of two or more chemical species; it may be gaseous, liquid, or solid. By mixture at the molecular level, we mean that, on traversing a distance of the order of molecular dimensions, the different types of molecules present will be encountered in proportion to the overall composition. If clusters different from average composition are present, then the distance required to be traversed to obtain an average sample will be larger. If this distance is of the order of 100 Å (10^{-6} cm) or more, the system is colloidal in nature; if it reaches 10^{-3}–10^{-4} cm, we speak of the mixture as a suspension, an emulsion, or an aerosol; and if it is larger than about 10^{-3} cm, then, for most purposes, we simply have a mechanical mixture of two or more bulk phases.

There are no sharp natural boundaries in this sequence, but there are practical ones. Most physical chemists have concentrated on the extremes, that is, on molecular solutions or on systems having well-defined bulk phases which themselves may be solutions. On the other hand, much of the biological and physical world involves mixtures of the colloidal or intermediate type of dispersity. The physical chemistry of these last systems is difficult, and its introduction is reserved for Chapter 20. We confine ourselves here to the simpler case of molecular solutions.

A solution or mixture of gases presents little problem, at least at the level of complexity of this text. Unless very dense, gases are always fully miscible and, in the usual laboratory pressure range of around 1 atm, form essentially ideal

339

solutions. Dalton's law of partial pressures [Eq. (1–18)] is well obeyed. We will consider the entropy and free energy of formation of gaseous mixtures in Section 9-4.

Solid solutions, that is, molecular dispersions of two or more species in a solid phase, are quite common. Alloys are one example; also, many ionic crystals are able to substitute one type of ion for another (of the same charge) almost randomly within their crystal lattices. Solid solutions are more difficult to study experimentally, however, and are less studied than liquid ones. Their behavior is also more subject to eccentricities. Most of our data are from, and most of our common experience is with, liquid solutions. For these reasons, the material that follows refers mainly to liquid solutions. It should be remembered, however, that the formal thermodynamics is the same for both types of solutions.

It is now desirable to define the term composition more precisely. A phase may consist of a number of molecular species and yet still qualify thermodynamically as a pure substance. Liquid water, for example, contains not only a large assortment of transient clusters (see Section 8-CN-2), but also definite concentrations of hydrogen and hydroxide ions. These are all in equilibrium with each other, however, and their relative proportions are not subject to arbitrary change. Composition with respect to these species is not an independent variable; once we fix the temperature and pressure of a sample of water, we automatically also fix the various equilibrium constants and hence compositions. It is therefore not necessarily the number of species present that serves to characterize a solution. Nor is it necessarily the number of *constituents*. By constituents, we mean chemical species that we can physically measure out in making up a solution. The term *formal* composition denotes the composition calculated in terms of what is weighed out and mixed. We may, for example, prepare a mixture of hydrogen, nitrogen, and ammonia. In the presence of a catalyst, these would be in equilibrium, and it would be sufficient to specify the formal composition with respect to only two of the three species. In the absence of the catalyst, however, all three compositions are independently variable, and the formal composition with respect to all three would have to be specified.

We meet this type of complication by using the term *component*. The number of components of a solution (or of any mixture) is the least number of independently variable chemical species required to define the composition of the solution (and of all phases present, if there is more than one). Hydrogen plus nitrogen plus ammonia plus catalyst is a two-component system; without the catalyst, it becomes a three-component system. Ordinary water is a one-component system; water plus solute is a two-component system, and so forth.

As to compositions themselves, various measures are used. A common one for this chapter will be the mole fraction, denoted by x_i for a liquid solution and, for clarity, by y_i for a gaseous solution. Mole fractions are strictly additive. That is, the total number of moles of a solution is just the sum of the numbers of moles of each species, and the mole fraction composition of a solution formed when two others are mixed is strictly obtainable on this basis. Volume fractions ϕ_i are sometimes used, but the volume of a solution is not in general equal to the sum of the volumes of the constituents mixed, and care must be taken in the definition of the exact experimental basis for a volume fraction.

The term molality, m, denotes a kind of mole fraction which is well suited to aqueous solutions. It means the number of moles of the dilute or solute component per 1000 g of the major or solvent component. Finally, it is convenient both for the laboratory chemist and in certain theoretical treatments to use volume concentration. The term molarity, M, will be used here to denote moles per liter of solution (not of solvent alone), and n to denote the rational concentration unit of molecules per cubic centimeter of solution.

Finally, we will deal with solutions mainly from the phenomenological or classical thermodynamic point of view. Much formal statistical thermodynamics has been developed for solutions, but the complications are such that this approach is not as yet a powerful one in actual application. The statistical thermodynamic point of view is therefore discussed only briefly, in the Commentary and Notes section.

9-2   The Vapor Pressure of Solutions. Raoult's and Henry's Laws

The vapor pressure and vapor composition in equilibrium with a solution of volatile substances constitute important and very useful information. The practical usefulness lies in the application to distillation processes, and the physical chemical importance, in the provision of a means of studying the thermodynamic properties of liquids and of testing models for the structure of liquids. One function of this section is therefore to introduce characteristic data and behavior as a preliminary to the thermodynamic treatments.

A.   Vapor Pressure Diagrams

Vapor pressure data are customarily displayed in the form of vapor pressure–composition diagrams for some particular temperature, as illustrated schematically in Fig. 9-1. Here P_{tot} is the total combined vapor pressure above varying compositions of a solution of liquids A and B. The liquids are, in this example, taken to be fairly similar, and the P_{tot} curve, although not linear, decreases steadily from $P_A°$, the vapor pressure of pure A, to $P_B°$, that of pure B, as x_B is varied from 0 to 1. The vapor is a mixture of gaseous A and B, and the variations of the partial pressures P_A and P_B are also shown. We assume that no other gases are present and that the vapors are ideal, so that

$$P_{tot} = P_A + P_B . \qquad (9-1)$$

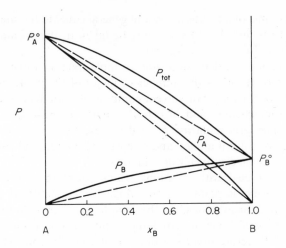

Fig. 9-1. *Vapor pressure–composition diagram.*

If A and B are very similar, the limiting case being one of two substances differing only in isotopic content, then the vapor pressure diagram takes on an especially simple appearance. A good example is provided by the benzene–toluene system, shown in Fig. 9-2. The values of P_{tot}, P_b, and P_t are now given by nearly straight lines. Thus we have

$$P_t = P_t^\circ x_t, \qquad P_b = P_b^\circ(1 - x_t) = P_b^\circ x_b, \tag{9-2}$$

where x_t and x_b denote the mole fractions of toluene and of benzene, respectively, and the degree superscript indicates a pure phase. Then P_{tot} is simply

$$P_{tot} = P_t + P_b = P_b^\circ + (P_t^\circ - P_b^\circ) x_t, \tag{9-3}$$

which is the equation of the straight line connecting P_b° with P_t°. A solution with this behavior is called an ideal solution, and the general form corresponding to Eqs. (9-2) is called *Raoult's law* (1884):

$$P_i = P_i^\circ x_i. \tag{9-4}$$

For simplicity, we will largely restrict the discussion to two-component systems, for which the Raoult's law statements are

$$P_1 = P_1^\circ x_1, \qquad P_2 = P_2^\circ x_2, \tag{9-5}$$

with the corollary that

$$P_{tot} = P_1^\circ + (P_2^\circ - P_1^\circ) x_2. \tag{9-6}$$

As will be seen in the Commentary and Notes section, Raoult's law corresponds to a particularly simple picture of a solution—essentially one in which the com-

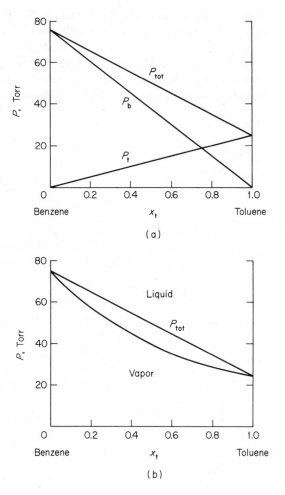

Fig. 9-2.   *The benzene–toluene system at 20°C: (a) vapor pressure–composition diagram; (b) liquid and vapor composition diagram.*

ponents are distinguishable, but just barely, so that their physical properties are virtually identical. The situation is rather analogous to that of the ideal gas; the ideal gas law also corresponds to a particular, very simple picture. The ideal gas law is, moreover, the limiting law for all real gases, and, in this respect, is not hypothetical or approximate at all. The same is believed to be true for Raoult's law. Experimental evidence indicates that Raoult's law is the limiting law for all solutions, approached by each component as its mole fraction approaches unity. That is, as a limiting law statement, Eq. (9-4) reads

$$\lim_{x_i \to 1} P_i = P_i^{\circ} x_i . \tag{9-7}$$

343

Notice that the curves for P_A and P_B are drawn in Fig. 9-1 so that they approach the Raoult's law line as x_A and x_B approach unity. The acetone–chloroform system shown in Fig. 9-3 provides a specific illustration. In this case, the partial pressure curves lie below the Raoult's law lines, whereas in Fig. 9-1, they lie above the Raoult's law lines. We speak of the first situation as one of negative deviation, and the second, as one of positive deviation (from ideality).

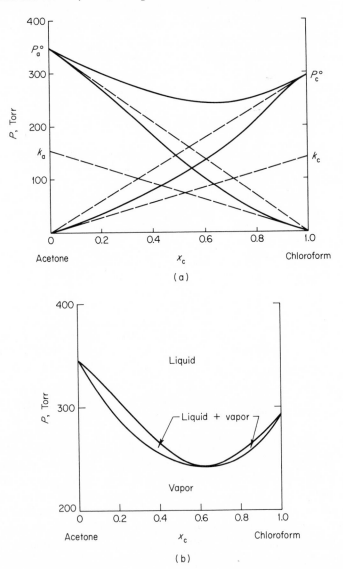

Fig. 9-3. *The acetone–chloroform system at 35°C, showing negative deviation from ideality: (a) vapor pressure–composition diagram; (b) liquid and vapor composition diagram.*

Although Raoult's law as a limiting law can be rationalized in terms of models, there is not quite the same intuitive basis for it as there is for the ideal gas law as a limiting law. A partial explanation follows. A molecule of species A becomes surrounded by like molecules as x_A approaches unity, that is, the presence of a few B molecules does not appreciably change the environment of the A molecules from that in pure A. Experimental observation affirms that the reduction in P_A from $P_A°$ now depends only on the mole fraction of B and not on its chemical nature. It is this attribute of Raoult's limiting law that gives the set of colligative properties such great importance (Chapter 10).

Acceptance of Raoult's limiting law provides a basis for the understanding of a second limiting law, *Henry's law*. Henry's law states that the partial pressure of a component becomes proportional to its mole fraction in the limit of zero concentration:

$$\lim_{x_i \to 0} P_i = k_i x_i .$$

(9-8)

This is illustrated in Fig. 9-4, in which the vapor pressure curves of Fig. 9-1 are shown approaching the limiting slopes k_A and k_B; these slopes define straight lines whose intercepts are k_A and k_B. Under the limiting Henry's law condition each molecule of component A has become surrounded by B molecules. The environment is thus not one of pure A, but another environment determined by the nature of the A–B interactions. We can regard k_A as the hypothetical vapor pressure that pure A would exert if the molecules all had this different environment, and similarly, k_B as the hypothetical vapor pressure that pure B would exert in an environment consisting of A molecules.

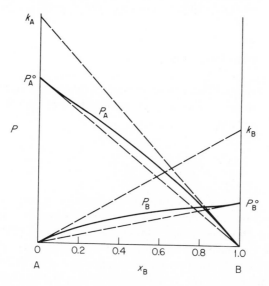

Fig. 9-4. *System showing positive deviation from ideality; illustration of Henry's and Raoult's laws.*

Like Raoult's law, Henry's law applies as a limiting law to systems of both positive and negative deviation from ideality. The partial pressure curves in Figs. 9-3 and 9-4 obey both limiting laws.

B.   Solubility of Gases

Henry's law is approximately valid for any solute in a dilute solution, and a particular application is to the solubility of gases in liquids. As an approximate law, Eq. (9-8) becomes

$$P_2 = k_2 x_2 , \qquad (9\text{-}9)$$

where species 2 in a two-component system will, by convention, be taken to refer to the solute. The solubilities of permanent, inert gases (such as N_2, O_2, CO, and CH_4) in water at 25°C give k_2 values of $\sim 10^5$ atm. Thus k_2 is 0.43×10^5 atm for O_2 in water; the solubility is then $x_{O_2} = 1/(0.43 \times 10^5) = 2.3 \times 10^{-5}$ at 1 atm. Since there are 55.5 moles of water per liter, this solubility corresponds to 1.23×10^{-3} M per atm at 25°C. The partial pressure of oxygen in air is 0.2 atm, so the actual concentration, due to equilibration with air, is $(1.23 \times 10^{-3})(0.2) = 2.5 \times 10^{-4}$ M. In this case, there will also be dissolved nitrogen present, corresponding to its k_2 value of 0.86×10^5 atm.

Some of the literature report Henry's law constants for gases in terms of the volume of gas dissolved, measured at the temperature and pressure in question, per unit volume of solvent. The Henry's law constant for oxygen becomes, on this basis, $(1.23 \times 10^{-3})(0.082)(298)/1.0$ or 0.030 liter of O_2 per liter of water.

C.   Vapor Composition Diagrams

A vapor pressure diagram also contains the information to give the composition of the vapor in equilibrium with a given composition of solution. Thus, for the system of Fig. 9-1, we have

$$y_A = \frac{P_A}{P_{tot}} = \frac{P_A}{P_A + P_B} , \qquad y_B = \frac{P_B}{P_{tot}} = \frac{P_B}{P_A + P_B} , \qquad (9\text{-}10)$$

where y_A and y_B denote the mole fractions of A and B in the vapor, respectively. A conventional way of supplying this information is to plot the vapor composition corresponding to each value of P_{tot}, along with P_{tot} versus liquid composition, as shown in Fig. 9-5. For example, for a liquid of composition x_1, P_{tot} has the value P_1, and the solution is in equilibrium with vapor of composition y_1. The corresponding vapor composition plots are included in Figs. 9-2(b) and 9-3(b).

Vapor composition diagrams are in effect phase maps or phase diagrams. If the system is contained in a piston and cylinder arrangement thermostated to the given

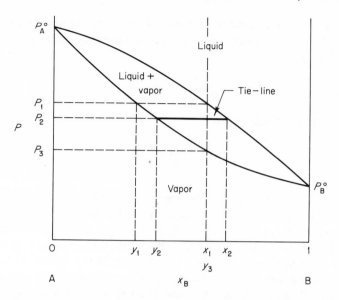

Fig. 9-5. *Use of vapor pressure and vapor composition diagrams—the lever principle.*

temperature, then from Fig. 9-5, liquid of composition x_1 cannot vaporize if the pressure is greater than P_1 ; the system will consist of liquid phase only. The same will be true for any composition and pressure defining a point lying above the liquid line. The upper region of the diagram is one of liquid phase only. Similarly, a system of composition x_1 at a pressure less than P_3 will consist of vapor phase only. The lower region of the diagram must be one of vapor phase only. The liquid and vapor composition lines thus mark the boundaries of the liquid-only and vapor-only regions, respectively. Finally, a system whose overall composition and pressure locate a point between the two lines will consist of a mixture of phases.

A diagram such as that of Fig. 9-5 allows a complete tracing of the sequence of events as the pressure of a system is changed at constant temperature. Suppose, for example, that a system of composition x_1 is initially under some high pressure. As the pressure is reduced vaporization will begin at P_1 , producing vapor of composition y_1 . With further decrease in pressure more and more vaporization must occur, and since the vapor is richer in A than is the liquid, the latter must move to the right in composition. When the pressure has reached P_2 , liquid of composition x_2 is now in equilibrium with vapor of composition y_2 . Finally, when the pressure has been reduced to P_3 all the liquid will be vaporized and further reduction in pressure will merely expand the mixed vapors.

Since the entire system is a closed one, the vapor and liquid phases are always of some uniform relative composition, and their relative amounts can be calculated by material balance. For example, if the system consists of n moles total, then at any point

$$n = n_v + n_l ,$$ (9-11)

347

where n_l and n_v are the number of moles of liquid phase and of vapor phase, respectively. Thus for a system of overall composition x_1 and at pressure P_2 the material balance in B is

$$nx_l = n_v y_2 + n_l x_2 = n_v y_2 + (n - n_v) x_2 . \qquad (9\text{-}12)$$

Equation (9-12) rearranges to give

$$\frac{n_v}{n} = \frac{x_2 - x_1}{x_2 - y_2} . \qquad (9\text{-}13)$$

Equation (9-13) can be given a very simple and useful graphical interpretation. The horizontal line connecting the points y_2 and x_2 is known as a *tie-line*. In general a tie-line connects the compositions of equilibrium phases. The difference $x_2 - y_2$ corresponds to the length of the tie-line at P_2 and the difference $x_2 - x_1$, the length of the right-hand section of the line. Alternatively, if the tie-line is regarded as a balance pivoted at the point x_1, then weights proportional to n_v and n_l will just balance if placed at the y_2 and x_2 ends, respectively. Equation (9-13) with its associated graphical interpretation is known as the *lever principle*.

D. Maximum and Minimum Vapor Pressure Diagrams

The acetone–chloroform system of Fig. 9-3 shows a minimum in P_{tot}. The physical interpretation is along the lines of Fig. 8-6, where for a pure liquid the energy of vaporization was attributed to $n\phi/2$, where n is the number of nearest neighbors and ϕ, is the interaction energy. A negative deviation then suggests that ϕ_{AB} is greater than ϕ_{AA} or ϕ_{BB}, so that the ease of vaporization is reduced if A and B molecules mutually surround each other.

Such an increase in interaction energy between unlike molecules would, as an extreme, lead to the formation of an actual compound. In the case of Fig. 9-3 the appearance is more that of a tendency toward association. The fact that the deviation of P_{tot} from the ideal or Raoult's law line is at a maximum at about 50 % mole fraction suggests that the association is of the AB type (and not A_2B or AB_2, and so on).

The extreme case, in terms of this picture, would be one in which a very stable AB compound actually formed, as illustrated in Fig. 9-6. Systems in which the overall composition x_B is less than 0.5 consist of a solution of A and AB, those of composition greater than 0.5 consist of a solution of B and AB. These two solutions are shown as ideal but need not be. Note that there is a discontinuity in the slope of the P_{tot} line at $x_B = 0.5$. In the acetone–chloroform system, however, the P_{tot} line is rounded at the minimum—an indication that no very stable AB complex forms. One may, in fact, estimate the dissociation constant of such a complex from the degree of curvature around this minimum.

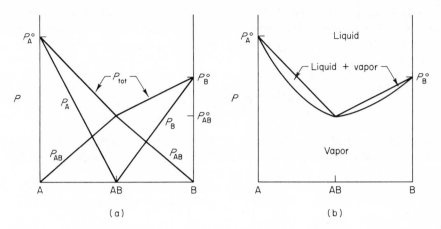

Fig. 9-6. *Formation of a stable compound* AB, *but with the solutions* A + AB *and* B + AB *ideal.*

Deviations from ideality may, of course, be positive. This is illustrated in Fig. 9-7 for the system benzene–ethanol. The physical argument is now reversed; we conclude that ϕ_{AB} is less than ϕ_{AA} or ϕ_{BB}. The extreme of this situation is that in which the two liquids have limited solubility in each other. This means that two phases α and β of different composition can coexist, and that therefore

$$P_A{}^\alpha = P_A{}^\beta = P_A^{\alpha\beta}, \qquad P_B{}^\alpha = P_B{}^\beta = P_B^{\alpha\beta}, \qquad P = P_A + P_B, \qquad (9\text{-}14)$$

where the superscript α or β refers to a quantity for a single phase and the super-

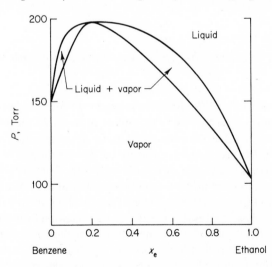

Fig. 9-7. *The benzene–ethanol system at 35°C.*

script $\alpha\beta$ for a quantity when both phases are present. This situation is shown in Fig. 9-8(a). The corresponding vapor composition diagram is given in Fig. 9-8(b). A mixture of the two mutually saturated phases produces a single vapor composition $y^{\alpha\beta}$:

$$y^{\alpha\beta} = \frac{P_B^{\alpha\beta}}{P_A^{\alpha\beta} + P_B^{\alpha\beta}} = \frac{P_B^{\alpha\beta}}{P^{\alpha\beta}}. \qquad (9\text{-}15)$$

This composition will often lie between x^α and x^β, as in the figure, but does not need to. If, say, a system of composition x_1 is placed in a piston and cylinder arrangement

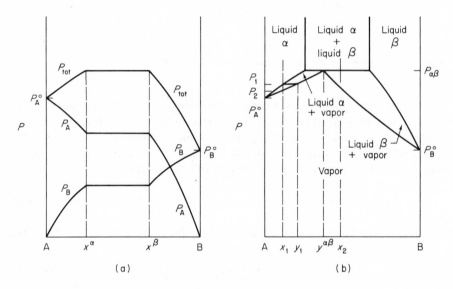

Fig. 9-8. *Partial miscibility. (a) Vapor pressure–composition diagram. (b) Corresponding phase diagram.*

at constant temperature and the pressure is gradually reduced, then at pressure P_1 vapor of composition y_1 begins to form, and at pressure P_2 the system is entirely vapor. On the other hand, if the system is initially of composition x_2 it will consist of phases α and β (in proportions given by the lever principle). At $P^{\alpha\beta}$ vapor of composition $y^{\alpha\beta}$ forms, and since this is the only vapor pressure possible so long as the two liquid phases are present, vaporization continues until one or the other phase is used up. In this particular example α phase is used up first and vaporization of the remaining β phase continues until the system is entirely gaseous.

The limiting situation of complete immiscibility is shown in Fig. 9-9. The only possible type of sequence is that for the system x_2. All systems now consist of two liquid phases initially, and when the pressure is reduced to P^{AB} vapor phase of composition y^{AB} forms and continues to do so until one liquid or the other is gone.

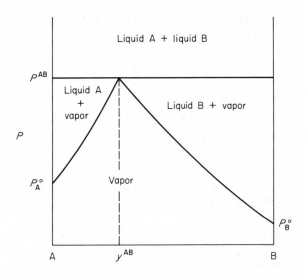

Fig. 9-9.   *Phase diagram for the case of complete immiscibility.*

The remaining liquid then continues to vaporize along the appropriate vapor composition line. The composition y^{AB} is in this case given by

$$y^{AB} = \frac{P_B{}^\circ}{P_A{}^\circ + P_B{}^\circ} = \frac{P_B{}^\circ}{P^{AB}}. \tag{9-16}$$

E.   A Model for Nonideal Solutions

A fairly simple treatment developed by M. Margules in 1895 is still a very useful one. The difference between ϕ_{AB} and ϕ_{AA} can be regarded as an energy term which enters as a Boltzmann factor modifying P_A over its ideal value. This energy difference should be approximately proportional to $x_B{}^2$ on the basis of arguments about the proportion of A–A and A–B interactions, and one writes

$$P_A = P_A{}^\circ x_A \exp(\alpha x_B{}^2), \tag{9-17}$$

where α is a characteristic constant (and is temperature-dependent). Since the A–B interaction is a mutual one, a similar equation applies to P_B :

$$P_B = P_B{}^\circ x_B \exp(\alpha x_A{}^2), \tag{9-18}$$

where α is the same constant as in Eq. (9-17). Notice the Eqs. (9-17) and (9-18) give Raoult's law as a limiting law, and reduce to Raoult's law for all compositions if $\alpha = 0$.

The model also provides a relationship between the Henry's law constants k_A and k_B [Eq. (9-8)]. Thus from Eq. (9-17) we have

$$\frac{dP_A}{dx_A} = P_A{}^\circ[\exp(\alpha x_B{}^2)](1 - 2\alpha x_A x_B) \tag{9-19}$$

and in the limit when $x_A \to 0$,

$$k_A = P_A{}^\circ e^\alpha. \tag{9-20}$$

The situation is symmetric, and so

$$k_B = P_B{}^\circ e^\alpha. \tag{9-21}$$

Thus the two Henry's law constants are predicted to be in the ratio of the P° values. This rule is obeyed reasonably well except for strongly associated liquids (α very negative).

In the case of positive deviation α is positive, and if sufficiently so, the curve calculated from Eq. (9-18) will show a maximum and a minimum, as illustrated in Fig. 9-10. The situation is reminiscent of that with respect to the van der Waals

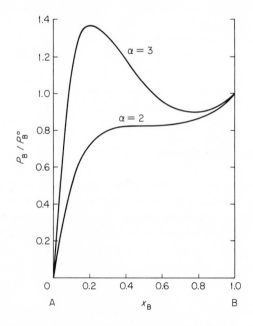

Fig. 9-10. *Plot of P_B according to the Margules equation (9-18). (The plot of P_A is similar, but increases from right to left, of course.)*

equation and the conclusion is that the experimental vapor pressure curve must show an equivalent horizontal portion and that the system is one of partial miscibility. The "critical temperature" is such that $\alpha = 2$. For this value of α the system just fails to show a miscibility gap.

9-3 The Thermodynamics of Multicomponent Systems

Some aspects of the more formal thermodynamics of solutions, gaseous, liquid, or solid, must now be taken up. An important result will be the introduction of a new quantity, the chemical potential, which plays much the same role for solutions as G does for pure substances. The criterion for phase equilibrium is then expanded to the case of phases that are solutions, and an important new relationship, the *Gibbs–Duhem equation*, is introduced. Further developments are given in the Special Topics section, including the thermodynamic treatment of the surface tension of solutions. The principal new concept to be understood is that of *partial molal quantities*. Thermodynamics has become more complicated, but unavoidably so.

A. The Chemical Potential

The various thermodynamic functions must now include the amount of each component as a variable. That is, we consider what is called an *open system*, or one which may gain or lose chemical species. Thus the total energy E is a function of S, v, and now n_i, where n_i denotes the number of moles of the ith species, and sans serif (E, S, and so on) denotes extensive quantities not on a per mole basis. The total differential for E is

$$dE = \left(\frac{\partial E}{\partial S}\right)_{v,n_i} dS + \left(\frac{\partial E}{\partial v}\right)_{S,n_i} dv + \left(\frac{\partial E}{\partial n_1}\right)_{S,v} dn_1 + \left(\frac{\partial E}{\partial n_2}\right)_{S,v} dn_2 + \cdots.$$

$$(9\text{-}22)$$

Comparison with Eq. (6-12), to which Eq. (9-22) should reduce if the dn_i are zero, gives

$$dE = T\,dS - P\,dv + \sum_i \left(\frac{\partial E}{\partial n_i}\right)_{S,v} dn_i. \qquad (9\text{-}23)$$

Similarly, free energy is now a function of T, P, and also n_i, so we have

$$dG = \left(\frac{\partial G}{\partial T}\right)_{P,n_i} dT + \left(\frac{\partial G}{\partial P}\right)_{T,n_i} dP + \sum_i \left(\frac{\partial G}{\partial n_i}\right)_{T,P} dn_i. \qquad (9\text{-}24)$$

Comparison with Eq. (6-43) identifies the first two coefficients, so that

$$dG = -S\,dT + v\,dP + \sum_i \left(\frac{\partial G}{\partial n_i}\right)_{T,P} dn_i. \qquad (9\text{-}25)$$

Alternatively, however, we have

$$dG = dH - d(TS) = dE + P\,dv + v\,dP - T\,dS - S\,dT,$$

so, in combination with Eq. (9-23), it must also be true that

$$dG = -S\,dT + v\,dP + \sum_i \left(\frac{\partial E}{\partial n_i}\right)_{S,v} dn_i. \qquad (9\text{-}26)$$

Thus we have

$$\mu_i = \left(\frac{\partial E}{\partial n_i}\right)_{S,v} = \left(\frac{\partial G}{\partial n_i}\right)_{T,P}, \qquad (9\text{-}27)$$

where μ_i is a new quantity called the *chemical potential*.

Equations (9-23) and (9-26) can now be written

$$dE = T\,dS - P\,dv + \sum_i \mu_i\,dn_i, \qquad (9\text{-}28)$$

$$dG = -S\,dT + v\,dP + \sum_i \mu_i\,dn_i. \qquad (9\text{-}29)$$

The second of these is perhaps the more useful since it identifies the chemical potential μ_i as the free energy change of a system per mole of added component i, with temperature, pressure, and the other mole quantities kept constant. The chemical potential is a coefficient (like heat capacity) and we are really talking about the change dG for a small increment dn_i. The added amount of the ith component should not be sufficient to change the composition of the system appreciably since μ_i will depend on composition as well as on temperature and pressure.

B. *Partial Molal Quantities*

The chemical potential is one of a family of partial molal quantities. If, in in general, we have some extensive property $\mathscr{P}$, then for a solution $\bar{\mathscr{P}}_i$ is the partial molal property for the ith component:

$$\bar{\mathscr{P}}_i = \left(\frac{\partial \mathscr{P}}{\partial n_i}\right)_{T,P_{\text{tot}}}. \qquad (9\text{-}30)$$

Thus

$$\bar{V}_i = \left(\frac{\partial v}{\partial n_i}\right)_{T,P}, \qquad (9\text{-}31)$$

$$\bar{H}_i = \left(\frac{\partial H}{\partial n_i}\right)_{T,P}, \qquad (9\text{-}32)$$

and

$$\bar{S}_i = \left(\frac{\partial S}{\partial n_i}\right)_{T,P}. \tag{9-33}$$

Further, the various thermodynamic coefficients that were derived for a single substance retain the same form for the ith component of a solution if the corresponding partial molal quantities are used. As useful examples, we have

$$\left(\frac{\partial \mu_i}{\partial P}\right)_T = \frac{\partial}{\partial P}\left(\frac{\partial G}{\partial n_i}\right)_{P,T} = \frac{\partial}{\partial n_i}\left(\frac{\partial G}{\partial P}\right)_T = \left(\frac{\partial v}{\partial n_i}\right)_{P,T} = \bar{V}_i \tag{9-34}$$

and, similarly,

$$\left(\frac{\partial \mu_i}{\partial T}\right)_P = -\bar{S}_i. \tag{9-35}$$

Equation (9-34) may be applied to a mixture of ideal gases. By Eq. (1-16), $(\partial v/\partial n_i)_{P,T} = RT/P_i$, where P_i is the partial pressure of the ith species. Then

$$\left(\frac{\partial \mu_i}{\partial P}\right)_T = \bar{V}_i = \frac{RT}{P_i} \quad \text{or} \quad d\mu_i = RT\frac{dP}{P_i}.$$

However, only that part of dP which corresponds to dP_i affects the chemical potential of an ideal gas species, so $dP = dP_i$ and

$$d\mu_i = RT\, d(\ln P_i) \quad \text{(ideal gas)} \tag{9-36}$$

or

$$\mu_i(g) = \mu_i^\circ(g) + RT \ln P_i \quad \text{(ideal gas)}, \tag{9-37}$$

where $\mu_i^\circ(g)$ is the chemical potential of the gas in its standard state, ordinarily taken to be 1 atm. (The same equation applies for a nonideal gas with fugacity f_i replacing P_i—see Section 6-ST-2.) Since $\mu_i^\circ(g)$ refers to pure component i, it could just as well have been written $G_i^\circ(g)$; it seems preferable, however, to keep the notation symmetric.

C.   Criterion for Phase Equilibrium

We are dealing with equilibrium systems, and hence with systems for which no spontaneous change in temperature or pressure occurs. Equation (9-29) then reduces to

$$dG = \sum_i \mu_i\, dn_i. \tag{9-38}$$

If the system consists of a single phase and is chemically isolated, that is, if no chemical species can enter or leave, then the criterion for equilibrium given by Eq. (6-42) applies, so we have

$$dG = 0, \qquad \sum_i \mu_i \, dn_i = 0. \tag{9-39}$$

Alternatively, the system might consist of two (or more) phases in equilibrium. For each phase there will be an equation of the form of Eq. (9-38):

$$dG^\alpha = \sum_i \mu_i{}^\alpha \, dn_i{}^\alpha, \qquad dG^\beta = \sum_i \mu_i{}^\beta \, dn_i{}^\beta, \tag{9-40}$$

and so forth, where

$$dG = dG^\alpha + dG^\beta + \cdots. \tag{9-41}$$

If the entire set of phases is in equilibrium and constitutes a chemically closed system overall, then again dG is zero, and we now have

$$0 = \sum_i \mu_i{}^\alpha \, dn_i{}^\alpha + \sum_i \mu_i{}^\beta \, dn_i{}^\beta + \cdots. \tag{9-42}$$

Suppose that some process occurs in this equilibrium system of phases whereby dn_i moles of the ith species is transferred from phase α to phase β; all other dn quantities are zero. For this process it follows that

$$\mu_i{}^\alpha \, dn_i{}^\alpha + \mu_i{}^\beta \, dn_i{}^\beta = 0. \tag{9-43}$$

Since $dn_i{}^\alpha = -dn_i{}^\beta$ (the total number of moles of the ith species remains the same in the overall system), we have

$$\mu_i{}^\alpha = \mu_i{}^\beta. \tag{9-44}$$

The very important conclusion is that for phase equilibrium between solutions the chemical potential of each species must be the same in every phase in which it is present. Equation (9-44) is a more general statement of the equilibrium condition condition for a pure substance, $G^\alpha = G^\beta$.

D.   The Gibbs–Duhem Equation

A very useful relationship may be obtained from Eq. (9-28). Since our applications will be restricted to two-component systems, we will make the derivation on that basis. The differentials of Eq. (9-28) are all of the form

$$(\text{intensive property}) \times d(\text{extensive property}).$$

We can therefore imagine that we introduce additional amounts of components 1 and 2, keeping the temperature, pressure, and composition (and hence μ_1 and μ_2) constant. The result amounts to an integration giving

$$E = TS - Pv + \mu_1 n_1 + \mu_2 n_2. \tag{9-45}$$

Since

$$G = E + Pv - TS,$$

we can write

$$G = n_1\mu_1 + n_2\mu_2. \tag{9-46}$$

Differentiation of Eq. (9-46) gives

$$dG = n_1\,d\mu_1 + \mu_1\,dn_1 + n_2\,d\mu_2 + \mu_2\,dn_2 \tag{9-47}$$

and comparison with Eq. (9-38) leads to the result

$$n_1\,d\mu_1 + n_2\,d\mu_2 = 0. \tag{9-48}$$

If we divide by the total number of moles, then an alternative form is

$$x_1\,d\mu_1 + x_2\,d\mu_2 = 0. \tag{9-49}$$

Equations (9-48) and (9-49) are alternative forms of the *Gibbs–Duhem equation*. Its great usefulness is in relating the chemical potential change of one component (for a constant-temperature, constant-pressure process) to that of the other. The next section provides some specific applications.

An alternative way of obtaining Eq. (9-48) is as follows. Equation (9-45) is of general validity and may be differentiated to give

$$dE = T\,dS + S\,dT - P\,dv - v\,dP + \mu_1\,dn_1 + n_1\,d\mu_1 + \mu_2\,dn_2 + n_2\,d\mu_2. \tag{9-50}$$

Comparison with Eq. (9-28) gives

$$0 = S\,dT - v\,dP + n_1\,d\mu_1 + n_2\,d\mu_2. \tag{9-51}$$

For a process at constant temperature and pressure, Eq. (9-51) reduces to Eq. (9-48). We will find this type of procedure useful in obtaining the Gibbs adsorption equation (see Special Topics section).

9-4   Ideal Gas Mixtures

The chemical potential of a component of an ideal gas mixture is given by Eq. (9-37),

$$\mu_i(g) = \mu_1°(g) + RT \ln P_i. $$

We can apply this equation to calculate the free energy and entropy change for the isothermal process

$$n_1(\text{gas 1 at } P) + n_2\,(\text{gas 2 at } P) = \text{mixture (at } P, \text{ with } P_1 = x_1 P \text{ and } P_2 = x_2 P). \tag{9-52}$$

357

The process, physically, corresponds to the procedure shown in Fig. 9-11. For pure gases, $G_1 = n_1[\mu_1^\circ(g) + RT \ln P]$ and $G_2 = n_2[\mu_2^\circ(g) + RT \ln P]$. The free energy of the mixture is, by Eq. (9-46),

$$G_{mix} = n_1[\mu_1^\circ(g) + RT \ln P_1] + n_2[\mu_2^\circ(g) + RT \ln P_2],$$

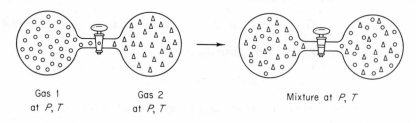

Gas 1   Gas 2   Mixture at P, T
at P, T at P, T

Fig. 9-11.

or, since $P_1 = x_1 P$ and $P_2 = x_2 P$, substitution gives

$$G_{mix} = n_1[\mu_1^\circ(g) + RT \ln P + RT \ln x_1] + n_2[\mu_2^\circ(g) + RT \ln P + RT \ln x_2].$$

The free energy change for process (9-52) is then $G_{mix} - G_1 - G_2$ or

$$\Delta G_M = n_1 RT \ln x_1 + n_2 RT \ln x_2 \qquad \text{(ideal gas).} \qquad (9\text{-}53)$$

The free energy of mixing per mole of mixture is

$$\Delta G_M = x_1 RT \ln x_1 + x_2 RT \ln x_2 \qquad \text{(ideal gas).} \qquad (9\text{-}54)$$

Since $\Delta S = -[\partial(\Delta G)/\partial T]_P$, the entropy of mixing per mole of solution is

$$\Delta S_M = -(x_1 R \ln x_1 + x_2 R \ln x_2) \qquad \text{(ideal gas).} \qquad (9\text{-}55)$$

Notice that the free energy of mixing is independent of P and that the entropy of mixing is independent of both P and T. The latter could have been obtained on the basis of the probability arguments of Section 6-8a (see Commentary and Notes section).

9-5   Ideal and Nonideal Solutions. Activities and Activity Coefficients

We can apply the criterion for equilibrium to the case of a solution and its vapor. The treatment will be in terms of a liquid solution, but it is equally applicable to solid solutions. The vapor phase is assumed, as usual, to be ideal, and for simplicity we consider only a two-component solution. The requirement that the chemical potential of a component be the same in two phases that are in equilibrium may be combined with Eq. (9-37) to give

$$\mu_1(l) = \mu_1(g) = \mu_1^\circ(g) + RT \ln P_1 . \tag{9-56}$$

In the case of a pure liquid $\mu_1(l)$ becomes $\mu_1^\circ(l)$ [or just $G_1^\circ(l)$] and Eq. (9-56) reduces to

$$\mu_1^\circ(l) = \mu^\circ_1(g) + RT \ln P_1^\circ. \tag{9-57}$$

Alternatively, we may add and subtract $RT \ln P_1^\circ$ on the right-hand side of Eq. (9-56) to obtain

$$\mu_1(l) = [\mu_1^\circ(g) + RT \ln P_1^\circ] + RT \ln \frac{P_1}{P_1^\circ}$$

or

$$\mu_1(l) = \mu_1^\circ(l) + RT \ln \frac{P_1}{P_1^\circ} . \tag{9-58}$$

We thus have two ways of expressing the chemical potential of component one. Equation (9-56) does so in terms of $\mu_1^\circ(g)$ and P_1, while Eq. (9-58) does so in terms of $\mu_1^\circ(l)$ and P_1/P_1°. In the first case the standard or reference state is the vapor at unit pressure, 1 atm, and in the second case it is the pure liquid. The equations are symmetric with respect to the components and so a parallel set of relationships applies for component 2:

$$\mu_2(l) = \mu_2^\circ(g) + RT \ln P_2 , \tag{9-59}$$

$$\mu_2(l) = \mu_2^\circ(l) + RT \ln \frac{P_2}{P_2^\circ} . \tag{9-60}$$

A.   Ideal Solutions

Equations (9-58) and (9-60) take on a very simple form if Raoult's law is obeyed, since then $P_1/P_1^\circ = x_1$ and $P_2/P_2^\circ = x_2$. Thus

$$\mu_1(l) = \mu_1^\circ(l) + RT \ln x_1 \qquad \text{(ideal solution)}, \tag{9-61}$$

$$\mu_2(l) = \mu_2^\circ(l) + RT \ln x_2 \qquad \text{(ideal solution)}. \tag{9-62}$$

We can use Eq. (9-46) to obtain the total free energy of the solution:

$$G = n_1\mu_1^\circ(l) + n_2\mu_2^\circ(l) + n_1RT \ln x_1 + n_2RT \ln x_2 \qquad \text{(ideal solutions)}. \tag{9-63}$$

If we now consider the process of preparing the solution by mixing the pure liquids,

$$n_1(\text{component 1}) + n_2(\text{component 2}) = \text{solution}, \tag{9-64}$$

the corresponding free energy change is

$$\Delta G_M = n_1 RT \ln x_1 + n_2 RT \ln x_2 \qquad \text{(ideal solution)}. \qquad (9\text{-}65)$$

or, per mole of solution,

$$\Delta G_M = x_1 RT \ln x_1 + x_2 RT \ln x_2 \qquad \text{(ideal solution)}. \qquad (9\text{-}66)$$

We can also obtain the entropy of mixing. From Eqs. (9-35) and (9-61),

$$-\bar{S}_1(l) = -S_1°(l) + R \ln x_1 \qquad \text{(ideal solution)}, \qquad (9\text{-}67)$$

and similarly for component 2. The total entropy of the solution is then

$$S = n_1 S_1°(l) + n_2 S_2°(l) - (n_1 R \ln x_1 + n_2 R \ln x_2), \qquad (9\text{-}68)$$

and, for the mixing process, per mole of solution,

$$\Delta S_M = -(x_1 R \ln x_1 + x_2 R \ln x_2). \qquad (9\text{-}69)$$

Note that Eqs. (9-66) and (9-69) are identical to Eqs. (9-54) and (9-55) for the mixing of ideal gases (see Commentary and Notes section).

Since $\Delta G = \Delta H - T \Delta S$ for a constant-temperature process, it follows from Eqs. (9-66) and (9-69) that

$$\Delta H_M = 0. \qquad (9\text{-}70)$$

The heat of mixing for an ideal solution (and for ideal gases) is zero.

B. Nonideal Solutions

Equations (9-58) and (9-60) could be used for nonideal solutions, but it would be inconvenient always to have to refer to vapor pressures. A more general form, preferably analogous to Eqs. (9-61) and (9-62) for ideal solutions, would be very advantageous. We obtain this form by introducing the effective or thermodynamic concentration, called the *activity*. Activity or effective mole fraction a is defined so as to retain the form of Raoult's law:

$$P_i = a_i P_i°. \qquad (9\text{-}71)$$

Equation (9-58) becomes

$$\mu_1(l) = \mu_1°(l) + RT \ln a_1, \qquad (9\text{-}72)$$

and similarly for component 2. Since Raoult's law is the limiting law for all solutions, as $x_1 \rightarrow 1$, a_1 must approach x_1. We may retain the Raoult's law form even more explicitly by using the term activity coefficient γ_i, defined as the factor by which a_i deviates from x_i:

$$a_i = \gamma_i x_i. \qquad (9\text{-}73)$$

Since $a_i \to x_i$, $\gamma_i \to 1$ as $x_i \to 1$. Equation (9-72) now becomes

$$\mu_1(l) = \mu_1^\circ(l) + RT \ln x_1 + RT \ln \gamma_1 . \tag{9-74}$$

The equation for the free energy of mixing, corresponding to the process of Eq. (9-64), can be put in a form that allows ΔG_M to be expressed as the sum of an ideal and a nonideal contribution. Equation (9-65) becomes

$$\Delta G_M = x_1 RT \ln a_1 + x_2 RT \ln a_2 \tag{9-75}$$

or

$$\Delta G_M = x_1 RT \ln x_1 + x_2 RT \ln x_2 + x_1 RT \ln \gamma_1 + x_2 RT \ln \gamma_2 .$$

Alternatively,

$$\Delta G_E = \Delta G_M - \Delta G_{M(ideal)} = x_1 RT \ln \gamma_1 + x_2 RT \ln \gamma_2 . \tag{9-76}$$

The difference $\Delta G_M - \Delta G_{M(ideal)}$ is known as the *excess free energy of mixing* ΔG_E. Similarly,

$$\Delta S_E = \Delta S_M - \Delta S_{M(ideal)} . \tag{9-77}$$

The evaluation of ΔS_E involves the change in activity coefficients with temperature or, alternatively, a measurement of ΔH_M (see Special Topics section). Also, $\Delta G_E = \Delta H_E - T \Delta S_E$, where

$$\Delta H_E = \Delta H_M \tag{9-78}$$

since $\Delta H_{M(ideal)}$ is zero.

Note that if the vapor pressure shows a positive deviation from ideality, then a_1 and a_2 will be greater than the corresponding mole fractions and the γ's will be greater than unity. Conversely, if the deviation is negative, the γ's will be less than unity. The Gibbs–Duhem equation provides some important conclusions in this respect. If we evaluate $d\mu_1(l)$ from Eq. (9-72), then, by Eq. (9-49),

$$x_1 \, d(\ln a_1) + x_2 \, d(\ln a_2) = 0 \tag{9-79}$$

or

$$\int d(\ln a_2) = - \int \frac{x_1}{x_2} \, d(\ln a_1). \tag{9-80}$$

Thus if the activities of component 1 are known for a range of concentrations, integration of Eq. (9-80) allows a calculation of the change in activity of component 2 (see Section 9-5C and Special Topics section). Further analysis shows that if component 1 has a positive deviation from ideality, so must component 2, and *vice versa*. That is, the deviation must be of the same type for both components.

C. Calculation of Activities and Activity Coefficients

The preceding material is sufficiently complicated that we now offer a detailed numerical example to help clarify just how the various definitions and procedures are implemented. The data of Fig. 9-3 for the acetone–chloroform system will be used. Values for the two partial pressures, interpolated from the original data, are given in Table 9-1. There are a number of regularities and interrelations to notice. First, the activity coefficients are given either by $\gamma_c = a_c/x_c$ and $\gamma_a = a_a/x_a$ (c = chloroform and a = acetone) or by $\gamma_c = P_c/P_{c\,(\text{ideal})}$ and $\gamma_a = P_a/P_{a\,(\text{ideal})}$, where P_{ideal} is the Raoult's law value for the partial pressure. The two calculations are equivalent.

Next, the plot of the activity coefficients given in Fig. 9-12 shows that $\gamma_c \rightarrow 1$ as $x_c \rightarrow 1$, and γ_c approaches the limiting value of 0.484 as x_c approaches zero. This limiting value is just the ratio of the Henry's law limiting slope to $P_c{}^\circ$; that is, from Fig. 9-3(a), $k_c = 142$ Torr and $P_c{}^\circ =$

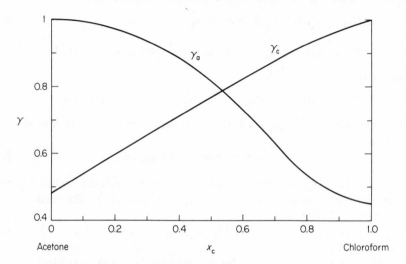

Fig. 9-12.   *Activity coefficient plot for the acetone–chloroform system at 35°C.*

Table 9-1.   *The Acetone (a)–Chloroform (c) System at 35°C*[a]

	Vapor pressure (Torr)						Activity coefficient[c]	
	Observed		Raoult's law		Activity[b]			
x_c	P_c	P_a	P_c	P_a	a_c	a_a	γ_c	γ_a
0.00	0	345	0	345	0	(1.00)	0.484	(1.00)
0.10	16.0	310	29.3	310	0.0546	0.900	0.546	1.00
0.20	35	270	59	276	0.120	0.782	0.595	0.978
0.30	57	227	88	242	0.195	0.657	0.650	0.939
0.40	82	185	117	207	0.280	0.536	0.700	0.894
0.50	112	140	147	173	0.382	0.407	0.763	0.810
0.60	142	102	176	138	0.485	0.296	0.809	0.740
0.70	180	65	205	104	0.613	0.189	0.875	0.630
0.80	219	37	234	69	0.747	0.107	0.933	0.535
0.90	257	16.5	264	34.5	0.877	0.048	0.973	0.477
1.00	293	0	293	0	(1.00)	0	(1.00)	0.450

[a] Data from the "International Critical Tables," Vol. 3. McGraw-Hill, New York, 1928.
[b] $a_c = P_c/P_c{}^\circ$, $a_a = P_a/P_a{}^\circ$.
[c] $\gamma_c = a_c/x_c$, $\gamma_a = a_a/x_a$.

293 Torr, so that the ratio is $142/293 = 0.484$. Similarly, $\gamma_a \to 1$ as $x_a \to 1$, and γ_a approaches the limiting value of 0.450 as $x_a \to 0$; here the ratio is $155/345$, where $k_a = 155$ Torr and $P_a{}^\circ = 345$ Torr.

The data serve to test the Margules model (Section 9-2E). By Eqs. (9-20) and (9-21), k_c/k_a should be equal to $P_c{}^\circ/P_a{}^\circ$ or $293/345 = 0.85$; the actual ratio is $142/155$ or 0.92. Alternatively, the model predicts that the limiting value of γ_c as $x_c \to 0$ should be the same as the limiting value of γ_a as $x_a \to 0$, and equal to e^α. The respective limiting values are actually 0.484 and 0.450, or about 8% different. The model is thus approximate in this case, but still is not too bad, considering its simplicity.

If an average limiting activity coefficient of 0.464 is used, then the value of α is -0.768. Equations (9-17) and (9-18) predict the variation of the activity coefficients with mole fraction to be

and

$$\gamma_A = \exp(\alpha x_B{}^2) \qquad \text{or} \qquad \ln \gamma_A = \alpha x_B{}^2 \tag{9-81}$$

$$\gamma_B = \exp(\alpha x_A{}^2) \qquad \text{or} \qquad \ln \gamma_B = \alpha x_A{}^2. \tag{9-82}$$

If the two lines of Fig. 9-12 are calculated with $\alpha = -0.768$, we find fair agreement with the data.

The data may also be used to illustrate the application of Eq. (9-80). Figure 9-13 shows the plot of x_a/x_c versus $\log a_a$. The shaded area corresponds to the integral between $x_c = 0.9$ and $x_c = 0.3$:

$$\log a_{c(x_c=0.9)} - \log a_{c(x_c=0.3)} = \int_{x_c=0.3}^{x_c=0.9} \frac{x_a}{x_c} \, d(\log a_a). \tag{9-83}$$

The area is approximately -0.66, so

$$\log a_{c(x_c=0.3)} = \log a_{c(x_c=0.9)} - 0.66.$$

As an approximation, we assume that γ_c has approached unity at $x_c = 0.9$, so that $a_c = x_c$,

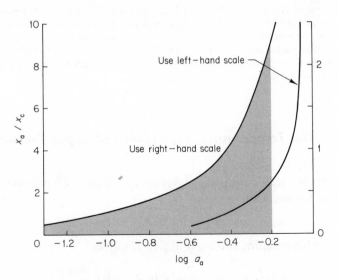

Fig. 9-13. *Application of the Gibbs–Duhem equation to the acetone–chloroform system at 35°C.*

and log a_c is then -0.0458. The value of a_c at $x_c = 0.3$ should then be the antilog of -0.71, or 0.195, in excellent agreement with the experimental value.

Finally, we can calculate the free energy and excess free energy of mixing, using Eqs. (9-75) and (9-76). We have

$$\Delta G_E = (2.303)(1.987)(308)(x_c \log \gamma_c + x_a \log \gamma_a)$$

$$= 1409(x_c \log \gamma_c + x_a \log \gamma_a).$$

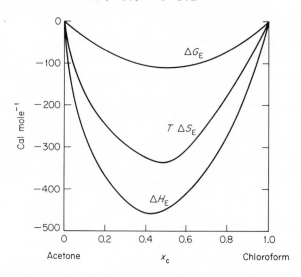

Fig. 9-14. *The acetone–chloroform system at 25°C. [Data from I. Prigogine and R. Defay, "Chemical Thermodynamics" (D. H. Everett, translator). Longmans, Green, New York, 1954.]*

The calculated values for ΔG_E are plotted in Fig. 9-14 for 25°C. Here ΔG_E is negative and goes through a minimum at about $x_c = 0.6$; it is zero, of course, for either pure liquid. We must know the temperature dependence of ΔG_E in order to obtain ΔS_M and hence ΔS_E or, alternatively, calorimetric heat of mixing data so as to obtain ΔH_E. These quantities have been obtained, and are included in the figure. Notice that $T \Delta S_E$ and ΔH_E are both relatively large but partially cancel to give a much smaller ΔG_E.

9-6 The Temperature Dependence of Vapor Pressures

We can obtain a relationship analogous to the Clausius–Clapeyron equation by proceeding as follows. Differentiation of

$$\mu_i(l) = \mu_i°(g) + RT \ln P_i \qquad [\text{Eq.}(9\text{-}56)],$$

with respect to temperature, and use of Eq. (9-35), gives

$$-\bar{S}_i(l) = -S_i°(g) + R \ln P_i + RT \frac{d(\ln P_i)}{dT}.$$

The term $R \ln P_i$ is replaced by $[\mu_i(l) - \mu_i°(g)]/T$ to give

$$RT \frac{d(\ln P_i)}{dT} = \frac{[\mu_i°(g) + TS_i°(g)]}{T} - \frac{[\mu_i(l) + T\bar{S}_i(l)]}{T}.$$ (9-84)

The defining equation for G,

$$G = H - TS \qquad \text{[Eq. (6-31)]}$$

becomes, for a component of a solution,

$$\mu_i = \bar{H}_i - T\bar{S}_i$$ (9-85)

[obtained by differentiating Eq. (6-31) with respect to dn_i at constant T and P]. The terms in brackets in Eq. (9-84) may next be replaced by the corresponding enthalpies to give, on rearrangement,

$$\frac{d(\ln P_i)}{dT} = \frac{\Delta \bar{H}_{v,i}}{RT^2},$$ (9-86)

where

$$\Delta \bar{H}_{v,i} = H_i°(g) - \bar{H}_i(l),$$ (9-87)

and is the partial molal heat of vaporization for the ith component. In the case of pure liquid $\bar{H}_i(l)$ becomes $H_i°(l)$ and Eq. (9-86) reduces to the Clausius–Clapeyron equation. The same is true for an ideal solution, since ΔH_M is zero.

The ideal solution form of Eq. (9-86) may be developed more explicitly. First, for a pure liquid the Clausius–Clapeyron equation can be written

$$P_i° = \exp\left[\frac{\Delta H_{v,i}°}{R}\left(\frac{1}{T_{b,i}°} - \frac{1}{T}\right)\right],$$ (9-88)

where $T_{b,i}°$ is the normal boiling point of liquid i; Eq. (9-88) follows from Eq. (8-10) when we set the vapor pressure equal to 1 atm at $T_b°$. For an ideal solution, $P_i = x_i P_i°$, so Eq. (9-88) becomes

$$P_i = x_i \exp\left[\frac{\Delta H_{v,i}°}{R}\left(\frac{1}{T_{b,i}°} - \frac{1}{T}\right)\right].$$ (9-89)

Equations (9-87) and (9-89) apply equally well to the vapor pressure of the ith component of a solid solution, ideal in the case of Eq. (9-89). The enthalpy quantities are then those for sublimation, of course.

9-7 Boiling Point Diagrams

A. General Appearance

The material of Section 9-2 is now extended to show the various types of boiling point diagrams that one finds for a solution of two volatile liquids. It is first necessary to consider how the total vapor pressure of the solution should vary with composition and temperature. This is most easily done for the case of an ideal solution, for which the two partial pressures are, from Eq. (9-89),

$$P_A = x_A \exp\left[\frac{\Delta H^\circ_{v,A}}{R}\left(\frac{1}{T^\circ_{b,A}} - \frac{1}{T}\right)\right] \qquad (9\text{-}90)$$

and

$$P_B = x_B \exp\left[\frac{\Delta H^\circ_{v,B}}{R}\left(\frac{1}{T^\circ_{b,B}} - \frac{1}{T}\right)\right]. \qquad (9\text{-}91)$$

The total pressure P is just

$$P = P_A + P_B. \qquad (9\text{-}92)$$

Substitution of the expressions for P_A and P_B into Eq. (9-92) gives the equation for the variation of P with composition and temperature.

The general appearance of this function is shown in Fig. 9-15; it is assumed that component A is the one with the lower boiling point.

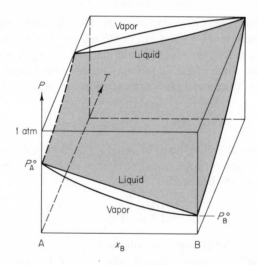

Fig. 9-15. *Variation of P with temperature and composition for an ideal solution.*

The upper surface gives the total vapor pressure and the lower one the vapor composition for solutions of a given composition and temperature. The front of the projection corresponds to a cross section at constant temperature, and thus constitutes the vapor pressure–composition diagram for that temperature, as shown in Fig. 9-16(a). The top surface in Fig. 9-15 corresponds to a cross section at constant pressure and therefore to the boiling point diagram for that pressure, as shown in Fig. 9-16(b). Notice that the liquid composition line is now curved and lies below rather than above the vapor composition line.

The normal boiling point diagram is given by a cross section at $P = 1$ atm.

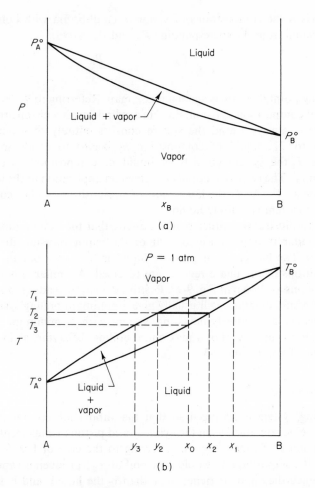

Fig. 9-16. *Two cross sections of Fig. 9-15. (a) At constant T, giving the vapor pressure and vapor composition diagram. (b) At constant P = 1 atm, giving the boiling point and vapor composition diagram.*

We can obtain the boiling point versus composition line analytically by setting $P = 1$ in Eq. (9-92):

$$1 = x_A\left\{\exp\left[\frac{\Delta H_{v,A}^\circ}{R}\left(\frac{1}{T_{b,A}^\circ} - \frac{1}{T_b}\right)\right]\right\} + x_B\left\{\exp\left[\frac{\Delta H_{v,B}^\circ}{R}\left(\frac{1}{T_{b,B}^\circ} - \frac{1}{T_b}\right)\right]\right\}.$$

$$(9\text{-}93)$$

Equation (9-93) reduces to two variables since $x_A + x_B = 1$. Since it is transcendental, it is best solved by picking successive choices for T_b and solving for corresponding x_A or x_B. The resulting plot is shown in Fig. 9-16(b). The vapor line gives the compositions of vapor in equilibrium with boiling solutions and is calculated from the corresponding P_A and P_B values:

$$y_A = \frac{P_A}{P}, \qquad y_B = \frac{P_B}{P}. \qquad (9\text{-}94)$$

The boiling point diagram is again a phase map. Referring to 9-16(b), we see that if a system of composition x_0 is contained in a cylinder with a piston arranged so that the pressure is always 1 atm, the system consists entirely of vapor if $T > T_1$. On cooling to T_1, liquid of composition x_1 begins to condense out and by temperature T_2 the system consists of liquid of composition x_2 and vapor of composition y_2. The relative amounts are given on application of the lever principle to the tie-line at T_2. At T_3 the last vapor, of composition y_3, has condensed, and below T_3 the system is entirely liquid.

Figure 9-16 illustrates another point, namely, that the boiling point diagram is (roughly) similar in appearance to that of the vapor pressure diagram turned upside down: The higher vapor pressure liquid is the lower boiling one, and the relative positions of the phase regions are reversed. A similar situation holds for nonideal systems as shown in Fig. 9-17. Positive deviation, leading to a maximum in the vapor pressure diagram, will usually give a minimum-boiling system as in Fig. 9-17(a), whereas a negatively deviating system with a minimum in the vapor pressure diagram usually shows maximum boiling behavior, as in Fig. 9-17(b). Compare with Figs. 9-7 and 9-3.

B. Distillation

If a boiling system is arranged so that the vapors are continuously removed rather than being contained as in the cylinder and piston arrangement, a somewhat different sequence of events occurs. Referring to the case of Fig. 9-16(b), we see that liquid of composition x_0 would first boil at T_3, producing vapor of composition y_3. Since the vapor is richer in A than is the liquid, and is steadily being removed, the liquid composition progressively becomes richer in B, passing compositions x_2 and x_1, respectively. Unlike the situation with the closed system, however, liquid remains when T_1 is reached. This is because the overall vapor composition is not x_0, but rather the average of the compositions of the succession of vapors produced, ranging from y_3 to x_0. For example, this average vapor composition might be about equal to y_2, in which case the relative amount of liquid remaining would be given by the lever $(y_2 - x_0)/(y_2 - x_1)$, or about 50%. Continued boiling would continue to shift the liquid composition to the right, and the last drop of liquid remaining would be essentially pure B.

A similar analysis applies to Fig. 9-17a. Liquids of composition either x_0 or x_0' produce initial vapors of composition y_1 or y_1'; in both cases the vapor composition is closer to the minimum-boiling composition than is the liquid composition. As a a consequence, continued boiling of system x_0 moves the liquid composition progressively toward pure benzene, and continued boiling of system x_0' moves it

9-7 Boiling Point Diagrams

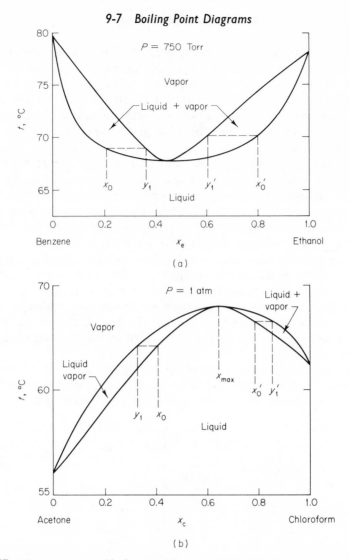

Fig. 9-17. *Vapor pressure and boiling point diagrams: (a) Positive deviation from Raoult's law, giving a minimum boiling diagram. (b) Negative deviation from Raoult's law, giving a maximum boiling diagram.*

toward pure ethanol. If there is a maximum boiling point, the vapor compositions lie away from the maximum, as compared to the liquid composition, as shown in Fig. 9-17(b). The result is that continued boiling of either liquid x_0 or x_0' eventually produces liquid of composition x_{max}, the maximum boiling composition. At this point the liquid and vapor compositions are the same and continued boiling produces no further change. The system now behaves as though it were a pure liquid and is called an *azeotropic mixture*. The value of x_{max} depends on the pressure; Fig. 9-17(b) is, after all, merely one particular isobaric cross section of a general diagram of the type shown in Fig. 9-15. It is possible, however, to use this maximum boiling feature as a means of preparing a standard solution. An example is the hydrochloric acid–water system, for which the maximum boiling composition is 20.222 % HCl at 760 Torr (but shifts to 20.360 % HCl at 700 Torr). The standardization procedure consists simply in boiling a solution until no further change in boiling point occurs and recording the concentration appropriate to the ambient or barometric pressure.

Fractional distillation comprises a series of evaporation–condensation steps. It is helpful at this point to refer to a diagram of the type shown in Fig. 9-18, in which vapor composition y is plotted against liquid composition x. The case illustrated is that of a relatively ideal solution. Liquid of composition x_0 produces some vapor of composition y_1. If this vapor is condensed, the effect is to locate a new liquid composition x_1 on the diagonal. Liquid x_1 produces vapor y_2 and on its condensation, liquid x_2 results. The series of steps gives the number of operations needed to reach the final liquid composition x_3. This analysis assumes that only a small amount of each liquid is vaporized; in actual practice the fraction is appreciable and so the vapor compositions are always less enriched in the more volatile component than in the ideal situation. The detailed treatment of fractional distillation constitutes a major subject in chemical engineering and is beyond the scope of this text.

A special case in distillation is that of two immiscible liquids. A mixture of two such liquids will boil when their combined vapor pressure reaches 1 atm. We thus write the separate Clausius–Clapeyron equations for each pure liquid:

$$P_A{}^\circ = \exp\left[\frac{\Delta H^\circ_{v,A}}{R}\left(\frac{1}{T^\circ_{b,A}} - \frac{1}{T}\right)\right], \tag{9-95}$$

$$P_B{}^\circ = \exp\left[\frac{\Delta H^\circ_{v,B}}{R}\left(\frac{1}{T^\circ_{b,B}} - \frac{1}{T}\right)\right]. \tag{9-96}$$

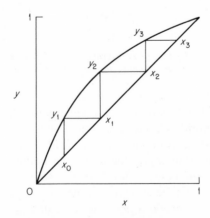

Fig. 9-18. *Plot of y versus x.*

The normal boiling point of the mixture of liquid phases is given by

$$1 = \exp\left[\frac{\Delta H^{\circ}_{v,A}}{R}\left(\frac{1}{T^{\circ}_{b,A}} - \frac{1}{T_b}\right)\right] + \exp\left[\frac{\Delta H^{\circ}_{v,B}}{R}\left(\frac{1}{T^{\circ}_{b,B}} - \frac{1}{T_b}\right)\right], \quad (9\text{-}97)$$

since we require that $P_A{}^{\circ} + P_B{}^{\circ} = 1$. The situation is illustrated in Fig. 9-19.

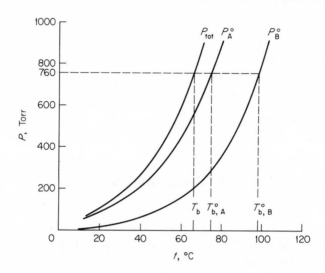

Fig. 9-19. *The case of two immiscible liquids.*

Boiling of such a mixture produces vapor of composition

$$y_B = \frac{P_B{}^{\circ}}{P_A{}^{\circ} + P_B{}^{\circ}} \quad (= P_B{}^{\circ} \text{ if } P = 1), \quad (9\text{-}98)$$

where $P_A{}^{\circ}$ and $P_B{}^{\circ}$ are the vapor pressures of the pure liquids at T_b. On continued boiling, one or the other liquid phase will eventually disappear and the boiling point will then revert to that of the remaining liquid.

A procedure of this type is often known as a steam distillation, since a frequent application is the distillation of a mixture of water and an insoluble organic liquid or oil. The advantage is that the oil is thereby distilled at a much lower temperature than would otherwise be needed and with less danger of decomposition. It is also possible to obtain the molecular weight of the oil from Eq. (9-98). If component A is water, then $P_A{}^{\circ}$ is given by the measured T_b and $P_B{}^{\circ}$ is then the ambient or barometric pressure minus $P_A{}^{\circ}$ and y_B is given by Eq. (9-98). With y_B and the weight fraction of the distillate known, M_B can be calculated.

As an example, suppose that a mixture of an insoluble organic liquid and water boiled at 90.3°C under a pressure of 740.2 Torr. The vapor pressure of pure water is 530.1 Torr at this temperature. The condensed distillate is 71 % by weight of the oil. Evidently $P_B°$ is 740.2 − 530.1 or 210.1 Torr; therefore $y_B = 210.1/740.2 = 0.2838$. Since

$$y_B = \frac{W_B/M_B}{(W_B/M_B) + (W_A/M_A)},$$

where W denotes weight of substance, or

$$\frac{W_B}{M_B} = \frac{y_B}{1 - y_B}\frac{W_A}{M_A},$$

then, per 100 g of distillate,

$$\frac{W_B}{M_B} = \frac{0.2838}{0.7161}\frac{29}{18} = 0.638$$

and $M_2 = 71/0.638 = 111.2$ g mole^{-1}.

9-8 Partial Miscibility

The equilibrium between a liquid solution and a pure solid phase of one of the components is treated in Chapter 10 and that between liquid and solid solutions in Chapter 11. There remains the case of two partially miscible liquid phases. If liquid phases α and β are in equilibrium, then if the system is one of two components A and B, the condition for equilibrium is that

$$\mu_A{}^\alpha = \mu_A{}^\beta \quad \text{and} \quad \mu_B{}^\alpha = \mu_B{}^\beta. \tag{9-99}$$

As discussed in the Special Topics section, this means that a plot of the molar free energy of the solution $G/(n_A + n_B)$ versus composition shows a double minimum, and therefore so, too, does a plot of ΔG_{mix} versus composition.

The situation is one in which there is a limited solubility of B in A, giving A-rich solutions designated as α phase, and a limited solubility of A in B, giving B-rich solutions designated as β phase. The maximum solubilities may then be designated as S^α and S^β, where S^α is the composition of a solution saturated with respect to B and S^β is that of a solution saturated with respect to A. The compositions S^α and S^β are not very dependent on pressure; quite large pressures are needed to change the free energies of liquids appreciably. They are temperature-dependent, however, and this dependence is customarily shown in plots of solubility versus temperature at 1 atm pressure.

Figure 9-20 shows a schematic temperature–composition plot for two liquids A and B. The left-hand line gives the variation with temperature of S^α and the right-hand line the variation of S^β. The behavior illustrated is the very common one in which both solubilities increase with increasing temperature. There is therefore a

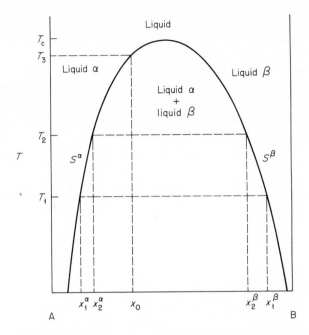

Fig. 9-20. *Miscibility gap between two liquids with an upper consolute temperature.*

temperature T_c at which they have become equal and above which the two liquids are completely miscible. The temperature T_c is known as a *consolute temperature*, in this case, an upper consolute temperature. The figure again has the properties of a phase map. Systems whose overall composition and temperature locate a point in the region between the S^α and S^β lines, such as system x_0 at T_1, will consist of two liquid phases. The compositions are given by the ends of the tie-line as $x_1{}^\alpha$ and $x_1{}^\beta$, and the relative amounts present may be obtained by means of the lever principle. Thus we have

$$\frac{n^\alpha}{n^\alpha + n^\beta} = \frac{x_0 - x_1{}^\beta}{x_1{}^\alpha - x_1{}^\beta}, \tag{9-100}$$

where n^α and n^β are, respectively, the number of moles of phase α of composition $x_1{}^\alpha$ and of phase β of composition $x_1{}^\beta$. When the system is warmed to T_2 the two phases are of composition $x_2{}^\alpha$ and $x_2{}^\beta$ and application of the lever principle shows that the proportion of phase α has increased. At T_3 phase β disappears and the system consists of phase α of composition x_0.

One may, alternatively, make a horizontal traverse of the diagram. Thus addition of liquid B to pure liquid A at T_1 gives a phase of increasing mole fraction of B. When composition $x_1{}^\alpha$ is reached phase of composition $x_1{}^\beta$ begins to appear, and further addition of B steadily increases the proportion of β phase. When the system composition reaches $x_1{}^\beta$ no more α phase remains and continued addition of B now merely increases the concentration of B in the β phase.

373

The phenol–water system shows this type of behavior, as illustrated in Fig. 9-21(a). The upper consolute temperature in this case is about 70°C. It can also happen that the solubilities increase with decreasing temperature, as illustrated by the water–triethylamine system of Fig. 9-21(b). There is now a *lower consolute temperature*. Finally, both types of behavior may be shown, as in the case of the water–nicotine system of Fig. 9-21(c). The compositions are given in weight fraction in all these figures and application of the lever principle will therefore give the relative weights of the two phases that are present.

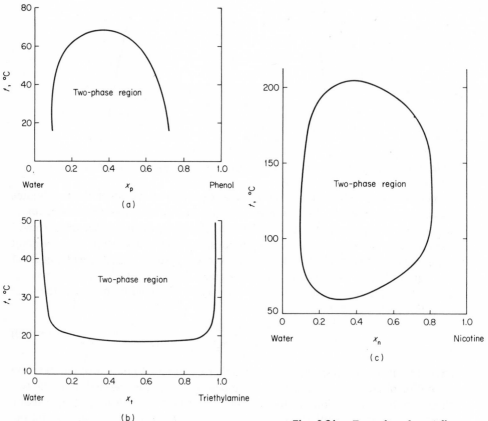

Fig. 9-21. *Examples of partially miscible liquid pairs.*

COMMENTARY AND NOTES

9-CN-1   Other Properties of Solutions

The emphasis of this chapter has been almost entirely on the vapor pressure of solutions. Vapor pressures provide experimental access to the thermodynamic quantities for solutions, solid or liquid, as well as vapor pressure and boiling point diagrams of great general utility. These topics have therefore received first priority. Unfortunately, anything approaching a complete outline of the physical chemistry of solutions would take entirely too much space. Actually, all of the various types of properties mentioned in previous chapters have been measured for solutions. Examples are molar refractions and polarizations, usually with additivity of the solvent and solute contributions assumed, density, compressibility, thermal expansion, and surface tension.

The molar volume of a solution might be discussed briefly, however. At constant temperature and pressure, volume is a function of composition only, and for a two-component system we have

$$dv = \left(\frac{\partial v}{\partial n_1}\right)_{T,P,n_2} dn_1 + \left(\frac{\partial v}{\partial n_2}\right)_{T,P,n_1} dn_2 \tag{9-101}$$

or

$$dv = \overline{V}_1 \, dn_1 + \overline{V}_2 \, dn_2 , \tag{9-102}$$

where $\overline{V}_1$ and $\overline{V}_2$ are the partial molal volumes. Integration at constant composition gives

$$v = n_1 \overline{V}_1 + n_2 \overline{V}_2 \quad \text{or} \quad V = x_1 \overline{V}_1 + x_2 \overline{V}_2 . \tag{9-103}$$

Differentiation, and subtraction of Eq. (9-102), leads to the important relation

$$n_1 \, d\overline{V}_1 + n_2 \, d\overline{V}_2 = 0 \tag{9-104}$$

or

$$x_1 \, d\overline{V}_1 + x_2 \, d\overline{V}_2 = 0. \tag{9-105}$$

The procedure is analogous to that used in obtaining the Gibbs–Duhem equation [Eq. (9-48)] and, in fact, is one that can be applied to any extensive property (see Special Topics section).

The partial molal volume of a component of an ideal solution will be the same as the molar volume of the pure substance. For most ordinary organic liquids the average molar volume V/n varies almost linearly with composition. In the acetone–chloroform system, for example, the volume change on mixing amounts to a few tenths of a percent at the most. The molar volume of acetone is 72.740 cm^3 mole^{-1} at 25°C and the partial molal volume increases slightly on dilution with chloroform to a limiting dilute solution value of 73.993 cm^3 mole^{-1}. Solutions involving water are often anomalous; there is almost a 3% volume change when a water–methanol solution is made up, and an actual shrinkage in total volume may occur when an electrolyte is dissolved in water. The explanation for this last is that ions attract water molecules so strongly that the resulting compaction more than compensates for the added volume of the ions themselves. The existence of negative partial molal volumes serves to emphasize that $\bar{V}_i$ and other partial molal quantities are coefficients rather than directly measured properties of a pure substance.

The viscosity of a solution of similar substances will again vary nearly linearly with composition; often a better straight line is obtained if the reciprocals or fluidities are used instead. Deviations from linearity in the plot of viscosity versus mole fraction tend to correlate with such deviations in the corresponding vapor pressure diagrams. The acetone–chloroform system, which shows a minimum in the vapor pressure diagram attributable to greater A–B than A–A or B–B types of interactions, has a maximum in the viscosity–composition plot. Diffusion has also been studied a good deal in binary liquid systems. There is a single mutual diffusion coefficient, but, in addition, self-diffusion coefficients may be obtained for each component separately by means of isotopic labeling. As with viscosity, there are a number of semiempirical models but no really satisfactory ones.

The surface tension of solutions constitutes a large subject. Figure 9-22 displays typical categories of surface tension versus composition plots. In the case of similar liquids the surface tension plot is roughly symmetric relative to a straight line connecting the values of γ for the pure liquids, as exemplified by the data shown in Fig. 9-22(a). If the molecular areas σ of the two species are similar, then a simple treatment based on the energy $\gamma\sigma$ required to bring a molecule into the surface gives the equation

$$e^{-\gamma\sigma/kT} = x_1 e^{-\gamma_1\sigma/kT} + x_2 e^{-\gamma_2\sigma/kT}. \tag{9-106}$$

The surface tensions of the respective pure liquids are given by γ_1 and γ_2. Another form, derived for regular solutions (Section 9-CN-2), is

$$\gamma = \gamma_1 x_1 + \gamma_2 x_2 - \beta x_1 x_2, \tag{9-107}$$

where β is an empirical constant related to the constant α of Eq. (9-17).

If the two liquids have rather different surface tensions, then the plot will look like that shown in Fig. 9-22(b) for the water–ethanol system. The surface tension drops rapidly over the first 10 or 20% of ethanol added and then approaches the value for pure ethanol more slowly. This type of behavior becomes accentuated in the case of a long-chain solutes having a polar end group, such as sodium lauryl

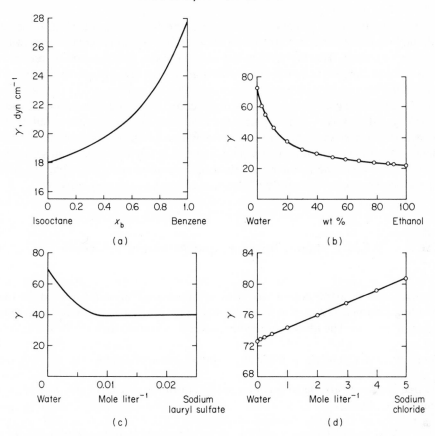

Fig. 9-22. *Surface tension–composition behavior: (a) similar liquids; (b) a high surface tension liquid and a low surface tension liquid; (c) an aqueous surfactant system; (d) an aqueous electrolyte system. [Part (a) from H. B. Evans, Jr. and H. L. Clever, J. Phys. Chem. 68, 3433 (1964). Copyright 1964 by the American Chemical Society. Reprinted by permission of the copyright owner.]*

sulfate. As illustrated in Fig. 9-22(c), there is a sharp drop in γ even for very dilute solutions. Such long-chain solutes include the common soaps and detergents and belong to the class of so-called surface-active agents (surfactants). As discussed in the Special Topics section, the thermodynamic implication is that the surfactant concentrates at the solution–air interface. With sodium lauryl sulfate, there is nearly a monolayer or complete film of the surfactant by 0.01 M concentration. With a higher molecular weight and less soluble surfactant, the monolayer is usually formed simply by adding the material directly to the surface. One may drop a hexane solution of stearic acid carefully onto a water surface and thus obtain a monolayer of the acid after the hexane has evaporated. The film may be compressed between movable barriers and its surface tension measured as a function of surface concentration.

A fourth category of system is that of an electrolyte solution such as aqueous sodium chloride, shown in Fig. 9-22(d). The surface tension increases somewhat with concentration. The thermodynamic implication is that the surface region is more dilute in electrolyte than the bulk solution, or that negative adsorption occurs at the interface.

To return to the general sequence of this section, we see that yet another aspect of the physical chemistry of solutions is the somewhat special behavior of solution–vapor and solution–solid equilibria when only one component is present in both phases. This subject is taken up in the Chapter 10. Finally, electrolyte solutions constitute a large topic in their own right and are discussed in Chapter 12. For these solutions, the new property of electrical conductivity is very important.

9-CN-2 Ideal, Regular, and Athermal Solutions

Several of the attributes of an ideal solution have been introduced in the preceding sections. These, plus some further ones, are assembled here to provide an overall picture. The ideal solution obeys Raoult's law, so that

$$\mu_i(l) = \mu_i°(l) + RT \ln x_i \qquad \text{[ideal solution, Eq. (9-61)]}.$$

The free energy of mixing to form an ideal solution is given, for the case of two components, by

$$\Delta G_M = x_1 RT \ln x_1 + x_2 RT \ln x_2 \qquad \text{[ideal solution, Eq. (9-65)]},$$

and the entropy of mixing by

$$\Delta S_M = -(x_1 R \ln x_1 + x_2 R \ln x_2) \qquad \text{[ideal solution, Eq. (9-69)]}.$$

By definition, of course, the excess free energy and entropy of mixing are zero. Since $\Delta H = \Delta G + T \Delta S$, it follows that the heat of mixing is zero for an ideal solution. Figure 9-14 showed the variations of ΔG_M, ΔS_M, and ΔH_M with composition for a nonideal solution. It is necessarily also true that $\bar{H}_i = H_i°$, that is, the partial molal enthalpy of an ideal solution component is equal to that of the pure species.

Differentiation of Eq. (9-61) with respect to P at constant T, and with the use of Eq. (9-34), gives

$$\bar{V}_i - V_i° = 0.$$

The partial molal volume of an ideal solution component is thus the same as that of the pure component. Consequently ΔV_M is zero.

Nonideal solutions may be viewed in terms of the excess quantities of mixing

ΔG_E, ΔS_E, and $\Delta H_E = \Delta H_M$. If, for example, Eqs. (9-17) and (9-18) are obeyed, then

$$\Delta G_E = x_1 x_2 \alpha RT. \tag{9-108}$$

Solutions obeying Eq. (9-108) have been called "*simple*" *solutions* by E. A. Guggenheim. If, further, α represents an energy divided by RT, $d(\Delta G_E)/dT$, and hence the excess entropy of mixing will be zero, but not ΔH_M. This type of solution is known, after J. H. Hildebrand, as a *regular solution*. The implication is that the two components are randomly distributed in the solution as though it were ideal, although their interaction energies with themselves and with each other are different.

Finally, an *athermal solution* is one for which $\Delta H_M = 0$, although ΔS_E and ΔG_E are not necessarily zero. This situation may occur with components rather similar in chemical nature but very different in molecular size. A simple treatment on this basis leads to the equation for the free energy of mixing:

$$\Delta G_M = x_1 RT \ln \phi_1 + x_2 RT \ln \phi_2, \tag{9-109}$$

where ϕ_1 and ϕ_2 are the volume fractions. There is some statistical thermodynamic basis for the supposition that for a solution to be ideal the molar volumes of the components should be about the same (see the next section) and Raoult's law may in fact be less general, even as a limiting law, than is customarily thought.

9-CN-3 Statistical Thermodynamics of Solutions

Needless to say, the statistical thermodynamic treatment of solutions is difficult and fragmentary in its achievements. One may, in principle, set up the partition functions, which now involve the chemical potential of a component as a weighting factor. Useful in this connection is what is called the *absolute* or *rational activity q*, given by

$$\mu_i = RT \ln q_i. \tag{9-110}$$

Like the chemical potential, the absolute activity of a species is the same in all equilibrium phases in which the species is present.

Certain simple entropy calculations can be made. One consideration is the following. It will be recalled that the translational partition function for a gas required the factor $1/N!$

$$\mathbf{Q}_{\text{tot}} = \frac{1}{N!} \mathbf{Q}^{N_0} \qquad \text{[Eq. (6-68)]}.$$

379

In the case of a crystalline solid each molecule is restricted to its own volume V/N_0 and the translational partition function becomes

$$Q'_{tot} = Q^{N_0}\left(\frac{V}{N_0}\right)^{N_0}.$$

(9-111)

Equation (9-111) follows from Eq. (4-68) if the volume is made V/N_0 rather than v, the volume of the whole system. The difference between the two corresponding entropies is, by Eq. (6-64), just $k \ln(Q/Q')$, since the energies for the two situations are the same. Thus

$$S(\text{gas}) - S(\text{lattice}) = k \ln\left(\frac{N_0^{N_0}}{N_0!}\right) = N_0 k$$

(9-112)

[using Stirling's formula for $\ln(N_0!)$].

This entropy factor is known as the *communal entropy*, and is thought to develop by stages as a solid melts and the liquid is heated. The lattice model may be approximately applicable to the liquid, in other words. Although absolute calculations of thermodynamic quantities are most difficult, we can obtain the entropy of mixing. We assume the solution to consist of lattice sites, all equivalent, which may be occupied either by a molecule of component 1 or by a molecule of component 2. In addition to all other contributions there is now one which has to do with the ways in which N_1 molecules of species 1 and N_2 molecules of species 2 may be distributed, where $N_1 + N_2 = N_0$. The reasoning at this point is very similar to that of Section 2-2. There are $N_0!$ ways in which N_0 molecules can be arranged among the sites, but we assume that those of component 1 are indistinguishable among themselves, and likewise for those of component 2. We must then divide by the number of ways in which N_1 molecules can be arranged among themselves, and similarly for the N_2 molecules. The thermodynamic probability of the solution is

$$W = \frac{N_0!}{N_1! \, N_2!}.$$

(9-113)

The relationship between entropy and thermodynamic probability [Eq. (6-66)] now gives for the mixing entropy of the solution

$$\Delta S_M = k \ln\left(\frac{N_0!}{N_1! \, N_2!}\right).$$

(9-114)

Use of Stirling's approximation for factorials and some straightforward algebraic maneuvering yields the final form

$$\Delta S_M = -(x_1 R \ln x_1 + x_2 R \ln x_2) \qquad \text{[Eq. (9-69)]},$$

which is the same as that previously obtained. The uniform lattice concept does seem to imply that the two species should be of about the same molecular size for ideal solution behavior to hold, as mentioned in the preceding section. This is only an implication, however, since the lattice picture is not essential to obtain a correct expression for the entropy of mixing. Thus Eq. (9-69) also applies to the mixing of two ideal gases, although the basis of obtaining it is through the Sackur–Tetrode equation [Eq. (6-78)], which gives the volume dependence of the entropy of an ideal gas to be $R \ln V$. Then ΔS for the mixing process of Eq. (9-52) is, per mole,

$$\Delta S_M = x_1 R \ln \frac{V}{V_1} + x_2 R \ln \frac{V}{V_2}, \tag{9-115}$$

where V_1 and V_2 are the initial volumes of the two gases and V is their common final volume. Since $V_1 = x_1 V$ and $V_2 = x_2 V$, Eq. (9-69) again results.

Thus two very different pictures have produced the same conclusion. One must be cautious in assuming that, simply because a particular model yields a correct equation, the model itself is therefore correct.

SPECIAL TOPICS

9-ST-1   Partial Molal Quantities

The derivations of the Gibbs–Duhem equation [Eq. (9-49)] and of Eq. (9-104) for volumes are specific examples of a more general procedure. If the independent variables of some function $y = f(u, v, w, ...)$ are extensive quantities, that is, ones which increase in proportion to the amount of the system, then by a theorem due to Euler, it must be true that

$$u\left(\frac{\partial f}{\partial u}\right)_{v,w,...} + v\left(\frac{\partial f}{\partial v}\right)_{u,w,...} + w\left(\frac{\partial f}{\partial w}\right)_{u,v,...} + \cdots = 0. \tag{9-116}$$

This theorem was invoked implicitly in integrating Eq. (9-28), with $E = f(S, v, n_i)$, to obtain Eq. (9-45).

In the case of partial molal quantities we restrict ourselves to a system at constant temperature and pressure, so that the amounts n_i of the various components are the only variables. Thus in the case of a two-component system, for some property $\mathscr{P}$, we have

$$d\mathscr{P} = \left(\frac{\partial \mathscr{P}}{\partial n_1}\right)_{n_2} dn_1 + \left(\frac{\partial \mathscr{P}}{\partial n_2}\right)_{n_1} dn_2 = \mathscr{P}_1 \, dn_1 + \mathscr{P}_2 \, dn_2, \tag{9-117}$$

where $\bar{\mathscr{P}}_1$ and $\bar{\mathscr{P}}_2$ are the partial molal values. Then, by Euler's theorem,

$$\mathscr{P} = n_1\bar{\mathscr{P}}_1 + n_2\bar{\mathscr{P}}_2 .\tag{9-118}$$

Differentiation and comparison with Eq. (9-117) gives

$$n_1 \, d\bar{\mathscr{P}}_1 + n_2 \, d\bar{\mathscr{P}}_2 = 0.\tag{9-119}$$

Equation (9-49) corresponded to the case of $\mathscr{P} = \mathsf{G}$ and Eq. (9-104) to that of $\mathscr{P} = v$. For $\mathscr{P} = \mathsf{H}$ we have

$$\mathsf{H} = n_1\bar{H}_1 + n_2\bar{H}_2\tag{9-120}$$

and

$$n_1 \, d\bar{H}_1 + n_2 \, d\bar{H}_2 = 0.\tag{9-121}$$

There are some useful special procedures for obtaining partial molal quantities from experimental data, which can be illustrated easily for volume. We define the average molar volume as

$$V_{\mathrm{av}} = \frac{v}{n_1 + n_2} .\tag{9-122}$$

Then

$$\bar{V}_1 = \left(\frac{\partial v}{\partial n_1}\right)_{n_2} = V_{\mathrm{av}} + (n_1 + n_2)\left(\frac{\partial V_{\mathrm{av}}}{\partial x_2}\right)\left(\frac{\partial x_2}{\partial n_1}\right)_{n_2} .$$

Since

$$\left(\frac{\partial x_2}{\partial n_1}\right)_{n_2} = -\frac{n_2}{(n_1 + n_2)^2} ,$$

it follows that

$$\bar{V}_1 = V_{\mathrm{av}} - x_2 \frac{dV_{\mathrm{av}}}{dx_2} .\tag{9-123}$$

Equation (9-123) has a simple geometric meaning. If V_{av} is plotted against mole fraction, then dV_{av}/dx_2 is the slope of the tangent at composition x_2, and the intercept of the tangent at $x_2 = 0$ then gives $\bar{V}_1$. Since the equation is symmetric, the intercept at $x_2 = 1$ gives $\bar{V}_2$. The situation is illustrated in Fig. 9-23 for the acetone–chloroform system. Also, of course, Eq. (9-105) may be used for the calculation of $\bar{V}_2$ if $\bar{V}_1$ is known as a function of composition.

The volume change when the pure components are mixed is

$$\Delta V_{\mathrm{M}} = V_{\mathrm{av}} - x_1 V_1^\circ - x_2 V_2^\circ,\tag{9-124}$$

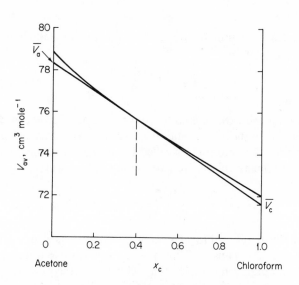

Fig. 9-23. *Variation of V_{av} with composition for the acetone–chloroform system at 25°C. The intercepts of the tangent give $\bar{V}_a$ and $\bar{V}_c$ for that composition.*

where $V_1{}^\circ$ and $V_2{}^\circ$ are the molar volumes of the pure species. Alternatively, using Eq. (9-103), we obtain

$$\Delta V_M = x_1(\bar{V}_1 - V_1{}^\circ) + x_2(\bar{V}_2 - V_2{}^\circ). \tag{9-125}$$

Enthalpies are treated somewhat similarly, but a complication is that, unlike volumes, absolute enthalpies are not known. It is necessary, then, to deal entirely with heats of mixing. The enthalpy change for the process

$$n_1 \text{ (component 1)} + n_2 \text{ (component 2)} = \text{solution}$$

is called the *integral heat of solution,* as an alternative expression to the heat of mixing ΔH_M. For this process

$$\Delta H_M = H_{soln} - n_1 H_1{}^\circ - n_2 H_2{}^\circ, \tag{9-126}$$

where $H_1{}^\circ$ and $H_2{}^\circ$ are the enthalpies of the pure components. Alternatively, using Eq. (9-120), we obtain

$$\Delta H_M = n_1(\bar{H}_1 - H_1{}^\circ) + n_2(\bar{H}_2 - H_2{}^\circ) \tag{9-127}$$

or

$$\Delta H_M = n_1\bar{Q}_1 + n_2\bar{Q}_2, \tag{9-128}$$

where $\bar{Q}$ denotes the enthalpy relative to the pure component. According to Eq. (9-128), $\bar{Q}_2$ is given by

$$\bar{Q}_2 = \left[\frac{\partial(\varDelta H_M)}{\partial n_2}\right]_{n_1} \tag{9-129}$$

and could be obtained experimentally from the slope of a plot of $\varDelta H_M$ versus n_2, from data on the heats of dissolution of various amounts of solute in a fixed amount of solvent. Therefore $\bar{Q}_2$ is called the *differential enthalpy of solution*.

Equation (9-128) may alternatively be written in the form

$$\varDelta H_M = \frac{\varDelta H_M}{n_1 + n_2} = x_1\bar{Q}_1 + x_2\bar{Q}_2. \tag{9-130}$$

The same graphical procedure may now be applied as was used for obtaining partial molal volumes. Thus if a plot of $\varDelta H_M$ versus mole fraction is constructed, then the tangent at a given composition will have intercepts at $x_1 = 1$ and $x_2 = 1$ of $\bar{Q}_1$ and $\bar{Q}_2$, respectively, as illustrated in Fig. 9-24.

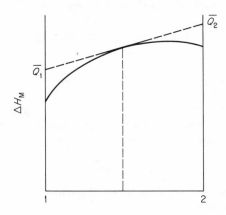

Fig. 9-24.   *Variation of the molar heat of mixing $\varDelta H_M$ with composition. The intercepts of the tangent give the differential heats of solution $\bar{Q}_1$ and $\bar{Q}_2$ for that composition.*

Many of the results on heats of solution are for electrolytes or other solid solutes, and for such systems it is customary to polarize the treatment around the solute species, component 2. One refers heats of solution of solutes to the value $\bar{Q}_2{}^\circ$ for an infinitely dilute solution by introducing a quantity called the relative enthalpy of solution $\bar{L}$:

$$\bar{L}_2 = \bar{Q}_2 - \bar{Q}_2{}^\circ = \bar{H}_2 - \bar{H}_2{}^\circ, \tag{9-131}$$

where $\bar{H}_2^\circ$ is the partial molal enthalpy of the solute at infinite dilution and $\bar{Q}_2^\circ = \bar{H}_2^\circ - H_2^\circ$. By definition $\bar{L}_2^\circ = 0$. Usually the pure liquid solvent is kept as the reference state for component 1, so we have

$$\bar{L}_1 = \bar{Q}_1 = \bar{H}_1 - H_1^\circ. \tag{9-132}$$

Since $\bar{H}_2^\circ$ and H_1° are constants, insertion of the definitions for $\bar{L}_1$ and $\bar{L}_2$ into Eq. (9-121) gives

$$n_1\, d\bar{L}_1 + n_2\, d\bar{L}_2 = 0. \tag{9-133}$$

The $\bar{L}$ quantities may thus be used in the same way as the $\bar{Q}$ quantities, or in general as ordinary partial molal quantities. We also have

$$\Delta H_{M,x_2} - \Delta H_M{}^\circ = L = n_1\bar{L}_1 + n_2\bar{L}_2, \tag{9-134}$$

where $\Delta H_{M,x_2}$ is the enthalpy of mixing of n_1 moles of solvent and n_2 moles of solute to give a solution of composition x_2, and $\Delta H_M{}^\circ$ is the heat of solution of n_2 moles of solute to give an infinitely dilute solution.

One may obtain $\bar{L}_1$ or $\bar{Q}_1$ experimentally as suggested by the equation analogous to Eq. (9-129), that is, from the variation of ΔH_M with n_1, as solvent is added to a fixed amount of solute. The alternative, and equivalent, measurement is that of the heat evolved on the addition of a small amount of solvent to a solution of a given composition. This last is known as a *heat of dilution*. One may also obtain $\bar{L}_1$ by the graphical method of Fig. 9-24 or indirectly from $\bar{L}_2$ values by the integration of Eq. (9-133).

As a numerical illustration, for a 1.11 m solution of sodium chloride $\bar{L}_1 = 4.0$ cal mole^{-1} and $\bar{L}_2 = -248$ cal mole^{-1}. The heat of solution at infinite dilution is, from Tables 5-2 and 5-3,

$$NaCl(s) + H_2O = NaCl(\text{infinitely dilute solution})$$
$$\Delta H = -97{,}302 - (-98{,}232) = 930 \quad \text{cal mole}^{-1}.$$

The heat of solution to give a 1.11 m solution differs from this value by

$$L = n_1\bar{L}_1 + n_2\bar{L}_2 \qquad [\text{Eq. (9-134)}],$$

or by $(55.5)(4.0) + (1.11)(-248) = 222 - 275 = -53$ cal per 1.11 mole or by -48 cal mole^{-1}. The actual heat of solution is then $930 - 48 = 882$ cal mole^{-1}.

Heats of mixing or of solution are direct, calorimetrically determined quantities, and the preceding framework of relationships and definitions has been developed with this in mind. Free energies of mixing are determined indirectly, through vapor pressure measurements, but may still be treated in just the same way. The equation analogous to Eq. (9-128) is

$$\Delta G_M = n_1\mu_{1(\text{rel})} + n_2\mu_{2(\text{rel})}, \tag{9-135}$$

where $\mu_{1(\text{rel})} = \mu_1 - \mu_1{}^\circ$ and $\mu_{2(\text{rel})} = \mu_2 - \mu_2{}^\circ$. Again, if ΔG_M is plotted against mole fraction, then the tangent line at a given composition has intercepts at $x_1 = 1$ and $x_2 = 1$ corresponding to $\mu_{1(\text{rel})}$ and $\mu_{2(\text{rel})}$ as shown in Fig. 9-25(a).

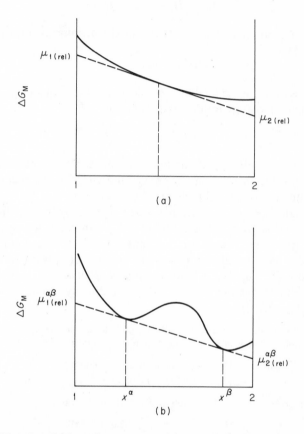

Fig. 9-25. *Variation of ΔG_M with composition. (a) A nearly ideal solution. (b) A system showing a miscibility gap. The intercepts of the tangent give $\mu_{1(\text{rel})}$ and $\mu_{2(\text{rel})}$.*

The plot in Fig. 9-25(b) shows two minima; there are thus two compositions x^α and x^β for which the $\mu_{1(\text{rel})}$ values are the same and the $\mu_{2(\text{rel})}$ values are the same. The situation is one of partial miscibility and a system of overall composition lying between x^α and x^β will spontaneously separate into phases of those two compositions. Figure 9-25(b) is thus the free energy plot corresponding to the vapor pressure plot of Fig. 9-8.

9-ST-2 The Surface Tension of Solutions. The Gibbs Equation

An important application of thermodynamics is to the variation of surface tension of a solution with its composition. The following derivation is essentially that of J. W. Gibbs, and the result is known as the *Gibbs adsorption equation*. We wish to deal with surface thermodynamic quantities and we must somehow separate their contribution from those of the bulk phases that form the interface. We do this by locating an arbitrary dividing plane S–S roughly in the interfacial region as shown in Fig. 9-26. We then assign a total energy and entropy to bulk phase α assuming it to continue unchanged up to this dividing plane, and similarly for bulk phase β. The actual total energy and enthalpy of the system are then written as

$$\mathsf{E} = \mathsf{E}^\alpha + \mathsf{E}^\beta + \mathsf{E}^\mathsf{s}, \qquad \mathsf{S} = \mathsf{S}^\alpha + \mathsf{S}^\beta + \mathsf{S}^\mathsf{s}, \tag{9-136}$$

where E^s and S^s are now called the surface *excess energy* and *entropy*. Similarly, we have

$$n_i = n_i{}^\alpha + n_i{}^\beta + n_i{}^\mathsf{s}. \tag{9-137}$$

For a small, reversible change $d\mathsf{E}$ in the energy of the whole system,

$$d\mathsf{E} = d\mathsf{E}^\alpha + d\mathsf{E}^\beta + d\mathsf{E}^\mathsf{s} = T\,dS^\alpha - P\,dv + \sum_i \mu_i\,dn_i{}^\alpha + T\,dS^\beta - P\,dv^\beta$$

$$+ \sum_i \mu_i\,dn_i{}^\beta + T\,dS^\mathsf{s} + \sum_i \mu_i\,dn_i{}^\mathsf{s} + \gamma\,d\mathscr{A} \tag{9-138}$$

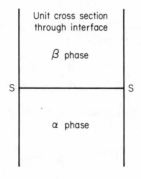

Unit cross section
through interface

β phase

S ———————— S

α phase

Fig. 9-26.

(the volume is entirely taken care of by $v^\alpha + v^\beta$). Equation (9-28) applies separately to phases α and β, so these terms all drop out, to leave

$$dE^s = T\,dS^s + \sum_i \mu_i\,dn_i{}^s + \gamma\,d\mathscr{A} \qquad (9\text{-}139)$$

The Euler theorem (preceding section) may now be applied; that is, Eq. (9-139) may be integrated, with T, μ_i, and γ kept constant, to give

$$E^s = TS^s + \sum_i \mu_i\,n_i{}^s + \gamma\mathscr{A}. \qquad (9\text{-}140)$$

Differentiation and comparison with the preceding equation gives

$$0 = S^s\,dT + \sum_i n_i{}^s\,d\mu_i + \mathscr{A}\,d\gamma. \qquad (9\text{-}141)$$

For a two-component system at constant temperature,

$$n_1{}^s\,d\mu_1 + n_2{}^s\,d\mu_2 + \mathscr{A}\,d\gamma = 0. \qquad (9\text{-}142)$$

It is convenient for us to divide through by the area $\mathscr{A}$ to obtain

$$d\gamma = -\Gamma_1\,d\mu_1 - \Gamma_2\,d\mu_2, \qquad (9\text{-}143)$$

where Γ_1 and Γ_2 are the excess quantities per unit area.

The exact position of the dividing surface shown in Fig. 9-26 is not specified; clearly the values of Γ will depend on this. We now specify the location to be such that $\Gamma_1 = 0$, so that Eq. (9-143) reduces to

$$\Gamma_2{}^1 = -\left(\frac{\partial\gamma}{\partial\mu_2}\right)_T, \qquad (9\text{-}144)$$

where the superscript is a reminder of the choice that has been made. The chemical potential may be expressed in terms of activity,

$$\Gamma_2{}^1 = -\frac{1}{RT}\frac{d\gamma}{d(\ln a_2)}. \qquad (9\text{-}145)$$

Finally, in dilute solution the activity will be proportional to concentration, so that an approximate form is

$$\Gamma_2{}^1 = -\frac{C}{RT}\frac{d\gamma}{dC}. \qquad (9\text{-}146)$$

The preceding are various forms of the Gibbs equation.

Figure 9-27 may help to explain the physical meaning of this conventional choice of location of the dividing surface. The figure shows schematically how the concentrations of solvent and of solute might vary across the interfacial region. The β phase is assumed to be vapor, so the concentrations in it are negligible. The surface excess is the difference between the amount actually present and that which would be present were the bulk phase to continue unchanged up to S–S so that the phase

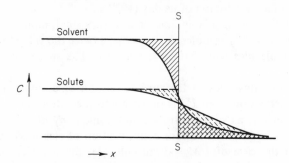

Fig. 9-27. *Illustration of the Γ_2^1 convention for the Gibbs equation. The dividing surface is located so that the shaded areas for the solvent curve balance. [From A. W. Adamson, "The Physical Chemistry of Surfaces." Copyright 1967, Wiley (Interscience), New York. Used with permission of John Wiley & Sons, Inc.]*

boundary became a step. The net shaded area for the solvent is then its surface excess, and S–S has been located so that this is zero. The surface excess of the solute is also given by its net shaded area and is positive in this example. An alternative, operational definition is as follows. If a sample of interface is taken, of 1 cm² area, and deep enough to include at least some bulk phase on either side, then Γ_2^1 is the (algebraic) excess of solute over the number of moles that would be present in a bulk region containing the same number of moles of solvent. The excess Γ_2^1 may be measured directly. In an experiment by J. W. McBain, a fast-moving knife blade (called a *microtome*) scooped a 3.2 g sample of solution at 20°C from the surface of a trough having a surface area of 310 cm². The solution contained 5 g of phenol ($M = 94$ g mole⁻¹) per 1000 g of water, that is, it was 0.053 m. It was found, by means of an interferometer, that the sample contained 2.52×10^{-6} g more of phenol per gram of water than did the bulk solution. The value of Γ_2^1 is thus $(2.52 \times 10^{-6})(3.2)/(94)(310) = 2.77 \times 10^{-10}$ mole cm⁻².

The Gibbs equation allows an indirect calculation of Γ_2^1 from surface tension data. Continuing with the preceding example, the surface tensions of 0.05 m and 0.127 m solutions were 67.7 and 60.1 dyn cm⁻¹, respectively, at 20°C. Thus $-d\gamma/dC$ was $(72.7 - 67.7)/0.05 = 100$ between 0 and 0.05 m and $(67.7 - 60.1)/$

$(0.127 - 0.05) = 92$ between $0.05 \, m$ and $0.127 \, m$. Using $C = 0.053 \, m$ and an average value for $-d\gamma/dC$ of 96, application of Eq. (9-146) gives

$$\Gamma_2^1 = \frac{(0.053)(96)}{(8.31 \times 10^7)(273)} = 2.1 \times 10^{-10} \quad \text{mole cm}^{-2}.$$

The two numbers agree fairly well—the microtome experiment is a very difficult one and was, in fact, a triumph of its day (1930's).

The value of Γ_2^1 obtained is, in one sense, a very small number. It corresponds, however, to about 80 Å² per molecule, or perhaps twice the value for a close-packed monolayer of molecules lying flat on the surface. The surface population is thus quite high.

As the example illustrates, if the surface tension of a solution decreases with increasing concentration, then Γ_2^1 is positive and the solute is concentrated at the interface. Conversely, as with electrolyte solutions, if $d\gamma/dC$ is positive, then Γ_2^1 is negative, meaning that the surface concentration of electrolyte is less than it is in solution. In the case of $1 \, M$ sodium chloride, the negative surface excess is equivalent to a surface layer of pure water about one molecule thick.

In sufficiently dilute solution, the surface tension will approach proportionality to concentration, that is,

$$\gamma = \gamma^\circ - bC, \tag{9-147}$$

where γ° is the surface tension of the pure solvent. The product $C \, d\gamma/dC$ is now just $-(\gamma^\circ - \gamma)$, so Eq. (9-146) reduces to

$$\Gamma_2^1 = \frac{\gamma^\circ - \gamma}{RT}.$$

It is now convenient to introduce the quantity π, called the *surface* pressure, and defined as

$$\pi = \gamma^\circ - \gamma. \tag{9-148}$$

Also $\Gamma_2^1 = 1/\sigma$, where σ is the area per mole. With these substitutions Eq. (9-146) becomes

$$\pi\sigma = RT. \tag{9-149}$$

This is the equation of state of a two-dimensional ideal gas! The film pressure does in fact correspond to a two-dimensional pressure. As illustrated in Fig. 9-28, if a flexible membrane separates pure solvent from solution, the floating barrier will experience a force πl, where l is its length. Returning to the numerical example, the film pressure of a $0.05 \, m$ solution of phenol was given as 7.6 dyn cm⁻¹. Again, this seems like a small number. The force is being exerted by a monolayer, however, and so we obtain the equivalent three-dimensional pressure by dividing by the

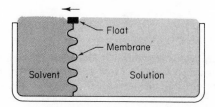

Fig. 9-28. *The PLAWM (Pockels–Langmuir–Adam–Wilson–McBain) trough—a means of measuring directly the film pressure π for a solution.*

depth of a molecule. In this case, the result is about $7.6/(4 \times 10^{-8})$ or 2×10^8 dyn cm^{-2}, which corresponds to 200 atm. Thus the lateral compression on the monolayer is quite appreciable at the molecular level.

More generally, the Gibbs equation allows surface tension–concentration data to be translated into values of π versus σ and such plots often look much like the ones of P versus V for a nonideal gas. A two-dimensional van der Waals equation may be used, for example,

$$\left(\pi + \frac{a}{\sigma^2}\right)(\sigma - b) = RT. \tag{9-150}$$

Such films are known as Gibbs monolayers, since they are normally studied through use of the Gibbs equation.

If the surfactant is quite insoluble, then, as mentioned in Section 9-CN-1, it may be spread directly onto the liquid surface, usually one of water. Now Γ_2^1 is known directly, as the amount placed on a known area of surface, and hence σ also is known. The film pressure is usually obtained from surface tension measurements, by the Wilhelmy slide method, although the force on a floating barrier may also be measured directly. The data are again usually reported as π versus σ plots.

GENERAL REFERENCES

General treatises cited in Chapter 1.

HILDEBRAND, J. H., AND SCOTT, R. L. (1950). "The Solubility of Nonelectrolytes," 3rd ed. Van Nostrand–Reinhold, Princeton, New Jersey.

ADAMSON, A. W. (1967). "The Physical Chemistry of Surfaces," 2nd ed. Wiley (Interscience), New York.

CITED REFERENCES

FRICKE, R., (1929). *Z. Elektrochem.* **35**, 631.

HILDEBRAND, J. H., AND SCOTT R. L. (1950). "The Solubility of Nonelectrolytes," 3rd ed. Van Nostrand–Reinhold. Princeton, New Jersey.

9 Solutions of Nonelectrolytes

Exercises

9-1 Assume that benzene and toluene form ideal solutions; the normal boiling point of benzene is 80°C and at this temperature the vapor pressure of toluene is 350 Torr. Calculate the separate partial pressures and the total vapor pressure at 80°C of a solution of $x_b = 0.2$. What composition of solution would boil at 80°C under the reduced pressure of 500 Torr?

Ans. $P_b = 152$ Torr, $P_t = 280$ Torr, $P_{tot} = 432$ Torr; $x_t = 0.634$.

9-2 Calculate the composition of the vapor in equilibrium with each of the two solutions of Exercise 9-1.

Ans. $y_b = 0.353$, $y_b = 0.556$.

9-3 The vapor pressure of propyl acetate (pa) is 21.5 Torr at 17°C. A mixture of 0.2 mole of pa with 0.5 mole of ipa (isopropyl acetate) has a total vapor pressure of 34.7 Torr at 17°C. Assuming ideal solution behavior, calculate the vapor pressure of ipa at this temperature and the composition of the vapor above the solution.

Ans. $P^\circ_{ipa} = 40.0$ Torr, $y_{pa} = 0.177$.

9-4 The molecular weight of substance B is 70 g mole^{-1} and dissolving 0.300 g in 2 mole of nonvolatile solvent A gives a solution of vapor pressure 2.50 Torr. Calculate the Henry's law constant for B dissolved in A.

Ans. 1170 Torr.

9-5 The Henry's law constant for Kr in water is 2.00×10^4 atm at 20°C. How many grams of Kr should dissolve in 1000 g of water at this temperature under pressure of 30 atm?

Ans. 6.95 g.

9-6 The Henry's law constant for H_2 in water is 5.51×10^7 Torr at 30°C. How many cubic centimeters of H_2, measured at 30°C and the pressure used, should dissolve in 1 cm^3 of water?

Ans. 0.0191 cm^3 of H_2 per cm^3 of water.

9-7 Two mole of toluene and 8 mole of benzene are introduced into a vessel at 20°C and the total vapor pressure is found to be 60 Torr. Using Fig. 9-2(b), estimate the number of moles of vapor formed and the compositions of the liquid and vapor phases present.

Ans. $x_t = 0.35$, $y_t = 0.18$, $n_v = 8.80$.

9-8 Water and toluene are essentially immiscible. The vapor pressures of the pure liquids at 90°C are 525 and 400 Torr, respectively. Calculate the composition of the vapor above a mixture of the two liquids.

Ans. $x_t = 0.43$.

9-9 Isopropyl alcohol (ipa) and benzene (b) form nonideal solutions. If x_{ipa} is 0.059, the partial pressure of ipa is 12.9 Torr at 25°C. The vapor pressures of the pure liquids are 44.0 and 94.4 Torr, respectively. Calculate k_{ipa} and α and estimate k_b.

Ans. $k_{ipa} = 219$ Torr, $\alpha = 1.60$, $k_b = 469$ Torr.

9-10 Calculate the free energy, enthalpy, and entropy of mixing for the process $0.2\ O_2$(1 atm, 25°C) $+ 0.8\ N_2$(1 atm, 25°C) $=$ air(1 atm, 25°C). Assume ideal gas behavior.

Ans. $\Delta G_M = -295$ cal, $\Delta H_M = 0$, $\Delta S_M = 0.991$ cal °K^{-1}.

9-11 Assuming ideal solution behavior, calculate the free energy, enthalpy, and entropy of mixing of 0.25 mole of benzene with 0.50 mole of toluene at 30°C.

Ans. $\Delta G_M = -287$ cal, $\Delta H_M = 0$, $\Delta S_M = 0.95$ cal °K^{-1}.

9-12 Determine the activity and the activity coefficient of ipa in the solution of Exercise 9-9 using pure ipa as the standard state.

Ans. $a_{ipa} = 0.293$, $\gamma_{ipa} = 4.97$.

9-13 Using the data of Exercise 9-9, calculate the excess free energy of mixing one mole of ipa with sufficient benzene to form a solution of $x_{ipa} = 0.059$ at 25°C.

Ans. 1009 cal.

9-14 A certain amount of an ethanol–benzene solution of $x_b = 0.20$ is introduced into a flask; some of it vaporizes and the residual solution has a total vapor pressure of 750 Torr at 72.5°C. Find the compositions of the final solution and of the vapor phase in equilibrium with it at 72.5°C.

Ans. x_b(final) $= 0.10$, $y_b = 0.30$.

9-15 The final solution as in Exercise 9-14 is boiled in an open flask until the boiling point (under 750 Torr pressure) rises from 72.5°C to 75°C. Estimate the number of moles of liquid remaining per mole originally present.

Ans. 0.71.

9-16 In a steam distillation of an insoluble oil the boiling point of the mixture is found to be 95°C and the distillate is found to contain 80 % by weight of the oil. Atmospheric pressure is 755 Torr, and the vapor pressure of water at 95°C is 634 Torr. Calculate the molecular weight of the oil.

Ans. 380 g mole^{-1}.

9-17 One hundred grams of a 60 mole % solution of phenol in water ($x_p = 0.60$) initially at 80°C is cooled. (a) At what temperature will the solution become turbid? (b) What are the amounts and compositions of the phases present at 40°C? (The abscissa scale of Fig. 9-21a is in mole fraction.)

Ans. (a) 55°C; (b) 95 g of phenol-rich phase with $x_p = 0.67$ and 5 g of water-rich phase with $x_p = 0.10$.

9-18 (a) Triethylamine is added to 0.2 mole of water at 30°C until the solution just becomes turbid. How many moles are added? (b) Water is added to 0.3 mole of triethylamine at 30°C until the solution just becomes turbid. How many moles are added? (c) The solutions of (a) and (b) are combined. Give the compositions and amounts of the phases present.

Ans. (a) 0.013 mole; (b) 0.013 mole; (c) 0.31 mole of triethylamine-rich phase with $x_t = 0.96$ and 0.21 mole of water-rich phase with $x_t = 0.06$.

Problems

9-1 Calculate the minimum work to "unmix" air, that is, to obtain 80 liter of pure nitrogen and 20 liter of pure oxygen, each at 25°C and 1 atm pressure, from 100 liter of air at this pressure and temperature. The ΔH_{M} may be assumed to be zero.

9-2 Calculate the total vapor pressure of solutions of toluene and benzene of compositions 0.2, 0.4, 0.6, and 0.8 (mole fraction) for the temperatures 85, 95, 100, 105°C. Assume Raoult's law to hold, and look up the necessary data. Plot the results as P (in atm) versus mole fraction and also calculate and plot the composition of vapor in equilibrium with each of the solutions at each temperature. Construct from this information a plot of the normal boiling point versus composition. Give also the vapor composition line.

A small amount of the vapor in equilibrium at 95°C with solution of $x_{\mathrm{t}} = 0.5$ condenses. What is the vapor pressure of the condensate at 95°C? What is the boiling point of the original solution? Of the condensate? What is the composition of the vapor in equilibrium with the original solution at 95°C and with the condensate at 95°C? If the original solution were boiled in an open vessel until the boiling point rose 5°C, what would be the composition of the remaining solution and the number of moles of each component present in it, assuming that the original solution contained one mole of benzene?

9-3 Liquids A and B form an ideal solution. A solution of mole fraction $x_{\mathrm{A}} = 0.4$ is treated as follows: (a) 0.30 mole is introduced into an evacuated vessel of volume such that, at 25°C, 15% of the liquid (mole %) evaporates. The final total pressure is 82.2 Torr at 25°C. (b) A portion of the equilibrium vapor is drawn off, condensed completely, and then found to have a total vapor pressure of 92.3 Torr at 25°C. Calculate the vapor pressures of pure liquids A and B at 25°C.

9-4 An aqueous solution of ammonia at 20°C has $x_{\mathrm{a}} = 0.0300$ and the equilibrium water and ammonia vapor pressures are 17.5 and 18.2 Torr, respectively. A vessel of two liters capacity contains one liter of water, and 1.35 mole of ammonia is introduced. Calculate the total equilibrium pressure in the vessel.

9-5 Calculate the total vapor pressure of solutions of water and methyl alcohol of compositions 20% (mole %), 40%, 60%, and 80% for the temperatures 70, 80, 85, and 90°C. Assume Raoult's law to hold, and use tables to look up the vapor pressures of the pure liquids at the various temperatures. Plot the results as P (in atm) versus mole fraction and also calculate and plot the composition of vapor in equilibrium with each of the solutions at each temperature. Construct a plot of the boiling point at 1 atm against composition. Give the vapor composition line.

A small amount of the vapor in equilibrium at 80°C with a solution containing 50% water is condensed. What is the vapor pressure of the condensate at 80°C? What is the boiling point of the original solution? Of the condensate? What is the composition of the vapor in equilibrium with the original solution at 80°C and with the condensate at 80°C? How many evaporation condensation steps would suffice to yield a small amount of final condensate containing 95% methyl alcohol?

9-6 *Para*-xylene and toluene form solutions which can be regarded as ideal. The vapor pressure of pure *p*-xylene is 34.0 mm and of pure toluene is 59.1 mm at 40°C. A liquid mixture of the two, containing 0.002 mole of each, is introduced in a previously evacuated 1-liter flask at 40°C. Neglecting the volume of the liquid phase in comparison with 1 liter, calculate the equilibrium composition of the liquid which remains after vaporization has occurred.

9-7 A solution of 1 mole of NaOH in 4.559 mole of water has a vapor pressure of 4.474 Torr at 15°C, whereas the vapor pressure of pure water is 12.788 Torr at 15°C. What is (a) the activity of water in the solution (that is, the effective mole fraction) and (b) the difference between the chemical potential (that is, molar free energy) of the water in the solution and in pure water (Fricke, 1929!)?

9-8 The total vapor pressure of a 5 mole % solution of NH_3 in water at 20°C is 51.78 Torr and the vapor pressure of pure water at the same temperature is 17.36 Torr. Apply Henry's and Raoult's laws to calculate the partial pressures and total vapor pressure of a 2 mole % solution at the same temperature.

9-9 A solution containing 20 mole % of phenol in water is cooled to 50°C and the phenol-rich layer which separates out is drawn off. This phenol-rich layer is then cooled to 30°C, and of the two layers present, the one richest in phenol is again drawn off. If 100 g of original solution were used, how many grams of the final phenol-rich layer are obtained and what is the composition of this layer?

9-10 Calculate the total vapor pressure of solutions of heptane and octane of compositions 0.2, 0.4, 0.6, and 0.8 (mole fraction) for the temperatures 100, 105, 110, and 120°C. Assume Raoult's law to hold, and look up the necessary data. Plot the results as P (in atm) versus mole fraction and calculate and plot on the same graph the composition of vapor in equilibrium with each of the solutions at each temperature. Construct a plot of the normal boiling point versus composition. Give the vapor composition line.

A small amount of the vapor in equilibrium at 110°C with a solution of $x_0 = 0.5$ is condensed. What is the composition of the condensate? What is the vapor pressure of the condensate? If the solution were boiled in an open vessel until the boiling point rose 5°C, what would be the compositions of the first vapor coming off and of the last vapor coming off? What would be the composition of the remaining solution? If the solution contained one mole of octane, how many moles of octane would be left in the solution after this boiling over the 5°C range? Insofar as possible, show your operations graphically and indicate on the graphs the source of the various data employed in answering the questions.

9-11 The accompanying diagram shows the activity coefficients versus composition for carbon disulfide–acetone solutions. (a) Calculate and plot the corresponding vapor pressure

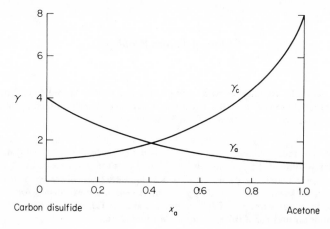

diagram. (b) Calculate and plot the partial molal free energies and the total excess free energy as functions of solution composition. Assume 25°C; look up necessary $P°$ values.

9-12 Construct an accurate diagram of the type of Fig. 9-9 for the water–toluene system at 90°C. (Use the data of Exercise 9-8.) Two-tenths mole of water and 0.3 mole of toluene are placed in a piston and cylinder arrangement kept at 90°C; the mixture is initially gaseous. The piston is gradually depressed so as to compress the mixture. At what pressure will liquid begin to condense? Which liquid? What will be the composition of the last vapor to condense as the pressure is further increased? What will this pressure be?

9-13 Demonstrate that the critical temperature for a system obeying the Margules equations is one for which $\alpha = 2$.

9-14 Mixtures of liquids A and B obey the Margules equations. Make an accurate set of plots corresponding to Fig. 9-8(a, b) if $\alpha = 4.0$ at 50°C. The constant α often varies inversely as T. Calculate the consolute temperature for this system. Is it an upper or a lower consolute temperature? Assume $P_A° = P_B°$.

9-15 The International Critical Tables (1928) give the following data for the partial pressure of acetic acid above acetic acid–benzene solutions at 50°C:

x_a (%)	1.60	4.39	8.35	11.38	17.14	29.79
P (Torr)	3.63	7.25	11.51	14.2	18.4	24.8
x_a (%)	36.96	58.34	66.04	84.35	99.31	
P (Torr)	28.7	36.3	40.2	50.7	54.7	

Calculate and plot the activities and activity coefficients of acetic acid as a function of composition. Apply the method of Fig. 9-13 to obtain the activities and activity coefficients of benzene for several concentrations and plot these results as well.

9-16 Calculate ΔG_M for various compositions of the acetone–chloroform system at 35°C and plot the results.

Special Topics Problems

9-1 The partial molal volumes for water and ethanol at 20°C are 17 and 57 cm³ mole⁻¹, respectively, for a solution of $x_e = 0.4$. Calculate the volume change on mixing sufficient ethanol with two moles of water to give this final composition.

9-2 The apparent molar volume ϕ_2 of a solute, is defined as $\phi_2 = (V - n_1 V_1)/n_2$, where V_1 is the molar volume of the pure solvent. It is found that for solutions of $CaCl_2$, ϕ_2 (in cm³) is closely approximated by $\phi_2 = 10.15 + 3.52\,m - 1.62\,m^2$, where m is the molality, or number of moles of $CaCl_2$ per 1000 g of water. Derive the expression for V as a function of m and thence an expression for $\bar{V}_2$ as a function of m. Calculate $\bar{V}_1$ and $\bar{V}_2$ for an infinitely dilute solution and for a 0.7 m solution. Assume 25°C.

9-3 The density of aqueous acetic acid solutions varies with composition at 20°C as follows:

density (g cm^{-3})	0.9982	1.0125	1.0263	1.0384	1.0488	1.0575
wt % acetic acid	0	10	20	30	40	50

density (g cm^{-3})	1.0642	1.0685	1.0700	1.0661	1.0498
wt % acetic acid:	60	70	80	90	100

Calculate V_{av} and plot it as a function of mole fraction of acetic acid. Determine the partial molal volumes of water and of acetic acid for nearly pure water, nearly pure acetic acid, and for several intermediate compositions. Plot these values against composition.

9-4 Show that $\bar{Q}_2 = \phi - x_1(d\phi/dx_1)$.

9-5 For the process

$$\text{NaCl (solution, } m) \rightarrow \text{NaCl (infinite dilution)},$$

$-\Delta H$ has been found to vary as follows at 25°C:

m	0.2	1.0	2.0	3.0	4.0	5.0	6.12
$-\Delta H$ (cal mole^{-1})	90	-23	-177	-304	-395	-453	-483

Calculate $\bar{L}_1$ and $\bar{L}_2$ for $2\,m$ NaCl and for the saturated solution (6.12 m), and find the value for ΔH for the process

$$\text{NaCl}(s) + \text{water} \rightarrow \text{saturated solution}$$

(remember Table 5-3).

9-6 Plot the data of Table 9-1 in the form of Fig. 9-25 and calculate $\mu_{1(rel)}$ and $\mu_{2(rel)}$ for solutions of $x_1 = 0.2$ and $x_1 = 0.8$ (species 1 being acetone).

9-7 The surface tension of an aqueous solution varies with concentration according to the equation $\gamma = 72 - 500C$, provided that C is less than 0.05. Calculate the surface excess of solute for a 0.02 M solution. Assume 25°C.

9-8 Find the expression for γ as a function of C if $\Gamma = aC/(1 + bC)$, where a and b are constants.

9-9 Find the expression for Γ as a function of C if Eq. (9-150) is obeyed.

10 DILUTE SOLUTIONS OF NONELECTROLYTES. COLLIGATIVE PROPERTIES

The material that follows has been separated from the preceding chapter primarily because a somewhat special emphasis is involved. A very important situation is that in which two phases are in equilibrium, one of which is a solution and the other of which is a *pure phase* of one of the components. The description is a general one of a system exhibiting a *colligative property* (from the Latin *colligatus* or collected together). The common feature of colligative properties is that, to a first approximation, the observed behavior depends on the mole fraction composition of the solution and on the physical properties of the component which is present in both phases but not on the nature of the second component. The former will be defined as the solvent and the latter as the solute.

This common feature is an exactly observed one if the solution phase is ideal in its behavior. What is actually required is that the activity coefficient of the solvent be independent of the chemical nature of the solute; this condition will always be approached as $x_1 \rightarrow 1$, since Raoult's law is the general limiting law for all solutions. Alternatively stated, it is usually desirable that the solution phase be dilute with respect to the solute. There is therefore considerable emphasis in this chapter on the behavior of dilute solutions.

The most important types of phase equilibria which give rise to colligative phenomena are given in Table 10-1. Other combinations are possible, of course, but are not encountered very often and are therefore ignored here.

One of the important applications of colligative phenomena is to the determination of the molecular weight of a solute present in dilute solution. There are a number of other methods for such a determination and these are reviewed in Section 10-7 so as to provide a general picture of this aspect of physical chemistry.

Table 10-1.

Phases in equilibrium	Restriction or condition	Name of resulting colligative property
Liquid solution ⇋ vapor	Solute must be nonvolatile	Vapor pressure lowering Boiling point elevation
Solid ⇋ liquid solution	Solid phase must consist of pure solvent	Freezing point depression
Liquid solution ⇋ liquid solvent	Semipermeable membrane prevents the solute from entering the pure solvent phase	Osmotic pressure

Colligative property measurements on nonideal solutions give the thermo-dynamic mole fraction or activity of the solvent and, indirectly, the activity and activity coefficient of the solute. This constitutes a second major application of colligative phenomena and is described in some detail in the Special Topics section. Although appropriate to this chapter, chemical equilibria involving nonelectrolytes are more conveniently discussed in Chapter 12 along with equilibria involving electrolytes.

10-1 Vapor Pressure Lowering

The general statement for the vapor pressure of the solvent component of a liquid solution is:

$$P_1 = a_1 P_1^\circ \qquad [\text{Eq. (9-71)}]$$

or

$$\frac{\Delta P_1}{P_1^\circ} = 1 - a_1, \tag{10-1}$$

where ΔP_1 is the vapor pressure lowering of the solvent, $P_1^\circ - P_1$. If the solute is nonvolatile, then P is the total vapor pressure above the solution and ΔP_1 is the total vapor pressure lowering ΔP.

If the solution is ideal, then Raoult's law, Eq. (9-4), holds, which means that $a_1 = x_1$. Equation (10-1) becomes

$$\frac{\Delta P}{P_1^\circ} = x_2, \tag{10-2}$$

still assuming the solute to be nonvolatile. Thus a measured behavior of the solvent has given the mole fraction of the solute, independent of the chemical nature of the latter. As will be illustrated later, if the weight composition of the solution is known, then the value of x_2 can be used for calculation of the molecular weight of the solute.

10-2   Boiling Point Elevation

We can use the procedures of Section 9-6 to relate the change in normal boiling point of a solution to the solvent activity if the solute is nonvolatile. The situation is that since $P = 1$ atm, $\mu_1(g) = \mu_1°(g)$, and for phase equilibrium $\mu_1(l)$ is therefore equal to $\mu_1°(g)$. Thus

$$\mu_1°(g) = \mu_1(l) = \mu_1°(l) + RT \ln a_1 \qquad (10\text{-}3)$$

[from the definition of a_1, Eq. (9-72)].

Differentiation with respect to temperature gives

$$-S_i°(g) = -S_i°(l) + R \ln a_i + RT \frac{d(\ln a_i)}{dT}, \qquad (10\text{-}4)$$

or as shown in Section 9-6,

$$\frac{d(\ln a_1)}{dT} = \frac{H_1°(l) - H_1°(g)}{RT^2} = -\frac{\Delta H_{v,1}°}{RT^2}, \qquad (10\text{-}5)$$

where $\Delta H_{v,1}°$ is the standard heat of vaporization of the pure solvent. Equation (10-5) may be integrated between limits, with $a_1 = 1$ at $T = T_{b,1}°$, the normal boiling point of the pure solvent:

$$\ln a_1 = \frac{\Delta H_{v,1}°}{R} \left(\frac{1}{T_b} - \frac{1}{T_{b,1}°} \right), \qquad (10\text{-}6)$$

with T_b denoting the normal boiling point of a solution of solvent activity a_1.

We next consider the solution to be ideal. Equation (10-6) becomes

$$\ln x_1 = \frac{\Delta H_{v,1}°}{R} \left(\frac{1}{T_b} - \frac{1}{T_{b,1}°} \right). \qquad (10\text{-}7)$$

Again, a measurement of a property due to the solvent has yielded the mole fraction composition of the solution: x_2 may, of course, be calculated from $\ln x_1$.

It was noted in the opening remarks that we obtain the condition of ideality in practice by using a dilute solution. Equation (10-7) undergoes considerable simplification under this condition. First, $\ln x_1$ may be expanded and only the first term of the series used, so that $\ln x_1 \simeq -(1 - x_1) = -x_2$. For example, if

$x_2 < 0.01$, the error in the approximation is less than 1 %. With this substitution, and after rearrangement, Eq. (10-7) becomes

$$\varDelta T_b = \frac{RT_{b,1}^{\circ} T_b}{\varDelta H_{v,1}^{\circ}} x_2, \qquad (10\text{-}8)$$

where $\varDelta T_b$ is the normal boiling point elevation of the solution, $T_b - T_{b,1}^{\circ}$.

The expansion of the $\ln x_1$ term has already limited the maximum value of x_2 to be tolerated, and no significant further error is introduced if T_b is approximated by $T_{b,1}^{\circ}$ in the numerator of Eq. (10-8). Also, we have

$$x_2 = \frac{n_2}{n_2 + n_1} = \frac{m}{m + (1000/M_1)}, \qquad (10\text{-}9)$$

where m is the molality of the solute and M_1 is the molecular weight of the solvent. The error due to neglecting m in the denominator of Eq. (10-9) is again not important. With these further approximations Eq. (10-8) becomes

$$\varDelta T_b = \left[\frac{R(T_{b,1}^{\circ})^2 M_1}{1000 \, \varDelta H_{v,1}^{\circ}} \right] m = K_b m, \qquad (10\text{-}10)$$

where K_b is called the *boiling point elevation constant*. K_b depends only on properties of the pure solvent. The value for water is 0.51; further values are given in Table 10-2 in Section 10-4.

10-3 Freezing Point Depression

The equilibrium between a solid phase consisting of pure solvent and a liquid solution is treated as follows. The condition of equilibrium is that $\mu_1^{\circ}(s) = \mu_1(l)$. Then, by Eq. (9-72), we have

$$\mu_1^{\circ}(s) = \mu_1^{\circ}(l) + RT \ln a_1. \qquad (10\text{-}11)$$

The rest is analogous to the preceding derivation. Differentiation with respect to temperature yields

$$-S_1^{\circ}(s) = -S_1^{\circ}(l) + R \ln a_1 + RT \frac{d(\ln a_1)}{dT}, \qquad (10\text{-}12)$$

and, on replacement of $R \ln a_1$ by $[\mu_1^{\circ}(s) - \mu_1^{\circ}(l)]/T$ and rearrangement, we have

$$\frac{d(\ln a_1)}{dT} = \frac{H_1^{\circ}(l) - H_1^{\circ}(s)}{RT^2} = \frac{\varDelta H_{f,1}^{\circ}}{RT^2}. \qquad (10\text{-}13)$$

Equation (10-13) is then integrated between limits, with $a_1 = 1$ at $T_{f,1}$, the melting (or freezing) point of the pure solvent, to give

$$\ln a_1 = \frac{\Delta H^{\circ}_{f,1}}{R} \left(\frac{1}{T^{\circ}_{f,1}} - \frac{1}{T_f} \right), \tag{10-14}$$

where T_f is the freezing point of the solution of solvent activity a_1. Notice the parallel that is developing between the boiling point elevation and freezing point depression effects.

If the solution is ideal, Eq. (10-14) becomes

$$\ln x_1 = \frac{\Delta H^{\circ}_{f,1}}{R} \left(\frac{1}{T^{\circ}_{f,1}} - \frac{1}{T_f} \right). \tag{10-15}$$

Again, the most valid application will be to dilute solutions, for which $\ln x_1$ may be approximated by $-x_2$, so that

$$\Delta T_f = \frac{R T^{\circ}_{f,1} T_f}{\Delta H^{\circ}_{f,1}} x_2, \tag{10-16}$$

and, by setting $T_f = T^{\circ}_{f,1}$ and neglecting m in the denominator of Eq. (10-9), we obtain

$$\Delta T_f = \left[\frac{R(T^{\circ}_{f,1})^2 M_1}{1000 \, \Delta H^{\circ}_{f,1}} \right] m = K_f m. \tag{10-17}$$

K_f is called the *freezing point depression constant*; its value depends only on properties of the solvent. For water, $K_f = 1.86$.

10-4   Summary of the First Three Colligative Properties

The preceding two derivations were made on a somewhat formal thermodynamic basis and it is possible to give a physical explanation of all of the effects so far discussed. This is done in Fig. 10-1, which shows schematic vapor pressure plots for pure solid and pure liquid solvent and for a dilute solution of a nonvolatile solute. The vapor pressure lowering follows directly. The boiling point elevation is the difference between the two temperatures at which the $P = 1$ atm line crosses the $P_1^{\circ}(l)$ and $P_1(l)$ curves.

As noted in Section 8-4, at the melting point of a pure substance the solid and liquid vapor pressures must be the same. Therefore $T^{\circ}_{f,1}$ is the temperature of crossing of the $P_1^{\circ}(s)$ and $P_1^{\circ}(l)$ curves. Since the solute is not present in the solid phase, the vapor pressure of the solid is not altered by the presence of solute, and T_f must therefore be the temperature of crossing of the $P_1^{\circ}(s)$ and $P_1(l)$ curves.

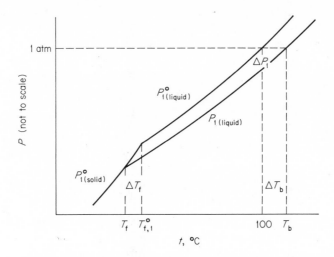

Fig. 10-1. *Explanation of boiling point elevation and freezing point depression effects in terms of vapor pressure changes. The solute is assumed to be nonvolatile.*

One objection to this last analysis is that it is not strictly necessary that the solute be nonvolatile in the freezing point depression effect. It is only necessary that it be insoluble in the solid solvent phase.

The boiling point elevation and freezing point depression effects are the more commonly used of the three, and some of the experimental aspects are as follows. Figure 10-2 shows a Cottrell boiling point apparatus, the main feature of which is the tubular yoke around the bulb of the thermometer. The purpose is to bathe the bulb in boiling solution; were vapor simply allowed to condense onto the bulb, the temperature registered would tend to be that of the boiling point of the solvent, since the vapor consists of pure solvent.

Freezing point depressions may be obtained with very simple equipment, often consisting merely of a Dewar flask equipped with a Beckmann thermometer and a stirrer. The freezing point of the pure solvent is first determined, as, for example, by using a mixture of ice and water if the system is aqueous or in general by gradual cooling of the solution until freezing sets in. The experiment is repeated with the solution. Liquids tend to supercool, and it is necessary to be sure that enough finely divided solid solvent is present to ensure equilibrium.

It is also essential to know the composition of the equilibrium solution that corresponds to the temperature measurement. This is not difficult in the case of boiling elevation; if the boiling solution is under reflux, its composition is essentially the same as that initially. In the freezing point depression experiment, however, there is apt to be appreciable freezing or melting before the final temperature reading, and a sample of the solution should be withdrawn for analysis at that point.

The vapor pressure lowering effect, while less frequently used, is actually quite

Fig. 10-2.   *Cottrell boiling point apparatus.*

important for very precise work. Rather than attempting direct vapor pressure measurements, however, one usually compares the unknown with a known solution by allowing the two solutions to come to vapor pressure equilibrium at a known temperature. For example, an open beaker of each solution might be placed in an otherwise empty desiccator, which is then thermostated. Solution A contains a known nonvolatile solute and solution B contains the nonvolatile one being studied. The solvent vapor pressures above the two solutions will initially not be the same. Suppose that at first $P_{1,A}$ is greater than $P_{1,B}$. Then solvent will distill from solution A to solution B, concentrating the former and diluting the latter. Eventually *isopiestic equilibrium* is reached, that is, $P_{1,A} = P_{1,B}$. The solutions must now have identical values for solvent activity a_1. Analysis of solution A then determines the actual value of $a_{1,A}$. Since the solutions are in equilibrium, $a_{1,A} = a_{1,B}$. If solution B is ideal or is dilute enough that Raoult's law has been reached as a limiting law, then $a_{1,B} = x_{1,B}$.

The isopiestic method has an advantage over the other two in being an isothermal

Table 10-2. *Boiling Point Elevation and Freezing Point Depression Constants*

Solvent	t_b (°C)	K_b	t_f (°C)	K_f
Ethyl ether	34.4	2.11	—	—
Chloroform	61.2	3.63	—	—
Ethanol	78.3	1.22	—	—
Benzene	80.2	2.53	5.6	5.12
Water	100.0	0.514	0.00	1.855
Acetic acid	118	2.93	17	3.90
Bromobenzene	155.8	6.20	—	—
Naphthalene	—	—	80.2	6.8
Camphor	—	—	178	40

one, so that corrections for changes in solvent properties with temperature are not needed. The isopiestic method is tedious, however, and is only used when very accurate results are wanted.

Representative values of K_b and K_f are given in Table 10-2; some are quite large and such solvents are often used in qualitative molecular weight determinations because of the ease of measuring ΔT_b or ΔT_f. It should be pointed out that both constants, but especially K_b, depend on the ambient pressure. Thus K_b for benzene changes by 0.025 % per Torr difference between 760 Torr and the actual barometric pressure.

The following calculation illustrates the three effects. Suppose that an aqueous solution of an organic compound is in isopiestic equilibrium with 0.1 m sucrose at 25°C. What is the vapor pressure of the solution if that of pure water is 23.76 Torr at 25°C? What would be the boiling point elevation and freezing point depression? If the solution contains 2.50 wt % of the compound, what is its molecular weight?

To answer the first question, we need the mole fraction of the sucrose solution: $x_2 = 0.1/[0.1 + (1000/18)] = 0.0018$. The vapor pressure lowering is then $(0.0018)(23.76) = 0.0428$ Torr. The solution of the compound must have the same value for a_1 as the sucrose solution and is dilute enough that we can use the dilute solution approximation; the molality of the two solutions is therefore also the same. The boiling point elevation is then $(0.514)(0.1) = 0.0514$°C, and the freezing point depression is $(1.855)(0.1) = 0.1855$°C.

We have 25 g of compound per 975 g of water or 25.6 g per 1000 g of water. Since the solution is 0.1 m, the molecular weight must be 256.

10-5 Osmotic Equilibrium

An osmotic equilibrium is one between a solution and pure solvent, both liquid. It is necessary to have a barrier between the liquids to separate them. The barrier must be impermeable to the solute, yet for equilibrium it must be permeable to the solvent. Such barriers or membranes (since they usually are thin) are called *semipermeable membranes*. The solvent activity is different in the two liquids, being lower in the solution than in the pure solvent; to bring the system to equilibrium, it is necessary to have the solution under mechanical pressure. The effect of such pressure on a pure liquid was shown in Section 8-5 to increase its vapor pressure or activity, and the same is true for a solution. The pressures involved can be considerable, and a semipermeable "membrane" usually must be either well supported or itself quite strong.

A schematic osmotic pressure apparatus is shown in Fig. 10-3. In the form

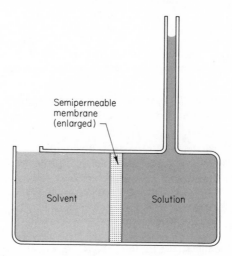

Semipermeable
membrane
(enlarged)

Solvent

Solution

Fig. 10-3.   *Schematic osmotic pressure apparatus.*

pictured, solvent passes through the semipermeable membrane until sufficient hydrostatic head develops on the solution side for the activity of water in the solution to be equal to that of the pure solvent. Alternatively, the solution may be placed under sufficient mechanical pressure to just prevent net flow of solvent.

A very simple illustration of the osmotic effect is given by Fig. 10-4. The end of a flared-out capillary tube is tightly covered with filter paper which is wet with water. The inside is filled with chloroform, and the tube dips into ether. The level in the tube will slowly rise; ether is somewhat soluble in water and the dissolved ether diffuses through to the chloroform side. Chloroform, however, is quite insoluble in water, and the wet filter paper is a barrier to its passage. This particular membrane would be a "leaky" one. Eventually enough chloroform would get through to establish the final equilibrium state of equal levels of identical solution inside and out.

Osmotic equilibrium is independent of how the membrane acts so long as it is in fact permeable only to the solvent. The condition for equilibrium is that $\mu_1^\circ(l) = \mu_1(l)$, where $\mu_1(l)$ is the chemical potential of the solvent in the solution. For a solution not under pressure,

$$\mu_1(l) = \mu_1^\circ(l) + RT \ln a_1 \qquad \text{[Eq. (9-72)]}$$

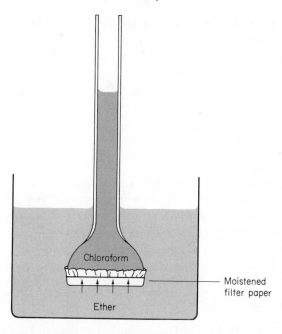

Fig. 10-4. *Filter paper moistened with water and acting as a "leaky" membrane between chloroform (in the tube) and ether.*

and the effect of pressure is, according to Eq. (8-22), to increase $\mu_1(l)$ by the integral of $\overline{V}_1\, dP$:

$$\mu_1(l) = \mu_1^\circ(l) + RT \ln a_1 + \int_{P_1^\circ}^{\Pi} \overline{V}_1\, dP. \tag{10-18}$$

At equilibrium the free energy of the solvent must be the same on both sides of the diaphragm, or

$$\mu_1^\circ(l) = \mu_1(l) = \mu_1^\circ(l) + RT \ln a_1 + \int_{P_1^\circ}^{\Pi} \overline{V}_1\, dP$$

or

$$-RT \ln a_1 = \int_{P_1^\circ}^{\Pi} \overline{V}_1\, dP. \tag{10-19}$$

The required mechanical pressure Π to produce equilibrium is known as the *osmotic pressure*. Ordinarily Π is large compared to P_1° and the change in $\overline{V}_1$ with pressure can be neglected, so Eq. (10-19) simplifies to

$$-RT \ln a_1 = \Pi \overline{V}_1. \tag{10-20}$$

If the solution is ideal, then $a_1 = x_1$ and

$$-RT \ln x_1 = \Pi \overline{V}_1. \tag{10-21}$$

407

If the solution has approached ideality by also being dilute, then $\ln x_1$ may be approximated by $-x_2$, as before. At the same level of approximation $x_2 \simeq n_2/n_1$, and so Eq. (10-21) takes the very simple form

$$RT \frac{n_2}{n_1} = \Pi \overline{V}_1^\circ.$$

In the case of a dilute solution $n_1 \overline{V}_1^\circ$ is essentially the volume of the solution, so

$$\Pi V = n_2 RT \quad \text{or} \quad \Pi = CRT. \tag{10-22}$$

The interesting final result is that in dilute solution osmotic pressure obeys the ideal gas law. The final approximation is unnecessarily severe, and a very useful dilute solution form is one in which C is the number of moles of solute per unit volume of solvent, rather than per unit volume of solution.

The numerical example of the preceding section may be extended to the calculation of the osmotic pressure of the solutions. The osmotic pressure Π must be the same for the sucrose solution and that of the unknown compound at 25°C since they are in isopiestic equilibrium. Then $C = 0.1$ mole liter^{-1} of solvent and $\Pi = (0.1)(0.0821)(298) = 2.45$ atm. Note how large the osmotic pressure is compared to the other colligative effects.

Some data due to Berkeley and Hartley in 1906 on the osmotic pressure of sucrose solutions are given in Table 10-3. The simple formula (10-22) fails badly by about 1 m sucrose concentration, and even the more exact form, Eq. (10-21), is inadequate; it would predict an osmotic pressure of 92 atm for the most concentrated solution, instead of the observed 134.7 atm. We have confidence in the thermodynamics, and evidently the solution must not be ideal, as assumed in writing Eq. (10-21). It turns out, however, that the quite excellent agreement shown by the last column of Table 10-3 results if one supposes that each sucrose molecule binds six molecules of water. The actual number of moles of solvent present is thus reduced by six per mole of sucrose present, and x_2 is correspondingly increased. This example is cited to illustrate one way in which a formal nonideality may be accounted for.

Table 10-3.   *Osmotic Pressure of Aqueous Sucrose at 0°C*[a]

Concentration (grams per liter of solution)	$(n_2/n_1) \times 10^4$	Osmotic pressure (atm)		
		Observed	Equation (10-22)	Modified Eq. (10-21)[b]
2.02	1.064	0.134	0.132	0.133
10.0	5.294	0.66	0.655	0.661
45.0	24.22	2.97	2.947	3.056
300	193.6	26.8	19.65	26.99
750	737.2	134.7	49.14	154.5

[a] Source: E. A. Moelwyn-Hughes, "Physical Chemistry," p. 803. Pergamon, Oxford, 1961.
[b] See text.

―

10-6   Activities and Activity Coefficients for Dilute Solutions

The use of activities and activity coefficients for solutions was discussed in Section 9-5. It will be recalled that activity a was defined as the effective mole fraction such as to keep the form of Raoult's law:

$$P_i = a_i P_i^\circ \qquad \text{[Eq. (9-71)]}.$$

The activity coefficient γ was defined as the factor whereby a differs from x,

$$a_i = \gamma_i x_i \qquad \text{[Eq. (9-73)]},$$

so that the chemical potential for the ith species is

$$\mu_i(l) = \mu_i^\circ(l) + RT \ln a_i \qquad \text{[Eq. (9-72)]}.$$

Since Raoult's law is approached by all solutions as $x_i \to 1$, it follows that in this limit $a_i \to x_i$ and $\gamma_i \to 1$.

This convention is fine for solutions of two liquids, whose compositions can range from pure component 1 to pure component 2. It is, however, very awkward for dilute solutions, and an alternative set of definitions has become customary for the solute. That for the solvent remains the same. Since Henry's law is the limiting law for the solute, we now define an activity a' such that Henry's law is obeyed,

$$P_2 = a_2' k_2. \qquad (10\text{-}23)$$

The corresponding activity coefficient γ_2' is given by

$$a_2' = \gamma_2' x_2. \qquad (10\text{-}24)$$

These conventions are to be applied only to the solute, and Eqs. (10-23) and (10-24) have been written on this basis. Since Henry's law is approached as $x_2 \to 0$, then $a_2' \to x_2$ and $\gamma_2' \to 1$ at this limit.

In the case of aqueous solutions, it is customary to express the concentration of solute as molality m rather than as x_2. Henry's law may still be used as a limiting law since by Eq. (10-9), m and x_2 become proportional as $x_2 \to 0$, and in this limit

$$P_2 = m k_m. \qquad (10\text{-}25)$$

Activity is now defined by

$$P_2 = a_m k_m \qquad (10\text{-}26)$$

and activity coefficient as

$$a_m = \gamma_m m. \qquad (10\text{-}27)$$

As x_2, and hence m, approaches zero, $a_m \to m$ and $\gamma_m \to 1$. Finally, x_2 or m becomes proportional to C, the concentration in moles per liter of solution, as the concentration approaches zero. Henry's law becomes $P_2 = Ck_C$, and a concentration-based activity a_C may be defined as

$$P_2 = a_C k_C. \tag{10-28}$$

The corresponding activity coefficient γ_C is

$$a_C = \gamma_C C. \tag{10-29}$$

Again, as x_2, and hence C, approaches zero, $a_C \to C$ and $\gamma_C \to 1$.

The subject is discussed in more detail in the Special Topics section, but it turns out that the effect of using the Henry's law conventions is to change the reference or standard state, and hence the value of $\mu_i°(l)$ of Eq. (9-72). All equations involving only changes in activity remain the same, but in using the Gibbs–Duhem equation, as in Section 9-5, the first integration limit is $x_2 = 0$ rather than $x_2 = 1$ since it is now the former condition for which $\gamma = 1$ and hence $\ln \gamma = 0$. Alternatively, γ_2' differs from γ_2 by a constant factor. However, mole fraction, molality, and concentration cease to be proportional in concentrated solutions, and as a consequence the three types of activity coefficient differ. The general relationship among them is

$$\gamma_2' = \gamma_m(1 + 0.001mM_1) = \gamma_C \frac{\rho + 0.001C(M_1 - M_2)}{\rho°}, \tag{10-30}$$

where M_2 is the solute molecular weight, ρ is the density of the solution, and $\rho°$ is the density of the pure solvent.

With the exception of the next chapter, all further treatments of solutions will be of dilute solutions and the conventions of Eq. (10-27) or (10-29) will be used. It is not at all necessary that the solute be volatile, since one may obtain a_m without the need to measure P_2 values. For example, colligative property measurements on sugar solutions will give $\ln a_1$ as a function of m and use of the Gibbs–Duhem equation then allows a calculation of a_m and γ_m. In Chapter 13 it will be seen that the emf of electrical cells can be used to obtain γ_m values for electrolytes.

10-7 Other Methods of Molecular Weight Determination

One of the important uses of colligative property measurements is to obtain the molecular weight of a solute. This is particularly true for new substances being characterized for the first time, including biological species such as proteins or nucleic acids. Polymer chemistry is also a highly developed field, and a central piece of information is again the molecular weight of a particular preparation. In this case there will usually be a mixture of various molecular weights and one seeks to determine the average value (as will be discussed later).

There are several other means whereby either the size or the molecular weight of a solute may be determined and it seems appropriate to include these in the present chapter. A more general discussion of the various methods will then be given in Section 10-CN-4.

A. Sedimentation Velocity

It is possible to estimate the size of a molecule by the speed with which it moves through a solution under the influence of some force. One such force is that due to gravity. A particle of mass m_2 experiences a downward pull of m_2g, opposed in solution by the buoyancy of the solvent. In effect, the particle displaces volume m_2/ρ_2, corresponding to a mass of solvent equal to $(m_2/\rho_2)\,\rho_1$, where ρ_2 and ρ_1 are the densities of the particle and of the solvent, respectively. The net force due to gravity is then

$$m_2 g \left(1 - \frac{\rho_1}{\rho_2}\right) = m_2 g(1 - \bar{V}_2\rho_1), \qquad (10\text{-}31)$$

where $\bar{V}_2$ is the partial specific volume of the particle.

The particle will fall through the solution if $\rho_2 > \rho_1$, but as it accelerates a viscous drag develops which is proportional to the velocity, or equal to $f v$, where v is the velocity and f is called the *friction coefficient*. A limiting or terminal velocity is reached when the force due to gravity and that of the viscous drag have become equal, or when

$$v = \frac{m_2 g(1 - \bar{V}_2\rho_1)}{f}. \qquad (10\text{-}32)$$

In liquids of ordinary viscosity, this terminal velocity is reached very quickly, and the experimental observation is that the particle immediately assumes a constant speed of fall.

The friction coefficient depends in a complicated way on the shape of the particle and on the viscosity of the solvent. However, if the particle is spherical, a simple formula due to Stokes applies:

$$f = 6\pi\eta r, \qquad (10\text{-}33)$$

where η is the viscosity of the medium and r is the radius of the particle. The velocity of fall is then

$$v = \frac{m_2 g}{6\pi\eta r}(1 - \bar{V}_2\rho_1). \qquad (10\text{-}34)$$

The particle is to be a solute molecule, although perhaps a large one such as a protein, and its rate of fall due to gravity will be extremely small—so small, in fact, that, as will be seen, it is quickly nullified by back-diffusion. It is therefore ordinarily necessary to increase the sedimentation force by using a centrifuge. Acceleration due to gravity is replaced by $\omega^2 x$, where ω is the angular velocity (in radians per second) and x is the distance from the center of rotation. Equation (10-32) becomes

$$\frac{dx}{dt} = \frac{m_2 \omega^2 x (1 - \bar{V}_2 \rho_1)}{f}, \tag{10-35}$$

or

$$s = \frac{m_2}{f}(1 - \bar{V}_2 \rho_1), \qquad s = \frac{dx/dt}{\omega^2 x}, \tag{10-36}$$

where s is called the *sedimentation coefficient* and is characteristic of a given solute and solvent.

In a typical laboratory centrifuge, x might be about 10 cm and the speed of rotation 50 rps. The force $\omega^2 x$ is then $(2\pi)^2(50)^2(10)$ or about 1×10^6 cm sec^{-2} or $10^3 g$. A protein molecule of molecular weight 100,000, or particle weight 1.66×10^{-19} g, and of specific volume 0.80 cm^3 g^{-1} would then sediment with a rate of $(1.66 \times 10^{-19})(1 \times 10^6)(1 - 0.8)/f$, or about $3.4 \times 10^{-14}/f$, in cm sec^{-1}. If the particle is spherical, we have

$$\tfrac{4}{3}\pi r^3 = (1.66 \times 10^{-19})(0.8) \simeq 1.3 \times 10^{-19},$$

from which r is found to be 3.14×10^{-7} cm. The viscosity of water is about 0.01 P and, by Stokes' law, $f = 6\pi(0.01)(3.14 \times 10^{-7}) = 5.8 \times 10^{-8}$ cm sec^{-2}. The velocity of sedimentation of the protein molecules would then be $(3.4 \times 10^{-14})/(5.8 \times 10^{-8})$, or about 5.9×10^{-6} cm sec^{-1}, a rather small number.

The calculation illustrates the difficulty in carrying out sedimentation experiments with ordinary centrifuges. A Swede, Thé Svedberg, pioneered in the 1920's the development of very high-speed centrifuges or *ultracentrifuges*. Forces as high as 300,000g have been obtained. The sedimentation rate would be 300 times larger than in the preceding example, or about 2×10^{-3} cm sec^{-1}, an easily measurable rate. Centrifuges of this type may be air-suspended and air-driven. More elegantly, the rotor can be suspended by a magnetic field and driven by induction. In the latter version, the rotor chamber is evacuated so that friction is virtually absent. The cell containing the solution is placed in the rotor and can be viewed through windows. Stroboscopic pictures of the boundary formed by sedimenting material can be obtained with the use of synchronous lighting, and the sedimentation velocity thus determined. The molecular weight may then be found, essentially by reversal of the preceding calculation.

B.   Diffusion

A second type of kinetic approach which yields information about molecular size is that of diffusion studies. The *coefficient of diffusion* is defined phenomenologically by Fick's law,

$$J = -\mathscr{D} \frac{d\mathbf{n}}{dx} \qquad \text{[Eq. (2-67)],}$$

where $\mathscr{D}$ is the diffusion coefficient and J is the molecular flux along the concentration gradient, in molecules per square centimeter per second. Diffusion occurs because molecules in solution drift around under random kinetic motion and more move from a high-concentration region than from a low-concentration region. It is purely as a statistical effect that net flow occurs down a concentration gradient. The flow may be treated as a net bias in the otherwise random motion, whereby molecules appear to exhibit a net velocity v in the direction of the concentration gradient. The flux J can therefore be represented as

$$J = \mathbf{n}v. \tag{10-37}$$

We now invoke a force to produce the velocity v, namely the gradient of chemical potential $-d\mu_2/dx$ or $-kT\,d(\ln a)/dx$. The velocity is then

$$v = -\frac{kT\,d(\ln a)/dx}{f}, \tag{10-38}$$

and combination of Eqs. (2-67), (10-37), and (10-38) gives

$$-\frac{kT\mathbf{n}\,d(\ln a)/dx}{f} = -\mathscr{D}\frac{d\mathbf{n}}{dx}$$

or

$$\mathscr{D} = \frac{kT}{f}\frac{d(\ln a)}{d(\ln \mathbf{n})}. \tag{10-39}$$

It is convenient to use the convention of a_C, so that $d(\ln a_C) = d(\ln C) + d(\ln \gamma_C)$ (see Section 10-6) and since $d(\ln \mathbf{n}) = d(\ln C)$ ($\mathbf{n}$ and C are proportional), Eq. (10-39) reduces to

$$\mathscr{D} = \frac{kT}{f}\left(1 + \frac{d(\ln \gamma_C)}{d(\ln C)}\right). \tag{10-40}$$

In the case of dilute nonelectrolyte solutions γ_C will approach unity, and Eq. (10-40) is often used in the limiting form

$$\mathscr{D} = \frac{kT}{f}. \tag{10-41}$$

Equation (10-40) was obtained by Einstein in 1905 (see Section 16-CN-1 for a historical sketch).

The formalism of the chemical potential gradient as a driving force in diffusion is just that—a formalism. It is a very convenient one, however, and more elaborate analyses based on the statistics of individual molecular motions give the same result.

As in the case of sedimentation rates, one may consider the diffusing molecule to be spherical and apply Stokes' law. The diffusion coefficient becomes

$$\mathscr{D} = \frac{kT}{6\pi\eta r}.\tag{10-42}$$

It is thus possible to obtain a molecular radius from diffusion data. Small molecules have diffusion coefficients in water of about 10^{-5} cm^2 sec^{-1} at room temperature and hence corresponding r values of about $(1.37 \times 10^{-16})(298)/(6\pi)(0.01)(10^{-5}) = 2.2 \times 10^{-8}$ cm, or of a few angstroms. The values obtained agree fairly well with estimates from van der Waals constants or from crystallographic determinations of molecular sizes. A molecule such as sucrose, however, departs from Stokes' law behavior since it is not spherical. Moreover, as noted in Section 10-5, the hydrodynamic size of a sucrose molecule is very likely increased by its having about six closely held water molecules. Long-chain molecules, such as *n*-alkanes, appear to diffuse link by link, so that $\mathscr{D}$ is not proportional to the length of the molecule. Diffusion studies have also been valuable in determining the hydrodynamic size of ions in solution; this aspect is taken up in Section 12-5. In general, even though the exact form of Stokes' law may not be correct, Eq. (10-42) is often obeyed to the extent that $\mathscr{D}\eta$ is a constant ; the observation is known as *Walden's rule*.

It is difficult to measure diffusion coefficients smaller than about 10^{-7} cm^2 sec^{-1}, so that the method begins to fail for molecular weights above 10^6 (see Table 10-4). In summary, diffusion coefficients provide a measure of the hydrodynamic radius of a molecule and thereby information about its molecular weight.

C. Sedimentation Equilibrium

We may now combine the two preceding subsections to treat sedimentation equilibrium. The dynamic picture is that a molecule under the influence of gravity or a centrifugal field will move in the direction of the force, so that a concentration gradient develops. Eventually the back-diffusion rate becomes equal to the sedimentation rate. That is, v in Eq. (10-32) and v in Eq. (10-38) may be equated to give

$$m_2 g(1 - \bar{v}_2\rho_1) = kT\frac{d(\ln a)}{dx}.\tag{10-43}$$

The friction coefficient is the same for both processes, and therefore cancels out. Rearrangement gives

$$\frac{d(\ln a)}{dx} = \frac{m_2 g}{kT}(1 - \bar{v}_2\rho_1),\tag{10-44}$$

or, in dilute solution

$$\frac{d(\ln C)}{dx} = \frac{m_2 g}{kT}(1 - \bar{v}_2\rho_1).\tag{10-45}$$

Except for the necessary buoyancy correction, Eq. (10-45) is the same as the barometric equation (1-34); if integrated, with $dx = -dh$, it yields

$$C = C_0 \exp\left(-\frac{m_2 g' h}{kT}\right),$$

where, to bring out the comparison, g has been replaced by the effective force due to gravity g', where $g' = g(1 - \bar{v}_2\rho_1)$.

Alternatively, Eq. (10-41) may be used to eliminate f in Eq. (10-36), to give

$$s = \frac{m_2 \mathcal{D}}{kT}(1 - \bar{v}_2\rho_1) \tag{10-46}$$

or

$$M_2 = \frac{RTs}{\mathcal{D}(1 - \bar{v}_2\rho_1)}. \tag{10-47}$$

Thus if both the sedimentation and diffusion coefficients are known, the molecular weight may be determined without any assumptions as to the size or shape of the molecule. This will be a true molecular weight; essentially that of the solute vapor above the solution. Even though the solute may not be appreciably volatile, Eq. (10-47) is a limiting form for infinite dilution. We reach this conclusion by tracing back through the way in which the reference state is defined.

To return to sedimentation equilibrium, we see that if g in Eq. (10-45) is replaced by $\omega^2 x$ and the equation is integrated between the limits C_1 at x_1 and C_2 at x_2, the result is

$$M = \frac{2RT \ln(C_2/C_1)}{\omega^2(x_2^2 - x_1^2)(1 - \bar{v}_2\rho_1)}. \tag{10-48}$$

Sedimentation equilibrium studies using ultracentrifuges have provided a great deal of information about the molecular weights of large molecules such as proteins, other biological substances, and polymers. The method is tedious in that considerable time is required to attain equilibrium. A modern variant involves the use of a gradient in the density of the medium. The effect is greatly to accentuate the equilibrium concentration distribution, and molecular weights as low as about 300 can be determined by this means.

The numerical example of Section 10-7A may be extended to Eq. (10-48). We take ω^2 to be 1×10^5, the molecular weight to be 100,000, and $\bar{v}_2$ to be 0.80, and assume that x_2 and x_1 are 4 and 3 cm, respectively. Then

$$\log \frac{C_2}{C_1} = \frac{(100,000)(1 \times 10^5)(4^2 - 3^2)(1 - 0.80)}{(2)(8.3 \times 10^7)(298)(2.303)} \simeq 0.010.$$

This is only about a 2% effect and again the higher speed centrifuge would be desirable.

Some assorted values for diffusion and sedimentation coefficients are given in Table 10-4.

Table 10-4.   *Diffusion and Sedimentation Coefficients (in Water at 25°C)*

Substance	Molecular weight (g mole^{-1})	$10^5 \times \mathcal{D}$ (cm^2 sec^{-1})	$10^{13} \times s$ (sec)	$\bar{v}_2$ (cm^3 g^{-1})
Water	18	2.14^a	—	—
Urea	60	1.18 (20°C)	—	—
Sucrose	342	0.52	—	—
Ovalbumin	44,000	0.078	3.6	0.75
Hemoglobin (man)	63,000	0.069	4.46	0.75
Urease	490,000	0.034	18.6	0.73
Tobacco mosaic virus	40×10^6	0.0053	185	0.72

^{a} This is a self-diffusion coefficient obtained by isotopic labeling.

D. Light Scattering

The subject of light scattering by small particles is a complicated one and will be treated here only in a superficial way. In terms of the electromagnetic theory of light, incident radiation induces an oscillating dipole in a molecule or particle, which in turn reradiates. The intensity of scattered light therefore depends on the polarizability α; it is also a function of angle, being a maximum in the direction of the incident beam.

The detailed analysis was begun by Lord Rayleigh in 1900, extended by G. Mie around 1908, and further extended by P. Debye in 1947. The intensity of unpolarized light scattered by a single molecule is given by

$$\frac{i}{I_0} = \frac{16\pi^4\alpha^2(1 + \cos^2 \theta)}{\lambda^4 r^2},$$
(10-49)

where, as illustrated in Fig. 10-5, I_0 is the incident light intensity per square centimeter, i is the intensity per square centimeter observed at scattering angle θ, α is the polarizability of the scattering molecule, λ is the wavelength of light, and r is the distance from the scattering particle. Some of the important features of Eq. (10-49) are as follows:

(1)   The intensity depends inversely on λ^4 and is therefore much stronger for blue than for red light. Small-molecule scattering in our atmosphere brings blue light to us from the sky and yellows or reddens direct sunlight, especially at sunset when the distance traveled through the atmosphere is larger than at other times.

(2)   The minimum scattering occurs at 90°. The qualitative reason is that the induced dipoles are oriented perpendicularly to the incident light and reradiate most strongly in the same direction.

(3)   The dependence on the polarizability has been accounted for. Since α and index of refraction n are related [Eq. (3-15)], it is possible to introduce the latter

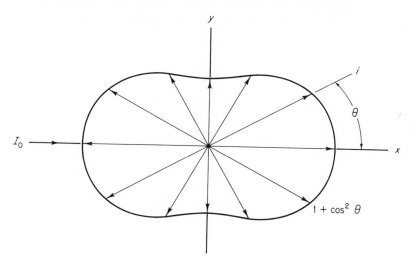

Fig. 10-5. *Intensity envelope for scattered light. The envelope is a figure of revolution about the axis defined by the incident light.*

into the equation. For a dilute gas or a dilute solution n can be approximated by $1 + c(dn/dc)$, where c is the concentration in grams per cubic centimeter and some manipulation of Eq. (3-15) then gives $\alpha = (M/2\pi N_0)(dn/dc)$. The resulting equation equation for i/I_0 is

$$\frac{i}{I_0} = \frac{4\pi^2 M^2 (1 + \cos^2 \theta)\, n_0^2 (dn/dc)^2}{N_0^2 \lambda^4 r^2}, \qquad (10\text{-}50)$$

where n_0 is the refractive index of the medium. Since the number of particles per cubic centimeter is cN_0/M, the total scattering is

$$\frac{i}{I_0} = \frac{4\pi^2 (1 + \cos^2 \theta)\, n_0^2 (dn/dc)^2}{N_0 \lambda^4 r^2}\, Mc. \qquad (10\text{-}51)$$

We next integrate the scattered intensity over all angles, to obtain the total proportion of light removed from the incident beam. The removal of light by scattering produces the same mathematical law as for the absorption of light (see Section 3-2),

$$I = I_0 e^{-\tau x}, \qquad (10\text{-}52)$$

where I is the intensity of unscattered light and τ is called the *turbidity*. The proportion of light that is scattered is then $(I_0 - I)/I_0$ and for small amounts of scattering this is equal to τ for a 1-cm path length. The result of the integration over all angles and the introduction of τ is

$$\tau = \frac{32\pi^3 n_0^2 (dn/dc)^2}{3 N_0 \lambda^4}\, Mc = HMc, \qquad (10\text{-}53)$$

where

$$H = \frac{32\pi^3 n_0^2 (dn/dc)^2}{3N_0\lambda^4}, \tag{10-54}$$

and therefore

$$M = \frac{\tau}{Hc}. \tag{10-55}$$

Actual practice is somewhat more complicated. Solution nonidealities cause deviation from Eq. (10-55), so the quantity Hc/τ is usually plotted against c and extrapolated to zero concentration. Further, the reduction in light intensity of the direct beam is rather small, so it is difficult to measure $I_0 - I$ accurately. A better procedure is to determine i at some definite angle, most commonly 90°, and use Eq. (10-49) to relate the scattering intensity at that angle to the total scattering corresponding to τ. A further complication is that if the particles are comparable in size to the wavelength of the light used, there will be interference effects arising from light scattered from different parts of the same particle. If this is a problem, then i/I_0 is measured at various angles and the calculated H values are extrapolated to $\theta = 0$, where such interference vanishes. This is done for each of several concentrations and the set of extrapolated points lies on a line which can in turn be extrapolated to zero concentration.

Light scattering can be used for any size molecule; one may, for example, observe scattering from a pure liquid due just to the fluctuations in density that occur, and the scattering by the atmosphere has already been mentioned. Equation (10-53) states, however, that for a given concentration in grams per cubic centimeter the larger the molecular weight, the greater the scattering. The method is then most sensitive for macromolecules and has been widely used in the study of biological and synthetic polymers.

E.   *Types of Molecular Weight Averages*

It is particularly true for polymer solutions (discussed further in Chapter 20) that a preparation will consist of a range of molecular weights. A molecular weight determination by one of the methods of this chapter will give an average value but, it turns out, not always the same average one as that given by some other method.

There are two principal ways in which one may average the molecular weight of a collection of solute molecules. The first is the intuitive one of simply dividing the total weight by the total number of particles. This is known as the *number average molecular weight* M_n and is defined formally as follows:

$$M_n = \frac{n_1 M_1 + n_2 M_2 + \cdots}{n_1 + n_2 + \cdots} = \frac{\sum_i n_i M_i}{\sum_i n_i} = \sum_i x_i M_i. \tag{10-56}$$

Thus a sample consisting of equal numbers of molecules of molecular weight 100, 1000, and 10,000 g mole^{-1} would have a number average molecular weight of

$$M_n = \frac{\frac{1}{3}(100) + \frac{1}{3}(1000) + \frac{1}{3}(10,000)}{1} = 3700.$$

In this case each molecular weight is weighted by the number of particles involved. An alternative weighting is by the weight of particles of a given molecular weight (or essentially by their size):

$$M_w = \frac{w_1 M_1 + w_2 M_2 + \cdots}{w_1 + w_2 + \cdots} = \frac{\sum_i w_i M_i}{\sum_i w_i}. \qquad (10\text{-}57)$$

M_w is known as the *weight average molecular weight*. Referring to the example just given, to obtain M_w, we observed that w_1 is proportional to $\frac{1}{3}(100)$, w_2 is proportional to $\frac{1}{3}(1000)$, and w_3, to $\frac{1}{3}(10,000)$. Thus

$$M_w = \frac{\frac{1}{3}(100)(100) + \frac{1}{3}(1000)(1000) + \frac{1}{3}(10,000)(10,000)}{\frac{1}{3}(100) + \frac{1}{3}(1000) + \frac{1}{3}(10,000)}$$

$$= \frac{1.0101 \times 10^8}{1.11 \times 10^4} = 9100.$$

In this case, as in general, the weight-average molecular weight is greater than the number average molecular weight. The ratio of the two gives a measure of the total spread of molecular weights in the sample.

The colligative property measurements essentially count the number of particles and one obtains the molecular weight by dividing the weight of material present by this number. The result is therefore a number average molecular weight. Sedimentation experiments weight each particle according to its mass and therefor give a weight average molecular weight. The same is true of light scattering measurements.

COMMENTARY AND NOTES

10-CN-1   Colligative Properties and Deviations from Ideality

The equations for the four colligative properties are summarized in Table 10-5. They group into three categories: (1) the forms that are strictly valid (except for the assumed constancy of heats of vaporization and freezing, and of activity coeffi-

Table 10-5. *Colligative Property Equations*

| Effect | Exact equation[a] | Equation assuming | |
		Ideal solution	Ideal and dilute solution
Vapor pressure lowering	$(\Delta P)/P_1{}^\circ = 1 - a_1$	$(\Delta P)/P_1{}^\circ = x_2$	—
Boiling point elevation	$\ln a_1 = (\Delta H_{v,1}^\circ/R)$ $\times [(1/T_b) - (1/T_{b,1}^\circ)]$	$\ln x_1 = (\Delta H_{v,1}^\circ/R)$ $\times [(1/T_b) - (1/T_{b,1}^\circ)]$	$\Delta T_b = K_b m$
Freezing point depression	$\ln a_1 = (\Delta H_{f,1}^\circ/R)$ $\times [(1/T_{f,1}^\circ) - (1/T_f)]$	$\ln x_1 = (\Delta H_{f,1}^\circ/R)$ $\times [(1/T_{f,1}^\circ) - (1/T_f)]$	$\Delta T_f = K_f m$
Osmotic pressure effect	$-RT \ln a_1 = \Pi \bar{V}_1$	$-RT \ln x_1 = \Pi \bar{V}_1$	$\Pi = CRT$

[a] The last three of these equations are not fully exact. Assumptions such as constancy of heat of vaporization or heat of freezing have been made in integration over ΔT_b or ΔT_f. In the case of osmotic pressure, other assumptions, noted in the text, have been made. These are not serious assumptions, and in this text the equations given are regarded as thermodynamically exact.

cients with temperature), (2) those that assume an ideal solution, and (3) those that assume an ideal and dilute solution. A number of systems have been studied very precisely, and there seems to be no question that Raoult's law is a valid limiting law, at least for solutions not involving molecules grossly different in size. Also, heats of fusion from K_f values agree well with those from direct calorimetric determinations.

Although these affirmations are important, it is also true that deviations from the simple behavior are common. We discount immediately cases in which the dilute solution forms have been misused in that the conditions for the mathematical approximations have not been met. There remain several explanations. One is that the solute is either associated or dissociated to some extent, so that its apparent molecular weight differs from its fomula weight. Remember that the colligative property effects are determined by x_2, the mole fraction of solute. This mole fraction is determined by the actual species present. As one example, the molecular weight of benzoic acid is just the formula weight of 122.1 in acetone solution, but in benzene, the apparent molecular weight is 242. That is, the colligative property measurement reports half as many solute molecules as expected from the amount weigned out in making up the solution. The explanation is that benzoic acid is largely dimerized in benzene solution.

Alternatively, if the freezing point depression is determined for an aqueous sodium chloride solution the result gives an apparent molecular weight that is about half the formula weight. In this case we have a strong electrolyte which has dissociated into two ions, each of which acts as a solute species with respect to a colligative property. The Dutchman van't Hoff, who contributed much to the physical chemistry of the osmotic pressure effect, defined a factor i as

$$\Pi v = i n_2 RT, \tag{10-58}$$

where the simple meaning of i is that it gives the average number of moles of particles produced per formula weight of solute. Thus i would be $\frac{1}{2}$ for benzoic acid in benzene and 2 for aqueous sodium chloride. The approach, while over-simplified, emphasizes the point that the colligative property measurement gives an average molecular weight. One may thus use the measurement to calculate the degree of association or, for a weak electrolyte, the degree of dissociation. In the case of polymer solutions, where a wide range of molecular weight species is present, the average molecular weight that results is known as a number average (see Section 10-7E).

Another source of deviation from ideal behavior is illustrated by the data of Table 10-3. It appears, from this as well as from other evidence, that sucrose tightly binds about six molecules of water. The situation is essentially one of com-pound formation between solute and solvent, and the effect on a colligative property measurement is that the effective value of x_1 is reduced while that of x_2 is increased. A fair measure of the departure from ideal behavior of electrolyte solutions can be accounted for if each ion, especially the positive ion, is assumed to bind a certain number of water molecules.

These explanations are real enough. They are couched in terms of clear-cut compound formation, however, and do not function well when weaker but still specific interactions between molecules are present. These are generally lumped together as an activity coefficient for the solvent γ_1 and one for the solute γ_2 (see Section 10-6 and Special Topics section). The acetone–chloroform system of the previous chapter is an example of a nonideal one which is treated in terms of activity coefficients. As discussed in somewhat more detail in the Special Topics section, colligative property measurements over a range of concentrations give a series of a_1 values. The value of a_2 for a particular solute concentration, and hence that of γ_2, may then be obtained by means of the Gibbs–Duhem integration (Section 9-5C).

10-CN-2 Relationship between Freezing Point Depression and Solubility

In dealing with colligative property effects, we have consistently applied the term solvent to that component which is present in both phases. Thus in the case of a freezing point depression Eq. (10-15) may be written

$$\ln x_A = \frac{\Delta H^\circ_{f,A}}{R} \left(\frac{1}{T^\circ_{f,A}} - \frac{1}{T_f} \right)$$

and applies to the equilibrium system

$$\text{pure solid A} \rightleftharpoons \text{ideal solution of A and B,} \tag{10-59}$$

where A denotes solvent, by the preceding convention, and B denotes solute. The laboratory appearance of such an equilibrium mixture is simply one of a suspension of a solid in a solution, and the system could just as well be described as a saturated solution of solid A in solvent B, with excess A present.

When viewed according to this alternative perspective, Eq. (10-15) gives the solubility of component A, now thought of as the solute, in solvent component B. Then T_f would no longer be described as a freezing point, but just as T, the temperature at which the solubility is measured. As an example, the freezing point of a 0.25 mole fraction solution of, say, ethanol, in acetic acid should be approximately 0°C (assuming ideal behavior). The calculation is made, from Eq. (10-15), with acetic acid as the solvent. Alternatively, the same value denotes the solubility of solid acetic acid in ethanol at 0°C (although it is not customary to speak of the solubility of such low-melting substances as acetic acid).

The same principle applies to any equilibrium of the type of Eq. (10-59). Equation (10-15) therefore provides some useful qualitative rules on solubility. (1) The solubility of a compound increases as temperature increases. General experience confirms this prediction. (2) The solubility of a series of compounds decreases as the melting point increases. This rule is fairly well obeyed provided that the heats of fusion are rrot very different. It should be remembered that in solubility situations x_A is usually relatively small, and Eq. (10-15) can be seriously in error if the solution is not reasonably ideal.

10-CN-3   Water Desalination

The material of this chapter has some bearing on the important subject of water desalination. This is at present accomplished mainly by distillation, and large-scale installations are found in the southwestern United States, in parts of South America, and in the Middle East. It seems inevitable that the coastal regions of the world will draw increasingly on this method as a source of both agricultural and potable water. The current prevalence of distillation may be largely a reflection of the fact that engineering is most highly developed for this type of process. Other methods may eventually dominate, and many are now under active investigation.

Sea water contains about 35,000 ppm of dissolved salts, mostly sodium chloride, with magnesium, calcium, and potassium following in order of importance; it is roughly equivalent to a 0.7 M sodium chloride solution, and the vapor pressure of sea water at 25°C averages about 0.78 Torr lower than that of pure water.

The basic desalination process is then

$$\text{sea water } (25°C, P_1 = 22.98 \text{ Torr}) = \text{pure water } (25°C, P_1° = 23.76 \text{ Torr}). \quad (10\text{-}60)$$

This supposes that the pure water is obtained from so large an amount of sea water that the concentration of the latter is not materially affected. The free energy change is

$$\Delta G = RT \ln \frac{P_1°}{P_1} = 1370 \log \frac{23.76}{22.98} = 19.4 \quad \text{cal.}$$

This is the reversible work required and is therefore the minimum possible. The free energy change ΔG would be somewhat larger for a process in which the products consisted of more highly concentrated sea water plus pure water. In either case, however, the minimum energy required is far less than the approximately 10,000 cal mole^{-1} needed to vaporize the water directly. The relatively high efficiency of contemporary distillation plants is a result of using very efficient multistep evaporation as well as heat exchangers. In effect, the 10,000 cal mole^{-1} needed for evaporation is largely recovered from the heat liberated on condensation. The heat "turnover" is very large, however, and it has seemed that some process whose direct energy requirement was closer to the minimum could be efficient without the large capital investment required by the complex engineering of distillation plants.

One proposal has been to produce pure water by partially freezing sea water and then separating out the ice. The heat investment in the initial step is now only about 1400 cal mole^{-1}. However, the refrigeration plant needed introduces a new fundamental inefficiency. More important, perhaps, is the finding that the ice so produced tends to occlude considerable salt so that more than one cycle of purification is necessary.

Osmotic devices have attracted much interest. If sea water is separated from fresh water by a semipermeable membrane, then application of mechanical pressure exceeding the osmotic pressure will cause water to pass to the pure water side. The process is one of *reverse osmosis*. The pressure could be applied by means of pumps. Conceivably a pipe could be lowered into the ocean to a depth such that the hydrostatic head exceeded the osmotic pressure. A semipermeable membrane covering the end of the pipe would pass fresh water. In effect, one would have a fresh water well for which the only work required would be that needed to pump the water to the surface.

The problem has been to find membranes that will not pass electrolytes but will pass water rapidly. The osmotic pressure of sea water is some thirty atmospheres, and either a membrane must be very strong or several stages would be needed. Some progress has been made in the use of electrical energy to do the osmotic work with ion-selective membranes in electrolyte cells. As illustrated in Fig. 10-6, cations may pass out of the central compartment at the right, but anions cannot enter; and anions may pass out at the left, but cations cannot enter. The

423

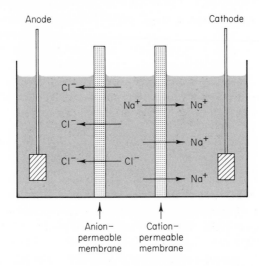

Fig. 10-6.   *Electrolytic method for water desalination.*

efficiency increases in proportion to the number of such units in parallel but other-wise decreases in proportion to the salt concentration. Cells of this type are being used for the desalination of very hard well water (in Israel) but do not appear so far to be economic for the treatment of sea water. Some recent developments with ion-exchange and clay-type membranes have given encouraging results in an ordinary reverse osmotic process but only in small-scale tests.

It should be pointed out that the problem is heightened by the economic require-ments. It is necessary to produce water at a cost of no more than about 35 cents per 1000 gal. This is a difficult accomplishment for what amounts to a chemical processing plant. Efficiency must be very high if power costs alone are not to exceed this cost figure, even with no allowance for capital investment. Large amounts of low-cost power are thus a vital ingredient—hence the emphasis on coupling desalination plants with nuclear power generators.

10-CN-4   Molecular Weight Determination

The preceding portions of the Commentary and Notes section have stressed various aspects of colligative phenomena. We now comment briefly on the general subject of molecular weight determination from the point of view of suitability of the different methods. Each has its difficulties if the solutions are not ideal or are not dilute; the thermodynamic methods are the most amenable to exact corrections for such deviations. These methods consist of the colligative effects and sedimentation equilibrium. The interpretation of sedimentation and diffusion rates is very difficult when it is necessary to consider interactions among solute particles or even that particles may be nonspherical. Use of Eq. (10-47) eliminates the latter complication but does not entirely eliminate the former. Light scattering becomes a fiercely complex phenomenon once the limiting conditions are exceeded.

If we assume that all methods are applied under their simplest theoretical condition of a very dilute solution, then our choice of method is controlled by considerations of inherent sensitivity and practical experimenal error. If we classify molecules as small if their molecular weight is less than about 300, large if it is between 300 and about 10^6, and colloidal if it is over 10^6 (or if a molecule is over about 100 Å in size), then we can make distinctions among the methods as follows. Vapor pressure lowering, boiling point elevation, and freezing point depression are best with small molecules, and we usually utilize them to obtain activity coefficient data or to study chemical equilibria (the molecular weight of most small molecules being already known). Diffusion gives hydrodynamic sizes and hence apparent molecular weights with good precision for both small and large molecules, but in practice it is employed mainly for small ones.

Sedimentation rate, sedimentation equilibrium, and light scattering are effective for both large and colloidal particles. Light scattering is fairly simple to use experimentally, and the theory is now so highly developed (and computerized) that even the more complicated equations that apply for colloidal particles approaching the wavelength of visible light in size have been worked out. The principal remaining method is that of conductivity or electrophoresis, and it is applicable to ions or charged particles. This subject is taken up in Chapter 12.

SPECIAL TOPICS

10-ST-1 Dilute Solution Conventions for Activities and Activity Coefficients

The concepts of activity and activity coefficient were introduced in Section 9-5B. Activity is defined by Eq. (9-71) as the effective mole fraction required to retain the form of Raoult's law and therefore that of the general thermodynamic treatment of ideal solutions. The effect of deviation from ideality is extracted yet more clearly by means of an activity coefficient, or the factor whereby the activity deviates from mole fraction. Since Raoult's law is obeyed as a limiting law for all solutions, it follows that $a_i \to 1$ and $\gamma_i \to 1$ as $x_i \to 1$. Thus by Eq. (9-72),

$$\mu_1(l) = \mu_1°(l) + RT \ln a_1 \,,$$

and $\mu_1(l) \to \mu_1°(l)$ as $x_1 \to 1$. The standard or reference state, for which $\mu_1°(l)$ is the chemical potential, is therefore the pure component 1. The same equations but with the subscript 2 apply to component 2.

The second important equation of the preceding chapter is the Gibbs–Duhem relationship, which allows the calculation of the activity of one component of a solution if that of the other component is known over a range of compositions,

$$x_1 \, d(\ln a_1) + x_2 \, d(\ln a_2) = 0 \qquad \text{[Eq. (9-79)]}$$

or

$$d(\ln a_2) = -\frac{x_1}{x_2} d(\ln a_1) \qquad \text{[Eq. (9-80)]}.$$

An example of the use of Eq. (9-80) is given in Section 9-5C.

It is now desirable to extend the applications of the Gibbs–Duhem equation to a two-component system. Since $a_1 = \gamma_1 x_1$,

$$x_1 \, d(\ln a_1) = x_1[d(\ln x_1) + d(\ln \gamma_1)] = dx_1 + x_1 \, d(\ln \gamma_1). \qquad (10\text{-}61)$$

Similarly,

$$x_2 \, d(\ln a_2) = dx_2 + x_2 \, d(\ln \gamma_2). \qquad (10\text{-}62)$$

Since $dx_1 = -dx_2$, substitution into Eq. (9-79) yields

$$x_1 \, d(\ln \gamma_1) = -x_2 \, d(\ln \gamma_2) \qquad (10\text{-}63)$$

or

$$\ln \gamma_2 = -\int_{x_2=1}^{x_2} \frac{x_1}{x_2} d(\ln \gamma_1), \qquad (10\text{-}64)$$

where the integration limits are from $x_2 = 1$ (and hence $\gamma_2 = 1$ and $\ln \gamma_2 = 0$) to some specific mole fraction x_2.

Returning to Eq. (9-79), we may divide the first term by dx_1 and the second term by $-dx_2$ (which is the same as dx_1) to get

$$\frac{d(\ln a_1)}{d(\ln x_1)} = \frac{d(\ln a_2)}{d(\ln x_2)}. \qquad (10\text{-}65)$$

This is known as the *Duhem–Margules equation*. It tells us, for example, that if component 1 obeys Raoult's law, so that $d(\ln a_1)/d(\ln x_1) = 1$, then it must also be true that $d(\ln a_2)/d(\ln x_2) = 1$. This condition is only required to hold in differential form, and on integration we find

$$\ln a_2 = \ln x_2 + \ln k_2'$$

or

$$a_2 = k_2' x_2 . \tag{10-66}$$

Since a_2 is defined as equal to $P_2/P_2°$, Eq. (10-66) can be written as

$$P_2 = k_2 x_2 \qquad [\text{Eq. (9-9)}],$$

which is a statement of Henry's law. The conclusion is that, in the case of a nonideal solution, as component 1 approaches Raoult's law behavior ($x_1 \to 1$), component 2 must approach Henry's law behavior ($x_2 \to 0$). Thus the validity of Raoult's law as $x_1 \to 1$ implies that of the Henry's law limiting behavior as $x_2 \to 0$.

The preceding framework of thermodynamic treatment is very useful in the case of solutions which can range in composition from pure component 1 to pure component 2 with both components volatile. More often, however, the solute is not a liquid in the pure state and is not volatile. Physical chemical studies are then restricted to the range of composition from $x_2 = 0$ up to the solubility of the solute, and therefore often to relatively dilute solutions. It has therefore been necessary to devise an alternative framework, and this has been done with Henry's law as a reference rather than Raoult's law. The procedure follows.

We start with Eq. (9-56),

$$\mu_2(l) = \mu_2(g) = \mu_2°(g) + RT \ln P_2 ,$$

but this time add and subtract $RT \ln k_2$ on the right-hand side to obtain

$$\mu_2(l) = \mu_2°(g) + RT \ln k_2 + RT \ln \frac{P_2}{k_2} \tag{10-67}$$

or

$$\mu_2(l) = \mu_2°{}' + RT \ln \frac{P_2}{k_2} \tag{10-68}$$

[we do not write $\mu_2°{}'(l)$ since the pure solute is not necessarily a liquid], where

$$\mu_2°{}' = \mu_2°(g) + RT \ln k = \mu_2°(l) + RT \ln \frac{k_2}{P_2°} . \tag{10-69}$$

A new activity a_2' is now defined as

$$P_2 = a_2' k_2 \qquad [\text{Eq. (10-23)}],$$

so that Eq. (10-68) becomes

$$\mu_2(l) = \mu_2^{\circ\prime} + RT \ln a_2'. \tag{10-70}$$

Also,

$$a_2' = x_2\gamma_2' \qquad \text{[Eq. (10-24)],}$$

so, alternatively,

$$\mu_2(l) = \mu_2^{\circ\prime} + RT \ln x_2 + RT \ln \gamma_2'. \tag{10-71}$$

Equations (10-70) and (10-71) have the same form as do Eqs. (9-72) and (9-74), but there has been a change in the standard or reference state, as given by Eq. (10-69). Henry's law is the limiting reference condition and $a_2' \rightarrow x_2$ and $\gamma_2' \rightarrow 1$ as $x_2 \rightarrow 0$. Alternatively, a_2' is now defined as P_2/k_2, whereas a_2 was defined as P_2/P_2°. A numerical illustration will be given later.

Mole fraction composition units are convenient for relatively symmetric systems, but where the emphasis is on dilute solutions and one of the components is always thought of as the solute it is more customary to use molalities. This is particularly true for electrolyte solutions. Molality and mole fraction are related by Eq. (10-9), which reduces to

$$x_2 = \frac{mM_1}{1000} \tag{10-72}$$

in the limit of infinite dilution. Henry's law may now be written

$$P_2 = \frac{k_2 M_1}{1000} m = mk_m. \tag{10-73}$$

We proceed as before, but now adding and subtracting $RT \ln k_m$ on the right-hand side of Eq. (9-56), to obtain

$$\mu_2(l) = \mu_2^{\circ}(g) + RT \ln k_m + RT \ln \frac{P_2}{k_m} \tag{10-74}$$

or

$$\mu_2(l) = \mu_m^{\circ} + RT \ln \frac{P_2}{k_m}, \tag{10-75}$$

where

$$\mu_m^{\circ} = \mu_2^{\circ\prime} + RT \ln \frac{M_1}{1000}. \tag{10-76}$$

A new activity a_m is then defined as

$$P_2 = a_m \left(\frac{M_1}{1000}\right) k_2 = a_m k_m \qquad \text{[Eq. (10-25)]}$$

so that

$$\mu_2(l) = \mu_m{}^\circ + RT \ln a_m . \tag{10-77}$$

Again, if

$$a_m = \gamma_m m \qquad [\text{Eq. (10-27)}],$$

then

$$\mu_2(l) = \mu_m{}^\circ + RT \ln m + RT \ln \gamma_m . \tag{10-78}$$

The form is the same as before, with the standard state given by Eq. (10-76). The reference condition is again that of infinite dilution, since as $m \to 0$, $a_m \to m$ and $\gamma_m \to 1$.

We must repeat the process once more. It is occasionally necessary to deal with molarity rather than molality concentrations in connection with nonideal solutions. Mole fraction and molarity C are related:

$$C = \frac{1000\rho n_2}{n_1 M_1 + n_2 M_2} = \frac{1000\rho x_2}{M_1 + x_2(M_2 - M_1)} , \tag{10-79}$$

where ρ is the density of the solution. The limiting relationship at infinite dilution is

$$x_2 = \frac{M_1 C}{1000\rho_0} , \tag{10-80}$$

where ρ_0 is the density of the pure solvent. The limiting Henry's law form becomes

$$P_2 = Ck_C = C \left(\frac{M_1}{1000\rho_0}\right) k_2 . \tag{10-81}$$

We add and subtract the quantity $RT \ln k_C$ on the right-hand side of Eq. (9-56) to give

$$\mu_2(l) = \mu_2{}^\circ(g) + RT \ln k_C + RT \ln \frac{P_2}{k_C} \tag{10-82}$$

or

$$\mu_2(l) = \mu_C{}^\circ + RT \ln \frac{P_2}{k_C} , \tag{10-83}$$

where

$$\mu_C{}^\circ = \mu_2{}^{\circ\prime} + RT \ln \frac{M_1}{1000\rho_0} . \tag{10-84}$$

A new activity a_C is defined as

$$P_2 = a_C k_C = a_C \left(\frac{M_1}{1000\rho_0}\right) k_2 , \tag{10-85}$$

so we have

$$\mu_2(l) = \mu_C{}^\circ + RT \ln a_C .$$ (10-86)

The corresponding activity coefficient is

$$a_C = \gamma_C C,$$ (10-87)

so that

$$\mu_2(l) = \mu_C{}^\circ + RT \ln C + RT \ln \gamma_C .$$ (10-88)

The three conventions give the following alternative expressions for $\mu_2(l)$:

$$\mu_2(l) = \mu_2{}^\circ + RT \ln a_2 = \mu_2{}^{\circ\prime} + RT \ln a_2{}'$$

$$= \mu_m{}^\circ + RT \ln a_m = \mu_C{}^\circ + RT \ln a_C .$$ (10-89)

Since the standard-state values are constants, we have

$$d\mu_2(l) = d \ln a_2 = d \ln a_2{}' = d \ln a_m = d \ln a_C$$ (10-90)

and substitution into the Gibbs–Duhem equation gives the same form, Eq. (9-80), in all three cases. The subsequent steps leading to Eq. (10-64) are exactly the same as for $\gamma_2{}'$, so that we have

$$\ln \gamma_2{}' = - \int_{x_2=0}^{x_2} \frac{x_1}{x_2} \, d(\ln \gamma_1).$$ (10-91)

The integration limit, however, is from $x_2 = 0$ (and hence $\gamma_2{}' = 1$ and $\ln \gamma_2{}' = 0$) to x_2. In the case of γ_m the convenient cancellation of the $d(\ln x_1)$ and $d(\ln x_2)$ terms does not occur. However, since $x_2/x_1 = m/(1000/M_1)$ and

$$d(\ln a_m) = d(\ln \gamma_m) + d(\ln m),$$

one obtains

$$d(\ln \gamma_m) = - \int_{m=0}^{m} \left[\frac{1000}{mM_1} \, d(\ln a_1) - d(\ln m) \right].$$ (10-92)

In actual practice, we make some further algebraic manipulations to facilitate the evaluation of the integral, but the point is that the Gibbs–Duhem equation still allows an evalutation of γ_m if the activity of the solvent is known over a range of concentration. Notice, incidentally, that the Raoult's law standard state is retained for the solvent; that is $\gamma_1 \to 1$ as x_2 or m approaches zero. The computation of γ_C values follows a similar procedure.

The complications of the preceding methods for changing standard state are regrettable but cannot be avoided. However, the operations are not difficult. The example of Section 9-5C may be extended to the calculation of a_2' and γ_2', with chloroform assumed to be the solute. We now add Table 10-6 to Table 9-1. Since k_c was found to be 142 Torr, $a_c' = P_c/142$ and $\gamma_c' = a_c'/x_2 = P_c/142x_2$.[†] The values of γ_c' differ from those of γ_c by the constant factor of $1/0.484$, reflecting the fact that only a change in the choice of reference state is involved. The acetone–chloroform system is a symmetric one, and a set of a_a' and γ_a' values could also be calculated. This is left as an exercise. Values of γ_m and γ_c are not given, but manipulation of the preceding equations gives

$$\gamma_2' = \gamma_m(1 + 0.001mM_1) = \gamma_c \frac{\rho + 0.001C(M_1 - M_2)}{\rho^\circ} \qquad \text{[Eq. (10-30)]}.$$

The preceding example was for a system of two volatile liquids. The values of a_2' and hence of γ_2' could be calculated from those of P_2. It is not necessary, however, that P_2 be measured or even that the solute be volatile. Equations (10-91) and (10-92) allow the calculation of γ_2' and γ_m through an integration of the Gibbs–Duhem equation. This may be done if the activity of the solvent is known over a range of concentration, as illustrated in Section 9-5C by the analogous calculation of

Table 10-6. *Extension of Table 9-1 to the Henry's Law Convention (The Acetone–Chloroform System at 35°C)[a]*

x_c	P_c (Torr)	Activity[b]		Activity coefficient[c]	
		a_c	a_c'	γ_c	γ_c'
0.00	0	0	0	0.484	(1.00)
0.10	16.0	0.056	0.116	0.546	1.16
0.20	35.0	0.120	0.248	0.595	1.24
0.30	57.0	0.195	0.403	0.650	1.34
0.40	82.0	0.280	0.579	0.700	1.45
0.50	112	0.382	0.789	0.763	1.58
0.60	142	0.485	1.00	0.809	1.67
0.70	180	0.613	1.27	0.875	1.81
0.80	219	0.747	1.54	0.933	1.93
0.90	257	0.877	1.81	0.973	2.01
1.00	298	(1.00)	2.07	(1.00)	2.07

[a] Subscript c denotes chloroform.
[b] $a_c = P_c/P_c^\circ = P_c/293$, $a_c' = P_c/k_c = P_c/142$.
[c] $\gamma_c = a_c/x_c$, $\gamma_c' = a_c'/x_c$.

[†] Subscript c denotes chloroform and subscript a denotes acetone.

=====

a_2 from the data for a_1. As summarized in Table 10-5 the exact equations for the colligative phenomena all involve a_1 or $\ln a_1$. The precise use of these equations involves obtaining a_1 values over a range of concentration and then calculating from them the activity or the activity coefficient of the solute for various concentrations. Depending on the way in which the Gibbs–Duhem integration is set up, one obtains γ_2, $\gamma_2{}'$, γ_m, or γ_C.

One final comment. The three Henry's law reference procedures introduce a slightly paradoxical situation. The reference condition is that of infinite dilution; it is at infinite dilution that γ', γ_m, and γ_C approach unity, so that this becomes the integration limit for relationships such as Eqs. (10-91) and (10-92). On the other hand, $\mu_2(l)$ in Eqs. (10-70) and (10-77) equals $\mu_2^{\circ\prime}$, $\mu_m{}^\circ$, or $\mu_C{}^\circ$ when the corresponding activities are *unity* (not zero!). In the acetone–chloroform system, for example, $a_2{}'$ is unity at $x_C = 0.60$. We speak of $\mu_2^{\circ\prime}$, $\mu_m{}^\circ$, and $\mu_C{}^\circ$ as, respectively, the *hypothetical unit mole fraction*, *unit molality*, and *unit molarity* standard states. The reason for the term hypothetical is that there is no condition in which the solute has both unit activity and unit activity coefficient. By contrast, in the Raoult's law system, the pure liquid does meet this condition. Hypothetical standard states are perfectly definite ones; the activities and activity coefficients are given by operational procedures. Their lack of simple physical meaning is therefore no handicap to their use.

10-ST-2   *Theoretical Treatment of Diffusion*

One of the important theoretical models for diffusion in liquids is due to H. Eyring and resembles closely that for the viscosity of liquids given in Section 8-ST-2. The material that follows is an extension of that section. The assumed molecular picture is that of Fig. 8-25 and the elementary process is that of a molecule jumping from one position to another at the rate given by Eq. (8-65).

The concentration gradient is taken to be in the direction of the spacing δ in Fig. 8-25, as is the jump direction. The rate of jumping from one layer to the next gives the forward diffusional flow:

$$\text{rate of diffusion in forward direction} = \delta\mathbf{n}\,\frac{kT}{h}\,\exp\!\left(-\frac{\epsilon^*}{kT}\right),$$

where $\mathbf{n}$ is the concentration at that layer level. The concentration at the next layer level is $\mathbf{n} + \delta(d\mathbf{n}/dx)$, and so the diffusional flow back to the first one is

$$\text{rate of diffusion in backward direction} = \mathbf{n} + \delta\,\frac{d\mathbf{n}}{dx}\,\frac{kT}{h}\,\exp\!\left(-\frac{\epsilon^*}{kT}\right).$$

=====

The net diffusional flow in the forward direction is

$$\text{net diffusional flow} = -\delta^2 \frac{kT}{h}\left[\exp\left(-\frac{\epsilon^*}{kT}\right)\right]\frac{d\mathbf{n}}{dx}.$$

Comparison with Eq. (2-67) gives

$$\mathscr{D} = \delta^2 \frac{kT}{h}\exp\left(-\frac{\epsilon^*}{kT}\right). \tag{10-93}$$

The exponential may be eliminated by means of Eq. (8-66):

$$\mathscr{D} = \delta^2 \frac{kT}{h}\frac{\delta h}{\eta \sigma \lambda^2} = \frac{\delta^3}{\sigma \lambda^2}\frac{kT}{\eta}. \tag{10-94}$$

Further simplification results if one takes $\sigma = \delta^2$ and also equates δ and λ:

$$\mathscr{D} = \frac{kT}{\eta \delta}. \tag{10-95}$$

This result is really for a self-diffusion coefficient. If we apply it to the self-diffusion of water, then from Table 10-4, $\mathscr{D} = 2.14 \times 10^{-5}\,\text{cm}^2\,\text{sec}^{-1}$ at 25°C and $\eta = 0.01$ P. The resulting value of δ is about 20 Å, or perhaps four times as great as it should be. This is not bad if we consider the simplicity of the theory as well as the approximations made in equating the various kinds of distances. On the other hand, there is evidence that diffusion (and viscous) flow in liquids more likely occurs by pairs of molecules moving past each other rather than by independent jumps of single molecules.

Ordinary diffusion involves two kinds of molecules as a minimum, solute and solvent. The driving force now is the activity rather than the concentration gradient, and a more elaborate derivation based on the preceding model does reproduce the activity coefficient term of Eq. (10-40). The problem of defining the various types of characteristic distances is too great, however, to allow more than qualitative conclusions. As with Eq. (10-95), one concludes that Walden's rule ($\mathscr{D}\eta = $ constant) should hold approximately.

GENERAL REFERENCES

HILDEBRAND, J. H., AND SCOTT, R. L. (1950). "The Solubility of Nonelectrolytes," 3rd ed. Van Nostrand–Reinhold, Princeton, New Jersey.

HIRSCHFELDER, J. O., CURTISS, C. F., AND BIRD, R. B. (1964). "Molecular Theory of Gases and Liquids," corrected ed. Wiley, New York.

LEWIS, G. N., AND RANDALL, M. (1961). "Thermodynamics," 2nd ed. (revised by K. S. Pitzer and L. Brewer). McGraw-Hill, New York.

MOELWYN-HUGHES, E. A. (1961). "Physical Chemistry," 2nd revised ed. Pergamon, Oxford.

CITED REFERENCES

BRØNSTED, J. N. (1906). *Z. Phys. Chem.* **55**, 371.

SCHRÖDER, I. (1893). *Z. Phys. Chem. (Leipzig)* **11**, 457.

SIMONS, J. H., AND POWELL, M. G. (1945). *J. Amer. Chem. Soc.* **67**, 77.

WALL, F. T., AND ROSE, P. E. (1941). *J. Amer. Chem. Soc.* **63**, 3302.

Exercises

10-1   An aqueous solution of cane sugar has a vapor pressure of 17.379 Torr at 20°C (the vapor pressure of pure water is 17.535 Torr). Calculate the molality of the solution.

Ans.   0.503 *m*.

10-2   What is the molecular weight of a solute which produces a vapor pressure lowering of 0.500 % when 20 g is dissolved in 1000 g of benzene at 25°C?

Ans.   310 g mole^{-1}.

10-3   Calculate the boiling point elevation for the solution of Exercise 10-1 by Eq. (10-7) and by Eq. (10-10).

Ans.   0.257°C, 0.255°C.

10-4   The normal boiling point elevation for a solution of 10 g of sucrose in 400 g of ethanol is 0.143°C, whereas 8 g of a substance of unknown molecular weight raises the boiling point by 0.250°C if dissolved in 400 g of ethanol. Calculate the molecular weight of the unknown and the value of K_b for ethanol.

Ans.   156 g mole^{-1}, 1.96 °K m^{-1}.

10-5   Calculate the freezing point depression for the solution of Exercise 10-1 by Eq. (10-15) and by Eq. (10-17).

A   0.928°C, 0.928°C.

10-6   Ethylene glycol, CH_2OHCH_2OH, is used as an antifreeze. Assuming ideal solutions, what weight per cent of ethylene glycol should be present in a car's radiator to protect it down to 0°F?

Ans.   41 %.

10-7   The density of the solution of Exercise 10-1 is 1.0575 g cm^{-3}. Calculate its osmotic pressure using Eq. (10-22), and then $\bar{V}_1$ using Eq. (10-21).

Ans.   11.0 atm, 20 cm^3 mole^{-1}.

10-8 Calculate the boiling point elevation and the freezing point depression of an $0.05\,m$ aqueous solution of sodium chloride, assumed to be ideal, and the vapor pressure lowering and osmotic pressure of this solution at 25°C.

Ans. 0.050°C, 0.186°C, 0.042 Torr, 2.44 atm.

10-9 How fast should an aqueous suspension of colloidal gold settle at 25°C if the particles are $1\,\mu m$ (10^{-4} cm) in diameter and the density of gold is 19.3 g cm^{-3}? Assume the particles to be spherical.

Ans. 1.11×10^{-3} cm sec^{-1}.

10-10 How fast should the suspension of Exercise 10-9 settle in a centrifuge operating at 50 rps and having a radius of 5 cm?

Ans. 0.561 cm sec^{-1}.

10-11 Calculate the diffusion coefficient in water at 25°C for a protein of molecular weight 200,000, assumed to be spherical, and of density 1.35 g cm^{-3}.

Ans. 6.06×10^{-7} cm^2 sec^{-1}.

10-12 Using data as needed from a handbook and from Table 10-4, calculate from Walden's rule the diffusion coefficient of aqueous urea at 50°C.

Ans. 2.16×10^{-5} cm^2 sec^{-1}.

10-13 A polymer consists of the following molecular weight fractions: $M = 2 \times 10^3$, 20%; $M = 1 \times 10^4$, 60%; $M = 3 \times 10^4$, 20% (percentages are by weight). Calculate the number and the weight average molecular weights.

Ans. $M_n = 6.0 \times 10^3$ g mole^{-1}, $M_w = 1.24 \times 10^4$ g mole^{-1}.

Problems

10-1 Calculate the freezing point versus composition plot for the system glycerol–water. Make a plot of your calculated freezing points versus mole fraction and give the temperature and composition of the eutectic (see Section 11-3B). Compare these results with the actual freezing point versus composition data. Assume that Raoult's law holds, the Clausius–Clapeyron equation holds, ΔH's are independent of T and composition, and the vapors are ideal. ΔH_f's for water and glycerol are 1.44 and 4.32 kcal mole^{-1}, respectively.

10-2 The vapor pressure of an aqueous solution of a nonvolatile solute is 4.550 Torr at 0°C, at which temperature the vapor pressure of water is 4.579 Torr. Calculate the freezing point of the solution. State all the assumptions and approximations involved in the calculation.

10-3 A flask contained 242.6 mg phenanthrene ($C_{14}H_{10}$) dissolved in benzene; another flask contained 323.8 mg of benzoic acid, also in benzene solution. The flasks were connected with a wide tube, evacuated, and immersed in a bath thermostated at 56.1°C. In the next few days the volumes of the solutions were slightly changed by benzene distilling from one flask to the other. After equilibrium had been reached the weight of the phenanthrene solution was 21.6805 g and that of the benzoic acid solution was 24.5475 g. Benzoic acid, but not phenanthrene, forms a dimer in benzene to some extent. Find the equilibrium constant for (Wall and Rose, 1941)

$$2(\text{benzoic acid}) = (\text{benzoic acid})_2 \quad (\text{in benzene}).$$

10-4 Calculate the freezing point versus composition plot for the system acetone–ethanol. Make a plot of your calculated freezing points versus mole fraction of the solution, locate the eutectic, and complete the phase diagram, labeling each region. Assume that the solutions (liquid) are ideal, that the Clausius–Clapeyron equation holds, and that the two solids are completely immiscible.

10-5 The freezing point of CCl_4 is lowered by $5.97°C$ if 66.83 g of VCl_4 is present per 1000 g of solvent. Find the equilibrium constant for the reaction $V_2Cl_8 = 2VCl_4$ at the temperature of the freezing solution. Carbon tetrachloride melts at $-22.9°C$ and its heat of fusion is 640 cal mole^{-1}. Assume ideal solution behavior. [See Simons and Powell (1945).]

10-6 The solubility of naphthalene in benzene at $21°C$ is 36.7% by weight. Calculate the solubility of naphthalene in CCl_4 at $4°C$ if the heat of fusion of naphthalene is 4800 cal mole^{-1}. Assume ideal solutions. [See Schröder (1893) (!).]

10-7 Sulfur is present as S_8 molecules in a variety of solvents (such as diethyl ether or benzene) and a series of measurements by Brønsted (1906) showed that in these solvents the solubility of monoclinic sulfur was always 1.28 times that of rhombic sulfur at $25°C$. Calculate ΔG for the conversion of one mole of monoclinic sulfur to rhombic sulfur at $25°C$. Explain which of the two forms is the more stable at $25°C$.

10-8 Calculate the solubility of phenanthrene in benzene at $25°C$ (in mole $\%$) if its heat of fusion is 4450 cal mole^{-1}. The melting point is $100°C$ and the solution is to be assumed ideal.

10-9 Naphthalene and diphenylamine form a eutectic mixture, melting at $32.45°C$. When 1.268 g of eutectic mixture were added to 18.43 g of naphthalene, the freezing point of the melt was $1.89°$ lower than the freezing point of pure naphthalene. What percentage by weight of naphthalene is there in the eutectic mixture if the molal freezing point lowering is 6.78 for naphthalene and 8.60 for diphenylamine. (If necessary supplement the data with additional physical constants for pure naphthalene and pure diphenylamine.)

10-10 A problem to which considerable attention is being devoted is the economic conversion of sea water to potable water. Sea water may be considered as an approximately $1\ m$ solution of NaCl, and two typical processes might be (each at $25°C$):

(a) H_2O (in infinite amount of sea water) $= H_2O$ (pure)
(b) $NaCl + 55.5H_2O = NaCl + 18H_2O + 37.5\ H_2O$ (pure).
     (as a solution)   (as a solution)

Calculate the minimum work for each process. The vapor pressure of sea water is 0.78 Torr lower than that of pure water (at $25°C$), and that of concentrated NaCl solution in (b) is 2.5 Torr lower than that of pure water. Calculate the cost per 1000 gal water (fresh) produced by each process, assuming 0.5 ¢ per kW hr. The approximate cost of water (wholesale) in this area is 15 ¢ per 1000 gal.

10-11 A suspension contains equal numbers of particles with molecular weights 20,000 and 30,000. Calculate the number and weight average molecular weights. Calculate the number and weight average molecular weights if the suspension instead contained equal weights of particles with molecular weights 20,000 and 30,000.

10-12 Calculate the molecular weight of a substance which in a concentration of 6 g per 1000 cm³ of solution exerts an osmotic pressure of 3 Torr at 25°C.

10-13 A suspension contains 30 wt % of particles having a radius of 5 μ and 70 wt % of particles having a radius of 2 μ. The density of the dispersed phase is 1.90 g cm⁻³ and that of the medium is 1.00 g cm⁻³ and the viscosity of the medium is 1 cP. The height of the column of suspension is 50 cm. Calculate the time in which the larger particle size fraction settles out completely, the fraction by weight of the suspension that settles out in this time, and the composition of the sediment.

10-14 The molecular weight of an albumin protein is determined by the sedimentation equilibrium method at a speed of 140 rps. The protein has a density of 1.35 g cm⁻³ and that of the aqueous medium is 1.00 g cm⁻³. The equilibrium concentration gradient is such that at 25°C the solution contains 0.65 wt % of protein at a distance of 4.30 cm from the axis of rotation and 1.300 wt % at a distance of 4.60 cm. Calculate the molecular weight.

10-15 Several ways of determining Avogadro's number are implicit in the material of this chapter: Describe specific illustrative experiments.

10-16 Consider the enclosed system shown in the accompanying diagram. Pure solvent (1) is separated from solution (2) by a semipermeable membrane, and at equilibrium the solution has risen up a tube to a point such that the hydrostatic pressure on the solution just equals the osmotic pressure. There appears to be a paradox here. The vapor pressure

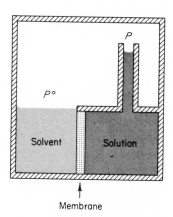

Membrane

of the solution (the solute being nonvolatile) is less than that of the pure solvent, yet both the surface of the solvent and that of the solution (at the end of the tube) are exposed to the same solvent vapor phase. To be in equilibrium with solvent, the vapor pressure should be that of the pure solvent $P°$, whereas to be in equilibrium with the solution, the vapor pressure should be that of the solution P. Resolve this contradiction.

10-17 The molecular weight of a particular DNA is found to be 4.00×10^6 g mole^{-1} and its sedimentation coefficient is 12.0×10^{-13} in cgs units. The product $\bar{v}_2 \rho$ is 0.52 (in water at 25°C). Calculate the diffusion coefficient for this DNA.

10-18 Calculate the molecular weight from the following light scattering data for an aqueous solution of a substance if the following turbidities are obtained (for 426 nm and 25°C; $dn/dc = 0.105$):

Concentration (g cm^{-3})	0.080	0.070	0.057	0.050	0.038	0.026	0.015	0.008
$10^3 \tau$ (cm^{-1})		0.700	0.633	0.544	0.492	0.394	0.286	0.174	0.096

10-19 Calculate the turbidity of a 0.100 M solution of sucrose in water at 20°C assuming the solution to be ideal. The refractive indices of 1.00, 2.00, 3.00, and 4.00 wt % sucrose solutions at 20°C are 1.3344, 1.3359, 1.3374, and 1.3388. Assume a wavelength of 546 nm.

Special Topics Problems

10-1 Derive Eq. (10-30).

10-2 Calculate a_a' and γ_a' from the data of Table 10-6 for each of the compositions and plot the results versus composition along with the corresponding values for chloroform.

10-3 Calculate γ_C and γ_m for chloroform from the data of Table 10-6 and plot the set of four kinds of activity coefficients versus composition.

10-4 Estimate the diffusion coefficient of CCl$_4$ in benzene at 25°C using the theory of Section 10-ST-2. Assume that the activation energy for the diffusion is one-third the heat of vaporization of the solvent, and make a reasonable estimate for δ.

10-5 The diffusion coefficient for naphthalene in benzene is 3.5×10^{-5} cm^2 sec^{-1} at 6°C; assume the relevant viscosity to be that of the solvent, 0.80 cP, and calculate the value of δ for the diffusion process.

11 HETEROGENEOUS EQUILIBRIUM

Equilibria involving two or more phases—heterogeneous equilibria—have been discussed at various points in preceding chapters. The function of the present chapter is to organize examples of such systems according to a more formal framework and to extend the complexity and variety of systems considered. The thermodynamic criterion for equilibrium finds a more general form known as the *Gibbs phase rule*. There will be considerable emphasis on graphical methods for representing phase equilibria. Graphs showing pressure–temperature–composition domains for phases were called phase maps in preceding chapters; the more common term of *phase diagram* will now be used.

11-1 The Gibbs Phase Rule

A. Analytical Derivation

The criterion for phase equilibrium was developed in Section 9-3C, where it was concluded that the chemical potential of each component must be the same in all phases. Thus for two phases in equilibrium the condition for the ith component is

$$\mu_i^\alpha = \mu_i^\beta = \cdots \qquad [\text{Eq. (9-44)}],$$

where α, β, and so on denote the various phases in equilibrium. The effect of this condition is to reduce the number of independent variables that are needed to specify the state of the system.

11 Heterogeneous Equilibrium

Consider first the case of a pure substance. If it is present as a single phase α, then we must specify pressure and temperature to fix the state of the substance. That is, we write

$$\mu^\alpha = f^\alpha(P, T) \tag{11-1}$$

and phase α will have a region of existence over some range of P and T, as is illustrated in Fig. 8-13. The same is true for some second phase β:

$$\mu^\beta = f^\beta(P, T). \tag{11-2}$$

(It would be perfectly acceptable to use G^α and G^β instead of μ^α and μ^β, since composition is not a variable, but it seems better to keep a uniform nomenclature.)

Equilibrium between the two phases corresponds to a line of crossing of the surfaces generated by f^α and f^β in the three-dimensional plots of μ versus P and T. In effect we solve Eqs. (11-1) and (11-2) simultaneously to obtain as the condition of phase equilibrium

$$f^\alpha(P, T) = f^\beta(P, T) \qquad \text{or} \qquad P = \phi^{\alpha\beta}(T). \tag{11-3}$$

This is essentially what was done in deriving the Clapeyron equation [Eq. (8-6)] and, from it, the Clausius–Clapeyron equation [Eq. (8-9)] for the equilibrium between a liquid and its vapor:

$$P = Ae^{-\Delta H_\mathrm{V}/RT} \qquad \text{[Eq. (8-9)]}.$$

If a third phase γ is possible, then for α–γ equilibrium we have

$$f^\alpha(P, T) = f^\gamma(P, T) \qquad \text{or} \qquad P = \phi^{\alpha\gamma}(T). \tag{11-4}$$

We now ask that all three phases be in equilibrium, that is, coexist at the same P and T. We obtain the condition by solving Eqs. (11-3) and (11-4) simultaneously. With two unknowns (P and T) and two equations, the solution gives unique values for pressure and temperature. As was pointed out in Section 8-4 in connection with the water phase diagram (Fig. 8-11), equilibrium between α and β phases and between α and γ phases implies equilibrium between β and γ phases.

We will designate the number of *degrees of freedom* of a system as the number of variables whose values may be chosen independently. With only α phase present there are two such variables, P and T, and the system has two degrees of freedom. If α and β phases are in equilibrium, then, by Eq. (11-3), we may choose P or T, the choice then fixing the other variable; the system has one degree of freedom. If three phases are in equilibrium, then P and T have unique values and neither can be chosen arbitrarily. The system has zero degrees of freedom. The regularity that emerges is that

$$F + \mathscr{P} = 3, \tag{11-5}$$

where $\mathscr{P}$ denotes the number of phases in equilibrium and F the number of degrees of freedom.

440

A system consisting of a single substance is called a *one-component* system, meaning that its composition is fixed. A system in which the amounts of two substances must be specified for composition to be fixed is called a *two-component* system. The statements of chemical potential for phase α are now

$$\mu_1^{\alpha} = f_1^{\alpha}(P, T, x_1^{\alpha}) \quad \text{and} \quad \mu_2^{\alpha} = f_2^{\alpha}(P, T, x_1^{\alpha}), \quad (11\text{-}6)$$

where the subscripts identify the components and x is mole fraction. Since $x_1 + x_2 = 1$, it is simpler to eliminate x_2 immediately in writing the second of Eqs. (11-6). There are three degrees of freedom in this case; we must specify P, T, and x_1 in order to define the state of the system.

If two phases α and β are in equilibrium, then

$$\mu_1^{\alpha} = \mu_1^{\beta} \quad \text{and} \quad \mu_2^{\alpha} = \mu_2^{\beta},$$

or

$$f_1^{\alpha}(P, T, x_1^{\alpha}) = f_1^{\beta}(P, T, x_1^{\beta}) \quad \text{and} \quad f_2^{\alpha}(P, T, x_1^{\alpha}) = f_2^{\beta}(P, T, x_1^{\beta}). \quad (11\text{-}7)$$

There are now four variables, P, T, x_1^{α}, and x_1^{β}, and two equations, so that two of the variables are no longer independent. In the case of an equilibrium between a solution and its vapor, we choose $x_1(l)$ and T as the independent variables. That is, for a given choice of T, the equilibrium vapor pressure P is determined by the composition of the liquid phase, as is also the vapor composition. An example is the benzene–toluene system of Fig. 9-2.

The number of degrees of freedom in this case is reduced to two, and if the analysis is extended to three and then to four coexisting phases, the rule for a two-component system is found to be

$$F + \mathscr{P} = 4. \quad (11\text{-}8)$$

The trend of Eqs. (11-5) and (11-8) may be extended to the general case as follows.

If a system has C components, then the number of variables required to define its state will be two (P and T), plus $(C - 1)$. That is, C mole fractions are involved, one of which is immediately eliminated by the condition that their sum must be unity. The total number of variables is

$$\text{number of variables} = \mathscr{P}(C - 1) + 2. \quad (11\text{-}9)$$

The condition for equilibrium generates the equations

$$\mu_1^{\alpha} = \mu_1^{\beta} = \mu_1^{\gamma} = \mu_1^{\delta} = \cdots,$$
$$\mu_2^{\alpha} = \mu_2^{\beta} = \mu_2^{\gamma} = \mu_2^{\delta} = \cdots,$$
$$\vdots$$

or $\mathscr{P} - 1$ equations for each component. The total number of equations is

$$\text{number of equations} = C(\mathscr{P} - 1). \quad (11\text{-}10)$$

The number of degrees of freedom is the difference between Eqs. (11-9) and (11-10),

$$F = \mathscr{P}(C - 1) + 2 - C(\mathscr{P} - 1),$$

or

$$F + \mathscr{P} = C + 2. \tag{11-11}$$

Equation (11-11) is known as the *Gibbs phase rule*.

The phase rule is useful in several ways. It tells us the maximum possible number of equilibrium phases that can coexist. In the more complex systems it helps to determine the number of components present and whether the phases present are well behaved. This aspect is discussed further in the Commentary and Notes section; for the present it is sufficient to make the following definitions:

Number of components: the minimum of compositions needed, along with pressure and temperature, to define the state of the system;

Number of phases: the number of different kinds of states of matter present.

B.   Graphical Interpretation

The phase rule was just derived on an analytical basis and it may be helpful to explain it in a more geometric fashion. This approach was suggested in connection with the one-component system when it was pointed out that Eqs. (11-1) and (11-2) correspond to surfaces in the three-dimensional plot of μ against P and T. Equating μ^α and μ^β, as in Eq. (11-3), corresponds graphically to finding the line of crossing of the two surfaces. Similarly, equating μ^α to μ^γ gives the line of equilibrium between α and γ phases, and equating μ^β to μ^γ gives the line of equilibrium between β and γ phases. The mutual crossing of these three possible two-phase lines then yields a point of three-phase equilibrium. The plot of the state variables, in this case P versus T, then shows areas of one-phase existence, lines of two-phase equilibrium, and triple points, The number of degrees of freedom thus corresponds to the dimensionality (area, line, point) of the domain for each situation.

A four-dimensional plot would be needed to display the equation of state of a two-component system, that is, to show $\mu = f(P, T, x_1)$; the region of existence of a given phase α would then be given by a solid figure in four-dimensional space. Alternatively, each phase occupies a volume domain in a graph of the state variables P, T, and x_1. The boundaries of two such domains give a surface of two-phase equilibrium, as in Fig. 9-15. Three such surfaces intersect at a line of three-phase equilibrium, and the six possible lines of three-phase equilibrium cross at a point of four-phase equilibrium. Again, the number of degrees of freedom drops from three to zero, in step with the dimensionality of the corresponding domain.

We will take up one-, two-, and three-component systems in order. It will become very apparent that as the number of components increases, more and more difficulties are encountered in the graphical display of phase equilibria. One is forced to deal with increasingly restrictive cross sections and projections of the complete phase diagrams.

11-2   One-Component Systems

One-component systems were largely summarized in Chapter 8. The phase rule reduces to Eq. (11-5). We may have single phases existing over a region of P and T, two-phase equilibria governed by the Clapeyron (or Clausius–Clapeyron) equation and thus defined by a P–T line, and three-phase equilibria characterized by a triple point, or unique values of P and T. If n phases are known, there will be $n(n-1)/2$ lines of two-phase equilibria; this is the number of distinguishable ways of picking two out of n objects. Also, there will be $n(n-1)(n-2)/3!$ possible triple points.

From the graphical point of view, a three-dimensional model is needed; one must show $\mu = f(P, T)$, as in Fig. 8-13, or the equation of state of each phase $V = g(P, T)$, as illustrated in Fig. 1-9. One may take various cross sections of the three-dimensional plot, usually either isothermal or isobaric ones, such as in Fig. 1-10. The surfaces of state for gaseous, liquid, and solid water intersect to give gas–liquid, gas–solid, and liquid–solid lines, which in turn intersect at the triple point.

Two-phase equilibria can, of course, be shown as P versus T plots, as in Fig. 8-3 for vapor pressures. A set of two-phase equilibrium lines constitutes a phase diagram, as in Figs. 8-10 and 8-12. Two additional systems are shown in Fig. 11-1.

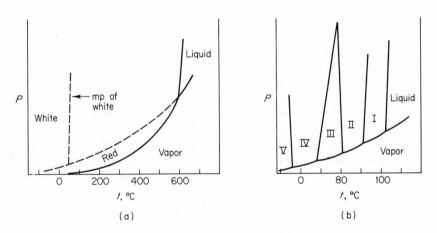

Fig. 11-1   (a) *Phase diagram for phosphorus.* (b) *Phase diagram for* NH_4NO_3 *[see R. G. Early and T. M. Lowry, J. Chem. Soc. 1387 (1919)].*

That for phosphorus (a) illustrates a case where, although two solid forms are known, only one is ever stable. White phosphorus may be prepared chemically but is always unstable with respect to red phosphorus. The ammonium nitrate system (b) is one in which a rather long succession of crystal modifications occur, each with a region of stability.

11-3   Two-Component Systems

The phase rule for a two-component system is given by Eq. (11-8). A four-dimensional plot would be needed to show the state of a two-component system, that is, to plot Eqs. (11-6) or to show $V = g(P, T, x_1)$. One must therefore proceed immediately to one or another cross section, or use tabulations. Our interest, however, is in phase equilibria. The equilibrium between two phases can be shown as a P–T-composition plot or three-dimensional model, as in Fig. 9-15. These are awkward to use, so in actual practice one customarily takes either isothermal or isobaric cross sections. The vapor pressure-composition diagrams of Chapter 9 are examples of the former, and the boiling point diagrams are examples of the latter. Figure 7-2 similarly shows isothermal and isobaric cross sections for the CaO–CO_2 system and Fig. 9-21 shows an isobaric cross section depicting the equilibrium between two partially miscible liquids. The freezing point depression equation (10-15) gives the line of equilibrium between a solution and a pure solid for a constant pressure of 1 atm.

These examples represent isolated portions of various phase diagrams, and the material that follows will assemble these various portions into a more complete picture. Two-phase equilibria are given by surfaces in the P–T-composition plot; the intersection of two such surfaces generates a line of three-phase equilibrium, that is, of the three variables, only one is now independent (usually taken to be the pressure). As in the one-component systems, the intersection of two two-phase equilibria implies the presence of a third one; a third surface must therefore be present at the intersection of the other two. Finally, it is possible, according to the phase rule, to have four phases in equilibrium, with P, T, and composition then defined. Such *quadruple points* are given by the intersection of two lines of three-phase equilibrium. Since four different three-phase combinations are possible, it follows that a total of four three-phase lines mutually intersect at a quadruple point.

The preceding discussion has been stated in rather abstract form. The ensuing examples should help to clarify matters. The examples are mostly schematic; it is not appropriate in a text such as this to deal with the subject at all exhaustively.

A.   Variation of Boiling Point Diagrams with Pressure

Figure 9-15 shows the P–T-composition plot for solution–vapor equilibrium in a relatively ideal system. A succession of lower and lower pressure cross sections would at first yield a series of diagrams of lower and lower general boiling points, as illustrated in Fig. 11-2(a,b). Suppose now that at a still lower temperature the liquids are only partially miscible. The region of partial miscibility, or miscibility gap, is shown as having an upper consolute temperature T_c ; the region is treated as invariant in the diagrams because applied pressure affects equilibrium between condensed phases only slightly.

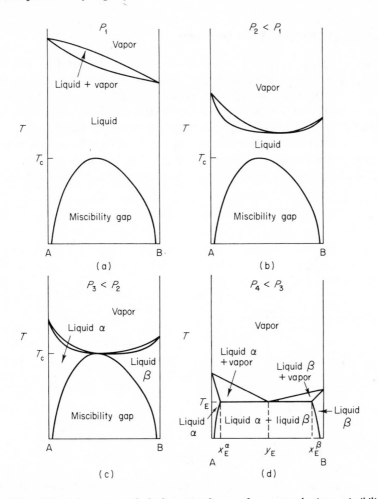

Fig. 11-2. *Effect of pressure on the boiling point diagram for a system having a miscibility gap.*

We now suppose the pressure to be reduced yet further so that the boiling point region approaches the miscibility gap. As shown in Fig. 11-2(b), a positive deviation from ideality develops, leading eventually to a minimum-boiling diagram. Finally, in Fig. 11-2(c) the boiling point region impacts on the miscibility gap and the diagram changes in appearance; three phases, vapor and two solutions, can coexist.

Since the one degree of freedom available has been used in setting the pressure, the compositions of the three phases are fixed, as is the temperature. Thus in Fig. 11-2(d) phases of composition y_E, x_E^α, and x_E^β are in equilibrium at T_E, where the subscript E stands for eutectic (Section 11-3B). Rather similar diagrams appear in the more important analogous situation of freezing point systems and these are discussed in detail in the Special Topics section.

B. Freezing (or Melting) Point Diagrams

Solution–solid equilibria are ordinarily shown only in terms of the isobaric diagram for 1 atm. High-pressure studies could yield sequences of the type shown in Fig. 11-2 but these are not of much present interest. We consider the simplest case first, namely, that in which the miscibility gap essentially coincides with the A and B sides of the diagram, that is, the case of complete immiscibility.

If the liquid solution is ideal, then the solution–solid equilibrium line is given by the freezing point depression equation (10-15). This equation is plotted in Fig. 11-3(a), assuming first that pure solid A separates out; line *ab* results. A system of

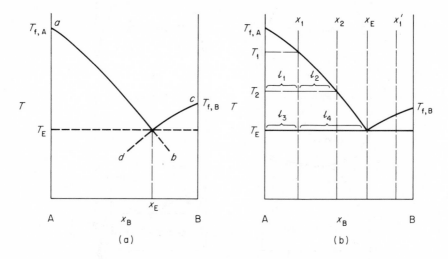

Fig. 11-3. *Freezing point diagram for an ideal solution.*

this type is symmetric, and the freezing point of liquid B will similarly be lowered by the presence of dissolved A. This second freezing point depression curve is shown by line *cd* in the figure. At the point of crossing of these two lines solution of composition x_E is simultaneously in equilibrium with pure solid A and pure solid B. On attempted cooling, the system can pursue neither the dashed extension of *ab* nor that of *cd* without departing from equilibrium with respect to either solid B or solid A. The consequence is that the temperature must remain invariant at T_E so long as the three phases are present. This invariance is demanded by the phase rule—the one degree of freedom having been used in setting the pressure at 1 atm.

The completed phase diagram is shown in Fig. 11-3(b); it is called a *eutectic diagram*. The temperature T_E is the *eutectic temperature* and x_E the *eutectic composition*. The phase map aspect may be developed as follows. A solution (or melt, if the system is a high-temperature one) of composition x_1 will begin to freeze at T_1. With further cooling, solid A appears, and at some temperature T_2 the system consists of solid A and liquid of composition x_2. The proportions are given by the lever principle (Section 9-2C). The lengths l_1 and l_2 of the two sections of the tie-line at T_2 are in the same proportion as are the amounts of solution and of solid:

$$l_1/l_2 = \text{(amount of solution)/(amount of solid)}.$$

If composition is plotted as mole fraction, the ratio will be of the number of moles of solution to the number of moles of solid; and if composition is in weight fraction or percent, the ratio will be that of weight of solution to weight of solid.

At T_E the solution has reached composition x_E, and further withdrawal of heat leads to the simultaneous freezing out of solid A and solid B. Since the solution cannot change composition, the proportion of A and B in the mixed solids must be given by x_E. The eutectic solid is thus one of definite composition, and perhaps for this reason it has sometimes been misnamed a *eutectic compound*. It is not a compound; its composition varies with pressure, for example. In the case of metal systems especially the superficial appearance of the eutectic mixture may be that of a single phase, but microscopic examination shows a mechanical mixture of small crystals of the two pure phases.

Eventually the liquid phase disappears and the system consists of solid A and solid B in overall proportion corresponding to x_1.

Cooling of a liquid of composition x_1' gives the same general sequence of changes. The first phase to separate out is now pure solid B, however. At T_E both A and B freeze out together, and when the liquid phase has disappeared one has the mixed solid phases of overall composition x_1'.

C. Cooling Curves for a Simple Eutectic System

The preceding system is called a simple eutectic one, for reasons that are made especially apparent in the Special Topics section; freezing point diagrams can take on a rather complicated appearance. Simple eutectic, as well as the more complex systems, may be studied by what is known as the method of *thermal analysis*. The experiment consists in placing the liquid solution or melt in a container from which heat is withdrawn at a steady rate. That is, dq/dt is kept approximately constant. The liquid has a certain heat capacity $C_P(l)$ and the rate of change of its temperature with time is

$$\frac{dT}{dt} = \frac{1}{C_P(l)} \frac{dq}{dt} \tag{11-12}$$

447

(*dq*, and hence dT/dt, is negative since the system is losing heat). If we suppose the solution to be of composition x_1 in Fig. 11-3(b), then at T_1 solid A begins to freeze out. This means that its latent heat of freezing $\Delta H^\circ_{f,A}$ is liberated. The shape of the line *ab* [Fig. 11-3(a)] determines dn_A/dT, that is, the number of moles of A appearing per unit temperature drop. Due to this effect, heat is supplied to the system at the rate

$$\frac{dq_f}{dT} = -\Delta H^\circ_{f,A}\,\frac{dn_A}{dT}.$$
(11-13)

The consequence is that the heat capacity of the system is increased by an amount $C_{P,f}$, and the net heat capacity becomes

$$C_P(\text{net}) = C_P(l)\,n_L + \Delta H^\circ_{f,A}\,\frac{dn_A}{dT} + C_A n_A,$$
(11-14)

where n_L and n_A are the number of moles of liquid and of solid A present respectively. The rate of cooling is therefore reduced.

A schematic cooling curve for composition x_1 is shown in Fig. 11-4(a). The slope of the first section is given by Eq. (11-12). At T_1 (see Fig. 11-3) the slope changes to

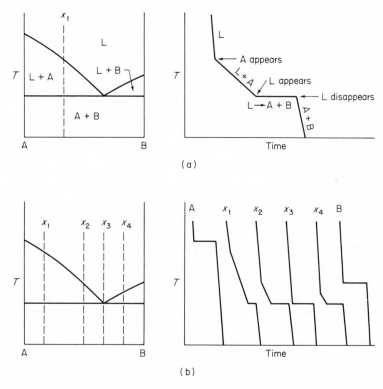

(a)

(b)

Fig. 11-4.   *Cooling curves for a simple eutectic system.*

one determined by C_P(net); the cooling line is now curved since C_P(net) changes with the relative amounts of liquid and solid phase. At T_E the temperature remains constant; the removal of heat now goes to freezing out A and B together, and the halt in the cooling curve lasts for a time given by

$$t_{halt} = \frac{n_E[x_E \, \Delta H^\circ_{f,B} + (1 - x_E) \, \Delta H^\circ_{f,A}]}{dq/dt} . \tag{11-15}$$

Equation (11-15) merely states that the average molar heat of freezing $\Delta H_{f,av}$ of a eutectic solution of composition x_E is $[x_E \, \Delta H^\circ_{f,B} + (1 - x_E) \, \Delta H^\circ_{f,A}]$, and that the total amount of heat required is the product of the number of moles of such solution n_E and this average heat.

At the end of the halt, liquid phase has disappeared, and cooling resumes, with dT/dt given by Eq. (11-12) but with a heat capacity corresponding to that of the mixture of solids:

$$C_P(A + B) = n[x_1 C_B + (1 - x_1) C_A], \tag{11-16}$$

where n denotes the total number of moles of the system. Experimental cooling curves may show small temperature minima at breaks and halts, due to supercooling.

It helps to define exactly what is happening along each section of a cooling curve if the phase or phases present are indicated as is done in Fig. 11-4(a). A halt corresponds to a so-called phase reaction, that is, to the physical process of inter-conversion of phases. In the present example, the phase reaction is $L \rightarrow A + B$. One should also show at each break what phase or phases are appearing or disappearing.

Figure 11-4(b) shows a series of cooling curves for various initial compositions of the system of Fig. 11-3. Notice that the locus of the temperatures of the first break defines the freezing point lines [ab and cd in Fig. 11-3(a)]. The unique halt temperature identifies the system as one having a single eutectic, and the cooling curve of composition labeled x_3 identifies the eutectic composition since preliminary separation of neither A nor B alone occurs.

The relative lengths of the various sections of the cooling curves should also be consistent with the phase diagram. Suppose, for simplicity, that there is always one mole total of system. The length of the halt for the cooling of pure liquid A is then $\Delta H^\circ_{f,A}/(dq/dt)$ and that for the cooling of pure liquid B is $\Delta H^\circ_{f,B}/(dq/dt)$. The length of the halt for the cooling of the solution of eutectic composition x_3 is similarly given by ΔH_{av}, defined in connection with Eq. (11-15). For intermediate compositions the length of the eutectic halt is proportional to n_E in Eq. (11-15). The amount of eutectic phase that must freeze out, n_E, is in turn determined by application of the lever principle. Returning to Fig. 11-3(b), we see that n_E for composition x_1 is given by the ratio of the lengths l_3/l_4. Clearly, the closer the initial composition is to x_E, the greater will be this proportion, and the longer will be the halt in the cooling curve. An alternative way for one to locate the eutectic composition is then to plot the length of halt against initial composition and extrapolate both sections to find the maximum, as shown in Fig. 11-5. One thus avoids having to hit the composition x_E exactly in a series of thermal analysis experiments.

Simple eutectic behavior is illustrated by the benzene–naphthalene system shown in Fig. 11-6. Details are entirely analogous to those already described and need not be elaborated.

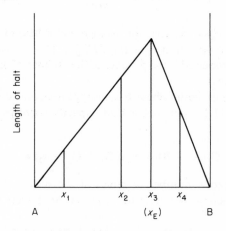

Fig. 11-5.   *Variation of length of eutectic halt with initial solution composition.*

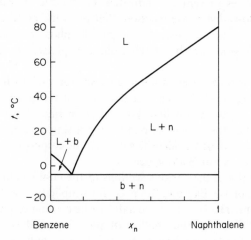

Fig. 11-6.   *The benzene–naphthalene system.*

D.   Compound Formation

It happens quite often that the two components form one or more solid compounds—AB, A_2B, AB_2, and so on. If these are stable, they show a normal melting point, or are said to melt congruently. The effect is simply to divide the phase diagram into as many separate sections. This is illustrated in Fig. 11-7 for the case of a compound AB_2. The two eutectics have no necessary connection with each other, nor, in fact, do any aspects of the two portions of the diagram. Each may be treated separately.

What sometimes happens, however, is that a compound decomposes to give liquid and one of the other solid phases. Figure 11-7 would now take on the appearance of Fig. 11-8, where compound AB_2 decomposes at T_{d,AB_2} to give liquid of composi-

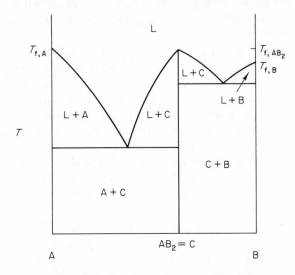

Fig. 11-7. *The case of compound formation.*

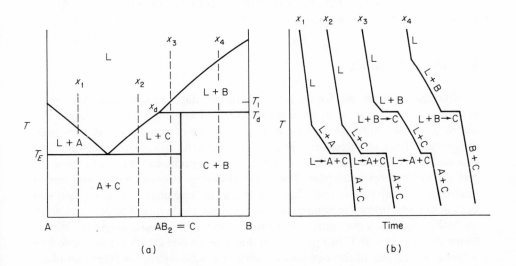

(a)   (b)

Fig. 11-8. *(a) Unstable compound formation. (b) Cooling curves.*

tion x_d and solid B. Such a decomposition is called an *incongruent melting*, meaning that the liquid is not of the same composition as the solid and avoiding the implication of irreversibility suggested by the term decomposition. It is helpful at this point to label the various phase regions. This not only clarifies the geography of the phase map but is of direct use in the construction or interpretation of cooling curves. The general rule is that a break occurs when, on cooling, the system composition line passes from one type of phase region to another, such as on cooling along the x_1 line shown in Fig. 11-8. A halt must occur when a line of three-phase equilibrium is reached, and cooling must resume when a two-phase or a one-phase region is entered.

Systems of composition x_1 and x_2 show normal eutectic cooling curves, but the behavior of the curve for x_3 is more complex. Solid B begins to separate out at T_1 and at T_d the solution has reached composition x_d and is now in equilibrium with both solid B and compound C ($= AB_2$). There must therefore be a halt in the cooling curve until at least one of the three phases disappears.

The phase reaction that occurs at T_d may be determined as follows. Just above T_d the phases present are L and B; just below T_d they are L and C. Evidently B disappears and C appears. However, B cannot by itself produce C, and the phase reaction is evidently $L + B \rightarrow C$. We may confirm this by noting that for composition x_3, use of the lever principle shows that the proportion of L present decreases when the three-phase line is traversed.

After the halt at T_d, the system x_3 consists of $L + C$, and further cooling freezes out more C until T_E is reached. At this point the liquid is at x_E and the rest of the cooling curve is the same as for the simple eutectic case.

Finally, a system of composition x_4 traverses the T_d line on cooling but then enters the $C + B$ phase region. The phase reaction is always the same anywhere along a three-phase line, but what now happens is that as the process $L + B \rightarrow C$ occurs it is the liquid phase which is used up first.

E. Rules of Construction

Although not important for the relatively simple diagrams considered here, there are some rules that assist in the construction and labeling of more complicated diagrams. A two-component phase diagram consists of one-phase and two-phase regions and lines of three-phase equilibria. The latter always connect the three compositions of the three phases that are in equilibrium and must, of course, be mathematically horizontal lines. There will always be two end phases and one of intermediate composition, and a first rule is that the end phases are always present both above and below the temperature of the three-phase line. The phase of intermediate composition may exist only above the line, as in eutectic diagrams, or only below the line, as with C in Fig. 11-8. In this case the line is called a *peritectic line*. Alternatively, a line of three-phase equilibrium is a boundary for three two-phase regions. There are two such regions above a eutectic line and one below it; conversely, there is one such region above a peritectic line and two regions below it.

A second rule is that a horizontal traverse must encounter alternate one-phase and two-phase regions. In applying the rule to a diagram such as that of Fig. 11-8, we regard pure A, pure C, and pure B as very narrow one-phase regions. The reader is encouraged to test the various two-component diagrams of this chapter against these rules.

11-4   Sodium Sulfate–Water and Other Systems

A specific system that both illustrates and extends a number of the points discussed in the preceding section is that for sodium sulfate and water. The usual phase diagram is shown in Fig. 11-9 and displays the following features. The lower

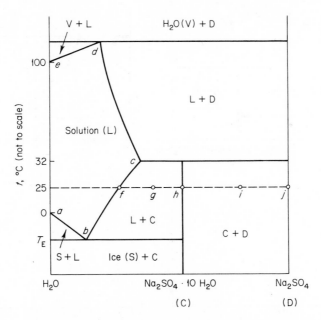

Fig. 11-9.   *The* H_2O–Na_2SO_4 *system for* 1 *atm pressure.*

left curve *ab* is the ordinary freezing point depression curve for aqueous sodium sulfate solutions. Curve *bc* is the solubility curve for $Na_2SO_4 \cdot 10H_2O$, showing a normal increasing solubility with increasing temperature. (The curve can be viewed alternatively as the freezing point depression curve of $Na_2SO_4 \cdot 10H_2O$, as discussed in Section 10-CN-2.) This region of the diagram then shows a simple eutectic behavior, T_E being at $-1.3°C$, and the eutectic solution being 0.33 *m* in sodium

453

sulfate. As an item of incidental information, a eutectic involving ice as one of the solid phases is often called a *cryohydric point*.

The decahydrate decomposes at 32.4°C to give the anhydrous salt whose solubility curve is given by *cd*. The situation is that of unstable compound formation and the three-phase line at 32.4°C is therefore of the peritectic type. The diagram is schematic in that both the temperature and the composition scales have been somewhat distorted so as to display the various phase regions more clearly. These are labeled, however, and a cooling curve, such as for the system of composition x_1, leads to the sequence of phase changes determined by the regions traversed; it will show the usual eutectic halt at T_E.

In a system of this type one of the components is relatively volatile, and one may consider an evaporation sequence. For example, if a dilute sodium sulfate solution is evaporated at 25°C the system will traverse the horizontal line shown in Fig. 11-9.

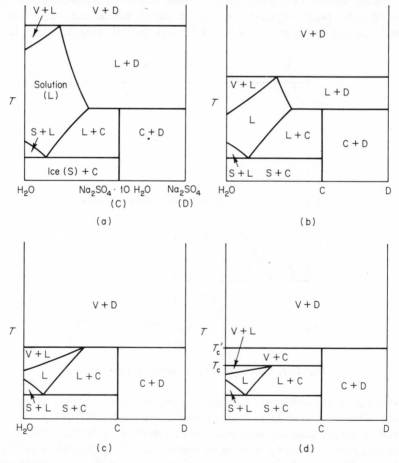

Fig. 11-10.   *Effect of successive reductions of pressure on the phase diagram for the* $H_2O-Na_2SO_4$ *system.*

Saturation with respect to $Na_2SO_4 \cdot 10H_2O$ occurs at system composition f, and continued evaporation deposits solid $Na_2SO_4 \cdot 10H_2O$ in increasing amounts. When the overall composition has reached point g, solution f and solid decahydrate are present in amounts given by the lever principle. At system composition h, solution has disappeared and only $Na_2SO_4 \cdot 10H_2O$ is present. Further evaporation—or removal of water—begins to transform the solid into anhydrous salt; at system composition i there would be about equal parts of $Na_2SO_4 \cdot 10H_2O$ and Na_2SO_4. At point j, of course, only the anhydrous salt is present.

We now turn to the higher-temperature region of the diagram. Pure water is in equilibrium with vapor at 100°C, this being the diagram for 1 atm pressure, and there is a boiling point elevation with increasing salt concentration, given by line de. At the intersection of lines de and cd, solution, vapor, and Na_2SO_4 are in equilibrium, and above T_c the solution has evaporated to give water vapor and solid Na_2SO_4. Although the lower part of the diagram is not sensitive to pressure, since only condensed phases are involved, the upper part is. Figure 11-10 shows the sequence of events on progressive lowering of the pressure. The effect at first is that the boiling point elevation line intersects the cd line at a lower and lower temperature. In Fig. 11-10(c) this intersection is at 32.4°C, at which temperature $Na_2SO_4 \cdot 10H_2O$ has just become stable. At this one temperature and pressure, therefore, four phases are in equilibrium: water vapor, solution, Na_2SO_4, and $Na_2SO_4 \cdot 10H_2O$. This is the quadruple point for the system; no degrees of freedom remain.

On further lowering of the pressure the quadruple point is passed and the boiling point elevation curve now begins to intersect the solubility curve bc. The three-phase line that is formed consists of water vapor, solution, and $Na_2SO_4 \cdot 10H_2O$ as shown in Fig. 11-10(d). Above this T_c water vapor and

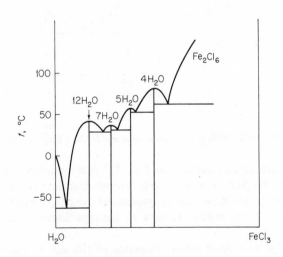

Fig. 11-11. *The H_2O–$FeCl_3$ system.*

455

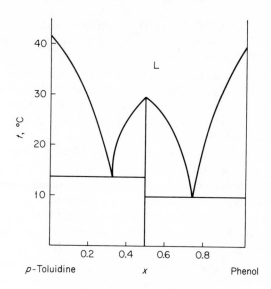

Fig. 11-12.   *The p-toluidine–phenol system.*

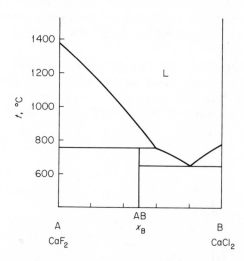

Fig. 11-13.   *The* CaF_2–$CaCl_2$ *system, showing unstable* $CaF_2 \cdot CaCl_2$ *compound formation.*

$Na_2SO_4 \cdot 10H_2O$ are in equilibrium, and at T_c' decomposition of the latter into water vapor and Na_2SO_4 occurs, to generate another line of three-phase equilibrium. Alternatively, the dissociation pressure of $Na_2SO_4 \cdot 10H_2O$ is now equal to the system pressure; the system is now of the type discussed in Section 7-5 on solid–gas equilibria.

There is a large variety of phase diagrams of the salt hydrate type. Another common one is for the H_2O–$FeCl_3$ system, shown in Fig. 11-11. A succession of hydrates exists, each melting congruently. An interesting exercise is to trace out the series of changes occurring on evaporation of a $FeCl_3$ solution at a temperature just below the melting point of the heptahydrate—the unsuspecting physical chemist who first chanced to do this could well have been quite puzzled. Not shown, but equally interesting is the H_2O–H_2SO_4 phase diagram. A very simple example of 1:1 compound formation involving organic compounds is provided by the *p*-toluidine–phenol system shown in Fig. 11-12; the CaF_2–$CaCl_2$ system shown in Fig. 11-13 illustrates unstable compound formation.

11-5 Three-Component Systems

A. Graphical Methods

Some formidable problems of representation develop with three-component systems. Graphing of the equation of state $V = g(P, T, x_1, x_2)$ now requires five-dimensional space! The requirement is reduced to a four-dimensional one if two-phase equilibria are to be shown over a region of existence. Fortunately, or perhaps because of this difficulty, most studies of three-component systems have been carried out with only condensed phases present so that pressure is not an important variable, and isobaric diagrams supply the important information. These are three-dimensional, and their use is awkward but feasible. The chemical engineer who deals with the distillation of multicomponent systems has a problem that we will not consider here.

In an isobaric phase diagram two coordinates are used to fix composition and a third is used to fix the temperature. There are various ways in which the composition of a ternary or three-component system may be plotted, the choice being made in terms of the type of system. A very convenient one makes use of the properties of an equilateral triangle. As illustrated in Fig. 11-14, one of these properties is that the sum of the perpendicular distances to an interior point, $ad + bd + cd$, is always equal to the altitude of the triangle h. Triangular graph paper is therefore ruled with three sets of lines, each set parallel to one of the bases. A point such as d may then be read as having the coordinates $50\% \, h_A$, $20\% \, h_B$, and $30\% \, h_C$. The coordinate system is then used to express composition. For example, point d would be the pivot or balance point for the triangle if weights in the proportion 50:20:30 were hung from the A, B, and C corners, respectively. Point d thus corresponds to a system of composition 50% A, 20% B, and 30% C.

A valuable feature of the triangular graph is that addition of one of the components will cause the system composition to move along the line drawn between it and that corner. Thus addition of C to a mixture of composition d will produce the succession of new compositions along the line dC. The lever principle applies. Thus at point e the ratio of the amount of added C to the amount of original mixture is l_1/l_2.

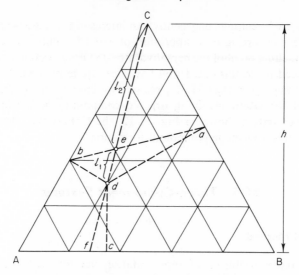

Fig. 11-14.   *Triangular coordinate paper.*

If C is removed from mixture *d* (by evaporation or freezing), the composition of the remaining mixture will move toward *f*, still on the *d*C line. It is not necessary that the added or removed material be pure component. The line connecting any two compositions is the locus of all mixtures of such compositions. For example, point *e* happens to be on the line connecting points *a* and *b*. Addition of mixture *a* to mixture *e* would move the system composition along the *aeb* line, toward *a*. Alternatively, mixture *e* could be made up by the combination of *a* and *b* in the proportions given by the lever principle.

B. The Simple Ternary Eutectic Diagram

Isobaric diagrams may be constructed with a coordinate system based on the equilateral triangular prism, with temperature measured along the prism axis. Each face of the prism constitutes a two-component system; the three faces thus show the A–B, B–C, and A–C phase diagrams. This is illustrated in Fig. 11-15 for a simple eutectic system, that is, one in which A, B, and C are fully miscible in the liquid phase but are essentially immiscible in the solid state.

Examination of the figure shows, for example, that the freezing point T_{AC} of the binary eutectic solution *ac* is further lowered on addition of B to the system. The composition of the series of freezing A–C eutectic solutions moves along the line *ac-abc*. There is a corresponding depression of the *bc* eutectic by the addition of A and of the *ab* eutectic by the addition of C. The three freezing point depression curves for the three binary eutectic solutions meet at point *abc* at T_{ABC}. This is the quadruple point of the diagram; at T_{ABC} solids A, B, and C are in equilibrium with solution of composition *abc*.

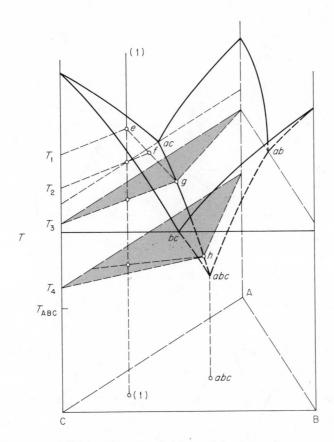

Fig. 11-15.   *A simple ternary eutectic system.*

The sequence of events on cooling of a solution of composition (1) is also shown. At temperature T_1, or point e on the diagram, C begins to freeze out, and the solution composition moves along the dashed line ef. When it reaches the ac-abc line and temperature T_3, solid A begins to freeze out as well, and with further cooling A and C freeze out together while the solution composition moves toward abc. At T_{ABC} the solution is of composition abc and is now also saturated with respect to B. The system is invariant at this point and the temperature remains constant while A, B, and C freeze out together. Cooling resumes when the solution has disappeared.

It is necessary to work with isothermal sections of the diagram if the analysis is to be more accurate. A succession of these is shown in Fig. 11-16; the temperatures correspond to those marked in Fig. 11-15. The section at T_1, Fig. 11-16(a), cuts the three "cloverleaves" of the solid model, the curved lines marking the intersection of the T_1 plane with each surface and hence giving the compositions of solutions saturated with respect to A, to B, and to C. The temperature T_1 is such

459

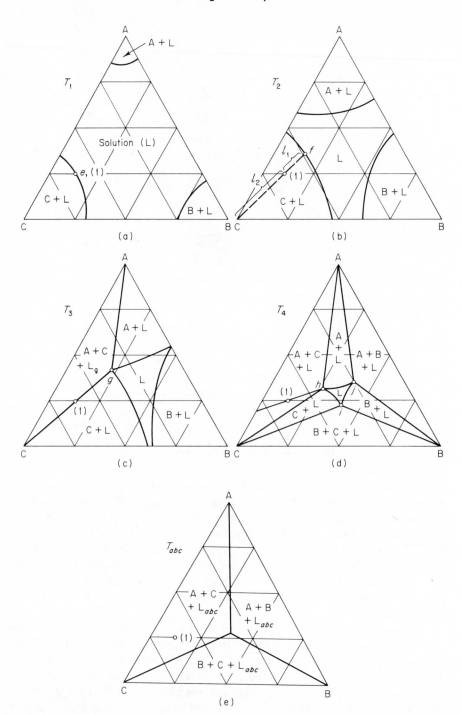

Fig. 11-16. *Cross sections taken at successively lower temperatures (see Fig. 11-15).*

that a system of composition (1) is just on the solubility curve for solutions saturated with respect to C.

The section at T_2, Fig. 11-16(b), is lower down, and so the three solubility curves have moved inward or in the direction of decreased solubility. Point (1) now lies within the pie-shaped region at the C corner. The system consists of solid C and solution of composition f in the ratio l_1/l_2. The pie-shaped regions are thus two-phase regions, as marked in the figure.

Figure 11-16(c), for T_3, shows that the system is now in equilibrium with solution g, which is on the tie-line to the A corner as well as on that to the C corner; the solution is therefore saturated with respect to both solids. At T_4 the system composition lies within the triangular region AhC; the system consists of solids A and C and solution h. The other two triangular regions that have also appeared consist, respectively, of A, B, and solution j, and of B, C, and solution i. We will return later to show how the proportion of each phase can be determined. Continuing to the final diagram of the sequence, at temperature T_{ABC} the three triangular regions have just joined to leave a vestigial point marking the composition of the ternary eutectic solution abc. The cross section at a yet lower temperature would show no features at all—the system consists of solids A, B, and C in amounts given by the overall composition.

We return now to Figure 11-16(d), the triangular region of which is reproduced in larger form in Fig. 11-17. To repeat, system of composition (1) is present as solid A, solid C, and solution of composition h. The relative amounts of these three phases are such that weights corresponding to them would, if placed at the A, C, and h corners, make point (1) a balance point for the triangle. The equivalent graphical procedure is as follows. We first divide the system into solution h and mixed solids A and C. The relative amounts are given as l_2/l_1 (and would be about 1:2 in this case). If the diagram were on a weight percent basis, this means that 100 g of the system would consist of 33.3 g of solution h and 66.6 g of mixed solids A and C.

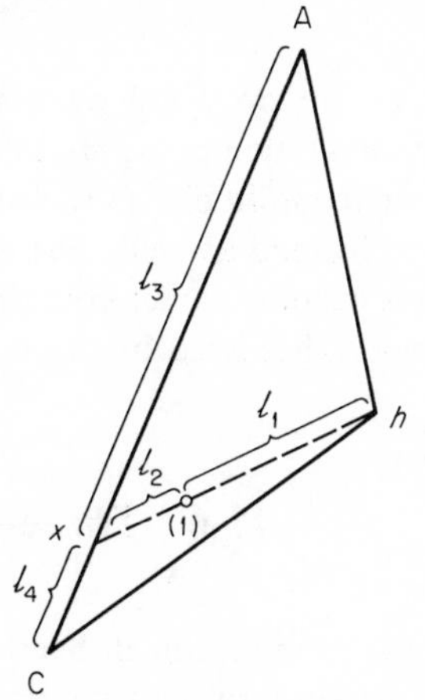

Fig. 11-17.   *Application of the lever principle.*

The proportion of A to C in the mixed solids is next given by the lever AxC; A/C = l_4/l_3, or about one-fifth in this example. The 66.6 g therefore is made up of 11.1 g of A and 55.5 g of C.

C. Ternary Eutectic Systems

There are a fair number of simple three-component eutectic systems known. A specific example is the Bi–Pb–Sn system shown in Fig. 11-18. Other types of

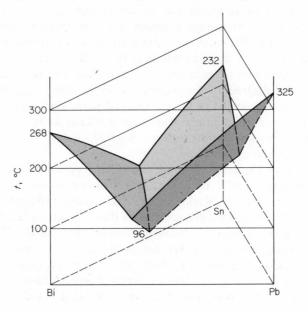

Fig. 11-18. *The* Bi–Pb–Sn *system.*

example are provided by trios of salts such as KCl–NaCl–CdCl$_2$ or of organic compounds such as *o*-, *m*-, and *p*-dichlorobenzene.

Often the solid phases will show some mutual solubility. Also, various compounds may be formed as well. The complete, three-dimensional phase diagrams for such systems become rather complicated; the simple treatment of particular isothermal sections is discussed briefly in the Special Topics section.

11-6   Three-Component Solubility Diagrams

It was pointed out in Section 10-CN-2 that the terms freezing point and solubility merely represent different emphases of the same phenomenon. Consider the system H$_2$O–NaCl–KCl. The respective melting points are 0°C, 1413°C, and 1500°C and the solids are mutually insoluble, so that the phase diagram is of the simple eutectic type but is highly distorted because of the large difference between the melting point for water and those for the salts. The diagram is sketched in Fig. 11-19 and the isothermal cross section at 25°C is shown in Fig. 11-20. The context is such

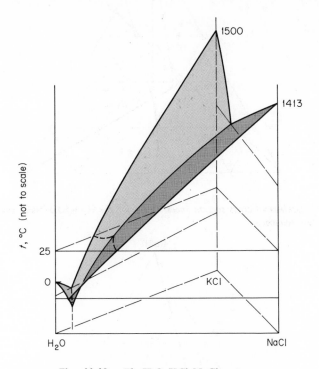

Fig. 11-19.   *The H$_2$O–KCl–NaCl system.*

that we prefer to call line *ab* the solubility curve for NaCl in mixed NaCl–KCl solutions rather than the freezing composition curve. Similarly, line *bc* gives the solubility curve for KCl in mixed NaCl–KCl solutions.

As in the case of the H$_2$O–Na$_2$SO$_4$ system, one may discuss evaporation sequences. Evaporation of a solution of composition (1) (Fig. 11-20) means that water is removed from the system, and the system composition therefore moves along the line drawn from the H$_2$O corner through point (1). When the system reaches composition *d* it is now saturated with respect to KCl, and further evaporation precipitates this salt. The solution composition moves along the *cb* line toward *b*, and at system composition *e* solution of composition *f* and solid KCl are present. The relative amounts are given, as usual, by the lever principle. At system composition *g* the solution is at *b* and has just become saturated with respect to NaCl as well. Since temperature as well as pressure is kept constant, the system has no further variance, and continued evaporation changes the proportions but not the compositions of the three phases present. For system composition *h* the lever

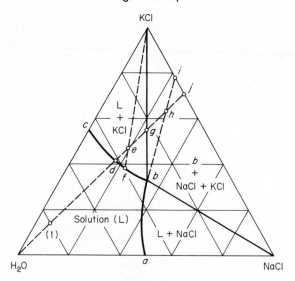

Fig. 11-20.   *Isothermal cross section (near 25°C) for the H_2O–KCl–$NaCl$ system. Illustration of an evaporation sequence.*

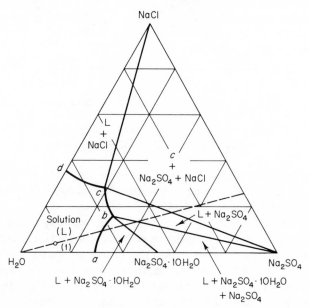

Fig. 11-21.   *The H_2O–$NaCl$–Na_2SO_4 system (near 25°C). Illustration of hydrate formation.*

bhi gives the relative amount of solution *b* and mixed solids KCl and NaCl. The lever KCl–*i*–NaCl then gives the proportion of KCl to NaCl in the mixed solids.

Another example is as follows. It will be recalled that compound formation occurred in the H_2O–Na_2SO_4 binary system; below 32°C the solid in equilibrium with saturated solution was $Na_2SO_4 \cdot 10H_2O$. It is of interest therefore to consider the ternary system H_2O–Na_2SO_4–$NaCl$. The 25°C cross section is shown in Fig. 11-21. The line *cd* is for solutions saturated with respect to NaCl. Something interesting has happened, however, along the section *bc*. This is now a solubility curve for anhydrous sodium sulfate. This equilibrium, not previously possible at 25°C, now occurs. The physical explanation is that addition of NaCl has reduced the activity of water in the solution sufficiently to make Na_2SO_4 the preferred solid phase. Further, at point *b* the solution is in equilibrium with both Na_2SO_4 and $Na_2SO_4 \cdot 10H_2O$, and water vapor pressure above this solution must be that of Fig. 11-10(d), since these two solids are in equilibrium with water vapor at this pressure and $T_c' = 25°C$.

The topology of the H_2O–Na_2SO_4–$NaCl$ diagram is such as to show the phenomenon of *retrograde solubility*. Evaporation of a solution of composition (1) leads first to precipitation of $Na_2SO_4 \cdot 10H_2O$, the composition moving toward *b*. When the solution composition reaches *b*, Na_2SO_4 is ready to precipitate, and further evaporation converts $Na_2SO_4 \cdot 10H_2O$ into Na_2SO_4 (plus solution). The decahydrate therefore *disappears* with further evaporation and the solution then moves toward composition *c*. From this point on NaCl and Na_2SO_4 precipitate out together until solution *b* has dried up.

A large number of salt solubility diagrams have been studied, and a concluding example illustrates a case of double salt formation, shown in Fig. 11-22. Here, the compound $Li_2SO_4 \cdot (NH_4)_2SO_4$ forms.

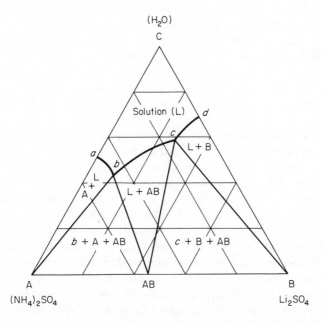

Fig. 11-22. *The* H_2O–Li_2SO_4–$(NH_4)_2SO_4$ *system (near 25°C), illustrating double salt formation.*

The more symmetric ternary eutectic systems are of great general importance in metallurgy. Salt solubility systems are similarly central to the understanding of the evaporative recovery of salts from brines. The evaporation of brines, either from sea water or from dissolved natural salt deposits, constitutes our major source of most of such minerals.

COMMENTARY AND NOTES

11-CN-1 Definitions of the Terms Component and Phase

The definitions given in Section 11-1 of the number of components of a system and of the number of phases present are adequate for the types of phase equilibria considered in this chapter. The subject is full of subtleties, however, and we now take a more careful look at what is meant by the terms component and phase.

Some explanation of the concept of a component was given in the introduction to Chapter 9. Briefly, a phase may contain a variety of molecular species but many of these will be in chemical equilibrium with each other and cannot therefore be varied independently. Pure liquid water has monomers, dimers and so on, and clusters, as well as H^+ and OH^- ions; it is a one-component system because these species are all in equilibrium with each other. Water plus alcohol has water–alcohol clusters and so on, but all compositions are fixed if the proportions of water-substance and alcohol-substance are given. The system is a two-component one.

The number of components is therefore the *minimum* number of formal compositions, such as mole fractions, needed to define the state of a system at a given T and P. A complication begins to develop in the case of electrolyte solutions. Aqueous sodium chloride is a two-component system; sodium and chloride ions cannot be varied independently because the system must remain electrically neutral. An aqueous mixture of NaCl and KNO_3 might be thought to constitute a three-component system. It is actually a special case of a four-component system. The solution contains Na^+, K^+, Cl^-, and NO_3^- ions; the four compositions are reduced by the electroneutrality requirement to three independent ones, plus water, for a total of four. Alternatively, the mole fraction of water, that of total salt, the Na^+/K^+ ratio, and the Cl^-/NO_3^- ratio define all possible compositions. As another example, aqueous sodium acetate appears to be a two-component system. Although the hydrolysis reaction

$$Ac^- + H_2O = OH^- + HAc$$

is present, its equilibrium constant defines the HAc concentration if that of sodium acetate is given. The system aqueous sodium acetate–benzene presents a complication, however. Acetic acid but virtually no sodium acetate extracts into the benzene. The composition of the benzene layer would have to be described in terms of the mole fractions of benzene and acetic acid present (plus trace amounts of water and of sodium acetate). That of the water layer would be expressed in terms of the mole fractions of water, sodium acetate, sodium hydroxide, and the small amount of dissolved benzene; The acetic acid concentration would still be determined by the hydrolysis equilibrium constant. It would appear that there are five components (water, benzene, NaAc, NaOH, and HAc), but on reflection we see that HAc can be expressed as (NaAc + H_2O − NaOH), so that by allowing for negative compositions, only four components are needed.

A second kind of problem is that the number of components may depend on whether or not a given chemical reaction is rapid within the time scale of the phase equilibrium studies. As mentioned in Section 9-1, the system hydrogen–nitrogen–ammonia consists of either two or three components according to whether or not chemical equilibrium is reached rapidly. In dealing with freezing point diagrams, we took up briefly cases of compound formation. If such formation is very slow, so that is the compound is not in equilibrium with the reactants that form it, then the compound must be treated as an additional component.

The reader can perhaps appreciate at this point why the phase rule often helps one decide just how many components are effectively present in a given system. We have mentioned the preceding complications in order to give depth to the definition of component. The actual systems described in this chapter present no such problems.

We next consider the definition of the term phase. A phase is first of all a homogeneous portion of matter, by which we mean that its time-average properties do not vary discontinuously from one spot to another. A phase region must be large enough that random, thermal fluctuations are small, otherwise the operational definition would become impossible to apply. Adjacent phase regions are marked by an interface or discontinuity in properties. The derivation of the phase rule is based on the further requirement that the chemical potentials of all components present are determined by the variables P, T, and $(C − 1)$ compositions. Neither these potentials nor any other molar thermodynamic properties ordinarily depend appreciably on the state of subdivision of the phase. Thus $H_2O(l)$ and one piece of ice is a two-phase system; likewise $H_2O(l)$ and two pieces of ice, and so on. The chemical potential of each piece of ice is the same and is independent of how many pieces are present.

A problem develops if the particles of a phase are so small that their chemical potential does depend appreciably on size owing to the surface energy contribution. The Kelvin equation (8-43) gives the free energy of a small particle as a function of T and of particle radius r. The molar free energy also depends on total mechanical pressure; it is therefore a function of P, T, and r. It is possible to derive a more general form of the phase rule which includes specific interfacial areas as state variables. It would apply, however, to the final equilibrium condition in which all condensed phases had collected into single individual regions. Thus the two pieces of ice in the preceding example should eventually become a single piece. The mechanism would probably be through the dissolving of the smaller piece (its free energy being greater because of the smaller r) and growth of the larger piece.

This matter is not a trivial one. A precipitate of AgCl, for example, initially consists of a dispersion of particle sizes. Is, now, the measured solubility that of the smaller or of the larger crystals? (It appears to be that of the smaller ones.) Such precipitates will usually age or equilibrate to what appears to be nearly the equilibrium solubility. In colloidal suspensions, however, the particles may be prevented from merging by interparticle repulsions (see Section 20-1) and may be too insoluble to age by a dissolution–reprecipitation process. The system is then metastable in this respect, even though a range of particle size is present. How many phases are present? In the case of aqueous colloidal electrolytes, there is a concentration above which aggregates of 50 to 100 monomer units, called *micelles*, form. This critical micelle concentration is not as sharply defined as is a solubility limit, but almost so. Do micelles represent a new phase?

Questions such as these arise in the study of phase equilibria, and in difficult situations the phase rule itself may be used as the criterion for establishing the number of phases present. That is, if one knows the number of components in a system and can determine the number of degrees of freedom one defines the number of phases present.

SPECIAL TOPICS

11-ST-1   Two-Component Freezing Point Diagrams. Partial Miscibility

The freezing point diagrams so far considered have all been ones for systems in which the solid phases were entirely immiscible. The other extreme is that of complete miscibility in both liquid and solid phases. The appearance would now be that of Fig. 11-2(a), repeated in Fig. 11-23(a) with the appropriate change in labeling of the phase regions. In the sequence of Fig. 11-2 a miscibility gap was made to intrude into the liquid–vapor equilibrium by gradual lowering of the pressure. In the case of liquid–solid systems we can accomplish the same result by imagining a progressive change in the properties of A and of B such that the

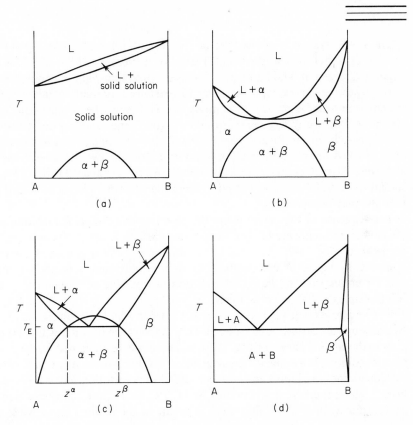

Fig. 11-23. *Progression of appearance of a freezing point diagram with increasing degree of immiscibility of the solid phases.*

miscibility in the solid state gradually decreases and the miscibility gap moves upward. The effect is to give essentially the same series of types of diagrams as before. In Fig. 11-23(b) the miscibility gap has come close to the melting points of A and B, and the incipient immiscibility is reflected in the minimum of the solid solution–liquid solution composition curves.

In Fig. 11-23(c) the miscibility gap has impacted the freezing point curves and the system is now of the eutectic type. Solution of composition x_E is in equilibrium at T_E with two solid phases. These are not pure A and B, but solid solutions of composition z^α and z^β. The letter z will be used to denote compositions of solid solutions and the Greek superscripts to indicate the type of phase. Thus an α phase is one that is rich in component A and a β phase one that is rich in component B. Further diminution of the degree of miscibility leads to Fig. 11-23(d), essentially the same as Fig. 11-3(b).

The Pb–Bi system is of the type of Fig. 11-23(c), as shown in Fig. 11-24. The cooling of a melt of composition (1) leads to a break at about 275°C as α phase begins to freeze out, and liquid and α phases would then vary in composition along their respective curves, with the latter increasing in amount. At about 175°C the system is entirely α phase [of composition (1)] and the cooling rate increases. At about 50°C the system composition line crosses the solubility curve for α phase, and β phase begins to form. There is a break in the cooling curve at this point, but not a marked one since the heat of separation into the two solid solutions is prob-ably not large. Cooling curves for compositions between 37 and 97% Bi are similar to those for a simple eutectic, except that the solid phases are α and β rather than the pure components.

The sequence of Fig. 11-23 is not the only possible one. If the melting points of the two components are fairly different and the miscibility gap is narrow, then the sequence of Fig. 11-25 may result. The diagram 11-25(b) is now of the peritectic type. At T_P liquid of composition x_P is in equilibrium with solid solutions z^α and z^β; notice that the liquid composition lies outside of those of the two solid solutions rather than between them.

Iron and gold form a peritectic system, shown in Fig. 11-26, and some representative cooling curves may be considered. That for a system of composition (1) is analogous to the cooling curve for Fig. 11-24 and need not be explained further. A system of composition (2) will show a break at about 1400°C, when α phase first forms. With continued cooling, liquid and α phase shift in composition along their respective lines, α phase increasing in amount. At 1170°C, or T_P, the solution is now also in equilibrium with β phase, and there is a halt in the cooling curve while α and β

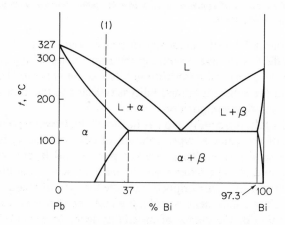

Fig. 11-24.   *The* Pb–Bi *system.*

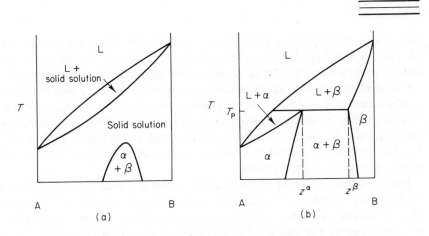

Fig. 11-25. *Development of peritectic type of freezing point diagram.*

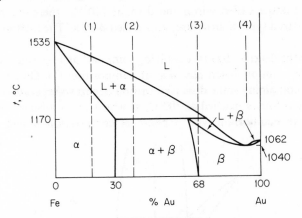

Fig. 11-26. *The* Fe–Au *system.*

phases (30 % Au and 65 % Au, respectively) crystallize out. The phase reaction is that of a peritectic system (see Section 11-3D), or L + α → β. In this case L phase is used up first, and at the end of the halt the system consists of α and β phases only.

The cooling curve for a system of composition (3) is similar to that for (2) up to the halt. Phase α is now used up first in the phase reaction, however, so L and β phase remain at the end of the halt. With further cooling, L and β phase compositions shift along their respective curves, with β phase increasing in proportion, and at about 1150°C only β phase remains. Compositions to the right of the three-phase line give cooling curves similar to (1), but with β phase forming rather than α

phase. Note that there is a slight minimum in the freezing point curve at (4), or
94% Au. A liquid of this composition freezes to β phase of the same composition,
and the cooling curve has the same appearance as that for a pure substance.

Partial miscibility may occur in the liquid region to give a phase diagram such
as illustrated in Fig. 11-27. The diagram is labeled, and one can work out the
various cooling curves by following a system composition line through the various
phase regions. A system of composition (1) would, for example, show one halt at
T_1 while L^α phase converted to L^β and α phase, and a second halt at T_E while L^β
phase converted to α and β phases.

Finally, no discussion of phase diagrams seems complete without a mention of
the iron–carbon system. The diagram, shown in Fig. 11-28, illustrates yet another
kind of partial miscibility—that between two different crystalline modifications
of a solid phase. The stable crystalline form of pure iron below 910°C is body-
centered cubic and is called α-iron. At 910°C α-iron changes to a face-centered
type of crystal lattice called γ-iron and then, at 1401°C, there is a reversion back
to a body-centered type of structure, now called δ-iron. The melting point of iron
is 1535°C.

We explore the diagram by first dissolving some carbon in γ iron at about 1200°C,
to give a solid solution called *austenite* of composition (1). On cooling to about
800°C α-iron containing some dissolved carbon begins to separate out. A eutectic-
type three-phase line is reached at 700°C, at which point austenite phase of composition a is in equilibrium with α phase of composition b and Fe_3C (called

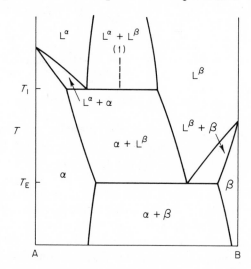

Fig. 11-27. *Partial miscibility in the liquid phases as well as in the solid phases.*

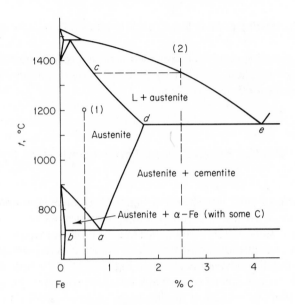

Fig. 11-28. *The Fe–C system.*

cementite). Below 700°C the system consists of α-iron (with some dissolved carbon) and cementite.

This sequence corresponds to the heat treatment of *steel.* Iron with less than about 2% carbon can be heated to the austenite single-phase region. It is then easily rolled or otherwise formed. On cooling, the separation into α-iron and cementite occurs, and the extreme hardness of cementite gives steel its strength. The rate of cooling affects the particle size of the two-phase mixture and hence the mechanical properties of the steel.

Consider next a system of composition (2) corresponding to about 2.5% C. On cooling of a molten iron–carbon solution, austenite phase of composition *c* begins to form, and with further cooling the liquid and solid solutions move in composition toward *e* and *d*, respectively, the proportion of the latter type of phase increasing. At 1125°C the eutectic is reached, and the system is now in equilibrium with Fe₃C; during the halt austenite phase of composition *d* and Fe₃C crystallize out together. Below 1125°C the system consists of Fe₃C and austenite phase of composition moving along the *da* line. At 700°C the α-iron–austenite–Fe₃C three-phase line is reached, and the further changes are as described earlier. An iron of this composition, unlike a steel, does not become a single phase until the melting point is reached. Such iron is called *cast iron*—it is not malleable when hot, but has valuable corrosion-resistant properties. If of composition close to the eutectic, its melting point is low enough to allow a fairly easy casting procedure.

The remaining small region in the upper left is of no great interest here. One can trace the details of its phase behavior by following system composition lines that pass through various portions of the region.

11-ST-2   Partial Miscibility in Three-Component Systems

The water–phenol system was shown in Fig. 9-21(a); there is an upper consolute temperature of about 70°C and around room temperature the miscibility is rather limited. Acetone is fully miscible with water and with phenol separately and when it is added to a water–phenol two-phase system the effect is to increase the mutual solubility. The solubility behavior is shown in Fig. 11-29 for a temperature of about 30°C. The tie-lines connect pairs of mutually saturated solutions. Thus a system of overall composition (1) consists of liquid phases of compositions a and b and in amounts given by the lever principle. Addition of acetone moves the system composition along the line drawn from point (1) to the acetone corner, the compositions

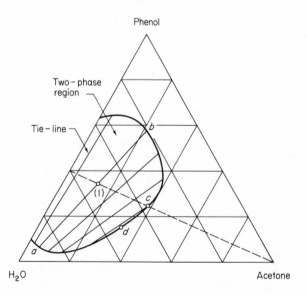

Fig. 11-29. *The three-component miscibility gap. The H_2O–acetone–phenol system.*

of the two liquid phases being given by the ends of each successive tie-line. When the system composition reaches *c* only a single phase is present and further addition of acetone merely dilutes the liquid solution. The tie-lines themselves reach a vanishing point at *d* called the *critical point.*

The whole region of partial miscibility diminishes in size with increasing temperature, and a set of isothermal cross sections generates a helmet-shaped two-phase region in the three-dimensional phase diagram, as illustrated in Fig. 11-30.

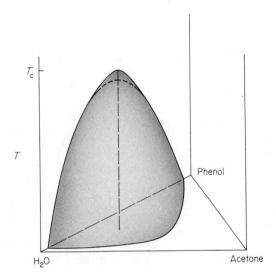

Fig. 11-30. *The three-component miscibility gap in three dimensions.*

The locus of successive critical points goes through the peak of the helmet (at 92°C, 59 % water and 29 % phenol), which is the *critical temperature* of the ternary system. Various cooling or dilution sequences may be traced out in the usual way by following the system composition line and, where it is in the two-phase region, using the ends of the tie-line through it to determine the compositions of the liquid phases present.

It must be remembered that while a tie-line is an isothermal line, there is no requirement that a set of lines such as for Fig. 11-29 be parallel. The ends of each successive line must be determined by individual experiment, and a set of tie-lines must be shown if the diagram is to be usable.

A number of types of miscibility gaps are possible for a ternary system, as illustrated in Fig. 11-31. Figure 11-31(d) represents the case of partial miscibility in all three binary systems and Fig. 11-31(e) shows the result of a further decrease in

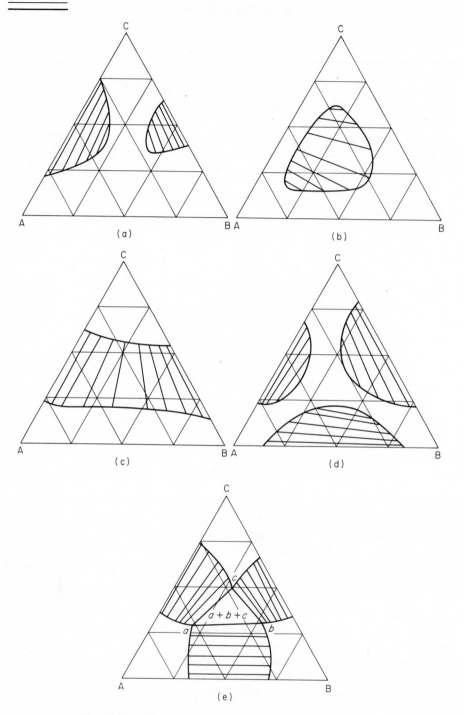

Fig. 11-31. *Various types of three-component miscibility gaps.*

miscibility, such as by lowering of the temperature. The three miscibility gaps have now merged to frame a central triangular region of three phase equilibrium.

Three-component freezing point diagrams with partial miscibility in the solid phases add partial miscibility regions to Fig. 11-15. A perspective drawing of such a model is shown in Fig. 11-32; the reader may enjoy working out the various phase

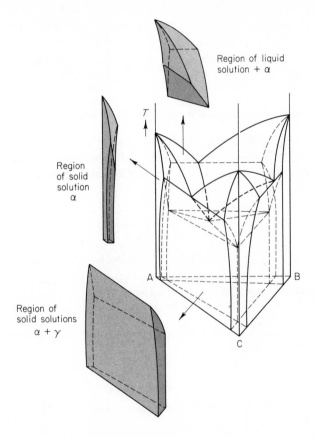

Region of liquid
solution + α

Region
of solid
solution
α

Region of
solid solutions
α + γ

Fig. 11-32. *Three-component eutectic system with partial miscibility in the solid phases.*

regions. As with all models based on the prismatic coordinate scheme, each side shows a two-component phase diagram. The various elementary types of two-component freezing point diagrams that have been described are given in Table 11-1. Other miscibility combinations are clearly possible, and the variety of standard types is rather large. Any combination of three of these may form the

Table 11-1.

General type	Miscibility characteristics Liquid region	Solid region	Example Fig. No.
Eutectic	Miscible	Immiscible	3, 7
	Miscible	Partially miscible	23(c, d), 24
	Miscible	Miscible	23(a)
	Partially miscible	Partially miscible	27
Peritectic	Miscible	Partially miscible	25, 26
Compound formation	Miscible	Immiscible	7, 11, 12
Unstable compound	Miscible	Immiscible	8, 9, 13
Polymorphism	Miscible	Partially miscible	28

three faces of the prismatic model of a ternary system, and so there are a formidable number of possible "simple" ternary systems. Most of these possibilities have been observed but their analysis is definitely beyond the scope of this text.

GENERAL REFERENCES

MARSH, J. S. (1935). "Principles of Phase Diagrams." McGraw-Hill, New York.
MASING, G. (1944). "Ternary Systems" (translated by B. A. Rogers). Dover, New York.
RICCI, J. E. (1951). "The Phase Rule and Heterogeneous Equilibrium." Van Nostrand–Reinhold, Princeton, New Jersey.
WETMORE, F. E. W., AND LeROY, D. J. (1951). "Principles of Phase Equilibria." McGraw-Hill, New York.

CITED REFERENCE

LIGHTFOOT, W. J., AND PRUTTON, C. F. (1947). *J. Amer. Chem. Soc.* **69**, 2098.

Exercises

11-1 How many degrees of freedom are present for the following systems: (a) ice plus a solution of alcohol and water; (b) a layer of water saturated with phenol plus a layer of phenol saturated with water plus equilibrium vapor, all at 25°C; (c) a solution of sodium chloride plus equilibrium vapor; (d) a solution of sodium chloride and potassium chloride at 25°C?

Ans. (a) 2; (b) 0; (c) 2; (d) 3.

Problems

11-2 In Fig. 11-3, composition x_2 is about 50% B and composition x_E is about 70% B. A liquid of composition x_2 is cooled to just above T_E; calculate the per cent that has frozen out at this point and give the composition of the remaining liquid.

Ans. 29%, 70% B.

11-3 As a continuation of Exercise 11-2, how long should the halt at T_E be if the heats of fusion of A and B are 5 and 7 kcal mole^{-1}, respectively, and the rate of removal of heat is 100 cal min^{-1}? One-tenth of a mole of system is present.

Ans. 4.5 min.

11-4 The break and halt temperatures for the cooling curves of solutions of metals A and B are given in the accompanying table. Construct a phase diagram consistent with these data and label the phase regions. Give the probable formulas for any compounds.

Mole % A	First break (°C)	First halt (°C)	Second halt (°C)
100	—	1100	—
90	1060	700	—
80	1000	700	—
70	940	700	400
60	850	700	400
50	750	700	400
40	670	400	—
30	550	400	—
20	—	400	—
10	—	400	—
0	—	500	—

Ans. The compound A_3B is suggested.

11-5 Explain at what temperature the evaporation of aqueous ferric chloride should lead to two successive solidifications and liquefactions of the system.

Ans. About 40°C (see Fig. 11-11).

11-6 Assume that Fig. 11-20 is scaled in weight percent. One hundred grams of solution of composition (1) is evaporated at 25°C until KCl first begins to precipitate. (a) How many grams of solution remain at this point? The system is then evaporated until NaCl begins to precipitate out. (b) How many grams of solution remain at this point? (c) Give the amounts and compositions of the phases present when 95% of the original water has been evaporated.

Ans. (a) 32 g; (b) 16 g; (c) 12 g of solution of composition (b), 1.4 g of NaCl and 9.6 g of KCl.

Problems

The general instruction for the following problems is to draw the simplest phase diagram consistent with the information given and to label the various phase regions as to the number and nature of the phases present. The instructor may ask for various cooling curves to be sketched and labeled.

		Melting points (°C)			
Al	658	Fe	1535	Ni	1452
Sb	630	Pb	327	Na	98
Bi	273	Mg	651	Tl	303
Ca	810	Hg	−39	Zn	420
Co	1480	Mo	2535		

11-1 Mercury and lead dissolve in all proportions in the liquid state and they form no compounds. A liquid phase is in equilibrium at −40°C with two crystalline phases containing 35% and 100% Hg, respectively.

11-2 Bismuth and lead form no compounds; solid solutions containing 1% and 63% lead are in equilibrium with a liquid containing 43% lead at 125°C.

11-3 Calcium and sodium mix in all proportions in the liquid state above 1150°C, the mutual solubilities are 33% Na and 82% Na at 1000°C, liquids of 14 and 93% Na are in equilibrium with solid calcium at 710°C; the eutectic temperature is 97.5°C and no compounds or solid solutions form.

11-4 Liquid and solid phases of the composition Hg_5Tl_2 are in equilibrium at 14°C; the phases at 0°C are a liquid of 40% Tl and solid solutions of 32% and 84% Tl; the phases at −59°C are Hg, a liquid of 8% Tl, and a solution of 22% Tl.

11-5 Solids A and B melt at 750 and 1280°C, respectively, and form no compounds. The melt is in equilibrium with solid solutions containing 20% A and 60% A at 900°C. Draw the phase diagram, and cooling curves for melts of the following compositions: 90% A, 50% A, 18% A, 5% A.

11-6 In the isothermal, isobaric system H_2O–NH_4Cl–$HgCl_2$ the compounds are [P] $(NH_4Cl)_2$ $(HgCl_2)H_2O$, [Q] $(NH_4Cl)(HgCl_2)H_2O$, [R] $(NH_4Cl)_2(HgCl_2)_3H_2O$, [S] $(NH_4Cl)_2(HgCl_2)_9$. Indicate and label the phase regions, and discuss the evaporation of the various solutions.

11-7 No compounds are formed in the system AgCl–LiCl. The solids are partially miscible, and at 480°C melt is in equilibrium with solid solutions containing 15% and 30% AgCl, respectively. The melting points are 455°C and 610°C for AgCl and LiCl, respectively.

11-8 Magnesium and nickel form a compound $MgNi_2$ that melts at 1145°C and a compound Mg_2Ni that decomposes at 770°C into a liquid containing 30 mole % nickel and the other compound. The eutectics are at 23% nickel and 510°C and 89% nickel and 1080°C.

11-9 Aluminum and cobalt form three compounds, of which AlCo melts at 1630°C, Al_5Co_2 decomposes at 1170°C, and Al_4Co decomposes at 945°C. AlCo and Co form an incomplete series of solid solutions, with solid containing 84 mole % Co, liquid containing 89 mole % Co, and solid containing 92 mole % Co in equilibrium at 1375°C.

Problems

11-10 Describe the nature and number of phases present on evaporating a dilute solution of sodium sulfate in water isothermally at 10°C. Describe the result when a solution initially saturated with sodium sulfate at 35°C is gradually cooled to 0°C.

11-11 The following data have been obtained for the isobaric system As_2O_5–K_3AsO_4. Compounds: As_2O_5 melts at 700°C, $KAsO_3$ melts at 650°C, $K_5As_3O_{10}$ melts at 650°C (unstable; ordinarily the compound decomposes at 630°C), $K_4As_2O_7$ melts at 996°C, K_3AsO_4 melts at 1310°C.

Eutectic mixture	t_E (°C)	Mole % K_3AsO_4
As_2O_5–$KAsO_3$	570	42
$K_4As_2O_7$–K_3AsO_4	965	86
$KAsO_3$–$K_5As_3O_{10}$	542	58

(a) Plot the phase diagram for this system; label each phase region. Express composition as mole % K_3AsO_4. (b) Describe what happens on slowly cooling melts of the compositions (1) 71.3 % K_3AsO_4, (2) 60 % K_3AsO_4, (3) 75 % K_3AsO_4. (c) Draw semiquantitative cooling curves for (b).

11-12 Nickel and molybdenum form one compound, MoNi, which decomposes at 1345°C into molybdenum and a liquid containing 53 % Mo. The phases at the only eutectic, 1300°C, are MoNi, a liquid of 48 % Mo, and a solid solution of 32 % Mo.

11-13 $MgZn_2$ melts at 590°C and there are four temperatures in the Mg–Zn system at which three phases exist, with percentages of Zn as follows: 340°C, α (8 %) + liquid (53 %) + MgZn; 354°C, liquid (55 %) + MgZn + $MgZn_2$; 380°C, liquid (96 %) + $MgZn_2$ + $MgZn_5$; 364°C, liquid (97 %) + $MgZn_5$ + Zn.

11-14 Iron and Fe_3Sb_2 (melting point 1015°C) form solid solutions in one another to a limited extent, and $FeSb_2$ decomposes at 728°C into a liquid and the other compound. The eutectics are at 1000 and 628°C.

11-15 The following data refer to the system K_2SO_4–$(NH_4)_2SO_4$–H_2O at 30°C. In each line of data are given the compositions of a saturated solution and of a moist solid (solid solutions are formed) (in weight per cent).

Saturated solution		Solid	
K_2SO_4	$(NH_4)_2SO_4$	K_2SO_4	$(NH_4)_2SO_4$
0	44.2	[only $(NH_4)_2SO_4$]	
1.2	42.7	1.6	90.3
2.4	40.9	22.1	69.3
4.1	37.8	33.9	57.8
4.9	33.5	50.8	42.3
6.4	31.0	62.2	30.0
9.1	18.5	84.0	12.7
10.7	8.4	93.2	3.1
11.2	0	(only K_2SO_4)	

Draw the triangular diagram and label all phase regions for the K_2SO_4–$(NH_4)_2(SO_4)$–H_2O system. A system containing 90 g of water and 10 g each of K_2SO_4 and $(NH_4)_2(SO_4)$ is evaporated isothermally at 42°. (a) What is the composition of the solution when a precipitate first appears and what is the composition of the precipitate? (b) What is the composition of the last solution to exist before the system solidifies? Give the compositions and amounts of the solid(s) present. (c) When the system reaches the point of containing 40% by weight of water what phases are present and in what amounts? Show your calculations and indicate them graphically on your diagram insofar as possible.

11-16 The following isothermal data are for the system CrO_3–Na_2O–H_2O; they give the solution compositions for each compound.

			Saturated solution	
Solid phase	Wt % CrO_3	Wt % Na_2O	g CrO_3 per 100 g H_2O	g Na_2O per 100 g H_2O
$NaOH \cdot H_2O$	0	42	0	72.4
	2.00	41.44	3.54	73.4
Na_2CrO_4	2.91	37.50	4.33	63.0
	4.23	35.51	7.01	58.9
	6.64	32.34	10.9	53.0
	10.21	29.70	17.0	49.4
(unstable)	15.19	27.06	26.3	46.8
	10.22	29.39	16.9	48.7
$Na_4CrO_5 \cdot 13H_2O$	8.93	28.49	14.4	45.5
	8.62	26.91	13.4	41.7
	10.74	25.55	16.9	40.2
	13.12	23.91	20.8	38.0
	17.73	23.13	30.0	39.1
	18.44	22.86	31.4	39.0
	19.26	22.98	33.4	39.8
$Na_2CrO_4 \cdot 4H_2O$ (unstable)	17.84	24.21	30.8	41.8
	20.06	22.03	34.6	38.1
	22.20	20.67	39.9	36.2
	28.82	17.88	54.0	33.5
	38.93	16.30	86.9	36.4
	48.7	16.49	139.8	47.3
$Na_2Cr_2O_7 \cdot 2H_2O$	50.68	15.72	150.8	46.8
	55.09	14.44	180.5	47.4
	58.08	13.89	207	49.5
	64.24	13.67	305	65.0
	66.13	13.70	328	67.8
$Na_2Cr_3O_{10} \cdot H_2O$	67.37	12.52	332	62.4
	68.46	10.95	336	53.7
$Na_2Cr_4O_{13} \cdot 4H_2O$	66.88	9.85	287	42.3
CrO_3	76.72	6.31	235	22.5
	64.48	4.51	208	14.6
	62.28	0	165	0

Problems

Make a triangular plot of this system. Label all phase regions. Locate on the triangular diagram the following points:

	CrO_3 (wt %)	Na_2O (wt %)		CrO_3 (wt %)	Na_2O (wt %)
a	5	25	d	2	35
b	6.1	3.9	e	7	78
c	40	10			

Describe what would happen when these solutions are evaporated at constant temperature.

11-17 The following data were obtained by W. J. Lightfoot and C. F. Prutton (1947) on the system $CaCl_2$–KCl–H_2O at 75°C:

Saturated solution (wt %)		
$CaCl_2$	KCl	Solid phase
0	33.16	KCl
11.73	21.62	KCl
18.27	16.00	KCl
28.47	9.62	KCl
37.65	6.77	KCl
47.65	8.43	KCl
50.19	10.32	KCl and $2KCl \cdot CaCl_2 \cdot 2H_2O$
50.92	9.36	$2KCl \cdot CaCl_2 \cdot 2H_2O$
53.85	6.21	$2KCl \cdot CaCl_2 \cdot 2H_2O$
56.33	4.51	$2KCl \cdot CaCl_2 \cdot 2H_2O$
57.62	3.60	$2KCl \cdot CaCl_2 \cdot 2H_2O$ and $CaCl_2 \cdot 2H_2O$
57.77	2.56	$CaCl_2 \cdot 2H_2O$
58.58	0	$CaCl_2 \cdot 2H_2O$

Construct the triangular plot for this system; label all phase regions. Describe what would happen on isothermal evaporation at 75°C of a solution initially containing 85 % water, 10 % $CaCl_2$ and 5 % KCl. Assume 100 g of solution. How many grams of H_2O have been evaporated when half the weight of the system is in solids?

11-18 Mercury and lead dissolve in all proportions in the liquid state and they form no compounds. A liquid phase is in equilibrium at −40°C with two crystalline phases containing 35 and 100 % Hg, respectively.

11-19 The following are phase diagrams for various binary systems; they are melting point diagrams in the sense that the upper regions generally contain only liquid phases. State the *number* and *type* of phases present in each *area* and *label each line of three-phase equilibrium*.

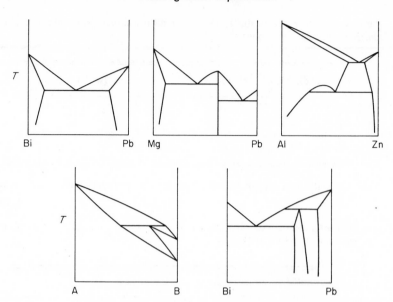

11-20 Construct the $Fe_2Cl_6 \cdot H_2O$ diagram given the following data. The headings give the solid phase in equilibrium with solution of indicated compositions (mole fraction of Fe_2Cl_6, right column) and temperatures (°C, left column).

Ice		$Fe_2Cl_6 \cdot 12H_2O$		$Fe_2Cl_6 \cdot 7H_2O$	
−55	0.0267	−55	0.0268	20	0.102
−40	0.0231	−41	0.0273	27.4	0.108
−27.5	0.0186	−27	0.0289	32	0.1195
−20.5	0.0162	0	0.0396	32.5	0.125
−10	0.0099	10	0.0434	30	0.131
0	0.0000	20	0.0485	25	0.1345
		30	0.0562		
		35	0.0635		
$Fe_2Cl_6 \cdot 5H_2O$		36.5	0.0736	$Fe_2Cl_6 \cdot 4H_2O$	
		37	0.0768		
12	0.1145	36	0.0847	50	0.1665
20	0.1225	33	0.0912	55	0.1685
27	0.1295	30	0.1005	60	0.172
30	0.1315	27.4	0.108	69	0.178
35	0.1355	20	0.114	72.5	0.192
45	0.149	10	0.116	73.5	0.200
55	0.1605	8	0.1205	72.5	0.207
56	0.167			70	0.218
55	0.169	Fe_2Cl_6		66	0.226
		66	0.225		
		70	0.224		
		75	0.2235		
		80	0.225		
		100	0.229		

Describe in detail the succession of phase changes that would occur on the isothermal evaporation at 32°C of a dilute solution of ferric chloride. What would happen on cooling a solution containing 15 mole % Fe_2Cl_6? (Be sure to label all regions of your diagram.)

11-21 Magnesium and antimony form a compound Mg_3Sb_2 which melts at 961°C; the eutectics are at 627°C and 39% Sb and at 594°C and 95% Sb. Draw the phase diagram; label the phase regions.

11-22 Calcium and sodium mix in all proportions in the liquid state above 1150°C. The mutual solubilities are 33% Na and 82% Na at 1000°C; liquids of 14% and 93% Na are in equilibrium with solid calcium at 710°C; the eutectic temperature is 97.5°C and no compounds or solid solutions form.

11-23 Iron and Fe_3Sb_2 (melting point 1015°C) form solid solutions to a limited extent and $FeSb_2$ decomposes at 728°C into a liquid and the other compound. The eutectics are at 1000°C and 628°C.

11-24 Metals A and B form ideal solutions and are completely immiscible in the solid phase. Calculate the simple eutectic diagram for this system using the freezing point depression equation of Chapter 10; the melting points are 500°C and 800°C, respectively, the pure metals both have 4.0 cal °K^{-1} $mole^{-1}$ entropy of fusion, and both obey the Dulong and Petit heat capacity relationship. Calculate and plot the actual cooling curves for solutions containing 100% A, 80% A, and of the eutectic composition, assuming 0.1 mole of solution is used in each case and that the rate of heat removal is 200 cal min^{-1}.

Special Topics Problems

11-1 Sketch and label a set of cooling curves for the system of Fig. 11-24; these should be for 10, 20, 30, 50, and 70% Bi.

11-2 Sketch and label the set of cooling curves for the marked compositions in Fig. 11-26.

11-3 Describe the sequence of phase changes when water is added to a system of composition (1) in Fig. 11-29. Calculate the amounts of acetone and of phenol that should be added to system (1) to bring it to composition d in the diagram.

11-4 For each of the systems of Fig. 11-31 describe the sequence of changes if B is added to a 1:1 mixture of A and C.

12 SOLUTIONS OF ELECTROLYTES

12-1 Introduction

The historical development of electrochemistry constitutes one of the more interesting stories of science. It begins, for us, with observations made in 1600 by W. Gilbert, physician to Queen Elizabeth, on the ability of amber to attract pith or other light objects when rubbed with a piece of fur. Gilbert coined the word *electric* (from the Greek for amber) in describing such behavior. Benjamin Franklin became interested in the subject and suggested, around 1750, that the different behavior of electrostatically charged glass and amber was not due to two kinds of electricity, but rather to an excess or deficiency of an electric "fluid." Thus began the subject of electrostatics, which culminated around 1890 with the identification of the electron as the unit of electricity.

Another chain of events led to the discovery of a second kind of electricity. The story traces back to 1678 when Swammerdam demonstrated before the Grand Duke of Tuscany that a frog's leg resting on a copper support would twitch when touched with a silver wire connected to the copper. We are more familiar with the experiments of L. Galvani in 1790, who observed that a frog's leg (again) would twitch when connected to a static electricity generator or when the nerve was merely touched with a metal strip which was connected to the end of the leg. The terms *galvanic electricity* and *galvanometer* honor this discovery. By 1800 A. Volta succeeded in producing visible sparks from a stack of alternate silver and zinc plates. This was the first battery, then called a *voltaic pile* or a *galvanic cell*. The first definite experiment in electrochemistry appears to have been made by W. Nicholson and A. Carlisle in 1800, who used a galvanic cell to electrolyze water. By 1807 H. Davy had isolated sodium and potassium by the electrolysis of their hydroxides.

The foundation of modern electrochemistry was laid by M. Faraday, working around 1830 at the Royal Institution. He showed that a given quantity of electricity produced a fixed amount of electrolysis and formulated the following now well-known laws:

1. The amount of chemical decomposition produced by a current is proportional to the quantity of electricity passed.
2. The amounts of different substances deposited or dissolved by a given quantity of electricity are proportional to their chemical equivalent weights.

Faraday's contribution is of an importance comparable to that of Joule in finding the mechanical equivalent of heat. In modern language, Faraday determined the electrochemical equivalence, or the amount of electricity corresponding to one mole of electrons. This equivalence, which we call the *Faraday constant* $\mathscr{F}$ is

$$\mathscr{F} = N_0 e = (6.02252 \times 10^{23})(1.6021 \times 10^{-19}) = 96,487 \quad \text{C mole}^{-1},$$

where N_0 is Avogadro's number and e is the charge on the electron; C is the abbreviation for the coulomb. Our name for the natural unit of charge, the *electron*, was proposed, incidentally, by G. Stoney in 1874.

A great number of interesting and perceptive experiments have been passed over in this account. Much of our basic nomenclature originated during Faraday's time: *anode* and *cathode* for the positive and negative pole, respectively, of a battery; *ion* (Greek for wanderer) for the carrier of electricity in solution; *ampere* for the unit of current; and *ohm* for the measure of electrical resistance. The latter two terms are, of course, in recognition of the pioneer investigations of A.M. Ampère and G.S. Ohm.

The mechanism whereby current is transported through solutions of salts took nearly a century to be understood after the first observations of the phenomenon by Davy and others. An early idea was that of T. von Grotthus, who suggested in 1805 that an electrolyte consisted of polar molecules which lined up in an electric field and, by exchanging ends, passed electricity down a chain. He was trying to explain how electricity could go through a solution and yet cause electrolysis only at the electrodes. As illustrated in Fig. 12-1, his thought was that application of a potential across the electrodes caused the polar molecules to break and reform in such a way as to leave a negative piece of one at the anode and a positive piece of another at the cathode. The idea was clever, and will be invoked in more modern language in explanation of the motion of hydrogen ions.

As originally stated, the Grotthus mechanism was untenable on various grounds: Electrolyte "molecules" are not that close together in solution; why should even the weakest potential be able to cause strong molecules to break up; and so on. The hypothesis was largely demolished in 1857 by R. Clausius. Clausius proposed instead that the positive and negative parts of the electrolyte molecule were always

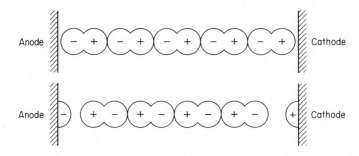

Fig. 12-1. *Illustration of the original Grotthus mechanism.*

partially present as fragments or ions, which then carried the current. We would call his proposal one of partial dissociation. It was a compromise in the sense that it was very difficult to accept that a molecule could break up or dissociate, and Clausius theorized that only a small fraction of the molecules actually did so.

We come now to the last quarter of the nineteenth century. J. van't Hoff and his group made colligative property measurements on sugar solutions and then on aqueous electrolytes, They reported large *i* factors [Eq. (10-58)] in the latter case. Thus *i* was close to two for NaCl solutions. S. Arrhenius drew heavily on van't Hoff's work in proposing the theory of electrolytic dissociation in 1883. The theory amounted to an assertion that electrolytes were mostly and not just partially dissociated into ions. During this last period the giants of electrochemistry were Arrhenius, F. Kohlrausch, W. Ostwald, and van't Hoff. Kohlrausch and his school carried out a monumental number of experiments on the conductance of electrolyte solutions, establishing that they obeyed Ohm's law. Thus the terms *specific conductivity* and *equivalent conductivity* were defined, and the major rules governing the variation of conductance with concentration were formulated. Ostwald did much to clarify the behavior of what we now call *weak electrolytes*, or ones which behave essentially as Clausius had proposed much earlier.

The basic framework of electrochemistry was thus in place by the turn of the century. The early 1900's were spent in more and more precise studies of electrolyte solutions. The next major advances were made in the 1920's, in the treatment of the forces between ions, which determined the quantitative aspects of their motion through a solvent and their thermodynamic properties. A major theory by P. Debye and E. Hückel led, in 1923, to an enduring picture of dilute electrolyte solutions. Each ion tends to have around it an excess concentration of oppositely charged ions, which form a statistical or diffuse *atmosphere*. This atmosphere contributes to the thermodynamic chemical potential of the ion and hence to its activity coefficient. At about the same time, J. Brønsted and N. Bjerrum (in Copenhagen) made lasting contributions both to the understanding of acid and base strengths and in establishing that ions could form *ion pairs* in more concentrated solutions.

Late in the same decade, L. Onsager extended the Debye–Hückel theory to treat dynamic effects such as conductance and diffusion, Later, with I. Prigogine, he was a leader in developing the general thermodynamic treatment of irreversible processes. Still later, R. Tolman and J. Kirkwood pioneered the development of the statistical mechanical theory of solutions—a task yet to be finished.

We begin the subject of electrochemistry with the important new property of electrolyte solutions—that of *conductance*. The separate behavior of each kind of ion is then discussed in terms of ionic mobilities and of transference numbers. The chapter moves on to a presentation of the Debye–Hückel treatment of the non-ideality of electrolyte solutions and concludes with a study of ionic equilibria.

12-2 Conductivity—Experimental Definitions and Procedures

A. Defining Equations

The various systems of electrical units were reviewed in Section 3-CN-2. It was noted there that international commissions have recommended the uniform adoption of the mksa/SI system of units, one of the advantages being that the esu and emu systems are merged into a single one. Experimental electrochemistry makes use of the volt (V), ampere (A), coulomb (C), and ohm (Ω)—all accepted in the mksa/SI recommendations.

As noted in Section 3-CN-2, the ampere is defined in terms of the magnetic field produced by current i flowing in a loop of wire. The coulomb is the quantity of electricity q corresponding to a current of 1 A flowing for 1 sec, or in general, $q = it$ (or $\int i \, dt$). The unit of potential V is the volt; it requires 1 J (joule) of energy to transport 1 C of charge across 1 V potential difference. Resistance R is defined in terms of Ohm's law,

$$V = iR. \tag{12-1}$$

A current of 1 A flowing through a resistance of one ohm produces a voltage drop of 1 V. The resistance R is, of course, a function of temperature and, in the case of electrolyte solutions, of concentration.

Ohm's law can be thought of both as an ideal law and as the limiting law for small V and i. It is well obeyed by all substances, provided the energy dissipated does not result in appreciable local heating and provided that the current-carrying species are not made to move much faster than their natural diffusion rates. In the case of electrolyte solutions Ohm's law begins to fail at high voltages because ionic velocities become large enough that the distortion of the diffuse ion atmosphere around each ion ceases to be proportional to its velocity. In the case of metals current is carried by electrons, and there is no problem in this last respect. The same is true for semiconductors, which differ from metals mainly in that the concentration of conduction electrons is small and increases exponentially with temperature so that the resistance is very temperature-dependent.

The resistance of a substance is proportional to its thickness l and inversely proportional to the cross-sectional area $\mathscr{A}$. One therefore generally reports a specific resistance or *resistivity* ρ defined by

$$R = \frac{l}{\mathscr{A}} \rho. \tag{12-2}$$

The resistivity ρ is given in ohm centimeter in the cgs system and ohm meter in the mksa/SI system. Although resistance is the measured quantity, its reciprocal, the *conductance*, is more useful in dealing with electrolyte solutions. Conductance L is defined as

$$L = \frac{1}{R} \tag{12-3}$$

and *specific conductivity* κ as

$$\kappa = \frac{1}{\rho} = \frac{l}{\mathscr{A}} \frac{1}{R}. \tag{12-4}$$

As will be seen later, the ratio $l/\mathscr{A}$ is usually treated as an apparatus or cell constant and is given the symbol k. Thus

$$R = k\rho, \tag{12-5}$$

$$\kappa = kL. \tag{12-6}$$

(A considerable range of symbols will be found for these quantities; the ones here are the mksa/SI ones, except that L rather than G is used to denote conductance.)

An electrolyte solution conducts electricity by several paths. Each ion contributes, including those from the self-ionization of the solvent. The situation is therefore one of resistances in parallel so that the total resistance obeys the law

$$\frac{1}{R_{obs}} = \frac{1}{R_1} + \frac{1}{R_2} + \frac{1}{R_3} + \cdots.$$

Conductances are thus additive:

$$L_{obs} = L_1 + L_2 + L_3 + \cdots. \tag{12-7}$$

Hence their great utility in this situation. One is ordinarily interested just in the contribution to the observed conductance by the electrolyte and therefore subtracts out that due to the medium L_0:

$$L = L_{obs} - L_0. \tag{12-8}$$

The same relation will, of course, apply to specific conductivities:

$$\kappa = \kappa_{obs} - \kappa_0. \tag{12-9}$$

One of the first quantitative observations was that the net specific conductivity of a solution is approximately proportional to the electrolyte concentration. It should be exactly so if each ion were a completely independent agent since each would then make its separate, additive contribution to κ. A very useful quantity is therefore the *equivalent conductivity*, Λ, which is the value of κ contributed by 1 equiv. of ions of either charge. We consider a portion of the electrolyte solution which is 1 cm deep and of area such that the volume contains one mole of charge due to the ions of the electrolyte (with only the positive or only the negative ions being considered). The number of moles of such charge per liter will be designated by C^*, the concentration in equivalents of ions per liter whenever we wish to emphasize the distinction between actual ion concentration and equivalents of electrolyte per liter, C. The volume (in cubic centimeters) required to contain one mole of ions is $1000/C^*$ and the area (in square centimeters) of the required portion of solution is then $1000/C^*$. It follows from Eq. (12-6) that

$$\Lambda \quad (= L \quad \text{for 1 equiv}) = \frac{\kappa}{k} = \kappa \frac{\mathscr{A}}{l},$$

or, since $\mathscr{A} = 1000/C^*$ and $l = 1$,

$$\Lambda = \frac{1000}{C^*} \kappa. \tag{12-10}$$

The above language is somewhat carefully phrased. We want Λ to be the conductivity ascribable to 1 equiv of actual ions. For a strong electrolyte, such as NaCl or Na_2SO_4, $C^* = M_{NaCl} = M_{Na_2SO_4}/2$, and so on, where M is the molarity. That is, C^* is the molarity divided by the number of positive ion charges (or the number of negative ion charges) per formula weight, and corresponds to the usual definition of equivalents per liter. In the case of a weak electrolyte, such as acetic acid, however, C^* should be the concentration of actual ions present per liter of solution; the concentration of undissociated acetic acid is not to be included. If the solute is not fully dissociated or if there is doubt on the matter, one may write

$$\Lambda_{\text{app}} = \frac{1000}{C} \kappa, \tag{12-11}$$

where Λ_{app} is the apparent equivalent conductivity, obtained with C, the formal concentration in equivalents per liter. "Formal" means the number of gram equivalent weights of the solute present.

The various defining equations are summarized in Table 12-1.

B. Measurement of Conductance

The actual quantity measured for an electrolyte solution is its electrical resistance R. This is usually done by means of a Wheatstone bridge, the basic scheme of which is shown in Fig. 12-2. In its simplest form, the galvanometer G shows no current flow when $R_x/R_1 = R_2/R_3$. In practice, it is very important first of all that

Table 12-1. *Definitions of Electrical Quantities*

Quantity	Symbol	Units Cgs	mksa/SI	Defining relationship[a]	Equation number
Resistance	R	ohm	ohm	$V = iR$	(12-1)
Specific resistance	ρ	ohm cm	ohm m	$\rho = \dfrac{\mathscr{A}}{l} R$	(12-2)
Conductance	L	ohm^{-1} (or mho)	ohm^{-1}	$L = \dfrac{1}{R}$	(12-3)
Specific conductivity	κ	ohm^{-1} cm^{-1}	ohm^{-1} m^{-1}	$\kappa = \dfrac{1}{\rho} = \dfrac{l}{\mathscr{A} R}$	(12-4)
Cell constant	k	cm^{-1}	m^{-1}	$k = \dfrac{l}{\mathscr{A}}$	
Equivalent conductivity	Λ	cm^2 equiv^{-1} ohm^{-1}	m^2 equiv^{-1} ohm^{-1}	$\Lambda = \dfrac{1000}{C^{*}} \kappa$	(12-10)

[a] Here V is the potential difference and i the current between electrodes of effective area $\mathscr{A}$ and separation l.

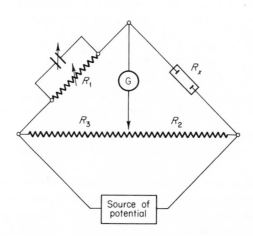

Fig. 12-2. *Schematic diagram of a Wheatstone bridge.*

the electrodes of the cell used have identical electrode potentials; otherwise a voltage change across the cell will be present in addition to the voltage drop due to Ohm's law. This requirement is usually met by the use of identical reversible electrodes, such as platinized platinum, and an alternating source of potential. This last avoids having any appreciable net electrolysis at the electrodes and hence buildup of electrolysis products. The use of the ac bridge introduces another problem, however, namely that due to the capacitance of the cell. There must now be a means for balancing out capacity differences across the two legs of the bridge, or otherwise the ac galvanometer (often an oscilloscope) will not register a point of zero current. The reader is referred to experimental texts for further details.

The typical measurement, then, is of R_x, the resistance of the cell, first when filled with the solvent medium and then when filled with the electrolyte solution. Application of Eq. (12-8) then gives the net conductance L due to the solute.

The second experimental problem is the reduction of L to a specific conductivity κ. The defining equation (12-4) is not easily applied in practice since l is not exactly the distance between the electrodes and $\mathscr{A}$ is not exactly the area of the electrodes. The reason is that ions lying outside of the cylinder defined by the two electrodes still experience potential gradients and contribute to the conductivity. Extensive and careful studies have allowed for this contribution, with the result that accurate specific conductivities are known for several standard electrolyte solutions. One such standard is a solution containing 0.74526 g KCl per 1000 g of solution, whose specific conductivity at 25°C is 0.0014088 ohm^{-1} cm^{-1}. [See Daniels *et al.* (1956) for further details.] Alternatively, the specific conductivities of 0.1 *M* and 0.01 *M* KCl are 0.012886 and 0.0014114 ohm^{-1} cm^{-1} at 25°C, respectively.

The availability of precise, absolute specific conductivities allows the problem of determining the l and $\mathscr{A}$ values for a cell to be by-passed. One measures the resistance of the cell when filled with a standard solution and calculates the cell constant k by means of Eq. (12-5). The same cell constant applies to a measurement with any other solution (in very precise work, the standard and unknown solutions should have about the same resistance). One then uses k to calculate ρ or κ from the measured resistance R or conductance L.

Resistances can be measured with great precision, and conductance determinations can therefore be extended to very dilute solutions. At this point, however, one must take major precautions to rinse the cell clean of any impurities adsorbed on the wall or on the electrodes and to free the solvent of all traces of electrolytes. Kohlrausch and co-workers, for example, were able to obtain water virtually free of ionic impurities and found a residual specific conductivity of 6.0×10^{-8} ohm^{-1} cm^{-1} at 25°C. As discussed in Section 12-4A this residual value is due to the $\sim 10^{-7}$ mole liter^{-1} of H$^+$ and OH$^-$ ions from the dissociation of the water itself. This concentration then represents the upper limit of dilution possible with an aqueous electrolyte before its contribution to the conductivity of the solution is swamped by that of the solvent water.

12-3 Results of Conductance Measurements

The decades preceding and following 1900 were ones in which the conductance of aqueous salt solutions was studied in great detail. Most soluble mineral salts, such as NaCl or KNO$_3$, show a pattern of behavior which led Arrhenius to propose his theory of electrolytic dissociation, namely that salts are largely dissociated in aqueous solution and fully dissociated at extreme dilution. We agree with this interpretation today and call such substances *strong electrolytes*.

Other salts, and especially some acids and bases, behave quite differently from strong electrolytes. It is necessary to suppose that only a small degree of dissociation takes place; such substances are known as *weak electrolytes*. We take up these two categories of electrolytes in turn and then consider some of the more modern treatments of their behavior.

A. Strong Electrolytes

It is typical of a strong electrolyte solution that its specific conductivity is proportional to its concentration, to a first approximation. This behavior is illustrated in Fig. 12-3(a), and its observation led to the introduction of equivalent conductivity Λ as a useful quantity. According to Eq. (12-10), κ should be a linear function of concentration if Λ is an intrinsic property of the electrolyte, independent of its concentration. The linearity law is not exact, however; as shown in Fig. 12-3(b), Λ for typical strong electrolytes decreases noticeably with increasing concentration. It was found very early that the decrease was proportional to $\sqrt{C}$; that is,

$$\Lambda = \Lambda_0 - A \sqrt{C^*}, \tag{12-12}$$

where, in the case of a strong electrolyte, we take $C = C^*$. Figure 12-3(c) shows that Eq. (12-12) is well obeyed up to about 0.1 M uni-univalent electrolyte concentration. Deviations set in much earlier, however, with more highly charged ions.

As is discussed in more detail in the Commentary and Notes and Special Topics sections, Eq. (12-12) has been explained theoretically as a consequence of interionic attractions and repulsions, that is, as a result of long-range Coulomb forces between ions. The effect is, in a sense, an incidental one arising from the charge on ions rather than from more chemical properties. The most important specific characteristic of an electrolyte is therefore Λ_0, its equivalent conductivity at infinite dilution, since in this limit interionic attraction effects have vanished. Table 12-2 summarizes some Λ_0 values for common electrolytes.

One of the early observations that helped to establish the concept of a strong electrolyte was that their Λ values are approximately additive. By this is meant that, for example, Λ_{KCl} is due to independent contributions from K^+ and Cl^- ions, and similarly for Λ_{NaNO_3} and Λ_{KNO_3}. An example of additivity behavior would then be

$$\Lambda_{NaCl} = \Lambda_{KCl} + \Lambda_{NaNO_3} - \Lambda_{KNO_3}. \tag{12-13}$$

Values at 25°C are

$$0.1\ M \qquad 106.74 \stackrel{?}{=} 128.96 + 98.7 - 120.40 = 103.66,$$

$$\Lambda_0 \qquad 126.45 \stackrel{?}{=} 149.86 + 121.55 - 144.96 = 126.45.$$

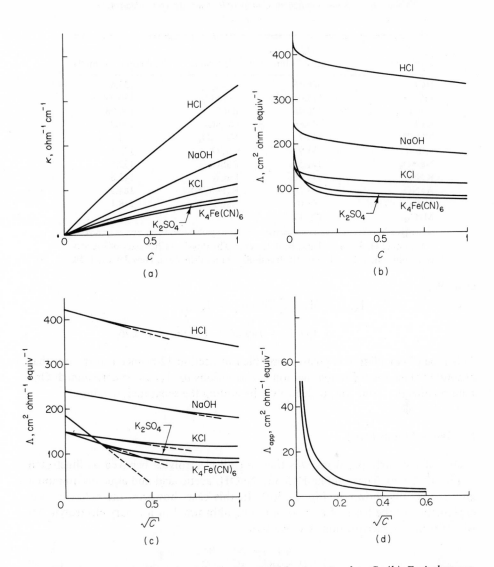

Fig. 12-3. *(a) Specific conductivity is approximately proportional to C. (b) Equivalent conductivity for strong electrolytes decreases with increasing C and (c) is nearly linear in $\sqrt{C}$. (d) Equivalent conductivity decreases strongly with increasing C in the case of a weak electrolyte. All data are for 25°C.*

The first line of these data shows that the additivity rule holds to within a few percent for 0.1 *M* solutions. Our interpretation of Λ_0 requires that the rule hold exactly at infinite dilution, and this expectation is confirmed by the second line.

The additivity rule allows the indirect calculation of Λ for an electrolyte. For

Table 12-2. *Some Equivalent Conductivities for Aqueous Electrolytes*
at 25°C[a]

Electrolyte	Λ_0 (cm² equiv⁻¹ ohm⁻¹)	Electrolyte	Λ_0 (cm² equiv⁻¹ ohm⁻¹)
HCl	426.16	$CaCl_2$	135.84
LiCl	115.03	$Ca(NO_3)_2$	130.94
NaCl	126.45	$BaCl_2$	139.98
KCl	149.86	Na_2SO_4	129.9
NH_4Cl	149.7	$Na_2C_2O_4$	124
KBr	151.9	$CuSO_4$	133.6
$NaNO_3$	121.55	$ZnSO_4$	132.8
KNO_3	144.96	$LaCl_3$	145.8
$AgNO_3$	133.36	$K_4Fe(CN)_6$	184.5
$NaOOCCH_3$	91.0	NaOH	248.1
$MgCl_2$	129.40		

[a] Source: H. S. Harned and B. B. Owen, "The Physical Chemistry of Electrolyte Solutions," 3rd ed. Van Nostrand–Reinhold, Princeton, New Jersey, 1958.

example,

$$\Lambda_{AgCl} = \Lambda_{AgNO_3} + \Lambda_{KCl} - \Lambda_{KNO_3}$$

$$= 133.36 + 149.86 - 144.96 = 138.26.$$

This type of calculation is greatly simplified in Section 12-6 since it turns out that absolute values for the individual ion contributions to Λ_0 can be determined. One then obtains the value for an electrolyte by adding the separate ion values.

B. Weak Electrolytes

One of the early problems was that not all electrolytes behaved as illustrated in Fig. 12-3(a–c). Thus, unlike HCl and NaOH, acetic acid and aqueous ammonia give the results shown in Fig. 12-3(d). In this case, however, the behavior was explainable on the basis of a dissociation equilibrium. For a binary electrolyte AB whose formal concentration is C we write

$$\begin{array}{ccc} AB & = A^+ + & B^- , \\ (1 - \alpha)C & \alpha C & \alpha C \end{array}$$

where α is the degree of dissociation. The equilibrium constant is then

$$K = \frac{(\alpha C)^2}{(1 - \alpha)C} = \frac{\alpha^2 C}{1 - \alpha} . \qquad (12\text{-}14)$$

Alternatively, the quotient of Eqs. (12-10) and (12-11) gives

$$\frac{\Lambda_{app}}{\Lambda} = \frac{C^*}{C} = \alpha. \qquad (12\text{-}15)$$

The ratio C^*/C is that of the concentration of ions, $\alpha C = C^*$, to the formal concentration C, and hence is equal to α. Substitution of this result into Eq. (12-14) gives

$$K = \frac{\Lambda_{\text{app}}^2 C}{\Lambda(\Lambda - \Lambda_{\text{app}})}. \tag{12-16}$$

If interionic attraction effects (see Section 12-3C) can be neglected, as is often true for weak electrolyte solutions if their actual ionic concentrations are low, then Λ is identified with Λ_0 ; Eqs. (12-15) and (12-16) then become

$$\frac{\Lambda_{\text{app}}}{\Lambda_0} = \alpha \tag{12-17}$$

and

$$K = \frac{\Lambda_{\text{app}}^2 C}{\Lambda_0(\Lambda_0 - \Lambda_{\text{app}})}. \tag{12-18}$$

Equation (12-18) is known as the *Ostwald dilution law*, after W. Ostwald, who proposed it. It allows a determination of the dissociation constant of a weak electrolyte from conductance data.

C. General Treatment of Electrolytes

The great success of Eq. (12-18) in accounting for the behavior of weak electrolytes such as acetic acid led Ostwald, Arrhenius, and others to apply the same equation to salts such as KCl and to acids such as HCl. The results were confusing. Although the K values computed on the basis of Eq. (12-18) were reasonably constant for a weak electrolyte, they would vary 10- or 20-fold when so computed for strong electrolytes.

It was eventually realized that two different effects are present. The predominant one in the case of a weak electrolyte is that of its partial dissociation into ions. Superimposed on this, however, is the effect of interionic attraction, which causes the value of Λ (as distinct from Λ_{app}) to vary with concentration. If the electrolyte is largely or fully dissociated, then the interionic attraction aspect becomes the dominant one. This is the situation with strong electrolytes.

Neither effect can be neglected for any electrolyte. In the case of a weak electrolyte the correct equation to use is Eq. (12-16), where Λ must have the value corresponding to the actual ionic environment that is present. That is, the dissociation produces an ion concentration C^*, which in turn affects Λ according to Eq. (12-12). The constant A of this equation,

$$\Lambda = \Lambda_0 - A \sqrt{C^*} \qquad \text{[Eq. (12-12)]},$$

has been evaluated theoretically (see Special Topics), and is given by

$$A = 0.2289\Lambda_0 + 60.19. \tag{12-19}$$

12 Solutions of Electrolytes

Equation (12-19) is valid for aqueous univalent ions at 25°C at concentrations below about 0.1 M. Its use is as follows. The measured L value gives Λ_{app} through Eqs. (12-6) and (12-11). Equation (12-17) is then used to calculate a first approximation to the degree of dissociation α_1, which in turn gives a first approximation to the actual ion concentration $C_1^* = \alpha_1 C$. Equation (12-12) is next used to obtain a better approximation Λ_1 for use in Eq. (12-17) in place of Λ_0. Insertion of Λ_1 in Eq. (12-15) then gives a second approximation to the degree of dissociation α_2 and hence to the actual ion concentration C_2^*. Then C_2^* is used for the calculation of a better value for the equivalent conductivity Λ_2, and so on. The cycle is repeated until self-consistent results are obtained. A numerical illustration is given later.

Not only must interionic attraction effects be allowed for in the calculation of a K value for a weak electrolyte, but, conversely, partial dissociation may be present in the case of a strong electrolyte. The equivalent conductivities of solutions of many so-called strong electrolytes deviate significantly from theoretical expectations and in a way that is consistent with incomplete dissociation. Thus a dissociation constant of about 1.4 has been estimated for aqueous KNO_3 at 25°C and of about 0.15 for the dissociation of KSO_4^- into K^+ and SO_4^{2-} ions. Salts involving higher charge types, such as $ZnSO_4$, are far from fully dissociated in moderately concentrated solution; K is about 5.3×10^{-3} at 25°C in this last case.

12-4 Some Sample Calculations

A. Calculation of Dissociation Constants

The first two examples are ones in which interionic attraction effects are neglected. That is, we assume that Λ_0 gives the equivalent conductivity of the ions. We obtain the data in Table 12-3.

We wish to calculate the dissociation constant of acetic acid. It is first necessary to obtain the cell constant. The net conductance due to the KCl is

$$\frac{1}{24.96} - \frac{1}{10^6} = 0.04006.$$

Table 12-3.

Solution	Measured resistance at 25°C (ohms)
Solvent water	1×10^6
0.1 M KCl	24.96
0.01 M acetic acid	1982

498

The specific conductivity of 0.1 M KCl is known to be 0.012886 ohm^{-1} cm^{-1}, and use of Eq. (12-6) gives the cell constant:

$$k = \frac{\kappa}{L} = \frac{0.012886}{0.04006} = 0.3217 \quad cm^{-1}.$$

The net conductance of the acetic acid is

$$L = \frac{1}{1982} - \frac{1}{10^6} = 5.035 \times 10^{-4},$$

from which we find

$$\kappa = (5.035 \times 10^{-4})(0.3217) = 1.620 \times 10^{-4}.$$

The apparent equivalent conductivity is therefore

$$\Lambda_{app} = \frac{1000}{0.01} 1.620 \times 10^{-4} = 16.35 \quad cm^2 \, equiv^{-1} \, ohm^{-1}.$$

We may obtain Λ_0 for the ions of acetic acid from the additivity rule, using the values 91.0, 426.1, and 126.5 for the Λ_0 values of sodium acetate (NaAc), HCl, and NaCl, respectively:

$$\Lambda_{0,HAc} = \Lambda_{0,NaAc} + \Lambda_{0,HCl} - \Lambda_{0,NaCl}$$
$$= 91.0 + 426.1 - 126.5 = 390.6.$$

The degree of dissociation is then

$$\alpha = \frac{16.35}{390.6} = 0.0419$$

and the dissociation constant is

$$K = \frac{(0.0419)^2(0.01)}{1 - 0.0419} = 1.83 \times 10^{-5}.$$

The resistance of 1×10^6 quoted for the solvent water was deliberately picked as a somewhat low value. It corresponds to a specific conductivity of

$$\kappa = (10^{-6})(0.3217) = 3.217 \times 10^{-7} \quad ohm^{-1} \, cm^{-1}.$$

The value for pure water was quoted in Section 12-2B as 6.0×10^{-8} ohm^{-1} cm^{-1}, and the difference, 2.60×10^{-7}, is therefore to be attributed to impurities. Taking NaCl as a typical impurity, we get the corresponding concentration from Eq. (12-10) using $\Lambda_0 = 126$:

$$C = \frac{1000}{\Lambda} \kappa = \frac{1000}{126} (2.60 \times 10^{-7}) = 2.06 \times 10^{-6} \quad M.$$

This concentration of ionic impurity is not likely to affect the dissociation of the 0.01 M acetic acid, so the slightly impure water used is acceptable for the particular experiment.

A value of 6.0×10^{-8} ohm^{-1} cm^{-1} for the specific conductivity of pure water at 25°C was obtained by Kohlrausch and co-workers in 1894; the measurement allows a calculation of the dissociation constant for water itself. We write

$$H_2O = H^+ + OH^-, \qquad K_w = (H^+)(OH^-). \qquad (12\text{-}20)$$

The concentration of water does not appear in K_w since we take pure liquid water to be the standard state for water substance, and hence of unit activity. The limiting equivalent conductivity for the electrolyte H^+, OH^- may again be calculated from the additivity rule:

$$\Lambda_{0,H^+,OH^-} = \Lambda_{0,HCl} + \Lambda_{0,NaOH} - \Lambda_{0,NaCl}$$

$$= 426.16 + 248.1 - 126.45 = 547.81.$$

Equation (12-10) then gives the concentration of ions present:

$$C = \frac{1000}{547.81} (6.0 \times 10^{-8}) = 1.03 \times 10^{-7}.$$

The value of K_w at 25°C is therefore

$$K_w = (1.03 \times 10^{-7})^2 = 1.05 \times 10^{-14}.$$

It is very difficult to remove the last traces of ionic impurities from water and this value for K_w is a little high; a better (modern) value is

$$K_w = 1.01 \times 10^{-14}. \qquad (12\text{-}21)$$

B.   Correction for the Interionic Attraction Effect

We can improve the preceding calculation of the dissociation constant for acetic acid can if we correct for the error introduced by using $\Lambda_{0,HAc}$ rather than Λ_{H^+,Ac^-} in determining it (we write Λ_{H^+,Ac^-} as a reminder that this is the actual equivalent conductivity of the ions H^+ and Ac^-). The value of 0.0419 for α is now regarded as a first approximation, giving an ion concentration

$$C^* = (0.0419)(0.01) = 4.19 \times 10^{-4} \, M.$$

The constant A of Eq. (12-12) is as given by Eq. (12-19),

$$A = (0.2289)(390.6) + 60.19 = 149.60.$$

Equation (12-12) then gives

$$\Lambda_{H^+, Ac^-} = 390.6 - (149.60)(4.19 \times 10^{-4})^{1/2} = 387.5.$$

The second approximation to α is therefore

$$\alpha = \frac{16.35}{387.5} = 0.0422.$$

The change is small enough in this case that another round of approximation is not needed (but may be carried out by the reader as an exercise). The final value for K is now

$$K = \frac{(0.0422)^2(0.01)}{1 - 0.0422} = 1.86 \times 10^{-5}. \tag{12-22}$$

C. Calculation of Solubility Products

A useful application of conductivity measurements is to the calculation of the solubility of slightly soluble salts. Consider the following set of data: The resistance of a cell is 227,000 ohms when filled with water and is 21,370 ohms when filled with saturated calcium oxalate solution. The cell constant is 0.25 cm^{-1}.

We calculate first the net specific conductivity of the calcium oxalate. The specific conductivity of the water is, by Eq. (12-4), $0.25/227,000 = 1.10 \times 10^{-6}$ (the water is again somewhat impure), and that of the saturated solution is $0.25/21,370 = 1.170 \times 10^{-5}$. The net value is 1.060×10^{-5} ohm^{-1} cm^{-1}. The value of Λ_0 for Ca^{2+} and oxalate, Ox^{2-}, ions is obtained through use of the additivity rule:

$$\Lambda_{0, Ca^{2+}, Ox^{2-}} = \Lambda_{0, Ca(NO_3)_2} + \Lambda_{0, Na_2Ox} - \Lambda_{0, NaNO_3}$$

$$= 130.94 + 124 - 121.55 = 133.$$

An equivalent conductivity for a salt such as $Ca(NO_3)_2$ will often be written as $\Lambda_{\frac{1}{2}Ca(NO_3)_2}$ as a reminder that 1 equiv. and not one mole of salt is present in the defining experiment for Λ. We will take this point to be implicit in the writing of a Λ value, and will insert such fractions only when the reminder seems desirable.

The concentration of Ca^{2+} and Ox^{2-} ions is then

$$C = \frac{1000}{133} 1.060 \times 10^{-5} = 7.98 \times 10^{-5} \ N.$$

The solubility product is, of course

$$CaOx(s) = Ca^{2+} + Ox^{2-}, \qquad K_{sp} = (Ca^{2+})(Ox^{2-}).$$

The concentration of $CaOx(s)$ does not appear in K_{sp} since solid calcium oxalate is in its standard state and hence has unit activity. The concentration is in equivalents per liter, so the molar concentration of ions in the saturated solution is 3.99×10^{-5} M. The value of K_{sp} is therefore $(3.99 \times 10^{-5})^2 = 1.59 \times 10^{-9}$ mole^2 liter^{-2}.

12-5   Ionic Mobilities

The conductance of an electrolyte solution is understood to be due to the motion of ions through the solution as a result of the applied potential. Positive ions move toward the electrode which is negatively charged in solution, or the cathode, and negative ions move toward the electrode which is positively charged in solution, or the anode. The current due to each ion is given by the product of the velocity of the ion and its charge. We consider first the quantitative aspect of this motion of ions under the influence of an applied potential, and then methods for measuring ion velocities.

A.   Defining Equations

The motion of a particle in solution when subjected to some force f was discussed in Section 10-7A. To review the situation, we recall that a limiting velocity v is quickly reached such that

$$v = \frac{f}{f'},\tag{12-23}$$

where f' is the friction coefficient. In the case of spherical particles, recall that a relationship due to Stokes gives $f' = 6\pi\eta r$, where η is the viscocity of the medium and r is the particle radius. It has become customary when dealing with ions to use the reciprocal of f', called the *mobility* ω. Equation (12-23) then becomes

$$v = \omega f.\tag{12-24}$$

We want now to consider the case of an ion in solution which experiences a force due to the imposed potential difference between the electrodes. The potential energy ϕ of a charge q in a potential V is, by the definition of potential, just qV (and will be in joules if q is in coulombs and V in volts). The force acting on a particle of this charge is then $d\phi/dx$ or $q\mathbf{F}$, where $\mathbf{F}$ is the field and is equal to dV/dx. The force in dynes is then

$$f = 10^7 \mathbf{F} z e,\tag{12-25}$$

where $\mathbf{F}$ is in volts per centimeter, z is the valence number of the ion, and e is the electronic charge in coulombs, $e = 1.602 \times 10^{-19}$ C. If the charge is given in esu, Eq. (12-25) becomes

$$f = \mathbf{F}z \frac{e}{300}. \qquad (12\text{-}26)$$

The velocity of the ith ion is

$$v_i = 10^7 \mathbf{F} z_i \omega_i e \qquad (12\text{-}27)$$

or

$$v_i = u_i \mathbf{F}, \qquad (12\text{-}28)$$

where u_i is called the *electrochemical mobility*, usually expressed as (cm sec^{-1})/ (V cm^{-1}) or cm^2 V^{-1} sec^{-1}, and

$$u_i = 10^7 z_i \omega_i e. \qquad (12\text{-}29)$$

We now want to determine the equivalent conductivity of this ion. According to the definition of equivalent conductivity, the electrodes are to be 1 cm apart and of area such that the enclosed volume contains 1 equiv. The conductance so measured is then the equivalent conductivity. In the present case the current carried will be

$$i_i = v_i \mathscr{F}, \qquad (12\text{-}30)$$

since Faraday's number gives the charge per equivalent. The potential difference is just $\mathbf{F}$, since the electrodes are 1 cm apart, and we find from Ohm's law

$$\lambda_i = \frac{1}{R_i} = \frac{i_i}{\mathbf{F}} = \frac{v_i \mathscr{F}}{\mathbf{F}} = \frac{u_i \mathbf{F} \mathscr{F}}{\mathbf{F}}$$

or

$$\lambda_i = u_i \mathscr{F}. \qquad (12\text{-}31)$$

It is customary to use the lower case lambda, λ, to designate the equivalent conductivity of an individual ion.

The equivalent conductivity for an electrolyte is the sum of the contributions of the separate ions. Ordinarily only one kind of positive and one kind of negative ion are involved, so

$$\Lambda = \lambda_+ + \lambda_-. \qquad (12\text{-}32)$$

Since Λ can be determined from conductance measurements, if λ_+ can be found by some independent means, then λ_- may be calculated, and vice versa. One way that this may be done is by measurement of the velocity u of an ion per unit field.

It should be emphasized that this velocity of an ion is not very large under ordinary potential gradients. The Λ values for electrolytes are around 100 cm^2 equiv^{-1} ohm^{-1} (Table 12-2) and λ values for individual ions are about 50 cm^2 equiv^{-1} ohm^{-1}.

A typical ion mobility is then 50/96,500 or about 5×10^{-4} cm² V⁻¹ sec⁻¹. The potential gradient is not apt to be more than perhaps 10 V cm⁻¹ in experimental conductance measurements and so actual ion velocities would be less than 5×10^{-3} cm sec⁻¹. Such a velocity is far less then the kinetic energy velocity at room temperature, about 10^4 cm sec⁻¹, and the effect of the imposed electric field is evidently to give a very minor net bias to the random motion of ions in solution.

B.   *Measurement of Ionic Mobilities*

The rate of motion of a given kind of ion under an imposed electric field may be observed directly if a boundary is present between two kinds of electrolytes. The method, called the *moving boundary method*, is illustrated schematically in Fig. 12-4.

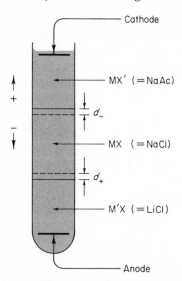

Fig. 12-4.   *Illustration of the moving boundary method.*

A vertical tube is layered with a solution of MX' (sodium acetate in this example) on top of one of MX (sodium chloride), which in turn is on top of one of M'X (lithium chloride). The concentrations are such that the solutions decrease in density upward, so that convectional mixing will not occur. The applied potential is such as to cause positive and negative ions to move in the directions shown. The lower boundary is one between M'X and MX, and hence between two types of positive ions, while the upper boundary is between MX and MX', or between two types of negative ions. The positions of these boundaries can be measured optically (and would also be visible to the eye) because of the change in refractive index.

A further requirement is that the mobility of M be greater than that of M' and that the mobility of X be greater than that of X'. In terms of the particular example, $u_{Na^+} > u_{Li^+}$ and $u_{Cl^-} > u_{Ac^-}$. If this condition is met, then M' cations will not overtake the M cations but will lag behind slightly until enough extra potential drop occurs locally to bring them just up to the velocity of the M cations. The boundary between MX and M′X then remains sharp and its motion is determined by the velocity of the cations M. Similarly, the upper boundary remains sharp and its motion is determined by that of the anions X.

On application of a potential across the electrodes, after a time t the lower boundary has moved up a distance d_+ and the upper one down a distance d_-. The The velocities of the M and X ions are then proportional to d_+ and d_-, respectively, and since the ions experience the same potential gradient, the velocities are in turn proportional to the respective mobilities, and, by Eq. (12-31), to the respective λ values. Thus

$$\frac{\lambda_M}{\lambda_X} = \frac{d_+}{d_-}. \tag{12-33}$$

By Eq. (12-32),

$$\Lambda_{MX} = \lambda_M + \lambda_X = \lambda_X \left(\frac{d_+}{d_-} + 1\right)$$

or

$$\lambda_X = \Lambda_{MX} \left(\frac{d_-}{d_+ + d_-}\right),$$

and

$$\lambda_M = \Lambda_{MX} \left(\frac{d_+}{d_+ + d_-}\right). \tag{12-34}$$

One can therefore determine λ_X and λ_M from the motions of the two boundaries if Λ_{MX} is known.

The restrictions on this type of procedure are somewhat severe, and act to limit the number of systems that can be studied. An alternative is to deal with just one boundary, say the one between MX and M′X. The motion of this boundary through distance d_+ sweeps out a volume $d_+\mathscr{A}$, where $\mathscr{A}$ is the cross-sectional area of the tube. If the concentration of MX is C equivalents per liter, then the total quantity of electricity carried by the M cations is

$$q_M = \frac{C_{MX}}{1000}(d_+\mathscr{A})\mathscr{F}. \tag{12-35}$$

Had the motion of the upper boundary been observed, then, similarly,

$$q_X = \frac{C_{MX}}{1000}(d_-\mathscr{A})\mathscr{F}. \tag{12-36}$$

It follows that

$$\lambda_M = \Lambda_{MX} \frac{q_M}{q_M + q_X} \tag{12-37}$$

since q_M and q_X are proportional to d_+ and d_-, respectively. However, $q_M + q_X = q_{tot} = it$, where i is the current through the system and t is the elapsed time. Equation (12-37) can therefore be written

$$\lambda_M = \Lambda_{MX} \frac{(C_{MX}/1000)(d_+\mathscr{A})\mathscr{F}}{it}. \tag{12-38}$$

It is thus possible to determine the ratio λ_M/Λ_{MX} from measurements of the motion of just one of the two boundaries. This ratio is known as the *transference number* for the ion M in salt MX (see Section 12-6).

C. *Experimental Results*

Ionic mobilities may be determined by the preceding method or indirectly, through the measurement of transference numbers, discussed in the next section. Some representative values are given in Table 12-4, extrapolated to infinite dilution. As suggested in the numerical example of Section 12-5A, the values are of the order of 10^{-4} cm^2 V^{-1} sec^{-1}. We can use Eq. (12-29) to relate u to the absolute mobility ω and if, further, we invoke Stokes' law so that $\omega = 1/f = 1/6\pi\eta r$, then we find

$$u_i = \frac{10^7 z_i e}{6\pi\eta r}, \tag{12-39}$$

where e is in coulombs. It is thus possible to calculate the radius of an ion from its mobility.

As an example, the mobility of Na$^+$ ion is 5.19×10^{-4} cm^2 V^{-1} sec^{-1}, and taking the viscosity of water to be 0.01 P at 25°C, we obtain

$$r_{Na^+} = \frac{(1)(1.602 \times 10^{-19})(10^7)}{(6)(3.142)(0.01)(5.19 \times 10^{-4})}$$

$$= 1.64 \times 10^{-8} \quad \text{cm.}$$

Table 12-4. *Mobilities of Aqueous Ions at Infinite Dilution at 25°C*

Cation	Mobility (cm^2 V^{-1} sec^{-1} × 10^4)	Anion	Mobility (cm^2 V^{-1} sec^{-1} × 10^4)
H$^+$	36.30	OH$^-$	20.50
Li$^+$	4.01	F$^-$	5.70
Na$^+$	5.19	Cl$^-$	7.91
K$^+$	7.62	Br$^-$	8.13
Rb$^+$	7.92	I$^-$	7.95
Ag$^+$	6.41	NO$_3^-$	7.40
Cs$^+$	7.96	CH$_3$COO$^-$	4.23
NH$_4^+$	7.60	CO$_3^{2-}$	7.46
Ca^{2+}	6.16	SO$_4^{2-}$	8.27
La^{3+}	7.21		

The radius of the Na^+ ion in a crystal of NaCl is found to be 0.95 Å, so, to the extent that Stokes' law is accurate, it appears that Na^+ ion is larger in solution than its true size. The accepted explanation is that the ion strongly binds a sphere of water molecules around it, so that the size of the hydrodynamic unit is thereby increased. This interpretation is supported by the fact that the corresponding calculation for a large ion such as $N(CH_3)_4^+$ gives essentially the crystallographic radius. Tetramethylammonium ion is large and nonpolar so that its interaction with water molecules is not expected to be so strong as to bind them to it as a kinetic unit.

This example illustrates that quite reasonable ionic radii result from calculations based on mobility measurements, provided that ions are regarded as capable of binding water molecules so as to increase the size of the effective hydrodynamic unit. Table 12-4 shows that the order of increasing mobility is

$$Li^+ < Na^+ < K^+ < Rb^+ < Cs^+.$$

Since by Eq. (12-39), mobility should vary inversely with the ion radius, the series is just opposite to what might be expected in terms of the actual ion sizes—Li^+ should be the smallest and the most mobile of the series. The accepted explanation is that the binding of water molecules by a cation is strongly affected by the charge density at the surface of the ion and therefore varies along the series. The potential of a point charge q is q/r at a distance r (as discussed in Section 8-ST-1), and is consequently larger at the surface of a Li^+ ion than at the surface of a Cs^+ ion, to consider the extremes. Aqueous Li^+ ion probably carries about six water molecules with it, tightly held by the strong local field. The surface potential for Cs^+ is small enough that it appears to carry few if any water molecules with it. The mobility series for the alkali metal ions thus provides one of the strong evidences for the hydration of ions in solution.

Independent methods confirm that aqueous ions hold or coordinate solvent water molecules around them. In the case of divalent and trivalent ions the rate of exchange between coordinated and free water is slow enough to be followed as a chemical reaction. The coordination chemist thus regards an aqueous cation in much the same light as any other complex ion; the ion holds water more or less tightly in its coordination sphere, and this water must leave if some other group or ligand is to be coordinated in its place.

Returning to the data of Table 12-4, we see that the radius of Cl^- ion as calculated from its mobility is about 2.5 Å, somewhat larger than the crystallographic value of 1.86 Å. Again, some water appears to be present in the hydrodynamic unit. However, the lack of variation of mobility in the series Cl^-, Br^-, I^- suggests that the amount of bound water is less than in the alkali metal series, so that its decrease with increasing anion size is just compensated for by the increase in size of the bare ion.

The case of the H^+ ion is a very interesting one. The simple ion, is, of course, just a proton, and its radius on this basis would be about 10^{-13} cm. We know that this is not the situation and that H^+ is coordinated to a water molecule, so that it is more appropriately written as H_3O^+. However, as discussed in Section 8-CN-2, liquid water is a very complex mixture of individual molecules and clusters of hydrogen-bonded molecules. These last were described as "flickering clusters" since they form, break up, and reform elsewhere very rapidly. It is therefore difficult to assign H^+ to any one single unit and the formulation H_3O^+ is used here in the same way that H_2O is used to describe the molecular unit of liquid water.

The formula H_3O^+ is, however, the minimum size of the positively charged unit, and the observed mobility for H^+ ion is much too large to be explainable in terms of Eq. (12-39). It seems very likely that a variation of the Grotthus mechanism of Fig. 12-1 is operative in this case. As an illustration of the proposed mechanism, one of the clusters of Fig. 8-22 may be stretched out in linear form and imagined to carry an extra proton:

$$
\begin{array}{cccccccc}
\text{H} & \text{H} & \text{H} & \text{H} & \text{H} & \text{H} & \text{H} & \text{H} \\
_+| & | & | & | & | & | & | & |_+ \\
\text{H--O--H-- --O--H-- --O--H-- --O--H} \rightarrow \text{H--O-- --H--O-- --H--O-- --H--O--H} .
\end{array}
$$

The long spacings represent hydrogen bonds, and the short ones, regular bonds. The proton is shown as first assigned to the left-hand oxygen, but hydrogen bonds are mobile in that the hydrogen atom can easily jump from a O—H——O to a O——H—O position. Such a shift down the chain then puts the extra proton on the right-hand oxygen. Thus in this case a unit of positive charge has moved four molecular distances without any appreciable molecular motion being required.

This process is not quite complete, however, since after the charge transfer each water molecule has, in effect, been rotated 180°. The following elementary step illustrates the point:

$$
\begin{array}{cccccc}
\text{H} & \text{H} & \text{H} & \text{H} & \text{H} & \text{H} \\
| & | & | & | & | & | \\
\text{H--O--H} + \text{O--H} \rightarrow \text{H--O} + \text{H--O--H} \rightarrow \text{O--H} + \text{H--O--H.} \\
_+ & & & _+ & & _+
\end{array}
$$

It may be that either the rotation time for a water molecule or the rate of formation and disruption of clusters determines the speed at which charge can move through the solution. M. Eigen, from his studies of very fast reactions in aqueous solutions, has been led to suggest that rather than being associated randomly with molecules and clusters, a special unit is the most stable one:

$$
\begin{array}{cc}
\text{H} & \text{H} \;_+ \\
| & | \\
\text{O} & \text{O} \\
\diagup \;\; \diagdown & \diagup \;\; \diagdown \\
\text{H} \quad\quad \text{H} \quad \text{H} \quad\quad \text{H} \\
& \text{O} \\
& | \\
& \text{H} \\
& | \\
& \text{O} \\
& \diagup \;\; \diagdown \\
& \text{H} \quad\quad \text{H}
\end{array}
$$

If so, the rate of reformation of $H_9O_4^+$ may be the slow step that determines the mobility of protons in water. The subject is as complicated as the structure of water itself.

The mobility of the OH^- ion is also unusually high, and mechanisms have been proposed that are similar to those for proton migration.

D. Electrophoresis

A special case of the moving boundary method should be discussed briefly. It has been very highly developed for use in the study of proteins and other large molecules and the process is now called *electrophoresis*. As an example, a boundary is formed between two buffer solutions, one of which contains protein. The boundary is observed to move on application of a potential between the electrodes and one thus obtains the rate of motion of the protein and, from the potential gradient, a value for its electrochemical mobility. The temperature is often set at about 4°C or at the point of maximum density of the solution. In this way convection currents due to temperature fluctuations are largely eliminated.

Electrophoresis measurements serve to distinguish protein molecules qualitatively since each shows a characteristic rate of motion. If a mixture is initially present as a thin band, separation into several distinct zones will occur. The method may thus be used for the analysis of a protein or other mixture. On a more quantitative level the determination of the mobility u allows us to estimate the charge z that is carried. If the size of the protein molecule is known, then Eq. (12-39) may be used for the calculation of z. The more elegant approach is to determine the friction coefficient f by means of sedimentation or diffusion measurements (see Section 10-7) and to write the more general expression

$$u_i = \frac{10^7 z_i e}{f}. \tag{12-40}$$

The charge may then be computed without making any assumptions about molecular size or shape.

A difficulty at this point is that the charge on a protein molecule is not a fixed and known quantity as in the case of a simple ion. The charge is determined mainly by the pH of the solution, which controls the extent of dissociation of protons from acidic groups and of hydrolysis of basic groups, and the net charge may thus range from positive to negative. Since it is an average value, it need not be in multiples of electronic charge. Since charge is a variable quantity in this type of system, one does not usually speak of the equivalent conductivity of the molecule.

Electrophoretic measurements may be extended to particles large enough to be visible under a microscope, that is, to colloidal systems. For reasons that are not discussed until Section 20-ST-1, the equipment is now called a *zetameter*, but the method is essentially the same as that just described. One applies a known potential gradient and observes the slow motion of the colloidal particle along the gradient. We can then calculate the mobility from the rate of such motion and the field and use Eq. (12-39) to obtain the total charge on the particle.

12-6 Transference Numbers—Ionic Equivalent Conductivities

The direct measurement of ionic mobilities was discussed in the preceding section. An alternative approach is to determine directly the fraction of current carried by a particular ion, rather than its actual velocity.

A. Defining Equations

The *transference* (or *transport*) *number* of an ion in an electrolyte solution is defined as the fraction of the total current which that ion carries when a potential gradient is applied. We can write Eq. (12-35) in the form

$$i_i = \frac{C_i}{1000} v_i \mathscr{A} \mathscr{F},$$ (12-41)

where $v_i = dd_i/dt$ and is the velocity of the ith ion. Since each velocity is proportional to the field, Eq. (12-41) reduces to the form

$$i_i = k u_i C_i,$$ (12-42)

where k is a proportionality constant common to all the ions present. The total current is then $\sum_i i_i = \sum_i u_i C_i$, so the transference number of the ith ion is

$$t_i = \frac{u_i C_i}{\sum_i u_i C_i}.$$ (12-43)

Further, the mobility of an ion is proportional to its equivalent conductivity, by Eq. (12-31), so that

$$t_i = \frac{\lambda_i C_i}{\sum_i \lambda_i C_i}.$$ (12-44)

Equation (12-44) is a general one, valid for a mixture of electrolytes. If a single electrolyte is present, then $C_+ = C_-$ and the special form for this case is therefore

$$t_+ = \frac{\lambda_+}{\lambda_+ + \lambda_-}$$

or

$$t_+ = \frac{\lambda_+}{\varLambda}, \qquad t_- = \frac{\lambda_-}{\varLambda}.$$ (12-45)

B.   The Hittorf Method

The fraction of current carried by each ion of an electrolyte, and hence the transference numbers, may be determined directly with a special type of electrolysis cell. The procedure is known as the *Hittorf method* (introduced in 1853) and a Hittorf cell is sketched in Fig. 12-5. The cell is constructed so that the three

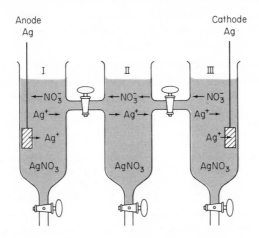

Fig. 12-5.   *Schematic drawing of a Hittorf transference cell.*

compartments may be isolated from each other and drained separately. The basis of the method is that the change in the amount of electrolyte in either end compartment depends both on the electrolysis reaction and on the number of ions that have migrated in or out in the process of carrying current.

The cell shown in the figure is filled with silver nitrate solution and has silver electrodes. The general situation is that since the mobilities of Ag^+ and NO_3^- ions are about equal, each carries about half the current. Thus for each faraday of electricity put through the cell, $\frac{1}{2}$ equiv of Ag^+ ions will pass from left to right across the dividing line I–II between cells I and II and $\frac{1}{2}$ equiv of NO_3^- ions will pass across the line I–II from right to left. Oxidation occurs at the anode, so that, per faraday, 1 equiv of Ag^+ ions is delivered into cell I by the silver electrode. Between the gain by electrolysis and the loss by migration, there is a net gain of $\frac{1}{2}$ equiv of Ag^+ ions in cell I. Since the NO_3^- ion is not involved in the electrode reaction, the gain of $\frac{1}{2}$ equiv by migration is net. Cell I will thus show a overall gain of $\frac{1}{2}$ equiv of silver nitrate per faraday.

The details of the analysis of the Hittorf method are given in the Special Topics section. It is sufficient here to note that analysis of the changes in amounts present in the electrode compartments of a Hittorf cell allows the calculation of the fraction of current carried by each ion, and hence the determination of its transference number.

C. Ionic Equivalent Conductivities

We have two methods for obtaining equivalent conductivities for individual ions. The first is by direct determination of the ionic mobility and the second is by direct determination of the transference number, which, by Eq. (12-45), gives λ if Λ is known. Although results of two methods agree, a complication should be mentioned. Not only does Λ vary with the concentration of an electrolyte, but also, of course, so do λ_+ and λ_- ; moreover, the two ionic equivalent conductivities do not vary in exactly the same way. Consequently, the result is that transference

Table 12-5.   *Cation Transference Numbers in Aqueous Solutions at 25°C[a]*

Concentration C	Cation transference number				
	HCl	NaCl	KCl	Na_2SO_4	$LaCl_3$
0.01	0.8251	0.3918	0.4902	0.3848	0.4625
0.02	0.8266	0.3902	0.4901	0.3836	0.4576
0.05	0.8292	0.3876	0.4899	0.3829	0.4482
0.10	0.8314	0.3854	0.4898	0.3828	0.4375
0.20	0.8337	0.3821	0.4894	0.3828	0.4233

[a] As determined by the moving boundary method. See H. S. Harned and B. B. Owen, "The Physical Chemistry of Electrolyte Solutions," 3rd ed. Van Nostrand–Reinhold, Princeton, New Jersey, 1958.

Table 12-6.   *Equivalent Conductivities of Aqueous Ions at 25°C[a]*

Cation	Equivalent conductivity (cm^2 $equiv^{-1}$ ohm^{-1})	Anion	Equivalent conductivity (cm^2 $equiv^{-1}$ ohm^{-1})
H^+	349.7	OH^-	198
Li^+	38.7	F^-	55
Na^+	50.1	Cl^-	76.3
K^+	73.5	Br^-	78.4
Rb^+	76.4	I^-	76.8
Cs^+	76.8	NO_3^-	71.44
Ag^+	61.9	HSO_3^-	50
NH_4^+	73.7	SO_3^{2-}	72
Be^{2+}	45	HCO_3^-	44.5
Mg^{2+}	53.06	CO_3^{2-}	72
Ca^{2+}	59.50	SO_4^{2-}	79.8
Ba^{2+}	63.7	$HCOO^-$	56
La^{3+}	69.6	$HC_2O_4^-$	40.2
$Co(NH_3)_6^{3+}$	102	$C_2O_4^{2-}$	74
		CH_3COO^-	40.9

[a] See D. MacInnes, "Principles of Electrochemistry." Van Nostrand–Reinhold, Princeton, New Jersey, 1939.

numbers as well as mobilities depend on the ionic environment. Some data on the variation of cation transference number with electrolyte concentration are given in Table 12-5.

As in the case of the equivalent conductivity of an electrolyte, the usual quantity tabulated is the equivalent conductivity of the ion at infinite dilution. This value is characteristic of the isolated ion free of long-range interionic attraction effects. A number of such values are given in Table 12-6. These are, of course, parallel to the mobilities in Table 12-4, being related by Faraday's number. The same general comments apply here as were made in Section 12-5C.

12-7 Activities and Activity Coefficients of Electrolytes

A. Introductory Comments

An electrolyte, like any other solute, tends to give nonideal solutions, approaching Henry's law behavior at infinite dilution. We know that at high dilution the positive and negative ions act independently. The colligative property effects report, for example, the number of particles expected from the complete dissociation of the electrolyte. On the other hand, it is not possible to vary a single ion concentration, keeping everything else constant. An attempt to do so would immediately result in the solution acquiring an enormous electrostatic charge. An excess of even 10^{-10} mole liter^{-1} of one kind of ion over another would result in a static charging of the solution to a potential of about 10^6 V! In other words, we cannot prepare a solution containing only one kind of ion and therefore cannot determine individual ion activities or activity coefficients; we can only observe a mean value for the positive and negative ions present.

The situation is illuminated if we consider the case of a solubility product equilibrium. We write for a slightly soluble salt MX the solubility equilibrium

$$MX(s) = MX(\text{solution}) = M^+ + X^-. \tag{12-46}$$

The thermodynamic criterion for equilibrium is satisfied if we write

$$\mu_{MX}(s) = \mu_{MX}(\text{solution})$$

as required by Eq. (9-44). We can introduce the activity of the electrolyte species:

$$\mu_{MX}(\text{solution}) = \mu_{MX}^{\circ}(\text{solution}) + RT \ln a_{MX}. \tag{12-47}$$

The activity a_{MX} corresponds to the solute activity a_2 in the equations of Chapter 10. It can be obtained, for example, by application of the Gibbs–Duhem integration procedure to solvent activities as determined from colligative property measurements. As with solutes generally, we use a Henry's law standard state, usually the one based on molality as a concentration unit (see Section 10-6).

The treatment up to this point is rather unsatisfactory, however. It does not tell us that the electrolyte is dissociated or how a_{MX} is apt to be influenced by the presence of a common ion in the solution. Returning to the solubility equilibrium, the normal way of writing the equilibrium constant for process (12-46) is in terms of a solubility product:

$$K_{sp} = (M^+)(X^-). \qquad (12\text{-}48)$$

We know that the constant K_{sp} is well–behaved in dilute solutions. For example, while we cannot avoid having essentially equal numbers of positive and negative ions present in any solution, we can, by using mixed electrolytes, vary the concentrations of specific kinds of ions, such as M^+ or X^-, independently. If S denotes the solubility of MX(s), then in pure water we have

$$K_{sp} = S^2. \qquad (12\text{-}49)$$

If added X^- ion is present, as in the form of a concentration C of NaX, then Eq. (12-48) becomes

$$K_{sp} = (S)(S + C). \qquad (12\text{-}50)$$

We now have the common ion effect whereby added X^- ion depresses the solubility of MX(s). Since the solution is still in equilibrium with the solid, a_{MX} must not have changed, even though the individual values of (M^+) and (X^-) are now quite different from before. Thus observation tells us that in dilute solution

$$a_{MX} = (M^+)(X^-). \qquad (12\text{-}51)$$

Use of Eq. (12-51) allows a more realistic treatment of colligative effects in dilute solution. The Gibbs–Duhem integration gives $\ln a_{MX}$, and for a single electrolyte solute MX, $(M^+) = (X^-) = m$. We then have $\ln a_{MX} = \ln m^2 = 2 \ln m$, and the experimentally observed factor of 2 has now appeared.

Consider, for example, the osmotic pressure effect. The basic equation is

$$-\ln a_1 = \frac{V_1}{RT} \Pi \qquad \text{[Eq. (10-20)]}$$

and this is to be used with the Gibbs–Duhem relation

$$x_1 \, d(\ln a_1) + x_2 \, d(\ln a_2) = 0 \qquad \text{[Eq. (9-79)]},$$

where x_1 and x_2 must denote the mole fraction of components 1 (solvent) and 2 (salt MX). It is simpler for the present illustration to use mole fraction rather than molality for the salt concentration, and so we write $a_{MX} = (x_M^+)(x_X^-) = x_2^2$ (rather than $a_{MX} = m^2$). This amounts to using the first of the Henry's law conventions of Section 10-6. Since $d(\ln a_{MX}) = 2\,d(\ln x_2)$, combination of Eqs. (10-20) and (9-79) gives

$$2x_2\,d(\ln x_2) = -x_1\,d(\ln a_1) = \frac{V_1}{RT}x_1\,d\Pi \qquad (12\text{-}52)$$

or

$$\frac{V_1}{RT}\Pi = 2\int_0^{x_2}\frac{x_2}{x_1}\,d(\ln x_2) = 2\int_0^{x_2}\frac{dx_2}{x_1}\,.$$

The integral of dx_2/x_1 is $-\ln(1 - x_2)$ and since the solution is to be dilute, this becomes just x_2. The final result is

$$\frac{V_1}{RT}\Pi = 2x_2\,. \qquad (12\text{-}53)$$

Thus the osmotic pressure is predicted to be twice the value expected just from the mole fraction of the salt, or the van't Hoff i factor comes out equal to 2, as observed.

B. Defining Equations for Activity and Activity Coefficient

The preceding analysis was presented to show that the activity of an electrolyte is equal to the product of the ion concentrations in very dilute solutions. For the more general case of a nonideal solution we therefore write

$$a_2 = a_+ a_-\,, \qquad (12\text{-}54)$$

where a_2 denotes the electrolyte activity and a_+ and a_- the individual ion activities, which become equal to m_+ and m_-, respectively, in the limit of infinite dilution. We then further define the activity coefficients γ_+ and γ_-:

$$a_+ = \gamma_+ m_+ \qquad \text{and} \qquad a_- = \gamma_- m_-\,. \qquad (12\text{-}55)$$

Since a_2 involves the square of a concentration, it is convenient to define a new activity $a_\pm$ as the square root of a_2:

$$a_2 = a_\pm{}^2. \qquad (12\text{-}56)$$

The activity $a_\pm$ is known as the *mean activity*. Similarly, $\gamma_\pm$ is called the *mean activity coefficient*:

$$\gamma_\pm{}^2 = \gamma_+ \gamma_-\,, \qquad (12\text{-}57)$$

and $m_\pm$ the *mean molality*:

$$m_\pm{}^2 = m_+ m_-\,. \qquad (12\text{-}58)$$

Then

$$a_\pm = \gamma_\pm m_\pm\,. \qquad (12\text{-}59)$$

This set of definitions is for the specific case of a 1–1 electrolyte, that is, for an electrolyte which produces 1 mole of ions of each kind per formula weight. The general treatment is suggested by consideration of the solubility product for a salt $M_{\nu+}X_{\nu-}$:

$$M_{\nu+}X_{\nu-}(s) = \nu_+M^{z+} + \nu_-X^{z-}, \qquad K_{sp} = (M^{z+})^{\nu+}(X^{z-})^{\nu-}, \qquad (12\text{-}60)$$

where z_+ and z_- are the respective ion charges and ν_+ and ν_- are the numbers of ions of each type. It follows that

$$\nu_+z_+ = \nu_-z_- . \qquad (12\text{-}61)$$

We want to define the activity of this general electrolyte in terms of individual ion activities such that in the limit of infinite dilution we obtain the expression on the right-hand side of Eq. (12-60). The definitions are then

$$a_2 = a_+^{\nu+}a_-^{\nu-}, \qquad (12\text{-}62)$$

$$a_\pm^{\nu} = a_+^{\nu+}a_-^{\nu-}, \qquad \text{where} \quad \nu = \nu_+ + \nu_- , \qquad (12\text{-}63)$$

$$a_+ = \gamma_+m_+ , \qquad a_- = \gamma_-m_- \qquad [\text{Eq. (12-55)}],$$

$$\gamma_\pm^{\nu} = \gamma_+^{\nu+}\gamma_-^{\nu-}, \qquad (12\text{-}64)$$

$$m_\pm^{\nu} = m_+^{\nu+}m_-^{\nu-}, \qquad (12\text{-}65)$$

and, as before,

$$a_\pm = \gamma_\pm m_\pm \qquad [\text{Eq. (12-59)}].$$

The complications introduced by these definitions are regrettable. They develop naturally, however, when we deal with nonideal electrolyte solutions.

C. Activity Coefficients from Solubility Measurements

The preceding material allows us to write the thermodynamic equilibrium constant for the solubility equilibrium of an electrolyte. Thus for AgCl we have

$$AgCl(s) = Ag^+ + Cl^-, \qquad (12\text{-}66)$$

$$K_{th} = a_{Ag^+}a_{Cl^-} = (Ag^+)(Cl^-)\,\gamma_{Ag^+}\gamma_{Cl^-} , \qquad (12\text{-}67)$$

or

$$K_{th} = K_{sp}\gamma_\pm^2, \qquad (12\text{-}68)$$

where K_{th} is the thermodynamic solubility product and K_{sp} is the usual form in which concentrations are used. The solubility of AgCl in water is about $10^{-5}\,m$

and it seems likely that $\gamma_\pm$ will be unity for so low a concentration. We can investigate the situation by adding some neutral or noncommon-ion electrolyte. We find experimentally that on doing so the solubility of AgCl increases, and hence so does its K_{sp} value. Evidently $\gamma_\pm$ is varying with the concentration of added neutral electrolyte, since K_{th} must remain a constant.

A useful way of graphing such data follows if we write Eq. (12-68) in the form

$$\log K_{sp} = \log K_{th} - 2 \log \gamma_t . \qquad (12\text{-}69)$$

We then plot $\log K_{sp}$ against some function of concentration. Figure 12-6 gives the

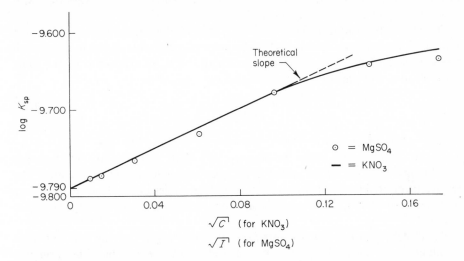

Fig. 12-6. *Variation of K_{sp} for* AgCl *at 25°C with increasing* KNO_3 *concentration (plotted as $\sqrt{C}$) and increasing* $MgSO_4$ *concentration (circles, plotted as $\sqrt{I}$).*

results of measurements that show the effect of added KNO_3 and $MgSO_4$ on the solubility and hence the K_{sp} for AgCl. As with equivalent conductivity, the experimental observation is that a plot is nearly linear if the square root of the added electrolyte concentration is used. The theoretical explanation is given in the next section.

Since we are using the Henry's law convention for activities and activity coefficients, $\gamma_\pm$ approaches unity at infinite dilution. The intercept of Fig. 12-6 therefore gives $\log K_{th} = -9.790$, or $K_{th} = 1.62 \times 10^{-10}$. We may then calculate $\gamma_\pm$ for the ions Ag^+ and Cl^- in the presence of added KNO_3 by inserting K_{th} and the measured K_{sp} into Eq. (12-69). Thus $\log K_{sp} = -9.645$ at $\sqrt{C} = 0.175$ or $C = 0.0306$; then $\log \gamma_\pm = [(-9.790) - (-9.645)]/2 = -0.0725$, whence $\gamma_\pm = 0.845$. The data allow a tabulation of $\gamma_\pm$ versus concentration of added KNO_3 (strictly speaking, C includes the contribution of the dissolved AgCl to the total salt concentration).

D. The Ionic Strength Principle

Studies such as the preceding were carried out for a number of systems, especially by V. LaMer and co-workers, and these confirmed an earlier observation by G. Lewis that the activity coefficient of an electrolyte depends mainly on the total concentration of ions and only secondarily on their specific chemical natures. Thus for concentrations below about 0.05 m, the data of Fig. 12-6 would be essentially the same if $NaNO_3$, $KClO_4$, and so on were used instead of KNO_3. The results, incidentally, would also have been the same if NaCl were the added electrolyte. Although there is now a common-ion effect, depressing the solubility of the AgCl, the experimental K_{sp} values will still show the same variation with concentration of total electrolyte present.

Empirical observation showed, however, that if other than uni-univalent salts were used, there was an increased effect on activity coefficients. It was found that all types of electrolytes can be put on a common basis by expression of the ionic concentration in terms of a quantity called the ionic strength I, where

$$I = \tfrac{1}{2} \sum_i C_i z_i^2. \tag{12-70}$$

In the case of a uni-univalent electrolyte, $I = C$, but for, say K_2SO_4, $I = \tfrac{1}{2}(2C + 4C) = 3C$, while for $MgSO_4$, $I = \tfrac{1}{2}(4C + 4C) = 4C$. The increase in solubility of a salt in the presence of any electrolyte is nearly the same if the results are plotted in terms of I rather than C. The circles in Fig. 12-6 are the points obtained with $MgSO_4$ as the neutral salt and with the abscissa reading $\sqrt{I}$ rather than $\sqrt{C}$.

The discovery of the *ionic strength principle* was a major step toward the understanding of nonideality effects in dilute electrolyte solutions. The principle constituted strong evidence that it was the charges on ions and not their particular chemical natures that determined activity coefficients. It paved the way for the development of the interionic attraction theory (described in Section 12-8).

E. Methods of Determining Activity Coefficients

The change in solubility of a salt with ionic strength provides one means for determination of the activity coefficient of the salt in the presence of some other electrolyte. The method is not applicable to soluble salts, and, moreover, necessarily gives activity coefficients in mixed electrolyte solutions. The activity coefficient of an electrolyte in solutions containing no other ionic species is of more general importance.

As indicated in Section 12-7A, a_2, the solute activity, may be obtained from colligative property measurements through use of the Gibbs–Duhem equation. Equation (12–52) would be written with $d(\ln a_2)$ rather than $d(\ln x_2)$, and then manipulated into the form of Eq. (9-80). The detailed procedures for simplifying the handling of this integration may be found in more specialized texts [for example, Lewis and Randall (1951)]. Much of our activity coefficient data comes from measurements of the emf of electrochemical cells. This approach is discussed in detail in Chapter 13 and will not be reviewed here.

Activity coefficients may also be obtained from a study of ionic equilibrium. As a specific example, Table 12-7 gives the concentration equilibrium constant for the dissociation of acetic acid as determined from conductivity measurements at various concentrations. The concentration equilibrium constant is

$$\text{HAc} = \text{H}^+ + \text{Ac}^-, \qquad K = \frac{\alpha^2 C}{1 - \alpha} \tag{12-71}$$

and α in the table has been corrected for the ion atmosphere effect on Λ, as described in Section 12-3C. The residual variation in K is attributed to nonideality, and Eq. (12-71) is written

$$K_{\text{th}} = K \frac{\gamma_{\text{H}^+} \gamma_{\text{Ac}^-}}{\gamma_{\text{HAc}}} = K K_\gamma . \tag{12-72}$$

The solutions are dilute enough that, as a nonelectrolyte, HAc is probably in the Henry's law region of behavior, so $\gamma_{\text{HAc}} = 1$. Therefore $K_\gamma = \gamma_\pm^2$, and Eq. (12-72) may be plotted according to the form

$$\log K = \log K_{\text{th}} - 2 \log \gamma_\pm . \tag{12-73}$$

The ionic strength derives entirely from the H^+ and Ac^- ions, whose concentration is αC, and the plot of $\log K$ versus $(\alpha C)^{1/2}$ is shown in Fig. 12-7. Extrapolation to zero αC gives $\log(10^5 K_{\text{th}}) = 0.2440$, or $K_{\text{th}} = 1.754 \times 10^{-5}$. Insertion of this value into Eq. (12-72) allows K_γ, and hence $\gamma_\pm$, to be calculated for each concentration. Thus for 0.050 m HAc, $\gamma_\pm^2 = 1.754 \times 10^{-5}/1.849 \times 10^{-5} = 0.949$, or $\gamma_\pm = 0.97$.

Table 12-7.   *Dissociation Constant of Acetic Acid at 25°C[a]*

$C \times 10^3$ (M)	$\alpha C \times 10^4$	$K \times 10^5$ (M)
0.028014	0.151	1.768
0.2184	0.540	1.781
2.4140	2.00	1.809
9.8421	4.12	1.834
20.000	5.96	1.840
50.000	9.50	1.849

[a] Adapted from S. Glasstone, "Textbook of Physical Chemistry," p. 955. Van Nostrand–Reinhold, Princeton, New Jersey, 1946.

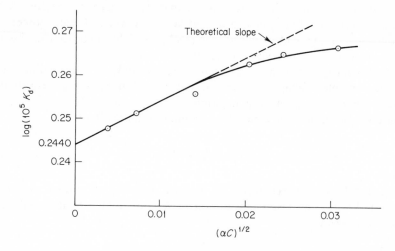

Fig. 12-7. *Variation of K_d for acetic acid with concentration at 25°C.*

The same approach would be used in the case of an equilibrium not involving ionic species. Thus for the esterification reaction in aqueous solution,

$$CH_3COOH + C_2H_5OH = CH_3COOC_2H_5 + H_2O,$$

one again writes

$$K_{th} = \frac{(CH_3COOC_2H_5)(H_2O)}{(CH_3COOH)(C_2H_5OH)} \frac{\gamma_{CH_3COOC_2H_5}\gamma_{H_2O}}{\gamma_{CH_3COOH}\gamma_{C_2H_5OH}} = KK_\gamma$$

and extrapolates the measured values of K to infinite dilution. Pure water is taken to be in its standard state so that γ_{H_2O} approaches unity at infinite dilution of the other species, and the extrapolated value of K is then equal to K_{th}. We are primarily concerned with rather dilute solutions in this chapter, and activity coefficients for nonionic species are close to unity. It is only in the case of ions that the long-range Coulomb interactions lead to nonideal behavior even in quite dilute solutions ($C < 0.1m$).

F. Activity Coefficients of Electrolytes

As noted earlier, a number of methods may be used for the determination of the activity coefficient of an electrolyte. The results have been collected and tables of standard activity coefficients are available. A selection of such results is given in Table 12-8 and the mean activity coefficients of some typical electrolytes are plotted against concentration in Fig. 12-8.

The points to notice are the following. First, of course, even 0.1 m solutions

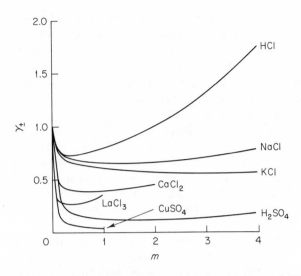

Fig. 12-8.   *Activity coefficient plots for various electrolytes at 25°C.*

can be drastically nonideal in their behavior. Second, electrolytes of a given charge type tend to show similar variations of $\gamma_\pm$ with concentration at first but deviate from each other at higher concentrations. Third, the higher the product $z_+ z_-$, the earlier the deviations from ideality set in. The differences within a given family of the same $z_+ z_-$ product appear to be due to several causes. Extensive hydration

Table 12-8.   *Mean Activity Coefficients for Aqueous Electrolytes at 25°C[a]*

	Mean molal activity coefficient								
Electrolyte	0.001 m	0.005 m	0.01 m	0.05 m	0.1 m	0.5 m	1.0 m	2.0 m	4.0 m
HCl	0.965	0.928	0.904	0.830	0.796	0.757	0.809	1.009	1.762
NaCl	0.966	0.929	0.904	0.823	0.778	0.682	0.658	0.671	—
KCl	0.965	0.927	0.901	0.815	0.769	0.650	0.605	0.575	0.582
HNO$_3$	0.965	0.927	0.902	0.823	0.785	0.715	0.720	0.783	0.982
KNO$_3$	—	—	—	—	0.733	0.542	0.548	0.481	—
AgNO$_3$	—	0.92	0.90	0.79	0.72	0.51	0.40	0.28	—
NaOH	—	—	—	0.82	—	0.69	0.68	0.70	0.89
H$_2$SO$_4$	0.830	0.639	0.544	0.340	0.265	0.154	0.130	0.124	0.171
K$_2$SO$_4$	0.89	0.78	0.71	0.52	0.43	—	—	—	—
BaCl$_2$	0.88	0.77	0.72	0.56	0.49	0.39	0.39	—	—
CuSO$_4$	0.74	0.53	0.41	0.21	0.16	0.068	0.047	—	—
K$_4$Fe(CN)$_6$	—	—	—	0.19	0.14	0.067	—	—	—

[a] Adapted from W. M. Latimer, "The Oxidation States of the Elements and Their Potentials in Aqueous Solutions," 2nd ed. Prentice-Hall, Englewood Cliffs, New Jersey, 1952, and H. S. Harned and B. B. Owen, "The Physical Chemistry of Electrolytic Solutions," 3rd ed. Van Nostrand–Reinhold, Princeton, New Jersey, 1958.

of the ions ties up the solvent water and makes the true mole fraction higher than the apparent one; a similar explanation was offered for the behavior of aqueous sucrose solutions (note Table 10-3). This may be a major reason for the rather high activity coefficients of electrolytes such as HCl in concentrated solutions. A second factor is that many electrolytes are not fully dissociated. Although a chemical bond is not ordinarily expected to form in the case of electrolytes involving a rare gas type of ion such as K^+, ions may associate strongly as an ion pair. Salts such as $CuSO_4$, however, may actually form a coordinate bond in their association. Acids such as H_2SO_4 are relatively weak, and are not fully dissociated except in dilute solution. If association occurs for any of these reasons, the result is generally to lower the activity coefficient of the electrolyte.

A less chemically specific effect is that the actual size of the ion becomes important in concentrated solutions. The result is an increase in activity coefficient over what it would otherwise be.

These various explanations are important in the sense that they provide some rationale for an otherwise bewildering variety of behavior. They are discussed in somewhat more detail in the Commentary and Notes section. On the other hand, an activity coefficient is a *phenomenological* quantity; when multiplied by the mean molality, it gives the mean activity of the electrolyte and therefore its chemical potential, regardless of explanation.

12-8   The Debye–Hückel Theory

Repeated remarks have been made throughout this chapter about the effect of the long-range Coulomb interactions between ions on both their transport behavior or mobilities and their activity coefficients. The theoretical approach to the former effect is mentioned further in the Special Topics section. The same interactions that affect ion mobilities also affect their activity coefficients, and the treatment of this second effect is important enough to cover here.

The theory of Debye and Hückel (1923) constituted a major breakthrough. Earlier observations, especially by G. Lewis, had shown that the activity coefficients of electrolytes were, in dilute solutions, determined more by ionic strength than by any specific chemical property. The implication that nonideality effects are due mainly to long-range Coulomb interactions between ions was accepted, but the problem of treating a collection of ions seemed insurmountable. The normal statistical mechanical approach would require one somehow to list the energy states of each ion while recognizing that its energy was affected by the location of all other ions.

The path that Debye and Hückel found was through the assumption that there exists some average potential around each ion and that each potential field is independent, that is, one does not perturb another. Further assumptions were that the electrolyte is completely dissociated and, at first, that the ions are of negligible size. It was also assumed that electrical interactions are solely responsible for deviations from nonideality. The treatment is therefore limited to rather dilute solutions.

We proceed as follows, taking for simplicity the electrolyte to be of the uni-univalent type. It is assumed that there is some average potential ψ which is a function of distance r from any particular ion. The potential energy of an ion in this potential is $e\psi$, where e is the electronic charge. Since we are dealing with Coulomb's law, ψ will be in esu units and likewise e. The probability of finding a positive ion in a region of potential ψ around a particular ion of like charge is given by the Boltzmann principle:

$$\mathbf{n}_+ = \mathbf{n}e^{-e\psi/kT}, \tag{12-74}$$

where $\mathbf{n}$ is the average concentration in molecules per cubic centimeter. Similarly

$$\mathbf{n}_- = \mathbf{n}e^{e\psi/kT}. \tag{12-75}$$

The net charge density ρ is then

$$\rho = (\mathbf{n}_+ - \mathbf{n}_-)e = \mathbf{n}e(e^{-e\psi/kT} - e^{e\psi/kT}). \tag{12-76}$$

The next major assumption, without which further progress would have stopped, was that a theorem from electrostatics, known as the Poisson equation, could be used. This states that the rate of change or the divergence of the gradient of the electrostatic potential at a given point is proportional to the charge density at that point. The equation is valid for a continuous medium of uniform dielectric constant D and the equation for spherical coordinates is

$$\nabla^2\psi = \frac{1}{r^2}\frac{d}{dr}\left(r^2\frac{d\psi}{dr}\right) = -\frac{4\pi\rho}{D}. \tag{12-77}$$

This implies that the random motion of ions gives a smeared-out charge density to which Eq. (12-77) can be applied.

We now combine Eqs. (12-76) and (12-77) to obtain what has come to be known as the *Poisson–Boltzmann equation*:

$$\nabla^2\psi = -\frac{4\pi\mathbf{n}e}{D}(e^{-e\psi/kT} - e^{e\psi/kT}). \tag{12-78}$$

The assumptions implicit up to this point (such as the independence of the potential fields around each ion) require that the effect not be a large one, that is, that $e\psi/kT$ be a small number. We therefore proceed to expand the exponentials, keeping only the first term, to obtain

$$\nabla^2\psi = \left(\frac{8\pi\mathbf{n}e^2}{DkT}\right)\psi. \tag{12-79}$$

523

The collection of quantities multiplying ψ on the right-hand side of Eq. (12-79) is assembled into a single parameter κ, defined as

$$\kappa^2 = \frac{4\pi e^2}{DkT} \sum_i z_i^2 \mathbf{n}_i .$$ (12-80)

Equation (12-80) applies to the general case of a collection of ions of charges z_i and reduces to $\kappa^2 = 8\pi \mathbf{n}e^2/DkT$ for a uni-univalent electrolyte. Equation (12-79) then becomes

$$\nabla^2 \psi = \kappa^2 \psi.$$ (12-81)

The solution to Eq. (12-81) is

$$\psi(r) = \frac{ze}{Dr} e^{-\kappa r}.$$ (12-82)

This may be verified by insertion of the expression for $\psi(r)$ back into Eq. (12-81). Thus

$$\frac{d\psi}{dr} = -\frac{ze}{Dr^2} e^{-\kappa r} - \frac{ze\kappa}{Dr} e^{-\kappa r},$$

$$r^2 \frac{d\psi}{dr} = -\frac{ze}{D} e^{-\kappa r} - \frac{ze\kappa r}{D} e^{-\kappa r},$$

$$\frac{d}{dr}\left(r^2 \frac{d\psi}{dr}\right) = \frac{ze\kappa}{D} e^{-\kappa r} - \frac{ze\kappa}{D} e^{-\kappa r} + \frac{ze\kappa^2 r}{D} e^{-\kappa r}$$

$$= \frac{ze\kappa^2 r}{D} e^{-\kappa r},$$

$$\frac{1}{r^2}\frac{d}{dr}\left(r^2 \frac{d\psi}{dr}\right) = \frac{ze\kappa^2}{Dr} e^{-\kappa r} = \kappa^2 \psi \qquad \text{Q.E.D.}$$

We again expand the exponential, keeping only the first terms, to get

$$\psi(r) = \frac{ze}{Dr} - \frac{ze}{D\epsilon} \kappa.$$ (12-83)

The first term on the right is just the potential due to the charge on the ion itself, and we are interested only in the second term, $-ze\kappa/D$, which gives the alteration in the potential due to the distribution of other ions around the given ion. Notice that this second term corresponds to the potential of a charge $-ze$ as observed at a distance $1/\kappa$. The quantity $1/\kappa$ has the dimensions of distance (centimeters in the cgs system) and has come to be known as the *effective* or *equivalent radius of the ion atmosphere*. The simple physical picture, illustrated in Fig. 12-9, is thus one of an ion of charge ze having a statistical excess of ions of opposite charge around it, the excess amounting to just $-ze$ and behaving as though it were located on a spherical shell of radius $1/\kappa$.

It is next necessary to find the free energy associated with this extra potential

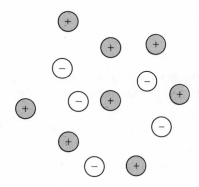

Fig. 12-9. *Illustration of the ion atmosphere effect.*

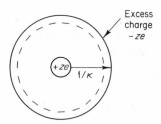

originating from the ion atmosphere. This is done by calculating the reversible work needed to form the atmosphere: We integrate the product of potential times charge as the ion is allowed to build up its charge from zero to the full value:

$$\text{electrical work} = \int_0^{ze} \psi_{\text{atm}}\, d(ze) = \int_0^{ze} \left(-\frac{ze\kappa}{D}\right) d(ze)$$

or

$$w_{\text{el}} = -\frac{1}{2}\frac{\kappa}{D}(ze)^2.$$

This electrical work then contributes to the chemical potential μ_i of the ith ion:

$$\mu_i = \mu_i{}^\circ + kT \ln a_i + w_{\text{el}}.$$

Since the whole derivation is for a very dilute solution, it seems safe to assume $a_i = m_i$, that is, that the ion obeys Henry's law *apart from the electrical contribution*. This last is the source of the observed deviation from ideality, reported experimentally in terms of an activity coefficient. The conclusion is then

$$w_{\text{el}} = kT \ln \gamma_i = -\frac{z_i{}^2 e^2 \kappa}{2D}$$

or

$$\ln \gamma_i = -\frac{z_i^2 e^2 \kappa}{2DkT}.$$ (12-84)

We next need to find the mean activity coefficient for the case of an electrolyte having just two kinds of ions. From Eq. (12-64) we have

$$\ln \gamma_\pm = \frac{\nu_+}{\nu} \ln \gamma_+ + \frac{\nu_-}{\nu} \ln \gamma_-.$$ (12-85)

Algebraic manipulation of Eqs. (12-85) and (12-61) gives

$$\ln \gamma_\pm = -|z_+z_-| \frac{e^2 \kappa}{2DkT}.$$ (12-86)

Finally, κ can be related to the ionic strength I [Eq. (12-70)] since $n_i = (C_i/1000) N_0$ and in dilute solution $C_i = m_i \rho_0$, where ρ_0 is the solvent density. Equation (12-80) becomes

$$\kappa^2 = \frac{8\pi e^2 N_0^2 \rho_0}{1000 DRT} I$$ (12-87)

and so Eq. (12-86) becomes

$$\ln \gamma_\pm = -|z_+z_-| \frac{e^3 N_0^2}{DRT} \left(\frac{2\pi\rho_0}{1000 DRT}\right)^{1/2} I^{1/2}$$ (12-88)

$$= -A |z_+z_-| I^{1/2}.$$

Insertion of the values for the general constants (e in esu and R in erg mole^{-1} $^\circ K^{-1}$) gives

$$\log \gamma_\pm = -1.823 \times 10^6 |z_+z_-| \left(\frac{\rho_0}{D^3 T^3}\right)^{1/2} I^{1/2}.$$ (12-89)

For water at 25°C, $D = 78.54$ and Eq. (12-89) reduces to

$$\log \gamma_\pm = -0.509 |z_+z_-| I^{1/2}.$$ (12-90)

The Debye–Hückel treatment leads, first of all, to a theoretical explanation of the empirical observation that the activity coefficient of an electrolyte is determined by the ionic strength I of the medium. The quantitative predictions, as for example, from Eq. (12-90), have been well verified for uni-univalent electrolytes. The theoretical slopes are included in Figs. 12-6 and 12-7, and the experimental points approach agreement at low concentrations. One may make a more direct check by plotting the activity coefficient data of Table 12-7 according to Eq. (12-90). This is done in Fig. 12-10, and it is apparent that the uni-univalent electrolytes approach agreement with theory. It is less clear whether accurate agreement occurs in the case of the higher charge types. Equation (12-90) is a limiting law in that

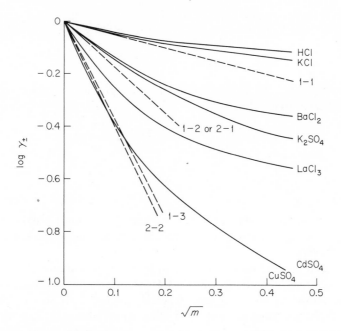

Fig. 12-10. *Plot of activity coefficient data at 25°C so as to test the Debye–Hückel theory. Dashed lines give the various limiting law slopes.*

various approximations restrict its validity to dilute solutions, and it has been assumed that activity coefficients for the more highly charged electrolytes will approach the theoretical predictions at sufficiently low concentrations. This aspect is discussed further in the Commentary and Notes section.

12-9 Ionic Equilibria

There are two somewhat separate aspects of the treatment of ionic equilibria. The first, introduced in Section 12-7, is that of the determination of the true or thermodynamic equilibrium constant. Recall that the basic procedure is the extrapolation of a concentration equilibrium constant, K_{sp} in the case of solubility and K in the case of homogeneous equilibrium, to infinite dilution. To review this aspect briefly, we write for each species $\mu_i = \mu_i{}^\circ + RT \ln a_i$, and, following the derivation of Eq. (7-10), obtain

$$\Delta G = (m\mu_M + n\mu_N + \cdots) - (a\mu_A + b\mu_B + \cdots)$$

or

$$\Delta G = \Delta G^0 + RT \ln Q_{th}, \qquad Q_{th} = \frac{a_M{}^m a_N{}^n \cdots}{a_A{}^a a_B{}^b \cdots}. \qquad (12\text{-}91)$$

At equilibrium $\Delta G = 0$, and Q_{th} becomes the thermodynamic equilibrium constant K_{th} :

$$\Delta G^0 = -RT \ln K_{th} . \tag{12-92}$$

It is convenient for us to write each activity as a product of concentration and activity coefficient, to obtain

$$K_{th} = \frac{(M)^m (N)^n \cdots}{(A)^a (B)^b \cdots} \frac{\gamma_M{}^m \gamma_N{}^n \cdots}{\gamma_A{}^a \gamma_B{}^b} = K K_\gamma ,$$

or

$$K = \frac{K_{th}}{K_\gamma} , \tag{12-93}$$

where K is the concentration equilibrium constant, using mole fraction, molality, or molarity, and K_γ is the activity coefficient constant using the corresponding activity coefficients.

Solution equilibria are usually studied in fairly dilute solutions, and one commonly assumes that nonionic species obey Henry's law, that is, have unit activity coefficients. However, we have seen that electrolytes show serious departures from ideality even at high dilution, and quite appreciable error can result if we treat ionic equilibria without considering K_γ . Several procedures are possible. First, as already discussed, one may extrapolate K values to infinite dilution so as to obtain K_{th} , and then back calculate the K_γ value for each equilibrium condition. One may estimate K_γ by evaluating each ion activity coefficient from the Debye–Hückel equation (12-89) or (12-90). One may, alternatively, use an experimental mean activity coefficient from some independent source. Thus if K_{th} is for a solubility equilibrium, then, as discussed in Section 12-7, K_γ will correspond to the mean activity coefficient of the electrolyte raised to the power ν, and standard tables of activity coefficients, such as Table 12-8, can be used. In the case of an equilibrium such as

$$Ac^- + H_2O = HAc + OH^-,$$

where ions of more than one electrolyte are involved, it is always possible to give K in terms of mean activity coefficient ratios. Thus in this case, we have

$$K_\gamma = \frac{\gamma_{OH^-}}{\gamma_{Ac^-}} \tag{12-94}$$

and if the cation present in the solution is Na^+, multiplication of the numerator and denominator of Eq. (12-94) gives

$$K_\gamma = \frac{\gamma_{\pm,NaOH}^2}{\gamma_{\pm,NaAc}^2} . \tag{12-95}$$

It is usually acceptable to take activity coefficients in mixed electrolytes, $\gamma_{\pm,NaOH}$ and $\gamma_{\pm,NaAc}$ in this case, to be the same as for the pure electrolyte species at the same overall ionic strength, although specific effects would have to be allowed for in accurate work.

A remaining device that is employed is to examine the equilibrium in the presence of a large excess of nonparticipating electrolyte, often $NaClO_4$. The nature of the solvent medium is in this way made essentially independent of the concentrations of the species and K_{th}/K_y is therefore constant. The use of a swamping electrolyte is very common, for example, in the study of reaction kinetics involving ionic species.

The second aspect of the treatment of ionic equilibria, and the principal subject of this section, is that of the algebraic relationships and manipulations that are useful. These are for the most part standard, and the discussion here will be cursory except for some special cases. Table 12-9 gives some representative ionic

Table 12-9. *Ionic Equilibrium Constants*[a]

Solubility products			
Salt	K_{sp}	Salt	K_{sp}
CuCl	1.0×10^{-6} [b]	$Ag(C_2H_3O_2)$	1.8×10^{-3} [b]
$PbCl_2$	1.0×10^{-4}	AgCl	1.55×10^{-10}
$PbCrO_4$	1.8×10^{-14} [b]	AgBr	7.7×10^{-13}
$Mg(C_2O_4)$	8.6×10^{-5} [b]	AgI	1.5×10^{-16}
$HgCl_2$	2.6×10^{-15}	Ag_2CrO_4	9×10^{-12}
HgCl	2×10^{-18}	TlCl	2.7×10^{-4}

Dissociation of simple acids and bases			
Acid	K_a	Base	K_b
H_2O	1.01×10^{-14}	NH_4OH	1.8×10^{-5}
CH_3COOH	1.75×10^{-5}	$C_6H_5NH_3OH$	3.8×10^{-10}
$CH_2ClCOOH$	1.38×10^{-3}	$C_2H_5NH_3OH$	5.6×10^{-4}
CCl_3COOH	0.13	—	—
C_6H_5COOH	6.3×10^{-5}	—	—
HCN	7.2×10^{-10}	—	—

Dissociation of polybasic acids			
Acid	K_1	K_2	K_3
H_2CO_3	4.31×10^{-7}	5.6×10^{-11}	—
$H_2C_2O_4$	6.5×10^{-2}	6.1×10^{-5}	—
$C_4H_4O_4$ (succinic acid)	6.4×10^{-5}	2.7×10^{-6}	—
H_2S	9.1×10^{-8}	1.2×10^{-15}	—
H_2SO_4	Strong	0.012	—
H_2SO_3	0.0172	6.24×10^{-8}	—
H_3PO_4	7.5×10^{-3}	6.2×10^{-8}	4.8×10^{-13}
H_3AsO_4	5×10^{-3}	8.3×10^{-6}	6×10^{-10}

[a] Aqueous solution at 25°C.   [b] 18°C.

equilibrium constants, and we now proceed to consider the use of solubility products in calculating solubilities under various circumstances, and then the treatment of simple acids and bases. A more detailed approach to acid–base equilibria is given in the Special Topics section.

A. Solubility Equilibria

The solubility product expression for a 1–1 electrolyte is

$$MX(s) = M^{z+} + X^{z-}, \qquad K_{sp} = (M^{z+})(M^{z-}),$$

and, for the general case,

$$M_{\nu_+}X_{\nu_-}(s) = \nu_+ M^{z+} + \nu_- X^{z-}, \qquad K_{sp} = (M^{z+})^{\nu_+}(X^{z-})^{\nu_-} \qquad \text{[Eq. (12-60)]}.$$

The solid salt is taken to be in its standard state and hence to have unit activity, but we must remember that for K_{sp} to apply, the solid must in fact be in equilibrium with the solution.

The solubility S of an electrolyte is defined as the number of gram formula weights that dissolve in the particular medium. If there is no added common ion, then $S = (M^{z+})/\nu_+ = (X^{z-})/\nu_-$, so in the general case

$$K_{sp} = (\nu_+)^{\nu_+}(\nu_-)^{\nu_-} S^{\nu}.$$

As an example, $K_{sp} = 9 \times 10^{-12}$ for Ag_2CrO_4 at 25°C, so we have

$$9 \times 10^{-12} = (2)^2 (1) S^3, \qquad S = 1.3 \times 10^{-4}.$$

If, however, an electrolyte is present which furnishes a common ion, say X^{z-}, then the solubility is given by $(M^{z+})/\nu_+$. The expression for K_{sp} becomes

$$K_{sp} = (\nu_+ S)^{\nu_+}(C + \nu_- S)^{\nu_-},$$

where C is the concentration of added X^{z-}.

Continuing this example, if 0.1 m Na_2CrO_4 is also present, then

$$9 \times 10^{-12} = (2S)^2(0.1 + S).$$

The resulting cubic equation is best solved by successive approximations:

$$S_1 \simeq \left(\frac{9 \times 10^{-12}}{(4)(0.1)}\right)^{1/2} = 4.7 \times 10^{-6}.$$

The first approximation, S_1, gives a result small compared to 0.1, and is therefore adequate. A more serious calculation would now proceed to the estimation of K_γ for a solution S molal in Ag_2CrO_4 and 0.1 m in Na_2CrO_4 as the medium, so as to obtain a more nearly correct K_{sp} using Eq. (12-93).

Another type of complication is that the dissolved salt may not be fully dissociated. For example, appreciable amounts of CoOx (where Ox denotes oxalate ion)
are present in solution as the undissociated molecule. If the solution is saturated
with respect to CoOx(s), the concentration S_0 of undissociated CoOx in solution
is a constant. The observed solubility S is then $S_0 + (Co^{2+})$, and if Na_2Ox is
added, then S decreases according to the equation

$$S = S_0 + \frac{K_{sp}}{C + (S - S_0)},$$

where C is the concentration of added common ion and $(S - S_0)$ that of the
oxalate ion from the dissolved solid. The concentration S_0 does not change. The
behavior is shown schematically in Fig. 12-11 by curve a; curve b shows the
behavior for $S_0 = 0$. A not uncommon added feature is that with further addition
of oxalate ion, the complex $Co(Ox)_2^{2-}$ begins to form. This has the effect of increasing the amount of Co^{2+} in solution and hence the measured solubility, whose
variation is now given by curve c. Algebraic analysis of data of this type gives
both S_0 and the formation equilibrium constant for any complex that may form.

Other cases of complex formation with slightly soluble salts include the well-
known example of $Ag(CN)_2^-$, as well as that of $AgCl_2^-$ and other silver halide
complexes.

Finally, if the anion of the slightly soluble salt is one of a weak acid, then the
solubility will depend on the pH of the solution. Thus in the case of silver acetate
the following simultaneous equilibria would hold:

$$AgAc(s) = Ag^+ + Ac^-, \qquad K_{sp} = 1.8 \times 10^{-3},$$

$$HAc = H^+ + Ac^-, \qquad K = 1.75 \times 10^{-5}.$$

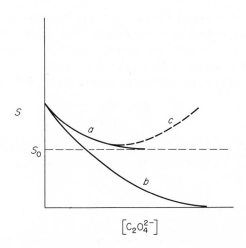

$$\left[C_2O_4^{2-}\right]$$

Fig. 12-11.   *Effect of complex formation on the solubility of* $Co(C_2O_4)$.

If the pH is known, this determines the degree of dissociation α of the acid, and

$$K_{\mathrm{sp}} = (\mathrm{Ag^+})(\mathrm{Ac^-}) = S(\alpha S).$$

In this case the total acetic acid substance is given by the solubility S, but the actual $\mathrm{Ac^-}$ concentration is only αS.

B. Equilibrium across a Semipermeable Membrane

An important type of ionic equilibrium is that across a membrane which is permeable only to certain of the ions present. The situation is known as one of *Donnan equilibrium*. As an example, consider the arrangement shown in Fig. 10-3, but now suppose that the "solution" side, side II, contains ions $\mathrm{M^+}$, $\mathrm{N^+}$, and $\mathrm{X^-}$, while the "solvent" side, side I, contains only ions $\mathrm{M^+}$ and $\mathrm{X^-}$. The membrane is permeable to solvent and to $\mathrm{M^+}$ and $\mathrm{X^-}$ ions, but *not to* $\mathrm{N^+}$ ions. Such selectivity is shown, for example, by the membranes of living nerve cells.

The condition for ionic equilibrium is that the activity a_2 [see Eq. (12-52)] be the same on both sides of the membrane for that electrolyte to which it is permeable, in this case $\mathrm{M^+}$, $\mathrm{X^-}$. Thus

$$a_{\mathrm{M^+}}^{\mathrm{I}} a_{\mathrm{X^-}}^{\mathrm{I}} = a_{\mathrm{M^+}}^{\mathrm{II}} a_{\mathrm{X^-}}^{\mathrm{II}} . \tag{12-96}$$

If the solutions are dilute, activities may be replaced by concentrations. Also, electroneutrality requires that $(\mathrm{M^+})^{\mathrm{I}} = (\mathrm{X^-})^{\mathrm{I}} = C$ and $(\mathrm{M^+})^{\mathrm{II}} + (\mathrm{N^+})^{\mathrm{II}} = (\mathrm{X^-})^{\mathrm{II}}$. Equation (12-96) thus reduces to

$$C^2 = (\mathrm{M^+})^{\mathrm{II}} [(\mathrm{M^+})^{\mathrm{II}} + (\mathrm{N^+})^{\mathrm{II}}]. \tag{12-97}$$

Suppose that $C = 0.01\ m$ and that $(\mathrm{N^+}) = 0.1\ m$. We find $(\mathrm{M^+})^{\mathrm{II}} = 9.9 \times 10^{-4}\ m$ and see that the Donnan effect acts to exclude $\mathrm{M^+}$ from side II. If C is $10^{-3}\ m$, $(\mathrm{M^+})^{\mathrm{II}}$ drops to $1 \times 10^{-5}\ m$, and the exclusion ratio $(\mathrm{M^+})^{\mathrm{I}}/(\mathrm{M^+})^{\mathrm{II}}$ increases from 10.1 to 100.

The physical basis for the exclusion effect is that a potential difference, the *Donnan potential* ϕ, makes side II positive relative to side I. It can be shown that

$$\phi = \frac{RT}{\mathscr{F}} \ln \frac{(\mathrm{M^+})^{\mathrm{I}}}{(\mathrm{M^+})^{\mathrm{II}}} , \tag{12-98}$$

where $\mathscr{F}$ is Faraday's number [see Eq. (13-12)]. In the numerical example, ϕ is 0.0594 V and 0.118 V for C values of 0.01 m and 0.001 m, respectively, for 25°C.

C. Weak Acids and Bases

The treatment of dissociation equilibria involving weak acids and bases will be limited here to the cases of a simple acid HA and a simple base BOH. Even so, the general solutions can involve rather complex algebraic manipulations. A powerful alternative approach is given in the Special Topics section.

We consider first the weak monobasic acid HA:

$$HA = H^+ + A^-, \qquad K_a = \frac{(H^+)(A^-)}{(HA)}. \qquad (12\text{-}99)$$

The general situation is one of a solution prepared by dissolving amounts of HA and of the salt MA so as to give the formalities f_{HA} and f_{MA}. The cation M^+ is assumed not to hydrolyze. With the solvent taken to be water, we have

$$H_2O = H^+ + OH^-, \qquad K_w = (H^+)(OH^-). \qquad (12\text{-}100)$$

The solution must be electrically neutral, and so

$$(M^+) + (H^+) = (A^-) + (OH^-), \qquad (12\text{-}101)$$

where $(M^+) = f_{MA}$. Finally, by material balance

$$(HA) + (A^-) = f_{HA} + f_{MA}. \qquad (12\text{-}102)$$

Note that (HA) and (A⁻) denote the actual concentrations of these species, whereas f_{HA} and f_{MA} are the amounts weighed out per 1000 g of water when the solution is made up.

The preceding four equations must be solved simultaneously, and it is helpful to reduce them as follows. From Eq. (12-101) we have

$$(A^-) = f_{MA} + (H^+) - (OH^-)$$

and insertion of this result into Eq. (12-102) gives

$$(HA) = f_{HA} - (H^+) + (OH^-).$$

Equation (12-99) then becomes

$$K_a = \frac{(H^+)[f_{MA} + (H^+) + (OH^-)]}{f_{HA} - (H^+) + (OH^-)}. \qquad (12\text{-}103)$$

The simultaneous solution of Eqs. (12-100) and (12-103) then gives (H^+) and (OH^-) for any formal composition.

Equation (12-103) simplifies considerably under various special conditions.

Case 1. $f_{MA} = 0$. Then

$$K_a = \frac{(H^+)[(H^+) - (OH^-)]}{f_{HA} - (H^+) + (OH^-)}. \qquad (12\text{-}104)$$

If $(OH^-) \ll (H^+)$, then $K_a = (H^+)^2/[f_{HA} - (H^+)]$. This condition holds if $(H^+)^2 > 10^{-12}$ and hence if $K_a f_{HA} > 10^{-12}$. If also $f_{HA} \gg (H^+)$, then $K_a = (H^+)^2/f_{HA}$. This condition holds if $f_{HA} > 100(H^+)$ and hence if $f_{HA} > 10^4 K_a$.

As examples, for 0.1 m HAc, $K_a f_{HA} = 1.75 \times 10^{-6}$ and is much greater than 10^{-12}. Since f_{HA} is about $10^4 K_a$, the last approximation can just be used (to 1 % error) and $(H^+)^2 = 1.75 \times 10^{-6}$, $(H^+) = 1.32 \times 10^{-3}$. However, if f_{HA} were 10^{-8} m, then $K_a f_{HA}$ would be 1.75×10^{-13}, and the full equation (12-103) would be needed.

Case 2. $f_{HA} = 0$. Then

$$K_a = \frac{(H^+)[f_{MA} + (H^+) - (OH^-)]}{-(H^+) + (OH^-)}.$$

If we divide K_a by K_w to give K_h, the hydrolysis constant, we obtain

$$K_h = \frac{K_w}{K_a} = \frac{(OH^-)[(OH^-) - (H^+)]}{f_{MA} + (H^+) - (OH^-)}. \tag{12-105}$$

This is of the same form as Eq. (12-104), and the same two types of approximation follow:

$$\text{If} \quad K_h f_{MA} > 10^{-12}, \quad \text{then} \quad K_h = \frac{(OH^-)^2}{f_{MA} - (OH^-)}.$$

$$\text{If} \quad f_{MA} > 10^4 K_h, \quad \text{then} \quad K_h = \frac{(OH^-)^2}{f_{MA}}.$$

For example, $K_h = 1.01 \times 10^{-14}/1.75 \times 10^{-5} = 5.77 \times 10^{-10}$. For 0.1 m NaAc, $K_h f_{MA} = 5.77 \times 10^{-11}$, or more than 10^{-12}, and $f_{MA} = 0.1$, or more than $10^4 K_h$. The simplest form may then be used and $(OH^-)^2 = (0.1)(5.77 \times 10^{-10})$, $(OH^-) = 7.6 \times 10^{-6}$, $(H^+) = 1.3 \times 10^{-9}$.

Case 3. If f_{MA} and f_{HA} are each greater than (H^+) or (OH^-), then Eq. (12-103) reduces to

$$K_a = \frac{(H^+) f_{MA}}{f_{HA}}. \tag{12-106}$$

The solution is now said to be *buffered*. That is, in order to change (H^+) appreciably, we must add sufficient acid or base to change f_{MA} or f_{HA} appreciably. Thus in a solution 0.1 f in HAc and 0.1 f in NaAc, (H^+) will be 1.75×10^{-5}. Addition of 0.01 f HCl changes f_{HAc} to 0.11 and f_{NaAc} to 0.09, and hence (H^+) only changes to 2.1×10^{-5}.

A parallel set of relationships holds for the weak base BOH:

$$BOH = B^+ + OH^-, \qquad K_b = \frac{(B^+)(OH^-)}{(BOH)}.$$

The analog of Eq. (12-103) is

$$K_b = \frac{(OH^-)[f_{BX} + (OH^-) - (H^+)]}{f_{BOH} - (OH^-) + (H^+)}, \tag{12-107}$$

where X^- is a nonhydrolyzing anion. The various special cases are similarly analogous to those for the weak acid.

We can find the equilibrium concentrations in a solution containing HA, MA, BOH, and BX, by solving Eqs. (12-100), (12-103), and (12-107) simultaneously. If all of the concentrations (HA), (A^-), (BOH), and (B^+) are much larger than that of (H^+) or (OH^-), then these ions may be ignored in the charge balance, and the simultaneous equations to be solved are

$$BOH + HA = B^+ + A^- + H_2O, \qquad K_{ab} = \frac{(B^+)(A^-)}{(BOH)(HA)} = \frac{K_a K_b}{K_w},$$

$$(B^+) + f_{MA} = (A^-) + f_{BX}, \qquad f_{HA} + f_{MA} = (HA) + (A^-),$$

$$f_{BOH} + f_{BX} = (BOH) + (B^+).$$

D. Titration Curves

An acid–base titration consists of adding successive amounts of a base to a solution of an acid, or of an acid to a solution of a base, and noting how the hydrogen ion concentration [or $pH = -\log(H^+)$] varies. We will consider only the first situation here.

The calculation of a titration curve is clarified if one recognizes that a solution which initially has a formality f_{HA} in acid is converted into one having formalities f'_{HA} and f'_{MA} by addition of a strong base, where f'_{MA} is the formality of the added base and $f'_{HA} + f'_{MA} = f_{HA}$. As a specific example, consider a solution that initially is $0.1 f$ in acetic acid. Addition of sodium hydroxide sufficient to make the solution $0.05 f$ in NaOH must yield an equilibrium mixture identical to that which would be obtained if the solution were $0.05 f$ in HAc and $0.05 f$ in NaAc. In effect, the formal composition of the solution may be expressed in two alternative ways:

$$\left.\begin{array}{l} 0.1 f \text{ in HAc} \\ 0.05 f \text{ in NaOH} \end{array}\right\} \sim \left\{\begin{array}{l} 0.05 f \text{ in HAc,} \\ 0.05 f \text{ in NaAc.} \end{array}\right.$$

Both statements specify the same amount of acetic acid substance and sodium ion.

The general procedure for finding such alternative ways of expressing a formal composition is to consider species that would tend to react and then to suppose that the reaction goes to completion. The new formal composition is expressed in terms of the products. Thus HAc and NaOH tend to react:

$$HAc + Na^+ + OH^- = Na^+ + Ac^- + H_2O. \tag{12-108}$$

The alternative expression of formal composition follows if we suppose that the neutralization of the $0.1\,m$ HAc by $0.05\,m$ NaOH goes to completion, giving $0.05\,m$ NaAc and residual $0.05\,m$ HAc. The reaction does not in fact go entirely to completion, but the formal composition can be given as $0.05 f$ NaAc and $0.05 f$ HAc.

With this preamble, the calculation of a titration curve reduces to the calculation of (H^+) from Eq. (12-103) for various ratios of f_{MA} to f_{HA}, with their total kept constant. The equivalence point is that for which $f_{HA} = 0$. The result of such a calculation for a $0.002\,m$ acetic acid solution is shown in Fig. 12-12, where F_N

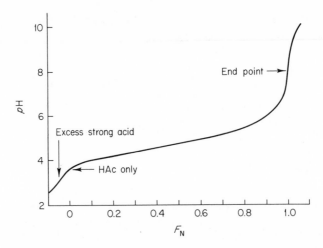

Fig. 12-12. *Titration curve for acetic acid using a strong base.*

is the degree of neutralization. (It has been assumed that the added sodium hydroxide solution is sufficiently concentrated that dilution effects can be neglected.)

Calculations of this type can be quite tedious, and as in the preceding subsection, the reader is reminded that a more general and powerful approach is given in the Special Topics section.

A titration may be followed conductimetrically. In a neutralization reaction such as that of Eq. (12-108), each portion of NaOH added converts an equivalent amount of HAc into $Na^+ + Ac^-$. The conductance of the solution therefore increases since a weak electrolyte is being replaced by a strong one. At the end point, further addition of NaOH adds Na^+ and OH^- ions to those of the NaAc, and the conductance increases more rapidly, as illustrated in Fig. 12-13. If the

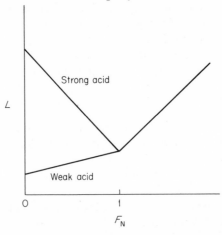

Fig. 12-13. *Conductimetric titration curves for a strong acid (upper left line) and a weak acid (lower left line).*

acid being titrated is a strong acid, then the neutralization converts the ions $H^+ + A^-$ into $Na^+ + A^-$ or, in effect, substitutes sodium ion for hydrogen ion. Since the equivalent conductivity of sodium ions is much less than that of hydrogen ions, the result is that the conductance drops during the titration until the end point is reached, and then rises as before.

Suppose that 0.1 m HCl is being titrated with concentrated NaOH (volume changes therefore being negligible) and that the conductance is followed using an immersion-type conductivity cell of cell constant 0.2. The initial conductance is $L_0 = (C\Lambda)/1000\kappa = (0.1)(426)/(1000)(0.2) = 0.213$ ohm^{-1}. When enough NaOH has been added to make the solution 0.05 f in NaOH or, alternatively, 0.05 m in NaCl and 0.05 m in residual HCl, the conductance L_1 is

$$L_1 = \frac{(0.05)(426) + (0.05)(126)}{(1000)(0.2)} = 0.138 \quad \text{ohm}^{-1}.$$

At the end point the formality of the added NaOH is 0.1, and the solution consists of just 0.1 m NaCl. The conductance $L_2 = (0.1)(126)/(1000)(0.2) = 0.063$ ohm^{-1}. When the end point is overshot with 0.15 f added NaOH, the system is 0.1 m in NaCl and 0.05 m in NaOH, and L_3 is now

$$L_3 = \frac{(0.1)(126) + (0.05)(248)}{(1000)(0.2)} = 0.125 \quad \text{ohm}^{-1}.$$

Thus the series of L values 0.213, 0.138, 0.063, and 0.125 goes through a minimum at the end point.

COMMENTARY AND NOTES

12-CN-1 Electrolytic Dissociation

A brief further discussion of the theory of electrolytic dissociation seems worthwhile. This is something we now take for granted, yet the reasons for the original resistance to Arrhenius' proposal were serious ones and should be appreciated. It must be remembered that in 1890 the electron as such had not yet been discovered; it would be many years before x-ray crystallography revealed the crystal structures of solids; and, of course, wave mechanics was not imagined. Mineral solids, such as NaCl, were known as hard, high-melting materials, similar in these respects to metals, and evidently held together by strong chemical forces. It seemed incredible that the mere dissolving of such a salt in water would break it up into fragments. The heat of solution of most salts is relatively small, and so it appeared that little play of energy was present; the most natural supposition was that solutions of mineral salts consisted of the molecular units.

Two types of observations led Arrhenius to attack this very reasonable picture. The first was the difficulty in accounting for Ohm's law being obeyed by electrolyte solutions. The original Grotthus idea of salt molecules exchanging polar parts (Fig. 12-1) implied that even the most minute applied potential would induce a chain of bond breaking and making. This was contrary to experimental evidence, which strongly indicated that electrical charge carriers were ever-present, waiting to carry current, and did not have to be created by an applied potential. The second type of observation was that of the colligative behavior of electrolyte solutions. Van't Hoff, in particular, had found it necessary to introduce his (now famous) i factor into the osmotic equation [Eq. (10-58)]. The experimental result is that $i \approx 2$ for aqueous NaCl and this was entirely mysterious until electrolytic dissociation was proposed. At that time, the situation was clouded by what we now understand to be combinations of interionic attraction and partial dissociation effects, and i values rarely came out as simple, rational fractions. At first, Arrhenius took all electrolytes to be partially dissociated except at extreme dilution, and the i factors were used to calculate the degree of dissociation. Thus a salt $M_{\nu_+} X_{\nu_-}$, producing ν ions on complete dissociation, would actually furnish only $[(1 - \alpha)m + \nu\alpha m]$ particles if the degree of dissociation were α. The i value is the ratio of the observed or colligative molality to the formality, so we have

$$i = \frac{(1 - \alpha)m + \nu\alpha m}{m} = (1 - \alpha) + \alpha\nu,$$

whence

$$\alpha = \frac{i - 1}{\nu - 1}.$$

Although we do not now accept such α values as correct for strong electrolytes, it was the combined impact of colligative property and conductance measurements that established the theory of electrolytic dissociation.

As noted in Section 12-3, it became necessary to class electrolytes as strong or as weak. Weak electrolytes obey the Ostwald dilution law well, and their behavior is thus determined primarily by a dissociation equilibrium. Strong electrolytes, however, do not obey a dissociation equilibrium constant at all well, and it was not until the development of interionic attraction theory that they could be understood.

We can also now explain how it is possible that strongly bonded salt crystals can so readily dissociate in water solution. X-ray crystallography tells us that crystalline NaCl consists of a closely packed array of alternate Na^+ and Cl^- ions and not of molecular Na—Cl units (Section 19-3). The strong forces that hold the crystal together are primarily Coulomb attractions between unlike charged ions. The Coulomb attractive potential between one Na^+ and an adjacent ion is

$$\phi = \frac{e^2}{r}, \qquad (12\text{-}109)$$

where r is the distance between the centers of the ions. The picture is essentially that of Fig. 8-6, and a summation of all of the mutual Coulomb interactions gives the total crystal or so-called lattice energy. Such calculations (see Section 19-ST-2) agree well with the observed heats of sublimation, 184 kcal mole^{-1} in the case of NaCl. As an approximate calculation, $r = 2.74$ Å in NaCl(s), so $\phi = (4.8 \times 10^{-10})^2/2.74 \times 10^{-8} = 8.41 \times 10^{-11}$ erg. This corresponds to 121 kcal mole^{-1} as the estimated energy of vaporization of Na$^+$ + Cl$^-$. More exact calculation gives 185.9 kcal mole^{-1}.

Equation (12-109) applies if the medium in which the ions are present is vacuum; otherwise the dielectric constant enters in the denominator. Water has a dielectric constant of about 80, so the energy to dissociate NaCl would be reduced to about 1.5 kcal mole^{-1}. Thus by inserting itself between the ions, water reduces their mutual attraction to a point where the gain in entropy on dissolution can make the process occur. The 125 kcal mole^{-1} or other analogous quantity has not disappeared. This much energy is still required to take the aqueous Na$^+$ and Cl$^-$ ions into the gas phase. In other words, the strong mutual binding in the crystal has, in solution, been replaced by a strong binding to water. We speak of this binding as the *hydration energy* and ionic crystals may be said to dissolve in water because the hydration energy nearly balances the lattice energy. It is interesting, for example, that the heat of solution of an anhydrous salt is generally more negative (more heat is evolved) than that of a corresponding hydrate. Thus the heat of solution of Na$_2$SO$_4$ is -0.5 kcal mole^{-1}, while that of Na$_2$SO$_4 \cdot$ 10H$_2$O is 19 kcal mole^{-1}; the presence of water of hydration in the crystal has noticeably diminished the amount of hydration energy available when the crystal dissolves.

The Coulomb forces between ions in aqueous solution, although greatly reduced from those between ions in the crystal, are still important; they give rise to the interionic attraction effects in conductance and in the Debye–Hückel treatment of nonideality. It seems certain that ion pairs and possibly ion clusters form in concentrated solutions as discussed in the next section.

12-CN-2 Activity Coefficients for Other than Dilute Aqueous Solutions

It was noted in Section 12-8 that the activity coefficients of uni-univalent electrolytes approach the Debye–Hückel limiting law in dilute solutions, and that the values for other valence types also would do so at extreme dilution. In effect, however, the simple Debye–Hückel treatment is valid only for slightly "contaminated" water, and a great deal of effort has been devoted to the physical chemical treatment of more concentrated aqueous solutions and of nonaqueous solutions. The first improvement was with the recognition of the finite size of ions, based on the assumption that there is some distance a of closest approach; the effect is to modify ψ in such a way as to lead to the following equation:

$$\ln \gamma_i = -\frac{z^2 e^2}{2DkT} \frac{\kappa}{1 + \kappa a} \tag{12-110}$$

or

$$\log \gamma_\pm = -\frac{AI^{1/2}}{1 + BI^{1/2}}, \tag{12-111}$$

where A is as defined in Eq. (12-88) and B is given by

$$B = \frac{35.56}{(DT)^{1/2}} \mathring{a} \tag{12-112}$$

where $\mathring{a}$ is now in Ångstroms. For water at 25°C, $B = 0.232\mathring{a}$. Equation (12-111) fits activity coefficient data for uni-univalent electrolytes, up to perhaps 0.1 m, with reasonable values for $\mathring{a}$.

The next efforts were in various different directions. V. LaMer and others attempted to solve the Poisson–Boltzmann equation (12-78) more exactly, but encountered great mathematical difficulties. Although major departures from the simple theory were shown to be expected, especially for asymmetric electrolytes, such as those of the 1–2 type, the extended terms that they obtained are hard to use and are not very satisfactory. A semiempirical equation due to Brønsted suggested that at higher concentrations $\log \gamma_\pm$ should be proportional to m, and a commonly used form today is

$$\log \gamma_\pm = -\frac{AI^{1/2}}{1 + BI^{1/2}} + Cm. \tag{12-113}$$

Now B and C are treated as empirical constants. A more stimulating approach was that of N. Bjerrum, also of the Copenhagen school, who pointed out that in terms of the Debye–Hückel model, the probability of finding an ion of opposite charge near a given ion went through a minimum at a characteristic distance q:

$$q = \frac{e^2 z_1 z_2}{DkT}. \tag{12-114}$$

For a 1–1 electrolyte at 25°C, q is about 3.5 Å and Bjerrum suggested that ions closer than this distance should be regarded as ion pairs. The existence of a distance q arises as somewhat of an accident, however; $\psi(r)$ decreases steadily outward, but the volume of space increases with r^3 and it is the combination of these opposite factors that leads to q as the radius of the spherical shell having a minimum probability of finding a counter ion. The approach, however, established a pattern of thought that has been very useful.

At this point a distinction should be made between ion pairing and chemical association. Acetic acid is highly associated, but as a result of chemical bond formation between H^+ and Ac^-. Transition metal ions form coordinate bonds (see Section 12-ST-3) with anionic ligands; the case of CoOx and $Co(Ox)_2^{2-}$ mentioned in Section 12-9A is but one example. As just one further example, the Fe^{3+} ion forms the complex FeX^{2+}, where X may be a halogen, pseudohalogen, or hydroxide ion. In fact, transition metal ions have a solvation shell of coordinated water, and the formation of FeX^{2+} would more properly be written

$$Fe(H_2O)_6^{3+} + X^- = Fe(H_2O)_5X^{2+} + H_2O.$$

Many of these ligand substitution reactions are in rapid equilibrium, and the apparent nonideality of, say, aqueous $FeCl_3$ is largely due to complex formation. On the other hand, an ion such as Na^+ does not have much ability to form coordinate bonds, and the attraction between Na^+ and Cl^- is, as noted in the preceding section, mainly of Coulombic origin. We speak of *ion association* (or ion pairing), then, when we wish to think of the unit as consisting of the intact ions. The distinction between ion pairing and coordinative association is not always easy to make. The association which occurs with, say, Zn^{2+} and SO_4^{2-} may be partly Coulombic and partly coordinative—Zn^{2+} does, after all, form well-known complex ions. In the case of $Co(NH_3)_6^{3+}$, however, the coordination sphere is saturated, and the association constant of 1000 observed between this ion and SO_4^{2-} is therefore spoken of confidently as due to ion pairing.

To return to the matter of activity coefficients, we find that there is no question that ion pairing does occur in more concentrated solutions, and even in dilute ones if the ions are highly charged. R. M. Fuoss and C. A. Kraus have estimated ion pair dissociation constants for a number of electrolytes from conductivity measurements. For uni-univalent electrolytes values are of the order of unity and for di-divalent ones such as $ZnSO_4$ values are around 0.01 or less. The general conclusion is that the simple Debye–Hückel theory must be used with considerable caution for other than dilute solutions of uni-univalent electrolytes. Semiempirical equations such as Eq. (12-113) are very helpful, but it must be remembered that the constants B and C of the equation depend on the total ionic makeup of a solution and not just on the particular electrolyte in question.

Ion pairing, important in aqueous solutions, becomes a dominant feature in nonaqueous systems. As the dielectric constant of a medium is reduced, the Coulomb forces between ions increase, and the degree of dissociation of an electrolyte drops dramatically. As an example, the dissociation constant of KI is only about 2×10^{-4} in pyridine as solvent. There are a few nonaqueous solvents, of fairly high dielectric constant, in which electrolytes having large ions may be moderately dissociated. The salt $K^+[Cr(NH_3)_2(NCS)_4]^-$ is fully dissociated in nitromethane, and similar complex ions are moderately dissociated in dipolar aprotic solvents such as dimethylsulfoxide, dimethylformamide, and the like.

12-CN-3   Acids and Bases

A.   Aqueous Solutions

There are many interesting regularities in the dissociation constants of weak acids and bases. The following are a few examples which draw on the data of Table 12-9. Carboxylic acids tend to have K_a values of around 10^{-5}, except that as the carbon atom adjacent to the carboxyl group is subsituted with electro-negative groups, such as halogens, the acidity increases. For CCl_3COOH, $K_a = 0.13$, for example. This appears to be an inductive effect by which the carboxyl carbon atom is made more positive and the O—H bond is electrostatically weakened. A large number of acids of this type have been studied, and L. P. Hammett has used the data to characterize substituents. Thus in the case of substituted benzoic acids a substituent is assigned a parameter σ, defined as $\sigma = pK_0 - pK_s$, where $pK_0 = -\log K_0$, with K_0 the dissociation constant of benzoic acid, and $pK_s = -\log K_s$, with K_s the dissociation constant of the sub-stituted acid. The σ values are then found to correlate with the behavior of the compounds in other equilibria or in their reaction kinetics.

The electrostatic effect appears to be very important in determining the pK values of oxyacids. The approximately 10^5-fold reduction in successive K values for H_3PO_4 is one example. The three protons should be essentially equivalent, except for the increased electrostatic work of dissociation in the series H_3PO_4, $H_2PO_4^-$, HPO_4^{2-}. A useful empirical rule is that for an oxyacid of the general formula $MO_m(OH)_n$, pK_1 is approximately $7 - 5m$, pK_2 is $12 - 5m$, and so on. Thus for H_3PO_4, pK_1 should be $7 - 5 = 2$, pK_2 should be about $12 - 5 = 7$, and so on; for H_2SO_4, pK_1 is predicted to be -3, in agreement with the observa-tion that the first dissociation is that of a strong acid, while pK_2 should be 2, again about as observed.

Another type of situation is that in which two acid functions are sufficiently separated in a molecule that they should be essentially free of the preceding electrostatic effects. An example is $HOOC-(CH_2)_n-COOH$, where n is two or more. It might be supposed that K_1 and K_2 should be the same since the two groups are independent. A statistical factor remains, however. If the acid is represented by H_1H_2A, there are two ways for the first-stage dissociation to occur, namely to give H_1A^- or H_2A^-. There is only one choice of hydrogen to dissociate in the second stage, but the association reaction $H^+ + A^{2-}$ can occur on either position. Thus K_1 is enhanced and K_2 is diminished by this effect. In the case of succinic acid, $HOOC-(CH_2)_2-COOH$, $K_1 = 6.4 \times 10^{-5}$, or somewhat more than twice K_a for acetic acid, and K_2 is 2.7×10^{-6}, or about half K_a for acetic acid.

A related behavior is that of amino acids, typifying electrolytes having separated weakly acidic and weakly basic groups. An amino acid is sometimes shown in the form $H_2N-R-COOH$, but it appears certain that internal proton transfer is largely complete, so that $^+H_3N-R-COO^-$ is the actual species in aqueous solution. This last is known as a *zwitterion*. The behavior of an amino acid is then represented in terms of the two stages of dissociation of a dibasic acid:

$$^+H_3N-R-COOH = H^+ + {^+}H_3N-R-COO^-, \qquad K_1 = \frac{(H^+)(A^\pm)}{(A^+)},$$
$$\qquad A^+ \qquad\qquad\qquad\qquad A^\pm$$

$$^+H_3N-R-COO^- = H^+ + H_2N-R-COO^-, \qquad K_2 = \frac{(H^+)(A^-)}{(A^\pm)}.$$
$$\qquad A^\pm \qquad\qquad\qquad\qquad A^-$$

In the case of glycine, H_2NCH_3COOH, $K_1 = 4.5 \times 10^{-3}$ and $K_2 = 2.24 \times 10^{-12}$ at 25°C.

The *isoelectric* point is a state of special importance for an amino acid. This is the pH value such that $(A^+) = (A^-)$. Acid–base equilibria are rapid, which means that an individual amino acid molecule rapidly samples all its possible states of dissociation and at the isoelectric point it therefore spends equal times as A^+ and as A^-. The effect is that the amino acid behaves as though it were electrically neutral, even though it is still a conducting electrolyte; it displays essentially no net motion in an electrophoresis experiment, for example. Analysis of the preceding equilibrium relationships shows that at the isoelectric point $(H^+) = (K_1K_2)^{1/2}$. It can also be shown that at this pH the total degree of ionization of the amino acid is at a minimum. For this reason many of the physical properties of an amino acid solution exhibit maxima or minima at the isoelectric point.

B. Brønsted Treatment of Acids and Bases

The phenomenology of electrolyte behavior in aqueous solutions made it natural for Arrhenius and Ostwald to define an acid as a substance furnishing H^+ ions and a base as one furnishing OH^- ions. Neutralization then consisted of the reaction of these ions to give water. This formalism is an adequate and functioning one for the treatment of acid–base equilibria in water solution, although it is somewhat misleading chemically. The H^+ ion exists in water at least as H_3O^+, if not in more complex forms, and the dissociation of a weak acid is more correctly written as

$$HA + H_2O = A^- + H_3O^+ \qquad\qquad (12\text{-}115)$$

than as $HA = H^+ + A^-$. Similarly, a weak base may produce OH^- ions by the reaction

$$H_2O + B = OH^- + HB^+ \qquad\qquad (12\text{-}116)$$

(as, for example, with $B = NH_3$).

Brønsted and Lowry illuminated the chemistry of weak acids and bases by recognizing (in 1923) that the degree of a reaction such as those given by Eqs. (12-115) and (12-116) must depend on the natures of both reactants and that the reactions are really symmetric. They introduced the more general definitions that an *acid* is a *proton donor* and a *base* is a *proton acceptor*. Equations (12-115) and (12-116) now fall into the common form

acid + base = conjugate base + conjugate acid

$$\text{HA} + \text{H}_2\text{O} = \quad \text{A}^- \quad + \quad \text{H}_3\text{O}^+$$

$$\text{H}_2\text{O} + \text{B} = \quad \text{OH}^- \quad + \quad \text{HB}$$

An acid, on yielding a proton, becomes its conjugate base, and a base, on accepting a proton, becomes its conjugate acid.

The Brønsted picture has been useful in two major ways. First, it emphasizes that the anion of a weak acid is a proton acceptor, or a base, as well as OH^- ion and may be capable of reacting directly with a proton donor without going through the route of accepting an H^+ ion released by it. There are a number of cases of acid- or base-catalyzed reactions in which direct reaction evidently occurs. The rate of reaction in such cases is found to depend on the specific acid or base present and not just on the pH of the solution.

The second important feature of the Brønsted picture is that it relates aqueous to nonaqueous systems. Other solvents can now be seen in striking analogy to water. Liquid ammonia, for example, autoionizes to give NH_4^+ and NH_2^- ions, in analogy to the H_3O^+ and OH^- ions of water. Acetic acid in liquid ammonia solution then dissociates according to the reaction

$$\text{HAc} + \text{NH}_3 = \text{Ac}^- + \text{NH}_4^+. \tag{12-117}$$

This dissociation is virtually complete. That is, acetic acid is a strong acid in liquid ammonia solvent, and the reason is clearly that NH_3 is a much better proton acceptor than is H_2O. Acids that are too weak to be studied in water solution can be observed easily in liquid ammonia.

Pure acetic acid may be used as a solvent, and the autoionization reaction gives $\text{CH}_3\text{CO}_2\text{H}_2^+$ and CH_3CO_2^- ions. Then HCl in acetic acid solution dissociates according to the reaction

$$\text{HCl} + \text{HAc} = \text{Cl}^- + \text{H}_2\text{Ac}^+. \tag{12-118}$$

However, HAc is a weak base and this dissociation is not complete. That is, HCl behaves as a weak acid in acetic acid solvent. In this solvent, the series of acid strengths

$$\text{HClO}_4 > \text{HBr} > \text{H}_2\text{SO}_4 > \text{HCl} > \text{HNO}_3$$

is established. All of these acids are so completely dissociated in water that distinctions among them cannot be made and it is only by balancing their proton-donating ability against a rather poor acceptor that the real differences become apparent.

Other acid–base systems have some value. In molten oxide mixtures an acid and a base may be defined as an acceptor and a donor, respectively, of oxide ion. In the reaction $BaO + CO_2 = BaCO_3$, BaO is then the base and CO_2 the acid. G. N. Lewis proposed the rather general definitions of an *acid* as an *electron pair acceptor* and a *base* as an *electron pair donor*. The designations are consistent with the Brønsted scheme in that a Brønsted base has an unshared pair of electrons capable of bonding with H^+. The Lewis definition also allows the reaction $BF_3 + (CH_3)_3N: = (CH_3)_3N:BF_3$ to be characterized as an acid–base one, BF_3 being the acid. The Lewis formalism does not provide the symmetry of the Brønsted formalism, however, and really is more a notation indicating that an important type of chemical bond is that in which the electron pair derives from one of the associating molecules. Such a bond is also often called a *coordinate bond*, and in the Lewis sense coordination chemistry is a study of acid–base reactions. More recently, Lewis acids and bases have been subdivided into categories A and B, alternatively known as "hard" and "soft," depending roughly on their charges and polarizabilities. This author feels that it is more profitable to study the coordinate bond as it is, rather than in terms of often hypothetical acid plus base reactions. Thus in the case of $Cr(CO)_6$, Cr is supposedly the acid and CO the base, but this approach does not seem very illuminating of the actual wave-mechanical description of the Cr—CO bond.

SPECIAL TOPICS

12-ST-1 Ionic Diffusion Coefficients

It was shown in Section 10-7B that the diffusion coefficient for a particle in solution is given by

$$\mathscr{D} = \frac{kT}{f} \quad \text{[Eq. (10-41)]},$$

where f is the friction coefficient. The same treatment applies to individual ions, and writing $\omega = 1/f$, Eq. (10-41) becomes

$$\mathscr{D}_i = \omega_i kT. \tag{12-119}$$

It is now possible to relate $\mathscr{D}_i$ and electrochemical mobility u_i, using Eq. (12-29):

$$\mathscr{D}_i = 10^{-7} \frac{u_i kT}{z_i e}$$

or, using Eq. (12-31),

$$\mathscr{D}_i = 10^{-7} \frac{\lambda_i kT}{z_i e \mathscr{F}} = \frac{\lambda_i RT}{z_i \mathscr{F}^2}, \tag{12-120}$$

where R is now in joules per degree Kelvin per mole.

Equation (12-120) gives the diffusion coefficient for a single ion, as might be observed in a self-diffusion experiment. Ordinarily, however, one studies the diffusion of an electrolyte as a whole, and the electroneutrality requirement enforces the same diffusional velocity on both ions. The intrinsically slower diffusing type of ion will lag behind the faster one until a local potential (called the *diffusion potential*) builds up. This potential ϕ acts to retard the faster ions and speed up the slower ones, and Eq. (2-67) for the diffusional flux therefore becomes:

$$J_1 = -\mathscr{D}_1 \frac{dC_1}{dx} + \phi \omega_1 C, \tag{12-121}$$

$$J_2 = -\mathscr{D}_2 \frac{dC_2}{dx} - \phi \omega_2 C, \tag{12-122}$$

where 1 and 2 denote the two kinds of ion present and C is the ion concentration assuming a 1–1 electrolyte. In other words, $\phi \omega$ gives the increment in velocity due to the local field and $\phi \omega C$ gives the corresponding increment to the molecular flow across a unit area. We require that $J_1 = J_2$, that is, that no excess of one ion build up over the other during the diffusion, and on equating (12-121) and (12-122), we obtain

$$\phi = \frac{(\mathscr{D}_1 - \mathscr{D}_2) \, dC/dx}{(\omega_1 + \omega_2)C}.$$

Substitution of this result into Eq. (12-121) [or (12-122)] gives

$$J_1 = -\left(-\mathscr{D}_1 + \frac{\mathscr{D}_1 - \mathscr{D}_2}{\omega_1 + \omega_2} \omega_1\right) \frac{dC}{dx}. \tag{12-123}$$

Since ω_i is proportional to $\mathscr{D}_i$ and J_1 is now the flux for the diffusion of the electrolyte as a whole, we have

$$J_1 = -\mathscr{D} \frac{dC}{dx}.$$

Equation (12-123) reduces to

$$\mathscr{D} = \frac{2\mathscr{D}_1\mathscr{D}_2}{\mathscr{D}_1 + \mathscr{D}_2} = \frac{2RT}{z\mathscr{F}^2}\frac{\lambda_1\lambda_2}{\Lambda}. \tag{12-124}$$

Equation (12-124) is known as the *Nernst diffusion equation*; it permits the calculation of the diffusion coefficient for an electrolyte if the equivalent conductivities are known.

The more complete form of Eq. (12-124) allows for nonideality in the same manner as does Eq. (10-40):

$$\mathscr{D} = \frac{2RT}{z\mathscr{F}^2}\frac{\lambda_1\lambda_2}{\Lambda}\left[1 + \frac{d(\ln \gamma_C)}{d(\ln C)}\right]. \tag{12-125}$$

Strictly speaking, interionic attractions affect the equivalent conductivities differently from the diffusional mobilities. In the former case the two kinds of ion are moving in opposite directions, whereas in diffusion they are moving in the same direction. In brief, two kinds of effects are recognized in conductance. The motion of a given ion a direction opposite to its atmosphere produces an electrical drag or *relaxation effect*, given by the first term of Eq. (12-19). In addition, the ion atmosphere entrains solvent, so that each ion is in effect swimming in a countercurrent of moving solvent. This is known as the *electrophoretic effect* and is given by the second term of Eq. (12-19). In diffusion, there is no relaxation effect, but there is still an electrophoretic one. The theories of these effects are approximate, and the treatment of the electrophoretic effect is open to certain objections, particularly for other than uni-univalent electrolytes. Also, the derivations are intimately tied to the Debye–Hückel assumptions, and show these approximations. [See Harned and Owen (1950) for further details.]

12-ST-2   The Hittorf Method

The analysis of the Hittorf method for the determination of transference numbers was greatly abridged in Section 12-6, and the more detailed presentation appears here.

We consider first the system shown in Fig. 12-5, for which a qualitative analysis was given. The more exact bookkeeping is as follows, based on 1 $\mathscr{F}$ of electricity passing through the cell.

Cell I.   Anode compartment

Anode reaction: Ag = Ag⁺ + e⁻:   gain of 1 equiv of Ag⁺
migration of Ag⁺:   loss of t_+ equiv of Ag⁺
migration of NO₃⁻:   gain of t_- equiv of NO₃⁻.

Net change: Gain of $1 - t_+$ or t_- equiv of Ag⁺, gain of t_- equiv of NO₃⁻;
or gain of t_- equiv of AgNO₃ .

Cell III.   Cathode compartment

Cathode reaction: Ag⁺ + e⁻ = Ag: loss of 1 equiv of Ag⁺
migration of Ag⁺:   gain of t_+ equiv of Ag⁺
migration of NO₃⁻:   loss of t_- equiv of NO₃⁻.

Net change: Loss of $1 - t_+$ or t_- equiv of Ag⁺, loss of t_- equiv of NO₃⁻;
or loss of t_- equiv of AgNO₃ .

The overall change per faraday is that the anode compartment gains t_- equiv of AgNO₃ and the cathode compartments loses t_- equiv. The middle compartment should not change in content since the gains and losses due to the migration of ions past the dividing lines I–II and II–III exactly compensate.

This analysis applies to any cell containing a single electrolyte and having electrodes that generate or consume the cation of the electrolyte. The cell of Fig. 12-5 might have been filled with CuSO₄ solution, for example, and have copper electrodes. We would conclude that, per faraday, the anode compartment would gain t_- equiv of CuSO₄ and the cathode compartment would lose t_- equiv.

Alternatively, the electrodes might be reversible to the anion, that is, the electrode reaction might produce and consume anion. This would be the case if, for example, the cell were filled with NaCl solution, and the electrodes were silver coated with silver chloride. The bookkeeping is now as follows:

Cell I.   Anode compartment

Anode reaction: Ag + Cl⁻ = AgCl + e⁻:   loss of 1 equiv of Cl⁻
migration of Na⁺:   loss of t_+ equiv of Na⁺
migration of Cl⁻:   gain of t_- equiv of Cl⁻.

Net change: Loss of t_+ equiv of Na⁺, loss of $1 - t_-$ or t_+ equiv of Cl⁻;
or loss of t_+ equiv of NaCl.

Cell III.   Cathode compartment

Cathode reaction: AgCl + e⁻ = Ag + Cl⁻:   gain of 1 equiv of Cl⁻
migration of Na⁺:   gain of t_+ equiv of Na⁺
migration of Cl⁻:   loss of t_- equiv of Cl⁻.

Net change: Gain of t_+ equiv of Na⁺, gain of $1 - t_-$ or t_+ equiv of Cl⁻;
or gain of t_+ equiv of NaCl.

The opposite working of the electrode reaction thus has the effect of making the anode compartment undergo a net loss of t_+ equiv of NaCl and the cathode compartment undergo a net gain of t_+ equiv of NaCl, in contrast to the preceding example.

It is not necessary, of course, that the electrode reaction involve either of the ions of the electrolyte. If platinum electrodes were used in the example just given, the analysis would be as follows:

Cell I. Anode compartment

Anode reaction: $\frac{1}{2}H_2O = \frac{1}{4}O_2 + H^+ + e^-$: gain of 1 equiv of H^+
migration of Na^+: loss of t_+ equiv of Na^+
migration of Cl^-: gain of t_- equiv of Cl^-.

Net change: Gain of 1 equiv of H^+, loss of t_+ equiv of Na^+, gain of t_- equiv of Cl^-; or gain of 1 equiv of HCl, loss of t_+ equiv of NaCl.

Cell III. Cathode compartment

Cathode reaction: $e^- + H_2O = \frac{1}{2}H_2 + OH^-$: gain of 1 equiv of OH^-
migration of Na^+: gain of t_+ equiv of Na^+
migration of Cl^-: loss of t_- equiv of Cl^-.

Net change: Gain of 1 equiv of OH^-, gain of t_+ equiv of Na^+, loss of t_- equiv of Cl^-; or gain of 1 equiv of NaOH, loss of t_- equiv of NaCl.

This last example illustrates some further points. First, the net change can be expressed either in terms of gains and losses of individual types of ions or in terms of gains and losses of complete electrolytes; the alternative statements are seen on examination to be entirely equivalent. The purpose of the middle compartment now becomes apparent. The analysis assumes that only Na^+ and Cl^- ions carry current past the I–II and II–III dividing lines. The electrode reactions are producing H^+ and OH^- ions, however, and if mixing occurs in compartments I and III during the electrolysis, then these electrode products will carry part of the current between compartments. The gains and losses of Na^+ and Cl^- ions would then be less than expected, and the overall analysis would be in error. The test of whether electrolysis products reached compartment II would, in this case, be whether the pH of II changed or not.

Notice that all of these analyses are couched in terms of amounts gained or lost during electrolysis. The concentrations present do not enter directly. The transference numbers are themselves concentration-dependent, however, since λ_+ and λ_- will in general change differently with concentration. It is desirable for this reason that no great change in composition occur during the electrolysis. Ordinarily, then, the amount of electricity passed through the cell will be some small fraction of a faraday.

It is, of course, necessary to measure the quantity of electricity involved in a

Hittorf experiment so that the results can be put on a per faraday basis. It is not necessary, however, to know the applied potential or the actual current—only the total quantity of electricity. One usually obtains this by determining the amount of an electrode reaction that has occurred. Thus in the first example, the loss in weight of the silver anode gives the number of faradays used. It would be possible in the third example to titrate the solution in the anode compartment to find the amount of H^+ ion produced. However, it is generally more convenient to have a second cell in series with the Hittorf cell, which functions as a *coulometer*. This might consist of a silver anode dipping into silver nitrate solution and a platinum cathode. Either the loss in weight of the anode or the amount of silver deposited on the cathode would show the number of faradays that had passed through the cell. A numerical example is as follows.

We can construct an illustrative problem around the last example, in which an NaCl solution was electrolyzed with platinum electrodes. Suppose that the initial NaCl solution is $0.1000\ m$, and thus contains 5.845 g of NaCl per 1000 g of water. The electrolysis is carried out until 1.92 g of silver have been deposited in a coulometer in series with the cell, at which point the anode compartment is drained and then rinsed with some of the *original* NaCl solution, so that a total of 301.3 g of solution results which is found to contain 0.02315 equiv of NaCl. Calculate t_+ and t_-.

First, 1.92 g of silver corresponds to $1.92/107.88 = 0.01779$ equiv so that $0.01779\ \mathscr{F}$ of electricity passed through the cell. At the end of the experiment, the 0.02315 equiv of NaCl present in the anode solution plus rinse corresponds to 1.3 g, and so the amount of water in the solution was $301.3 - 1.3 = 300.0$ g. Now the amount of NaCl associated originally with 300 g of water is $(0.1)(300)/1000 = 0.03000$ equiv. There has been a loss of $0.03000 - 0.02315 = 0.00685$ equiv of NaCl.

This loss becomes, per faraday, $0.00685/0.01779 = 0.385$. From the earlier bookkeeping analysis, the loss should be t_+ equiv of NaCl per faraday. The transference number of Na^+ is therefore 0.385 and that of Cl^- is 0.615. The equivalent conductivity of $0.1\ m$ NaCl is 106.74, so that $\lambda_{Na^+} = (0.385)(106.74) = 41.09$ and $\lambda_{Cl^-} = (0.615)(106.74) = 65.65$.

The use of a rinse of original solution is a characteristic procedure in a transference experiment. The purpose of the rinsing, of course, is to displace all of the electrolyzed solution, and the use of original solution for the rinse simplifies the ensuing calculation. We are not interested in concentrations and need only to compare the amount of NaCl present in electrolyzed solution plus rinse with the amount originally associated with the quantity of water in the combined solutions. It is thus not necessary to know exactly how much solution was originally present in the anode compartment.

An alternative but less accurate procedure would have been to fill the anode compartment with a known volume of the $0.1\ m$ solution and to determine the change in concentration resulting from the electrolysis. For example, had the anode compartment originally contained 200 cm³ of solution, or approximately 0.02 equiv of NaCl, then at the end of the electrolysis the amount remaining would have been $0.02 - 0.00685 = 0.00315$ equiv, corresponding to a $0.0157\ m$ NaCl solution. The solution would also have contained 0.01779 equiv of HCl, or $0.0889\ m$ HCl.

When we calculate transference numbers by the Hittorf method we implicitly assume that the solvent water does not migrate during the electrolysis. The water of hydration of the ions should move with them, however, and Washburn suggested the ingenious experiment of adding a sugar to the solutions in a Hittorf cell and referring the calculations to the sugar as the non-migrating species. The result showed that several molecules of water do in fact migrate with each ion.

12-ST-3 Treatment of Complex Ionic Equilibria

The treatment of the dissociation of a weak acid or a weak base is developed along standard lines in Section 12-9 but stops at the point of simple acids and bases, HA and BOH. The solution of the simultaneous equations for (H^+) or (OH^-) becomes very unwieldy if more than one stage of dissociation can occur or if there is a mixture of weak electrolytes. An alternative procedure becomes much more practical.

A. Acid HA or Base BOH

We first illustrate the method for a monobasic acid HA before proceeding to more complex situations. The material balance equation (12-102) is now written in the form

$$f_{\text{tot}} = f_{\text{HA}} + f_{\text{MA}} = (\text{HA}) + \frac{(\text{HA})\,K_a}{(H^+)},$$

using Eq. (12-99) to eliminate (A^-). Rearrangement gives

$$F_{\text{HA}} = \frac{1}{[K_a/(H^+)] + 1},\qquad(12\text{-}126)$$

where $F_{\text{HA}} = (\text{HA})/f_{\text{tot}}$ and is the fraction of the total acid-substance which is present as undissociated acid HA. Alternatively, we may eliminate (HA) to obtain

$$F_{A^-} = \frac{1}{1 + [(H^+)/K_a]}.\qquad(12\text{-}127)$$

Equations (12-126) and (12-127) are usually displayed as a plot of $\log F$ versus $p\text{H}$. Such a plot is called a *logarithmic diagram*. That for acetic acid is shown in Fig. 12-14. Notice that if the $p\text{H}$ is much less than pK_a, Eq. (12-127) reduces to

$$\log F_{A^-} = p\text{H} - pK_a$$

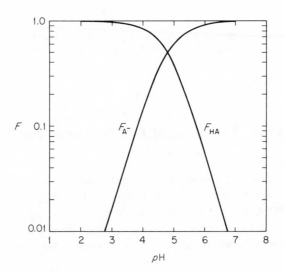

Fig. 12-14.   *Logarithmic diagram for acetic acid at 25°C.*

and so the plot of $\log F_{A^-}$ versus pH becomes a straight line of slope $+1$ and intercept $-pK_a$ in the region of high acidity. Similarly, if $pH \gg pK_a$, then the plot of $\log F_{HA}$ versus pH becomes a straight line of slope -1 and intercept pK_a.

The logarithmic diagram for a weak electrolyte resembles a phase diagram. It provides a map of the pH domain of each species so that one can tell at a glance the general makeup of a solution at any given pH. The diagram is used quantitatively as follows. The charge balance equation

$$(M^+) + (H^+) = (A^-) + (OH^-) \qquad \text{[Eq. (12-101)]}$$

can be put in the form

$$(M^+) + (H^+) = F_{A^-} f_{tot} + (OH^-). \qquad (12\text{-}128)$$

One knows f_{HA} and f_{MA} and hence f_{tot} and (M^+), and Eq. (12-128) is solved by successive approximations. A first guess at (H^+) allows F_{A^-} to be read off the logarithmic diagram, and substitution into the equation will indicate whether the value is too high or too low. This guides a second choice of (H^+), and so on, until a self-consistent answer is reached.

As an example, we calculate the pH of a solution which is $0.002 f$ in HAc and $0.001 f$ in NaAc; f_{tot} is then 0.003 and Eq. (12-128) becomes

$$0.001 + (H^+) = F_{A^-}(0.003) + (OH^-)$$

or

$$F_{A^-} = 0.333 + \frac{(H^+) - (OH^-)}{0.003}.$$

We can guess immediately a pH of 4.45, at which $F_{A^-} = \frac{1}{3}$. The test of the equation is then

$$0.333 \overset{?}{=} 0.333 + \frac{3.54 \times 10^{-5}}{0.003} = 0.345.$$

F_{A^-} is slightly too small, and we next try a pH of 4.46, $F_{A^-} = 0.345$. The test is now

$$0.345 \overset{?}{=} 0.333 + \frac{3.45 \times 10^{-5}}{0.003} = 0.345.$$

The desired pH is then close to 4.46.

One may also calculate a titration curve. In Eq. (12-128), f_{tot} is now the initial formality of the acid, and (M^+) gives the concentration of added strong base. One may now insert successive choices for (H^+) and calculate (M^+) for each. The fraction of neutralization F_N is just

$$F_N = \frac{(M^+)}{f_{tot}}.$$

Several points on the titration curve for $0.002\,f$ HAc are summarized thus. Equation (12-128) becomes $(M^+) + (H^+) = 0.002 f_{A^-} + (OH^-)$, or $F_N = f_{A^-} - \{[(H^+) - (OH^-)]/0.002\}$; some sample calculations are given in Table 12-10. The calculation illustrates several items. The first two values for F_N are negative, meaning that excess strong acid must be present. The third line gives the actual starting point of the titration; the relatively rapid change in F_N between pH 4 and 6 characterizes the buffer region, and the asymptotic approach to $F_N = 1$ marks the endpoint. The last entry shows that 5.1% excess base has been added. The curve is plotted in Fig. 12-12.

The logarithmic diagram approach offers little advantage in speed over the straight attack in the case of a simple acid. Being graphical, it is also less precise,

Table 12-10.

pH	(H^+)	(OH^-)	f_{A^-}	$[(H^+) - (OH^-)]/0.002$	F_N
2	0.01	—	1.7×10^{-3}	5	-5
3	0.001	—	1.7×10^{-2}	0.5	-0.483
3.69	1.78×10^{-4}	—	0.089	0.089	0
4	1×10^{-4}	—	0.147	0.05	0.097
4.76	1.73×10^{-5}	—	0.500	0.009	0.491
6	1×10^{-6}	1.05×10^{-8}	0.91	—	0.91
8	1×10^{-8}	1.05×10^{-6}	$1 - (6 \times 10^{-4})$	—	0.9994
10	1×10^{-10}	1.05×10^{-4}	1.000	-0.051	1.051

but this is not a matter of great importance since the overriding uncertainty will be in the value for K_y, that is, in the size of the activity coefficient correction.

The treatment of a simple weak base BOH is analogous to that just given:

$$F_{\text{BOH}} = \frac{1}{[K_b/(\text{OH}^-)] + 1}, \qquad F_{\text{B}^+} = \frac{1}{1 + [(\text{OH}^-)/K_b]}. \qquad (12\text{-}129)$$

The logarithmic diagram is still a plot of $\log F$ versus pH, and the associated charge balance equation is

$$F_{\text{B}^+} f_{\text{tot}} + (\text{H}^+) = (\text{X}^-) + (\text{OH}^-), \qquad (12\text{-}130)$$

where $f_{\text{tot}} = f_{\text{BOH}} + f_{\text{BX}}$, where X is a nonhydrolyzing anion. The plots for ammonium hydroxide are included in Fig. 12-17.

Logarithmic diagrams may be used for any mixture of weak electrolytes. Thus, for a mixture which contains both a weak acid and a weak base, the charge balance equation becomes

$$(\text{M}^+) + F_{\text{B}^+} f_{(\text{BOH}+\text{BX})} + (\text{H}^+) = (\text{X}^-) + F_{\text{A}^-} f_{(\text{HA}+\text{MA})} + (\text{OH}^-) \quad (12\text{-}131)$$

and the correct pH for a given mixture is found by trial-and-error solution. As an example, a solution which is $0.002\,f$ in HAc, $0.001\,f$ in NaAc, $0.003\,f$ in NH_4OH, and $0.005\,f$ in NH_4Cl would have a pH such that the equation

$$0.001 + 0.008 F_{\text{NH}_4^+} + (\text{H}^+) = 0.005 + 0.003 F_{\text{Ac}^-} + (\text{OH}^-)$$

is obeyed. In this case, (H^+) and (OH^-) will be negligible compared to the other terms, and so

$$F_{\text{NH}_4^+} = 0.05 + 0.375 F_{\text{Ac}}.$$

A few successive choices of pH should serve to locate the value such that $F_{\text{NH}_4^+}$ and F_{Ac^-} as read off the logarithmic diagrams satisfy the equation.

B. Successive Dissociations of a Weak Acid

In the case of a dibasic acid H_2A the equilibrium constants are

$$K_1 = \frac{(\text{H}^+)(\text{HA}^-)}{(\text{H}_2\text{A})} \quad \text{and} \quad K_2 = \frac{(\text{H}^+)(\text{A}^{2-})}{(\text{HA}^-)}, \qquad (12\text{-}132)$$

and substitution into the material balance statement $f_{tot} = (H_2A) + (HA^-) + (A^{2-})$ gives

$$F_{H_2A} = \frac{1}{1 + [K_1/(H^+)] + [K_1K_2/(H^+)^2]} \,, \qquad (12\text{-}133)$$

$$F_{HA^-} = \frac{1}{[(H^+)/K_1] + 1 + [K_2/(H^+)]} \,, \qquad (12\text{-}134)$$

$$F_{A^{2-}} = \frac{1}{[(H^+)^2/K_1K_2] + [(H^+)/K_2] + 1} \,. \qquad (12\text{-}135)$$

The logarithmic diagram for H_2CO_3 is shown in Fig. 12-15. Its use follows the

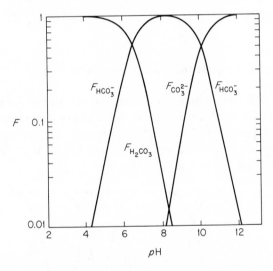

Fig. 12-15. *Logarithmic diagram for H_2CO_3 at 25°C.*

same scheme as before, the charge balance equation now being

$$(M^+) + (H^+) = F_{HA^-} f_{tot} + 2F_{A^{2-}} f_{tot} + (OH^-). \qquad (12\text{-}136)$$

Figure 12-16 shows the titration curve for $0.1\ M\ H_2CO_3$ calculated by the same procedure as before. That is, each assumed pH provides a value for (M^+) through Eq. (12-136) and hence for the degree of neutralization.

The treatment for a tribasic acid H_3A yields the equation

$$F_{H_3A} = \frac{1}{1 + [K_1/(H^+)] + [K_1K_2/(H^+)^2] + [K_1K_2K_3/(H^+)^3]} \,, \qquad (12\text{-}137)$$

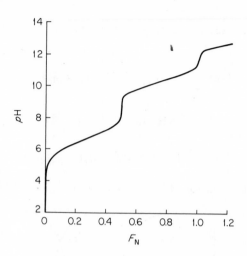

Fig. 12-16. *Titration curve for* H_2CO_3.

and so on. The logarithmic diagram for phosphoric acid is given in Fig. 12-17. Phosphate buffers are much used and the figure allows the calculation of the pH of any mixture of phosphoric acid and its various salts. The dashed curves are for ammonium hydroxide, so the combined plots can be used for mixtures that include ammonium salts as well as phosphates.

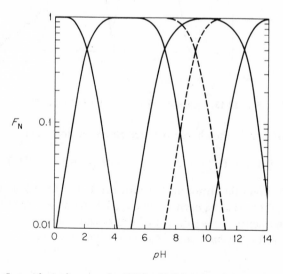

Fig. 12-17. *Logarithmic diagrams for* H_3PO_4 *(full lines) and* NH_4OH *(dashed lines).*

C. Complex Ions

The logarithmic diagram approach is not limited to weak acids and bases but may be applied to any set of successive dissociations. For example, Co^{2+} forms a succession of ammine complexes:

$$H_2O + Co(NH_3)_6^{2+} = Co(NH_3)_5(H_2O)^{2+} + NH_3, \qquad pK_6 = -0.74,$$

$$H_2O + Co(NH_3)_5(H_2O)^{2+} = Co(NH_3)_4(H_2O)_2^{2+} + NH_3, \qquad pK_5 = 0.06,$$

and so on. The values of pK_1, pK_2, pK_3, and pK_4 are 1.99, 1.51, 0.93, and 0.64, respectively. Note that the reactions have been written as interchanges of water for ammonia in the coordination sphere, in recognition of our belief that Co^{2+} is octahedrally coordinated.

Application of the standard procedure leads to

$$F_{Co(NH_3)_6^{3+}} = \frac{1}{1 + [K_6/(NH_3)] + [K_5K_6/(NH_3)^2] + [K_4K_5K_6/(NH_3)^3] + \cdots},$$

and similarly for the other species. The logarithmic diagram now consists of plots of the log F's against $p(NH_3)$, that is, against $-\log(NH_3)$. Application of the charge balance equation then allows the calculation of the composition of any mixture of ammonia and a cobalt salt.

GENERAL REFERENCES

HARNED, H. S., AND OWEN, B. B. (1950). "The Physical Chemistry of Electrolyte Solutions." Van Nostrand–Reinhold, Princeton, New Jersey.

BOCKRIS, J. O'M., AND CONWAY, B. E. (eds.) (1954). "Modern Aspects of Electro-Chemistry." Butterworths, London and Washington, D.C.

LEWIS, G. N., AND RANDALL, M. (1961). "Thermodynamics," 2nd ed. (revised by K. S. Pitzer and L. Brewer). McGraw-Hill, New York.

ROBINSON, R. A., AND STOKES, R. H. (1959). "Electrolyte Solutions." Academic Press, New York.

MACINNES, D. A. (1939). "The Principles of Electrochemistry." Van Nostrand–Reinhold, Princeton, New Jersey.

Exercises[†]

12-1 The measured resistance of a 0.02 M solution of NaCl is 793 ohm in a cell whose path length can be taken to be 10 cm. Calculate (a) the specific conductivity of the solution,

---

[†] Neglect interionic attraction effects in the following Exercises and Problems unless specifically directed otherwise.

(b) its conductance, (c) the effective area of the electrodes, and (d) the cell constant.

Ans. (a) 2.53×10^{-3} ohm^{-1} cm^{-1}, (b) 1.26×10^{-3} ohm^{-1},
(c) 5.0 cm^2, (d) 2.00 cm^{-1}.

12-2 The resistance of electrolyte solution A is 45 ohm in a given cell and that of electrolyte solution B is 100 ohm in the same cell. Equal volumes of solutions A and B are then mixed. Calculate the resistance of this mixture, again in the same cell.

Ans. 62.1 ohm.

12-3 Calculate the resistance of a 0.03 M solution of Na$_2$SO$_4$ in a cell of cell constant 1.50 cm^{-1}.

Ans. 192 ohm.

12-4 The specific conductivity of a saturated solution of AgCl in pure water at 25°C is 1.79×10^{-6} ohm^{-1} cm^{-1} while that of the water used is 6.0×10^{-8} ohm^{-1} cm^{-1}. From Table 12-2, calculate Λ for Ag$^+$, Cl$^-$ and thence the solubility of AgCl.

Ans. 138.26 cm^2 ohm^{-1} equiv^{-1}, 1.25×10^{-5} M.

12-5 Calculate Λ for (a) Na$_4$Fe(CN)$_6$, (b) Cu(NO$_3$)$_2$, and (c) the double salt (Na)(NH$_4$)SO$_4$, using the data of Table 12-2.

Ans. (a) 161.1, (b) 125.3, (c) 141.3 (cm^2 ohm^{-1} equiv^{-1}).

12-6 The solubility product for barium oxalate is 2.0×10^{-7} at 25°C. Calculate the specific conductivity of the saturated solution.

Ans. 1.23×10^{-4} ohm^{-1} cm^{-1}.

12-7 The dissociation constant for NH$_4$OH is 1.80×10^{-5} at 25°C. Calculate Λ_{app} and the specific conductivity of a 0.02 M solution.

Ans. 8.0 cm^2 ohm^{-1} equiv^{-1}, 1.63×10^{-4} ohm^{-1} cm^{-1}.

12-8 Calculate the specific conductivity of 0.05 M sodium chloride at 25°C, allowing for interionic attraction effects.

Ans. 5.33×10^{-3} ohm^{-1} cm^{-1}.

12-9 The equivalent conductivity of a cation M$^+$ is determined at 25°C by means of a moving boundary experiment. A 0.005 M solution of MCl is used, and after 30 min of passing a current of 0.2 mA the cation boundary has moved 0.208 cm; the area of the column of solution is 1.5 cm^2. Calculate λ_{M^+} .

Ans. 55.0 cm^2 ohm^{-1} equiv^{-1}.

12-10 Calculate the electrochemical mobility and the effective radius of (a) an ion M$^+$ whose equivalent conductivity is 55.0 cm^2 ohm^{-1} equiv^{-1}, and (b) Fe(CN)$_6^{4-}$, whose λ value is 95.0 cm^2 ohm^{-1} equiv^{-1} (both for 25°C).

Ans. (a) 5.70×10^{-4} cm^2 V^{-1} sec^{-1} and 1.67 Å,
(b) 9.84×10^{-4} cm^2 V^{-1} sec^{-1} and 6.45 Å.

12-11 Calculate the transference number at 25°C for NO$_3^-$ in 0.1 M KNO$_3$ and in a solution which is also 0.05 M in NaCl.

Ans. 0.493, 0.343.

Problems

12-12 The solubility of $Pb(IO_3)_2$ in water at 25°C is 4.00×10^{-5} m and the $K_{sp} = 5.00 \times 10^{-13}$ in an aqueous KNO_3 solution. Calculate (a) the solubility product, (b) the mean molarity of the saturated solution, (c) the solubility in the KNO_3 solution, (d) the mean activity coefficient for the electrolyte Pb^{2+}, IO_3^- in the KNO_3 solution.

> *Ans.* (a) 2.56×10^{-13}, (b) 6.35×10^{-5} m, (c) 5.00×10^{-5} m, (d) 0.800.

12-13 If the aqueous KNO_3 solution of Exercise 12-12 was 0.02 m, in what concentration of $LaCl_3$ should the solubility of $Pb(IO_3)_2$ be 5.00×10^{-5} m, according to the ionic strength principle?

> *Ans.* 0.00333 m.

12-14 Calculate $\gamma_\pm$ for 0.02 m acetic acid at 25°C using Table 12-7.

> *Ans.* 0.977.

12-15 Assuming the ionic strength principle, calculate $\gamma_\pm$ for 0.0333 m $Cu(NO_3)_2$ using the data of Table 12-8 (and assuming that the principle is obeyed by each ion separately).

> *Ans.* 0.52.

12-16 Calculate γ_{K^+} and $\gamma_{SO_4^{2-}}$ (separately) at 25°C in 0.05 m K_2SO_4 using the Debye–Hückel theory and compare the resulting $\gamma_\pm$ with the value in Table 12-8.

> *Ans.* 0.4566, 0.0435, 0.2085.

12-17 What is the Debye–Hückel value for $\gamma_\pm$ of 0.5 m NaCl at 50°C?

> *Ans.* 0.42.

12-18 The solubility product of Ag_2CrO_4 is 2.0×10^{-7} at 25°C; calculate the solubility of this salt in 0.1 m silver nitrate.

> *Ans.* 2.0×10^{-5} m.

12-19 Obtain the degree of dissociation of 0.1 m chloroacetic acid in 0.05 m HCl at 25°C.

> *Ans.* 0.0255.

12-20 What would the pH of the solution in Exercise 12-19 be if 0.06 mole liter^{-1} of NaOH were added to it?

> *Ans.* 1.91.

Problems

12-1 The following data apply to aqueous solutions of sodium propionate at 25°C:

Concentration ($M \times 10^3$)	2.1779	4.1805	7.8705	14.272	25.973
Λ (cm^2 ohm^{-1} equiv^{-1})	82.53	81.27	79.72	77.88	76.64

Find the limiting equivalent conductivity of (a) sodium propionate, (b) propionic acid.

12 Solutions of Electrolytes

12-2 A conductivity cell has a resistance of 3736 ohm when filled with 0.028 m H_2S solution and of 59.0 ohm when filled with 0.0100 m KCl. The measurements are made at 18°C, at which temperature the equivalent conductivity for HS$^-$ is 62 cm^2 ohm^{-1} equiv^{-1}. Calculate K_a for H_2S (relevant data are available in the text, but should be corrected to 18°C with the use of Walden's rule).

12-3 The specific conductivity of a saturated solution of silver iodate at 80°C is 1.25×10^{-5} ohm^{-1} cm^{-1}; that of the water used is 1.4×10^{-6} ohm^{-1} cm^{-1} and the equivalent conductivity of silver iodate is 89 cm^2 ohm^{-1} equiv^{-1}. Calculate the solubility product for silver iodate.

12-4 The specific conductivities at 25°C were measured for the following solutions:

Solution	Specific conductivity (ohm^{-1} cm^{-1})
10^{-3} M Phenanthrolinium chloride (BHCl)	1.360×10^{-4}
10^{-3} M BHCl plus a large excess of phenanthroline (B)	1.045×10^{-4}
10^{-3} M HCl	4.21×10^{-4}

Phenanthrolinium chloride is a strong electrolyte, that is, it exists as BH$^+$ and Cl$^-$ ions. Phenanthroline is a nonelectrolyte. Calculate K_a for the acid dissociation BH$^+$ = B + H$^+$.

12-5 Chlorine dissolved in water reacts according to the equation

$$Cl_2(aq) + H_2O = H^+ + Cl^- + HClO.$$

Since all the forms present are essentially nonconducting with the exception of the HCl, the concentration of this last may be determined by measuring the conductance of the solution. If the total dissolved chlorine is known, then the equilibrium constant for the reaction may be determined. Given the following data, calculate this equilibrium constant: The specific conductivity of 0.01 M Cl_2 solution is 0.00351 ohm^{-1} cm^{-1}. The equivalent conductivities of 0.01 M HCl and 0.005 M HCl solutions are 412 and 415.6, respectively. Using Eq. (12-12) and the data given, calculate the hydrolysis constant (do not use conductivity values other than the ones given).

12-6 One hundred cubic centimeters of 0.10 N sodium acetate solution is titrated with 0.1 N HCl solution. Calculate the specific conductivity of the resulting solution when 90, 99, 101, and 110 cm^3 of the HCl solution has been added. Bear in mind that acetic acid is only slightly ionized in the presence of HCl and NaAc; in these calculations neglect the variation of equivalent conductivity with concentration and use the value for infinite dilution. Your answers need be correct to only 1 %. Make a semiquantitative plot of your calculated specific conductivities (as ordinate) versus the volume of HCl solution added.

12-7 If pure water has a conductivity of 4.5×10^{-8} ohm^{-1} cm^{-1} at 20°C, calculate the specific conductivity of a saturated solution of CO_2 in water at 20°C if the CO_2 pressure is maintained at 20 Torr and the equilibrium constant for the reaction $H_2O(l) + CO_2(aq) = HCO_3^- + H^+$ is 4.35×10^{-7}. The solubility of CO_2 in water follows Henry's law with a constant of 0.03353 mole liter^{-1} atm^{-1}.

12-8 Given the following information:

Salt	Λ
NaCl	126.4
KNO_3	144.9
KCl	149.8

and t_+ for Na^+ in NaCl is 0.39, calculate Λ for $NaNO_3$ and t_+ for Na^+ in $NaNO_3$ solution.

12-9 For an incompletely dissociated electrolyte the Onsager equation is

$$\Lambda = \alpha[\Lambda_0 - (A + B\Lambda_0)(\alpha C)^{1/2}] = \alpha\Lambda',$$

where $A = 82.4/\eta(DT)^{1/2}$, $B = 8.2 \times 10^5/(DT)^{3/2}$, D is the dielectric constant, and η is the viscosity. The equivalent conductivity of dichloroacetic acid in 0.03 M solution is 273 ohm^{-1} cm^{-1}. For dichloroacetic acid, $\Lambda_0 = 388.5$. Calculate the degree of dissociation α from the Onsager equation. [*Hint*: use a procedure of successive approximations, starting with $\alpha = \Lambda/\Lambda_0$.] Assume 25°C.

12-10 In a transport experiment in 0.02 M NaCl solution at 25°C, using the moving boundary method, Longsworth found the boundary between NaCl and $CdCl_2$ solutions to move 6.0 cm in 2070 sec with a current of 0.00160 A. Tube cross section was 0.12 cm². Calculate t_+.

12-11 Longsworth determined the transference number of sodium ion by the following moving boundary experiment. The data refer to the movement of a rising boundary between solutions of sodium and cadmium chlorides; the lower electrode was a cadmium anode and the upper a silver/silver chloride cathode. The temperature was 25°C, the current was maintained constant at 16.00×10^{-4} A, the cross section of the tube was 0.1115 cm², and the concentration of the sodium chloride 0.02 mole liter^{-1}. The table gives some corresponding readings of the time t and the distance of traverse of the boundary x:

t (sec)	172	344	2757	3104	3454
x (cm)	0.5	1.0	8.0	9.0	10.0

Calculate the transference number of sodium ion. [*Note*: For the most accurate value of x/t divide the difference between the average of the last three distances and that of the first two by the difference between the average of the last three values of t and that of the first two.]

12-12 At high temperatures solid $PbCl_2$ and solid AgCl are ionic conductors. In AgCl the silver ions are almost the only mobile ones ($t_+ = 1$). The transference numbers in $PbCl_2$ were found in the following way. $PbCl_2$ or AgCl was pressed into rods which were laid in a row and pressed together:

$$\text{Ag} \left| \begin{array}{c} \text{rod I} \\ (PbCl_2) \end{array} \right| \begin{array}{c} \text{rod II} \\ (PbCl_2) \end{array} \left| \begin{array}{c} \text{rod III} \\ (PbCl_2) \end{array} \right| \begin{array}{c} \text{rod IV} \\ (AgCl) \end{array} \right| \text{Ag.}$$

The rods and electrodes were kept at 250°C and current was sent through them for a few hours in the direction I to IV. The rods were then separated and weighed. The anode had lost 211.9 mg, rod I had gained 281.5 mg, II and III had not changed weight, IV had lost 280.9 mg, and the cathode had gained 211.6 mg. After the passage of the current I also contained some AgCl, at the end toward the anode; II and III still consisted of pure $PbCl_2$ and IV of pure AgCl. In a silver coulometer connected in series, 211.7 mg of Ag had separated or deposited. Find the transference numbers of the ions in solid $PbCl_2$.

12-13 Calculate the concentration of H_2S, HS^-, S^{2-}, and H^+ in a 0.200 M NaHS solution (to an accuracy of about 1 %). [*Note:* The solution to this problem can be much simplified by making judicious approximations at each stage.]

12-14 Calculate the concentrations of acetate ion, benzoate ion, and H^+ in a solution made up of 0.0100 mole of acetic acid and 0.0100 mole of benzoic acid dissolved in water and then diluted to 1 liter.

12-15 A total of 0.01 mole of NaCl and 0.01 mole of solid Ag_2CrO_4 are shaken with a liter of water. Calculate the equilibrium constant for the reaction

$$Ag_2CrO_4 + 2Cl^- = 2AgCl + CrO_4^{2-}.$$

Calculate also the concentrations of each ion at equilibrium and the number of moles of any solids present. The K_{sp} values are 1.8×10^{-10} for AgCl and 1.2×10^{-12} for Ag_2CrO_4.

12-16 Derive Eq. (12-90) from Eq. (12-84).

12-17 The following are mixed until equilibrium is achieved: 0.02 mole of AgCl, 0.02 mole of AgCN, 0.01 mole of NaCN, and 1 liter of water. Calculate within 1 or 2 % relative accuracy the final concentration of each species in solution and the amounts of each solid present given the following data: final pH is 7.00; K_{sp} for AgCl is 1.8×10^{-10}; K_{sp} for AgCN is 7×10^{-15}; K_a for HCN is 1×10^{-10}; $K = (Ag(CN)_2^-)/(Ag^+)(CN^-)^2$ is 2.6×10^{18}.

12-18 Solid NaOH is added to 1 liter of a 0.1 f solution of H_2S until the pH rises to 12. Taking K_1 and K_2 as 10^{-9} and 10^{-14}, respectively, (a) calculate the initial pH and (b) calculate the number of moles of NaOH added and the concentration of all species present in this final solution.

12-19 Leucylglycine is an amino acid which dissociates into both hydrogen and hydroxide ions. At 25°C the constant for the dissociation into anions and hydrogen ions is 1.51×10^{-8}. The apparent dissociation constant for the dissociation into cations and hydroxyl ions is 3.02×10^{-11}. Calculate the pH at which the degree of dissociation into hydrogen ions and hydroxyl ions is the same.

12-20 How many millimoles of HA should be added to 100 cm^3 of a 0.01 M solution of base BOH in order to give a solution with a pH of 8.90? pK_a for HA is 4.76, pK_b for BOH is 5.40. How many cubic centimeters of 0.01 M HA would one have to add to 100 cm^3 of 0.01 M BOH to obtain this pH?

12-21 One hundred cubic centimeters of 0.1 f H_2SO_4 is mixed with 100 cm^3 of 0.025 f NaOH.

Calculate the pH of the resulting solution. The second dissociation constant of sulfuric acid is 0.015 and the first corresponds to a strong acid.

12-22 Barney *et al.* obtained data on the solubility of cobaltous oxalate (CoOx) as a function of added potassium oxalate concentration. The solubility is at first depressed due to the common ion effect, then increased, due to the complex formation:

$$Co^{2+} + 2Ox^{2-} \overset{K}{=} Co(Ox)_2^{2-} .$$

The minimum in solubility occurs at $S = 9.2 \times 10^{-5}$ and $(K_2Ox) = 4.5 \times 10^{-4}$; the solubility of CoOx in pure water is 1.44×10^{-4}. Derive the equation whereby K can be calculated from the solubility minimum, and calculate K.

12-23 The solubility of lead chloride is 0.005 mole liter^{-1} at 25°C. Calculate the activity product (that is, make correction for activity coefficients). Calculate also the solubility of $PbCl_2$ in 0.02 m sodium nitrate solution.

12-24 At 25°C, 162.1 mM of HCN dissolves 2.45 mM of AgCN per liter. The equilibrium constant for $AgCl(s) + 2HCN = Ag(CN)_2^- + 2H^+ + Cl^-$ is 1.9×10^{-9}. The solubility product for AgCl is 1.7×10^{-10} and K_a for HCN is 2.06×10^{-9}. Find pK for the reactions (a) $Ag(CN)_2^- = Ag^+ + 2CN^-$; (b) $AgCN(s) = Ag^+ + CN^-$; and (c) $2AgCN(s) = Ag^+ + Ag(CN)_2^-$.

12-25 At 25°C, pK for the dissociation of $Ag(NH_3)_2^+$ into its components is 7.22. For AgCl, AgBr, and AgI, pK_{sp} is 9.77, 12.48, and 16.07, respectively. Calculate how many milligrams of these salts are dissolved by 1 liter of 1.0 m NH_3. Neglect $Ag(NH_3)^+$, NH_4^+, and OH^-.

Special Topics Problems

12-1 Calculate the limiting value for the diffusion coefficient of aqueous NaCl at 25°C.

12-2 The equivalent conductivity for 0.01 m KCl is 146 cm^2 ohm^{-1} equiv^{-1} at 25°C. Calculate the diffusion coefficient for 0.01 m KCl using Eq. (12-125).

12-3 A solution containing 0.14941 wt % KCl is electrolyzed in a Hittorf cell at 25°C with silver/silver chloride electrodes. After the electrolysis, which deposits 0.16024 g of silver in a silver nitrate coulometer, one of the end cells is analyzed and found to contain 120.99 g of solution of 0.19404 wt % KCl. Calculate the transference number for K$^+$.

12-4 A 0.01 m solution of HCl is electrolyzed in a Hittorf cell with a Pt/H$_2$ anode and a silver/silver chloride cathode. Each compartment contains 50 cm^3 of solution. A current of 2 mA is passed through the cell for 1 hr. Calculate the final concentrations of the various species present in the anode and cathode compartments.

12-5 A famous early experiment by Washburn attempted to find the amount of water of hydration carried by ions. The procedure was to carry out an electrolysis in a Hittorf cell

12 Solutions of Electrolytes

with solutions containing a sugar. The sugar, being neutral, was assumed not to move during the electrolysis (an assumption later found not to be quite correct). In one experiment a solution contained 4.939 wt % of LiCl and 4.73 % of a sugar and an amount of electricity corresponding to 0.0464 $\mathscr{F}$ was passed through the cell with a silver/silver chloride cathode and a silver anode. After the electrolysis the cathode solution weighed 81.47 g and contained 5.565 % of LiCl and 4.619 % of sugar, while the anode solution weighed 104.4 g and contained 4.440 % of LiCl and 4.806 % of sugar. Find n_c as a function of n_a, the number of water molecules bound per cation and per anion, respectively.

12-6 By means of a logarithmic diagram, find the pH of a solution 0.1 M in ammonia and 0.1 M in $KHCO_3$.

12-7 The acid dissociation constants for monochloroacetic acid (HM) and acetic acid (HAC) are 1.55×10^{-3} and 1.8×10^{-5}, respectively.
   (a)   Make a semilogarithmic plot of the fractions of HM, M^-, HAc, and Ac^- versus pH.
   (b)   Using this plot, calculate the pH of a solution 0.01 m in HM (total concentration of acid) and 0.02 m in HAc (again total concentration of acid).
   (c)   Calculate the pH if 0.01 mole of solid NaOH is added to a liter of the solution in (b).
   (d)   Calculate the pH if 0.02 mole of solid NaOH is added to a liter of the solution in (b).

12-8 The acids HA and HB have pK_a values of 4.5 and 7.5; pK_w is 14.0. Find by means of a logarithmic diagram the pH for solutions that have been mixed so as to contain: (a) 10 mM of HA; (b) 10 mM of HA, 5 mM of HB; (c) 10 mM of NaA, 5 mM of HB; (d) 10 mM of NaA, 5 mM of NaB, 5 mM of NaOH; (e) 5 mM of HB, 10 mM of HA, 2 mM of HCl. (These are formalities.)

12-9 By means of a logarithmic diagram, find the pH of a solution whose formalities are 100 mM NH_3, 100 mM $KHCO_3$.

12-10 Solution A contains 9.08 g liter^{-1} of KH_2PO_4; solution B contains 11.88 g liter^{-1} of $Na_2HPO_4 \cdot 2H_2O$. Calculate the pH of the solution that results when 95 cm³ of A are mixed with 5 cm³ of B.

12-11 Ethylenediaminetetraacetic acid is a tetrabasic acid H_4Y. The successive pK's are 2.00, 2.67, 6.16, and 10.26. It forms a stable complex with Co ion, $Co^{2+} + Y^{4-} = CoY^{2-}$.
   For this complex formation $K = 10^{16}$; Ba^{2+} forms a similar complex with $K = 10^7$. Both CoY^{2-} and BaY^{2-} are the anions of strong acids, that is, one does not get H_2CoY and so on in acid solution (although the solids are known). Calculate and plot the logarithmic diagram for the various forms of ethylenediaminetetraacetic acid for the pH range from 0 to 7, and the similar diagram for the distribution of cobalt and barium between Co^{2+} and Ba^{2+} and CoY^{2-} and BaY^{2-} as a function of pC, where C is the concentration of Y^{4-}. Calculate the percentage of complexing of Co^{2+} and Ba^{2+} in solutions of (a) 0.01 f $Co(NO_3)_2$, 0.01 f $Ba(NO_3)_2$, 0.1 f Na_2H_2Y; (b) the same as (a) but also 0.1 f in NaOH. Also give the pH's of these solutions.

12-12 Derive Eq. (12-98). Calculate the osmotic pressure at 25°C if $C = 0.01$ m and $(N^+) = 0.1m$, neglecting activity coefficient effects.

13 ELECTROCHEMICAL CELLS

The preceding chapter dealt primarily with the physical chemistry of electrolyte solutions; we now concern ourselves with the overall chemical process that occurs when electricity is passed through a conducting solution. The emphasis will be on the work associated with this overall change, as measured by the reversible cell potential. Since reversible work at constant temperature and pressure corresponds to a free energy change, we will thus be able to bring the emf of cells into the general scheme of thermodynamics. The chapter concludes with a discussion of irreversible electrode processes, that is, with the physical chemistry of the approach of ions to, and their reaction at, the surface of an electrode.

13-1 Definitions and Fundamental Relationships

A. Cell Conventions

An electrochemical cell has, as essential features, a current-carrying solution and two electrodes at which oxidation and reduction processes occur, respectively, as current flows. Figure 13-1 gives a schematic example of a fairly typical cell for this chapter; we have hydrogen and silver–silver chloride electrodes dipping into an aqueous solution of HCl. The hydrogen electrode, incidentally, typically consists of a platinized platinum metal surface arranged so that hydrogen gas bubbles past as it dips partly into the solution, the object being to provide the most intimate possible gas–solution–metal contact. Platinized platinum is merely

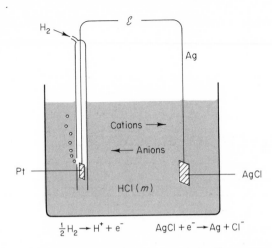

$$\tfrac{1}{2}H_2 \rightarrow H^+ + e^- \qquad AgCl + e^- \rightarrow Ag + Cl^-$$

Fig. 13-1. *Schematic diagram of an electrochemical cell. The cell reaction is given by Eq. (13-2).*

platinum metal on which additional, very finely divided platinum has been deposited electrolytically; the result is a high area, catalytically active surface. A silver–silver chloride electrode consists of silver on which a fine-grained, adherent deposit of silver chloride has been placed, again electrolytically. The terminals of the cell might be connected to a motor, so as to provide electrochemical energy, or, in the laboratory, to a potentiometer circuit (see Section 13-2), so that the potential difference could be measured.

It is awkward to describe cells in a pictorial manner, and the conventional representation of the cell of Fig. 13-1 is

$$Pt/H_2(P \text{ atm})/HCl(m)/AgCl/Ag. \qquad (13-1)$$

Equation (13-1) is known as a *cell diagram*. The rule is that one writes in order each successive phase that makes up the electrical circuit of the cell, using a diagonal bar to separate phases. One should in general specify not only the temperature of the cell, but also the composition of each condensed phase and the partial pressure of any gaseous one; we assume the general mechanical pressure to be 1 atm.

A potentiometric measurement on a cell will report a potential difference between the electrode terminals, and the second convention needed is that to specify the sign of this cell potential $\mathcal{E}$. There is some variation in practice and consequent ambiguity, and the least confusing way of stating the convention used here seems to be the following. We first define the cell reaction as the chemical change that occurs per faraday of electricity passed through the cell in the direction such that oxidation occurs at the left-hand electrode of the cell diagram. This electrode will be called the *anode*; it is also the electrode toward which anions migrate in the cell solution as they carry current. The right-hand electrode of the cell diagram is then the one at which reduction occurs, and it is called the *cathode*;

it is also the electrode toward which cations migrate as they carry current. The cell reaction corresponding to (13-1) is

anode $\quad\quad\quad \frac{1}{2}H_2(1\ atm) = H^+(m) + e^-$

cathode $\quad\quad\quad AgCl + e^- = Ag + Cl^-(m)$ $\quad\quad\quad\quad$ (13-2)

net $\quad\quad\quad \frac{1}{2}H_2(1\ atm) + AgCl = Ag + H^+(m) + Cl^-(m)$.

Since the potential is a function of concentration as well as of the chemical species involved, statements of cell reactions should include the concentration or partial pressure of each substance.

The sign of $\mathscr{E}$ is now defined to be positive if the cell reaction occurs spontaneously in the direction written and to be negative if the reverse direction of reaction is the spontaneous one. In this particular example $\mathscr{E}$ would be positive. That is, silver chloride is spontaneously reduced by hydrogen gas. Although the mechanical arrangement of the cell is such that the direct chemical reaction is prevented from occurring, the process will take place spontaneously when the electrode terminals are connected.

This last is an important feature of electrochemical cells. The cell reaction has to be spontaneous in one direction or the other, and the cell must always be so designed that the direct chemical reaction is physically prevented from occurring. In the case of the cell of Eq. (13-1) the reactants H_2 and AgCl are isolated at the separate electrodes. Another way in which direct chemical reaction is prevented is illustrated by the *Daniell cell* shown in Fig. 13-2; this consists of a zinc anode

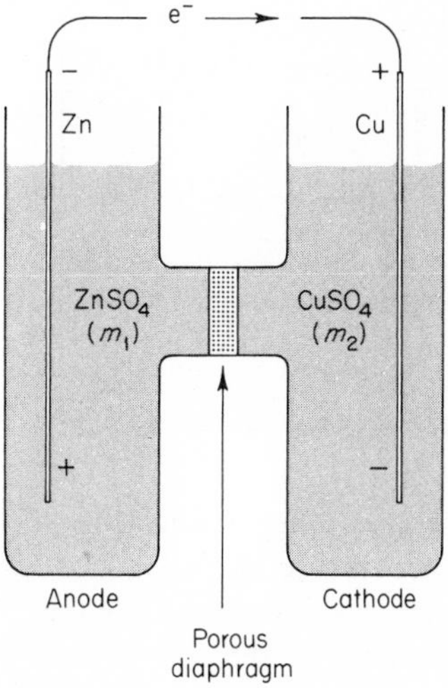

Fig. 13-2. *The Daniell cell.*

dipping into $ZnSO_4$ solution and a copper cathode dipping into $CuSO_4$ solution. The two solutions are separated by a porous diaphragm which allows electrical contact but prevents gross mixing. The cell diagram is then

$$Zn/ZnSO_4(m_1)\ /\ CuSO_4(m_2)/Cu, \quad\quad\quad\quad (13\text{-}3)$$

where the dashed diagonal conventionally is used to indicate two miscible phases that are physically prevented from mixing. This situation will later be referred to as one of a *liquid junction*. The cell reaction is

$$\begin{array}{lll}
\text{anode} & \tfrac{1}{2}Zn = \tfrac{1}{2}Zn^{2+}(m_1) + e^- & \\
\text{cathode} & \tfrac{1}{2}Cu^{2+}(m_2) + e^- = Cu & \text{(13-4)} \\
\text{net} & \tfrac{1}{2}Zn + \tfrac{1}{2}Cu^{2+}(m_2) = \tfrac{1}{2}Zn^{2+}(m_1) + \tfrac{1}{2}Cu. &
\end{array}$$

Again, the cell has been written in such a way that the cell reaction occurs spontaneously—if placed directly into the $CuSO_4$ solution, the zinc electrode would react as shown—and so the measured emf of this cell would be reported as positive.

To return to the matter of sign convention, we note that the usual source of confusion is in the plus and minus markings of electrodes. The cells of Figs. 13-1 and 13-2 are drawn so that in spontaneous action the left-hand electrode is the anode. This means that the anode bears a positive charge relative to the cathode *at the solution end* and a negative charge relative to the cathode *at the exposed terminals*. It is the terminals that are marked, hence it is the spontaneously operating anode of a cell that bears the negative sign. To repeat, when we write a cell reaction the various signs and directions of flow are taken to be as shown in Fig. 13-3. If

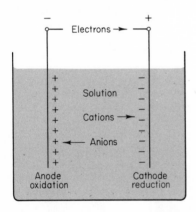

Fig. 13-3. *Cell conventions. The cell diagram is anode/solution/cathode.*

this is the spontaneous direction of flow, the $\mathscr{E}$ is reported as a positive number.

A further feature of electrochemical cells that are used in precise measurements is that they are *reversible*. That is, the cell reaction must take place readily in either direction. If the cell is short-circuited, the reaction should proceed in its spontaneous direction; and if an external potential is applied which overrides the natural cell potential, then the reaction should just as readily proceed in the opposite direction. The reversible electrochemical cell is thus one which may be held in a state of dynamic balance by application of an external counterpotential just equal to $\mathscr{E}$. For example, in the case of the Daniell cell $\mathscr{E}$ is about 1.1 V if $m_1 = m_2 = 1$. External application of an opposing 1.1 V will just prevent reaction from occurring; a slightly smaller opposing potential will allow the cell reaction to occur as written, and a slightly larger opposing potential will make the reaction go in the opposite direction.

The customary way of determining $\mathscr{E}$ for a cell is, in fact, to find that opposing emf which puts the cell in balance. The procedure thus defines $\mathscr{E}$ as the reversible emf of the cell. If current is allowed to flow through the cell under conditions such that applied potential remains essentially equal to $\mathscr{E}$, then the work done is a reversible work. From the definition of potential, work in joules is given by qV, where q is the amount of charge carried through potential difference V. The reversible work for an electrochemical cell is then $n\mathscr{F}\mathscr{E}$, where n is the number of faradays passed through the cell.

For the Daniell cell as written in Eq. (13-4), the reversible work is $(96,480(1.1) = 1.06 \times 10^5 \text{ J}$ $(m_1 = m_2 = 1$, and 25°C). Had the reaction been written for $2\mathscr{F}$,

$$Zn + Cu^{2+}(m_2) = Zn^{2+}(m_1) + Cu,$$

the reversible work would be 2.12×10^5 J, and had the reaction been written in the opposite direction, $\mathscr{E}$ would be reported as -1.1 V and the corresponding reversible work would be -1.06×10^5 J. Thus the sign of $\mathscr{E}$ and both the sign and magnitude of the reversible work depend on how the cell reaction is written. A useful conversion factor is that for $n = 1$ an emf of 1 V = 23.06 kcal. This unit is sometimes called the *electron-volt*: 1 eV = 23.06 kcal mole^{-1}.

B. Thermodynamics of Cells

The reversible emf that is measured for a cell gives the reversible work associated with the cell reaction. Since this is reversible work at constant temperature and pressure, it is therefore the free energy change and, by Eq. (6-34), the sign convention is such that we must write

$$\Delta G = -n\mathscr{F}\mathscr{E}; \tag{13-5}$$

that is, a positive cell emf corresponds to a spontaneous cell reaction and hence to a negative free energy change.

We may now rewrite several important equations of Section 7-4 in terms of emf's. Thus Eqs. (7-23) and (7-24) become

$$\Delta S = n\mathscr{F} \left(\frac{\partial \mathscr{E}}{\partial T} \right)_P, \tag{13-6}$$

$$\Delta S^0 = n\mathscr{F} \left(\frac{\partial \mathscr{E}^0}{\partial T} \right)_P, \tag{13-7}$$

and, since $G = H - TS$ by definition, for a constant-temperature process we have

$$\Delta H = \Delta G + T \Delta S, \tag{13-8}$$

$$\Delta H = -n\mathscr{F} \left[\mathscr{E} - T \left(\frac{\partial \mathscr{E}}{\partial T} \right)_p \right], \tag{13-9}$$

$$\Delta H^0 = -n\mathscr{F} \left[\mathscr{E}^0 - T \left(\frac{\partial \mathscr{E}^0}{\partial T} \right)_p \right]. \tag{13-10}$$

Equation (13-9) or (13-10) is known as the *Gibbs–Helmholtz equation.*

As an example, the emf of the cell Cd/solution saturated with $CdCl_2 \cdot 2.5H_2O/AgCl/Ag$ is 0.6753 V at 25°C, and $d\mathscr{E}/dT = -0.00065$ V °K^{-1}. If we write the cell reaction as Cd + 2AgCl = $CdCl_2$(sat. soln.) + 2Ag, then $\Delta S = (2)(96,487)(-0.00065) = -125$ J or -29.9 cal °K^{-1} mole^{-1}, $\Delta H = -(2)(96,487)[0.6753 - (298.1)(-0.00065)] = -1.677 \times 10^5$ J or -40.08 kcal (as compared with -39.5 kcal from thermochemical measurements), and $\Delta G = -(2)(96,487)(0.6753) = -1.303 \times 10^5$ J or -31.14 kcal.

An interesting point is that the q for a reversibly operating cell is given by $T \Delta S$; q would be $-(29.9)(298.1)$ or -8.91 kcal in the example. In terms of Eq. (13-8) the measured q is given by ΔH when the reaction occurs directly, as in a thermochemical experiment; in the reversible cell the energy ΔG goes to do useful work, and the observed q is then determined by the entropy change. Thus the statement $\Delta H = \Delta G + T \Delta S$ amounts to saying:

$$(\text{total energy change}) = \binom{\text{energy available}}{\text{to do work}} + \binom{\text{energy not available}}{\text{to do work}}.$$

C. The Nernst Equation

A very important relationship is obtained as follows. For a general cell reaction

$$aA + bB + \cdots = mM + nN + \cdots,$$

we have from Eq. (12-91) that

$$\Delta G = \Delta G^0 + RT \ln Q_{th} \qquad [\text{Eq. (12-91)}],$$

where, it will be remembered, Q_{th} has the same form as an equilibrium constant but contains the activities of the products and reactants as arbitrarily specified by the stated reaction. If the system is at equilibrium, however, $\Delta G = 0$, and we then obtain

$$\Delta G^0 = -RT \ln K_{th} \qquad [\text{Eq. (12-92)}],$$

where K_{th} is the thermodynamic equilibrium constant.

Combination of Eqs. (13-5) and (12-91) gives the Nernst equation:

$$\mathscr{E} = \mathscr{E}^0 - \frac{RT}{n\mathscr{F}} \ln Q_{th} . \tag{13-11}$$

Insertion of the numerical constants for 25°C yields

$$\mathscr{E} = \mathscr{E}^0 - \frac{0.05917}{n} \log Q_{th} . \tag{13-12}$$

Equation (13-11) is the central equation of electrochemistry. By means of it we can determine how the emf of a cell should vary with composition, and we can also determine $\mathscr{E}^0$ for a cell reaction, which in turn enables us to obtain activity coefficients for electrolytes.

An example of its use is the following. The Nernst equation for the cell reaction of Eq. (13-2) is

$$\mathscr{E} = \mathscr{E}^0 - 0.059 \log \frac{a_{H^+} a_{Cl^-}}{P_{H_2}^{1/2}} . \tag{13-13}$$

Ag and AgCl are in their standard states and hence have unit activity. The hydrogen pressure will be 1 atm, and, for the moment, we neglect activity coefficient effects, so Eq. (13-13) reduces to

$$\mathscr{E} = \mathscr{E}^0 - 0.059 \log[(H^+)(Cl^-)] = \mathscr{E}^0 - 0.118 \log m. \tag{13-14}$$

The observed emf of this cell is 0.49844 at 25°C and $m = 0.005$ and we may use the Nernst equation to calculate $\mathscr{E}$ for some other concentration, say 0.01 m. Since $\mathscr{E}^0$ is a constant, it follows from Eq. (13-14) that

$$\mathscr{E}_{0.01m} = \mathscr{E}_{0.005m} - 0.118 \log \frac{0.01}{0.005}$$

or

$$\mathscr{E}_{0.01m} = 0.49844 - (0.118)(0.30103) = 0.46292.$$

The observed value is 0.46419, a difference we will shortly be attributing to the nonideality of aqueous HCl.

As a different kind of example, for the reaction of the Daniell cell, Eq. (13-4), we have

$$\mathscr{E} = \mathscr{E}^0 - 0.059 \log \frac{a_{Zn^{2+}}^{1/2}}{a_{Cu^{2+}}^{1/2}} = \mathscr{E}^0 - 0.0295 \log \frac{a_{Zn^{2+}}}{a_{Cu^{2+}}} .$$

If Zn^{2+} and Cu^{2+} are at unit activity (or, very roughly, 1 m), $\mathscr{E} = 1.10$ V at 25°C. This means that $\mathscr{E}^0$ is also 1.10 V, since the log term is zero. If an excess of zinc metal is placed in a solution of copper sulfate which is initially at unit activity, the direct spontaneous reaction will occur to form copper metal and zinc ion. Eventually the solution will consist of roughly 1 m or unit activity Zn^{2+} and some small equilibrium concentration of Cu^{2+}. We can use the Nernst equation to calculate this last. Since the final state is at equilibrium, ΔG and hence $\mathscr{E}$ must be zero, and so

$$\mathscr{E}^0 = 1.10 = 0.0295 \log \left(\frac{a_{Zn^{2+}}}{a_{Cu^{2+}}} \right)_{equil}$$

$$= 0.0295 \log \left(\frac{1}{a_{Cu^{2+}}} \right)_{equil} .$$

The equilibrium (Cu^{2+}) is then antilog$(-1.10/0.0295)$, or about 10^{-37} m (!).

13-2   Experimental Procedures

A.   The Potentiometer

The reader is referred to experimental texts for details, but the principle employed in the measurement of emf's of cells should be described at least briefly. An elementary potentiometer arrangement is shown in Fig. 13-4. One sets up a closed

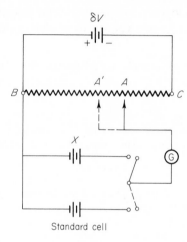

Fig. 13-4.   *A potentiometer circuit.*

circuit involving a working battery, usually a wet cell capable of delivering a reasonable amount of current without changing its voltage. The circuit contains a moderately high resistance, perhaps 1000 ohms, which is either in the form of a slide wire, or which may be tapped at close intervals. This resistance R then has an ohmic drop in potential iR across it. The electrochemical cell is connected as shown, with the electrodes in the same direction as for the working cell. One now moves the point of contact A until the galvanometer G shows no current flow. At this point the potential drop AB is the same as $\mathscr{E}$ for the cell.

The circuit is usually calibrated by means of a standard cell, or one of accurately known emf $\mathscr{E}_{ref}$. By determining point A' when the standard cell is in balance, one therefore knows the voltage drop $A'B$. The desired emf is then $\mathscr{E}_{ref}(R_{AB}/R_{A'B})$. In actual practice one adjusts subsidiary resistances in the circuit (not shown) in calibrating with the standard cell so that the tapped or slide wire resistance position A will read directly in volts.

Potentiometric measurements are among the most accurate of physical chemistry. Cell potentials may be measured to about 10^{-5} V, the limiting accuracy usually being that of the voltage of the reference cell. If the unknown cell is one of very high resistance, then the sensitivity of the galvanometer may become the limiting factor. In the case of a pH meter, for example, the glass electrode may have

10^5 ohms resistance, and one must use a vacuum-tube null-meter to detect the balance point (early users of pH meters struggled with quadrant electrometers).

The potentiometric method is a null method—when the circuit is balanced the galvanometer shows no current flow, and a slight shift in the position of the contact A to one side or the other causes a galvanometer deflection in one direction or the other. A barely detectable galvanometer deflection need correspond to no more than perhaps 10^{-12} A, so the change in condition needed to reverse the current flow is very small and the measured potential is essentially the reversible one. If a relatively large current, say 10^{-3} A, is drawn through a cell, then the potential drops as various irreversible processes occur, such as polarization, discussed in Section 13-9. The magnitude of the measured potential is therefore at a maximum at zero current.

B. Standard Cells

The most widely accepted reference cell is the *Weston cell*, illustrated in Fig. 13-5.

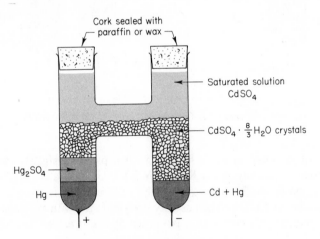

Fig. 13-5. *The Weston cell.*

The anode consists of a layer of solid cadmium amalgam containing 12.5% cadmium, and the cathode consists of a pool of mercury layered with a thick paste of Hg_2SO_4. The solution is saturated with $CdSO_4 \cdot \frac{8}{3}H_2O$, with some excess crystals present on both sides, to maintain saturation. The cell diagram is

$$Pt/Cd(Hg)/\text{saturated } CdSO_4 \cdot \tfrac{8}{3}H_2O/Hg/Pt$$

and the corresponding cell reaction is

$$\tfrac{8}{3}H_2O + Cd(\text{amalgam}) + Hg_2SO_4(s) = CdSO_4 \cdot \tfrac{8}{3}H_2O(s) + 2 Hg.$$

The emf at 25°C is 1.01463 V; the temperature dependence is small, -4.05×10^{-5} V °K^{-1}.

C. Reference Electrodes

An electrochemical cell consists essentially of the two parts defined by the two electrodes, and one often constructs a cell in which one electrode is that under investigation and the other is a conventional electrode of known properties. This last is called a *reference electrode*. A very common and easily constructed one is the *calomel reference electrode*, illustrated in Fig. 13-6(a). Platinum wire dips

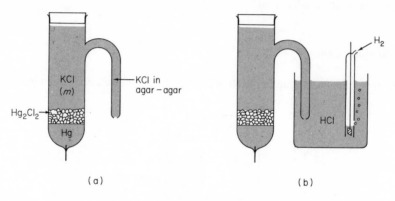

(a)   (b)

Fig. 13-6. *Reference electrodes. (a) Calomel half cell. (b) Complete cell that includes a calomel half cell.*

into a pool of mercury which is layered with a paste of Hg_2Cl_2, followed by a solution which is usually 0.1 N KCl, 1 N KCl, or saturated KCl. Electrolytic connection must be made to the rest of the cell, and this is done through a side arm in which the KCl solution has usually been stiffened with agar-agar or gelatine. This type of electrolytic connection is known as a *salt bridge* (see Special Topics section).

A complete cell might then appear as in Fig. 13-6(b). The cell diagram is

$$Pt/Hg/Hg_2Cl_2(s)/1 \ N \ KCl \text{ or saturated KCl} / HCl(m)/H_2(1 \text{ atm})/Pt.$$

If the HCl is at unit activity, then

$$\mathscr{E}_{298} = -0.280 \quad V \quad (1 \ N \ KCl) \quad \text{and} \quad \mathscr{E}_{298} = 0.242 \quad V \quad \text{(saturated KCl).}$$

The boundary between the KCl solution and that of the electrolyte of the second part of the cell is known as a *liquid junction*. Since ions are carrying the current in solution, passage of electricity means that ions move across the junction, just as in a transference experiment. In terms of this cell some K^+ ions must move from the KCl solution into the HCl one, and some Cl⁻ ions must move from a concentration m in the HCl to that in the KCl. Some net changes thus occur at the liquid junction, whose free energy requirement contributes to the emf of the cell as a whole. This contribution is known as the *junction potential*, and fortunately it is small if the bulk of the current is carried by oppositely charged ions of the same mobility. This is essentially the situation in the case of a KCl salt bridge; K⁺ and Cl⁻ do have nearly the same mobility. The more detailed treatment of junction potentials is given in the Special Topics sections, and it is sufficient here to note that for most purposes the junction potential for a saturated KCl (or a concentrated NH_4NO_3) salt bridge can be neglected. However, this effect does impair the accuracy of a cell involving a calomel reference electrode.

Other reference electrodes include the hydrogen electrode itself, which is very accurate but somewhat inconvenient to use, and well-known reversible electrodes such as the silver–silver ion or the silver–silver chloride ones. For accurate work a reference electrode should be a direct part of the cell, but it may be more convenient to connect the electrode being studied to the reference electrode via a salt bridge and to either neglect or try to estimate the value of the junction potential.

13-3   Determination of $\mathscr{E}^0$ Values and Activity Coefficients

Equation (13-11) may be written in the form

$$\mathscr{E} = \mathscr{E}^0 - \frac{RT}{n\mathscr{F}} \ln Q - \frac{RT}{n\mathscr{F}} \ln Q_\gamma, \qquad (13\text{-}15)$$

where

$$Q_{th} = \frac{a_M{}^m a_N{}^n \cdots}{a_A{}^a a_A{}^b \cdots} = \frac{(M)^m(N)^n \cdots}{(A)^a(B)^b \cdots} \frac{\gamma_M{}^m \gamma_N{}^n \cdots}{\gamma_A{}^a \gamma_B{}^b \cdots} = QQ_\gamma . \qquad (13\text{-}16)$$

We now write

$$\mathscr{E}' = \mathscr{E} + \frac{RT}{n\mathscr{F}} \ln Q = \mathscr{E}^0 - \frac{RT}{n\mathscr{F}} \ln Q_\gamma . \qquad (13\text{-}17)$$

The quantity $\mathscr{E}'$ is determined for a series of concentrations and plotted against concentration. At infinite dilution the activity coefficients and hence Q_γ approach unity, and $\ln Q_\gamma$ approaches zero; the extrapolated value of $\mathscr{E}'$ is thus equal to $\mathscr{E}^0$.

The procedure may be illustrated for the cell corresponding to reaction (13-2) at 25°C. We write Eq. (13-14) in the form

$$\mathscr{E} = \mathscr{E}^0 - 0.1183 \log m - 0.1183 \log \gamma_\pm$$

or

$$\mathscr{E}' = \mathscr{E} + 0.1183 \log m = \mathscr{E}^0 - 0.1183 \log \gamma_\pm. \qquad (13\text{-}18)$$

According to the Debye–Hückel limiting law, Eq. (12-89), $\log \gamma_\pm$ should be proportional to $\sqrt{m}$, so $\mathscr{E}'$ is plotted against $\sqrt{m}$ as shown in Fig. 13-7. Extrapolation to zero concentration gives $\mathscr{E}^0_{298} = -0.22239$ V. Having determined the $\mathscr{E}^0$ for the

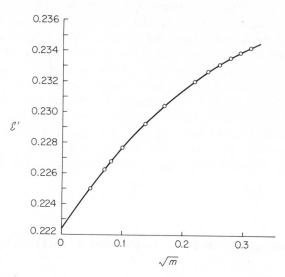

Fig. 13-7. *Determination of $\mathscr{E}^0_{298}$ for the cell* Pt/H$_2$(*1 atm*)/HCl(*m*)/AgCl/Ag.

cell reaction, one may then insert its value back into Eq. (13-18) and thus obtain $\gamma_\pm$ for HCl at each concentration.

This procedure illustrates how a number of very accurate values of $\mathscr{E}^0$ and of activity coefficients have been obtained. One may also, of course, estimate Q_γ either theoretically or from other activity coefficient data and thus calculate $\mathscr{E}^0$ from the measured $\mathscr{E}$.

13-4 Additivity Rules for Emf's. Standard Oxidation Potentials

Since the $\mathscr{E}$ or $\mathscr{E}^0$ for a cell reaction is just the free energy change per equivalent, emf's obey essentially the same additivity rules as do free energies. For example,

(a)	$\text{Zn} + 2\text{H}^+ = \text{Zn}^{2+} + \text{H}_2,$
(b)	$\text{Cu} + 2\text{H}^+ = \text{Cu}^{2+} + \text{H}_2,$

(c) = (a) − (b) $\text{Zn} + \text{Cu}^{2+} = \text{Zn}^{2+} + \text{Cu}.$

We know that $\Delta G^0_{(c)} = \Delta G^0_{(a)} - \Delta G^0_{(b)}$, hence

$$-n\mathscr{F}\mathscr{E}^0_{(c)} = -n\mathscr{F}\mathscr{E}^0_{(a)} - (-n\mathscr{F}\mathscr{E}^0_{(b)}),$$

or $\mathscr{E}^0_{(c)} = \mathscr{E}^0_{(a)} - \mathscr{E}^0_{(b)}$. In general, if two cell reactions are added (subtracted), the resultant emf is the sum (difference) of those for the two reactions.

We make use of this attribute in much the same way as is done in formulating enthalpies and free energies of formation. First, all emf data are expressed as $\mathscr{E}^0$ relative to the hydrogen electrode as cathode. Second, a cell reaction is expressed as a combination of two *half-cells*. For example, reaction (a) is broken down as

$$\begin{array}{ll} Zn = Zn^{2+} + 2e^- & \mathscr{E}^0_{Zn/Zn^{2+}} \\ \underline{H_2 + 2e^- = 2H^+} & \underline{-\mathscr{E}^0_{H_2/H^+}} \\ Zn + 2H^+ = Zn^{2+} + H_2 & \mathscr{E}^0 = \mathscr{E}^0_{Zn/Zn^{2+}} - \mathscr{E}^0_{H_2/H^+} \end{array}$$

Thus any cell reaction may be written as the difference between two half-cell oxidation reactions and any $\mathscr{E}^0$ as the difference between two standard half-cell oxidation potentials. This combination of equations may therefore be written as

$$\mathscr{E}^0_{(c)} = (\mathscr{E}^0_{Zn/Zn^{2+}} - \mathscr{E}^0_{H_2/H^+}) - (\mathscr{E}^0_{Cu/Cu^{2+}} - \mathscr{E}^0_{H_2/H^+})$$

$$= \mathscr{E}^0_{Zn/Zn^{2+}} - \mathscr{E}^0_{Cu/Cu^{2+}} .$$

Some indirect estimates suggest that the absolute standard half-cell potential for H_2/H^+ is small, but it is apparent that its actual value is immaterial in combining equations, since it cancels out. The third step is, accordingly, to make the convenient, arbitrary assignment that $\mathscr{E}^0_{H_2/H^+} = 0$ and to report the measured $\mathscr{E}^0$ values for reactions such as (a) and (b) as the actual values for the half-cells. Thus $\mathscr{E}^0_{298} = 0.763$ and -0.337 for reactions (a) and (b), respectively, and we report that

$$\mathscr{E}^0_{Zn/Zn^{2+}} = 0.763 \quad \text{and} \quad \mathscr{E}^0_{Cu/Cu^{2+}} = -0.337.$$

Then $\mathscr{E}^0_{298}$ for reaction (c) is $0.763 - (-0.337) = 1.10$ V; this result is independent of the assumption regarding $\mathscr{E}^0_{H_2/H^+}$.

The convention is that the emf of a cell is given by

$$\mathscr{E}^0 = \mathscr{E}^0_{left} - \mathscr{E}^0_{right} , \tag{13-19}$$

where $\mathscr{E}^0_{left}$ and $\mathscr{E}^0_{right}$ are the *standard oxidation potentials* of the half-cells corresponding to the anode and cathode of the full cell, respectively.

The general mass of emf data has been reduced by means of this formalism and a number of standard half-cell potentials are given in Table 13-1. Their use follows the example just given. Each value is actually the $\mathscr{E}^0$ for the cell whose anode is the stated half-cell and whose cathode is the standard hydrogen electrode.

Table 13-1. *Standard Oxidation Potentials at 25°C[a]*

Half-cell reaction	$\mathscr{E}^0_{298}$	$\mathscr{V}^0_{298}$ [b]
$Li = Li^+ + e^-$	3.045	−3.045
$K = K^+ + e^-$	2.925	−2.925
$Ca = Ca^{2+} + 2e^-$	2.87	−2.87
$Na = Na^+ + e^-$	2.714	−2.714
$Mg = Mg^{2+} + 2e^-$	2.52	−2.52
$Al = Al^{3+} + 3e^-$	1.66	−1.66
$Zn = Zn^{2+} + 2e^-$	0.763	−0.763
$Fe = Fe^{2+} + 2e^-$	0.440	−0.440
$Cd = Cd^{2+} + 2e^-$	0.402	−0.402
$Pb + SO_4^{2-} = PbSO_4 + 2e^-$	0.356	−0.356
$Pb = Pb^{2+} + 2e^-$	0.126	−0.126
$Tl = Tl^+ + e^-$	0.3363	−0.3363
$Ag + I^- = AgI + e^-$	0.126	−0.126
$Fe = Fe^{3+} + 3e^-$	0.036	−0.036
$H_2 = 2H^+ + 2e^-$	0.0000	0.0000
$Ag + Br^- = AgBr + e^-$	−0.0713	0.0713
$Cu^+ = Cu^{2+} + e^-$	−0.153	0.153
$Ag + Cl^- = AgCl + e^-$	−0.22239	0.22239
Saturated calomel	−0.242	0.242
$2Hg + 2Cl^- = Hg_2Cl_2 + 2e^-$	−0.2676	0.2676
Normal calomel	−0.280	0.280
0.1 N calomel	−0.3358	0.3358
$Cu = Cu^{2+} + 2e^-$	−0.337	0.337
$Cu = Cu^+ + e^-$	−0.521	0.521
$2I^- = I_2 + 2e^-$	−0.5355	0.5355
$Fe^{2+} = Fe^{3+} + e^-$	−0.771	0.771
$2Hg = Hg_2^{2+} + 2e^-$	−0.789	0.789
$Ag = Ag^+ + e^-$	−0.7991	0.7991
$Hg_2^{2+} = 2Hg^{2+} + 2e^-$	−0.920	0.920
$2Br^- = Br_2 + 2e^-$	−1.0652	1.0652
$Tl^+ = Tl^{3+} + 2e^-$	−1.25	1.25
$2Cl^- = Cl_2 + 2e^-$	−1.36	1.36
$PbSO_4 + 2H_2O =$		
$\quad PbO + SO_4^{2-} + 4H^+ + 2e^-$	−1.685	1.685
$2F^- = F_2 + 2e^-$	−2.87	2.87
Basic solutions		
$SO_3^{2-} + 2OH^- = SO_4^{2-} + H_2O + 2e^-$	0.93	−0.93
$H_2 + 2OH^- = 2H_2O + 2e^-$	0.8281	−0.8281
$Ni + 2OH^- = Ni(OH)_2 + 2e^-$	0.72	−0.72
$3OH^- = H_2O + HO_2^- + 2e^-$	−0.88	0.88

[a] Largely adapted from G. N. Lewis and M. Randall, "Thermodynamics," 2nd ed. (revised by K. S. Pitzer and L. Brewer). McGraw-Hill, New York, 1961.

[b] See Commentary and Notes section.

As one other further example, the reaction

(c) $2Hg + 2AgCl = Hg_2Cl_2 + 2Ag$

can be written as the difference between

(a) $2Hg + 2Cl^- = Hg_2Cl_2 + 2e^-$, $\mathscr{E}^0_{298} = -0.2676$

and

(b) $Ag + Cl^- = AgCl + e^-$, $\mathscr{E}^0_{298} = -0.2224$.

Then $\mathscr{E}^0_{(c)} = -(0.2676) - (-0.2224) = -0.0452$. Note that although we must multiply reaction (b) by 2 before subtracting it from reaction (a) in order to obtain reaction (c), we subtract the emf's directly. This is because an emf corresponds to the free energy change *per faraday*, so that all emf's are on the same basis.

There is one situation where the additivity procedure must be handled with care, namely in the combining of two half-cell reactions to give a third half-cell reaction. Each emf should be weighted by the number of faradays for which the half-cell reaction is written. As an example, consider the case

(a) $Fe = Fe^{2+} + 2e^-$, $\Delta G^0_{(a)} = -2\mathscr{F}\mathscr{E}^0_{(a)}$,

(b) $Fe^{2+} = Fe^{3+} + e^-$, $\Delta G^0_{(b)} = -\mathscr{F}\mathscr{E}^0_{(b)}$,

(c) $Fe = Fe^{3+} + 3e^-$, $\Delta G^0_{(c)} = -3\mathscr{F}\mathscr{E}^0_{(c)}$.

Since $\Delta G^0_{(c)} = \Delta G^0_{(a)} + \Delta G^0_{(b)}$, it follows that $\mathscr{E}^0_{(c)} = (2\mathscr{E}^0_{(a)} + \mathscr{E}^0_{(b)})/3$. At 25°C, we get $\mathscr{E}^0_{(c)} = [(2)(0.440) + (-0.771)]/3 = 0.036$. The general equation is

$$\mathscr{E}^0_{(c)} = \frac{n_{(a)}\mathscr{E}^0_{(a)} + n_{(b)}\mathscr{E}^0_{(b)}}{n_{(c)}}, \tag{13-20}$$

where n denotes number of faradays. Whenever one has any question about combining cell reactions, he should always do so first in terms of ΔG's since these are always additive.

13-5   Emf and Chemical Equilibria

A.   Thermodynamic Relationships

Combination of Eqs. (13-5) and (12-92), $\Delta G^0 = -RT \ln K_{th}$, gives an important relationship between the $\mathscr{E}^0$ for a cell and the equilibrium constant for the cell reaction:

$$\mathscr{E}^0 = \frac{RT}{n\mathscr{F}} \ln K_{th} \tag{13-21}$$

or, for 25°C

$$\log K_{th} = \frac{n}{0.05917}\,\mathscr{E}^0. \tag{13-22}$$

Thus for $n = 1$, 0.059 V corresponds to one power of ten in K.

B. Direct Applications

A very direct and useful application of $\mathscr{E}^0$ values is to the treatment of oxidation–reduction equilibria in solution. The following examples illustrate typical situations.

EXAMPLE 1. To what extent will Zn reduce 0.01 m Fe^{2+} at 25°C? The reaction is

$$Zn + Fe^{2+} = Zn^{2+} + Fe$$

and, from Table 13-1, $\mathscr{E}^0_{298} = 0.763 - 0.440 = 0.323$. Then $K_{th} = \text{antilog}[2/(0.05917)(0.323)] = 8.3 \times 10^{10}$, or

$$8.3 \times 10^{10} = \frac{a_{Zn^{2+}}}{a_{Fe^{2+}}}.$$

The reaction will go virtually to completion, or, if activity coefficients are neglected, until (Zn^{2+}) is essentially 0.01 m; the equilibrium (Fe^{2+}) is then $0.01/8.3 \times 10^{10} = 1.2 \times 10^{-13}$.

EXAMPLE 2. What is the equilibrium concentration of Cu^+ in a 0.01 m Cu^{2+} solution at pH 3 and saturated with respect to $H_2(g)$ at 1 atm and 25°C? The reaction is

$$Cu^{2+} + \tfrac{1}{2}H_2 = Cu^+ + H^+$$

and the $\mathscr{E}^0$ is just that for the Cu^+/Cu^{2+} half-cell, -0.153 V; K_{th} is therefore antilog$(-0.153/0.05917) = 2.6 \times 10^{-3}$. Then

$$2.6 \times 10^{-3} = \frac{(Cu^+)(H^+)}{(Cu^{2+})}, \qquad \frac{(Cu^+)}{(Cu^{2+})} = 2.6$$

(neglecting activity coefficients), or $(Cu^+)/[0.01 - (Cu^+)] = 2.6$ and $(Cu^+) = 0.00722$ m.

The next question would be whether the hydrogen would further reduce the Cu^+ to Cu. From Table 13-1, $\mathscr{E}^0$ must be -0.521, and the equilibrium constant for

$$Cu^+ + \tfrac{1}{2}H_2 = Cu + H^+$$

is therefore antilog$(-0.521/0.05917)$ or about 10^{-9}. It would require about 10^6 m (!) Cu^+ for Cu metal to deposit.

EXAMPLE 3. To what extent should 0.01 m Hg_2^{2+} disproportionate into Hg and Hg^{2+} at 25°C? We combine the following half-cell reactions:

(a)	$\tfrac{1}{2}Hg_2^{2+} = Hg^{2+} + e^-$,	$\mathscr{E}^0_{(a)} =$	-0.920,
(b)	$\tfrac{1}{2}Hg_2^{2+} + e^- = Hg(l)$,	$\mathscr{E}^0_{(b)} =$	0.789,
(c)	$Hg_2^{2+} = Hg^{2+} + Hg(l)$,	$\mathscr{E}^0_{(c)} =$	-0.131.

$K_{th} = $ antilog$(-0.131/0.05917) = 6.1 \times 10^{-3}$, so we have

$$6.1 \times 10^{-3} = \frac{(Hg^{2+})}{(Hg_2^{2+})} = \frac{(Hg^{2+})}{0.01 - (Hg^{2+})},$$

from which $(Hg^{2+}) = 6.0 \times 10^{-5}$. The calculation supposes that some $Hg(l)$ is formed or is present.

C. Determination of Solubility Products

Several of the half-cell reactions of Table 13-1 are written as the reaction of a metal with an anion to give a slightly soluble salt. The potential for such a half-cell reaction may be combined with the one for the simple oxidation of the metal to give the solubility product of the salt. If we have

(a) $\qquad M + X^- = MX(s) + e^-, \qquad \mathscr{E}^0_{(a)}$,

(b) $\qquad M = M^+ + e^-, \qquad \mathscr{E}^0_{(b)}$,

$\overline{\text{(c)} = \text{(b)} - \text{(a)} \quad MX(s) = M^+ + X^-, \qquad \mathscr{E}^0_{(c)} = \mathscr{E}^0_{(b)} - \mathscr{E}^0_{(a)}}$,

then, neglecting activity coefficients, $K_{sp} = $ antilog$(\mathscr{E}^0_{(c)}/0.05917)$ at 25°C.

An alternative and sometimes very useful approach is the following. We write the Nernst equation for reaction (b):

$$\mathscr{E}_{(b)} = \mathscr{E}^0_{(b)} - 0.05917 \log a_{M^+}. \tag{13-23}$$

The potential at a metal–metal ion electrode must always reflect the chemical potential of that ion; in the presence of X^-, $MX(s)$ forms, which decreases a_{M^+} according to the solubility constant, $a_{M^+} = K_{th}/a_{X^-}$. The standard potential of reaction (a) must therefore be the same as the potential of the metal–metal ion electrode for that value of a_{M^+} which is present when a_{X^-} is unity. Thus when a_{X^-} is unity $\mathscr{E}_{(b)}$ in Eq. (13-23) may be replaced by $\mathscr{E}^0_{(a)}$ and a_{M^+} by K_{th} :

$$\mathscr{E}^0_{(a)} = \mathscr{E}^0_{(b)} - 0.05917 \log K_{th} , \qquad K_{th} = \text{antilog} \frac{\mathscr{E}^0_{(b)} - \mathscr{E}^0_{(a)}}{0.05917},$$

which is the same result as before. This alternative treatment, although longer as presented here, becomes very advantageous when one is dealing with more complicated situations.

Calculate the solubility product for Ag_2SO_4 if $\mathscr{E}^0_{298} = -0.627$ V for the cell

$$Ag/Ag_2SO_4/H_2SO_4(m)/H_2/Pt.$$

The $\mathscr{E}^0$ is that for the half-cell reaction

$$2Ag + SO_4^{2-} = Ag_2SO_4 + 2e^-, \qquad \mathscr{E}^0_{298} = -0.627.$$

Subtraction of this from

$$2Ag = 2Ag^+ + 2e^-, \qquad \mathscr{E}^0_{298} = -0.799$$

gives

$$Ag_2SO_4 = 2Ag^+ + SO_4^{2-}, \qquad \mathscr{E}^0_{298} = -0.172.$$

The solubility product is then antilog$[(2)(-0.172)/0.05917] = 1.54 \times 10^{-6}$. Note that $n = 2$ in this case.

Application of the alternative procedure is as follows. We write

$$\mathscr{E} = -0.799 - \tfrac{1}{2}(0.05917) \log a^2_{Ag^+}.$$

When $a_{SO_4^{2-}}$ is unity, $\mathscr{E} = -0.627$ V, and $a^2_{Ag^+} = K/a_{SO_4^{2-}} = K$, so

$$-0.627 = -0.799 - \tfrac{1}{2}(0.05917) \log K,$$

which gives the same result as before.

D. Determination of Dissociation Constants

The alternative procedure described in the treatment of solubility equilibria may be applied to a homogeneous equilibrium in solution. If a metal ion is complexed in solution, then the half-cell potential M/M^{z+} gives the activity of that ion, and this often allows the calculation of the equilibrium constant for complexation.

As an example, the potential for the cell

$$Cu/0.02 f \, Cu(II) \text{ in } 0.5 f \, NH_3/\text{normal calomel electrode}$$

is 0.26 V at 25°C. [We use formalities since the copper is largely present as the complex $Cu(NH_3)_4^{2+}$ and we wish merely to describe the overall makeup of the solution.] We treat the left-hand electrode as a Cu/Cu^{2+} electrode whose emf is determined by $a_{Cu^{2+}}$ in the solution: The emf of the cell is therefore written

$$\mathscr{E} = \mathscr{E}^0_{Cu/Cu^{2+}} - \mathscr{E}_{ref} - \tfrac{1}{2}(0.05917) \log a_{Cu^{2+}}$$

or

$$0.26 = -0.337 - (-0.280) - \frac{0.05917}{2} \log a_{Cu^{2+}},$$

$$a_{Cu^{2+}} = \text{antilog} \frac{(2)(-0.317)}{0.05917} = 1.9 \times 10^{-11}.$$

Virtually all of the Cu^{2+} is in the form of $Cu(NH_3)_4^{2+}$; therefore $(NH_3) = 0.5 - (4)(0.02) = 0.42$, and we evaluate the equilibrium constant as

$$K = \frac{(Cu(NH_3)_4^{2+})}{(Cu^{2+})(NH_3)^4} = \frac{0.02}{(2.8 \times 10^{-11})(0.42)^4} = 3.4 \times 10^{10}$$

(neglecting activity coefficients).

582

A number of equilibrium constants for the dissociation of complex ions have been determined in this way. We see in Section 13-8 that an analogous procedure may be applied to the determination of a_{H^+} in a solution.

13-6 . Concentration Cells

The term *concentration cell* is used to designate a cell whose net reaction involves only changes in composition of species (or of gas pressures) and no *net* oxidation or reduction. The $\mathscr{E}^0$ for such a cell must be zero since all species in the cell reaction are then to be at unit activity, in which case no change at all accompanies the passage of electricity.

A. Electrode Concentration Cells

A very straightforward type of concentration cell is the following:

$$Pt/H_2(P_1)/HCl(m)/H_2(P_2)/Pt,$$

for which the cell reaction is

anode $\qquad\qquad H_2(P_1) = 2H^+(m) + 2e^-,$
cathode $\qquad 2H^+(m) + 2e^- = H_2(P_2),$
net reaction $\qquad H_2(P_1) = H_2(P_2),$

with

$$\mathscr{E}_{298} = -\frac{0.05917}{2} \log \frac{P_2}{P_1}.$$

In the case of a metal electrode the metal may be present as an amalgam:

$$Cd(x_1 \text{, in Hg})/CdSO_4(m)/Cd(x_2 \text{, in Hg}),$$

with

$$\mathscr{E}_{298} = -\frac{0.05917}{2} \log \frac{a_{x_2}}{a_{x_1}}.$$

B. Simple Electrolyte Concentration Cells

In a simple electrolyte concentration cell liquid junctions are avoided by setting up two opposing cells which differ only in their electrolyte concentration. The following is an example:

$$Ag/AgCl/HCl(m_1)/H_2(1\ atm)/Pt\!-\!Pt/H_2(1\ atm)/HCl(m_2)/AgCl/Ag,$$

first anode	$Ag + Cl^-(m_1) = AgCl + e^-,$
first cathode	$H^+(m_1) + e^- = \frac{1}{2}H_2(1\ atm),$
second anode	$\frac{1}{2}H_2(1\ atm) = H^+(m_2) + e^-,$
second cathode	$AgCl + e^- = Ag + Cl^-(m_2),$
net reaction	$H^+(m_1) + Cl^-(m_1) = H^+(m_2) + Cl^-(m_2).$

Note that it is important to write each ionic species separately if the electrolyte is in fact treated as fully dissociated. The emf for this cell is

$$\mathscr{E}_{298} = -0.05917 \log \frac{a_{H^+,m_2}a_{Cl^-,m_2}}{a_{H^+,m_1}a_{Cl^-,m_1}},$$

$$\mathscr{E}_{298} = -0.1183 \log \frac{m_2}{m_1} - 0.1183 \log \frac{\gamma_{\pm,m_2}}{\gamma_{\pm,m_1}}.$$

Cells of this type may be used to obtain the ratio of activity coefficients of an electrolyte at two different concentrations.

Electrolyte concentration cells having a liquid junction are discussed in the Special Topics section.

13-7   Oxidation–Reduction Reactions

We consider here the situation in which both the oxidized and reduced forms of the half-cell couple are solution species. Examples are the couples Fe^{2+}/Fe^{3+} and Cu^+/Cu^{2+}. Both partners of the redox couple are in solution, and since they can be exposed only to one of the electrodes (or else the cell would be short-circuited), it is mandatory that the second electrode be connected by means of a salt bridge. Thus we have

$$Pt/Cu^+(m_1),\ Cu^{2+}(m_2)/standard\ calomel\ electrode.$$

The potential of such a cell is given by the general form

$$\mathscr{E} = \mathscr{E}^0_{anode} - \mathscr{E}_{ref} - \frac{0.05917}{n} \log \frac{a_{oxid}}{a_{red}}, \tag{13-24}$$

where the anode reaction is

$$M(red) = M(oxid) + ne^-$$

and a_{oxid} and a_{red} refer to the activities of the oxidized and the reduced forms of the species of the redox couple, respectively. As mentioned in Section 13-2C, the presence of a liquid junction introduces some unavoidable inaccuracy in the measured emf. (See also the Special Topics Section.)

Cells of this type have been used in the determination of the redox emf not only for metal ion couples but also for a variety of inorganic coordination compounds and for many organic systems. An example of the second type is the $Fe(CN)_6^{4-}/Fe(CN)_6^{3-}$ couple, for which $\mathscr{E}_{298}^0 = -0.36$ V, and an example of the latter is the couple

$$[HO-C_6H_4-OH] = [O=C_6H_4=O] + 2H^+ + 2e^-, \qquad \mathscr{E}_{293}^0 = -0.6994. \qquad (13\text{-}25)$$

It will be seen in the next section that the quinone–hydroquinone couple is useful in pH determinations.

Returning to inorganic examples, we note that most elements exist in several oxidation states and that the potentials between these states are generally determined by cells of the type represented by Eq. (13-24). Table 13-2 summarizes a few of these emf relationships. The number between oxidation states is the standard oxidation potential at 25°C. We assume acid solutions and use H^+ and H_2O as needed in writing the balanced half-cell reactions.

A cell corresponding to Eq. (13-24) may also be used to follow a redox titration. Let us say that ion M_1 is initially present in reduced form and that an oxidizing agent, ion M_2, is added progressively. The reaction

$$M_1(red) + M_2(oxid) = M_1(oxid) + M_2(red)$$

occurs. We assume that the reaction is rapid so that at each stage of the titration the system is in equilibrium. Since there can be only one potential at the platinum anode, this means that $a_{M_1(oxid)}/a_{M_1(red)}$ is always equal to $a_{M_2(oxid)}/a_{M_2(red)}$.

The situation is most easily delineated by means of a concrete example. Consider the titration of Cu^+ with Fe^{3+}:

$$Cu^+ + Fe^{3+} = Cu^{2+} + Fe^{2+}. \qquad (13\text{-}26)$$

Table 13-2.   *Selected Standard Oxidation Potentials for the Elements in Their Various Valence States[a]*

$$Cr \xrightarrow{\ 0.91\ } Cr^{2+} \xrightarrow{\ 0.41\ } Cr^{3+} \xrightarrow{\ -1.33\ } Cr_2O_7^{2-}$$

$$Mn \xrightarrow{\ 1.1\ } Mn^{2+} \xrightarrow{\ -1.51\ } Mn^{3+} \xrightarrow{\ -0.95\ } MnO_2 \xrightarrow{\ -2.26\ } MnO_4^{2-} \xrightarrow{\ -0.564\ } MnO_4^{-}$$

$$Fe \xrightarrow{\ 0.44\ } Fe^{2+} \xrightarrow{\ -0.771\ } Fe^{3+}$$

$$Co \xrightarrow{\ 0.277\ } Co^{2+} \xrightarrow{\ -1.82\ } Co^{3+} \xrightarrow{\ <-1.8\ } CoO_2^{-}$$

$$Ni \xrightarrow{\ 0.250\ } Ni^{2+} \xrightarrow{\ -1.78\ } NiO_2$$

$$Cu \xrightarrow{\ -0.521\ } Cu^+ \xrightarrow{\ -0.153\ } Cu^{2+}$$

$$Cl^- \xrightarrow{\ -1.3595\ } Cl_2 \xrightarrow{\ -1.63\ } HClO \xrightarrow{\ -1.645\ } HClO_2 \xrightarrow{\ -1.21\ } ClO_3^- \xrightarrow{\ -1.19\ } ClO_4^{-}$$

$$Br^- \xrightarrow{\ -1.07\ } Br_2 \xrightarrow{\ -1.59\ } HBrO \xrightarrow{\ -1.49\ } BrO_3^{-}$$

$$I^- \xrightarrow{\ -0.535\ } I_2 \xrightarrow{\ -1.45\ } HIO \xrightarrow{\ -1.14\ } IO_3^- \xrightarrow{\ (-1.7)\ } H_5IO_6$$

[a] Adapted from W. M. Latimer, "The Oxidation States of the Elements and Their Potentials in Aqueous Solution," 2nd ed. Prentice-Hall, Englewood Cliffs, New Jersey, 1952.

The cell would be

Pt/Cu⁺(plus Cu^{2+}, Fe^{3+}, Fe^{2+} as the titration proceeds)/calomel reference electrode.

The cell potential is $\mathscr{E}_{cell} = \mathscr{E}_{Pt} - \mathscr{E}_{ref}$, where $\mathscr{E}_{Pt}$ is the half-cell potential at the platinum electrode. The statement is that at all stages of the titration

$$\mathscr{E}_{Pt} = \mathscr{E}_{Fe^{2+}/Fe^{3+}} = \mathscr{E}_{Cu^+/Cu^{2+}},\tag{13-27}$$

or

$$\mathscr{E}_{Pt} = \mathscr{E}^0_{Cu^+/Cu^{2+}} - 0.05917 \log \frac{(Cu^{2+})}{(Cu^+)} = \mathscr{E}^0_{Fe^{2+}/Fe^{3+}} - 0.05917 \log \frac{(Fe^{3+})}{(Fe^{2+})},\tag{13-28}$$

where, for simplicity, activity coefficients are neglected. Equation (13-28) rearranges to

$$\mathscr{E}^0_{Fe^{2+}/Fe^{3+}} - \mathscr{E}^0_{Cu^+/Cu^{2+}} = 0.05917 \log \frac{(Cu^+)(Fe^{3+})}{(Cu^{2+})(Fe^{2+})} = -0.771 - (-0.153) = -0.618.\tag{13-29}$$

Equation (13-29) defines the equilibrium constant for reaction (13-26) and may be solved for each stage of the titration. One then inserts the equilibrium ratio of $(Cu^{2+})/(Cu^+)$ or that of $(Fe^{3+})/(Fe^{2+})$ in Eq. (13-28) to give $\mathscr{E}_{Pt}$ and thence $\mathscr{E}_{cell}$.

At the end point, $Fe_{tot} = Cu_{tot}$, and since $(Fe^{2+}) = (Cu^{2+})$ by the stoichiometry of Eq. (13-26), it follows that $(Fe^{3+}) = (Cu^+)$. Equation (13-29) then reduces to

$$\mathscr{E}^0_{Fe^{2+}/Fe^{3+}} - \mathscr{E}^0_{Cu^+/Cu^{2+}} = 0.1183 \log \left[\frac{(Fe^{3+})}{(Fe^{2+})} \right]_{endpoint}.$$

Insertion of this relationship into the right-hand side of Eq. (13-28) to eliminate the log term leads to

$$\mathscr{E}_{Pt,endpoint} = \tfrac{1}{2}(\mathscr{E}^0_{Fe^{2+}/Fe^{3+}} + \mathscr{E}^0_{Cu^+/Cu^{2+}}).\tag{13-30}$$

Equation (13-30) gives the value of $\mathscr{E}_{Pt}$ and hence of $\mathscr{E}_{cell}$ at the end point. The plot of this particular titration is shown in Fig. 13-8.

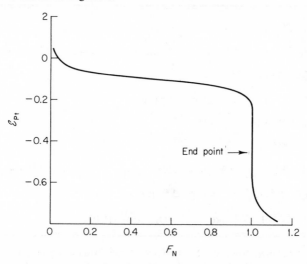

Fig. 13-8. *Potentiometric titration curve for* $Cu^+ + Fe^{3+} = Cu^{2+} + Fe^{2+}$.

13-8   Determination of pH

The term pH was coined by S. Sorensen in 1909 to mean $-\log(H^+)$, and we have come to use the symbol $p(X)$ as an operator meaning $-\log X$, where X may be a concentration, an activity, or an equilibrium constant; pK_a means $-\log K_a$, for example. A potential measurement always reflects the activity of the species present, and only at infinite dilution can activity be equated with concentration. Potentiometric methods for pH determination therefore measure some type of hydrogen ion activity, although it turns out that the exact nature of what is measured depends on the cell that is used. The modern procedure is to define pH as essentially

$$pH = -\log a_{H^+} \qquad (13\text{-}31)$$

but with the exact meaning of a_{H^+} determined by the cell used.

Consider first a cell such as (13-1):

$$\text{Pt/H}_2(1\ \text{atm})/\text{HCl}(m)/\text{AgCl/Ag.}$$

The corresponding Nernst equation is

$$\mathscr{E} = \mathscr{E}^0 - 0.1183 \log a_{\pm,\text{HCl}} . \qquad (13\text{-}32)$$

The procedure described in Section 13-3 allows the determination of $\mathscr{E}^0$, and so the cell measurements provide values for the mean activity of HCl in any solution, which might be thought to correspond to a_{H^+}. Suppose that now we replace the electrolyte by $[\text{HAc}(m_1) + \text{KCl}(m_2)]$. The $\mathscr{E}^0$ remains the same, as does Eq. (13-32). However, the calculated mean activity for HCl will now depend on both m_1 and m_2. Thus such a cell is not suited for pH determination.

Next, consider the cell

$$\text{Pt/H}_2(1\ \text{atm})/\text{solution}\,/\,\text{calomel electrode.}$$

This emf is

$$\mathscr{E}_{298} = -\mathscr{E}_{\text{ref}} - 0.05917 \log a_{H^+} = -\mathscr{E}_{\text{ref}} + 0.05917\, pH \qquad (13\text{-}33)$$

and it appears that out goal is achieved. The problem is that $\mathscr{E}_{\text{ref}}$ contains the junction potential at the solution/KCl interface (see Section 13-2C and Special Topics section) and is not rigorously measurable. What is actually done is to determine $\mathscr{E}_{\text{ref}}$ such that a_{H^+} corresponds to $(H^+)\, \gamma_\pm$ as observed, by independent means, to apply to various solutions of weak acids. In effect, it is assumed, not quite correctly, that $\gamma_{H^+} = \gamma_\pm$; it is also assumed, not quite correctly, that the junction potential incorporated in $\mathscr{E}_{\text{ref}}$ will not vary with the nature of the solution studied.

The result of all this is that the operational definition of pH is given by Eq. (13-33) with the $\mathscr{E}_{\text{ref}}$ values of Table 13-1 for the various calomel reference electrodes.

The definition allows very precise pH measurements, but ones whose accuracy is subject to some, but probably not much uncertainty so long as fairly dilute solutions are involved. The determination of pH in concentrated solutions or in nonaqueous solvents can be quite a problem.

The hydrogen electrode is a demanding one to use experimentally; the platinized platinum can be poisoned (lose its catalytic ability due to adsorption of solution components), so that the electrode fails to function well. An alternative pH-determining cell is that corresponding to Eq. (13-25):

Pt/solution with quinone (Q) plus hydroquinone (H$_2$Q) $/$ calomel electrode.

One convenience is that quinone forms a 1:1 compound with hydroquinone, *quinhydrone*, so that by dissolving the compound in the solution to be tested, one establishes equal concentrations of both species. With the added assumption that, being nonelectrolytes, their activity coefficients will be unity, the Nernst term, $(RT/n\mathscr{F}) \ln(a_Q/a_{H_2Q})$, drops out and one has

$$\mathscr{E}_{298} = -0.06994 - \mathscr{E}_{ref} + 0.05917\,pH \qquad (13\text{-}34)$$

(subject to the same reservations about liquid junctions as stated earlier).

The most widely used pH-determining cell is that known as the pH *meter* or *glass electrode*. The cell diagram is

$$\begin{array}{c} \text{glass membrane} \\ \text{reference electrode } // \\ \text{in solution A } // \end{array} \text{ unknown solution } / \text{ calomel electrode}, \qquad (13\text{-}35)$$

where the anode may be either Ag/AgCl or a calomel electrode, but with the solution buffered at some constant pH. The glass membrane has the property of passing essentially only hydrogen ions, and, per faraday, the cell reaction is

$$H^+(\text{solution A}) = H^+(\text{unknown solution})$$

so

$$\mathscr{E}_{298} = \text{constant} + 0.05917\,pH, \qquad (13\text{-}36)$$

where the constant contains $\mathscr{E}^0$ for the cell, a constant Nernst term, and the junction potential. In practice, one calibrates the pH meter scale by measuring the emf when a known buffer solution is used in place of the unknown solution, and one finds that it gives almost the same pH values for other solutions as a hydrogen electrode does [see Dole (1941) and Bates (1954) for details].

Recently other ion-selective membranes have been developed that pass only one or another cation or anion, and an electrode incorporating such a membrane allows the determination of a pM or a pX, where M or X is the ion passed. The selectivity is not always rigorous, however, and one must test such electrodes carefully in the actual situation before accepting the results of their use.

13-9   Irreversible Electrode Processes

The material so far has dealt with reversible emf's, the experimental measurements being made under conditions of virtually no current flow through the cell. Practical applications of electrochemistry, except for standard reference cells, involve appreciable current flows and we now encounter a new set of phenomena which involve irreversible processes. One is that of overvoltage, important in electrodepositions and also in the study of the kinetics of electrode reactions. Another is polarography, discussed in the Special Topics section.

A.   Electrodeposition

Electrodeposition is the production of an electrolysis product, usually a metal, on a preparative scale. The situation is illustrated in Fig. 13-9. When a potential is applied across the

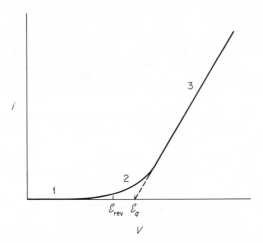

Fig. 13-9.   *Variation of current i with voltage V. 1–2: current determined by diffusion of electrode products away from the electrode region; 2–3 current determined by Ohm's law.*

terminals of a cell very little happens until a critical voltage is reached, beyond which the current increases about linearly with potential. This is what occurs: Suppose that we have two platinum wires dipping in an HCl solution. The cell reaction and reversible potential are

$$\text{anode} \qquad 2Cl^-(m) = Cl_2(P) + 2e^-,$$
$$\text{cathode} \qquad 2H^+(m) + 2e^- = H_2(P),$$

and

$$\mathscr{E} = \mathscr{E}^0 - \frac{RT}{2\mathscr{F}} \ln \frac{1}{a_{\pm,\text{HCl}}^4} - \frac{RT}{2\mathscr{F}} \ln(a_{H_2}a_{Cl_2}), \qquad (13\text{-}37)$$

where $\mathscr{E}^0 = -1.3595$ V at 25°C. This would, in principle, be established if hydrogen and chlorine gas were bubbling past the respective electrodes, so that a_{H_2} and a_{Cl_2} corresponded to a P of 1 atm. In the present experiment, however, no gases are being supplied, and P is initially zero, so that $\mathscr{E}$ is

589

some large positive number, infinity in theory. When the electrodes are inserted into the solution and connected, but with no potential applied some fluctuation will decide one to be the anode and the other the cathode, and some minute amount of electrolysis will occur, forming a little dissolved hydrogen and chlorine next to the electrodes and bringing their local activities up to some low, but nonzero value. The activity of the dissolved gases is far below that for 1 atm pressure and no bubbles can form, but the dissolved gases will diffuse steadily away from the electrodes into the solution. The result is that a small current will flow, and if a very sensitive probe could be used, each electrode would be observed to have some potential relative to the probe. The electrodes are said to be *polarized*, and the small current is called the *residual polarization current*.

If we now apply a small potential V between the electrodes, additional electrolysis will take place, building up a_{H_2} and a_{Cl_2} so that a back emf $\mathscr{E}_q$ develops in opposition to the applied potential difference. The increased hydrogen and chlorine activities lead to an increased diffusion rate away from the electrodes and a consequent increase in the very low steady-state current. We thus observe section 1–2 of the curve shown in Fig. 13-9. With continued increase in applied voltage a_{H_2} and a_{Cl_2} will become equal to the value of the gases at 1 atm, and actual bubble formation will occur. Then $\mathscr{E}_q$ is at its maximum value $\mathscr{E}_{q(max)}$ and cannot increase further, and beyond this point the increase in applied potential goes into an ohmic potential drop through the solution, that is, $V - \mathscr{E}_{q(max)} = iR$. The section 2–3 of the plot is thus linear.

This analysis indicates that extrapolation of the linear portion of the plot of Fig. 13-9 gives $\mathscr{E}_{q(max)}$; this is called the *decomposition potential*. Ideally, $\mathscr{E}_{q(max)}$ is equal to $\mathscr{E}_{rev}$ for the cell, but in practice it may be more positive, and the difference between the two is then called the *overvoltage*. In electrodeposition one is operating in this linear region, and although the reversible potential is the ideal decomposition potential, in practice one must know what the overvoltage will be.

Suppose that we wish to deposit cadmium from a 0.1 m solution of a cadmium salt at pH 7. The reversible potential for the reaction $Cd^{2+} + 2e^- = Cd$ will be, at 25°C and with activity coefficient effects neglected,

$$\mathscr{E}_{Cd} = -0.402 - \frac{0.05917}{2} \log \frac{1}{0.1} = -0.432 \quad V.$$

The value for hydrogen, that is, $\mathscr{E}$ for evolving hydrogen gas, is

$$\mathscr{E}_{H_2} = 0 - \frac{0.05917}{2} \log \left(\frac{1}{10^{-7}} \right)^2 = -0.414 \quad V.$$

One thus expects the evolution of hydrogen to occur first as potential is applied to the electrolysis cell and that, in fact, it would be virtually impossible to cause cadmium metal to deposit on the electrode. The actual situation is just the reverse because the overvoltage for hydrogen evolution from a cadmium surface is about 0.5 V; as a consequence, the cadmium deposits and no hydrogen evolution occurs.

Some representative hydrogen evolution overvoltages are as follows: platinized platinum, zero or small; smooth platinum, 0.09; silver, 0.15; copper, 0.23; lead, 0.64; zinc, 0.70; and mercury, 0.78 (for zero current). An interesting observation is that the hydrogen overvoltage parallels the heat of adsorption of atomic hydrogen on the metal. The overvoltage thus seems to be related to the energy required to produce surface hydrogen atoms as the intermediate to H_2 formation.

B. Theory of Overvoltage

The excess of an applied potential over the reversible decomposition potential, or the overvoltage, is usually given the symbol η, and Fig. 13-9 could be redrawn so as to show a plot of i

versus η. However, there are three general types of contribution to an observed overvoltage, only two of which are of fundamental interest. As mentioned earlier, the linear portion of Fig. 13-9 arises primarily from the Ohm's law drop in potential across the solution and is trivial from a theoretical point of view. Second, as active decomposition occurs, electrolysis products accumulate and reactants are depleted in the vicinity of the electrode; the effect is to change $\mathscr{E}_q$ from the reversible value calculated for the average compositions. This contribution to η is known as *concentration polarization*, and is of practical but not much theoretical interest (see Special Topics section). We wish to concentrate on that portion of η due to the intrinsic chemistry of the electrode process itself, often called *activation polarization*.

The experimental method is illustrated in Fig. 13-10. The desired current i is passed through

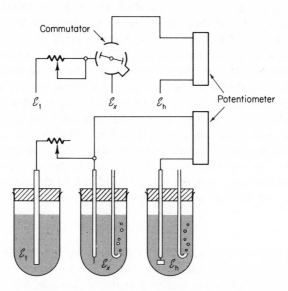

Fig. 13-10. *Apparatus for measuring overvoltages. [From A. W. Adamson, "Physical Chemistry of Surfaces," 2nd ed. Copyright 1967, Wiley (Interscience), New York. Used by permission of John Wiley & Sons, Inc.]*

the electrode to be studied $\mathscr{E}_x$ by means of the circuit $\mathscr{E}_1 - \mathscr{E}_x$ and the potential variation at $\mathscr{E}_x$ is measured by means of the separate potentiometer circuit $\mathscr{E}_x - \mathscr{E}_h$. Thus the ohmic contribution is essentially eliminated, and, with good stirring, most of the concentration polarization. The commutator device shown allows η to be measured either during current flow or immediately after cessation of flow; in this last case that portion of η due to activation polarization will often decay exponentially with time.

Activation polarization usually obeys an equation due to J. Tafel in 1905, known as the first law of electrode kinetics:

$$\eta = a + b \ln i. \tag{13-38}$$

A derivation of Eq. (13–38) is given in the Special Topics section, but the qualitative basis for it is that there is some slow step in the electrode process which involves an energy barrier, so that a Boltzmann factor $\exp(-\Delta G^*/RT)$ determines i. The applied potential acts to lower the level of this barrier, and hence the increased current is logarithmically related to η.

COMMENTARY AND NOTES

13-CN-1   Standard Oxidation Potential $\mathscr{E}^0$ and Standard Electrode Potential $\mathscr{V}^0$

We have used the standard oxidation potential $\mathscr{E}^0$ throughout this chapter, and an alternative quantity, the standard electrode potential $\mathscr{V}^0$, should be mentioned. This last is defined according to the recommendations of an international commission of 1953 as follows. A cell is made up of the particular electrode and a hydrogen electrode, and the half-cell electrode potential is that of the reversible potential difference between the terminals of the electrodes. Referring to Fig. 13-3, we see that if the half-cell operates spontaneously as the anode, the potential at its terminal is negative, and its electrode potential is therefore reported as negative. The standard electrode potential is defined the same way as to sign, but, of course, with all species now in their standard states.

The standard electrode potential is, by this definition, a property of the half-cell (relative to the hydrogen electrode), and its sign is therefore independent of the direction in which one writes the half-cell reaction. In determining $\mathscr{E}^0$ for a cell, one writes the cell diagram as usual, and, by definition,

$$\mathscr{E}^0 = \mathscr{V}^0_{\text{right}} - \mathscr{V}^0_{\text{left}} . \tag{13-39}$$

By this definition $\mathscr{E}^0$ is positive if the cell reaction, with the left-hand electrode taken to be the anode, is spontaneous; there is no change in this respect.

The system used here compares with that just given as follows. The standard oxidation potential is positive for a half-cell if, relative to the hydrogen electrode, the spontaneous reaction of the half-cell is one of oxidation. For some other cell $\mathscr{E}^0$ is, by this definition,

$$\mathscr{E}^0 = \mathscr{E}^0_{\text{left}} - \mathscr{E}^0_{\text{right}} \qquad \text{[Eq. (13-19)].}$$

The standard oxidation potential is always associated with the half-cell reaction written as an oxidation; the standard potential for a half-cell written as a reduction is called the standard reduction potential. In effect, $\mathscr{V}^0$ values are the same in sign and in use as standard reduction potentials. Their values, included in Table 13-1, are thus always the negative of the $\mathscr{E}^0$ values.

The system used in this chapter, that of $\mathscr{E}^0$ values, is the one employed by Latimer (1952) in his definitive book on oxidation potentials and is the traditional one in the United States. The $\mathscr{V}^0$ system conforms more to the European tradition of signing an electrode according to the potential at its terminal. This writer feels that the first convention, the one used here, is better suited to the physical chemist interested in electrode reactions and in viewing the potential of an electrode in solution rather that at its terminal. It is also consistent with the sign convention for the emf of a whole cell. Both these potentials are positive if the cell reaction proceeds spontaneously with the left-hand electrode as anode. Likewise, the $\mathscr{E}^0$ for a half-cell is positive if the cell reaction is spontaneous with the half-cell written as the left-hand electrode or anode and the hydrogen half-cell as the cathode.

13-CN-2   Storage Batteries

Electrochemical cells have great practical application. They are called *primary cells* if electrical energy is supplied on a one-time basis and *secondary cells* or *storage batteries* if an external source of energy is required to charge them.

One common type of storage battery is the lead–sulfuric acid cell for which the electrode reactions are

anode $\qquad\qquad\qquad$ $Pb + H_2SO_4 = PbSO_4(s) + 2H^+ + 2e^-$,

cathode $\qquad$ $PbO_2(s) + H_2SO_4 + 2H^+ + 2e^- = Pb + PbSO_4(s) + 2H_2O$.

The net reaction is

$$PbO_2(s) + PbSO_4 + 2H_2SO_4 = 2PbSO_4(s) + 2H_2O.$$

The potential is about 2 V; most lead storage batteries consist of several cells in series. The Leclanché dry cell has a potential of about 1.6 V and consists of a carbon electrode surrounded by manganese dioxide and graphite immersed in a starch paste containing zinc chloride and excess solid ammonium chloride. The electrode reactions of this cell are

anode $\qquad\qquad$ $Zn + 2NH_3 = Zn(NH_3)_2^{2+} + 2e^-$,

cathode $\qquad$ $2MnO_2 + 2NH_4^+ + 2e^- = Mn_2O_3 + H_2O + 2NH_3$.

The lead storage battery loses a good deal of power under high loads and, of course, is very heavy. A more expensive, but otherwise very attractive storage battery has been in use in Europe for many years, and, more recently, in the United States. This is the Jungner nickel–cadmium battery, which consists of nickel and cadmium electrodes and a KOH or other alkali electrolyte. The cell reactions are

anode $\qquad$ $Cd + 2OH^- = Cd(OH)_2 + 2e^-$,

cathode $\qquad$ $Ni(OH)_3 + e^- = Ni(OH)_2 + OH^-$.

The net reaction is

$$Cd + 2Ni(OH)_3 = Cd(OH)_2 + 2Ni(OH)_2.$$

Notice that the electrolyte serves merely as a vehicle for the transportation of

OH⁻ ions. The Ni–Cd battery is rechargeable and can deliver very high currents without appreciable loss of power. An important use is in battery-powered tools and appliances.

An important type of primary cell is the fuel cell. A simple example is the cell

$$Pt/H_2(g)/\text{electrolyte}/O_2(g)/C,$$

for which the net reaction is just $H_2 + \frac{1}{2}O_2 = H_2O$. Much current research is being carried out on the development of suitable electrodes for the reversible combustion of hydrocarbons so as to obtain electrical energy directly from a reaction such as $CH_4 + 2O_2 = CO_2 + 2H_2O$. The electrode reactions should be nearly reversible, high current densities are desirable, and a means must be provided for removing the products of the electrode reaction. It has not yet been possible to meet these requirements in a fully satisfactory manner, although results with experimental fuel cells have been encouraging.

13-CN-3 Thermodynamic Quantities for Aqueous Ions

We have completed, with this chapter, the presentation of the various experimental approaches by which we obtain thermodynamic quantities for aqueous electrolytes. The thermochemical approach is summarized in Section 5-5B and standard enthalpies of formation of aqueous electrolytes and of individual ions are given in Table 5-3; it will be recalled that these latter are based on the convention that $\Delta \overline{H}^0_{f,298} = 0$ for H⁺ ion.

The free energy of formation of an aqueous electrolyte may be determined from either solubility or emf data. As an example of the first method, the solubility of KCl is 4.82 M at 25°C and the mean activity coefficient in the saturated solution is 0.588; the standard free energy of solution is the solubility equilibrium constant, or

$$\Delta \mu^0 = -RT \ln K = -2RT \ln a_{\pm(\text{sat})}$$
$$= -(2)(1.98)(298) \ln[(4.82)(0.588)] = -1.26 \quad \text{kcal mole}^{-1}.$$

The value of ΔH^0 of solution (at infinite dilution since this is the reference condition) is 4.11 kcal mole⁻¹, and on combination of the two results, ΔS^0 of solution is 18.0 cal °K⁻¹ mole⁻¹. In the case of AgCl the corresponding calculation might be based on the thermodynamic solubility constant, as determined from emf data, whose temperature dependence would give ΔS^0 directly.

Absolute standard entropies for a number of electrolytes have been determined by one or another of these methods and one now adopts the convention that S^0 of H⁺ ion is zero. This allows the entropy data to be reported for individual ions, and a selection of such values is given in Table 13-3. The standard free energies

Table 13-3. *Standard Free Energies of Formation and Absolute Entropies of Aqueous Ions at 25°C[a]*

Ion	$\bar{S}^0$ (cal °K^{-1} mole^{-1})	$\Delta\mu_f^0$ (kcal mole^{-1})
H$^+$	(0.0000)	(0.0000)
Li$^+$	3.4	−70.22
Na$^+$	14.4	−62.59
K$^+$	24.5	−67.46
Ag$^+$	17.67	18.43
OH$^-$	−2.52	−37.59
F$^-$	−2.3	−66.08
Cl$^-$	13.2	−31.35
Br$^-$	19.29	−24.57
I$^-$	26.14	−12.35
ClO$_4^-$	43.2	−2.47
SO$_4^{2-}$	4.1	−177.34
CO$_3^{2-}$	−12.7	−126.22

[a] Adapted from G. N. Lewis and M. Randall, "Thermodynamics," 2nd ed. (revised by K. S. Pitzer and L. Brewer). McGraw-Hill, New York, 1961.

of formation of the various ions are included in the table; again that for H$^+$ ion is taken to be zero. One may use tables such as Table 13-3 in combination with those for standard entropies and free energies of formation of pure compounds to obtain $\mathscr{E}^0$ values for half-cells not previously measured.

As an alternative, one might assemble the value of the entropy of an ion by calculating the value for the gaseous ion using the Sackur–Tetrode equation (6-78) and adding the value for immersion of the ion into water. This last cannot be calculated exactly, but it should be related to the electrostatic potential of the ion, ze/r (note Section 12-8). It is not too surprising, therefore, that ionic entropies have been found to be well represented by the empirical equation

$$\bar{S}_{298}^0 = \frac{3}{2} R \ln M - \frac{270z}{(r+x)^2} + 37, \qquad (13\text{-}40)$$

where M is the molecular weight (the same term occurs in the Sackur–Tetrode equation), z is the ionic valence number, and r is the crystallographic radius in angstroms. We have some leeway in proportioning distances between ions in a crystal, and also we expect that the effective radius in solution might be different from that in the crystal. At any rate, it is necessary to correct r by an additive constant x equal to 2.00 for a positive ion and to 1.00 for a negative ion. The excellence of the correlation is illustrated in Fig. 13-11.

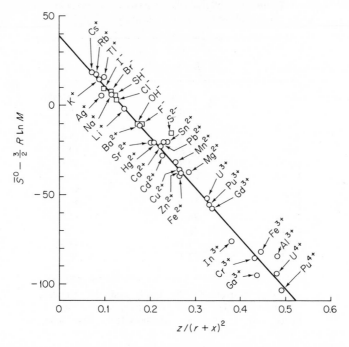

Fig. 13-11. *Corrected ionic entropies versus $z/(r + x)^2$ (r corrected as described in the text).*
[From Wendell M. Latimer, "The Oxidation States of the Elements and Their Potentials in Aqueous Solution," 2nd ed., © 1952. By permission of Prentice-Hall, Inc., Englewood Cliffs, New Jersey.]

13-CN-4   Electrocapillarity. Absolute Electrode Potentials

There has been a perhaps unfortunate tendency to concentrate on just a few properties of electrolyte solutions in this and the preceding chapter. Granted, these are the properties of central importance, yet the resulting impression may be a distorted one. A great variety of physical attributes of electrolyte solutions have been studied—density, viscosity, magnetic susceptibility, optical absorption, heat capacity, light scattering, compressibility, thermal expansion, surface tension, and so on. It seems worthwhile to introduce one variant from the usual at this point.

A very interesting electrochemical effect is that of the change in interfacial tension with applied potential. Not many interfaces allow an accurate study of this effect, however, because an attempt to apply a potential difference often results in electrolysis or in electrolytic transport across the interface. An especially well-adapted system is that of the mercury–electrolyte solution interface. This is highly polarizable, meaning that applied potentials result in little electrolysis in the absence of easily reducible ions, and, since mercury is a liquid, the interfacial tension can be observed by the methods of capillarity.

The typical experimental observation is illustrated in Fig. 13-12, which shows the mercury–solution interfacial tension to increase, go through a maximum, and then decrease as potential is applied. The experimental arrangement is that depicted in Fig. 13-13; a mercury reservoir terminates in a fine capillary tube and the position of the meniscus is viewed through a traveling microscope. Since the contact angle glass–mercury–solution is obtuse, there is a capillary depression

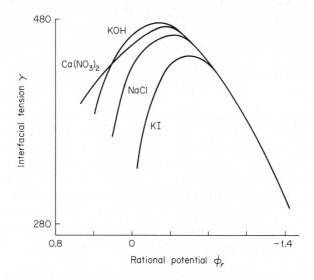

Fig. 13-12. *Electrocapillarity curves. [From D. C. Grahame, Chem. Rev.* **41**, *441 (1947).* © *1947, The Williams and Wilkins Co., Baltimore, Maryland.]*

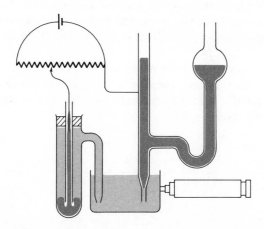

Fig. 13-13. *The Lippmann apparatus for observing the electrocapillary effect. [From A. W. Adamson, "Physical Chemistry of Surfaces," 2nd ed. Copyright 1967, Wiley (Interscience), New York. Used with permission of John Wiley & Sons, Inc.]*

[note Eq. (8-37)], so a positive head of mercury is needed to force the meniscus toward the end of the tapering capillary tube. The electrical connection is from the mercury through a source of potential to a calomel electrode and thence to the electrolyte solution. Measurement of the head required to maintain the meniscus yields the capillary depression and hence the surface tension at the mercury–solution interface. It is the variation of this surface tension with applied potential that is reported in Fig. 13-12; the abscissa is the potential relative to that at the maximum, called the *rational potential.*

The thermodynamic explanation of the electrocapillarity effect is that the derivative of surface tension with respect to potential gives the surface charge density σ:

$$\frac{\partial \gamma}{\partial V} = -\sigma. \tag{13-41}$$

Just as the adsorption of a surfactant at an interface lowers the interfacial tension, so does the concentration of charge at an interface. At the maximum the derivative in (13-41) is zero and so therefore must be the surface charge density; this suggests that the absolute potential difference across the interface is also zero. The voltage applied to reach this electrocapillarity maximum therefore just balances the natural potential difference between the phases. This applied potential difference is 0.48 V if the electrolyte is one not apt to interact with the mercury surface, such as potassium carbonate or sulfate, which implies that the absolute half-cell potential of the calomel electrode is -0.48 V (as compared to -0.28 V on the hydrogen scale).

The problem is that even though the charge density must be zero at the electrocapillarity maximum, there will still be adsorbed and polarized solvent and solute molecules, so that $\Delta\phi$, the galvanic potential difference across the interface, is not necessarily zero. Notice, for example, that the position of the electrocapillarity maximum shown in Fig. 13-12 varies with the nature of the electrolyte as the anion is changed; the same happens if the cation is varied or if the solvent medium is altered.

Various other attempts have been made to determine absolute half-cell potentials, but, as in this case, certain unprovable assumptions are always involved. It does seem likely, though, that the absolute values are not greatly different from those reported on the hydrogen scale.

SPECIAL TOPICS

13-ST-1 Liquid Junctions

The existence and importance of the potential at a liquid junction have been noted in several places in this chapter. The detailed treatment is somewhat specialized, however, and has therefore been placed in this section. We consider first the potential of a cell having a liquid junction and then some aspects of the electrochemistry of the liquid junction itself.

A. Concentration Cells with a Liquid Junction

The least complicated type of cell which has a liquid junction is a concentration cell since the electrode reactions are then the same, except for a difference in concentration of the electrolyte across the junction. The general cell diagram is

$$\text{anode/solution at } m_1 \,/\, \text{solution at } m_2/\text{cathode,}$$

where the dashed line means that the two solutions are in electrolytic contact but are somehow prevented from mechanical mixing. This may be by means of a porous diaphragm, as in the Daniell cell of Fig. 13-2, or by a stiffening of one of the solutions at its point of contact with the other by agar-agar or gelatine, as is done in a salt bridge.

An example of a concentration cell with a liquid junction is the following:

$$\text{Pt/H}_2(1 \text{ atm})/\text{HCl}(m_1) \,/\, \text{HCl}(m_2)/\text{H}_2(1 \text{ atm})/\text{Pt,} \tag{13-42}$$

anode reaction	$\frac{1}{2}\text{H}_2(1 \text{ atm}) = \text{H}^+(m_1) + \text{e}^-,$
cathode reaction	$\text{H}^+(m_2) + \text{e}^- = \frac{1}{2}\text{H}_2(1 \text{ atm}),$
net reaction	$\text{H}^+(m_2) = \text{H}^+(m_1).$

$$\tag{13-43}$$

The emf of a cell corresponds to the free energy change associated with the sum of *all* processes occurring per faraday of electricity passed through the cell. Current is carried by the ions in the solution, which means that t_+ equiv of hydrogen ion must cross the junction from left to right and t_- equiv of chloride ion must do so from right to left, where t denotes transference number (see Section 12-6). The changes that occur in addition to the electrode reactions are then

$$t_+H^+(m_1) = t_+H^+(m_2), \qquad t_-Cl^-(m_2) = t_-Cl^-(m_1). \tag{13-44}$$

The sum of process (13-43) and processes (13-44) is

$$t_-H^+(m_2) + t_-Cl^-(m_2) = t_-H^+(m_1) + t_-Cl^-(m_1), \tag{13-45}$$

bearing in mind that $t_+ + t_- = 1$. The corresponding Nernst equation is

$$\mathscr{E} = -\frac{RT}{\mathscr{F}} \ln \frac{a_{H^+,m_1}^{t_-} a_{Cl^-,m_1}^{t_-}}{a_{H^+,m_2}^{t_-} a_{Cl^-,m_2}^{t_-}}$$

or

$$\mathscr{E} = -2t_- \frac{RT}{\mathscr{F}} \ln \frac{a_{\pm,m_1}}{a_{\pm,m_2}}. \tag{13-46}$$

If m_1 and m_2 are 0.1 and 0.01, respectively, then the $\gamma_\pm$ values are 0.796 and 0.904, respectively, and the t_- values are 0.1686 and 0.1749, respectively. The average value of t_- is 0.1717, and the emf of the cell at 25°C is calculated to be

$$\mathscr{E} = -(2)(0.1717)(0.05917) \log \frac{(0.1)(0.796)}{(0.01)(0.904)}$$

$$= (2)(0.1717)(0.05590) = -0.01920 \quad V.$$

The overall cell reaction is the sum of processes (13-43) and (13-44), and the separate Nernst expressions for these are

$$\mathscr{E}_E = -\frac{RT}{\mathscr{F}} \ln \frac{a_{H^+,m_1}}{a_{H^+,m_2}} \tag{13-47}$$

and

$$\mathscr{E}_J = -t_+ \frac{RT}{\mathscr{F}} \ln \frac{a_{H^+,m_2}}{a_{H^+,m_1}} - t_- \frac{RT}{\mathscr{F}} \ln \frac{a_{Cl^-,m_1}}{a_{Cl^-,m_2}}. \tag{13-48}$$

Inspection confirms that the sum of Eqs. (13-47) and (13-48) gives Eq. (13-46); thus

$$\mathscr{E} = \mathscr{E}_E + \mathscr{E}_J.$$

The emf for the cell can therefore be viewed as made up of two terms: that due to the electrode reactions $\mathscr{E}_E$, and the junction potential $\mathscr{E}_J$, which gives the work associated with the transport of ions across the liquid junction.

We can extend the preceding numerical example to the calculation of $\mathcal{E}_E$ and $\mathcal{E}_J$ only by making some assumption regarding individual ionic activity coefficients. If, for example, we assume that $\gamma_{H^+} = \gamma_{Cl^-} = \gamma_\pm$, then Eqs. (13-47) and (13-48) give

$$\mathcal{E}_E = -0.05590 \quad V, \qquad \mathcal{E}_J = 0.03670 \quad V.$$

The junction potential represents a major correction in this case.

In using Eq. (13-46), an average value of t_- for the two concentrations was used. It turns out that the correct average is not the simple arithmetic one, and the work done in transporting an ion across the junction actually involves the integral

$$RT \int_{m_1}^{m_2} t_i \, d(\ln a_i), \tag{13-49}$$

so that the corrected version of Eq. (13-46) is

$$\mathcal{E} = -2 \frac{RT}{\mathscr{F}} \int_{m_1}^{m_2} t_- \, d(\ln a_\pm). \tag{13-50}$$

A study of cells of this type evidently permits the determination of transference numbers as a function of concentration.

As a last point, the overall cell reaction will depend on whether the electrodes are reversible to the anion or to the cation. Thus for the cell

$$\text{Ag/AgCl/HCl}(m_1) \,/ \text{HCl}(m_2)/\text{AgCl/Ag}$$

Eqs. (13-46) and (13-50) would have t_+ rather than t_-, and $\mathcal{E}_E$ would have the opposite sign. The numerical example would then give

$$\mathcal{E} = \mathcal{E}_E + \mathcal{E}_J, \qquad \text{or} \qquad 0.09260 = 0.05590 + 0.03670.$$

The sign of the junction potential remains the same. Thus, although we analyze in detail each specific concentration cell to determine the correct overall cell reaction, the junction potential remains the same for any given junction.

B. Junction Potentials

Equation (13-48) simplifies considerably if activity coefficient effects are neglected. We then obtain

$$\mathcal{E}_J = (t_+ - t_-) \frac{RT}{\mathscr{F}} \ln \frac{m_1}{m_2}. \tag{13-51}$$

This form brings out the important point that $\mathscr{E}_\text{J}$ depends on $t_+ - t_-$. It is largely with this factor in mind that one expects the junction potential to be small in the case of a KCl bridge; t_+ for 1 m KCl is 0.488, and so $t_+ - t_-$ is only 0.024. The same situation applies in the case of NH_4NO_3, an electrolyte that is used in a salt bridge if it is not desirable that Cl^--ion-containing solution have contact with the electrolyte of the half-cell being studied.

If various electrolytes are present on either side of a liquid junction, then the total work of transporting ions across the junction per faraday, which gives $\mathscr{E}_\text{J}$, depends on weighted averages or integrals such as that of Eq. (13-49). By using concentrated KCl in the salt bridge, one ensures that the important t_i will be those of K^+ and Cl^-, so that $\mathscr{E}_\text{J}$ will not be very sensitive to the nature of the more dilute electrolyte solution of the half-cell into which the salt bridge dips. The analysis makes it clear, however, that although we can reduce a junction potential to a fairly small value, cells with liquid junctions retain a residual uncertainty in the interpretation of their emf's and one which is difficult to analyze exactly.

13-ST-2 Polarization at Electrodes. Polarography

Three types of polarization effects were noted in Section 13-9: ohmic, concentration, and activation. We now discuss these last two in more detail.

A. Activation Polarization

The Tafel equation (13-38), which relates the activation polarization component of the overvoltage to the current i, may be accounted for in terms of the following analysis. Consider a general electrode reaction

$$e^- + O \text{ (oxidized state)} = R \text{ (reduced state)},$$

where, as illustrated in Fig. 13-14, the oxidized state must pass through some high-energy intermediate I in the process of being reduced. We write an equation analogous to Eq. (8-65) for the rate of the forward process:

$$R_\text{f} = \left[\frac{kT}{h} \exp\left(\frac{-\Delta G_\text{f}^{0\ddagger}}{RT} \right) \right] \quad (O), \qquad (13\text{-}52)$$

where $\Delta G_\text{f}^{0\ddagger}$ is the standard free energy change to go from O to I. It will be known

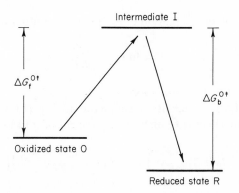

Fig. 13-14. *Mechanism for activation polarization.*

in the next chapter as the free energy of activation. Similarly, the rate of the back reaction is

$$R_b = \left[\frac{kT}{h} \exp\left(\frac{-\Delta G_b^{0\ddagger}}{RT}\right)\right] \quad (R). \tag{13-53}$$

The presence of a potential difference ϕ between the electrode and the solution contributes to $\Delta G_f^{0\ddagger}$ and we write this last as the sum of a chemical component and an electrical one:

$$\Delta G_f^{0\ddagger} = \Delta G_{f,\text{chem}}^{0\ddagger} - \alpha\mathscr{F}\phi, \tag{13-54}$$

which allows that only some of this potential difference is effective; this fraction is called the *transfer coefficient* α. The current part due to the forward reaction is then

$$i_f = \left[\frac{kT}{h} \exp\left(\frac{-\Delta G_{f,\text{chem}}^{0\ddagger}}{RT}\right) \exp\left(\frac{\alpha\mathscr{F}\phi}{RT}\right)\right] \quad (O), \tag{13-55}$$

where current is in faradays per square centimeter per second. At equilibrium there will be equal and opposite currents in the two directions, or $i_f^\circ = i_b^\circ = i^\circ$, where i° is known as the exchange current, and ϕ has the value ϕ° and corresponds to $\mathscr{E}^0$. Then

$$i^\circ = \left[\frac{kT}{h} \exp\left(\frac{-\Delta G_{f,\text{chem}}^{0\ddagger}}{RT}\right) \exp\left(\frac{\alpha\mathscr{F}\phi^\circ}{RT}\right)\right] \quad (O). \tag{13-56}$$

Combination of Eqs. (13-55) and (13-56) gives

$$i_f = i^\circ \exp\frac{\alpha\mathscr{F}(\phi - \phi_0)}{RT} = i^\circ \exp\frac{\alpha\mathscr{F}\eta}{RT}, \tag{13-57}$$

where η is the overvoltage. Equation (13-57) may be written in the form

$$\ln i = \ln i^\circ + \frac{\alpha \mathscr{F} \eta}{RT},$$

which rearranges to the Tafel equation.

In a stricter analysis, an equation analogous to Eq. (13-55) is written for i_b, with $i = i_t - i_b$; the effect is to alter the coefficient of η in Eq. (13-57) to give

$$i = i_0 \left[\exp\left(\frac{\alpha \mathscr{F} \eta}{RT}\right) - \exp\left(-\frac{(1-\alpha)\mathscr{F} \eta}{RT}\right) \right]. \tag{13-58}$$

As the equation suggests, the situation is symmetric; η may be positive or negative, so that the electrode reaction is driven either forward or backward. Figure 13-15 shows the general behavior of Eq. (13-58).

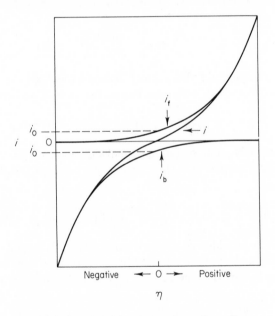

Fig. 13-15. *A general current versus voltage diagram.*

This treatment, although somewhat sketchy, is designed to indicate how the detailed study of overvoltage effects can lead to information about the intrinsic rate of the electrode reaction, through i°, and the energy of the reaction barrier. As an example, although the mechanism for the reduction of H^+ ion at a metal electrode is still not fully elucidated, the evidence suggests that the rate-determining step is probably the reaction of H_3O^+ with the metal surface to give adsorbed hydrogen atoms and water:

$$H_3O^+ + M + e^- = M-H + H_2O.$$

B. Concentration Polarization

The preceding analysis was based on the assumption that the rate-limiting step of the electrode process was some activated chemical reaction at the electrode surface. Another process must become rate-controlling at sufficiently high current densities, namely the rate of diffusion of reactant to and of product away from the electrode surface. If the reaction is one of the deposition of a metal from solution, only the rate of diffusion of the metal ion to the electrode is to be considered. Recalling Eq. (2-67) and the discussion of Section 10-7B, we can write

$$J = -\mathscr{D}\frac{dC}{dx}, \tag{13-59}$$

where J is now in moles per square centimeter per second. If there is an excess of inert electrolyte in the solution so that the ion being reduced carries little of the current, the potential term in Eq. (12-121) will not be important and $\mathscr{D}$ will be a constant, equal to the ion diffusion coefficient as given by Eq. (12-119). Further, a reasonable approximation to the physical situation is that the stirring conditions leave a thin stagnant layer of thickness δ within which C varies linearly from C, the bulk solution concentration, to C^s, the concentration at the electrode surface. We expect the linear variation of C with x since in a steady-state condition J is constant, and since $\mathscr{D}$ is constant, so must be dC/dx. Equation (13-59) then becomes

$$i_d = zJ = -\frac{z\mathscr{D}(C^s - C)}{\delta}, \tag{13-60}$$

where i_d is the diffusion current density in faradays per square centimeter per second and z is the valence number of the metal ion being discharged. Under the conditions of the preceding subsection it is assumed that $\mathscr{D}/\delta$ is large enough that $C^s = C$, and the observed current is determined by the rate of the chemical reduction reaction at the electrode, i_a . That is, under steady-state conditions there is no accumulation of material in the diffusion zone and $i_d = i_a$. As the overvoltage is increased, i_a increases by Eq. (13-58), and C^s drops enough for i_d to match the increase in i_a. The maximum possible diffusion rate $i_{d(max)}$ is reached when C^s has dropped to zero. Further increase in the overvoltage cannot increase the current any further, and the plot of i versus V must level off at $i_{d(max)}$, or at

$$i_{d(max)} = \frac{z\mathscr{D}C}{\delta}.\qquad(13\text{-}61)$$

Thus the effect of concentration polarization is to give a maximum current which is proportional to the concentration of the ion being discharged.

If a mixture of potentially reducible ions is present, again with a supporting electrolyte, that is, an excess of inert electrolyte, present, then as the applied reducing potential is increased the first metal ion begins to deposit, reaches its i_{max}, and the second metal ion begins to deposit at some higher potential, and reaches *its* i_{max}, so that the plot of i versus V is as shown in Fig. 13-16. The

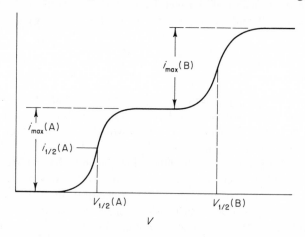

Fig. 13-16. *Current versus voltage in the region of concentration polarization.*

characteristic deposition potential for each ion could be identified as in Fig. 13-9 but when one is operating in the diffusion-controlled region C^s and hence $\mathscr{E}_{rev}$ is changing with V so that one obtains a sinusoidal rather than a linear i versus V plot. Consequently, it is much more accurate to pick the potential at the half-way point of the step, or the half-wave potential $V_{1/2}$, as the characteristic one.

Since the overvoltage η is given by

$$\eta = \mathscr{E}_i - \mathscr{E}_{rev} = -\frac{RT}{z\mathscr{F}}\ln\frac{C^s}{C},\qquad(13\text{-}62)$$

where ohmic polarization is neglected, as are activity coefficient terms, we can solve for C^s/C. Also, combination of Eqs. (13-60) and (13-61) gives

$$i_d = i_{d(max)} \left(1 - \frac{C^s}{C}\right). \tag{13-63}$$

The result is

$$\frac{i_d}{i_{d(max)}} = 1 - \exp - \frac{z\mathscr{F}\eta}{RT} . \tag{13-64}$$

Equation (13-64) gives a symmetric curve such as shown in Fig. 13-16, for which $V_{1/2}$ occurs at the inflection point.

C. Polarography

The preceding analysis suggests that we could analyze for metal ions in solution by obtaining experimental i versus V curves, each limiting diffusion current giving the concentration of a particular ion, the ion being identified by its $V_{1/2}$. This procedure is indeed used. To maintain δ more constant than is possible by stirring the solution, a common practice is to use a rotating electrode. There is still a problem with accumulation of reduction products, and a very ingenious alternative procedure was devised by J. Heyrovsky in 1922.

The basic experimental features of the *Heyrovsky polarograph* are shown in Fig. 13-17. The cathode is a mercury drop that is steadily growing at the tip of a capillary immersed in the electrolyte solution, and the anode is a large pool of mercury. By having a tiny drop as the anode surface, concentration polarization

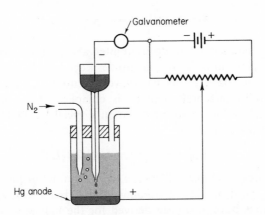

Fig. 13-17. *Schematic diagram of a polarographic cell.*

effects can be made to develop at relatively small currents; the large area of the anode pool of mercury essentially eliminates concentration polarization at its surface. As each drop grows and falls the anode surface is steadily kept fresh and reproducible, and with a supporting electrolyte the same general analysis applies as for a stationary electrode.

A typical polarogram is shown in Fig. 13-18. The oscillations are a result of

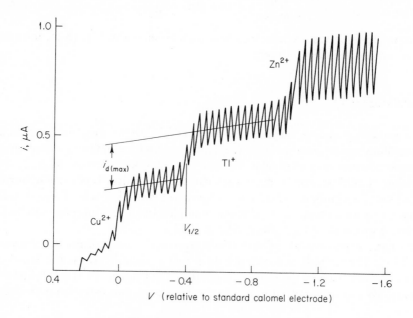

Fig. 13-18. *A typical polarogram.*

the successive appearance of new drops at intervals of a few seconds; currents may be only microamperes in order of magnitude. Each step is called a *polarographic wave* and is characterized by its half-wave potential $V_{1/2}$ and *diffusion current* $i_{d(max)}$. The detailed algebraic analysis is complicated by the situation of an expanding cathode surface, and an equation derived by D. Ilkovic in 1938 will be given without the derivation:

$$i_{d(max)} = 70.82 zw(\tfrac{2}{3}t)(\tfrac{1}{6}\mathscr{D})(\tfrac{1}{2}C),\qquad(13\text{-}65)$$

where z is the valence number of the ion, w is the flow of the mercury in grams per second, t is the drop time in seconds, and C is the concentration in moles per liter. Equations have also been derived for the half-wave potential, but this remains essentially an empirically determined quantity for each species.

===

Polarography is capable of measuring ion concentrations as low as 10^{-4} M and is a rapid as well as a sensitive analytical tool. The physical chemist uses it to study the chemistry of reduction (or of oxidation) processes. One can determine from the diffusion current whether the reduction occurs as a one- or as a two-electron step. If complexing ions are added to the solution, both the reduction potentials and the formation constants of complex ions can be found. With a commutator to interrupt the applied voltage, chemical rate processes can be followed.

===

GENERAL REFERENCES

ADAMSON, A. W. (1967). "The Physical Chemistry of Surfaces," 2nd ed. Wiley (Interscience), New York.

DANIELS, F., MATHEWS, J. H., WILLIAMS, J. W., BENDER, P., AND ALBERTY, R. A. (1956). "Experimental Physical Chemistry," 5th ed. McGraw-Hill, New York.

DOUGLAS, B. E., AND MCDANIEL, D. H. (1965). "Concepts and Models of Inorganic Chemistry." Ginn (Blaisdell), Boston, Massachusetts.

KORTUM, G. (1965). "Treatise on Electrochemistry." Elsevier, Amsterdam.

LATIMER, W. M. (1952). "The Oxidation States of the Elements and Their Potentials in Aqueous Solution," 2nd ed. Prentice-Hall, Englewood Cliffs, New Jersey.

LEWIS, G. N., AND RANDALL, M. (1961). "Thermodynamics," 2nd ed. (revised by K. S. Pitzer and L. Brewer). McGraw-Hill, New York.

CITED REFERENCES

BATES, R. G. (1954). "Electrometric pH Determinations." Wiley, New York.

DOLE, M. (1941). "The Glass Electrode." Wiley, New York.

HARNED, H. S., AND EHLERS, R. W. (1932). *J. Amer. Chem. Soc.* **54**, 1350.

LATIMER, W. M. (1952). "The Oxidation States of the Elements and Their Potentials in Aqueous Solution," 2nd ed. Prentice-Hall, Englewood Cliffs, New Jersey.

Exercises†

13-1 The emf of the cell $Pb/PbCl_2(s)/KCl(m)/Hg_2Cl_2(s)/Hg$ is 0.5357 V at 25°C and increases with temperature by 1.45×10^{-4} V °K^{-1}. Write the electrode and overall cell reactions and calculate ΔG^0, ΔH^0 ΔS^0, and q_{rev}.

Ans. $Pb + Hg_2Cl_2 = PbCl_2 + 2Hg(l)$, $\Delta G^0 = -103.4\,kJ$, $\Delta S^0 = 28.0\,J\,°K^{-1}$, $\Delta H^0 = -95.1\,kJ$, $q_{rev} = 8.34\,kJ$.

† Activity coefficient effects are to be neglected in Exercises and Problems unless specifically noted otherwise. Assume 25°C unless otherwise specified.

13 Electrochemical Cells

13-2 The emf for the cell $Cd/0.1\ m\ Cd(NO_3)_2,\ 0.01\ m\ AgNO_3/Ag$ is -0.446 V at 25°C. Calculate $\mathscr{E}^0$ for this cell.

Ans. -0.357 V.

13-3 Calculate $\mathscr{E}_{298}$ for the cell $Ag/AgI(s)/0.1\ m\ HI/H_2(1\ atm)/Pt$.

Ans. 0.008 V.

13-4 Calculate $\mathscr{E}^0$ and K at 25°C for the reaction $Tl + Ag^+ = Tl^+ + Ag$.

Ans. $\mathscr{E}^0 = 1.135$ V, $K = 1.51 \times 10^{19}$.

13-5 Calculate K for the reaction $\frac{1}{2}Cd + Tl^+ = \frac{1}{2}Cd^{2+} + Tl$ and the ratio $(Cd^{2+})/(Tl^+)$ if excess Cd is added to a solution which is 0.1 m in Tl^+.

Ans. $K = 13.2\ M^{-1/2}$; 2.70.

13-6 Calculate $\mathscr{E}^0_{298}$ for the half-cell reaction $Tl = Tl^{3+} + 3e^-$.

Ans. -0.720 V.

13-7 Obtain $\mathscr{E}^0_{298}$ for the half-cell $Mg + C_2O_4^{2-} = Mg(C_2O_4) + 2e^-$ given that $K_{sp} = 9.0 \times 10^{-6}$ for $Mg(C_2O_4)$.

Ans. 2.67 V.

13-8 What fraction of $Ag(CN)_2^-$ is dissociated into Ag^+ in $1 \times 10^{-3}\ M\ CN^-$ if $\mathscr{E}^0_{298} = 0.289$ V for the half-cell $Ag + 2\ CN^- = Ag(CN)_2^- + e^-$? (Neglect the hydrolysis of CN^-.)

Ans. 4.9×10^{-13} (!).

13-9 Calculate $\mathscr{E}_{298}$ for the following concentration cells: (a) $Na(Hg, x_{Na} = 0.1)/NaCl(m = 0.1)/Na(Hg, x_{Na} = 0.01)$; (b) $Pt/H_2(P = 0.1\ atm)/HCl(m = 0.1)/H_2(P = 0.01\ atm)/Pt$; (c) $Ag/AgBr(s)/HBr(m = 0.1)/H_2(1\ atm)/Pt—Pt/H_2(1\ atm)/HBr(m = 0.01)/AgBr(s)/Ag$.

Ans. (a) 0.059 V, (b) 0.0295 V, (c) 0.118 V.

13-10 Calculate $\mathscr{E}_{350}$ for the cell in Exercise 13-9(b).

Ans. 0.0346 V.

13-11 Calculate $\mathscr{E}_{298}$ for the cell $Ag/AgCl(s)/0.1\ m\ HCl/H_2(1\ atm)/Pt$, using activity coefficient data from Chapter 12.

Ans. -0.352 V.

13-12 A pH meter gives a reading of 200 mV when measuring a solution whose hydrogen ion activity is considered to be 10^{-4}; what is the hydrogen ion activity of a solution for which the meter reads 100 mV? (Assume 25°C.)

Ans. $pH = 2.31$.

Problems

13-1 If copper and silver are negligibly soluble in each other as solids, approximately what must be the concentration of Ag^+ in a solution in which Cu^{2+} is at unit activity in order that the two metals may be plated out together in electrolysis? At what potential will this occur, on the assumption that oxygen is formed at the anode at an overvoltage of 0.50 V at 1 atm pressure from a solution of pH 5? Assume 25°C.

13-2 Calculate the equilibrium concentration of ferric ion at 25°C in a solution which is 0.01 f in $Hg(NO_3)_2$ and 0.01 f in $Fe(NO_3)_2$. Use the Debye–Hückel limiting law to estimate activity coefficients.

13-3 The cell $Cu/CuCl(s)/KCl(0.100\ m)/Cl_2(1\ atm)/C$ has a potential of 1.234 V at 25°C.
(a) Calculate the solubility product for CuCl in water at 25°C.
(b) What is the concentration of cuprous ion at the anode of this cell?

13-4 At 25°C, $\mathscr{E}$ for the cell

$$Ag/AgCl/NaCl(m)/NaHg(amalgam)\text{—}NaHg\ (amalgam)/NaCl(0.100\ m)/AgCl/Ag$$

is as follows:

m	0.200	0.500	1.000	2.000	3.000	4.000
$\mathscr{E}_{298}$ (V)	0.03252	0.07584	0.10955	0.14627	0.17070	0.19036

The mean activity coefficient of 0.100 m NaCl is 0.773. Calculate the mean activity coefficients of NaCl in solutions of these concentrations and plot the values against the square root of m.

13-5 At 25°C, $\mathscr{E}$ for the cell $Pb/PbSO_4(s)/H_2SO_4(m)/H_2(1\ atm)/Pt$ changes with the molality of the sulfuric acid as follows:

m	0.00100	0.00200	0.00500	0.0100	0.0200
$\mathscr{E}_{298}$ (V)	0.1017	0.1248	0.1533	0.1732	0.1922

By the extrapolation method, obtain $\mathscr{E}^0$ for this cell. From this value calculate the thermodynamic solubility product for $PbSO_4$.

13-6 The voltage of the cell $Ag/Ag_2SO_4(s)/$saturated solution of Ag_2SO_4 and $Hg_2SO_4/Hg_2SO_4/$ Hg is 0.140 V at 25°C and its temperature coefficient is 0.00015 V °C^{-1}.

(a) Give the cell reaction.
(b) Calculate the free energy change for the cell reaction.
(c) Calculate the enthalpy change for the cell reaction.
(d) Calculate the entropy change for the cell reaction.
(e) Does the cell absorb or emit heat as the cell reaction occurs? Calculate the number of calories per mole of cell reaction.
(f) One mole each of Hg, $Ag_2SO_4(s)$, $Hg_2SO_4(s)$, and some saturated solution of the two salts are mixed. What solid phases finally will be present and in what amounts?

13-7 Given that $\mathscr{E}^0 = 0.152$ for $Ag + I^- = AgI + e^-$ at 25°C and is -0.800 for $Ag = Ag^+ + e^-$, calculate the solubility product for AgI.

13-8   At 25°C, $\mathscr{E}$ for the cell Pt/H₂(1 atm)/ m Ba(OH)₂/Ba(amalgam)/0.1200 m Ba(OH)₂/H₂ (1 atm)/Pt is as follows:

1000 m	2.45	7.93	15.09	49.70	199.60
$\mathscr{E}$ (V)	−0.1245	−0.0840	−0.0630	−0.0254	+0.0144

(a)   Write the cell reaction (each electrode separately and then the net reaction).
(b)   By means of the appropriate extrapolation procedure, calculate the mean activity coefficient for 0.1000 m Ba(OH)₂ .

13-9   Given the cell

$$\text{Ag/AgNO}_3(0.00100\ m)\ /\ \text{AgNO}_3(0.00100\ m),\ \text{KCN}\ (0.004\ m)/\text{Ag},$$

whose emf is −0.767 V at 25°C:

(a)   Write the electrode and net cell reactions.
(b)   Calculate the equilibrium constant for Ag⁺+ 2CN⁻ = Ag(CN)₂⁻ (neglect activity coefficient effects).

13-10   At 25°C, $\mathscr{E}$ for the cell Pt/H₂(1 atm)/HCl(m)/AgCl/Ag is as follows (Harned and Ehlers, 1932):

m	0.01002	0.01010	0.01031	0.04986	0.05005	0.09642
$\mathscr{E}$ (V)	0.46376	0.46331	0.46228	0.38582	0.38568	0.35393
m	0.09834	0.2030				
$\mathscr{E}$ (V)	0.35316	0.31774				

Calculate $\mathscr{E}^0$ for the cell by the extrapolation method, and then the activity coefficients for HCl at these concentrations and plot them against $\sqrt{m}$; compare the limiting slope with the value from theory.

13-11   At 25°C, $\mathscr{E}$ for the cell Pb/PbSO₄(s)/H₂SO₄(0.00200 m)/H₂(1 atm)/Pt is 0.125 V. Calculate the solubility product of PbSO₄ at 25°C.

13-12   Calculate the percentage of mercury in the mercuric state in a solution of mercuric nitrate that is in equilibrium with liquid mercury.

13-13   Calculate the solubility product of ferrous hydroxide from the cell Fe(s)/Fe(OH)₂(s)/ Ba(OH)₂(0.05 m)/HgO(s)/Hg. $\mathscr{E}_{298}$ = 0.973 V.

13-14   A thallous (Tl⁺) solution is titrated with ceric (Ce⁴⁺) solution. The reaction is

$$\text{Tl}^+ + 2\text{Ce}^{4+} = \text{Tl}^{3+} + 2\text{Ce}^{3+}.$$

Calculate the half-cell potential at 25°C for the reaction Tl⁺ = Tl³⁺ + 2e⁻ at the end point (that is, the equivalence point of the titration) given

$$\text{Ce}^{3+} = \text{Ce}^{4+} + \text{e}^-, \qquad \mathscr{E}^0 = -1.60\ \text{V},$$
$$\text{Tl}^+ = \text{Tl}^{3+} + 2\text{e}^-, \qquad \mathscr{E}^0 = -1.23\ \text{V}.$$

As a calculator problem, obtain the titration curve for 0.1 m Tl⁺ titrated with 0.1 m Ce⁴⁺.

13-15   The mean activity coefficient for the ions in 7 m HCl is 4.66 at 25°C. The partial pressure of HCl(g) over this solution is 0.348 Torr. The standard potential for Pt/Cl₂/Cl⁻ is $\mathscr{E}^0$ = −1.3594 V. Find (a) the equilibrium constant for the dissociation of two moles of gaseous

HCl to the elements (at 25°C), and (b) the number of single hydrogen and single chlorine molecules at equilibrium in 1 cm³ of HCl gas at 1 atm and 25°C.

13-16 In chemical engineering it is sometimes convenient to use molecular weights on a pound basis, that is, the molecular weight of O_2 would be 32 lb rather than 32 g. In going from the gram atomic weight scale to the pound atomic weight scale, state whether the numerical value of each of the following is changed, and if it is, calculate the new value. (a) Avogadro's number. (b) Faraday's number. (c) $\mathscr{E}^0$ for the cell $Pt/H_2(1 \text{ atm})/HCl/AgCl/Ag$. (d) ΔG^0 for the cell reaction in (c). (e) $\mathscr{E}$ at 25°C for the cell $Pt/H_2(1 \text{ atm})/HCl(0.001 \text{ } m)/AgCl/Ag$. (Assume that m on the pound system denotes pound molecular weights per 1000 lb of solvent.)

13-17 It is desired to separate Cd^{2+} from Pb^{2+} by electrodeposition from a solution which is 0.1 m in each ion and at pH 2. Calculate the sequence in which Cd and Pb metals and H_2 are produced and the concentrations of the various species in solution when a new stage of electrolysis occurs. Include overvoltage effects in considering H_2 evolution.

13-18 R. Ogg found $\mathscr{E} = -0.029$ V at 25°C for the cell

$$Hg \left/ \left(\begin{array}{c} \text{mercurous nitrate (0.01 } N) \\ HNO_3 \text{ (0.1 } m) \end{array} \right) \right/\!\!\left/ \left(\begin{array}{c} \text{mercurous nitrate (0.001 } N) \\ HNO_3 \text{ (0.1 } m) \end{array} \right) \right/ Hg.$$

What is the formula for mercurous ion? Show how your conclusion follows from this information.

The actual dissociation constant for $Hg_2^{2+} = 2Hg^+$ is not known, but suppose that $\mathscr{E}$ for this cell is found to be -0.059 V when the higher and lower mercurous nitrate normalities are 2×10^{-4} and 3×10^{-6}, respectively. Calculate K_{diss} for Hg_2^{2+} from this data. (In both parts of the problem neglect any junction potential.)

13-19 The pH of a solution may be found with the use of a hydrogen electrode and a calomel half-cell. Suppose that the pH of a certain buffer solution is measured at a high altitude such that the ambient pressure is 600 Torr but that the observer neglects this aspect and calculates the pH assuming the pressure of the hydrogen bubbling past the electrode to be 1 atm. If he reports a pH of 5.50, what is the correct pH of the solution?

13-20 Calculate the free energy of formation of $AgCl(s)$ using the solubility product for AgCl and data from Table 13-3.

13-21 Calculate ΔG^0 for the reaction $H_2O(l) = H^+ + OH^-$ at 25°C given that the free energy of formation of liquid water is -56.69 kcal mole^{-1} and using Table 13-3.

13-22 Calculate the emf of the following cells (neglect activity coefficient effects):

(a) $Pt/H_2(0.1 \text{ atm})/H_2SO_4(1 \text{ } m) \left/ \left/ \left(\begin{array}{c} H_2SO_4(1 \text{ m}) \\ K_4Fe(CN)_6(0.01 \text{ } m) \\ K_3Fe(CN)_6(0.01 \text{ } m) \end{array} \right) \right/ \right/ Au.$

(b) $Au/O_2(0.2 \text{ atm}) \left/ \left(\begin{array}{c} H_2SO_4(1 \text{ } m) \\ H_2O_2(0.1 \text{ } m) \end{array} \right) \right/ \!\!\left/ H_2SO_4(1 \text{ } m)/H_2(1 \text{ atm})/Pt. \right.$

(c) $Ag/AgBr/HBr(0.01 \text{ } m)/H_2(0.5 \text{ atm})/Pt.$

Neglect junction potentials.

13-23 Suppose that the atomic weight of carbon is defined as 12 kg mole^{-1}. Explain whether this redefinition would affect the values of $\mathscr{E}$ and $\mathscr{E}^0$ for the cell $Pb/PbCl_2(s)/KCl(10$ g liter$^{-1})/$ $Hg_2Cl_2(s)/Hg$ at 25°C.

Special Topics Problems

13-1 Calculate $\mathscr{E}$, $\mathscr{E}_E$, and $\mathscr{E}_J$ at 25°C for the cell

$$Na(\text{dilute Hg amalgam})/NaCl(0.01\ m) \;/\; NaCl(0.001\ m)/Na(\text{dilute Hg amalgam}).$$

13-2 Calculate the emf's of concentration cells with transference for the following electrolytes in 0.01 m and 0.001 m solution, respectively, with appropriate silver chloride or mercurous sulfate electrodes: (a) $CaCl_2$; (b) $La_2(SO_4)_3$.

13-3 Calculate the emf of the following cells with transference at 25°C:

(a) $Ag/AgCl/CaCl_2(0.01\ m) \;/\; CaCl_2(0.001\ m)/AgCl/Ag.$

(b) $Hg/Hg_2SO_4/K_2SO_4(0.01\ m) \;/\; K_2SO_4(0.001\ m)/Hg_2SO_4/Hg.$

14 KINETICS OF GAS-PHASE REACTIONS

14-1 Introduction

The emphasis up to this point has been on the equilibrium properties of substances in pure or solution form. The rate processes considered have been restricted to transport phenomena such as diffusion and conductance. Chemical kinetics is a more complicated subject than that of chemical equilibrium because time is now a variable in the description of the state of a system and because there may be more than one reaction path whereby reactants become products. The theory is difficult because such paths involve molecules in energetic and otherwise unusual states; these states can rarely be studied by themselves independently, so theoretical models contain assumptions which cannot be corroborated in detail.

There are three major facets to the study of chemical kinetics. The first might be termed the experimental side but involves not only the measurement of reaction rates but also their reduction to what we will call a *rate law*. In chemical kinetics we retain the historic mass action rate law (Section 7-1) by expressing the rate R of a reaction at constant temperature as a function of the composition of the system,

$$R = -\frac{d(A)}{dt} = f[(A), (B), (C), ...]. \tag{14-1}$$

The complete function can be complicated, but it is often of the form

$$R = k(A)^x(B)^y(C)^z \cdots, \tag{14-2}$$

where A, B, and C are reactants. This may come about either naturally or by

615

deliberate choice of experimental conditions, such as having one reagent in great excess so that its concentration is constant. Thus if the complete rate law were either

$$R = \frac{k(A)(B)}{1 + k'(C)} \qquad \text{or} \qquad R = k(A) + k'(A)(C),$$

it would reduce to one of the preceding type if (C) were constant; one could then carry out a series of experiments in which the constant level of (C) was varied. The constant k in Eq. (14-2) is called the *rate constant*, and the expression which gives R as a function of concentrations is the *rate law*. The first goal of the experimental stage is then to devise and carry out experiments that will establish the algebraic form of a mass action type of expression for R and to evaluate the rate constant or constants that it contains. The next experimental stage is that of determining how such constants vary with temperature and with the nature of the reaction medium.

The second facet of chemical kinetics is that of reaction mechanism. It turns out that with few exceptions the fundamental act of chemical change involves just one or two molecules at a time; that is, *elementary reactions* in kinetics are nearly always *unimolecular* or *bimolecular*. The overall reaction that is being studied may, however, occur through a series of such elementary steps, which then gives the experimental rate law some complicated form. The steps, typically, will involve transient chemical species or reaction intermediates whose presence is not always independently provable. The reaction between H_2 and Br_2, for example, is considered to occur through hydrogen and bromine atoms as intermediates, and steps in the overall reaction include $H + Br_2 = HBr + Br$.

It is this detailing of the intermediate bimolecular steps constituting the path for the overall reaction that is known as the *reaction mechanism*. One uses mainly the experimentally observed rate law, but in general all available information, to infer a reaction mechanism that is consistent with the kinetics of the system. The study of reaction mechanisms is the final goal of the more chemically oriented investigator; the field can be a very controversial one because it has happened that two or more mechanisms, each equally capable of explaining the data, have each received strong partisan support.

Third, the theoretical study of elementary reactions is now highly developed. It is concerned with the detail of how molecules approach each other, what their special requirements are for reaction—for example, with respect to energy—and with just how the crucial act of chemical bond making or breaking occurs. The two principal theoretical models of current importance differ considerably in flavor. If the elementary reaction is one of A with B to give products, and we suppose that state [AB]* is that in which the two reactants have come together with the necessary energy and so on for reaction, but have not yet fallen apart into products, we can write

$$A + B \underset{k_{-2}}{\overset{k_2}{\rightleftharpoons}} [AB]^* \overset{k_1}{\rightarrow} \text{products.} \qquad (14\text{-}3)$$

The first model, that of collision theory, deals with the rate at which A and B can form [AB]* and thus emphasizes k_2, and, in its simpler form, ignores k_{-2} so that [AB]* is considered always to go on to products. The second model, that of transition-state theory, treats [AB]* as being in equilibrium with A and B, so that the reaction rate is determined by the [AB]* concentration and by the frequency or rate constant k_1.

The two models approach each other when pursued to a more sophisticated level, but each in its simple form has provided a framework or a language for qualitative explanations as to why a given reaction is fast or slow. Both are therefore presented.

Although chemical kinetics can be outlined as a unified general subject, as has been done here, when details are explored facets of the treatment of gaseous and solution systems tend to separate as distinguishable subfields. The three aspects just described develop different emphases and different bodies of empirical fact. For this reason the material has been separated into two chapters. We first take up the subject of rate laws and their algebraic manipulation and then that of some important mechanisms of gas-phase reactions. The two major theories are next presented, with emphasis on their application to gaseous systems. Chapter 15 covers some of the experimental techniques special to solution systems and then proceeds to a discussion of how both collision and transition-state theory are modified in the case of solutions.

14-2 Rate Laws and Simple Mechanisms

A rate law is conventionally presented in the form of Eq. (14-1), that is, as a differential equation, and the principal concern at the moment is with the mathematical characteristics of specific functions $f[(A), (B), (C), ...]$, including their integrated forms. There is virtually no limit to the complexity of functions that may be encountered, and only the more important ones are taken up here. Also, we will consider only reactions that go to completion, deferring the more general case until Chapter 15.

A major category of rate laws is that for which R is given by an expression of the form of Eq. (14-2). We then speak of the *order* of the rate law as the sum of the exponents $(x + y + z \cdots)$, the important cases being those of first- and second-order reactions, Although the rate law bears no *a priori* relationship to the chemical equation for the overall reaction, the *stoichiometry* of this last must always be kept in mind; this point will be illustrated in Section 14-2B.

A. The First-Order Rate Law

Suppose that the forward rate R_f of a reaction is found to depend only on the concentration of some reactant A.

The rate law is then

$$\frac{d(A)}{dt} = -k(A) \tag{14-4}$$

and the overall reaction may be condensed to the form

$$A + \text{other reactants} \xrightarrow{R_f} \text{products,} \tag{14-5}$$

where R_f is the forward reaction rate. If the reaction goes to completion, then Eq. (14-4) provides the complete description of the rate behavior since R_b, the rate of the back reaction, is zero. Integration gives

$$\int \frac{d(A)}{(A)} = -k \int dt$$

or

$$\ln(A) = -kt + \text{constant.} \tag{14-6}$$

Thus a plot of $\ln(A)$ versus t gives a straight line of slope equal to $-k$, as in Fig. 14-1(a), where k is the rate constant, usually given in sec^{-1}.

It may be convenient to evaluate the constant of integration by setting $(A) = (A)_0$ at $t = 0$. Equation (14-6) then becomes, in exponential form,

$$(A) = (A)_0\, e^{-kt} \tag{14-7}$$

and the graphical appearance is illustrated in Fig. 14-1(b). A characteristic time is that at which $(A)/(A)_0 = \frac{1}{2}$; this is called the *half-life* $t_{1/2}$ of the reaction, and is very simply related to k:

$$\frac{(A)}{(A)_0} = \frac{1}{2} = e^{-kt_{1/2}}\ldots, \qquad \ln\frac{1}{2} = -kt_{1/2} \tag{14-8}$$

or

$$kt_{1/2} = 0.6931. \tag{14-9}$$

Thus either k or $t_{1/2}$ defines the rate of a first-order reaction. Note that if $t = 2t_{1/2}$, the effect is to double the exponential in Eq. (14-8), so that $(A)/(A)_0 = (\frac{1}{2})^2 = \frac{1}{4}$. In general, if $t = nt_{1/2}$,

$$\frac{(A)}{(A)_0} = \left(\frac{1}{2}\right)^n. \tag{14-10}$$

This is illustrated in Fig. 14-1(b): $(A)/(A)_0 = \frac{1}{2}$ at $t_{1/2}$, $\frac{1}{4}$ at $2t_{1/2}$, $\frac{1}{8}$ at $3t_{1/2}$, and so on.

There is nothing unique about the time for half reaction—any other fraction could be picked. Were we to speak of $t_{1/3}$, the analog of Eq. (14-8) would be $kt_{1/3} = -\ln\frac{1}{3}$, and in general if $t_{1/r}$ is the time for (A) to drop to the fraction $1/r$ of its initial value,

$$\frac{(A)}{(A)_0} = \frac{1}{r} = e^{-kt_{1/r}}, \qquad kt_{1/r} = -\ln\frac{1}{r} \tag{14-11}$$

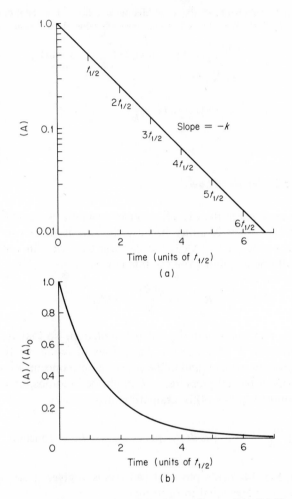

Fig. 14-1.   *The first-order rate law. (a) Plotted according to Eq. (14-6). (b) $(A)/(A)_0$ as a function of time, showing the constancy of $t_{1/2}$.*

and

$$\frac{(A)}{(A)_0} = \left(\frac{1}{r}\right)^{n_r}, \tag{14-12}$$

where n_r is the time expressed in multiples of $t_{1/r}$. An important feature of an exponential function is then that if it takes a time $t_{1/r}$ for (A) to decrease by factor $1/r$, then in a second such interval of time a further decrease by the same factor will occur, or an overall decrease of $(1/r)^2$, and so on. A numerical illustration is given in Section 14-3.

It is sometimes useful to take $1/r = 1/e$, in which case $t_{1/r}$ is given the special symbol τ and is known as the *mean lifetime* for the reaction since it is, in fact, the average time elapsed before a molecule of A reacts. Substitution into Eq. (14-11) gives $1/e = e^{-k\tau}$, or $-1 = -k\tau$, whence

$$k\tau = 1. \tag{14-13}$$

619

The quantity τ can be shown to be the mean lifetime as follows. For the moment let the mean lifetime be denoted by $\bar{t}$, which we define by weighting each value of t by the amount of A present:

$$\bar{t} = \frac{\int_{(A)=(A)_0}^{(A)=0} t\, d(A)}{\int_{(A)=(A)_0}^{(A)=0} d(A)} = \frac{[(A)_0/k]\int_{t=0}^{t=\infty} (kt)\, e^{-kt}\, d(kt)}{(A)_0},$$

$$\bar{t} = \frac{1}{k}| -e^{-kt}(1+kt)|_0^\infty = \frac{1}{k}.$$

Thus $\bar{t}$ is identical to τ.

B. The Second-Order Rate Law

Consider the case where the overall order of reaction in Eq. (14-2) is found to be two, that is $(x + y) = 2$, either because the rate is proportional to $(A)^2$ or because it is proportional to $(A)(B)$. In the first case we can use Eq. (14-5) as giving the overall process, and write the rate law as

$$R_f = -\frac{d(A)}{dt} = k(A)^2. \tag{14-14}$$

We again assume that the reaction goes to completion, so that R_b is zero. Note that the rate constant k now has the dimensions of $(\text{concentration})^{-1} (\text{time})^{-1}$; time is usually given in seconds, and in the case of gases, concentration is commonly expressed in terms of partial pressure, so k might be in atmosphere^{-1} second^{-1}.

The integration of Eq. (14-14) is straightforward:

$$\int \frac{d(A)}{(A)^2} = -\int k\, dt \quad \text{or} \quad \frac{1}{(A)} = kt + \text{constant}. \tag{14-15}$$

As illustrated in Fig. 14-2(a), a plot of $1/(A)$ versus t gives a straight line, with intercept $1/(A)_0$ and slope equal to k, so that

$$\frac{1}{(A)} = \frac{1}{(A)_0} + kt. \tag{14-16}$$

One may again use the concept of half-life, and setting $(A)/(A)_0 = \frac{1}{2}$ at $t_{1/2}$ in Eq. (14-16) gives

$$2 - 1 = (A)_0\, kt_{1/2} \quad \text{or} \quad t_{1/2} = \frac{1}{k(A)_0}. \tag{14-17}$$

However, unlike the case of a first-order reaction, the time for successive diminutions in (A) by a factor of one-half is not a constant, but doubles with each decrement. Thus $t_{1/4} = 3/k(A)_0$ and $t_{1/8} = 7/k(A)_0$, so that, as illustrated in Fig. 14-2(b), the first interval is $t_{1/2}$, the second $2t_{1/2}$, and so on.

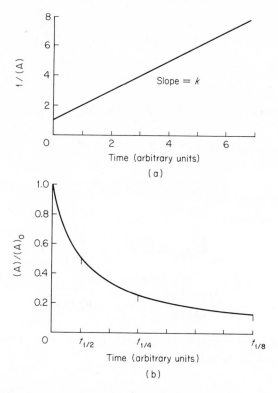

Fig. 14-2. *The second-order rate law. (a) Plotted according to Eq. (14-16). (b)* (A)/(A)₀ *as a function of time, showing the successive doubling of* $t_{1/2}$.

If the rate law is second order but of the form

$$R_f = -\frac{d(A)}{dt} = k(A)(B), \qquad (14\text{-}18)$$

the reaction type becomes

$$aA + bB + \text{other reactants} \overset{R_f}{\to} \text{products}. \qquad (14\text{-}19)$$

We again assume that there is no back reaction, but note that R_f could equally well be expressed in terms of $d(B)/dt$, from the stoichiometry of the reaction,

$$b\frac{d(A)}{dt} = a\frac{d(B)}{dt}. \qquad (14\text{-}20)$$

A notation that is convenient at this point is that of defining x as the decrease in concentration in A at time t, $x = (A)_0 - (A)$, and similarly, $y = (B)_0 - (B)$. We then have

$$-\frac{d(A)}{dt} = \frac{dx}{dt}, \qquad -\frac{d(B)}{dt} = \frac{dy}{dt},$$

and

$$b\frac{dx}{dt} = a\frac{dy}{dt}, \qquad bx = ay.$$

The rate law becomes

$$\frac{dx}{dt} = k[(A)_0 - x][(B)_0 - y] \quad \text{or} \quad \frac{dx}{dt} = k[(A)_0 - x]\left[(B)_0 - x\frac{b}{a}\right]. \qquad (14\text{-}21)$$

The simplest case is that for which $b = a$, so that

$$\frac{dx}{[(A)_0 - x][(B)_0 - x]} = k\,dt.$$

On integrating, we obtain

$$\frac{1}{(A)_0 - (B)_0}\ln\frac{(B)_0[(A)_0 - x]}{(A)_0[(B)_0 - x]} = kt$$

or

$$\ln\frac{(B)_0(A)}{(A)_0(B)} = [(A)_0 - (B)_0]\,kt. \qquad (14\text{-}22)$$

We can simplify the graphical presentation of this result by defining $p = (B)_0/(A)_0$, and F_A as $(A)/(A)_0$, to obtain

$$\ln\frac{pF_A}{(p-1) + F_A} = (1 - p)\,k(A)_0t = \frac{1-p}{p}\,k(B)_0t. \qquad (14\text{-}23)$$

Equation (14-23) is plotted in Fig. 14-3 as F_A versus $k(B)_0\,t$. In effect, $(B)_0$ is regarded as constant, and as p increases $(A)_0$ varies from being greater than $(B)_0$ to being smaller than $(B)_0$.

The sequence in the figure is worth some study. First, the initial rate is in each case $R_{in} = k(A)_0(B)_0$ and since F_A is the quantity plotted, the consequence is that $dF_A/dt = k(B)_0$; the initial slopes are therefore independent of the value of p. If p is small, so that $(A)_0 > (B)_0$, the reaction necessarily terminates at $(A)_\infty = (A)_0 - (B)_0$ or at $F_A = 1 - p$, as illustrated by the first two curves of the figure. If p is greater than one, the reaction proceeds to completion, that is, all of A is used up, and the more rapidly the larger the value of p.

There are two special cases of interest. First, if $(A)_0 \ll (B)_0$, then very little B is consumed so that (B) is essentially constant and equal to $(B)_0$. The effect is that Eq. (14-18) reduces to the form

$$-\frac{d(A)}{dt} = [k(B)_0](A) = k_{app}(A), \qquad (14\text{-}24)$$

or to the same form as the first-order rate law, Eq. (14-5). Thus the curve for $p = \infty$ in Fig. 14-3 is simply that for a first-order reaction; note that $F_A = 0.5$

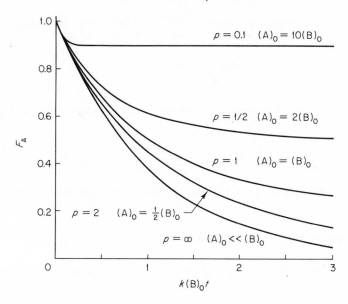

Fig. 14-3.   *Behavior of the rate law $R = k(A)/(B)$ for various ratios $p = (B)_0/(A)_0$.*

at $k(B)_0 t = 0.69$ and that the time for successive decrements of one-half is constant.

Since k_{app} is not a true rate constant but the product of k and the concentration $(B)_0$, it is customary to call Eq. (14-24) a *pseudo-first-order* rate law. This term is applied whenever a first-order rate expression has been obtained by virtue of some concentration or concentrations being held constant. The distinction is important to the mathematics of the situation, in that k_{app} will vary with $(B)_0$. Thus Eq. (14-24) gives the *time* rate law for a particular experiment, but not the *full concentration* rate law. The distinction can also be quite important in any theoretical interpretation of the rate constant.

The second special case is that for $p = 1$. Equation (14-23) becomes indeterminate, and it is necessary (as always in such a circumstance) to return to the original differential equation. The situation is now that $(A)_0 = (B)_0$, and since we are still assuming that $a = b$, it follows that $(A) = (B)$ at all times during the reaction. Equation (14-18) therefore reduces to

$$\frac{d(A)}{dt} = -k(A)^2,$$

or to Eq. (14-14).

These two special cases illustrate an important point for the experimentalist. By choosing $(A)_0 \ll (B)_0$, we reduce the rate law to a first-order one, and by choosing $(A)_0 = (B)_0$, we reduce it to a much simpler mathematical form of a second-order rate law. Part of the art of experimental chemical kinetics lies in the designing of experimental conditions so that the mathematical complexity of the *time* rate law is reduced.

We return briefly to the general case of $a \neq b$, or to Eq. (14-21). The integration is still that of a standard form, and with some algebraic manipulation, the result is

$$\ln \frac{(B)_0(A)}{(A)_0(B)} = \frac{b(A)_0 - a(B)_0}{a} kt. \tag{14-25}$$

Again, a suitable choice of experimental conditions can greatly simplify matters. If p is made equal to b/a, then Eq. (14-21) becomes

$$\frac{dx}{dt} = k \frac{b}{a} [(A)_0 - x]^2 \quad \text{or} \quad \frac{d(A)}{dt} = -k \frac{b}{a} (A)^2, \tag{14-26}$$

so that the simpler form of Eq. (14-14) has been regained, with $k_{\text{app}} = kb/a$.

C.   The Zero-Order and Other Rate Laws

The term "zero order" is applied to a reaction whose rate is independent of time, that is,

$$R = -\frac{d(A)}{dt} = k \tag{14-27}$$

or

$$(A) = (A)_0 - kt. \tag{14-28}$$

Such rate laws are more properly called pseudo-zero-order, since Eq. (14-27) gives the time dependence of (A) but cannot be the full description of the factors affecting the rate.

This point may be illustrated as follows. First, in photochemical reactions if the entire incident radiation is absorbed by the reacting species, then the rate of reaction will not depend on concentration and hence will be of zero order. However, the complete rate law is actually $R = I_{\text{abs}} \phi$, where I_{abs} is the intensity of the absorbed light and ϕ is an efficiency factor called the quantum yield for the reaction (see Section 18-4E); in the form written I_{abs} would be expressed as quanta of light per unit volume per second. Thus although the rate does not depend on (A), it does depend on I_{abs} ; at a sufficiently low concentration of A, I_{abs} will become proportional to (A), and the rate law will revert to first order in (A).

Second, many examples of zero-order reactions occur in heterogeneous catalysis. The situation is one in which the reaction takes place on the surface of the catalyst so that $R = k'\theta\mathscr{A}$, where θ is the fraction of surface covered by the adsorbed reactant and $\mathscr{A}$ is the total catalyst surface area. If the concentration or pressure of A is large enough, $\theta = 1$, and the reaction is zero order; at sufficiently low pressures, however, θ becomes proportional to (A) and the reaction reverts to first order. Note that R will depend on the amount of catalyst, that is, on the area $\mathscr{A}$, as well. See the Special Topics section for further details.

These two illustrations depict a fairly general situation, that is, one in which the reaction is zero order at large (A) and first order at small (A). The intermediate behavior is often given by the form

$$-\frac{d(A)}{dt} = \frac{k_1(A)}{1 + k_2(A)}.$$

(14-29)

Integration is straightforward, giving

$$\ln \frac{(A)}{(A)_0} + k_2[(A) - (A)_0] = -k_1 t.$$

(14-30)

Equation (14-29) reverts to Eq. (14-7) if $k_2(A)_0$ is small compared to the logarithmic term, and it reverts to Eq. (14-28) if the reverse is true.

Experimental rate laws may be of some general order n, the simplest case of which is

$$-\frac{d(A)}{dt} = k(A)^n.$$

(14-31)

Integration gives

$$\frac{1}{(A)^{n-1}} - \frac{1}{(A)_0^{n-1}} = (n-1)\,kt,$$

(14-32)

provided that $n \neq 1$. Some examples are the interconversion of *ortho-* and *para-* hydrogen, for which $n = \frac{3}{2}$, the formation of phosgene ($CO + Cl_2 = COCl_2$), for which $n = \frac{5}{2}$, and a variety of reactions for which $n = 3$.

14-3   Experimental Methods and Rate Law Calculations

A.   Use of Additive Properties

As stated earlier, an important goal of the experimentalist is that of establishing the rate law which governs a given reaction. The initial task is very similar to that in the study of chemical equilibrium—one needs some way of following the degree of reaction. As discussed in Section 7-3, one may quench or otherwise stop a reaction and then proceed at one's leisure to analyze chemically for reactants or products. However, very often some specific physical property of one or more of the species may be measured *in situ*, so that one may follow the reaction continuously as it proceeds. If one of the reactants has a characteristic light absorption, for example, the optical density of the solution may be monitored at a particular wavelength. In the case of a gas-phase reaction the change in the total pressure may be used as a measure of the degree of reaction (provided the number of moles of gaseous products differs from that of the reactants).

These last two quantities, optical density and total pressure, are examples of additive properties $\mathscr{P}$ discussed in Chapter 3. There is a very useful relationship whereby $\mathscr{P}$ for a reacting mixture may be used to give the degree of advancement of the reaction. Consider the general reaction

$$aA + bB + \cdots = mM + nN + \cdots .$$

Initially $(A)_0$ moles of A, $(B)_0$ moles of B, and so on are present per unit volume, and we have

$$\mathscr{P}_0 = (A)_0 \mathscr{P}_A + (B)_0 \mathscr{P}_B + \cdots .$$

We now define v as the degree of advancement of the reaction, where av is the number of moles of A reacted, bv the number of moles of B reacted, and so on, and mv is the number of moles of M produced, nv is the number of moles of N produced, and so on. After some time t we then have

$$\mathscr{P}_t = [(A)_0 - av]\mathscr{P}_A + [(B)_0 - bv]\mathscr{P}_B + \cdots + mv\mathscr{P}_M + nv\mathscr{P}_N + \cdots ,$$

so that

$$\mathscr{P}_0 - \mathscr{P}_t = av\mathscr{P}_A + bv\mathscr{P}_B + \cdots - mv\mathscr{P}_M - nv\mathscr{P}_N - \cdots . \tag{14-33}$$

At infinite time, or on completion of the reaction, v has the value v_∞, and so

$$\mathscr{P}_\infty = [(A)_0 - av_\infty]\mathscr{P}_A + [(B)_0 - bv_\infty]\mathscr{P}_B + \cdots + mv_\infty\mathscr{P}_M + nv_\infty\mathscr{P}_N + \cdots ,$$

so that

$$\mathscr{P}_0 - \mathscr{P}_\infty = av_\infty\mathscr{P}_A + bv_\infty\mathscr{P}_B + \cdots - mv_\infty\mathscr{P}_M - nv_\infty\mathscr{P}_N - \cdots \tag{14-34}$$

and therefore

$$\frac{\mathscr{P}_0 - \mathscr{P}_t}{\mathscr{P}_0 - \mathscr{P}_\infty} = \frac{v}{v_\infty} , \tag{14-35}$$

the term $(a\mathscr{P}_A + b\mathscr{P}_B + \cdots - m\mathscr{P}_M - n\mathscr{P}_N - \cdots)$ being a common factor to both Eqs. (14-33) and (14-34). Alternatively, we have

$$\frac{\mathscr{P}_t - \mathscr{P}_\infty}{\mathscr{P}_0 - \mathscr{P}_\infty} = 1 - \frac{v}{v_\infty} = \frac{(A)_t - (A)_\infty}{(A)_0 - (A)_\infty} . \tag{14-36}$$

We see that the second part of Eq. (14-36) is correct by writing $(A)_t$ as $[(A)_0 - av]$ and so on, and observing that the result simplifies to $1 - (v/v_\infty)$.

As a specific example, paraldehyde, $(CH_3CHO)_3$, dissociates into acetaldehyde, the overall reaction being of the form

$$A = 3B.$$

The change in total pressure with time at 260°C is given in Table 14-1 and application of Eq. (14-36), with $\mathscr{P} = P_{tot}$ (total pressure), then gives $P_A/P_{0,A}$, or the fraction of paraldehyde remaining ($P_{\infty,A}$ being zero in this case since the reaction goes to completion). The results are plotted in Fig. 14-4(a), according to Eq. (14-6), and the linearity of the plot indicates that the reaction is first order. As a check, the data are also plotted according to Eq. (14-16), which tests for possible obedience

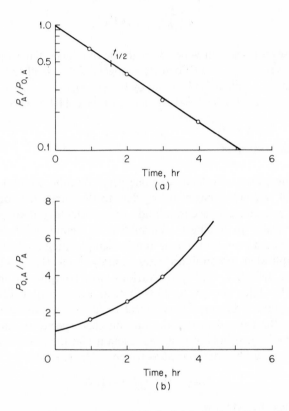

Fig. 14-4. *The thermal dissociation of paraldehyde. (a) Data plotted according to the first-order rate law. (b) Data plotted according to the second-order rate law.*

Table 14-1. *Thermal Dissociation of Paraldehyde at 260°C*

Time (hr)	P_{tot} (Torr)	$P_A/P_{0,A}$
0	100	1.00
1	173	0.64
2	218	$0.41 = (0.64)^2$
3	248	$0.26 = (0.64)^3$
4	266	$0.17 = (0.64)^4$
∞	300	0.00

to the second-order rate law, but the points now fall on a curved line. As indicated in the table itself, one could determine the first-order character directly by noting that $P_A/P_{0,A}$ drops by the constant factor 0.64 with each interval of 1 hr.

The rate law for the reaction is therefore

$$\frac{dP_A}{dt} = -kP_A ,$$

and there are several ways in which k might be obtained. The slope of the line in Fig. 14-4(a) gives $k = -2.303[\log(0.1) - \log(1)]/5.2 = 0.44$ hr^{-1}. Alternatively, $t_{1/2}$ is read from the graph as 1.57 hr, and by Eq. (14-9), $k = 0.693/1.57 = 0.44$ hr^{-1}. Finally, $kt_{0.64} = -2.3 \log 0.64 = 0.44$, and so $k = 0.44/1 = 0.44$ hr^{-1}.

B.   The Isolation Method

The preceding subsection dealt with one very common method of determining an experimental rate law—that of fitting data to the integrated form of a specific rate law. This procedure is accurate and very satisfactory if the reaction rate is some integral order in a single reactant, or a second-order reaction in two reactants. If the data do not fit one or another simple integrated form, the number of more complicated possibilities rises rapidly, and the approach becomes increasingly less definitive, that is, the various more complicated integrated forms may not actually differ enough to allow a clear experimental distinction among them. At this point it becomes very useful to fix one or another concentration so as to *isolate* the dependence of the rate on each species in turn. One usually does this using a large excess of first one reactant and then another.

An illustration may be constructed as follows. The reaction

$$2NO + H_2 = N_2O + H_2O \tag{14-37}$$

is known to obey the rate law

$$\frac{dP_{N_2O}}{dt} = kP_{NO}^2 P_{H_2} , \tag{14-38}$$

with $k = 1.00 \times 10^{-7}$ Torr^{-2} sec^{-1} at 820°C. Let us examine how this conclusion might have been arrived at by the isolation method. Suppose that first the reaction was studied with a large excess of NO: $P_{0,NO} = 600$ Torr and $P_{0,H_2} = 10$ Torr. P_{NO} will be virtually constant, and the rate law becomes pseudo first order:

$$-\frac{dP_{H_2}}{dt} = \frac{dP_{N_2O}}{dt} = [kP_{0,NO}^2] P_{H_2} = k_{app}P_{H_2} ,$$

where $k_{app} = (1.00 \times 10^{-7})(600)^2 = 0.036$ sec^{-1}. The reaction would be found to obey Eq. (14-6) or Eq. (14-7), with $t_{1/2} = 0.693/0.036 = 19.3$ sec, and the experimenter would therefore conclude that the rate law contains P_{H_2} as a term. We confirm this by observing that $t_{1/2}$ does not depend on P_{0,H_2} so long as NO is in large excess.

The next step would be to reverse the situation and use a large excess of $H_2 : P_{0,NO} = 10$ Torr and $P_{0,H_2} = 600$ Torr. The reaction would now be pseudo second order:

$$-\frac{1}{2}\frac{dP_{NO}}{dt} = \frac{dP_{N_2O}}{dt} = (kP_{0,H_2})\,P_{NO}^2 = k_{app}P_{NO}^2$$

or

$$\frac{dP_{NO}}{dt} = -k_{app}P_{NO}^2\,,$$

with k_{app} now equal to $2(1.00 \times 10^{-7})(600) = 1.20 \times 10^{-4}\,\text{Torr}^{-1}\,\text{sec}^{-1}$. Note the presence of the stoichiometry factor of 2. The rate data would now obey Eq. (14-16), and would show $t_{1/2} = 1/(1.20 \times 10^{-4})(10) = 833$ sec. As a check, one would find that varying P_{NO} would give the same k_{app}, or that doubling $P_{0,NO}$ would halve the value of $t_{1/2}$. The reaction would then be identified as second order in NO, and Eq. (14-38) could then be written as the complete rate law. As a further check, k would then be calculated from all the various sets of data, and found to be the same. At this point final confirmation could be made with the use of intermediate compositions and the integrated form of the full rate law.

C. Use of Initial Rates

The procedures so far have made use of integrated rate laws. One must obtain data over a sufficient degree of reaction to establish agreement with one or another particular form. Considerable difficulties can develop with this procedure, however. The reaction may not be clear-cut, so that side reactions obscure the true course of the process being studied. Or the reaction may not proceed to completion, so that the term for the back reaction has mistakenly been omitted from the rate laws tested. It must be emphasized that quite different appearing algebraic forms will often fit a given set of data equally well, especially if the results are of the usual accuracy of about 1%.

In either case, the difficulty is avoided if the reaction is studied during its initial stages only. The experimental problem is that the analytical procedure must now be one suited to determining small amounts of a product in large amounts of reactants. Conventional quenching techniques followed by specific product analysis are often best. A nonvolatile product might be selectively condensed out of the reaction mixture or separated from it by gas chromatography, for example. If a product has a distinctive absorption spectrum, then even small amounts may be measured *in situ*. General additive properties such as total pressure are not very sensitive to small degrees of reaction, however, and become difficult to use.

The measurement of an initial reaction rate provides no information in itself as to the form of the rate law; it is necessary to make several experiments in which the initial concentrations are varied. In terms of the previous example, $(dP_{N_2O}/dt)_{initial}$ would have been found to be 0.36 Torr sec^{-1} with $P_{0,NO} = 600$ Torr and $P_{0,H_2} = 10$ Torr (at 820°C) and 0.72 Torr sec^{-1} if P_{0,H_2} had been increased to 20 Torr. Thus, doubling (H$_2$) at constant (NO) doubled the initial rate, and on the assumption that the rate law was of the form

$$\frac{dP_{N_2O}}{dt} = kP_{NO}^x P_{H_2}^y ,$$

one would write

$$\frac{0.72}{0.36} = \frac{k(600)^x(20)^y}{k(600)^x(10)^y} = 2^y \quad \text{or} \quad 2 = 2^y, \quad y = 1.$$

The conclusion would thus again have been that the reaction was first order in H$_2$. Had $P_{0,NO}$ been 300 Torr and P_{0,H_2} 10 Torr, the initial rate would have been 0.090 Torr sec^{-1} and the corresponding quotient of rate expressions would be

$$\frac{0.36}{0.090} = \frac{k(600)^x(10)^y}{k(300)^x(10)^y} = (2)^x \quad \text{or} \quad 4 = 2^x, \quad x = 2.$$

The reaction would thus have been shown to be second order in NO.

D. Fast Reaction Techniques

The analytical techniques so far mentioned require from a few seconds to carry out, as with optical density determinations, to minutes or hours, for chemical procedures. Many reactions are much faster than this, and a number of ingenious methods have been developed for such cases. For example, reaction times of as low as a few milliseconds can be studied with fast-mixing reactors. As illustrated in Fig. 14-5, the separate reactant gases are jetted into a chamber so designed that mixing is rapid and complete, and the mixed gases exit into a viewing chamber. One then determines optical density of the mixture by allowing a steady light beam to shine through the chamber and measuring its reduction in intensity. The average lifetime of the mixture can be estimated from the inlet flow rates and the volume of the mixing chamber, and each measurement is thus for one particular time of reaction. One varies the inflow rates to vary the reaction time.

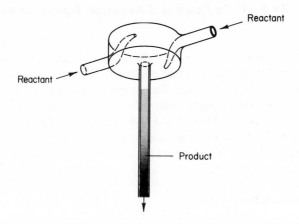

Fig. 14-5. *Mixing cell for the study of fast reactions.*

A difficulty with this procedure is in the calculation of the average lifetime and in the fact that each measurement gives only one point on the plot of amount of reaction versus time. An alternative procedure is to stop the flow of the mixed gases (such as by means of an electrically operated gate) and then to observe the progress of the reaction in the now stationary mixture in the viewing chamber. To do this, the monitoring light beam must impinge on a light detector, such as a photomultiplier tube, whose output can go to an oscilloscope. The sweep of the oscilloscope then traces the decay of the reactants with time. Reactions involving NO_2 have been much studied by this type of technique since its intense brown color makes its disappearance very easy to follow.

A very closely related photochemical technique is that of flash photolysis. The reactive species is now produced by a short, intense flash of light, and its decay is followed by the same monitoring light beam–oscilloscope method as before. Light flashes containing perhaps 10^{-7} mole of light quanta can be made to occur within a few microseconds by triggering of the discharge of high-voltage capacitors through a gas-filled tube; xenon at about 10 Torr is often used. Many reactions involving free radicals and other reactive species have been studied by this means. More recently laser flashes of a few nanoseconds have become possible, so that reaction times of this order of magnitude can now be studied.

These methods may be used for either gas- or solution-phase kinetics, and additional methods specially suited for solution work are described in Section 15-3. A remaining technique that is special for gaseous mixtures is that of the shock tube. The reaction mixture is separated by means of a diaphragm from some inert gas which is at a high pressure. On rupture of the diaphragm, a shock wave passes down the reaction mixture, rapidly heating it by hundreds of degrees. As a result of the change in temperature, reaction occurs, and it is followed, again by the monitoring light beam–oscilloscope technique. Reaction times of the order of microseconds may thus be studied.

14-4   Rate Laws and Reaction Mechanisms

Once an experimental rate law has been determined attention turns to the actual sequence of chemical steps that produces the reaction, that is, to the nature of the reaction path or mechanism. Such steps are known as *elementary chemical reactions*, as distinguished from the overall reaction. With two exceptions, discussed further in Sections 14-7 and 14-CN-1, we take *all* elementary reactions to be bimolecular, that is, to involve the reaction together of just two molecules. We proceed in this section to see how various overall rate laws can result.

A.   Simple Reactions

A *simple reaction* is defined here as one for which the overall process and the elementary reaction are the same. The simple reactions that have been studied fall into perhaps three categories, summarized in Table 14-2. *Association reactions*, as the name implies, involve the combining of two molecules to give a single product. *Exchange reactions* are ones in which an atom or a group is transferred from one molecule to another. A very large number of such reactions have been studied; for example, many organic molecules and radicals can exchange hydrogen or halogen atoms. *Decomposition reactions* may be ones in which two molecules of a species combine to then break up into simpler products. These are often exchange reactions.

The experimental observation is that the mass action law, in its historic form, applies to simple reactions. That is, the rate law corresponds to the overall chemical reaction. Thus for the exchange reaction

$$NO + ClNO_2 = NOCl + NO_2,$$

Table 14-2.   *Some Simple Reactions*

Type	Example
Association	$2NO_2 \rightarrow N_2O_4$
	$2CH_3 \rightarrow C_2H_6$
Exchange	$NO + ClNO_2 \rightarrow NOCl + NO_2$
	$NO_2 + O_3 \rightarrow NO_3 + O_2$
	$CO + Cl_2 \rightarrow COCl + Cl$
	$H + D_2 \rightarrow HD + D$
	$H + HCl \rightarrow H_2 + Cl$
	$CH_3 + H_2 \rightarrow CH_4 + H$
	$CH_3 + NH_3 \rightarrow CH_4 + NH_2$
Decomposition	$C_3H_7I \rightarrow C_3H_6 + HI$

the rate law is

$$R_f = -\frac{d(NO)}{dt} = k(NO)(ClNO_2).$$

B.   Two-Step Mechanisms. Rules for Obtaining a Rate Law from a Mechanism

A rather frequent situation is that in which a bimolecular reaction produces an intermediate which in turn reacts with itself or with one of the original reactants. The reaction $2NO + H_2 \rightarrow N_2O + H_2O$ [Eq. (14-37)] is one example. The mechanism seems likely to be

$$2NO \overset{K}{=} N_2O_2 \qquad \text{(rapid equilibrium)},$$

$$N_2O_2 + H_2 \overset{k}{\rightarrow} N_2O + H_2O \qquad \text{(slow step)}.$$

The rules for constructing the rate law from a reaction mechanism are that, first, the mass action principle is applied to each elementary step, or to the slow step if all others are fast. This slow step determines the overall reaction rate, but it is then conventional to use the equilibrium constants and the stoichiometry of the other steps of the mechanism to express the rate law purely in terms of species that appear in the overall reaction.

The example provides an illustration of these rules. We first apply the mass action law to the slow step:

$$\frac{d(N_2O)}{dt} = -\frac{d(N_2O_2)}{dt} = k(N_2O_2)(H_2).$$

However, N_2O_2 does not appear in the overall equation (14-37), and we may eliminate it by using the equilibrium constant expression $K = (N_2O_2)/(NO)^2$ to get

$$\frac{d(N_2O)}{dt} = kK(NO)^2(H_2), \tag{14-39}$$

which is the observed rate law [Eq. (14-38)].

Note, however, that the alternative mechanism

$$NO + H_2 \overset{K}{=} NO \cdot H_2 \qquad \text{(rapid equilibrium)},$$

$$NO \cdot H_2 + NO \overset{k}{\rightarrow} N_2O + H_2O \qquad \text{(slow step)},$$

where $NO \cdot H_2$ is an association complex, equally well reproduces the experimental rate law (the reader might verify this statement). Thus even in this simple situation at least two alternative paths can be thought of, both chemically reasonable and both agreeing with the kinetic results. The similar type of reaction

$2NO + X_2 = 2NOX$ is known, with $X_2 = O_2$, Cl_2, or Br_2, and the same ambiguity of mechanism is present. One of the applications of fast reaction techniques has been to the identification of reaction intermediates so as to allow a decision to be made between alternative mechanisms. It has not yet been determined, however, whether in the cases cited the intermediate is N_2O_2 or $NO \cdot X_2$.

A further point is that by either mechanism the experimental rate constant is seen to be a product of a true rate constant and the equilibrium constant for the precursor reaction. This type of situation presents a very real problem in the theoretical analysis of rate data; reaction rate theories deal with elementary reactions and can easily lead to erroneous conclusions if applied to composite rate constants.

C.   The Stationary-State Hypothesis

The two-step mechanism just discussed is a special case of a more general situation. It was assumed that the first step consisted of a rapid equilibrium, but the more complete analysis would be as follows:

$$2NO \underset{k_{-1}}{\overset{k_1}{\rightleftharpoons}} N_2O_2 ,$$

$$N_2O_2 + H_2 \overset{k_2}{\rightarrow} N_2O + H_2O.$$

We now write the sum of the mass action rate expressions for *each* process whereby a given species should change in concentration with time:

$$\frac{1}{2}\frac{d(NO)}{dt} = -k_1(NO)^2 + k_{-1}(N_2O_2), \tag{14-40}$$

$$\frac{d(N_2O_2)}{dt} = k_1(NO)^2 - k_{-1}(N_2O_2) - k_2(N_2O_2)(H_2), \tag{14-41}$$

$$\frac{d(N_2O)}{dt} = k_2(N_2O_2)(H_2). \tag{14-42}$$

The set of three differential equations must now be solved simultaneously. Although this can be done in the present case, the mathematics of such situations rapidly becomes intractable, and a very useful approximation is usually made so as to simplify matters. If an intermediate I, in this case N_2O_2, is being produced and consumed in such a manner that its concentration never becomes appreciable, this means that the total reaction "traffic" is large compared to the amount of intermediate and hence that the latter rapidly attains a steady level of concentration which then slowly drops as the reactants are consumed. The further implication is that, in this case, $d(N_2O_2)/dt$ is small compared to $d(NO)/dt$ or $d(N_2O)/dt$; if (N_2O_2) is, say, $10^{-3}(NO)$, then $d(N_2O_2)/dt$ should be about $10^{-3}\, d(NO)/dt$, and hence 10^{-3} times each of the terms of Eq. (14-41). The approximation that is therefore made is to set $d(\mathrm{I})/dt$ equal to zero. This is known as the *steady-* or *stationary-state approximation*.

Application of the stationary-state approximation to the present example sets $d(\mathrm{N_2O_2})/dt = 0$ and allows Eq. (14-41) to be solved for $(\mathrm{N_2O_2})$:

$$(\mathrm{N_2O_2}) = \frac{k_1(\mathrm{NO})^2}{k_{-1} + k_2(\mathrm{H_2})} . \tag{14-43}$$

Insertion of this result into Eq. (14-42) gives

$$\frac{d(\mathrm{N_2O})}{dt} = \frac{k_2 k_1(\mathrm{NO})^2(\mathrm{H_2})}{k_{-1} + k_2(\mathrm{H_2})} . \tag{14-44}$$

Notice that if k_{-1} is large compared to $k_2(\mathrm{H_2})$, then Eq. (14-44) reduces to Eq. (14-39), since $K = k_1/k_{-1}$. On the other hand, at very large $(\mathrm{H_2})$, it should be possible to obtain the other limiting form:

$$\frac{d(\mathrm{N_2O})}{dt} = k_1(\mathrm{NO})^2. \tag{14-45}$$

Were the alternative mechanism, involving $\mathrm{NO \cdot H_2}$ as intermediate, the correct one, then at large (NO), the limiting form should be

$$\frac{d(\mathrm{N_2O})}{dt} = k_1(\mathrm{NO})(\mathrm{H_2}). \tag{14-46}$$

Investigators have attempted such studies as a means of distinguishing between the two mechanisms, but without success in that they could not reach sufficiently high pressures to observe departures from the normal rate law. However, success in this respect has been achieved in some related situations that will be discussed in Section 14-7.

D. Chain Reactions

A chain reaction is one in which some intermediate or intermediates are consumed and regenerated in a cycle of reactions the net result of which is to carry forward the overall reaction. Analysis of such systems can be quite complicated, and the following example will serve to illustrate both the type of mechanism encountered and a further application of the stationary-state hypothesis.

The reaction

$$\mathrm{H_2 + Br_2 = 2HBr} \tag{14-47}$$

has been extensively studied f. n the time of M. Bodenstein around 1906. Unlike the situation with the seemingly analogous reaction $H_2 + I_2 = 2HI$, the experimental rate law is very complex:

$$\frac{d(HBr)}{dt} = \frac{k_t(H_2)(Br_2)^{1/2}}{1 + [k_i(HBr)/(Br_2)]}, \tag{14-48}$$

where k_i has been called the inhibition constant and the term in the denominator reflects the inhibition of the reaction rate by the product HBr. The mechanism for this reaction seems now well established as the following:

$$Br_2 + M \xrightarrow{k_1} 2Br + M \qquad \text{(chain initiation)},$$

$$2Br + M \xrightarrow{k_2} Br_2 + M \qquad \text{(chain termination)},$$

$$Br + H_2 \underset{k_4}{\overset{k_3}{\rightleftharpoons}} HBr + H \qquad \text{(chain propagation)},$$

$$H + Br_2 \xrightarrow{k_5} HBr + Br \qquad \text{(chain propagation)}.$$

(M is any gaseous species, and serves to supply the energy for the dissociation—see Section 14-CN-1.) Note that the last two reactions together constitute a cycle, the net effect of which is to carry out the overall reaction [Eq. (14-47)]; this pair then constitutes the chain reaction.

The stationary state assumption is now applied to the intermediates H and Br[†]:

$$\frac{d(Br)}{dt} = 0 = 2k_1(Br_2)(M) - k_2(Br)^2(M) - k_3(Br)(H_2) + k_4(HBr)(H) + k_5(H)(Br_2)$$

$$\tag{14-49}$$

and

$$\frac{d(H)}{dt} = 0 = k_3(Br)(H_2) - k_4(HBr)(H) - k_5(H)(Br_2) \tag{14-50}$$

or

$$(H) = \frac{k_3(Br)(H_2)}{k_4(HBr) + k_5(Br_2)}. \tag{14-51}$$

Also, addition of Eqs. (14-49) and (14-50) leads to

$$(Br) = \left[\frac{2k_1(Br_2)}{k_2} \right]^{1/2} = K_{1,2}^{1/2}(Br_2)^{1/2}, \tag{14-52}$$

where $K_{1,2}$ is the equilibrium constant for the dissociation of Br_2 into atoms; notice that (M) has cancelled out.

The rate of production of HBr is given by

$$\frac{d(HBr)}{dt} = k_3(Br)(H_2) - k_4(HBr)(H) + k_5(H)(Br_2) \tag{14-53}$$

[†] Rate constants conventionally refer to a *process*, so if, as in this case, two moles of product are formed per process, the rate expression for the formation of product contains a factor of 2.

and replacement of (H) and (Br) by the appropriate expressions yields

$$\frac{d(\text{HBr})}{dt} = \frac{2k_3 K_{1,2}^{1/2}(\text{H}_2)(\text{Br}_2)^{1/2}}{1 + [k_4(\text{HBr})/k_5(\text{Br}_2)]},$$ (14-54)

which is the same as the observed rate law [Eq. (14-48)].

Many oxidation reactions proceed through a chain mechanism, and a particular example, $\text{H}_2 + \frac{1}{2}\text{O}_2 = \text{H}_2\text{O}$, is discussed in Section 14-CN-5 as illustrative of systems that can lead to explosions. In addition, the thermal decomposition of many gaseous organic molecules involves free radical chains. Usually, however, thermal decomposition or *pyrolysis* is complicated by the presence of a large variety of products due to the various types of decomposition reactions that can occur. It has therefore been useful to initiate such decompositions photochemically; the first step is then more apt to be a simple one, and the whole reaction sequence can be followed at a low enough temperature that intermediates and reaction products do not themselves pyrolyze.

Perhaps the most studied system of this last type is that of the photodecomposition of acetone. Hundreds of publications have appeared on the subject, and it must suffice here to sketch the main conclusions. Irradiation of acetone vapor with light of around 254 nm wavelength results in its fragmentation to give CH_3CO, CH_3, and CO:

$$\text{CH}_3\text{COCH}_3 \xrightarrow{h\nu} \begin{cases} \text{CH}_3\text{CO} \cdot + \cdot \text{CH}_3 \\ \text{CO} + 2 \cdot \text{CH}_3. \end{cases}$$

The following reactions then appear to be important:

$$
\begin{array}{ll}
2 \cdot \text{CH}_3 \rightarrow \text{C}_2\text{H}_6 & \text{(association)}, \\
2 \cdot \text{COCH}_3 \rightarrow (\text{CH}_3\text{CO})_2 & \text{(association)}, \\
\cdot \text{CH}_3 + \cdot \text{COCH}_3 \rightarrow \text{CH}_3\text{COCH}_3 & \text{(recombination)}, \\
\cdot \text{CH}_3 + \cdot \text{COCH}_3 \rightarrow \text{CH}_4 + \text{CH}_2{=}\text{CO} & \text{(H exchange)}, \\
\cdot \text{COCH}_3 + \text{M} \rightarrow \text{CO} + \cdot \text{CH}_3 + \text{M} & \text{(decomposition)}, \\
\cdot \text{CH}_3 + \cdot \text{CH}_2\text{COCH}_3 \rightarrow \text{CH}_3\text{CH}_2\text{COCH}_3 & \text{(association)}, \\
\cdot \text{CH}_3 + \text{CH}_3\text{COCH}_3 \rightarrow \text{CH}_4 + \cdot \text{CH}_2\text{COCH}_3 & \text{(H exchange)}, \\
\cdot \text{CH}_2\text{COCH}_3 \rightarrow \cdot \text{CH}_3 + \text{CH}_2{=}\text{CO}. &
\end{array}
$$

(For clarity radicals are marked with an electron dot.) The products thus include CO, CH_4, C_2H_6, $\text{C}_2\text{H}_5\text{COCH}_3$, and $\text{CH}_2{=}\text{CO}$, with the various indicated radicals as chain carriers. Notice that all but one of the elementary reactions are bimolecular. The last reaction, however, shows a unimolecular decomposition process.

14-5 Temperature Dependence of Rate Constants

The preceding material has presented the customary procedure of expressing a reaction rate in terms of a rate law, or function of concentrations of species, and the concept of reaction mechanism, whereby the mass action principle is applied to the one or more elementary reactions that are responsible for the overall process. All dependences of a reaction rate other than on concentration are thus contained in the rate constant (or constants if the rate law is a complex one). We now examine the temperature dependence of reaction rates, that is, of rate constants.

A preliminary historical review seems appropriate at this point. The mass action principle developed during the period 1850–1890, beginning with the observation by L. Wilhelmy that the rate of inversion of cane sugar was proportional to the amount of unconverted sugar, the reaction being

$$H_2O + C_{12}H_{22}O_{11} \rightarrow C_6H_{12}O_6 \text{ (glucose)} + C_6H_{12}O_6 \text{ (fructose)}.$$

Wilhelmy integrated the first-order rate equation and, in effect, developed much of the material of Section 14-2A. The first emphasis on chemical equilibrium as the result of a dynamic balance of equal forward and reverse rates came from C. Guldberg and P. Waage in 1867, who also clearly formulated the law of mass action. Later, van't Hoff added that the equilibrium constant should then be given by $K = k_f/k_b$. It was not until 1865, however, that the first second-order reaction was clearly defined experimentally, by Harcourt and Essen (1865, 1866, 1867), in a study of the reaction between permanganate and oxalate ions. Thus the subject of reaction kinetics evolved through the study of solution rather than gas-phase reactions, although we will see that it is for the latter that theory is best developed today.

The preceding developments set the stage for Arrhenius to observe in 1889 that rate constants showed much the same temperature dependence behavior as did equilibrium constants, namely,

$$\frac{d(\ln k)}{dT} = \frac{\text{constant}}{T^2}.$$

By analogy with the second law equation, Eq. (7-29), for equilibrium constants, it was then natural to write

$$\frac{d(\ln k)}{dT} = \frac{E^*}{RT^2}, \tag{14-55}$$

where E^* represents some characteristic energy that must be added to the reactants for reaction to occur. We call E^* the *activation energy* of the reaction.

Equation (14-55) has the usual alternative forms. Integration gives

$$\ln k = \text{constant} - \frac{E^*}{RT}, \tag{14-56}$$

so that a plot of $\ln k$ versus $1/T$ should give a straight line of slope $-E^*/R$.

An equivalent form is

$$k = A\, e^{-E^*/RT} \tag{14-57}$$

and integration between limits gives

$$\ln \frac{k_2}{k_1} = \frac{E^*}{R}\left(\frac{1}{T_1} - \frac{1}{T_2}\right).$$ (14-58)

These various forms are all known as the *Arrhenius equation* for rate constants; the constant A is called the *preexponential* or *frequency factor*.

As the equations imply, reaction rates increase as temperature increases; around 25°C, for example, a doubling of k with a 10°C rise in temperature corresponds to about 12 kcal mole^{-1} for E^*, and a quadrupling of the rate, to 24 kcal mole^{-1}, and so on. The factor by which k increases over a 10°C interval is known as the *temperature coefficient*.

The Arrhenius equation is amazingly well obeyed by systems showing a rate law of the type of Eq. (14-2). The reaction $2HI \rightarrow H_2 + I_2$ obeys second-order kinetics over a wide range of conditions and some of Bodenstein's data (1894–1899) are plotted in Fig. 14-6 according to the form of Eq. (14-56). The values of k are given in Table 14-3 along with those calculated from the best-fitting straight line

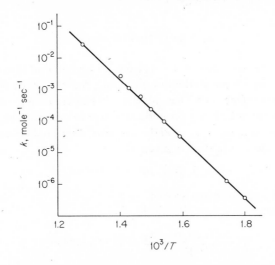

Fig. 14-6. *Arrhenius plot for the reaction* $2HI \rightarrow H_2 + I_2$.

in the Arrhenius plot. The agreement is within about 25 % over five orders of magnitude variation in k. This best straight line is given by

$$k_f = 9.17 \times 10^{10} e^{-44,450/RT},$$ (14-59)

where k_f is in liters per mole per second.

Excellent though this agreement is, there is some systematic deviation of the data from the straight line; a better fit is obtained by an equation of the form

$$k_f = A'T^{1/2}\, e^{-E^*/RT}$$ (14-60)

Table 14-3. *The Reaction* $2HI \longrightarrow H_2 + I_2$ [a]

T (°K)	k (liter mole^{-1} sec^{-1})	
	Observed	Calculated from Arrhenius equation
556	3.52×10^{-7}	3.11×10^{-7}
575	1.22×10^{-6}	1.18×10^{-6}
629	3.02×10^{-5}	3.33×10^{-5}
647	8.59×10^{-5}	8.96×10^{-4}
666	2.19×10^{-4}	1.92×10^{-4}
683	5.12×10^{-4}	5.53×10^{-4}
700	1.16×10^{-3}	1.21×10^{-3}
716	2.50×10^{-3}	2.53×10^{-3}
781	3.95×10^{-2}	3.33×10^{-2}

[a] Adapted from E. A. Moelwyn-Hughes, "Physical Chemistry." Pergamon, Oxford, 1961.

or

$$k_f = 2.04 \times 10^9 T^{1/2} e^{-42,500/RT} . \qquad (14\text{-}61)$$

As will be seen in the next section, Eq. (14-60) is suggested on theoretical grounds to be better than the simple Arrhenius equation. An important point to note is that the slight improvement in fit has resulted in rather different A and E^* parameters; kineticists are not always properly sensitive to this situation.

The reverse reaction, $H_2 + I_2 \rightarrow 2HI$, has also been studied extensively, and the second-order rate constant k_b is given by

$$k_b = 3.30 \times 10^9 T^{1/2} e^{-38,900/RT}, \qquad (14\text{-}62)$$

where k_b is in liters per mole per second.

According to the mass action relationship,

$$K = \frac{(H_2)(I_2)}{(HI)^2} = \frac{k_f}{k_b} = 0.727 e^{-3600/RT}. \qquad (14\text{-}63)$$

That is, ΔH^0 for the reaction is 3600 according to the kinetic data. Table 5-2 gives 6.20 kcal mole^{-1} as the heat of formation of HI [from $I_2(s)$], so the corresponding thermochemical $\Delta H^0 = -(2)(6.20) + 14.88 = 2.48$ kcal [where 14.88 is the heat of sublimation of $I_2(s)$]. The agreement is quite good, especially if the thermochemical ΔH is corrected by the (small) ΔC_P of reaction to the temperature region of the kinetic studies. The absolute values of K as determined directly and as found by the mass action equation also agree well.

Application of the van't Hoff and Arrhenius equations to the mass action expression $K = k_f/k_b$ thus leads to the conclusion that

$$\Delta E = E_f^* - E_b^*, \qquad (14\text{-}64)$$

as confirmed by the example. (The distinction between ΔH and ΔE is unimportant in the present case since for $H_2 + I_2 = 2HI$ the two are equal.) The picture that emerges is one of a critical energy content of reacting species which is the same for either direction of reaction as illustrated in Fig. 14-7. This conclusion is in

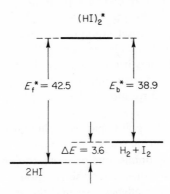

Fig. 14-7. *Relationship among $E_f{}^*$, $E_b{}^*$, and ΔE.*

accord with the principle of microscopic reversibility (see Section 7-CN-1). The nature of the common high-energy state will be the subject of discussion in Sections 14-6 and 14-8.

This presentation has left the implication that the $H_2 + I_2 \rightarrow 2HI$ reaction is a simple one, that is, one that proceeds by the single-step, bimolecular path indicated by the overall equation. The reaction has, in fact, been cited in countless texts as the clearest and best understood example of a bimolecular reaction. It was a shock to many persons (including this writer) to learn that work by Sullivan (1966) has shown the actual mechanism probably to be either

$$I_2 \overset{K_1}{=} 2I, \tag{14-65}$$

$$H_2 + 2I \underset{k_{-2}}{\overset{k_2}{\rightleftharpoons}} 2HI, \tag{14-66}$$

or the preequilibrium (14-65) followed by

$$H_2 + I \overset{K_3}{=} H_2I, \tag{14-67}$$

$$H_2I + I \underset{k_{-4}}{\overset{k_4}{\rightleftharpoons}} 2HI. \tag{14-68}$$

The first mechanism gives (after the procedure of Section 14-4B)

$$k_f = K_1 k_2, \qquad k_b = k_{-2}$$

and the second gives

$$k_f = K_1 K_3 k_4, \qquad k_b = k_{-4}.$$

Notice that the *rate law* remains second order in both directions. Only the interpretation of k_f and of k_b has changed—the former now contains either one or two preequilibrium constants. None of the earlier mass action analysis is invalidated—k_f/k_b still gives the correct equilibrium constant—but the detailed picture of the reaction path has changed profoundly. The revised mechanisms were arrived at, incidentally, by the photochemical generation of iodine atoms. By this means, their concentration could be varied independently of that of I_2. The same series of investigations also indicated that above 600°K an increasing proportion of the reaction goes through a short chain mechanism similar to that for the reaction of hydrogen with bromine. Thus the period from Bodenstein to the present has barely sufficed to unravel the detailed mechanism of an apparently very simple reaction!

This example illustrates the point that even though the Arrhenius equation is well obeyed, detailed mechanistic studies may indicate the apparent rate constant to be composite, that is, to contain one or more equilibrium constants. In some instances the situation is obvious. Thus the reaction $2NO + O_2 \rightarrow 2NO_2$ shows a small *negative* temperature coefficient, so that the apparent activation energy is negative. The mechanism is thought to be analogous to that giving Eq. (14-39), so that the observed rate constant is really equal to kK, where K is the equilibrium constant for the preequilibrium step. One thus has

$$E^*_{\text{app}} = E^*_{\text{true}} + \Delta E_{\text{preequil}} .$$

The preequilibrium involves an association, probably $2NO = N_2O_2$, and is therefore likely to be exoergic, with ΔE negative. It appears in this case that ΔE is sufficiently negative to give a net negative apparent activation energy.

The foregoing situation is one that clearly invites the indicated conclusion; more often, as in the $H_2 + I_2 \rightarrow 2HI$ reaction, E^*_{app} will be positive even though the rate constant is composite.

In summary, if rate data do *not* obey the Arrhenius equation reasonably well, it is an indication that the apparent rate constant is a sum or some other more complicated function of rate and equilibrium constants. If the Arrhenius equation *is* obeyed, the observed rate constant may still be a product of equilibrium and true rate constants and the apparent activation energy a corresponding sum of energy quantities. The molecular interpretation of an observed activation energy can thus only be made in terms of a specific reaction mechanism.

14-6 Collision Theory of Gas Reactions

The mass action background to the treatment of reaction rates made it natural for Arrhenius to associate E^* with a critical energy for reaction and to suggest that there might be an equilibrium between ordinary and "active" molecules, with only the latter reacting. This approach was not very fruitful for some time because it provided no detailed explanation of how molecules become activated or of the frequency factor A in the Arrhenius equation; it reappeared, however, in transition state theory (Section 14-8), but only much later. Perhaps the early emphasis on solution kinetics retarded the advance of theory because of the great difficulty in treating liquids on a molecular basis. At any rate, the first major theoretical advance was based on the kinetic molecular theory of gases.

During the period around 1920, M. Trautz, W. Lewis, C. Hinshelwood, and others developed a quantitative treatment of gas-phase reactions on the basis that only colliding molecules could react and then only if their combined kinetic energy of impact equaled or exceeded a critical energy E^*. The rate of a bimolecular reaction should then be

$$\text{rate} = (\text{collision frequency}) \left(\begin{array}{c} \text{(fraction of impact pairs} \\ \text{expected to have } E \geqslant E^* \end{array} \right). \qquad (14\text{-}69)$$

The first quantity is given by[†]

$$Z_{12} = 2\sqrt{2}\, \sigma_{12}^2 \left(\frac{\pi \mathbf{k} T}{\mu_{12}} \right)^{1/2} \mathbf{n}_1 \mathbf{n}_2 \qquad \text{[Eq. (2-54)]},$$

where, we recall, σ_{12} is the average collision diameter, μ_{12} is the reduced mass, and $\mathbf{n}_1$ and $\mathbf{n}_2$ are the concentrations in molecules per cubic centimeter, so that Z is in collisions per cubic centimeter per second. Thus Z_{12} can be written as

$$Z_{AB} = (\text{constant})\, T^{1/2}(\text{A})(\text{B})$$

for a reaction between molecules A and B. The numerical example of Section 2-6 gives typical Z_{AB} values of about 6×10^5 moles of collisions cm^{-3} sec^{-1} for A and B each at 1 atm pressure and 25°C, or about 3×10^{11} moles of collisions liter^{-1} sec^{-1} if A and B are each at a concentration of 1 mole liter^{-1}.

The second factor of Eq. (14-69) is arrived at as follows. We consider that E^* is to be provided by the kinetic energy of relative motion of two molecules making a head-on collision. This is equivalent to asking that a velocity c (in two dimensions) be such that $\frac{1}{2}mc^2 \geqslant E^*$, and we may therefore turn to Eq. (2-29):

$$\frac{dN(c)}{N_0} = \frac{m}{\mathbf{k}T}\, e^{-mc^2/2\mathbf{k}T} c\, dc.$$

That is, the probability that a single molecule will have one-dimensional velocities u and v such that $u^2 + v^2 = c^2$ is the same as the probability that two colliding molecules will have separate one-dimensional velocities such that $u_A{}^2 + u_B{}^2 = c^2$. If we make the change of variable $x = mc^2/2\mathbf{k}T$, Eq. (2.29) becomes

$$\frac{dN}{N_0} = e^{-x}\, dx.$$

[†] We write the Boltzmann constant as $\mathbf{k}$ in this chapter to avoid confusion with a rate constant.

This is now integrated from $x = x^*$ to $x = \infty$ to give

$$\frac{\Delta N}{N_0} = e^{-E^*/kT} \; ,$$

where $\Delta N/N_0$ is the fraction of molecules taken two at a time that have an impact kinetic energy equal to or greater than E^*.

Equation (14-69) now reads

$$\text{rate} = (\text{constant}) \; T^{1/2} \, e^{-E^*/RT} \, (\text{A})(\text{B})$$

and the corresponding bimolecular rate constant is then

$$k = A \, e^{-E^*/RT} = A' T^{1/2} \, e^{-E^*/RT} \; , \tag{14-70}$$

where

$$A' = 2 \sqrt{2} \, \sigma_{12}^2 \left(\frac{\pi \mathbf{k}}{\mu_{12}} \right)^{1/2} \left(\frac{N_0}{1000} \right)$$

(A' is reduced by a factor of 2 in the case of collisions between like molecules).

Equation (14-70) represents the initial achievement of collision theory and one which was at first very successful. It is the same as Eq. (14-60), which fits the temperature dependence data for the HI decomposition very well. Moreover the calculated A' value is remarkably close to the experimental one; if one takes σ to be 3.5 Å, one obtains 2.13×10^9 as compared to the experimental value of 2.06×10^9. Considering the sensitivity of A' and of E^* to small variations in the fitting of a best straight line to the plot of $\ln(k/T)$ versus $1/T$, agreement within even a factor of two or three would justify concluding that the collision theory was correct.

Data for a number of simple bimolecular reactions are summarized in Table 14-4 and the agreement between experimental and calculated A' values can be quite good. In many cases, however, the observed rate is definitely too small. This problem of "slow" reactions was recognized by around 1925, and Eq. (14-70) was modified by the addition of an empirical factor P called the *steric factor*, where $P = A_{\text{obs}}/A_{\text{calc}}$:

$$k = PA \, e^{-E^*/RT} \; . \tag{14-71}$$

The factor was justified qualitatively on the grounds that colliding molecules might not be suitably oriented for reaction; P then represents the fraction of energetically suitable collisions for which the orientation is also favorable.

The orientation explanation is perhaps acceptable for P values not much below about 0.1, but as shown in the last column of Table 14-4, there are many instances of much lower values, as low as 10^{-6}. There are in fact enough of such cases to put simple collision theory into serious difficulty. The matter is discussed further in the Commentary and Notes section.

Table 14-4. *Some Simple Bimolecular Reactions*[a]

Reaction	E^* (kcal mole^{-1})	log A' (liter mole^{-1} sec^{-1}) Observed	log A' (liter mole^{-1} sec^{-1}) Calculated	P
$2NO_2 \rightarrow 2NO + O_2$	26.6	8.42	9.85	0.038
$2NOCl \rightarrow 2NO + Cl_2$	25.8	9.51	9.47	1.1
$NO + ClNO_2 \rightarrow NOCl + NO_2$	6.6	7.73	9.76	0.01
$NO + O_3 \rightarrow NO_2 + O_2$	2.3	7.80	9.90	0.008
$NO_2 + O_3 \rightarrow NO_3 + O_2$	6.7	8.60	9.84	0.06
$NO + Cl_2 \rightarrow NOCl + Cl$	19.6	8.00	9.87	0.014
$CO + Cl_2 \rightarrow COCl + Cl$	51.3	8.5	9.87	0.04
$H + D_2 \rightarrow HD + H$	6.5	9.00	10.45	0.035
$Br + H_2 \rightarrow HBr + H$	17.6	9.31	10.23	0.12
$H + HBr \rightarrow H_2 + Br$	0.9	8.91	10.39	0.033
$H + Br_2 \rightarrow HBr + Br$	0.9	9.83	10.65	0.15
$Br + HBr \rightarrow Br_2 + H$	41.8	9.13	9.83	0.20
$CH_3 + H_2 \rightarrow CH_4 + H$	10.0	7.25	10.27	0.00095
$CH_3 + CHCl_3 \rightarrow CH_4 + CCl_3$	5.8	6.10	10.18	8.3×10^{-5}
2-Cyclopentadiene $\rightarrow$ dimer	14.5	3.39	9.91	3×10^{-7}

[a] Adapted from S. W. Benson, "Foundations of Chemical Kinetics." McGraw-Hill, New York, 1960.

14-7 Unimolecular Reactions

The considerable success of collision theory in the period 1910–1920 seemed to establish that elementary gas-phase reactions were always bimolecular, with the colliding molecules supplying the necessary activation energy. A puzzling difficulty developed, however, with the finding that many decomposition reactions were first-order kinetically, which implied that the reaction was unimolecular. Yet the Arrhenius equation was well obeyed, giving quite respectable activation energies. How, then, could a molecule undergoing unimolecular decomposition acquire the necessary energy to react? An early proposal was that radiation absorbed and emitted between molecules provided the activation energy, but this hypothesis did not stand up to detailed inspection—molecules often would not have an absorption band in the wavelength region for which light quanta would have the requisite energy, for example.

The solution to the problem came through a recognition that there could be a lag between the time a molecule gains energy E^* and its decomposition. The decomposition reaction is essentially one of the breaking of a particular chemical bond, and if the energy E^* were distributed among various vibrational degrees of freedom, only after a number of vibrational cycles might it happen to concentrate on a particular bond vibration. The picture is difficult to present graphically, but suppose that a molecule has four bonds, each with its own potential energy curve, as illustrated in Fig. 14-8(a), and that as a result of a collision the vibrational quantum states of the molecule are populated as shown. Bond 3 has the smallest dissociation limit, and we take this to be the one that will break first. Although bond 3 does not initially have sufficient vibrational energy for dissociation, the various vibrational modes are coupled to some extent, with the result that various redistributions of energy can occur. Eventually a situation such as shown in

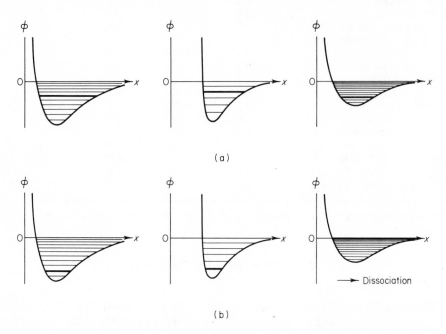

(a)

(b)

Fig. 14-8. *A molecule with three vibrational modes. (a) As populated immediately after a collision. (b) After energy redistribution has occurred, leading to bond breaking along mode 3.*

Fig. 14-8(b) occurs, in which bond 3 gains sufficient energy to dissociate on the next vibrational swing, and reaction occurs. During this waiting period the molecule has a total energy E^* or more, which is much above the average molecular energy, and if a second collision occurs, it will most probably take energy away rather than add to it. Thus if reaction is to occur, it must do so between the time of the collision which has brought the energy up to E^* and that of the next collision, and if the probability of this happening is small, then in effect a Boltzmann distribution of molecules of energy E^* or more is present, only slightly distorted by the disappearance of some molecules through reaction.

The kinetic scheme corresponding to this picture was proposed by F. Lindemann and J. Christiansen in 1922 and is as follows. The activating and deactivating processes are written

$$A + A \underset{k_{-2}}{\overset{k_2}{\rightleftharpoons}} A + A^*, \tag{14-72}$$

where A^* is a molecule which is sufficiently energized to react, and which does so with a certain probability, and hence according to the rate law

$$A^* \xrightarrow{k_1} P \text{ (products).} \tag{14-73}$$

Equations (14-72) and (14-73) may be treated according to the stationary state approximation described in Section 14-4C to give

$$\frac{d(P)}{dt} = \frac{k_1 k_2 (A)^2}{k_1 + k_{-2}(A)}. \tag{14-74}$$

If $k_{-2}(A) \gg k_1$, then Eq. (14-74) reduces to

$$\frac{d(P)}{dt} = k_1 K_2 (A) = k_{app}(A), \tag{14-75}$$

where K_2 is the equilibrium constant for process (14-72), and $K_2(A)$ is therefore the equilibrium concentration of A^*. This corresponds to the situation mentioned earlier, in which the rate of decomposition of energized molecules is slow enough that their distribution is the equilibrium or Boltzmann one. Equation (14-75) is pseudo first order, and thus accounts for the existence of first-order decomposition reactions.

A crucial test of the Lindemann–Christiansen mechanism lies in its prediction that at sufficiently small (A), Eq. (14-74) becomes

$$\frac{d(P)}{dt} = k_2 (A)^2 \tag{14-76}$$

or second order. The actual test is usually made in the following way. We write Eq. (14-74) in the form

$$\frac{d(P)}{dt} = \frac{k_1 k_2 (A)}{k_1 + k_{-2}(A)} (A) = k_{uni}(A). \tag{14-77}$$

That is, the initial rate of decomposition is reported as though it were a unimolecular reaction with rate constant k_{uni}. One then determines k_{uni} for various pressures and plots $k_{uni}/k_{uni,\infty}$ versus pressure, where $k_{uni,\infty}$ is the limiting value at high pressures [given by Eq. (14-75)]. This ratio should decrease toward zero at low pressures, and such behavior has indeed been found in a number of well-substantiated cases. Some data on the isomerization of cyclopropane are shown in Fig. 14-9.

It is not necessary that A collide with a second molecule of its own kind in order to be energized, and Eq. (14-72) may be written in the more general form

$$A + M \underset{k_{-2}}{\overset{k_2}{\rightleftharpoons}} A^* + M,$$

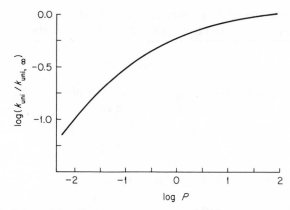

Fig. 14-9. *Variation of $k_{uni}/k_{uni,\infty}$ versus pressure for the isomerization of cyclopropane. P is in cm Hg and temperature is 490°C. [From H. Pritchard, R. Sowden, and A. Trotman-Dickenson, Proc. Roy. Soc.* **A217**, *563 (1953).]*

which leads to

$$\frac{d(P)}{dt} = \frac{k_1 k_2(M)}{k_1 + k_{-2}(M)} \text{(A)},$$

(14-78)

where M denotes some nonreactive gas present in large excess over A, so that A–A collisions are unimportant. The decomposition will now be first order at all pressures, since (M) in Eq. (14-78) is constant, but k_{uni} will vary as the pressure of (M) is altered in successive experiments. Most studies of the Lindemann–Christiansen mechanism are made in this manner nowadays, and collisional efficiencies as given by k_2 have been studied for a large number of inert gases.

The Arrhenius parameters for the high-pressure limiting rates of some unimolecular reactions are given in Table 14-5. In the case of the cyclopropane isomerization, investigators have compared k_2 for various inert gases with that for cyclopropane itself to obtain relative efficiencies of activation. Some values are He, 0.060; N_2, 0.060; CO, 0.072; H_2O, 0.79; and toluene, 1.59. It appears

Table 14-5. *Arrhenius Parameters for Some Unimolecular Reactions[a]*

Reaction	log A (sec^{-1})	E^* (kcal mole^{-1})
Cyclopropane → propylene	15.17	65.0
cis-Isostilbene → *trans*-isostilbene	12.78	42.8
$CH_3CH_2Cl \rightarrow C_2H_4 + HCl$	14.6	60.8
$CCl_3-CH_3 \rightarrow CCl_2=CH_2 + HCl$	12.5	47.9
t-Butyl alcohol → isobutene + H_2O	14.68	65
$ClCOOC_2H_5 \rightarrow C_2H_5Cl + CO_2$	10.7	29.4

[a] Adapted from S. W. Benson, "Foundations of Chemical Kinetics." McGraw-Hill, New York, 1960.

that the more internal degrees of freedom a molecule has, the greater is its ability to transfer energy in a collision, which supports the idea that internal energy as well as translational energy transfers are important.

A numerical illustration of the treatment presented here is as follows. The high-pressure limiting rate for the decomposition of azomethane is found to obey the Arrhenius equation with $A = 9.228 \times 10^{15}$ and $E^* = 51.130$ kcal mole^{-1}. At $603°K$ $k_{uni}/k_{uni,\infty} = 0.10$ at $P = 0.2$ Torr. First, from Eq. (14-75),

$$k_{app} = k_{uni,\infty} = k_1 K_2 = 9.228 \times 10^{15} e^{-51,130/(1.987)(603)}$$

or $k_1 K_2 = 0.00273$ sec^{-1}. Then from Eq. (14-77),

$$\frac{k_{uni}}{k_{uni,\infty}} = 0.10 = \frac{0.2}{(k_1/k_{-2}) + 0.2}$$

or $k_1/k_{-2} = (0.2/0.10) - 0.2 = 1.8$ Torr. Alternatively, $k_2 = (k_1 K_2)(k_{-2}/k_1) = 0.00273/1.8 = 1.52 \times 10^{-3}$ Torr^{-1} sec^{-1}. Thus the experimental data give values for $k_1 K_2$ and for k_2 or k_1/k_{-2}; it is not possible to obtain k_1 or K_2 alone, however, unless some assumptions are made. One could, for example, assume that k_1 corresponds to a single vibrational frequency, or to about 10^{13} sec^{-1}, in which case $K_2 = 2.73 \times 10^{-16}$ and $k_{-2} = 5.5 \times 10^{12}$ Torr^{-1} sec^{-1}.

An interesting point now arises. One might expect K_2 to be given simply by the Boltzmann factor for the probability of a molecule of A having energy E^*, or $\exp(-E^*/RT)$. The observed activation energy of 51 kcal mole^{-1} then leads to a theoretical value for K_2 of 3.0×10^{-19}, or much smaller than the estimate based on $k_1 = 10^{13}$ sec^{-1}. It is not reasonable to take k_1 as any larger than this estimate, so it appears that the population of energized molecules is at least 1000 times that expected. The qualitative explanation is that the energized state is more probable than otherwise expected because of the many degrees of freedom among which E^* can be distributed; that is, its entropy as well as its energy must be taken into account. Some further discussion of this aspect is given in the Commentary and Notes section.

14-8 Absolute Rate Theory. The Activated Complex

A. The Reaction Profile

The material of the preceding section leads rather naturally into an alternative treatment of reaction rates. The Lindemann–Christiansen mechanism deals with molecules A* having within them enough energy to react but able to do so only at some rate k_1 determined by the speed with which E^* can localize on the particular bond that is to break. We now consider the simplest possible situation, namely a reaction of the type $A' + A-A \rightarrow A'-A + A$, where A is an atom and the prime might denote isotopic labeling that distinguishes A' from A. There is now only one bond in the reacting molecule, and if sufficient energy is present, it should break on the next vibrational swing. Further, the concentration of energized molecules should now be given by a simple Boltzmann factor. There is thus the possibility of making an absolute calculation of a reaction rate.

A theory along these lines was developed by H. Eyring and M. Polanyi in the period 1930–1935. Consider the reaction

$$H' + H-H \rightarrow H'-H + H,$$

where H′ might in fact be a deuterium atom. Assume that colliding H′ and H_2 molecules approach along a common line through the centers, so that various stages of reaction would be

$$H' + H-H \rightarrow H'---H--H \rightarrow H'--H--H \rightarrow H'--H---H \rightarrow H'-H + H.$$
$$\quad 1 \qquad\quad 2 \quad 3 \quad 1 \qquad 2 \quad 3 \quad 1 \qquad 2 \qquad 3$$

As atom 1 approaches, or the distance r_{12} decreases, the bond length between atoms 2 and 3, or r_{23}, begins to increase. The maximum potential energy must be at a point such that $r_{12} = r_{23}$, corresponding to the energized molecule which, being symmetric, might break up either to return to H′ + H_2 or to give the product H′H + H. Essentially, the kinetic energy of approach of H′ and H_2 is converted into potential energy, and it is possible to construct a diagram illustrating the situation as shown in Fig. 14-10. The skewed coordinates are used as a clever

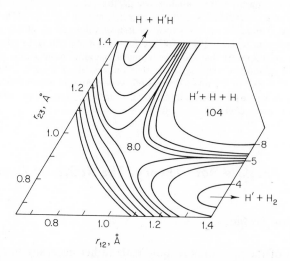

Fig. 14-10. *Interconversion of relative translational and vibrational energy in the* H + H_2 *system.* [*From R. E. Weston, Jr., J. Chem. Phys.* **31**, *892 (1959).*]

graphical device whereby the interconversion of kinetic and potential energy in the H′—H—H system exactly corresponds to that for a frictionless ball rolling on the surface shown. A three-dimensional model of the surface would have the appearance of two valleys which interconnect through a high saddle point. The approach of H′ to H_2 would be given by motion from right to left up the r_{12} valley. If the atoms of H_2 were vibrating as well, then r_{23} would be oscillating, and the approach path would be given by the wavy line shown in Fig. 14-11(a). In this

H + H'H

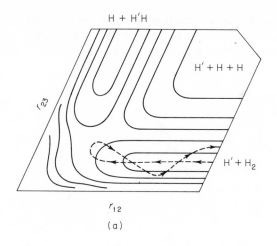

H' + H + H

H' + H$_2$

r_{23}

r_{12}

(a)

H + H'H

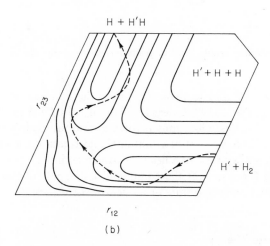

H' + H + H

H' + H$_2$

r_{23}

r_{12}

(b)

Fig. 14-11. *Possible trajectories (see Fig. 14-10).*

case there is insufficient energy to reach the saddle point, and the system would be "reflected" back on itself, the motions being the same as for a marble which is impelled up the valley, reaches its highest point, and then rolls back.

The contours of Fig. 14-10 are theoretical ones—the system is simple enough to allow reasonably accurate quantum mechanical calculations. The saddle point is placed at 8.0 kcal energy above that for separated H' and H$_2$, so that if the two molecules approach with slightly more than this kinetic energy, a simple path leading to reaction would be that illustrated in Fig. 14-11(b)—note that the product H'H has in this case retained some vibrational energy. Such a detailed analysis of how an elementary reaction occurs will be called the *intimate mechanism* of a reaction. The reaction profile is the plot of potential energy against degree of advancement of the elementary reaction; in the present case the degree of advancement might be given by $\nu = r_{12} - r_{23}$, so that a plot for each ν of the minimum potential energy versus ν would look as shown in Fig. 14-12.

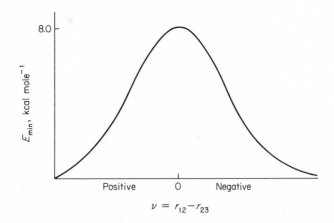

Fig. 14-12. *The reaction profile. Plot of minimum energy versus degree of advancement of reaction.*

At the saddle point the system corresponds to the molecule $H'-H-H$, where each bond length is about 0.93 Å instead of the usual 0.74 Å in H_2. The species $H'-H-H$ is stable against vibrations involving motions against the walls of the saddle point; it should have a set of vibrational and rotational energy states. It is, however, a compound with an Achilles heel—there is one mode of vibration that meets no restoring force so that the compound falls apart in this mode. Such a compound is called a *transition state* or an *activated complex*.

B. Transition-State Theory

The relatively pure theoretical approach that can be made to the $H + H_2$ system is simply not possible with more complicated systems; it is difficult even to treat the $H + H_2$ case if the approach paths of the molecules are at an angle to each other. However, H. Eyring and others have developed this picture into a form that provides a framework for treating reactions generally. Although detailed reaction trajectories are abandoned, it is assumed that the activated complex is a distinct chemical species in equilibrium with the reactants, but a special kind of species in which one degree of vibrational freedom has become open, that is, corresponds to translation along the reaction coordinate (a parameter equivalent to $r_{12} - r_{23}$ in the $H + H_2$ case). The activated complex is not the same as the energized molecule of the preceding section; the latter possessed the energy E^* but might be anywhere on a reaction coordinate system, such as high on the side of a valley in Fig. 14-10, while the activated complex has the configuration corresponding to the saddle point.

The procedure is to write the intimate mechanism for an elementary reaction as

$$A + B \overset{K^\ddagger}{=} [AB]^\ddagger,$$

(14-79)

where $[AB]^\ddagger$ denotes the activated complex, which then gives products

$$[AB]^\ddagger \overset{k_1}{\to} \text{products}.$$

(14-80)

In the case of the Lindemann–Christiansen mechanism, k_1 could not be determined *a priori*, but the special nature of $[AB]^\ddagger$ now makes it possible for us to do so. The more rigorous treatment is given in the Special Topics section, but essentially k_1 is the frequency with which the open vibrational mode of the activated complex can lead to reaction and is approximated by $\mathbf{k}T/h$.

The rate of process (14-80) is then

$$\frac{d[AB]^\ddagger}{dt} = -\frac{\mathbf{k}T}{h}[AB]^\ddagger.$$

(14-81)

The overall reaction rate is then

$$R_f = -\frac{d(A)}{dt} = \frac{\mathbf{k}T}{h}K^\ddagger(A)(B),$$

(14-82)

and the rate constant for an elementary reaction becomes

$$k = \frac{\mathbf{k}T}{h}K^\ddagger.$$

(14-83)

$K^\ddagger$ is regarded as a normal equilibrium constant, and Eq. (7-11) therefore gives

$$k = \frac{\mathbf{k}T}{h}\exp\left(-\frac{\Delta G^{0\ddagger}}{RT}\right)$$

(14-84)

or

$$k = \frac{\mathbf{k}T}{h}\exp\left(\frac{\Delta S^{0\ddagger}}{R}\right)\exp\left(-\frac{\Delta H^{0\ddagger}}{RT}\right).$$

(14-85)

C.   Applications of Transition-State Theory

The statistical mechanical methods of Chapter 6 can be applied to estimate $\Delta G^{0\ddagger}$, that is, the standard free energy of the activated complex. One needs to list the number of rotational and vibrational degrees of freedom and make a guess as to the characteristic rotational and vibrational temperatures or the moment of inertia of the activated complex and the spacings of its vibrational levels. The same can be done for the reactants, so it is possible to make reasonable calculations of $\Delta G^{0\ddagger}$ in simple cases. The procedure is developed in more detail in the Special Topics section.

More often, one uses the experimental rate constant and activation energy to calculate $\Delta S^{0\ddagger}$ from Eq. (14-85). The resulting value then allows some conclusions to be drawn about the structure and general chemical nature of the activated complex. Note first that according to Eq. (14-85) a plot of $\ln k$ versus $1/T$ gives $\Delta H^{0\ddagger}$ rather than the E^* of the Arrhenius equation. This might be thought to be a distinguishing feature between the collision and transition-state theories, but apart from more subtle aspects, the formal difference between the two is only RT, and in the absence of accurate independent means of determining the minimum energy for reaction, the distinction is essentially useless.

We can illustrate the application of statistical thermodynamics to transition-state theory by means of the following sample calculation. Experiment gives $\log A' = 9.52$ for the reaction $H_2 + I_2 \rightarrow 2HI$, or $A = 7.94 \times 10^{10}$ mole liter^{-1} sec^{-1} at 575°K, and according to transition state theory,

$$A = \frac{\mathbf{k}T}{h} \exp\left(\frac{\Delta S^{0\ddagger}}{R}\right), \tag{14-86}$$

where $\Delta S^{0\ddagger}$ is the standard entropy change for the reaction

$$H_2 + I_2 = [(HI)_2]^{\ddagger}. \tag{14-87}$$

The questions of mechanism discussed earlier do not enter into the picture at the moment; entropy being a state function, the value of $\Delta S^{0\ddagger}$ does not depend on the path whereby the transition state $[(HI)_2]^{\ddagger}$ is formed. The quantity $\mathbf{k}T/h$ has the value 1.20×10^{13} sec^{-1} at 575°K and we calculate the experimental $\Delta S^{0\ddagger}$ to be -9.97 cal °K^{-1} mole^{-1}.

Alternatively, $\Delta S^{0\ddagger}$ may be estimated from statistical thermodynamics as a sum of translational, rotational, and vibrational contributions. First, the translational contribution is obtained from the Sackur–Tetrode equation

$$S^0_{\text{trans}} = R \ln(T^{5/2} M^{3/2}) - 2.31 \qquad \text{[Eq. (6-80)]}.$$

Substitution of $T = 575$°K and of the appropriate molecular weights gives 31.3, 35.8, and 35.8 cal °K^{-1} mole^{-1} for the entropies of H_2, I_2, and $[(HI)_2]^{\ddagger}$ at 1 atm pressure. We want, however, to use a standard state of 1 mole liter^{-1} rather than the 47.2 liter mole^{-1} for 1 atm at 575°K. The correction is then $R \ln(1/47.2) = -7.66$ cal °K^{-1} mole^{-1} and yields 23.7, 28.1, and 28.1 cal °K^{-1} mole^{-1} for the corrected entropies. Then $\Delta S^{0\ddagger}_{\text{trans}} = -23.7$ cal °K^{-1} mole^{-1}.

We proceed to obtain the rotational entropies. The entropy S_{rot} is given by

$$S_{\text{rot}} = R + R \ln \frac{T}{\sigma \theta_{\text{rot}}} \qquad \text{[Eq. (6-84)]},$$

where, for completeness, σ is a degeneracy factor given by the number of equivalent ways of orienting the molecule in space; $\sigma = 2$ for each of the molecules involved here. From Table 6-1, $\theta_{\text{rot}} = 87.5$°K for H_2 and 0.0538°K for I_2, giving 4.4 and 19.0 cal °K^{-1} mole^{-1} for the respective rotational entropies at 575°K.

14-8 Absolute Rate Theory. The Activated Complex

We have now reached a point where some specific structure must be assumed for the activated complex $[(HI)_2]^{\ddagger}$. Equation (14-66) suggests that the structure may be the linear molecule $I-H-H-I$. We expect the bonds to be somewhat longer than normal and guess the $I-H$ bond to be about 1.75 Å and the $H-H$ bond to be 0.97 Å, so that the iodine and hydrogen atoms are 2.23 Å and 0.48 Å from the center of mass, respectively. The moment of inertia of the molecule is then

$$I^{\ddagger} = \frac{2}{N_0}\,[(127)(2.23 \times 10^{-8})^2 + (1)(0.48 \times 10^{-8})^2] = 2.09 \times 10^{-37} \quad \text{g cm}^2.$$

Recalling Eq. (4-74), we obtain $\theta_{rot} = 0.0193°K$ and thence $S^{\ddagger}_{rot} = 22.5$ cal $°K^{-1}$ mole^{-1}. Therefore $\Delta S^{\ddagger}_{rot} = 22.5 - 4.4 - 19.0 = -0.9$ cal $°K^{-1}$ mole^{-1}.

The vibrational entropy of a molecule is given by

$$S_{vib} = R\left[\frac{x}{e^x - 1} - \ln(1 - e^{-x})\right] \qquad \text{[Eq. (6-86)]},$$

where $x = \theta_{vib}/T$. Table 6-1 gives θ_{vib} as $5986°K$ and $306.8°K$ for H_2 and I_2, respectively. For H_2, S_{vib} is negligible in view of the large θ_{vib} and for I_2, $S_{vib} = 3.2$ cal $°K^{-1}$ mole^{-1}. The molecule $I-H-H-I$, being linear, has $(3)(4) - 3 - 2 = 7$ degrees of vibrational freedom, of which, however, one is open or corresponds to translation along the reaction coordinate. We guess that at least three of the remaining six vibrational degrees of freedom are low in fundamental frequency ($I-H-H-I$ is, after all, a rather weakly bonded molecule at best) and assign them a frequency of 100 cm^{-1} each; the other three frequencies we assume to be high enough that their contribution to the entropy of the molecule is small. From Section 4-12, $\theta_{vib} = h\nu_0/k$, so that for the low-energy vibrations $\theta_{vib} = 144°K$; x is then 0.25 and application of Eq. (6-86) yields $S_{vib} = (3)(4.76) = 14.3$ cal $°K^{-1}$ mole^{-1}. Then $\Delta S^{\ddagger}_{vib} = 14.3 - 3.2 = 11.1$ cal $°K^{-1}$ mole^{-1}.

We now assemble $\Delta S^{0\ddagger}$ as $-23.7 - 0.9 + 11.1 = -13.5$ cal $°K^{-1}$ mole^{-1}. We have thus calculated a value for $\Delta S^{0\ddagger}$ which is within about 3 cal $°K^{-1}$ mole^{-1} of the experimental value, which corresponds to a factor of 5 in A. This example illustrates both the power and the weakness of the approach.

We are able to explain experimental activation entropies theoretically. Herschbach et al. (1956) have carried out a number of similar calculations of $\Delta S^{0\ddagger}$ for various reactions of the type listed in Table 14-4 and again were able to obtain order-of-magnitude agreement with the experimental frequency or Arrhenius A factors in almost every case. The reactions treated included several with very low steric or P factors and the effect could be seen to arise as a natural consequence of the structure and degree of stiffness of the activated complex as compared to that of the reactants.

On the other hand, the example also illustrates that there is a considerable degree of latitude in the choice of moments of inertia and vibrational frequencies for the activated complex, so that agreement of theory with experiment can be rather subjective. For example, it was thought for many years that the activated complex in the $H_2 + I_2 \rightarrow 2HI$ reaction was a four-centered molecule

and about equally successful statistical calculations were made on this assumption.

One other example might be given. In the case of a unimolecular reaction one has, in terms of transition-state theory,

$$A \overset{K}{=} [A]^{\ddagger}, \qquad [A]^{\ddagger} \overset{k_1}{\to} \text{products,}$$

where k is still given by Eq. (14-85). From the example of the preceding section $k = 0.00273$ sec^{-1} for the decomposition of azomethane at 603°K, and the Arrhenius constant $A = 9.23 \times 10^{15}$. Equation (14-86) then gives $\Delta S^{0\ddagger} = 13.2$ cal °K^{-1} mole^{-1}—a fairly positive value. From the statistical thermodynamic point of view, $\Delta S^{0\ddagger}_{\text{trans}}$ should be zero since there is no change in the number of species in the formation of the activated complex. Since A and $[A]^{\ddagger}$ must be very similar in moment of inertia, $\Delta S^{\ddagger}_{\text{rot}}$ should also be zero, or at best a small positive number if $[A]^{\ddagger}$ is somewhat expanded in size over A as a result of its high energy content. The main contribution to $\Delta S^{0\ddagger}$ must then come from $\Delta S^{\ddagger}_{\text{vib}}$. This last should be negligibly small for A, but evidently the activated complex must have one or more vibrational modes of very low θ_{vib} value, that is, some low-frequency vibrations corresponding to very weak bonds.

COMMENTARY AND NOTES

14-CN-1   Termolecular Reactions

All elementary reactions considered so far have been bimolecular or unimolecular, and even the so-called unimolecular processes are explained physically on the basis of activation by bimolecular collisions. The reason elementary reactions of a higher order are not usually important is simply that their frequency factor is expected to be small. The situation may be examined from either the point of view of collision theory or from that of transition-state theory.

Simple collision theory treats molecules as hard spheres so that the duration of a collision is so very short that the chance of a third molecule hitting a colliding pair is small. Thus we have a problem in defining exactly what is meant by a triple collision; roughly, we want the chance of three molecules being within a molecular diameter of each other. One way of estimating this is to assume that a collision between two molecules lasts about one vibrational period, or 10^{-13} sec. The collision frequency Z_{12} for two molecules is about 10^{11}(A)(B), in liter mole^{-1} sec^{-1}, and the concentration of a collision complex (AB) is then (rate of formation of AB) $\times$ (lifetime of AB) $= 10^{-13}Z_{12}$. The frequency of collisions between (AB) and another molecule C is then about 10^{11}(AB)(C) or $(10^{-13})(10^{11})^2$(A)(B)(C) $= 10^{9}$(A)(B)(C). The frequency factor A for a termolecular reaction should then be about 10^{9} liter^2 mole^{-2} sec^{-1} as compared to the value of 10^{11} liter mole^{-1} sec^{-1} for a bimolecular reaction. The rate constant for a termolecular reaction is thus expected to be about one-hundredth that for a bimolecular one, others factors being the same.

According to transition-state theory, the elementary process is

$$A + B + C = [ABC]^{\ddagger}$$

and $\Delta S^{0\ddagger}$ is expected to be more negative than usual simply because of the loss in translational entropy. The numerical example of the preceding section gave S^0_{trans} as about 36 cal $°K^{-1}$ mole^{-1}, so the translational entropy contribution to $\Delta S^{0\ddagger}$ for a termolecular reaction should be about $36 - (36 + 36 + 36) = -72$ cal $°K^{-1}$ as compared to -36 cal $°K^{-1}$ in the case of a bimolecular reaction. The difference, -36 cal $°K^{-1}$ mole^{-1}, corresponds to a factor of 10^{-7} in the $\exp(-\Delta S^{0\ddagger}/R)$ term. However, $[ABC]^{\ddagger}$ has rotational and vibrational entropy, and more detailed calculations again indicate that A for a termolecular reaction should be about 10^{-2}–10^{-3} that for a bimolecular reaction.

Termolecular reactions should thus be considerably slower than bimolecular reactions of the same activation energy, and it is for this reason that the elementary reactions making up a reaction mechanism are ordinarily restricted to bimolecular ones. There is one type of reaction that can *only* occur as a termolecular one, however. If two atoms are to combine to give a molecule,

$$A + A = A_2 ,$$

a third body must be present to carry off the energy of the A—A bond—otherwise the atoms can only fly apart again. The process must then be

$$A + A + M = A_2 + M.$$

For example, in writing the mechanism for reaction (14-47), the step

$$2Br + M \rightarrow Br_2 + M \qquad (14\text{-}88)$$

was involved. Further, by the principle of microscopic reversibility (see Section 7-CN-1), the reverse process must occur by the same path:

$$Br_2 + M \rightarrow 2Br + M.$$

The rates of a number of termolecular reactions have been measured. That for reaction (14-88), for example, shows nearly zero activation energy (as expected, since the two atoms need only proceed to form the Br—Br bond) and a frequency factor $A = 10^9$ liter^2 mole^{-2} sec^{-1} dependent somewhat on the nature of M. For the reaction $O + O_2 + M \rightarrow O_3 + M$ the activation energy is again virtually zero but A is only about 10^8. Collision theory would explain the lower value in terms of a steric factor. The frequency factor may be quite low if M is also a reactant; thus for $2NO + O_2 \rightarrow 2NO_2$, A is only 10^3. At this point a transition state theory examination of the rotational and vibrational entropies of the reactants and the activated complex would be needed.

14-CN-2 Collision versus Transition-State Theory

The collision theory for gas-phase reactions presents a very direct, indisputable physical picture of how molecules react—they must collide and must do so with the proper orientation and with a certain minimum energy E^*. One difficulty is in treating the so-called steric factor P. Not only does the simple geometric interpretation become implausible in the case of very small P values such as 10^{-6}, but this interpretation provides virtually no way to make calculational estimates or correlations.

A major further development of collision theory took place as a result of some observations of the rates of unimolecular reactions. According to the Lindemann mechanism, the maximum possible rate for a unimolecular reaction would be observed if each energized molecule decomposed on the next vibrational swing, which means that

$$k_{\text{uni},\infty} = \frac{\mathbf{k}T}{h} e^{-E^*/RT}.$$

Thus the maximum possible frequency factor for a unimolecular reaction should be about 10^{13} sec^{-1}. However, the observed Arrhenius A parameter is over 10^{15} for cyclopropane isomerization (see Table 14-5) and is 9.23×10^{15} for the decomposition of azomethane (from the numerical illustration in Section 14-7). It appeared at first that something was seriously wrong.

The explanation that was developed by O. Rice, H. Ramsperger, and L. Kassel around 1930 is the following. G. Lewis had pointed out several years previously that it was not necessarily true that E^* came only from the kinetic energy of relative motion of the colliding molecules, since it would also be supplied by their internal energy. The resulting modification of Eq. (14-70) gives

$$k = A \frac{(E^*/RT)^{(f/2)-1}}{(\tfrac{1}{2}f - 1)!} e^{-E^*/RT}, \qquad (14\text{-}89)$$

where f is the number of degrees of freedom available to supply E^*. The equation reduces to the usual one if $f = 2$, but has the effect of increasing the apparent A value for larger values of f. It should be mentioned that f is actually the number of so-called square terms, that is, terms contributing to the equipartition energy, so that each vibrational degree of freedom contributes 2 toward f. Thus the cases of very high preexponential or A factors could easily be explained—in the cyclopropane case it would only be necessary to say that about one-third of the molecular vibrations contribute to E^* in addition to the impact kinetic energy.

There remained some discrepancies between the Lindemann mechanism and the experimentally observed variation of $k_{\text{uni}}/k_{\text{uni},\infty}$ with pressure, and one of the contributions of Rice *et al.* was to further suppose that k_1 of Eq. (14-73) depended on the actual energy possessed by A^*. That is, the greater it was in excess of the minimum amount E^*, the greater the probability of the necessary energy localizing on the particular bond that was to break before a deactivating collision occurred.

Thus if energy E was distributed among s vibrational degrees of freedom, $s \leqslant f$, the conclusion was that for that particular molecule

$$k_1 = k_1' \left(\frac{E - E^*}{E} \right)^{s-1}.$$

An elaborate integration procedure is necessary to sum this expression over all possible E values, that is, from E^* to infinity, but the results have given reasonably good detailed agreement with experiment.

There appear to remain no fundamental difficulties with collision theory—only the problem that it is rather difficult to estimate steric factors, that is, very low Arrhenius A values.

Transition state theory draws its justification from the type of absolute rate calculations that can be made on simple reactions such as that of $H' + H_2 \rightarrow H'H + H$. In actual practice one is dealing with reactions for which the exact structure of the activated complex can only be guessed. There is generally sufficient flexibility to account for any observed $\Delta S^{0\ddagger}$, and it is therefore difficult to say that the theory has really been verified. On the other hand, its formalism is very convenient and allows for a pleasing structural approach to the detailed reaction path.

One or two ambiguities might be mentioned. If we have a reaction

$$A + B = C + D,$$

then for the forward rate

$$A + B \overset{K^{\ddagger}}{=} [AB]^{\ddagger} \overset{k_1}{\rightarrow} C + D, \qquad R_f = \frac{kT}{h}([AB]^{\ddagger}).$$

Similarly, for the reverse rate,

$$C + D \overset{K'^{\ddagger}}{=} [CD]^{\ddagger} \overset{k_1'}{\rightarrow} A + B, \qquad R_b = \frac{kT}{h}([CD]^{\ddagger}).$$

Yet, according to the principle of microscopic reversibility (Section 7-CN-1), the forward and back reactions should follow the same detailed path, which seems to imply that $[AB]^{\ddagger}$ is the same as $[CD]^{\ddagger}$, yet if this is so, R_f should always equal R_b, which cannot be true. It has been argued that $[AB]^{\ddagger}$ and $[CD]^{\ddagger}$ are perhaps the same structurally but differ in their directions of motion along the reaction path. The analogy can be made to two billiard balls in collision. If ball A has been propelled to a head-on collision with stationary ball B, the two balls at the moment of collision would look the same as if ball B had been propelled against stationary ball A. Yet in the first case A remains stationary after the collision, whereas in the second case B remains stationary, as illustrated in Fig. 14-13.

A second question is that of whether an activated complex can really be in thermodynamic equilibrium with its surroundings. Collision theory certainly implies that the energized molecules which react do not necessarily have an equilibrium distribution of energy among the internal degrees of freedom, although they can proceed to react. It has been suggested that a species [AB] of energy

659

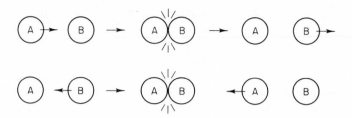

Fig. 14-13.

just below E^* cannot react, so that its population *will* be given by equilibrium thermodynamics, and that the perturbation from equilibrium when [AB] gains a further small increment of energy to become [AB] is negligibly small. To decide this question we must find some independent means of measuring the free energy of $[AB]^\ddagger$, and this does not seem possible to do. One other ambiguity is mentioned in the Special Topics section.

On the whole, it appears that because of the desirable features of each, both theories will remain in active use. Very likely, as each is developed further the differences between them will diminish. Thus the introduction of Eq. (14-89) adds to collision theory some of the flavor of the statistical mechanical calculation of $\Delta S_{\text{vib}}^\ddagger$, while for the reaction $H' + H_2 \rightarrow H'H + H$ absolute rate theory is not really very different from collision theory.

14-CN-3 *Molecular Beam and Related Studies*

Equation (14-70) was derived on the assumption that molecules whose mutual kinetic energy of approach exceeds a critical energy E^* react whereas if the energy is less than E^* no reaction occurs. A more general treatment of the rate constant k of a bimolecular reaction is

$$k = \left[\frac{8}{\pi\mu(\mathbf{k}T)^3}\right]^{1/2} \int_0^\infty e^{-E/RT}\sigma(E, T)E\, dE, \qquad (14\text{-}90)$$

where σ denotes the effective cross section or target area of a molecule for a reactive collision and is considered to be a function of the relative kinetic energy E and of temperature.

Molecular beam experiments have made possible the determination of $\sigma(E, T)$ for some simple reactions of the $A + BC \rightarrow AB + C$ type. A molecular beam, that is, a collimated beam of molecules, can be formed if vapor from a (usually hot) reservoir is allowed to escape into an evacuated chamber through a pin hole and series of slits. A velocity selector, which might be of the type illustrated schematically in Fig. 2-12, then selects or permits to pass only molecules of a predetermined velocity. A second molecular beam of some other type of molecule is allowed to cross the first beam, and detectors scan for both the angular direction and the energy of the product molecules. The active region of the apparatus must, of course, be under high vacuum so that the beams are not scattered by adventitious molecules.

Experimental difficulties have limited the number and type of systems studied. Much work has been done, for example, with alkali metal vapors and halide-containing molecules because of the ease with which the products are produced and detected. Reactions that have been investigated include

$$K + HBr \rightarrow H + KBr, \qquad K + Br_2 \rightarrow Br + KBr,$$
$$Cs + RbCl \rightarrow Rb + CsCl, \qquad Ar^+ + D_2 \rightarrow D + ArD^+.$$

The angular distribution of the products or the *reactive scattering* is often such that the product AB moves in the same general direction as did the reactant BC. Sometimes, however, a collision complex is formed, as with the reaction of an alkali metal atom with an alkali halide molecule; the complex rotates sufficiently before breaking up that the departure directions of the products lose correlation with the approach directions of the reactants.

Since the kinetic energy of the product AB can be measured, one learns what fraction of the reaction energy appears as kinetic energy and what fraction remains as vibrational excitation. Also, by introducing a small amount of inert gas into the reaction chamber so that the escaping product is apt to make one or more collisions before being detected, one can learn about the way in which vibrational excitation energy is lost in collisions. These and other types of studies have indicated that molecules, especially polyatomic ones, tend to lose their excess vibrational energy in a few large increments rather than in many small ones. Current research is thus providing a great deal of detailed information about how gas-phase molecules interact with each other.

14-CN-4 Chemical Estimation of Arrhenius Parameters

We can often use a somewhat chemical approach to estimate Arrhenius A factors and energies of activation. This is especially true for gas-phase reactions involving small molecules and molecular fragments or free radicals. Thus recombination reactions of the type of Eq. (14-88) generally have zero activation energy, so that their rates can be estimated from the collision theory value of A for a termolecular reaction. Conversely, the activation energy for the reverse reaction must simply be the dissociation or bond energy for Br_2, and its rate can therefore be estimated either directly or from the equilibrium constant and the calculation for the forward rate.

Reasoning of this type serves to eliminate a reaction such as $H_2 + M \rightarrow 2H + M$ from consideration in the mechanism for the formation of HBr discussed in Section 14-4D. The bond energy for H_2 is 104 kcal mole^{-1}, which gives the *minimum* activation energy for the dissociation reaction; its rate is thus calculated to be negligibly small.

More general application of this approach by Benson (1968) has allowed the estimation of what amounts to energies of formation of various reactive intermediate species, such as free radicals. Thus the activation energy for the dissociation of ethane gives an approximate value for the energy of formation of $CH_3\cdot$, confirmed by a zero activation energy for recombination of the radicals. This energy may then be used in connection with any other reaction producing $CH_3\cdot$ to estimate the minimum activation energy. This approach is of great help in the working out of mechanisms for complex reactions since it permits a semiquantitative estimate of the rate constants for the various imaginable elementary reactions with the result that a number of otherwise plausible steps are eliminated from consideration.

14-CN-5 Explosions

An explosion is a reaction which proceeds at an accelerating rate; once initiated it goes to completion very quickly and essentially cannot be stopped. The subject is obviously one of very great practical importance, ranging from the engineering of internal combustion engines to the devising of commercial and military explosives. The subject is also a very difficult one for the gas kineticist. A mixture of hydrogen and oxygen at about 500°C will react slowly and in a well-behaved way at a low pressure, say a few Torr. If the pressure is raised to about 10 Torr, an explosion occurs and this behavior continues up to a pressure of perhaps 20 Torr, above which the mixture again reacts in a normal, nonexplosive fashion. If the pressure is raised further to about 10 atm pressure, the mixture is again explosive! A diagram showing these explosion limits is given in Fig. 14-14. The problem is to explain the behavior.

One general explanation for explosive reaction is simply that if the process is exothermic, the heat released may not be able to escape rapidly enough, and so the reaction mixture heats up, thereby increasing all reaction rates, which then increases the rate of heat production, which further accelerates the rise in temperature and speed of reaction. Such an explosion is called a *thermal explosion*. There is no doubt that this is one important mechanism, but it cannot explain the complexity of behavior shown in the figure.

A very common characteristic of systems which can produce explosions is that a so-called *branching chain reaction* is present. Thus in the reaction between H_2 and O_2 some of the postulated steps are

(1) $H_2 + wall \rightarrow H (on wall) + H,$

(2) $H + O_2 \rightarrow HO + O,$

(3) $O + H_2 \rightarrow HO + H,$

(4) $HO + H_2 \rightarrow HOH + H.$

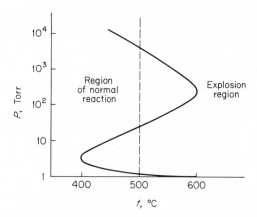

Fig. 14-14. *Explosion limits of a stoichiometric mixture of* $H_2 + O_2$. *(From S. W. Benson, "The Foundations of Chemical Kinetics," Copyright 1960, McGraw-Hill, New York. Used with permission of McGraw-Hill Book Co.)*

Steps 2 and 3 are said to be branching in that one radical produces two new ones, so that the effect is to multiply the number of chain-carrying intermediates present. All of the various radicals may recombine at the wall of the container to give stable species, and the geometry and nature of the vessel is therefore very important.

The general explanation of Fig. 14-14 seems to be that the first explosion limit is reached because, as pressure is increased at constant temperature, the concentration of radicals has become high enough that their diffusional deactivation at the walls is insufficient to control the reaction. The reaction becomes ordinary again at a still higher pressure, perhaps because of the onset of a termolecular process which interferes with the chain, such as the reaction

$$H + O_2 + M \rightarrow HO_2 + M,$$

which replaces the very active radical H by the much less active one HO_2. The final high-pressure explosion region is then probably a thermal explosion one.

14-CN-6   Free Radicals

A number of the reaction mechanisms cited invoke free radical species, that is, chemically unsaturated atoms or molecules such as $H\cdot$, $Br\cdot$, $CH_3\cdot$, and so on. Many of these are quite definite chemical substances in the sense that independent measurement of their physical and chemical properties is possible. The ion Br_2^- for example, may be detected in flash photolysis studies as a transient absorbing species, and its absorption spectrum has been determined.

There is both direct and indirect independent evidence for the existence of hydrocarbon free radicals. Around 1930 F. Paneth and co-workers showed that the thermal decomposition of lead tetraethyl or mercury dimethyl produced a gaseous product which, on being swept downstream by a flow of inert gas such as nitrogen, was capable of reacting with a film of lead to regenerate the lead alkyl compound. With other metals the corresponding metal alkyl would be produced. There is no doubt that methyl and ethyl radicals were present. Some organic radicals are, in fact, quite stable; the best-known case is perhaps that of triphenylmethyl, produced by the dissociation of hexaphenylethane, and stable enough in solution to be observed both spectrophotometrically and by means of its paramagnetism. Nitrogen dioxide, NO_2, is a common, very stable free radical.

The number of ordinary, stable compounds must be vastly exceeded by the number which are sufficiently unstable that they are difficult to study but which are just as much a part of the world of chemistry. As one further example, modern mass spectrometers routinely measure trace quantities of all kinds of molecular fragments produced either in a chemical reaction or by induced decomposition by light or by electron impact. In this last approach one determines the energy of impinging electrons needed to produce a given fragment, the threshold value being called the appearance potential. Methane produces CH_4^+ when 12-V electrons are passed through the gas, and at 14 V, CH_3^+ results. Methyl radicals generated in a chemical reaction and then electron bombarded give CH_3^+ again, but now with only 10 V electrons and the difference between 14 and 10 V must correspond to the energy for the process $CH_4 \rightarrow CH_3 + H$. Thus the energies of formation of unstable species can be estimated.

SPECIAL TOPICS

14-ST-1   Heterogeneous Catalysis. Chemisorption of Gases

It was mentioned in Section 14-2C that zero-order reactions may be observed under conditions of heterogeneous catalysis; a brief presentation of this general subject seems worthwhile. Many commercially important gas-phase processes depend on heterogeneous catalysis to make the reaction proceed more cleanly to desired products or at a lower temperature than otherwise feasible. Often the equilibrium is favorable only at such a low temperature that the reaction rate is very slow, and it is only by catalytic means that the reaction can be made to occur on a practical basis.

Several examples of important catalyzed reactions were mentioned in Section 7-CN-2. Iron oxide (with added aluminum and potassium oxides) catalyzes the formation of ammonia from hydrogen and nitrogen; mixed cobalt thorium oxides catalyze the Fischer–Tropsch reaction whereby hydrocarbons are produced from CO and H_2; nickel and platinum metals catalyze various hydrogenation reactions; various aluminas and other acidic oxides are widely used in the catalytic cracking of hydrocarbons, and so forth. In all of these cases the role of the catalyst is that of stabilizing some intermediate, which then takes part in reactions on the catalyst surface or with a molecule from the gas phase which collides with the surface. Hydrogenation catalysts may dissociate hydrogen into atoms to give $M-H$, where M denotes a surface metal atom. Thus a mechanism for the hydrogenation of ethylene is

$$(1) \qquad C_2H_4 + M = \begin{matrix} H_2C--CH_2 \\ | \qquad | \\ M \qquad M \end{matrix},$$

$$(2) \qquad H_2 + M \rightarrow \begin{matrix} H_2 \\ | \\ M \end{matrix} \rightarrow 2\begin{matrix} H \\ | \\ M \end{matrix},$$

$$(3) \quad \begin{matrix} H_2C--CH_2 \\ | \qquad | \\ M \qquad M \end{matrix} + \begin{matrix} H_2 \\ | \\ M \end{matrix} \rightarrow \begin{matrix} CH_3 \\ | \\ CH_2 \\ | \\ M \end{matrix} + \begin{matrix} H \\ | \\ M \end{matrix},$$

$$\begin{matrix} CH_3 \\ | \\ CH_2 \\ | \\ M \end{matrix} + \begin{matrix} H \\ | \\ M \end{matrix} \rightarrow C_2H_6.$$

That for catalytic cracking probably involves the step

$$RH + SH^+ \rightarrow \begin{matrix} R^+ \\ | \\ S \end{matrix} + H_2,$$

where SH^+ denotes an acidic surface site, perhaps an $Al-OH$ function, and R^+-S is a surface-adsorbed carbonium ion, which then fragments or undergoes surface reactions with other adsorbed carbonium ions.

Heterogeneous catalysis, then, is intimately related to adsorption processes in which the absorbed species, or adsorbate, forms a chemical bond with the adsorbent. Such adsorption is called *chemisorption*, as contrasted to the much weaker adsorption of vapors on a surface due to secondary or van der Waals forces. This second kind of adsorption is more like a condensation process, and is called *physical adsorption* (or, sometimes, physisorption). It is necessary first to discuss chemisorption as a phenomenon before proceeding to the subject of the kinetics of heterogeneous catalysis.

A.   Chemisorption. The Langmuir Equation

Chemisorption may be studied as a separate phenomenon from catalysis simply by using a single adsorbate species which is stable toward reaction. Examples would be the chemisorption of nitrogen on tungsten, of hydrogen on nickel, and of ammonia on carbon black. The adsorption process can be slow and temperature-dependent, that is, increase in rate with increasing temperature, indicating an activation energy for adsorption; it may not always be possible to attain a reversible equilibrium. The better-behaved systems, however, show rapid adsorption and for each pressure of adsorbate gas there will be an equilibrium amount of adsorption. The data are conventionally plotted as an *adsorption isotherm*, that is, as amount adsorbed v (usually measured as cubic centimeters STP of gas adsorbed per gram of adsorbent) versus pressure, as shown in Fig. 14-15. The normal behavior is for v to approach a limiting value v_m with increasing pressure, and, as shown in Fig. 14-16(a), for the amount adsorbed to decrease with increasing

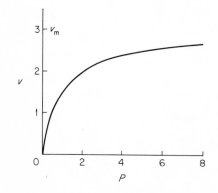

Fig. 14-15.   *Adsorption isotherm. Units for v and P are arbitrary.*

temperature at constant pressure. One may alternatively plot equilibrium pressure versus T at constant amount adsorbed, that is, *isosteres*, as is done in Fig. 14-16(b).

A very straightforward treatment of chemisorption was given by I. Langmuir in 1918. The picture is one of a surface having a certain number of adsorption sites S of which S_1 may be occupied by adsorbate and $S_0 = S - S_1$ is then bare.

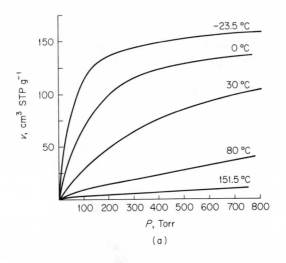

(a)

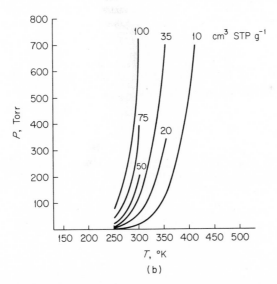

(b)

Fig. 14-16. *(a) Adsorption isotherms for ammonia on charcoal. (b) Adsorption isosteres for ammonia on charcoal. [From Vol. I, "Physical Adsorption" of Stephen Brunauer, "The Adsorption of Gases and Vapors" (copyright 1943 © 1971 by Princeton University Press). Reprinted by Permission of Princeton University Press, Princeton, New Jersey.]*

Adsorption equilibrium is treated as a dynamic state in which the rate of adsorption is equal to the rate of desorption. The former rate is taken to be nonactivated and just proportional to the surface collision frequency of the gaseous adsorbate on the bare sites, which, by Eq. (2-46), is proportional to the pressure P:

$$\text{rate of adsorption} = k_2 P S_0 = k_2 P(S - S_1).$$

The rate of desorption is proportional to the number of occupied sites S_1 :

$$\text{rate of desorption} = k_1 S_1 .$$

The two rates are set equal, and on solving for S_1 we obtain

$$\frac{S_1}{S} = \theta = \frac{bP}{1 + bP} , \tag{14-91}$$

where θ is the fraction of surface covered and $b = k_2/k_1$. The limiting value v_m of Fig. 14-15 corresponds to $\theta = 1$, hence $v/v_\mathrm{m} = \theta$, and we can write

$$v = \frac{v_\mathrm{m} bP}{1 + bP} . \tag{14-92}$$

Equations (14-91) and (14-92) are known as the Langmuir adsorption isotherm. The latter may be rearranged to the form

$$\frac{P}{v} = \frac{1}{bv_\mathrm{m}} + \frac{P}{v_\mathrm{m}} , \tag{14-93}$$

which states that a plot of P/v versus P should be linear. The isotherm of Fig. 14-15 is plotted in this manner in Fig. 14-17.

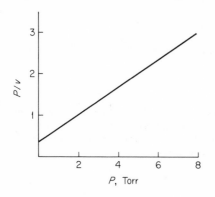

Fig. 14-17. *Plot of isotherm of Fig. 14-15 in the form of Eq. (14-93).*

Although the adsorption process is not considered to be activated, that for desorption must be, since there will be an adsorption energy Q which the adsorbate must gain if it is to desorb; k_1 must therefore be of the form $k_1 = k_1'e^{-Q/RT}$, and the constant b consequently can be written

$$b = b_0 e^{Q/RT}. \qquad (14\text{-}94)$$

Equation (14-91) reduces to the form

$$\theta = bP, \quad \text{or} \quad v = v_m bP \qquad (14\text{-}95)$$

at low pressure, so that the Langmuir model requires that the adsorption isotherm be linear at low pressures; the isosteres for this region obey a Clausius–Clapeyron type of equation:

$$\left(\frac{d \ln P}{dT}\right)_{v \text{ or } \theta} = \frac{Q}{RT^2}. \qquad (14\text{-}96)$$

From its nature, Q must be a positive number, and so pressure must increase with temperature. Alternatively, at constant pressure,

$$\left(\frac{d \ln \theta}{dT}\right)_P = \frac{d \ln b}{dT} = -\frac{Q}{RT^2}. \qquad (14\text{-}97)$$

Finally, if more than one species is competing for adsorption, the adsorption isotherm for some one of them is given by the Langmuir derivation as

$$\theta_i = \frac{b_i P_i}{1 + \sum b_j P_j}, \qquad (14\text{-}98)$$

where the summation is over all species.

Relatively few chemisorption systems obey the simple Langmuir model really well; the data may not fit the Langmuir equation, especially at the extremes, or if they do, the variation of the b parameter with temperature may fail to obey the simple exponential law. The basic model seems sound, however, and such difficulties can often be attributed to nonuniformity of the surface so that Q varies with degree of surface occupancy. The adsorbate adsorbs first on the more active sites, with highest Q, and then on progressively less active ones. Hydrogen appears to be present on the surface as individual atoms, so that the desorption process requires a recombination of two surface atoms, and is therefore bimolecular. Analysis leads to an isotherm of the form

$$\theta = \frac{bP^{1/2}}{1 + bP^{1/2}}. \qquad (14\text{-}99)$$

The derivation assumes that the adsorbing gas requires two adjacent sites, which has the effect of making the rate of adsorption proportional to $S_0{}^2$.

As may well be imagined, there are a number of sophisticated treatments both of the Langmuir derivation and of variants such as that just given. Equation (14-91) may be obtained, for example, by means of a statistical thermodynamic derivation in which the adsorbed gas has the partition function

$$Q^s = Q^s_{site}\, Q^s_{int}\, e^{Q/RT}\,,$$

where $e^{Q/RT}$ allows for the change in zero-point energy on adsorption; Q^s_{int} may be taken to be the same as for the free gas, and Q^s_{site} is given by the number of distinguishable ways of arranging N molecules on S sites. Our present use of the Langmuir model, however, is simply as a convenient basis for treating the kinetics of hererogeneous catalysis.

B. Kinetics of Heterogeneous Catalysis

A number of simple catalytic systems can be reasonably well treated on the basis that the reactants adsorb on the catalyst surface, to react according to a mass action type of rate law.

Suppose that the reaction is $A \rightarrow C + D$ and that the surface reaction proceeds according to the rate law $dn_A/dt = -kS_A$, where S_A is the surface covered by adsorbed A, or, by Eq. (14-98),

$$\frac{dn_A}{dt} = -kS\,\frac{b_A P_A}{1 + b_A P_A + b_C P_C + b_D P_D}\,. \qquad (14\text{-}100)$$

If the products C and D are weakly adsorbed, then Eq. (14-100) reduces to

$$\frac{dn_A}{dt} = -kS\,\frac{b_A P_A}{1 + b_A P_A}\,,$$

which means that at low P_A the rate should be proportional to P_A , while at high P_A the rate levels off at the maximum value kS, and hence is independent of P_A . This last situation is then one of a zero-order reaction. Behavior of this type has been observed for the decomposition of HI on gold and platinum and of N_2O on indium sesquioxide.

If the reaction is of the type $A + B \rightarrow C + D$ and the surface reaction obeys the rate law $dn_A/dt = -kS_A S_B$, then the general expression for the apparent rate law is

$$\frac{dn_A}{dt} = -kS\frac{b_A b_B P_A P_B}{(1 + b_A P_A + b_B P_B + b_C P_C + b_D P_D)^2} . \qquad (14\text{-}101)$$

If both products and reactants are weakly adsorbed, this reduces to

$$\frac{dn_A}{dt} = -kSb_A b_B P_A P_B = -k_{app} P_A P_B .$$

Examples are the reaction between nitric oxide and oxygen on glass and the low-pressure, low-temperature hydrogenation of ethylene on active carbon. If reactant A and the products are weakly adsorbed but B is strongly adsorbed, then

$$\frac{dn_A}{dt} = -kS\frac{b_A P_A}{b_B P_B} = -\frac{k_{app} P_A}{P_B} .$$

It is thus possible for a reactant to inhibit a reaction.

We return to Eq. (14-100) to make a final observation. At low P_A, the equation becomes

$$\frac{dn_A}{dt} = -kSb_A P_A = -k_{app} P_A .$$

The reaction is first order, and its temperature dependence could be written as

$$\frac{d(\ln k_{app})}{dT} = \frac{E^*_{app}}{RT^2} .$$

However, k_{app} contains the product of b_A and the true rate constant k and by Eq. (14-97), it follows that

$$E^*_{app} = E^*_{true} - Q_A .$$

Thus the apparent activation energy is less than the true one by the heat of adsorption. There is not only this effect, of course, but the true activation energy may be less than that for the bulk-phase reaction. Thus the true activation energy for the tungsten-catalyzed decomposition of ammonia is only 39 kcal mole^{-1} as compared to the value of about 90 kcal mole^{-1} for the gas-phase reaction. One reason a catalyst is effective, then, is because of a reduction in the activation energy for reaction.

14-ST-2   Statistical Thermodynamic Treatment of Transition-State Theory

The application of statistical thermodynamics to the calculation of $\Delta S^{0\ddagger}$ was illustrated in Section 14-8C. This in fact represents the practical approach that is the most useful. It is possible, however, to arrive at Eq. (14-81) or Eq. (14-82) on a more formal basis and one which sheds some light on the fundamental assumptions of transition-state theory. We must first develop a certain formalism for the general treatment of an equilibrium constant, which will then be applied to $K^{\ddagger}$.

A.   Statistical Thermodynamic Treatment of Equilibrium Constants

The statistical thermodynamic expression for the free energy of an ideal gas can be reduced to a very simple form. Equation (6-76) reads

$$G = -RT(\ln \mathbf{Q}) + RTV\left[\frac{\partial(\ln \mathbf{Q})}{\partial V}\right]_T + RT \ln N_0 - RT.$$

However, only $\mathbf{Q}_{\text{trans}}$ depends on V, and for an ideal gas it is proportional to V by Eq. (4-68), so that $[\partial(\ln \mathbf{Q})/\partial V]_T$ is just $1/V$ and the second and fourth terms of Eq. (6-76) cancel. Also, Eq. (6-76) was derived on the assumption that H_0, the absolute enthalpy at $0°K$, was set equal to zero. We now want to retain this reference point, and since for an ideal gas at $0°K$ $H_0 = E_0$, we obtain

$$G = E_0 - RT \ln \mathbf{Q} + RT \ln N_0 \tag{14-102}$$

or

$$G = E_0 - RT \ln \frac{\mathbf{Q}}{N_0}. \tag{14-103}$$

We now define a subsidiary partition function ϕ defined as $\mathbf{Q} = \phi V$, that is, ϕ contains all the terms of $\mathbf{Q}$ except the volume factor. If the standard state is taken to be 1 atm pressure, then $V = N_0 \mathbf{k}T$, and Eq. (14-103) becomes

$$G^0 = E_0 - RT \ln(\phi \mathbf{k}T). \tag{14-104}$$

From our standard chemical reaction

$$aA + bB + \cdots = mM + nN + \cdots,$$

for which

$$\Delta G^0 = -RT \ln K_P \qquad [\text{Eq. (7-11)}].$$

If the standard state is 1 atm, substitution of Eq. (14-104) gives

$$K_P = (\mathbf{k}T)^{\Delta n} K_\phi e^{-\Delta E_0/RT}, \qquad (14\text{-}105)$$

where Δn is the number of moles of products minus moles of reactants and K_ϕ is the quantity

$$K_\phi = \frac{\phi_M{}^m \phi_N{}^n \cdots}{\phi_A{}^a \phi_B{}^b \cdots}.$$

[Note the resemblance to Eq. (7-48).] Since by Eq. (7-14) $K_C = K_P(RT)^{-\Delta n}$, or $K_n = K_P(\mathbf{k}T)^{-\Delta n}$, where K_n is the concentration equilibrium constant using the concentration in molecules per unit volume $\mathbf{n}$, Eq. (14-104) can be put in the final form

$$K_n = K_\phi e^{-\Delta E_0/RT}. \qquad (14\text{-}106)$$

An equilibrium constant can thus be expressed as the product and quotient of the slightly modified partition functions ϕ multiplied by the term $e^{-\Delta E_0/RT}$, which involves the change in zero-point energy accompanying the chemical reaction.

B. Application to Transition-State Theory

We first calculate the concentration of activated complex $[AB]^{\ddagger}$ as

$$([AB]^{\ddagger}) = K_n{}^{\ddagger}(A)(B) = K_\phi{}^{\ddagger}\, e^{-\Delta E_0^{\ddagger}/RT}(A)(B).$$

A special assumption has been made regarding Q or ϕ for $[AB]^{\ddagger}$, however, namely that one of its degrees of freedom is in translation along the reaction coordinate; this particular component of $\phi^{\ddagger}$ is then to be expressed separately with Eq. (4-67) for the translational partition function in one dimension, leaving $\phi^{\ddagger}$ containing the usual three degrees of translational freedom but one less than the normal number of vibrational contributions. We therefore write

$$([AB]^{\ddagger}) = \frac{(2\pi m^{\ddagger}\mathbf{k}T)^{1/2}}{2h} \frac{a^{\ddagger}\phi^{\ddagger}}{\phi_A \phi_B}\, e^{-\Delta E_0^{\ddagger}/RT}(A)(B),$$

where $a^{\ddagger}$ must be some characteristic linear dimension associated with the saddle point of Fig. 14-10 and the factor of $\frac{1}{2}$ is present since only forward translation along the reaction path is being considered.

The frequency with which molecules of [AB]‡ will pass over the saddle is next expressed as in terms of a velocity $v^\ddagger$:

$$\text{rate} = \frac{v^\ddagger([AB]^\ddagger)}{a^\ddagger} = v^\ddagger \frac{(2\pi m^\ddagger \mathbf{k}T)^{1/2}}{2h} \frac{\phi^\ddagger}{\phi_A \phi_B} e^{-\Delta E_0^\ddagger/RT}(A)(B).$$

The velocity $v^\ddagger$ is now supposed to have a Boltzmann distribution of values given by the treatment for a one-dimensional gas, Eq. (2-29). The average velocity for a three-dimensional gas is $(8\mathbf{k}T/\pi m)^{1/2}$ [Eq. (2-38)]; for a one-dimensional gas it turns out to be $(2\mathbf{k}T/\pi m)^{1/2}$, and this result is inserted in place of $v^\ddagger$ to obtain

$$\text{rate} = \frac{\mathbf{k}T}{h} \frac{\phi^\ddagger}{\phi_A \phi_B} e^{-\Delta E_0^\ddagger/RT}(A)(B),$$

from which the rate constant, expressed in molecules per cubic centimeter, is

$$k = \frac{\mathbf{k}T}{h} \frac{\phi^\ddagger}{\phi_A \phi_B} e^{-\Delta E_0^\ddagger/RT}. \tag{14-107}$$

One may, of course, factor the partition function ϕ in the usual manner, writing $\phi = \phi_{trans}\phi_{rot}\phi_{vib}$, and evaluate the terms from the standard expressions of Chapter 4, remembering that V is dropped out of $\mathbf{Q}_{trans}$ and [AB]‡ has one less than the usual number of vibrations; otherwise the ϕ's are the same as the $\mathbf{Q}$'s.

C.   Discussion

The preceding derivation has led to an equation of the same form as Eq. (14-85) but shows more specifically the assumptions that are made in transition-state theory. There is a certain artificiality to the treatment of the rate of passage over the saddle point, but the more interesting aspect is the following. Although the ϕ's are temperature-dependent, the major temperature term is $\exp(-\Delta E_0^\ddagger/RT)$. The experimental activation energy, as obtained by means of the Arrhenius equation, is thus largely identified with the difference in *zero-point energy* between [AB]‡ and the reactants A and B. Thus [AB]‡ is treated as a definite chemical species and not just as some special energized association of A and B. Its translational, rotational, and vibrational partition functions are treated as though [AB]‡ were in *ordinary thermal equilibrium* with its surroundings; that is, the ambient temperature is used in their evaluation.

The contrast with collision theory is especially striking in the case of a unimolecular reaction. Collision theory treats such a reaction in terms of a molecule

A* which is essentially the same molecule as A but in a highly vibrationally excited state. Transition-state theory says that $[A]^{\ddagger}$ is a new chemical species of extra zero-point energy $\Delta E_0^{\ddagger}$ whose vibrations are those corresponding to equilibrium with the ambient temperature. The writer must confess a reluctance to accept this second picture.

The case of an elementary bimolecular reaction is somewhat different. Here we do rather expect that A and B will form some new kind of molecule (as in the $H_2 + I_2$ reaction), and it makes sense to regard this as having a real $\Delta E_0^{\ddagger}$. There is still a question as to whether those molecules of $[AB]^{\ddagger}$ that pass on to reaction do, in reality, have vibrations (and rotations) corresponding to the ambient temperature. These questions are rather subtle ones and are brought up here mainly to give some perspective to the two theories of reaction rates.

GENERAL REFERENCES

BENSON, S. W. (1960). "The Foundations of Chemical Kinetics." McGraw-Hill, New York.
FROST, A. A., AND PEARSON, R. A. (1961). "Kinetics and Mechanism." Wiley, New York.
GARDINER, W. C., JR. (1969). "Rates and Mechanisms of Chemical Reactions." Benjamin, New York.

CITED REFERENCES

BENSON, S. (1968). "Thermochemical Kinetics." Wiley, New York.
HARCOURT, A., AND ESSEN, W. (1865). *Proc. Roy. Soc. (London)* **14**, 470.
HARCOURT, A., AND ESSEN, W. (1866). *Phil. Trans. Roy. Soc. (London)* **156**, 193.
HARCOURT, A., AND ESSEN, W. (1867). *Phil. Trans. Roy. Soc. (London)* **157**, 117
HERSCHBACH, D., *et al.* (1956). *J. Chem. Phys.* **25**, 737.
KUNSMAN, C. H. (1928). *J. Amer. Chem. Soc.* **50**, 2100.
SULLIVAN, J. (1966). *J. Chem. Phys.* **46**, 73.

Exercises

14-1 Calculate k, τ, and $t_{1/2}$ for a first-order reaction for which $t_{1/3} = 25$ min.

Ans. 0.044 min^{-1}, 22.7 min, 15.7 min.

14-2 The disappearance of a reactant is at the rate of 0.25% min^{-1}. Calculate the half-life if the reaction is first order.

Ans. 277 min.

14-3 A plot of $1/(A)$ versus t gives a straight line of intercept 150 atm^{-1} and slope 2×10^{-3} atm^{-1} sec^{-1}. Calculate the half-life for this reaction.

Ans. 7.5×10^4 sec.

14-4 A gas-phase reaction has the stoichiometry $A + 2B \rightarrow$ products and obeys the rate law $d(A)/dt = -k(A)(B)$ with $k = 2 \times 10^{-4}$ liter mole^{-1} sec^{-1} at 25°C. A reaction mixture at 25°C initially contains 20 % A and 80 % B at a total pressure of 2 atm. Calculate the percentage of A and of B that have reacted after 1 hr.

Ans. 4.79% A, 2.40% B.

14-5 Calculate the half-life for the reaction of Exercise 14-4 if (a) $(A)_0 = 0.02\ M$ and $(B)_0 = 0.5\ M$, (b) if $(A)_0 = 0.5\ M$ and $(B)_0 = 0.02\ M$, and (c) if $(A)_0 = 0.02\ M$ and $(B)_0 = 0.04\ M$. (Half-life is the time for half of that reactant not in excess to have reacted.)

Ans. (a) 6930 sec, (b) 3460 sec, (c) 1.25×10^5 sec.

14-6 Suppose that A and B are volatile solids and that the reaction of Exercise 14-4 is carried out in a five-liter flask at 25°C in the presence of excess solid A and B. If the vapor pressures of A and B are 0.1 atm and 0.02 atm, respectively, how long should it take for 0.5 mole of A to be converted to products?

Ans. 1.50×10^8 sec.

14-7 A catalyzed reaction obeys Eq. (14-29). If (A) is expressed in atmospheres and t in seconds, what are the dimensions of k_1 and of k_2 ? The rate reaches a maximum, limiting value of 10 atm sec^{-1} and is at half of this value when the pressure of A is 100 atm. Calculate k_1 and k_2.

Ans. $k_1 = 0.1$ sec^{-1}, $k_2 = 0.01$ atm^{-1}.

14-8 Under certain conditions the reaction $H_2 + Br_2 = 2HBr$ obeys a rate law of the form $d(HBr)/dt = k(H_2)^a(Br_2)^b(HBr)^c$. At a certain temperature T the reaction rate is found to be R when (HBr) is 2 M and (H_2) and (Br_2) are both 0.1 M. The rate varies with concentration as follows:

Concentration (M)			
(H_2)	(Br_2)	(HBr)	Rate
0.1	0.1	2	R
0.1	0.4	2	$8R$
0.2	0.4	2	$16R$
0.1	0.2	3	$1.88R$

Find the exponents a, b, and c.

Ans. $1, \frac{3}{2}, -1$.

14-9 Consider the reaction $A_2 + B_2 \rightarrow 2AB$. Explain what the rate law for each of the following mechanisms should be: (a) $A_2 \xrightarrow{k_1} 2A$ (slow step), $B_2 \xrightarrow{K_2} 2B$ (rapid equilibrium highly displaced toward B_2) and $A + B \xrightarrow{k_3} AB$ (fast). (b) $A_2 \stackrel{K_1}{=} 2A$, $B_2 \stackrel{K_2}{=} 2B$ (both rapid equilibria, highly displaced toward A_2 and B_2, respectively), $A + B \xrightarrow{k_3} AB$ (slow step). (c) $A_2 + B_2 \xrightarrow{k_1} A_2B_2$ (slow step), $A_2B_2 \xrightarrow{k_2} 2AB$ (fast).

> *Ans.* (a) $R = k_1(A_2)$; (b) $R = k_{app}(A_2)^{1/2}(B_2)^{1/2}$, where $k_{app} = K_1^{1/2}K_2^{1/2}k_3$; (c) $R = k_1(A_2)(B_2)$.

14-10 Derive the steady-state rate law for the mechanism:

$$NO + H_2 \underset{k_{-1}}{\overset{k_1}{\rightleftharpoons}} NO \cdot H_2$$

$$NO \cdot H_2 + NO \xrightarrow{k_2} N_2O + H_2O.$$

Show under what condition this reduces to the form of Eq. (14-39).

> *Ans.* $R = k_1k_2(NO)^2(H_2)/[k_{-1} + k_2(NO)]$.

14-11 Verify the expressions for k_f that follow Eq. (14-68).

14-12 Calculate the activation energy for the reaction $2HI \rightarrow H_2 + I_2$ using the first and last entries of Table 14-3. Obtain also the frequency factor A.

> *Ans.* 44.6 kcal mole^{-1}, 1.19×10^{11} liter mole^{-1} sec^{-1}.

14-13 Calculate the rate constant for the reaction $CH_3 + H_2 \rightarrow CH_4 + H$ at 100°C.

> *Ans.* 460 liter mole^{-1} sec^{-1}.

14-14 Calculate $\log A'$ for the reaction of Exercise 14-13, assuming a collision diameter of 3 Å.

> *Ans.* 10.27.

14-15 The reaction cyclopropane $\rightarrow$ propylene conforms (approximately) to the simple Lindemann mechanism. The limiting rate constant has the parameters $\log A = 15.2$ (A in sec^{-1}) and $E^* = 65$ kcal mole^{-1} and at 765°K, $k_{uni} = 10^{-4}$ sec^{-1} at a pressure of 1 Torr. Calculate $k_{uni,\infty}$ at 765°C and the ratio k_1/k_{-2} .

> *Ans.* 4.0×10^{-4} sec^{-1}, 3.0 Torr.

14-16 Calculate $\Delta S^{0\ddagger}$ and $\Delta H^{0\ddagger}$ for the decomposition of N_2O_5 . At high pressures the reaction is first order with $k = 3.35 \times 10^{-5}$ sec^{-1} at 25°C and 0.0048 sec^{-1} at 65°C.

> *Ans.* 24.9 kcal mole^{-1}, 2.2 cal °K^{-1} mole^{-1}.

14-17 The entropy of activation is -20 cal °K^{-1} mole^{-1} for the reaction $CH_3 + NH_3 \rightarrow CH_4 + NH_2$, thought to be a simple reaction. Estimate the translational contribution to this entropy and hence, by difference, that from rotation and vibration. Assume 25°C.

> *Ans.* $\Delta S^{0\ddagger}_{trans} = -25.8$ cal °K^{-1} mole^{-1}, $(\Delta S^{\ddagger}_{rot} + \Delta S^{\ddagger}_{vib}) = 5.8$ cal °K^{-1} mole^{-1}.

Problems

14-1   The following mechanism is proposed for the formation of ammonia:

(1) $H_2 \rightleftharpoons H + H$,   (4) $N + H_2 \rightleftharpoons NH_2$,
(2) $N_2 + H \rightleftharpoons NH + N$,   (5) $NH_2 + H \rightleftharpoons NH_3$.
(3) $NH + H \rightleftharpoons NH_2$,

All are gas-phase reactions. Show that the equilibrium constant derived from the mass action principle has the same form as the thermodynamic one.

14-2   A reaction obeys the rate law of Eq. (14-31). How should (A) be plotted as a function of time so as to give a straight line plot? Relate the slope of this plot to k, $t_{1/2}$, and n.

14-3   (Calculator problem)   Obtain a set of curves for the system of Fig. 14-3 but plotted as F_A versus $k(A)_0 t$.

14-4   The half-life for the decomposition of NH_3 as catalyzed by a hot tungsten filament (at about 1100°C) is found to vary with the initial NH_3 pressure as follows:

P (Torr)	300	100	30
$t_{1/2}$ (min)	8.4	2.8	0.84

[see Kunsman (1928)]. Show what the order of the reaction is (in P_{NH_3}) and calculate the rate constant.

14-5   The reaction $4A(g) \rightarrow B(g) + 6C(g)$ is studied, and the following data are obtained, where P is the total pressure. Assume that no products are present initially and that the reaction goes to completion. Show what the order of the reaction is and calculate the rate constant.

P (Torr)	500	687.5	781.3
t (sec)	0	60	120

14-6   The decomposition $ClCOOCCl_3 \rightarrow 2COCl_2$ goes to completion, and the total pressure is found to vary with time (at 280°C) as follows:

t (sec)	0	500	800	1300	1800
P (Torr)	15.0	18.9	20.7	23.0	24.8

Show what the order of the reaction is and calculate the rate constant.

14-7   The reaction $2NOCl \rightarrow 2NO + Cl_2$ is studied at 200°C. The concentration of a sample initially consisting of NOCl only changes with time as follows:

t (sec)	0	200	300	500
C_{NOCl} (M)	0.02	0.0159	0.0144	0.0121

Assuming that the reaction goes to completion as stated, show what the order is and calculate the rate constant.

14-8   A reaction between the substances A and B is represented stoichiometrically by the equation $A + B \rightarrow C$. Observations on the rate of this reaction are obtained as follows (figures are "rounded" values):

Initial concentration (M)			Concentration of A at end of interval (M)
A	B	t (hr)	
0.1	1.0	0.5	0.095
0.1	2.0	0.5	0.080
0.1	0.1	1000	0.05
0.2	0.2	500	0.10

Formulate the differential equation that expresses the rate of this reaction and calculate the specific rate constant. Indicate your reasoning.

14-9 The following reaction sequence is proposed:

$$NO_2Cl \underset{k_{-1}}{\overset{k_1}{\rightleftharpoons}} NO_2 + Cl,$$

$$NO_2Cl + Cl \overset{k_2}{\rightarrow} NO_2 + Cl_2 .$$

Show what the overall reaction is and derive the stationary-state rate law.

14-10 R. Ogg proposed the following mechanism for the reaction $N_2O_5 \rightarrow N_2O_4 + \frac{1}{2}O_2$:

$$N_2O_5 \underset{k_{-1}}{\overset{k_1}{\rightleftharpoons}} NO_2 + NO_3 ,$$

$$NO_2 + NO_3 \overset{k_2}{\rightarrow} NO + O_2 + NO_2 ,$$

$$NO + NO_3 \overset{k_3}{\rightarrow} 2NO_2 .$$

Derive the stationary-state rate law for this mechanism. (Both NO_3 and NO are treated as stationary-state intermediates.)

14-11 Sullivan (1966) reported that k_2 of reaction (14-66) is 1.12×10^5 liter^2 mole^{-2} sec^{-1} at 418°K. Calculate K_1 and k_{-2} .

14-12 For the decomposition of N_2O_5 the following is observed:

t (°C)	25	35	45	55	65
$10^5 \, k$ (sec^{-1})	1.72	6.65	24.95	75	240

Calculate $\Delta H^{0\ddagger}$ and the frequency factor. Calculate $\Delta G^{0\ddagger}$ and $\Delta S^{0\ddagger}$ for the reaction at 50°C.

14-13 For unimolecular gas reactions the activation entropy can often be neglected. Assuming the activation entropy to be exactly zero, calculate the rate constant and half-life at room temperature (25°C) for a reaction with a heat of activation of (a) 15 kcal and (b) 20 kcal.

14-14 (Calculator problem) Askey and Hinshelwood obtained the following data for the pyrolysis of dimethyl ether at 777°K:

Initial concentration ($M \times 10^3$)	0.58	1.20	1.89	3.12	5.01
$k_{uni} \times 10^4$ (sec^{-1})	1.88	2.48	3.26	4.12	5.57
Initial concentration ($M \times 10^3$)	6.48	8.18	13.21	16.61	18.57
$k_{uni} \times 10^4$ (sec^{-1})	5.58	6.29	6.90	6.64	7.45

The system was believed to conform to the general Lindemann mechanism. Plot the data in a linear form so as to obtain values for k_2 and k_{-2}/k_1 from the best least-squares slope and intercept. The observed activation energy for $k_{uni,\infty}$ is 65.5 kcal mole^{-1}. Estimate the value of f in Eq. (14-89) that will account for the experimental $k_1 K_2$.

14-15 Estimate the value of $k_1 K_2$ and k_{-2}/k_1 for the isomerization of cyclopropane (using Fig. 14-9) and also the best value of f in Eq. (14-89).

14-16 The rate constants for the second-order reaction $CH_3CHO + I_2 \rightarrow CH_4 + CO + I_2$ vary with temperature as follows:

T (°K)	63	645	660	675	695
k (liter mole^{-1} sec^{-1})	12	22	41	76	140

Calculate A and E^*, and, using transition-state theory, $\Delta S^{0\ddagger}$. (Optional: make a least-squares fit of the data to an Arrhenius plot in evaluating the above quantities.) Assume 630°K in the calculations.

14-17 Before some recent new developments (see Section 14-5) the $H_2 + I_2 = 2HI$ reaction was thought to be a simple one, the probable transition state being

(distances in angstroms). Calculate the value of $\Delta S^{0\ddagger}$ at 575°K assuming that the three moments of inertia are 921.5, 6.9, and 928.4 (in units of 10^{-40} g cm^2) [note that $\sigma = 2$; see Eq. (4-90)], and that the vibrational frequencies are 994, 86, 1280, 1400, and 1730 (all in cm^{-1}).

14-18 (Calculator problem)   Calculate k for activation enthalpies varying from 10 to 60 kcal mole^{-1} in increments of 10 kcal mole^{-1}, and activation entropies varying from -20 to 20 cal °K^{-1} mole^{-1} in increments of 5 cal °K^{-1} mole^{-1}. Plot the results (a) as log k versus $\Delta H^{0\ddagger}/RT$ for various $\Delta S^{0\ddagger}/R$ and (b) $\Delta S^{0\ddagger}/R$ versus $\Delta H^{0\ddagger}/RT$ for various k. Assume $\mathbf{k}T/h = 10^{13}$ sec.

Special Topics Problems

14-1 The Pt-catalyzed decomposition of NO (into N_2 and O_2) is found to obey the experimental rate law $dP_{NO}/dt = -kP_{NO}/P_{O_2}$. Assuming adsorbed gases obey the Langmuir equation, derive this rate law starting with some reasonable assumed mechanism for the surface reaction.

If the heat of adsorption of NO is 20 kcal mole^{-1} and that of O_2 is 25 kcal mole^{-1}, show what the actual activation energy for the surface reaction should be, given that the apparent activation energy is 15 kcal mole^{-1} (as found from the temperature variation of k).

14-2 Gases A and B chemisorb according to the Langmuir model. The adsorbent has a specific surface area of 50 m^2 g^{-1} and the area occupied by an A or B molecule is 20 Å^2. The gas

A reaches one-half of its maximum adsorption at 10 Torr while B, in a separate experiment, reaches the half adsorption point at 20 Torr (at 50°C). (a) Calculate v_m in cubic centimeters STP per gram. (b) Calculate b for gas A and b for gas B. (c) Calculate θ_A and θ_B if adsorption occurs at 50°C from a mixture of the two gases each at 10 Torr pressure.

14-3 Derive the relationship between K_q of Eq. (7-48) and K_ϕ of Eq. (14-106).

14-4 If the transition state for a reaction is one in which some bond $M-X$ is stretched essentially to the point of dissociation, then the dissociation energy is regarded as making a direct contribution to the activation energy. Consider the case where M is a heavy atom and X is hydrogen or deuterium. The bond dissociation energy is less for the $M-H$ case than for the $M-D$ one since this energy is the difference between the potential energy of the separated atoms and the zero-point energy of the $M-X$ vibration. This last is smaller for $M-D$ than for $M-H$ [note Eq. (4-78)]. Assuming the mass of M to be effectively infinite and the $M-H$ vibrational frequency to be 3300 cm^{-1}, calculate the zero-point energies for $M-H$ and $M-D$, the difference in their dissociation energies, and the resulting difference in the rate constant for the reaction. The effect is known as the *primary isotope effect*.

14-5 For the case of the reaction $A + B \rightarrow AB$, where A and B are atoms, Eq. (14-107) reduces to

$$k = \left[\frac{8\pi(m_A + m_B)\,kT}{m_A m_B} \right]^{1/2} r_{AB}^2 \exp\left(-\frac{\Delta E_0^{\ddagger}}{RT} \right) \quad \text{cm}^3 \text{ molecule}^{-1} \text{ sec}^{-1},$$

where r_{AB} is the $A-B$ bond distance. Derive this result; also, compare the equation with the corresponding one from collision theory and comment on the similarities.

15 KINETICS OF REACTIONS IN SOLUTION

Much of the material of Chapter 14 is needed as a foundation for this chapter. Particularly important are the sections on reaction rate laws, the relationship between reaction mechanism and rate law, and the collision and transition-state theories. We proceed to consider some aspects of rate laws that were omitted before and which are often encountered in solution kinetics, as well as experimental approaches that are now more relevant. Collision and transition-state theories are discussed again in terms of their special applications to solutions, and the main portion of the chapter concludes with a discussion of a number of types of reaction mechanisms.

The flavor of this chapter differs noticeably from that of Chapter 14. There is less emphasis on detailed, quantitative theories and more on reaction mechanisms. One reason lies in the far greater variety of reactions in solution than in the gas phase. There are perhaps 30 important types of gas-phase reactions as compared to 1000 or more in solution. Gas-phase reactions are restricted to small (volatile) molecules and ions. Solution studies extend to protein and other macromolecular species. Reactions involving ions are rarely studied in the gas phase, but dominate large areas of kinetics in solution.

An important and recurring theme, again special to this chapter, will be that of the role of solvent. The solvent affects the manner in which reacting molecules can come together and, further, it not only may specifically alter the structure or other properties of the reactants but often is itself a reactant. In fact, one of the difficulties of solution kinetics is the distinction between solvent as a medium and solvent as a direct participant in a rate-controlling step. Mechanistic schemes involving solvent are for this reason often more difficult to establish and more subject to controversy than gas-phase reactions, hence the relatively high degree of preoccupation with them by solution kineticists.

15-1 **Additional Comments on Rate Laws. Reversible Reactions**

It will be recalled that in Section 14-2 a detailed presentation was made of the mathematical behavior of first- and second-order rate laws. Some minor additional types of rate laws were mentioned, and the stationary-state hypothesis was developed in detail.

All of these treatments assume that the reaction goes to completion. It is entirely possible, however, for the equilibrium constant to be such that equilibrium is reached before the reactants are entirely consumed. In effect this means that the back reaction must be included in the rate equation. Although this situation can, of course, occur with either gas- or solution-phase reactions, it is perhaps more often encountered in the latter case; its consideration is therefore appropriate at this point.

A. **Reversible First-Order Reaction**

Consider the reaction

$$\text{A + other reactants} \underset{k_2}{\overset{k_1}{\rightleftharpoons}} \text{B + other products,} \tag{15-1}$$

where we suppose either that A is actually the only reactant and B the only product or that the concentrations of other reactants and products are kept constant. In either case, we take the consequence to be that the forward rate is first order in A and the reverse rate first order in B. If, as in Section 14-2A, only the forward reaction is considered, then the rate equation is

$$R_\mathrm{f} = -\frac{d(\text{A})}{dt} = k_1(\text{A}) \qquad \text{[Eq. (14-4)]}$$

and, on integration, we obtain

$$(\text{A}) = (\text{A})_0\, e^{-k_1 t} \qquad \text{[Eq. (14-7)],}$$

where $(\text{A})_0$ is the initial concentration, with the half-life $t_{1/2}$ given by

$$k_1 t_{1/2} = 0.693 \qquad \text{[Eq. (14-9)].}$$

The reaction thus goes to completion; (A) approaches zero as $t \to \infty$.

We next allow the reverse reaction to be significant, so that if one starts with no B present, R_f is at first large but decreases as A is consumed, and R_b, zero initially, gradually increases as B is formed. The net rate of reaction at any time is thus

$$\frac{d(\text{A})}{dt} = -k_1(\text{A}) + k_2(\text{B}) \tag{15-2}$$

683

or, since $(B) = (A)_0 - (A)$,

$$\frac{d(A)}{dt} = -k_1(A) + k_2[(A)_0 - (A)].$$

Separation of the variables leads to

$$\frac{d(A)}{k_2(A)_0 - (k_1 + k_2)(A)} = dt,$$

which gives, on integration,

$$-\frac{1}{k_1 + k_2} \ln[k_2(A)_0 - (k_1 + k_2)(A)] = t + \text{constant}.$$

On setting $(A) = (A)_0$ at $t = 0$, we obtain

$$A = \frac{(A)_0}{k_1 + k_2} (k_2 + k_1 e^{-kt}), \tag{15-3}$$

where $k = k_1 + k_2$. Equation (15-3) may be put in a more elegant form as follows. At $t = \infty$ we have equilibrium, so that $d(A)/dt = 0$, and Eq. (15-2) gives

$$K = \frac{k_1}{k_2} = \frac{(B)_\infty}{(A)_\infty}$$

or, since $(B)_\infty = (A)_0 - (A)_\infty$, rearrangement yields

$$\frac{(A)_\infty}{(A)_0} = \frac{1}{1 + K} = \frac{k_2}{k_1 + k_2}, \tag{15-4}$$

where K is the mass action law equilibrium constant. Since $(A)_0 k_2/(k_1 + k_2) = (A)_\infty$ and $(A)_0 k_1/(k_1 + k_2) = (A)_0 \{1 - [k_2/(k_1 + k_2)]\} = (A)_0 - (A)_\infty$, Eq. (15-3) becomes

$$\frac{(A) - (A)_\infty}{(A)_0 - (A)_\infty} = e^{-kt}. \tag{15-5}$$

It follows from Eq. (14-35) that if $\mathscr{P}$ is any additive property, then

$$\frac{\mathscr{P} - \mathscr{P}_\infty}{\mathscr{P}_0 - \mathscr{P}_\infty} = e^{-kt}. \tag{15-6}$$

Two alternative forms of Eq. (15-5) are

$$\frac{(A)}{(A)_\infty} = 1 + Ke^{-kt} \tag{15-7}$$

and

$$\frac{(A)}{(A)_0} = \frac{1}{1 + K} + \frac{K}{1 + K} e^{-kt}, \tag{15-8}$$

or

$$\frac{(A)}{(A)_0} = \frac{1}{1+K} + \frac{K}{1+K} e^{-[(1+K)/K]k_1 t}.$$ (15-9)

Equation (15-5) makes clear the point that the rate law will still be first order in nature, provided that the quantity $(A) - (A)_\infty$ is used rather than just (A). Thus a plot of $\ln[(A) - (A)_\infty]$ versus t will be a straight line of slope $-k$. The usual half-life relationships are obeyed, with $kt_{1/2} = 0.693$. Notice, however, that the observed rate constant is k and not k_1. The experimental rate data thus give $k = k_1 + k_2$, and $(A)_\infty/(A)_0 = k_2/(k_1 + k_2)$, and these two pieces of information allow k_1 and k_2 to be calculated separately. If the reaction goes to completion, so that $(A)_\infty = 0$ and $k_2 \ll k_1$, Eq. (15-5) reduces to Eq. (14-6).

The set of curves shown in Fig. 15-1 is calculated from the alternative equation

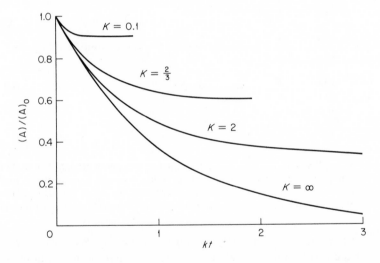

Fig. 15-1. *Rate of approach to equilibrium for the case* A $\leftrightarrows$ B, *for varying K. For K* $= 0.1$ $(A)_\infty/(A)_0 = 0.91$; $K = \frac{2}{3}$, $(A)_\infty/(A)_0 = \frac{3}{5}$, $K = 2$, $(A)_\infty/(A)_0 = \frac{1}{3}$; $K = \infty$, $(A)_\infty/(A)_0 = 0$.

(15-9), which brings out more explicitly the effect of allowing the back reaction to assume increasing importance. As K decreases from infinity, $(A)/(A)_0$ approaches a larger and larger limiting $(A)_\infty/(A)_0$ value, and the approach, while always exponential, is increasingly rapid. That is, although the initial rates are all the same, the back reaction comes in earlier and earlier to cause $(A)/(A)_0$ to level off at the equilibrium value.

A pointer for the experimentalist is the following. It may not always be possible to determine $(A)_\infty$—the reaction may take inconveniently long to go to completion or other reactions may begin to perturb the results at long times. One may still determine whether the reaction is a reversible first-order one by observing the change in $(A)/(A)_0$ for successive equal time intervals.

That is, $(A)/(A)_0$ is measured at $t = 0$, $t = \Delta t$, $t = 2\,\Delta t$, $t = 3\,\Delta t$, and so on. By Eq. (15-8) we have

$$t = 0 \qquad \frac{(A)_0}{(A)_0} = 1 = \frac{1}{1 + K} + \frac{K}{1 + K},$$

$$t = \Delta t \qquad \frac{(A)_1}{(A)_0} = \frac{1}{1 + K} + \frac{K}{1 + K}\,e^{-k\Delta t},$$

$$t = 2\,\Delta t \qquad \frac{(A)_2}{(A)_0} = \frac{1}{1 + K} + \frac{K}{1 + K}\,e^{-2k\Delta t},$$

$$t = 3\,\Delta t \qquad \frac{(A)_3}{(A)_0} = \frac{1}{1 + K} + \frac{K}{1 + K}\,e^{-3k\Delta t},$$

and so on. The successive changes in $(A)/(A)_0$ are

$$1 - \frac{(A)_1}{(A)_0} = \frac{K}{1 + K}\,(1 - e^{-k\Delta t}) = \alpha,$$

$$\frac{(A)_1}{(A)_0} - \frac{(A)_2}{(A)_0} = \frac{K}{1 + K}\,(e^{-k\Delta t} - e^{-2k\Delta t}) = \frac{K}{1 + K}\,(1 - e^{-k\Delta t})\,e^{-k\Delta t} = \alpha e^{-k\Delta t},$$

$$\frac{(A)_2}{(A)_0} - \frac{(A)_3}{(A)_0} = \frac{K}{1 + K}\,(e^{-2k\Delta t} - e^{-3k\Delta t}) = \frac{K}{1 + K}\,(1 - e^{-k\Delta t})\,e^{-2k\Delta t} = \alpha e^{-2k\Delta t},$$

$$\frac{(A)_i}{(A)_0} - \frac{(A)_{i+1}}{(A)_0} = \alpha e^{-ik\Delta t}.$$

Thus a plot of $\log\{[(A)_i/(A)_0] - [(A)_{i+1}/(A)_0]\}$ versus i should give a straight line if the reaction is a reversible first-order one. The slope and intercept give $-kt$ and α, respectively, from which k_1 and k_2 can be calculated. Even if $(A)_\infty$ can be determined, the use of Eq. (15-5) places undue emphasis on this single point, while the procedure just given weights each experimental datum equally.

Similar but more complex analyses can be made for cases where either the forward or the reverse reaction is second order or where both are. Some of these are given in the Special Topics section. However, such treatments are difficult to use and to fit accurately to data, and it is good practice to try to establish experimental conditions such that the rate law is made pseudo first order.

B.   Kinetics of a Small Perturbation from Equilibrium

An important type of method for studying fast reactions, discussed in Section 15-2B, consists in making a sudden change in the physical state of a system at equilibrium, such as a sudden jump in temperature, so that a different equilibrium constant applies and the system seeks its new equilibrium state. If the perturbation is relatively small, then the kinetics of this relaxation to the new equilibrium position takes on a rather simple mathematical form.

While the treatment may be generalized, it is best illustrated in terms of a specific example. Consider the dissociation of a weak acid

$$HA \underset{k'_{-1}}{\overset{k'_1}{\rightleftharpoons}} H^+ + A^-, \qquad K' = \frac{k'_1}{k'_{-1}}, \tag{15-10}$$

with $(H^+) = (A^-) = x_e'$ and $(HA) = a - x_e'$ initially, where a is the total formality of the acid present. As a result of a sudden temperature jump, the equilibrium constant takes on a new value K, where $K = k_1/k_{-1}$, for which the corresponding equilibrium concentrations are x_e and $a - x_e$, so that the system has been displaced from equilibrium by $\Delta x_0 = x_e - x_e'$. Net reaction will now occur with x at some subsequent time t equal to $x_e + \Delta x$. If the reaction is a simple one, that is, if Eq. (15-10) is also the mechanism for the reaction, then the reaction will take place according to the mass action rate law:

$$\frac{dx}{dt} = k_1(a - x) - k_{-1}x^2 \tag{15-11}$$

or

$$\frac{d(\Delta x)}{dt} = k_1(a - x_e - \Delta x) - k_{-1}(x_e + \Delta x)^2,$$

$$\frac{d(\Delta x)}{dt} = k_1(a - x_e) - k_1 \Delta x - k_{-1}x_e^2 - 2k_{-1}x_e \Delta x - k_{-1}(\Delta x)^2. \tag{15-12}$$

Since x_e *is* the new equilibrium value, it must be true that

$$k_1(a - x_e) = k_{-1}x_e^2,$$

so Eq. (15-12) reduces to

$$\frac{d(\Delta x)}{dt} = -k_1 \Delta x - 2k_{-1}x_e \Delta x - k_{-1}(\Delta x)^2. \tag{15-13}$$

At this point the characteristic assumption is made that Δx is sufficiently small that square or higher-power terms in Δx can be dropped. In the present case the result is

$$\frac{d(\Delta x)}{dt} = -(k_1 + 2k_{-1}x_e) \Delta x = -k_r \Delta x. \tag{15-14}$$

Equation (15-14) is first order in Δx and integrates to give

$$\Delta x = \Delta x_0 e^{-k_r t}, \qquad k_r = \frac{1}{\tau}, \tag{15-15}$$

where k_r, the relaxation rate constant, is often reported as its reciprocal τ, the *relaxation time*. From Eq. (15-14) we have

$$k_r = k_1 + 2k_{-1}x_e = k_1 \left(1 + \frac{2x_e}{K}\right). \tag{15-16}$$

Thus if K is known, k_1 and k_{-1} may be calculated.

The general derivation is somewhat complicated, but the result is that regardless of mechanism or actual rate law, the dropping of all terms higher than first power in Δx leads to Eq. (15-16), where k_r will have some specific relationship to the actual rate constants and various equilibrium concentrations. If the mechanism is in doubt, the form of the rate law may be deduced from a study of the variation of k_r (or of τ) with system composition.

As a numerical illustration, a $0.010 f$ solution of NH_4OH experiences a temperature jump terminating at $25°C$, at which temperature $K = 1.8 \times 10^{-5}$ mole liter^{-1} for the equilibrium $NH_4OH = NH_4^+ + OH^-$, so that $x_e = 4.1 \times 10^{-4} M$. The observed relaxation time is 1.09×10^{-7} sec, corresponding to $k_r = 9.2 \times 10^6$ sec^{-1}. From Eq. (15-16) we have

$$k_1 = \frac{9.2 \times 10^6}{1 + [(2)(4.1 \times 10^{-4})/(1.8 \times 10^{-5})]} = 2 \times 10^5 \quad \text{sec}^{-1}$$

and $k_{-1} = 2 \times 10^5/1.8 \times 10^{-5} = 1.1 \times 10^{10}$ liter mole^{-1} sec^{-1}. Note how a knowledge of k_1 has allowed the indirect determination of an extremely large k_{-1}. If there were any doubt about the correct rate law, it could be verified that k_1 and k_{-1} were in fact independent of the ammonia concentration used.

15-2   Experimental Methods

A.   General

Most of the experimental techniques described in Section 14-3 are applicable to reactions in solution. The system may be quenched, either by cooling or by removal of a catalyst, and then analyzed chemically. Or an additive property may be used such as optical density at a suitable wavelength. A technique special to solutions is that of following the change in volume; the partial molal volumes of the reactants and products generally will differ, with the consequence that the total volume of the solution will increase or decrease as the reaction proceeds. The change is usually not large but can be followed accurately if the system is in a *dilatometer*, or essentially a flask capped with a capillary tube (see Fig. 15-2) and well thermostated. The level of the meniscus in the tube is then measured periodically with a traveling microscope. The method is often resorted to if, as in the case of polymerization reactions, no very characteristic optical density changes occur. Equation (15-38) was followed dilatometrically, for example.

One does not, however, follow solution reactions by means of pressure change at constant volume. In the case of liquids the pressure necessary to maintain constant volume in the face of even a small partial molal volume change would be quite large—large enough to affect the rate constant itself (see Special Topics section).

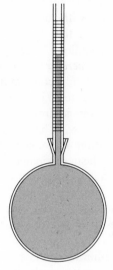

Fig. 15-2.   *Dilatometer.*

B.   *Fast Reaction Techniques*

The types of methods just cited are applicable to reactions whose half times are 1 min or more. Reaction times as short as 0.1 sec can be investigated by means of rapid mixing devices such as illustrated in Fig. 14-5. The reacting solutions enter a mixing chamber and then travel down a small-bore tube; it is necessary that some color change accompany the reaction so that the light absorption at a suitable wavelength can be used in the determination of the degree of reaction at various positions down the tube and hence for various times of reaction.

A number of additional methods have come into use in recent years which allow the time scale to be shortened considerably. An important one of these is called the *stop-flow method*—reacting solutions are again delivered into a mixing chamber, now usually by means of motor-driven syringes. After an interval sufficient to establish a steady-state condition in the exit tube the flow is stopped abruptly and the optical absorption is determined as a function of time thereafter. The associated equipment is as described in Section 14-3D. A monitoring light beam passes through the solution and impinges on a photomultiplier tube whose response actuates an oscilloscope. The progress of the reaction, following stoppage of the flow, then appears as a time trace on the oscilloscope. Reaction times of the order of milliseconds can be handled by this technique.

The subject of photochemistry is discussed in Section 18-4D, but it might be mentioned here that, as with gas-phase reactions, flash photolysis allows reaction times of as small as a few microseconds to be studied. Current developments forecast routine extension of the time scale down to the nanosecond region. The same is true for pulse radiolysis, in which reacting intermediates are formed by means of very short bursts of electrons or of other high-energy radiation.

A somewhat different family of techniques is that known as *relaxation methods*. One now starts with an equilibrium mixture and subjects it to some physical perturbation such that the system must adjust or relax to a new equilibrium condition. A technique largely developed by M. Eigen and co-workers is known as the *T-* or *temperature-jump method*. By discharging a large condenser across electrodes placed in a conducting solution, one achieves a quick, ohmic heating. If R denotes the resistance of the solution, then the power dissipated, iV, or current times voltage drop, can be written alternatively as V^2/R for a solution obeying Ohm's law. The condenser may be charged to perhaps 40,000 V and a typical solution resistance of 1000 ohm would then lead to 1.6×10^6 W or J sec^{-1} of heat dissipated in the solution. With the volume restricted to, say, 20 cm^3, a heat capacity of about 80 J °C^{-1} would apply, and so the temperature rise becomes about 2×10^5 °C sec^{-1}. The voltage pulse from the condensers might last 2×10^{-5} sec, so the actual temperature rise would be perhaps 4°C. As a result of the temperature jump, the system is no longer in equilibrium, and one uses the usual monitoring light–oscilloscope technique to follow the rate of reequilibration. As pointed out in Section 15-2B, if the perturbation is small, the relaxation to the new equilibrium state will follow first-order kinetics and is thus easily analyzed; by carrying out experiments at different concentrations, one may then determine the complete rate law. Even shorter times can be explored if the behavior of the system is studied during the buildup of the applied potential.

Another type of relaxation method makes use of sound waves. The absorption of sound by a medium is a consequence of various irreversible, essentially frictional processes that take place during the compression–rarefaction cycles that occur as a sound wave passes through the solution. If a chemical reaction system is present, its position of equilibrium is cyclically perturbed by the sound wave, with the frequency of the sound. If the rate of reaction is slow, then the chemical system cannot follow the changing equilibrium constant, and the solution behaves

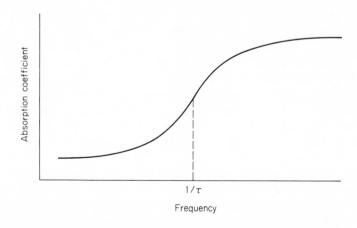

Fig. 15-3. *Dispersion curve for the absorption of sound waves.*

simply as a nonreacting mixture of solutes. If the reaction rate is fast compared to the sound frequency, then the reacting system does follow the changing equilibrium position, with the result that energy is taken from the sound wave to supply the heat of reaction; the absorption coefficient or rate of attenuation of the sound wave is thereby increased. The transition between the two extremes of no effect and maximum effect occurs fairly narrowly at a frequency corresponding to the relaxation time of the chemical system. Thus, as shown in Fig. 15-3, the variation in the absorption coefficient of the sound with its frequency—known as the *dispersion curve*—has an inflection point at the frequency equal to $1/\tau$, where τ is the relaxation time as given by Eq. (15-15). By using high-frequency sound, one can observe reaction times of as short as perhaps ten microseconds.

15-3   Kinetic-Molecular Picture of Reactions in Solution

A.   Encounters

The physical picture of molecular motions in a liquid is rather different from that in a gas. The molecules of a liquid are about as close together as in the crystalline solid—there is usually about a 10% expansion on melting (water being an exception because of its unusually open crystal structure) which allows some looseness and randomness in the liquid structure. As illustrated in Fig. 8-8(b), it seems likely that molecules of a liquid are in a potential well, but a somewhat flattened one so that vibrations against immediate neighbors are of low energy. There is, nonetheless, a confinement which is usually referred to as the *solvent cage effect*. The physical picture is then one of a molecule vibrating a number of times against the walls of its cage, that is, against its immediate neighbors, with occasional escapes to some adjacent position. The situation is illustrated in Fig. 15-4, where the molecules are shown as roughly spherical and in a somewhat expanded but essentially close-packed arrangement.

Fig. 15-4.   *The solvent "cage."*

The cage model is supported by the fairly successful treatment of diffusion in liquids (see Section 10-ST-2) in which the random diffusional motion of molecules in a liquid is taken to occur as a sequence of jumps from one molecular position to the next. This elementary jump distance λ is about $2r$, where r is the radius of the molecule. By Eq. (2-69),

$$\mathscr{D} = \frac{\lambda^2}{2\tau}.$$

The average time between jumps should then be

$$\tau = \frac{\lambda^2}{2\mathscr{D}}. \tag{15-17}$$

Equation (2-69) assumes a continuous medium, and since we are treating a liquid as having a quasi-crystalline structure, with more or less definite molecular sites, it turns out that a somewhat more accurate statement should be

$$\mathscr{D} = \frac{\lambda^2}{6\tau} \quad \text{or} \quad \tau = \frac{\lambda^2}{6\mathscr{D}}. \tag{15-18}$$

For small molecules a reasonable value of λ is about 4 Å, and, from Table 10-4, $\mathscr{D}$ at 25°C would be about 1×10^{-5} cm^2 sec^{-1}; τ is then about $(4 \times 10^{-8})^2/(6)(1 \times 10^{-5}) \approx 2.5 \times 10^{-11}$ sec. We next guess that the solvent cage is sufficiently loose that the average vibrational energy is about $\mathbf{k}T$, corresponding to a frequency $h\nu = \mathbf{k}T$ or $\nu = \mathbf{k}T/h$. Vibrations against the wall of the cage then occur at intervals of $h/\mathbf{k}T$ or about 1.5×10^{-13} sec at 25°C. We conclude that a typical molecule in solution vibrates about $2.5 \times 10^{-11}/1.5 \times 10^{-13}$ or about 200 times against its immediate neighbors before escaping to a new position and new neighbors.

The same analysis applies to solute molecules, and the next task is to estimate the frequency with which two solute molecules A and B will, by diffusion, accidentally become neighbors (Fig. 15-5). Such a process is called an *encounter*

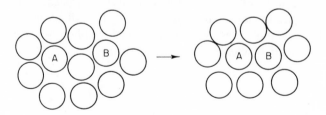

Fig. 15-5. *Diffusional encounter between* A *and* B.

and the estimation of encounter frequencies is central to much of solution kinetics. The problem is a difficult one, complicated by the present impossibility of describing the structure of a liquid with any great accuracy. As an approximation, we assume the molecules of solvent and of A and B to be about the same size and to be spherical. Each A molecule should then have about 12 nearest neighbors, so that on each diffusional jump it should find 6 new ones. The chance that one of these will be a molecule of B is given by the mole fraction of B in the solution,

$$x_B = \frac{\text{molecules of B cm}^{-3}}{\text{molecules of solvent cm}^{-3}} = \frac{n_B}{1/\gamma\lambda^3}, \quad (15\text{-}19)$$

where γ is a geometric factor which reflects the way in which molecules are packed in the liquid and λ^3 is the molecular volume. Substitution into Eq. (15-18) gives the frequency $1/\tau_{AB}$ of encounters of A with B as

$$\frac{1}{\tau_{AB}} = \frac{6\mathscr{D}}{\lambda^2}\,(n_B\gamma\lambda^3)(6) = 36\gamma\lambda n_B\mathscr{D}.$$

If we take the effective $\mathscr{D}$ to be the sum of $\mathscr{D}_A$ and $\mathscr{D}_B$, γ to be about 0.7, and λ to be the sum of the molecular radii r_{AB},

$$\frac{1}{\tau_{AB}} = 25 r_{AB}\mathscr{D}_{AB} n_B. \quad (15\text{-}20)$$

The total number of encounters per cubic centimeter per second is this value multiplied by n_A or, in moles per liter units,

$$Z_{e,AB} = \frac{25 r_{AB}\mathscr{D}_{AB}N_0}{1000}\,(A)(B), \quad (15\text{-}21a)$$

where $Z_{e,AB}$ is the A–B encounter frequency. The corresponding frequency factor is

$$A_e = \frac{25 r_{AB}\mathscr{D}_{AB}N_0}{1000}. \quad (15\text{-}21b)$$

For $\mathscr{D}_A = \mathscr{D}_B = 1 \times 10^{-5}$ cm^2 sec^{-1} and $r_{AB} = 4$ Å, $A_e = 1.2 \times 10^9$ liter mole^{-1} sec^{-1}.

A very simple and useful approximation results if $\mathscr{D}$ is estimated by means of Eq. (10-42) so that r_{AB} cancels out. The result is

$$A_e = 1.1 \times 10^5 \frac{T}{\eta} \quad \text{liter mole}^{-1}\text{ sec}^{-1}. \quad (15\text{-}22)$$

In summary, for a solution 1 M in A and 1 M in B the encounter frequency at 25°C is about 1.5×10^9 mole liter^{-1} sec^{-1}. Having made an encounter, A and B remain in their solvent cage for some 200 vibrational periods. We next contrast this picture with that provided by gas collision theory.

B. Application of Collision Theory to Reactions in Solution

It would seem that collision theory, based on the kinetic molecular theory of gases, would be totally inapplicable to reactions in solution. The surprising and very significant fact is that a number of solution reactions do have an Arrhenius frequency factor A [Eq. (14-57)] which is very close to that expected from collision theory—recall that Eq. (14-70) leads to a theoretical A value of about 3×10^{11} liter mole^{-1} sec^{-1} at 25°C. Some representative data are given in Table 15-1. In other cases, although the frequency factor may be smaller than the theoretical value, it is not affected by the nature of the medium, as illustrated by the data of Table 15-2. More qualitatively, a number of other reactions have been found to have the same rate in the gas phase as in solution; for example, the rate of decomposition of N_2O_5 is about the same in the gas phase as in nitromethane solution.

These examples are ones in which there is probably not a great deal of specific interaction between the solvent and the reacting solutes, and it seems necessary to conclude that at least in such cases the bimolecular collision frequency is about the same as in the gas phase. This conclusion, incidentally, provides a qualitative rationale for the fact that the osmotic pressure equation (10-22) has the same form as the ideal gas law. The frequency of solute collision against the semipermeable membrane appears to be the same as for gaseous solute at the

Table 15-1. *Some Second-Order Reactions in Solutions[a]*

Reactants	Solvent	A (liter mole^{-1} sec^{-1})	E^* (kcal mole^{-1})
$CH_3Br + I^-$	CH_3OH	2.26×10^{10}	18.25
	H_2O	1.68×10^{10}	18.26
$I_2 + N_2CHCOOC_2H_5$	CCl_4	2.21×10^{11}	20.23
$C_2H_5Br + (C_2H_5)_2S$	$C_6H_5CH_2OH$	1.40×10^{11}	25.47

[a] See E. A. Moelwyn-Hughes, "Physical Chemistry," 2nd ed. Pergamon, Oxford, 1961.

Table 15-2. *Dimerization of Cyclopentadiene[a]*

Medium	log A (liters mole^{-1} sec^{-1})	E^* (kcal mole^{-1})
Gas	6.1	16.7
C_2H_5OH	6.4	16.4
CS_2	6.2	16.9
C_6H_6	6.1	16.4

[a] Source: S. W. Benson, "The Foundations of Chemical Kinetics." McGraw-Hill, New York, 1960.

same volume and temperature, thus making the osmotic pressure equal to the corresponding gas-phase pressure.

We can also return to Fig. 8-8(b) for a rationalization of this conclusion. If the potential well has a flat bottom, the vibrations of a molecule against its neighbors may be of low enough energy that there is an equipartition distribution among vibrational states (note Section 8-CN-1). The degrees of freedom of such vibrations will then be rather like three degrees of translational freedom insofar as the frequency of intermolecular impacts is concerned. Thus if a molecule having a room-temperature gas-kinetic theory velocity of 10^5 cm sec^{-1} were simply bouncing back and forth in a box of about 4 Å on the side, its collision frequency with the walls would be about 2.5×10^{13} sec^{-1}, or about the same as the vibrational frequency kT/h.

C. Encounters versus Collisions

The previous discussion about encounters does tell us, however, that although the collision frequency may be the same in the gas phase and in solution, the pattern of collisions must be quite different. Consider the case of molecules A and B both 1 M in concentration. The gas collision frequency at 25°C would be about 3×10^{11} liter^{-1} sec^{-1} and, as illustrated in Fig. 15-6(a), if each A–B collision could be marked on a time scale, their pattern would be a random one.

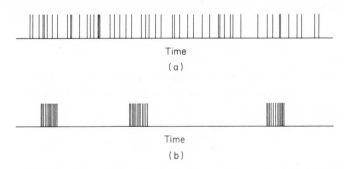

Time

(a)

Time

(b)

Fig. 15-6. *(a) Pattern of* A–B *collisions according to collision theory and (b) pattern of* A–B *collisions according to encounter picture.*

The encounter frequency would be about 1.5×10^9 liter^{-1} sec^{-1}, or 1/200 as often. The two molecules would stay in their mutual solvent cage for about 2.5×10^{-11} sec, however, or long enough to make about 200 collisions with each other. The collision pattern is therefore as shown in Fig. 15-6(b)—occasional encounters with many collisions during each encounter.

The activation energies cited in Table 15-1 are around 20 kcal mole^{-1}, which means that at 25°C the chance of a collision leading to reaction is about $\exp(-20,000/298R)$ or about 10^{-15}. Thus only after 10^{15} collisions, or 5×10^{12}

encounters, does reaction occur, on the average. The difference in pattern between Fig. 15-6(a) and Fig. 15-6(b) is thus unimportant in such cases. If, however, the activation energy is small so that reaction should occur after only a few collisions at the most, then *every* encounter should result in reaction. Conversely, the frequency factor for the reaction is now limited by the encounter frequency. Reactions which occur with every encounter are said to be *diffusion-controlled*. Their observed activation energy will not be zero, however, but will be determined by the temperature dependence of $\mathscr{D}_{AB}$ [in Eq. (15-21b)] and hence by that of the viscosity of the solvent since by Walden's rule (Section 10-7B), $\mathscr{D}\eta$ is approximately a constant. From Table 8-4, this means that diffusion or encounter-controlled reactions should show activation energies of 3–4 kcal mole^{-1} in common solvents. Reactions of this type are discussed in somewhat more detail in the next section.

There is a problem in the theoretical treatment of encounter frequencies that should be mentioned at this point. In deriving Eq. (15-21a), we assumed that the distribution of A and of B in solution was random. If we focus on A as the species making the encounter, the derivation also assumes that as A diffuses away after an encounter it remains available to make new encounters with the same or nearby B molecules. If, however, chemical reaction takes place with every encounter, then B acts as a sink into which A disappears and there is therefore on the average a depletion of A in the vicinity of B (and vice versa, of course). A simple treatment given by Smoluchowski in 1917 applies ordinary diffusion theory to this situation. By Fick's law [Eq. (2-67); see also Section 10-7B] the total flux of A flowing toward a B molecule is

$$J = \left(-\frac{d\mathbf{n}_A}{dr} \right)_r \mathscr{D}\mathscr{A} = -4\pi r^2 \mathscr{D}_A \left(\frac{d\mathbf{n}_A}{dr} \right)_r, \qquad (15\text{-}23)$$

where $\mathscr{A}$ is the area of the spherical surface around B at a distance r. We now assume a steady-state condition, that is, that $d\mathbf{n}_A/dr$ is independent of time, so that Eq. (15-23) has the form

$$\frac{d\mathbf{n}_A}{dr} = -\frac{J}{4\pi r^2 \mathscr{D}_A}$$

and integrates to give

$$\mathbf{n}_A = \frac{J}{4\pi r \mathscr{D}_A} + a,$$

where a is a constant of integration. We then set $\mathbf{n}_A = 0$ at $r = r_{AB}$ and $\mathbf{n}_A = \mathbf{n}_A{}^\circ$, the average concentration, at $r = \infty$, which allows a to be evaluated. On solving for J, we obtain

$$J = -4\pi r_{AB}\mathscr{D}_A \mathbf{n}_A{}^\circ. \qquad (15\text{-}24)$$

We allow for the diffusion of B by using $\mathscr{D}_{AB}$ instead of just $\mathscr{D}_A$, and multiply by $\mathbf{n}_B{}^\circ$ to get the total encounter frequency.

$$Z_{\bar{e},AB} = 4\pi r_{AB}\mathscr{D}_{AB}\mathbf{n}_A\mathbf{n}_B \qquad (15\text{-}25)$$

(dropping the superscript degree as no longer necessary), or the frequency factor

$$A_e = \frac{4\pi r_{AB}\mathscr{D}_{AB}N_0}{1000}.$$ (15-26)

The frequency factor as given by Eq. (15-26) is about half of that from Eq. (15-22), and although both derivations are approximate, this comparison is probably about right. That is, the encounter frequency for a diffusion-controlled reaction is about half that expected in the absence of reaction.

There is a rather interesting (and perhaps somewhat controversial) implication in the comparison of frequency factors. Suppose that molecules B can react only if put into an excited state by the absorption of a quantum of light—that is, that the A–B reaction is a photoinduced one. When the solution is first illuminated the B molecules that become activated find themselves in an unperturbed A environment and react at the rate given by Eq. (15-21a). After a short time, however, the distribution of A goes over to that assumed by Smoluchowski and the photoreaction should obey Eq. (15-25). The same switchover should occur if the reaction is suddenly made to occur by a T-jump or other relaxation method. The effect should be observable only over a time period corresponding to A_e, or about 10^{-9} sec, and at present there are only qualitative indications that it really does take place.

D.   Collision Theory as Modified for Solution Reactions

There are two limiting situations. The first, treated earlier, is that in which reaction occurs on every encounter, so that the rate constant is given by Eq. (15-26) and the activation energy is that for diffusion (see Section 15-4). The second is that in which the chemical activation energy is large enough that reaction occurs only after many encounters. Practically speaking, this means that E^* should be more than about 10 kcal mole^{-1}. It is this second situation to which collision theory seems to apply about equally well in gas and solution reactions. We can write

$$k = A_e f_e \, e^{-E^*/RT},$$ (15-27)

where A_e is the encounter frequency factor, now given by Eq. (15-21b), and f_e is the number of collisions that occur during an encounter; $A_e f_e$ then gives the total collision frequency, or A in the Arrhenius equation,

$$k = Ae^{-E^*/RT} \qquad \text{[Eq. (14-57)]}.$$

One complicating factor to be considered in the case of solution reactions is that the lifetime of the encounter complex [AB] may be altered by the presence of attractive or repulsive forces between A and B. In the formation of [AB] the van der Waals forces of attraction (see Section 8-ST-1) between A and B will be balanced against those between A and solvent and B and solvent, since solvent is displaced in forming [AB]; the net effect could be either a repulsion or an attraction. In addition, of course, hydrogen bonding may be present. If w is the work of separating A from B, then Eq. (15-18) should now be

$$\tau = \frac{\lambda^2}{6\mathscr{D}} \, e^{w/kT}.$$ (15-28)

If w is positive, the encounters will last longer and more collisions will occur during each one. A way of treating the situation is as follows. The concentration of encounter complexes is given by the product (rate of encounter) × (lifetime of encounter). In the absence of any net force between A and B, we can write Eq. (15-27) as

$$k = \frac{kT}{h} \frac{([AB])}{(A)(B)} e^{-E^*/RT}, \qquad (15\text{-}29)$$

where ([AB]) is the concentration of encounter complexes. We can now generalize by writing for the process

$$A + B \rightleftharpoons [AB], \qquad K_e = \frac{([AB])}{(A)(B)},$$

where K_e is the equilibrium constant for forming [AB]. We then have

$$k = \frac{kT}{h} K_e \, e^{-E^*/RT} \qquad (15\text{-}30)$$

or

$$k = \frac{kT}{h} e^{\Delta S_e^0/R} \, e^{-H_e^0/RT} e^{-E^*/RT}. \qquad (15\text{-}31)$$

In the absence of any net interaction between A and B, K_e is determined by the simple statistical chance of A and B being adjacent to each other, or approximately by $6/C_s$, but the formalism of Eq. (15-30) allows for more complicated specific effects. The experimental activation energy is now $E_{exp} = \Delta H_e^0 + E^*$, that is, one cannot from rate measurements alone distinguish between ΔH_e^0 and E^*.

15-4   Diffusion-Controlled Reactions

According to the treatment of the preceding section, a diffusion-controlled reaction should have a rate constant of around 10^9 liter mole^{-1} sec^{-1} at 25°C and show an activation energy corresponding to that for diffusion or for the solvent viscosity, namely of 3–4 kcal mole^{-1} for ordinary solvents. An implied condition is that the chemical activation energy be small enough that reaction occur within the first few collisions. This last condition is often met in the case of the recombination of free radicals and in what is known as *fluorescence quenching*. This last is discussed in more detail in Section 18-4C, and consists of a reaction whereby a molecule in an electronically excited state is induced to return to the ground state by collision with some other molecule B. As illustrated in Fig. 15-7, the excited-state molecules may also return to the ground state by emitting a quantum of light, or fluorescing. The chemical deactivation by B competes with the radiative deactivation, and so as B is added to the solution there is a quenching or reduction in fluorescence. The rate constant for fluorescence can often be estimated independently, and the rate constant for the chemical deactivation can then be calculated from the concentration of B that produces a given degree of quenching.

Some examples of what appear to be diffusion-controlled processes are given

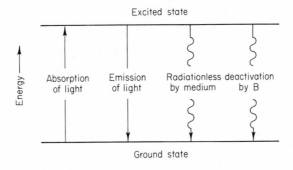

Fig. 15-7.   *Various deactivation processes for a molecule in an excited state.*

in Table 15-3. Note that the rate constants are around 10^9 liter $mole^{-1}$ sec^{-1}, depending somewhat on the solvent and on the size of the reactants. Equally important, the activation energies are only a few kcal $mole^{-1}$, or about that expected for diffusion in the solvents in question.

A number of acid–base type of reactions appear to be diffusion-controlled. Table 15-4 gives the rate parameters for several reactions of the type

$$HA + H_2O \rightleftharpoons A^- + H_3O^+, \tag{15-32}$$

which are believed to be simple reactions, that is, the overall reaction also constitutes the mechanism. These reactions have been studied by one or another fast reaction techniques of the type mentioned in Section 15-2B. Notice that in all cases it is the back reaction, or the transfer of a proton from H_3O^+ to A^-, that is in the diffusion-controlled region of rate constant value; k_1 for each forward reaction is then proportional to K, the equilibrium constant (see also Section 15-7).

The values of k_{-1} are distinctly larger than the 10^9 figure arrived at earlier for a diffusion-controlled reaction and at least two possible additional factors may be present over the usual situation. It will be recalled that the mobility of H^+ ion

Table 15-3.   *Some Diffusion-Controlled Reactions*[a]

Reaction	Solvent	$10^{-9} k$ (liter $mole^{-1}$ sec^{-1})	t (°C)	E^* (kcal $mole^{-1}$)
$I + I \rightarrow I_2$	Vapor phase	7	23	3.2
	n-Hexane	18	50	—
$2CCl_3 \rightarrow C_2Cl_6$	Cyclohexene + CCl_3Br	0.05	30	<6
	Vinyl acetate + CCl_3Br	0.05	30	<6
β-Naphthylamine +	Cyclohexane	6	20	2.5
$CCl_4 \rightarrow$ fluorescence quenching	Isooctane	13	20	1.6

[a] Source: S. W. Benson, "The Foundations of Chemical Kinetics." McGraw-Hill, New York, 1960.

Table 15-4. *Fast Reactions of the Type*

$$HA + H_2O \underset{k_{-1}}{\overset{k_1}{\rightleftharpoons}} A^- + H_3O^{+\ a}$$

HA	pK_a	$\log k_1$	$\log k_{-1}$
H_2O	15.7[b]	−4.6	11.1
H_2S	7.0	3.9	10.9
HF	3.3	7.7	11.0
HSO_4^-	1.6	9.4	11.0
CH_3COOH	4.8	5.9	10.7
CH_3COCH_3	20	−9.3	10.7
$(CH_3)_3NH^+$	9.8	1.0	10.8
β-Naphthol[c]	3.1	7.6	10.7

[a] Source: E. F. Caldin, "Fast Reactions in Solutions." Wiley, New York, 1964. The k values are in liter mole^{-1} sec^{-1} at 25°C.

[b] K_w has been put on a basis consistent with other weak acids by writing it as $(H^+)(OH^-)/(H_2O)$, that is, the usual value for K_w has been divided by 55.5, the number of moles of H_2O per liter.

[c] The reaction is one of deactivation of the first electronic excited state of β-naphthol by proton transfer, as observed by fluorescence quenching.

is unusually large and that a Grotthus-type mechanism is presumably responsible. As discussed in Section 12-5C, the hydrogen-bonded structure of water makes it possible for charge to move from one end of a chain of water molecules to the other by hydrogen bond shifts, the effect being the same as if a proton moved the length of the chain. It may then be that A^- can acquire a proton from other than nearest-neighbor H_3O^+ molecules by means of a similar mechanism, so that A^- and H_3O^+ do not have to diffuse as close to each other as in a normal bimolecular reaction. Their effective encounter rate would therefore be increased.

The second factor is that the reactants, being oppositely charged, experience an electrostatic attraction which enhances their diffusion toward each other. It is a rather difficult problem to treat theoretically, but, qualitatively, the encounter frequency equation (15-26) is modified by an exponential term:

$$A_e = \frac{4\pi r_{AB} \mathscr{D}_{AB} N_0}{1000} e^{-\phi/kT}, \tag{15-33}$$

where ϕ should be proportional to $z_A z_B$, the algebraic product of the charges on the reactants. Since $z_A z_B = -1$ in the present case, the exponential term acts to increase A_e over its normal value.

15-5 Transition-State Theory

The formal statement of transition-state theory is the same for solution as for gas-phase reactions. An elementary bimolecular reaction is given the intimate mechanism

$$A + B \overset{K^{\ddagger}}{\rightleftharpoons} [AB]^{\ddagger} \qquad \text{[Eq. (14-79)]},$$

$$[AB]^{\ddagger} \overset{k_1}{\rightarrow} \text{products} \qquad \text{[Eq. (14-80)]},$$

where $k_1 = \mathbf{k}T/h$. The rate constant is then

$$k = \frac{\mathbf{k}T}{h} K^{\ddagger} = \frac{\mathbf{k}T}{h} \exp\left(\frac{\Delta S^{0\ddagger}}{R}\right) \exp\left(\frac{\Delta H^{0\ddagger}}{RT}\right) \qquad \text{[Eq. (14-85)]}.$$

The equilibrium constant for forming the activated complex $[AB]^{\ddagger}$ or, alternatively, $\Delta S^{0\ddagger}$ and $\Delta H^{0\ddagger}$, must reflect not only the changes in chemical bonding that occur but also any changes in solvation. As a consequence, the complete statistical mechanical evaluation of $K^{\ddagger}$ is too complicated to be of practical use in the case of solution systems. Portions of the partition functions can be estimated, however. For example, the translational entropy change can be calculated approximately from the change in the entropy of mixing accompanying Eq. (14-79) if ideal solutions are assumed. By Eq. (9-69), the entropy of mixing of a solution of A and B for the standard state of 1 m is $-(R \ln x_A + R \ln x_B)$ and that of 1 m $[AB]^{\ddagger}$ is $-R \ln x_{[AB]^{\ddagger}}$, where each mole fraction is just $1/n_s$, n_s being the number of moles of solvent per 1000 g. We are neglecting some change in entropy of the solvent, and on this basis

$$\Delta S^{0\ddagger}_{\text{trans}} = -R \ln x_{[AB]^{\ddagger}} + R \ln x_A + R \ln x_B = R \ln \frac{1}{n_s}. \qquad (15\text{-}34)$$

In the case of water $n_s = 55.5$, which gives $\Delta S^{0\ddagger}_{\text{trans}} = -4R$ and $\exp(\Delta S^{0\ddagger}/R) = 0.02$. This value, although obtained by a very different route, is essentially the same quantity as the purely statistical part of K_e of Eq. (15-30), which was found to be $6/C_s$, or about 0.1 for water. The difference between 0.02 and 0.1 merely reflects the different approximations and further aspects of the comparison between collision and transition-state theory as applied to solutions are taken up in the Commentary and Notes section.

15-6   Linear Free Energy Relationships. Reactions Involving an Acid or a Base

A.   Acid–Base Systems

A rather interesting observation is that if some particular reaction is studied for a series of related compounds, then it will often be true that log k will vary linearly with log K, where k is the rate constant and K the equilibrium constant.

The actual relationship, proposed by Brønsted, is

$$k = \text{(constant)}\, K_a{}^\alpha,\tag{15-35}$$

or

$$\log k = b + \alpha \log K_a,\tag{15-36}$$

where b and α are constants. The data of Table 15-4 for the reaction $HA + H_2O \xrightarrow{k_1} A^- + H_3O^+$ are plotted in this manner in Fig. 15-8, and indeed, give a reasonably straight line, whose slope (and hence α) is 1.03. All this is rather misleading, however, since for these cases k_2 is essentially constant, being at the diffusion-controlled limit; and if k_2 is constant, then k_1 *must* be proportional to K_a, so that on the $\log k_1$ versus $\log K_a$ plot a straight line of slope unity is auto-

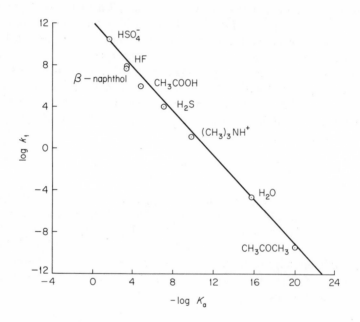

Fig. 15-8. *Data of Table 15-4 plotted according to the Brønsted equation (15-36).*

matically expected. The more complete picture is as shown in Fig. 15-9. Thus k_1 should increase with K_a until the diffusion-controlled limit is reached and thereafter should be constant. Conversely, k_2 should increase with decreasing K_a again until the diffusion-controlled limit is reached. When one k is at this limit, so that for it $\alpha = 0$, then the other k must obey the Brønsted equation with $\alpha = 1$. Thus α varies from 0 to 1 (or -1) along each curve. The two curves need not be symmetric, although they have to cross at $\log K = 0$. Also, there can be regions where neither k is at the diffusion limit, so that there can be an intermediate region for which both α's lie between zero and unity. It happened that the early studies

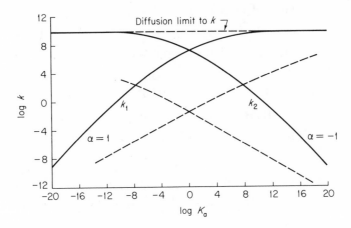

Fig. 15-9. *Brønsted plot showing both diffusion-controlled limits.*

on rates of dissociation lay in this intermediate region and that the range of values that was experimentally accessible was small enough that α appeared to be a characteristic constant for each acid.

Equation (15-32) is merely a special case of an acid–base reaction

$$HA + B^- = A^- + HB.$$

That is, bases other than water may be used, in which case the more general form of Eq. (15-36) is

$$\log k = b + \alpha(\log K_{HA} - \log K_{HB}) \tag{15-37}$$

and a number of systems have been studied in which B^- is varied with behavior analogous to that shown in Fig. 15-9 [the abscissa now being $(\log K_{HA} - \log K_{HB})$]. The results may sometimes appear as indicated by the dashed lines in the figure, however. That is, it is not always possible to reach the diffusion limit for either k. For more detailed discussion see Eigen (1963).

B. Acid and Base Catalysis

A somewhat more complex situation is that in which a reaction is acid- or base-catalyzed. For example, the acid-catalyzed dehydration of acetaldehyde hydrate,

$$CH_3CH(OH)_2 \overset{(HA)}{\rightleftharpoons} CH_3CHO + H_2O, \tag{15-38}$$

703

appears to occur through the mechanism

$$
\underset{\substack{|\\ \text{OH}\\ \text{(B)}}}{\overset{\text{OH}}{\text{CH}_3\text{CH}}} + \text{HA} \underset{}{\overset{K_1}{\rightleftharpoons}} \underset{\substack{|\\ \text{OH}\\ \text{(HB)}^+}}{\overset{\text{H H}}{\text{CH}_3\text{C}-\overset{+}{\text{O}}-\text{H}}} + \text{A}^- \quad \text{(fast)},
$$

$$
\underset{\substack{|\\ \overset{+}{\text{OH}}}}{\overset{\text{H H}}{\text{CH}_3-\text{C}-\text{O}-\text{H}}} + \text{A}^- \overset{k_2}{\to} \underset{\substack{|\\ \text{O}^-}}{\overset{\text{H H}}{\text{CH}_3-\text{C}-\overset{+}{\text{O}}-\text{H}}} + \text{HA} \;\text{(slow)},
$$

$$
\underset{\substack{|\\ \overset{+}{\text{O}^-}}}{\overset{\text{H H}}{\text{CH}_3-\text{C}-\text{OH}}} \to \underset{}{\overset{\text{H}}{\text{CH}_3-\text{C}=\text{O}}} + \text{H}_2\text{O} \quad \text{(fast)},
$$

where HA is some acid. The rate law for this mechanism is

$$
\frac{dR}{dt} = -k_2K_1(\text{B})(\text{HA}) = -k_{\text{app}}(\text{B})(\text{HA}), \tag{15-39}
$$

where B denotes acetaldehyde hydrate [the student should verify Eq. (15-39)].

Brønsted and co-workers studied a number of reactions of this type in the 1920's and found, as an empirical observation, that Eq. (15-36) again applied, with α values between zero and unity, depending on the system. Some data on reaction (15-38) are plotted according to Eq. (15-36) in Fig. 15-10; the straight line relationship is obeyed reasonably well with $\alpha = 0.53$ [see Bell and Higginson (1949)].

There are a large number of acid- or base-catalyzed reactions, and the following examples are merely illustrative. First, the following type of mechanism may be observed:

$$
\text{S} + \text{H}^+ \overset{K_1}{\rightleftharpoons} \text{SH}^+ \qquad \text{(fast)}, \tag{15-40}
$$

$$
\text{SH}^+ + \text{R} \overset{k_2}{\to} \text{products} \qquad \text{(slow)}, \tag{15-41}
$$

$$
\frac{d(\text{S})}{dt} = -k_{\text{app}}(\text{S})(\text{H}^+)(\text{R}) = -k_2K_1(\text{S})(\text{H}^+)(\text{R}), \tag{15-42}
$$

where S is the main reactant and R some additional one, often the solvent. The hydrolysis of esters, acetals, and ethers, as well as the inversion of sucrose, follow this type of mechanism. Alternatively, the mechanism may be of the type

$$
\text{S} + \text{HA} \overset{K_1}{\rightleftharpoons} \text{S} \cdot \text{HA} \qquad \text{(fast)}, \tag{15-43}
$$

$$
\text{S} \cdot \text{HA} + \text{R} \overset{k_2}{\to} \text{products} \qquad \text{(slow)}, \tag{15-44}
$$

$$
\frac{d(\text{S})}{dt} = -k_2K_1(\text{S})(\text{HA})(\text{R}). \tag{15-45}
$$

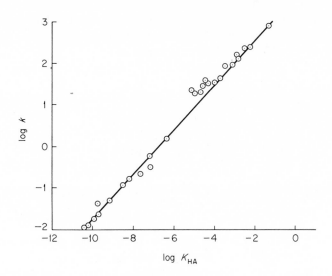

Fig. 15-10.   *Brønsted plot for the acid-catalyzed dehydration of* $CH_3CH(OH)_2$. *[Data from R. Bell and W. Higginson, Proc. Roy. Soc.* **A197**, *141 (1949).]*

An example is the hydrolysis of ethylorthoacetate (with R = water). Yet another example is

$$HS + H^+ \overset{K_1}{\rightleftharpoons} HSH^+ \qquad \text{(fast)}, \tag{15-46}$$

$$HSH^+ + B \overset{k_2}{\rightarrow} BH^+ + SH \qquad \text{(slow)}, \tag{15-47}$$

$$SH \rightarrow \text{products},$$

$$\frac{d(HS)}{dt} = -k_2 K_1 (HS)(H^+)(B) = k_2 K_1 K_{BH^+}(HS)(BH^+), \tag{15-48}$$

where BH^+ is some acid; HS and SH differ in the location of the proton. Note that in the final form of the rate law $(H^+)(B)$ has been replaced by $K_{BH^+}(BH^+)$. The addition of aldehydes and ketones to hydrazine or hydroxylamine, as well as the dehydration of acetaldehyde hydrate discussed earlier, appear to follow this mechanism.

Analogous base-catalysis mechanisms occur. Thus

$$HS + B \overset{K_1}{\rightleftharpoons} S^- + BH^+ \qquad \text{(fast)}, \tag{15-49}$$

$$S^- + R \overset{k_2}{\rightarrow} \text{products} \qquad \text{(slow)}, \tag{15-50}$$

$$\frac{d(R)}{dt} = -\frac{k_2 K_1 (HS)(B)(R)}{(BH^+)} = \frac{k_2 K_1}{K_B}(HS)(R)(OH^-), \tag{15-51}$$

where K_B is the base constant for $B + H_2O = BH^+ + OH^-$. Many of the condensation reactions of organic chemistry seem to follow this last mechanism, such as the Claisen, Michael, Perkin, and aldol condensations. The base-catalyzed reactions of many transition metal ammine complexes follow Eq. (15-51), with $B = OH^-$ and $R = H_2O$. Another mechanism is

$$S + B \overset{K_1}{\rightleftharpoons} S \cdot B \qquad \text{(fast)}, \tag{15-52}$$

$$S \cdot B \overset{k_2}{\rightarrow} \text{products} \qquad \text{(slow)}, \tag{15-53}$$

$$\frac{d(S)}{dt} = -k_2 K_1(S)(B). \tag{15-54}$$

The base-catalyzed hydrolysis of esters follows this mechanism, with $B = OH^-$:

$$
\begin{array}{ccc}
\overset{\displaystyle O}{\underset{\displaystyle \|}{}} & & \overset{\displaystyle O^-}{\underset{\displaystyle |}{}} \\
R-C-O-R' + OH^- & \overset{K_1}{\rightleftharpoons} & R-C-O-R', \\
& & \underset{\displaystyle OH}{|}
\end{array}
\tag{15-55}
$$

$$
\begin{array}{c}
\overset{\displaystyle O^-}{\underset{\displaystyle |}{}} \\
R-C-O-R' \overset{k_2}{\rightarrow} RCOO^- + R'OH, \\
\underset{\displaystyle OH}{|}
\end{array}
\tag{15-56}
$$

$$\frac{d(\text{ester})}{dt} = -k_2 K_1(\text{ester})(OH^-). \tag{15-57}$$

A distinction is usually made as to whether the catalysis is a general acid or base one or is specifically by H^+ or OH^- ions. Thus Eqs. (15-42), (15-51), and (15-57) contain the specific ion H^+ or OH^-. On the other hand, Eqs. (15-45) and (15-48) involve the acid concentrations (HA) and (BH$^+$), respectively, and the rate depends on these rather than on (H$^+$). Experimental distinction is possible since solutions can be made up which, say, vary in (H$^+$) at constant (HA), or vice versa. Similarly, Eq. (15-54) contains (B). It is the cases of general acid or base catalysis to which the Brønsted equation (15-36) applies.

C.   A Further Application of the Brønsted Equation

If a series of reactions obeys Eq. (15-36) so that b is the same for each, an alternative approach developed by Hammett (1940) is to take one specific reaction as a reference, with rate constant k_0 and acid constant K_0, and write

$$\log \frac{k}{k_0} = \rho \log \frac{K}{K_0}, \tag{15-58}$$

where, by convention, ρ is used in place of α. The quantity $\log(K/K_0)$ is taken to be a characteristic of the system being studied and is denoted by σ, so Eq. (15-58) becomes

$$\log \frac{k}{k_0} = \rho\sigma. \tag{15-59}$$

The application has been largely to reactions of substituted benzoic acids, with benzoic acid itself taken as the reference. Various types of reactions each have a characteristic ρ value, whereas σ, of course, depends only on the nature of the substituent on the benzoic acid. [See Hammett (1940) for more details.]

D. Linear Free Energy Relationships

The Brønsted equation (15-36) and its progeny, such as Eq. (15-59), are examples of what is called a *linear free energy relationship*. The basis for this phrase is that $\log K$ is proportional to ΔG^0 for the reaction while, by transition-state theory, $\log k$ is proportional to $\Delta G^{0\ddagger}$. Equation (15-36) can thus be written

$$\Delta G^{0\ddagger} = b' + \alpha \, \Delta G^0. \tag{15-60}$$

This type of relationship is so often obeyed that it amounts to one of the empirical laws of kinetics, and it is important to inquire into possible explanations. It has already been pointed out that in a series of simple reactions (so that $K = k_1/k_2$) Eq. (15-37) must be obeyed by k_1 with $\alpha = 1$ for systems such that k_2 is at the diffusion-controlled limit, and with $\alpha = 0$ for those such that k_1 is at this limit. Intermediate values of α then arise naturally for cases lying in the transition region between these extremes. Certain sets of reactions may then appear to have an intermediate and constant value of α simply because an insufficient range of k or K values is experimentally accessible.

Data such as those of Fig. 15-10 seem to require a different explanation—the linearity extends over too large a range of values for the constancy of α to be an artifact. The alternative possibility is that there is in fact an intrinsic proportionality between $\Delta G^{0\ddagger}$ and ΔG^0 for a series of related reactions. A simple exposition is the following.

If the reactions, being related, have a constant $\Delta S^{0\ddagger}$, then the proportionality is actually between $\Delta H^{0\ddagger}$ and ΔH^0, or between the activation energy and the overall energy of reaction. Suppose, for example, that the reaction is one of proton transfer,

$$HA_1 + A_2^- \rightarrow A_1^- + HA_2.$$

The reaction could proceed by the mechanism

$$
\begin{array}{lll}
HA_1 \rightarrow H^+ + A_1^-, & \Delta H_1^0 & \text{(rate determining)}, \\
H^+ + A_2^- \rightarrow HA_2 & & \text{(fast)},
\end{array}
$$

707

for which the activation energy would be ΔH_1^0. If, however, the reaction takes place by the route

$$HA_1 + A_2^- \rightarrow [A_1 \cdots H \cdots A_2]^- \rightarrow A_1^- + HA_2,$$

then, as illustrated in Fig. 15-11, the activation energy should be smaller since

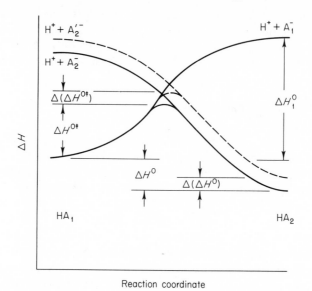

Reaction coordinate

Fig. 15-11. *Possible explanation for the existence of linear free energy relationships.*

complete breaking of the $H-A_1$ bond is not required. If now some second reactant HA_2' is employed and the general shape of the energy curves remains the same, as illustrated by the dashed line in the figure, then the geometry of the situation indicates that the change in activation enthalpy, $\Delta(\Delta H^{0\ddagger})$ should be proportional to the change in overall reaction enthalpy, $\Delta(\Delta H^0)$, which leads to Eq. (15-37) if the entropies do not change. This last assumption may be a poor one, but it turns out that very often ΔS and ΔH quantities for a given process are linearly related to each other, and so Eq. (15-37) is still obeyed.

15-7 Ionic Reactions. Role of Activity Coefficients

Reactions in the gas phase are generally at pressures of 1 atm or less so that the species are essentially ideal in their behavior. By contrast, solution systems are often distinctly nonideal, and this is true for electrolytes even at quite low concentrations. An important question is then whether the mass action law is correctly applied to elementary reactions when concentrations rather than activities are used in the rate expression. Alternatively, if we retain the mass action law, then does the rate constant contain activity coefficient quantities?

Both transition-state theory and collision theory as modified for solutions affirm that rates should depend on activity coefficients. Considering the former first, we see that the derivation of Eq. (14-82) (repeated in Section 15-5) should really be

$$\text{rate} = \frac{\mathbf{k}T}{h}([\text{AB}^\ddagger]) = \frac{\mathbf{k}T}{h}\frac{\gamma_A\gamma_B}{\gamma_{[\text{AB}]^\ddagger}}K^\ddagger(\text{A})(\text{B})$$

or

$$k = \frac{\mathbf{k}T}{h}\frac{\gamma_A\gamma_B}{\gamma_{[\text{AB}]^\ddagger}}\exp\left(\frac{\Delta S^{0\ddagger}}{R}\right)\exp\left(-\frac{\Delta H^{0\ddagger}}{RT}\right)$$

$$= \frac{\mathbf{k}T}{h}\frac{1}{K_\gamma^\ddagger}\exp\left(\frac{\Delta S^{0\ddagger}}{R}\right)\exp\left(-\frac{\Delta H^{0\ddagger}}{RT}\right). \tag{15-61}$$

The difficulty, of course, is in the evaluation of $\gamma_{[\text{AB}]^\ddagger}$, and for neutral molecules the activity coefficient factor $1/K_\gamma^\ddagger$ is generally ignored—one can argue that in dilute solutions each activity coefficient is close to unity and further that small departures from unity will tend to cancel each other.

The remaining situation is that of a reaction involving ions, and here the Debye–Hückel theory allows estimation of each γ purely on the basis of the charge of the species. Consider the elementary reaction

$$A^{z_A} + B^{z_B} \rightarrow [\text{AB}]^{\ddagger z_A + z_B} \rightarrow \text{products},$$

for which the activity coefficient factor $1/K_\gamma^\ddagger$ is given by

$$\frac{1}{K_\gamma^\ddagger} = \frac{\gamma_A\gamma_B}{\gamma_{[\text{AB}]^\ddagger}}. \tag{15-62}$$

The Debye–Hückel limiting law is

$$\log \gamma_i = -pz_i^2 \qquad [\text{Eq. (12-84)}],$$

where the constant $p = e^2\kappa/2D2.303\mathbf{k}T$ and κ is proportional to the square root of the ionic strength I [by Eq. (12-87)], where

$$I = \tfrac{1}{2}\sum C_i z_i^2 \qquad [\text{Eq. (12-70)}].$$

It follows that

$$\log \frac{1}{K_\gamma^\ddagger} = -[z_A^2 + z_B^2 - (z_A + z_B)^2]\alpha\sqrt{I} = 2z_Az_B\alpha\sqrt{I},$$

where for water as solvent $\alpha = 0.509$ at 25°C. Equation (15-61) may then be written

$$\log k = \log k_0 + 2z_Az_B\alpha\sqrt{I}, \tag{15-63}$$

where k_0 is the rate constant if $K_\gamma^\ddagger$ is unity—for example, at infinite dilution. Note that the same result follows from collision theory as phrased in the form of Eq. (15-30). We now deal with $\gamma_{[AB]}$, but the Debye–Hückel theory involves only the net charge on a species, and the distinction makes no difference.

Equation (15-63) predicts a linear relationship if $\log k$ is plotted against $\sqrt{I}$, with a slope proportional to $z_A z_B$. The qualitative prediction has been confirmed in that with increasing ionic strength reactions between like charged ions increase in rate constant and those between oppositely charged ions decrease in rate constant. It is questionable, however, whether Eq. (15-63) has ever been verified quantitatively. The difficulty is that the effect predicted is not very large relative to the precision of rate data until such ionic strengths are reached that serious departure from the Debye–Hückel limiting law occurs and Eq. (15-63) should not hold anyway. The reader is referred to Section 12-CN-2 for a discussion of activity

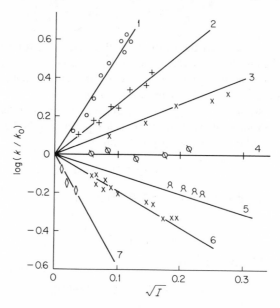

Fig. 15-12. *Effect of ionic strength on the rates of some ionic reactions.*

(1) $Co(NH_3)_5Br^{2+} + Hg^{2+} + H_2O \rightarrow Co(NH_3)_5(H_2O)^{3+} + HgBr^+$.

(2) $S_2O_8^{2-} + I^- \rightarrow (ISO_4^- + SO_4^{2-}) \rightarrow I_3^- + 2SO_4^{2-}$.

(3) $O_2N-N-COOC_2H_5 + OH^- \rightarrow N_2O + CO_3^{2-} + C_2H_5OH$.

(4) *cane sugar* $+ OH^- \rightarrow$ *invert sugar.*

(5) $H_2O_2 + H^+ + Br^- \rightarrow H_2O + \frac{1}{2}Br_2$ *(not balanced).*

(6) $Co(NH_3)_5Br^{2+} + OH^- \rightarrow Co(NH_3)_5(OH)^{2+} + Br^-$.

(7) $Fe^{2+} + Co(C_2O_4)_3^{3-} \rightarrow Fe^{3+} + Co(C_2O_4)_4^{3-}$.

[Adapted from "The Foundations of Chemical Kinetics," by S. W. Benson, Copyright 1960, McGraw-Hill, New York (Used with permission of McGraw-Hill Book Company) in which the detailed references may be found. The interested reader should also refer to A. Olson and T. Simonson, J. Chem. Phys. 17, 1167 (1949) for some adverse comments, and also to M. Kilpatrick, Ann. Rev. Phys. Chem. 2, 269 (1951).]

coefficients of electrolytes in more concentrated solutions. There is no doubt, however, that nonparticipating electrolytes or "neutral" salts do affect reaction rate constants. Figure 15-12 shows a traditional plot of rate constants for various types of charge reactions.

Reaction not involving ions or between a neutral molecule and an ion are also subject to ionic strength effects, but now higher concentrations are needed. Figure 15-13 illustrates the effect of ionic strength on the hydrolysis of γ-butyrolac-

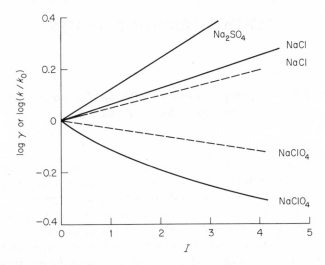

Fig. 15-13. *Effect of ionic strength on the activity coefficient (solid lines) and the relative rate of hydrolysis (dashed lines) of γ-butyrolactone. (From A. A. Frost and R. G. Pearson, "Kinetics and Mechanism," 2nd ed. Copyright 1961, Wiley, New York. Used with permission of John Wiley & Sons, Inc.)*

tone (and the solid lines give the variation of the activity coefficient of the lactone). The reaction is acid-catalyzed, with the rate proportional to the lactone and H^+ concentrations, and the fact that the ionic strength effect on the rate constant is in the same direction as, but smaller than, that on the activity coefficient of the reacting lactone suggests that the latter is being only partly compensated by a similar but smaller departure from ideality of the transition state (or of the encounter complex).

The determination of a rate law usually involves changes in concentrations of reactants, as in the usual procedure of fitting data to an integrated expression, and hence changes in the ionic makeup of the solution. The consequent activity coefficient changes can be severe enough to lead to error in the determination of the actual form of the rate law. An example is the reaction

$$Co(NH_3)_5(H_2O)^{3+} + X^- \rightarrow Co(NH_3)_5X^{2+} + H_2O,$$

where X^- denotes a halogen ion. Activity coefficient (or, alternatively, ion pairing) effects are so large that early studies appeared to give first-order kinetics, although the reaction is actually second order. One can reduce such effects by conducting the reaction in a medium having a high concentration of nonreactive salt such as 1 *M* sodium perchlorate. The activity coefficients of the reactants may then be nearly independent of their concentration.

COMMENTARY AND NOTES

15-CN-1 Comparison of Collision–Encounter and Transition-State Theories

It turns out to be quite difficult to devise a means of distinguishing experimentally between collision theory (as modified for solutions) and transition-state theory. In the case of the usual reaction of activation energy greater than about 10 kcal mole^{-1}, both treatments lead essentially to the experimentally observed Arrhenius equation. Both predict about the same frequency factor to be the "normal" one. The activity coefficient formulations are indistinguishable.

There seems no doubt, however, that the collision–encounter picture is essentially correct, at least with respect to the sequence of events up to actual chemical change. There are many substantiations of the cage model for liquids, and we have seen that bimolecular reactions in solution *do* reach a diffusion-controlled limit. Further, the existence of reactions showing the same rate constant in a solvent as in the gas phase indicates that collision frequencies, as distinct from encounter frequencies, are about the same in the two phases, provided that specific molecular interactions in the encounter complex are weak.

Transition-state theory, of course, offers a most appealing formalism in ascribing essentially well-behaved thermodynamic properties to a transition state or activated complex. The formalism leads naturally to pleasing explanations of the existence of linear free energy relationships. Also, the term $\exp(\Delta S^{0\ddagger}/R)$ is amenable to some very useful structural interpretations.

For example, the denaturation of proteins—in everyday experience, the cooking of an egg—is enormously temperature-sensitive. The denaturation rate doubles with about every 1° rise in temperature (the boiling point of water has dropped by about 10°C at 14,000 ft elevation and the time to boil an egg has increased perhaps 70-fold) corresponding to an activation energy of about 130 kcal mole^{-1}. The term $\exp(-E^*/RT)$ is then about 10^{-75} (!) at 100°C, so that the rate of denaturation should be negligible on this basis. The reaction does in fact occur, of course, and the transition-state formalism leads to a calculated compensating entropy of activation of about 300 cal $°K^{-1}$ mole^{-1}. This is understandable since denaturation corresponds to an unraveling of the secondary, helical coil of the protein to a far more random structure. If the transition state is one of partial unraveling, then $\Delta S^{0\ddagger}$ should indeed be a large positive number.

Although this is an extreme example, the point is that $\Delta S^{0\ddagger}$ often lies between zero and ΔS^0 for the overall reaction. The ratio $\Delta S^{0\ddagger}/\Delta S^0$ then appears to be a useful indication of the extent to which the transition state resembles either reactants or products. These are esthetic arguments, however. Their acceptance is more a matter of taste than of scientific necessity since comparable and not much more contrived rationalizations can be made in terms of the collision–encounter model.

An important point concerning reactions in solution has to do with the manner of energy acquisition. Transition-state theory is silent on this matter since it begins with the assumption that the activated complex is in equilibrium with its surroundings. Collision theory, however, suggests the following important difference between solution- and gas-phase reactions. In the latter case activation energy E^* is gained from the collisions of the reactants, drawing on their kinetic energy of impact and on the energy distributed among various internal degrees of freedom. In solution, however, the reactants that diffuse together to form the encounter complex are essentially of normal energy content. The activation energy must then be supplied by collisions of surrounding solvent molecules. Perhaps more accurately, the Boltzmann distribution of energies in a liquid is present as regions of extravibrational energy; these regions move around rapidly and can be thought of as soundlike waves in the liquid—called *phonons*. The activation of an encounter complex probably occurs when a confluence of phonon waves momentarily concentrates an unusually large amount of energy in the vicinity of the complex.

Such energy can hardly reside very long in any one locale, however. We know from fluorescence studies, for example, that an important competing process is one of radiationless deactivation by the solvent medium. In this case the entire energy of the excited state (see Fig. 15-7) is delivered to the molecule and surrounding solvent as vibrational energy, and this energy can amount to 50–100 kcal mole^{-1}, the usual energy content of fluorescing excited states. The molecule can be one which is unstable toward some chemical reaction with adjacent solvent molecules and the ordinary activation energy might be, say 25 kcal mole^{-1}. The experimental observation is that the 50–100 kcal mole^{-1} can often be dumped into molecular vibrations with little if any chemical reaction resulting. Thus, a complex such as $Co(NH_3)_5Cl^{2+}$ has an excited state lying about 54 kcal mole^{-1} above the ground state, corresponding to absorption of light of 530 nm wavelength. There is no fluorescence in room-temperature solution, so this energy is entirely dissipated by radiationless processes. The complex ion is unstable toward the aquation reaction

$$Co(NH_3)_5Cl^{2+} + H_2O \rightarrow Co(NH_3)_5(H_2O)^{3+} + Cl^-,$$

for which the activation energy is only 24 kcal mole^{-1}. Yet absorption of 530-nm light leads to virtually no chemical reaction at all!

Activation via the photochemical route need not give the same distribution of vibrational energies as phonon activation. The point remains that a large excess of vibrational energy, no matter how acquired, need not dwell long enough in the vicinity of the complex for its mere presence to ensure chemical reaction. In terms of the preceding example it seems likely that some one water molecule must be in just the right position to allow reaction to proceed within a few vibrational swings if the energy is available.

In summary, in the collision–encounter model, the encounter complex replaces the activated complex of transition-state theory; the two "complexes" are similar in concept except that the former possesses no unusual energy. The principal question, not yet answered, is whether the energized complex may have too short a period of existence to be regarded as a species in a definite thermodynamic state.

15-CN-2   Relationship between the Equilibrium Constant for a Reaction and Its Rate Constants

The statement has been made several times in this and the preceding chapter that the equilibrium constant K for a chemical reaction is equal to k_f/k_b, the ratio of the forward and backward rate constants. This is strictly true only for a simple reaction, that is, one for which the mechanism is the same as the overall reaction, and it is now time to take a closer look at the situation.

If the reaction is a simple one, such as

$$A + B = C + D, \qquad K = \frac{(C)(D)}{(A)(B)},$$

then $R_f = k_f(A)(B)$ and $R_b = k_b(C)(D)$, and at equilibrium $R_f = R_b$, so that

$$\frac{k_f}{k_b} = K. \tag{15-64}$$

Further, we have from Eq. (15-61) that

$$k_f = \frac{k_{0,f}\gamma_A\gamma_B}{\gamma_{[AB]^\ddagger}}, \qquad k_b = \frac{k_{0,b}\gamma_C\gamma_D}{\gamma_{[CD]^\ddagger}},$$

so that

$$\frac{k_{0,f}}{k_{0,b}} = \frac{(C)(D)}{(A)(B)} \frac{\gamma_C\gamma_D}{\gamma_A\gamma_B} \frac{\gamma_{[AB]^\ddagger}}{\gamma_{[CD]^\ddagger}}.$$

If we assume that $\gamma_{[AB]^\ddagger} = \gamma_{[CD]^\ddagger}$ or, in the collision–encounter model, that $\gamma_{[AB]} = \gamma_{[CD]}$, then

$$\frac{k_{0,f}}{k_{0,b}} = K_{th},\qquad(15\text{-}65)$$

where K_{th} is the thermodynamic equilibrium constant. This is the usual statement, in somewhat more elegant form.

Quite apart from activity coefficients, a complication arises if the reaction is complex, that is, if the reaction mechanism does not coincide with the statement of the overall reaction. Neglecting activity coefficients, it turns out that the correct general statement of Eq. (15-64) is

$$\frac{k_f}{k_b} = K^n,\qquad(15\text{-}66)$$

where n is an integer or rational fraction. The conclusion is perhaps best demonstrated by means of a specific example.

Consider the reaction

$$2Fe^{2+} + 2Hg^{2+} = 2Fe^{3+} + Hg_2^{2+}\qquad(15\text{-}67)$$

for which

$$K = \frac{(Fe^{3+})^2\,(Hg_2^{2+})}{(Fe^{2+})^2\,(Hg^{2+})^2}.\qquad(15\text{-}68)$$

The experimentally observed forward rate law is

$$R_f = k_f(Fe^{2+})(Hg^{2+}),\qquad(15\text{-}69)$$

which can be explained by the mechanism

$$\text{(a)}\quad Fe^{2+} + Hg^{2+} \underset{k_{-1}}{\overset{k_1}{\rightleftharpoons}} Fe^{3+} + Hg^+ \qquad\text{(slow)},$$

$$\text{(b)}\qquad\qquad 2Hg^+ \overset{K_2}{\rightleftharpoons} Hg_2^{2+} \qquad\qquad\text{(rapid equilibrium)}.$$

Then R_f is as given by Eq. (15-69) with $k_f = k_1$, and R_b is

$$R_b = k_{-1}(Fe^{3+})(Hg^+),$$

or, on elimination of (Hg^+) by means of the expression for K_2,

$$R_b = \frac{k_{-1}}{K_2^{1/2}}\,(Fe^{3+})(Hg_2^{2+})^{1/2} = k_b(Fe^{3+})(Hg_2^{2+})^{1/2}.\qquad(15\text{-}70)$$

On equating R_f to R_b at equilibrium, we obtain

$$\frac{k_f}{k_b} = \frac{(Fe^{3+})(Hg_2^{2+})^{1/2}}{(Fe^{2+})(Hg^{2+})}.\qquad(15\text{-}71)$$

The ratio k_f/k_b is thus the *square root* of K as defined by Eq. (15-68).

We can now generalize somewhat. Suppose that for some reaction the mechanism is such that

$$R_f = \theta_f(k)\ \phi_f(C),\tag{15-72}$$

where $\theta_f(k)$ denotes some function of rate constants and $\phi_f(C)$ some function of concentrations, and, similarly,

$$R_b = \theta_b(k)\ \phi_b(C).\tag{15-73}$$

At equilibrium R_f must equal R_b and therefore $\theta_f(k)\ \phi_f(C) = \theta_b(k)\ \phi_b(C)$ or $\theta_f(k)/\theta_b(k) = \phi_b(C)/\phi_f(C)$. The right-hand side of this last equation is a function of C only and must be identifiable with K^n, that is,

$$K^n = \frac{\theta_f(k)}{\theta_b(k)} = \frac{\phi_b(C)}{\phi_f(C)}.\tag{15-74}$$

If, now, the expression for R_f has been determined experimentally, it follows that the expression for R_b must be

$$R_b = K^n \theta_b(k)\ \phi_f(C).\tag{15-75}$$

The exponent n is not known *a priori*, and could be any rational number. Thus even though the forward rate law is known, as well as the overall reaction (and hence K), an indefinite number of possible expressions for R_b remain. Each is generated through Eq. (15-75) by making some particular choice for n.

Returning to the example, we see that R_f is given by Eq. (15-69) and K by Eq. (15-68), so that

$$R_b = \left[\frac{(\mathrm{Fe}^{3+})^2\ (\mathrm{Hg}_2^{2+})}{(\mathrm{Fe}^{2+})^2\ (\mathrm{Hg}^{2+})^2}\right]^n \theta_b(k)(\mathrm{Fe}^{2+})(\mathrm{Hg}^{2+}).\tag{15-76}$$

If n is set equal to $\frac{1}{2}$, Eq. (15-70) results, with $\theta_b(k) = k_b$, consistent with the mechanism given by reactions (a) and (b). Suppose, however, that we set $n = 1$. Now R_b must be

$$R_b = \theta_b(k)\frac{(\mathrm{Fe}^{3+})^2\ (\mathrm{Hg}_2^{2+})}{(\mathrm{Fe}^{2+})(\mathrm{Hg}^{2+})}.\tag{15-77}$$

Such a reverse rate law cannot be explained by the first mechanism, but does result from the following one [where (a) is as before]:

(a) $\mathrm{Fe}^{2+} + \mathrm{Hg}^{2+} \underset{k_{-1}}{\overset{k_1}{\rightleftharpoons}} \mathrm{Fe}^{3+} + \mathrm{Hg}^+$ (slow),

(b) $\mathrm{Fe}^{2+} + \mathrm{Hg}^+ \overset{K_3}{\rightleftharpoons} \mathrm{Fe}^{3+} + \mathrm{Hg}^\circ$ (rapid equilibrium),

(c) $\mathrm{Hg}^\circ + \mathrm{Hg}^{2+} \overset{K_4}{\rightleftharpoons} \mathrm{Hg}_2^{2+}$ (rapid equilibrium).

R_b is still

$$R_b = k_{-1}(\mathrm{Fe}^{3+})(\mathrm{Hg}^+),$$

but on eliminating (Hg^+) by means of K_3 and K_4, we obtain

$$R_b = \frac{k_{-1}}{K_3 K_4} \frac{(Fe^{3+})^2 (Hg_2^{2+})}{(Fe^{2+})(Hg^{2+})}, \tag{15-78}$$

which is the form required by Eq. (15-77).

Thus in the study of the rate of oxidation of ferrous by mercuric ion experimental knowledge of the forward rate law does not allow unambiguous selection among various possible mechanisms. The mass action relation between forward and reverse rate laws does serve to reduce the alternatives to a limited set. In practice, n can be expected to be a rather simple number such as 1, 2, or $\frac{1}{2}$. One therefore rarely proceeds further in considering possible mechanisms in cases where the forward rate law but not the reverse one has been determined experimentally.

15-CN-3 The Composition of the Encounter or Activated Complex

A consideration that is very useful in formulating a mechanism to account for observed rate data is the following. By either the collision–encounter or transition-state theories, the rate of reaction is determined by some step of the type $[XY]^{\ddagger} \rightarrow$ products, where $[XY]^{\ddagger}$ is the activated complex (or, alternatively, we would write $[XY]$, the encounter complex). We can show that the chemical composition of $[XY]^{\ddagger}$ (or of $[XY]$) is deducible from the experimentally observed rate law.

If the reaction is simple so that the mechanism is

$$A + B \rightleftharpoons [AB]^{\ddagger} \rightarrow \text{products},$$

then obviously the composition of $[XY]^{\ddagger}$ is just $A + B$. (The parallel phrasing in terms of $[XY]$ will be assumed henceforth.) Suppose, however, that the slow step is preceded by various rapid preequilibria, so that the rate law is of the form

$$R = k_{\text{slow}} f(K_1, K_2, \dots) \phi(C) \tag{15-79}$$

[or similar to Eq. (15-72) or Eq. (15-73)]. The composition of $[XY]^{\ddagger}$ is necessarily just $X + Y$, but X, Y, or both do not occur in the overall reaction

$$aA + bB + \cdots = mA + nN + \cdots$$

and $K_1, K_2, \dots$ allow the rephrasing of (X) and (Y) in terms of (A), (B), (M), and (N), as was done in the derivation of Eq. (15-78). Since an equilibrium constant is always written for a balanced equation, the total content of elements of the species in the numerator must be equal to that of the species in the denominator.

The consequence is that any alternative statement of (X) or of (Y) through the use of equilibrium constants must lead to an expression giving the same elemental composition.

Conversely, then, if the observed rate law is of the form

$$R = (\text{constant})(A)^x(B)^y(M)^z(N)^w \cdots,$$

then the composition of the activated complex must be given by

[x(elemental composition of A) + y(elemental composition of B)

+ z(elemental composition of M) + w(elemental composition of N) + $\cdots$].

Thus we know from Eq. (15-78) that the activated complex has the composition (2Fe + 2Hg − Fe − Hg) or (Fe + Hg). A check on the mechanism is that its slow step should indeed involve an activated complex of this composition [as step (a) in the example does]. Note that we are dealing with *elemental* composition —thus valence states and chemical structures are ignored.

SPECIAL TOPICS

15-ST-1   *Integrated Forms for Some Additional Rate Laws*

There are a few additional cases which occur often enough to warrant inclusion in this text. More extensive coverage can be found in monographs such as that by Benson (1960).

A. *Branching First-Order Reactions*

A compound may be able to react in two different ways. An example from coordination chemistry is

$$\text{Co(en)}_2(X)(Y)^+ + \text{H}_2\text{O} \quad \overset{k_1}{\underset{k_2}{\diagdown}} \quad \begin{array}{l} \text{Co(en)}_2(\text{H}_2\text{O})(X)^{2+} + X^- \\[1em] \text{Co(en)}_2(\text{H}_2\text{O})(Y)^{2+} + Y^- \end{array} \tag{15-80}$$

where "en" denotes the bidentate ligand ethylenediamine and X and Y are halogens or pseudohalogens. If both reactions are first order, then the rate of disappearance of reactant A is

$$\frac{d(A)}{dt} = -(k_1 + k_2)(A), \tag{15-81}$$

or still first order, but with $k_{app} = k_1 + k_2$. The rates of formation of the alternative products B and C are

$$\frac{d(B)}{dt} = k_1(A), \qquad \frac{d(C)}{dt} = k_2(A).$$

Thus the ratio of (B) to (C) at any time must be k_1/k_2, and their sum, of course, must be $(A)_0 - (A)$. If, for example, k_1 and k_2 were 0.1 hr^{-1} and 0.2 hr^{-1}, respectively, the plots of concentrations versus time would look as shown in Fig. 15-14.

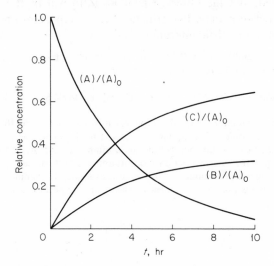

Fig. 15-14. *The case*

with $k_1 = 0.1$ hr^{-1} and $k_2 = 0.2$ hr^{-1}.

The products B and C will have some equilibrium ratio themselves, and this in general will not be the same as k_1/k_2. The example of Fig. 15-14 is based on the assumption that the B–C equilibration is slow, so that the product ratio (B)/(C) is kinetically determined. The general situation is

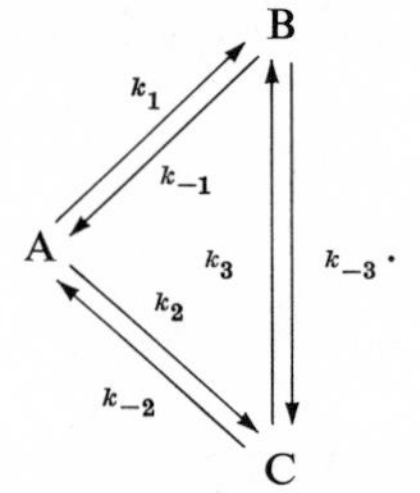

$$(15\text{-}82)$$

If k_3 and k_{-3} are large compared to $k_1 + k_2$, then B and C will equilibrate as they are produced, and the observed product ratio will be the equilibrium one. The distinction between these two situations is an important one if the rate data are to be used in mechanistic interpretations.

As an example, if X and Y in Eq. (15-80) are Cl$^-$ and NCS$^-$, respectively, it turns out that k_1 is much larger than k_2, so the reaction is exclusively

$$Co(en)_2(NCS)(Cl)^+ + H_2O \rightarrow Co(en)_2(H_2O)(NCS)^{2+} + Cl^-. \qquad (15\text{-}83)$$

The equilibration between the two possible products is slow, so that in this case the product ratio is kinetically determined. The equilibrium also strongly favors the product $Co(en)_2(H_2O)$ $(NCS)^{2+}$, so that the rate constants parallel the equilibrium constants K_1 and K_2, that is, $k_1 \gg k_2$ and $K_1 \gg K_2$. A linear free energy relationship thus appears to be present.

This need not be the case. Continuing with the same example, the complex $Co(en)_2(NCS)(Cl)^+$, being octahedral, has *cis* and *trans* isomers as shown in the accompanying diagram. The *cis*

Trans   Cis

isomer is the thermodynamically favored one, and if allowed to aquate according to Eq. (15-83), the product is entirely *cis*-$Co(en)_2(H_2O)(NCS)^{2+}$. However, if the *trans* isomer is the starting material, then about 60% *cis* and 40% *trans* product results. In this last instance, then, the reaction is definitely subject to some kinetic, stereospecific control. If $X = Cl^-$ and $Y = NO_2^-$ the chloride aquation reaction, which again dominates, is 100 % stereospecific, *cis* starting material giving *cis* product only and *trans* starting material giving *trans* product only.

The reaction scheme of Eq. (15-82) is the classic one of a triangular reaction system. The mathematics was investigated extensively in the 1920's and for a while it appeared that if an equilibrium system were perturbed by, say, the sudden addition of more A, then the concentrations of A, B, and C could undergo oscillation. This has never been observed experimentally, and more modern calculations suggest that there is no combination of k values that could sustain oscillations.

B. Sequential First-Order Reactions

The reaction sequence

$$A \xrightarrow{k_1} B \xrightarrow{k_2} C \tag{15-84}$$

occurs often enough that its mathematical behavior should be explored. Each reaction is first order or pseudo first order and each goes to completion. The equations for (A) are as before,

$$\frac{d(A)}{dt} = -k_1(A) \qquad \text{[Eq. (14-3)]},$$

$$(A) = (A)_0 \, e^{-k_1 t} \qquad \text{[Eq. (14-6)]}.$$

For (B), however, we have

$$\frac{d(B)}{dt} = k_1(A) - k_2(B) = k_1(A)_0 \, e^{-k_1 t} - k_2(B). \tag{15-85}$$

Equation (15-85) may be put in integrable form by a change of variable,

$$R = (B) \, e^{k_1 t} \qquad \text{or} \qquad (B) = R e^{-k_1 t} \qquad \text{and} \qquad \frac{d(B)}{dt} = e^{-k_1 t} \frac{dR}{dt} - k_1 R e^{-k_1 t}.$$

Substitution into Eq. (15-85) introduces $e^{-k_1 t}$ into each term, so that it may be canceled out, leaving, on rearrangement,

$$\frac{dR}{dt} = k_1(A)_0 + (k_1 - k_2)R, \qquad \text{or} \qquad \int \frac{dR}{k_1(A)_0 + (k_1 - k_2)R} = t,$$

and

$$\frac{1}{k_1 - k_2} \ln[k_1(A)_0 + (k_1 - k_2)R] = t + \text{constant}.$$

We now replace R by $(B)\, e^{k_1 t}$ and solve for (B), evaluating the constant of integration by setting $(B) = 0$ at $t = 0$, to obtain

$$(B) = \frac{k_1(A)_0}{k_2 - k_1}\, (e^{-k_1 t} - e^{-k_2 t}). \tag{15-86}$$

If (C) is the final product, then, by material balance,

$$(C) = (A)_0 - (A) - (B). \tag{15-87}$$

The behavior of the reaction sequence of Eq. (15-84) is somewhat complex since, although (A) is always given by Eq. (14-6), there is a qualitative difference in the behavior of (B) and hence of (C) for $k_2 > k_1$ versus $k_2 < k_1$.

CASE 1. $k_2 > k_1$.   Equation (15-86) may be put in the form

$$(B) = \frac{k_1(A)_0}{k_2 - k_1}\, e^{-k_1 t}(1 - e^{-(k_2 - k_1)t}) = \frac{k_1(A)}{k_2 - k_1}\, (1 - e^{-(k_2 - k_1)t}). \tag{15-88}$$

The second exponential term of Eq. (15-88) goes to zero at times long compared to $1/(k_2 - k_1)$, and in this limit

$$\left(\frac{(B)}{(A)}\right)_{\text{lim}} = \frac{k_1}{k_2 - k_1} \quad \text{or} \quad (B)_{\text{lim}} = \frac{k_1}{k_2 - k_1}\, (A)_0\, e^{-k_1 t}. \tag{15-89}$$

Thus (B) eventually must parallel (A), differing from it by the constant factor $k_1/(k_2 - k_1)$. This limiting condition is known as one of *transient equilibrium*, a name given by early radiochemists; sequences such as Eq. (15-84) are especially common with radioactive species (see Section 21-5). Since $(B) = 0$ at $t = 0$ and returns toward zero as (A) goes to zero, we conclude that (B) must have a maximum value, as is indeed the case. At the maximum $d(B)/dt = 0$, and so, by Eq. (15-85), $k_1(A) = k_2(B)$. Insertion of this relationship into Eq. (15-88) gives

$$e^{-(k_2 - k_1)t_{\max}} = \frac{k_1}{k_2}, \qquad t_{\max} = \frac{\ln(k_2/k_1)}{k_2 - k_1}. \tag{15-90}$$

Figure 15-15(a) shows the variation of (A), (B), and (C) with time for the case of $k_1 = 0.1$ hr^{-1} and $k_2 = 0.3$ hr^{-1}. Note that (B) never exceeds (A); in general,

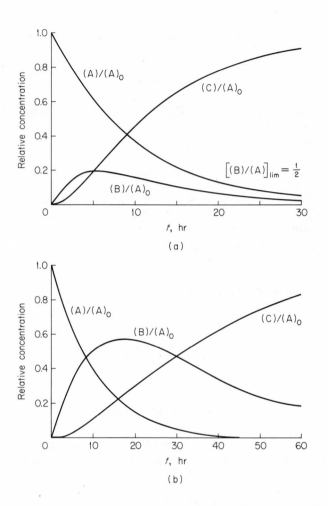

Fig. 15-15. *Sequential first-order reactions. (a) The case of transient equilibrium, $k_2 > k_1$ (b) The case of no equilibrium, $k_2 < k_1$.*

the mathematics of this case does not allow B ever to be the majority species. Note also that (C) shows a time lag or induction period before beginning to rise rapidly; the inflection point is at t_{max} of Eq. (15-90).

CASE 2 $k_1 > k_2$. We now write Eq. (15-86) in the form

$$(B) = \frac{k_1(A)_0}{k_1 - k_2} e^{-k_2 t}(1 - e^{-(k_1 - k_2)t}). \tag{15-91}$$

The second exponential term goes to zero at times long compared to $1/(k_1 - k_2)$, to give

$$(\text{B})_{\text{lim}} = \frac{k_1}{k_1 - k_2} (\text{A})_0 \, e^{-k_2 t}. \tag{15-92}$$

The previous condition of secular equilibrium is not present—(B) simply disappears according to its own rate constant k_2. If $k_1 \gg k_2$, (A) disappears very quickly, leaving only (B), which then reacts at its own slower rate:

$$(\text{B})_{\text{lim}} = (\text{A})_0 \, e^{-k_2 t}.$$

An illustrative set of curves is shown in Fig. 15-15(b) for $k_1 = 0.1 \text{ hr}^{-1}$ as before, but now with $k_2 = 0.0333 \text{ hr}^{-1}$. The concentration (B) goes through a maximum as before, with t_{max} again given by Eq. (15-90), and for a time B is the dominant species. Again, there is an induction period for (C).

C. Reversible Second-Order Reactions

We consider the simple reaction

$$\text{A} + \text{B} \overset{k_1}{\underset{k_2}{\rightleftharpoons}} \text{C} + \text{D},$$

for which the rate law is

$$\frac{d(\text{A})}{dt} = -k_1(\text{A})(\text{B}) + k_2(\text{C})(\text{D}).$$

If a and b denote the initial concentrations of A and B, respectively, and x denotes the degree of advancement of the reaction, so that $(\text{A}) = (a - x)$ and $(\text{B}) = (b - x)$, then we have

$$\frac{dx}{dt} = k_1(a - x)(b - x) - k_2 x^2$$

(supposing no C or D to be present initially), or

$$\frac{dx}{\alpha + \beta x + \gamma x^2} = dt, \tag{15-93}$$

where $\alpha = k_1 ab$, $\beta = -k_1(a + b)$, and $\gamma = k_1 - k_2$. Equation (15-93) integrates to give

$$\ln \frac{\gamma x + \frac{1}{2}(\beta - q^{1/2})}{\gamma x + \frac{1}{2}(\beta + q^{1/2})} = q^{1/2} t + \delta, \tag{15-94}$$

where $q = \beta^2 - 4\alpha\gamma$ and δ is the constant of integration, determined by setting $x = 0$ and $t = 0$. Equation (15-94) is difficult to use experimentally. A problem is that, given some experimental error in the data points and a limited range of t, it may be possible to find choices of k_1 and k_2 that appear to fit the results even though some other rate law is actually the correct one. We should either choose experimental conditions such that the system becomes a reversible first-order one (such as by having excess B and D present) or, at least, obtain an independent relation between k_1 and k_2 (such as from the equilibrium constant). Figure 15-16

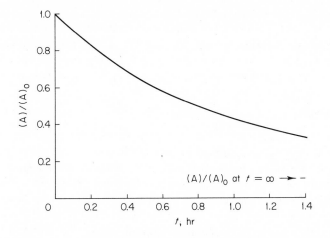

Fig. 15-16. *The case* $A + B \underset{k_2}{\overset{k_1}{\rightleftharpoons}} C + D$; *illustration of Eq. (15-94).*

illustrates the relatively uninformative shape of an $(A)/(A)_0$ versus time plot given by Eq. (15-94); it is calculated for $a = 0.1\ M$ and $b = 0.2\ M$.

D. Rate Law for Isotopic Exchange

A type of kinetic approach that has been widely deployed in the study of reaction mechanisms is isotopic labeling to follow the exchange of an atom or group between two chemical states. An example of an exchange reaction is

$$RBr + {}^{80}Br^- = R^{80}Br + Br^-, \tag{15-95}$$

where R might be an alkyl group, and radioactive ^{80}Br is used as a label. Other examples are

$$SO_4^{2-} + H_2{}^{18}O = SO_3{}^{18}O^{2-} + H_2O, \tag{15-96}$$

where oxygen exchange is studied with the use of the stable isotope ^{18}O and

$$Ni(CN)_4^{2-} + {}^{14}CN^- = Ni(CN)_3({}^{14}CN)^{2-} + CN^-, \tag{15-97}$$

$$^{55}Fe^{3+} + Fe^{2+} = {}^{55}Fe^{2+} + Fe^{3+}, \tag{15-98}$$

in which radiocarbon and iron are tracers.

The normal exchange procedure consists of establishing an equilibrium system containing the two chemical species AX and BX, having atom X in common and exchange between which is to be studied, and following the rate of appearance of labeled BX if the labeling was originally present in AX. That is, the reaction type is

$$AX^* + BX \rightleftharpoons AX + BX^*, \tag{15-99}$$

where the asterisk denotes the presence of a radioactive atom or an excess of some stable isotope of the atom. Samples of the system are taken periodically, compounds A and B are physically separated by some procedure (such as precipitation or solvent extraction), and the content of labeled atom in each is determined. It is ordinarily assumed that different isotopes of the same atom have essentially identical chemistry, which means that at exchange equilibrium the proportion of labeled X atoms must be the same in compound AX as in compound BX.

It turns out that these conditions imply that the kinetics of an exchange reaction will always be of the first-order reversible type, regardless of the actual mechanism whereby the exchange occurs. The demonstration of this conclusion is as follows. Since the system of Eq. (15-99) is at chemical equilibrium—that is, the amounts of AX and BX are not changing with time—it follows that R_f, the rate at which chemical species AX forms chemical species BX, is just equal to R_b, the rate of the back reaction. We denote the total amounts of AX and of BX by a and b, respectively, and the amount of AX* and BX* by x and y, respectively,

$$AX^* + BX \rightleftharpoons AX + BX^*,$$
$$x \quad\ b \quad\ a \quad\ y$$

and suppose that x_0 is the initial amount of AX* (and $y_0 = 0$). Then the rate of appearance of BX* must be

$$\frac{dy}{dt} = R\frac{x}{a} - R\frac{y}{b}, \tag{15-100}$$

where $R = R_f = R_b$. That is, the rate of appearance of BX* is the overall chemical rate R times the fraction of atoms X in compound AX that are labeled, and the rate of back exchange is R times the fraction of atoms X in compound BX that are labeled. Since $x_0 = x + y$, Eq. (15-100) can be written

$$\frac{dy}{dt} = \frac{Rx_0}{a} - R\left(\frac{1}{a} + \frac{1}{b}\right)y.$$

Separation of variables and integration gives

$$\frac{Rx_0}{a} - cy = (\text{constant}) \, e^{-ct}, \qquad \text{where} \quad c = R\left(\frac{1}{a} + \frac{1}{b}\right). \qquad (15\text{-}101)$$

The constant of integration is evaluated from $y = 0$ at $t = 0$, and rearrangement leads to

$$cy = \frac{Rx_0}{a}(1 - e^{-ct}).$$

However at exchange equilibrium, $y_\infty = x_0 b/(a + b)$, so

$$\frac{Rx_0}{a} = \frac{Ry_\infty}{ab/(a+b)} = cy_\infty,$$

and the final form of the exchange rate equation is

$$1 - \frac{y}{y_\infty} = e^{-ct}, \qquad (15\text{-}102)$$

which is a special case of Eq. (15-5). Thus a plot of $\ln[1 - (y/y_\infty)]$ versus t should give a straight line of slope $-c$.

Each exchange experiment provides a value of the exchange rate constant c for some particular set of values of a and b. Use of Eq. (15-101) then gives the rate R of the chemical reaction responsible for the exchange. The rate law for the chemical reaction is then explored by repetition of the exchange study with varying concentrations of (AX) and (BX).

By way of example, the exchange of n-C_4H_9I with I^- was followed at 50°C with radioiodide ion as tracer. Samples were withdrawn periodically and the amount of radioactivity associated with the butyl iodide determined. The plots of $[1 - (y/y_\infty)]$ versus t for three sets of concentrations are shown in Fig. 15-17. Thus for (RX) = 0.1 M and (I^-) = 0.2 M, the exchange half-life is 0.588 hr, or $c = 1.178$ hr^{-1}. From Eq. (15-101), we find the rate of reaction $R = 1.178/[(1/0.1) +$

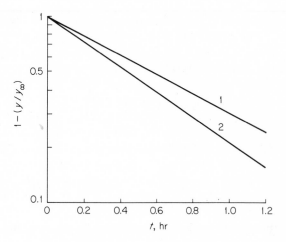

Fig. 15-17. *Exchange of n-C₄H₉I(RI) with I⁻. (1) (RI) = 0.1 M, (I⁻) = 0.2 M, or (RI) = 0.2 M, (I⁻) = 0.1 M. (2) (RI) = (I⁻) = 0.2 M.*

$(1/0.2)] = 0.0785$ liter mole⁻¹ hr⁻¹. The same slope and R value are obtained if $(RX) = 0.2$ and $(I⁻) = 0.1$. If both concentrations are $0.2\ M$, then the exchange half-life becomes 0.441 hr, which leads to an R value of 0.157. Thus doubling (RX) at constant $(I⁻)$ doubles the rate, indicating the rate law to be first order in (RX), and doubling (RX) while halving $(I⁻)$ does not change the rate, implying first-order dependence on $(I⁻)$ as well.

The rate then appears to be given by $R = k(RI)(I⁻)$, with $k = 0.0785/(0.1)(0.2) = 3.92$ liter mole⁻¹ hr⁻¹ [or $k = 0.157/(0.2)(0.2) = 3.9$ liter mole⁻¹ hr⁻¹]. The exchange of one halogen for another in alkyl iodides is believed to occur by the bimolecular process

$$CHR_1R_2I + X⁻ \rightarrow CHR_1R_2X + I⁻.$$

Exchange studies have, in fact, provided strong confirmatory support for this *Walden inversion mechanism*.

Some further points are the following. The quantities a and b refer to the amounts (or concentrations) of labeled element, so that in a case such as that of Eq. (15-97), $a = 4[Ni(CN)_4^{2-}]$ and $b = (CN⁻)$. The rate law, or expression for R, remains, of course, in terms of the concentrations of the molecular species, $[Ni(CN)_4^{2-}]$ and $(CN⁻)$.

It was assumed in the derivation that $x \ll a$ and $y \ll b$, that is, that the amounts of labeled elements were small compared to those of the normal ones. This is generally true in the case of radioactive labeling but is usually not so if labeling is by means of a stable isotope. The writing of Eq. (15-100) is altered, but the final result is still Eq. (15-102).

15-ST-2 Enzyme Catalysis

A very important family of catalytic reactions comprises those involving an enzyme. Enzymes are biologically developed catalysts, each usually having some one specific function in a living organism. Pepsin, secreted by the stomach, catalyzes the hydrolysis of proteins; urease, that of urea; others are involved in the mechanism of blood clotting, in the fixation of nitrogen by legumes, and so on. Some 150 different types of enzymes have been isolated in crystalline form; many others remain to be well characterized. Enzymes themselves may have molecular weights of 15,000 or more but in the living organism may be associated with a large protein or other molecule.

A rather widely applicable kinetic framework for enzymatic action is that known as the *Michaelis mechanism*. If an enzyme E acts to catalyze the reaction of some species, called the substrate S, then the first step is an association:

$$S + E \underset{k_{-1}}{\overset{k_1}{\rightleftharpoons}} S \cdot E. \qquad (15\text{-}103)$$

The enzyme–substrate complex then breaks up into products plus free enzyme,

$$S \cdot E \overset{k_2}{\rightarrow} E + P \text{ (products)}. \qquad (15\text{-}104)$$

The steady-state approximation (Section 14-4C) is made:

$$\frac{d(S \cdot E)}{dt} = k_1(S)(E) - k_{-1}(S \cdot E) - k_2(S \cdot E) = 0. \qquad (15\text{-}105)$$

Since by material balance, $(E) + (S \cdot E) = (E)_0$, where $(E)_0$ is the total enzyme concentration, Eq. (15-105) may be solved for $(S \cdot E)$ to give

$$(S \cdot E) = \frac{k_1(S)(E)_0}{k_1(S) + k_{-1} + k_2}.$$

The rate of formation of products is then obtained from Eq. (15-104) as

$$\frac{d(P)}{dt} = k_2(S \cdot E) = \frac{k_2(S)(E)_0}{(S) + [(k_{-1} + k_2)/k_1]}. \qquad (15\text{-}106)$$

The quantity $(k_{-1} + k_2)/k_1$ is called the Michaelis constant; for a given enzyme, it will be characteristic of the substrate.

A plot of Eq. (15-106) is shown in Fig. 15-18(a). Note that $d(P)/dt$ reaches a limiting value equal to $k_2(E)_0$, from which k_2 follows. Catalase, for example,

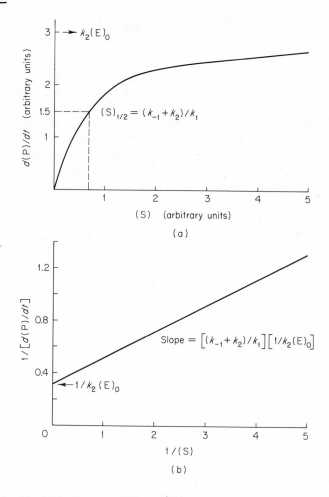

Fig. 15-18. *The Michaelis mechanism. (a) Plot according to Eq. (15-106). (b) Plot according to Eq. (15-107) (same data).*

catalyzes the decomposition of hydrogen peroxide into water and oxygen with a k_2 value of about 10^8 min^{-1}. Further, when the rate is just half of the maximum or limiting rate, then $(k_{-1} + k_2)/k_1 = (S)_{1/2}$, so that the ratio k_1/k_{-1} can be calculated on introduction of the value for k_2.

A more elegant approach follows from the writing of Eq. (15-106) in the form

$$\frac{1}{d(P)/dt} = \frac{1}{k_2(E)_0} + \frac{k_{-1} + k_2}{k_1} \frac{1}{k_2(E)_0} \frac{1}{(S)}. \qquad (15\text{-}107)$$

As illustrated in Fig. 15-18(b), a plot of $1/[d(P)/dt]$ versus $1/(S)$ should then give a straight line whose slope and intercept allow evaluation of k_2 and of k_1/k_{-1} [if $(E)_0$ is known].

15-ST-3 Effect of Mechanical Pressure on Reaction Rates

It is easiest to approach the effect of pressure on reaction rates through the formalism of transition-state theory, whereby we can write

$$k = \frac{kT}{h} \exp\left(-\frac{\Delta G^{0\ddagger}}{RT}\right) \qquad \text{or} \qquad \ln k = \ln \frac{kT}{h} - \frac{\Delta G^{0\ddagger}}{RT}.$$

It follows from Eq. (6-47) that

$$\left(\frac{\partial(\ln k)}{\partial P}\right)_T = -\frac{\Delta \bar{V}^{0\ddagger}}{RT}. \tag{15-108}$$

Strictly speaking, the effect of pressure on activity coefficients is being neglected, but this contribution should be small compared to the $\Delta \bar{V}^{0\ddagger}$ term if the system is dilute, so that departures from ideality are not large.

Partial molal volume changes for a reaction are generally small—of the order of 20 cm³ mole⁻¹, and pressures of thousands of atmospheres are needed to make an appreciable change in k. Experiments therefore require special high-pressure equipment. Some representative data are given in Fig. 15-19. It appears that $\Delta \bar{V}^{0\ddagger}$ values tend to lie between zero and $\Delta \bar{V}^0$, the value for the overall reaction. The results also tend to make qualitative sense in terms of structural considerations. If a reaction involves bond breaking, it seems reasonable that $\Delta \bar{V}^{0\ddagger}$ should be positive, corresponding to an expanded or loose activated complex structure relative to that of the reactants, as in the case of the decomposition of benzoyl peroxide (curve 1 in the figure). Conversely, $\Delta \bar{V}^{0\ddagger}$ should be negative for an association reaction since the transition state should now involve incipient bond formation and hence a compaction. This case is illustrated by curve 2 in the figure. An ionization reaction also tends to give a negative $\Delta \bar{V}^{0\ddagger}$, presumably as a consequence of the electrostatic compaction of solvent around ions; that is, one assumes the transition state to correspond to incipient ionization.

As a numerical illustration, we read from curve 2 of Fig. 15-19 that $\log(k_P/k)$ at 50°C is about 1.0 at $P = 2000$ atm for the dimerization of cyclopentadiene, where k_P and k are the rate constants at P and at 1 atm, respectively. Therefore $\partial(\ln k)/\partial P = 5 \times 10^{-4}$ atm⁻¹. From Eq. (15-108),

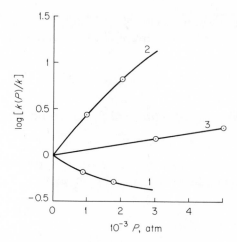

Fig. 15-19. *Variation of some rate constants with pressure. Curve 1: rate of decomposition of benzoyl peroxide at 70°C; curve 2: rate of dimerization of cyclopentadiene at 50°C (in monomer as solvent); curve 3: rate for $C_2H_5I + C_2H_5O^- \rightarrow C_2H_5OC_2H_5 + I^-$ in ethanol at 25°C. (From "The Foundations of Chemical Kinetics." by S. W. Benson. Copyright 1960, McGraw-Hill, New York. Used with permission of McGraw-Hill Book Company.)*

$\Delta \bar{V}^{0\ddagger}$ is then $-(82)(323)(5 \times 10^{-4}) = -13 \text{ cm}^3$. For comparison, $\Delta \bar{V}^0$ for the overall reaction can be estimated to be about -30 cm^3.

GENERAL REFERENCES

BASOLO, F., AND PEARSON, R. G. (1967). "Mechanisms of Inorganic Reactions," 2nd ed. Wiley New York.
BENSON, S. W. (1960). "Foundations of Chemical Kinetics." McGraw-Hill, New York.
BRESLOW, R. (1969). "Organic Reaction Mechanisms," 2nd ed. Benjamin, New York.
CALDIN, E. F. (1964). "Fast Reactions in Solution." Wiley, New York.
FROST, A. A., AND PEARSON, R. G. (1961). "Kinetics and Mechanism," 2nd ed. Wiley, New York.
LANGFORD, C. H., AND GRAY, H. B. (1965). "Ligand Substitution Processes." Benjamin, New York.
NORTH, A. M. (1964). "The Collision Theory of Chemical Reactions in Liquids." Methuen, London.

CITED REFERENCES

BELL, R., AND HIGGINSON, W. (1949). *Proc. Roy. Soc.* **A197**, 141.
BENSON, S. W. (1960). "Foundations of Chemical Kinetics." McGraw-Hill, New York.
EIGEN, M. (1963). *Angew. Chem.* **75**, 498.
HAMMETT, L. P. (1940). "Physical Organic Chemistry." McGraw-Hill, New York.

Exercises

15-1 The initial rate of the reaction

$$A \underset{k_2}{\overset{k_1}{\rightleftharpoons}} B$$

is 0.2% A reacted per minute; at equilibrium 80% of A is converted to B. Calculate the half time of the reaction.

Ans. 277 min.

15-2 The dissociation constant of a weak acid HA is 3×10^{-6} mole liter^{-1} and the relaxation time observed in a temperature-jump experiment using a 2×10^{-3} M solution is 6.5 μsec. Calculate the rate constants for dissociation and association, k_1 and k_{-1}.

Ans. 3.0×10^3 sec^{-1}, 1.00×10^9 liter mole^{-1} sec^{-1}.

15-3 Consider the reaction $CH_3Br + I^-$ occurring in aqueous solution (see Table 15-1). Assume both species to be 4 Å in diameter and that Eq. (10-42) applies. Taking 25°C and the solution to be 1 M in each species, calculate (a) the reaction rate, (b) the frequency factor A, (c) the encounter rate, (d) the encounter frequency factor A_e, (e) the collision frequency from collision theory, and (f) the value of K_e assuming that ΔH_e^0 is zero.

Ans. (a) 6.96×10^{-4} mole liter^{-1} sec^{-1}, (b) 1.68×10^{10} liter mole^{-1} sec^{-1} (from Table 15-1), (c) 7.4×10^9 mole liter^{-1} sec^{-1}, (d) same as encounter rate in this case, (e) 1.02×10^{11} mole liter^{-1} sec^{-1}, (f) 2.7×10^{-3} liter mole^{-1}.

15-4 Verify (a) Eq. (15-39), (b) Eq. (15-42), (c) Eq. (15-48), (d) Eq. (15-51), and (e) Eq. (15-57).

15-5 For chloroacetic acid $K_a = 1.38 \times 10^{-3}$ mole liter^{-1}. Estimate the rate constant for the dissociation of this acid at 25°C.

Ans. 1.4×10^8 sec^{-1}.

15-6 The equilibrium constant for the reaction $Co(NH_3)_5(H_2O)^{3+} + Br^- = Co(NH_3)_5Br^{2+} + H_2O$ is 0.37 liter mole^{-1} and the rate constant for the back reaction is 6.3×10^{-6} sec^{-1} (both values for 25°C). Calculate the rate constant for the forward or anation reaction (a) in a low-ionic-strength medium and (b) in 0.1 M NaClO$_4$.

Ans. (a) 2.33×10^{-6} liter mole^{-1} sec^{-1}, (b) 2.5×10^{-7} liter mole^{-1} sec^{-1}.

Problems

15-1 Find the rate law for the reaction $3HNO_2 = H_2O + 2NO + H^+ + NO_3^-$ if the actual mechanism is the following, where the first two steps rapidly attain equilibrium and the third step is slow:

(1) $2HNO_2 = NO + NO_2 + H_2O$

(2) $2NO_2 = N_2O_4$,

(3) $N_2O_4 + H_2O \overset{k}{\rightarrow} HNO_2 + H^+ + NO_3^-$.

15-2 The reaction $2Fe^{2+} + 2Hg^{2+} = Hg_2^{2+} + 2Fe^{3+}$ has been studied by measurement of the optical density of the solution at various times. The initial solutions contained only ferrous and mercuric ions, and at the wavelength employed the optical density D increased owing to the increased absorption of the products. The following two runs are given: Run 1, initially $(Fe^{2+}) = 0.1$, $(Hg^{2+}) = 0.1$; run 2, initially $(Fe^{2+}) = 0.1$, $(Hg^{2+}) = 0.001$.

Run 1			Run 2	
t (sec)	D	$(Hg^{2+})/0.1$	t (sec)	$(Hg^{2+})/0.001$
0	0.100	—	0	1.000
1×10^5	0.400	—	0.5×10^5	0.585
2×10^5	0.500	—	1.0×10^5	0.348
3×10^5	0.550	—	1.5×10^5	0.205
∞	0.700	—	2.0×10^5	0.122
			∞	0

(a) Calculate the ratios $(Hg^{2+})/0.1$ for run 1, that is the fraction of Hg^{2+} remaining at the various times.
(b) Show what the order of the reaction is in run 1 and in run 2.
(c) If the rate equation is written in the form: $Rate = k(Fe^{2+})^p(Hg^{2+})^q$, what are the values of p and q?
(d) Write a possible mechanism which would give this rate law.

15-3 The kinetics of the reaction $S_2O_8^{2-} + 2I^- \rightarrow 2SO_4^{2-} + I_2$ is being studied. A solution was made up which was 0.1 M in KI and 0.001 M in $K_2S_2O_8$, and the concentration of iodine was measured at 3 min intervals with the following results:

t (min)	0	3	6	9	12
(I_2) (mole liter^{-1})	0	0.00010	0.00019	0.00027	0.00034

The rate of the reaction will be some function of the concentrations of the species appearing in the overall equations, such as

$$d(I_2)/dt = k(S_2O_8^{2-})^a(I^-)^b(SO_4^{2-})^c(I_2)^d.$$

(a) Derive from the data as much information as you can about the values of the exponents a, b, c, and d. (b) The following mechanism is proposed for the reaction:

$$S_2O_8^{2-} + I^- = SO_4I^- + SO_4^{2-} \quad \text{(rapid equilibrium)},$$

$$I^- + SO_4I^- \xrightarrow{k} I_2 + SO_4^{2-} \quad \text{(slow)}.$$

Show what the values of a, b, c, and d are that would be predicted by this proposed mechanism. Discuss whether the rate data are compatible with the mechanism.

15-4 The following data are obtained on the kinetics of the lactonization of hydroxyvaleric acid. The overall reaction is

$$CH_3CHOHCH_2CH_2COOH \rightarrow CH_3-CH-CH_2-CH_2-C=O + H_2O.$$
$$\underset{O}{||}$$

	25°C				50°C	
(H+) = 0.025 M			(H+) = 0.050 M		(H+) = 0.025 M	
t (min)	Concentration of acid (M)		t (min)	Concentration of acid (M)	t (min)	Concentration of acid (M)
0	0.080		0	0.100	0	0.080
2	0.0570		2	0.0510	1	0.0408
4	0.0408		4	0.0260	2	0.0210
6	0.0295		6	0.0133	3	0.0107
8	0.0210					

The rate is to be expressed by the equation $d(\text{hydroxyvaleric acid})/dt = k(\text{H}^+)^a(\text{hydroxy-}$ valeric acid)^b. Calculate the values of a and b and the value of the rate constant k at 25°C and 50°C, and the activation energy. Estimate the entropy of activation.

15-5 Cobaltic trioxalate undergoes a thermal decomposition into cobaltous dioxalate and carbon dioxide. The following mechanism is assumed;

$$\text{Co(Ox)}_3^{3-} \underset{k_2}{\overset{k_1}{\rightleftharpoons}} \text{Co(Ox)}_2^{2-} + \text{C}_2\text{O}_4^-,$$

$$\text{C}_2\text{O}_4^- + \text{Co(Ox)}_3^{3-} \overset{k_3}{\rightarrow} \text{Co(Ox)}_2^{2-} + 2\text{CO}_2 + \text{C}_2\text{O}_4^{2-}.$$

Derive the corresponding rate expression if (a) the first reaction is assumed to be a rapid reversible equilibrium, and the second reaction is rate determining, (b) the forward direction of the first reaction is rate determining, and (c) a stationary state is assumed. Derive likewise the three cases if instead of the second reaction, the assumed reaction is

$$2\text{C}_2\text{O}_4^- \overset{k_4}{\rightarrow} 2\text{CO}_2 + \text{C}_2\text{O}_4^{2-}.$$

15-6 A mixed ethanol–water solvent is 0.0677 M in formic acid (plus some added HCl as catalyst) and the esterification reaction is followed by periodic titration of 5 cm³ aliquots by 0.010 m base. The following data (for 25°C) are obtained:

Time (min)	0	50	100	160	290	∞
Amount of base (cm³)	43.52	40.40	37.75	35.10	31.09	24.29

Calculate the rate constants k_1 and k_{-1} for the formation and decomposition of the ester and the equilibrium constant K. If the rate law is written to include (H+) (as catalyst), what are the values of k_1 and k_{-1} ?

15-7 The aquation reaction $\text{Co(NH}_3)_5\text{Br}^{2+} + \text{H}_2\text{O} = \text{Co(NH}_3)_5(\text{H}_2\text{O})^{3+} + \text{Br}^-$ is followed spectrophotometrically at 25°C by monitoring of the optical density of a 0.001 M solution at 370 nm. Added Br$^-$ is present, and also other absorbing but inert species, so that the measured optical density does not directly give the concentration of the reactant, nor is the value at infinite time known. Obtain the aquation rate constant.

t (min)	0	10	20	30	40	50
D (at 370 nm)	1.03	0.91	0.81	0.730	0.665	0.615

15-8 Calculate k_1 and k_2 for the curve labeled $K = 2$ of Fig. 15-1. At a different temperature, k_1 is doubled and K increases by 20%. Calculate the new half-time.

15-9 Find the constants b and α of the Brønsted relation given the following data for the general base-catalyzed reaction of nitramide, $H_2NNO_2 \rightarrow H_2O + N_2O$:

Base	Pyridine	Acetate ion	Formate ion	Dichloracetate ion
k (liter mole^{-1} min^{-1})	4.6	0.50	0.082	7×10^{-4}
K_b	2.3×10^{-9}	5.5×10^{-10}	4.8×10^{-11}	2.0×10^{-13}

Estimate k in water (K_w must be in liter mole^{-1} for consistency).

15-10 The exchange reaction

$$*Ce^{4+} + Ce^{3+} = *Ce^{3+} + Ce^{4+}$$

is a simple one, with $\Delta S^{0\ddagger} = -40$ cal °K^{-1} mole^{-1} and $\Delta H^{0\ddagger} = 7.7$ kcal mole^{-1}. Calculate k at (a) 25°C, at negligible ionic strength, (b) 25°C and $I = 0.1$, and (c) 35°C and $I = 0.1$.

15-11 Calculate A_e at 25°C for the dimerization of cyclopentadiene, assuming that the molecular diameter is 4.5 Å and that Eq. (10-42) applies. Compare A_e with the experimental A factor; alternatively, calculate K_e. Assume the solvent to be benzene, obtain necessary data from a handbook and from Table 15-2.

15-12 The reaction $CH_3I + C_2H_5O^- = CH_3OC_2H_5 + I^-$ is second order and k varies with temperature as follows:

t (°C)	0	12	18	24
k (liter mole^{-1} sec^{-1})	5.60×10^{-5}	24.4×10^{-5}	48×10^{-5}	100×10^{-5}

Calculate A, E^*, $\Delta S^{0\ddagger}$, and $\Delta H^{0\ddagger}$.

15-13 The first-order catalyzed decomposition of H_2O_2 in aqueous solution is followed by titration of the undecomposed H_2O_2 with $KMnO_4$ solution. By plotting the proper function, ascertain from the following data the value of the rate constant.

t (min)	0	5	10	20	30	50
cm^3 $KMnO_4$ per given amount of H_2O_2 solution	46.1	37.1	29.8	19.6	12.3	5.0

15-14 A reaction between the substances A and B is represented stoichiometrically by the equation $A + B \rightarrow C$. Observations on the rate of this reaction are obtained as follows (figures are "rounded" values):

Initial concentration (M)		t	Concentration of A at end of interval
A	B	(hr)	(M)
0.1	1.0	0.5	0.095
0.1	2.0	0.5	0.080
0.1	0.1	1000	0.05
0.2	0.2	500	0.10

Formulate the differential equation that expresses the rate of this reaction and calculate the rate constant. Indicate your reasoning.

15-15 A solution at 25°C initially contains 0.063 M $FeCl_3$ and 0.0315 M $SnCl_2$. After the elapsed times given, the concentration of the ferrous chloride produced is determined by a titration procedure:

t (min)	1	3	7	17	40
Fe^{2+} (M)	0.0143	0.0259	0.0361	0.0450	0.0506

Determine the reaction order and the rate constant. (This one is hard!)

15-16 A proposed mechanism for the reaction

$$2Cr(VI) + 3As(III) = 2Cr(III) + 3As(V)$$

is the following:

$$Cr(VI) + As(III) \underset{k_{-1}}{\overset{k_1}{\rightleftharpoons}} Cr(IV) + As(V),$$

$$Cr(IV) + Cr(VI) \underset{k_{-2}}{\overset{k_2}{\rightleftharpoons}} 2Cr(V),$$

$$Cr(V) + As(III) \underset{k_{-3}}{\overset{k_3}{\rightleftharpoons}} Cr(III) + As(V).$$

The observed forward rate law is $R = k_{app}[Cr(VI)][As(III)]$. What are possible rate laws for the reverse reaction?

Special Topics Problems

15-1 Referring to the reaction scheme of Eq. (15-82), suppose that $k_1 = 0.01$ min^{-1}, $k_{-1} = 2 \times 10^{-4}$ min^{-1}, $k_3 = 1 \times 10^{-7}$ min^{-1}, $k_{-3} = 5 \times 10^{-7}$ min^{-1}, and k_2 and k_{-2} are very small. Calculate the composition of a system consisting initially of A only after 10 min, 100 min, 10^3 min, 10^5 min, and 10^7 min. Also, find the ratio k_2/k_{-2}.

15-2 A sequential reaction, such as given by Eq. (15-84) is being studied. It is found that (B) reaches a maximum at 200 min and eventually disappears with a half time of 345 min, which is also the half-life with which (A) decreases with time. Calculate k_1 and k_2 and plot $(A)/(A)_0$ and $(B)/(A)_0$ as a function of time up to 1000 min.

15-3 Calculate k_1, k_2, and K from the plot of Fig. 15-16.

15-4 A study of the kinetics of the exchange of radiocyanide ion with the hexacyanomanganate (III) ion, $Mn(CN)_6^{3-}$, gave the following values for the slope c of the exchange plot.

Concentration (M)		pH	c (min^{-1})
CN^-	$Mn(CN)_6^{3-}$		
0.0596	0.0199	10	1.31×10^{-2}
0.0571	0.0102	10	0.883×10^{-2}
0.104	0.0199	10	0.943×10^{-2}
0.0596	0.0199	9	1.33×10^{-2}

Determine the form of the kinetic equation for the reaction leading to exchange and calculate the rate constant. On the basis of these results suggest a possible mechanism for the exchange.

15-5 The rate of exchange between I_2^* and IO_3^- is studied with $0.00050\ M\ I_2$ and $0.00100\ M$ HIO_3. The radioactivity of the IO_3^- at various subsequent times is given (corrected for radioactive decay). The total radioactivity of the system (or that initially present as I_2) is 1650.

t (hr)	19.1	47.3	92.8	169.2	∞
Radioactivity of IO_3^-	107	246	438	610	819

Calculate c of Eq. (15-101) and the rate R of the exchange reaction.

15-6 A series of solutions is made up which have the same concentration of the enzyme saccharase (E) but different initial concentrations of substrate saccharose (S). The enzyme E is present in some small (unknown) concentration and catalyzes the hydrolysis of the saccharose, and the rate is measured from the change in optical rotation of the solutions. With increasing (S) the rate reaches a maximum R_∞ ; it is half of this value when (S) is 1.1 % by weight. Assuming the Michaelis mechanism, calculate as much information as you can about k_1, k_{-1}, and k_2.

15-7 The treatment for the sequence of Eq. (15-84) yields an indeterminate result if $k_1 = k_2$. Redo the derivation so as to obtain (B) and (C) as functions of time.

15-8 Find the integrated expression for (C) as a function of time for the case $A + B \underset{k_2}{\overset{k_1}{\rightleftharpoons}} C$.

15-9 A type of enzyme mechanism is the following:

$$E + S \overset{K_1}{\rightleftharpoons} ES,$$

$$ES + S \overset{K_2}{\rightleftharpoons} ES_2,$$

$$ES \overset{k}{\rightarrow} \text{products} + E.$$

The first two equilibria are rapid; only ES reacts to give products, regenerating E. If (S) ≫ (E) and the total concentration of S is varied at constant (E), find an expression for (S) when the rate of decomposition is at a maximum.

16 WAVE MECHANICS

16-1 Introduction

The chapter on wave mechanics is probably subject to more variation in style and content than any other in a textbook of physical chemistry. Wave mechanics is of central importance to the physical chemist: Many of its results are of great utility, as in statistical thermodynamics, chemical bonding, and molecular spectroscopy. It is also the most nearly correct theory of mechanics that we have and its very language has permeated chemistry. On the other hand, it is difficult to present. Wave mechanics is virtually unique in the history of scientific theories in that it introduces a mathematical rather than a physical model of nature—and its mathematics becomes so fiercely complicated for systems of chemical interest that its practice has developed into the very specialized field of discovering and evaluating various approximation methods. It is simply not possible to do more than describe such methods qualitatively in an introductory physical chemistry text.

It is true, however, that the wave equation can be solved exactly for certain simple or model cases: A particle confined to a box or potential well, the hydrogen atom, and the harmonic oscillator are important illustrations. Most of the approximation methods use combinations or modifications of the exact solutions for such cases, and the procedure in this chapter will be to describe some of these exact solutions in sufficient detail that the rationale of the more advanced approaches can be appreciated. Moreover, most of the language and qualitative thinking in wave mechanics draws on the results for the simple situations, as, for example, in chemical bonding and molecular spectroscopy.

The detailed treatment of the important model situations is thus both highly utilitarian and within the spirit of a course in physical chemistry. It might be thought, from all this, that the older quantum chemistry, as exemplified by the Bohr model, would be useless. However, the Bohr theory does give rough descriptions of the quantum states of an atom and also provides some of the terminology of modern spectroscopy. Spectroscopy, as part of the physical chemistry of electronic excited states, is taken up in Chapter 18. For the moment, we shall content ourselves with a brief review of Bohr's picture for the hydrogen atom. Also, although the origins of quantum theory lie in the development of the quantum treatment of blackbody radiation by Max Planck (around 1900), that subject itself is not ordinarily of great utility to the physical chemist and its outline is placed in the Special Topics section. It is of importance, however, to note here that Planck proposed and successfully defended the hypothesis that molecular oscillators can only have frequencies that are integral multiples of a fundamental, and that the energy of the oscillator is given by

$$\epsilon = h\nu, 2h\nu, 3h\nu, ...,\tag{16-1}$$

where ν is the fundamental frequency and h is a proportionality constant, now called Planck's constant. In the cgs system, $h = 6.6252 \times 10^{-27}$ erg sec. Planck's ideas marked the beginning of quantum theory.

Einstein added a vital complement to Planck's hypothesis in explaining how it was that in the photoelectric effect the energy of electrons ejected from a metal by incident light had a definite energy which was independent of the energy flux of the light. Einstein (1905) proposed that light comes in units of energy, or quanta, of value given by the following equation, with ν now the frequency of the light radiation:

$$\epsilon = h\nu.\tag{16-2}$$

Each quantum ejects one electron and since the energy of the quantum is definite, so also is the energy of the electron. Increasing the flux of incident light merely increases the number of photoelectrons, their energy being determined by the wavelength or the frequency of the radiation. Wavelength and frequency are related, of course, by the equation

$$\lambda\nu = c,\tag{16-3}$$

where λ is the wavelength and c the velocity of light (3.00×10^{10} cm sec^{-1} in vacuum). Later, in the period 1908–1912, Einstein extended his law to photochemistry, saying that the absorption of each quantum of light results in the activation or excitation of a molecule by an energy corresponding to that of the quantum. This law of *photochemical equivalence* is honored by the unit called the *einstein*; an einstein is one mole of light quanta.

Equation (16-2) is sometimes called the *Planck–Einstein equation*, in reflection of its general implications. An oscillation of frequency ν, associated with atomic oscillators, electrons, or electromagnetic radiation, has energy $h\nu$. Absorption of a quantum of light changes the energy of an atom or molecule by $h\nu$, and, conversely, if an atom or molecule changes energy by an amount $\Delta\epsilon$ and thereby radiates light, that light will be of frequency given by

$$\Delta\epsilon = h\nu. \tag{16-4}$$

The origins of wave mechanics trace back to Einstein's special theory of relativity, which led him to conclude that mass m and energy ϵ are interconvertible,

$$\epsilon = mc^2. \tag{16-5}$$

One of the important implications of Eq. (16-5) was perceived by L. de Broglie in 1923 as he puzzled over the fact that electromagnetic radiation sometimes appears to behave as particles or quanta, as, for example, illustrated by the law of photochemical equivalence, and yet also appears to behave as waves, as in diffraction effects. Equation (16-5) provided a connection between these two aspects; if a light quantum has energy $h\nu$, then it must have mass, given by $mc^2 = h\nu$, and momentum p,

$$p = mc = \frac{h\nu}{c} = \frac{h}{\lambda}. \tag{16-6}$$

The intuitional leap made by de Broglie was to see that if radiation could have this duality, so might particles as well. Equation (16-6) provided the connecting link. Although light must always have velocity c (in vacuum, at least), a particle may have some arbitrary velocity v. The generalization of Eq. (16-6) to both radiation and particles is

$$p = \frac{h}{\lambda}, \tag{16-7}$$

where, for a particle, $p = mv$. Dramatic verifications of de Broglie's equation (16-7) followed. It was found, for example, that electrons show diffraction effects and therefore a wave nature, and today, even neutrons are used in the study of crystal structures by diffraction, their wavelengths being determined by their velocities through Eq. (16-7). Many qualitative features of the wave mechanical theory that followed are derivable just from de Broglie's equation.

The remaining principle that completes the foundations of wave mechanics was formulated by Heisenberg (1927). It is called the *uncertainty principle* or, sometimes, the *principle of indeterminancy*. The principle states that neither the position nor the momentum of a particle (or of a light quantum) can be determined with unlimited accuracy, and that if the two quantities are determined simultaneously, the *minimum* uncertainty in each is such that

$$\Delta p\, \Delta x \simeq h. \tag{16-8}$$

Equation (16-8) refers to the ultimate obtainable accuracy; any actual experiments will, of course, probably be far less accurate. When the principle was first introduced, a number of attempts were made to disprove it by means of experiments, either real or hypothetical, that would violate Eq. (16-8). There is a certain parallelism with the situation concerning the second law. It, too, is a negative statement, in certain of its phrasings, and many attempts were made to test it through finding real or hypothetical perpetual motion machines of the second kind. Einstein himself had a disastrous encounter with the uncertainty principle (see Commentary and Notes section). It is hard—perhaps logically impossible—to prove a negative statement, but the repeated failures to disprove the uncertainty principle have given it its present unchallenged acceptance.

The uncertainty principle may be stated in alternative ways, since there are other pairs of quantities which determine the state of a particle and whose product has the dimensions of h. The product of the minimum uncertainty in each will then be equal to h (or $h/4\pi$). For example, a very useful alternative form states that

$$\Delta\epsilon\,\Delta t = h \quad \left(\text{or } \frac{h}{4\pi}\right), \tag{16-9}$$

where Δt is the uncertainty in the time at which a measurement of energy is made. Equation (16-9) can be applied to a fluorescing excited state (see Section 18-4). Quite apart from instrument error, there is always some finite range of frequencies or linewidth for the fluorescent emission of light, which makes the energy of the emitting excited state somewhat uncertain. The rate constant for fluorescent emission gives the *average* lifetime of the state [see Eq. (14-13)] and this lifetime is a measure of the uncertainty as to just how long a particular excited molecule has lived before emitting. The product of these two uncertainties is h.

The Planck–Einstein, de Broglie, and Heisenberg principles largely demolished the philosophy of the classical physics of mechanics (Newton's laws), optics, and electricity and magnetism. Neither energy nor momentum were any longer infinitely divisible; the state of a particle could no longer be described exactly, but only in terms of probabilities. It is important to remember, however, that it is the *philosophy* and not the *laws* of classical physics that are affected. The laws, being phenomenological, remain as useful as ever in the macroscopic world although we now regard them as approximations or as limiting forms derivable from the more exact theory of wave mechanics.

It is appropriate that we conclude this introduction with a review of perhaps the most dramatic early success of quantum theory, namely the model proposed by Bohr in 1913 for an atom—at first applied to the hydrogen atom, but almost immediately generalized to other atoms, especially those of the alkali metals. One of the mysteries of his day was the emission spectrum of hot hydrogen atoms, consisting of groups of sharp lines when registered on the photographic plate of a spectrograph. By contrast, a hot object or blackbody merely emits a broad, continuous spectrum of radiation. Groups of hydrogen lines were found, first in the visible (the Balmer series), then in the ultraviolet by T. Lyman, and then in the infrared, by F. Paschen and others. W. Ritz found, in 1908, geometric regularities in each series which we nowadays summarize by the equation

$$\bar{\nu} = \mathcal{R} \left(\frac{1}{n_2{}^2} - \frac{1}{n_1{}^2} \right), \tag{16-10}$$

where $\bar{\nu}$ is the reciprocal of the wavelength of the emitted light corresponding to a particular line and is called the *wavenumber* and n_1 and n_2 are integers. The Balmer series is accurately given by $n_2 = 2$ and $n_1 = 3, 4, 5, \ldots$; the Lyman series, by $n_2 = 1$ and $n_1 = 2, 3, 4, \ldots$; and the Paschen series by $n_2 = 3$ and $n_1 = 4, 5, 6, \ldots$. The same constant $\mathcal{R}$ applies to all the series, and is called the *Rydberg constant*. The modern value for $\mathcal{R}$ is 109,677.581 cm^{-1}.

Bohr had available in 1913 this very precise, very regular, and as yet mysterious spectral data, although by 1912 J. Nicholson and N. Bjerrum had arrived at the point of explaining line spectra as due to transitions between atomic or molecular states of definite energies with the frequencies of the emitted light governed by the Planck–Einstein principle, or Eq. (16-4). Bohr was the first, however, to assemble a quantitative model. He made use of the nuclear model for the atom arrived at by E. Rutherford from the then rather new phenomenon of natural radioactivity and from observations on the way in which alpha particles are scattered by matter (see Section 21-4). According to Rutherford, the mass of an atom was concentrated in a small nucleus of charge Z surrounded by electrons at a much greater distance. Bohr also retained the classical Coulomb law and the laws of mechanics but added the quantum principle of discrete, rather than continuous, energy states and the ideas of Planck and Einstein.

He then proposed the very specific picture of a hydrogen atom as consisting of an electron orbiting around a nucleus of equal and opposite charge. To make his model work, however, he had to postulate that it was not the energy of the electron that was quantized, that is, varied in simple steps, but rather its angular momentum. By classical mechanics, the angular momentum of an orbiting electron is given by mvr, where m is the mass of the electron and r is the radius of its circular orbit. Bohr's postulate was that mvr can only have simple multiples of some minimum value, the necessary specific assumption being that

$$mvr = \frac{nh}{2\pi}, \tag{16-11}$$

where n is an integer having the values $1, 2, 3, \ldots$. We call n the *principal quantum number*.

By classical mechanics and electrostatics, the centrifugal force on the electron mv^2/r must be balanced by the Coulomb force of attraction to the nucleus Ze^2/r^2, where e is the charge on the electron and Z is the positive charge on the nucleus expressed in units of e. On balancing these two forces, one obtains

$$r = \frac{Ze^2}{mv^2}, \tag{16-12}$$

or, in combination with Eq. (16-11) so as to eliminate v,

$$r = \frac{n^2 h^2}{4\pi^2 m e^2 Z}. \tag{16-13}$$

For the lowest quantum state $n = 1$, and for the hydrogen atom $Z = 1$, so the corresponding radius, given the special symbol a_0, is

$$a_0 = \frac{h^2}{4\pi^2 m e^2}. \tag{16-14}$$

The total energy of an electron in its orbit is the sum of its kinetic energy $\frac{1}{2}mv^2$ and its potential energy $-Ze^2/r$, and with the use of Eq. (16-12) to eliminate mv^2, the result is

$$E = \frac{1}{2}mv^2 - \frac{Ze^2}{r} = -\frac{Ze^2}{2r}. \tag{16-15}$$

The negative sign of E reflects the fact that it takes energy to remove the electron an infinite distance away from the nucleus. One next eliminates r by means of Eq. (16-13) to obtain

$$E = -\frac{2\pi^2 m e^4 Z^2}{h^2}\frac{1}{n^2} \tag{16-16}$$

for the energies of successive quantum states.

The emission spectrum of an atom was then explained as due to the transition from one energy state E_i to a lower one E_j, the emitted radiation being of frequency given by Eq. (16-4):

$$E_i - E_j = h\nu = \frac{2\pi^2 m e^4 Z^2}{h^2}\left(\frac{1}{n_j{}^2} - \frac{1}{n_i{}^2}\right).$$

It is customary for spectroscopists to deal with wave numbers, and from Eq. (16-3) the wavenumber of the emitted light is

$$\bar{\nu} = \frac{2\pi^2 m e^4 Z^2}{h^3 c}\left(\frac{1}{n_j{}^2} - \frac{1}{n_i{}^2}\right). \tag{16-17}$$

Equation (16-17) predicts that for the hydrogen atom, with $Z = 1$, the value of the Rydberg constant should be given by $2\pi^2 m e^4/h^3 c$, which comes out to be 109,737 cm^{-1}. It was a major triumph for Bohr not only to have arrived at the form of Eq. (16-10), but also to have produced so accurate a value for $\mathscr{R}$ from a simple model.

As an incidental point, the system (electron plus nucleus) really revolves around its center of gravity rather than the center of the nucleus. If this is taken into account, then μ, the reduced mass, replaces m in the preceding equations, where μ is given by $m m_A/(m + m_A)$, m_A being the mass of the nucleus. The correction is small; for example, the atomic weight of the electron is 0.00055, or about 1/2000 of that of the nucleus of the hydrogen atom, so $\mu = 0.9995m$. For the hydrogen atom, $\mathscr{R}$ is therefore actually 109,678 cm^{-1}.

A pleasing relationship is found if one combines Eqs. (16-7) and (16-11) so as to eliminate the momentum mv. The result is

$$2\pi r = n\lambda. \tag{16-18}$$

That is, a Bohr orbit has a circumference which is an integral number of de Broglie wavelengths. The picture of the electron is thus one of a standing or stationary wave. One achievement of the Schrödinger wave equation, discussed in this chapter, is to give the amplitude of such a standing wave at every point in space and as a function of time.

16-2   Energy Units

We pause to review at this point some of the characteristic units of atomistics and spectroscopy as well as certain simple but instructive relationships among the various quantities described in the Section 16-1. Coulomb's law is the only classical law of electricity that we will need in this and succeeding chapters, and it is therefore easy and rather natural to use the esu system. The increasing appearance of mksa/SI units (see Section 3-CN-2) makes it desirable, however, for us to illustrate the application of this system as well.

There is also a considerable variety of energy units in use. The fundamental unit is, of course, the erg in the cgs system, or the joule in the mksa/SI system. However, since charged particles are often accelerated experimentally by an electric field, it is convenient to take as a unit the energy necessary to transport 1 electronic charge across a potential difference of 1 V. The charge on the electron is 1.6021×10^{-19} C (coulomb), and from the definition of the volt, the required energy is just 1.6021×10^{-19} J (joule). Thus

$$1 \text{ electron-volt} \quad \text{or} \quad 1 \text{ eV} \sim 1.6021 \times 10^{-19} \quad \text{J}.$$

The energy acquired by a particle carrying Z units of electronic charge falling through a potential difference of V volts is then $1.6021 \times 10^{-19} ZV$. Chemists often prefer to consider 1 mole of electrons and to express the result in calorie units:

$$1 \quad \text{eV} \sim \frac{(1.6021 \times 10^{-19})(6.0226 \times 10^{23})}{4.18400} \sim 23,061 \quad \text{cal mole}^{-1}.$$

The spectroscopist is interested in energies associated with light quanta. Although the energy of a light quantum is given by Eq. (16-2), the practice has been to use wavenumbers rather than frequency, and the energy per wavenumber is

$$1 \text{ wavenumber} \sim hc = (6.6256 \times 10^{-27})(2.99793 \times 10^{10})$$
$$\sim 1.9863 \times 10^{-16} \quad \text{erg} = 1.9863 \times 10^{-23} \quad \text{J}.$$

Alternatively,

$$1000 \text{ wavenumbers} \sim 0.12398 \quad \text{eV} \sim 2.8591 \quad \text{kcal mole}^{-1}.$$

The unit of 1 wavenumber is sometimes called a *kayser*; 1000 wavenumbers is then a kilokayser or 1 kK.

Finally, it is sometimes convenient to express atomic energy states in units of the potential energy of an electron in the first Bohr orbit, called the *atomic unit* (of energy) or a.u. The radius of the first Bohr orbit is given by Eq. (16-14), and insertion of numerical values for the constants gives

$$a_0 = 0.52917 \quad \text{Å}.$$

The potential energy of the electron is then e^2/a_0, with e in esu units, or $(4.8030 \times 10^{-10})^2/0.529 \times 10^{-8}$, so we have

$$1 \text{ a.u.} \sim 4.361 \times 10^{-11} \quad \text{erg} = 4.361 \times 10^{-18} \quad \text{J}.$$

Alternatively,

$$1 \text{ a.u.} \sim 27.22 \quad \text{eV}.$$

Alternative units are the hartree and the rydberg; 1 hartree = 1 a.u. and 1 rydberg = $\frac{1}{2}$ a.u. Various equations may be considerably simplified if expressed in terms of atomic units. Thus Eq. (16-15) becomes

$$E_{\text{a.u.}} = -\frac{Z^2}{2n^2}. \qquad (16\text{-}19)$$

Use of the mksa/SI system may be illustrated as follows. Coulomb's law is now given by Eq. (3-41), so that the potential energy of an electron in the first Bohr orbit for hydrogen is $e^2/4D_0 a_0$, where e is now in coulombs and the dielectric constant of vacuum has become $10^7/4\pi c^2 = 8.854 \times 10^{-12}$. The result in joules is, of course, the same as before.

Interconversions between the various energy units may be summarized as follows:

$$1 \quad \text{eV} = 1.6021 \times 10^{-19} \quad \text{J} = 1.6021 \times 10^{-12} \quad \text{erg} = 8.066 \quad \text{kK}$$
$$= 0.03674 \quad \text{a.u.} = 23.061 \quad \text{kcal mole}^{-1}.$$

16-3   Hydrogen and Hydrogen-Like Atoms

The energy states of a hydrogen atom are summarized diagrammatically in Fig. 16-1; the three scales allow conversion from one energy unit to another. The energies are given by Eq. (16-16) or Eq. (16-19) and the energy change accompanying a transition between two states is given by Eq. (16-10) or Eq. (16-17). Several of the series observed in spectroscopy are indicated in the figure. Notice that the states become more and more closely spaced as n approaches infinity.

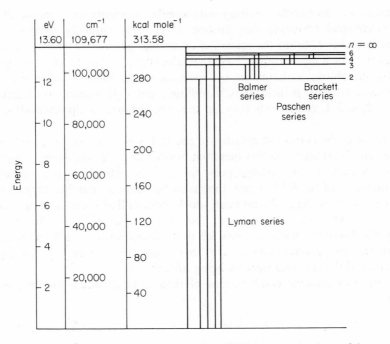

Fig. 16-1.   *The hydrogen atom spectrum (and energy conversion scale).*

An electron of energy greater than that corresponding to $n = \infty$ is free or is said to be dissociated. Thus the energy to dissociate an electron is 13.6 eV (or 109,727 cm^{-1} or 300 kcal mole^{-1}) if the initial state is the $n = 1$ or *ground state*. Alternatively, this energy is called the ionization energy or the ionization potential.

Equations (16-16) and (16-19) apply to one-electron atoms other than the hydrogen atom if the appropriate value of Z is used. Thus for He$^+$ the ground state is still that with $n = 1$, but the ionization energy is given by Eq. (16-19) with $Z = 2$; this energy is thus 2^2 times that for a hydrogen atom, or is 2 a.u. (54.4 eV). The ionization energy for Li^{2+} is 3^2 times that for a hydrogen atom, or 4.5 a.u.

The same equations may be applied to multielectron atoms if it is recognized that the inner electrons partially shield the outer ones from the full nuclear charge. As a consequence, the ionization energy of an outer electron can be regarded as corresponding to the presence of an effective nuclear charge (or atomic number) Z_{eff}. Although modern wave mechanics allows calculation of Z_{eff}, it is often treated as a semiempirical parameter. For example, in the case of He the ionization energy of the first electron is only 0.92 a.u. so that by Eq. (16-19), $Z_{\text{eff}} = [(0.92)(2)]^{1/2} = 1.36$ (instead of 2). Before considering atoms beyond He it is necessary to review the additional quantum numbers that are involved.

The rules for placing further electrons around a nucleus developed as the Bohr theory was applied to atoms other than hydrogen. First, it was necessary to allow elliptical as well as circular orbits, whose angular momenta were quantized. The wave mechanical treatment (see Section 16-7) leads naturally to this second quantum number ℓ, called the *azimuthal* or *angular quantum number*, and further specifies that for a given n, ℓ can have the values $0, 1, ..., n - 1$. As a consequence of early descriptive assignments by spectroscopists, these ℓ states are often designated s (sharp), p (principal), d (diffuse), and f (fundamental), referring to $\ell = 0, 1, 2$, and 3, respectively (beyond this, the lettering is alphabetical: s, p, d, f, g, h, i, j, ...).

Second, the observation of splitting of spectral lines in a magnetic field (called the Zeeman effect) led to another quantum number m, called the *magnetic quantum number*, which gives the possible projections of the orbital angular momentum in the direction of the field. Again, the magnetic quantum number appears naturally in the wave mechanical treatment, which specifies that m can have the integral values $-\ell, -(\ell - 1), ..., 0, ..., \ell - 1$, and ℓ, or a total of $2\ell + 1$ values in all. Finally, the discovery of electron spin led to the introduction of a fourth quantum number, the *spin quantum number* δ, whose value can be $\frac{1}{2}$ or $-\frac{1}{2}$, the angular momentum of the spinning electron being $\delta(h/2\pi)$.

The first few possible combinations of these four quantum numbers are as follows:

$$
\begin{array}{llll}
n = 1: & \ell = 0\ (\text{s}) & m = 0 & \delta = \tfrac{1}{2}, -\tfrac{1}{2} \\[4pt]
n = 2: & \ell = 0\ (\text{s}) & m = 0 & \delta = \tfrac{1}{2}, -\tfrac{1}{2} \\
 & \ell = 1\ (\text{p}) & m = -1 & \delta = \tfrac{1}{2}, -\tfrac{1}{2} \\
 & & m = 0 & \delta = \tfrac{1}{2}, -\tfrac{1}{2} \\
 & & m = 1 & \delta = \tfrac{1}{2}, -\tfrac{1}{2} \\[4pt]
n = 3: & \ell = 0\ (\text{s}) & m = 0 & \delta = \tfrac{1}{2}, -\tfrac{1}{2} \\
 & \ell = 1\ (\text{p}) & m = -1 & \delta = \tfrac{1}{2}, -\tfrac{1}{2} \\
 & & m = 0 & \delta = \tfrac{1}{2}, -\tfrac{1}{2} \\
 & & m = 1 & \delta = \tfrac{1}{2}, -\tfrac{1}{2} \\[4pt]
 & \ell = 2\ (\text{d}) & m = -2 & \delta = \tfrac{1}{2}, -\tfrac{1}{2} \\
 & & m = -1 & \delta = \tfrac{1}{2}, -\tfrac{1}{2} \\
 & & m = 0 & \delta = \tfrac{1}{2}, -\tfrac{1}{2} \\
 & & m = 1 & \delta = \tfrac{1}{2}, -\tfrac{1}{2} \\
 & & m = 2 & \delta = \tfrac{1}{2}, -\tfrac{1}{2}.
\end{array}
$$

Experimental spectroscopy led Pauli (1925) to conclude that no two electrons may have the same four quantum numbers. By this *Pauli exclusion principle* only 2 electrons can be in the $n = 1$ state, 8 in the $n = 2$ state, 18 in the $n = 3$ state, and so on, For example, the ground- or lowest-energy state of Li has the electron configuration $1s^2 2s$, the first number denoting the principal quantum number and the superscript the number of electrons of the indicated ℓ value. Table 16-1 lists the outer electron configurations for a number of elements, along with their energies for the ionization of successive electrons.

Table 16-1. *Ionization Energies*

Element	Z	Outer electron configuration	Ionization energy I for successive electrons (a.u.)							
			I_1	I_2	I_3	I_4	I_5	I_6	I_7	I_8
H	1	1s	0.50	—	—	—	—	—	—	—
He	2	1s²	0.90	2.00	—	—	—	—	—	—
Li	3	1s²2s	0.20	2.78	4.5	—	—	—	—	—
Be	4	...2s²	0.35	0.67	5.65	8.0	—	—	—	—
B	5	...2s²2p	0.31	0.93	1.4	9.53	12.5	—	—	—
C	6	...2s²2p²	0.42	0.90	1.76	2.37	14.4	17.9	—	—
N	7	...2s²2p³	0.53	1.09	1.74	2.84	3.60	18.6	24.4	—
O	8	...2s²2p⁴	0.50	1.29	2.02	2.84	4.18	5.06	27.0	32
F	9	...2s²2p⁵	0.64	1.29	2.30	3.20	4.20	5.75	6.8	35
Ne	10	...2s²2p⁶	0.79	1.51	—	—	—	—	—	—
Na	11	...2s²2p⁶3s	0.19	1.74	2.62	—	—	—	—	—
Mg	12	...3s²	0.28	0.55	2.95	—	—	—	—	—
Al	13	...3s²3p	0.22	0.69	1.05	4.41	—	—	—	—
Si	14	...3s²3p²	0.30	0.60	1.23	1.66	6.12	—	—	—
P	15	...3s²3p³	0.41	0.73	1.11	1.89	2.39	—	—	—
S	16	...3s²3p⁴	0.38	0.86	1.29	1.74	2.66	3.22	—	—
Cl	17	...3s²3p⁵	0.48	0.88	1.47	2.00	2.50	3.56	4.18	—
Ar	18	...3s²3p⁶	0.58	1.02	1.51	2.20	—	—	—	—
K	19	...3s²3p⁶4s	0.16	1.17	1.75	—	—	—	—	—
Ca	20	...4s²	0.23	0.44	1.88	—	—	—	—	—
Sc	21	...4s²3d	0.24	0.48	0.91	2.72	—	—	—	—
Ti	22	...4s²3d²	0.25	0.50	1.04	1.59	3.67	—	—	—
V	23	...4s²3d³	0.25	0.52	1.09	1.79	2.35	4.88	—	—
Cr	24	...4s3d⁵	0.25	0.61	—	—	—	—	—	—
Mn	25	...4s²3d⁵	0.28	0.58	—	—	—	—	—	—

We can now proceed with some further examples of Z_{eff} calculations. The first ionization energy for Li is 0.20 a.u., and since $n = 2$ for this electron, Eq. (16-19) gives $Z_{\text{eff}} = [(0.20)(2)(2)^2]^{1/2} = 1.26$. For Na the outer electron is 3s and its ionization energy is 0.19 a.u., giving $Z_{\text{eff}} = 1.85$ as compared to the actual $Z = 11$. It requires 1.75 a.u. to remove a second 2p electron, however, and now $Z_{\text{eff}} = [(1.75)(2)(2)^2]^{1/2} = 3.7$. Thus the electrons in the $n = 2$ shell of Na are exposed to about one-third the full nuclear charge. The difference between Z and Z_{eff} is called the *screening constant s*. This constant is 7.3 for Na⁺ and 9.15 for Na, for example.

16-4   The Schrödinger Wave Equation

The Bohr model encountered increasing difficulties as attempts were made to apply it to atoms other than hydrogen; furthermore, it failed to account for the de Broglie principle that particles behave as though they had characteristic wavelengths. The de Broglie hypothesis was quantitatively confirmed by the second half of the 1920's through experiments, such as those of C. Davisson and L. Germer and G. Thomson, that showed that electrons produce x-ray-like diffraction patterns on striking a gold foil. The hypothesis is also consistent with the Heisenberg uncertainty principle that the position of a particle can not be stated exactly but only as a probability. A new model was needed that would unite all the aspects of the behavior of atoms and electrons; this was provided in 1926 by E. Schrödinger and W. Heisenberg, somewhat independently.

Schrödinger used the mathematical framework that had been developed for periodic motions such as those of waves. For a plane wave of electromagnetic radiation, the classical equation is of the form

$$\Psi = A \exp\left[2\pi i\left(\frac{x}{\lambda} - \nu t\right)\right], \tag{16-20}$$

where Ψ is the amplitude of the wave at point x and time t, λ is its wavelength and ν is its frequency; the constant A determines the maximum amplitude. Equations of the form of Eq. (16-20) will appear frequently in the following material and an important identity to keep in mind is

$$e^{\pm ix} = \cos x \pm i \sin x \tag{16-21}$$

(as one can verify by writing out the respective series expansions). Equation (16-20) may then be written as

$$\Psi = A \left\{\cos\left[2\pi\left(\frac{x}{\lambda} - \nu t\right)\right] + i \sin\left[2\pi\left(\frac{x}{\lambda} - \nu t\right)\right]\right\}. \tag{16-22}$$

The intensity of a wave is given by the square of its amplitude, and if the latter is complex, by $\Psi\Psi^*$, where Ψ^* is the complex conjugate of Ψ, in this case $A \exp[-2\pi i(x/\lambda - \nu t)]$. By using Eq. (16-22), we can see that the intensity for a plane wave is just A^2. Also, by using the real part of Eq. (16-22), we can plot amplitude as a function of x and t; this is just a cosine function oscillating between A and $-A$, with a wavelength λ if plotted against x with t constant, or of frequency ν if plotted against time with x constant. Figure 16-2 shows such plots.

Equation (16-20) is a solution to the second-order partial differential equation

$$\frac{\partial^2 \Psi}{\partial x^2} = \left(\frac{1}{v^2}\right)\frac{\partial^2 \Psi}{\partial t^2}, \tag{16-23}$$

where v is the velocity $\lambda\nu$ of the wave, as one can verify by carrying out the differentiations. One may then put the corpuscular nature of light quanta into Eq. (16-23) by replacing λ by h/p [Eq. (16-7)] and ν by ϵ/h [Eq. (16-2)], whence $\lambda\nu = \epsilon/p$:

$$\frac{\partial^2 \Psi}{\partial x^2} = \frac{p^2}{\epsilon^2}\frac{\partial^2 \Psi}{\partial t^2}. \tag{16-24}$$

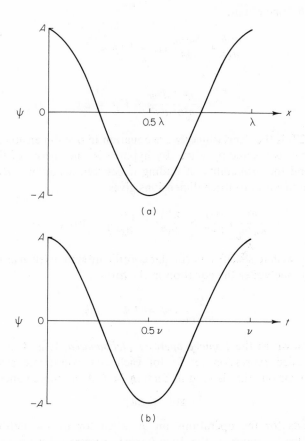

Fig. 16-2. *The amplitude of a wave. (a) As a function of distance at a given time and (b) as a function of time at a given position.*

The next step is to restrict the situation to standing waves, that is, waves whose amplitude at a given x is not a function of time. This is done by writing Eq. (16-20) as

$$\Psi = \psi e^{-2\pi i \nu t}, \qquad \psi = A e^{2\pi i x/\lambda}. \tag{16-25}$$

One then deals only with the ψ function, for which the differential equation is

$$\frac{d^2\psi}{dx^2} = -\frac{4\pi^2 p^2}{h^2}\,\psi \tag{16-26}$$

(obtained by differentiating $\psi = A e^{2\pi i x/\lambda}$ twice and replacing λ by h/p).

Schrödinger modified equations of this type to apply to a particle. The kinetic energy of a particle is $\frac{1}{2}mv^2$, or $p^2/2m$, and kinetic energy can be regarded as the total energy E minus the potential energy V. On substituting $p^2 = 2m(E - V)$

751

into Eq. (16-26), one obtains

$$\frac{d^2\psi}{dx^2} + \frac{8\pi^2 m}{h^2}(E - V)\psi = 0$$

or

$$-\frac{h^2}{8\pi^2 m}\frac{d^2\psi}{dx^2} + V\psi = E\psi. \tag{16-27}$$

Equation (16-27) is the Schrödinger wave equation in one dimension for a particle which is present as a standing wave. By hypothesis, the energy of the particle is given by E, and the probability of finding it between x and $x + dx$ is given by $\psi^*\psi\, dx$. Generalization to three dimensions gives

$$-\frac{h^2}{8\pi^2 m}\left(\frac{\partial^2\psi}{\partial x^2} + \frac{\partial^2\psi}{\partial y^2} + \frac{\partial^2\psi}{\partial z^2}\right) + V\psi = E\psi. \tag{16-28}$$

If one does not wish to specify a particular coordinate system (such as the Cartesian one used here), one writes the equation in the form

$$-\frac{h^2}{8\pi^2 m}\nabla^2\psi + V\psi = E\psi, \tag{16-29}$$

where ∇^2 is known as the *Laplace operator*, *del squared*. It is then necessary to derive the detailed expression for ∇^2 for each new coordinate system, as, for example, the polar one that is used in Section 16-7. A yet more concise form is

$$\mathbf{H}\psi = E\psi, \tag{16-30}$$

where $\mathbf{H}$ stands for the operations on ψ called for by the left-hand side of Eq. (16-29). This is known as the *Hamiltonian operator* (of wave mechanics), so named by analogy with a similar function that appears in the classical equations of motion.

Schrödinger pursued the analogy to classical wave equations further by postulating the more general equation

$$-\frac{h^2}{8\pi^2 m}\nabla^2\Psi + V\Psi = -\frac{h}{2\pi i}\frac{\partial\Psi}{\partial t}, \tag{16-31}$$

where Ψ is a function of both position and time. As was done with Eq. (16-25), we assume the special case in which Ψ can be written as a product $\psi\phi$, where ϕ is a function of time alone (and ψ has already been taken to be a function of position alone). If this substitution is made into Eq. (16-31), then $\nabla^2\Psi$ becomes $\phi\nabla^2\psi$ (since ϕ is not a function of coordinates) and $\partial\Psi/\partial t$ becomes $\psi\,\partial\phi/\partial t$ (since ψ is not a function of time). On dividing through by $\psi\phi$, we obtain

$$\frac{1}{\psi}\left(-\frac{h^2}{8\pi^2 m}\nabla^2\psi + V\psi\right) = -\frac{h}{2\pi i}\frac{1}{\phi}\frac{\partial\phi}{\partial t}. \tag{16-32}$$

The left-hand side of Eq. (16-32) is a function of coordinates only [assuming that $V \neq f(t)$] and the right-hand side is a function of time only; consequently the quantity to which both sides are equal cannot be a function either of time or of coordinates—it must be a constant. Another way of phrasing one of Schrödinger's hypotheses is to say that we take this constant to be E, the total energy. Equation (16-32) then separates into two equations, Eq. (16-29) and the time-dependent equation

$$\frac{d\phi}{dt} = - \frac{2\pi i}{h} E\phi, \tag{16-33}$$

which integrates to

$$\phi = (\text{constant}) \, e^{-(2\pi i E/h)t}. \tag{16-34}$$

Notice the analogy to Eq. (16-25), for which the time-dependent part is $\cdot e^{-2\pi i \nu t}$. This is the same as Eq. (16-34) if we write $E = h\nu$. Remembering relationship (16-21), ϕ is evidently a function which oscillates with time.

Nearly all of the applications of wave mechanics treated in this text will be in terms of ψ rather than Ψ. The typical application of Eq. (16-29) will be to an electron under the influence of some potential V, usually a potential well. In the case of the hydrogen atom, for example, $V = -e^2/r$. The solutions to Eq. (16-29) then give the various energies which an electron can have if it is to act as a standing or stationary wave. Such a stationary state is possible only for certain wavelengths, depending on the nature of V, and hence only for certain energies. It will turn out, in other words, that discrete or quantized energy states appear as a natural consequence of our asking for stationary solutions to the wave equation. The stationary-state solutions are the appropriate ones for an atom or molecule which does not change with time. Rate processes, such as the emission of radiation (fluorescence), require the use of the full equation, (16-31), a use which is largely beyond the scope of this text; see, however, Section 18-ST-1.

A remaining point is that while Eq. (16-29) is the wave equation for a single particle, in this case, an electron, obeying a potential energy function V and having total energy E, there is a simple recipe for constructing the wave equation for a system of particles. The first term of Eq. (16-29) plays the role of the kinetic energy of the particle and if more than one particle is involved, an analogous term is written for each of them. That is, the first term becomes $\sum_i -[(h^2/8\pi^2 m_i) \nabla_i^2 \psi]$ if i particles are present. Then V becomes the function giving all the mutual interactions between the particles; E is still the energy of the system.

In concluding this section, it should be emphasized that while the Schrödinger equation can be obtained by means of certain analogies with classical wave equations, there does not exist a rigorous derivation. The Schrödinger equation is taken to be correct *by hypothesis*, and therefore is itself the starting point of wave mechanics. The various analogies are useful in trying to attach some physical picture to the solutions obtained; they are also dangerous because wave mechanics does not rest on a physical picture (as does the Bohr theory)—it is a purely mathematical model [see Bridgman (1961)].

16-5 Some Simple Choices for the Potential Function V

A. The Free Particle

One of the simplest applications of the Schrödinger wave equation is to a particle for which the potential function is a constant. It is customary to take $V = 0$; if V has some other value, it merely changes the energy of the system accordingly. Equation (16-28) therefore becomes

$$-\frac{h^2}{8\pi^2 m}\left(\frac{\partial^2 \psi}{\partial x^2} + \frac{\partial^2 \psi}{\partial y^2} + \frac{\partial^2 \psi}{\partial z^2}\right) = E\psi \qquad (16\text{-}35)$$

or

$$\mathbf{H}_x\psi + \mathbf{H}_y\psi + \mathbf{H}_z\psi = E\psi. \qquad (16\text{-}36)$$

Any wave equation such as Eq. (16-36), in which **H** can be written as a sum of terms that do not share coordinates, can be resolved into the set

$$\mathbf{H}_x\psi_x = E_x\psi_x, \qquad \mathbf{H}_y\psi_y = E_y\psi_y, \qquad \mathbf{H}_z\psi_z = E_z\psi_z, \qquad (16\text{-}37)$$

where $\psi = \psi_x\psi_y\psi_z$ and $E = E_x + E_y + E_z$. The procedure for demonstrating this conclusion is entirely analogous to that used in obtaining Eqs. (16-32) and (16-34). One substitutes $\psi_x\psi_y\psi_z$ for ψ in Eq. (16-35) and then divides through by $\psi_x\psi_y\psi_z$. The left-hand side then consists of a sum of terms in x only, y only, and z only, and therefore separates into the three equations (16-37).

In the present case, the x, y, and z equations are identical in form, so that only one need be solved:

$$-\frac{h^2}{8\pi^2 m}\frac{d^2\psi_x}{dx^2} = E_x\psi_x. \qquad (16\text{-}38)$$

A stationary-state solution to Eq. (16-38), that is, one for which E is not a function of time, is

$$\psi_x = A_x \sin\left[\left(\frac{8\pi^2 m E_x}{h^2}\right)^{1/2} x\right], \qquad (16\text{-}39)$$

as we can verify by substituting back into Eq. (16-38); A_x is an integration constant (note Problem 16-4). Since the wave is not confined, there are no restrictions on its wavelength and E_x can have any positive value. The total ψ is then the product

$$\psi = A \sin\left[\left(\frac{8\pi^2 m E_x}{h^2}\right)^{1/2} x\right] \sin\left[\left(\frac{8\pi^2 m E_y}{h^2}\right)^{1/2} y\right] \sin\left[\left(\frac{8\pi^2 m E_z}{h^2}\right)^{1/2} z\right] \qquad (16\text{-}40)$$

and corresponds to an infinite sinusoidal wave.

The wavelength in, say, the x direction is given by

$$\lambda = \frac{2\pi}{(8\pi^2 m E_x/h^2)^{1/2}} , \tag{16-41}$$

since for this value of x we have $\sin 2\pi$, which completes one cycle. Equation (16-41) simplifies to $\lambda = h/(2mE_x)^{1/2}$, but E_x is also equal to $p_x^2/2m$, so the final result is just the de Broglie equation, $\lambda = h/p$. This result is not too surprising in view of analogies made when writing down the wave equation.

B. The Particle in a Box

We may next stipulate that the particle has zero potential energy over a region defined by $0 < x < a$, $0 < y < b$, and $0 < z < c$, but that beyond these boundaries the potential energy is infinite. That is, V_x is zero for $0 < x < a$ and is infinite for $x < 0$ and $x > a$, and similarly for V_y and V_z; hence the term "box." Equation (16-28) is now

$$-\frac{h^2}{8\pi^2 m}\left(\frac{\partial^2\psi}{\partial x^2} + \frac{\partial^2\psi}{\partial y^2} + \frac{\partial^2\psi}{\partial z^2}\right) + V\psi = E\psi. \tag{16-42}$$

The situation is the same as for Eq. (16-35) in that the substitution $\psi = \psi_x\psi_y\psi_z$ allows the equation to be separated into three separate ones:

$$-\frac{h^2}{8\pi^2 m}\frac{\partial^2\psi_x}{\partial x^2} + V_x\psi_x = E_x\psi_x \tag{16-43}$$

and similarly for y and z, where $V = V_x + V_y + V_z$ and $E = E_x + E_y + E_z$. Alternatively, Eq. (16-43) may be viewed as the wave equation for a particle in a one-dimensional box.

The solution to Eq. (16-43) is the same as that for Eq. (16-38) for the region inside the box, since $V_x = 0$. However, the solution outside the box, where $V = \infty$, must be that $\psi_x = 0$. This conclusion can be reached on both physical and mathematical grounds. Physically, it should be impossible for the particle to escape the box, and since $\psi_x\psi_x^*\, dx$ gives the probability of finding the particle in the region dx at each x, it follows that $\psi_x\psi_x^* = 0$ and hence $\psi_x = 0$ for $x < 0$ and $x > a$. The mathematical reasoning is that the curvature of the plot of ψ_x versus x, $\partial^2\psi_x/\partial x^2$, is proportional to $(V_x - E_x)\,\psi_x$; if $V_x = \infty$ and $\psi_x \neq 0$, then the curvature must be infinite and ψ_x must increase to infinity itself. This is an impossible catastrophe—it is not acceptable that ψ_x, and hence the probability function for the particle, be infinite anywhere. This catastrophe can be avoided only if ψ_x is zero (and hence the curvature is zero) for $x < 0$ and $x > a$.

We also do not expect ψ_x to change discontinuously, that is, to have two values at a given x. There should be only one probability for the particle being at any one position. Since ψ_x must be zero just outside the box, it must therefore also be zero just inside the box. The consequence is that only those values of E_x in Eq. (16-39) are acceptable which make ψ_x zero at $x = 0$ and at $x = a$, which means that the wave must have a node at these boundaries. In other words, there must be an integral number n_x of half-wavelengths in the distance a, as illustrated in Fig. 16-3. As applied to Eq. (16-41), the condition is that $a = n_x\lambda/2$, or, on

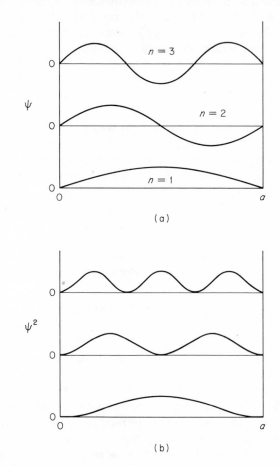

Fig. 16-3. ψ *and* ψ^2 *functions for a particle in a one-dimensional box.*

rearrangement,

$$E_x = \frac{h^2 n_x^2}{8ma^2}, \qquad n_x = 1, 2, 3, \dots . \tag{16-44}$$

Also, substitution of this expression for E_x into Eq. (16-39) gives

$$\psi_x = A_x \sin\left(\frac{n_x\pi x}{a}\right). \tag{16-45}$$

One further step is usually taken with a solution to the wave equation. The solution will contain a constant of integration, A_x in Eq. (16-45), and the value of A_x is usually set so that the probability of the particle being somewhere is unity. The function is then said to be *normalized*. In the present case this condition is

$$\int \psi_x \psi_x^* \, d\tau = 1 = A_x^2 \int_0^a \left[\sin\left(\frac{n_x \pi x}{a}\right) \right]^2 dx, \qquad (16\text{-}46)$$

where the first integral is the formal statement that the integral of $\psi_x \psi_x^*$ over all space is to be unity and the second integral is the specific one involved here. The integral is a standard one, equal to $a/2$ for the given integration limits. The constant A_x is therefore $(2/a)^{1/2}$ and the normalized solution is

$$\psi_x = \left(\frac{2}{a}\right)^{1/2} \sin\left(\frac{n_x \pi x}{a}\right). \qquad (16\text{-}47)$$

The preceding illustrates a fairly typical procedure in obtaining wave mechanical solutions. One uses the requirement that ψ be everywhere finite and single-valued if the solution is to have physical meaning, and this requirement then limits the possible number of solutions and hence of energy states. Quantization thus appears naturally and not as an *ad hoc* assumption.

To continue with the particle-in-a-box treatment, we see that the solutions for the y and z coordinates are the same as that for the x coordinate, so the complete solution for a three-dimensional box is

$$\psi = \left(\frac{8}{abc}\right)^{1/2} \sin\left(\frac{n_x \pi x}{a}\right) \sin\left(\frac{n_y \pi y}{b}\right) \sin\left(\frac{n_z \pi z}{c}\right), \qquad (16\text{-}48)$$

and

$$E = \frac{h^2}{8m} \left(\frac{n_x^2}{a^2} + \frac{n_y^2}{b^2} + \frac{n_z^2}{c^2} \right), \qquad (16\text{-}49)$$

where, for generality, the x, y, and z dimensions of the box are taken to be a, b, and c, respectively. Alternatively, for a two-dimensional square and a three-dimensional cubic box,

$$E_{\text{square}} = \frac{h^2}{8ma^2} (n_x^2 + n_y^2), \qquad (16\text{-}50)$$

$$E_{\text{cube}} = \frac{h^2}{8ma^2} (n_x^2 + n_y^2 + n_z^2). \qquad (16\text{-}51)$$

C. Some Applications

The equations for the particle in a box have several important applications. One of these is the use of Eq. (16-51) to supply the energy states for a gaseous molecule in a container of volume V, thereby leading to the translational partition function for an ideal gas (see Sections 4-10 and 6-9C). The spacing of these energy states is quite small if the side a is of macroscopic size or if the particle is massive. On insertion of numerical constants, Eq. (16-44) becomes

$$E = \frac{(6.6252 \times 10^{-27})^2 (6.0226 \times 10^{23})(10^{16})}{8} \frac{n_x{}^2}{M\hat{a}^2}$$

$$= 3.304 \times 10^{-14} \frac{n_x{}^2}{M\hat{a}^2} \text{ (erg molecule}^{-1}) = 475 \frac{n_x{}^2}{M\hat{a}^2} \text{ (cal mole}^{-1}), \quad (16\text{-}52)$$

where M is the molecular weight of the particle and $\hat{a}$ is the length of the box in angstroms. For hydrogen gas in a 1 cm box, the first energy level would be at 2.37×10^{-14} cal mole^{-1} (!), the second at 2^2 times this, and so on.

The spacing becomes quite respectable, however, for a light particle such as an electron in a box of atomic dimensions. The atomic weight of the electron is 0.000546 g mole^{-1}, so that E is

$$E = 867.0 \frac{n_x{}^2}{\hat{a}^2} \text{ kcal mole}^{-1} = 303.3 \frac{n_x{}^2}{\hat{a}^2} \text{ kK} = 37.59 \frac{n_x{}^2}{\hat{a}^2} \text{ eV.} \quad (16\text{-}53)$$

Equation (16-53) may be applied in an approximate treatment of certain types of molecules which have electrons that can oscillate over the whole structure. The electrons which form the double bond in ethylene probably behave in this way. A more interesting example is butadiene, $H_2C{=}CH{-}CH{=}CH_2$, in which each carbon atom contributes one electron to the double bond system, and these four electrons probably can oscillate over the entire length of the chain. That is, the double bonds are not really localized to the particular pairs of atoms shown. In effect, then, the four electrons are in a one-dimensional box equal in length to that of the chain. This last can be estimated as equal to two $C{=}C$ bond lengths or 2(1.35) Å, plus one $C{-}C$ bond or 1.54 Å, plus the distance of a carbon atom radius at each end or another 1.54 Å, for a total of 5.78 Å. Equation (16-53) then gives the energy states in eV as $[37.59/(5.78)^2] n_x{}^2 = 1.12 n_x{}^2$. By the Pauli exclusion principle, each state can hold two electrons (with spins opposed), and so the four electrons fill the first two levels as illustrated in Fig. 16-4(a).

The energy of the first excited state of this system of four electrons is that for having one electron in the $n = 3$ level, and the energy to produce this state is $E = 1.12(3^2 - 2^2) = 5.60$ eV or 45,000 cm^{-1}. Butadiene does have an absorption band at 46,100 cm^{-1} (217 nm), and the very simple free-electron model, as this is called, has been fairly successful.

As a further example, hexatriene, $H_2C{=}CH{-}CH{=}CH{-}CH{=}CH_2$, should have six delocalized electrons in the double bond system, in a box of length 8.67 Å. The energy for the $n = 1$ state is then $37.59/(8.67)^2 = 0.500$ eV, and as shown in Fig. 16-4(b), the six electrons fill the first three levels. The first excited state should now have one electron in the $n = 4$ state, and ΔE for the transition should therefore

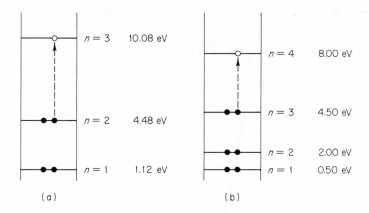

Fig. 16-4.   *Particle-in-a-box energy level scheme for (a) butadiene and (b) hexatriene.*

be $0.500(4^2 - 3^2) = 3.50$ eV or 28,000 cm^{-1}. The experimental value is 38,500 cm^{-1}, and although the agreement is rather poor, the model has correctly predicted that the frequency of the absorption band should decrease with increasing chain length.

The free-electron model is a semiempirical one—one does not know, for example, just how much "end space" to allow in calculating the length of the box. The uncertainty becomes less important with longer chains, and with carotene, which has alternating single and double bonds in an 11 carbon atom chain, one estimates about 25,000 cm^{-1} for the transition to the first excited state, as compared to 22,200 cm^{-1} observed. The model may also be applied to two-dimensional boxes, such as benzene or fused aromatic ring systems, with Eq. (16-50). A more sophisticated treatment is given in Section 17-ST-1.

It may happen that two or more solutions to the wave equation for a system have *identical* energy. Such solutions and the corresponding states of the system are said to be *degenerate*. Consider, for example, a two-dimensional box for which the energy states are given by Eq. (16-50). The energy for a state $(n_x = 1, n_y = 2)$ is identical to that for a state $(n_x = 2, n_y = 1)$ and the state of this energy is said to be doubly degenerate.

16-6   The Harmonic Oscillator

The *harmonic oscillator* represents the simplest possible model for an atom vibrating in a potential well. The force on the atom is in this case $-kx$, that is, proportional to the displacement x from the equilibrium position, and is negative since it is a restoring force. The potential energy is then $\frac{1}{2}kx^2$, corresponding to the parabolic curve in Fig. 16-5, and the wave equation is

$$\frac{d^2\psi}{dx^2} + \frac{8\pi^2 m}{h^2}(E - \tfrac{1}{2}kx^2)\psi = 0. \tag{16-54}$$

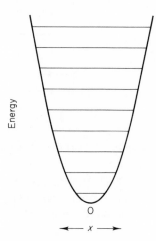

Fig. 16-5. *The potential energy function for a harmonic oscillator.*

We let $\alpha = (8\pi^2 m/h^2)E$ and $\beta = 2\pi\sqrt{mk}/h$, so that Eq. (16-54) becomes

$$\frac{d^2\psi}{dx^2} + (\alpha - \beta^2 x^2)\psi = 0$$

and then further make the change of variable $q = \sqrt{\beta}\, x$, to get

$$\frac{d^2\psi}{dq^2} + \left(\frac{\alpha}{\beta} - q^2\right)\psi = 0. \tag{16-55}$$

The solution is of the form

$$\psi = \phi(q)e^{-q^2/2} \tag{16-56}$$

and substitution back into Eq. (16-55) gives the equation

$$\frac{d^2\phi}{dq^2} - 2q\frac{d\phi}{dq} + \left(\frac{\alpha}{\beta} - 1\right)\phi = 0, \tag{16-57}$$

which is identical in form to a standard differential equation known as *Hermite's equation*,

$$\frac{d^2\phi}{dq^2} - 2q\frac{d\phi}{dq} + 2n\phi = 0. \tag{16-58}$$

The admissible (see end of this section) solutions to Eq. (16-58) are in the form of polynomials whose nature depends on the value of n. If n is an integer, the first few are as follows:

$$H_{n=0} = 1, \qquad H_{n=3} = 8q^3 - 12q,$$
$$H_{n=1} = 2q, \qquad H_{n=4} = 16q^4 - 48q^2 + 12,$$
$$H_{n=2} = 4q^2 - 2, \qquad H_{n+1} = 2qH_n - 2nH_{n-1}.$$

The solutions to Eq. (16-55) are then

$$\psi_n = \left[\frac{(\beta/\pi)^{1/2}}{2^n n!} \right]^{1/2} H_n(q) e^{-q^2/2}, \qquad (16\text{-}59)$$

where n may be 0, 1, 2, 3, ... The factor in front of the right-hand term serves to normalize the wave function. Substitution of the expressions for q and for β then allow ψ to be plotted as a function of x for various n values. This is done in Fig. 16-6 for the first three energy levels. Notice the wave nature of the solutions

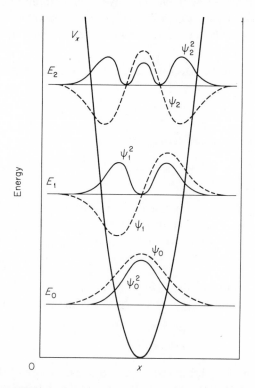

Fig. 16-6. *Energy levels for a harmonic oscillator, with superimposed plots of corresponding* ψ *and* ψ^2. *(Adapted from K. S. Pitzer, "Quantum Chemistry,"* © *1953. By permission of Prentice-Hall, Inc., Englewood Cliffs, New Jersey.)*

and also the fact that those for n even are symmetric about the middle line while those for n odd are antisymmetric or inverted across the line. The probability of finding the atom at a given x is obtained from $\psi\psi^*$, or ψ^2 in this case, and, except for $n = 0$, is greater at the extremes of the oscillation than in the middle. Also, although ψ falls off rapidly with large x, because of the $\exp(-q^2/2)$ term, there is always a finite probability of finding the particle at any x, however large.

The energy of the various states is obtained as follows. The matching of Eqs. (16-57) and (16-58) requires that

$$\frac{\alpha}{\beta} = 2n + 1, \qquad (16\text{-}60)$$

or, on substitution of the expressions for α and β and simplification,

$$E = \frac{h}{2\pi}\left(\frac{k}{m}\right)^{1/2}(v + \tfrac{1}{2}) = h v_0(v + \tfrac{1}{2}), \qquad (16\text{-}61)$$

where n has been replaced by the more conventional vibrational quantum number symbol v. The quantity $(h/2\pi)(k/m)^{1/2}$ has the dimensions of energy, and is conventionally set equal to $h v_0$, since v_0 would be the natural frequency of oscillation of a classical harmonic oscillator.

The classical treatment writes mass times acceleration as equal to the force, or

$$m\frac{d^2x}{dt^2} = -kx$$

and the solution to this differential equation is

$$x = a\cos(2\pi v_0 t), \qquad (16\text{-}62)$$

where $v_0 = (1/2\pi)(k/m)^{1/2}$.

It turns out that the same treatment applies to the case of two atoms vibrating against each other, provided that the restoring force is still $-kx$. The only modification is that m becomes the reduced mass $\mu = m_1 m_2/(m_1 + m_2)$. With this modification, Eq. (16-61) is identical to Eq. (4-77), used in calculating the vibrational partition function.

According to Eq. (16-61), the lowest energy state is not zero, but $\tfrac{1}{2}h v_0$; this is known as the zero-point energy. Also, the E for the transition from one state to another is given by

$$\Delta E = h v_0(v_2 - v_1). \qquad (16\text{-}63)$$

Because of the alternating symmetric–antisymmetric nature of the wave functions, it further turns out that the probability of making a transition by emission or absorption of light is large only if the change in quantum number is ± 1; other transitions are said to be *forbidden*, that is, improbable (see Section 18-ST-1).

As a numerical illustration, force constants $\not k$ are about 10^5 dyn cm^{-1} for typical diatomic molecules, and are therefore often expressed in this unit. We then have

$$h\nu_0 = \frac{h}{2\pi}\left(\frac{\not k}{\mu}\right)^{1/2} = \frac{6.6256 \times 10^{-27}}{2\pi}(10^5 \times 6.0226 \times 10^{23})^{1/2}\left(\frac{\not k'}{\mu'}\right)^{1/2}$$

or

$$h\nu_0 = 2.57 \times 10^{-13}\left(\frac{\not k'}{\mu'}\right)^{1/2} \quad \text{erg,} \tag{16-64}$$

where $\not k'$ is in units of 10^5 dyn cm^{-1} and μ' is in atomic weight units. For $h\nu_0$ in eV the proportionality constant is 0.162, and for $h\nu_0$ in kK it is 1.30.

The first vibrational transition for HCl is at 2886 cm^{-1}, so $\not k'/\mu' = (2886/1300)^2 = 4.928$. The reduced mass is $(1)(35)/(1 + 35) = 0.972$, so $\not k' = 4.790$ and $\not k = 4.790 \times 10^5$ dyn cm^{-1}.

Vibrational potential energy curves and energy states are often shown as in Fig. 4-11(a); such a figure is somewhat misleading since it implies that the atoms are bounded in position by the the potential energy curve. It must be remembered that the actual situation is as shown in Fig. 16-6. Second, the harmonic oscillator model appears to be satisfactory for treating the first few vibrational levels, but a much more correct potential function is that shown in Fig. 4-11(b). That is, the restoring force that keeps atoms from separating gradually weakens with higher and higher vibrational energy until a dissociation limit is reached. The wave equation has been solved for potential functions of this shape, and as also illustrated in Fig. 4-11(b), the vibrational energy levels tend to come closer together with increasing quantum number. For example, a convenient algebraic form which approximates that shown in Fig. 4-11(b) is due to P. Morse,

$$V = D(1 - e^{-a(r-r_e)})^2, \tag{16-65}$$

where D is the depth of the potential well at the equilibrium separation r_e. Use of this potential function in the wave equation leads to a better approximation for vibrational levels:

$$E = w_e(\nu + \tfrac{1}{2}) - x_e w_e(\nu + \tfrac{1}{2})^2, \tag{16-66}$$

where $w_e = (ah/\pi)(D/2\mu)^{1/2}$ and $x_e = w_e/4D$. The levels now converge slowly, although the dissociation limit is still reached after a finite number of states.

Finally, as with the particle in a box, the quantization of vibrational energy occurs in a natural way in the wave mechanical treatment. First, at large x, E drops out of Eq. (16-54) and the limiting solution is of the form $\exp(\pm q^2/2)$; however, only the minus sign is physically acceptable since otherwise the catastrophe of ψ going to infinity would occur. This conclusion then leads to Eqs. (16-56) and (16-57), the latter being Hermite's equation. Only integral values of n are allowed in the solution to Eq. (16-58) if the polynomials satisfying the equation are to have a finite number of terms and not themselves lead to a catastrophe. The quantization thus arises from restriction of the mathematical possibilities to physically acceptable solutions.

16-7 Solutions of the Wave Equation for the Hydrogen Atom

The most complete application of wave mechanics is undoubtedly to the case of the hydrogen atom. Not only can exact solutions be obtained, but these solutions are then widely used in approximate treatments of heavier atoms. We proceed in this section to the formal solutions for the hydrogen atom and will discuss the behavior of these solutions in detail in the following section. The derivation that follows is more frightening in appearance than actually difficult!

A. The Schrödinger Equation for the Hydrogen Atom

The potential function for the electron is now $-e^2/r$, where r is its distance from the nucleus, and Eq. (16-29) becomes

$$-\frac{h^2}{8\pi^2 m} \nabla^2 \psi - \frac{e^2}{r} \psi = E\psi. \tag{16-67}$$

The presence of r as a parameter in the potential function makes it awkward for one to work in Cartesian coordinates and it turns out to be very convenient to use the polar coordinate system shown in Fig. 16-7. A point at (x, y, z) is now given

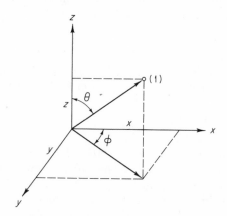

Fig. 16-7. *The polar coordinate system used for the hydrogen atom.*

by its radial distance r and the two angles θ and ϕ. In sweeping out all of space r varies from 0 to ∞, θ varies from 0 to π, and ϕ varies from 0 to 2π.

The two coordinate systems are related. The projection of r onto the z axis gives

$$z = r \cos \theta \tag{16-68}$$

and $r \sin \theta$ gives the projection onto the xy plane, so that

$$x = r \sin \theta \cos \phi, \tag{16-69}$$

$$y = r \sin \theta \sin \phi. \tag{16-70}$$

By inserting these relationships into the expression for ∇^2 in Cartesian coordinates, one obtains (finally) for Eq. (16-67):

$$\frac{1}{r^2}\frac{\partial}{\partial r}\left(r^2\frac{\partial\psi}{\partial r}\right) + \frac{1}{r^2 \sin \theta}\frac{\partial}{\partial \theta}\left(\sin\theta\,\frac{\partial\psi}{\partial\theta}\right) + \frac{1}{r^2 \sin^2\theta}\frac{\partial^2\psi}{\partial\phi^2} + \frac{8\pi^2 m}{h^2}\left(E + \frac{e^2}{r}\right)\psi = 0 \tag{16-71}$$

[see, for example, Eyring *et al.* (1944)].

One advantage of the new coordinate system is that it allows the variables to be separated. We do this by writing $\psi(r, \theta, \phi) = R(r)\,\Theta(\theta)\,\Phi(\phi)$, that is, as a product of three functions each having only one variable. The procedure is much the same as that used with Eq. (16-42); we substitute $\Theta(\theta)\,\Phi(\phi)[\partial R(r)/\partial r]$ for $\partial\psi/\partial r$, and so on and then divide through by $R(r)\,\Theta(\theta)\,\Phi(\phi)$ to obtain (dropping the arguments of R, Θ, and Φ for convenience)

$$\frac{1}{r^2 R}\frac{d}{dr}\left(r^2\frac{dR}{dr}\right) + \frac{1}{r^2(\sin\theta)\Theta}\frac{d}{d\theta}\left(\sin\theta\,\frac{d\Theta}{d\theta}\right)$$

$$+ \frac{1}{r^2(\sin^2\theta)\Phi}\frac{d^2\Phi}{d\phi^2} + \frac{8\pi^2 m}{h^2}\left(E + \frac{e^2}{r}\right) = 0,$$

where the partial differentiation signs are no longer needed since each function is of a single variable only. We multiply through by $r^2 \sin^2\theta$ and rearrange to obtain

$$\frac{\sin^2\theta}{R}\frac{d}{dr}\left(r^2\frac{dR}{dr}\right) + \frac{\sin\theta}{\Theta}\frac{d}{d\theta}\left(\sin\theta\,\frac{d\Theta}{d\theta}\right)$$

$$+ \frac{8\pi^2 m}{h^2}\left(E + \frac{e^2}{r}\right)(r^2\sin^2\theta) = -\frac{1}{\Phi}\frac{d^2\Phi}{d\phi^2}. \tag{16-72}$$

The left-hand side of Eq. (16-72) is a function of r and θ only, and the right-hand side is a function of ϕ only, so neither can depend on the other's variable(s); each side must therefore be equal to some common constant, which we take to be m^2. The right-hand side of Eq. (16-72) then gives

$$\frac{1}{\Phi}\frac{d^2\Phi}{d\phi^2} = -m^2, \tag{16-73}$$

which we will call the Φ equation.

The left-hand side of Eq. (16-72) is likewise equal to m^2; we divide through by $\sin^2\theta$ and rearrange to obtain

$$\frac{1}{R}\frac{d}{dr}\left(r^2\frac{dR}{dr}\right) + \frac{8\pi^2 m}{h^2}\left(E + \frac{e^2}{r}\right)r^2 = \frac{m^2}{\sin^2\theta} - \frac{1}{\sin\theta}\frac{1}{\Theta}\frac{d}{d\theta}\left(\sin\theta\,\frac{d\Theta}{d\theta}\right). \tag{16-74}$$

By the same argument as before, each side must equal some common constant, which is taken to be λ. The resulting two equations are, with some rearrangement,

$$\frac{1}{r^2}\frac{d}{dr}\left(r^2\frac{dR}{dr}\right) - \frac{\lambda}{r^2}R + \frac{8\pi^2 m}{h^2}\left(E + \frac{e^2}{r}\right)R = 0 \tag{16-75}$$

and

$$\frac{1}{\sin\theta}\frac{d}{d\theta}\left(\sin\theta\frac{d\Theta}{d\theta}\right) - \frac{m^2\Theta}{\sin^2\theta} + \lambda\Theta = 0. \tag{16-76}$$

These will be called the R and Θ *equations*, respectively.

The problem is now reduced to the solution of three separate equations, each in one variable only. Before proceeding to these solutions, it should be mentioned that, strictly speaking, the mass of the electron m in the $8\pi^2 m/h^2$ term should be replaced by the reduced mass $mm_n/(m + m_n)$, where m_n is the nuclear mass. The correction is a small one, however.

B. Solution of the Φ Equation

Since m is a constant that can have various values, there is a family of solutions to Eq. (16-73), of the form

$$\Phi_m = \frac{1}{\sqrt{2\pi}}e^{im\phi} = \frac{1}{\sqrt{2\pi}}(\cos m\phi + i\sin m\phi). \tag{16-77}$$

One can easily verify that Eq. (16-77) is a solution for any m by differentiating twice and comparing with Eq. (16-73). By now it should be no surprise that the physically acceptable solutions are limited to those for which $m = 0, \pm1, \pm2, \dots$. The reason is simply that the solution must be for a stationary state or a standing wave and consequently cannot depend on how many times one cycles ϕ around a circle. Φ_m must be the same for $\phi = 0$, $\phi = 2\pi$, $\phi = 4\pi$, and so on, and this is possible only if m is an integer or zero. As was anticipated, m turns out to be the magnetic quantum number of the Bohr theory. Finally, the factor $1/\sqrt{2\pi}$ is a normalization factor, such that $\int_0^{2\pi}\Phi_m\Phi_m{}^*\,d\phi = 1$.

The expression for Φ_m is just $1/\sqrt{2\pi}$ if $m = 0$. For other m values it is awkward to deal with an imaginary exponential. Use is therefore made of a general property of solutions of a differential equation of this type. It is that any linear combination of solutions must also be a solution. For any given m we can take the sum and difference of the solutions for m and $-m$ to obtain two new ones. Thus for $m = 1$,

$$\Phi_1 = A(\cos\phi + i\sin\phi), \qquad \Phi_{-1} = A(\cos\phi - i\sin\phi),$$

and $\Phi_1 + \Phi_{-1} = 2A\cos\phi$, $\Phi_1 - \Phi_{-1} = 2iA\sin\phi$. It is customary to drop the factor i in the second of these combinations, since it disappears when we write

$\Phi\Phi^*$. Also, the constant $2A$ must be reevaluated if the new functions are to be normalized, and is then found to be just $1/\sqrt{\pi}$. In summary, the solutions of the equation are usually written

$$\Phi_0 = \frac{1}{\sqrt{2\pi}}, \qquad \Phi_m = \begin{cases} \dfrac{1}{\sqrt{\pi}}\cos(|\,m\,|\,\phi)\,, \\[2mm] \dfrac{1}{\sqrt{\pi}}\sin(|\,m\,|\,\phi). \end{cases} \tag{16-78}$$

Their graphical appearance is discussed in the next section.

The solutions of the wave equation for the various cases that we deal with are called *eigenfunctions*, and the corresponding energy values are called *eigenvalues*. An important property of the set of eigenfunctions for a particular system is that they are *orthogonal*. By orthogonal we mean that $\int \psi_1^*\psi_2\,dx = 0$, where the integral is over the entire range of the variable and ψ_1 and ψ_2 are two different eigenfunctions. In the present case, the statement is that $\int_0^{2\pi} \Phi_{m_1}^* \Phi_{m_2}\,d\phi = 0$, $m_1 \neq m_2$. In addition, since the product $\psi^*\psi\,dx$ gives the probability of finding the particle in the region between x and $x + dx$, it is convenient to adjust the coefficients of the eigenfunctions so that $\int \psi^*\psi\,dx = 1$. A set of eigenfunctions is said to be *orthonormal* if $\int \psi_i^*\psi_j\,dx = \delta$, where $\delta = 0$ for $i \neq j$ and $\delta = 1$ for $i = j$.

C. Solution of the Θ Equation

The general solution of Eq. (16-76) requires considerations whose details are beyond the scope of this text. As with the Φ equation, the solution is in the form of a polynomial, but now in θ, and the requirement that it be cyclic in θ restricts the values of λ to $\ell(\ell + 1)$, where ℓ is an integer. That is, in order for the solutions to represent stationary states, they must be the same for $\theta = 0, \pi, 2\pi, \dots$. The integer ℓ, as may be guessed, functions as the azimuthal or angular momentum quantum number of the Bohr theory. The requirement that the polynomial solution have a finite number of terms further requires that m in Eq. (16-76) also be an integer, but not exceeding ℓ. Once again, imposition of the physical condition of a stationary-state solution introduces integral values for constants of integration, thus converting them into quantum numbers.

The polynomials that are stationary-state solutions of Eq. (16-76) are known as *associated Legendre polynomials*; Table 16-2 lists a sufficient number of them to meet most needs. They are normalized and orthogonal. There is a somewhat tricky point here. The element of volume in polar coordinates is $r^2 \sin\theta\,dr\,d\theta\,d\phi$; this is the expression equivalent to $dx\,dy\,dz$ in Cartesian coordinates. The normalization integral for the Θ function is therefore

$$\int_0^\pi \Theta_{\ell,m}^* \Theta_{\ell,m} \sin\theta\,d\theta$$

Table 16-2. *Solutions to the Θ Function*

$\ell = 0, m = 0$ (s orbitals)		$\Theta_{0,0} = \frac{1}{2}\sqrt{2}$
$\ell = 1$ (p orbitals)	$m = 0$	$\Theta_{1,0} = \frac{1}{2}\sqrt{6}\cos\theta$
	$\lvert m \rvert = 1$	$\Theta_{1,1} = \frac{1}{2}\sqrt{3}\sin\theta$
$\ell = 2$ (d orbitals)	$m = 0$	$\Theta_{2,0} = \frac{1}{4}\sqrt{10}\,(3\cos^2\theta - 1)$
	$\lvert m \rvert = 1$	$\Theta_{2,1} = \frac{1}{2}\sqrt{15}\sin\theta\cos\theta$
	$\lvert m \rvert = 2$	$\Theta_{2,2} = \frac{1}{4}\sqrt{15}\sin^2\theta$
$\ell = 3$ (f orbitals)	$m = 0$	$\Theta_{3,0} = \frac{3}{4}\sqrt{14}\,(\frac{5}{3}\cos^3\theta - \cos\theta)$
	$\lvert m \rvert = 1$	$\Theta_{3,1} = \frac{1}{8}\sqrt{42}\,(\sin\theta)(5\cos^2\theta - 1)$
	$\lvert m \rvert = 2$	$\Theta_{3,2} = \frac{1}{4}\sqrt{105}\sin^2\theta\cos\theta$
	$\lvert m \rvert = 3$	$\Theta_{3,3} = \frac{1}{8}\sqrt{70}\sin^3\theta$

or, since the solutions are real,

$$\int_0^\pi \Theta_{\ell,m}^2 \sin\theta\, d\theta = 1. \tag{16-79}$$

Similarly, the orthogonality integral is

$$\int_0^\pi \Theta_{\ell,m}\Theta_{\ell',m'} \sin\theta\, d\theta = 0, \tag{16-80}$$

where either ℓ and ℓ' or m and m' (or both) are different. Equations (16-79) and (16-80) might be verified by the reader for the first few entries in Table 16-2 as well as the fact that the latter are indeed solutions to Eq. (16-76).

The principal regularity in the Θ functions to be noticed at the moment is that they are all polynomials whose highest term is of the form $(\cos\theta)^a (\sin\theta)^b$, where $a + b = \ell$ and $b = \lvert m \rvert$. Within a given ℓ set, the progression is from an expression containing $\cos\theta$ terms only to one containing only $\sin\theta$. Also, Θ for $\lvert m \rvert = \ell$ is always $(\sin\theta)^\ell$ and Θ for $\lvert m \rvert = \ell - 1$ is always $(\sin\theta)^{\ell-1}(\cos\theta)$. These functions are very important in the applications of wave mechanics to chemical bonding and are sufficiently limited in number that the reader should familiarize himself with them.

D. Solution of the R Equation

Equation (16-75) again can be reduced to a standard differential equation, and, as with the Θ equation, the solutions are in the form of polynomials—this time in r and known as the *associated Laguerre polynomials*. To avoid a catastrophe at $r \to \infty$, it is again necessary that the polynomials terminate after a finite number of terms; the requirement for this to happen is that λ or $\ell(\ell + 1)$ be an integer. This defines a quantum number n, the same as the principal quantum number of the Bohr theory.

It is convenient to generalize a little by replacing the potential function of Eq. (16-75), e^2/r, by Ze^2/r, to allow for a nuclear charge other than unity. Also, the polynomials are much simplified in appearance if written in terms of

$$\rho = \frac{2Z}{na_0} r, \qquad (16\text{-}81)$$

where a_0 is the radius of the first Bohr orbit, as given by

$$a_0 = \frac{h^2}{4\pi^2 \mu e^2} \qquad \text{[Eq. (16-14)]}$$

(in the more accurate form using μ rather than m).

The most commonly needed solutions of the R equation are given in Table 16-3. These are again normalized and orthogonal. (Remember that the integrals involved are of the form $\int_0^\infty R_1 R_2{}^* r^2 \, dr$; these are equal to unity if $R_1 = R_2$ and zero otherwise.) The principal regularities of these solutions are the following. Each contains the exponential $e^{-\rho/2}$ preceded by a polynomial in ρ. The highest term in the polynomial, that is, the order of the polynomial, is $n - 1$, and the polynomial is of the form

$$(a + b\rho + c\rho^2 + \cdots + \rho^{n-1-\ell})(\rho)^{(n-1+\ell)/2}.$$

This general term looks complicated, and it is easier to perceive what is being said by studying the actual polynomials. Although the numerical coefficients are unimportant for our purposes, it is again very desirable to become familiar with the progression in *form* of these solutions.

E. *Energy Levels for the Hydrogen Atom*

The energy corresponding to a given set of quantum numbers may be obtained by substituting the corresponding solution of the R equation back into the differential equation, that is, into Eq. (16-75), and solving for E [remembering that $\lambda = \ell(\ell + 1)$]. This procedure may be followed for each of the functions in Table 16-3, and the results are summarized by the expression

$$E = -\frac{2\pi^2 \mu e^4 Z^2}{h^2 n^2} \qquad \text{[Eq. (16-16)]}.$$

This is exactly the result obtained by the simple Bohr theory (in the more accurate version with μ replacing m)!

Table 16-3.   *Solutions to the R Equation*

$n = 1$

$\ell = 0$ (1s) $R_{1,0} = \left(\dfrac{Z}{a_0}\right)^{3/2}(2)(e^{-\rho/2})$

$n = 2$

$\ell = 0$ (2s) $R_{2,0} = \dfrac{(Z/a_0)^{3/2}}{2\sqrt{2}}(2 - \rho)e^{-\rho/2}$

$\ell = 1$ (2p) $R_{2,1} = \dfrac{(Z/a_0)^{3/2}}{2\sqrt{6}}\rho e^{-\rho/2}$

$n = 3$

$\ell = 0$ (3s) $R_{3,0} = \dfrac{(Z/a_0)^{3/2}}{9\sqrt{3}}(6 - 6\rho + \rho^2)e^{-\rho/2}$

$\ell = 1$ (3p) $R_{3,1} = \dfrac{(Z/a_0)^{3/2}}{9\sqrt{6}}(4 - \rho)\rho e^{-\rho/2}$

$\ell = 2$ (3d) $R_{3,2} = \dfrac{(Z/a_0)^{3/2}}{9\sqrt{30}}\rho^2 e^{-\rho/2}$

$n = 4$

$\ell = 0$ (4s) $R_{4,0} = \dfrac{(Z/a_0)^{3/2}}{96}(24 - 36\rho + 12\rho^2 - \rho^3)e^{-\rho/2}$

$\ell = 1$ (4p) $R_{4,1} = \dfrac{(Z/a_0)^{3/2}}{32\sqrt{15}}(20 - 10\rho + \rho^2)\rho e^{-\rho/2}$

$\ell = 2$ (4d) $R_{4,2} = \dfrac{(Z/a_0)^{3/2}}{96\sqrt{5}}(6 - \rho)\rho^2 e^{-\rho/2}$

$\ell = 3$ (4f) $R_{4,3} = \dfrac{(Z/a_0)^{3/2}}{96\sqrt{35}}\rho^3 e^{-\rho/2}$

The more elegant approach of advanced texts is to express R in a general form and to substitute this into Eq. (16-75); one then obtains Eq. (16-16) as the general result, the quantum number ℓ canceling out. It is sufficient here to point out that the reader can verify Eq. (16-16) as the correct result for specific n and ℓ values.

16-8   The Graphical Appearance of Hydrogen-Like Orbitals

The solutions of the R, Θ, and Φ equations were given in analytical form in the preceding section. Their product is ψ, and the particular function for a given n, ℓ, and m is commonly called an orbital when used as a one-electron wave function. We now explore their semiquantitative graphical appearance. The natural division at this point is into the R solutions and the product of the Θ and Φ solutions.

The first contains the principal quantum number n explicitly and the nuclear charge Z and determines the energy of the ψ wave function. That is, the energy of a given $\psi = R(r)\,\Theta(\theta)\,\Phi(\phi)$ is determined by the $R(r)$ function alone. Thus for the hydrogen atom, states of the same n but different ℓ or m are degenerate. This function is crucial in quantitative calculations. The product $\Theta(\theta)\,\Phi(\phi)$ establishes the *angular* dependence of the solution and plays a key role with respect to the symmetry or geometric appearance of the ψ function. Sometimes the term orbital is applied to this product rather than to the complete ψ function.

To make the point in a somewhat different way, it will be emphasized in the next chapter that a chemical bond develops if two atoms have orbitals that suitably overlap in space. Although the degree of such overlap is determined by the overall ψ function, the $R(r)$ component of ψ determines how close the atoms must come and the $\Theta(\theta)\,\Phi(\phi)$ component determines the most suitable bond angles. It is therefore this latter portion of ψ that is of central importance to the qualitative understanding of molecular geometry.

The functions to be discussed are called hydrogen-like since, although they derive from the solutions for the hydrogen atom, they apply approximately to the outer electrons of any atom. That is, only the $R(r)$ function contains Z, and for other than hydrogen, it is a fairly good approximation to use a Z_{eff} or a screening constant just as was done in the Bohr model. The $\Theta(\theta)\,\Phi(\phi)$ functions do not contain Z and thus are independent of the nature of the atom. This last is true only in first approximation, of course, and a sketch of the problems encountered in more exact treatments is given in the Commentary and Notes section. Qualitative descriptions of the wave functions for atoms in general are almost invariably made in terms of the hydrogen-like functions, however, and these therefore are of prime importance unless a person enters the discipline of chemical physics in a serious, professional way.

A. The R(r) Functions

Figure 16-8 presents the first few $R(r)$ functions of Table 16-3. At large r, all approach zero as a consequence of the exponential factor, but notice the presence of nodes or points at which $R(r)$ is zero, representing r values at which the polynomial portion is zero. The number of such nodes is simply the degree of the polynomial, and inspection of either the analytical or the graphical presentation leads to the general formula

$$\text{number of nodes} = n - \ell - 1. \tag{16-82}$$

The probability of one's finding an electron as one goes out along a particular radius line is proportional to $[R(r)]^2$. Right now, however, it is of more interest to deal with the probability of finding an electron at a distance r from the nucleus, regardless of direction. What is now in question is the relative density of electrons

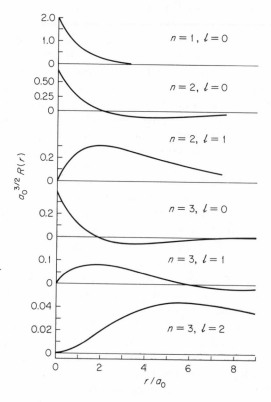

Fig. 16-8. *The R functions. (Adapted from H. Eyring, J. Walter, and G. E. Kimball, "Quantum Chemistry," Copyright 1960, Wiley, New York. Used with permission of John Wiley & Sons, Inc.)*

in a spherical shell lying between r and $r + dr$, which means that $[R(r)]^2$ must be weighted by the area of a sphere of radius r, $4\pi r^2$. Figure 16-9 plots $4\pi r^2[R(r)]^2$ against ρ for various n and ℓ values, and Fig. 16-10 makes the same presentation in terms of a polar plot of the electron density intercepted by a plane through the nucleus.

Either of the figures makes the point that the $R(r)$ function leads to peaks in electron density, the number of which is given by $n - \ell$. There is only one such maximum for the function having the largest possible ℓ for the given n value, and within the family having the same n the number of maxima then increases stepwise with decreasing ℓ. This nodal aspect of the electron density distribution will not be referred to much henceforth but should be kept in mind. One is usually concerned mainly with the outermost maximum, which is the most important one with respect to chemical bonding, and it is important in this respect to note that its radial position increases with increasing n value, and within a given n set, with decreasing ℓ value, the first dependence being the more significant of the two.

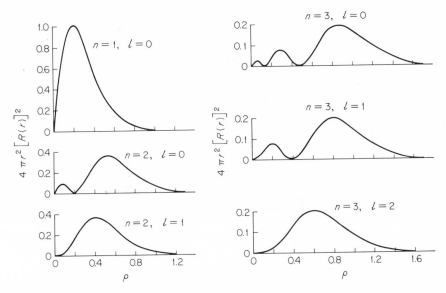

Fig. 16-9. *Radial probability functions for the hydrogen atom.*

B. The Angular Dependence Function

The total angular dependence function $\Theta(\theta)\,\Phi(\phi)$ modulates the $R(r)$ functions shown in Fig. 16-8–16-10 according to direction in space. It has become customary to show these as three-dimensional polar plots, or as two-dimensional polar plots for some particular plane. It is necessary to keep in mind that in such plots distance out from the center is proportional to the numerical value of $\Theta(\theta)\,\Phi(\phi)$ and is *not* distance from the center of the nucleus. Also, although strictly speaking the term orbital refers to a particular one-electron ψ function, it is often used to designate the $\Theta(\theta)\,\Phi(\phi)$ function for a given ℓ and will be so used in this section. An s orbital thus refers to this function for $\ell = 0$, a p orbital to the function for $\ell = 1$, and a d orbital to this function for $\ell = 2$. For simplicity of notation the product $\Theta(\theta)\,\Phi(\phi)$ will be designated as $A(\theta, \phi)$.

Let us now examine a few of these polar plots for particular $A(\theta, \phi)$ functions. We obtain the function for an s orbital by multiplying the $\Theta(\theta)$ function for $\ell = 0$ (from Table 16-2) by that for the $\Phi(\phi)$ function for $m = 0$ [Eq. (16-78)]:

$$A_{\text{s}} = \frac{\sqrt{2}}{2\sqrt{2\pi}} = \frac{1}{2\sqrt{\pi}}. \tag{16-83}$$

This is obviously independent of direction and merely modifies the appropriate radial function by the constant $1/2\sqrt{\pi}$. The three-dimensional polar plot of an s orbital is then just a sphere of radius $1/2\sqrt{\pi}$, and the two-dimensional plot for any plane is just a circle, again of radius $1/2\sqrt{\pi}$, as illustrated in Fig. 16-11(a).

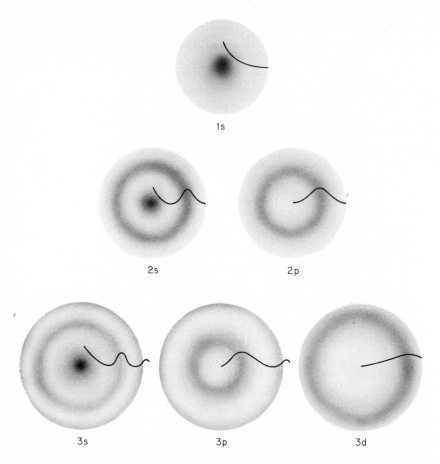

Fig. 16-10. *Pictorial representation of radial probability functions.*

There are three p orbitals, corresponding to the three possible values of m for $\ell = 1$. Thus for $\ell = 1$ and $m = 0$,

$$A_{p_z} = \frac{\sqrt{6}}{2} (\cos\theta) \frac{1}{\sqrt{2\pi}} = \frac{1}{2}\sqrt{\frac{3}{\pi}} \cos\theta. \qquad (16\text{-}84)$$

This is known as a p_z orbital since $\cos\theta$ gives the projection of a unit vector on the z axis (see Fig. 16-7). The other two are for $|m| = 1$:

$$A_{p_x} = \left(\frac{\sqrt{3}}{2}\sin\theta\right)\left(\frac{1}{\sqrt{\pi}}\cos\phi\right) = \frac{1}{2}\sqrt{\frac{3}{\pi}}\sin\theta\cos\phi, \qquad (16\text{-}85)$$

$$A_{p_y} = \left(\frac{\sqrt{3}}{2}\sin\theta\right)\left(\frac{1}{\sqrt{\pi}}\sin\phi\right) = \frac{1}{2}\sqrt{\frac{3}{\pi}}\sin\theta\sin\phi, \qquad (16\text{-}86)$$

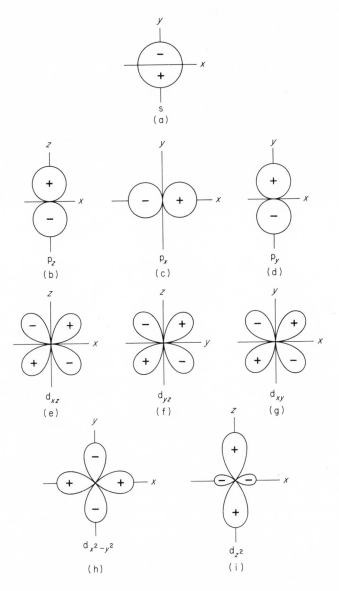

Fig. 16-11.   *Polar plots for various A functions.*

and are designated as the p_x and p_y orbitals, respectively, since by Eqs. (16-69) and (16-70), the trigonometric functions correspond to the x and y projections of a unit vector.

The p_z orbital is independent of ϕ and is therefore symmetric about the z axis. A polar plot in any plane containing the z axis there has the appearance shown in Fig. 16-11(b) (the actual plane being taken to be the *xz* plane). The polar plot of cos θ is a circle tangent to the *xy* plane at the origin, and from a consideration of the sign of cos θ for various quadrants the upper circle or *lobe* is positive and the lower one is negative.

The p_x and p_y orbitals have their maximum values at $\theta = 90°$ and their polar plots in the *xy* plane are shown in Fig. 16-11(c, d). The three p orbitals are identical except for their orientation in space; each is a figure of revolution, so that in a three-dimensional polar plot each consists of a pair of spheres, as shown in Fig. 16-12(b–d).

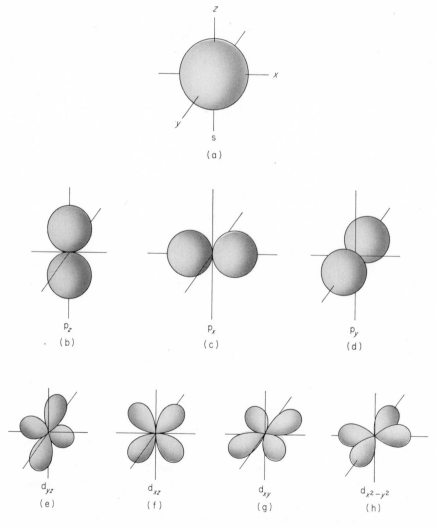

Fig. 16-12. *Pictorial representations of A functions.*

Finally (for us), there are five d orbitals, one for each of the possible m values for $\ell = 2$. Again using Eqs. (16-78) and Table 16-2, one obtains for $A(\theta, \phi)$, when $m = 0$,

$$A d_{z^2} = \left(\frac{\sqrt{10}}{4}(3\cos^2\theta - 1)\right)\frac{1}{\sqrt{2\pi}} = \frac{1}{4}\sqrt{\frac{5}{\pi}}(3\cos^2\theta - 1), \quad (16\text{-}87)$$

when $|m| = 1$,

$$A d_{xz} = \left(\frac{\sqrt{15}}{2}\sin\theta\cos\theta\right)\left(\frac{1}{\sqrt{\pi}}\cos\phi\right) = \frac{1}{2}\sqrt{\frac{15}{\pi}}\sin\theta\cos\theta\cos\phi, \quad (16\text{-}88)$$

$$A d_{yz} = \left(\frac{\sqrt{15}}{2}\sin\theta\cos\theta\right)\left(\frac{1}{\sqrt{\pi}}\sin\phi\right) = \frac{1}{2}\sqrt{\frac{15}{\pi}}\sin\theta\cos\theta\sin\phi, \quad (16\text{-}89)$$

and when $|m| = 2$,

$$A d_{x^2-y^2} = \left(\frac{\sqrt{15}}{4}\sin^2\theta\right)\left(\frac{1}{\sqrt{\pi}}\cos 2\phi\right) = \frac{1}{4}\sqrt{\frac{15}{\pi}}\sin^2\theta\cos 2\phi, \quad (16\text{-}90)$$

$$A d_{xy} = \left(\frac{\sqrt{15}}{4}\sin^2\theta\right)\left(\frac{1}{\sqrt{\pi}}\sin 2\phi\right) = \frac{1}{4}\sqrt{\frac{15}{\pi}}\sin^2\theta\sin 2\phi. \quad (16\text{-}91)$$

The designations d_{xz} and d_{yz} are fairly obvious since by Eqs. (16-68)–(16-70), the respective trigonometric functions are the product of the x and z and of the y and z projections of a unit vector. The d_{xz} orbital has its maximum value for $\phi = 0$ (or π), and, correspondingly, the polar plot in the xz plane is that shown in Fig. 16-11(e). The d_{yz} orbital has its maximum extent in the yz plane and is shown in Fig. 16-11(f). Since the product $\sin\theta\cos\theta$ is a maximum at 45°, the lobes now point midway between the axes and carry alternate plus and minus signs, as determined from the signs of the functions for the various quadrants. They are no longer circular, but each lobe is a figure of revolution about its axis, and the three-dimensional polar plots are as illustrated in Fig. 16-12(e, f).

The d_{xy} orbital has its maximum extension in the xy plane and the $\sin 2\phi$ function produces four lobes as shown in Figs. 16-11(g) and 16-12(g). Since $\sin 2\phi = 2\sin\phi\cos\phi$, the trigonometric function of Eq. (16-91) corresponds to the product of the x and y projections of a unit vector, hence the name d_{xy}. The d_{xz}, d_{yz}, and d_{xy} orbitals form a group; they are identical in three-dimensional shape, differing only in their spatial orientation; each d_{ij} orbital lies in the plane defined by the i and j axes and the members of the set are thus mutually perpendicular.

There remain the $d_{x^2-y^2}$ and d_{z^2} functions. The first again has its maximum extension in the xy plane ($\sin^2\theta = 1$) and the $\cos 2\phi$ term produces four lobes with maxima at 0°, 90°, 180°, and 270°, or as shown in Figs. 16-11(h) and 16-12(h). It further turns out that the $d_{x^2-y^2}$ orbital is identical in shape to those of the d_{ij} set. The first four so far discussed are thus equivalent except for spatial orientation.

Since an atom has no preferred direction in space, it might be thought that the situation should be symmetric, and that there should be $d_{z^2-x^2}$ and $d_{z^2-y^2}$ orbitals to complete a set of three, as with the d_{ij} ones. There can only be five independent orbitals, however, corresponding to the five possible m values; that is, the $\ell = 2$ set is just fivefold degenerate. What is done therefore is to pick the z axis as unique (with respect to the orbitals but not with respect to space) and to use a linear combination of the $d_{z^2-x^2}$ and $d_{z^2-y^2}$ pair. From Eqs. (16-68)–(16-70) these should be of the form

$$d_{z^2-x^2} \propto \cos^2 \theta - \sin^2 \theta \cos^2 \phi, \qquad d_{z^2-y^2} \propto \cos^2 \theta - \sin^2 \theta \sin^2 \phi$$

and their sum is then

$$d_{z^2-x^2} + d_{z^2-y^2} \propto 2 \cos^2 \theta - (\sin^2 \theta)(\cos^2 \phi + \sin^2 \phi)$$

or, since $\cos^2 \phi + \sin^2 \phi = 1$ and $\sin^2 \theta = 1 - \cos^2 \theta$,

$$d_{z^2-x^2} + d_{z^2-y^2} \propto 3 \cos^2 \theta - 1.$$

Except for the numerical coefficient, this is the expression for d_{z^2} given by Eq. (16-87); because of its origin, an alternative designation sometimes seen is $d_{2z^2-x^2-y^2}$.

The graphical operation corresponding to the preceding is illustrated in Fig. 16-13; what happens is that the lobes along the z axis reinforce, and the four negative lobes in the xy plane combine to give a doughnut-shaped region. The cross section shown in Fig. 16-11(i) also illustrates the point that the node between the z lobes and the doughnut lobe is at $\cos^2 \theta = \frac{1}{3}$ or at a θ of about 54°.

The functions for the set of seven $\ell = 3$ or f orbitals may be assembled from Eq. (16-78) and Table 16-2 in the same manner as was done for the d orbitals. The cross section for the $m = 0$ or f_{z^3} will, for example, resemble d_{z^2} in having large lobes on the z axis, but will now have *two* small lobes in the equatorial region. The pair for $m = 3$ will have six rather than four lobes in the xy plane, and so on.

It turns out that the f orbital set obtained in this way is not very convenient in its

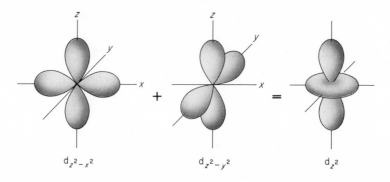

Fig. 16-13. *Illustration of the construction of the d_{z^2} orbital.*

geometric properties. Fortunately, if one has a set of solutions to a partial differential equation, any new set constructed by independent linear combinations of the old one will also constitute a set of solutions. A more useful set of f orbitals may thus be obtained, designated as f_{z^3}, f_{x^3}, f_{y^3}, f_{xyz}, $f_{x(z^2-y^2)}$, $f_{y(z^2-x^2)}$, and $f_{z(x^2-y^2)}$. The corresponding trigonometric functions follow immediately from Eqs. (16-68)–(16-70); the qualitative appearances of f_{xyz} and $f_{x(z^2-y^2)}$ are shown in Fig. 16-14.

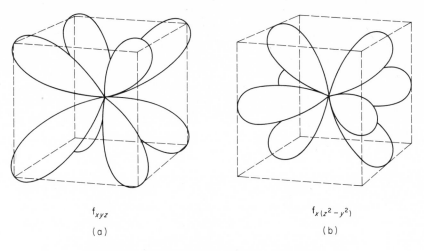

$$f_{xyz}$$

$$(a)$$

$$f_{x(z^2-y^2)}$$

$$(b)$$

Fig. 16-14.   *Plots of f orbitals. (a) f_{xyz} and (b) $f_{x(z^2-y^2)}$.*

16-9   Graphical Appearance of the Electron Density around a Hydrogen-Like Atom

A.   The Angular Portion. Ünsold's Theorem

The preceding section dealt only with $A(\theta, \phi)$, and this function must be squared to obtain the corresponding probability or electron density functions. The effect is to elongate all lobes, and, of course, to remove their sign designation. Figure 16-15 shows the appearance of A^2 for s, p, and d electrons as the usual polar plots in the plane of maximum electron density.

There is a useful and instructive rule known as Ünsold's theorem. It states that the sum of A^2 for the orbitals making up the set of a particular ℓ value is a constant. Thus

$$A_s^2 = \frac{1}{\pi},$$

$$A_{p_x}^2 + A_{p_y}^2 + A_{p_z}^2 = \frac{3}{4\pi} \sin^2 \theta \cos^2 \phi + \frac{3}{4\pi} \sin^2 \theta \sin^2 \phi + \frac{3}{4\pi} \cos^2 \theta$$

$$= \frac{3}{4\pi} \sin^2 \theta + \frac{3}{4\pi} \cos^2 \theta = \frac{3}{4\pi}.$$

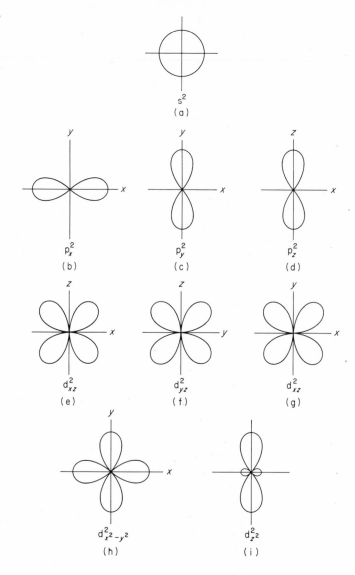

Fig. 16-15. *Polar plots of A^2 functions.*

The demonstration of Ünsold's theorem for the set of five d orbitals is left as an exercise.

The significance of the theorem is that with two electrons in each orbital of a set the total electron density is independent of angle, that is, is spherically symmetric. We often speak of such a set as a closed or filled shell. Thus Ne has a closed shell of six 2p and Ar a closed shell of six 3p electrons; therefore each has a spherically symmetric electron density. The outer electrons of Kr constitute closed shells of 3d and of 4p electrons, and again give a spherically symmetric total electron density. This point has been stressed to counteract the impression given by the various preceding polar plots of orbitals that an atom with a filled set would be "bumpy," with orbitals sticking out in various directions. In a sense, a set of orbitals (of a given ℓ value) represents one way of dividing a spherically symmetric electron density into a set of standing waves. Such a set of waves is known, incidentally, as one of *spherical harmonics*. Thus a sphere of electron density may be left as such, and called an s orbital. It may be divided into a set

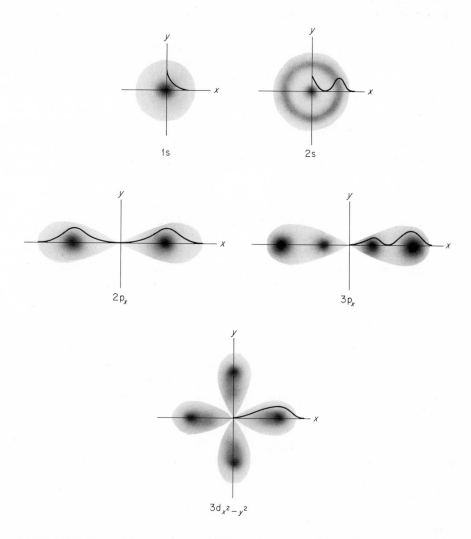

Fig. 16-16. *Pictorial representations of electron density as a function of radius and of angle, for various ψ^2 functions.*

of three p orbitals or a set of five d orbitals. As we will see in the next section, yet other ways are possible and useful.

B.   The Complete Wave Function

It is important to appreciate that the polar plots of the A^2 functions are *not* representations of how the electron density actually looks; distance out from the origin of such plots is *not* distance from the nucleus but only the measure of the value of A^2 in that direction. To obtain representations of electron density, each A^2 function must be multiplied by the appropriate $R^2(r)$. In a polar plot of the electron density for a given ψ^2, distance out from the origin is now distance from the nucleus, and no coordinates are left to give the electron density. A qualitative graph can be constructed, however, in which the density of shading indicates the electron density. This is done in Fig. 16-16 for several cases. Thus although the 1s and 2s cases are both spherically symmetric, the radial wave function introduces a node in the latter. Similarly, the $2p_x$ and $3p_x$ differ in that the latter has a node, and so on. An alternative way of modeling the electron density around an atom, by means of *domains*, is discussed in the Special Topics section.

16-10   Hybrid Orbitals

Hydrogen-like orbitals may be used as a basis for the treatment of directional bonding between atoms. From the wave mechanical point of view a bond develops as two atoms A and B approach if their wave functions reinforce each other. One requirement is that both have appreciable amplitude in some common region of space, a convenient index of this being that $\int \psi_A \psi_B \, d\tau$ is large. The orbitals thus should overlap. The wave functions must also have the proper phase relationships to reinforce and in simple situations this will be the case if the overlapping orbitals have the same sign so that the integral is positive. Since individual orbitals are directional (except for s orbitals), so therefore are the bonds that an atom forms.

Conversely, knowing the geometry of a molecule, one looks for correspondingly oriented orbitals. Thus in CH_4 the four C—H bonds point to the corners·of a tetrahedron; in BF_3 the three B—F bonds lie in a plane and are 120° apart. The problem that now arises is that the s and p orbitals available to light elements do not have this angular relationship to each other. One therefore looks for linear combinations of orbitals that will produce a new set having the desired directional properties.

In the case of BF_3 one asks what combination of 2s and 2p orbitals produces lobes 120° apart and lying in a plane. We can assume the plane to be the xy one, which restricts the choice to s, p_x, and p_y orbitals (the p_z orbital being zero in this plane). The following set has the desired properties:

$$A_1 = \frac{1}{\sqrt{3}} A_s + \sqrt{\frac{2}{3}} A_{p_x}, \qquad A_2 = \frac{1}{\sqrt{3}} A_s - \frac{1}{\sqrt{6}} A_{p_x} + \frac{1}{\sqrt{2}} A_{p_y},$$

$$A_3 = \frac{1}{\sqrt{3}} A_s - \frac{1}{\sqrt{6}} A_{p_x} - \frac{1}{\sqrt{2}} A_{p_y}.$$

(16-92)

A plot of these functions is shown in Fig. 16-17. Not only do they have the desired directional properties; but also the coefficients of Eq. (16-92) are such that each is normalized; the set is mutually orthogonal. Further, the sum $A_1{}^2 + A_2{}^2 + A_3{}^2$ is identical to the sum $A_s{}^2 + A_{p_x}^2 + A_{p_y}^2$ and equal to a constant. That is, $A_s{}^2$ is

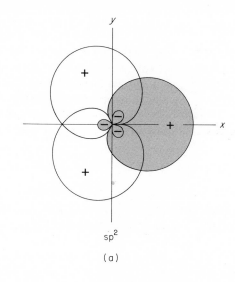

sp^2

(a)

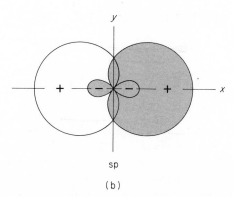

sp

(b)

Fig. 16-17. *Hybrid orbitals. (a)* sp^2 *and (b)* sp.

circularly symmetric and so is $A_{p_x}^2 + A_{p_y}^2$ so that the sum of electron densities in the xy plane is independent of direction. The new set, A_1, A_2, A_3, represents an alternative way of dividing the circle. Strictly speaking, one should use the full wave functions ψ in constructing such new sets of orbitals, but the coefficients remain the same if the $R(r)$ functions are the same or can be adjusted to nearly compensate if they are not.

The combinations of s and p orbitals of Eq. (16-92) are known as *hybrid orbitals*, after L. Pauling, or as sp² hybrids.

A set of tetrahedrally oriented orbitals can similarly be constructed from s, p_x, p_y, and p_z. These are

$$A_1 = \tfrac{1}{2}(A_s + A_{p_x} + A_{p_y} + A_{p_z}), \qquad A_2 = \tfrac{1}{2}(A_s + A_{p_x} - A_{p_y} - A_{p_z}),$$

$$(16\text{-}93)$$

$$A_3 = \tfrac{1}{2}(A_s - A_{p_x} + A_{p_y} - A_{p_z}), \qquad A_4 = \tfrac{1}{2}(A_s - A_{p_x} - A_{p_y} + A_{p_z}).$$

The new set is normalized and orthogonal. Again, one usually makes the assumption that $R(r)$ is the same for each wave function, and so Eq. (16-93) can be written in terms of the complete ψ functions rather than just the angular parts. Orbitals such as A_1, ..., A_4 are known as sp³ hybrid orbitals.

The third and very simple case of hybrid bond formation is the sp hybrid, formed by a linear combination of an s orbital and a p orbital. For example, the set

$$A_1 = \tfrac{1}{2}(A_s + A_{p_x}), \qquad A_2 = \tfrac{1}{2}(A_s - A_{p_x}) \qquad (16\text{-}94)$$

gives lobes lying on the x axis, as shown in Fig. 16-17(b).

A number of other hybrid bond combinations are known; these will be discussed in more detail in Chapter 17 using the more powerful group-theoretical approach.

COMMENTARY AND NOTES

16-CN-1   *Albert Einstein*

Albert Einstein is the third great man of science that we attempt to describe. Benjamin Thompson (see Section 4-2) had a multifaceted brilliance and, as an individual, was effectively self-serving in a scoundrely way. Willard Gibbs (see Section 6-CN-2) had a tremendous depth and rigor of thought; as an individual he was austere and retiring but kindly. Einstein resembled Thomson in the variety of his brilliance and Gibbs in its depth; as a person he resembled neither.

The general sequence of Einstein's life is as follows.

1879 Born on March 14 in the small Swabian Jewish community of Ulm, on the Danube. His father was the manager of a small electrochemical works and his mother an able *hausfrau* and fine pianist. The family left for Munich shortly after his birth.

1894 Completed studies at the Luitpold Humanistische Gymnasium in Munich, mainly on the basis of mathematical achievement. He then joined his family, which at this time was residing in Milan.

1895 Flunked the entrance examination of the Polytechnic Academy in Zurich but the examiners were so impressed by his mathematics that they enrolled him in a small liberal arts school in Aarau, and a year later he gained admission to the Academy.

1900 Graduated in physics but failed to receive a staff appointment. He did odd jobs, was a relief mathematics teacher in a technical school in Winterthur (and wrote an essay on capillarity), and then worked in the Swiss Patent Office in Berne until 1905. By then he was a Swiss citizen.

1902 Married Mileva, a small dark-haired girl from the Serbian town of Novi. A son, Hans Albert, was born in 1904, and then a second son, Edward. Some intensely personal troubles, unknown in detail to this day, seem to have clouded the marriage. In 1902 he published a paper on the second law of thermodynamics and thermal equilibrium—apparently unaware of Gibbs' work, he essentially rediscovered statistical thermodynamics.

1905 In an amazing volume of *Annalen der Physik* Einstein published his paper on Brownian motion [note Eqs. (2-69) and (10-41)]; the Nobel-prize-winning paper on the quantum theory of light, based on photo-electric and photochemical behavior (see Section 16-1); *and* the first paper on the special theory of relativity (while still working in the patent office).

1907 Was offered an unpaid lectureship (privatdozent) at the University of Zurich. He rejected the offer but did take such a position at the University of Berne. By 1909 his accomplishments were being recognized worldwide, and, over some political infighting, the University of Zurich offered him a professorship (an *extraordinary* or nonadministrative chair), which he accepted.

1910 Was offered and accepted the chair in theoretical physics at the University of Prague—the oldest university in central Europe. At Zurich and then at Prague he continued working on relativity theory. One of his important papers on general relativity was published in 1911. That year he attended the first of several Solvay Conferences (all-expense-paid gatherings of topflight physicists and chemists, supported by a wealthy scientific hobbyist). This was Einstein's first opportunity to meet such people as Rutherford, Poincaré, Langevin, Planck, Nernst, Lorentz, and Marie Curie.

1912   Returned to Zurich as professor of theoretical physics at the Polytechnic Academy.

1913   Went to Berlin as director of a specially created research institute for physics and as a member of the Royal Prussian Academy of Science. He remained there until the rise of Hitler. In 1919 he divorced Mileva and married a second cousin, Elsa Rudolph, who had two daughters from a previous marriage.

1933   Joined the Institute for Advanced Studies at Princeton. (By this time the position of most Jews in Germany was untenable.)

1939   Wrote a letter supporting the position of Leo Szilard (and of R. Sachs, an advisor to President Roosevelt) who urged the President to begin work on an atomic bomb, pointing out that the Germans had already started.

1955   Died in Princeton Hospital on April 18 from a massive failure of the aorta.

The above factual summary cries for amplification. Einstein was perhaps the first scientist to catch the public imagination. In the 1920's he gave popular lectures to packed houses in England and on the Continent; relativity became a household word. He was a scientist's genius as well, until perhaps the Solvay Conference of 1928. Much of Einstein's contributions were in the area of statistics —statistical thermodynamics, Brownian motion, blackbody radiation—and even though he was responsible for establishing the corpuscular and hence dual nature of electromagnetic radiation, he never accepted Heisenberg's uncertainty principle. He felt this to be a reflection of an inadequacy of wave mechanics rather than a fundamental limitation of nature. The whole matter came to a head at the 1928 Solvay Conference. Einstein proposed a violation of the uncertainty principle. Briefly, it should be possible to have a mechanism that would allow one photon to escape from a box at a precisely determined time. The change in mass determined by weighing the box before and after should give the exact energy of the photon that was lost. The story is that Bohr came away from that session deeply worried, but toward the end of a sleepless night perceived an answer (which had to do with the fact that the impulse given to the box by the photon would change the rate of running of the clock and hence make the precise determination of time impossible). He presented this solution the next day—and essentially defeated Einstein. This event, it appears, began the decline of Einstein as the head of the scientific world. Einstein worked until his death on an attempt to formulate a general (unified-field) theory that would contain within it both the corpuscular and wave aspects of photons and of matter. He never fully succeeded, but continued strongly to believe that wave mechanics was an incomplete model and that the search for a more complete one should continue. While the support is unneeded, this writer agrees.

As a person, Einstein seems to have had an inner reserve that prevented him from making any close personal ties. As a teacher he could be enthusiastic and inspiring, but on specific occasions and subjects. It appears that, overall, it was difficult for students to learn from him. This conclusion is supported by the fact that there was and is no "Einstein" school of physicists—he was a loner.

He could be passionate in causes, as with regard to the League of Nations. As a pacifist, he refused any war-related work during World War I. In New York in 1930, he rousingly called upon true pacifists to refuse to take up arms under any circumstances, asserting that if only 2% of the populace would do this any country's war effort would be doomed. Communists (at that time in alliance with Hitler) applauded. He was not a Communist, however. While he was "open" to the left, seeing less danger from communist than from capitalist societies, Einstein was also quite capable of walking out of an association if he perceived it to be primarily a Communist political front. His abhorrence of fascism (that is, Hitlerism) was special; it led him to promote the United States atomic bomb program. Later, in 1945, he urged the country to outlaw voluntarily use of atomic bombs and campaigned strenuously for the Emergency Committee of Atomic Scientists (along with Bethe, Pauling, and Urey).

Einstein was a Jew by descent and by culture, but not in a synagogue-attending way. His God made the universe orderly but did not inquire into the activities of individuals. He was an ardent Zionist. He toured the United States with Chaim Weizmann in 1921 to help raise money for the Palestine Foundation Fund. Israel owes much to him. [Interesting accounts of Einstein's life include the books by Schilpp (1963), and Frank (1947).]

Surely the trio Thompson, Gibbs, and Einstein illustrate the point that genius in science imposes no bounds on diversity in all other respects.

16-CN-2 Steps beyond Hydrogen-Like Wave Functions

Very extensive advances have been made in the direction of obtaining more accurate solutions to the wave equation for multielectron atoms. The detailed methodology of advanced treatments must be left to subsequent elective or graduate courses. We can, however, outline the directions taken and summarize qualitatively the degree of progress made.

The difficulty of dealing with multielectron atoms becomes apparent even with the helium atom. The wave equation is now

$$-\frac{h^2}{8\pi^2 m}(\nabla_1{}^2 + \nabla_2{}^2)\psi - \left(\frac{Ze^2}{r_1} + \frac{Ze^2}{r_2} - \frac{e^2}{r_{12}}\right)\psi = E\psi, \qquad (16\text{-}95)$$

where the subscripts refer to electrons 1 and 2; that is, the Hamiltonian is [see Eq. (16-30)]

$$\mathbf{H} = -\frac{h^2}{8\pi^2 m}(\nabla_1{}^2 + \nabla_2{}^2) - \frac{Ze^2}{r_1} - \frac{Ze^2}{r_2} + \frac{e^2}{r_{12}}. \qquad (16\text{-}96)$$

One now has a second-order partial differential equation in six variables—three coordinates for each electron. The real difficulty is in the e^2/r_{12} term, which gives the interelectronic repulsion. Were it not for this, the wave equation could be separated into two, one for each electron. Put another way, the helium atom is the wave mechanical three-body problem. It has not been solved explicitly, but successive approximation methods aided by high-speed computers have led to solutions which appear to be exact theoretically and which agree well with experiment (with respect to, say, the spectrum of helium).

One approach is to start with the hydrogen-like wave functions and introduce the e^2/r_{12} term as a correction; one does this by expanding the term by means of associated Legendre polynomials and evaluating the resulting integral term by term. The first approximation for the ground-state energy is $E_{He} = (2Z^2 - \frac{5}{4}Z) E_H$. The ionization energy of the first electron of He is then $\frac{3}{2}E_H = 20.40$ eV, as compared to the experimental value of 24.49 eV. Further approximations can be made, but with a cascading increase of effort.

Another approach is to consider that the electron of He which is to ionize is in a nuclear field corresponding to charge Z_{eff}, where Z_{eff} lies between 1 and 2, and to write the corresponding hydrogen-like wave function for this electron. The value of Z_{eff} which makes the energy of this electron a minimum gives $E = 23.05$ eV, or much closer to the experimental value than the other method does in its first approximation. The hydrogen-like wave function with Z_{eff} can next be modified by trial and error until a yet lower or more stable energy for the electrons is found. In this manner a calculated ionization energy agreeing with experiment to within 0.002 eV has been obtained.

Neither of these methods is sufficiently efficient to be very useful for atoms beyond helium, and two further developments are as follows. J. Slater pursued the approach of using a Z_{eff} plus an n_{eff} to make hydrogen-like wave functions give a better approximation to observed ionization energies and other behavior. The results of a great deal of effort in this direction have led to rules such as the following:

1. Values of n_{eff} are given by

n	1	2	3	4	5	6
n_{eff}	1	2	3	3.7	4.0	4.2

2. To determine the screening constant s (see Section 16-3), electrons are divided into the groups (1s), (2s, 2p), (3s, 3p), (3d), (4s, 4p), (4d, 4f) and so on. Then (a) electrons outside the group containing the one in question contribute nothing to s; (b) each electron in the group being considered contributes 0.35 to s, except that if a 1s electron is involved, the other one contributes 0.30 to s; and (c) if the shell considered is an s or p shell, an amount 0.85 is contributed from each electron with principal quantum number less by 1, and an amount 1.00 from each electron still further in; but if the shell is a d or an f shell, an amount 1.00 is contributed from each electron of that shell.

For example, carbon has the configuration $1s^2 2s^2 2p^2$. The 1s electrons are described by the hydrogen-like wave function with $Z_{eff} = 5.70$. The 2s and 2p electrons are approximated by the hydrogen-like wave function for $n = 2$, but with $Z_{eff} = 6 - 2(0.85) - 3(0.35) = 3.25$. Insertion of $n = 2$ and $Z = 3.25$ into Eq. (16-19) gives 0.41 a.u. for the first ionization energy, as compared to the observed value of 0.42 (from Table 16-1).

The alternative of the more advanced approaches has been to say that as a first approximation, one can estimate the interaction of a particular electron with all other electrons by taking the latter to obey hydrogen-like wave functions (perhaps with Slater corrections). The wave function for the particular electron is then solved and this is done for each electron in turn. The process is repeated with the new set of wave functions. That is, one estimates the interaction of a particular electron by using the new wave functions for all the others. Eventually, a convergence is reached in which no further change in the functions occurs. The potential energy function for the electrons is now said to be *self-consistent*. This method, due to D. Hartree (and further improved by V. Fock) is the basis for many modern calculations of the energies of low-atomic-number atoms.

The struggle in all of these approximation procedures is to find wave functions that reproduce the experimental ionization and total energies for atoms. If wave functions that do this can be found, then one has some confidence in their application to other calculations.

16-CN-3 Chemical Bonding from the Atomic Orbital Point of View. The Variation Method

The problem of solving the wave equation for a molecule is similar to but fiercer than that for an atom. The Hamiltonian for the hydrogen molecule *ion* is, for example,

$$-\frac{h^2}{8\pi^2 m} \nabla^2 - \frac{e^2}{r_A} - \frac{e^2}{r_B} + \frac{e^2}{r_{AB}}, \tag{16-97}$$

where the last term is the Coulomb repulsion between nuclei A and B. For the hydrogen *molecule*, we have

$$\mathbf{H} = -\frac{h^2}{8\pi^2 m}(\nabla_1^2 + \nabla_2^2) - \frac{e^2}{r_{1,A}} - \frac{e^2}{r_{2,A}} - \frac{e^2}{r_{1,B}} - \frac{e^2}{r_{2,B}} + \frac{e^2}{r_{12}} + \frac{e^2}{r_{AB}}, \tag{16-98}$$

where subscripts 1 and 2 refer to the electrons and subscripts A and B to the atoms. An approximation known as the Born–Oppenheimer separation has been made in writing Eqs. (16-97) and (16-98). The motion of nuclei is slow compared to that of electrons and the approximation is that of solving the wave equation for the electrons only, assuming particular, fixed nuclear positions.

Equations such as (16-97) and (16-98) are obviously not very easily solved; the cross terms prevent separation of the variables. One approach to the hydrogen molecule case (applicable to any diatomic molecule in principle) is to start with the wave function for the two separated atoms

$$\psi = \psi_A(1)\,\psi_B(2),$$

but to recognize that as the atoms approach each other, the identity of electrons 1 and 2 is lost, so that the function $\psi = \psi_A(2)\,\psi_B(1)$ is just as likely. The approximate complete wave function is then guessed to be, in the case of H_2,

$$\psi = \psi_{1S,A}(1)\,\psi_{1S,B}(2) + \psi_{1S,A}(2)\,\psi_{1S,B}(1). \tag{16-99}$$

This is known as the *valence bond method* (of W. Heitler and F. London).

If we now go back to Eq. (16-30), $H\psi = E\psi$, multiplication of both sides by ψ (or ψ^* if ψ is complex) gives, on rearrangement (and recognition that E is a constant),

$$E = \frac{\int \psi^* H\psi\,d\tau}{\int \psi^* \psi\,d\tau}, \tag{16-100}$$

which is a formal way of expressing the energy solution to a wave equation. The integrals are over $d\tau$, or over all space, and so if the ψ's are normalized the denominator is unity. An important theorem in wave mechanics is that if some incorrect wave function ϕ is used in Eq. (16-100), the resulting E',

$$E' = \frac{\int \phi^* H\phi\,d\tau}{\int \phi^* \phi\,d\tau}, \tag{16-101}$$

may be greater than the correct E but never less than it. A trial function such as Eq. (16-99), if inserted into Eq. (16-101) with H as given by Eq. (16-98), will then give an approximate E'. Some variation in the trial wave function which gives a lower E is then better; one seeks that trial function which gives the lowest possible value for the energy. The method is known as the *variation method* (see also Section 17-CN-1).

By putting ψ from Eq. (16-99) into Eq. (16-100) and minimizing the energy with respect to varying the internuclear distance r_{AB}, one obtains approximate values for both r_{AB} and E. This is essentially the procedure used in applying wave mechanics to molecules.

As a wave function, Eq. (16-99) places a great deal of electron density between the two hydrogen atoms, and since two electrons with spins opposed can be assigned to this valence bond orbital, the qualitative picture is just that of an electron pair bond. Wave mechanics aside, much of the stability of the H_2 molecule arises from there being a pair of negatively charged electrons between two positively charged nuclei. The interchange of electrons in the second term of Eq. (16-99) leads to additional stability—the effect is known as the *exchange energy*. Finally, there is an alternative linear combination to Eq. (16-99),

$$\psi' = \psi_{1s,A}(1)\,\psi_{1s,B}(2) - \psi_{1s,A}(2)\,\psi_{1s,B}(1).\qquad (16\text{-}102)$$

The function ψ' is antisymmetric in that it changes sign if the electron identities are interchanged; a consequence derivable from the Pauli exclusion principle is that the electron spins are now parallel. The wave function ψ' corresponds to an excited, paramagnetic state of H_2 (see Section 17-CN-1C).

The approach of writing linear combinations of atomic orbital products is widely used in describing a chemical bond. It may be used with hybrid orbitals, such as those described in Section 16-10, to provide a wave mechanical description of, say, CH_4, BF_3, and so on. The availability of high-speed computers has made fairly accurate calculations possible for a number of small molecules with this approach. In addition, very useful qualitative conclusions can be reached from consideration of the symmetry properties of hybrid orbitals. Chapter 17 proceeds in this direction.

SPECIAL TOPICS

16-ST-1 Quantum Theory of Blackbody Radiation

The period around 1890–1900 was one of fairly intensive study of the radiation emitted by hot objects. An important, essentially thermodynamic argument is that if an object is placed in a box or other isolated system and comes to equilibrium with the ambient temperature, then it must be emitting and absorbing radiant energy at the same rate. This equivalence must apply at each wavelength, on the basis that it would otherwise be possible for the object to have a different equilibrium temperature than its surroundings. It is commonplace that different surfaces have greater or lesser ability to reflect light—some are bright, some are dull, and others are colored. They must then also have correspondingly different abilities to absorb light. Further, the most perfectly absorbing material should also be the most perfectly emitting one.

The concept of the *blackbody* emerges from such considerations. A box lined in deep black material with only a small hole for light to enter should absorb virtually all light incident on the hole. That which is not absorbed immediately should be absorbed after a few reflections around the inside of the box. Such a box should then also be an essentially perfect emitter of radiation, hence the term blackbody radiation. The achievement by 1900 was to measure accurately the spectral distribution of blackbody radiation as a function of temperature, with results as illustrated by Fig. 16-18. Several laws developed as regularities were discovered. Wien (1894) found that the short-wavelength portion of the spectral distribution could be represented by a function of the form

$$E_\nu \, d\nu = a\nu^3 e^{-b\nu/T} \, d\nu, \tag{16-103}$$

where E_ν is the emissive power (radiant energy of frequency ν per unit frequency interval emitted per unit time by unit area of a blackbody) and a and b are constants. The law implies that the frequency ν_{max} at the maximum of the distribution is proportional to T, or

$$\lambda_{max} = \frac{A}{T}. \tag{16-104}$$

The constant A has the observed value of 0.290 cm °K.

Further, the total emissive power is $E_{tot} = \int_0^\infty E_\nu \, d\nu$, or, alternatively, $E_{tot} = \int_\infty^0 (-c/\lambda^2) E_\lambda \, d\lambda$, since $\lambda\nu = c$. That is, the emissive power per unit wavelength interval is proportional to $1/\lambda^2$ times that per unit frequency interval. If this conclusion plus Eq. (16-104) is substituted into Eq. (16-103), the result is

$$E_{\lambda_{max}} = BT^5, \tag{16-105}$$

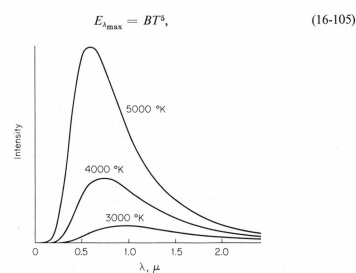

Fig. 16-18. *Energy distribution for a blackbody radiator according to Planck's equation.*

or the maximum in E_λ should be proportional to the fifth power of the temperature. Earlier, Boltzmann had shown by a thermodynamic argument that the total emitted energy obeyed the equation

$$E_{tot} = \sigma T^4, \tag{16-106}$$

where σ is now generally known as the Stefan–Boltzmann constant; its value is 5.670×10^{-5} erg cm^{-2} sec^{-1} °K^{-4}.

Finally, Lord Rayleigh and J. Jeans were able to obtain an alternative expression to Eq. (16-103) by supposing that the equilibrium radiation in a black box must consist of standing waves. Suppose the box to be of side a, so that $n\lambda = 2a$ for standing waves, or $nc/v = 2a$. If v_0 is some observed frequency of wavelength small compared to a, then the number of possible other frequencies is of order $N = 2a/\lambda_0$. Extension of the analysis of the three-dimensional box gives

$$N = \frac{4V}{3\lambda_0^3} = \frac{4\pi V}{3} \frac{v_0^3}{c^3},$$

where $V = a^3$ and is the volume of the box. The distribution function for N is then

$$N_v \, dv = \frac{4\pi V}{c^3} v_0^2 \, dv, \tag{16-107}$$

or, assuming equipartition so that each frequency has associated energy kT,

$$\rho_v \, dv = \frac{8\pi v^2 kT}{c^3} \, dv, \tag{16-108}$$

where ρ_v is the energy density of the radiant energy (ergs per cubic centimeter); also a factor of two has entered to allow for the magnetic as well as electric oscillations present in electromagnetic radiation. The total emissive power E_{tot} can be shown to be

$$E_{tot} = \tfrac{1}{4}c\rho, \tag{16-109}$$

where E_{tot} is given in ergs per square centimeter per second. Equation (16-108) then becomes

$$E_v \, dv = \frac{2\pi v_0^2 kT \, dv}{c^2} . \tag{16-110}$$

This equation works well for the long wavelength side of the distribution function but leads to infinite emission as $\lambda \to 0$ (called the ultraviolet catastrophe). By about 1900 it was becoming necessary to question the equipartition principle itself. M. Planck suggested that the difficulty with the Rayleigh–Jeans law could be eliminated if it were supposed that an oscillating system (such as atoms in a solid) could only acquire energy in steps, rather than by infinitesimal degrees. In this way the equipartition principle would gradually come into being as kT became large compared to such steps or quanta. If ν_0 were the fundamental frequency of the oscillators responsible for the radiation, then they could only emit radiation proportional to ν_0 or to some integral multiple of it. This proportionality factor is, of course, now called Planck's constant h.

Planck was then able to derive the distribution law for blackbody radiation. He assumed that the Boltzmann principle applied so that the number of oscillators of energy ϵ_i was given by $N_i = N^0 e^{-\epsilon_i/kT}$. The total number becomes

$$N = N^0 + N^0 e^{-h\nu_0/kT} + N^0 e^{-2h\nu_0/kT} + \cdots = N^0 \sum_{i=0}^{\infty} e^{-ih\nu_0/kT},$$

where N^0 is the number of oscillators in the lowest energy state ($\epsilon = 0$). The total energy for oscillators in their various quantum states is therefore

$$E_{\text{tot}} = N^0(0) + N^0(h\nu_0)\, e^{-h\nu_0/kT} + N^0(2h\nu_0)\, e^{-2h\nu_0/kT} + \cdots$$

$$= N^0(h\nu_0) \sum_{i=0}^{\infty} i e^{ix},$$

where $x = h\nu_0/kT$, and the average energy is

$$\bar{\epsilon} = h\nu_0 \frac{\sum_{i=0}^{\infty} i e^{ix}}{\sum_{i=0}^{\infty} e^{ix}}.$$

The sums are standard ones which, on evaluation, give

$$\bar{\epsilon} = \frac{h\nu_0}{e^x - 1} = \frac{h\nu_0}{e^{h\nu_0/kT} - 1}. \tag{16-111}$$

Note that if $kT \gg h\nu_0$, Eq. (16-111) gives $\bar{\epsilon} = kT$, or the classical equipartition law.

On substituting the expression for $\bar{\epsilon}$ into Eq. (16-110) in place of kT, Planck obtained the distribution law

$$E_\nu\, d\nu = \frac{2\pi h\nu^3}{c^2} \frac{1}{e^{h\nu/kT} - 1}\, d\nu \tag{16-112}$$

or

$$E_\lambda\, d\lambda = \frac{2\pi hc^2}{\lambda^5} \frac{1}{e^{ch/\lambda kT} - 1}\, d\lambda \tag{16-113}$$

(the subscript zero usually being dropped).

Equations (16-112) and (16-113) reduce to the Rayleigh–Jeans equation (16-110) at large wavelengths and to Wien's law, Eq. (16-103), at short wavelengths. The amazing success of Planck's treatment went far to guarantee acceptance of the then revolutionary idea of energy quanta.

We conclude with a numerical exercise. We wish to calculate $E_{\lambda_{max}}$ for a black body at 1646°K and λ_{max}. Differentiating Eq. (16-113) with respect to λ and setting $dE_\lambda/d\lambda = 0$ leads to the equation $5 - x = 5e^{-x}$, where $x = ch/\lambda_{max}kT$. The solution is $x = 4.97$, whence

$$\lambda_{max} = \frac{(3.00 \times 10^{10})(6.63 \times 10^{-27})}{(4.97)(1.38 \times 10^{-16})(1646)} = 1.78 \times 10^{-4} \quad cm = 1.78 \quad \mu.$$

[The same answer is obtained using Eq. (16-104) with $A = 0.290$.]
   Substitution of this result into Eq. (16-113) gives

$$E_{\lambda_{max}} = \frac{2\pi(6.63 \times 10^{-27})(3.00 \times 10^{10})^2}{(1.78 \times 10^{-4})^5} \frac{1}{144 - 1} = 1.46 \times 10^{12} \quad erg \ cm^{-2} \ sec^{-1}.$$

16-ST-2 The Rigid Rotator

The case of a diatomic molecule which can rotate, but whose bond length is fixed, is treated as follows. The wave equation is Eq. (16-71) but with $V = 0$ since the rotation is free. If r is distance from the center of mass, then it is a constant, so the terms involving differentiation with respect to r drop out; also, in this coordinate system, mr^2 becomes I, the moment of inertia of the molecule. Equation (16-71) then reduces to

$$\frac{1}{\sin\theta}\frac{\partial}{\partial\theta}\left(\sin\theta\frac{\partial\psi}{\partial\theta}\right) + \frac{1}{\sin^2\theta}\frac{\partial^2\psi}{\partial\phi^2} + \frac{8\pi^2 IE}{h^2}\psi = 0.$$

This separates into $\psi = \Theta(\theta)\,\Phi(\phi)$ as before, and the solution to $\Phi(\phi)$ is given by Eq. (16-77). The solutions to $\Theta(\theta)$ are analogous to those for Eq. (16-76), and on inserting them back into the $\Theta(\theta)$ equation, one obtains for the energy

$$E = \frac{h^2}{8\pi^2 I} J(J + 1), \tag{16-114}$$

where J plays the same role in the solutions to $\Theta(\theta)$ as does ℓ in the case of the hydrogen-like atom.

The actual wave functions ψ for the rigid rotator are thus very similar to the angular wave functions for the hydrogen atom. Their form is not ordinarily of much interest; so far as this text is concerned, Eq. (16-114) is the important one.

16-ST-3   Domain Representation of Hydrogen-Like Orbitals

It seems worthwhile to make a brief mention of an alternative way of showing the spatial disposition of electron density due to the various hydrogen-like orbitals. Figure 16-19 illustrates three conventional methods of depicting p_x and p_y orbitals

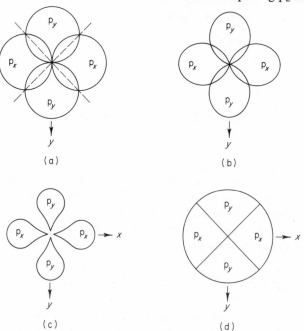

Fig. 16-19.   *Ways of showing p_x and p_y orbitals. (a) Polar plot of A_{p_x} and of A_{p_y}. (b) Polar plot of $A_{p_x}^2$ and of $A_{p_y}^2$. (c) Isodensity contours for $\psi_{p_x}^2$ and $\psi_{p_y}^2$. (d) Domain plot.*

in the xy plane. The first two are polar plots of the angular portion of the wave function; the third is an attempt to show density in real space, with r being actual distance from the nucleus [but with $R(r)$ assumed to be constant].

An alternative approach is to assign to p_x that area in the xy plane in which

$\psi_{p_x}^2$ is greater than $\psi_{p_y}^2$, and analogously for p_y. The result is shown in Fig. 16-19(b). This demarks regions in space for which the indicated orbital has the major electron density. The boundary lines are at the angles defined by $\psi_{p_x}^2 = \psi_{p_y}^2$ and are the same as the dotted lines in Fig. 16-19(a). Such regions have been called *domains* [see Adamson (1965)].

The extension to three dimensions of the set of p_x, p_y, and p_z domains yields three pairs of sectors of a sphere—each pair being the domain of one of the orbitals. The domains have also been worked out for the set of d orbitals and that of f orbitals. Advantages of the domain models are that they deal with actual electron densities as functions of distance out from the nucleus, they show the regions in space where given orbitals are dominant, and they make quite clear the fact that the sum of electron densities of a set of orbitals has spherical symmetry (Ünsold's theorem).

16-ST-4 First-Order Perturbation Theory

A very important method is that which treats a small perturbation to a system. The wave equation for the actual system is

$$\mathbf{H}\psi - E\psi = 0, \tag{16-115}$$

and we suppose that the Hamiltonian $\mathbf{H}$ is only slightly different from some other one, $\mathbf{H}°$, for which the equation

$$\mathbf{H}°\psi° - E°\psi° = 0 \tag{16-116}$$

has known solutions, the set of solutions and corresponding energy states being

$$\psi_0°, \psi_1°, \psi_2°, ..., \psi_k°; \qquad E_0°, E_1°, E_2°, ..., E_k°.$$

Since the perturbation is small, we write

$$\mathbf{H} = \mathbf{H}° + \alpha\mathbf{H}',$$

where α is the measure of the perturbation.

For example, in the case of the harmonic oscillator $\mathbf{H}°$ would be

$$-\frac{h^2}{8\pi^2 m}\frac{d^2}{dx^2} + \tfrac{1}{2}kx^2.$$

If the oscillator is not quite harmonic, so that $V(x)$ is $\frac{1}{2}kx^2 + bx^4$, then $\mathbf{H}'$ is simply $-bx^4$. In the case of Eq. (16-95), the (rather large) perturbation to $V(r)$ is e^2/r_{12}. A very common situation, then, is that in which $\mathbf{H}'$ equals some additional or perturbing terms in the potential energy function.

The next step is to assume that since the perturbation is to be small, the solutions to Eq. (16-115) involve only a small correction to those for the unperturbed case, Eq. (16-116), so that for the kth state

$$\psi_k = \psi_k{}^\circ + \alpha\psi_k{}', \qquad E_k = E_k{}^\circ + \alpha E_k{}'.$$

If these expressions for $\mathbf{H}$, ψ_k, and E_k are substituted into Eq. (16-115), one obtains

$$\mathbf{H}^\circ\psi_k{}' - E_k{}^\circ\psi_k{}' = (E_k{}' - \mathbf{H}')\,\psi_k{}^\circ \qquad (16\text{-}117)$$

[Eq. (16-116) has been used to cancel some terms, and also those in α^2 have been dropped]. It is further true that the correction wave function $\psi_k{}'$ can itself be expressed as some linear combination of the solutions $\psi_0{}^\circ$, $\psi_1{}^\circ$, and so on,

$$\psi_k{}' = \sum_i a_i\psi_i{}^\circ \qquad (16\text{-}118)$$

or

$$\mathbf{H}^\circ\psi_k{}' = \sum_i a_i\mathbf{H}^\circ\psi_i{}^\circ = \sum_i a_iE_i{}^\circ\psi_i{}^\circ.$$

Substitution of this last equation into Eq. (16-117) gives

$$\sum_i a_i(E_i{}^\circ - E_k{}^\circ)\,\psi_i{}^\circ = (E_k{}' - \mathbf{H}')\,\psi_k{}^\circ. \qquad (16\text{-}119)$$

Finally, Eq. (16-119) is multiplied by $\psi_k^{\circ*}$ and integrated:

$$\sum_i a_i(E_i{}^\circ - E_k{}^\circ)\int \psi_k^{\circ*}\psi_i{}^\circ\,d\tau = \int \psi_k^{\circ*}(E_k{}' - \mathbf{H}')\,\psi_k{}^\circ\,d\tau, \qquad (16\text{-}120)$$

where $d\tau$ represents the element of volume (and would be just dx in the case of the harmonic oscillator). The left-hand term of Eq. (16-120) is zero; the ψ° functions are all orthogonal so that $\int \psi_k^{\circ*}\psi_i{}^\circ\,d\tau = 0$ if $k \neq i$, and $E_i{}^\circ = E_k{}^\circ$ if $k = i$. The right-hand side can be separated into two integrals and solved for $E_k{}'$ (remembering that $\int \psi_k^{\circ*}\psi_k{}^\circ\,d\tau = 1$), to give

$$E_k{}' = \int \psi_k^{\circ*}\mathbf{H}'\psi_k{}^\circ\,d\tau. \qquad (16\text{-}121)$$

Equation (16-121) gives E_k' and hence $\alpha E_k'$, the first-order perturbation theory correction to the energy $E°$. The constant α is usually incorporated into E_k' and $\mathbf{H}'$ or, in effect, treated as equal to unity. For the kth energy state E' is obtained by averaging the perturbation function $\mathbf{H}'$ over the unperturbed state of the system. Thus for the $n = 1$ state of a harmonic oscillator and with $\mathbf{H}' = bx^4$, the correction would be

$$E'_{n=1} = b \int_{-\infty}^{\infty} \psi_{n=1} x^4 \psi_{n=1} \, dx, \qquad (16\text{-}122)$$

where $\psi_{n=1}$ is given by Eq. (16-59). In the case of the helium atom, for which $\mathbf{H}' = e^2/r_{12}$, the correction to the ground-state energy is

$$E' = \int | \psi_{1s}^* |^2 (e^2/r_{12}) | \psi_{1s} |^2 \, d\tau_1 \, d\tau_2 \, .$$

Finally, one may determine the coefficients a_i in Eq. (16-118) which define ψ_k' one at a time by multiplying Eq. (16-119) by a particular ψ_i^* and integrating. On utilizing the orthogonality and normalization properties of the $\psi°$ functions, the result is that a particular coefficient a_i is given by

$$a_i = - \frac{\int \psi_i^* \mathbf{H}' \psi_k° \, d\tau}{E_i° - E_k°} \qquad (i \neq k). \qquad (16\text{-}123)$$

The procedure as outlined must be modified if the energy level of the unperturbed system is degenerate. We assume in this derivation that the perturbed wave function differs only slightly from some function $\psi_k°$, that is, from a solution of the unperturbed wave equation for a certain energy. If there are two or more wave functions belonging to the same energy level, we do not know which one, if any, approximates the solution of the perturbed wave equation.

GENERAL REFERENCES

ANDERSON, J. M. (1969). "Introduction to Quantum Chemistry." Benjamin, New York.
COULSON, C. A. (1961). "Valence." Oxford Univ. Press, London and New York.
DAUDEL, R., LEFEBVRE, R., AND MOSER, C. (1959). "Quantum Chemistry, Methods and Applications." Wiley (Interscience), New York.
EYRING, H., WALTER, J., AND KIMBALL, G. E. (1944). "Quantum Chemistry." Wiley, New York.
HANNA, M. W. (1969). "Quantum Mechanics in Chemistry," 2nd ed. Benjamin, New York.
OFFENHARTZ, P. O'D. (1970). "Atomic and Molecular Orbital Theory." McGraw-Hill, New York.
PITZER, K. S. (1953). "Quantum Chemistry." Prentice-Hall, Englewood Cliffs, New Jersey.
TAYLOR, H. S., AND GLASSTONE, S., Eds. (1942). "A Treatise on Physical Chemistry." Van Nostrand–Reinhold, Princeton, New Jersey.

CITED REFERENCES

ADAMSON, A. W. (1965). *J. Chem. Ed.* **42**, 140.
BOHR, N. (1913). *Phil. Mag.* **26**, 140.
BRIDGMAN, P. W. (1961). "The Logic of Modern Physics." Macmillan, New York.
EINSTEIN, A. (1905). *Ann. Phys.* (4) **17**, 132.
EYRING, H., WALTER, J., AND KIMBALL, G. E. (1944). "Quantum Chemistry." Wiley, New York.
FRANK, P. (1947). "Einstein—His Life and Times." Knopf, New York.
HEISENBERG, W. (1927). *Z. Phys.* **43**, 172.
MICHELMORE, P. (1963). "Einstein—Profile of the Man." Muller, London.
SCHILPP, P. A. (1949). "Albert Einstein: Philospher–Scientist." Library of Living Philosophers, Evanston, Illinois.
SCHRÖDINGER, E. (1926). *Ann. Phys.* **79**, 361.
WIEN, W. (1894). *Wied. Ann.* **52**, 132.

Exercises

16-1 Calculate (a) the radius of the Bohr orbit with $n = 2$, (b) the potential energy in atomic units of the electron in this orbit, (c) the energy difference in electron volts between the $n = 2$ and $n = 3$ Bohr orbits, and (d) the frequency in wavenumbers of the light emitted when a hydrogen atom in the $n = 3$ state returns to the ground state.

Ans.   (a) $4a_0$ or 2.12 Å, (b) -0.25 a.u., (c) 1.89 eV, (d) 97,500 cm^{-1}.

16-2 Estimate the uncertainty in the energy (in electron-volts) of (a) an electron confined to a 2-Å-radius sphere and (b) a hydrogen atom so confined. Estimate (c) the uncertainty in the energy (in wavenumbers) of an excited state of 1×10^{-8} sec lifetime and (d) the lifetime of a rotational state whose energy is uncertain by 3×10^{-18} cm^{-1}.

Ans.   (a) 37.5, (b) 0.0207, (c) 2.6×10^{-4}, (d) 9×10^5 sec (not realizable in the laboratory, as collisions and other effects intervene).

16-3 Derive Eq. (16-19).

16-4 Calculate the wavelength of (a) a 1-keV electron and (b) a 1-keV proton.

Ans.   (a) 0.39 Å, (b) 9.1×10^{-11} cm.

16-5 Calculate Z_{eff} for the outer electron of (a) K and (b) Be$^+$. Calculate the ionization energy for the outer electron of (c) Cs and (d) La^{2+} if the respective screening constants are 51.8 and 49.9.

Ans.   (a) 2.26, (b) 2.31, (c) 0.14 a.u., (d) 0.700 a.u.

16-6 Verify that Eq. (16-20) is a solution to Eq. (16-23).

16-7 Verify that Eq. (16-39) is a solution to Eq. (16-38).

Problems

16-8 Benzene may be regarded as a two-dimensional box of side about 3.5 Å and containing six π electrons. What wavelength of light should be required to promote an electron from the ground to the first excited state?

Ans. 135 nm.

16-9 Plot ψ_n for $n = 1$ as a function of x.

16-10 Calculate the force constant for HBr (use Table 6-1) and, assuming it not to change, the fundamental frequency for DBr.

Ans. 3.81×10^5 dyn cm^{-1}, 1820 cm^{-1}.

16-11 The vibrational energy levels of HCl can be accurately reproduced by the equation $E\,(\text{cm}^{-1}) = 2988.95(\nu + \frac{1}{2}) - 51.65(\nu + \frac{1}{2})^2$. Calculate the dissociation energy of HCl in kcal mole^{-1}. What is the value of ν for the last vibrational state before dissociation occurs?

Ans. 123.6 kcal mole^{-1} (the actual value is 103 kcal mole^{-1}), $\nu = 28$ or 29.

16-12 Verify that Eq. (16-77) is a solution to Eq. (16-73).

16-13 Verify that $\Theta_{1,0}$ is a solution to Eq. (16-76).

16-14 Verify that $R_{2,0}$ is a solution to Eq. (16-75) (take $\mu = m$ and $Z = 1$).

16-15 Demonstrate Ünsold's theorem for the set of five d orbitals.

16-16 Calculate the velocity of an electron in the first Bohr orbit as a fraction of the velocity of light.

16-17 Calculate the normalization constant A for the wave function describing a particle in a two-dimensional square box.

16-18 The ground-state energy for an electron in a 3-Å one-dimensional box is about 100 kcal mole^{-1}. For what size three-dimensional box would the ground-state energy be equal to the average kinetic energy of the electron from thermal motion at 25°C?

Problems

16-1 Naphthalene may be considered to be roughly a rectangle of side 4 Å and length 7 Å. Derive the appropriate particle-in-a-box equation and calculate the expected frequency (in wavenumbers) for absorption to give the first excited state of naphthalene.

16-2 Calculate Z_{eff} and the screening constant for Cs.

16-3 The gravitational force between two masses m_1 and m_2 is given by $f = k m_1 m_2 / r^2$, where r is the separation and in the cgs system k has the value of 6.67×10^{-8}. Assume that the hydrogen atom is held together by gravity, that is, assume the proton and the electron to be neutral and apply the Bohr treatment to calculate the radius of the first "gravitational" orbit and the energy of an orbit in terms of its quantum number. Determine also if an integral number of de Broglie wavelengths of the electron would make up the circumference of the first gravitation orbit.

16-4 Show that $\psi = Ae^{iy} + Be^{-iy}$, $y = (2\pi/h)(2mE)^{1/2}(x)$, is also a solution to Eq. (16-38). Expand this into a cos y and a sin y term and explain why the cos y portion is not used in the treatment of the particle in a box. (Consider the graphical nature of the solution involving the cos y term.)

16-5 Show that the solutions for the harmonic oscillator are orthogonal for the case of $v_1 = 1$ and $v_2 = 2$; that is, show that $\int_{-\infty}^{\infty} \psi_{v=1}\psi_{v=2}\, dx = 0$. Similarly, show that $\psi_{v=1}$ is normalized, that is, $\int_{-\infty}^{\infty} \psi^2_{v=1}\, dx = 1$.

16-6 (Calculator problem) Plot Eq. (16-65) for the case of $H^{35}Cl$ given the information in Exercise 16-11, including each vibrational level up to the dissociation limit.

16-7 Show that the Φ_m functions of Eq. (16-77) are normalized and orthogonal.

16-8 Show that the $\ell = 1\ \Theta$ functions are normalized and orthogonal.

16-9 Derive the functional form of the f_{z^3} orbital and make a polar plot of this function in the xz plane.

16-10 Calculate the values of the three A functions of the sp^2 set and plot them on polar coordinate paper. Show that the lobes are indeed 120° apart.

16-11 Calculate values for the A_1 function of the sp^3 set to show its cross section in the plane containing the bond direction, which is $\theta = 54°44'$, $\phi = 45°$.

16-12 The bonding strength of an orbital is essentially the value of $\Theta\Phi$ in the direction of its maximum extension in the polar plot. Thus for an s orbital the strength is $(\sqrt{2}/2)(1/\sqrt{2\pi})$; usually, however, the values for other orbitals are written as relative to that for the s orbital. On this basis, the bonding strength of a p orbital is $\sqrt{3}$ or 1.73. Calculate the bonding strength of a sp^2 hybrid orbital.

16-13 Make a plot of the electron density for a 2s electron of Li as a function of radial distance r measured in units of a_0. What is wanted is that quantity which gives the chance of finding the electron in a spherical shell of radius between r and $r + dr$.

16-14 Calculate the per cent change in wavenumber for the transition from the ground to the first vibrational state for the stretching of the $C=O$ bond for free CO as compared to CO chemisorbed on a metal surface such as Ni. Assume that (a) no change in force constant occurs and (b) the $C=O$ force constant is reduced by 20% as a result of the adsorption bonding. Do each calculation assuming, first, that the adsorption bond is metal–carbon and second, that it is metal–oxygen. The effective mass of that atom which is bonded to Ni is to be regarded as infinite.

16-15 In what plane does the 4f orbital, $n = 4$, $\ell = 3$, $m = 3$, lie, that is, have its maximum extension? Make a polar plot of the angular dependence of this orbital in this plane.

Special Topics Problems

16-16 Show that the set of 2p hydrogen-like orbitals are mutually orthogonal.

16-17 The difference in energy ΔE between the ground and first excited state of amidinium polymethylene dyes,

$$(CH_3)_2\overset{+}{N}{=}CH(-CH{=}CH-)_n\overset{..}{N}(CH_3)_2 ,$$

has been treated according to the one-dimensional particle-in-a-box model. Let a be the C—C bond length and d the end space or distance due to each nitrogen. Derive a general formula for ΔE in electron volts. Calculate ΔE expressed in angstroms for the case of $n = 3$; assume $a = 1.24$ Å and $d/a = 1.5$. The observed wavelength of the first absorption band is 3290 Å in this case.

16-18 Verify Eq. (16-16) for the case of $n = 2$, $\ell = 1$.

16-19 The Bohr quantization principle may be applied to systems other than that of the nuclear atom; in its more general form, the principle is that $\oint p \, dq = nh$, where p is momentum, q a distance, and the integral is over one cycle of whatever the repetitive action is. Show that application of this principle to the harmonic oscillator leads to the quantized energy state $\epsilon = nh\nu$. [*Note*: the classical equation for the harmonic oscillator is obtained from Newton's law, $f = ma$, where $f = -kx$, or $m(d^2x/dt^2) + kx = 0$. Integration gives an equation of the form of Eq. (16-20), with x replacing Ψ; taking $x = 0$ at $t = 0$, the solution reduces to $x = A \sin(2\pi\nu t)$, with $2\pi\nu = (k/m)^{1/2}$. Substitute into the momentum integral; remember that at $t = 0$ the energy is all kinetic and hence equal to $p^2/2m$.]

Special Topics Problems

16-1 Calculate from Planck's law the relative intensities of the radiation from a blackbody at 2500°K at wavelength 4500 ± 10 Å and 8500 ± 10 Å.

16-2 Calculate the emissive power E at λ_{max} for a blackbody at 4000°K.

16-3 If 2×10^4 cal min^{-1} is lost by radiation from the door of an electrically heated furnace at 950°K, how much additional electrical power must be supplied to offset the increased loss due to radiation if the furnace is heated to 1150°K?

16-4 Calculate the distribution curve for $T = 5000°$K (Fig. 16-18).

16-5 Construct, with explanation, the cross section in the xy plane of the domain diagram for d orbitals. (Only the d_{xy} and $d_{x^2-y^2}$ orbitals need be considered.)

16-6 Evaluate $E'_{n=1}$ of Eq. (16-122).

17 MOLECULAR SYMMETRY AND BONDING

17-1 Introduction

The chemical bond presents quite a problem to the writer of a physical chemistry text. The numerous rather empirical rules that exist and are useful do not have enough solid theoretical content to be transferred out of their organic or inorganic chemical context and treated as true theory. Yet the exact wave mechanical approach becomes hopelessly bogged in mathematical complexities if one departs from diatomic molecules of the lightest elements. What, then, should be done?

It turns out that if we know the geometry of a molecule, it is much easier to set up the wave mechanical treatment; also, a number of qualitative results can be demonstrated without calculation. The emphasis of this chapter is therefore on that discipline of mathematics which allows a concise and penetrating description of the essential elements of molecular geometry, that is, *group theory*. As a branch of mathematics, group theory requires serious and extensive study. There are numerous theorems and lemmas to be proved and many special cases to be examined in detail. We will take a very pragmatic approach here, however. Theorems will be stated rather than rigorously proved; their validity will lie in the success of their practical as opposed to their abstract demonstration. By allowing ourselves this latitude, it will be possible to present the group-theoretical approach to the symmetry properties of molecules in a rather efficient, and, this writer hopes, a stimulating way.

We proceed therefore to describe symmetry operations and to develop the concept of a set of such operations as defining a symmetry group. Some of the basic attributes of groups necessarily are introduced. The result will be a compact description of those aspects of molecular geometry that determine the qualitative application of wave mechanics to a set of chemical bonds. Although beyond the scope of this text, the group-theoretical approach also provides a means for simplifying quantitative wave mechanical calculations.

The Special Topics section contains, in addition, a presentation of the molecular orbital approach to molecular bonding. This is an approach which, in essence, attempts to formulate standing electron waves which are distributed over the entire molecule rather than being located on particular atoms. It, too, makes heavy use of molecular symmetry as a guide to how hydrogen-like wave functions may be combined to give a molecular wave function.

17-2 Symmetry and Symmetry Operations

A. Symmetry Elements and Stereographic Projection Diagrams

The objects that we shall be dealing with, namely simple molecules, will generally have a considerable degree of symmetry. The ammonia molecule, for example, can be viewed as a triangular pyramid whose base is formed by the hydrogen atoms and whose apex is a nitrogen atom, as illustrated in Fig. 17-1(a). There is an axis of symmetry, labeled C_3, in recognition of the fact that if the molecule were

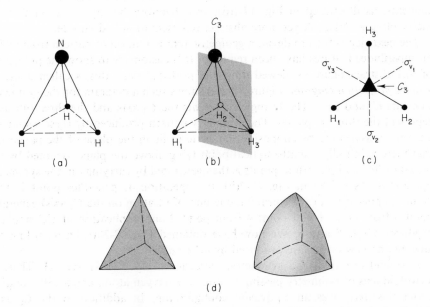

Fig. 17-1. *(a–c) Symmetry elements for the molecule* NH_3. *(d) Other objects having the same symmetry.*

rotated 120° about this axis, the result would be an equivalent configuration. That is, if the rotation were performed while the observer's eyes were closed, on looking again he could not tell that anything had occurred. The rotation is a symmetry operation—it gives an *equivalent configuration*. Were each hydrogen atom labeled, however, one could then tell that the rotation had been made. Only a rotation of 0°, 360°, and so on, would lead to a totally unobservable change; such an operation is called the *identity operation E*, since it results in a configuration *identical* to the starting one.

The ammonia molecule has other symmetry elements. A plane passing through the nitrogen and H_3 atoms and midway between H_1 and H_2 is a plane of symmetry. As illustrated in Fig. 17-1(b), if some molecular feature, such as H_1, occurs at a perpendicular distance x in front of the plane, then an equivalent feature is found by extending the perpendicular to a distance $-x$ to the other side of the plane, which in this case locates H_2. A plane of symmetry is designated by the symbol σ, and if it contains the principal axis of symmetry, C_3 in this case, it is called a *vertical plane* and written σ_v. There are evidently three equivalent such planes in the case of NH_3.

Three-dimensional perspective drawings are difficult to work with, and it has become conventional to use a projection down the principal axis of symmetry of the object. The ammonia molecule then looks as in Fig. 17-1(c), where the triangle imposed on the nitrogen atom stands for a C_3 rotation axis and the lines labeled σ_v locate the vertical planes of symmetry. Even Fig. 17-1(c) is too specific; quite a variety of objects would have C_3 and three σ_v's as the only symmetry elements, as illustrated in Fig. 17-1(d), and therefore belong to the same symmetry class as NH_3. A yet more abstract representation is desirable.

The next step is then to devise a geometric representation or pattern from which all superfluous features have been removed. It is customary to show the projection of this abstract figure as viewed down the principal axis—this is called a *stereographic projection diagram*. Figure 17-2(a) shows such a diagram for the symmetry elements C_3 and $3\sigma_v$. The triangle represents the C_3 axis and the three full lines represent the three σ_v planes. The symmetry pattern produced by these symmetry elements is generated by supposing the circle to lie in the plane of the paper and that there is initially a mathematical point lying above the plane, denoted by the plus sign. The full pattern of points is then generated by carrying out the symmetry operations. As shown in Fig. 17-2(b), the operation σ_v generates point 2 from point 1; application of C_3^1 (meaning one unit of rotation on the C_3 axis) generates point 3 from point 1 and point 4 from point 2 and application of C_3^2 similarly produces points 5 and 6. We now have obtained Fig. 17-2(a). Disregarding the labeling, no new points are produced by σ_v' or σ_v''.

A second example of a symmetric molecule is H_2O, or $H-O-H$. There is a twofold axis of symmetry passing through the oxygen atom, and a 180° rotation about this axis gives an equivalent configuration. In addition to the C_2 axis, there are two σ_v planes. Both contain the C_2 axis, and one is just the $H-O-H$ plane, while the other is perpendicular to it, as illustrated in Fig. 17-3(a). The

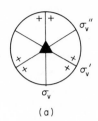

(a)

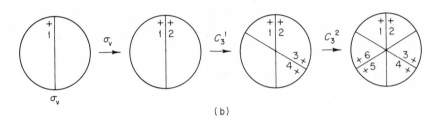

(b)

Fig. 17-2. *Stereographic projection showing the symmetry features of* NH_3.

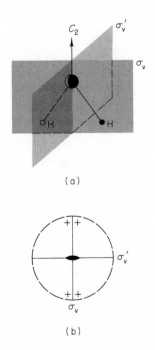

(a)

(b)

Fig. 17-3. *Stereographic projection showing the symmetry features of* H_2O.

stereographic projection diagram for an object having just these symmetry elements is shown in Fig. 17-3(b), the lens denoting a twofold rotation axis. The four plus points are generated from a single initial point by application of σ_v and then C_2 (or vice versa).

A square planar molecule, such as $PtCl_4^{2-}$, possesses a number of symmetry features. There is a fourfold rotation axis C_4 passing through the platinum atom and perpendicular to the molecular plane—successive rotations of 90° give equivalent configurations. As illustrated in Fig. 17-4(a), there are also two pairs of C_2

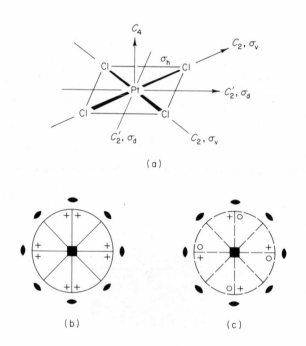

(a)

(b) (c)

Fig. 17-4. *(a) Symmetry elements of* $PtCl_4^{2-}$ *and (b) corresponding stereographic projection. (c) Stereographic projection if no* σ_h *and no* σ_v's *are present.*

axes, labeled C_2 and C_2'. The fourfold axis, being the highest-order one, is called the *principal axis*. The two pairs of σ_v planes contain the C_4 axis and either the C_2 or the C_2' ones; in addition, the molecular plane itself is a plane of symmetry. This last is a plane perpendicular to the principal axis, and is denoted σ_h.

The stereographic projection diagram generated by the symmetry features C_4, C_2, C_2', $2\sigma_v$, $-2\sigma_v'$ (or $2\sigma_d$), and σ_h is shown in Fig. 17-4(b). The set of plus points is generated by carrying out σ_v on the initial one, followed by the successive C_4 operations. The circles denote mathematical points lying *below* the plane of the paper and are produced by the σ_h operation. The set of points implies all of the symmetry features—none of the other operations generate any further points. Figure 17-4(b) also illustrates some additional conventions. The presence of σ_h is signified by drawing the projection as a full rather than a dashed circle. The secondary axes C_2 and C_2' are indicated by the lenses located radially around the circle; the fact that the lines to the lenses are full means that corresponding σ_v's are also present; were they not, the lines would be dashed. Thus Fig. 17-4(c) shows the presence of the symmetry elements C_4, C_2, and C_2' only (no σ_h and no σ_v's). A few remaining conventions will be illustrated later as they come up.

B. Symmetry Operations

A given symmetry element may generate more than one symmetry operation, and these will now be spelled out.

E: The identity operation has already been described; it is that which leaves the figure in an identical configuration to the initial one.

C_n :   A rotation axis is one about which the molecule may be rotated to give equivalent positions, *n* denoting the number of positions. Thus C_4 denotes a fourfold rotation axis; it generates the individual symmetry operations C_4^1, C_4^2, C_4^3, and C_4^4, the superscript denoting the number of rotational increments of $2\pi/n$ degrees each. Since C_4^2 is the same as C_2 and $C_4^4 = E$, this sequence would usually be written C_4^1, C_2, C_4^3, E.

If a molecule has more than one rotation axis, then the one of largest *n* is called the *principal* axis and the others the *secondary* axes.

σ: The symbol σ denotes a plane of symmetry, that is, a plane passing through the molecule such that matching features lie on opposite sides of, or are "reflected" by, the plane. A plane perpendicular to the principal axis is denoted σ_h (for horizontal) and one which contains the principal axis is called σ_v (for vertical). Finally, if a molecule has secondary rotation axes, a vertical-type plane of symmetry which bisects the angle between two such axes is called σ_d (for dihedral).

i: An inversion center is denoted by *i*. If present, matching features lie equidistant from a point or inversion center. Alternatively, if a feature has the coordinates (x, y, z), then an equivalent feature is present at $(-x, -y, -z)$. Thus $PtCl_4^{2-}$ has an inversion center but H_2O and NH_3 do not.

S_n :   This symbol stands for an *improper rotation axis*. An improper rotation may be thought of as taking place in two steps. First, a proper rotation and then, a reflection through a plane perpendicular to the rotation axis, usually a σ_h plane. The subscript *n* again denotes the order of the axis. By way of illustration, consider the triangular antiprism shown in Fig. 17-5(a). We are looking along the prism axis and see the staggered triangular ends. Rotation by 60° gives Fig. 17-5(b) and reflection in a plane perpendicular to the axis gives Fig. 17-5(c). The result is equivalent to the starting figure if the labeling is ignored, and hence is a symmetry operation. The figure therefore has the symmetry element S_6, the operation being S_6^1. The complete set of operations would be S_6^1, C_3^1, i, C_3^2, S_6^5, E (note that $S_6^2 = C_3^1$, that is, gives the identical change, and similarly, $S_6^4 = C_3^2$; also

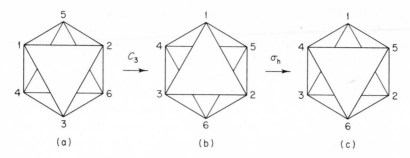

Fig. 17-5. *Illustration of the symmetry operation $S_6{}^1$.*

$S_6{}^3 = i$). As an exercise, the reader should examine the series $S_5{}^1, S_5{}^2, \ldots$ for similar alternative statements—it is now necessary to go to S_5^{10} before the series repeats.

C. Naming of Symmetry Groups

Any object or molecule has some certain set of symmetry features and this set accordingly characterizes its symmetry. Each distinctive such set is called a *point group*. As is seen in the next section, the set of symmetry operations has the property of a mathematical group and the term "point" refers to the fact that no translational motions are being considered. In the case of a crystal lattice, the addition of translations generates what are then called *space groups.*

Some easily recognizable, either very simple or highly symmetric, cases are summarized later, but the following is the general procedure for classifying a point group. The names or point group symbols used are those introduced by Schoenflies.

One first looks for rotation axes. If there is only one, then the naming is as follows:

C_n No other symmetry features are present.

C_{nh} There is also a σ_h plane.

C_{nv} There is no σ_h plane but there is a σ_v plane. (There must then be n such planes.)

If the molecule or object possesses more than one rotation axis, the one of higher order becomes the principal axis, of order n. We will only consider cases where the secondary axes are perpendicular to the principal one. The naming is now as follows:

D_n No other symmetry features are present.

D_{nh} A σ_h is present.

D_{nd} There is no σ_h but there is a σ_d (necessarily n σ_d's).

If there is an S_{2n} axis collinear with the principal C_n axis and no other symmetry features, the group is then S_{2n}. If there is only a plane of symmetry, the group is C_s, and if there is only an inversion center, it is C_i. If no symmetry elements at all are present, the group is named C_1.

D. Special Groups

There are some further groups whose symmetry properties can usually be recognized on sight. An A—B type of molecule has a σ_v and can be thought of as having a rotation axis of infinite order; this combination of symmetry elements is called $C_{\infty v}$; an A—A type of molecule has a σ_h and a twofold secondary axis, and the corresponding group name is $D_{\infty h}$.

Easily recognizable but more complicated to describe in terms of symmetry are tetrahedral and octahedral molecules, for which the corresponding point group names are T_d and O_h. The tetrahedral case is best constructed by using a cubic framework, as illustrated in Fig. 17-6. The symmetry elements and opera-

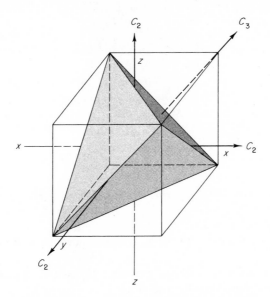

Fig. 17-6. *Some symmetry elements of a tetrahedron.*

tions are as follows.

1. The identity operation E.
2. Three C_2 axes coinciding with the x, y, and z axes of the figure. The operations characteristic of equivalent symmetry elements are often just totaled, and could be reported as $3C_2$ in this case.
3. Three S_4 axes collinear with the preceding C_2 ones. These generate the

operations $3S_4^1$ and $3S_4^3$. There is a total of $6S_4$ operations, excluding the S_4^2 ones already accounted for (being identical to C_2).

4. Four C_3 axes, each coinciding with a body diagonal of the cube. Counting C_3^1 and C_3^2 for each, the total is $8C_3$.

5. There is a plane of symmetry containing each pair of apexes of the tetrahedron and bisecting the opposite edge, and examination of the figure shows six equivalent such planes. The symmetry operations are then 6σ, usually reported as $6\sigma_d$.

The T_d group then has a total of 24 distinct symmetry operations.

Examination of the regular octahedron shown in Fig. 17-7 yields the following symmetry aspects.

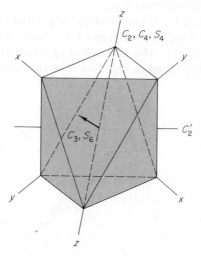

Fig. 17-7. *Symmetry elements of an octahedron.*

1. The identity operation E.
2. Three C_2 axes collinear with the x, y, and z coordinates of the figure, or $3C_2$ operations.
3. Three C_4 axes collinear with the preceding C_2 axes, each generating C_4^1 and C_4^2 new operations, for a total of $6C_4$.
4. Three S_4 axes collinear with the preceding and generating S_4^1 and S_4^3 new operations, or a total of $6S_4$.
5. Six C_2' axes each bisecting opposite edges. The total is then $6C_2'$.
6. Four C_3 axes each passing through the center of opposite triangular faces, and giving $8C_3$ operations in all.
7. Four S_6 axes collinear with the C_3 ones (note Fig. 17-5!). Each generates the operations S_6^1, S_6^2 ($= C_3^1$), S_6^3 ($= i$), S_6^4 ($= C_3^2$), S_6^5, or two new ones, for a total of $8S_6$.
8. An inversion center i.

9. Three planes of symmetry each of which passes through four of the six apices, or $3\sigma_h$.
10. Six planes of symmetry each of which passes through two apices and bisects two opposite edges, or $6\sigma_d$.

The total number of symmetry operations for the octahedron is 48.

E. Some Illustrations of Point Groups

The stereographic projection diagrams for a number of point groups are shown in Fig. 17-8. The only additional convention to be noted is that an open geometric

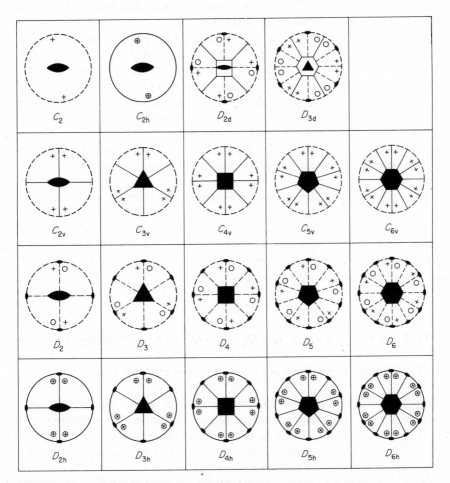

Fig. 17-8. *Stereographic projection diagrams for various point groups. (From H. Eyring, J. Walter, and G. E. Kimball, "Quantum Chemistry." Copyright 1960, Wiley, New York. Used with permission of John Wiley & Sons, Inc.)*

figure in the center of the diagram indicates a corresponding improper axis of rotation.

Some molecular examples are collected in Table 17-1 [for additional ones see Adamson (1969)]. The Schoenflies designation for each can be obtained by following the procedure described in Section 17-2C. A useful point to remember is that it is not necessary to identify all the symmetry elements present in order to determine the point group designation. Thus in the case of NH_3 it is sufficient to determine that there is a C_3 axis and no secondary axes and that there is a σ_v but no σ_h, to establish the group as C_{3v}. The D_{2h} designation for $H_2C{=}CH_2$ follows on observing that there are two mutually perpendicular C_2 axes and a σ_h plane —the presence of σ_v planes is automatically assured. Dibenzene chromium is D_{6h} since the principal axis is C_6, there is at least one secondary axis, and a σ_h plane. The remaining symmetry features are implicit.

The entries for H_2O_2 illustrate another point. The molecule has C_{2v} symmetry if it is in the *cis* configuration with all atoms coplanar. Keeping this plane as a reference, one may then twist the molecule about the O−O axis, thus rotating one O−H bond forward above the plane and the other backward below the plane. A 90° rotation makes the molecule planar and *trans*; it now has C_{2h} symmetry. The actual configuration in the crystal is in between these positions, and for any such intermediate angle the symmetry is reduced to C_2. Thus the symmetry group of a molecule varies with molecular motions; one ordinarily takes the most probable positions of the atoms in the lowest vibrational energy state. In the case of $Co(NH_3)_6^{3+}$ the hydrogens are ignored in giving the symmetry as O_h; were they included, then, depending on their assumed configuration, some much lower symmetry would be reported.

The symmetry properties of a molecule are thus not absolutely invariant or unique. We will be using symmetry to draw conclusions about chemical bonding and it is well to realize that assumptions as to what is important are inherent in most statements of molecular symmetry.

17-3   A Set of Symmetry Operations as Constituting a Group

A. The Multiplication Table for a Set of Symmetry Operations

The term "multiplication" has the meaning in group theory of sequential performance of designated operations. Thus AB means *first* operation B, *then* operation A. With this definition in mind one can construct a "multiplication table" for the set of symmetry elements possessed by any particular object, each symmetry operation being entered separately.

Table 17-2 shows the multiplication table for the point group C_{3v}. The procedure for developing this table is as follows. It is simplest to make use of the stereographic projection diagram (Fig. 17-2 or Fig. 17-8), but with each plus identified by a

Table 17-1. *Molecular Examples of Various Point Groups*

Molecule	Structure	Symmetry elements and operations	Point group
CH_4		$E, 8C_3, 3C_2, 6S_4, 6\sigma_d$	T_d
$Co(NH_3)_6^{3+\ a}$		$E, 8C_3, 6C_2', 6C_4, 3C_2, i,$ $6S_4, 8S_6, 3\sigma_h, 6\sigma_d$	O_h
HCl	H — Cl	E, C_∞, σ_v	$C_{\infty v}$
H_2	H — H	$E, C_\infty, C_2, \sigma_h, \sigma_v$	$D_{\infty h}$
H_2O_2	(planar) (planar)	$E, C_2, \sigma_v, \sigma_v'$ E, C_2, i, σ_h E, C_2	C_{2v} C_{2h} C_2
C_6H_6		$E, 2C_6, 2C_3, C_2, 3C_2',$ $3C_2, i, 2S_3, 2S_6, \sigma_h,$ $3\sigma_d, 3\sigma_v$	D_{6h}
$Cr(NH_3)_2(NCS)_4^-$		$E, 2C_4, C_2, 2C_2', 2C_e,$ $i, 2S_4, \sigma_h, 2\sigma_v, 2\sigma_d$	D_{4h}
$(C_6H_5)_2Fe$ (ferrocene)		$E, 2C_5, 2C_5^2, 5C_2, i,$ $2S_{10}, 2S_{10}, 5\sigma_d$	D_{5d}
$XeOF_4$		$E, 2C_4, C_2, 2\sigma_v, 2\sigma_d$	C_{4v}

^{a} As is customary with such complex ions, only the central metal ion and the atoms directly bonded to it are considered.

Table 17-2.   *Multiplication Table for the C_{3v} Group*

	E	C_3^{1}	C_3^{2}	σ_v	σ_v'	σ_v''
E	E	C_3^{1}	C_3^{2}	σ_v	σ_v'	σ_v''
C_3^{1}	C_3^{1}	C_3^{2}	E	σ_v'	σ_v''	σ_v
C_3^{2}	C_3^{2}	E	C_3^{1}	σ_v''	σ_v	σ_v'
σ_v	σ_v	σ_v''	σ_v'	E	C_3^{2}	C_3^{1}
σ_v'	σ_v'	σ_v	σ_v''	C_3^{1}	E	C_3^{2}
σ_v''	σ_v''	σ_v'	σ_v	C_3^{2}	C_3^{1}	E

number. As illustrated in Fig. 17-9, the effect of each separate symmetry operation is first diagrammed. Each possible symmetry operation is then performed
again. Thus C_3^{1} followed by C_3^{1} gives the identical result as C_3^{2}; C_3^{1} followed by
σ_v gives the identical result as σ_v', and so on. In this way a table of all possible

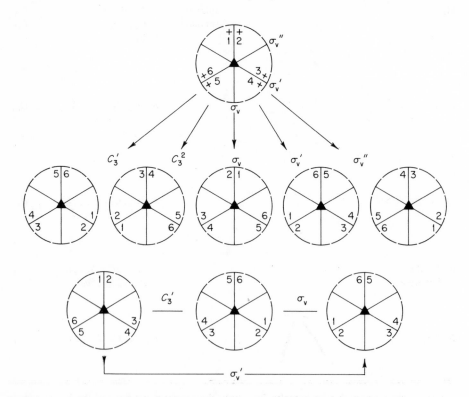

Fig. 17-9.   *Demonstration that $\sigma_v C_3^{1} = \sigma_v'$ in the C_{3v} group.*

products is worked out. The convention we will follow is that in a multiplication table such as Table 17-2 the operation in the left-hand column is performed first, followed by that indicated by the top row.

There are several important features to notice in the table. First, each product gives a result identical to the result of some single symmetry operation of the set. Second, each symmetry operation occurs just once in each row and in each column. Each operation has a *reciprocal*, that is, for each A there exists a B such that $AB = E$ (and we then say that $A = B^{-1}$). The *associative law* of multiplication holds, that is, $A(BC) = (AB)(C)$. For example,

$$C_3^1(C_3^2\sigma_v) = C_3^1\sigma_v'' = \sigma_v \quad \text{and} \quad (C_3^1C_3^2)\,\sigma_v = E\sigma_v = \sigma_v. \quad (17\text{-}1)$$

These features characterize a mathematical group, by definition; they hold for the multiplication tables of all of the point groups discussed here.

The multiplication of symmetry operations differs from ordinary multiplication in not being *commutative*, that is, the order of operation makes a difference. Thus AB is not in general the same as BA. For example, $C_3^1\sigma_v = \sigma_v'$, while $\sigma_v C_3^1 = \sigma_v''$. Finally, notice that the identity operation E occurs either along the diagonal of the multiplication table or is symmetrically disposed to it. This behavior will be a general one of symmetry point groups.

B. Some Properties of Groups

Some general definitions and theorems for groups are now useful; we omit proofs for the latter, although in many cases the exercise is not difficult [see Cotton (1963)]. The *order h* of a symmetry group is the number of distinct symmetry operations, or captions to the rows and columns of the multiplication table; the order of the C_{3v} group is six, for example. A group may have subgroups; thus the set E, C_3^1, C_3^2 obeys the rules for a group. It can be shown that the order g of any subgroup must be an integral divisor of the group order h.

An important item is that the symmetry operations of a group will generally subdivide into *classes*. Before defining the term class we must first consider an operation known as a *similarity transformation*.

If A and X are two elements of a group and X^{-1} is the reciprocal of X, that is, $X^{-1}X = E$, then the product $X^{-1}AX$ will in general give some other element B of the group. For example, in the C_{3v} group if X is C_3^1, then X^{-1} is C_3^2; then $C_3^2\sigma_v C_3^1 = C_3^2\sigma_v'' = \sigma_v'$. Thus if A is σ_v, its similarity transformation by C_3^1 is σ_v'.

We next take as X each element of the group in turn and apply the operation $X^{-1}AX$; if this is done for the C_{3v} group, with $A = \sigma_v$, the result is always σ_v, σ_v', or σ_v''. The same result obtains if A is σ_v' or σ_v''. The last three elements are then said to be conjugate with each other and constitute a *class* of the group. If the procedure is repeated with $A = C_3^1$ or C_3^2, the result of the similarity transformation (with X equal to *any* element of the group) is always C_3^1 or C_3^2, and these two symmetry operations constitute a second class. The identity operation always is a class by itself.

An important theorem is that the order of any class of a group must be an integral divisor of the order h of the group. We will henceforth group symmetry operations by classes—those for C_{3v} are E, $2C_3^1$, and $3\sigma_v$. Note that this has been done in Table 17-1.

17-4   Representations of Groups

Just as the set of symmetry elements is an abstraction of the symmetry properties of an object, there is a very useful abstraction of a group multiplication table known as a *representation*. A representation of a group is a set of numbers (or, as seen in the next section, of matrices) which if assigned to the various symmetry operations, will obey or be consistent with the group multiplication table. It turns out that all of the symmetry operations of a given class must be given the same number if the set of assignments is to work as a representation.

Two representations for the C_{3v} group are

(1) $E = 1,$ $C_3^1 = C_3^2 = 1,$ $\sigma_v = \sigma_v' = \sigma_v'' = 1;$

(2) $E = 1,$ $C_3^1 = C_3^2 = 1,$ $\sigma_v = \sigma_v' = \sigma_v'' = -1.$

If these simple designations are substituted into Table 17-2, then a self-consistent multiplication table is obtained. Considering representation 2, $\sigma_v C_3^2 = \sigma_v'$ and $(-1)(1) = (-1)$. It will be customary to show a representation in the more compact form given in Table 17-3, where Γ is the general symbol for a representation.

As a second example, the multiplication table for the group C_{2v} is given by Table 17-4. In this case each symmetry operation constitutes a separate class (as may be verified as an exercise). A set of simple representations for this group turns out to be as shown in Table 17-5. The designations A_1, A_2, and so on will be discussed later.

The concept of a representation as developed so far seems rather trivial. It provides, however, the key to using the symmetry properties of a molecule in wave mechanical treatments. To develop this application, we proceed to examine how representations may be generated.

A.   Geometric Transformations; Matrix Notation

An important method of generating a representation will be to carry out the symmetry operations of a group on some elementary object such as a point or a

Table 17-3. *Two Representations of C_{3v}*

	E	$2C_3$	$3\sigma_v$
Γ_1	1	1	1
Γ_2	1	1	-1

Table 17-4. *Multiplication Table for the C_{2v} Group*

	E	C_2	σ_v	σ_v'
E	E	C_2	σ_v	σ_v'
C_2	C_2	E	σ_v'	σ_v
σ_v	σ_v	σ_v'	E	C_2
σ_v'	σ_v'	σ_v	C_2	E

Table 17-5. *Representations for C_{2v}*

	E	C_2	σ_v	σ_v'
$\Gamma_1 = A_1$	1	1	1	1
$\Gamma_2 = A_2$	1	1	-1	-1
$\Gamma_3 = B_1$	1	-1	1	-1
$\Gamma_4 = B_2$	1	-1	-1	1

vector. Suppose a point is located at (x_1, y_1, z_1) and we apply the symmetry operations of the C_{2v} group to it. These consist of E, a C_2 axis collinear with the z axis, a σ_v in the xz plane, and a σ_v' in the yz plane. As illustrated in Fig. 17-10(a), application of this last changes the point to $(-x_1, y_1, z_1)$, or

$$x_2 = -x_1 + 0y_1 + 0z_1, \qquad y_2 = 0x_1 + y_1 + 0z_1,$$
$$z_2 = 0x_1 + 0y_1 + z_1. \tag{17-2}$$

As shown in Fig. 17-10(b), the operation C_2 gives

$$x_2 = -x_1 + 0y_1 + 0z_1, \qquad y_2 = 0x_1 - y_1 + 0z_1,$$
$$z_2 = 0x_1 + 0y_1 + z_1. \tag{17-3}$$

In these cases the new coordinates are just 1, 0, or -1 times the old ones, with no mixing—that is, x_2 does not depend on y_1 or z_1, and so on. This will not in general be true. For example, were the C_{3v} group involved, the operation C_3^1 would be as shown in Fig. 17-10(c), leading to

$$x_2 = x_1 \cos(\tfrac{2}{3}\pi) - y_1 \sin(\tfrac{2}{3}\pi) + 0z_1,$$
$$y_2 = x_1 \sin(\tfrac{2}{3}\pi) + y_1 \cos(\tfrac{2}{3}\pi) + 0z_1, \tag{17-4}$$
$$z_2 = 0x_1 + 0y_1 + z_1.$$

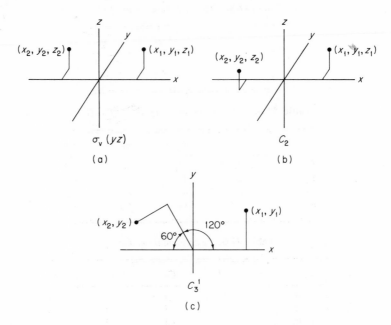

Fig. 17-10. *The C_{2v} point group.(a) The $\sigma_v(yz)$ operation on a general point and (b) the C_2 operation. (c) The C_3^1 operation of the C_{3v} group as applied to a general point.*

Here the x and y coordinates mix with each other but not with the z coordinate.

A set of transformation equations such as Eqs. (17-2), (17-3), or (17-4) may be expressed in matrix notation. Equation (17-2) becomes

$$\begin{bmatrix} -1 & 0 & 0 \\ 0 & 1 & 0 \\ 0 & 0 & 1 \end{bmatrix} \begin{bmatrix} x_1 \\ y_1 \\ z_1 \end{bmatrix} = \begin{bmatrix} x_2 \\ y_2 \\ z_2 \end{bmatrix}. \qquad (17\text{-}5)$$

·That is, multiplication of the matrix

$$\begin{bmatrix} x_1 \\ y_1 \\ z_1 \end{bmatrix} \qquad \text{by} \qquad \begin{bmatrix} -1 & 0 & 0 \\ 0 & 1 & 0 \\ 0 & 0 & 1 \end{bmatrix}$$

yields the new set

$$\begin{bmatrix} x_2 \\ y_2 \\ z_2 \end{bmatrix}.$$

Similarly, Eqs. (17-3) and (17-4) become

$$\begin{bmatrix} -1 & 0 & 0 \\ 0 & -1 & 0 \\ 0 & 0 & 1 \end{bmatrix} \begin{bmatrix} x_1 \\ y_1 \\ z_1 \end{bmatrix} = \begin{bmatrix} x_2 \\ y_2 \\ z_2 \end{bmatrix}. \qquad (17\text{-}6)$$

and

$$\begin{bmatrix} \cos(\tfrac{2}{3}\pi) & -\sin(\tfrac{2}{3}\pi) & 0 \\ \sin(\tfrac{2}{3}\pi) & +\cos(\tfrac{2}{3}\pi) & 0 \\ 0 & 0 & 1 \end{bmatrix} \begin{bmatrix} x_1 \\ y_1 \\ z_1 \end{bmatrix} = \begin{bmatrix} x_2 \\ y_2 \\ z_2 \end{bmatrix}. \tag{17-7}$$

The preceding statements follow from the rules for matrix multiplication. If we have the product $\mathscr{A}\mathscr{B} = \mathscr{C}$ when a capital script letter denotes a matrix, or, for example,

$$\underset{\mathscr{A}}{\begin{bmatrix} a_{11} & a_{12} \\ a_{21} & a_{22} \\ a_{31} & a_{32} \end{bmatrix}} \underset{\mathscr{B}}{\begin{bmatrix} b_{11} & b_{12} & b_{13} & b_{14} \\ b_{21} & b_{22} & b_{23} & b_{24} \end{bmatrix}} = \underset{\mathscr{C}}{\begin{bmatrix} c_{11} & c_{12} & c_{13} & c_{14} \\ c_{21} & c_{22} & c_{23} & c_{24} \\ c_{31} & c_{32} & c_{33} & c_{34} \end{bmatrix}},$$

then the rule is

$$c_{il} = \sum_k a_{ik} b_{kl} . \tag{17-8}$$

That is, the entry in row i and column l of the product matrix is the sum of the products of row i of matrix $\mathscr{A}$ with column l of matrix $\mathscr{B}$, with the restriction that the column number of a must match the row number of b. The idea of rows "into" columns may by illustrated more explicitly:

$$c_{11} = \sum_k a_{1k} b_{k1} = a_{11} b_{11} + a_{12} b_{21} ,$$

$$c_{21} = \sum_k a_{2k} b_{k1} = a_{21} b_{11} + a_{22} b_{21} ,$$

$$c_{34} = \sum_k a_{3k} b_{k4} = a_{31} b_{14} + a_{32} b_{24} ,$$

and so on. A requirement implicit in Eq. (17-8) is that in order to multiply two matrices, the number of columns of the left-hand one must equal the number of rows of the right-hand one.

Application of the multiplication rule to Eq. (17-8) yields

$$x_2 = c_{11} = [\cos(\tfrac{2}{3}\pi)] \, x_1 + [-\sin(\tfrac{2}{3}\pi)] \, y_1 + 0z_1 ,$$

$$y_2 = c_{21} = [\sin(\tfrac{2}{3}\pi)] \, x_1 + [\cos(\tfrac{2}{3}\pi)] \, y_1 + 0z_1 ,$$

$$z_2 = c_{31} = 0x_1 + 0y_1 + 1z_1 ,$$

or Eq. (17-4) again.

To return to the C_{2v} case, the matrices which transform the point (x_1, y_1, z_1) into a point (x_2, y_2, z_2) are, for the various symmetry operations,

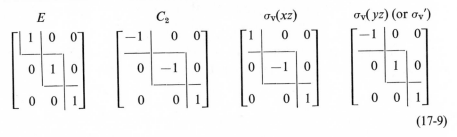

$$
\begin{array}{cccc}
E & C_2 & \sigma_v(xz) & \sigma_v(yz)\ (\text{or } \sigma_v')
\end{array}
$$

$$(17\text{-}9)$$

These matrices will turn out to be representations of the C_{2v} group. Referring to Table 17-4, $C_2\sigma_v = \sigma_v'$ and multiplication of the matrix for the σ_v transformation by that for the C_2 one will yield the matrix for the σ_v' transformation.

A further point is that the matrices of Eq. (17-9) can all be blocked into smaller matrices, outside of which the only entries are zeros. A check on the application of Eq. (17-8) will confirm that the products of such matrices are just the separate products of the blocked-out areas. In this case these are just matrices of dimension one. Where such blocking reduces a set of matrices to ones of lower dimension, then, necessarily, each of these last must be a representation of the group if the original matrices were. As a confirmation, representations A_1, B_1, and B_2 of Table 17-5 correspond to the three blocked-out sets of Eq. (17-9).

The set of matrices for the transformations of a point in the C_{3v} group are

$$
\begin{array}{ccc}
E & C_3^1 & C_3^2
\end{array}
$$

$$
\begin{bmatrix} 1 & 0 & 0 \\ 0 & 1 & 0 \\ \hline 0 & 0 & 1 \end{bmatrix}
\quad
\begin{bmatrix} \cos(\tfrac{2}{3}\pi) & -\sin(\tfrac{2}{3}\pi) & 0 \\ \sin(\tfrac{2}{3}\pi) & \cos(\tfrac{2}{3}\pi) & 0 \\ \hline 0 & 0 & 1 \end{bmatrix}
\quad
\begin{bmatrix} \cos(\tfrac{4}{3}\pi) & -\sin(\tfrac{4}{3}\pi) & 0 \\ \sin(\tfrac{4}{3}\pi) & \cos(\tfrac{4}{3}\pi) & 0 \\ \hline 0 & 0 & 1 \end{bmatrix}
$$

$$(17\text{-}10)$$

$$
\begin{array}{ccc}
\sigma_v(xz) & \sigma_v' & \sigma_v''
\end{array}
$$

$$
\begin{bmatrix} 1 & 0 & 0 \\ 0 & -1 & 0 \\ \hline 0 & 0 & 1 \end{bmatrix}
\quad
\begin{bmatrix} -\sin(\tfrac{1}{6}\pi) & -\cos(\tfrac{1}{6}\pi) & 0 \\ -\cos(\tfrac{1}{6}\pi) & +\sin(\tfrac{1}{6}\pi) & 0 \\ \hline 0 & 0 & 1 \end{bmatrix}
\quad
\begin{bmatrix} -\sin(\tfrac{1}{6}\pi) & \cos(\tfrac{1}{6}\pi) & 0 \\ \cos(\tfrac{1}{6}\pi) & \sin(\tfrac{1}{6}\pi) & 0 \\ \hline 0 & 0 & 1 \end{bmatrix}
$$

Remember that in C_{3v}, σ_v' is a plane rotated 120° from $\sigma_v(xz)$ and σ_v'' is one rotated 240° from $\sigma_v(xz)$. This set of matrices is a representation of the C_{3v} group, that is, the matrices obey the group multiplication table. They may be blocked off into a 2 × 2, or two-dimensional, set and a 1 × 1, or one-dimensional, set of matrices; each set is then also a representation of the group. The 1 × 1 matrices constitute the representation Γ_1 given in Table 17-3.

B.   The Trace of a Matrix

We have shown that while a set of simple numbers may constitute a representation of a group, one may also have a set of matrices. This last is the more general situation. In fact, an infinite number of matrix representations may be generated for a given symmetry group merely by taking more and more complicated functions through the symmetry transformations. In the C_{2v} group, for example, the molecule H_2O (or any A_2B molecule) could be taken through the transformations by locating the oxygen atom at the origin and assigning x, y, and z coordinates to each hydrogen. The original six coordinates would then transform into six others upon application of a symmetry operation, thus producing a 6×6 matrix. The set of these would again be a representation of the C_{2v} group. Such transformation matrices are always square ones, that is, they have the same number of rows as of columns.

It is unnecessarily cumbersome to write down complete matrices for a representation since it turns out that the sum of the diagonal elements sufficiently characterizes a matrix for our purposes. This sum is called the *trace* χ of a matrix. In the case of a 1×1 matrix χ is just the matrix itself, of course. For the set of 2×2 matrices of Eqs. (17-10) the traces are

$$E: 2, C_3^1: \quad (-0.5) + (-0.5) = -1, \qquad C_3^2: \quad (-0.5) + (-0.5) = -1,$$
$$\sigma_v(xz): \qquad (1) + (-1) = 0, \qquad \sigma_v': \qquad (-0.5) + (0.5) = 0, \quad (17\text{-}11)$$
$$\sigma_v'': \qquad (-0.5) + (0.5) = 0.$$

An important point is that while the matrices for the symmetry operations *within a given class* may differ in detail, their traces are the *same*. Also, the matrix corresponding to the identity operation must consist of just ones along the diagonal, so its trace *must* be equal to the dimension of the matrix.

It is customary to describe a representation of a group by giving just the traces of the matrices involved. Thus for C_{3v}, the result is as shown in Table 17-6. The symbols A_1, A_2, and so on used to label the representations will be described later. In the case of a representation which is higher than one-dimensional, such as that for E, it is important to remember that matrices are involved. While the traces serve to characterize them, it is the *actual matrices* that must be multiplied in verifying that they obey the group multiplication table.

Table 17-6.   *Representations for C_{3v}*

	E	$2C_3$	$3\sigma_v$
A_1	1	1	1
A_2	1	1	-1
E	2	-1	0

C. Reducible and Irreducible Representations

The concept of a similarity transformation discussed in Section 17-3B may also be applied to square matrices. The reciprocal of a matrix $\mathscr{Q}$, denoted by $\mathscr{Q}^{-1}$, is defined by $\mathscr{Q}^{-1}\mathscr{Q} = \mathscr{E}$, where $\mathscr{E}$ is the identity matrix, that is, a matrix having ones on its diagonal and zeros elsewhere. The similarity transformation on a matrix $\mathscr{A}$ is then written

$$\mathscr{B} = \mathscr{Q}^{-1}\mathscr{A}\mathscr{Q}. \tag{17-12}$$

A theorem which we will not prove is that the resultant matrix $\mathscr{B}$ must have the same trace as does $\mathscr{A}$ (but may otherwise be different). A related consequence is that if the set of matrices $\mathscr{A}_1$, $\mathscr{A}_2$, ... constitute a representation of a group, so also will the set $\mathscr{B}_1$, $\mathscr{B}_2$, ...

The importance of the similarity transformation is that it is usually possible to find one which reduces some set $\mathscr{A}_1$, $\mathscr{A}_2$, ... to a new set which has blocked-out sections and therefore decomposes into simpler matrices which are also representations. A representation which can be so simplified is termed *reducible*. There will remain, however, certain sets of matrices which cannot be simplified further by any possible similarity transformations. Such a set is then an *irreducible representation*, hereafter abbreviated IR, of the group. It is the irreducible representations of a group which are of fundamental importance. The set of traces which a representation has for the various symmetry operations is called the *character* of the representation. Also, the tabular listing of the characters of the IR's of a group is called a *character table*.

There are several important theorems concerning the irreducible representations of a group which we will state without derivation.

1. The sum of the squares of the dimensions l of the irreducible representations of a group is equal to the order h of the group. Thus

$$\sum l_i^2 = h. \tag{17-13}$$

For example, the representations A_1, A_2, and E given by Table 17-6 for the C_{3v} group constitute the complete set of irreducible representations (and the display is just the character table for that group). The group is of order 6 (the total number of symmetry operations) and the dimension of each representation is given by the trace for the E symmetry operation. We see that $1^2 + 1^2 + 2^2 = 6$, as required by Eq. (17-13). A corollary is evidently that the sum of the squares of the traces of the irreducible representations for the E operation also be equal to h, or

$$\sum \chi_i^2(E) = h. \tag{17-14}$$

2. The number of irreducible representations of a group is equal to the number of classes in the group. The C_{3v} group has three classes and just three irreducible representations.

3. The sum of the squares of the traces of any IR is equal to h. In applying this rule, we sum the squares of the traces over all the symmetry operations R:

$$\sum_R \chi^2(R) = h. \tag{17-15}$$

Again referring to the C_{3v} group, we have

$$
\begin{aligned}
A_1 &: & 1^2 + (2)(1^2) + 3(1^2) &= 6, \\
A_2 &: & 1^2 + (2)(1^2) + 3(-1)^2 &= 6, \\
E &: & 2^2 + (2)(-1)^2 + (3)(0) &= 6.
\end{aligned}
$$

4. It will be recalled that if a representation is reducible, there will be some similarity transformation that will convert it into a set of matrices having blocked-out areas. The ultimate case is one in which each set of blocked-out areas constitutes an irreducible representation. In general, not all of the possible irreducible representations will appear, or a given one may show up in two or more sets of blocked-out areas. There is a very useful rule which determines the number of times, a_i, the ith IR occurs in a given reducible representation:

$$a_i = \frac{1}{h} \sum_R \chi(R)\,\chi_i(R). \tag{17-16}$$

The statement is that one sums over all symmetry operations the product of the trace of the IR and that of the reducible one in question. Using the C_{3v} group as an example, Eqs. (17-10) provide an obviously reducible representation (the matrices being already blocked out). The traces for the *whole* matrices are

E	$2C_3$	$3\sigma_v$
3	0	1

Application of Eq. (17-16) gives

$$
\begin{aligned}
a_{A_1} &= \tfrac{1}{6}[(3)(1) + 2(0)(1) + 3(1)(1)] = 1, \\
a_{A_2} &= \tfrac{1}{6}[(3)(1) + 2(0)(1) + 3(1)(-1)] = 0, \\
a_E &= \tfrac{1}{6}[(3)(2) + 2(0)(-1) + 3(1)(0)] = 1,
\end{aligned}
$$

which confirms that the set of matrices (17-10) consists of the irreducible representations $A_1 + E$.

17-5 Atomic Orbitals as Bases for Representations

It was demonstrated in the preceding section that a general point (x_1, y_1, z_1) generates a representation of a symmetry group when carried through the various symmetry operations. The same is true of wave functions of an atom when all symmetry operations are about the nucleus. Since symmetry properties involve the angular rather than the radial aspect of an object, it is only necessary to consider the former portion of a wave function; we will further restrict ourselves to the hydrogen-like set of functions derived in Chapter 16.

An s function is angularly symmetric, and hence is unchanged by any symmetry operation. From Eq. (16-84), the A_{p_z} function is proportional to $\cos \theta$, which is just the projection of a vector on the z axis; A_{p_x} is proportional to $\sin \theta \cos \phi$ [Eq. (16-85)] or to the x projection of a vector, and A_{p_y} is proportional to the y projection [Eq. (16-86)]. If, for example, these vectors are put through the operations of the C_{2v} group, we obtain

$$C_2: \quad p_x = -p_x; \quad p_y = -p_y; \quad p_z = p_z;$$

or the transformation matrix

$$\begin{bmatrix} -1 & 0 & 0 \\ 0 & -1 & 0 \\ 0 & 0 & 1 \end{bmatrix}.$$

The operation $\sigma_v(xz)$ leads to the matrix

$$\begin{bmatrix} 1 & 0 & 0 \\ 0 & -1 & 0 \\ 0 & 0 & 1 \end{bmatrix}.$$

The identity operation E leads, of course, to

$$\begin{bmatrix} 1 & 0 & 0 \\ 0 & 1 & 0 \\ 0 & 0 & 1 \end{bmatrix}.$$

The set of matrices for the transformations

$$\begin{bmatrix} p_x \\ p_y \\ p_z \end{bmatrix}$$

is thus blocked out into three one-dimensional matrices, and a check with Table 17-5 identifies the matrix for p_x to be the same as B_1, that for p_y as B_2, and that for p_z as A_1. We therefore say that p_x transforms as does the B_1 irreducible representation, or forms a basis for it, p_y transforms as does B_2, and so on.

Similarly, each d wave function will transform as one or another irreducible representation of a group, or is said to form a basis for it. Thus d_{xz} has the angular nature of the product of the x and z projections of a vector. Since the z projection is unchanged by any of the operations of the C_{2v} group, d_{xz} transforms as does p_x, and thus is a basis for the B_1 irreducible representation.

17-6   Character Tables

It is customary to assemble the basic information concerning each symmetry point group in what is called a character table. Several such tables are given in Table 17-7. Their organization is as follows. The first column designates each irreducible representation, the naming scheme being outlined shortly. The next group of columns lists the traces of each representation for each class of symmetry operation. The next to last column lists the types of vectors which form a basis for each representation. Thus for the C_{2v} group, the row designated A_1 shows that the z projection of a vector is appropriate, which means that the p_z wave function will form a basis for this representation. The last column lists products of vectors which are appropriate. The designation yz after the B_2 representation then means that d_{yz} orbitals will form a basis for the B_2 representation, and so on. There are occasional entries R_x, R_y, or R_z in the next to last column. These refer to a circular vector whose plane is perpendicular to the named axis. Although such vectors will not be of direct interest to us, they also form a basis for a representation.

It should be mentioned that several complexities have been side-stepped in the presentation of symmetry groups and their character tables. As a consequence a number of types have been omitted from Table 17-7 as involving entries which there is insufficient space to explain. The omissions are not of vital importance here, however; the omitted aspects have more the nature of complications than of new principles.

Returning to the first column, the naming scheme is one developed by R. Mulliken. Irreducible representations of a group may be one-, two- or three-dimensional (we will not encounter any of higher dimension), and may also possess various symmetry properties themselves.

One-dimensional representations are named A if they are symmetric to rotation by $2\pi/n$ about the principal or C_n axis, and B if antisymmetric to such rotation. They have subscripts 1 or 2 to designate whether they are symmetric or antisymmetric to rotation about a secondary C_2 axis, or if this is missing, to a vertical plane of symmetry.

For example, the A_1 representation in C_{2v} [Table 17-5] is generated by a vector on the z axis, and such a vector is unchanged by C_2 and σ_v. The A_2 representation is generated by a circular vector in the xy plane, centered at the origin; it is unchanged by rotation but inverted on reflection by σ_v. The B_1 representation is like a vector on the x axis; it is inverted by C_2 but unchanged by σ_v (taken to be the xz plane), and B_2 is like a vector on the y axis and is inverted by both C_2 and σ_v.

In more complicated symmetry groups primes and double primes are attached to all letters to indicate symmetry or antisymmetry with respect to σ_h. Also the subscripts g and u (from the German *gerade* and *ungerade*) may be present to show whether the representation is symmetric or antisymmetric with respect to inversion.

Table 17-7.   *Character Tables*

C_2

C_2:	E	C_2		
A	1	1	z, R_z	x^2, y^2, z^2, xy
B	1	-1	x, y, R_x, R_y	yz, xz

D_n

D_2:	E	$C_2(z)$	$C_2(y)$	$C_2(x)$		
A	1	1	1	1		x^2, y^2, z^2
B_1	1	1	-1	-1	z, R_z	xy
B_2	1	-1	1	-1	y, R_y	xz
B_3	1	-1	-1	1	x, R_x	yz

D_3:	E	$2C_3$	$3C_2$		
A_1	1	1	1		$x^2 + y^2, z^2$
A_2	1	1	-1	z, R_z	—
E	2	-1	0	$(x, y)(R_x, R_y)$	$(x^2 - y^2, xy)(xz, yz)$

D_4:	E	$2C_4$	$C_2 (=C_4^2)$	$2C_2'$	$2C_2''$		
A_1	1	1	1	1	1		$x^2 + y^2, z^2$
A_2	1	1	1	-1	-1	z, R_z	—
B_1	1	-1	1	1	-1		$x^2 - y^2$
B_2	1	-1	1	-1	1		xy
E	2	0	-2	0	0	$(x, y)(R_x, R_y)$	(xz, yz)

D_5:	E	$2C_5$	$2C_5^2$	$5C_2$		
A_1	1	1	1	1		$x^2 + y^2, z^2$
A_2	1	1	1	-1	z, R_z	—
E_1	2	$2 \cos 72°$	$2 \cos 144°$	0	$(x, y)(R_x, R_y)$	(xy, yz)
E_2	2	$2 \cos 144°$	$2 \cos 72°$	0		$(x^2 - y^2, xy)$

D_6 :	E	$2C_6$	$2C_3$	C_2	$3C_2'$	$3C_2''$		
A_1	1	1	1	1	1	1	—	$x^2 + y^2,\ z^2$
A_2	1	1	1	1	-1	-1	z, R_z	—
B_1	1	-1	1	-1	1	-1	—	—
B_2	1	-1	1	-1	-1	1	—	—
E_1	2	1	-1	-2	0	0	$(x, y)(R_x, R_y)$	(xy, yz)
E_2	2	-1	-1	2	0	0	—	$(x^2 - y^2, xy)$

C_{nv}

C_{2v} :	E	C_2	$\sigma_v(xz)$	$\sigma_v'(yz)$		
A_1	1	1	1	1	z	x^2, y^2, z^2
A_2	1	1	-1	-1	R_z	xy
B_1	1	-1	1	-1	x, R_y	xz
B_2	1	-1	-1	1	y, R_x	yz

C_{3v} :	E	$2C_3$	$3\sigma_v$		
A_1	1	1	1	z	$x^2 + y^2,\ z^2$
A_2	1	1	-1	R_z	—
E	2	-1	0	$(x, y)(R_x, R_y)$	$(x^2 - y^2, xy)(xz, yz)$

C_{4v} :	E	$2C_4$	C_2	$2\sigma_v$	$2\sigma_d$		
A_1	1	1	1	1	1	z	$x^2 + y^2,\ z^2$
A_2	1	1	1	-1	-1	R_z	—
B_1	1	-1	1	1	-1	—	$x^2 - y^2$
B_2	1	-1	1	-1	1	—	xy
E	2	0	-2	0	0	$(x, y)(R_x, R_y)$	(xz, yz)

C_{5v} :	E	$2C_5$	$2C_5^2$	$5\sigma_v$		
A_1	1	1	1	1	z	$x^2 + y^2,\ z^2$
A_2	1	1	1	-1	R_z	—
E_1	2	$2\cos 72°$	$2\cos 144°$	0	$(x, y)(R_x, R_y)$	(xz, yz)
E_2	2	$2\cos 144°$	$2\cos 72°$	0	—	$(x^2 - y^2, xy)$

Table 17-7 (cont.).

C_{6v} :	E	$2C_6$	$2C_3$	C_2	$3\sigma_v$	$3\sigma_d$		
A_1	1	1	1	1	1	1	z	x^2+y^2, z^2
A_2	1	1	1	1	-1	-1	R_z	—
B_1	1	-1	1	-1	1	-1	—	—
B_2	1	-1	1	-1	-1	1	—	—
E_1	2	1	-1	-2	0	0	$(x,y)(R_x, R_y)$	(xz, yz)
E_2	2	-1	-1	2	0	0	—	(x^2-y^2, xy)

C_{nh}

C_{2h} :	E	C_2	i	σ_h		
A_g	1	1	1	1	R_z	x^2, y^2, z^2, xy
B_g	1	-1	1	-1	R_x, R_y	xz, yz
A_u	1	1	-1	-1	z	—
B_u	1	-1	-1	1	x, y	—

D_{nh}

D_{2h} :	E	$C_2(z)$	$C_2(y)$	$C_2(x)$	i	$\sigma(xy)$	$\sigma(xz)$	$\sigma(yz)$		
A_g	1	1	1	1	1	1	1	1	—	x^2, y^2, z^2
B_{1g}	1	1	-1	-1	1	1	-1	-1	R_z	xy
B_{2g}	1	-1	1	-1	1	-1	1	-1	R_y	xz
B_{3g}	1	-1	-1	1	1	-1	-1	1	R_x	yz
A_u	1	1	1	1	-1	-1	-1	-1	—	—
B_{1u}	1	1	-1	-1	-1	-1	1	1	z	—
B_{2u}	1	-1	1	-1	-1	1	-1	1	y	—
B_{3u}	1	-1	-1	1	-1	1	1	-1	x	—

D_{3h} :	E	$2C_3$	$3C_2$	σ_h	$2S_3$	$3\sigma_v$		
A_1'	1	1	1	1	1	1	—	x^2+y^2, z^2
A_2'	1	1	-1	1	1	-1	R_z	—
E'	2	-1	0	2	-1	0	(x, y)	(x^2-y^2, xy)
A_1''	1	1	1	-1	-1	-1	—	—
A_2''	1	1	-1	-1	-1	1	z	—
E''	2	-1	0	-2	1	0	(R_x, R_y)	(xz, yz)

D_{4h}	E	$2C_4$	C_2	$2C_2'$	$2C_2''$	i	$2S_4$	σ_h	$2\sigma_v$	$2\sigma_d$		
A_{1g}	1	1	1	1	1	1	1	1	1	1		$x^2+y^2,\ z^2$
A_{2g}	1	1	1	-1	-1	1	1	1	-1	-1	R_z	
B_{1g}	1	-1	1	1	-1	1	-1	1	1	-1		x^2-y^2
B_{2g}	1	-1	1	-1	1	1	-1	1	-1	1		xy
E_g	2	0	-2	0	0	2	0	-2	0	0	(R_x, R_y)	(xz, yz)
A_{1u}	1	1	1	1	1	-1	-1	-1	-1	-1		
A_{2u}	1	1	1	-1	-1	-1	-1	-1	1	1	z	
B_{1u}	1	-1	1	1	-1	-1	1	-1	-1	1		
B_{2u}	1	-1	1	-1	1	-1	1	-1	1	-1		
E_u	2	0	-2	0	0	-2	0	2	0	0	(x, y)	

D_{5h}	E	$2C_5$	$2C_5^2$	$5C_2$	σ_h	$2S_5$	$2S_5^3$	$5\sigma_v$		
A_1'	1	1	1	1	1	1	1	1		$x^2+y^2,\ z^2$
A_2'	1	1	1	-1	1	1	1	-1	R_z	
E_1'	2	$2\cos 72°$	$2\cos 144°$	0	2	$2\cos 72°$	$2\cos 144°$	0	(x, y)	
E_2'	2	$2\cos 144°$	$2\cos 72°$	0	2	$2\cos 144°$	$2\cos 72°$	0		(x^2-y^2, xy)
A_1''	1	1	1	1	-1	-1	-1	-1		
A_2''	1	1	1	-1	-1	-1	-1	1	z	
E_1''	2	$2\cos 72°$	$2\cos 144°$	0	-2	$-2\cos 72°$	$-2\cos 144°$	0	(R_x, R_y)	(xz, yz)
E_2''	2	$2\cos 144°$	$2\cos 72°$	0	-2	$-2\cos 144°$	$-2\cos 72°$	0		

D_{6h}	E	$2C_6$	$2C_3$	C_2	$3C_2'$	$3C_2''$	i	$2S_3$	$2S_6$	σ_h	$3\sigma_d$	$3\sigma_v$		
A_{1g}	1	1	1	1	1	1	1	1	1	1	1	1		$x^2+y^2,\ z^2$
A_{2g}	1	1	1	1	-1	-1	1	1	1	1	-1	-1	R_z	
B_{1g}	1	-1	1	-1	1	-1	1	-1	1	-1	1	-1		
B_{2g}	1	-1	1	-1	-1	1	1	-1	1	-1	-1	1		
E_{1g}	2	1	-1	-2	0	0	2	1	-1	-2	0	0	(R_x, R_y)	(xz, yz)
E_{2g}	2	-1	-1	2	0	0	2	-1	-1	2	0	0		(x^2-y^2, xy)
A_{1u}	1	1	1	1	1	1	-1	-1	-1	-1	-1	-1		
A_{2u}	1	1	1	1	-1	-1	-1	-1	-1	-1	1	1	z	
B_{1u}	1	-1	1	-1	1	-1	-1	1	-1	1	-1	1		
B_{2u}	1	-1	1	-1	-1	1	-1	1	-1	1	1	-1		
E_{1u}	2	1	-1	-2	0	0	-2	-1	1	2	0	0	(x, y)	
E_{2u}	2	-1	-1	2	0	0	-2	1	1	-2	0	0		

Table 17-7 (cont.).

D_{2d} :	E	$2S_4$	C_2	$2C_2'$	$2\sigma_d$		
A_1	1	1	1	1	1		$x^2+y^2,\ z^2$
A_2	1	1	1	-1	-1	R_z	—
B_1	1	-1	1	1	-1		x^2-y^2
B_2	1	-1	1	-1	1	z	xy
E	2	0	-2	0	0	$(x,y)(R_x, R_y)$	(xz, yz)

D_{3d} :	E	$2C_3$	$3C_2$	i	$2S_6$	$3\sigma_d$		
A_{1g}	1	1	1	1	1	1		$x^2+y^2,\ z^2$
A_{2g}	1	1	-1	1	1	-1	R_z	—
E_g	2	-1	0	2	-1	0	(R_x, R_y)	$(x^2-y^2,\ xy),\ (xz, yz)$
A_{1u}	1	1	1	-1	-1	-1		—
A_{2u}	1	1	-1	-1	-1	1	z	—
E_u	2	-1	0	-2	1	0	(x,y)	—

D_{4d} :	E	$2S_8$	$2C_4$	$2S_8^3$	C_2	$4C_2'$	$4\sigma_d$		
A_1	1	1	1	1	1	1	1		$x^2+y^2,\ z^2$
A_2	1	1	1	1	1	-1	-1	R_z	—
B_1	1	-1	1	-1	1	1	-1		—
B_2	1	-1	1	-1	1	-1	1	z	—
E_1	2	$\sqrt{2}$	0	$-\sqrt{2}$	-2	0	0	(x,y)	—
E_2	2	0	-2	0	2	0	0		$(x^2-y^2,\ xy)$
E_3	2	$-\sqrt{2}$	0	$\sqrt{2}$	-2	0	0	(R_x, R_y)	(xz, yz)

D_{5d} :	E	$2C_5$	$2C_5^2$	$5C_2$	i	$2S_{10}^3$	$2S_{10}$	$5\sigma_d$		
A_{1g}	1	1	1	1	1	1	1	1		$x^2+y^2,\ z^2$
A_{2g}	1	1	1	-1	1	1	1	-1	R_z	—
E_{1g}	2	$2\cos 72°$	$2\cos 144°$	0	2	$2\cos 72°$	$2\cos 144°$	0	(R_x, R_y)	(xz, yz)
E_{2g}	2	$2\cos 144°$	$2\cos 72°$	0	2	$2\cos 144°$	$2\cos 72°$	0		$(x^2-y^2,\ xy)$
A_{1u}	1	1	1	1	-1	-1	-1	-1		—
A_{2u}	1	1	1	-1	-1	-1	-1	1	z	—
E_{1u}	2	$2\cos 72°$	$2\cos 144°$	0	-2	$-2\cos 72°$	$-2\cos 144°$	0	(x,y)	—
E_{2u}	2	$2\cos 144°$	$2\cos 72°$	0	-2	$-2\cos 144°$	$-2\cos 72°$	0		—

D_{6d} :	E	$2S_{12}$	$2C_6$	$2S_4$	$2C_3$	$2S_{12}^5$	C_2	$6C_2'$	$6\sigma_d$		
A_1	1	1	1	1	1	1	1	1	1	—	$x^2 + y^2, z^2$
A_2	1	1	1	1	1	1	1	-1	-1	R_z	—
B_1	1	-1	1	-1	1	-1	1	1	-1	—	—
B_2	1	-1	1	-1	1	-1	1	-1	1	z	—
E_1	2	$\sqrt{3}$	1	0	-1	$-\sqrt{3}$	-2	0	0	(x, y)	—
E_2	2	1	-1	-2	-1	1	2	0	0	—	$(x^2 - y^2, xy)$
E_3	2	0	-2	0	2	0	-2	0	0	—	—
E_4	2	-1	-1	2	-1	-1	2	0	0	—	—
E_5	2	$-\sqrt{3}$	1	0	-1	$\sqrt{3}$	-2	0	0	(R_x, R_y)	(xz, yz)

The cubic groups

T_d :	E	$8C_3$	$3C_2$	$6S_4$	$6\sigma_d$		
A_1	1	1	1	1	1	—	$x^2 + y^2 + z^2$
A_2	1	1	1	-1	-1	—	—
E	2	-1	2	0	0	—	$(2z^2 - x^2 - y^2, x^2 - y^2)$
T_1	3	0	-1	1	-1	(R_x, R_y, R_z)	—
T_2	3	0	-1	-1	1	(x, y, z)	(xy, xz, yz)

O_h :	E	$8C_3$	$6C_2$	$6C_4$	$3C_2$ $(=C_4^2)$	i	$6S_4$	$8S_6$	$3\sigma_h$	$6\sigma_d$		
A_{1g}	1	1	1	1	1	1	1	1	1	1	—	$x^2 + y^2 + z^2$
A_{2g}	1	1	-1	-1	1	1	-1	1	1	-1	—	—
E_g	2	-1	0	0	2	2	0	-1	2	0	—	$(2z^2 - x^2 - y^2, x^2 - y^2)$
T_{1g}	3	0	-1	1	-1	3	1	0	-1	-1	(R_x, R_y, R_z)	—
T_{2g}	3	0	1	-1	-1	3	-1	0	-1	1	—	(xz, yz, xy)
A_{1u}	1	1	1	1	1	-1	-1	-1	-1	-1	—	—
A_{2u}	1	1	-1	-1	1	-1	1	-1	-1	1	—	—
E_u	2	-1	0	0	2	-2	0	1	-2	0	—	—
T_{1u}	3	0	-1	1	-1	-3	-1	0	1	1	(x, y, z)	—
T_{2u}	3	0	1	-1	-1	-3	1	0	1	-1	—	—

17-7   *Bonds as Bases for Reducible Representations*

We have pointed out that the hydrogen-like wave functions have trigonometric factors which correspond to various projections of a vector and that such projections if carried through the symmetry operations of a group, generate a representation. We may also take a set of vectors through the symmetry operations of a group, thus generating matrices which will again be representations, usually reducible ones. The detailing of such matrices is lengthy and, fortunately, it turns out that a simple rule allows the determination of the *trace* of the matrix for each symmetry operation.

The rule is that any vector of the set which remains unchanged by the symmetry operation contributes unity to the trace. A vector which is unchanged in position but reversed in sign contributes -1. These rules will always work for the cases considered here, but it should be mentioned that they have been simplified. If, for example, a set of vectors is rotated, each into the other's position, by a symmetry operation, then it may be necessary to assign appropriate fractional numbers in adding up the trace of the matrix.

A.   Sigma Bonds

The term *sigma bond* is conventionally used to describe a type of bond between two atoms which results from the overlap of an atomic orbital of each atom. The further requirement is that the orbitals and hence their region of overlap be a figure of revolution about the line between the two nuclei. As illustrated in Fig. 17-11, two s orbitals can form a sigma bond, and if the atoms A and B lie on the x axis, then the sigma-bonding combination $s_A p_{x,B}$ is possible, as well as $p_{x,A} p_{x,B}$, $s_A d_{x^2-y^2,B}$, and $p_{x,A} d_{x^2-y^2,B}$.

The orbital pictures shown in the figure are just the polar plots of the angular portions—these must be multiplied by the radial function $R(r)$ to give the corresponding electron density. As two atoms are brought together, the product of the electron amplitudes determines what is called the overlap; the mathematical operation is the evaluation of the integral $\int \psi_1 \psi_2 \, d\tau$ for the atoms at some given distance of separation, where $d\tau$ is the element of volume (note Section 16-10). This integral normally provides a guide to the degree of bonding that is expected. For two atoms to bond, it is first necessary that their respective orbitals overlap, that is, have appreciable values in some common region of space. There must also be a reinforcement of the two orbital wave functions; their phase relation must be suitable. First, it is conventional to indicate the phase relationships between the lobes of the angular portion of a given orbital by plus and minus signs. These signs are usually chosen so that if the orbitals of two atoms overlap in regions for which their sign is the same, then a bonding interaction is indicated —the potential energy of the atoms close together should be less than when sepa-

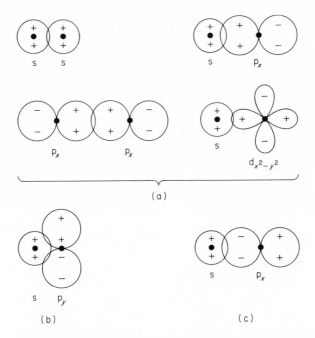

Fig. 17-11. *Arrangements of orbitals showing (a) sigma bonding, (b) nonbonding, and (c) anti-bonding for the case of an* A—B *molecule.*

rated. Conversely, if the overlapping orbitals are of opposite sign, the potential energy of the system is higher than for the separated atoms. The two situations are referred to as *bonding* and *antibonding*, respectively.

It may happen alternatively that the overlap integral is small or zero either because the overlap is small or because positive and negative domains of the integral cancel. The usual consequence is that neither bonding or repulsion is expected and the situation is called one of *nonbonding*. The three cases are illustrated in Fig. 7-11.

It should be emphasized that the overlap integral does not *in itself* give the degree of bonding; as discussed in Section 16-CN-3, the actual integrals involve the Hamiltonian of the system. However, the preceding qualitative use of the overlap idea will usually work—it is a convenient quantum mechanical rule of thumb.

By using group theory, it is possible to determine which pairs of wave functions can give a nonzero overlap integral. The approach is the following. The symmetry properties of the set of sigma bonds form a representation of the symmetry group of the molecule and one which will contain various irreducible representations of the group, as determined by the use of Eq. (17-16). The wave functions which are bases for these irreducible representations will have the necessary symmetry properties for the overlap integral to be nonzero and either positive or negative, depending on the signs given to the orbital lobes.

As illustrated in Fig. 17-12, we draw a set of vectors corresponding to the sigma bonds of the molecule. The trace of the matrix generated by each symmetry operation is then determined by applying the rule described at the beginning of this section. Equation (17-16) gives the irreducible representations contained by, or "spanned" by, the reducible one, and consultation of the character table for the group determines which hydrogen-like orbitals have the right symmetry for bonding.

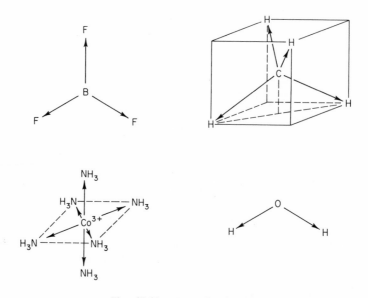

Fig. 17-12. *Sigma bond vectors.*

The following examples should help to clarify matters. The planar BF_3 molecule has D_{3h} symmetry. Consultation of Table 17-7 gives the symmetry classes as E, $2C_3$, $3C_2$, σ_h, $2S_3$, and $3\sigma_v$. The operation E leaves all three bond vectors unchanged, C_3 changes all of them, C_2 leaves one unchanged, σ_h leaves all unchanged, S_3 changes all, and σ_v leaves one unchanged. The character for the reducible representation $\Gamma_{3\sigma}$ generated by the set of bonds is therefore

	E	$2C_3$	$3C_2$	σ_h	$2S_3$	$3\sigma_v$
$\Gamma_{3\sigma}$	3	0	1	3	0	1

Application of Eq. (17-16) gives

$$a_{A_1'} = \tfrac{1}{12}[(3)(1) + 2(0)(1) + 3(1)(1) + (3)(1) + 2(0)(1) + 3(1)(1)] = 1.$$

The A_1' irreducible representation is thus contained once. On repeating the calculation for each irreducible representation of the D_{3h} group in turn, it is found that the coefficient is zero for all except E', for which it is again unity. Thus $\Gamma_{3\sigma}$ spans the $A_1' + E'$ irreducible representations. Consultation of the last two columns of the character table shows that the algebraic functions of the correct symmetry are $(x^2 + y^2)$ or z^2 for A_1' and (x, y) or $(x^2 - y^2, xy)$ for E'. The E' irreducible representation is a two-dimensional one and the functions *must* be taken together. The function $(x^2 + y^2)$ corresponds to a circle, and since the molecule is planar, this is the projection of an s orbital. Thus a combination s, p_x, p_y would do for bonding—this is just the hybrid bond combination discussed in Section 16-10. Another possibility is s, $d_{x^2-y^2}$, d_{xy}. The choice between these two combinations is made on the basis of whether it is the p or d orbitals that are the more stable. This is easy in the case of BF_3 since the outer electrons of boron occupy 2p orbitals, and the lowest d ones, 3d, would be very high in energy. In a less extreme case it may be appropriate to use a linear combination of the two sets of orbitals.

Notice that in this approach the fluorine atoms are really irrelevant. We are determining what orbital combinations for the central atom will have the proper symmetry to form sigma bonds in the observed bonding directions.

A second example is CH_4 (or any tetrahedral molecule), for which the point group is T_d. Turning to the character table for this group, we find

	E	$8C_3$	$3C_2$	$6S_4$	$6\sigma_d$
$\Gamma_{4\sigma}$	4	1	0	0	2

Application of Eq. (17-16) gives $\Gamma_{4\sigma} = A_1 + T_2$. The IR A_1 corresponds to $x^2 + y^2 + z^2$, or to a sphere, and hence to an s orbital. The IR T_2 is generated by (x, y, z) or (xy, xz, yz). The bonding can thus be $sp_x p_y p_z$ or $sd_{xy}d_{xz}d_{yz}$; it can be some combination of both types if the p and d orbitals are similar in energy. The first choice is obvious in the case of CH_4 and is the set given in Section 16-10 in the discussion of hybrid orbitals. The tetrahedral molecule $CoCl_4^{2-}$ might, however, use the $sd_{xy}d_{xz}d_{yz}$ combination, in view of the availability of cobalt d orbitals. Decisions of this type rest on quantitative calculations.

For a molecule having O_h symmetry, such as $Co(NH_3)_6^{3+}$ (considering only the Co and N atoms) the result is

	E	$8C_3$	$6C_2$	$6C_4$	$3C_2$	i	$6S_4$	$8S_6$	$3\sigma_h$	$6\sigma_d$
$\Gamma_{6\sigma}$	6	0	0	2	2	0	0	0	4	2

We now find $\Gamma_{6\sigma} = A_{1g} + T_{1u} + E_g$, which corresponds to the orbital set $sd_{z^2}d_{x^2-y^2}p_x p_y p_z$ (often reported as just d^2sp^3). A linear combination of these orbitals will indeed generate a set of new orbitals having lobes pointing to the corners of an octahedron.

As a final example, consider the molecule H_2O. This belongs to the C_{2v} group, and the procedure yields

	E	C_2	$\sigma_v(xz)$	$\sigma_v'(yz)$
$\Gamma_{2\sigma}$	2	0	2	0

with the conclusion that $\Gamma_{2\sigma} = A_1 + B_1$. From the character table the bonding might involve some combination of s, p_x, and p_z. This answer does not seem very helpful, that is, it does not suggest why the experimental bond angle in water is 104°27′. It should be recognized at this point that the oxygen atom has two additional pairs of electrons; these are not used in bonding in H_2O but are used, for example, in the hydrogen-bonded structures present in liquid water and in ice (see Section 8-CN-2). Since the treatment centers on the oxygen atom it is more realistic to view it as having four more or less tetrahedrally disposed pairs of electrons, of which two happen to be shared in a bond. The point is that the treatment described here works best for coordinatively saturated atoms; a useful alternative approach for an AB_2 type of molecule is given in Section 17-CN-2.

B. Pi Bonds

The term pi bond applies to a bonding overlap where there is a node along the bonding axis, that is, the electron density is zero along the line of the sigma bond. Figure 17-13 illustrates some typical pi bonding orbital combinations, assuming

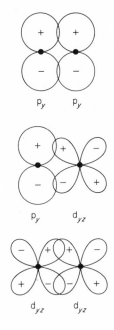

Fig. 17-13. *Arrangements of orbitals showing pi bonding for the case of an A—B molecule.*

the bond to lie on the x axis. The figures suggest, and calculation confirms, that the value of a pi-bonding overlap integral is in general smaller than that of a sigma-bonding one (see Section 17-CN-1). As a consequence, pi bonding is considered not so much as providing the primary bonding holding a molecule together as supplementing an already present sigma bond.

The symmetry approach may again be used. As shown in Fig. 17-14, pi bonds

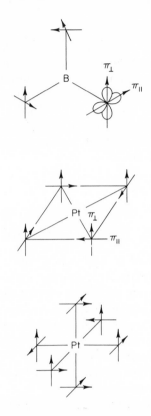

Fig. 17-14.   *Pi bonding vectors.*

must be represented by vectors since there is a plus-to-minus direction. Usually, two such vectors at right angles to each other must be considered. Various symmetry operations of the molecular point group may now leave pi bond vectors unchanged in position but reversed in sign; as noted at the beginning of this section, the rule is then that -1 is contributed to the trace of the representation generated by the pi bonding set. Also, one may consider each set of mutually perpendicular vectors separately.

For example, a D_{3h} molecule such as BF_3 or NO_3^- generates the traces shown in Table 17-8, where $\Gamma_{3\pi\parallel}$ and $\Gamma_{3\pi\perp}$ denote the sets of pi bonding vectors parallel to and perpendicular to the molecular plane, respectively. Application of Eq. (17-16) leads to the result

$$\Gamma_{3\pi\perp} = A_2'' + E'', \qquad \Gamma_{3\pi\parallel} = A_2' + E',$$

Table 17-8.

	E	$2C_3$	$3C_2$	σ_h	$2S_3$	$3\sigma_v$
$\Gamma_{3\pi\perp}$	3	0	-1	-3	0	1
$\Gamma_{3\pi\parallel}$	3	0	-1	3	0	-1

which gives $p_x p_y$ as suitable bonding orbitals. We exclude d_{xz}, d_{yz}, listed for E'', as energetically unavailable, and the other irreducible representations do not correspond to any hydrogen-like orbitals. However, $p_x p_y$ is also suitable for sigma bonding, and we assume that this type of overlap will take precedence over the pi bonding type. It appears that molecules such as BF_3 have mainly sigma bonding.

Turning next to the D_{4h} molecule $PtCl_4^{2-}$, we find the situation shown in Table 17-9. Application of Eq. (17-16) yields

$$\Gamma_{4\sigma} = A_{1g} + B_{1g} + E_u \qquad \text{or} \qquad d_{z^2}, d_{x^2-y^2}, (p_x p_y),$$

$$\Gamma_{4\pi\parallel} = A_{2g} + B_{2g} + E_u \qquad \text{or} \qquad d_{xy}, (p_x p_y),$$

$$\Gamma_{4\pi\perp} = A_{2u} + B_{2u} + E_g \qquad \text{or} \qquad p_z, (d_{xz} d_{yz}).$$

The sigma bonds are thus dsp^2 in type, leaving the d_{ij} set and p_z available for some pi bonding. We assume in the latter case that the ligands are suitably disposed, that is, have available electrons in pi bonding orbitals to enter empty metal orbitals, or vice versa. Since Pt(II) has eight d electrons of its own and chloride ion has a full octet of electrons, neither the ligands nor the central metal ion has empty pi-type orbitals to accommodate the other's electrons. The conclusion, in the case of $PtCl_4^{2-}$, is that pi bonding is unimportant. Cyanide ion, however, does have some empty pi bonding type orbitals, and the $Pt(CN)_4^{2-}$ complex is considered to have both sigma and pi bonding.

Finally, and in abbreviated fashion, the situation for the combined sets of pi bonds of an O_h complex is

	E	C_3	$6C_2'$	$6C_4$	$3C_2$	i	$6S_4$	$8S_6$	$3\sigma_h$	$6\sigma_d$
$\Gamma_{12\pi}$	12	0	0	0	-4	0	0	0	0	0

This corresponds to $T_{1g} + T_{2g} + T_{1u} + T_{2u}$ or $(d_{xy} d_{xz} d_{yz})$, $(p_x p_y p_z)$. There are only six appropriate orbitals, of which the set $(p_x p_y p_z)$ is preempted by sigma

Table 17-9.

	E	$2C_4$	C_2	$2C_2'$	$2C_2''$	i	$2S_4$	σ_h	$2\sigma_v$	$2\sigma_d$
$\Gamma_{4\sigma}$	4	0	0	2	0	0	0	4	2	0
$\Gamma_{4\pi\parallel}$	4	0	0	-2	0	0	0	4	-2	0
$\Gamma_{4\pi\perp}$	4	0	0	-2	0	0	0	-4	2	0

bonding. We conclude that only the set d_{ij} is available for pi bonding in an O_h complex. The actual degree of such bonding will depend on the particular central metal ion and the ligands. The ion Cr(III) has only three d electrons and could accept or donate pi bonding electron density from or to ligand pi-type orbitals. If the ligand is NH_3, as in $Cr(NH_3)_6^{3+}$, the nitrogen is surrounded by hydrogen atoms, so no pi bonding at all is possible. Ligands such as Cl^- might donate some pi bonding electrons to Cr(III) and ligands such as CN^- might accept some.

These examples illustrate how symmetry plus ancillary considerations allow the physical chemist to draw qualitative conclusions as to the bonding in coordination compounds. The treatment of pi bonding in organic molecules generally involves multicenter situations, as in $CH_2=CH_2$ or benzene, and these are usually treated by a molecular orbital approach (see Commentary and Notes and Special Topics sections).

COMMENTARY AND NOTES

17-CN-1   The Chemical Bond. The Valence Bond Method

The group-theoretical approach makes it possible to determine what mixture of hydrogen-like orbitals a central atom should use in forming bonds with its neighbors, given a known molecular geometry. As outlined in Section 17-7, this information is enough for many purposes; also, some further discussion of the application of group theory to coordination compounds is given in Section 17-CN-3.

Numerical calculations of optimum bond distances and corresponding bond dissociation energies constitute a much more formidable task, even for diatomic molecules. Consider, for example, two hydrogen atoms or any two atoms A and B which are treated as hydrogen-like. The complete Hamiltonian is†

$$\mathbf{H} = -\frac{h^2}{8\pi^2 m}\left[\nabla^2(1) + \nabla^2(2)\right] - e^2\left(\frac{Z_A}{r_{A,1}} + \frac{Z_B}{r_{B,1}} + \frac{Z_A}{r_{A,2}} + \frac{Z_B}{r_{B,2}}\right)$$

$$+ e^2\left(\frac{Z_A Z_B}{r_{AB}} + \frac{1}{r_{12}}\right). \tag{17-17}$$

† The ∇^2 terms for the two nuclei have been omitted; this can be shown to be a reasonable approximation because nuclear masses are so large compared to the electron mass that the electrons adjust instantaneously to the nuclear motions. As a consequence, we treat the energy of nuclear motions separately as vibrational energy (note Sections 16-6 and 18-5) and assume that the amount of vibrational energy present simply adds to the energy of the electronic state.

The potential energy terms include the Coulomb attraction of electron 1 to atoms A and B, and likewise that of electron 2. The remaining terms give the internuclear repulsion and the interelectronic repulsion. The factors Z_A and Z_B are the nuclear charges—in general the effective charges, or the respective atomic numbers corrected by screening constants (Section 16-CN-2). While Eq. (17-17) has not been solved exactly in explicit form, approximation methods allow accurate solutions in the case of low atomic number diatomic molecules.

The two principal approaches are known as the *valence bond* and the *molecular orbital* methods, and we consider each in turn. In the valence bond method one considers a pair of atoms at a time and writes an approximate wave function as follows. If atoms A and B are separated, two possible wave functions are

$$\psi_1 = \psi_A(1)\,\psi_B(2), \qquad \psi_2 = \psi_A(2)\,\psi_B(1).$$

That is, electron 1 may stay with atom A and electron 2 with atom B, or vice versa. The approximate wave function is taken to be a linear combination of the two possibilities, that is,

$$\phi = a\psi_1 + b\psi_2 . \tag{17-18}$$

The approximate wave function in the valence bond method is thus assembled as a linear combination of the products of the wave functions for the separated atoms.

In the molecular orbital approach we construct an approximate wave function for the molecule as a whole. Thus for a diatomic molecule we may write

$$\phi = a\psi_A + b\psi_B , \tag{17-19}$$

where ψ_A and ψ_B are suitable atomic orbitals for atoms A and B; in the case of H_2 the 1s orbitals of each hydrogen atom would be used. The principle of this approach is thus to obtain orbitals for the molecule as a whole, into which electrons may then be placed or assigned.

A. Application of the Variation Principle

As discussed in Section 16-CN-3, if some approximate wave function ϕ (which meets the physical boundary conditions) is used as a trial function, then

$$E' = \frac{\int \phi^* H\phi \, d\tau}{\int \phi^* \phi \, d\tau} \qquad \text{[Eq. (16-101)]}.$$

Here **H** is the exact Hamiltonian, and according to the variation theorem, the calculated energy E' may be greater than the true energy but never less than it. If atoms A and B are the same, then it can be shown (by the method outlined in Section 17-ST-1) that the lowest E' is obtained if coefficients a and b of Eq. (17-18) are unity, or

$$\phi_1 = \psi_1 + \psi_2 . \tag{17-20}$$

Equation (16-101) then becomes

$$E_1 = \frac{\int (\psi_1^* + \psi_2^*) \, \mathbf{H}(\psi_1 + \psi_2) \, d\tau}{\int (\psi_1^* + \psi_2^*)(\psi_1 + \psi_2) \, d\tau}. \qquad (17\text{-}21)$$

We now simplify the notation by the introduction of the definitions

$$H_{11} = \int \psi_1^* \mathbf{H} \psi_1 \, d\tau, \qquad H_{12} = \int \psi_1^* \mathbf{H} \psi_2 \, d\tau, \qquad \text{and so on,}$$

$$\qquad (17\text{-}22)$$

$$S_{11} = \int \psi_1^* \psi_1 \, d\tau, \qquad S_{12} = \int \psi_1^* \psi_2 \, d\tau, \qquad \text{and so on.}$$

Since A and B are the same, $H_{12} = H_{21}$ and $S_{12} = S_{21}$, so

$$E_1 = \frac{H_{11} + H_{12}}{1 + S_{12}}. \qquad (17\text{-}23)$$

Integrals of the type H_{11} are known as *Coulomb integrals* (two-center in this case since **H** involves both atoms); those of the type H_{12} are called exchange or *resonance integrals*; and those of type S_{12} are called *overlap integrals*. Since ψ_A and ψ_B are assumed to be normalized, S_{11} and S_{22} are equal to unity.

These three types of integrals have been evaluated rather accurately for pairs of hydrogen-like atoms using modern computer methods. Calculations for the case of two hydrogen atoms give the results shown in Fig. 17-15, for example. The integrals H_{11} and H_{12} are negative for most interatomic distances, the latter

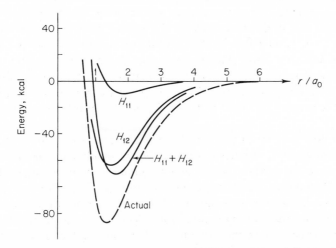

Fig. 17-15. *Plots of the total energy, Coulomb energy, and exchange energy for* H_2 *as a function of internuclear distance. The upper, repulsive curve corresponds to the second possible linear combination,* $\psi_1 - \psi_2$ *[see Eq. (17-25)]. The energy scale is actually* $E/(1 + S^2)$. *(From C. A. Coulson, "Valence," 2nd ed. Oxford Univ. Press, London and New York, 1961.)*

more so; the sum goes through a minimum around $1.7a_0$, where a_0 is the radius of the first Bohr orbit. The integral S_{12} may be written S^2, where S is the one-electron overlap integral,

$$ S = \int \psi_A(1)\, \psi_B(1)\, d\tau = \int \psi_A(2)\, \psi_B(2)\, d\tau. \qquad (17\text{-}24) $$

In the actual evaluation of S (and of the H's), one uses the elliptical coordinate system shown in Fig. 17-16. The angle ϕ is that between the xz plane and the

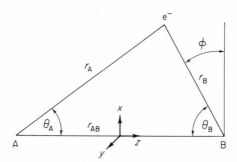

Fig. 17-16.   *The elliptical coordinate system.*

plane defined by A, B, and the electron. The calculation of S is relatively straight-forward and has been made for hydrogen-like wave functions for a variety of n and ℓ values [see Mulliken *et al.* (1949)]. Some representative results are shown in Fig. 17-17 for the case of two carbon atoms (using the appropriate Z_{eff}). There is not a great deal of difference in S for the various types of orbitals beyond about 1.5 Å (the C—C bond length is 1.54 Å), although that for the two pi-bonding type orbitals is distinctly lower than the rest. The 2s–2pσ and 2pσ–2pσ integrals go through a maximum, and the latter can actually be negative because at small distances oppositely signed lobes of the p orbitals begin to overlap (these are p$_x$ orbitals if x denotes the bond axis, that is, they are p orbitals of sigma bonding symmetry).

We can now see that in terms of Eq. (17-23) it is the Coulomb and exchange integrals that make E_1 negative (corresponding to bonding in our sign convention) and that while the overlap integral acts to diminish the denominator (S_{12} always being less than unity), it does not determine the sign of E_1. However, as discussed in Section 17-7, one often uses the rule of thumb that a proper overlap of bonding orbitals is needed for a strong bond to form. The rule is a good one in spite of the preceding comment, since the Coulomb and exchange integrals are often roughly proportional to the overlap integral.

This qualitative use of the overlap idea was extended by L. Pauling to the case of hybrid orbitals. The maximum value of the trigonometric portion gives a measure of the "reach" of an orbital in the direction of its greatest amplitude.

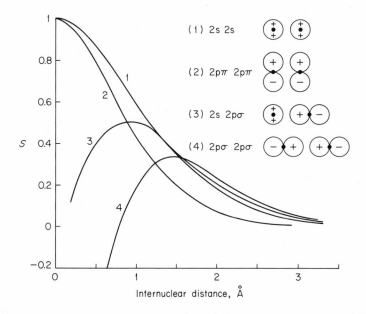

Fig. 17-17. *Overlap integrals S for various pairs of orbitals. [See R. S. Mulliken, C. A. Rieke, D. Orloff, and H. Orloff, J. Chem. Phys.* **17**, *1248 (1949).]*

The more precise observation is that for a given bond distance, S for sp^3, sp^2, and sp hybrid orbitals increases in that order.

Returning to Eq. (17-20), a second combination of ψ_1 and ψ_2 is possible,

$$\phi_2 = \psi_1 - \psi_2. \tag{17-25}$$

This leads to the energy

$$E_2 = \frac{H_{11} - H_{12}}{1 - S_{12}}. \tag{17-26}$$

Figure 17-15 shows that for H_2 the quantity $H_{11} - H_{12}$ is positive at all internuclear distances, so ϕ_2 corresponds to a repulsion between the atoms. We speak of ϕ_1 as a *bonding* wave function and ϕ_2 as an *antibonding* wave function. The result is characteristic: For every combination of atomic wave functions that leads to bonding there is always a related antibonding combination.

B. Results for H_2

The valence bond method, as it is now called, was originally developed by W. Heitler and F. London in their treatment of the hydrogen molecule. Again, Fig. 17-15 summarizes the results. [It should now be noted that H_{11}, H_{12}, and their sum and difference have been divided by $1 - S_{12}$ so that the energy scale should be read with this in mind.] The minimum energy occurs at 0.80 Å and -74 kcal mole^{-1}, as compared with the experimental values (dashed curve) of 0.74 Å and 108.9 kcal mole^{-1}. Note that it is the exchange integral H_{12} that supplies over 90% of the bond energy. The physical explanation of this integral is that the electrons, being indistinguishable, are not localized about the nuclei with which they were associated in the separated atoms, but expand over the system of both atoms. Without this exchange effect only a rather weak bond (given by the H_{11} contribution) would be expected.

C. The Spin Function

Complete wave functions will include the spin wave function—an item not so far mentioned. This function is essentially an algebraic mnemonic device for the automatic remembering that each electron has two states of angular momentum: either $\frac{1}{2}(h/2\pi)$ or $-\frac{1}{2}(h/2\pi)$, or ω and $-\omega$. The energies of these states are unaffected by the potential energy function for the atom or molecule although they are altered by an external magnetic field (see Sections 3-ST-2 and 18-CN-1).

The spin wave function is, accordingly, a rather peculiar one. There are really two functions, α and β, defined as having the values 1 or 0 according to the convention

$$\alpha(\omega) = 1, \quad \alpha(-\omega) = 0; \quad \beta(-\omega) = 1, \quad \beta(\omega) = 0. \quad (17\text{-}27)$$

The probability associated with the spin functions is treated in the same manner as for ordinary wave functions, and using the preceding conventions we have

$$\int \alpha(\omega)^2 \, d\omega = 1, \quad \int \alpha(\omega)\,\beta(\omega)\, d\omega = 0, \quad \int \beta(\omega)^2 \, d\omega = 1.$$

These integrals imply a summation over the two possible values of the ω products.

In writing a complete wave equation, one then includes $\alpha(\omega)$ or $\beta(\omega)$ as a factor. For example, ψ_{1s} becomes $\psi_{1s}\alpha$ or $\psi_{1s}\beta$. In the case of a molecule such as H_2 there are two electrons to consider, and the possible combinations of the spin functions are

$$\alpha(1)\,\alpha(2), \quad \beta(1)\,\beta(2), \quad [\alpha(1)\,\beta(2) + \alpha(2)\,\beta(1)] \quad \text{symmetric,}$$
$$(17\text{-}28)$$
$$[\alpha(1)\,\beta(2) - \alpha(2)\,\beta(1)] \quad \text{antisymmetric.}$$

These correspond to the four different ways of assigning electrons 1 and 2 between two atoms. Three of the combinations are unchanged in sign if the coordinates of the electrons are exchanged, and are therefore said to be symmetric; one function is antisymmetric.

We can now return to Eqs. (17-20) and (17-25) to write

$$[\psi_A(1)\,\psi_B(2) + \psi_A(2)\,\psi_B(1)][\alpha(1)\,\beta(2) - \alpha(2)\,\beta(1)] \qquad \text{singlet,}$$

$$[\psi_A(1)\,\psi_B(2) - \psi_A(2)\,\psi_B(1)] \begin{cases} \alpha(1)\,\alpha(2) \\ \beta(1)\,\beta(2) \\ \alpha(1)\,\beta(2) + \alpha(2)\,\beta(1) \end{cases} \qquad \text{triplet.} \qquad (17\text{-}29)$$

The restriction of choice to these combinations follows from an alternative state-ment of the *Pauli exclusion principle*: Every allowable wave function for a system of two or more electrons must be antisymmetric for the simultaneous interchange of the position and spin coordinates of any pair of electrons. This statement implies the usual one that no two electrons can have the same four quantum numbers. The first function of Eqs. (17-29) is symmetric in the spatial wave func-tions, and so must be antisymmetric in the spin function; as only one possible spin function of this type is available, there is only one complete wave function, and the state is called a *singlet* state. The *triplet* state is so called because it is triply degenerate in the spin function; since the wave function is antisymmetric, any one of the three possible symmetric spin functions may be used.

It is customary to designate the spin *multiplicity* or degeneracy by a left super-script to the symbol describing the state. Thus the singlet and triplet states of H_2 are designated $^1\Sigma_g$ and $^3\Sigma_u$, respectively. The symbol Σ is used to mean that the angular momentum of the state is zero about the internuclear axis, and g and u inform us that the wave functions are symmetric and antisymmetric with respect to inversion, respectively. It will be recalled that the triplet state is a high-energy, repulsive one, while the singlet state is the bonding and lowest-energy or ground state of H_2. There are, of course, many yet more energetic states than the $^3\Sigma_u$ one; these can be regarded as involving the mixing of 2s, 2p, ... orbitals (see Sec-tion 18-2).

D. Inclusion of Other Configurations

Somewhat improved results can be obtained for H_2 if ϕ is taken to be

$$\phi = \psi_A(1)\,\psi_B(2) + \psi_A(2)\,\psi_B(1) + \alpha[\psi_A(1)\,\psi_A(2) + \psi_B(1)\,\psi_B(2)]. \quad (17\text{-}30)$$

The last two terms correspond to H^-H^+ and H^+H^-, respectively. The variation method is used to find the optimum value for α, and the best calculated value for E_1 is now -94 kcal mole^{-1}.

The inclusion of such ionic configurations is often needed in the valence bond method. A molecule is sometimes said to resonate among various structures, the so-called *resonance* structures. It must be remembered, however, that a *single* wave function describes the state of the molecule. The so-called resonance struc-tures are merely the components of a linear combination of wave functions that has been assembled in an effort to approximate the correct one. It is particularly important not to be misled into supposing that the molecule is somehow flickering between different electronic configurations. Thus when one writes the valence bond structures for CO_2,

$$O=C=O, \qquad O^+\equiv C-O^-, \qquad O^--C\equiv O^+,$$

the actual structure is being taken to be their superposition. The structures need not include ionic ones; in the case of benzene, the various forms include ones such as

17-CN-2   The Molecular Orbital Method

A.   Diatomic Molecules

As noted in the preceding section, an alternative and very useful way of generating an approximate wave function for use in applying the variation method to molecules is the *molecular orbital* method. It will be recalled that in the valence bond approach the approximate wave function for a diatomic molecule ϕ was obtained as a linear combination of the products of the atomic wave functions for the two separate atoms [Eq. (17-18)]. In the molecular orbital approach we construct an approximate wave function for the molecule as a whole and write for a diatomic molecule

$$\phi = a\psi_A + b\psi_B = n(\psi_A + \lambda\psi_B), \qquad (17\text{-}31)$$

where n is a normalization factor and λ is an adjustable constant. The ψ_A and ψ_B are suitable combinations of atomic orbitals on atoms A and B. This means of constructing ϕ is known as the *LCAO* approximation—*linear combination of atomic orbitals*. If the molecule is H_2^+ or H_2, the 1s orbitals of each hydrogen atom are the appropriate ones to use in obtaining the lowest-energy molecular orbitals (and in this case $\lambda = \pm 1$ since the atoms are the same).

In general, ψ_A and ψ_B are not the same functions and the variation method is used to find an optimum value for the mixing coefficient λ. On doing this (and eliminating λ), we find

$$(E - E_A)(E - E_B) = (H_{AB} - ES_{AB})^2, \qquad (17\text{-}32)$$

where E_A and E_B are the energies associated with the atomic orbitals (and are equal to the integrals $\int \psi_A^* H\psi_A \, d\tau$ and $\int \psi_B^* H\psi_B \, d\tau$, also called Coulomb integrals, although not the same ones as in the valence bond method); E is the energy of the best molecular orbital function ϕ. The quantity H_{AB} is the integral $\int \psi_A * H \psi_B \, d\tau$ (also called a resonance integral, although again not the same one as described in the preceding section) and S_{AB} is the overlap integral $\int \psi_A \psi_B \, d\tau$, which is the same as the S integral described earlier. Equation (17-32) has two roots, so that two combinations of ψ_A and ψ_B in Eq. (17-31) are indicated, a bonding and an antibonding molecular orbital. In the case of H_2^+ these two states are called $1s\sigma_g$ and $1s\sigma_u*$ where σ denotes the symmetry of the molecular orbital relative to the bond axis and $1s$ the atomic orbital used. The contours for the corresponding ϕ^2's are shown in Fig. 17-18.

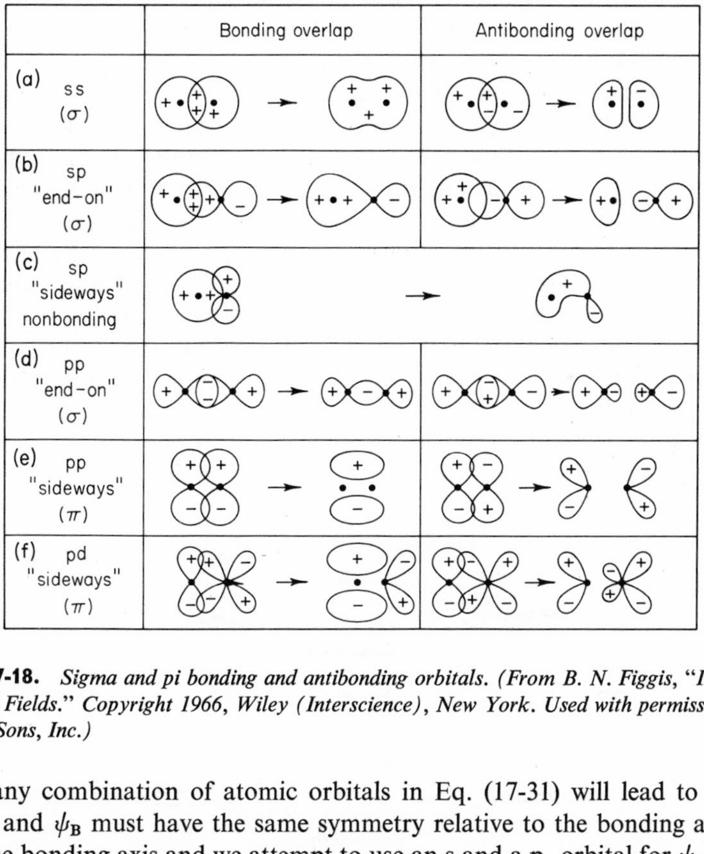

		Bonding overlap	Antibonding overlap
(a)	ss (σ)		
(b)	sp "end-on" (σ)		
(c)	sp "sideways" nonbonding		
(d)	pp "end-on" (σ)		
(e)	pp "sideways" (π)		
(f)	pd "sideways" (π)		

Fig. 17-18. *Sigma and pi bonding and antibonding orbitals. (From B. N. Figgis, "Introduction to Ligand Fields." Copyright 1966, Wiley (Interscience), New York. Used with permission of John Wiley & Sons, Inc.)*

Not any combination of atomic orbitals in Eq. (17-31) will lead to bonding. The ψ_A and ψ_B must have the same symmetry relative to the bonding axis. Thus if x is the bonding axis and we attempt to use an s and a p_y orbital for ψ_A and ψ_B, the molecular orbital energy turns out to be just E_A or E_B; that is, no interaction results. This is a consequence of the fact that H_{AB} and S_{AB} are separable into integrals of equal magnitude and opposite sign and are therefore zero (note Fig. 17-11). As noted earlier, the situation is known as nonbonding. Pairs of orbitals which behave this way are also called orthogonal.

Proceeding further, one may construct molecular orbitals from p-type atomic orbitals. If p_x orbitals are used, the resulting bonding and antibonding molecular orbitals are again of the sigma type, and are called pσ and pσ*, respectively. If, however, two p_y or two p_z atomic orbitals are used, the resulting molecular orbitals appear as shown in Fig. 17-18(e); they have a node along the bonding axis and are called pi-type orbitals, pπ and pπ*. A useful point is that a molecular orbital will always transform as one of the irreducible representations of the point group to which the molecule belongs.

A particular collection of molecular orbitals is shown in Fig. 17-19, ordered approximately as to energy. The designations g and u are applied if the molecule is a homonuclear one; g if the orbital is symmetric to inversion and u if it is anti-symmetric. As discussed later, molecular orbital diagrams of this type are useful in determining the electronic configuration of diatomic molecules.

At the moment, however, we consider another aspect, illustrated in Fig. 17-20. The right side of the figure shows the energy levels for the separated atoms and the middle shows the molecular orbitals arising from pairs of like atomic orbitals. The abscissa scale is one of internuclear distance, and at the extreme left the two atoms have merged to a single nucleus or *united atom* (He if two H atoms merge, for example), with corresponding energy levels. Such a diagram is known as a *correlation* diagram. A rule that we will not prove here is that states of the same orbital symmetry cannot cross; thus a σ_g can never cross another σ_g, and so on; a qualitative physical explanation is that at such a crossing one has two states of the same symmetry and the same energy, and a new linear combination must occur such that one state is raised and the other lowered in energy, the effect being that such lines in a correlation diagram must avoid each other.

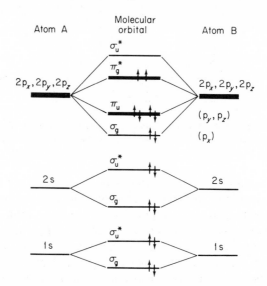

Fig. 17-19.   *Molecular orbital energy level diagram for O_2.*

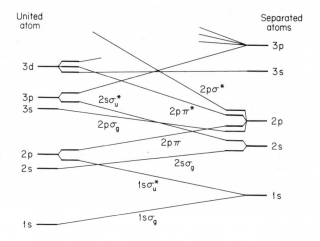

Fig. 17-20. *Correlation diagram showing how molecular orbital energies change with inter-nuclear distance in an A—A-type molecule. (From C. A. Coulson, "Valence," 2nd ed. Oxford Univ. Press, London and New York, 1961.)*

Note in Fig. 17-20 that bonding orbitals drop in energy as the united atom state is approached, while antibonding orbitals increase in energy. Of course, two atoms will not spontaneously fuse into a united atom! The internuclear repulsion has been omitted in the diagram; the actual equilibrium internuclear distance can be obtained (in principle) if this repulsion is included in the calculation.

We now return to Fig. 17-19 to discuss the electronic configuration of homonuclear diatomic molecules. The procedure is to fill the molecular orbitals with the requisite number of electrons, each orbital accomodating a pair with opposed spins. The H_2 molecule has the configuration $(1s\sigma_g)^2$ and He_2 has $(1s\sigma_g)^2 (1s\sigma_u{}^*)^2$. In this last case there are two electrons in a bonding and two in a nonbonding orbital; the net situation is equivalent to one of essentially no bonding, as observed—He_2 is not a stable molecule. However, an electronically excited He_2 molecule of configuration $(1s\sigma_g)^2 (1s\sigma_u{}^*)(2s\sigma_g)$ should have a net bonding, as is actually found to be the case.

Moving to second-row elements of the periodic table, Li_2 has the configuration $(2s\sigma_g)^2$ (the inner electrons make no net contribution and therefore are ignored); the molecule should exist, and does—its dissociation energy is about 1 eV. The Be_2 molecule should be like He_2—it is, in fact, not known. The next elements now involve 2p orbitals, which may be either $2p\sigma$ or $2p\pi$ in type.

The cases of N_2 and O_2 are especially interesting. The first has the configuration $(2s\sigma_g)^2 (2s\sigma_u{}^*)^2 (2p\sigma)^2 (2p\pi_u)^4$. There are two $2p\pi_u$ orbitals of equal energy (or degenerate) so that four electrons may be accommodated; they are bonding, so N_2 has a net of six bonding electrons, corresponding to the triple bond in the usual formula. The O_2 molecule is $(2s\sigma_g)^2 (2s\sigma_u{}^*)^2 (2p\sigma_g)^2(2p\pi_u)^4 (2p\pi_g)^2$ and therefore has a net of four bonding electrons, corresponding to a double bond ($2p\pi_g$ being antibonding). Since the $2p\pi_g$ set is only half filled, the pair of electrons in it are not required to pair their spin and, by Hund's rule (see Section 18-ST-4), do not. As a consequence, the ground state of oxygen is a paramagnetic one, called $^3\Sigma$, corresponding to two unpaired electrons. The situation is illustrated in Fig. 17-19.

These examples illustrate one important application of the molecular orbital approach. If one neglects interelectronic repulsions, a set of molecular orbital states is obtained into which the proper number of electrons are fed. One thus obtains a good qualitative understanding of the geometry of the filled orbitals and, as in the case of O_2, can predict cases of paramagnetism. In addition, it is easy to describe excited states as configurations in which one or more electrons are promoted to higher-energy molecular orbitals. This aspect will be discussed further in Chapter 18.

B. Triatomic Molecules. Walsh Diagrams

The bonding in triatomic and in MX_n-type molecules may be treated in terms of atomic orbitals suitably hybridized so as to give a maximum overlap in the bonding directions. The use of group theory for determining what combinations of orbitals should be hybridized for the central atom is discussed earlier in this chapter (Section 17-7) and the bonding can then be treated in terms of molecular orbitals formed between the hybrid orbital and an orbital on each of the X atoms.

While absolute bonding energies are very difficult to calculate, it is possible to reach qualitative conclusions about how the energies of the various molecular orbitals vary with geometry. The simplest case is that of the MH_2 molecule. If it is linear, the molecular orbitals may be of the sigma type, formed between the 1s hydrogen atomic orbitals and the sp_x hybrid orbital of the M atom (x being the H—M—H axis). One then obtains a pair of orbitals σ_g and σ_u, the first being lower in energy. The remaining p_y and p_z orbitals of M are pi in type and nonbonding; the molecular orbital is designated π_u and is twofold degenerate.

Consider next the situation if the H—M—H angle is 90°. The molecule is now C_{2v} in symmetry, with irreducible representations A_1, A_2, B_1, and B_2. A sigma M—H bond can be formed by the overlap of a pure p orbital on M with the 1s orbital on H, and the two M—H bonds would then involve the p_z and p_y M orbitals. These are equivalent, however, and the corresponding molecular orbitals are formed by taking the in-phase and the out-of-phase combinations of the two localized orbitals. The symmetry properties of these two molecular orbitals identify them as belonging to the a_1 and b_2 irreducible representations. (It is customary to use lower case letters in giving the IR to which a molecular orbital belongs.) The remaining p orbital is nonbonding and belongs to the b_1 irreducible representation. Finally, the s orbital on M is also nonbonding and has the symmetry designation a_1.

One may now assemble the correlation diagram shown in Fig. 17-21 [see Walsh (1953)]. As the H—M—H angle is increased from 90° the a_1 and b_2 bonding orbitals must eventually become the σ_g and σ_u orbitals, respectively, of the linear molecule. At the same time the binding energy of the orbitals must increase—one way of seeing this is that increasing s character develops in the bonds and sp hybrid orbitals give rise to a stronger bond than do those for pure p. Figure 17-21 is obtained from such considerations plus the no-crossing rule mentioned in connection with Fig. 17-20.

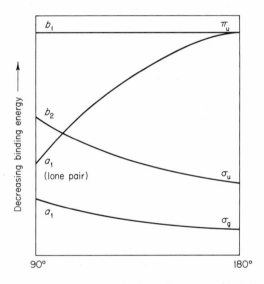

Fig. 17-21. *Qualitative variation of molecular orbital energies with bond angle for an* MH_2*-type molecule.* [*From A. D. Walsh, J. Chem. Soc.* **1953**, *2260 (1953).*]

While the energy scale is qualitative, the figure does allow some conclusions as to molecular geometry. A given MH_2 molecule will have a certain number of outer electrons, to be placed in the lowest possible molecular orbitals; each orbital has a capacity of two electrons (with spins opposed). A molecule such as BeH_2 or HgH_2 has four outer electrons, so that the σ_g and σ_u orbitals are just filled. The linear configuration is the lowest-energy one, so these molecules are predicted to be linear. On the other hand, MH_2 molecules having five, six, seven, or eight valence electrons should be bent. This is the case with H_2O, for example. The actual angle cannot be obtained from Fig. 17-21; it would be determined as the optimum compromise between the opposite trends of the a_1 (s) orbital and the a_1 and b_1 orbitals. Similarly, the molecule CH_2 should be bent, but less so in that excited state which has an electron promoted to the b_1 orbital (why?). Walsh diagrams thus also allow predictions of how molecular geometry should change in excited states (see also Section 18-CN-2); more complex diagrams are available for MA_2 (A $\neq$ H) molecules, and so on.

The molecular orbital method has been applied to polyatomic molecules, especially to conjugated organic ones. A rather crude version was discussed in Section 16-5, in which the conjugated system is treated as a box in which pi electrons are confined. A more refined, although still approximate approach is again to construct molecular orbitals by the LCAO method. The treatment is described in the Special Topics section.

17-CN-3   Crystal Field Theory

An important application of group theory is to the case of a transition metal ion which is in an environment of octahedral symmetry. The ion may be held in a crystal lattice, as is the case for Cr^{3+} in aluminium oxide (ruby is an example), or it may be a complex ion having six ligands in octahedral coordination.

We can now use a set of metal orbitals as the basis for a representation in the O_h point group. A metal s orbital is unchanged by all of the symmetry operations, and hence belongs to the A_{1g} IR (see Table 17-7). The set of three p orbitals ($4p_x, 4p_y, 4p_z$ for a first-row transition metal) generates the traces shown in Table 17-10. (As in Section 17-7B, 1 is entered if the orbital is unchanged, -1 if it is inverted, and 0 otherwise.) The set of traces for Γ_{p^3} is just that for the T_{1u} IR. Finally, if the process is repeated for the set of five d orbitals ($3d_{xy}, 3d_{yz}, 3d_{xz}, 3d_{x^2-y^2}, 3d_{z^2}$ for a first-row transition metal), one obtains for Γ_{d^5}: $(5, 1, 1, -1, 1, 5, -1, -1, 1, 1)$. On applying Eq. (17-16), we find that this corresponds to $E_g + T_{2g}$.

We found in Section 17-7 that a set of six sigma bonds corresponds to the $A_1 + T_{1u} + E_g$ irreducible representations, which are compatible with the s, $p_x p_y p_z$, and $d_{x^2-y^2} d_{z^2}$ hydrogen-like orbital functions. The bonding was thus d^2sp^3 in type. The remaining d_{ij} orbitals belong to the T_{2g} IR; they are not suitable for sigma bonding.

From a geometric point of view, the p- and d-bonding orbitals have lobes directed toward the apexes of the octahedron. The d_{ij} set have lobes directed toward the midpoint of edges, or away from the apexes.

One of the first treatments of this situation was in terms of a transition metal ion in an ionic crystal lattice such that the ion is octahedrally surrounded by negative

Table 17-10.

	E	$8C_3$	$6C_2'$	$6C_4$	$3C_2$	i	$6S_4$	$8S_6$	$3\sigma_h$	$6\sigma_d$
p_x	1	0	0	0	-1	-1	0	0	1	0
p_y	1	0	0	0	-1	-1	0	0	1	0
p_z	1	0	-1	1	1	-1	-1	0	-1	1
Γ_{p^3}	3	0	-1	1	-1	-3	-1	0	1	1

ions. The effect is to create an electrostatic *crystal field* of O_h symmetry, and the model used is one in which point charges are brought up to the apexes of an octahedron centered on the metal ion. As illustrated in Fig. 17-22, several work terms are involved. The point charges are attracted (a) by the nuclear charge of the metal ion and repelled (b) by its electrons. Further, the repulsion is less for electrons in the T_{2g} set (or in t_{2g} orbitals—the d_{ij} ones) than for those in the E_{2g} set. The consequence is that the metal d orbitals are separated (c) into a threefold degenerate set of t_{2g} types and a twofold degenerate set of e_g types. For example,

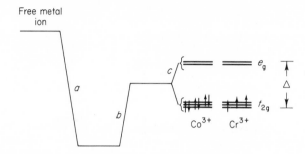

Fig. 17-22. *Schematic illustration of energy contributions as six point charges are brought up to a transition metal ion. (a) Stabilization by attraction between the charges and the metal ion, (b) destabilization due to mutual repulsion between the charges, and (c) splitting of the d-orbital energy levels in the O_h field of the charges.*

Cr^{3+} has three 3d electrons and, as indicated by the arrows, these would be placed in the lower-energy t_{2g} orbitals. An observation, known as *Hund's rule*, is that it takes energy to pair electron spins, so that electrons tend to remain unpaired.

The ion Co^{3+} has six electrons and these all pair up in the t_{2g} set of orbitals—it evidently takes more energy to promote an electron to the e_g orbitals than to pair its spin. The resulting state is therefore diamagnetic.

While the original crystal field treatment due to H. Bethe was applied to ions in a crystal lattice, it became evident that octahedral complexes showed much the same electronic behavior. The six ligands now furnish the octahedral crystal field. The energy Δ to promote an electron from a t_{2g} to an e_g orbital (see Fig. 17-22) can be determined from the absorption spectrum of the complex. The parameter Δ (sometimes referred to as $10Dq$) is a measure of the *crystal field strength*.

As one further example, the empirical observation is that Co^{2+} complexes exhibit a smaller crystal field strength than do Co^{3+} complexes. One consequence is that the separation Δ is now less than the spin pairing energy, so that the seven d electrons of Co^{2+} remain unpaired insofar as possible. The result is to leave three unpaired, so that the complex is paramagnetic. The contrasting situations for Co^{3+} and Co^{2+} with respect to spin pairing are known as the *strong-field* (large-Δ) and *weak-field* (small-Δ) cases.

The purely electrostatic crystal field picture has now given way largely to what is called *ligand field theory*. Perhaps the main change is that bonding is now recognized as occurring between the ligands and the central metal ion. On making up a linear combination of six ligand sigma bonding orbitals and the s, p, $d_{x^2-y^2}$, and d_{z^2} metal orbitals, one, as usual, obtains a bonding and an antibonding set. This is illustrated in Fig. 17-23; the asterisks denote antibonding orbitals. The t_{2g} orbitals are not suited for sigma bonding and therefore do not participate, that is, are nonbonding. Since a set of bonds for the whole molecule is involved, Fig. 17-23

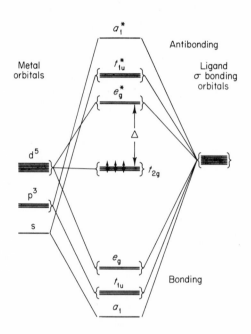

Fig. 17-23. *Sigma bonding molecular orbital diagram for an octahedral transition metal complex.*

is usually called a *molecular orbital diagram*. The small letters a, t_{2g}, and so on are used as a reminder that the energy levels are those which a single electron could have. The bonding levels are, of course, actually occupied by 12 electrons, two from each ligand, and, in the case chosen here, Cr(III), the t_{2g} set is occupied by three electrons, thought of as belonging to the central metal ion.

A point that should be mentioned is that the *set* of nonbonding metal electrons also has a symmetry designation, in this case $^4A_{2g}$. The superscript gives the spin multiplicity or number of energetically equivalent ways in which the spin $S = \frac{3}{2}$ may combine with the orbital angular momentum (see Section 18-ST-4). In the case of Co(III) complexes, the symmetry designation of the *set* of six t_{2g} nonbonding metal electrons is $^1A_{1g}$.

Returning to the figure, the quantity Δ, now called the ligand field strength, is the separation between the t_{2g} and the e_g* sets—it functions in much the same way as in crystal field theory. Its value, however, is now treated as primarily dependent on the strength of the bonding rather than as arising from the octahedrally disposed charges of crystal field theory. We find, for example, that various ligands produce an effective ligand field strength in the order $NH_3 > H_2O > OH^- > Cl^- > Br^-$.

Recalling Section 17-7B, the d_{ij} or t_{2g} set of metal orbitals is suited for pi bonding, the set of 12 pi bonding ligand orbitals also generating the t_{1g}, t_{1u}, and t_{2u} representations in O_h symmetry. One may next obtain bonding and corresponding antibonding combinations of pi symmetry orbitals to give the yet more complete molecular orbital diagram shown in Fig. 17-24. The pi bonding orbitals

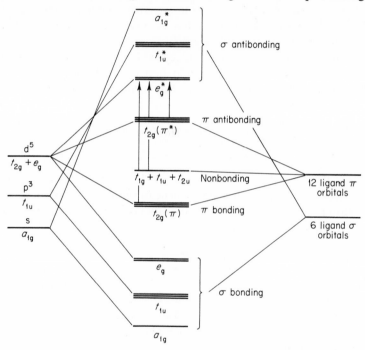

Fig. 17-24. *Same as Fig. 17-23, but also showing pi bonding.*

can hold up to six electrons and the nonbonding ones up to 18. It is not easy to determine the actual degree of pi bonding in a complex ion, and diagrams such as this one are necessarily rather schematic in nature. It is clear, however, that the energy separation Δ between the highest occupied level and the lowest unoccupied level must in reality be a rather complicated quantity.

SPECIAL TOPICS

17-ST-1   *Molecular Orbitals. The Hückel Method*

A number of rather approximate, semiempirical methods have been developed in an effort to calculate or at least to organize in a reasonable way the experimental properties of molecules in which pi bonding seems to be present. A rather useful and widely used approach is the following.

Starting with the variation method (Section 17-CN-1), one way of making a choice for ϕ is to take a linear combination of the lowest occupied atomic orbitals of the set of atoms involved. For two atoms we might then try $\phi = a\psi_1 + b\psi_2$, to obtain

$$\epsilon = \frac{\int (a\psi_1 + b\psi_2)^* \, \mathbf{H}(a\psi_1 + b\psi_2) \, d\tau}{\int (a\psi_1 + b\psi_2)^* \, (a\psi_1 + b\psi_2) \, d\tau} \tag{17-33}$$

(ψ_1 and ψ_2 are the ψ_A and ψ_B of Section 17-CN-1; the change in nomenclature is for convenience). At this point it is convenient to simplify the notation by means of the definitions of Eq. (17-22). Equation (17-33) becomes, on multiplying out the numerator and denominator,

$$\epsilon = \frac{a^2 H_{11} + 2ab H_{12} + b^2 H_{22}}{a^2 S_{11} + 2ab S_{12} + b^2 S_{22}} \tag{17-34}$$

(The distinction between H_{12} and H_{21} is not necessary here.) The next step is to obtain the minimum possible ϵ for the given choice of ψ_1 and ψ_2 as basis functions; this is done by setting $(\partial \epsilon / \partial a)_b = 0$ and $(\partial \epsilon / \partial b)_a = 0$. On carrying out the first differentiation, we obtain

$$\left(\frac{\partial \epsilon}{\partial a} \right)_b = \frac{2a H_{11} + 2b H_{12}}{a^2 S_{11} + 2ab S_{12} + b^2 S_{22}} - \epsilon \frac{2a S_{11} + 2b S_{12}}{a^2 S_{11} + 2ab S_{12} + b^2 S_{22}}$$

$$= \frac{2a(H_{11} - \epsilon S_{11}) + 2b(H_{12} - \epsilon S_{12})}{a^2 S_{11} + 2ab S_{12} + b^2 S_{22}}$$

or, on setting the derivative equal to zero,

$$a(H_{11} - \epsilon S_{11}) + b(H_{12} - \epsilon S_{12}) = 0. \tag{17-35}$$

Similarly, on setting the derivative $(\partial \epsilon / \partial b)_a = 0$, we obtain

$$a(H_{21} - \epsilon S_{21}) + b(H_{22} - \epsilon S_{22}) = 0. \tag{17-36}$$

As simultaneous equations in a and b, the solution is given by the determinant

$$\begin{vmatrix} (H_{11} - \epsilon S_{11}) & (H_{12} - \epsilon S_{12}) \\ (H_{12} - \epsilon S_{12}) & (H_{22} - \epsilon S_{22}) \end{vmatrix} = 0. \tag{17-37}$$

An equation such as (17-37) is called a *secular equation*; its solution is at the heart of methods involving the use of combinations of atomic orbitals to find the lowest possible energy orbital for the molecule as a whole, or *molecular orbital*. Clearly, if three atoms and three atomic wave functions had been used, three simultaneous equations in coefficients would result, yielding a 3×3 determinant.

A. The Hückel Approximations

We will now solve Eq. (17-37) by making some rather drastic-appearing approximations. In the case of molecules which are held together by a framework of sigma bonds but which also have available pi bonding orbitals, a set of pi-bonding molecular orbitals can be developed by taking ψ_1, ψ_2, and so on to be the wave functions on each atom which are of symmetry suitable for pi bonding. The usual situation is one of a chain or ring of carbon atoms, and each ψ is then a carbon p orbital perpendicular to the sigma bond. In ethylene, for example, the

sigma bonding framework might be regarded as provided by sp² hybrid bonds of each carbon atom. The remaining carbon p orbitals then overlap to give some pi bonding,

In this case, which is typical, one then takes ψ_1, ψ_2, and so on to be the same, that is, one p orbital per carbon. The specific further approximations made in the treatment by E. Hückel is then to assume that all integrals of the type H_{ii} are the same and equal to a constant α; as mentioned earlier (Section 17-CN-1), these are called *Coulomb integrals*. Integrals of the type H_{ij}, called *resonance integrals*, are taken to be the same and equal to a constant β if i and j refer to adjacent atoms and to be zero otherwise. The atomic p orbitals are assumed to be orthonormal, so that all $S_{ii} = 1$ and all $S_{ij} = 0$.

Equation (17-37), which applies to ethylene, then becomes

$$\begin{vmatrix} (\alpha - \epsilon) & \beta \\ \beta & (\alpha - \epsilon) \end{vmatrix} = 0. \qquad (17\text{-}38)$$

For butadiene, $H_2C{=}CH{-}CH{=}CH_2$, the secular equation is

$$\begin{vmatrix} (H_{11} - \epsilon S_{11}) & (H_{12} - \epsilon S_{12}) & (H_{13} - \epsilon S_{13}) & (H_{14} - \epsilon S_{14}) \\ (H_{12} - \epsilon S_{12}) & (H_{22} - \epsilon S_{22}) & (H_{23} - \epsilon S_{23}) & (H_{24} - \epsilon S_{24}) \\ (H_{13} - \epsilon S_{13}) & (H_{23} - \epsilon S_{23}) & (H_{33} - \epsilon S_{33}) & (H_{34} - \epsilon S_{34}) \\ (H_{14} - \epsilon S_{14}) & (H_{24} - \epsilon S_{24}) & (H_{34} - \epsilon S_{34}) & (H_{44} - \epsilon S_{44}) \end{vmatrix} = 0$$

or

$$\begin{vmatrix} (\alpha - \epsilon) & \beta & 0 & 0 \\ \beta & (\alpha - \epsilon) & \beta & 0 \\ 0 & \beta & (\alpha - \epsilon) & \beta \\ 0 & 0 & \beta & (\alpha - \epsilon) \end{vmatrix} = 0 \quad (17\text{-}39)$$

since, for example, $H_{14} = 0$ and $S_{14} = 0$, and so on. The solution to the ethylene secular equation is simply $\epsilon = \alpha + \beta$ and $\epsilon = \alpha - \beta$ [note Eqs. (17-23)and (17-26)]. Since α corresponds to the energy for the isolated atom, it is customary to take this as a point of reference, and the solutions for ethylene are as shown in Fig. 17-25. The β integrals are negative in value, so that $\alpha + \beta$ is the lower lying of the two. There are two pi electrons to place and since they may occupy the same level if their spins are opposed, this is the assumed configuration for ethylene.

The solutions for butadiene are[†]

$$\alpha + \tfrac{1}{2}(\sqrt{5} + 1)\beta, \quad \alpha + \tfrac{1}{2}(\sqrt{5} - 1)\beta, \quad \alpha - \tfrac{1}{2}(\sqrt{5} - 1)\beta, \quad \alpha - \tfrac{1}{2}(\sqrt{5} + 1)\beta.$$

There are now four electrons to place and these fill the first two levels in pairs. In the case of *cyclobutadiene*, integrals such as H_{14} are equal to β since these atoms are now adjacent; solution of the resulting equation gives $\alpha + 2\beta$, α, α, and $\alpha - 2\beta$. That is, there are two solutions with $\epsilon = \alpha$; such a case is called one of *degeneracy*. There are again four electrons to place and therefore two must go

[†] Divide every row by β and let $m = (\alpha - \epsilon)/\beta$, to give the determinant

$$\begin{vmatrix} m & 1 & 0 & 0 \\ 1 & m & 1 & 0 \\ 0 & 1 & m & 1 \\ 0 & 0 & 1 & m \end{vmatrix},$$

which expands to $m^4 - 3m^2 + 1 = 0$. If now $y = m^2$, the equation becomes $y^2 - 3y + 1 = 0$, which is easily solved.

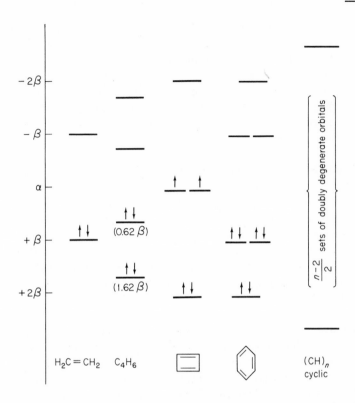

Fig. 17-25. *Pi electron molecular orbital levels according to the Hückel model.*

into the degenerate pair of $\epsilon = \alpha$ levels. As noted in Section 17-CN-2, an empirical rule of spectroscopy is that it takes energy to pair electrons, that is, to oppose their spins. The rule, known as *Hund's rule*, then calls for the two electrons to have their spins parallel. Cyclobutadiene should thus be a paramagnetic molecule with magnetic susceptibility corresponding to two unpaired electrons (Section 3-ST-2).

In terms of the assumptions made, the energy of the pi orbitals would be just $n\alpha$, where n is the number of pi electrons, if no mixing or linear combination is used. The difference between this and the calculated energy is then the stabilization (or destabilization) due to molecular orbital formation; it is called the *delocalization energy*. This energy is -2β for ethylene and -4.47β for butadiene. The fact that this last is more than twice the value for ethylene suggests that in butadiene the molecular orbitals extend over the whole molecule, or that one does not simply have two connected ethylene units, as the usual formula $H_2C{=}CH{-}CH{=}CH_2$

might suggest. The delocalization energy for cyclobutadiene is 4β, however, or just that of two ethylenes, which indicates that the ring structure provides no added stability. Cyclobutadiene has in fact been very difficult to synthesize, its existence seems at best to be transient, and the Hückel treatment does indicate that the molecule should be unstable since no extra delocalization energy is present to offset the strain energy of coercing the sigma bond framework to a four-membered ring.

B. *Evaluation of the Resonance Integral* β

The integrals H_{ij} can be estimated theoretically, but it is relatively easy to evaluate β experimentally, and this is what is usually done. For example, the heat of hydrogenation of ethylene is 32.8 kcal mole^{-1} and were butadiene just two noninteracting ethylene units, the value should be 65.6 kcal mole^{-1}. The observed value is 57.1, so butadiene appears to be more stable than expected by 8.5 kcal mole^{-1}. The extra delocalization energy from the Hückel treatment is 0.47β, which makes $\beta = 18$ kcal mole^{-1}.

The case of benzene is an important one, and solution of the appropriate secular equation gives the molecular orbital levels shown in Fig. 17-25; the pi bonding energy is 8β, as compared to 6β were benzene simply three ethylenes linked together. The extra stabilization is then 2β. Either from bond energies (Section 5-ST-1) or comparison of heats of hydrogenation of ethylene and of benzene, the experimental delocalization energy is 35–40 kcal mole^{-1}, again giving a β value of 18–20 kcal mole^{-1}.

If β is taken to be generally about 18–20 kcal mole^{-1} for carbon–carbon bonded systems, then application of the Hückel approach allows at least approximate delocalization energies to be calculated for a variety of linear and cyclic molecules. Included are rings of the type C_5H_5 and $C_5H_5^-$, C_7H_7, and other unstable species. The method has been extended to heterocyclic rings, to peroxo rings (where each carbon atom of the ring is also bonded to an oxygen), and so forth.

One may also estimate the energy to put a molecule in an excited state. That is, the lowest-lying electronic excited state is very likely that corresponding to promoting an electron to the first unoccupied pi molecular orbital. This energy should then be 2β for ethylene, 1.24β for butadiene, and so on. As shown in Fig. 17-26, a plot of the frequency of the first absorption band against the calculated energy in units of β is reasonably linear. The slope yields $\beta = 60$ kcal mole^{-1}.

This last value for β is, of course, quite different from that of about 20 kcal mole^{-1} from the thermochemical data. The probable reason is that in the thermo-

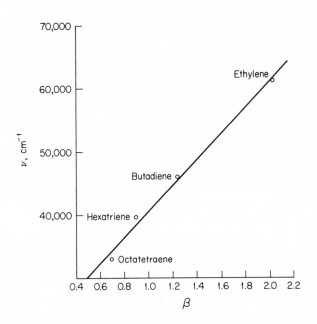

Fig. 17-26. *Spectroscopic evaluation of β (frequency of the first π → π* transition of various polyenes against energy in units of β). (From A. Streitweiser, Jr., "Molecular Orbital Theory for Organic Chemists." Copyright 1961, Wiley, New York. Used with permission of John Wiley & Sons, Inc.)*

chemical approach one is comparing actual heats of hydrogenation with those for a hypothetical structure of alternate single and double bonds, each of its natural bond length. The reference structure for, say, benzene is thus

It is first necessary to stretch the double bonds to the structure

before considering delocalization energy. The energy for this bond length changing has been estimated to be about 37 kcal mole^{-1}. The experimental delocalization energy of about 40 kcal mole^{-1} thus represents an excess over the 37 kcal mole^{-1} for bond distortion, so that the corrected experimental value becomes about

77 kcal mole^{-1}, making β about 38 kcal mole^{-1}, or considerably closer to the spectroscopic value.

The discussion illustrates the fact that thermochemical values include various contributions, such as bond length changes, not present in the spectroscopic values. The consequence is that β values are best used only in the context of the manner in which they were obtained.

C. Hückel Wave Functions

The coefficients a and b in Eq. (17-33) or, in general, the coefficients of a Hückel molecular orbital

$$\phi_j = c_{1j}\psi_1 + c_{2j}\psi_2 + c_{3j}\psi_3 + \cdots, \tag{17-40}$$

where ψ_1, ψ_2, ... are the atomic orbitals, may be obtained as follows. If we take the molecular orbital ϕ's to be normalized, then

$$\int \phi_j{}^*\phi_j \, d\tau = 1 = c_{1j}^2 \int \psi_1{}^*\psi_1 \, d\tau + c_{2j}^2 \int \psi_2{}^*\psi_2 \, d\tau + \cdots,$$

all the cross terms $\int \psi_i{}^*\psi_j \, d\tau$ vanishing if the ψ functions are orthogonal. If the functions are also normalized, then the remaining integrals are unity, so we have

$$c_{1j}^2 + c_{2j}^2 + c_{3j}^3 + \cdots = 1. \tag{17-41}$$

We find additional relationships between the c_{ij} as follows. The precursor equation to Eq. (17-33), Eq. (16-30), is $\mathbf{H}\phi_j = \epsilon\phi_j$, or $(\mathbf{H} - \epsilon)\,\phi_j = 0$. Suppose we are considering ϕ_1; then substitution of $\phi_1 = c_{11}\psi_1 + c_{21}\psi_2 + \cdots$, multiplication by $\psi_1{}^*$, and integration gives

$$c_{11} \int \psi_1{}^*(\mathbf{H} - \epsilon)\,\psi_1 \, d\tau + c_{21} \int \psi_1{}^*(\mathbf{H} - \epsilon)\,\psi_2 \, d\tau + \cdots = 0,$$

or, on insertion of the Hückel assumptions regarding H_{11} and H_{12},

$$c_{11}(\alpha - \epsilon) + c_{21}\beta = 0 \tag{17-42}$$

(assuming only atoms 1 and 2 are adjacent). Similar equations follow for the other coefficients on repeating the operation with $\psi_2{}^*$, ...

Thus in the case of butadiene, Eq. (17-42) applies, and since for the lowest energy state $\epsilon = \alpha + \frac{1}{2}(\sqrt{5} + 1)\beta$, the result is $c_{21} = \frac{1}{2}(\sqrt{5} + 1)\,c_{11}$. Pursuing the procedure, we find that $c_{31} = \frac{1}{2}(\sqrt{5} + 1)\,c_{41}$ and $c_{11} = c_{41}$. All the c_{ij} may then be expressed in terms of c_{11}, and insertion of these relationships into Eq. (17-37) gives $c_{11} = 0.37$; it then follows that $c_{41} = 0.37$, $c_{21} = c_{31} = 0.60$. Thus for the lowest molecular orbital $\phi_1 = 0.37(\psi_1 + \psi_4) + 0.60(\psi_2 + \psi_3)$. The whole process can then be repeated for the other three molecular orbital states. The results are summarized in Fig. 17-27. A minus sign means that the pi bonding

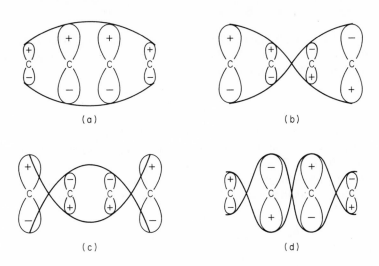

Fig. 17-27. *Hückel molecular orbitals for butadiene.*

p orbital (or pπ orbital) is inverted, and schematically, ϕ_1 corresponds to a simple standing wave, ϕ_2 to one with a single node, ϕ_3 to one with two nodes, and ϕ_4 to one with three nodes.

D. Application of Group Theory to Carbon Rings

Somewhat of a shortcut may be taken in evaluating the ϕ's if the carbon chain forms a ring. In the case of a six-membered ring (benzene) the molecular point group is D_{6h}. We can then find the traces for the reducible representation generated by a set of six pπ orbitals and then the irreducible representations to which the set corresponds. Each irreducible representation will have the symmetry of one of the molecular orbital energy states.

If we only want to know signs of the pπ orbitals for each solution, then it is only necessary to look at the symmetry of each irreducible representation with respect to the C_6^n operations. It is therefore easier to fall back to the C_{6v} group, for which the irreducible representations are half in number, but otherwise the same as far as the traces for the C_n operations. In C_{6v}, the traces for the set of six pπ bonds are

	E	$2C_6$	$2C_3$	C_2	$3\sigma_v$	$3\sigma_d$
pπ	6	0	0	0	2	0

Application of Eq. (17-16) gives $\Gamma_{6\pi p} = A_1 + B_1 + E_1 + E_2$. The A_1 IR is totally symmetric, and so must correspond to the pπ orbitals having all plus lobes on one side (and all minus lobes on the other). Thus

$$\phi_1 = (1/\sqrt{6})(\psi_1 + \psi_2 + \psi_3 + \psi_4 + \psi_5 + \psi_6);$$

the factor $1/\sqrt{6}$ is a normalization coefficient. The B_1 IR is antisymmetric to the operation C_6 (and C_6^5) and this as well as its other properties means that the signs of the ψ's must alternate. Then $\phi_2 = (1/\sqrt{6})(\psi_1 - \psi_2 + \psi_3 - \psi_4 + \psi_5 - \psi_6)$. The E_1 and E_2 IR are two-dimensional, and a somewhat more lengthy procedure is needed to find the coefficients of the ϕ's; only the results are given here:

$$E_1: \quad \phi_3 = \frac{1}{\sqrt{12}}(2\psi_1 + \psi_2 - \psi_3 - 2\psi_4 - \psi_5 + \psi_6),$$

$$\phi_4 = \frac{1}{2}(\psi_2 + \psi_3 - \psi_5 - \psi_6),$$

$$E_2: \quad \phi_5 = \frac{1}{\sqrt{12}}(2\psi_1 - \psi_2 + 2\psi_4 - \psi_5 - \psi_6),$$

$$\phi_6 = \frac{1}{2}(\psi_2 - \psi_3 + \psi_4 - \psi_5).$$

The various ϕ functions correspond to sets of standing molecular orbital waves as illustrated in Fig. 17-28.

E.   *The 4x + 2 rule. Bonding, Nonbonding, and Antibonding Molecular Orbitals*

The Hückel treatment leads to a simple rule which states that a ring $(CH)_n$ will have aromatic character if $n = 4x + 2$, x being an integer. The qualitative reasoning behind this rule is the following. Referring to Fig. 17-25, molecular orbitals lower in energy than α are said to be *bonding* since electrons placed in them are lower in potential energy than in the absence of the molecular orbital

ϕ_1 ϕ_2

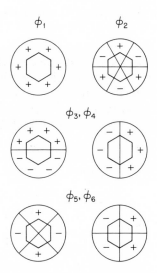

ϕ_3, ϕ_4

ϕ_5, ϕ_6

Fig. 17-28. *Hückel molecular orbitals for benzene.*

formation. Orbitals equal in energy to α are said to be *nonbonding*, or neutral in this respect, and those lying above α are then *antibonding*. On placing n electrons in the set of molecular orbitals, the molecule is stabilized as a result of molecular orbital formation, that is, of delocalizing the atomic orbitals, to the extent that the total energy is less than $n\alpha$.

It is clearly undesirable to have to place electrons in nonbonding or antibonding orbitals. If $(CH)_n$ is to be aromatic or extra stable, it is first of all necessary that n be even; since there are n pi electrons, the molecule would otherwise be a free radical. Second, the molecular orbital energy level scheme must be such that all n electrons can be accommodated, in pairs, in *bonding* orbitals. As may be inferred from Fig. 17-25 the pattern of molecular orbitals given by the Hückel treatment for n even is one of a single lowest-lying orbital and a single highest-lying one, and then one or more sets of doubly degenerate orbitals. That is, there will be $n - 2$ degenerate orbitals occurring in $(n - 2)/2$ pairs. If $(n - 2)/2$ is an odd number, then one of the sets of degenerate orbitals will be nonbonding, as in the case of $(CH)_4$. Since the $n/2$ pairs of electrons must just half fill the set of orbitals, this means that two must be nonbonding. To avoid this situation, $(n - 2)/2$ must be an even number, or $2x$, where x is an integer. It then follows that $n = 4x + 2$ if all electrons are to be paired and all to be in bonding orbitals.

According to this rule, C_4H_4 is not aromatic, C_6H_6 is, C_8C_8 is not, $C_{10}H_{10}$ is, and so on. This is the experimental observation.

17-ST-2   Orbital Symmetry Rules in Concerted Organic Reactions

An interesting observation is that reactions effecting ring closure of a conjugated chain are rather stereospecific. As illustrated in Fig. 17-29, the closure may result in isomers I or II. The $p\pi$ orbitals of the terminal carbon atoms must rotate so as to give a positive overlap, and may do so in the same direction or in opposite directions. The two modes are called *conrotatory* and *disrotatory*, respectively.

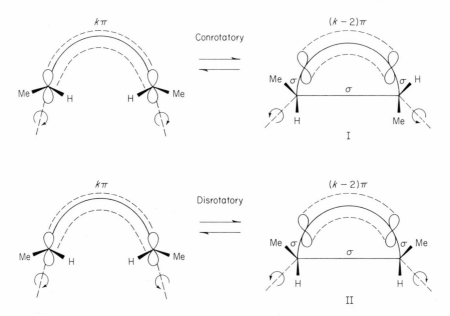

Fig. 17-29. *Rotatory modes for a concerted ring closure. [See G. B. Gill, Quart. Rev. **22**, 340 (1968).]*

The experimental observation is that if the ring closure is by means of a thermal reaction, the conrotatory isomer results if the chain has $4n$ pi electrons, while the disrotatory isomer is obtained if there are $4n + 2$ pi electrons. Just the opposite result is found if the ring closure is induced photochemically, that is, by promoting an electron to the first empty pi orbital.

R. Woodward and R. Hoffmann proposed an ingenious and appealing explanation. As illustrated in Fig. 17-30, if the terminal $p\pi$ orbital lobes are oppositely oriented as to sign, then the least motion to bring about positive overlap will be of the conrotatory type. Conversely, if the terminal $p\pi$ lobes have the same sign

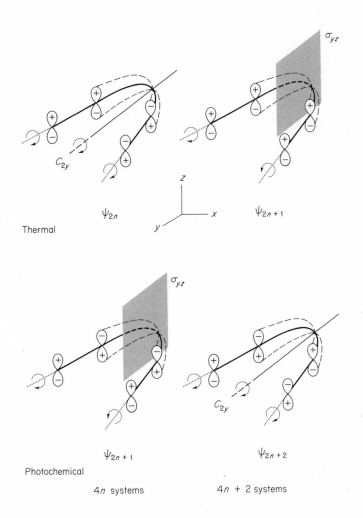

Fig. 17-30. *Orbital symmetry rules for a concerted ring closure. Ilustration of the differences in symmetry between the 4n and 4n + 2 cases and between ground-state and first Hückel excited-state systems. [See G. B. Gill, Quart. Rev. **32**, 340 (1968).]*

orientation, the disrotatory mode should be the most direct one to forming the new bond.

The pattern of molecular orbitals according to the Hückel treatment, was shown in Fig. 17-27 for butadiene. Essentially the same pattern prevails for any polyene, C_nH_{2n+2}. That is, successive molecular orbitals have 0, 1, 2, 3, 4, ... nodes. Those with 0, 2, 4, ... nodes have terminal $p\pi$ orbitals opposed in sign. Since electrons fill these orbitals in pairs, it means that $n/2$ orbitals are filled. If $n/2$ is even, or if $n = 4x$ (x an integer), then the highest filled orbital will have an odd number of nodes; if $n/2$ is odd or $n = 4x + 2$, then the highest filled orbital will be one with an even number of nodes. Thus the ring closure should be conrotatory in the first case and disrotatory in the second case, as illustrated in Fig. 17-30.

The conclusion is just reversed for the photochemical ring closure, since now the highest-energy electron is in the next higher molecular orbital. This has one more node, and the sign relationship of the terminal $p\pi$ orbitals is reversed.

Some further generalizations appear to be possible. The $4n$ case has a C_2 axis of symmetry when in position for ring closure (see Fig. 17-30), while the $4n + 2$ case has instead a σ_V plane. The conrotatory and disrotatory motions have these same symmetries. The generalization that is emerging is that the most effective path for concerted reactions may be that one whose intimate mechanism conforms to at least some one symmetry operation of the molecule.

GENERAL REFERENCES

ADAMSON, A. W. (1969). "Understanding Physical Chemistry," 2nd ed., Chapter 21. Benjamin, New York.
COTTON, F. A. (1963). "Chemical Applications of Group Theory." Wiley (Interscience), New York.
COULSON, C. A. (1961). "Valence," 2nd ed. Oxford Univ. Press, London and New York.
DAUDEL, R. LEFEBVRE, R., AND MOSER, C. (1959). "Quantum Chemistry." Wiley (Interscience), New York.
FIGGIS, B. N. (1966). "Introduction to Ligand Fields." Wiley (Interscience), New York.
EYRING, H., WALTER, J., AND KIMBALL, G. E. (1960). "Quantum Chemistry." Wiley, New York.
HALL, L. H. (1969). "Group Theory and Symmetry in Chemistry." McGraw-Hill, New York.
HANNA, M. W. (1969). "Quantum Mechanics in Chemistry," 2nd ed. Benjamin, New York.
OFFENHARTZ, P. O'D. (1970). "Atomic and Molecular Orbital Theory." McGraw-Hill, New York.
PITZER K. S. (1953). "Quantum Chemistry." Prentice-Hall, Englewood Cliffs, New Jersey.
STREITWEISER, A., JR. (1961). "Molecular Orbital Theory for Organic Chemists." Wiley, New York.

CITED REFERENCES

ADAMSON, A. W. (1969). "Understanding Physical Chemistry," 2nd ed. Benjamin, New York.
COTTON, F. A. (1963). "Chemical Applications of Group Theory." Wiley, New York.
MULLIKEN, R., RIEKE, C. A., ORLOFF, D., AND ORLOFF, H. (1949). *J. Chem. Phys.* **17**, 1248.
WALSH, A. D. (1953). *J. Chem. Soc.* **1953**, 2260, 2266.

Exercises

17-1 Write out the series of symmetry operations associated with an S_5 axis, that is, show with explanation alternative designations wherever possible.

> *Ans.* $S_5{}^1$, $S_5{}^2 = C_5{}^2$, $S_5{}^3$, $S_5{}^4 = C_5{}^4$, $S_5{}^5 = \sigma_h$,
> $S_5{}^6 = C_5$, $S_5{}^7$, $S_5{}^8 = C_5{}^3$, $S_5{}^9$, $S_5^{10} = E$.

17-2 Explain the symmetry elements present and the point group designation for the following: (a) A book with blank pages; (b) a normally printed book; (c) a tennis ball, including the seam; (d) Siamese twins; (e) an ash tray in the shape of a round bowl and with four equally spaced grooves in the rim for holding cigarettes.

> *Ans.* (a) C_{2v} ; (b) C_1 ; (c) D_{2d} ; (d) C_{2v} ; (e) C_{4v}.

17-3 Explain what symmetry elements are present and the point group designation for the following molecules: (a) Pyridine; (b) acetylene; (c) $H_2C=C=CH_2$; (d) C_2H_6 in the staggered configuration; (e) PCl_5 (a trigonal bipyramid); (f) $AuCl_4^-$ (a square planar ion); (g) ruthenocene (a pentagonal prism); (h) *trans*-$Co(NH_3)_4Br_2{}^+$ (ignore the H's); (i) *trans*-$Co(NH_3)_4ClBr^+$ (ignore the H's); (j) chloroform.

> *Ans.* (a) C_{2v} ; (b) $D_{\infty h}$; (c) D_{2d} ; (d) D_{3d} ; (e) D_{3h} ;
> (f) D_{4h} ; (g) D_{5h} ; (h) D_{4h} ; (i) C_{4v} ; (j) C_{3v}.

17-4 Work out the multiplication table for the C_{2v} group, showing each multiplication in the manner of Fig. 17-9.

> *Ans.* See Table 17-4.

17-5 Referring to Exercise 17-4, show that $\sigma(xz)$ and $\sigma'(yz)$ belong to separate classes by carrying out the similarity transformations $X^{-1}\sigma(xz)X$ and $X^{-1}\sigma'(yz)X$, where X is each symmetry operation.

> *Ans.* $X^{-1}\sigma(xz)X$ is $\sigma(xz)$ for $X = E$ ($X^{-1} = E$), $X = C_2$ ($X^{-1} = C_2$),
> $X = \sigma(xz)$ [$X^{-1} = \sigma(xz)$], and $X = \sigma'(yz)$ [$X^{-1} = \sigma'(yz)$];
> similarly $X^{-1}\sigma'(yz)X$ is $\sigma'(yz)$ for each case.
> Thus $\sigma(xz)$ and $\sigma'(yz)$ do not mix and therefore belong to separate classes.

17-6 Complete the example in connection with Table 17-2, which showed that σ_v, σ_v', and σ_v'' belong to the same class.

17-7 Carry out the matrix multiplication

$$\begin{bmatrix} 1 & 0 \\ 2 & 1 \end{bmatrix} \begin{bmatrix} 1 & 4 \\ 2 & 3 \end{bmatrix}.$$

> *Ans.* $\begin{bmatrix} 1 & 4 \\ 4 & 11 \end{bmatrix}.$

17-8   Carry out the matrix multiplication

$$\begin{bmatrix} 1 & 2 & | & 0 \\ 0 & 2 & | & 0 \\ \hline 0 & 0 & | & 3 \end{bmatrix} \begin{bmatrix} 3 & 2 & | & 0 \\ 1 & 1 & | & 0 \\ \hline 0 & 0 & | & 2 \end{bmatrix}.$$

Ans. $\begin{bmatrix} 5 & 4 & | & 0 \\ 2 & 2 & | & 0 \\ \hline 0 & 0 & | & 6 \end{bmatrix}.$ (Notice that the product matrix is blocked out in the same way as are those multiplied.)

17-9   Show what irreducible representations in C_{3v} are spanned by the reducible representation

	E	$2C_3$	$3\sigma_v$
Γ	5	-1	-1

Ans. $\Gamma = 2E + A_2$.

17-10   Find the traces of the reducible representation $\Gamma_{5\sigma}$ generated by the set of five sigma bonds in PCl_5 (a triangular bipyramid), the irreducible representations spanned by $\Gamma_{5\sigma}$, and the types of hydrogen-like orbitals that might be used for bonding.

Ans. $\Gamma_{5\sigma} \approx 2A_1' + E' + A_2''$, corresponding to $s(p_xp_y)p_zd_{z^2}$ or $s(d_{x^2-y^2}d_{xy})p_zd_{z^2}$.

17-11   Referring to Exercise 17-10 and PCl_5, find the traces for the reducible representation $\Gamma_{3\pi\perp}$ of the set of pi bonds for the three chlorines in the trigonal plane, whose lobes lie above and below the plane. Find also the irreducible representations spanned by $\Gamma_{3\pi\perp}$ and the types of hydrogenlike orbitals that might be used for pi bonding.

Ans. $\Gamma_{3\pi\perp} \sim A_2'' + E''$, corresponding to p_z (already used in sigma bonding) and $(d_{xz}d_{yz})$.

Problems

17-1   Show what the point group designations are for (a) ferrocene (iron sandwiched between two cyclopentadienyl rings, which are staggered; see the accompanying diagram), (b)

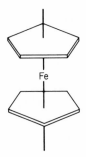

ethane in the eclipsed configuration, (c) $Cr(NH_3)_5Cl^{2+}$, (d) *cis*-$Co(NH_3)_4Cl_2^+$, (e) CH_2ClCH_2Cl in the staggered configuration, (f) naphthalene, (g) cyclohexane in the chair form. (List all symmetry elements; ignore H's in the ammine complexes.)

17-2 Show what the point group designations are for (a) $Fe(CN)_6^{4-}$, (b) HOCl (a bent molecule), (c) $(HNBH)_3$ (a planar six-membered ring with alternating N and B), (d) C_5H_8, spiro-pentane (two mutually perpendicular triangles joined apically), (e) CO, (f) $UO_2F_5^{3-}$ (a pentagonal bipyramid with apical oxygens), (g) diborane, B_2H_6 (two hydrogens are bridging and lie in a plane perpendicular to that of the other four hydrogens), (h) CH_2ClBr. (List all symmetry elements.)

17-3 Show what the point group designations are for (a) a triangular antiprism, (b) *trans*-$Pt(NH_3)_2Cl_2$ (ignore the H's), (c) IF_5 (four F's in a square plane and one apical·F), (d) Dewar benzene. (List all the symmetry elements.)

17-4 Work out the multiplication table for the D_{3h} group. Show which are the various classes, that is, carry out the necessary similarity transformations.

17-5 Equation (17-10) gives a set of matrices which simplify to a set of two-dimensional ones and a set of one-dimensional ones. Show that the first set does in fact obey the C_{3v} multiplication table.

17-6 Carry out the matrix multiplication

$$\begin{bmatrix} 1 & 3 & 2 \\ 1 & 2 & 1 \\ 4 & 0 & 1 \end{bmatrix} \begin{bmatrix} 0 & 2 & 1 \\ 3 & 0 & 2 \\ 2 & 0 & 1 \end{bmatrix}.$$

17-7 Determine what sets of orbitals should be appropriate for sigma bonding in a hypothetical $Cr(NH_3)_7^{3+}$ (a pentagonal bipyramid).

17-8 A reducible representation in the T_d point group has the traces: $E = ?, C_3 = 1, C_2 = -1$, $S_4 = -3$, and $\sigma_d = 1$. The trace under the symmetry operation E is missing. Explain what is the simplest choice for this missing number and what irreducible representations are spanned.

17-9 If an object has a C_2 axis and a σ_v plane but no other types of symmetry, show that a second σ_v plane must also be present.

17-10 Verify Eq. (17-10) by carrying out the transformations of a point according to the symmetry operations of C_{3v}.

17-11 Find the traces of the reducible representations in D_{4h} which are generated by carrying the set of (a) p orbitals and (b) d orbitals through the various symmetry operations. What irreducible representations are spanned in the two cases?

17-12 Show what combinations of s, p, and d orbitals are suitable for sigma bonding of n atoms to a central one if (a) $n = 2$ and the molecule is angular, (b) $n = 3$ and the symmetry is D_{3h}, (c) $n = 4$ and the n atoms lie at the corners of a square, $n = 5$ and the molecules have C_{4v} symmetry, (d) $n = 6$ and the n atoms lie at the corners of a triangular prism.

17-13 The following are the angular portions of 4f hydrogen-like orbitals. Determine the irreducible representations to which these orbitals belong in point groups T_d, O_h, D_{4h}.

$|m|$	Function	$|m|$	Function
3	$(\sin^3 \theta)\, e^{\pm 3i\phi}$	1	$(\sin \theta)(5\cos^2 \theta - 1)e^{\pm i\phi}$
2	$(\sin^2 \theta)(\cos \theta)\, e^{\pm 2i\phi}$	0	$\frac{5}{3}\cos^3 \theta - \cos \theta$

17-14 Determine the hydrogen-like orbitals which are of the proper symmetry for pi bonding in a tetrahedral molecule.

17-15 List the symmetry operations in the group D_6 and construct the group multiplication table.

17-16 Consider the overlap integral S for two ψ_{1s} functions located on hydrogen atoms a distance R apart. Demonstrate that S is $e^{-\alpha R}(1 + \alpha R + \frac{1}{3}\alpha^2 R^2)$; plot S as a function of R. [*Notes*: We find ψ_{1s} from Chapter 16, and substitution into Eq. (17-24) gives

$$ S = \frac{\alpha^3}{\pi} \int e^{-\alpha r_A}\, e^{-\alpha r_B}\, d\tau = \frac{\alpha^3}{\pi} I, $$

where $\alpha = 1/a_0$. We now go over to elliptical coordinates, defining $\lambda = (r_A + r_B)/R$ and $\mu = (r_A - r_B)/R$; $d\tau = (R^3/8)(\lambda^2 - \mu^2)\, d\mu\, d\lambda\, d\phi$. The ψ_{1s} function is symmetric with respect to ϕ and the integral I reduces to

$$ I = \tfrac{1}{4}\pi R^3 \int_{-1}^{1} d\mu \int_{1}^{\infty} e^{-\alpha R\lambda}(\lambda^2 - \mu^2)\, d\lambda. $$

The integral $\int_{x}^{\infty} t^n e^{-\alpha t}\, dt$ is known as an incomplete gamma function and is equal to

$$ \frac{n!\, e^{-\alpha x}}{\alpha^{n+1}}\left(1 + \alpha x + \frac{1}{2!}(\alpha x)^2 + \cdots + \frac{1}{n!}(\alpha x)^n\right).] $$

17-17 Explain whether the molecule PH_2 should be bent or linear.

Special Topics Problems

17-1 Write the secular determinant in the Hückel treatment of cyclopropenyl, C_3H_3, and solve for its roots. Construct the molecular orbital scheme in the manner of Fig. 17-25 and place the pi electrons of the molecule.

17-2 Carry out the same procedure as in the preceding problem but now for allyl radical, C_3H_5.

17-3 Verify the solutions for the Hückel method as applied to butadiene. Calculate the delocalization energy for butadiene in kilocalories per mole using spectroscopic data.

18 MOLECULAR SPECTROSCOPY AND PHOTOCHEMISTRY

==

18-1   Introduction

The field of molecular spectroscopy is a very large and a very popular one. Much of the present effort of chemical physicists is devoted to the study of the electronic, vibrational, rotational, and nuclear excited states of atoms and molecules. The great scope of the material is suggested by the rather lengthy list of references at the end of the chapter. The presentation here necessarily is severely limited; primary emphasis is given to electronic states of molecules—as physical chemists, we are very interested in the major changes in energy and in chemical nature that occur with electronic excitation. More than just a gain in energy is involved; an excited molecule may have a new geometry and it can undergo a variety of processes, such as emission, radiationless changes, and chemical reaction. We are beginning to see, in fact, the emergence of a distinct chemistry of excited states. We attempt therefore to present aspects of the chemical as well as of the wave mechanical approach to the subject.

The rest of molecular spectroscopy is largely concerned with phenomena whose primary interest to the physical chemist is that they provide information about the size and shape of a molecule or about the nature of the bonding in the electronic ground state. Thus analysis of vibrational and rotational spectra allows estimations of the force constants of bonds and of bond lengths. Nuclear magnetic resonance gives a special kind of information about the electronic environment of an atom, as does electron paramagnetic resonance. Such spectroscopy has become a major tool for the structural and analytical chemist. The detailed theories are of less interest, however, in a text such as this; we will present only the simplest model for each phenomenon.

18-2   Excited States of Diatomic Molecules

A.   The Hydrogen Molecule and Molecular Ion

The excited states of diatomic molecules are usually treated wave mechanically in terms of linear combinations of ψ functions for the separate atoms, as discussed in Sections 17-CN-1 and 17-CN-2. The molecular orbital method is commonly used and, as the simplest example, the ground and first excited states of H_2^+ are described in terms of the linear combinations

$$\phi_g = \psi_{1s,A} + \psi_{1s,B} \quad \text{and} \quad \phi_u = \psi_{1s,A} - \psi_{1s,B},$$

where A and B denote the two hydrogen atoms whose 1s orbitals are used; the subscripts g and u designate whether the ϕ function is symmetric or antisymmetric with respect to inversion through the center of symmetry. The energy can be calculated as a function of internuclear distance by means of the variation method (see Section 17-CN-1) and the result is shown in Fig. 18-1. Notice that the lower

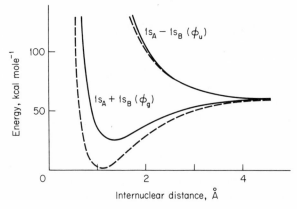

Fig. 18-1.   *Energy of the H_2^+ molecular ion as a function of the internuclear distance; solid lines are calculated by the variation method and dashed lines calculated by an exact method. (From W. Kauzmann, "Quantum Chemistry." Academic Press, New York, 1957.)*

curve, for ϕ_g, has a minimum, indicating that the H_2^+ molecule is stable, the depth of the minimum giving the dissociation energy. The first excited state, whose molecular orbital is ϕ_u, has no minimum; as a consequence, absorption of light by H_2^+ to put it in this excited state leads to prompt dissociation into H and H^+. There are further excited states, representable in first approximation by linear combinations of 2s, 2p, 3s, and so on atomic wave functions; these give a progression of states (called a *Rydberg progression*) leading eventually to ionization of the electron.

The next case, H_2, already presents a fairly difficult calculational problem. The approach is much the same as before, however, in that linear combinations of atomic orbitals are used, along with the variation method. The resulting states may be described in terms of the molecular orbitals occupied. Thus the ground state of H_2 is $(1s\sigma_g)^2$; the designation $1s\sigma_g$ refers to the molecular orbital formed from 1s atomic orbitals, or the ϕ_g orbital just given. The superscript 2 means that both electrons occupy this orbital.

The first excited state is $1s\sigma_g 2p\sigma_u*$; one electron is in the $1s\sigma_g$ molecular orbital and the other in the $2p\sigma_u*$ one. This last is formed from two 2p orbitals, which must be p_x (x being the bonding axis) since the molecular orbital is of the sigma type; the asterisk means that it is an antibonding orbital. Further excited states are listed in Table 18-1 and the calculated variation of energy with internuclear distance for several of them is shown in Fig. 18-2.

These designations give the molecular orbitals into which each of the two electrons is placed. One may alternatively describe each state by a new set of symbols. A quantity Λ is used to indicate the component of the total electronic orbital angular momentum L along the internuclear axis of a diatomic molecule. States of Λ number 0, 1, 2, 3, ... are called $\Sigma, \Pi, \Delta, \Phi, ...$, respectively, in capital Greek letters analogous to s, p, d, f, ... Right superscripts plus and minus denote whether or not the wave function for a Σ state changes sign on reflection in a plane through the two nuclei. If the molecule is homonuclear so that there is an inversion center, then subscripts g and u appear, to indicate whether the wave

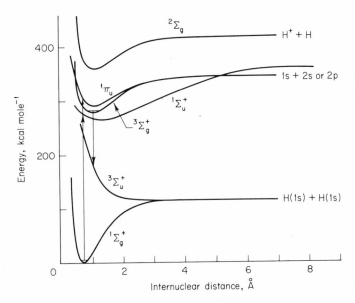

Fig. 18-2. *Potential energy curves for various electronic states of H_2 and H_2^+. The transitions $^1\Sigma_u^+ \leftarrow {}^1\Sigma_g^+$ and $^1\Pi_u \leftarrow {}^1\Sigma_g^+$ correspond to important absorption bands, while the transition $^3\Sigma_g^+ \rightarrow {}^3\Sigma_u^+$ is responsible for the continuous emission of a hydrogen arc lamp. (From E. J. Bowen, "Chemical Aspects of Light," 2nd ed. Oxford Univ. Press (Clarendon), London and New York, 1946.)*

Table 18-1.   *Energy States of* H_2 [a]

Electronic configuration	Energy of the minimum (cm^{-1})[b]		Internuclear distance at the minimum (Å)	
	Singlet	Triplet	Singlet	Triplet
$(1s\sigma_g)^2\,{}^1\Sigma_g{}^+$	124,429	—	0.742	—
$(1s\sigma_g 2p\sigma_u{}^*)\,{}^{1,3}\Sigma_u{}^+$	32,739	$\sim$68,000[c]	1.29	unstable
$(1s\sigma_g 2p\pi_u)\,{}^{1,3}\Pi_u$	24,386	28,685	1.033	1.038
$(1s\sigma_g 2s\sigma_g)\,{}^{1,3}\Sigma_g{}^+$	24,366	28,491	1.012	0.989
$1s\sigma_g\,(H_2{}^+)\,{}^2\Sigma_g{}^+$	0	—	1.06	—

[a] Adapted from J. G. Calvert and J. N. Pitts, Jr., "Photochemistry." Wiley, New York, 1966.
[b] Energies relative to the minimum of $H_2{}^+$.
[c] Energy at internuclear distance of 1.29 Å (note from Fig. 18-2 that this state has no energy minimum).

function for the state is symmetric or antisymmetric with respect to inversion (as noted in Section 17-6, the symbols stand for the German words *gerade* and *ungerade*). Finally, the left superscript gives the spin multiplicity, that is, whether the spin function is antisymmetric (spins paired and multiplicity 1) or symmetric (spins parallel and multiplicity 3) (see Section 17-CN-1).

The particular series of excited states of H_2 given in Table 18-1 is such that for each, one electron remains in the $1s\sigma_g$ molecular orbital. The schematic electron configurations of the separated atoms and of each molecular orbital are shown in Fig. 18-3. The plus and minus signs give the sign of the wave function in the indicated region of space, and the arrows show the directions of the electron spins.

There are certain rules, called *selection rules*, which state whether a given transition may occur or not, in first-order approximation. The physical basis is that the transition must involve a nonzero displacement of electronic charge if it is to be stimulated by the oscillating electric field of a light wave. The wave mechanical formulation discussed in Section 18-ST-1 leads to the statement

$$\text{probability} \propto \left(\int \psi_2 \overrightarrow{ex} \psi_1 \, d\tau \right)^2, \tag{18-1}$$

where $\overrightarrow{ex}$ is a vector representing the charge displacement in the x direction (in this case); it behaves like a vector in the operations of the symmetry group of the molecule. One concludes that in order for the integral to be nonzero, ψ_1 and ψ_2 must have certain relative symmetry properties. The requirement reduces to the statement or selection rule that possible transitions are ones for which $\Delta\Lambda = 0, \pm 1$, and $\Delta S = 0$, and for which the parity change must be $g \leftrightarrow u$ (if the molecule has a center of symmetry); also $+ \leftrightarrow +$ and $- \leftrightarrow -$ but $+ \not\leftrightarrow -$.

† Note that a reverse arrow has been used in writing a transition. It is an international convention among spectroscopists that the higher or more excited state be written first regardless of the direction of the process.

18-2 Excited States of Diatomic Molecules

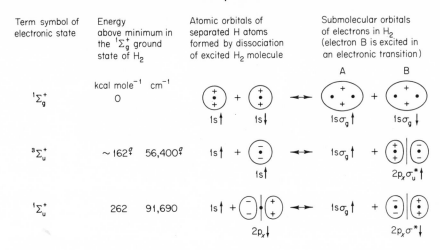

Term symbol of electronic state	Energy above minimum in the $^1\Sigma_g^+$ ground state of H_2		Atomic orbitals of separated H atoms formed by dissociation of excited H_2 molecule	Submolecular orbitals of electrons in H_2 (electron B is excited in an electronic transition)

Fig. 18-3. *The molecular orbitals for three photochemically important excited states of H_2 and the dissociation products of these excited molecules. (From J. G. Calvert and J. N. Pitts, Jr., "Photochemistry." Copyright 1966, Wiley, New York. Used with permission of John Wiley & Sons, Inc.)*

Referring to Fig. 18-2, the consequence is that the ground state should only undergo the processes $^1\Sigma_u^+ \leftarrow {}^1\Sigma_g^+$ and $^1\Pi_u \leftarrow {}^1\Sigma_g^+$.† These two transitions are responsible for the important absorptions of hydrogen at 110.0 nm and 100.2 nm.

Selection rules are never absolute, however, and other states may be obtained either through low-intensity absorptions or by indirect means. Once formed, the $^3\Sigma_g^+$ state can emit light to drop to the $^3\Sigma_u^+$ state, for example. This last state has no potential energy minimum and therefore dissociates on the next vibration to produce two ground-state hydrogen atoms (the energy appearing as kinetic energy). As indicated in Fig. 18-2, dissociation from higher excited states may produce electronically excited hydrogen atoms. The photochemistry of hydrogen (and of diatomic molecules generally) thus consists in the production of either ground-state or excited-state atoms.

In summary, excited states of H_2 differ not just in energy but also in equilibrium internuclear distance, in dissociation energy to give atoms, and in the states of the atoms produced.

B. Other Diatomic Molecules

The same general theoretical approach applies to other diatomic molecules, now using hydrogen-like orbital functions. Oxygen excited states have been mentioned briefly (Section 17-CN-2), and we show instead the somewhat analogous energy level diagram for S_2 in Fig. 18-4. The ground state, $^3\Sigma_g^-$, is paramagnetic with two unpaired spins, like that of O_2. The most probable transition is to the $^3\Sigma_u^-$ state. Notice the crossing point C in the figure where the potential energy

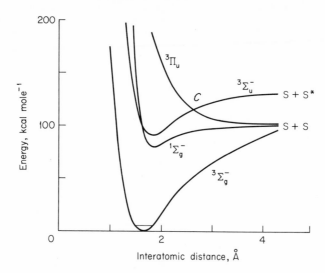

Fig. 18-4. *Potential energy curves for various electronic states of* S_2. *[From E. J. Bowen, "Chemical Aspects of Light," 2nd ed. Oxford Univ. Press (Clarendon), London and New York, 1946.]*

curve for $^3\Sigma_u^-$ is intersected by that for the $^3\Pi_u$ state. If S_2 has sufficient vibrational energy in the $^3\Sigma_u^-$ state for the atoms to reach the internuclear distance corresponding to this point, then it is possible for the molecule to change to the $^3\Pi_u$ potential energy curve. Since this has no minimum, the atoms dissociate on the next vibrational swing. This type of process is called *predissociation*; it provides an explanation of how excitation to a dissociatively stable excited state can in fact lead to a prompt breakup of the molecule.

We next consider the case of a heteronuclear diatomic molecule, HI. The potential energy curves are given in Fig. 18-5. Notice that the g and u designations have now disappeared; there is no longer an inversion center. The first few excited states are all dissociative. Irradiation of HI gas with light quanta of 5 or 6 eV energy (corresponding to about 40,000 cm^{-1} or 250 nm wavelength) leads to the production of hydrogen and iodine atoms, both with considerable excess kinetic energy. Depending on the wavelength used, the iodine atoms may be in the $^2P_{1/2}$ excited state (see Section 18-ST-4 for the significance of the notation).

The photochemically produced hydrogen atoms may then react with HI,

$$H + HI \rightarrow H_2 + I,$$

and this as well as recombination reactions

$$2I + M \rightarrow I_2 + M, \qquad 2H + M \rightarrow H_2 + M$$

(where molecule M carries off the recombination energy, note Section 14-CN-1)

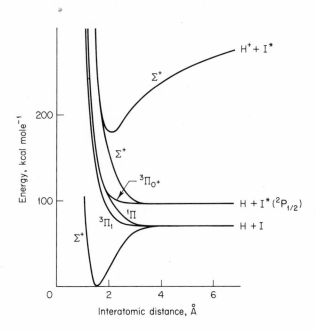

Fig. 18-5.   *Potential energy curves for low-lying electronic states of* HI. *(From J. G. Calvert and J. N. Pitts, Jr., "Photochemistry." Copyright 1966, Wiley, New York. Used with permission of John Wiley & Sons, Inc.)*

lead to the photochemical formation of H_2 and I_2. The physical chemist makes an important distinction between *primary* photochemical processes, such as

$$HI \xrightarrow{h\nu} H + I, \tag{18-2}$$

which show the immediate chemical change following excitation, and *secondary processes*, such as the other reactions just given, which the primary products undergo. These last are interesting, of course, not only for their chemistry but also in that they determine the overall photochemical change. A primary process has the special importance, however, in that it describes the chemistry of a particular excited state.

18-3   Electronic, Vibrational, and Rotational Transitions

A.   The Franck–Condon Principle

The discussion of the preceding section dealt only with electronic states, and we now consider how changes in vibrational and rotational energy may be included. The usual assumption is that electronic and vibrational–rotational energy states do not "mix," or that the total wave function can be written as

$$\psi = \psi_e \psi_{v,J},$$ (18-3)

where the subscripts stand for the separate wave functions. That is, we assume vibrational and rotational energies to simply superimpose on that of the electronic state. The separation of ψ_e from $\psi_{v,J}$ constitutes what is known as the *Born–Oppenheimer* approximation; the essential argument is that the nuclei, being massive, move slowly compared to electrons and may be considered at rest in solving for ψ_e. Further, rotational energies are so small that changes in them are usually neglected in considering electronic transitions, and we will do so here.

Figure 18-6 shows the hypothetical potential energy curves for the ground and first excited electronic states of a diatomic molecule. The horizontal lines indicate qualitatively the progression of vibrational states for each electronic state and, as in Fig. 16-6, the approximate appearance of the actual wave functions

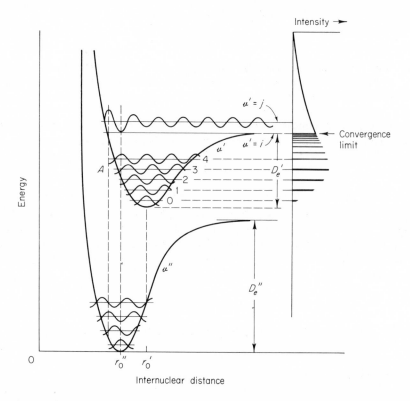

Fig. 18-6. *Illustration of the Franck–Condon principle: transitions between the ground state and excited state of a diatomic molecule. [From E. J. Bowen, "Chemical Aspects of Light," 2nd ed. Oxford Univ. Press (Clarendon), London and New York, 1946.]*

is included. An important implication of the Born–Oppenheimer approximation is that the transition probability expression (18-1) now has the form

$$\text{probability} \propto \left(\int \psi_{e'} \overrightarrow{ex} \psi_{e''} \, d\tau_e \int \psi_{v'} \psi_{v''} \, d\tau_v \right)^2, \qquad (18\text{-}4)$$

where prime and double prime denote final and initial state, respectively, and τ is a general symbol denoting the appropriate coordinates. That is, one separates out an explicit dependence on the overlap integral of the initial and final vibrational wave functions. Now, the time for an electronic transition is about 10^{-15} sec (about that for a train of electromagnetic radiation to pass an atom), or very small compared to vibrational times, which are about 10^{-13} sec. As a consequence, nuclei do not move appreciably during an electronic excitation. The integral $\int \psi_{v'} \psi_{v''} \, d\tau_v$ is therefore to be evaluated at *constant* internuclear distance, or for what is shown in Fig. 18-6 as a *vertical* transition. The idea is known as the *Franck–Condon principle*. Consider the transition from the ground electronic state to the first excited state. At ordinary temperatures most of the molecules will be in the $v'' = 0$ vibrational level. For the overlap integral to have a large value it is first of all necessary that $\psi_{v''}$ be large, which means that it is only those transitions occurring when r is near r_0'' that will be probable. It is next necessary that $\psi_{v'}$ be large for r around r_0'', which means that the most favored transition is to about the $v' = 3$ level in the figure. Transitions to various other v' levels retain some probability, however, as indicated by the satellite diagram in the right margin of the figure. In fact, the transition can be along line A, which means the excited molecule has enough energy to dissociate on the next vibration.

There being no barrier above D_e', the "vibrational" energy levels are essentially those of a free wave and are so close together that one sees a continuum rather than discrete energy levels.

The iodine molecule presents an example of this situation. As shown in Fig. 18-7, the first electronic transition shows as a series of lines corresponding to the spacing of vibrational states, and reaches a convergence limit or continuum. Clearly, the detailed appearance of such spectra will be sensitive to the relative shapes and positions of the potential curves for the ground and excited states. The reader

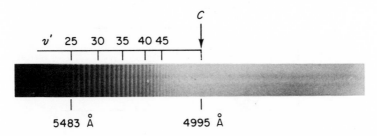

Fig. 18-7.   *Absorption spectrum of* I_2 *vapor. (From G. Herzberg, "Spectra of Diatomic Molecules," 2nd ed. Van Nostrand–Reinhold, Princeton, New Jersey, 1950.)*

might consider, for example, what the situation should be if the excited-state potential curve were very similar in shape and in r_e value to that of the ground state.

An absorption spectrum may become diffuse or blurred if a predissociation situation (see preceding section) exists. The vibrational energies of the excited state are, in effect, no longer well defined since on the first vibration the system may cross to a dissociative excited state. This is the case, for example, with the molecule S_2 (see Fig. 18-4).

Blurring also occurs often if the species is in solution or, if gaseous, is at a high pressure. Thus the absorption spectrum of I_2 in, say CCl_4, merely shows a single broad band. The qualitative reason is that collisions with gas or solvent molecules have become so frequent that a given vibrational state again has a very short life before being disturbed. Its energy is thereby made indefinite. In solution, the degree of this blurring is greater the more the molecule is solvated or highly interacting with solvent.

B. Emission

The discussion so far has been mainly in terms of excitation, but it is, of course, also possible for an excited state to return to some lower state, ordinarily the ground state, with the emission of light. Figure 18-8 illustrates the situation with I_2. In the excitation to one component of the $^3\Pi$ state the most probable value of v' is about 26, and in the dilute gas the return is largely from this same v' state back to the ground state. The process is known as *resonance emission*. At higher pressures or in solution what happens instead is that gas or solvent collisions

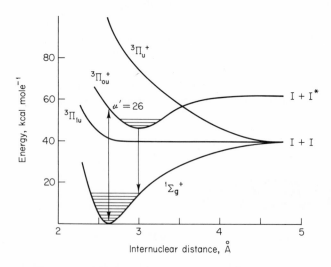

Fig. 18-8. *Potential energy diagram for various states of gaseous I_2.*

remove the excess vibrational excitation so quickly that when emission does occur it is mainly from the $v' = 0$ level. This is the more usual situation and, as indicated in the figure, the Franck–Condon principle now implies that the emission will be to a high vibrational level of the ground state. The consequence is that the emission is at a *longer* wavelength than is the absorption—an observation made by Stokes in 1852.

18-4 Electronic Excited States of Polyatomic Molecules

A. Localized States

It is very often possible to assign features of the absorption spectrum of a polyatomic molecule to excitations that are largely localized to some particular set of atoms or bonds. A carbonyl group will, for example, usually provide rather

Table 18-2. *Spectral Characteristics of Organic Chromophores[a]*

| Chromophore | Example | Absorption maximum | | Approximate extinction coefficient |
		ν (kK)	λ (Å)	ϵ (liter mole^{-1} cm^{-1})
C=C	$H_2C=CH_2$	55	1825	250
		57.3	1744	16,000
		58.6	1704	16,500
		62	1620	10,000
C≡C	$HC≡C-CH_2-CH_3$	58	1720	2500
C=O	H_2CO	34	2950	10
		54	1850	strong
C=S	$\begin{matrix} S \\ \| \\ CH_3C-CH_3 \end{matrix}$	22	4600	weak
$-NO_2$	CH_3NO_2	36	2775	15
		47.5	2100	10,000
$-N=N-$	$CH_3-N=N-CH_3$	28.8	3470	15
		>38.5	<2600	strong
Benzene		39	2550	200
		50	2000	6300
		55.5	1800	100,000
C—Cl	CH_3Cl	58	1725	
C—Br	CH_3Br	49	2040	1800
C—OH	CH_3OH	55	1500	1900
		67	1830	200

[a] Data from J. G. Calvert and J. N. Pitts, Jr., "Photochemistry." Wiley, New York, 1966.

characteristic absorption bands only secondarily modified by the rest of the molecule to which it is attached. Such groups are called *chromophores*, and a few, with their characteristic absorptions, are listed in Table 18-2. Many of these chromophores are diatomic ($R_2C=O$, $RC\equiv CR$, RCH_2X, and so on), and their theoretical treatment is that of a modified diatomic molecule. Figure 18-9 shows the set of

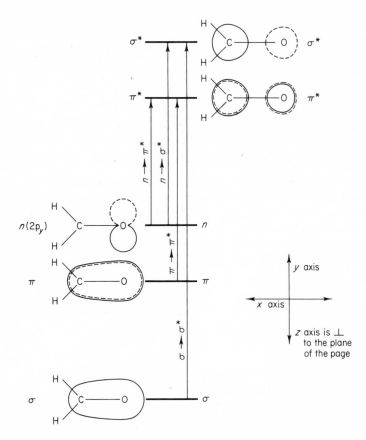

Fig. 18-9. *Molecular orbitals for formaldehyde and their approximate relative energies. (From J. G. Calvert and J. N. Pitts, Jr., "Photochemistry." Copyright 1966, Wiley, New York. Used with permission of John Wiley & Sons, Inc.)*

"molecular" orbitals for formaldehyde; these are not for the molecule as a whole, but really just for the C=O moiety. The excited states of the C—H bonds are higher enough in energy that the approximation of ignoring their mixing in with those of the C=O portion works fairly well.

There are several ways of describing the ground and excited states of a chromophore such as the C=O group in formaldehyde. One is in terms of the atomic orbitals involved. Thus the ground state of formaldehyde is $\sigma^2\pi^2p_y^2$, meaning that there are two electrons in a sigma bond and two in a pi bond; the p_y orbitals of the oxygen are perpendicular to the $C=O$ axis and are not involved in bonding; their two electrons are therefore nonbonding. As indicated in the discussion of Section 17-CN-1, for every bonding combination of atomic orbitals, there is an antibonding one, and Fig. 18-9 shows schematically the orbital appearance of the σ^* and π^* antibonding states. One then speaks of $\sigma \rightarrow \sigma^*$ and $\pi \rightarrow \pi^*$ transitions. In addition, an electron from the nonbonding p_y orbital of the oxygen may be promoted to the σ^* or a π^* level of the carbonyl "molecular" orbitals; the transitions are then called $n \rightarrow \sigma^*$ and $n \rightarrow \pi^*$, respectively.

In the case of simple molecules, a formal group-theoretic designation of the ground and excited-state wave functions may be useful. That is, the wave function for a given state will form the basis for one of the irreducible representations of the symmetry group to which the molecule belongs (Section 17-5). As an example, the $n \rightarrow \pi^*$ transition in formaldehyde has the group-theoretical designation $^1A_2 \leftarrow {}^1A_1$.

One may, alternatively, describe the excitation in a manner which emphasizes the change in polarity of the molecule. The term *charge transfer* was introduced by R. S. Mulliken for transitions in which a significant shift in electron density occurs between atoms or groups of atoms. In simple molecules or chromophores such transitions often involve the promotion of an electron from a bonding to the corresponding antibonding orbital. The hydrogen molecule, for example, has an absorption at 110.9 nm to an excited state whose orbital picture is approximately H^+H^-. Also, the gaseous alkali halide molecules show a charge transfer absorption, as in the continuous absorption band for $CsI(g)$ around 200 nm—the result of the absorption being to yield Cs and I atoms. The aqueous or hydrated halide ions show an absorption in which an electron is transferred to the solvent,

$$I^-(aq) \xrightarrow{h\nu, 232nm} I(aq) + e^-(aq), \qquad (18\text{-}5)$$

and similarly for metal ions such as $Fe^{2+}(aq)$ and coordination compounds such as $Fe(CN)_6^{4-}(aq)$. The $e^-(aq)$ species is a solvated electron; it reduces water in about 1 msec (millisecond) and other scavengers more quickly, but its transient absorption spectrum is well known. (There is a maximum at 680 nm and a concentrated solution of electrons would appear blue.)

The assignment of a particular absorption band as charge transfer is not so easy with polyatomic molecules. Two criteria are as follows. First, charge transfer excitations are usually facile, that is, the extinction coefficient for the transition is large, and an intense band not otherwise identifiable will generally be so classed. Second, the photochemistry of a charge transfer excited state is usually one of redox decomposition, as in Eq. (18-5). As a further example, Fig. 18-10 shows the absorption spectra for acetophenone, $CH_3CO\phi$, and benzophenone, $\phi CO\phi$ ($\phi = C_6H_5$). The intense absorption around 240 nm is attributed to charge transfer and, in the former case in particular, one reason for doing so is that the products CH_3CO and C_6H_5 are observed, indicative of an electron density shift from the

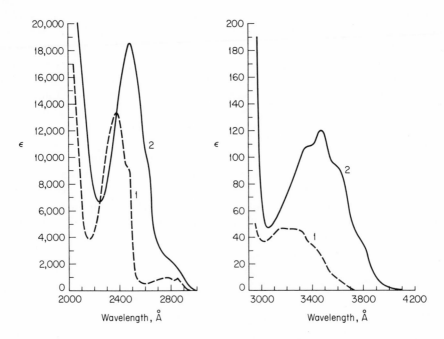

Fig. 18-10. *Absorption spectra for (1) acetophenone* $(CH_3COC_6H_5)$ *and (2) benzophenone* $(C_6H_5COC_6H_5)$ *(in cyclohexane at 25°C). (From J. G. Calvert and J. N. Pitts, Jr., "Photochemistry." Copyright 1966, Wiley, New York. Used with permission of John Wiley & Sons, Inc.)*

acetyl to the phenyl group in the excited state. Finally, the first intense absorption band of $Co(NH_3)_6^{3+}$ is classed as charge transfer (from ligand to metal), consistent with the photochemical observation that Co^{2+} and oxidized ammonia are produced.

B. Delocalized States

Electronic transitions may be between states whose wave functions are best described as encompassing a number of atoms. Examples are the conjugated polyenes and aromatic compounds. Both cases may be treated (rather crudely) by the particle-in-a-box model (Section 16-5) whereby the pi electrons are assigned in pairs to the successive energy levels of the set of standing waves. Such wave functions are truly molecular ones in that no use is made of atomic wave functions, the wave equation being solved for the molecule as a whole.

The Hückel treatment (Section 17-ST-1) makes use of combinations of atomic orbitals to formulate wave functions for the whole conjugated system. The result is again a set of standing waves distributed over the entire molecule, the corresponding energy states being populated by the available pi electrons.

C. Excited-State Processes

We have so far stressed the wave mechanical description of excited states in terms of their energies and electron distributions. The photochemist is also interested in the various processes which an excited state can undergo, and a generalized scheme is shown in Fig. 18-11. We suppose the molecule to be polyatomic, with several internuclear distances, so that simple potential energy diagrams such as Fig. 18-6 are no longer possible. The various families of energy levels are instead assembled in vertical arrays, the secondary lines indicating the superimposed vibrational and rotational fine structure.

The figure contains a great deal of detail which needs explanation. First, organic molecules generally have an even number of electrons, that is, they are not free radicals. Further, the spins are all paired in the ground state, which is therefore a singlet state, labeled S_0 in the figure. The more prominent absorptions are to excited singlet states, shown as S_1 and S_2. One expects a second series of states, similar to the singlet ones, but in which an electron has inverted its spin so that the molecule has a net spin of unity, and is therefore in a *triplet* state. Direct transitions such as $T_1 \leftarrow S_0$ are relatively improbable because of the symmetry selection rule mentioned in Section 18-2. Typically, then, one sees various absorp-

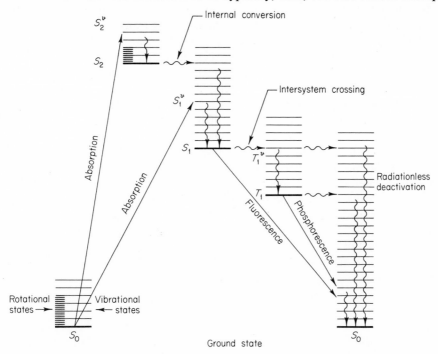

Fig. 18-11.   *Various photophysical processes. Radiative transitions are given by solid lines, and radiationless ones, by wavy lines. The fine structure of lines indicates schematically vibrational and rotational excitations.*

tion bands due to singlet–singlet transitions, usually with most or all of the vibrational–rotational detail washed out.

The actual absorptions are shown in the figure as $S_1^v \leftarrow S_0$ and $S_2^v \leftarrow S_0$, the superscript meaning that the transition terminates at some high vibrational level of the excited state. The situation is similar to that shown in Fig. 18-6; we assume the transitions to be vertical and that the S_1 and S_2 states are distorted relative to S_0.

A number of secondary processes may now take place. If the molecule is in solution, it is very likely that the S_2^v or S_1^v state will lose its vibrational energy or *thermally equilibrate* to the S_2 or S_1 true electronic state, the energy being dissipated into the solvent. Then S_2 may pass to the vibrationally excited state $S_1^{v'}$; the process is known as *internal conversion*. It may happen because of a crossing of the potential energy surfaces for the two states, or some interaction with solvent can be involved. The consequence is that regardless of which singlet excited state is first populated, a molecule usually ends up in the lowest excited singlet state as a result of internal conversion and rapid thermal equilibration.

The S_1 state may return to the ground state S_0 by emission. We will use the term *fluorescence* for emission between states of the same spin multiplicity. Alternatively, the S_1 state may go to S_0 by *radiationless deactivation*. As the name implies, no radiation is emitted, the excess energy appearing either as vibrational excitation of S_0 or of adjacent solvent. Finally, the S_1 state may transform to a more or less vibrationally excited triplet state. The act is radiationless, the difference in energy between S_1 and T_1 appearing in vibrational excitation of T_1 or, possibly, in solvent vibrations; we call such a transition an *intersystem crossing*. If the produced state is T_1^v, it is assumed to thermally equilibrate rapidly to T_1, which may then return to the ground state either by emission or by radiationless deactivation. Such emission now involves states of differing spin multiplicity and is called *phosphorescence*.

Processes of the preceding type have been termed *photophysical*, meaning that they leave the molecule intact. *Photochemical* change is, of course, that whereby an excited state undergoes isomerization, fragmentation, or reaction with solvent or a solute. A common observation with organic systems is that chemical change is largely associated with the T_1 state. For example, if a solution of *trans*-stilbene, $\phi-CH{=}CH-\phi$, is irradiated, one observes some fluorescence from the S_1 state, but a good deal of intersystem crossing to T_1 also occurs. The T_1 state is probably π^* in type, and the weakening of the double bond allows easy isomerization. The consequence is that irradiation of the *trans*-stilbene absorption band at about 290 nm, corresponding to $S_1^v \leftarrow S_0$, results in a fairly efficient *trans* to *cis* isomerization.

A very important type of process is that of *photosensitization*, whereby an excited molecule transfers its excitation energy to some second species. Thus the T_1 state of biacetyl,

$$\underset{\displaystyle CH_3CCCH_3,}{\overset{\displaystyle \overset{O\ O}{\| \ \|}}{}}$$

is about 55 kcal mole^{-1} above the ground state S_0. Irradiation of biacetyl in the presence of stilbene induces isomerization of the latter, and it appears that the process

$$^3D^* + {}^1A \rightarrow {}^1D + {}^3A^* \tag{18-6}$$

has occurred, where D denotes *donor* (biacetyl) and A *acceptor* (stilbene). The energy transfer very likely occurs during an encounter between $^3D^*$ and ^1A species. Often a reaction of this type occurs on the first encounter, or with a rate constant of about 10^{10} liter mole^{-1} sec^{-1} (see Section 15-4).

If the $^3D^*$ state shows an observable phosphorescence, then the competition of process (18-6) leads to phosphorescence *quenching*. That is, the intensity of phosphorescence, on irradiating the system, is progressively reduced by increasing concentrations of the acceptor. The same may happen to fluorescence emission. The situation may be treated by conventional stationary-state kinetic analysis.

To summarize, we have considered the following typical processes.

1. Absorption, usually $S_1^v \leftarrow S_0$ or $S_2^v \leftarrow S_0$.
2. Thermal equilibration: $S_1^v \rightarrow S_1$, $T_1^v \rightarrow T_1$, and so on.
3. Internal conversion: $S_2 \rightarrow S_1^v$, $T_2 \rightarrow T_1^v$.
4. Radiationless deactivation: $S_1 \rightarrow S_0$, $T_1 \rightarrow S_0$.
5. Intersystem crossing: $S_1 \rightarrow T_1^v$.
6. Fluorescence: $S_1 \rightarrow S_0^v + h\nu$.
7. Phosphorescence: $T_1 \rightarrow S_0^v + h\nu$.
8. Chemical reaction: S_1 or $T_1 \rightarrow$ chemical change.
9. Sensitization.
10. Quenching of emission.

D.   Photochemical Processes

The photochemistry of organic compounds is now a rather large subject, and that of coordination compounds is becoming so. Only a few examples can be given here.

Ketones are generally photosensitive, the primary reactions being

$$RCOR' \xrightarrow{h\nu} \begin{array}{c} R + COR' \\ RCO + R' \end{array} \tag{18-7}$$

where R and R' are alkyl groups. The RCO or R'CO fragment may then dissociate to carbon monoxide; the radicals R and R' undergo, of course, various further reactions until stable products eventually are reached. The bond that breaks tends to be the weaker of the two, the degree of discrimination being greater the longer the wavelength of the light used. Thus with gaseous $CH_3COC_2H_5$ the ratio of ethyl to methyl radicals formed in the primary dissociation reaction is about 40 with light of 313 nm but only 5.5 with light of 265 nm. The overall efficiency or quantum yield (see next subsection) varies greatly from one ketone to another, ranging from about 0.001 to nearly unity.

An alternative mode of reaction is exhibited by benzophenone, ϕ_2CO. Irradiation of the first singlet–singlet absorption band [believed to be an (n, π^*) transition] is followed by intersystem crossing to a lower-lying triplet state T_1, which now efficiently abstracts a hydrogen atom from the solvent:

$$\phi_2\text{CO} \xrightarrow{h\nu} \phi_2\text{CO*} (S_1) \rightarrow \phi_2\text{CO*} (T_1) \ ,$$

$$\phi_2\text{CO*} (T_1) + \text{RH} \rightarrow \phi_2\dot{\text{C}}\text{OH} + \text{R} \ , \tag{18-8}$$

$$2\phi_2\dot{\text{C}}\text{OH} \rightarrow \phi_2\text{COHCOH}\phi_2 \ .$$

The resulting ketyl radicals then combine to yield benzpinacol.

The alkyl halides RX, if irradiated in their first absorption band, usually give the radicals R and X with high efficiency. Irradiation of the second, higher-energy band may, however, yield an olefin plus HX,

$$\text{RCH}_2\text{CH}_2\text{X} \xrightarrow{h\nu} \text{RCH}{=}\text{CH}_2 + \text{HX}. \tag{18-9}$$

Examples are ethyl and *n*-propyl iodides. One thus observes *spectrospecificity*, that is, wavelength-dependent photochemistry.

Photoisomerization constitutes another important class of reactions. It was mentioned earlier in this section that the stilbenes photoisomerize, mainly from the first triplet excited state. The spiropyrans form an interesting class of *photoreversible* systems. The normal form is usually colorless (depending on the ring substituents) and irradiation in the ultraviolet converts form I to colored form II. There is a return in the dark which is accelerated photochemically on irradiation with light in the visible range.

Important primary photochemical processes in organic chemistry thus include homolytic bond breaking to yield radical species, bond weakening of a double bond to give *cis-to-trans* isomerization as well as more complex rearrangements, and excited-state reactions with solvent or solute molecules.

Coordination compounds also have a photochemistry. For example, irradiation of the first charge transfer band of a Co(III) complex such as $\text{Co(NH}_3)_6^{3+}$ leads to Co^{2+} and nitrogen, and that of $\text{Co(NH}_3)_5\text{Br}^{2+}$, to Co^{2+} and bromine atoms (which then undergo further reaction). Irradiation of a ligand field band generally leads to a substitution reaction. Thus visible light produces the reaction

$$\text{Cr(NH}_3)_5(\text{NCS})^{2+} + \text{H}_2\text{O} \xrightarrow{h\nu} \text{Cr(NH}_3)_4(\text{H}_2\text{O})(\text{NCS})^{2+} + \text{NH}_3 \tag{18-10}$$

with high efficiency. The ordinary thermal reaction of this complex ion is one of replacement of the NCS^- group, so in this case the photochemical and thermal reactions are distinctly different.

E. Kinetics of Excited-State Processes

The overall efficiency of an excited-state process is usually described by a *quantum yield* ϕ. This may be defined as

$$n = I_\text{a}\phi, \tag{18-11}$$

where n denotes the number of events which occur and I_a is the number of light quanta absorbed by the system in the irradiation. One may speak, for example, of a fluorescence yield ϕ_f, where the event is the emission of a light quantum from the S_1 state. Similarly, ϕ_p denotes a phosphorescence quantum yield. In the case of chemical reaction, an alternative form of Eq. (18-11) is

$$m = E\phi, \tag{18-12}$$

where m is the number of moles of photochemical reaction which occurs and E is the number of einsteins of light absorbed (an *einstein*, abbreviated E, is one mole of light quanta). If more than one product is formed, one may assign partial quantum yields ϕ_1, ϕ_2, ... to each.

A quantum yield usually refers to one or another of a set of mutually exclusive primary events such as emission or chemical reaction, and the set of quantum yields for all possible events should then total unity. However, if a photochemical quantum yield is an apparent one, being based on the amount of some final product, then values exceeding unity may be found. Thus in the case of photochemically initiated chain reactions quantum yields of several hundred or thousand may be found. Finally, it is clear from the material of this section that quantum yields are in general wavelength-dependent; they are therefore not very meaningful unless reported for at least a fairly narrow range of wavelengths.

Quantum yields refer to overall efficiencies, and one also assigns individual rate constants to separate, individual processes such as those shown in Fig. 18-11. Thus, referring to the S_1 state, the fluorescence process ($S_1 \rightarrow S_0{}^v$) will have a rate constant k_f; that of radiationless deactivation, k_d; and that of intersystem crossing, k_c. The total rate constant for disappearance of S_1 is then, the sum $k = k_f + k_d + k_c$, and the average life of S_1 is, correspondingly, $\tau = 1/k$ [Eq. (14-13)]. Under some conditions only the emission is important, and one speaks of $1/k_f$ as the *natural lifetime* of the state.

A fairly common situation is that in which an excited state is deactivated as the result of an encounter with some solute species. Dissolved oxygen is very effective in deactivating or quenching organic triplet excited states, for example. Other substances may be effective in quenching either singlet or triplet states; the complex ion $Cr(NH_3)_5(NCS)^{2+}$ quenches the fluorescence emission of acridinium ion as well as the phosphorescence emission of biacetyl.

A simple kinetic scheme for such quenching is the following:

$$S_0 \xrightarrow{h\nu} S_1, \qquad S_1 \xrightarrow{k_f} S_0 + h\nu, \qquad S_1 \xrightarrow{k_d} S_0, \qquad S_1 + M \xrightarrow{k_q} S_0 + M,$$

where M is the quenching species. We apply the stationary-state hypothesis (Section 14-4C),

$$\frac{d(S_1)}{dt} = 0 = I_a - k_f(S_1) - k_d(S_1) - k_q(S_1)(M),$$

to obtain for the rate of fluorescence

$$\frac{d(h\nu)}{dt} = k_f(S_1) = \frac{k_f I_a}{k_f + k_d + k_q(M)}$$

or

$$\phi_f = \frac{k_f}{k_f + k_d + k_q(M)}. \tag{18-13}$$

Equation (18-13) may be put in the linear form

$$\frac{1}{\phi_f} = \frac{k_f + k_d}{k_f} + \frac{k_q}{k_f}(M), \tag{18-14}$$

so that a plot of $1/\phi_f$ versus (M) allows a determination of the ratios k_d/k_f and k_q/k_f. The natural fluorescence rate k_f can be estimated from the area under the absorption band (see Section 18-ST-1) and can sometimes be determined directly. The other processes tend to decrease in importance as the temperature is lowered and if S_1 is produced at, say, liquid nitrogen temperature (77°K) by a sudden pulse of light in a flash photolysis experiment, then the decay rate of the subsequent fluorescence emission may closely approximate k_f. One can then calculate k_d and k_q from the k observed in, say, room-temperature solution, since k_f should be nearly independent of external conditions. The k_q values so calculated often correspond to the rate constant for a diffusion-controlled reaction (Section 15-4). Fluorescence lifetimes are usually quite small, 10^{-9}–10^{-6} sec, while phosphorescence lifetimes may range from 10^{-4} sec to minutes.

As an illustration, 1×10^{-3} M $Cr(NH_3)_5(NCS)^{2+}$ reduces the fluorescence emission of acridinium ion by 20%, the system being irradiated at 410 nm and the emission occurring around 500 nm. Equation (18-14) can be put in the form

$$\frac{\phi_f{}^\circ}{\phi_f} = 1 + \frac{k_q}{k_f}\phi_f{}^\circ(M), \tag{18-15}$$

whence $(k_q/k_f)\phi_f{}^\circ = (1.25 - 1)/(10^{-3}) = 250$. The fluorescence yield in the absence of quencher, $\phi_f{}^\circ$, is known from separate studies to be 0.77, and $\tau_f = 4 \times 10^{-8}$ sec. The quenching rate constant k_q is thus about 8×10^9 liter mole^{-1} sec^{-1}, or about the value for a diffusion-controlled reaction. Incidentally, the quenching largely results in an excitation of the complex ion, which then undergoes photochemical aquation of an ammonia group [Eq. (18-10)].

18-5   Vibrational Spectra

A.   Diatomic Molecules

Most vibrational spectra are treated in terms of a set of harmonic oscillators, both for diatomic and polyatomic molecules. The case of a single harmonic oscillator was treated wave mechanically in Section 16-6, with the result given by Eq. (16-61). There is a single characteristic frequency ν_0 and the quantized energy states are

$$\epsilon = h\nu_0(\nu + \tfrac{1}{2}) \qquad \text{[Eq. (16-61)]},$$

where ν may be 0, 1, 2, ... By analogy with the equivalent mechanical system, Eq. (16-64) gives

$$h\nu_0 = 2.57 \times 10^{-13} \left(\frac{k'}{\mu'}\right)^{1/2} \qquad \text{erg},$$

where k' is the restoring force constant, in units of 10^5 dyn cm^{-1}, and μ' is the reduced mass of the diatomic molecule, in mass units.

The symmetry requirement implicit in Eq. (18-1) imposes the further condition that the probability of light absorption to produce a change in vibrational energy will be zero unless $\Delta v = \pm 1$. (A slightly more detailed group-theoretical explanation is given in Section 18-ST-1.) It further turns out that even if the symmetry requirement is met, the probability of light absorption will be zero unless some change in molecular dipole moment accompanies the transition. The consequence is that vibrational intensities are theoretically zero for homopolar or A–A-type molecules; harmonic oscillations of such a molecule may vary in amplitude but cannot produce a dipole moment.

These rules are based on the assumption of the harmonic oscillator; an actual molecule will have a potential energy versus nuclear separation curve such as shown in Fig. 18-6, and in this case the $\Delta v = \pm 1$ rule is voided. In practice, this means that while the change $\Delta v = \pm 1$ remains the most probable, other values can occur as well. The requirement that a change in dipole moment occur is a quite stringent one, however, and the consequence is that the vibrational absorption spectrum of an A–A-type molecule is very weak indeed. Heteronuclear diatomic molecules, however, show fairly intense absorptions. As noted in Section 16-6, HCl absorbs at 2886 cm^{-1}, corresponding to the $v = 0$ to $v = 1$ transition. The corresponding frequencies for HF, HBr, and HI are at 4141, 2650, and 2309 cm^{-1}, respectively. These absorptions all lie in the infrared, of course.

B.   Raman Spectroscopy

A molecule may reveal its vibrational energy states by an inelastic scattering of a light photon. The experimental observation is that a small fraction of the incident light is scattered and that the scattered light may differ in energy from that of the incident light by an amount corresponding to a vibrational spacing. Usually this spacing is that for which $\Delta v = \pm 1$.

The whole effect is a second-order one, and might be rather unimportant except that its probability depends on the polarizability of the molecule rather than on its dipole moment. As a consequence, molecules of the A–A type will show a Raman spectrum even though the usual infrared vibrational absorption spectrum is forbidden. Thus Raman spectroscopy is a valuable supplement to the usual infrared absorption measurements.

From the experimental point of view, a very intense and highly monochromatic light source is needed, the first requirement to produce appreciable scattered light and the second so that the small change in frequency can be measured accurately. For example, if light of 254 nm, or about 39,000 cm^{-1}, is used to irradiate oxygen, the Raman scattered light differs in frequency by only 1600 cm^{-1}, corresponding to the difference between the $v = 0$ and $v = 1$ vibrational levels. A recent and important development is the use of laser light; this provides both the high-intensity and, more importantly, the highly monochromatic light needed. To repeat, it is not necessary that the wavelength used correspond to an actual electronic transition; the physical picture given here is merely a way of visualizing the inelastic collision of the light quantum with a molecule.

C. Polyatomic Molecules

   The equipartition principle (Section 4-8) informs us of the number of vibrational degrees of freedom for any molecule, namely $3n - 6$ for a nonlinear one and $3n - 5$ for a linear one, n being the number of atoms in the molecule. We should therefore expect to observe this number of distinct vibrational frequencies, each having a value determined by the force constant and reduced mass appropriate for the particular motion involved. These frequencies bear no rational relationship to each other, and if a polyatomic molecule could be observed in some ultra-microscope, its atoms would appear to be undergoing complicated, never-repeating oscillations. These complex oscillations are, however, the result of the super-position of various primitive vibrations, and an important theoretical problem is the prediction of what these last should be.

   The primitive vibrations are known as the *normal (vibrational)* modes of the molecule, and it turns out that the motions of each normal mode must form the basis for one of the irreducible representations of the point group to which the molecule belongs (Section 17-2). Consider, for example, the molecular ion CO_3^{2-}. The normal modes are depicted in Fig. 18-12. Carbonate ion, being planar, has the point group symmetry D_{3h}, for which the irreducible representations are A_1', A_2', E', A_1'', A_2'', and E'' (Table 17-7). It is easy to see that the v_1 mode of Fig. 18-12 is totally symmetric with respect to the operations of the group, and hence belongs to the A_1' representation. The v_2 mode is unchanged by the E, C_3, and σ_v operations but is put into the negative of itself by the C_2, S_3, and σ_h operations, thus identifying it as belonging to the A_2'' representation. The v_{3a} and v_{3b} modes *together* form the basis for the E' representation, and so on. One expects a total of $4 \times 3 - 6 = 6$ normal modes, which is just the sum of the orders of the irreducible representations involved.

   While it is relatively easy to see that the indicated normal modes for CO_3^{2-} do belong to certain representations, the reverse type of analysis is much more difficult. That is, considerable effort may be required to deduce what types of motions constitute the normal modes for some arbitrary molecule. We will not attempt to explore the problem here, except to mention that the procedure involves assigning x, y, and z vectors to each atom and carrying the set of vectors through the symmetry operations of the group. To give a brief example, the resulting reducible representation in the case of CO_3^{2-} gives

$$\Gamma = A_1' + A_2' + 3E' + 2A_2'' + E''.$$

   The translation of the molecule as a whole must involve representations carrying x, y, and z designations (see Table 17-7), or $A_2'' + E'$. Rotation corresponds to R_x, R_y, and R_z, so that A_2' and E'' are so assigned, leaving A_1', $2E'$, and A_2'' for vibrations.

   It would be convenient if infrared absorption spectra simply showed the separate frequencies for each normal mode. Several complications enter, unfortunately. First, only those modes that involve a change in dipole moment will be infrared-active; the others will usually be Raman-active. This means that certain fundamental frequencies, such as the v_1 mode for CO_3^{2-}, will be absent. Second,

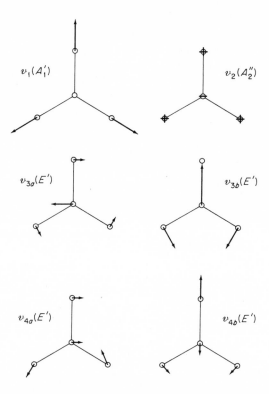

$v_1(A_1')$

$v_2(A_2'')$

$v_{3a}(E')$

$v_{3b}(E')$

$v_{4a}(E')$

$v_{4b}(E')$

Fig. 18-12. *The normal modes of vibration of* CO_3^{2-}; *plus and minus denote motion in and out of the plane of the paper, respectively. (After F. A. Cotton, "Chemical Applications of Group Theory." Copyright 1963, Wiley (Interscience), New York. Used with permission of John Wiley & Sons, Inc.)*

the normal modes interact, so that various combinations of changes in vibrational quantum numbers may be involved. Thus CO_2 has four normal modes, of which only three are infrared-active; these have fundamental frequencies of 667 cm^{-1} (twofold degenerate) for v_2 and 2349 cm^{-1} for v_3. The symmetric, Raman-active vibration v_1 is at 1384 cm^{-1}. The observed infrared spectrum shows absorptions at wavelengths corresponding to $\Delta v = 1$ for v_2 and v_3, but also for $v_3 - v_2$, $v_3 - 2v_2$, and other combinations, as well as for overtones, or larger Δv values. The consequence is that it can be very difficult to disentangle or assign infrared absorption frequencies to specific quantum transitions.

Fortunately, combination and overtone absorptions tend to be weaker than the fundamental ones, especially if the various normal mode frequencies are well separated in value. Furthermore, the normal modes will at least approximately correspond to simple motions of the molecular framework, with the result that to a first approximation the vibrations of a molecule may be regarded as simple stretchings or bendings of individual bonds. The consequence is that in polyatomic organic molecules characteristic functional group frequencies are found. Some of these are listed in Table 18-3. One can thus identify the presence of $C-H$, $C-C$, $C-O$ bonds and so on in a molecule from the appearance of characteristic infrared absorption peaks. In a very real sense, the infrared spectrum of a molecule identifies or "fingerprints" it; the presence of a particular molecule in a mixture can thus be identified or even determined quantitatively. The spectra of two simple molecules are shown in Fig. 18-13; the reader can test the extent to which frequencies listed in Table 18-3 are present.

If an atom has several equivalent bonds, as in a CH_3 group, then, of course, a collection of normal modes is involved rather than just a superposition of independent $C-H$ vibrations. The resulting spectral detail is itself a characteristic of the group of atoms, and in fact, the symmetry of a group of atoms may sometimes be deduced from the splittings of the bond frequencies of the group. As an example, irradiation of the carbonyl complex $Cr(CO)_6$ produces the fragment $Cr(CO)_5$, and the splitting of the CO frequencies determines that the geometry is that of a trigonal bipyramid.

Table 18-3. *Some Characteristic Bond Force Constants and Frequencies*[a]

	Stretching			Bending	
Bond	Force constant $(\times 10^5 \text{ dyn cm}^{-1})$	Frequency (cm^{-1})		Motion	Frequency (cm^{-1})
$\equiv C-H$	5.85	3300		$\equiv C \overset{\frown}{-} H$	700
$>C-H$	4.79	2960		$-C\overset{H}{\underset{H}{\overset{\frown}{<}}}{}^H$	1000
$-C\equiv C-$	15.59	2050		$>C\overset{H}{\underset{H}{\overset{\frown}{<}}}$	1450
$>C=C<$	9.6	1650		$-C\overset{H}{\underset{H}{\overset{H}{\underset{}{<}}}}$	1450
$-C\equiv N$	17.73	2100			
$>C=O$	12.1	1700			
$-O-H$	7.66	3680			
$>C-Cl$	3.64	650			

[a] Data from G. Herzberg, "Infrared and Raman Spectra of Polyatomic Molecules." Van Nostrand–Reinhold, Princeton, New Jersey, 1945.

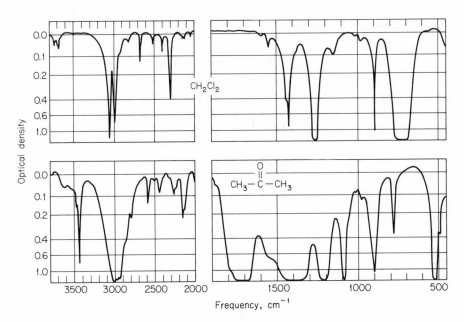

Fig. 18-13. *Infrared absorption spectra of* CH_2Cl_2 *(top) and acetone (bottom). (From W. J. Potts, Jr., "Chemical Infrared Spectroscopy." Copyright 1963, Wiley, New York. Used with permission of John Wiley & Sons, Inc.)*

COMMENTARY AND NOTES

18-CN-1   Geometric and Electronic Nature of Ground-State Molecules

There are several spectroscopic phenomena which yield valuable information about the geometry or the bonding of molecules in their lowest electronic or ground state. The detailed theory is beyond the scope of this text, but the final equations and their applications are definitely of interest. We have already considered vibrational spectra (Section 18-5) and now turn to pure rotational spectra and magnetic resonance phenomena. Mössbauer spectroscopy is mentioned in Section 21-CN-6.

A. Microwave Spectroscopy

Transitions from one rotational state to another may be observed directly with radiation of the appropriate wavelength (the molecule must have a permanent dipole moment). The energy levels of a diatomic rigid rotator are given by

$$\epsilon = \frac{h^2}{8\pi^2 I} J(J + 1) \qquad \text{[Eq. (16-114)]},$$

where J may be 0, 1, 2, ... The moment of inertia I is defined by $I = \sum m_i r_i^2$, where r_i is the distance of atom i from the center of mass, and for a diatomic molecule I values are around 10^{-40} g cm^2 (corresponding to m about 3×10^{-23} g and r about 10^{-8} cm).[†] Rotational energies are therefore about 5×10^{-15} erg molecule^{-1}, or about 0.1 kT at room temperature.

The symmetry properties of rotational wave functions (see Sections 18-ST-1 and 18-ST-3) lead to the rule that transitions are favored only if $\Delta J = \pm 1$, and for a transition from J to $J + 1$, Eq. (16-114) yields

$$\bar{\nu} = 2B(J + 1), \tag{18-16}$$

where $\bar{\nu}$ is frequency in wavenumbers and B, called the *rotational constant*, is $h/8\pi^2 Ic$. Usual values of B are around 1 to 100 cm^{-1}, corresponding to wavelengths of 0.5–0.005 cm in rotational spectra.

These numbers reveal several important qualitative aspects of rotational spectroscopy. The wavelength of the electromagnetic radiation involved approaches that of shortwave radio or radar waves. It was, in fact, the development of radar and the availability of surplus equipment after World War II that brought rotational or *microwave spectroscopy* into prominence. A second comment is that the rotational energy level spacings are so close together that a molecule at room temperature will most probably be in a fairly high rotational level; the observed spectrum is then one involving transitions from one excited state to another, unlike most other spectroscopy. It should be noted that polyatomic molecules have three moments of inertia and a correspondingly more complex set of energy states. Finally, rotational absorptions are relatively weak in intensity and the absorption bands must be quite sharp to be detected with precision. The consequence is that experiments are largely limited to rather dilute gases to minimize the line broadening which results from molecular collisions. The experimental equipment is rather special in nature; microwaves are best "conducted" in tubes or hollow rectangular pipes, and one looks for attenuation of the radiation by a gaseous sample admitted to a section of the pipe. The radiation is provided by a klystron or magnetron tube and is frequency modulated so as to sweep the range of frequencies where absorption should occur. An oscilloscope display then shows the strength of the signal received by a crystal detector as a function of frequency.

Perhaps the most important application of microwave spectroscopy is the determination of B and hence of the three (in general) moments of inertia of a molecule (see Section 4-CN-2). By isotopically labeling various atoms of the

---

[†] An equivalent statement for a diatomic molecule is that $I = \mu r^2$, where μ is the reduced mass and r the bond length.

molecule, individual bond lengths can be determined rather accurately, as can bond angles. Further, on application of an electric field, both changes and splittings in rotational energies result if the molecule has a dipole moment. As a consequence, it has been possible to obtain dipole moments for simple molecules from this effect, known as the *Stark effect*. Finally, a polyatomic molecule is difficult to treat theoretically unless two of its three moments of inertia are equal so that the molecule behaves as a symmetric "top"; examples are ammonia, CH_3Cl, and $CHCl_3$. Data for some symmetric top molecules are given in Table 18-4.

B. Nuclear Magnetic Resonance

A rather different type of spectroscopy is that which is based on the splitting of otherwise degenerate *nuclear* energy states which occurs in a magnetic field. The fundamental nuclear particles, the proton and the neutron, have intrinsic angular momenta of $\frac{1}{2}h/2\pi$, usually reported as just $\frac{1}{2}$. These combine in a nucleus to give a net nuclear spin which is an even integral number of units of $\frac{1}{2}$ if there are an even number of fundamental nuclear particles, and an odd integral number of units of $\frac{1}{2}$ otherwise. For example, the even nuclei ^2H, ^{12}C, and ^{16}O have nuclear spins of 1, 0, and 0, respectively, while the odd nuclei ^1H, ^7Li, ^{15}N, and ^{19}F have spins of $\frac{1}{2}$, $\frac{3}{2}$, $\frac{1}{2}$, and $\frac{1}{2}$, respectively. This net nuclear spin is given the symbol I (not to be confused with a molecular moment of inertia).

Nuclei have, of course, a net electric charge, and a nonzero nuclear spin implies a motion of this charge or a current, hence an associated nuclear magnetic moment μ_n. The theoretical magnetic moment for a proton, treated as a spinning spherical shell of charge, is given by the nuclear magneton β_n, defined as

$$\beta_n = \frac{eh}{4\pi Mc}. \tag{18-17}$$

Table 18-4. *Geometry of Some Symmetric Tops from Microwave Spectroscopy[a]*

Molecules	d_{12} (Å)	d_{23} (Å)	θ
CH_3F	1.11	1.39	110°
CH_3Cl	1.113	1.781	110°31'
CH_3I	1.113	2.1392	111°14'
CCl_3H	1.767	1.073	110°24'
SiH_3Cl	1.44	2.050	110°

[a] Data from C. H. Townes and A. L. Schawlow, "Microwave Spectroscopy." McGraw-Hill, New York, 1955. The molecules are all of the C_{3v} point group; the bond lengths and angles are as shown in the diagram.

The nuclear magneton is just m/M times the Bohr magneton (Section 3-ST-2), where m and M are the electron and proton mass, respectively, and its numerical value is 5.0493×10^{-24} erg G^{-1} (G is the abbreviation for the unit of magnetic field, gauss). Actual nuclear magnetic moments differ from this value, and it has become customary to express them as

$$\mu_n = g_n \beta_n I, \qquad (18\text{-}18)$$

where g_n is a number of the order of unity, called the *nuclear g factor*. {In a stricter presentation $[I(I + 1)]^{1/2}$ would be used instead of I.}

If a magnetic field **H** is present, then the energy of a nucleus having spin I becomes dependent on its orientation with respect to the field. The quantum restriction is that the component of μ_n in the direction of the field μ be

$$\mu = m_n g_n \beta_n, \qquad (18\text{-}19)$$

where m_n is a quantum number which may have the values $I, I - 1, I - 2, ..., -I$, or $2I + 1$ values in all. The energy of each orientation depends on the field strength,

$$\epsilon = -\mu H = -m_n g_n \beta_n H. \qquad (18\text{-}20)$$

Since our presentation is to be a brief one, we now restrict our examples to the proton, with $I = \frac{1}{2}$ and magnetic moment 2.79270 in units of β_n (corresponding to a g factor of 5.5854). According to Eq. (18-19), the energies of the two states are then $\pm \mu H$, and, as shown in Fig. 18-14, they are separated by an energy $2\mu H$.

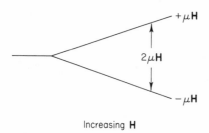

Increasing **H**

Fig. 18-14. *Splitting of the proton spin states in a magnetic field.*

This is a very small energy for ordinary values of **H**. Thus if the field is 10,000 G (gauss), we obtain

$$\Delta\epsilon = 2\mu H = 2(2.79270)(5.0493 \times 10^{-24})(10^4) = 2.820 \times 10^{-19} \quad \text{erg.} \quad (18\text{-}21)$$

This is to be compared with a kT value of 4.12×10^{-14} erg at 25°C. The population of the two states will therefore be almost equal, their ratio being given by the Boltzmann factor $\exp(2\mu H/kT)$. The exponential can be expanded to yield the probabilities of a given proton being in the upper or lower state as $\frac{1}{2}[1 \mp (\mu H/kT)]$, respectively, or about $\frac{1}{2}(1 - 10^{-5})$ and $\frac{1}{2}(1 + 10^{-5})$.

The natural time for nuclei to reach the equilibrium or Boltzmann distribution depends on the various processes present whereby nuclei exchange energy with their surroundings and is called the *spin–lattice relaxation time* T_1 (this is the reciprocal of the rate constant for the approach to the equilibrium distribution). Values of T_1 depend on the chemical (and magnetic) nature of the molecules present in the medium, but usually are in the range of 10^{-2}–10^2 sec for liquids. For water T_1 is about 3.6 sec and for ethanol the value is 2.2 sec. Thus when the external magnetic field is turned on the protons present in a sample will adjust very quickly to the Boltzmann distribution of their two energy states.

An experimental means of measuring $\Delta\epsilon$ might be through the absorption of a light quantum. A typical frequency is found by dividing the result of Eq. (18-21) by h to obtain $2.820 \times 10^{-19}/6.6256 \times 10^{-27} = 42.56 \times 10^6$ sec^{-1} or 42.6 kHz (kilohertz). The wavelength of radiation of this frequency would be $2.998 \times 10^{10}/42.56 \times 10^6 = 704$ cm, corresponding to the shortwave radio region. The problem is that while nuclei in the lower-energy state would absorb such radiation, those in the upper state would be stimulated to emit the same wavelength radiation and return to the ground state. The theoretical probabilities for absorption and stimulated emission are identical (see Section 18-ST-1), and since there are virtually equal numbers of nuclei in the two states, the *net* absorption of radiation will be very small. It is possible to measure it by equipment of the type shown in Fig. 18-15. First, it is easier and therefore customary to use a fixed

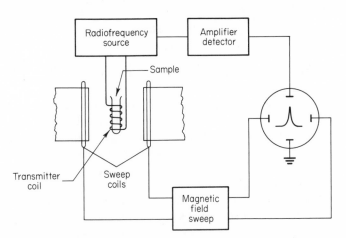

Fig. 18-15. *Schematic diagram of apparatus of an nmr experiment. (After J. A. Pople, W. G. Schneider, and H. J. Bernstein, "High Resolution Nuclear Magnetic Resonance." Copyright 1959, McGraw-Hill, New York. Used with permission of McGraw-Hill Book Company.)*

radiofrequency source and to put the magnetic field through a small variation— one only needs perhaps 100 parts per million (ppm) change in a field of 10,000 G. When the field is such that the frequency is just right, then a minute net energy dissipation occurs in the sample around which the transmitter coil is located and if the rf circuit is delicately tuned, a drop in its output voltage will occur and can be shown on an oscilloscope or, for a single sweep of the magnetic field, on a chart recorder.

The *nuclear magnetic resonance* (nmr) effect would be no more than a somewhat obscure aspect of physics were it not that the resonance energy depends on the exact value of the *local* field **H** at the nucleus and that **H** is affected by the electron distribution in the molecule containing the nucleus. For example, the orbital electrons of each atom themselves precess in the applied field $\mathbf{H_0}$ to give rise to diamagnetism (Section 3-ST-2), that is, to an induced field which opposes the applied one and is proportional to it. One then writes

$$\mathbf{H} = \mathbf{H_0}(1 - \sigma),\qquad(18\text{-}22)$$

where σ is often called the *screening constant* since its effect is to reduce the effective field at the nucleus; its value is around 10^{-5} for protons. The effect is called a *chemical shift*.

Since **H**, and therefore σ, is not directly determinable, the usual procedure is to compare the value of $\mathbf{H_0}'$ needed to produce resonance (at a given radio frequency) in some standard compound with the value $\mathbf{H_0}$ needed for the one being studied. The standard may be any liquid substance giving a simple resonance behavior— water, $CHCl_3$, and $Si(CH_3)_4$ have been used, for example, in the case of *proton magnetic resonance* (pmr). The chemical shifts involved are so small that it is convenient to report them as

$$\delta = \frac{\mathbf{H_0} - \mathbf{H_0}'}{\mathbf{H_0}'}\, 10^6,\qquad(18\text{-}23)$$

that is, δ is reported as the parts per million shift in the applied field needed to produce resonance.

We come now to actual pmr spectra. Each proton in some pure compound will have its own electron environment and hence chemical shift. Thus as shown schematically in Fig. 18-16, liquid ethanol shows resonances at three values of $\mathbf{H_0}$, corresponding to the $-OH$ proton, the two equivalent CH_2 protons, and the three equivalent CH_3 protons; the areas under the absorption peaks are in the ratio 1:2:3. One of the major values of pmr (and of nmr in general) is that it allows an identification of the nuclei in a molecule in terms of their various chemical environments. The chemical shifts for some compounds having only one kind of

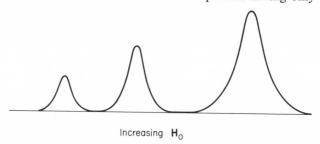

Increasing H_0

Fig. 18-16.   *The pmr spectrum of liquid ethanol.*

proton are given in Fig. 18-17, relative to cyclohexane. There are extensive tables of chemical shifts for protons in various chemical environments, and the pmr spectrum of a molecule not only serves to "fingerprint" it but usually allows quite detailed conclusions as to its isomeric structure. If doubts are left, deuteration of known functional groups eliminates those hydrogen atoms from pmr resonance, so that the peaks due to them in the original spectrum can be identified.

Fig. 18-17. *Observed chemical shifts at room temperature of some liquids that give a single proton signal; cyclohexane is taken as an arbitrary reference point.*

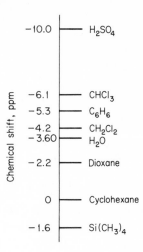

There are a large number of important effects and hence of nmr applications, two of which are illustrated in Fig. 18-18. In pure ethanol the OH, CH_2, and CH_3 peaks are seen to be split if measured with higher resolution than used for Fig. 18-16. This is due to the mutual interactions of the proton spins on neighboring groups; thus the hydroxyl proton resonance is split into three (an unresolved central one and two satellites) by the various ways in which spin–spin interaction can occur. The second effect illustrated is that in the presence of

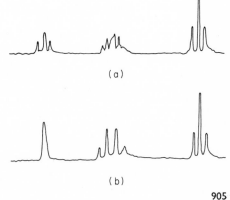

Fig. 18-18. *The pmr spectrum of liquid ethanol: (a) pure dry alcohol; (b) alcohol plus a small amount of* HCl.

905

hydrochloric acid the splitting of the $-OH$ peak disappears and the shape of the CH_2 peak is greatly simplified. The reason is that the hydroxyl proton is now exchanging so rapidly with that of neighboring molecules that only its average local magnetic field is being observed. The time scale for such averaging to occur is, in simple cases, of the order of T_1.

The spin–spin interactions which split the CH_2 peak into four components and the CH_3 peak into three components (Fig. 18-18) arise as follows. The principle is that the field at a CH_2 proton is perturbed slightly by the net field of the CH_3 protons and, similarly, the field at a CH_3 proton is affected by the net field of the CH_2 protons; the number of components into which the peaks split is the number of possible values of these net fields. Thus the three CH_3 protons may have their spins in the relative arrangements (↑↑↑), (↑↑↓, ↑↓↑, ↓↑↑), (↑↓↓, ↓↑↓, ↓↓↑), or (↓↓↓), and a given CH_2 proton then "sees" one of four possible perturbing net fields in the relative probabilities 1:3:3:1. Similarly, the two CH_2 protons may have their spins in the relative arrangements (↑↑), (↑↓, ↓↑), and (↓↓); a CH_3 proton then "sees" one of three perturbing fields in the relative probabilities 1:2:1.

Even a brief presentation of nmr would be inadequate without some mention of an alternative picture of the effect. The discussion has so far been in terms of energy levels, but a more detailed physical picture is as follows. If the magnetic moment of a proton is represented by a vector, then application of an external field causes this vector to precess at an angle to the field direction which is determined by I. The two energy states then correspond to the two vector orientations shown in Fig. 18-19. The precession, known as the Larmor precession, occurs with a *frequency* which is proportional to the field and equal to that of radiation corresponding to ϵ in Eq. (18-20)

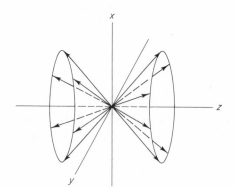

Fig. 18-19.   *Larmor precession of a magnetic moment along the z axis.*

The collection of protons in the sample will all be undergoing this precession, but not in unison as indicated schematically in Fig. 18-20(a). If, now, an rf field of resonance frequency is applied along the x axis, its oscillating magnetic field applies a small acceleration or retardation to the precessing magnetic moment vectors until they all come into phase, as indicated in Fig. 18-20(b). A precessing moment constitutes a source of electromagnetic radiation emitted along the y axis; since all of the nuclei are precessing together, the emission from them is in phase and so has a nonzero net amplitude. A detector coil placed perpendicular to the x axis then registers a signal. This is, in fact, an alternative method for obtaining an nmr spectrum—that is, one uses an rf emitting coil and a second, receiving coil at right angles to it, the two coils directed at axes perpendicular to that of the applied magnetic field.

Some additional phenomena may now be observed. The dynamic equilibrium between the two nuclear states N and N* may be written as a balance of several rates

$$(N)(k_r + k_a) = (N^*)(k_{se} + k_e + k_r^*), \qquad (18\text{-}24)$$

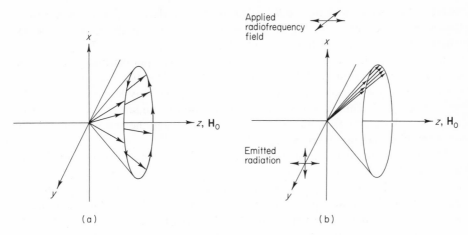

Fig. 18-20. *Effect of a perpendicular rf field in bringing precessing magnetic moments into phase.*

where k_a and k_{se} are the rate constants for absorption and stimulated emission, respectively. These are equal to each other and proportional to the intensity of the rf field; k_e is the rate constant for spontaneous or ordinary emission. The rate constants k_r and k_r^* are those for radiationless activation and deactivation processes. If the rf intensity is zero, then the various rate constants are such as to make $(N^*)/(N)$ equal to the Boltzmann ratio, as evaluated earlier. If, however, the rf intensity is made very large, so that k_a and k_{se} dominate, then, since they are equal, $(N^*)/(N)$ becomes unity—that is, in the limit one has an equal population in the two states. There will be no nmr resonance signal at all.

If now the rf intensity is returned to its normal low value, the Boltzmann population will reestablish itself, and the nmr signal will grow back in. The reciprocal of the first-order rate constant for this return is called the *spin-lattice* or *longitudinal relaxation time* T_1. Its value is primarily a measure of that of k_r and k_r^* since k_e is generally negligibly small. The presence of paramagnetic ions in the solution will, for example, greatly reduce T_1; the magnetic susceptibility of such ions may actually be measured by this means.

There is a second relaxation time, called T_2 or the *transverse relaxation time*. This has to do with the speed with which the aligned moments of Fig. 18-20(b) would drift out of phase in the absence of an rf field, due to the different local magnetic fields that individual nuclei experience. The relaxation time T_2 can be estimated from the width of the resonance line as well as by other, somewhat more complicated experiments. In liquids the mechanism for the T_1 and T_2 relaxations are often essentially the same, so the two times are about equal. In a solid, however, T_1 may become quite large while T_2 remains small. This is because the rate constant for energy exchange with the medium, k_r or k_r^* in Eq. (18-24), has become small, but the local field inhomogeneities remain to make the different nuclei precess at slightly different natural rates, and thus still produce the transverse relaxation effect.

C. Electron Spin Resonance

The general principle of electron spin resonance is the same as for nmr; the relevant equation is analogous to Eq. (18-20),

$$\epsilon = -g_e m_e \beta_e \mathbf{H}, \tag{18-25}$$

where g_e is called the *Landé splitting factor* and is about 2 for a free electron. The magnetic moment $m_e = \frac{1}{2}$ for a free electron and β_e is the Bohr magneton, whose value is about 2000 times that of the nuclear magneton β_n. The first consequence of these changes is that the splitting of the two spin orientations of a free electron is about a thousand times that for a nucleus. The difference in Boltzmann population of the upper and lower states is correspondingly larger, and so is the resonance signal. Thus a much lower concentration of unpaired electrons can be detected with *electron spin resonance, esr,* than of nuclei in the nmr method; smaller or more dilute samples therefore suffice.

The esr measurement is, of course, generally applied to molecules having an unpaired electron. It has been extremely useful in detecting small concentrations of free radicals, for example. Further, if the nucleus of the atom has a nonzero nuclear spin, then interaction with the odd electron leads to a fine structure or additional splitting of the esr spectrum. It is thus possible to determine with which nucleus the unpaired electron is primarily associated.

18-CN-2   Structure and Chemistry of Excited States

A.   Structure

Excited states do not survive long enough for conventional structure determinations but there is no doubt that major changes from the ground state may occur. In the case of diatomic molecules, the bond length is expected to increase in an excited state and this is confirmed by calculations for H_2 (note Fig. 18-2). The bond angle in a triatomic molecule may change greatly; as examples, it has been suggested that the $^2A_1$ state of NO_2 is linear and that the first excited state of NH_3 is planar. Conversely, the first singlet excited state of formaldehyde is known to be bent (deduced from an analysis of the rotational and vibrational structure of the fluorescence spectrum). In the case of states localized on a double bond, there is effectively weaker bonding in a π^* state and therefore easier rotation about the bond. It is possible that benzene is no longer planar in some of its excited states.

Considerable changes in geometry have been postulated for the ligand field excited states of coordination compounds. One of the singlet excited states of $Ni(CN)_4^{2-}$ (square planar in the ground state) is thought to have D_{2d} symmetry. Complexes such as $Cr(NH_3)_5 X^{2+}$ (where X is a halogen or pseudohalogen) may change from essentially octahedral geometry to that of a pentagonal pyramid.

One indication that an excited state is significantly different in geometry from the ground state is that the emission from the former is strongly shifted to lower energies relative to the absorption band. Recalling Fig. 18-11, the energy for the $S_1^v \leftarrow S_0$ process is shown as much greater than that for the $S_1 \rightarrow S_0^v$ fluorescent emission. As indicated in Fig. 18-6, this means that for a diatomic molecule, the bond length in the excited state is different from that in the ground state. In the case of polyatomic molecules, angle as well as bond length changes are likely.

An interesting example is that of $Cr(urea)_6^{3+}$, whose absorption and emission spectra are shown in Fig. 18-21. The main absorption band involves the process $^4T_{2g} \leftarrow {}^4A_{2g}$, and the narrower, lower-energy band involves the process $^2E_g \leftarrow {}^4A_{2g}$. The phosphorescence emission from the ^2E_g state is almost superimposed on the absorption band in its wavelength distribution, which strongly implies that the ^2E_g state has essentially the same bond lengths and the same O_h symmetry as the ground state. However, the fluorescence emission from the $^4T_{2g}$ state is broad, like the absorption band, but shifted to much longer wavelengths. The peak of the fluorescence emission is in fact at a *longer* wavelength than that of the phosphorescence emission. It seems evident that major bond length and perhaps bond angle changes have occurred in the $^4T_{2g}$ state.

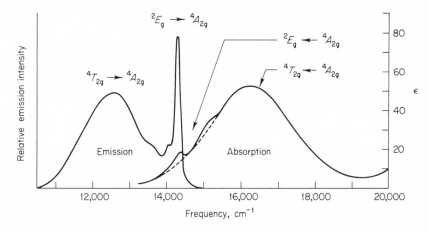

Fig. 18-21. *Absorption and emission spectra for* $Cr(urea)_6^{3+}$ *(in a glassy matrix at 77°K).* [*From G. B. Porter and H. L. Schläfer, Z. Phys. Chem.* **37**, *110 (1963).*]

B. Excited-State Chemistry

The chemical nature of an excited state is in general different from that of the ground state. We refer now not to prompt molecular cleavages, but to cases where the excited state lasts long enough to function as a chemical substance, and one in thermodynamic equilibrium with its environment (except for the electronic excitation energy). This is the situation with many of the triplet states of organic molecules; these may survive one or more encounters with other solute molecules. As examples, the triplet state of coumarin, undergoes a dimerization, and that of cyclopentadiene undergoes a Diels–Alder-type reaction with a second molecule to give endodicyclopentadiene:

A rather interesting case is that of singlet oxygen. Ordinary oxygen has a triplet ground state $^3\Sigma_g^-$ and is, perhaps for this reason, an unusually reactive molecule. It is known to photochemists for its very efficient quenching of triplet excited states—a process that usually occurs on every encounter. It is possible, however, to generate oxygen in the singlet excited state $^1\Delta_g$ lying about 22 kcal mole^{-1} above the ground state. This is a less reactive species than ground-state oxygen but shows a selective ability to add to organic dienes. Singlet oxygen may be prepared, incidentally, either by the reaction of hydrogen peroxide with metal hypochlorites or by using the triplet excited state of certain dyes such as methylene blue or eosin to sensitize the excitation $^1\Delta_g \leftarrow {}^3\Sigma_g^-$. [See Foote (1968).]

An example from coordination chemistry is that of $Cr(NH_3)_5(NCS)^{2+}$, which aquates in aqueous solution to give exclusively $Cr(NH_3)_5(H_2O)^{3+}$ and free NCS^- ion. However, on irradiation of the visible absorption bands, to produce the $^4T_{2g}$ excited state, the product is primarily $Cr(NH_3)_4(H_2O)(NCS)^{2+}$ (Zinato *et al.*, 1969).

18-CN-3 Smog

A great deal of popular discussion now exists on atmospheric pollution. Such pollution is of many types; it may be due to particulate matter such as dust and soot or to the presence of noxious gases such as sulfur dioxide. A rather special type of pollution, and one relevant to this chapter, is that known as *smog*. The term has come to have the special technical meaning of tissue irritants produced photochemically from hydrocarbons. It is a rather specific by-product of gasoline fumes and other automotive engine exhausts.

A complete discussion of the constituents of smog and of atmospheric photochemistry is not appropriate here, but the type of reaction sequence is the following. First, oxides of nitrogen assist in producing oxygen atoms, ozone, and hydroxyl radicals:

$$NO_2 \xrightarrow{h\nu} NO + O, \quad O + O_2 + M \rightarrow O_3 + M,$$

$$O + H_2O \rightarrow 2 \cdot OH \quad (NO + \tfrac{1}{2}O_2 = NO_2).$$

Hydrocarbons appear also to be involved in an ozone-producing chain reaction

$$RH + O \rightarrow R\cdot + \cdot OH, \quad RH + \cdot OH \rightarrow R\cdot + H_2O,$$

$$R\cdot + O_2 \rightarrow RO_2\cdot, \quad RO\cdot + O_2 \rightarrow RO\cdot + O_3$$

(and other reactions). Finally, product-forming reactions include

olefin + O_2 → products,   2RO· → aldehyde + alcohol, RO_2· + NO → RO_2NO.

A particularly obnoxious product is *peracetylnitrate*,

$$\begin{array}{c} O \\ \parallel \\ CH_3C\text{-}O\text{-}ONO_2 \, . \end{array}$$

Smog production thus requires three ingredients—oxides of nitrogen, hydrocarbons, and sunlight. Atmospheric inversion conditions help in confining and concentrating the reaction mixture. A less generally appreciated consequence of the smog-producing mechanism is that to obtain really significant inhibition one must reduce not only the amount of hydrocarbon vapor in the atmosphere but also the nitrogen oxides.

SPECIAL TOPICS

18-ST-1   Emission and Absorption of Radiation.
Transition Probability

A.   Absolute Absorption Coefficients

The physical picture of the absorption of a light quantum is illustrated in Fig. 18-22. Electromagnetic radiation consists of an oscillating electric field (and a magnetic field at right angles to it) and absorption occurs through an interaction of the field with the electrons of the molecule. In the particular example shown an electron in an s orbital is excited to a p orbital. Note the *polarization*—the particular p orbital is the one that is aligned with the plane of the electric field.

In the theoretical treatment one assumes the train of radiation to be long enough that the atom or molecule can be regarded as immersed in an oscillating electric field. A time-dependent perturbation $\mathbf{H}(t)$ gives rise to a probability for transition from state m to state n which involves the integral

$$H_{nm} = \int \psi_n \mathbf{H}(t) \, \psi_m \, d\tau.$$

The method is that of perturbation theory, and, from Eq. (16-121), H_{nm} is of the

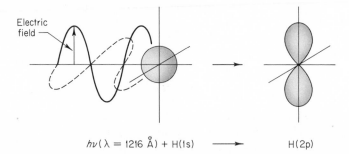

$$h\nu(\lambda = 1216 \text{ Å}) + \text{H(1s)} \longrightarrow \text{H(2p)}$$

Fig. 18-22. *Orbital representation of* H *atom undergoing the* 1s → 2p *transition (left to right). (After J. G. Calvert and J. N. Pitts, Jr., "Photochemistry." Copyright 1966, Wiley, New York. Used with permission of John Wiley & Sons, Inc.)*

nature of an energy, and in the case of absorption of radiation, is essentially the product of the oscillating electric field strength of the radiation and a dipole moment associated with the electron to be excited. Note from Table 8-6 that the product of dipole moment times field is an energy.

The general procedure for calculating the dipole moment associated with a particular state or wave function involves evaluation of the integral

$$(\mu_x)_{nn} = \int \psi_n^* \mu_x \psi_n \, d\tau, \tag{18-26}$$

where μ_x is the component of the instantaneous dipole moment given by

$$\mu_x = \sum e\vec{x}.$$

That is, one sums over the product of electronic charge and the displacement $\tilde{x}$ of each electron. The integral of Eq. (18-26) is zero for an atom—atoms cannot have a net dipole moment.

One may also calculate a dipole moment associated with the change from state m to state n,

$$(\mu_x)_{nm} = \int \psi_n^* \mu_x \psi_m \, d\tau. \tag{18-27}$$

This is now called a *transition dipole moment*, and in general, it need not be zero. It is this dipole moment that is used in formulating H_{nm}. The probability of absorption of radiation is then proportional to $(\mu_x)_{nm}^2$; the actual expression is

$$B_{nm} = \frac{8\pi^2}{h^2} (\mu_x)_{nm}^2, \tag{18-28}$$

assuming that only the transition dipole in the x direction need be considered. Here, B_{nm} is known as the *Einstein absorption coefficient*, defined as the probability of absorption in unit time with unit radiation density. The more general expression is

$$B_{nm} = \frac{8\pi^2}{3h^2} [(\mu_x)^2_{nm} + (\mu_y)^2_{nm} + (\mu_z)^2_{nm}], \qquad (18\text{-}29)$$

which allows for transition dipole components in the x, y, and z directions.

B_{nm} may be related to the ordinary molar extinction coefficient ϵ as defined by Eq. (3-7). Since an actual absorption is spread over a band or region of wavelength, it is necessary to use the integrated intensity $\int \epsilon \, d\bar{\nu}$, where $\bar{\nu}$ is the frequency in wavenumbers. The derivation requires several steps and leads to

$$\int \epsilon \, d\bar{\nu} = \frac{hN_0\nu_0 B_{nm}}{(2.303)(1000)\, c^2}, \qquad (18\text{-}30)$$

where ν_0 is the frequency at the band maximum. It is conventional to take as the "ideal" case the transition between the $v = 0$ and $v = 1$ states of a harmonic oscillator of electronic mass and if the corresponding wave functions from Eq. (16-59) are substituted into Eq. (18-28), one obtains

$$B_{nm} = \frac{\pi e^2}{hm\nu_0}.$$

Substitution of this result into Eq. (18-30) gives

$$\int \epsilon \, d\bar{\nu} = \frac{\pi e^2 N_0}{2303mc^2} = 2.31 \times 10^8. \qquad (18\text{-}31)$$

We take this transition probability as a reference and define the *oscillator strength* f as the actual transition probability relative to this ideal. Thus

$$f = 4.33 \times 10^{-9} \int \epsilon \, d\bar{\nu}. \qquad (18\text{-}32)$$

The area under an experimental absorption band gives either B_{nm} through Eq. (18-30) or f through Eq. (18-32). For example, the area under the intense absorption band of benzene, centered at 180 nm, gives an f of about 0.7. We speak of such a transition as an allowed one. By contrast, the visible absorption band of $Co(NH_3)_6^{3+}$ due to the ligand field transition $^1T_{1g} \leftarrow {}^1A_{1g}$ has a maximum extinction coefficient of about 100 liter mole^{-1} cm^{-1} at 20,000 cm^{-1} (500 nm); the bandwidth is such that the area is about $(100)(2000) = 2 \times 10^5$, so f is about 10^{-3}. This transition is thus forbidden, that is, it is of much less intensity than that of the maximum possible.

B.   Spontaneous Emission

We next consider the situation in which a collection of absorbing atoms or molecules has come to equilibrium with radiation. The system is dilute enough that no collisional processes are involved, that is, no radiationless deactivations occur. Only three types of things can occur: absorption of radiation, stimulated emission of radiation, and spontaneous emission of radiation. Stimulated emission is the reverse of absorption, that is, an excited atom or molecule interacts with a radiation field with a resultant probability of undergoing a transition from excited state n to ground state m. The analysis is entirely symmetric to that for absorption, and the probability coefficient for the process, B_{mn}, is equal to B_{nm} as given by Eq. (18-27). Spontaneous emission does not depend on the presence of a radiation field, however, and has some intrinsic probability A_{mn}. The theoretical treatment of spontaneous emission requires rather advanced wave mechanics.

At equilibrium the rates of population and depopulation of the excited state have become equal, and we write

$$\text{rate of population} = B_{nm}N_m\rho_{nm},$$
$$\text{rate of depopulation} = B_{mn}N_n\rho_{mn} + A_{mn}N_n,$$

where N_m and N_n are the numbers of ground- and excited-state atoms, and $\rho_{nm} = \rho_{mn} = \rho$ is the radiation density of frequency ν_{nm} corresponding to the difference in energy between states n and m. Since $B_{nm} = B_{mn}$, we obtain

$$\frac{A_{mn}}{B_{nm}} = \rho_{nm}\left(\frac{N_m}{N_n} - 1\right).$$

Since the two states are in equilibrium, the Boltzmann expression applies,

$$\frac{N_n}{N_m} = e^{-h\nu_{nm}/kT}.$$

Also, from Eqs. (16-109) and (16-112) the energy density of radiation, our ρ, is

$$\rho = \frac{8\pi h\nu_{nm}^3}{c^3}\frac{1}{e^{h\nu_{nm}/kT}-1}.$$

On combining these relationships, we obtain

$$\frac{A_{mn}}{B_{nm}} = \frac{8\pi h\nu_{nm}^3}{c^3}. \tag{18-33}$$

The coefficient A_{mn} is mathematically equivalent to a first-order rate constant and could be written as k_e, the rate constant for spontaneous emission. The reciprocal $1/k_e$ is the (mean) lifetime for spontaneous emission; these are experimentally measurable quantities, given by the rate of decay of fluorescent or phosphorescent emission under conditions such that radiationless deactivation processes are not important.

Alternatively, since B_{nm} can be determined from the area under the absorption band, Eq. (18-33) can be used to calculate A_{mn} or k_e. If the observed lifetime of the excited-state emission is shorter than so calculated, one then writes $k_{e(obs)} = k_{e(natural)} + k_q$, where k_q is the sum of rates of radiationless processes. Values of k_q are often determined indirectly in this manner.

One danger that should be mentioned is the following. The preceding derivation is based on a detailed balancing of forward and reverse rates. If the actual situation is that shown in Fig. 18-11, an irreversible process, namely thermal equilibration, intervenes between the absorption act and that of either spontaneous or natural emission. The absorption and stimulated emission steps do not retrace each other, and the derivation is not strictly valid. In fact, if the thermally equilibrated excited state such as S_1 in the figure is quite different in geometry from S_1^v, a calculation of k_e from B_{nm} can be very seriously in error.

C. Selection Rules

The exact evaluation of the integral of Eq. (18-27) requires the use of the detailed wave functions for the ground and excited states. It is possible, however, to determine on symmetry grounds whether an integral of the type

$$\int f_A f_C f_B \, d\tau$$

should be nonzero.

We first consider the simpler integral

$$\int f_A f_B \, d\tau,$$

where f_A and f_B might be two wave functions for a molecule. It turns out that such an integral *must* be zero unless the integrand is invariant under all operations of the symmetry group to which the molecule belongs. What this means specifically is that the product $f_A f_B$ must form the basis for the totally symmetric irreducible representation (IR) of the group—the one for which all the traces for the various symmetry operations are unity.

The procedure for determining whether or not this requirement is met is as follows. First, the traces of the representation of a product $f_A \times f_B$, called a *direct product*, are, for each symmetry operation R,

$$\chi(R) = \chi_A(R)\,\chi_B(R). \tag{18-34}$$

Consider, for example, a molecule in the C_{4v} point group. Table 18-5 gives the character table and the traces for the direct products of various IR's. Thus the direct product $A_1 \times A_2$ is just A_2, and likewise $B_1 \times B_2$. The direct product E^2 or $E \times E$ does not correspond to any of the IR's, but on application of Eq. (17-16), one finds it to contain the IR's $A_1 + A_2 + B_1 + B_2$. We conclude that an integral involving functions which are bases for the first three direct products in the table must be zero since the direct products do not contain the totally symmetric IR, in this case A_1. An integral based on the direct product E^2 would be nonzero, however, since it contains the A_1 IR.

The principle may be extended to three functions. One simply takes the direct product of the representations for which f_C and f_B are bases, and then the direct product of the result with the representation for which f_A is a basis. Again, unless the final result is or contains the totally symmetric IR of the point group, the integral must be zero.

We now return to Eq. (18-27). Since μ_x is essentially a constant e times the "x" coordinate, the IR for which μ_x is a basis will be that listed opposite the function "x" in the character table for the point group.

As an example, for the D_{2h} group, μ_x corresponds to the B_{3u} IR (see Table 17-7). In order for the integral to be nonzero, the functions ψ_n and ψ_m must have symmetry properties such that $\psi_n \mu_x \psi_m$ contains the A_g IR of the group. For example, if ψ_n belongs to or transforms like A_g, then ψ_m must belong to B_{3u}; that is,

Table 18-5. *Direct Products in C_{4v} Symmetry*

C_{4v}:	E	C_2	$2C_4$	$2\sigma_v$	$2\sigma_d$
A_1	1	1	1	1	1
A_2	1	1	1	-1	-1
B_1	1	1	-1	1	-1
B_2	1	1	-1	-1	1
E	2	-2	0	0	0
$A_1 \times A_2$	1	1	1	-1	-1
$B_1 \times B_2$	1	1	1	-1	-1
$B_1 \times E$	2	-2	0	0	0
$E \times E$	4	4	0	0	0
$A_1 \times E \times B_2$	2	-2	0	0	0

$B_{3u} \times A_g \sim B_{3u}$ and $B_{3u} \times B_{3u} \sim A_g$. The transition is then *allowed* for radiation along the x axis. For the same ground state the transitions to states belonging to B_{2u} and B_{1u} are allowed along the y and z axes, respectively.

Notice that in this example the IR's all have a g or u designation and that the allowed combinations are of the type g $\times$ u $\times$ u. A corollary of the general symmetry requirement is that the direct product $f_A \times f_B \times f_C$ must be g in nature (provided the molecule does have a center of symmetry so that g and u are meaningful). Since μ_x is always u (the sign of a dipole inverts on reflection through the center of symmetry), it follows that ψ_n and ψ_m *must* be of opposite parity. Otherwise the transition is said to be *parity-forbidden*; this is the case for the $^1T_{1g} \leftarrow {}^1A_{1g}$ transition of $Co(NH_3)_6^{3+}$ mentioned earlier. Similar considerations generate the rule that in vibrational absorption Δv must be odd; this follows directly from observing that if one state is odd, that is, has an odd number of nodes in the vibrational wave function, then the other state must be even. Ordinarily, one only observes transitions for which $\Delta v = \pm 1$.

Most of the simple selection rules that have been mentioned stem from such symmetry arguments. The rules are not absolute, but where they are violated one finds that the oscillator strength of the transition is greatly reduced from the allowed value of Eq. (18-31).

Returning to Fig. 18-22, we can now see an advantage to measuring the absorption spectrum of a crystal using plane-polarized radiation. The molecules will be fixed in definite orientations with respect to the crystal axes and if the crystal structure is known, then the incident radiation can be aligned with one or another symmetry axis of the molecule. Certain absorptions will then be strong in one direction but not in another, and such information is very helpful in assigning the various excited states to specific symmetry classes.

D. Lasers

Consider the two-state system described in Section 18-ST-1B. We can write the rate of population of excited state n as $k_a N_m$, where $k_a = B_{nm}\rho_{nm}$, and the rate of its depopulation as $k_d = k_{sa}N_n + k_{mn}N_n$ where $k_{sa} = B_{mn}\rho_{mn}$. If the radiation density is sufficiently high, k_d approaches $k_{sa}N_n$ and since $B_{nm} = B_{mn}$, the consequence is that $N_n = N_m$. Under this condition the rates of absorption and of stimulated emission are equal.

Suppose now that there exists some higher excited state n' which can undergo a conversion or crossing to excited state n. We can now populate state n *indirectly* by using radiation of frequency $\nu_{n'm}$. If A_{mn} is small enough, it will be possible to make N_n exceed N_m—after all, there is no radiation of frequency ν_{nm} to depopulate state n by stimulated emission. A system having such an *inverted* population is capable of laser (light amplification by stimulated emission of radiation) action.

Suppose further that this system is established in a cavity having reflecting walls, as, for example, a cylindrical space having mirrors at each end. If some radiation of frequency ν_{nm} is introduced along the cylinder axis (there will always be some from spontaneous emission), then it will stimulate further emission of the same frequency, in phase and in the same direction. Light of this frequency then reflects back and forth, gathering intensity as more and more stimulated emission occurs. The process is on the speed-of-light time scale, and the effect is that a short, intense pulse of radiation is produced. Various arrangements, such as use of a partially silvered mirror at one end, allow the escape of this pulse. Because it is in phase or coherent and accurately collimated, the beam diverges very little; laser beams can be reflected back from the moon and still be detected, for example. They may be focused down to an area comparable in dimensions to that of their wavelength to give enormous energy densities, and, a focused laser beam can be used for microsurgery. Laser beams are highly monochromatic, and this has made them very useful in spectroscopy, as, for example, in Raman spectroscopy; also, their high intensity and short (nanosecond) pulse duration allows experiments in flash photolysis where a short-lived excited state is produced in sufficient amount for its absorption spectrum and other properties to be measured.

Lasing systems are now commercially available which operate in the microwave, the infrared, and the visible wavelength regions. They may be pulsed or continuous; in some cases they can be tuned or varied in wavelength continuously over a region of values. A clever use of their property of coherence allows a doubling of their frequency so that lasers producing in the near ultraviolet are possible. In brief, lasers are becoming a common and indispensable tool for the chemist, the physicist, and the engineer.

18-ST-2 Optical Activity

This topic is taken up here rather than in Chapter 3 because modern applications lead to useful information about excited states. The traditional aspect, however, is that of the rotation of the plane of polarization of light by an optically active substance. The optical activity may result from a crystalline arrangement of atoms or molecules in a right- or left-handed spiral, as in quartz, in which case the optical activity disappears on melting. Alternatively, the individual molecules may be asymmetric, in which case the activity is retained in all physical states and in solution.

A. Rotation of Plane-Polarized Light

The usual experimental arrangement makes use of a *polarimeter*. Incident mono-chromatic light is plane-polarized by means of a special prism (as discussed later), passes through the material to be studied, and then through a second prism. The relative angular position of the two prisms for maximum (or minimum) transmission of light of a given wavelength is observed with and without the active substance, the difference in angle being the *optical rotation* α. It is customary to reduce α to *specific* rotation $[\alpha]$ by the definition

$$[\alpha]_\lambda^t = \frac{\alpha}{l\rho} = \frac{100\alpha}{lc}, \tag{18-35}$$

where l is the path length in decimeters, ρ is the density of the substance, if neat, c is the number of grams of substance per 100 cm³ of solution. The superscript and subscript give the temperature (in degrees Celsius) and wavelength; if the sodium D line is used, the subscript may be written as D. *Molar rotation* is defined as

$$[M]_\lambda^t = \frac{[\alpha]_\lambda^t M}{100}, \tag{18-36}$$

where M is the molecular weight. Recently more rational units have been proposed: 1 biot = 10^{-3} rad cm² g⁻¹ instead of $[\alpha]$ and 1 cotton = 0.1 rad cm² mole⁻¹ instead of $[M]$.

If a substance rotates the plane of polarized light clockwise as viewed looking toward the light source, it is said to be *dextrorotatory* and α is reported as positive; if the rotation is to the left or counterclockwise, the substance is *levorotatory* and α is reported as negative.

Specific rotations for small organic molecules range up to about 50°; $[\alpha]_D^{25}$ is $-39°$ for L-histidine, $[\alpha]_D^{20}$ is $-12°$ for (−)-tartaric acid and $+66°$ for sucrose (all in aqueous solution). Rather larger values may be found for optically active coordination compounds; the value of $[\alpha]_{600nm}^{25°}$ is 600° for $Cr(C_2O_4)_3^{3-}$, for example. Optical rotation is an additive property in dilute solutions, and polarimetry is therefore quite useful as an analytical tool. Molar rotations are to some extent constitutive (and thus resemble molar refractions, see Section 3-3) and structural conclusions may sometimes be reached on the assumption that the observed rotation is a sum of contributions from independent asymmetric centers.

B. Theory of Optical Activity

A beam of plane or linearly polarized light may be represented by a wave equation such as Eq. (16-39), corresponding to a sine wave of varying electric field. The accompanying magnetic field oscillates in phase and with the same amplitude, but in the plane at right angles to that of the electric field. Considering only the electric field, if two beams are polarized at right angles to each other and both are in phase and of the same amplitude, then as illustrated in Fig. 18-23(a), the resultant will be equivalent to a plane-polarized beam at an inclination of 45° to the other two. If one beam is a quarter of a wavelength out of phase with the other, then the maximum net amplitude rotates with distance, either clockwise or counterclockwise, as shown in Fig. 18-23(b). Such a beam is said to be *circularly polarized.*

The theory of optical activity is based on the behavior of circularly polarized light. A ray of plane-polarized light may be regarded as equivalent to two circularly polarized beams which are in phase and of equal amplitude but have opposite senses of rotation [Fig. 18-23(c)]. The right- and left-handed spirals cancel except for their x components, so the resultant is plane-polarized light vibrating along the x direction. The velocities of the two circularly polarized components are the same in an inactive substance, so the angle of the equivalent plane-polarized beam does not change with distance. In an optically active material, however, the two circularly polarized components have different velocities, with the consequence that the equivalent plane-polarized beam rotates as it passes through the substance [Fig. 18-23(d)].

The velocity of light is inversely proportional to the index of refraction of the medium, and an equation due to A. Fresnel (1825) gives

$$\alpha = \frac{\pi}{\lambda} (n_l - n_r), \tag{18-37}$$

where α is now the rotation in radians per centimeter and n_l and n_r are the indices of refraction for left and right circularly polarized light, respectively. Since the wavelength λ is a small number in the case of visible light, an appreciable value of α results even with very small differences in the refractive indices. Thus optical rotation is a second-order effect, dependent on the small difference between relatively large numbers.

The theoretical treatment involves integrals resembling those of Eq. (18-27). No effect results, however, if only the oscillating electric field of the light is considered; it is necessary to include the oscillating magnetic field as well. The symmetry properties of the integrals are such that the effect is still zero if the molecule possesses either a plane or a center of symmetry. It may be shown that the sufficient requirement for optical activity is that the molecule and its mirror image not be superimposable. A molecule may be transformed into its mirror image by reflection of its coordinates in any given plane; this reflection is equivalent to changing

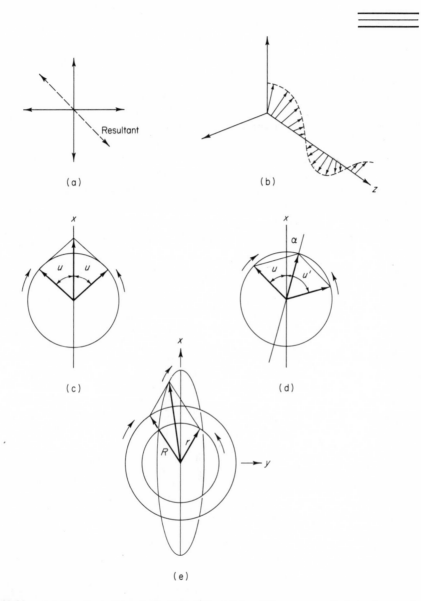

Fig. 18-23. *(a) Resultant of two beams of polarized light of the same amplitude in phase and with planes of polarization perpendicular to each other. (b) Resultant if the beams are a quarter of a wavelength out of phase. (c) Plane-polarized light as the resultant of two oppositely circularly polarized components. (d) Rotation of plane of polarized ion as a consequence of two circularly polarized components having different velocities in a medium. (e) Elliptically polarized light as a consequence of two circularly polarized beams having different extinction coefficients.*

from a right-handed to a left-handed coordinate system. An optically active molecule must behave differently toward right and left circularly polarized light.

C.   Rotatory Dispersion and Circular Dichroism

An important experimental observation is that α as well as the index of refraction $n = (n_l + n_r)/2$ and the separate indices n_l and n_r vary with the wavelength of the light used. The effect may be quite dramatic as the wavelength is varied through the region of an adsorption band. This behavior is illustrated in Fig. 18-24, where the curve labeled $n_l - n_r$ is proportional to α, by Eq. (18-37). The variation of α with wavelength is known as *optical rotatory dispersion*, ORD. Note that α

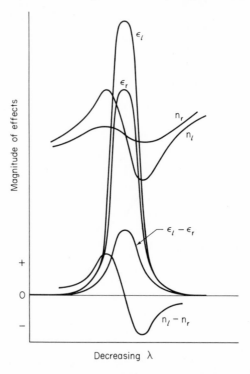

Fig. 18-24. *Schematic illustration of dispersion of index of refraction for right and left circularly polarized light and of the corresponding extinction coefficients. [After F. Woldbye, in "Technique of Inorganic Chemistry" (H. B. Jonassen and A. Weissberger, eds.), Vol. 4. Copyright 1965, Wiley (Interscience), New York. Used with permission of John Wiley & Sons, Inc.]*

changes sign in the vicinity of the absorption maximum, the ordinary absorption curve being given by $(\epsilon_l + \epsilon_r)/2$, where ϵ denotes extinction coefficient (Section 3-2).

An approximate expression for this behavior was given by Drude in 1900:

$$[\alpha] = \frac{k}{(\lambda^2 - \lambda_0{}^2)}\,,\qquad (18\text{-}38)$$

where k is a constant characteristic of the substance and λ_0 is the wavelength of the absorption maximum. Sometimes a sum of terms with different k and λ_0 values is needed to fit a rotatory dispersion curve; the implication is that two or more overlapping absorption bands are actually present. An important point is that the sign of α is not in itself a characteristic of an optically active substance; the sign depends on which side of an absorption band the measurement is made. It was perhaps fortunate for early investigators that their polarimetry was done mostly on compounds which absorb mainly in the ultraviolet, so that use of the sodium D line gives α values corresponding to the long-wavelength side of the first electronic absorption band. As a consequence, a related series of compounds, as of sugars, tend to have the same sign for α if the absolute configuration or *chirality* is the same. It is thus relatively safe to draw conclusions from how the sign of α behaves as to whether the "handedness" or chirality of an asymmetric center is retained in a chemical reaction; this rather simple approach can lead to serious errors, however.

The phenomenon of rotatory dispersion is connected with the fact that the absorption coefficients are different for right and left circularly polarized light in the case of an optically active substance. The effect is known as *circular dichroism*, CD. Both absorption coefficients are appreciable, of course, in the region of an absorption band, as illustrated in Fig. 18-24, and if they are different, the consequence is that *elliptically* polarized light results. As shown in Fig. 18-23(e), the y components of the amplitudes of two circularly polarized beams no longer cancel.

It is possible to measure these separate absorption coefficients to obtain the *coefficient of dichroic absorption* $\Delta\epsilon$:

$$\Delta\epsilon = \epsilon_l - \epsilon_r\,,\qquad (18\text{-}39)$$

or the *anisotropy* or *dissymmetry factor* $g = \Delta\epsilon/\epsilon$. The quantity $\Delta\epsilon$ varies with wavelength in the region of an absorption band, as shown in Fig. 18-24, or is said to exhibit dispersion. The dispersion of ORD and of CD constitute the *Cotton effect* (the name is French and should be pronounced accordingly).

Both ORD and CD spectra are fast becoming routine adjuncts to regular absorption spectra when dealing with optically active compounds. Rather undistinguished absorption spectra may reveal themselves as consisting of more than one absorption band by showing complicated ORD and CD behavior. Also, absorption bands not showing Cotton effects probably involve chromophores which are not themselves centers of optical activity or near such a center. Finally, if the symmetry designations of the ground and excited states are known, the CD spectrum may allow the assignment of the absolute configuration, that is, the chirality of the molecule. An example is given in Fig. 18-25; the tris-orthophenan-

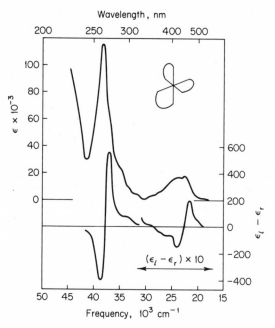

Fig. 18-25. *Circular dichroism spectrum of aqueous* $(+)$-$[\mathrm{Ru(phen)_3}](\mathrm{ClO_4})_2$. *[From B. Bosnich, Accounts Chem. Res.* **2**, *266 (1969).]*

throline complex of Ru(II), $\mathrm{Ru(phen)_3^{2+}}$, is basically octahedral in geometry, but the three bidentate *phen* ligands make the molecule resemble a three-bladed propeller. There are two ways for the blades to be pitched, corresponding to the two optical isomers, and the deduced absolute configuration is shown in the figure (Bosnich, 1969).

D. Instrumentation

Plane-polarized light may be produced by passing light through a suitable prism of calcite ($\mathrm{CaCO_3}$) or quartz. Such prisms have been cut in a plane tilted to the direction of the incident light beam and then cemented together. Ordinary light can be treated as consisting of two mutually perpendicular plane-polarized beams, and the two beams will transmit differently through a properly prepared split prism and are therefore separated. Various prism constructions, such as the Nicol, Glan, and Rochan prisms, have been designed. A Polaroid sheet has a layer of oriented crystals which polarize the transmitted light.

Circularly polarized light may be obtained by passing suitably oriented plane-polarized light through a quartz prism known as a *Fresnel* rhomb. The Fresnel rhomb is cut in such a way that the beam undergoes internal reflections before emerging, so as to cause just the right time lag between vibrations parallel and perpendicular to the plane of incidence.

Modern recording spectropolarimeters make the obtaining of ORD and CD spectra relatively easy. Just as the appearance of the recording spectrophotometer gave great stimulus to spectrophotometry, so has the appearance of ORD and CD automatic instruments led to great expansion of the study of optical activity.

18-ST-3 Vibrational–Rotational Spectra

The detailed spectrum of a molecule consists in principle of transitions between states whose complete description includes the electronic, vibrational, and rotational components of the wave functions. As discussed in Section 18-3, we assume that these types of functions do not interact appreciably. Thus as in Fig. 18-11, close-lying rotational states are superimposed on vibrational states which in turn are superimposed on electronic states.

The actual degree of detail that is seen in a spectrum depends on several factors. First, of course, is the resolution of the equipment used. Second, however, vibrational and rotational states have sufficiently long natural lifetimes for their energy to be made uncertain by collision processes. Thus in solution vibrational detail tends to be washed out and rotational detail disappears completely. This happens even with gases at high pressures.

If, however, one examines the infrared spectrum of a dilute gas, then rotational as well as vibrational detail is seen. It is such spectra that we consider briefly at this point. On combining Eqs. (16-61) and (16-114), the general expression for the vibrational–rotational energy of a diatomic molecule becomes

$$\epsilon_{vJ} = h\nu_0(v + \tfrac{1}{2}) + BhcJ(J + 1), \tag{18-40}$$

where $B = h/8\pi^2 Ic$ and is called *the rotational constant* (units are cm^{-1}).

The selection rules for a transition are that first, $\Delta v = \pm 1$ [and the molecule must have a dipole moment or else μ_x in Eq. (18-27) vanishes, so the intensity becomes zero], and second, $\Delta J = \pm 1$. We then write

$$\epsilon_{vJ} = (v' - v'')\,h\nu_0 + B'hcJ'(J' + 1) - B''hcJ''(J'' + 1) \qquad (18\text{-}41)$$

for a transition between two vibrational–rotational states. In general the rotational constant changes on going to a different vibrational state since the vibrational amplitude is different and hence so is the moment of inertia of the molecule. If this point is ignored, Eq. (18-41) simplifies to

$$\epsilon_{vJ} = h\nu_0 + 2BhcJ', \qquad\qquad J' - J'' = 1,$$
$$\epsilon_{vJ} = h\nu_0 + 2Bhc(J' + 1), \qquad J' - J'' = -1, \qquad (18\text{-}42)$$

where $v' - v''$ is taken to be unity, and ΔJ may be ± 1, primes and double primes denoting the final and initial states, respectively.

It is important to remember that at ordinary temperatures most molecules will be in the $v = 0$ vibrational state, but that the separation of rotational levels is so small that by the Boltzmann principle, an average molecule is apt to be in a $J = 10$ to 20 level. Thus the usual transition is from $v = 0$ to $v = 1$ in a diatomic molecule, but the rotational quantum number, being large, has scope to decrease as well as to increase. The consequence is that a vibrational–rotational spectrum has two branches. The R branch contains the transitions whereby the distribution of rotational states present in the collection of molecules changes by $\Delta J = 1$ and the P branch contains the transitions for which $\Delta J = -1$. These two branches are illustrated in the spectrum for the fine structure of the $v = 2$ fundamental of HCN shown in Fig. 18-26; the short-wavelength branch is, of course, that for R. In

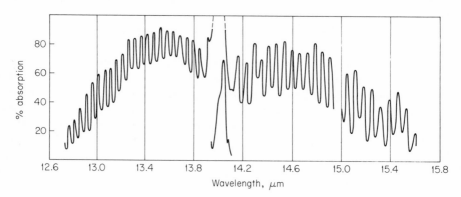

Fig. 18-26. *Fine structure of the ν_2 fundamental of* HCN. *(See G. Herzberg, "Infrared and Raman Spectra of Polyatomic Molecules." Van Nostrand–Reinhold, Princeton, New Jersey, 1945.)*

polyatomic molecules, transitions with $\Delta J = 0$ may also be observed; giving a third set of lines known as the Q branch.

Analysis of spectra of this type yield more information than analysis of pure rotational spectra since the intensities and spacings reflect the degree of interaction between the two forms of excitation. As mentioned earlier, the moment of inertia changes with the vibrational quantum number. Also, vibrational levels are affected by the rotational energy—essentially because the vibrating atoms are now in a centrifugal field.

18-ST-4   Atomic Energy States

The treatment of atomic energy states was by-passed in the main part of the text not because it is unimportant but because of the level of detail required. The energy states of the hydrogen atom are, of course, given by the Bohr theory and wave mechanics. Energies of states of hydrogen-like atoms may be estimated by rules such as given in Sections 16-3 and 16-CN-2. Those for atoms having two or more outer electrons involve rather high-level wave mechanics for their treatment but it is very useful at least to see how the various excited states are *named*. It is this nomenclature and the various combining rules on which it is based that we outline here.

In general the state of a multielectron atom is given by three angular momentum designations, S, L, and J. The number S gives the net spin quantum number, L is the net orbital angular momentum, and J is the vector sum of the spin and orbital angular momenta. Both S and L are zero for closed shells and only the outer electrons have to be considered. Each individual outer electron has some particular ℓ value and its spin is $\pm\frac{1}{2}$; there are various ways in which the orbital angular momenta can combine to give a net L, and the spin angular momenta to give a net S. A particular set of individual electron ℓ values thus gives rise to a number of L and S states for the atom as a whole. For each L and S state the possible J values are $L - S, L - S + 1, ..., L + S$.[†]

[†] The scheme whereby the individual electron orbital angular momenta combine to give L and the spins to give S, which then determine the possible J values, is known as Russell–Saunders coupling. An alternative combining rule, more valid for heavy atoms, is that of first obtaining the possible net angular momenta j for each electron, where $j = \ell - \delta, \ell - \delta + 1, ..., \ell + \delta$, and then combining these j values vectorially to obtain J values.

The detailed procedure for obtaining the possible L and S states may be outlined as follows. Each outer electron has $2\ell + 1$ possible values of the magnetic quantum number, $m_\ell = 0, \pm 1, ..., \pm\ell$ (corresponding to the various allowed projections of the ℓ vector); the sum of a possible combination of the m_ℓ for the outer electrons then gives a particular M_L value. Likewise, a spin of $\pm\frac{1}{2}$ may be assigned to each electron, bearing in mind the Pauli exclusion principle, to yield various M_S. One thus obtains an array of all the M_L and M_S generated by vectorial combinations of the individual electron ℓ and δ values. One now looks for a set of L and S states that will produce this same array. Each L state implies M_L values of $0, \pm 1, ..., L$ and each S state implies M_S values of $-S, -S + 1, ..., S$.

An example should be helpful at this point. We consider first the case of an atom with two outer electrons of the same principal quantum number n and of the same ℓ value, namely $\ell = 1$. The configuration is thus $(np)^2$. Table 18-6 lists the various assignments of m and of δ and the corresponding M_L and M_S values, and Table 18-7(a) summarizes the number of times each M_L and M_S combination occurs. We observe that the maximum M_L value is 2, which means that the state with $L = 2$ is present; since $M_L = 2$ occurs only with $M_S = 0$, the state is one of $S = 0$. The next step is to draw up the array for this state, given in Table 18-7(b), and to subtract it from the initial array, to give array (c).

The largest M_L value in array (c) is 1 and the largest M_S value is 1, corresponding to the state $L = 1$, $S = 1$. The array for this state is (d), which is then subtracted from (c) to give array (e). This last corresponds to the $L = 0$, $S = 0$ state.

Table 18-6. *Orbital Configurations for a p^2 Case*

m_ℓ				
1	0	−1	$M_L = \sum m_\ell$	$M_S = \sum m_\delta$
××	—	—	2	0^a
—	××	—	0	0^a
—	—	××	−2	0^a
×	×	—	1	$-1, 0, 0, 1^b$
×	—	×	0	$-1, 0, 0, 1^b$
—	×	×	−1	$-1, 0, 0, 1^b$

^{a} Only $M_S = 0$ is possible; since both electrons have the same three quantum numbers n, ℓ, and m_ℓ, their spins must be opposed.

^{b} The restriction in footnote a now does not apply; each electron can have $\delta = \frac{1}{2}$ or $\delta = -\frac{1}{2}$ independently. Zero is entered twice since the first electron may have its spin up or down and the case for the second electron is reversed; since the m values are different, these are not identical configurations.

Table 18-7. *Orbital Configurations for a p² Case*

(a)

M_L	-1	0	1
2		1	
1	1	2	1
0	1	3	1
-1	1	2	1
-2		1	

M_S

or

(b) ^1D

M_L	0
2	1
1	1
0	1
-1	1
-2	1

M_S

$+$

(c)

M_L	-1	0	1
1	1	1	1
0	1	2	1
-1	1	1	1

M_S

or

$^1D \; + \;$ (d) ^3P

M_L	-1	0	1
1	1	1	1
0	1	1	1
-1	1	1	1

M_S

$+$ (e) ^1S

M_L	1
0	1

M_S

or

$$p^2 \sim {}^1D + {}^3P + {}^1S$$

The naming system for L states is the same as that for ℓ ones, that is, $S, P, D, F, G, \ldots$ for $L = 0, 1, 2, 3, 4, \ldots$. It is customary to designate the S state by writing its number of possible M_S values, $2S + 1$, as an upper left superscript. Thus array (b) corresponds to a ^1D state, array (c) to a ^3P state, and array (e) to a ^1S state. The possible configurations for $(np)^2$ are thus $^1D + {}^3P + {}^1S$.

As one further example, we consider the case of $(nd)^3$. The display of possible m_ℓ, M_L, and M_S assignments is given in Table 18-8 and the tabulated array in Table 18-9. The reader can verify that this array is the sum of those for the states $^2H, {}^2G, {}^4F, {}^2F, {}^2D$ twice, ^4P, and ^2P. The general procedure can be extended to states involving more than one partially filled subshell, such as $(ns)^1(np)^1$.

Table 18-8.   *Orbital Configurations for a* d^3 *Case*

2	1	0	−1	−2	$M_L = \Sigma\, m_\ell$	$M_S = \Sigma\, m_s$
××	×	—	—	—	5	
××	—	×	—	—	4	
××	—	—	×	—	3	
××	—	—	—	×	2	
×	××	—	—	—	4	
—	××	×	—	—	2	
—	××	—	×	—	1	
—	××	—	—	×	0	
×	—	××	—	—	2	
—	×	××	—	—	1	$\dfrac{1}{2},\ -\dfrac{1}{2}$
—	—	××	×	—	−1	
—	—	××	—	×	−2	
×	—	—	××	—	0	
—	×	—	××	—	−1	
—	—	×	××	—	−2	
—	—	—	××	×	−4	
×	—	—	—	××	−2	
—	×	—	—	××	−3	
—	—	×	—	××	−4	
—	—	—	×	××	−5	
×	×	×	—	—	3	
×	×	—	×	—	2	
×	×	—	—	×	1	
×	—	×	×	—	1	
×	—	×	—	×	0	$\dfrac{3}{2},\dfrac{1}{2},\ -\dfrac{1}{2},\ -\dfrac{3}{2}$ [a]
×	—	—	×	×	−1	
—	×	×	×	—	0	
—	×	×	—	×	−1	
—	×	—	×	×	−2	
—	—	×	×	×	−3	

[a] Note that for this group of configurations there are three ways of assigning spins to give an M_S of $\frac{1}{2}$, and similarly for $M_S = -\frac{1}{2}$.

Hund's rule now appears in the form of the statement that the state of lowest energy will be that of largest S value and, within this restriction, of largest L value. Thus for $(np)^2$ the ground state is ^3P, while for $(nd)^3$ it is ^4F. A further rule is that for shells less than half filled, states with lower J values are lower in energy, and the reverse is true for shells more than half filled.

Table 18-9. *Orbital Configurations for a d^3 Case[a]*

M_L	$-\frac{3}{2}$	$-\frac{1}{2}$	$\frac{1}{2}$	$\frac{3}{2}$
5		1	1	
4		2	2	
3	1	4	4	1
2	1	6	6	1
1	2	8	8	2
0	2	8	8	2
		M_S		

[a] The array is symmetric to negative M_L, so only the positive ones need be listed.

GENERAL REFERENCES

BECKER, R. S. (1969). "Theory and Interpretation of Fluorescence and Phosphorescence." Wiley (Interscience), New York.

CALVERT, J. G., AND PITTS, J. N., JR. (1966). "Photochemistry." Wiley, New York.

COTTON, F. A. (1963). "Chemical Applications of Group Theory." Wiley (Interscience), New York.

DAUDEL, R., LEFEBVRE, R., AND MOSER, C. (1959). "Quantum Chemistry, Methods and Applications." Wiley (Interscience), New York.

EYRING, H. (1944). "Quantum Chemistry." Wiley, New York.

HERZBERG, G. (1967). "Molecular Spectra and Molecular Structure. III. Electronic Spectra and Electronic Structure of Polyatomic Molecules." Van Nostrand–Reinhold, Princeton, New Jersey.

PITZER, K. S. (1953). "Quantum Chemistry." Prentice-Hall, Englewood Cliffs, New Jersey.

POPLE, J. A., SCHNEIDER, W. G., AND BERNSTEIN, H. J. (1959). "High Resolution Nuclear Magnetic Resonance." McGraw-Hill, New York.

POTTS, W. J., JR. (1963). "Chemical Infrared Spectroscopy." Wiley, New York.

STREITWEISER, A., JR. (1964). "Molecular Orbital Theory for Organic Chemists." Wiley, New York.

SZYMANSKI, H. A. (1964). "Theory and Practice of Infrared Spectroscopy." Plenum, New York.

TOWNES, C. H., AND SCHAWLOW, A. L. (1955). "Microwave Spectroscopy." McGraw-Hill, New York.

CITED REFERENCES

BOSNICH, B. (1969). *Accounts Chem. Res.* **2**, 266.

FOOTE, C. S. (1968). *Accounts Chem. Res.* **1**, 104.

ZINATO, E., LINDHOLM, R. D., AND ADAMSON, A. W. (1969). *J. Amer. Chem. Soc.* **91**, 1076.

Exercises

18-1 Estimate, with explanation, the energy difference between the ^1D and ^3P states of atomic sulfur.

> *Ans.*   About 25 kcal mole^{-1}, as read off Fig. 18-4 (rest of explanation to be supplied by the student).

18-2 (a) Estimate the minimum frequency in cm^{-1} of light needed to dissociate H_2 into a ground-state and an excited-state atom. (b) Estimate the energy to produce H_2^+ from H_2.

> *Ans.*   (a) About 11.5×10^4 cm^{-1}, as read off Fig. 18-2. (b) About 13×10^4 cm^{-1}. (The student should supply more detail as to the states involved in both cases.)

18-3 Estimate the wavelength of the absorption maximum of the first absorption band of I_2 and the wavelength of maximum intensity of the fluorescent emission.

> *Ans.*   From Fig. 18-8 the absorption maximum should be at about 20,000 cm^{-1} or 500 nm; the most probable fluorescent emission should be at about 12,000 cm^{-1} or 830 nm.

18-4 Make a guess as to the probable absorption spectrum of ethyl formate.

> *Ans.*   The only significant chromophoric group is the carbonyl group; from Table 18-2 there should be an intense band at around 1900 Å (it is actually around 2100 Å).

18-5 In a photochemical experiment an intensity of 5×10^{-9} E sec^{-1} is incident on a cell containing 20 cm^3 of 0.01 M solution of $Cr(NH_3)_5(NCS)^{2+}$. It is estimated that 90 % of the incident light is absorbed and after 10 min of irradiation analysis shows that 0.6 % of the complex has photoaquated to give $Cr(NH_3)_4(H_2O)(NCS)^{2+}$. Calculate the quantum yield.

> *Ans.*   0.44.

18-6 Benzene vapor absorbs at 254 nm to give the first excited singlet state S_1, whose radiative lifetime is 6.2×10^{-7} sec. S_1 disappears by intersystem crossing to the first triplet excited state T_1 with a rate constant of $k_4 = 4.7 \times 10^6$ sec^{-1}, and S_1 is quenched by collisions with ground-state benzene with a rate constant of 1.00×10^9 liter mole^{-1} sec^{-1}, both rate constants being for 25°C. Calculate (a) the fluorescence quantum yield at low pressures and (b) the yield at a 0.1 atm pressure (25°C).

> *Ans.*   (a) $\phi_f{}^\circ = 0.24$; (b) $\phi_f = 0.15$.

18-7 A commonly used chemical actinometer is the ferrioxalate one, for which the photochemical reaction is

$$Fe(C_2O_4)_3^{3-} \xrightarrow{h\nu} Fe(II) + \text{oxalate} + \text{oxidized oxalate};$$

after the irradiation the Fe(II) is complexed with 1, 10-phenanthroline (neglect dilution at this point) and its concentration determined from the optical density at 510 nm, at which wavelength the extinction coefficient of the complex is 1.10×10^4. In a particular experiment 20 cm^3 of ferrioxalate solution was irradiated with light at 480 nm for 10 min and an optical density of 0.35 was subsequently found at 510 nm. The quantum yield at the irradiating wavelength is known to be 0.93. Calculate the light intensity in einsteins absorbed per second. A 1 cm cell is used.

> *Ans.* 1.14×10^{-9} E sec^{-1}.

Problems

18-8 The normal vibrational modes for C_2H_2 are as shown in the accompanying diagram. Explain which are infrared-active and -inactive and which are Raman-active and -inactive.

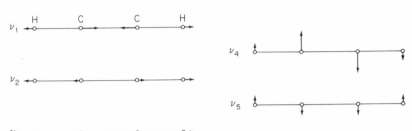

Ans. Only ν_3 and ν_5 are infrared-active; ν_1, ν_2, and ν_4 are Raman-active. (The student should explain these answers in reasonable detail.)

18-9 Identify some of the characteristic bond or group frequencies in the infrared spectrum for acetone (Fig. 18-13).

$\qquad\qquad$ *Ans.* $>\!\!C\!\!=\!\!O$ at 1700 cm^{-1} and so on.

Problems

18-1 Suppose that the equilibrium internuclear distance is essentially the same for the ground state and a certain excited state of a diatomic molecule (as for the $^1\Delta_g \leftarrow {}^3\Sigma_g^-$ transition of O_2). Explain what the qualitative appearance of the absorption spectrum of the dilute gas should be like. Pay particular attention to the relative intensities of transitions involving different vibrational states, that is, the general intensity contour of the absorption band, as well as how it is centered with respect to the energy for the pure electronic transition.

18-2 The strong Schumman–Runge absorption band of O_2 starts at about 200 nm and gradually increases in intensity to a continuum which begins at about 176 nm. Sketch the probable appearance of the ground- and excited-state potential energy curves (that is, produce a pair of plots similar to those of Fig. 18-6 but consistent with the data for O_2). Explain what happens when absorption is in the region of the continuum—is the excited state produced stable against dissociation, and if not, what might the products be? [*Note:* the energy to dissociate O_2 into two ground-state atoms is about 40,000 cm^{-1}.]

18-3 H_2 excited to the $^1\Pi_u$ state may under some conditions cross to the $^3\Sigma_g^+$ state. Light emission then occurs. Explain what happens in terms of Fig. 18-2 and estimate the range of wavelengths of the emitted light.

18-4 Sketch a guessed appearance of the absorption spectrum of (a) methyl ethyl ketone, (b) azobenzene, $\phi\!-\!N\!\!=\!\!N\!\!-\!\phi$, and

$$\text{(c)} \quad C_6H_5\!-\!CH_2\overset{\overset{\displaystyle S}{\|}}{C}\!-\!CH_3 .$$

Explain the basis for your spectra.

18-5 The following data were obtained for the benzophenone—sensitized decomposition of $Co(NH_3)_6^{3+}$. Assume that absorption of light by the benzophenone leads to its first triplet excited state in quantum yield $\phi°$ and that each encounter with a complex ion which transfers energy produces photochemical decomposition of the complex and deexcitation of the benzophenone with 100 % efficiency. Derive the kinetics for this situation and plot the data so as to obtain a straight line graph. If the lifetime of the benzophenone triplet state is 1.0×10^{-8} sec, calculate k_q, the bimolecular quenching rate constant; compare the result with an estimate of the encounter rate constant.

Complex (M)	0.01	0.005	0.002	0.001
ϕ for sensitized decomposition	0.46	0.25	0.10	0.064

18-6 An alternative actinometer to the ferrioxalate one is that which makes use of the reaction

$$Cr(NH_3)_2(NCS)_4^- \xrightarrow{h\nu} Cr(NH_3)_2(H_2O)(NCS)_3 + NCS^-.$$

The photoproduced NCS^- is determined spectrophotometrically by forming a complex with Fe(III) of extinction coefficient 4.3×10^3 liter mole^{-1} cm^{-1} at 450 nm. The quantum yield for the photochemical reaction is 0.29 at 520 nm. What is the absorbed light intensity in einsteins per second if irradiation of 25 cm^3 of a 0.02 M solution of the complex for 15 min produces a solution which when treated with the Fe(III) reagent has an optical density of 0.25 at 450 nm in a 1-cm cell? (Neglect any dilution due to the reagent.) A companion dark (nonirradiated) aliquot gives an optical density of 0.05 when treated with the Fe(III) reagent.

18-7 The quantum yield for the photoisomerization of *trans*-4, 4'-dinitrostilbene is 0.27 at 366 nm, at which wavelength the extinction coefficient is 3.0×10^4 liter mole^{-1} cm^{-1}. What absorbed light intensity in einsteins per liter per second is required to cause a 10^{-3} M solution to isomerize at the rate of 1 % min^{-1}? With continued irradiation the *cis* form builds up; this photoisomerizes back to the *trans* with a quantum yield of 0.34 at 366 nm. Assuming the extinction coefficient to be half that of the *trans* form, what stationary state ratio of *trans/cis* should result (what is the limiting value of this ratio on sufficiently prolonged irradiation)?

18-8 Biacetyl exhibits a phosphorescence in room-temperature aqueous 0.1 N H_2SO_4 solution, the quantum yield in this medium being 2.7×10^{-3} and the phosphorescence lifetime 6.2×10^{-5} sec. Addition of the complex ion $Cr(NH_3)_5(NCS)^{2+}$ progressively quenches this phosphorescence; thus 5×10^{-4} M complex reduces the phosphorescence yield tenfold and 1×10^{-3} M complex reduces it 18-fold. Set up the kinetic scheme for this situation. Calculate k_p, the rate constant for phosphorescent decay to the ground state, and k_q, the bimolecular quenching rate constant; compare the value of the latter to that estimated for diffusional encounters (at 25°C). The biacetyl emitting state is produced in 10 % yield.

18-9 In the experiments described in Problem 18-8 the quenching of the biacetyl phosphorescence was accompanied by a sensitized aquation of the complex to yield $Cr(NH_3)_4(H_2O)(NCS)^{2+}$. Assuming that each quenching act by a complex ion led to aquation, show that the aquation quantum yield obeys an equation of the form $1/\phi_{NH_3} = \alpha + (\beta/C)$, where C is the complex concentration. Remember that in this situation the incident light is absorbed by the sensitizer biacetyl, and ϕ_{NH_3} is the number of moles of aquated ammonia divided by the number of einsteins of light absorbed by the sensitizer.

18-10 Absorption of light by an organic molecule A leads to phosphorescence with a quantum yield ϕ_p of 0.30 in a particular solvent. Show that the relation $\phi_p/\tau_p = k_p$ holds, where τ_p is the experimentally observed lifetime of the phosphorescence and k_p is the rate constant for phosphorescent emission. The value of ϕ_p is for a deaerated solution; a solution in equilibrium with air has 3.0×10^{-4} mole liter^{-1} dissolved oxygen. Encounters between dissolved oxygen and A occur with a rate constant of 5×10^9 liter mole^{-1} sec^{-1}. Calculate ϕ_p' in this aerated solution; $k_p = 1.0 \times 10^5$ sec^{-1}.

18-11 Explain what wavelength of light should be effective in the photoproduction of atoms on irradiation of (a) S_2, (b) HI, (c) the molecule of Fig. 18-6 assuming that D_e'' is 55 kcal mole^{-1}, and (d) I_2.

18-12 The normal modes for the H_2O molecule are as shown in the accompanying diagram. Explain which should be infrared-active and -inactive and Raman-active and -inactive.

Carry the set of motion vectors through the symmetry operations of the H_2O point group and determine to what irreducible representation each mode belongs. (The answer may be arrived at by considering what vectors are left unchanged or are put into their opposites and comparing with the traces of the various irreducible representations.)

18-13 The normal modes for formaldehyde are as follows: (a) $\nu_1 = 2766$ cm^{-1}, CH_2(sym) stretch; (b) $\nu_2 = 1746$ cm^{-1}, $C=O$ stretch; (c) $\nu_3 = 1501$ cm^{-1}, CH_2 deformation; (d) $\nu_4 = 2843$ cm^{-1}, CH_2(asym) stretch; (e) $\nu_5 = 1247$ cm^{-1}, CH_2 rock, (f) $\nu_6 = 1164$ cm^{-1}, CH_2 wag. One corresponds to the B_2 irreducible representation, two to the B_1, and three to the A_1. Explain which is which. In the actual infrared spectrum of formaldehyde, absorptions are observed at 3930 cm^{-1}, 2910 cm^{-1}, 2665 cm^{-1}, and 4013 cm^{-1} (among others). Explain how these frequencies arise.

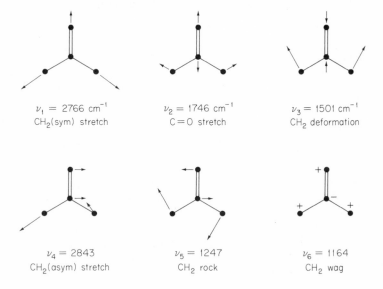

$\nu_1 = 2766$ cm^{-1}
CH_2(sym) stretch

$\nu_2 = 1746$ cm^{-1}
$C=O$ stretch

$\nu_3 = 1501$ cm^{-1}
CH_2 deformation

$\nu_4 = 2843$
CH_2(asym) stretch

$\nu_5 = 1247$
CH_2 rock

$\nu_6 = 1164$
CH_2 wag

18-14 Assign, with explanation, the origin of the various major absorptions in the infrared spectrum of CH_2Cl_2 (Fig. 18-13).

18-15 Explain what difference you might expect to see in the intensities of the $C{\equiv}C$ stretching vibration in an infrared absorption spectrum as compared to a Raman spectrum of (a) $HC{\equiv}CH$ and (b) $HC{\equiv}CCl$.

18-16 One of the fundamental vibration modes of CO gives rise to an infrared absorption at 2144 cm^{-1}. Calculate the vibration frequency (in hertz), the force constant, and the zero-point energy of CO in kilocalories per mole (for this vibrational mode).

Special Topics Problems

18-1 Estimate by a calculation the oscillator strength of the absorption bands of benzophenone in cyclohexane at (a) about 250 nm and (b) 350 nm (Fig. 18-10). Also calculate the emission rate constant A_{mn} for these excited states.

18-2 Assuming that the ordinate scale of Fig. 18-13 is for 0.1 mm path length, estimate the oscillator strength of the absorption feature for acetone at 900 cm^{-1}.

18-3 Estimate the oscillator strength of the absorption band of $Cr(urea)_6^{3+}$ centered at (a) about $16,250 \text{ cm}^{-1}$ and (b) $14,400 \text{ cm}^{-1}$. Also calculate the emission rate constant A_{mn} for these excited states and the corresponding lifetimes for emission.

18-4 Find what irreducible representations are spanned in C_{3v} by the direct product $E \times E$.

18-5 Find what irreducible representations are spanned in D_{3h} by the direct products $A_2' \times E'$ and $E' \times E'$.

18-6 Referring to Fig. 17-22, for an octahedral complex having just one d electron the first ligand field transition is from a state of symmetry T_{2g} to a state of symmetry E_g (in O_h). Explain whether or not this transition is allowed by (a) parity and (b) orbital symmetry, that is, by whether the appropriate direct product contains the totally symmetric irreducible representation.

18-7 The specific rotation $[\alpha]_D$ of a compound in aqueous solution is $33°$ at $25°C$. Calculate the concentration of this compound in grams per liter in a solution which has a rotation of $3.05°$ when measured in a polarimeter in which the tube of solution of 20 cm long.

18-8 The specific rotation of saccharose in water at $20°C$ is $66.42°$. Calculate the observed rotation using a polarimeter tube of 20 cm length filled with a 23.5% by weight solution of this sugar. The density of the solution is 1.108 g cm^{-3}.

18-9 A solution of 30 g of a substance of molecular weight 350 in 1 liter of water rotates the plane of polarized light by $10.5°$ (sodium D line, $25°C$) with a 30 cm polarimeter tube. Calculate the specific and the molar rotation of the substance.

18-10 Calculate $n_l - n_r$ for the solution of Special Topics Problem 18-7. The sodium D line is at 589 nm.

18-11 Read data off Fig. 18-25 to make a semiquantitative plot of g versus wavenumber for $Ru(phen)_3^{2+}$.

18-12 Estimate the moment of inertia of HCN from the spectrum shown in Fig. 18-26.

18-13 Find the set of free ion terms for a d^2 system. Explain which term should be that for the ground state.

19 THE SOLID STATE

We consider four more or less distinct aspects of the physical chemistry of the solid state. The emphasis is on crystalline as opposed to glassy phases, and the first topic is that of the perfect crystal as a regular, infinitely repeating structure. A special field of geometry informs us that only certain symmetry properties are possible if space is to be filled by a repeating structure or *lattice*. We then introduce some very simple examples of such lattices, involving the ways in which spherical atoms or ions can pack. This leads us to the structure of alkali metal halide and other ionic crystals and, in the Special Topics section, to calculations of the total cohesive energy of a crystal, called the *lattice energy*.

We consider next the use of x-ray diffraction as a means of determining the symmetry class of a crystal, and then its actual structure. Modern x-ray crystallography is a rather specialized subject and only the introductory aspects of it will be presented. Most crystal structures of interest today are rather complex ones, and a few examples of this type are described in the Commentary and Notes section. The main part of the chapter concludes with some material on imperfect crystals. Actual crystals have defects and dislocations, the presence of which can be quite important to their physical properties.

19-1 Space-Filling Lattices

There is an interesting history to the development of the awareness that the external regularity of crystals implies an inner regularity of structure. A beautifully perceptive intuition on this subject was that of Johannes Kepler. In a presen-

938

tation to his benefactor, Counsellor Wackher, Kepler (1611) ponders the questions: Why should a snowflake have just six sides? Is it because this is a two-dimensional space-filling geometry? Is it significant that spheres on a flat surface pack to give a hexagonal pattern?

Topologists have since greatly developed the subject of *mosaics*, or infinitely repeating two-dimensional patterns; as illustrated in Fig. 19-1, the hexagonal unit

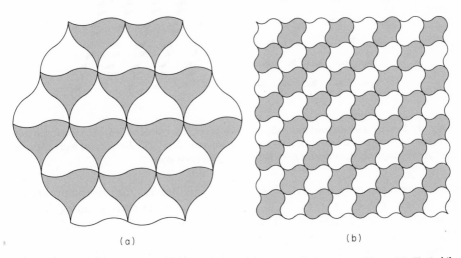

(a)   (b)

Fig. 19-1. *Mosaics of (a) modified triangles and (b) modified squares. (From M. Kraitchik, "Mathematical Recreations." Dover, New York, 1942.)*

is but one of many possibilities. The possibilities are not infinite, however. They can be shown to be limited by asking what symmetry operations can be applied at a point that will generate a lattice. It turns out that the only types possible are (a) mirror reflections across a line and (b) one-, two-, three-, four-, or sixfold axes. A square lattice has a fourfold axis and mirror plane along each axis. An oblique lattice, such as shown in Fig. 19-2(a), has only a twofold rotation axis. There are in fact only five possible area-filling lattices: oblique, rectangular, centered rectangular, square, and hexagonal. These are known as *Bravais lattices*, after A. Bravais (1848).

A Bravais lattice is not in itself a crystal or, in two dimensions, a mosaic. It is a geometric construct—a repeating frame of reference. It can be described by the various symmetry operations which put the lattice into an equivalent configuration. These will be point symmetry operations since one given lattice point remains unchanged. The *unit cell* of a lattice is the smallest portion of it exhibiting the symmetry features of the whole.

Not all of the point groups mentioned in Chapter 17 are possible for lattices. In the case of a two-dimensional lattice, we are restricted to just principal axes and vertical symmetry planes; further, as mentioned before, the order of the prin-

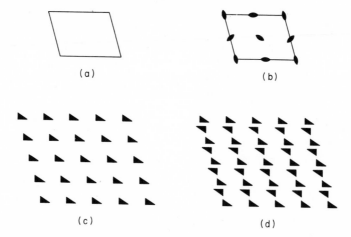

Fig. 19-2. *(a) Two-dimensional oblique lattice having C_1 symmetry. (b) The same, but with C_2 symmetry as indicated by the symbols for a twofold axis (lens). (c) Lattice plus basis belonging to C_1 point group. (d) Lattice plus basis belonging to C_2 point group.*

cipal axes can only be 1, 2, 3, 4, or 6. This leaves the 10 point groups C_1, C_2, C_3, C_4, C_6, C_s, C_{2v}, C_{3v}, C_{4v}, and C_{6v}. (The corresponding designations in the international crystallographic notation are 1, 2, 3, 4, 6, *m*, *2mm*, *3m*, *4mm*, and *6mm*—see Section 19-ST-1.)

The unit cell of a Bravais lattice may have certain but not all of these point group symmetries. The unit cell of a two-dimensional oblique lattice may have C_1 or C_2 symmetry but not others, for example. The former is illustrated in Fig. 19-2(a) and the latter in Fig. 19-2(b), where a lens denotes a twofold rotation axis.

As an exercise the reader might convince himself that the presence of *one* twofold axis at a lattice corner implies the presence of *all* of the others shown. For example, place an asymmetric object near one corner and carry out the twofold rotation—this places a second object in the adjacent cell. The existence of the lattice implies, however, that the object can be moved about by unit translations along the lattice directions; the object produced in the adjacent cell must also appear in the original cell.

The various possible combinations of the ten point group symmetries with the five Bravais lattices generate 12 lattice types, two of which are shown in Fig. 19-2(a, b). However, because one is dealing with a lattice rather than with a single object such as a molecule, some additional symmetry operations are possible which combine rotation or reflection with translation (see Section 19-ST-1). On inclusion of possible combinations of these new operations, a final total of 17 two-dimensional lattice types are possible. These are called *space groups*. The space group designations for the lattices of Fig. 19-2(a,b) are oblique, PC_1 and PC_2 or, in crystallographic symmetry notation, $P1$ and $P2$, where P denotes a primitive as opposed to a face-centered lattice.

In any actual crystal (or mosaic) some pattern of atoms is superimposed on a particular Bravais lattice. This pattern is called the *basis* and repeats with the unit cell of the lattice. Another way of seeing how the various space groups come about is as follows. The basis will have its own symmetry properties; if it is asymmetric, then the only symmetry of the repeating pattern is that of the lattice framework itself, as illustrated in Fig. 19-2(c). If, however, the basis has a higher symmetry, then it may conform to a more symmetric space group. Thus in Fig. 19-2(d) the basis consists of paired triangles, the pair having a C_2 axis. The presence of this axis then generates the pattern shown in the figure. The same higher lattice symmetry would be present if the basis were still more symmetric, as, for example, if it is consisted of just an atom at each lattice point. Thus the space group designation implies a certain *minimum* symmetry for the basis or, conversely, one can determine the space group if the lattice and the basis are known.

The analysis of the situation in three dimensions is similar to that for two dimensions. There are 14 Bravais lattices, however, as summarized in Table 19-1. The possible point groups now include those with secondary axes and σ_h planes, but are still restricted to C_1, C_2, C_3, C_4, and C_6 principal axes. The various combinations of symmetry elements consistent with each Bravais lattice give rise to 32

Table 19-1. *The Bravais Lattices*

System	Number of lattices	Lattice symbol[a]	Unit cell axes and angles	Symmetry designation[b]
Cubic	3	P I F	$a = b = c$ $\alpha = \beta = \gamma = 90°$	$m3m$
Tetragonal	2	P I	$a = b \neq c$ $\alpha = \beta = \gamma = 90°$	$4/mmm$
Orthorhombic	4	P C I F	$a \neq b \neq c$ $\alpha = \beta = \gamma = 90°$	mmm
Monoclinic	2	P C	$a \neq b \neq c$ $\alpha = \gamma = 90° \neq \beta$	$2/m$
Rhombohedral (or trigonal)	1	P	$a = b = c$ $\alpha = \beta = \gamma \neq 90°$	$3m$
Hexagonal	1	P	$a = b \neq c$ $\alpha = \beta = 90°; \gamma = 120°$	$6/mmm$
Triclinic	1	P	$a \neq b \neq c$ $\alpha \neq \beta \neq \gamma \neq 90°$	$m3m$

[a] The symbols stand for: *P*, primitive, with lattice points only at the corners of the unit cell; *C*, base centered; *I*, interior or body centered; *F*, centered on all faces, or face-centered.
[b] See Section 19-ST-1.

lattice types or lattice point groups. If combined rotation–translation and reflection–translation operations are included, then a total of 230 space groups are obtained. A three-dimensional crystal *must* belong to one of these space groups. Clearly, the detailed treatment of all of these symmetry combinations is too long to be practical here, and we will confine ourselves almost entirely to some important examples in the cubic system.

We will, in fact, deal mainly with rather simple crystals—ones having atoms or ions at lattice corners or in lattice faces. Figure 19-3 shows the unit cell for a

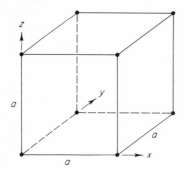

Fig. 19-3. *Simple cubic lattice having one atom at each lattice point.*

simple cubic lattice whose basis consists of an atom at each lattice point. A distinction to emphasize is that the unit cell is not necessarily the repeating unit. In Fig. 19-3 each corner atom is shared with eight adjacent unit cells and an attempt to generate the complete crystal by translations of this unit would superimpose atoms on each other. The repeating unit is in this case just the atom at the origin, that is, at position $(0, 0, 0)$. If this atom is translated by all possible combinations of the unit lattice distance a, then the crystal *is* generated.

The number of atoms or ions in a unit cell is, of course, just the number present in the repeating unit. The same answer can be obtained from a diagram of the unit cell provided that corner atoms are counted as one-eighth of an atom each, face atoms as one-half, and so on. That is, each atom or ion is weighted according to the number of adjacent unit cells which share it.

Figure 19-4 shows the unit cells for the 14 Bravais lattices. These can be described by specifying the unit lengths a, b, and c and the angles α, β, and γ as indicated in Fig. 19-5. The positions of the lattice points are then given in terms of this coordinate system. Thus the simple cubic unit cell has points (or atoms in the corresponding simplest possible crystal) at $(0, 0, 0)$, $(1, 0, 0)$, $(0, 1, 0)$, $(1, 1,.0)$, $(0, 0, 1)$, $(1, 0, 1)$, $(0, 1, 1)$, and $(1, 1, 1)$, the numbers giving positions in terms of (a, b, c); similar coordinates would likewise locate the atoms in the primitive tetragonal, orthorhombic, hexagonal, and triclinic lattices, measured in units of (a, b, c) and along the required axis directions. The body-centered cubic lattice has the same positions as does the simple cubic lattice plus one at $(\frac{1}{2}, \frac{1}{2}, \frac{1}{2})$; the face-centered cubic lattice has the additional points $(\frac{1}{2}, \frac{1}{2}, 0)$, $(0, \frac{1}{2}, \frac{1}{2})$, $(1, \frac{1}{2}, \frac{1}{2})$, $(\frac{1}{2}, 1, \frac{1}{2})$, $(\frac{1}{2}, 0, \frac{1}{2})$, and $(\frac{1}{2}, \frac{1}{2}, 1)$. In these last two cases the repeating units consist

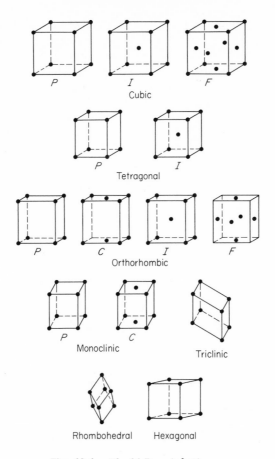

Fig. 19-4. *The 14 Bravais lattices.*

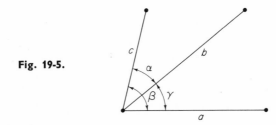

Fig. 19-5.

of the points $(0, 0, 0)$ and $(\frac{1}{2}, \frac{1}{2}, \frac{1}{2})$, and $(0, 0, 0)$, $(\frac{1}{2}, \frac{1}{2}, 0)$, $(0, \frac{1}{2}, \frac{1}{2})$, and $(\frac{1}{2}, 0, \frac{1}{2})$, respectively. Thus the body-centered cubic repeating unit has two points and the face-centered unit has four points. The same numbers would result if the unit cell points shown in Fig. 19-4 were counted as one-eighth if at a corner, one-half if on a face, and full weight if in the interior.

It is to be remembered that there will be actual crystals such that each point in Fig. 19-4 is occupied by a single atom, as just assumed, but many other crystals where each point is occupied by some molecule or grouping of atoms—a grouping whose symmetry is reduced from that of a sphere. Thus the lattice of crystalline carbon dioxide is face-centered cubic, but the basis consists of variously oriented CO_2 molecules, as illustrated in Fig. 19-6.

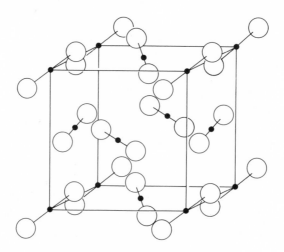

Fig. 19-6.   *The CO_2 unit cell.*

19-2   Crystal Planes; Miller Indices

Any actual crystal is finite in extent and its surfaces are made up of planes that pass through lattice points. Thus *ideal* physical crystals are bounded by planes which are lattice or *rational* planes; the inverse reasoning was made by Haüy in 1784, namely that the regular shapes of crystals imply an inner regularity. However, the *appearance* of a crystal is very dependent on which planes bound it, as illustrated in Fig. 19-7 for a crystal whose lattice is cubic. As we truncate the corners of a simple cube progressively, surfaces corresponding to planes of the type indicated in Fig. 19-8(a) increase in extent until the crystal is bounded only by such planes. These different appearances are called crystal *habits*. It was gradually appreciated that it is not the crystal habit that is in itself fundamental, but rather its symmetry, especially the angles between crystal faces, and hence between crystal planes. One may often determine the point group to which a crystal belongs just from its external symmetry.

A system for characterizing rational planes was developed by W. H. Miller in 1839, using what are now called Miller indices. If we locate an origin at some

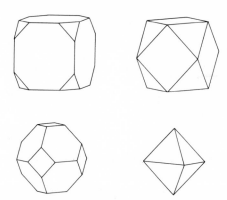

Fig. 19-7. *Some crystal habits for a cubic crystal.*

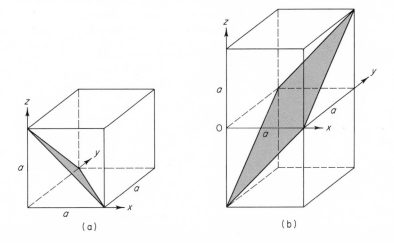

Fig. 19-8. *(a) The* (111) *plane of a cubic lattice. (b) The* (11$\bar{1}$) *plane of a cubic lattice.*

lattice point, then any crystal plane must intercept the crystal axes originating from this point, as illustrated in Fig. 19-9. A theorem which we will not prove is that the three intercepts of any rational plane must be in the ratio of integers. This is known as the *law of rational intercepts*, due to Haüy. Parallel to any such plane there is a whole set of planes which may be generated from it by application of unit translations along the axes of the lattice. If we now consider that plane of the set which is closest to the origin (without actually containing it), then the Miller indices (*hkl*) are the reciprocals of the intercepts, expressed in units of the lattice distances. In practice the indices (*hkl*) may refer either to this particular plane or to the whole set of equivalent ones.

To illustrate, the plane shown in Fig. 19-8(a) is the closest of its set to the origin and has the intercepts (1, 1, 1), expressed in units of *a*. The Miller indices are

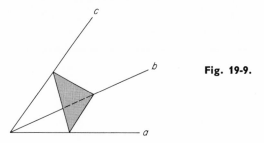

Fig. 19-9.

therefore the reciprocals, or (111). Other orientations are possible. Thus the plane shown in Fig. 19-8(b) has the intercepts $(1, 1, -1)$, and corresponding indices $(11\bar{1})$. Similarly, the planes $(\bar{1}11)$, $(1\bar{1}1)$, and so on exist. We will class all of these as just (111) planes in dealing with crystals in the cubic system.

Figure 19-10(a) shows a nearest-origin plane whose intercepts are $(1, 1, \infty)$ and corresponding Miller indices, (110). Planes parallel to one of the axes are more easily shown by means of a projection down that axis, as illustrated in Fig. 19-10(b), where the (110) planes now appear as set I. The intercepts for the nearest-origin

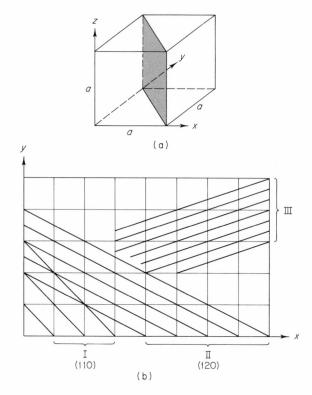

Fig. 19-10. *Various planes of a cubic lattice. (a) (110) plane. (b) Various (hk0) planes viewed down the z axis.*

plane of set II are $(1, \frac{1}{2}, \infty)$, giving the indices (120). Those for the planes of set III are left for the reader to determine.

19-3 Some Simple Crystal Structures

A. Close Packing of Spheres

Many of the elements assume a crystal structure which corresponds to the closest possible packing of spheres. As illustrated in Fig. 19-11(a), a single layer of spheres forms a pattern having triangular pockets. There are two equivalent ways of locating the second layer, namely by placing the spheres either in the set of first layer pockets labeled A or in the set labeled B. If the A set is used, as in Fig. 19-11(b), then the B set is excluded. The second layer again has two kinds of

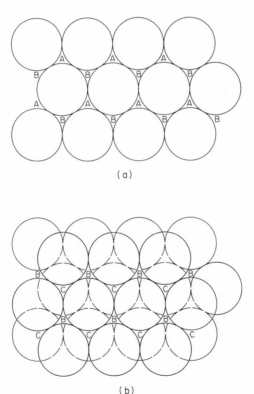

(a)

(b)

Fig. 19-11. *Close packing of spheres. (a) First layer. (b) Second layer located with centers above A-type pockets of the first layer.*

947

triangular pockets, those labeled B, which lie above the B pockets of the first layer, and those labeled C, which lie above the centers of the first-layer spheres.

There are now two *distinguishable* ways of placing a third layer. If the spheres are put in the set of C-type pockets, they will lie directly above the first-layer spheres. The structure then repeats, the types of pockets in which successive layers rest being in the sequence ACACAC..., as shown in Fig. 19-12. The resulting symmetry is easier to visualize if the spheres are replaced by points at their centers, as in Fig. 19-13(a); the structure can now be seen to have hexagonal symmetry. This arrangement is, accordingly, called *hexagonal close packing*, or *hcp*.

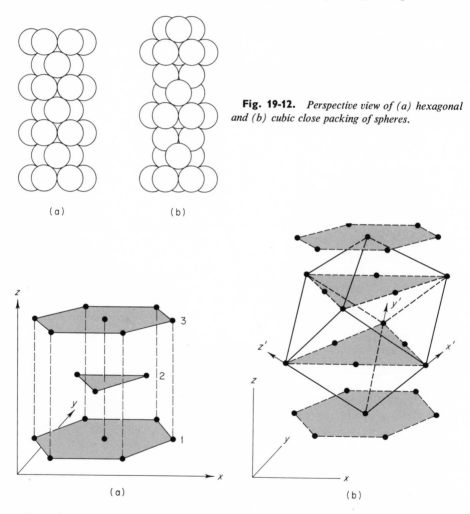

Fig. 19-12. *Perspective view of (a) hexagonal and (b) cubic close packing of spheres.*

(a)   (b)

(a)   (b)

Fig. 19-13. *Perspective view of the positions of sphere centers in (a) hexagonal close packing, ACACAC sequence, and (b) cubic close packing, ABCABC sequences. Note in (b) the pattern that forms a face-centered cube with axes x', y', and z'.*

Returning to Fig. 19-11(b), if the third-layer spheres are placed in the B-type pockets, this third layer will now have pockets of the A and C types. The next simplest repeating unit is then obtained by placing the *fourth* layer in the C pockets, so as to be directly above the first layer (Fig. 19-12). The symmetry of the ABCABC arrangement is somewhat difficult to see. As shown in Fig. 19-13(b), we can trace the pattern of a face-centered cube by connecting points between the successive layers. Figure 19-14 shows the cube in a normal orientation; we now

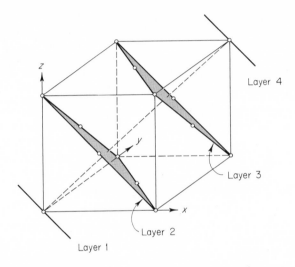

Fig. 19-14. *Cubic close packing drawn so as to show the face-centered cubic lattice.*

see more clearly that the successive layers of Figs. 12 and 13 correspond to (111) planes of a face-centered cubic lattice. The ABCABC arrangement is for this reason called *cubic close packing*, or *ccp*. Alternatively, of course, the structure is *face-centered cubic*, or *fcc*.

It must be remembered that it is the *symmetry* and not the density of packing that differs between the hcp and ccp structures. In both cases (but most easily seen in the hcp symmetry), each sphere in a close-packed plane has six neighbors which are touching. There is a triangle of three nearest neighbors above and one below, to give 12 neighbors in all. In the hcp structure the above and below triangles are oriented in the same way, while in the ccp structure they are rotated 120° relative to each other. It may be shown, incidentally, that the close packing of spheres leaves 26% void space.

Many metals crystallize in either the hcp or the ccp structure, the choice apparently being determined by relatively weak directional preferences in the metal–metal bonding. Metals having the hcp structure include γ-Ca, Cd, α-Co, β-Cr, Mg, and Zn, while those having the ccp structure are Cu, Ag, Au, Al, Pb, β-Ni, and γ-Fe. The rare gases Ar, Ne, and Xe also crystallize in the ccp structure.

A definite tendency toward directed bonding appears with Zn and Cd; although the structure is approximately hcp, the axial ratio c/a is 1.856 for Zn and 1.885 for Cd, as compared to 1.633 for closest packing. In other metals, this tendency leads to some other crystal structure, often *body-centered cubic*, or *bcc*. Metals showing bcc structures include Ba, α-Cr, Cs, α-Fe, δ-Fe, K, Li, Mo, Na, and β-W. Notice that a given element may show more than one crystal modification, as in the case of Cr and Fe.

While hcp and ccp structures both represent the closest packing of spheres, the physical properties of metals can be sharply dependent on which structure is present. Thus ccp metals tend to be much more ductile than hcp ones. The reason is as follows. For crystals in general it is those planes that are the most closely packed which slip past each other most easily [note Eq. (19-5)]. There is only one such set of planes in the hcp structure—namely the basal or hexagonal planes shown in Fig. 19-13(a). In the ccp structure, however, the close-packed planes are the (111) planes, and there are four of these, that is, there is a set of (111) planes, one normal to each of the four cube diagonals. In practice, one deals with metals which are polycrystalline, or have randomly oriented and mutually reinforcing crystal domains. As a consequence, the hcp metals tend to resist distortion in any given direction since most of the crystallites will not be properly oriented for slip to occur. A much smaller fraction will be able to oppose slip in the case of a ccp metal.

B. Alkali Metal Halide and Other MX Structures

One of the early triumphs of x-ray diffraction was the determination of the crystal structure of sodium chloride. It consists of two interpenetrating fcc lattices, as shown in Fig. 19-15, where, for clarity, the spherical ions are located by points

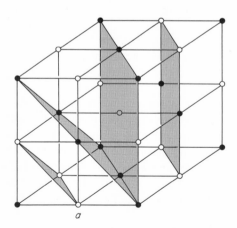

Fig. 19-15. *The NaCl structure of two interpenetrating face centered cubic lattices.*

marking their centers. It must be remembered, however, that in any lattice whose positions are occupied by spheres, nearest neighbors are in contact (see Special Topics section). Thus Na^+ and Cl^- ions are touching along the a axes, and the sum of the two ionic radii $r_{Na^+} + r_{Cl^-}$ is $a/2$.

The NaCl type of structure is a fairly common one for MX-type salts. It is the structure of most of the other alkali halides (M = Na$^+$, K$^+$, and Rb$^+$, and X = F$^-$, Cl$^-$, Br$^-$, and I$^-$, and CsF), as well as for compounds such as BaO, BaS, CaO, CaS, CdO, FeO, and other divalent metal oxides and sulfides. Ammonium ion acts like a spherical ion and NH$_4$I also has the NaCl structure.

The figure gives the unit cell for NaCl; this is not, however, the repeating unit, which consists of four Na$^+$ ions, at $(0, 0, 0)$, $(\frac{1}{2}, 0, \frac{1}{2})$, $(\frac{1}{2}, \frac{1}{2}, 0)$, and $(0, \frac{1}{2}, \frac{1}{2})$, and four Cl$^-$ ions, at $(\frac{1}{2}, 0, 0)$, $(0, \frac{1}{2}, 0)$, $(0, 0, \frac{1}{2})$, and $(\frac{1}{2}, \frac{1}{2}, \frac{1}{2})$. If this set is translated by all possible combinations of multiples of a in the x, y, and z directions, the entire crystal is generated. The same count of ions can be obtained from Fig. 19-15.

$$\text{Na}^+ \text{ ions:} \quad \begin{array}{ll} (8 \text{ corner})\frac{1}{8} & = 1 \\ (6 \text{ face})\frac{1}{2} & = 3 \\ \hline & 4 \end{array}$$

$$\text{Cl}^- \text{ ions:} \quad \begin{array}{ll} (12 \text{ edge})\frac{1}{4} & = 3 \\ (1 \text{ interior})1 & = 1 \\ \hline & 4 \end{array}$$

As a check in the counting of atoms, the proportion of each kind must always correspond to the stoichiometry of the formula of the compound. Notice also, as one characteristic of the NaCl structure, that each ion has six nearest neighbors, in an octahedral arrangement.

A second, and quite common, structure for MX salts is that of two interpenetrating simple cubic lattices, as illustrated in Fig. 19-16 for the best-known

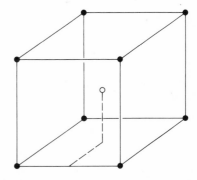

Fig. 19-16. *The* CsCl *structure of two interpenetrating simple cubic lattices.*

case, CsCl. The CsCl structure is also found for CsBr and CsI, as well as for other MX compounds, such as NH$_4$Cl and NH$_4$Br, and various intermetallic compounds, such as AgCd, AuZn, and CuZn. Each ion or atom has eight nearest neighbors, in square symmetry.

The NaCl and CsCl structures are only two of a number that MX compounds have been found to exhibit. Most such compounds, however, crystallize in one or the other of the structures shown in Fig. 19-17, each labeled according to its most prominent example. Notice that not all of the structures are cubic and that

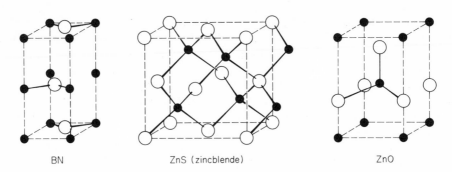

BN   ZnS (zincblende)   ZnO

Fig. 19-17. *Typical* MX *lattices.*

the number of nearest neighbors to a given kind of atom, or its coordination number, diminishes in the sequence:

lattice type	CsCl	NaCl	ZnO	ZnS	BN
coordination number	8	6	4	4	3

It should be apparent at this point that crystal structure does not correlate with the chemistry of a compound, nor with the atomic weights of the constituents *per se*. V. Goldschmidt, who determined many of the simple crystal structures around 1925, concluded that the structure of such crystals is determined by the stoichiometry of the compound, the ratio of atomic radii, and the polarizability of the units.

C. MX₂ Structures

Two of the important structures for MX_2 compounds are shown in Fig. 19-18. For example, the form of TiO_2 known as rutile crystallizes in the tetragonal system, with $c = 4.58$ Å and $a = b = 2.98$ Å. The unit cell contains two Ti atoms and four O atoms and is thus consistent with the formula of the compound. Each

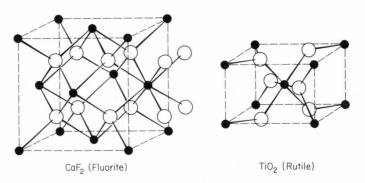

CaF₂ (Fluorite)   TiO₂ (Rutile)

Fig. 19-18. *Common* MX₂ *structures.*

Ti has six O nearest neighbors and each O has three Ti nearest neighbors. If C denotes the coordination number in an $M_a X_b$ compound, a useful rule of stoichiometry is that

$$C_M a = C_X b. \tag{19-1}$$

D. Covalent Crystals. Diamond and Graphite

We next consider briefly two examples of covalent crystals, diamond and graphite. In the case of diamond, the C—C bonds are of the covalent, sigma-bonded type, and show the tetrahedral bond angle of 109°28′. In a sense a diamond crystal is a single large molecule; the crystal structure, however, has a cubic unit cell, displayed in Fig. 19-19. As one way of visualizing the structure, notice that there

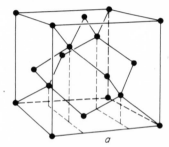

Fig. 19-19. *The diamond structure.*

is an atom at each corner, in the center of each face, and in the centers of alternate small cubes; one set of bonds is shown (the bond distance is 1.542 Å). Germanium, silicon, and gray tin have the same structure.

The diamond structure may also occur with covalent AB-type compounds, such as ZnS (zincblende) (see Fig. 19-17), AgI, CuBr, and BN. The atoms alternate in type, so each A and B atom has four tetrahedrally disposed nearest neighbors. Again, it is not the chemistry of the compound but primarily the relative size of the atoms and the geometry of their bonding that determine crystal structures in these cases.

Graphite serves as an example of a layer crystal. The structure is shown in Fig. 19-20 and is seen to consist of layers having a hexagonal tile pattern. The layers are aromatic in character; the C—C distance is 1.42 Å, or not much greater than the value of 1.397 Å for benzene. The distance between layers is relatively large, 3.40 Å, and the layer–layer bonds are consequently rather weak.

The high electrical conductivity of graphite can be regarded as due to the conjugation or aromaticity of the planes, which permits electrons to move through the crystal easily. The lubricating property has been thought to stem from the ease of slippage of one layer over the next, but the actual situation has been found to be somewhat more complex. If graphite is thoroughly degassed, its coefficient of friction rises about sixfold, and it appears that gases adsorbed between layers are responsible for the very low friction ordinarily observed. The same may be true for a

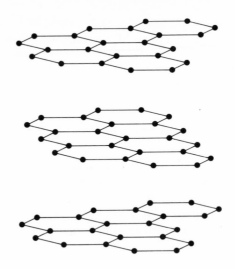

Fig. 19-20.   *The graphite structure.*

useful modern lubricant, MoS_2, whose structure is analogous to that of graphite, as well as for other layer crystals, such as talc.

E. Molecular Crystals

The substances considered so far—metals, alkali metal halides and other ionic crystals, and covalent crystals—all have high melting points. This is a reflection of the strong bonds—metallic, ionic, or covalent—between the atoms of the lattice. A rather different situation exists in the case of crystals whose basis consists of stable molecules and which are therefore held together by secondary or van der Waals forces (note Table 8-8). Figure 19-21 shows the structure of crystalline benzene. This is a low-melting (6°C) white solid; it is soft and is not electrically conducting and clearly is made up of only weakly interacting benzene molecules.

The crystals of most simple molecules, such as O_2, N_2, CO, CO_2, CH_4, are of this type. Most nonionic organic substances also crystallize by virtue of van der Waals forces only, except where hydrogen bonding is involved.

F. Hydrogen-Bonded Crystals. Ice

We conclude this section with a brief discussion of a remaining type of crystal structure, namely that in which hydrogen bonding is present. The most important example is undoubtedly that of ice, whose ordinary structure is shown in Fig. 19-22. It will be recalled from Fig. 8-10 that ice exhibits a number of crystal modifications, but only two, tetrahedral and hexagonal ice, are stable under atmo-

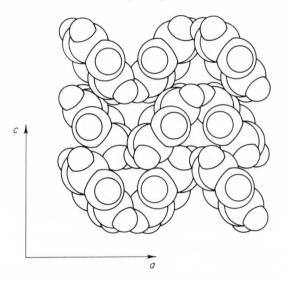

Fig. 19-21. *The benzene structure.* [*From E. G. Cox, D. W. J. Cruickshank, and J. A. S. Smith, Proc. Roy. Soc.* **247**, *1 (1958).*]

spheric pressure. It is the latter modification that is shown in Fig. 19-22. The basic structure is determined by the positions of the oxygen atoms; each is surrounded tetrahedrally by four nearest neighbors at a distance of 2.67 Å. Only recently have advanced techniques using neutron diffraction (see Section 19-CN-1)

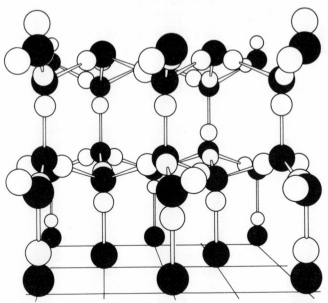

Fig. 19-22. *Hexagonal (ordinary) ice. (Courtesy of N. H. Fletcher.)*

established that the hydrogen atoms are located on the lines between oxygen atoms but asymmetrically placed; each oxygen is coordinated to two close hydrogen atoms and to two that are further away. The assignment of close versus far hydrogens is random, however, and in this respect the structure is disordered.

Hydrogen bonding is important in molecular crystals in which electronegative atoms, such as fluorine, oxygen, and nitrogen, can interact with an acidic proton of a neighboring molecule. This type of interaction becomes extremely important in crystals of biologically important substances, such as proteins and nucleic acids.

19-4   Some Geometric Calculations

The following types of calculations can be performed on any crystal but the geometric expressions rapidly become complicated as one departs from the cubic system. The general expression for the density of a crystal is, for example,

$$\rho = \frac{\sum n_i M_i}{N_0 V_c},$$
(19-2)

where n_i is the number of the ith kind of atom (or molecule) of molecular weight M_i in the unit cell, and V_c is the cell volume. In the case of a cubic crystal V_c is just a^3, while for a tetragonal unit cell V_c is $a^2 c$, and so on.

Two illustrations of the use of Eq. (19-2) follow. Iron (α-Fe) crystallizes in the bcc system with $a = 2.861$ Å; the eight corner and one interior atom in the unit cell give a net of two atoms, so

$$\rho = \frac{2(55.85)}{6.02 \times 10^{23}(2.861 \times 10^{-8})^3} = 7.92 \quad \text{g cm}^{-3}.$$

Reference to Fig. 19-4 shows that each atom in a body-centered cubic lattice has eight nearest neighbors; the center atom, for example, must therefore be in contact with the eight corner ones and the body diagonal of the cube must equal two atomic diameters. The radius of each Fe atom is therefore

$$r_{Fe} = \tfrac{1}{4}\sqrt{3}\,(2.861 \times 10^{-8}) = 1.24 \quad \text{Å}.$$

Iron also crystallizes in the fcc structure, and a reasonable assumption is that the *radius* of the atom does not change. In the cubic close-packed arrangement each atom has twelve nearest neighbors, and examination of either Fig. 19-4 or Fig. 19-14 shows that for a face-centered atom four of these neighbors consist of the atoms at the corners of the face. The face diagonal now contains two atomic diameters, or $r_{Fe} = \tfrac{1}{4}\sqrt{2}\,a$. On setting $r_{Fe} = 1.24$ Å, we obtain $a = 3.50$ Å for the fcc structure. The unit cell has eight corner and six face atoms, or a net of four atoms, so the density of fcc iron should be

$$\rho = \frac{4(55.85)}{6.02 \times 10^{23}(3.50 \times 10^{-8})^3} = 8.66 \quad \text{g cm}^{-3}.$$

As a second illustration, the density of NaCl is 2.165 g cm^{-3}. There are four Na$^+$ and four Cl$^-$ ions per unit cell, so we have

$$2.165 = \frac{4(22.99) + 4(35.45)}{6.02 \times 10^{23}a^3},$$

whence $a = 5.64$ Å. Reference to Fig. 19-15 shows that the closest distance between ions is that along a cube edge, so that $a = 2r_{Na^+} + 2r_{Cl^-}$. The sum of the two ionic radii is then $a/2 = 2.82$ Å. As discussed in the Special Topics section, only sums of ionic radii may be determined from a crystal structure, but there are various schemes whereby individual ionic radii can be assigned.

Another important type of calculation is that of the interplanar distances in a crystal. In the case of a two-dimensional, square lattice, illustrated in Fig. 19-23,

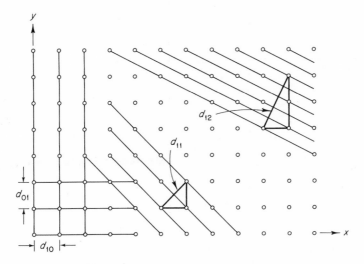

Fig. 19-23. *Interplanar distances for a square lattice.*

it is obvious that (10) and (01) planes are spaced just a units apart, or that $d_{10} = d_{01} = a$, and likewise that $d_{11} = \frac{1}{2}\sqrt{2}\,a = 0.707a$. The direction perpendicular to (12) planes is evidently that of the diagonal of a rectangle of sides 1 and 2 in the x and y directions, respectively. The particular diagonal shown is of length $\sqrt{5}\,a$ and spans five interplanar distances, so $d_{12} = (1/\sqrt{5})a$. The general formula is $d_{hk} = a/(h^2 + k^2)^{1/2}$. Extension to a three-dimensional cubic lattice gives

$$d_{hkl} = \frac{a}{(h^2 + k^2 + l^2)^{1/2}}, \tag{19-3}$$

or, for a lattice with $\alpha = \beta = \gamma = 90°$ but with $a \neq b \neq c$

$$\frac{1}{d_{hkl}^2} = \frac{h^2}{a^2} + \frac{k^2}{b^2} + \frac{l^2}{c^2}. \tag{19-4}$$

Equation (19-3) gives the interplanar distance for planes of specified Miller indices, but it is sometimes convenient to class as belonging to a given *type* all planes which are parallel to each other, regardless of actual Miller index. Thus (100) and (200) planes may be called (100)-type planes, (111) and (222) planes may be called (111)-type planes, and so on. The distinction is illustrated further as follows. The largest interplanar distances for a simple cubic crystal are, in order, d_{100}, d_{110}, and d_{111}, and their ratios are given by Eq. (19-3) as

$$\text{simple cubic:} \quad d_{100} : d_{110} : d_{111} = 1 : \frac{1}{\sqrt{2}} : \frac{1}{\sqrt{3}}.$$

The largest interplanar distances for a bcc lattice are, again in order, d_{110}, d_{200}, and d_{222} (see Fig. 19-24):

$$\text{bcc:} \quad d_{110} : d_{200} : d_{222} = \frac{1}{\sqrt{2}} : \frac{1}{2} : \frac{1}{2\sqrt{3}}.$$

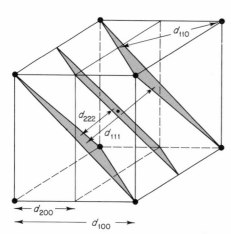

Fig. 19-24. *Interplanar distances in a bcc lattice.*

These latter two planes may be referred to as (100)- and (111)-*type* planes, however, and the ratios reported as

$$\text{bcc (type planes):} \quad d_{100} : d_{110} : d_{111} = \frac{1}{2} : \frac{1}{\sqrt{2}} : \frac{1}{2\sqrt{3}} = 1 : \frac{2}{\sqrt{2}} : \frac{1}{\sqrt{3}}.$$

Similarly,

$$\text{fcc (type planes):} \quad d_{100} : d_{110} : d_{111} = 1 : \frac{1}{\sqrt{2}} : \frac{2}{\sqrt{3}}$$

(the demonstration is left to the reader). As will be seen in the next section, x-ray diffraction studies may in some cases yield an interplanar spacing where the type but not the actual Miller index of the planes is known.

A final point of geometry is the following. In the case of simple structures it will often be true that a set of planes contains all of the atoms or ions of the crystal. Thus if a metal crystallizes in the bcc structure, the (200) planes as a set pass through or contain all of the atoms of the crystal. The same is true for the sets of (110) and (222) planes. The crystal can thus be viewed as consisting of layers of (200) planes having a surface concentration σ_{200} atoms cm^{-2} and separated by d_{200} cm. The quotient σ_{200}/d_{200} must therefore equal the volume concentration of atoms in the crystal, C atoms cm^{-3}. The crystal can alternatively be regarded as consisting of layers of (110) planes separated by d_{110}, so that $\sigma_{110}/d_{110} = C$. Thus for any set of planes which contains all the atoms of the crystal, it follows that

$$\frac{\sigma_{hkl}}{d_{hkl}} = C. \tag{19-5}$$

Equation (19-5) is often quite useful. It tells us that the highest surface density of atoms will occur on that set of planes of largest interplanar spacing. These are the (110) planes in the bcc structure and the (111) planes in the fcc case, for example. Such planes tend to have the lowest surface free energy and therefore tend to be prominent faces in actual crystals. They also tend to slip or to cleave the most easily, as is noted in Section 19-3A.

19-5 Diffraction by Crystals

X rays were first observed in experiments around 1890 with cathode ray tubes (see Section 21-1); by 1895 J. J. Thomson was describing the effect of this penetrating radiation on the electrical properties of gases. Later, in 1898, G. G. Stokes and G. J. Stoney suggested that x rays were electromagnetic in nature and the classic first experiment establishing x-ray diffraction was done in Munich in 1912 at the suggestion of M. von Laue.

X rays are produced by atoms which have lost a K or L electron as a result of a collision with some high-energy particle. Referring to Eq. (16-19), if a K, or $n = 1$, electron is lost from, say, a copper atom ($Z = 29$) and an L, or $n = 2$, electron falls into the vacancy, the energy of the emitted radiation is $0.5(29)^2[(1/1^2) - (1/2^2)] = 315$ a.u. or 8584 eV of energy. The wavenumber of radiation of this energy per quantum is

$$(8584)(8.066) = 6.92 \times 10^4 \quad \text{kK} = 6.92 \times 10^7 \quad \text{cm}^{-1},$$

corresponding to 1.44 Å. X-ray wavelengths are thus comparable to atomic radii. Modern equipment still consists essentially of a Crookes tube, in which a beam of perhaps 20-kV electrons impinges on a target, usually copper, iron, or tungsten. The emitted x-radiation is generally filtered (see Section 21-4 on the critical absorption of x rays) and then collimated by means of slits so as to produce a narrow, monochromatic beam.

Before discussing three-dimensional diffraction effects it should be explained why it is that x rays act as though they are reflected specularly from each plane of a crystal. The interaction of an x-ray quantum with an atom may be regarded as an absorption followed by resonance emission (Section 18-3), that is, by emission at the same wavelength. This process is a *virtual* one; it constitutes a hypothetical mechanism yielding the same result as does the wave mechanical treatment of scattering. The effect is that each atom becomes a secondary, isotropic emitter of the x-radiation, as illustrated in Fig. 19-25 for a single line of atoms.

A more detailed analysis is as follows. We suppose there to be incident radiation at angle θ to the line of atoms ABC. The radiation first hits atom A, which then emits isotropically, and by the time the wavefront reaches atom B the secondary radiation from atom A has a wavefront given by circle 1A. When the radiation reaches atom C the wavefronts of secondary radiation for atoms A and B are now given by circles 2A and 2B. Still later the reemitted radiation has reached circles 3A, 3B, and 3C. Where similarly numbered circles cross, the emitted radiation is in phase, as for example, at point a, the crossing between circles 2A and 2B, and point b, the crossing between circles 3A and 3B. As the circles move outward with time, the line along which the radiation is in phase is that given by the line ab. Alternatively, points b and c represent concurrent in-phase conditions and define the wavefront of the secondary radiation. Either reasoning leads to the conclusion that the direction of the secondary radiation is at the same angle θ to ABC as is the incident radiation, independent of the spacing between atoms, provided it is uniform.

This analysis is geometric and qualitative but serves to explain the rigorous result that the secondary radiation is mutually interfering except in the direction of specular reflection. We may now proceed to the three-dimensional situation.

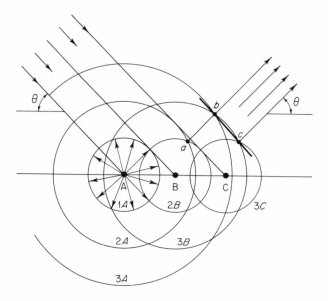

Fig. 19-25. *Scattering of x rays from a single line of atoms.*

A.   The Bragg Equation

The first diffraction experiment was made with the use of "white" x radiation, that is, radiation having a range of wavelengths, and a single crystal (of copper sulfate). Later, around 1912, W. Bragg and his son developed an approach which was, at that time, much easier to apply and to interpret. This consisted in using monochromatic x radiation and varying the orientation of the crystal.

The situation is illustrated in Fig. 19-26. We take each ray of incident radiation

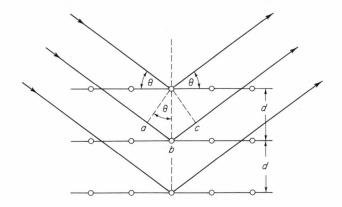

Fig. 19-26.   *The Bragg scattering condition.*

to be specularly "reflected" by a given layer of atoms, shown end-on in the figure. Reflections then occur from the successive layers, and we now ask what condition must be met for the reflected radiation to be in phase. Considering just the first two layers, the difference in path length for the respective rays is the distance *abc*. From the construction, this distance is 2*ab* or 2*d* sin θ. Thus 2*d* sin θ must be an integral number of wavelengths if the reflected radiation is to be in phase. The *Bragg condition* is thus

$$n\lambda = 2d \sin \theta, \tag{19-6}$$

where *n* is an integer. If $n = 1$, the reflection is called first order, if $n = 2$, second order, and so on. Note, however, that a second-order reflection for a given spacing *d* is at the same angle as a first-order reflection from planes of spacing *d*/2. Thus second-order reflections from (100) planes of a simple cubic crystal should be indistinguishable from first-order reflections from a hypothetical set of (200) planes. It is more convenient to treat the order of a reflection in this alternative way and to write Eq. (19-6) as simply

$$\lambda = 2d_{hkl} \sin \theta. \tag{19-7}$$

For cubic crystals combination with Eq. (19-3) gives

$$\sin^2 \theta = \frac{\lambda^2}{4a^2} (h^2 + k^2 + l^2). \tag{19-8}$$

961

B.   Bragg Diffraction Patterns

Figure 19-27 shows schematic plots of reflected intensity I versus θ for KCl and NaCl. A single crystal is oriented so that (100)-, (110)-, or (111)-type planes (or crystal faces) are perpendicular to the x-ray beam and the crystal is then rotated so that the angle of incidence θ is varied. As the angles for successive Bragg conditions are met, an increase in intensity of scattered radiation is observed by means of a detector whose angular position is also rotated so that it always "sees" radiation at the specular angle. The schematic arrangement is shown in Fig. 19-28.

In the case of NaCl the first-order peaks are found in a particular experiment to occur at 5°18′, 7°31′, and 4°36′ for reflections from (100)-, (110)-, and (111)-type planes, respectively. The interplanar distances are then in the ratio of the reciprocals of the sin θ values, or $d_{100} : d_{110} : d_{111} = 1/0.0924 : 1/0.1307 : 1/0.0801 = 1 : 0.707 : 1.154 = 1 : 1/\sqrt{2} : 2/\sqrt{3}$. This is just the ratio predicted in the preceding section for a fcc structure. The early experimentalists knew from the symmetry of NaCl crystals that they were in the cubic system and from the ratio test could determine which type. By reversing the density calculation of the preceding section, a could be calculated, and from this the wavelength of the x rays used.

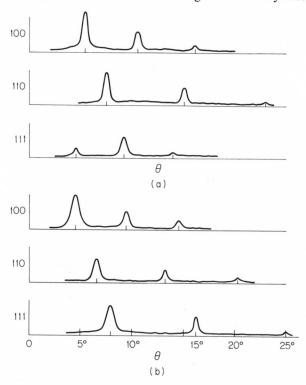

Fig. 19-27.   *Intensity versus θ for Bragg scattering from (100)-, (110)-, and (111)-type planes of* (a) NaCl *and* (b) KCl.

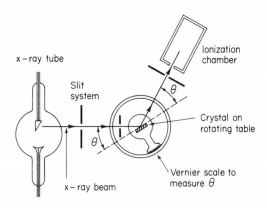

Fig. 19-28. *A Bragg x-ray spectrometer.*

Most other alkali halide crystals show an analogous set of intensity patterns but, as illustrated in Fig. 19-27(b), that for KCl gives $\sin\theta$ values of 0.0811, 0.1145, and 0.1405 for reflections from (100)-, (110)-, and (111)-type planes, respectively, using the same x rays. This yields a set of ratios $d_{100} : d_{110} : d_{111} = 1 : 0.707 : 0.577 = 1 : 1/\sqrt{2} : 1/\sqrt{3}$, or that corresponding to a simple cubic structure. Referring to Fig. 19-15, the explanation lies in the nature of the (111)-type planes. In the case of NaCl the Na^+ ions are contained by one set of (111) actual planes and the Cl^- ions, by a second set lying midway between. The reflections from the (111) actual planes are partially but not completely canceled by the out-of-phase reflections from the planes containing the other kind of ion. Thus in Fig. 19-27 the first peak for (111)-type planes for NaCl is weaker than usual. In the case of KCl the two ions are isoelectronic and scatter x rays about equally; the effect is that K^+ and Cl^- ions appear to be identical in the diffraction experiment. Reflections from the Cl^- (111)-type planes therefore cancel those from the K^+ (111)-type planes. The result is that the largest interplanar distance showing a net diffraction intensity is that for (222) actual planes. Alternatively expressed, x rays do not distinguish K^+ from Cl^- and KCl appears as a simple cubic lattice of side $a/2$, where a is the side of the actual fcc unit cell.

The example is introduced to illustrate the point that the intensity of Bragg reflections from a given (hkl) set of planes depends on the densities and nature of atoms on these and on intervening planes as well. A more formal approach is given in Section 19-ST-2.

C. *Powder Patterns*

The Bragg method is not only historic but is also of current usefulness. The application is mainly to a crystalline powder. The individual particles are assumed to be in random orientation, so that the monochromatic x rays will always find some particle with the correct orientation for reflection from each (*hkl*) set of planes. The experiment consists in irradiating a thin tube filled with the powdered sample, using a collimated beam of monochromatic x rays. Those crystals whose particular (*hkl*) planes are at the Bragg angle θ to the beam then give a reflection at an angle θ to the crystal planes, or 2θ to the incident beam. As illustrated in Fig. 19-29, one may use a circular strip of photographic film to intercept the diffracted radiation, which then shows as curved lines on the film. Alternatively, a traveling radiation counter may be used. The sin θ value for each line is calculated from the apparatus geometry.

The next task is to assign (*hkl*) values to the lines. This can be done if the crystal is known to be in the cubic, tetragonal, or orthorhombic class but is otherwise rather difficult. Often the "powder pattern" is used much as are infrared absorption spectra, namely as a kind of fingerprinting of the particular substance. A mixture of materials may then be analyzed semiquantitatively by calculating in what proportion pure substance powder patterns are present.

The procedure for assigning actual (*hkl*) values to individual lines can be illustrated fairly easily if the crystal is in the cubic system. From Eq. (19-8) the $\sin^2\theta$ values are proportional to $h^2 + k^2 + l^2$. The first step is to tabulate the film data in order of increasing $\sin^2\theta$. Since $h^2 + k^2 + l^2$ must be an integer, we then look for the smallest set of integers that are in the ratios of the $\sin^2\theta$ values. Only certain integral values for $h^2 + k^2 + l^2$ are possible for each type of cubic crystal. In the case of a simple cubic crystal, the sum cannot have the values 7, 15, or 23, for example, since there are no three integers the sum of the squares of which equals one of these numbers. The sum can only have the values 2, 4, 6, 8, ... for a bcc crystal and only the values 3, 4, 8, 11, 12, ... for a fcc one, as summarized in Table 19-2. We can then determine which set the observed series of $\sin^2\theta$ values matches.

An example should be helpful at this point. We suppose that a particular sample of finely divided lead shows the following $\sin^2\theta$ values with x rays of 1.54 Å : 0.0729, 0.0972, 0.194, 0.267, 0.292, and 0.389. The procedure is shown in Table 19-3. We first divide each number by 0.0729 and observe that the result is

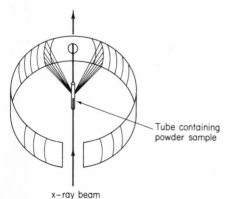

Fig. 19-29. *Schematic drawing of a powder method apparatus.*

Tube containing powder sample

x–ray beam

Table 19-2. *Indices of Cubic Crystals[a]*

Indices (hkl)	$h^2 + k^2 + l^2$	Simple cubic	bcc	fcc
			Allowed reflection	
100	1	×	—	—
110	2	×	×	—
111	3	×	—	×
200	4	×	×	×
210	5	×	—	—
211	6	×	×	—
220	8	×	×	×
300, 221	9	×	—	—
310	10	×	×	—
311	11	×	—	×
222	12	×	×	×
320	13	×	—	—
321	14	×	×	—
400	16	×	×	×

[a] The sum of the squares of three integers cannot have the values $(7 + 8m)4^n$, where m and n are arbitrary integers.

Table 19-3. *Sample Treatment of Powder Diffraction Data for Lead*

Observed $\sin^2 \theta$	Result of dividing by 0.073	Integers having these ratios	(hkl)
0.0729	1	3	(111)
0.0977	1.33	4	(200)
0.194	2.65	8	(220)
0.267	3.65	11	(311)
0.291	4.01	12	(222)
0.389	5.33	16	(400)

not a set of integers. Examination indicates that multiplying each number by three will yield integers, as shown in the third column. These integers are just those allowed by Table 19-2 for a fcc structure, and we then index each entry accordingly. In an actual experiment each $\sin^2 \theta$ value would now be divided by the assigned $h^2 + k^2 + l^2$ value to obtain a series of values of $\lambda^2/4a^2$, which would be averaged. In the present example we take this average to be $0.0729/3 = 0.0243$, and from the known λ of 1.54 Å calculate a to be 4.94 Å. We could proceed to check the result by calculating the density of lead.

COMMENTARY AND NOTES

19-CN-1   *Modern Crystal Structure Determination*

The presentation in Section 19-5 emphasized the Bragg method and powder patterns as a straightforward yet actively useful approach to x-ray diffraction. It is not, however, the method used for crystal structure determination where any degree of complexity exists. The difficulty with the Bragg method is that of indexing the diffraction lines (such as shown in Fig. 19-29). If the crystal unit cell contains many atoms and especially if it is not cubic, it can be virtually impossible to find a unique set of assignments. Alternative methods are available which avoid the loss of information in the powder method which occurs through not knowing the orientation of the crystals that give a particular reflection. These methods are described briefly later.

Once a set of reflections has been indexed and their intensities measured, the next problem is that of deducing the crystal structure. The lattice type or symmetry can often be determined from an examination of a crystal under a polarizing microscope. The symmetry of the crystal habit helps to establish the Bravais lattice involved; the behavior under polarizing light may suffice to limit the space group to at least a few possibilities. The presence or absence of certain reflections is usually sufficient to complete the assignment.

A.   *Rotation–Oscillation Methods*

One gains enormously in ability to index diffractions by using monochromatic x radiation *and* a single crystal which can be mounted so that one of its crystal axes is perpendicular to the x-ray beam. In the rotating crystal method, as the crystal turns various planes come into the Bragg angle with respect to the incident beam. The diffraction consists of spots generated in a series of horizontal layers on the film, as illustrated in Fig. 19-30. Those reflections at the same level as the crystal arise from planes parallel to the rotation axis, and those reflections above and below arise from planes whose inclination to the axis can be calculated. Thus each spot can immediately be assigned one index. The remaining indexing can still be very difficult if the crystal has many atoms in the unit cell, and a yet better procedure is available.

The next step is to displace the film synchronously with what is usually an oscillation rather than a continuous rotation of the crystal. In this way the *orientation* of the crystal is known for each diffraction spot. The *Weissenberg method*, as it is called, thus allows each spot to be fully indexed. The method produces series of diffraction spots which lie on curved lines, however, and in the *precession*

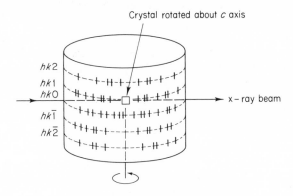

Crystal rotated about *c* axis

x – ray beam

Fig. 19-30. *Rotating crystal method.*

method, the motions of the crystal and the film are so regulated that the spots lie on straight lines.

B. Electron Density Projections

A crystal appears to x rays as a collection of scattering centers, each of intensity approximately proportional to the number of electrons possessed by a particular atom in the unit cell. The information provided by x-ray diffraction is therefore that of the distribution of electron density $\rho(x, y, z)$ in the crystal. Since this distribution is a periodic one, it is very convenient to represent it as a set of cosine and sine terms—that is, as a Fourier series.

The formal expansion of $\rho(x, y, z)$ is

$$\rho(x, y, z) = \frac{1}{V} \sum_h^\infty \sum_k^\infty \sum_l^\infty F_{hkl} \exp\left[-2\pi i\left(\frac{hx}{a} + \frac{ky}{b} + \frac{lz}{c}\right)\right], \qquad (19\text{-}9)$$

where V is the volume of the unit cell and F_{hkl} is called the structure factor (see Section 19-ST-3). This form recognizes that the electron density is periodic with repeat distances of a, b, and c. If one could evaluate each term from the diffraction data, the resulting $\rho(x, y, z)$ would *be* the crystal structure. The problem is that the intensity measurements yield $|F_{hkl}|^2$ but not the sign of F_{hkl} itself.

A number of rather sophisticated procedures have been developed to help get around the problem. It is possible, for example, to determine the distribution of interatomic distances from the indexed intensity data alone. With this information and some educated guesses the crystallographer may be able to arrive at a trial structure. Even if approximate, such a structure will allow a calculation of the *sign* of each F_{hkl}, and now the experimental intensity data can be used to calculate an actual $\rho(x, y, z)$. The result usually appears as electron density contour maps

967

calculated for one or another projection. Such a result for anthracene is shown in Fig. 19-31.

Another "trick" is to incorporate very heavy atoms (such as iodine) in the molecule. The intense scattering by such atoms dominates the diffraction pattern and it may be possible to determine the positions of the heavy atoms and thus the sign of their F factor. Sometimes a natural grouping, such as a benzene ring, can be recognized in the diffraction pattern and subtracted from it.

Fig. 19-31. *Electron density contours for anthracene. [From V. L. Sinclair, J. M. Robertson, and A. McL. Mathieson, Acta Crystallogr.* **3**, *254 (1950).]*

C.   Use of Radiation Other than X Rays

The fundamental equations of this chapter are not restricted to any particular kind of radiation. The main restriction is that inherent in the Bragg equation, namely that since $\sin \theta$ cannot exceed unity, λ must be less than $d_{hkl}/2$. Thus the wavelength of the radiation used must be less than half of the interplanar spacings to be determined. This means that radiation of no more than about 1 Å can be used.

In view of the de Broglie relationship (16-7), particles have a wave nature and should also exhibit diffraction effects. Thus 40,000-eV electrons would have $(4 \times 10^4)(1.602 \times 10^{-12}) = 6.408 \times 10^{-8}$ erg kinetic energy, corresponding to a momentum of

$$p = (2mE)^{1/2} = [2(9.0190 \times 10^{-28})(6.408 \times 10^{-8})]^{1/2} = 1.075 \times 10^{-17} \text{ g cm sec}^{-1}.$$

The wavelength is then $6.625 \times 10^{-27}/1.075 \times 10^{-17} = 0.0616$ Å. Electrons of this energy do indeed show diffraction effects and may be used for structure determinations. Electrons, being charged, interact more strongly with matter and are more rapidly absorbed than is x radiation. As a consequence, very thin samples must be used. Standard electron microscopes may, for example, be put in a diffraction mode of operation so as to show the diffraction pattern for very thinly sliced samples. Alternatively, one may obtain electron diffraction patterns from a gaseous sample. The situation is similar to that of the powder method since each individual molecule is in random orientation. The lack of a repeating lattice means that only intramolecular distances are involved and this makes the diffraction pattern rather diffuse.

Alternatively, neutron scattering may be employed. The same calculation as the preceding applies but now with m equal to the neutron mass, about 2000 times larger than that of the electron. Neutrons of momentum 1.08×10^{-17} g cm sec^{-1}, and hence wavelength 0.0616 Å, have 1/2000 the energy or about 3×10^{-11} erg molecule^{-1}, corresponding to a "temperature" of about 1000°K. Neutrons of thermal or room-temperature energy have wavelengths, then, of around 1 Å and such neutrons may be provided by nuclear reactors (see Section 21-CN-2). A velocity selector (such as illustrated in Section 2-CN-2) may then be used to provide a monoenergetic beam. The technique is a relatively difficult one, and the chief advantage in using it is that, unlike the case with x rays, the scattering of neutrons is large for light atoms. Neutron diffraction has, for example, been used to locate protons in ice, a very difficult task with x rays.

19-CN-2   Some Structures of Biological Importance

It is, of course, beyond the scope of this text to delve into the determination of complex crystal structures, but it seems worthwhile to illustrate the extent to which modern crystallography has been developed. A number of high-molecular-weight biological materials can be obtained in crystalline form, and some extremely difficult structure analyses have been made on such crystals.

One of the great triumphs of x-ray crystallography is the determination of the structure of vitamin B_{12} by Dorothy Hodgkin and her co-workers. The formula of this very complex molecule is shown in Fig. 19-32; it consists of two

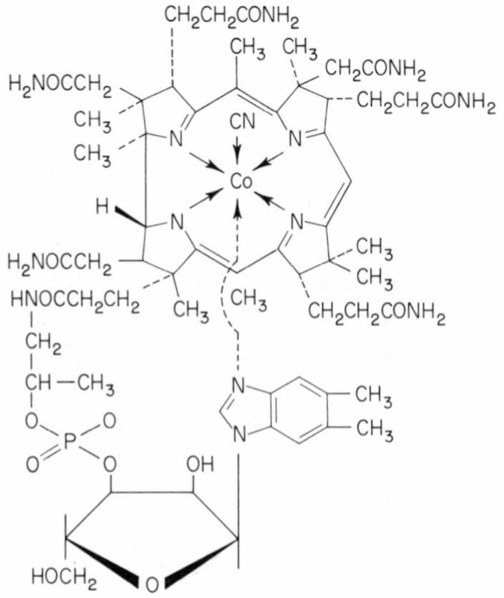

Fig. 19-32. *Structure of vitamin* B_{12} . *The cyanide attached to the* Co *atom is introduced during the isolation and crystallization procedure.*

principal parts, a nucleotide and a coordination complex of Co(III). The cobalt ion is chelated to four nitrogen atoms in a square planar ring and to cyanide ion and another nitrogen atom along the axis perpendicular to the ring. The entire structure, except for the cyanide, is called *cobalamin*. The analysis of the many thousands of individual diffraction spots to finally obtain the three-dimensional structure of vitamin B_{12} required the joint effort of a large international team of investigators.

A second crystallographic triumph was the determination of the structure of hemoglobin, illustrated in Fig. 19-33. This is, of course, a large protein molecule, a principal function of which is to coordinate an iron atom (shown in the figure). The iron reversibly takes up a molecule of oxygen, thus giving hemoglobin its oxygen-carrying property. More recently, a great deal of crystallographic work has been done on the structure of nucleic acids, RNA (ribonucleic acid) and DNA (deoxyribonucleic acid). We are now dealing with molecular weights up to several million, and while x-ray diffraction has confirmed the double helical structure, complete structural analyses have not so far been possible (see Section 20-6).

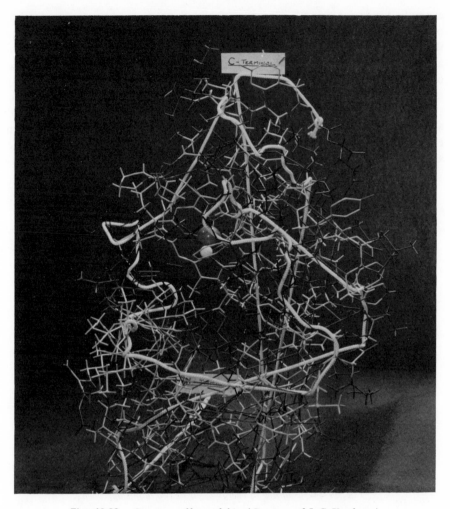

Fig. 19-33. *Structure of hemoglobin. (Courtesy of J. C. Kendrew.)*

19-CN-3   The Band Model for Solids. Semiconductors

We have so far considered a crystal to be made up of discrete atoms in a repeating structure. The wave mechanical picture, while basically not much different, does introduce an aspect of great importance with respect to the energy levels of electrons in a crystal. The point is that while completely isolated atoms would have energy levels as described in Chapters 17 and 18, when these are brought into proximity in a crystal, electron exchange begins to be possible. Suppose, for example, we had a crystal consisting of hydrogen atoms, or, more realistically, of hydrogen-like atoms, such as lithium. Considering first just one pair of atoms, then, as given by Eqs. (17-20) and (17-25), the single equal energy states of each atom combine to give a bonding and antibonding pair. In terms of the present discussion the point is that the mixing of wave functions between two atoms generates a pair of new states, one above and one below the original isolated atom state. In a crystal some number N of atoms mix their electrons wave mechanically, and the result is N states distributed in a band roughly centered at the original isolated atom state. The degree of this mixing increases as the atoms approach, and the situation is shown schematically in Fig. 19-34. In the case of a crystal of

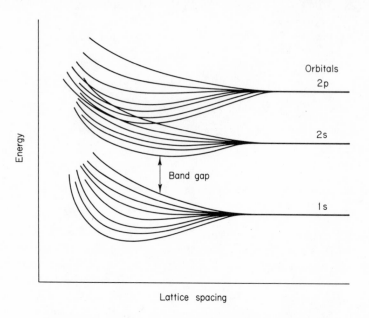

Fig. 19-34. *Splitting of energy levels as two atoms approach.*

lithium the band due to the 1s states does not span enough range of energy to overlap with that from the 2s ones. The 1s band will have N states and just $2N$ electrons, that is, two 1s electrons from each atom, to exactly fill it.

The 2s band is only half-filled, however, since only N outer electrons are present. There are thus many close-lying excited states accessible to these electrons, with the consequence that they have a Boltzmann-type distribution of kinetic energies and can move easily from one point to another. Hence the electrical conductivity of lithium.

A metal such as beryllium would exactly fill its 2s band, but it turns out that the 2p overlaps with it, so that again the outer electrons are able to move freely. The wave mechanical picture of metallic conduction is thus one of bands only partially filled with electrons. The *mobility* of the electrons is adversely affected by the thermal vibrations of the lattice, which disrupt its regularity. As a consequence, metallic conductivity tends to decrease with increasing temperature.

The profile of a band, that is, the plot of $N(E)$, the number of energy states, versus energy E, might look as in Fig. 19-35. Metals correspond to the situation

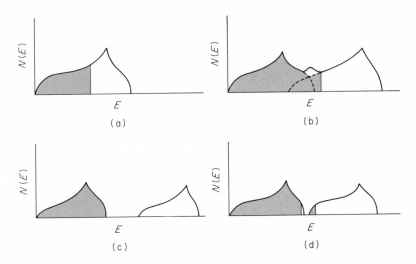

Fig. 19-35. *Distribution of energy states (shading indicates occupied states): (a, b) metals; (c) insulator; (d) semiconductor.*

shown in Fig. 19-35(a,b), that is, to an incompletely filled band or to overlapping bands. If, however, the highest energy band is completely filled and well separated from the next one, then electrons cannot move since there are no easily accessible excited states; the substance is then an insulator. An example is diamond, which has a completely filled band well separated from the next higher one, as in Fig. 19-35(c). Finally, it may happen that while a band is filled, the next higher one is so close that little additional energy is needed to promote electrons to it, as illustrated in Fig. 19-35(d). Such a substance will show an electrical conductivity which strongly increases with temperature, as the electron population of the upper band increases and leaves vacancies in the lower one. Such materials are called *intrinsic semiconductors*. Germanium has an energy gap of 0.72 eV, and gray tin one of only 0.1 eV; both behave in this manner.

It is also possible to produce electron mobility by incorporating suitable impurities in the lattice of an insulator or intrinsic semiconductor. The impurity should be able to substitute for one of the regular lattice atoms so as not to distort the lattice appreciably. Suppose, for example, a boron atom is substituted for carbon in the diamond lattice or for silicon or germanium in their crystals. The boron atoms act as C^+, Si^+, or Ge^+ ions, being one electron short, and the effect is to produce holes or vacancies in the highest energy band. The energy match is not exact, and while the boron atoms act as acceptors of electrons, some promotion energy is needed. Similarly, if P atoms are introduced, these act like C⁻, Si⁻, or Ge⁻ atoms, and with a little additional energy the extra electron can be promoted into the next higher unfilled band of the crystal. The effect of either impurity is to greatly increase the semiconductor property of the crystal. Such crystals also tend to exhibit *photoconductivity* since light energy can also promote electrons to allow conduction.

It might be mentioned that the bands in an insulator (which do not overlap) are not uniform through the crystal but are bounded geometrically by zones called *Brillouin zones* the shapes of which are determined by the crystal symmetry. The situation can be viewed as a confinement of electrons due to their reflection by crystal planes. In conductors, the Brillouin zones overlap, so that free motion through the crystal is possible.

19-CN-4   Crystal Defects

Actual crystals do not consist of the perfect lattice array implicit in the discussion so far. First, many apparently crystalline materials are actually microcrystalline, that is, they consist of small crystalline domains or grains welded together at their boundaries. This is often true of metals and especially of alloys, which may really be eutectic mixtures. The presence of such domains affects the mechanical and electrical properties of the crystal. The x-ray diffraction pattern becomes essentially that for a powder, and if the domains are very small, the diffraction lines will also be diffuse.

This is a macroscopic, adventitious imperfection. There are two other types which are always present in an otherwise perfect crystal. First, atoms or ions may be missing from various individual lattice sites, as illustrated in Fig. 19-36(a) for the case of an ionic crystal. The crystal as a whole remains electrically neutral so that positive and negative ion vacancies must occur in pairs. (An excess of even 10^{-10} mole of one over the other would give a crystal an electrostatic charge of

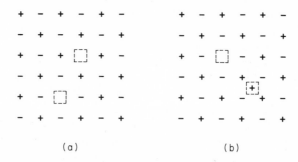

(a)   (b)

Fig. 19-36.   *Point defects: (a) Schottky defects; (b) Frenkel defects.*

perhaps one million volts!) This type of imperfection is known as a *Schottky defect*. The second situation is that in which an extra atom or ion has found an abnormal or interstitial position, as in Fig. 19-36(b); the particular situation shown is that in which a positive ion has left its lattice site, leaving a vacancy. Such defects are called *Frenkel defects*.

These two types of imperfection are known as *point defects*. Individual atom or ion displacements are involved and there is a definite energy requirement to be met. The population of point defects in a crystal is therefore governed by the Boltzmann principle, and any crystal is expected to have some equilibrium concentration of them. The fraction of such lattice vacancies will be about 10^{-5} at $1000°K$, corresponding to a typical energy of 20 kcal mole^{-1}. More detailed treatments estimate the entropy as well as the energy requirement.

A second major type of imperfection is that known as a *dislocation*. This is an organized concentration of point defects and is also termed a *lattice defect*. The presence of such defects does not represent a thermodynamic equilibrium but rather is a consequence of the history of formation of the crystal and of its subsequent mechanical experience.

One important type of lattice defect is that known as an *edge dislocation*, illustrated in Fig. 19-37. Here an extra lattice half-plane is present; the crystal below

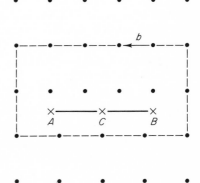

Fig. 19-37. *An edge dislocation. [From A. W. Adamson, "Physical Chemistry of Surfaces," 2nd ed. Copyright 1967, Wiley (Interscience), New York. Used with permission of John Wiley & Sons, Inc.]*

the *slip plane AB* is in tension and above it the crystal is in compression. The *dislocation line* is the slip plane at *C* (perpendicular to the plane of the figure). The dislocation emerges at the surface as a step or, conversely, pressure applied at the surface above *AB* has caused a slip of one lattice unit; the surface layers are in register, but the compression has localized around the dislocation line *C*. Continued motion of *C* to the left would result eventually in its emergence and the whole upper half of the solid would then have flowed one lattice unit. The process is much like moving a rug by pushing a crease down it.

This dislocation may be characterized by tracing a counterclockwise circuit around *C*, counting the same number of lattice points in the plus and minus directions along each axis or row. Such a circuit closes if the crystal is perfect but if a dislocation is present, it does not, as illustrated in the figure. This circuit is known as a *Burgers circuit*; its failure to close distinguishes a dislocation from a point defect. The ends of the circuit define a vector, the *Burgers vector b*, and the magnitude and angle of the Burgers vector are used to define the magnitude and type of dislocation.

The second major type of dislocation is the *screw dislocation*, illustrated in Fig. 19-38; each cube represents an atom or lattice site. The geometry of this may

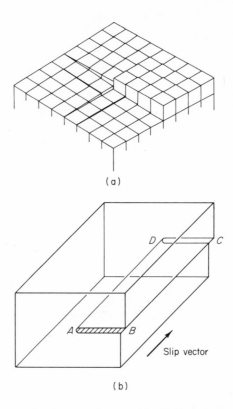

(a)

(b)

Fig. 19-38. *(a) Screw dislocation. (b) The slip that produces a screw-type dislocation. Unit slip has occurred over ABCD. The screw dislocation AD is parallel to the slip vector. (From W. T. Read, Jr., "Dislocations in Crystals." Copyright 1953, McGraw-Hill, New York. Used by permission of McGraw-Hill Book Company.)*

be imagined by supposing that a block of rubber has been sliced part way through and one section bent up relative to the other. A screw dislocation can be produced by slip on any plane containing the dislocation line *AB* [Fig. 19-38(b)], and the effect is that the crystal plane involved takes the form of a spiral ramp. A photomicrograph of a carborundum crystal is shown in Fig. 19-39, illustrating emergent screw dislocations on the surface of the crystal. The presence of dislocations is

Fig. 19-39. *Screw dislocation in a carborundum crystal. [From A. R. Verma, Phil. Mag.* **42,** *1005 (1951).]*

often made evident by an examination of the crystal surface; it may help to subject it to a mild etching.

The density of dislocations is usually stated in terms of the number of dislocation lines intersecting unit area in the crystal; it ranges from about 10^8 cm^{-2} for "good" crystals to perhaps 10^{12} cm^{-2} in cold-worked metals. Thus, dislocations are separated by 10^2–10^4 Å; every crystal grain larger than about 100 Å will normally have dislocations; one surface atom in 1000 is apt to be near a dislocation.

Dislocations greatly reduce the mechanical strength of a crystal; a normal specimen of metal has an experimental elastic limit about 1000 times smaller than the value for the perfect crystal. Also, the presence of emergent dislocations on crystal surfaces is very important to crystal growth. A saturated melt or solution can form new crystals only with difficulty, because of the Kelvin effect (Section 8-9) whereby the surface energy of a small crystal adds to its molar free energy and hence changes its melting temperature or solubility. It is much easier for the atoms or ions to deposit on an existing crystal surface, and especially so if they can locate at a step. Crystals often grow by successive new layers starting and then sweeping across the surface. A screw dislocation is also very effective as a site for crystal growth since crystal units depositing at an emergent screw step merely rotate it. Surface screw dislocations have been observed to be turning slowly as a crystal grows, in direct confirmation of this mechanism.

SPECIAL TOPICS

19-ST-1   Symmetry Notation for Crystals

The crystallographer deals with the same symmetry operations as were defined in Chapter 18 in connection with molecular symmetry. The nomenclature is somewhat different, however. A rotation axis is designated by the number giving its order, or relative to the Schoenflies symbols (Section 17-2), $1 = C_1$, $2 = C_2$, and so on. A rotation followed by an inversion through a center of symmetry is written $\bar{1}$, $\bar{2}$, and so on. The symbol m denotes a plane of symmetry or *mirror plane*; thus $2/m$ means the symmetry elements C_2 and σ_h. A succession of m's means mutually perpendicular planes of symmetry; mmm denotes three mutually perpendicular planes.

The lattice symmetries of the seven primitive lattices are given in the last column of Table 19-1. Not all the symmetry elements are generally listed, only those sufficient to define the lattice. Thus, for a primitive cubic lattice all other symmetry elements are implied by the designation $m3m$, which means a mirror plane, a threefold axis lying in the mirror plane, and a second mirror plane perpendicular to the first.

The 32 point groups may be generated by considering the various symmetry operations consistent with each type of lattice. For example, the monoclinic lattice has the symmetry elements $2/m$ and the possible point groups are 2, m (or $\bar{2}$), and $2/m$. The orthorhombic lattice has the symmetry $2/mm$ or mmm, and comprises the point groups $2m$ ($mm2$ or $\bar{2}m$), 22 (same as 222), and $2/mm$. The lattice of the triclinic system has the full symmetry $\bar{1}$ but need have only the symmetry 1. Each lattice type thus has a certain maximum possible point group symmetry, with various lesser sets of symmetry features also being consistent with it.

From the point of view of a real crystal, the basis (see Section 19-1) may be consistent with the full lattice symmetry—a simple example being the case where an atom occupies each lattice point—or may be consistent with only some of the possible symmetry features. In this second case the crystal will belong to one of the less symmetric point groups for the lattice.

A complication is that it is not sufficient to consider only point group symmetry elements. Some new symmetry operations enter which involve translation. The first is called a *screw axis*, designated by the integers p_q, where p is the order of the axis (1, 2, 3, 4, or 6) and q/p is the fraction of a unit cell length whereby the point is translated following the rotation. Points 1, 2, and 3 in Fig. 19-40(a) show the operation 3_2. Points 2 and 3 are obtained by two successive 120° rotations and advancements of two-thirds of the unit distance. Points 1', 1", 2', and 3' follow on carrying out unit translations.

The second principal space symmetry element is that called a *glide plane*, which combines reflection in a mirror plane and translation parallel to the plane. A glide plane is designated by a, b, or c if the translation is $a/2$, $b/2$, or $c/2$. An a glide operation is shown in (010) in Fig. 19-40(b). A particular combination of lattice symmetry and point group symmetry, including translational operations, is called a *space group*, and the addition of the latter operations combines the 32 point groups and the 14 Bravais lattices to yield 230 space groups.

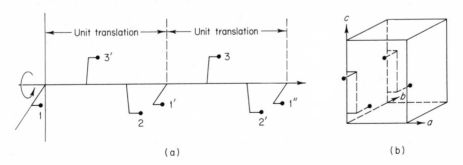

Fig. 19-40. *Illustration of (a) the screw axis operation 3_2 and (b) a glide plane operation.*

The nomenclature for space groups cannot be pursued very far here, but we can describe one scheme briefly. The first symbol is P, C, F, or I, designating the Bravais lattice type (see Table 19-1). This is followed by the point group symbol modified by the introduction of translational symmetry elements if needed. Thus $P2_1/c$ is related to the point group $2/m$, and the space group is therefore in the monoclinic system. The designation indicates a primitive monoclinic lattice with a twofold screw axis and a glide plane perpendicular to it.

19-ST-2   X-Ray Diffraction Intensities

We discussed in Section 19-5B how intervening (111)-type planes of Cl^- ions reduce, by interference, the intensity of scattering from the planes of Na^+ ions in NaCl, and essentially cancel the intensity for K^+ ion planes in KCl. The analysis can be put on a more general and a more quantitative basis as follows.

We consider first a simple rectangular lattice with incident radiation such that reflections from (21) planes are in phase, as shown in Fig. 19-41(a), that is, the phase difference is 2π. Recalling Eq. (16-25), the wave may be described by the mathematical form

$$\psi = Ae^{2\pi iq/\lambda},$$

where, to avoid confusion, we use q to denote distance; A is the amplitude of the wave. For the set of rays shown as solid lines in Fig. 19-41, $q = \lambda$, hence the statement that the phase difference is just 2π. Alternatively, if the point of reflection of the rays moves from (1) to (2), the phase of the reflected radiation changes by 2π. We can prorate this change; the distance from (1) to (2) is a/h, where h is the Miller index of the plane. A reflection from some intermediate plane, such as the dashed one shown, would be shifted in phase by the fraction $x/(a/h)$ times 2π or $P_x = (hx/a)\, 2\pi$, where P_x is the x component of the phase shift. The dashed plane also lies a distance y from the origin and, similarly, $P_y = (ky/b)2\pi$. The total phase shift is then $P_x + P_y = 2\pi[(hx/a) + (ky/b)]$. On extension to three dimensions, the result is

$$P_{\text{tot}} = 2\pi\left(\frac{hx}{a} + \frac{ky}{b} + \frac{lz}{c}\right). \tag{19-10}$$

This turns out to be general for any lattice of unit lengths a, b, and c and any plane displaced from the point of origin of the lattice by lengths (x/a), (y/b), and (z/c).

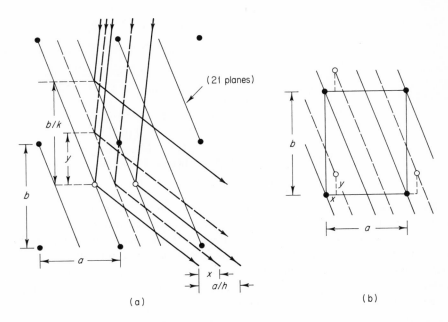

(a)

(b)

Fig. 19-41. *(a) Phase relation for scattering by a set of planes lying between (21) planes. (b) Scattering by an atom at position (x/a, y/b).*

The actual scattering is done by individual atoms of the lattice, and a unit cell having two kinds of atoms might appear as shown in Fig. 19-41(b). A plane of index (*hkl*) or, in the two-dimensional case, (*hk*) can then be passed through each atom, and the scattering amplitude per unit cell due to *that atom* is given by its *atomic scattering factor f*. The phase shift associated with reflections from the plane is given by Eq. (19-10), and the net *amplitude* for all reflections from the unit cell is obtained by summing each contribution to ψ in Eq. (16-25),

$$F_{hkl} = \sum_j f_j \, e^{2\pi i[(hx/a)+(ky/b)+(lz/c)]} \, . \tag{19-11}$$

The quantity F_{hkl} is called the *structure factor* of a crystal. The *intensity* of the diffracted radiation [due to that incident on (*hkl*) planes with the proper Bragg angle] is given by $|F_{hkl}|^2$. Thus if an x-ray diffraction pattern can be indexed as to *hkl* values for each reflection, the measured intensity gives $|F_{hkl}|^2$.

We illustrate the use of Eq. (19-11) to calculate F_{hkl} as follows. Consider first the case of α-Fe, which crystallizes in the bcc system. The *repeating unit* (which is what must be used) consists of iron atoms at positions $(0, 0, 0)$ and $(\frac{1}{2}, \frac{1}{2}, \frac{1}{2})$, in units of the lattice unit distance a. Substitution into Eq. (19-11) gives

$$F_{hkl} = f_{Fe}\{e^{2\pi i[(h)(0)+(k)(0)+(l)(0)]} + e^{2\pi i[(h)(\frac{1}{2})+(k)(\frac{1}{2})+(l)(\frac{1}{2})]}\}. \tag{19-12}$$

We can now calculate F for particular planes, remembering that $e^{ix} = \cos x + i \sin x$. For example, the amplitude of scattering from (100) planes will be

$$\begin{aligned}
F_{100} &= \{f_{Fe} \cos[2\pi i[(1)(0) + (0)(0) + (0)(0)]] \\
&\quad + i \sin[2\pi i[(1)(0) + (0)(0) + (0)(0)]] \\
&\quad + \cos[2\pi i[(1)(\tfrac{1}{2}) + (0)(\tfrac{1}{2}) + (0)(\tfrac{1}{2})]] \\
&\quad + i \sin[2\pi i[(1)(\tfrac{1}{2}) + (0)(\tfrac{1}{2}) + (0)(\tfrac{1}{2})]]\} \\
&= f_{Fe}[1 + (i)(0) + (-1) + (i)(0)] = 0.
\end{aligned}$$

Thus the intensity of reflections from (100) planes should be zero. This particular result could have been arrived at by qualitative reasoning, since in a bcc structure (100) planes would contain only half of the atoms, the rest lying on a second set of planes half way in between. Reflections from this second set would be exactly out of phase with those from the first set, so intensity cancellation should be complete.

We next consider (200) planes and obtain

$$F_{200} = f_{Fe}[1 + (i)(0) + (1) + (i)(0)] = 2f_{Fe}.$$

The amplitude is just that for the two atoms of iron in the unit cell. The amplitude for any other Miller index plane can be obtained by inserting the desired (hkl) values in Eq. (19-12).

As a second example, we can use NaCl. The Na^+ ions are at the positions $(0, 0, 0)$, $(\frac{1}{2}, 0, \frac{1}{2})$, $(\frac{1}{2}, \frac{1}{2}, 0)$, and $(0, \frac{1}{2}, \frac{1}{2})$ in the repeating unit and those of Cl^- are at $(\frac{1}{2}, 0, 0)$, $(0, \frac{1}{2}, 0)$, $(0, 0, \frac{1}{2})$, and $(\frac{1}{2}, \frac{1}{2}, \frac{1}{2})$. Equation (19-11) becomes

$$\begin{aligned}
F_{hkl} &= f_{Na^+}\{e^{2\pi i[(h)(0)+(k)(0)+(l)(0)]} + e^{2\pi i[(h)(\frac{1}{2})+(k)(0)+(l)(\frac{1}{2})]} \\
&\quad + e^{2\pi i[(h)(\frac{1}{2})+(k)(\frac{1}{2})+(l)(0)]} + e^{2\pi i[(h)(0)+(k)(\frac{1}{2})+(l)(\frac{1}{2})]}\} \\
&\quad + f_{Cl^-}\{e^{2\pi i[(h)(\frac{1}{2})+(k)(0)+(l)(0)]} + e^{2\pi i[(h)(0)+(k)(\frac{1}{2})+(l)(0)]} \\
&\quad + e^{2\pi i[(h)(0)+(k)(0)+(l)(\frac{1}{2})]} + e^{2\pi i[(h)(\frac{1}{2})+(k)(\frac{1}{2})+(l)(\frac{1}{2})]}\}. \tag{19-13}
\end{aligned}$$

The amplitude for (111) planes becomes

$$\begin{aligned}
F_{111} &= f_{Na^+}[1 + (i)(0) + (1) + (i)(0) + 1 + (i)(0) + 1 + (i)(0)] \\
&\quad + f_{Cl^-}[-1 + (i)(0) + (-1) + (i)(0) + (-1) + (i)(0) + (-1) + (i)(0)] \\
&= 4f_{Na^+} - 4f_{Cl^-}.
\end{aligned}$$

There will be a net intensity, but one proportional to $(f_{Na^+} - f_{Cl^-})^2$, and thus reduced in value. This is illustrated in Fig. 19-27, which shows the Bragg intensity pattern for reflections from (111)-type planes of NaCl. In the case of KCl, f_{K^+} is about equal to f_{Cl^-}, hence the nearly zero intensity of first-order reflections from (111)-type planes in this case.

Returning to the NaCl case, note that F_{111} could be either positive or negative, depending on the relative values of f_{Na^+} and f_{Cl^-}, but also on which set of ions is taken to be sodium. Standard tables of f values for atoms and ions allow the first point to be determined, but the sign of F_{111} is needed to establish which ions are which in the unit cell. A basic problem in crystal diffraction measurements is that intensities give only $|F_{hkl}|^2$ values and not the signs of the structure factors. As discussed in the Commentary and Notes section, it is the latter that are needed to obtain the actual assignment of atoms in the unit cell.

It should be mentioned that the intensity of a diffraction line or spot depends not only on the F_{hkl} value for each plane but also on some essentially trivial geometric factors which have to do with the general angular dependence of diffraction. First, the intensity of scattering of electromagnetic radiation is intrinsically angle-dependent [note Eq. (10-49)]. As a consequence, the intensity will, for this reason alone, vary as $(1 + \cos^2 2\theta)$. Second, if we imagine a crystal being rotated through the Bragg angle for a given reflection, the time spent in the region of this angle is a function of θ. For powders we can speak alternatively of the fraction of randomly distributed crystals which are properly oriented for a given reflection. The factor allowing for this effect is of the form $1/(\sin^2 \theta \cos \theta)$. The general scattering intensity will fall off with increasing θ as a result of these factors, and the Bragg reflections thus appear as peaks on a descending curve of intensity. It is after correction for these geometric effects that one obtains actual F_{hkl}^2 values.

19-ST-3 Lattice Energies

A. Rare Gas Crystals

The total cohesive energy of a crystal may in principle be calculated if one has detailed knowledge of the forces of attraction and of repulsion between molecules. In practice, the calculation has been limited almost entirely to lattices whose points are occupied by atoms or ions.

A rare gas crystal represents about the simplest possible case. The structure is fcc and the usual assumption is that the Lennard–Jones potential function

$$\epsilon(r) = -\alpha r_r^{-6} + \beta r^{-12} \qquad \text{[Eq. (1-71)]}$$

is applicable. The first term on the right gives the attractive potential due to dispersion (Section 8-ST-1), and the second amounts to a mathematically convenient way of providing a rapidly increasing potential at small distances. In the case of a square lattice, the distance d from an origin to some other point is just

$$d = (x^2 + y^2 + z^2)^{1/2} \quad \text{or} \quad d = a(m_1{}^2 + m_2{}^2 + m_3{}^2)^{1/2}, \quad (19\text{-}14)$$

where a is the side of the unit cell and the m's are integers. The potential energy ϵ of an atom in the interior is obtained by summing the interaction potential over all lattice sites,

$$2\epsilon = -\alpha a^{-6} \sum_{(m_1+m_2+m_3)\text{even}} \frac{1}{(m_1{}^2 + m_2{}^2 + m_3{}^2)^3}$$

$$+ \beta a^{-12} \sum_{(m_1+m_2+m_3)\text{even}} \frac{1}{(m_1{}^2 + m_2{}^2 + m_3{}^2)^6}$$

or

$$2\epsilon = -\alpha a^{-6} A_a + \beta a^{-12} B_a . \quad (19\text{-}15)$$

The sums are restricted to even values of $(m_1 + m_2 + m_3)$ since a fcc structure corresponds to a simple cubic one in which every other site is vacant; this means, however, that a is taken to be one-half the side of the full fcc unit cell. The sums are set equal to 2ϵ to compensate for the double counting of atoms, that is, each interaction is a mutual one, only half of which should be assigned to the particular atom in question. It is apparent that ϵ is just the energy of vaporization of an atom, that is, the energy to remove one atom entirely from the lattice, the structure then closing up to eliminate the vacancy created.

The sums A_a and B_a in Eq. (19-15) are geometric ones whose values are independent of a, and the coefficients α and β may be estimated from the nonideality of the behavior of the corresponding gas (Section 1-ST). It has been possible to make in this way fairly good calculations of energies of vaporization.

B.   Ionic Crystals

The application of the foregoing procedure to ionic crystals has been of much more interest and importance. One now usually neglects the dispersion term, considering that the Coulombic attraction between unlike ions dominates the attractive part of the potential, which may be written as

$$\epsilon(r) = \frac{z_1 z_2 e^2}{r} + \frac{be^2}{r^n}, \quad (19\text{-}16)$$

where z_1 and z_2 are the charges on the ions in question and the repulsion term is left open as to the exponent of r. The constant for this latter term is written as be^2 purely as a matter of algebraic convenience.

In the case of NaCl, a sodium ion experiences repulsions from other sodium ions as given by

$$2\epsilon_{Na^+-Na^+} = e^2 a^{-1} \sum_{(m_1+m_2+m_3)_{even}} \frac{1}{(m_1^2 + m_2^2 + m_3^2)^{1/2}}$$

$$+ \, be^2 a^{-n} \sum_{(m_1+m_2+m_3)_{even}} \frac{1}{(m_1^2 + m_2^2 + m_3^2)^{n/2}} \cdot \qquad (19\text{-}17)$$

The attraction between Na^+ and Cl^- ions is given by a similar sum, but now restricted to $(m_1 + m_2 + m_3)_{odd}$ (why ?). Again the sums are geometric ones which can be evaluated, and the total potential energy for a pair of Na^+, Cl^- ions is usually written in the form

$$\epsilon = -\frac{Ae^2}{a} + \frac{Be^2}{a^n}, \qquad (19\text{-}18)$$

where A and B are essentially these geometric sums, A being known as the *Madelung constant* and B also containing the constant b. Unlike the case with a rare gas crystal, it is difficult to evaluate b directly, and we therefore treat a as a parameter which is at the equilibrium value when $d\epsilon/da = 0$. On carrying out the differentiation, an expression for B in terms of A is found, whereby the former may be eliminated from Eq. (19-18) to give

$$\epsilon_0 = -\frac{Ae^2}{a_0}\left(\frac{1}{n} - 1\right), \qquad (19\text{-}19)$$

where ϵ_0 and a_0 are now the equilibrium energy and distance (again a_0 is half the side of the unit cell). The lattice energy E_0 is defined as the energy released in the formation of one mole of the crystal from the gaseous ions, $E_0 = -N_0\epsilon_0$.

This approach may be extended to any ionic crystal, A now being the geometric sum appropriate for the lattice type,

$$E_0 = \frac{N_0 Ae^2 Z^2}{a_0}\left(1 - \frac{1}{n}\right), \qquad (19\text{-}20)$$

where Z is defined as the highest common factor of the ionic charges (one for NaCl, Na_2O, Al_2O_3, ..., and two for MgO, TiO_2, ...). Table 19-4 gives the Madelung constants of several common minerals. The repulsion exponent n may be estimated from the compressibility of the crystal; values range from 6 to 10 for various

Table 19-4.   *Madelung Constants*

Structure	Madelung constant	Structure	Madelung constant
NaCl	1.7476	TiO_2 (rutile)	4.816
CsCl	1.7627	TiO_2 (anatase)	4.800
ZnS (zincblende)	1.6381	CdI_2	4.71
ZnS (wurzite)	1.641	SiO_2 (β quartz)	4.4394
CaF_2 (fluorite)	5.0388	Al_2O_3 (corundum)	25.0312

substances. A slightly better treatment appears to result if the repulsion term is written as the exponential $be^{-r/\rho}$, in which case the procedure yields

$$E_0 = \frac{N_0 A e^2 Z^2}{a_0} \left(1 - \frac{r}{\rho}\right).$$ (19-21)

Of course, a_0 is obtainable from x-ray diffraction studies, so the lattice energies of simple crystals may be calculated absolutely. Strictly speaking, the result is for $0°K$; the differential dG/da rather than $d\epsilon/da$ is needed otherwise to give the equilibrium condition, G being the lattice free energy.

C.   The Born–Haber Cycle

Lattice energies can be related to other thermodynamic quantities by means of a cycle known as the *Born–Haber cycle*. The formation of a solid salt MX from the elements may be formulated in two alternative ways:

$$\begin{array}{ccc} MX(c) & \xleftarrow{\quad -E_0 \quad} & M^+(g) + X^-(g) \\ {\scriptstyle \Delta H_f}\Big\uparrow & & \Big\uparrow {\scriptstyle I+A} \\ M(c) + \tfrac{1}{2}X_2(g) & \xrightarrow{\quad S+\frac{1}{2}D \quad} & M(g) + X(g) \end{array}$$ (19-22)

where I is the ionization potential of the gaseous metal atom, A the electron affinity of the gaseous halogen atom, D the dissociation energy of $X_2(g)$, S the sublimation energy of the metal, and ΔH_f the heat of formation of $MX(c)$ from the elements. The change in energy must be independent of path, so ΔH_f is equal to the algebraic sum of the other quantities:

$$\Delta H_f = S + \tfrac{1}{2}D - I + A - E_0.$$ (19-23)

The quantities I and E_0 are given a negative sign in the equation since they are

Table 19-5. *Thermochemical Data and Electron Affinities at* $0°K^{a,b}$

Salt	$-\Delta H_f$ (298°K)	S (298°K)	$\frac{1}{2}D$ (298°K)	$H_1{}^c$	$H_2{}^d$	I	E_0 (Theory)	A [from Eq. (19-22)]
NaF	136.3	25.9	18.9	3.0	1.9	118.4	218.7	79.7
KF	134.5	21.5	18.9	3.0	2.3	100.0	194.4	79.8
LiCl	96.0	38.4	28.9	3.0	1.8	124.4	202.0	84.5
NaCl	98.2	25.9	28.9	3.0	2.5	118.4	185.9	85.1
KCl	104.2	21.5	28.9	3.0	2.8	100.0	169.4	85.1
RbCl	103.4	19.5	28.9	3.0	3.0	96.3	164.0	84.2
CsCl	106.9	18.7	28.9	3.0	3.3	89.7	155.9	88.7
NaBr	86.0	25.9	26.8	3.0	2.8	118.4	176.7	80.2
KBr	93.7	21.5	26.8	3.0	3.0	100.0	162.4	79.6
NaI	68.8	25.9	25.5	3.0	3.1	118.4	165.4	73.3
KI	78.3	21.5	25.5	3.0	3.2	100.0	153.0	72.5

[a] Data given in kilocalories per mole.

[b] Adapted from B. E. Douglas and D. H. McDaniel, "Concepts and Models of Inorganic Chemistry." Ginn (Blaisdell), Boston, Massachusetts, 1965.

[c] Enthalpy to take $M(g)$ and $X(g)$ from 298°K to 0°K.

[d] Enthalpy to take $MX(c)$ from 298°K to 0°K.

usually reported as positive numbers although they correspond to exoergic processes.

Equation (19-23) may be used in various ways. Since the electron affinity A is the least accurately known, one use of the equation is to obtain an indirect value for it. The various quantities are given in Table 19-5 for several alkali metal halides. Note that all of the quantities make an appreciable contribution to E_0.

19-ST-4 Ionic Radii

It was pointed out in Section 19-4 that nearest-neighbor atoms or ions in a crystal are regarded as being in contact; the more correct statement is that they have approached to the point of being at the potential minimum or balance between attraction and repulsion. In effect, we *define* the crystal size of atoms or ions on this basis. Thus in NaCl the side of the unit cell is, by definition, equal to $2r_{Na^+} + 2r_{Cl^-}$; the body diagonal in CsCl is, again by definition, equal to $2r_{Cs^+} + 2r_{Cl^-}$.

Crystal lattice dimensions thus in general give a sum of radii for a pair of oppositely charged ions and some additional information is needed if individual ionic radii are to be obtained. Since molar refraction is a measure of atomic or ionic volume (Section 3-3), one method has been to use this as a basis for dividing the internuclear distance. The currently accepted procedure, however, is one due to Pauling whereby isoelectronic ions (such as K^+ and Cl^-, or Na^+ and F^-) are taken to have radii inversely proportional to their effective nuclear charge (Section 16-3). Thus for NaF, $r_{Na^+} + r_{F^-} = 2.31$ Å and the screening constant σ is taken from spectroscopy to be 4.5, so that the respective Z_{eff} values are $11 - 4.5 = 6.5$ and $9 - 4.5 = 4.5$. We write $(C/6.5) + (C/4.5) = 2.31$, whence the constant $C = 6.14$ for ions of the neon configuration. The radius of Na^+ is then $6.14/6.5 = 0.95$ Å and that of F^- is $6.14/4.5 = 1.36$ Å. One may proceed to estimate radii for a hypothetical ion, such as O^-; Z_{eff} is now $8 - 4.5 = 3.5$, so $r_{O^-} = 6.14/3.5 = 1.75$ Å.

By applying these assumptions to crystallographic data for sums of radii, Pauling has calculated a number of crystal radii for ions of various charges, a selection of which is given in Table 19-6. It is to be remembered that these rules are semi-empirical, so that particular sums of radii may come close to but will not in general give the measured crystallographic sum exactly.

Points to notice are that in an isoelectronic series of ions the radius decreases steadily with increasing net positive charge, attributed to the increasing mutual attraction of the electrons. Conversely, ions increase in size with increasing net negative charge. The comparison between M^{5+} and M^{3-} for the Group V ions dramatically illustrates this charge effect. Note, too, that the radius of O^{2-} is 1.40 Å as compared to 1.75 Å for O^-.

Table 19-6. *Crystal Radii* [a,b]

Li^+	Be^{2+}	B^{3+}	C^{4+}	N^{5+}	N^{3-}	O^{2-}	F^-	Ne
0.60	0.31	0.20	0.15	0.11	1.71	1.40	1.36	1.22
Na^+	Mg^{2+}	Al^{3+}	Si^{4+}	P^{5+}	P^{3-}	S^{2-}	Cl^-	Ar
0.95	0.65	0.50	0.41	0.34	2.12	1.84	1.81	1.54
K^+	Ca^{2+}	Sc^{3+}	Ti^{4+}	V^{5+}	—	Cr^{6+}	Mn^{7+}	—
1.33	0.99	0.81	0.68	0.59	—	0.52	0.46	—
Cu^+	Zn^{2+}	Ga^{3+}	Ge^{4+}	As^{5+}	As^{3-}	Se^{2-}	Br^-	Kr
0.96	0.74	0.62	0.53	0.47	2.22	1.98	1.95	1.69

[a] Data given in angstroms.

[b] See L. Pauling, "The Nature of the Chemical Bond," 3rd ed. Cornell Univ. Press, Ithaca, New York, 1960.

Knowledge of the individual ionic radii helps to understand why certain MX crystals have the NaCl structure, others the ZnS one, and still others that of CsCl. Considering first the NaCl structure, the face of the unit cell appears as shown in Fig. 19-42(a), where r_2 is the radius of the smaller of the two ions, ordinarily that of the cation. The oppositely charged ions are in contact, but not the like charged ones. However, as r_2 is decreased relative to r_1 a point is reached, shown in Fig. 19-42(b), such that the larger, like charged ions have just come in

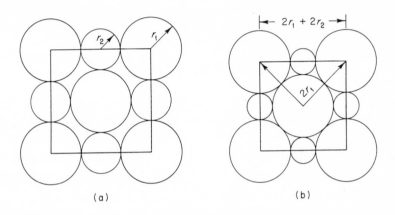

(a)   (b)

Fig. 19-42. *(a) Face of the unit cell of the NaCl structure. (b) Condition of double repulsion—negative ion–negative ion contact just occurs.*

contact. This condition is known as one of *double repulsion*, meaning that further approach will be resisted not only by Coulombic repulsion but also by the general strong repulsion of the electronic clouds [as given by the $1/r^n$ term in Eq. (19-16)]. One would expect the lattice energy of the crystal to decrease dramatically from this point on. The radius ratio r_2/r_1 for this critical condition can be calculated from the geometry of the situation. The right angle triangle shown in the figure yields the relationship $(2r_1)^2 + (2r_1)^2 = (2r_1 + 2r_2)^2$, whence $r_2/r_1 = 0.41$.

The condition for double repulsion in the CsCl structure may similarly be calculated to be $r_2/r_1 = 0.73$, and that for the ZnS structure to be 0.22. The energetics of the situation is illustrated in Figure 19-43. In the absence of double repulsion the CsCl structure should have the largest lattice energy since each ion has eight nearest neighbors. However, when the radius ratio drops to 0.73, double repulsion sets in, and the CsCl structure becomes unstable relative to the NaCl one, with six nearest neighbors. This in turn yields to the ZnS structure with four nearest neighbors when r_2/r_1 drops below 0.22.

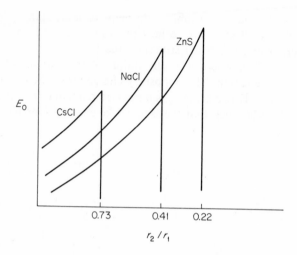

Fig. 19-43. *Qualitative variation of lattice energy with radius ratio for* CsCl, NaCl, *and* ZnS *structures.*

These radius ratio effects, as they are called, can be invoked in explanation of a number of the shifts in structure that occur in the various series of MX, MX_2, ... ionic lattices.

GENERAL REFERENCES

BUERGER, M. J. (1963). "Elementary Crystallography." Wiley, New York.
BUERGER, M. J. (1964). "X-ray Crystallography." Wiley, New York.
EITEL, W. (1954). "The Physical Chemistry of the Silicates." Univ. of Chicago Press, Chicago, Illinois.
PHILLIPS, F. C. (1946). "An Introduction to Crystallography." Longmans Green, New York.
STOUT, G. H., AND JENSEN, L. H. (1968). "X-ray Structure Determination." Macmillan, New York.
WELLS, A. F. (1950). "Structural Inorganic Chemistry," 2nd ed. Oxford Univ. Press, London and New York.
WYCKOFF, R. W. G. (1931). "The Structure of Crystals," 2nd ed. Chem. Catalog Co. (Tudor), New York.

CITED REFERENCES

KEPLER, J. (1611). "A New Year's Gift, Or On the Six-Cornered Snowflake" (translated from the Latin by C. Hardie). Oxford Univ. Press (Clarendon), London and New York, 1966.
WYCKOFF, R. W. G. (1931). "The Structure of Crystals," 2nd ed. Chem. Catalog Co. (Tudor), New York.

Exercises

19-1 Explain what the Miller indices are for the planes of set III in Fig. 19-10.

Ans. (130).

19-2 Explain how many ions of each kind are present in the unit cell of (a) BN, (b) ZnS, and (c) ZnO.

Ans. (a) two of each, (b) four of each, (c) two of each.

19-3 Explain how many ions of each kind are present in the unit cell of (a) CaF_2, (b) TiO_2, and (c) diamond.

Ans. (a) four Ca, eight F; (b) two Ti, four O; (c) eight.

19-4 The element Po has a simple cubic structure of side $a = 3.34$ Å. Calculate the density of Po.

Ans. 9.4 g cm^{-3}.

19-5 The density of solid Xe is 2.7 g cm^{-3} at $-140°C$, the unit cell being ccp. Assuming no change in the radius of Xe, calculate the density of a bcc crystalline form.

Ans. 2.47 g cm^{-3}.

19-6 Show that $d_{100} : d_{110} : d_{111} = 1 : 1/\sqrt{2} : 2/\sqrt{3}$, referring to type planes of a fcc structure.

19-7 Calculate the surface density of ions of either kind in (110)-type planes of NaCl; $a = 5.627$ Å.

Ans. 8.88×10^{14} ions cm^{-2}.

19-8 If a fcc crystal of an element gives a diffraction peak at $\theta = 6°30'$ for (120) planes (actual), at what angle will a peak occur for diffraction from (233) planes?

Ans. 13°40′.

19-9 Calculate the density of Pb from the data of Section 19-5C.

Ans. 11.4 g cm^{-3}.

19-10 Extend the listing of $h^2 + k^2 + l^2$ values of Table 19-2 up to 35, giving for each the possible (hkl) value(s).

19-11 Show that the close packing of spheres leaves 26% void space.

19-12 Show that the diamond structure given in Fig. 19-19 does indeed lead to a C—C—C angle of 109°28′.

19-13 The density of CaO is 3.35 g cm^{-3}. The oxide crystallizes in one of the cubic systems, with $a = 4.80$ Å. How many molecules of CaO are in the unit cell and which type of cubic system is it?

Ans. four; NaCl type.

19-14 The element Mo crystallizes in one of the cubic systems. A diffraction experiment using 1.541 Å x rays and a powdered sample showed reflections at 9°58′, 14°14′, 17°31′, 20°18′, 22°50′, 25°13′, 27°19′ (and further ones at higher angles). Show which cubic system is involved and calculate the value of a (the side of the unit cell) and the density of Mo.

Ans. bcc, 3.14 Å, 10.4 g cm⁻³.

Problems

19-1 The repeating unit for KIO_3 is a cube with edge $a = 4.46$ Å. The atoms occupy the following points: K in (0, 0, 0); I in $(\frac{1}{2}, \frac{1}{2}, \frac{1}{2})$; O in $(0, \frac{1}{2}, \frac{1}{2})$, $(\frac{1}{2}, 0, \frac{1}{2})$, and $(\frac{1}{2}, \frac{1}{2}, 0)$. The values give the coordinates of the center of the atom in fractions of a. How many oxygen atoms are the closest neighbors of each I? Of each K? What spatial figure is formed by those oxygen atoms that surround an I atom? Find the shortest distance between I and O; between K and O.

19-2 BeS is found to be cubic from microscopic examination. A powder pattern obtained with Cu x rays (1.539 Å) gives lines at the following values of $\sin^2 \theta$: 0.0746; 0.0992; 0.2011; 0.2767; 0.3019; 0.4030; 0.4786; 0.5027; 0.6038; 0.6789. Show which type of cubic lattice is present (index the $\sin^2 \theta$ values; that is, assign values of hkl to each). Calculate the side of the unit cell and the number of atoms per unit cell (the density is 2.36).

19-3 The mineral spinel contains 37.9 % Al, 17.1 % Mg, and 45% oxygen. The density is 3.57 g cm⁻³. The smallest unit (unit cell) in the crystal is a cube of edge 8.09 Å. How many atoms of each kind are in the unit cell?

19-4 A motorist is driving past an orchard which appears to be laid out in some form of square pattern. As he approaches his angle of vision becomes such that the trees line up in rows, and he observes that it takes him 2 sec to travel past each row. Driving on, this arrangement disappears, and a little later the trees again line up in rows which require 4 sec to travel past. Still later, a new pattern of alignment occurs, with the rows 2 sec apart. Make a drawing of an overhead airplane view of the orchard. Assume the motorist is driving at constant speed along a straight road which parallels one of the sides of the orchard.

19-5 Cuprous chloride (CuCl) forms an NaCl-type lattice. Its density is 4.135 g cm⁻³ and the strongest reflection of x rays was obtained from the set of (111)-type planes at an angle of 6°30′. Calculate the wavelength of the x rays.

19-6 The distance between d_{231} planes in tantalum is 1.335 Å. Tantalum forms a face-centered lattice. Calculate the density of tantalum.

19-7 Calculate the size of the sphere which can be accommodated in the octahedral hole of the fcc structure; cube edge $= a$, atom radius $= r$.

19-8 Calculate the structure factors for the (111) and (213) planes of NaCl in terms of the atomic structure or scattering coefficients. See Section 19-ST-2.

Special Topics Problems

19-9 Show that the presence of one twofold axis at a lattice point of the two-dimensional oblique lattice implies all the other axes shown in Fig. 19-2(b).

19-10 List the symmetry elements of a square lattice. Indicate these in the manner of Fig. 19-2(b). (See also Section 19-ST-1.)

19-11 Explain to what point group the mosaics of Fig. 19-1 belong.

19-12 What is the highest order diffraction line of (100) that can be observed from a CsCl crystal with x radiation of 1.54 Å? (Remember that $\sin \theta$ cannot exceed unity.)

19-13 The $\sin^2 \theta$ values observed on a sample of MgO powder with 0.710 Å x rays are as follows: 0.02134, 0.02857, 0.05734, 0.07846, 0.08613, 0.11437, 0.13671, 0.14358, 0.17219, 0.22939, 0.25836. Show to which type of MX cubic lattice the data correspond and the side of the unit cell. The density of MgO is 3.58 g cm^{-3}. [Data from Wyckoff (1931).]

19-14 Using Eq. (19-4), calculate d_{hkl}/a as a function of c/a for a tetragonal lattice. Cover the range $c/a = 2$ to $c/a = 0.2$, and $h^2 + k^2 + l^2$ values up to 10. Plot the results as log (d_{hkl}/a) versus c/a, using semilogarithmic graph paper. Graphs of this kind are useful in fitting powder diffraction data. As an example, the data of Problem 19-13 can be converted to a series of numbers proportional to the corresponding d's. If these numbers are marked on a strip of the same semilogarithmic scale, the strip can be slid up and down along the $c/a = 1$ line until a match is obtained; the (hkl) values can then be assigned directly.

19-15 Calculate F_{hkl} for $h^2 + k^2 + l^2 = 1, 2, 3, 4, 5$ for a fcc metal whose atomic scattering factor is 11. See Section 19-ST-2.

19-16 Spheres of 1.5 Å diameter are in a close-packed arrangement. Calculate the side of the unit cell if the arrangement is ccp and the values of a and c if it is hcp.

19-17 Calculate F_{hkl} for the first four diffraction lines (of nonzero intensity) for diamond. See Section 19-ST-2.

Special Topics Problems

19-1 Explain the alternative symmetry notation for the point groups (a) C_{2h}, (b) $2\,mm$, (c) $2/m, 2/m, 2/m$, (d) C_{4v}.

19-2 Calculate the lattice energy for NaCl assuming $n = 8$.

19-3 Calculate the lattice energy for CaF$_2$ assuming $n = 8$. The parameter a_0 is taken to be the Ca-F distance.

19-4 Calculate the lattice energy of AgCl from the following data. Heat of vaporization to give AgCl(g) is 54; heat of reaction Ag(g) + Cl(g) = AgCl(g) is −72; electron affinity of Cl is 84; ionization energy of Ag(g) is 174 (all values in kilocalories).

19-5 Calculate the proton affinity for ammonia, that is, E for the process $NH_3(g) + H^+(g) = NH_4^+(g)$, from the following data. Heat of vaporization of $NH_4Cl(s)$ to $NH_4^+(g)$ and $Cl^-(g)$ is 153; proton affinity of $Cl^-(g)$ is 327; heat of formation of $NH_4Cl(s)$ from $HCl(g)$ and $NH_3(g)$ is -42 (values in kilocalories).

19-6 Show that the value of the radius ratio r_2/r_1 for onset of double repulsion in CsCl is 0.73.

19-7 Estimate from the data of Table 19-6 the screening constant that is used in proportioning ionic radii between ions isoelectronic with argon.

19-8 ScN crystallizes in the NaCl structure. Calculate the side of the unit cell and the expected density.

19-9 (Calculator problem) Evaluate the sums A_a and B_a of Eq. (19-15) using a sufficient number of terms to be reasonably assured of convergence. Using estimated values of α and β (note Section 1-ST-1), calculate the heat of vaporization of argon.

19-10 (Calculator problem) Calculate the relative intensities for the NaCl reflections $h^2 + k^2 + l^2 = 1, 2, 3, 4, 5, 6, 7, 8, 9, 10$. Include angular dependence factors of Section 19-ST-2; assume x rays of 1.54 Å and that the atomic scattering factors are 4 and 8 for Na^+ and Cl^-, respectively.

20 COLLOIDS AND MACROMOLECULES

The twin topics of this chapter have vast extensions into applied areas, ranging from the behavior of detergents, emulsions, suspensions, and gels, to the properties of synthetic and biological polymers. We will be dealing with particles small enough or molecules large enough that their size, shape, and interfacial properties play a major role in determining behavior. Particle–particle interactions may be of great importance; these will be of the van der Waals type, including hydrogen bonding. One of the very significant contributions of colloid chemistry to fundamental science has been to the elucidation of the nature and manner of propagation of such secondary interactions. Modern colloid chemistry is in fact far more interesting and important than the meaning of the word *colloid*—gluelike— would imply!

The physical chemistry of macromolecules overlaps with that of colloidal systems. There are many experimental techniques which are common to the two subjects. In addition, however, polymer chemistry is concerned with reaction kinetics and with the stereochemistry of the primary or chemical bonding of the molecule.

The plan of the chapter is as follows. We take up first the topic of lyophobic colloids—a more complex subject than might at first be imagined—then lyophilic colloids and an excursion into rheology. Because of the difficulty in covering the field in any really adequate way, only a few rather descriptive aspects of polymer chemistry are presented. We conclude with a Special Topics section on electrokinetic phenomena, a part of surface chemistry not so far considered.

20-1 Lyophobic Colloids

The term "lyophobic" means solvent-hating, and the class of lyophobic colloids includes all dispersed systems in which the dispersed material is neither in true solution nor aggregated. A gold or silver iodide *sol* (a sol being a suspension of solid particles in a liquid medium) is an example of a lyophobic system. The particles tend to stay separated from each other; they are not strongly solvated nor do they otherwise interact with the solvent, in contrast to gel-forming substances. We consider here only one aspect of the subject, namely the theoretical explanation of why it is that lyophobic colloids are fundamentally unstable toward flocculation on the one hand, and why, on the other hand, the rate of flocculation may be very slow. As an example of this last point, some of Michael Faraday's gold sols—not yet flocculated—are still to be seen in the British Museum. There must evidently be present forces both of attraction and of repulsion.

The attraction is due to van der Waals forces, often mainly dispersion in type (see Section 8-ST-1), and the repulsion is due to the electric field around each particle. Both forces can be long-range, that is, extend over hundreds of angstroms. Being quite general in nature, these forces play an important role in any nonideal condensed system, which, incidentally, means virtually all biological ones. The importance of lyophobic colloids is partly that their study has served as a means for the experimental characterization of long-range forces.

A. Long-Range Dispersion Forces

The dispersion attraction between two like atoms is given by Eq. (8-61), which we will write in the simplified form

$$\epsilon(x) = -\frac{A}{x^6}, \tag{20-1}$$

where $A = \frac{3}{4}h\nu_0\alpha^2$, α being the polarizability of the atom and $h\nu_0$, its ionization potential. This is a general force of attraction, largely independent of the chemical nature of the atom; it arises from small, mutually induced perturbations in the electron clouds and is additive (to a first approximation). A representative value of A would be 10^{-60} erg cm^6.

A consequence of the additive nature of dispersion interactions is that an atom near a large body of matter experiences a total attraction given by integrating Eq. (20-1) over the length, breadth, and depth of the body. For a semi-infinite slab, the result is

$$\epsilon(x)_{\text{atom–slab}} = -\frac{\pi \mathbf{n} A}{6x^3}, \tag{20-2}$$

where $\mathbf{n}$ is the number of atoms in the slab per cubic centimeter. To get the attractive force between two slabs, we must consider a column of atoms in the second one, as illustrated in Fig. 20-1, and integrate over its depth. The result for two infinitely thick slabs is

$$\epsilon(x)_{\text{slab–slab}} = -\frac{1}{12\pi} \frac{H}{x^2}, \qquad (20\text{-}3)$$

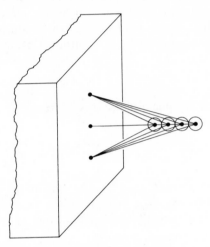

Fig. 20-1. *Van der Waals forces between a surface and a column of molecules.* [From A. W. Adamson, "Physical Chemistry of Surfaces," 2nd ed. Copyright 1967, Wiley (Interscience), New York. Used by permission of John Wiley & Sons, Inc.]

where H is called the *Hamaker* constant (alternatively given the symbol A), and is equal to $\pi^2 \mathbf{n}^2 A$. For two closely approaching spheres,

$$\epsilon(x) = -\frac{aH}{12x}, \qquad (20\text{-}4)$$

where a is the radius and x is the surface-to-surface distance, assumed to be small compared to a. A typical value for H is about 10^{-13} erg. These interaction potentials are long-range in the sense that they fall off only slowly with distance, that is, as $1/x^2$ or as $1/x$.

Consider two spherical colloidal particles of $1\,\mu\ (10^{-4}\,\text{cm})$ radius, for which H is 10^{-13} erg, so that from Eq. (20-4) $\epsilon(x) = -10^{-18}/x$ erg. At 100 Å or 10^{-6} cm separation, $\epsilon(x)$ is therefore -10^{-12} erg. This is a small quantity, but much larger than the kinetic energy of the particles kT, which is 4×10^{-14} erg at 25°C.

As the example demonstrates, once two colloidal particles are in each other's vicinity, either as a result of diffusion or of the action of convection currents, they should drift together and seize. The repulsive potential that prevents this is now discussed.

997

B. Electrostatic Repulsion. The Diffuse Double Layer

We consider first a single particle, large enough for its surface to be treated as flat, and having a surface charge σ_0 per square centimeter and corresponding potential ψ_0. The particle is in a liquid medium containing an electrolyte of concentration n_0, which we take to be uni-univalent in type. We further assume ψ_0 to be positive so that negative ions of the electrolyte are attracted to the surface and positive ions are repelled. The potential energy of an ion in a potential ψ is just $e\psi$, so by the Boltzmann principle the concentration of ions in a region near the surface is

$$n^- = n_0 e^{e\psi/kT}, \qquad n^+ = n_0 e^{-e\psi/kT}, \tag{20-5}$$

where ψ is the potential at some distance x away from the surface. The net charge density at this point is then

$$\rho = e(n^+ - n^-) = -2n_0 e \sinh \frac{e\psi}{kT} \tag{20-6}$$

[remembering that $\sinh x = \frac{1}{2}(e^x - e^{-x})$]. The derivation is so far entirely analogous to that of the Debye–Hückel theory [compare Eq. (12-76)], and we proceed to invoke the Poisson equation (12-77), thus obtaining

$$\nabla^2 \psi = \frac{8\pi n_0 e}{D} \sinh \frac{e\psi}{kT} \qquad \text{[Eq. (12-78)]},$$

where D is the dielectric constant of the medium.

The derivation now takes a turn from the Debye–Hückel one since in the present case $\nabla^2\psi$ is just $d^2\psi/dx^2$ and Eq. (12-78) can be integrated directly. The result is somewhat complicated, but if $e\psi/kT$ (for ions of charge z, $ze\psi/kT$) is small compared to unity, one obtains the simple result

$$\psi = \psi_0 e^{-\kappa x}, \tag{20-7}$$

where κ is the Debye–Hückel constant, defined for a uni-univalent electrolyte by Eq. (12-80),

$$\kappa^2 = \frac{8\pi n_0 e^2}{DkT}. \tag{20-8}$$

The potential thus decays exponentially with distance into the solution.

The behavior of Eq. (20-7) is illustrated in Fig. 20-2 for $\psi_0 = 25\,\text{mV}$ ($1\,\text{mV} = 0.001\,\text{V}$); for a singly charged ion the corresponding potential energy is 23 cal mole^{-1}; 25 mV therefore corresponds to about kT at 25°C. Notice that the range of ψ is about 100 Å for fairly typical electrolyte concentrations, and that ψ drops off more rapidly the higher the concentration and the higher the valence of the electrolyte ions.

The physical situation is that for a surface of potential ψ_0; the nearby solution has an excess of negative over positive ions, or a net charge density ρ which, along

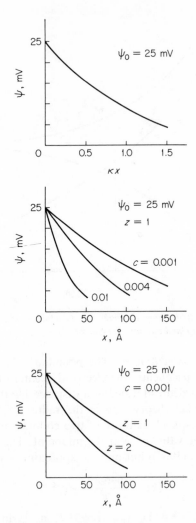

Fig. 20-2. *The diffuse double layer. [Courtesy K. J. Mysels.]*

with ψ, diminishes approximately exponentially with distance. The system as a whole is electrically neutral, so that the surface of the solid must have a surface charge density as illustrated in Fig. 20-3,

$$\sigma_0 = -\int_0^\infty \rho \, dx. \tag{20-9}$$

The picture is one of a positively charged surface and a counterbalancing net excess of negative charge in the neighboring solution. This last is diffuse, and the

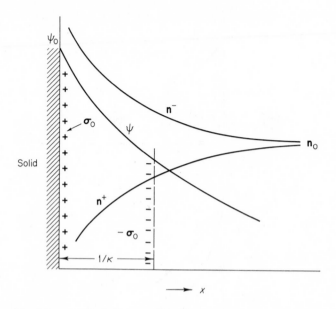

Fig. 20-3. *The diffuse double layer as equivalent to a plane of excess charge in solution at distance $1/\kappa$ from a surface of equal but opposite charge.*

system is called a *diffuse double layer*. The potential ψ has decayed to $1/e$ of ψ_0 at a distance $1/\kappa$, and consequently the electrical "center of gravity" of charge in the solution may be regarded as located at a distance $1/\kappa$ from the surface. In the case of the Debye–Hückel theory, $1/\kappa$ is the radius of the ionic atmosphere.

If two charged surfaces, such as those of two colloidal particles, approach, the repulsion depends on the value of ψ at the midpoint. The derivation will not be given here [see Adamson (1967)] but only an approximate result:

$$\epsilon(x) = \frac{64 \mathbf{n}_0 kT}{\kappa} \gamma^2 e^{-2\kappa x}, \tag{20-10}$$

where $\gamma = (e^{y_0/2} - 1)/(e^{y_0/2} + 1)$, $y_0 = ze\psi_0/kT$, $\mathbf{n}_0$ is in molecules per cubic centimeter, and $\epsilon(x)$ is the repulsion potential in ergs per square centimeter.

Suppose that $y_0 = 1$, $x = 10^{-6}$ cm, and the concentration of uni-univalent electrolyte is 0.001 M, so that κ is about 10^6 cm^{-1} (and $\kappa x = 1$). We then obtain

$$\epsilon(x) = \frac{64(0.001)(10^{-3})6.02 \times 10^{23} \, kT}{10^6} \left(\frac{1.65 - 1}{1.65 + 1}\right)^2 0.135 = 3.13 \times 10^{11} \, kT \quad \text{erg cm}^{-2}.$$

C. Flocculation of Colloidal Suspensions

The flocculation or coming together of colloidal particles can be examined in the light of the preceding estimates of the attraction and repulsion potentials. The approximate net potential is given by the sum of Eq. (20-3) or Eq. (20-4) and Eq. (20-8),

$$\epsilon(x) = \frac{64\mathbf{n}_0 kT}{\kappa}\, \gamma^2 e^{-2\kappa x} - \frac{1}{12\pi}\frac{H}{x^2}. \tag{20-11}$$

The function $\epsilon(x)$ is illustrated in Fig. 20-4. We assume particles of radius about

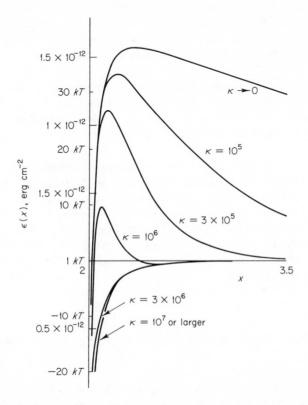

Fig. 20-4. *The effect of electrolyte concentration on the interaction potential energy between two spheres. (From E. J. W. Verwey and J. Th. G. Overbeek, "Theory of Lyophobic Colloids." Elsevier, Amsterdam, 1948.)*

10^{-5} cm or area about 3×10^{-10} cm^2 in applying Eq. (20-3). At small κ or low electrolyte concentration the electrostatic repulsion is strong and the colloidal particles will be virtually unable to approach each other; the suspension should be relatively stable. The barrier diminishes with increasing electrolyte concentration and eventually disappears.

One may, in fact, calculate the critical electrolyte concentration such that the barrier is just zero from the condition that $\epsilon(x) = 0$ and $d\epsilon(x)/dx = 0$. The resulting equation gives $\mathbf{n}_{0(\text{crit})}$ as proportional to $1/z^6$. Thus for a z–z electrolyte, equivalent conditions with respect to producing flocculation should be in the order

$1 : (\frac{1}{2})^6 : (\frac{1}{3})^6$ or $100 : 1.6 : 0.13$ for 1–1, 2–2, and 3–3 electrolytes, respectively. This is essentially the experimental observation as embodied in what is known as the *Schulze–Hardy rule*.

Another factor, not explicitly mentioned so far, is that while ψ_0 reflects the intrinsic nature of the particle–medium interface, it may be modified by adsorbed ions. The potential of colloidal AgI particles is, for example, very dependent on the concentration of Ag^+ or I^- ions in the solution and in general would be affected by the presence of any other adsorbable ions. One may thus vary ψ_0 as well as electrolyte concentration, and studies of this type have allowed approximate experimental values of the Hamaker constant H to be calculated from flocculation rates.

The basis of the calculation is that the flocculation rate should be just the encounter rate given by Eq. (15-25) modified by the factor $\exp(-\epsilon^*/kT)$, where ϵ^* is the height of the barrier (such as shown in Fig. 20-4). Thus ϵ^* may be calculated from the measured flocculation rate and, by means of Eq. (20-11), related to H.

It should be mentioned that H has been measured directly as a weak force of attraction between a spherical surface and a plate. The force is very small, of the order of 0.01 dyn for a separation of about 10^{-4} cm and the required apparatus is quite ingenious in design—the measurements come from the laboratories of J. Th. Overbeek in Holland and B. V. Derjaguin in the USSR. It is quite a triumph that the approximate wave mechanical theory, the direct measurements, and the indirect calculation through flocculation rates agree in value of H to within at least an order of magnitude.

20-2   Association Colloids. Colloidal Electrolytes

A solution of a soap or in general of a detergent will exhibit colloidal behavior under certain conditions. The qualitative phase diagram shown in Fig. 20-5 is typical for ordinary soaps (that is, sodium or potassium salts of long-chain fatty acids such as stearic or oleic acid). Below a certain temperature T_K, known as the *Kraft temperature*, the soap exhibits a fairly normal solubility behavior, but above T_K, there is a critical concentration beyond which the solution consists of colloidal aggregates plus free ions. These aggregates are called *micelles* and consist of 50 to 100 monomer molecules in a more or less spherical unit, with about half of the cations bound and the rest present in an electrical double layer. A schematic illustration of a micelle is shown in Fig. 20-6.

Micelles are in thermodynamic equilibrium with the monomer electrolyte and their formation occurs over a rather narrow range of concentration (as shown in Fig. 20-5); one therefore speaks of the *critical micelle concentration*. The presence of micelles seems to be necessary for, or at least to correlate with, detergent action.

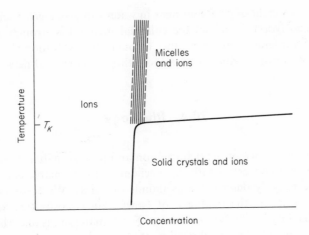

Concentration

Fig. 20-5. *Phase map for a colloidal electrolyte. [From W. C. Preston, J. Phys. Colloid Chem* **52**, *84 (1948). Copyright 1948 by the American Chemical Society. Reproduced by permission of the copyright owner.]*

Fig. 20-6. *Schematic representation of a spherical micelle.*

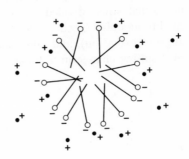

A soap below its Kraft temperature does not function well, for example. One explanation is that micelles are able to absorb or "solubilize" oily material such as present in dirt and one function of a soap in washing is in detaching dirt particles from the fabric and then keeping them in suspension.

20-3   Gels

A semisolid system having either a yield value (see Section 20-4) or a very high viscosity is called a gel, jelly, or paste. It is easily understandable that very concentrated suspensions should be semisolid or very viscous in behavior. It is possible, however, for quite dilute colloidal systems to show such properties also;

a few percent by weight of gelatin or agar in water can give a gel. Such systems are properly termed lyophilic in that the colloidal material is strongly solvated and individual units interact with each other through their solvation sheaths. Weakly bound aggregates result, which form a loose three-dimensional network.

20-4   Rheology

Rheology is the science of the deformation and flow of matter. It is that branch of physics which is concerned with the mechanics of deformable bodies, primarily those that are roughly describable as liquids or solids. We considered a simple rheological situation in the treatment of Newtonian viscosity (see Sections 2-7A and 8-10) defined by Eq. (2-59). An ideal or Newtonian fluid is one whose viscosity coefficient η is independent of the value of dv/dx, that is, independent of *shear*.

Another type of limiting behavior is that of an *ideal elastic* body. Such a body deforms or shows *strain* which is proportional to the applied unbalanced force or *stress*. The ratio of stress over strain is called the *elastic modulus*, and a crystal of cubic symmetry has three kinds of elastic modulus: Young's modulus Y (change in normal stress divided by the resulting relative change in length), shear or rigidity modulus G (change in tangential stress divided by change in the resulting angle of extension), and bulk modulus K (change in hydrostatic pressure divided by resulting change in volume). These deformations are illustrated in Fig. 20-7.

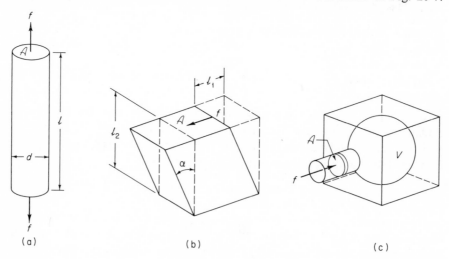

Fig. 20-7.   *Diagrams explaining the definitions of the elastic constants. (a) Young's modulus Y; (b) shear modulus G; and (c) bulk modulus K. ($\mathscr{A}$ is area, d is diameter, l is length, V is volume, and f is force.) [From J. R. Van Wazer, J. W. Lyons, K. Y. Kim, and R. E. Colwell, "Viscosity and Flow Measurement." Copyright 1963, Wiley (Interscience), New York. Used by permission of John Wiley & Sons, Inc.]*

A less isotropic solid has moduli that are different for different directions of stress—up to a maximum of 21 in all.

The subject of rheology is made considerably more complicated by nonideal behavior. A liquid whose viscosity decreases with increasing stress (such as increasing rate of flow or of stirring) is called *pseudoplastic*; if the viscosity increases with stress, the liquid is *dilatant*. These cases are illustrated in Fig. 20-8, in which *rate*

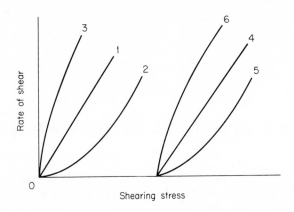

Fig. 20-8. *Shear versus stress plots. (1) Newtonian fluid; (2) pseudoplastic fluid; (3) dilatant fluid; (4) Bingham plastic; (5) pseudoplastic with a yield value; and (6) dilatant material with a yield value.*

of shear is plotted against the *shearing stress*. Referring to Eq. (2-59), $f = \eta \mathscr{A}\, dv/dx$, the quantity dv/dx is the rate of shear, and $f/\mathscr{A}$, the force differential per unit area, is the shearing stress.

An ideal elastic solid shows no shear at any shearing stress, but actual solids will have a *yield point* beyond which flow begins to occur. A solid is known as a *Bingham plastic* if, once flow takes place, the rate of shear is proportional to the shearing stress in excess of the yield value, illustrated by curve 4 in the figure. Curves 5 and 6 are those for pseudoplastic and dilatant materials showing a yield value.

The measured viscosity of a system is given by the ratio $(f/\mathscr{A})/(dv/dx)$. Thus Bingham and pseudoplastic solids as well as non-Newtonian liquids have viscosities that are dependent on the rate of shear.

The situation is yet worse than that described since the measured viscosity can vary with time as well as with shearing stress. A liquid which becomes more fluid with increasing time of flow is said to be *thixotropic*, while if the opposite is true, we say it exhibits *rheopexy*.

Examples of these types of behavior are as follows. Gases and pure single-phase liquids exhibit Newtonian viscosity, while suspensions, slurries, and emulsions are apt to show dilatant behavior—a common example being that of a thick starch paste. It is often difficult to distinguish between behaviors 2 and 5 of Fig. 20-8, that is, between a pseudoplastic fluid and a pseudoplastic solid with yield value; the term pseudoplastic is therefore often applied without attempting to make the distinction. Materials in this general category include melts or solutions of high molecular weight solutes. Household paints are often pseudoplastic so as to brush easily, yet not run; the same is true for printing inks.

Ordinary crystalline solids will always have a yield value, but often a very high one. That for metals is around 10–50 kg mm^{-2}, for example—flow begins to occur once this yield pressure is exceeded.

Some gels are thixotropic—they will liquify on shaking. Conversely, certain types of suspensions, such as of bentonite clay, are rheopectic. They settle very slowly on standing, but rapidly if tapped gently.

20-5   Liquid Crystals. Mesophases of Matter

There are a number of crystalline substances which show a very peculiar behavior on warming. For example, the compound 5-chloro-6-*n*-heptyloxy-2-naphthoic acid,

exists in ordinary crystalline form. On heating to 165.5°C, the crystals collapse to a turbid, viscous melt which adheres to the walls of the container. If this is spread on a flat plate, one may see steps or ridges; it is birefringent, showing colored areas under polarized light and having different optical properties parallel and perpendicular to the plate. Further heating of the compound produces a second change, at 176.5°C, to a fluid but turbid liquid. Only at 201°C does final true melting to a clear liquid occur.

This type of behavior is called *liquid crystalline* because of the combination of properties exhibited, and the phases involved are called *mesophases* (lying between crystalline and liquid). Liquid crystals tend to occur with compounds that are highly asymmetric in shape, often having well-separated polar and nonpolar portions to the molecule. The two types of mesophases described here are called *smectic* and *nematic*, and the type of order present is illustrated in Fig. 20-9. In the smectic phase the molecules have retained their parallel orientation but have lost the crystalline regularity in the spacing between them so that successive layers no longer match. In the nematic phase the molecules, while still parallel, have further lost their planar array.

A great many biological structures might be called liquid crystalline—there is

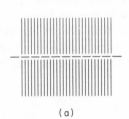  

(a) (b) (c)

Fig. 20-9. *Molecular arrangements for (a) smectic mesophase, (b) nematic mesophase, and (c) isotropic liquid.*

partial but not complete ordering between molecular units. Muscle fibers show double refraction; sperm cells may possess a truly liquid crystalline state; a solution of tobacco mosaic virus contains nematic-type micellar units. At a simpler level, cholesterol and its derivatives may show both a smectic and a so-called cholesteric mesophase, the transition from the latter to isotropic melt occurring at around body temperature.

20-6 Polymers

The great importance of polymers hardly needs to be stressed. Biological polymers such as proteins and nucleic acids are central to the functioning of living things. Natural polymers such as rubber and the host of synthetic ones such as polytetrafluoroethylene ("Teflon"), polyethylene, and polystyrene are vital materials to our technology.

There are perhaps three major aspects to the general subject. The first is that of the chemistry of polymers—their synthesis and degradation reactions; the second important subject is the physical chemistry of polymer solutions; and the third is that of the overall configurational structure of polymers. The material that follows is intended merely to be illustrative of each of these very large fields.

A. Polymerization Chemistry and Kinetics

The characteristic feature of a polymer is that it is composed of a large number of identical or at least similar units which are chemically bonded together. The compound which forms the "repeating" unit is called the *monomer*. Thus in polystyrene,

$$-\underset{\phi}{CH}-CH_2-(\underset{\phi}{CH}-CH_2)_n-\underset{\phi}{CH}-CH_2-,$$

the monomer unit is styrene, $C_6H_5CH_2=CH_2$. Polymers of this type are called *linear polymers*. Other examples include polyethylene, polyvinyl chloride, polyacrylic esters and biological polymers such as proteins and polysaccharides. If more than two polymer forming functions are present, as with divinyl benzene $(CH_2=CH-C_6H_4-CH=CH_2)$, then cross-linked chains form, yielding a three-dimensional network. Cross-linking may also be induced to occur in an already formed linear polymer. Thus in the case of rubber,

$$-CH_2-\underset{\underset{CH_3}{|}}{CH}=CH-CH_2-CH_2-\underset{\underset{CH_3}{|}}{C}=CH-CH_2-,$$

the natural linear polymer chains may be tied at random positions by mixing in sulfur and heating to form $C-S-C$ bonds bridging two chains. Irradiation of polyethylene with gamma rays knocks off hydrogen atoms at random points and the resulting active carbon atoms can then bond to a neighboring chain.

Polymerization reactions generally occur by one of two types of mechanism. Vinyl monomers are polymerized by a free radical process such as that for ethylene,

$$R_0\cdot + CH_2=CH_2 \rightarrow R_0-CH_2-CH_2\cdot$$
$$R_0-CH_2-CH_2\cdot + CH_2=CH_2 \rightarrow R_0-CH_2-CH_2-CH_2-CH_2\cdot \qquad (20\text{-}12)$$
$$\vdots$$

where $R_0\cdot$ is an initiating radical produced by some catalyst such as a peroxy acid,

$$\overset{\overset{\text{O}}{\|}}{R}COOH,$$

or photochemically. Styrene will polymerize just on heating in the presence of oxygen.

The formal kinetic scheme for the radical mechanism is as follows:

$$R_0 + M \xrightarrow{k_i} M_1\cdot \qquad \text{(initiation)}, \qquad (20\text{-}13)$$

$$M_1\cdot + M \xrightarrow{k_1} M_2\cdot, \qquad M_2\cdot + M \xrightarrow{k_2} M_3\cdot \qquad \text{(propagation)}, \qquad (20\text{-}14)$$

$$M_n\cdot + M_t\cdot \xrightarrow{k_t} M_n + M_s \,(\text{or } M_{n+s}) \qquad \text{(termination)}. \qquad (20\text{-}15)$$

Application of the stationary-state hypothesis (Section 14-4C) yields

$$R_i = R_t = k_t\left[\sum_{n=1}^{\infty} (M_n\cdot)\right]^2 = k_t(M\cdot)^2, \qquad (20\text{-}16)$$

where R_i and R_t are the initiation and termination rates, respectively, it being assumed that any two radical chains react to terminate with the same rate constant k_t; $(M\cdot)$ denotes the total radical concentration, $\sum_n (M_n\cdot)$. If we further assume that $k_1 = k_2 = k_n = k_p$ for the reactions of Eq. (20-14), where k_p is the common propagation rate constant, then the rate of disappearance of monomer is

$$-\frac{d(M)}{dt} = (M) k_p \sum_n (M_n \cdot).$$ (20-17)

On substitution for $(M \cdot)$ from Eq. (20-16), we obtain

$$-\frac{d(M)}{dt} = k_p \left(\frac{R_i}{k_t}\right)^{1/2} (M).$$ (20-18)

In general each polymerization system must be subjected to separate kinetic analysis since the appropriate set of approximations may vary. A particularly simple special case of Eq. (20-18), however, is that in which R_i is photochemical and therefore given by ϕI_a, where ϕ is the quantum yield for radical production and I_a is the number of quanta of light absorbed per unit volume and time. A point implicit in schemes such as this is that after some time t there will be a distribution of polymer molecular weights. A more detailed analysis would predict both the average molecular weight and the breadth of the distribution.

A second type of mechanism is that in which a Lewis acid such as $AlCl_3$ or an ordinary strong protonic acid such as H_2SO_4 adds a proton to the monomer. A typical sequence is that for the production of butyl rubber by the polymerization of isobutylene,

$$H^+\text{---}CH_2{=}\underset{\underset{CH_3}{|}}{\overset{\overset{CH_3}{|}}{C}}\frown CH_2{=}\underset{\underset{CH_3}{|}}{\overset{\overset{CH_3}{|}}{C}}\frown CH_2{=}\underset{\underset{CH_3}{|}}{\overset{\overset{CH_3}{|}}{C}} \rightarrow CH_3{-}\underset{\underset{CH_3}{|}}{\overset{\overset{CH_3}{|}}{C}}{-}CH_2{-}\underset{\underset{CH_3}{|}}{\overset{\overset{CH_3}{|}}{C}}{-}CH_2{-}\underset{\underset{CH_3}{|}}{\overset{\overset{CH_3}{|}}{C}} \cdots .$$ (20-19)

More recently, transition metal ions have been found to be excellent catalysts for polymerization reactions, often giving highly stereoregular or *isotactic* polymers. (A polymer such as polystyrene is isotactic if, when the chain is stretched out, all of the phenyl groups are on one side.)

A related mechanism is that whereby water is eliminated between two functional groups. Thus a protein chain,

$$H{-}\underset{\underset{H}{|}}{\overset{\overset{R}{|}}{C}}{-}\underset{\underset{H}{|}}{\overset{}{N}}{-}\overset{\overset{O}{\|}}{C}{-}(\underset{\underset{H}{|}}{\overset{\overset{R}{|}}{C}}{-}\underset{\underset{H}{|}}{\overset{}{N}}{-}\overset{\overset{O}{\|}}{C}{-})_n{-}\underset{\underset{H}{|}}{\overset{\overset{R}{|}}{C}}{-}\underset{\underset{H}{|}}{\overset{}{N}}{-}\overset{\overset{O}{\|}}{C}{-}H,$$

forms on elimination of water between RCOOH and RNH_2 groups. The R's vary down the chain in natural proteins but may be the same in synthetic polypeptides. As another illustration, nylon results from the condensation of adipic acid $(HOOC(CH_2)_4{-}COOH)$ with hexamethylenediamine $(H_2N(CH_2)_6NH_2)$. These various polymerizations follow kinetic schemes similar to that of Eqs. (20-13)–(20-15).

B. Polymer Solutions

The study of polymer solutions can be regarded as a branch of colloid chemistry. As with colloidal suspensions, one is interested in the distribution of particle sizes (in this case, polymer molecular weights), in the shape of the particles, in their interaction with the solvent medium, and in the general physical properties of the system.

1. MOLECULAR WEIGHT. The general methods for molecular weight determination are discussed in Section 10-7. For polymers these include measurement of osmotic pressure, diffusion rate, sedimentation equilibrium and sedimentation rate, and light scattering. If a range of molecular weights is present, a given method will yield either a number-average or a weight-average molecular weight; if both types of average molecular weight can be determined, their ratio provides a measure of the broadness of the molecular weight distribution.

2. VISCOSITY. There is an additional method of molecular weight estimation which makes use of viscosity measurements. Einstein showed in 1906 that for a dilute suspension of spheres in a viscous medium

$$\lim_{\phi \to 0} \frac{(\eta/\eta_0) - 1}{\phi} = 2.5, \tag{20-20}$$

where η and η_0 are the viscosities of the solution or suspension and pure solvent, respectively, and ϕ is the volume fraction of the solution occupied by the spheres. The fraction η/η_0 is called the viscosity ratio or *relative viscosity* η_r, and $[(\eta/\eta_0) - 1]$ is called the *specific viscocity* η_{sp}. In the case of a polymer solution the concentration C is usually given as grams per cubic centimeter and $\eta_{sp}/100\ C$ is called the *reduced viscosity* and its limiting value as C approaches zero is the *intrinsic viscosity* $[\eta]$. Since $\phi = v_2 C$, where v_2 is the specific volume (strictly, the partial specific volume) of the polymer in cubic centimeters per gram, it follows from Eq. (20-20) that $[\eta] = 0.025v_2$. The specific volume as determined from $[\eta]$ will in general be larger than that obtained from the density of the dry polymer, the difference being attributed to bound solvent.

The factor 2.5 in Eq. (20-20) applies to the case of spheres, and linear polymers are, of course, not spherical, in the sense of the molecule being a long chain. On the other hand, the completely extended configuration is a very improbable one, and the situation is more like that illustrated in Fig. 20-10, which shows various *random coils*. The problem is essentially the statistical one of calculating the most probable end-to-end distance d assuming the polymer to consist of n flexible links; d, as might be expected, turns out to be proportional to the square root of the chain length. The proportionality constant depends, however, on the balance between solvent–chain and chain–chain interactions. In a "good" solvent, the random coil will be very extended, while in a "poor" solvent, the chain prefers

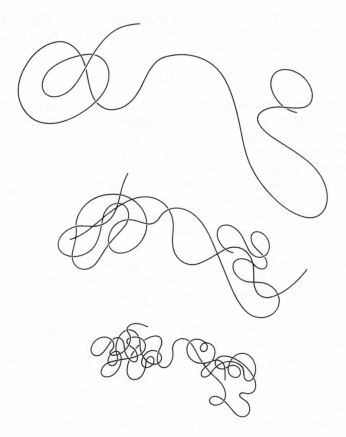

Fig. 20-10. *Random coils of the same length and same general configuration but of increasing tightness or in successively poorer solvents.*

its own environment and therefore assumes a compact configuration. While none of these configurations is exactly spherical, Eq. (20-20) can still be used, but with an empirical parameter ν in place of the Einstein coefficient 2.5, and ν evidently will depend on the nature of the solvent as well as on that of the polymer.

An alternative development of Eq. (20-20) is the following. If ϕ_0 denotes the volume fraction calculated using v_2 for the dry polymer, then the correct ϕ is given by $\phi_0\beta$, where β is the ratio of the hydrated to dry specific volumes. The dry volume of a polymer is, of course, proportional to its molecular weight M. The hydrated volume will be proportional to d^3, or to $M^{3/2}$, so β should be proportional to $M^{1/2}$. Thus Eq. (20-20) can be put in the form

$$[\eta] = KM^{1/2}. \tag{20-21}$$

If, however, the polymer were a rigid rod of length d, its effective volume would be that swept out by the tumbling of the rod. The "hydrated" volume is now proportional to M^3, and β is proportional to M^2.

The exponent in Eq. (20-21) can thus be expected to vary depending on the stiffness of the polymer, and in an equation proposed by M. Staudinger in 1932 it is treated as an empirical parameter:

$$[\eta] = KM^a. \tag{20-22}$$

The experimental observation is that K and a are approximately constant for a given type of polymer and a given solvent. Polymers of about the same chemical composition may differ greatly in molecular weight and Eq. (20-22) allows the relative molecular weights of different preparations to be determined. If two preparations of different known molecular weight can be obtained, then K and a can be evaluated, and absolute molecular weights may then be found for any other sample. It might be mentioned that if a range of molecular weights is present in the sample, then the value calculated by means of Eq. (20-22) will be an average lying between the number- and weight-average values.

This type of study has been made for a number of types of polymer and values of a are usually in the range 0.5–1.1. As expected, a decreases if one goes from a good to a poor solvent. That is, the relatively compact configuration present in a poor solvent behaves more like a sphere than a rod.

3. THERMODYNAMICS.   One approach to the statistical treatment of polymer solutions is to consider the solution as consisting of a number of cells or sites. Each site may be occupied by a solvent molecule or by one link or monomer unit of the polymer; as illustrated in Fig. 20-11, the requirement is that successive links occupy adjacent sites. One then treats the "solution" of links as a regular one (Section 9-CN-2) or essentially according to the model of Section 9-2E, but with the added aspect that the entropy of the links is reduced because of their having to remain connected.

The vapor pressure or activity of the polymer is then given by an equation

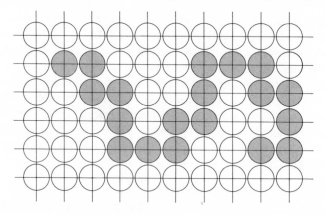

Fig. 20-11. *Illustration of the statistical fitting of solvent molecules (open circles) and monomer units (shaded circles) on a two-dimensional lattice.*

similar to Eq. (9-18) and varies with solution composition in a way similar to that shown in Fig. 9-10. Thus for $\alpha > 2$, there is a maximum and a minimum, corresponding to partial miscibility; however, the effect of the entropy complication is to distort the behavior in the direction of making intermediate compositions less probable than for an ordinary regular solution. As a consequence, one finds that for $\alpha > 2$, the dilute solution tends to be very dilute and the concentrated solution very concentrated, corresponding to slightly solvated polymer in equilibrium with a dilute solution. This explains the experimental observation that polymers tend to be either slightly soluble or quite soluble in a given solvent.

The quantity α in Eq. (9-18) is actually an interaction energy ω divided by kT. The critical condition is therefore that $\alpha = \omega/kT_c = 2$, or $T_c = \omega/2k$. This relationship accounts for the common observation that below a critical temperature a polymer will not be very soluble, whereas above this temperature it is almost completely miscible with the solvent.

4. SECONDARY STRUCTURE.   The primary structure of a polymer is that of the chemically bonded chain itself, including its stereochemistry. Since we are dealing with a macromolecule, there is a second level of structure, namely that of the polymer chain as a whole. We saw in the preceding section that linear polymers in solution assume a random coil configuration, for example. The coil becomes tighter the poorer the solvent or the more strongly interacting the polymer chain is with itself.

As a limiting case of this last situation, amino acid polymers, that is, proteins, can form hydrogen bonds between various portions of the chain. L. Pauling proposed a now widely accepted structure known as the *α-helix*. The helix makes one turn for every 3.7 amino acid residues, thus allowing hydrogen bonding between the CO and NH groups of adjacent coils.

In the case of the nucleic acids, the primary structure is that of a linear polymer in which adenine (A), guanine (G), cytosine (C), and thymine (T) rings are linked by phosphate groups; adjacent chains are hydrogen bonded as shown in Fig. 20-12. The secondary structure is that of a double helix in which C–G and A–T pairs form hydrogen bonds. The detailed configuration of these hydrogen bonds is at present subject to some controversy.

The ordinary denaturation of proteins and nucleic acids generally consists of a loss of the secondary structure but not of the primary structure. Intermediate situations are possible, too, in which part of the polymer has the helical configuration and part that of random coils. It has been possible in some cases to observe helix–coil transitions.

Finally, one may speak of a tertiary structure. A protein helix is still a long unit and one which may fold in on itself. Regions which have few polar groups find water a poor solvent, and hence tend to approach each other—the effect has been rather misnamed as *hydrophobic bonding*. The consequence is that native proteins tend to form a tertiary structure which is more or less globular and with the nonpolar groups in the interior.

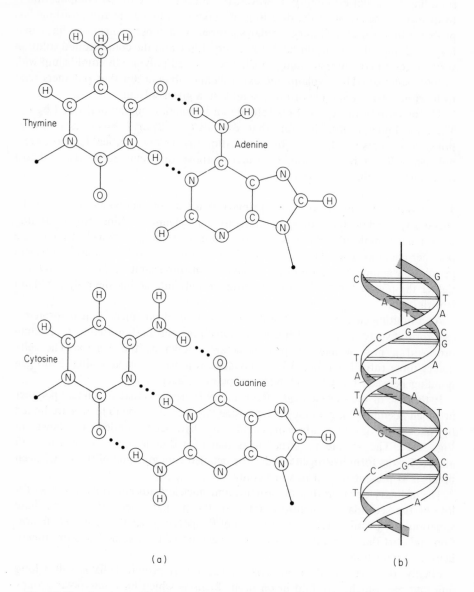

(a)   (b)

Fig. 20-12. *Structure of DNA. (a) Hydrogen bonding between adenine* (A) *and thymine* (T) *and between cytosine* (C) *and guanine* (G). *(b) Two strands held in a double helix by* C–G *and* T–A *hydrogen bonds. [See M. H. F. Wilkins and S. Arnott, J. Molec. Biol.* **11**, *391 (1965).] [Part (b) from A. White, P. Handler, and E. L. Smith, "Principles of Biochemistry," 4th ed. Copyright 1968, McGraw-Hill, New York. Used with permission of McGraw-Hill Book Company.]*

SPECIAL TOPICS

20-ST-1   Electrokinetic Effects

Several very interesting phenomena may occur if there is relative motion between a charged surface and an electrolyte solution; these are called *electrokinetic effects*. The surface is ordinarily either that of a solid particle suspended in the solution or the solid wall of tube down which the solution flows. What happens is essentially that a charged surface experiences a force in an electric field or, conversely, that a field is induced by the motion of such a surface relative to the solution. Thus if a field is applied to a suspension of colloidal particles, these will move or, alternatively, if a solution is made to flow down a tube an electric field develops. In each case there is a plane of shear between the surface and the solution, a plane which lies within the electrical double layer. The potential at this plane will not be ψ_0, but some lower value called the *zeta potential* ζ. The zeta potential does give a measure of ψ_0, however, and one important application of electrokinetic phenomena is to the measurement of ζ and hence estimation of ψ_0.

There are four types of electrokinetic effect, depending on whether the solid surface is stationary (as a wall) or moves (as a particle) and whether the field is applied or induced. In *electrophoresis* an applied field causes suspended particles to move, while in the *sedimentation potential effect* the motion of the particles in a centrifugal field induces a field. If the solid surface is that of the wall of a tube, application of a potential gradient or field induces a flow of solution, or *electroosmosis*, while a forced flow of solution induces a potential gradient or *streaming potential*. The four effects are summarized in Table 20-1. We will consider only two of them, however, namely electrophoresis and the streaming potential effect.

Table 20-1.   *Electrokinetic Effects*

	Nature of solid surface	
Potential	Stationary[a]	Moving[b]
Applied	Electroosmosis	Electrophoresis
Induced	Streaming potential	Sedimentation potential

[a] For example, a wall or apparatus surface.
[b] For example, a colloidal particle.

A. Electrophoresis

The most familiar type of electrokinetic experiment consists of setting up a potential gradient in a solution containing charged particles and determining their rate of motion. If the particles consist of ordinary small ions, the phenomenon is one of *ionic conductance*, treated in Chapter 12. As shown in Section 12-5, the velocity of an ion in a field $\mathbf{F}$ is

$$v_i = z_i e \omega_i \mathbf{F} \qquad [\text{Eq. (12-27)}],$$

where ω_i is the mobility and v_i will be in centimeters per second if e is in esu and $\mathbf{F}$ in esu volts per centimeter. Alternatively, by Eq. (12-28), $v_i = u_i \mathbf{F}$, where u_i is the electrochemical mobility and $\mathbf{F}$ is now given in ordinary volts per centimeter; also, by Eq. (12-31), $\lambda_i = u_i \mathbf{F}$.

In the case of a macromolecule, the total charge z_i is not known, and it is customary to refer to the motion of such molecules in an electric field as *electrophoresis*.

However, if the molecular weight is known, then the radius can be calculated assuming the shape to be spherical. This allows estimation of the friction factor f from Stokes' law, Eq. (10-33), and hence of $\omega = 1/f$. Alternatively, if the diffusion coefficient can be measured, then f can be obtained without any geometric assumptions from Eq. (10-41). The charge on the polymer molecule may then be calculated from the electrophoretic velocity using Eq. (12-27).

As would be expected from the discussion of the acid–base equilibria of amino acids (Section 12-CN-3), the net charge on a protein is very pH-dependent. For each protein there will be some one pH at which z and hence the electrophoretic velocity is zero. Conversely, at a given pH each protein will have a characteristic velocity in an electric field, depending both on its molecular weight and on its net charge. A mixture of proteins will therefore separate into different velocity groups in an electrophoresis experiment. In a typical procedure, a protein solution containing a buffer at a definite pH is placed at the bottom of a U-tube. Some of the buffer solution is then layered over so there is a sharp boundary between the two solutions. Nongassing electrodes are placed at each end and the whole apparatus is usually thermostated at around 4°C (this being the temperature of maximum density of water, small temperature changes will not produce appreciable thermal convection currents). An optical system may be used to observe the various bands or velocity groups of proteins that migrate. The concentration profile might look as in Fig. 20-13, each peak representing a particular protein or related group of proteins.

We turn now to colloidal particles. As with macromolecules, the charge is not known; in addition, the size cannot be determined very accurately, although it

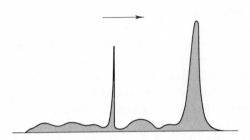

Fig. 20-13. *Electrophoretic pattern of a mixture of proteins.*

may be possible to estimate particle radii from microscopic (optical or electron) examination. Ordinary molecular weight determination is, of course, not possible (why?) nor is the diffusion rate fast enough for a determination of f. As noted in the introduction to this section, we assume instead that the particle is large enough for its interface with the solution to be treated as planar, and apply electrical double layer theory.

The complication mentioned at the beginning of this section is that, as illustrated in Fig. 20-14, there is undoubtedly a layer of solvent molecules and electrolyte

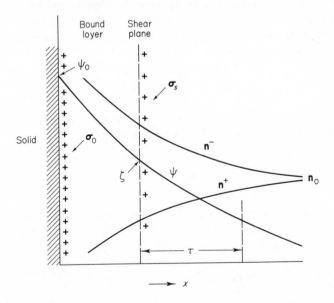

Fig. 20-14. *The diffuse double layer, showing the plane of shear at which ψ has the value ζ, the zeta potential.*

ions which is strongly enough held that it moves with the particle rather than with the solution. We must deal, therefore, with the plane of *shear* rather than with the actual interface; the potential ψ_0 is reduced to some value $\psi = \zeta$ at this plane, called the zeta potential, and σ_0, to some value σ_s. The remainder of the diffuse double layer must still balance σ_s, or, by Eq. (20-9), $\sigma_s = \int_{x=s}^{\infty} \rho \, dx$. The "center of gravity" of this portion of the double layer is taken to be at the point where ψ has dropped to $1/e$ of ζ, at distance τ from the plane of shear.

As a first approximation, the situation is likened to that of a parallel plate condenser, for which the standard formula gives $\Delta V = 4\pi q d / D \mathscr{A}$, where ΔV is the potential difference across the plates, d is their separation, $\mathscr{A}$ is their area, and D is the dielectric constant. One plate carries charge $+q$ and the other carries $-q$. We now equate ΔV to ζ, d to τ, and $q/\mathscr{A}$ to σ_s to obtain

$$\sigma_s = \frac{D\zeta}{4\pi\tau}.$$
(20-23)

We next proceed to balance the electrical force acting per square centimeter of the particle with that due to viscous drag. The first is just $\sigma_s \mathbf{F}$, where $\mathbf{F}$ is the field, and the second may be obtained from the defining equation for viscosity, Eq. (2-59). We assume that the relative velocity between the particle and the solution drops linearly with distance from v at $x = s$ to 0 at $x = \tau$ and therefore write $dv/dx = v/\tau$, which gives the viscous force or drag per square centimeter as $\eta v / \tau$. On equating the two forces, we obtain

$$v = \frac{\sigma_s \mathbf{F} \tau}{\eta} = \frac{\sigma_s \mathbf{F} \tau}{300\eta},$$
(20-24)

where in the second form, $\mathbf{F}$ is expressed in volts per centimeter. An alternative form results on combination with Eq. (20-23):

$$v = \frac{\zeta D \mathbf{F}}{4\pi\eta}.$$
(20-25)

All of the fundamental statements have been written in the esu system insofar as electrical quantities are involved, but one usually reports ζ in volts (actually, millivolts), having measured $\mathbf{F}$ in volts per centimeter. If one converts ζ to millivolts by means of the factor $1000/300$ and $\mathbf{F}$ to volts per centimeter by the factor $1/300$, one obtains a more practical form of Eq. (20-25):

$$\zeta = 12.9 \frac{v}{\mathbf{F}},$$
(20-26)

where, in addition, v is in microns per second and D and η have been taken to be for water at 25°C. Thus if a colloidal particle moves $50\,\mu$ sec^{-1} in a field of 10 V cm^{-1}, its zeta potential is 65 mV, positive or negative depending on the direction of motion relative to the field. The field may be applied by means of nongassing electrodes at each end of a tube containing the colloidal suspension and the rate of motion of individual particles observed under a microscope; the instrument is called a *zetameter*.

Most measured zeta potentials are in the range of ± 100 mV for lyophobic colloids, but with actual values dependent on the nature and concentration of the electrolyte. Table 20-2 gives some data on a gold sol which show that the charge decreases and then reverses with increasing Al^{3+} ion concentration. Note that the sol is stable if the particles are charged but flocculates rapidly if the zeta potential is small.

B. Streaming Potential

If an electrolyte solution flows through a tube, one observes a potential difference between the inflowing and outflowing solution. The physical basis for the effect is that the flowing solution carries with it the charge density σ_s in the diffuse double layer, so that there is in effect an electrical current at the wall. The current is just $i = 2\pi r \sigma_s v_\tau$, where v_τ is the streamline velocity at distance τ from the wall; it is thus proportional to the surface area and, by Eq. (20-23), to the zeta potential. A potential drop $\mathbf{E}$ develops in the electrolyte solution until a counter current $i = \mathbf{E}/R$, develops, where R is the resistance of the solution, such as to just balance the wall current. It is this steady-state potential that is called the *streaming potential*.

The actual derivation is somewhat in the same vein as that of the Poiseuille

Table 20-2. *Flocculation of Gold Sol*

Concentration of Al^{3+} (equiv liter^{-1} $\times$ 10^6)	Electrophoretic velocity (cm V^{-1} sec^{-1} $\times$ 10^6)	Stability
0	3.30 (toward anode)	Indefinitely stable
21	1.71	Flocculates in 4 hr
—	0	Flocculates spontaneously
42	0.17 (toward cathode)	Flocculates in 4 hr
70	1.35	Incompletely flocculated after 4 days

equation given in Section 8-10. Assuming streamline flow, the velocity at a radius x from the center of the tube is

$$v = \frac{P(r^2 - x^2)}{4\eta l} \quad \text{[Eq. (8-64)]},$$

where P is the pressure drop and r the radius of the tube, which is of length l. The double layer is centered at $x = r - \tau$, and substitution into Eq. (8-64) gives

$$v_d = \frac{\tau r P}{2\eta l} \tag{20-27}$$

if the term in τ^2 is neglected. The current due to the motion of the double layer is then

$$i = 2\pi r \sigma_s v_d \tag{20-28}$$

or

$$i = \frac{\pi r^2 \sigma_s P}{\eta l}. \tag{20-29}$$

If κ is the specific conductivity of the solution, then the actual conductivity of the liquid in the tube is $C = \pi r^2 \kappa / l$ and, by Ohm's law, the streaming potential is just $\mathbf{E} = i/C$. Combining these equations, we have

$$\mathbf{E} = \frac{\tau \sigma_s P}{\eta \kappa} \tag{20-30}$$

or, using Eq. (20-23),

$$\mathbf{E} = \frac{\zeta P \epsilon}{4\pi \eta \kappa}. \tag{20-31}$$

A practical form of Eq. (20-31) is

$$\mathbf{E} = 8.0 \times 10^{-5} \frac{\zeta P}{C \Lambda}, \tag{20-32}$$

where ζ is now in millivolts and P in atmospheres; C is the electrolyte concentration in equivalents per liter and Λ is the equivalent conductivity. Water at 25°C is assumed. Thus for a pressure drop of 10 atm, a zeta potential of 50 mV, and 10^{-5} N aqueous NaCl at 25°C (equivalent conductivity 126), $\mathbf{E} = 32$ V. As this example illustrates, the electrolyte must be quite dilute if an appreciable effect is to occur.

Streaming potentials may cause trouble in the filtering of dilute electrolyte solutions, especially nonaqueous ones whose electrolyte concentration and hence specific conductivity may be quite small. A quite real hazard developed in the early days of jet aircraft—the high pumping rate of the kerosene fuel led to streaming potentials large enough to cause sparks. The problem has since been eliminated by incorporating small amounts of conducting solutes in the fuel.

20-ST-2   Rubber Elasticity

Much of the discussion on polymers in the main part of this chapter is either phenomenological in nature or in a rather qualitative structural vein. A good example of polymer physical chemistry at the *molecular* level is the treatment of rubber elasticity. Rubber and rubbery materials in general consist of long-chain polymer molecules with sufficient cross-linking between chains that no actual flow can occur. The material stretches, of course, and it is possible to explain rubber elasticity in terms of a rather simple statistical thermodynamic model.

We write the first law of thermodynamics in the form

$$dE = T\,dS - P\,dV + f\,dx, \qquad (20\text{-}33)$$

where $f\,dx$ represents the work done on the polymer material by stretching it an increment dx against restoring force f. Assuming constant volume (a good approximation), Eq. (20-33) can be put in the differential form

$$\left(\frac{\partial E}{\partial x}\right)_{T,V} = T\left(\frac{\partial S}{\partial x}\right)_{T,V} + f.$$

The internal energy of a rubbery material is essentially that of the individual bond vibrations and it is reasonable to suppose that stretching the rubber does not affect the fundamental frequencies of these vibrations appreciably, so that E should not be very sensitive to x at constant T. If this is true, the force is just

$$f = -T\left(\frac{\partial S}{\partial x}\right)_{T,V} \qquad (20\text{-}34)$$

and rises from the change in entropy of the material with length.

We proceed now to formulate an expression for that part of the entropy which should vary with x. We chose a very simple model—each chain acts independently and consists of n links, each of length l; if fully extended, its overall length would then be $R = nl$. This is a very improbable configuration, however, since we assume that the chain is freely able to fold back on itself from one link to the next. As illustrated in Fig. 20-15 a particular chain will have n_+ links carrying it in the forward direction and n_- carrying it in the back direction, or a net length $x = (n_+ - n_-)l$, or $r = ml$, where $m = n_+ - n_-$. There are then $(n + m)/2$ for-

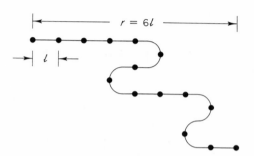

Fig. 20-15.

ward links and $(n - m)/2$ backward links. The probability that any particular link will be in the given direction is $\frac{1}{2}$, so the probability of a particular configuration such as shown in the figure is $(\frac{1}{2})^n$. We actually want the probability of having any sequence that will give a net length r, and to get at this, we imagine a collection of n loose links to be picked one at a time in assemblying the chain. There will be n ways of picking the first link, $n - 1$ ways of picking the second, and so on, and therefore a total of $n!$ ways of picking n links. We assume, however, that all forward-directed links form an indistinguishable group and so do all backward-directed ones. The permutations within each group must therefore be divided out, giving a net probability

$$p(x) = \frac{n!}{[\frac{1}{2}(n + m)]! \, [\frac{1}{2}(n - m)]!} \left(\frac{1}{2}\right)^n.$$

This equation is simplified with the use of Stirling's formula, an approximate version of which is $\ln n! = n \ln n - n$, to give

$$\ln p(x) = n \ln n - \frac{n + m}{2} \ln \frac{n + m}{2} + \frac{n + m}{2}$$
$$- \frac{n - m}{2} \ln \frac{n - m}{2} + \frac{n - m}{2} - n \ln 2.$$

This reduces to

$$\ln p(x) = n \ln n - \frac{n + m}{2} \ln\left[\frac{n}{2}\left(1 + \frac{m}{n}\right)\right] - \frac{n - m}{2} \ln\left[\frac{n}{2}\left(1 - \frac{m}{n}\right)\right] - n \ln 2$$

or

$$\ln p(x) = \text{constant} - \frac{n+m}{2} \ln\left(1 + \frac{m}{n}\right) - \frac{n-m}{2} \ln\left(1 - \frac{m}{n}\right).$$

We consider n to be much greater than m, and therefore expand $\ln[1 \pm (m/n)]$ as $\pm(m/n) - (m^2/2n^2) \cdots$ to obtain

$$\ln p(x) = \text{constant} - \frac{m^2}{2n},$$

or, since m is proportional to r,

$$p(x) = c \exp(-b^2 r^2).$$

The derivation has been abbreviated since for the present purpose it is necessary only to obtain the proper form, leaving the detailed expressions for the constants c and b undeveloped. The net chain length r is a vector which may point in any direction with equal probability if the rubber is unstretched, and the probability of finding a given r without regard to direction is obtained by weighting $p(x)$ by $4\pi r^2$,

$$p(r) = 4\pi r^2 c \exp(-b^2 r^2). \tag{20-35}$$

Note that if $dp(r)/dr$ is set equal to zero, one obtains the most probable net chain length r_p as just $1/b$. We will need the value of $\overline{r^2}$ as given by the expression

$$\overline{r^2} = \frac{\int_0^\infty r^2 p(r)\, dr}{\int_0^\infty p(r)\, dr} = \frac{3}{2b^2}. \tag{20-36}$$

The quantity which is related to the entropy of a rubber is the thermodynamic probability W of an ensemble (Section 6-CN-2) of N polymer chains, where

$$W = \prod_{i=1}^{N} p(r_i),$$

and $p(r_i)$ is the probability for the ith chain to have a net extension r_i. We assume that N is large enough that W peaks very sharply at a certain average value of r and, using Eq. (6-66), write

$$S_{\text{config}} = \text{constant} + k \ln W_{\text{max}}$$

or

$$S_{\text{config}} = \text{constant} - k \sum_{1}^{N} b_i^2 r_i^2 = \text{constant} - kNb^2\overline{r^2}.$$

Initially, all directions for r are equally probable; the set of r vectors for the ensemble fill a sphere if all are given the same point of origin. We now suppose that elongation of the rubber occurs in the x direction, so that the x component of all r's is increased by a factor α. The geometric equivalent of this change is that of an elongation of a sphere to an ellipse of the same volume (called an *affine transformation*) and one finds from analytical geometry that the new average radius squared $\overline{(r')^2}$ is

$$\overline{(r')^2} = \frac{1}{3}\overline{r^2}\left(\alpha^2 + \frac{2}{\alpha}\right).$$

The same result applies to $\overline{r^2}$ for a polymer and the entropy as a function of α is therefore

$$S = \text{constant} - \frac{k}{3}\sum_1^N b_i^2 r_i^2\left(\alpha^2 + \frac{2}{\alpha}\right)$$

$$= \text{constant} - \frac{Nk}{3}(b^2\overline{r^2})\left(\alpha^2 + \frac{2}{\alpha}\right).$$

However, $\overline{r^2}$ was found to be $3/2b^2$, so the final result is simply

$$S = \text{constant} - \frac{kN}{2}\left(\alpha^2 + \frac{2}{\alpha}\right). \tag{20-37}$$

Returning to Eq. (20-34), the average extension in the x direction as a result of force f is $x = x_0$, where x_0 is the initial length of the sample, so that

$$f = -\frac{T}{x_0}\left(\frac{\partial S}{\partial \alpha}\right)_{T,V}, \tag{20-38}$$

or, from Eq. (20-37),

$$f = \left(\frac{NkT}{x_0}\right)\left(\alpha - \frac{1}{\alpha^2}\right). \tag{20-39}$$

Alternatively, if $\mathscr{A}$ is the unstretched cross-sectional area of the sample, V is the volume per chain, and $\mathbf{n}$ is the number of chains per unit volume, we have

$$\frac{f}{\mathscr{A}} = \frac{kT}{V}\left(\alpha - \frac{1}{\alpha^2}\right) = \mathbf{n}kT\left(\alpha - \frac{1}{\alpha^2}\right) \tag{20-40}$$

Equation (20-40), due to P. Flory, agrees fairly well with experiment, confirming the entropic nature of rubber elasticity. If, for example, the molar volume of a particular polymer is 10^4 cm^3 mole^{-1},

$$f/\mathscr{A} = 10^{-4}(6.02 \times 10^{23})(1.38 \times 10^{-16})(298)[\alpha - (1/\alpha^2)]$$
$$= 2.5 \times 10^6[\alpha - (1/\alpha^2)] \quad \text{dyn cm}^{-2} \text{ at } 25°C.$$

This is a reasonable experimental value. The rather special functional dependence on α also is confirmed experimentally.

A rather interesting situation is that in which the rubber is stretched under adiabatic conditions, so that $\delta q = 0$ and $dE = f\,dx$. In this case the internal energy and hence the temperature must increase. The effect is easily observable. The warming of a rubber band on stretching may be felt by holding the band against one's lips. Also, if the tension is relieved, one can sense the cooling of the rubber as it contracts.

GENERAL REFERENCES

ADAMSON, A. W. (1967). "The Physical Chemistry of Surfaces," 2nd ed. Wiley (Interscience), New York.
BILLMEYER, F. W., JR. (1962). "Textbook of Polymer Science." Wiley (Interscience), New York.
GRAY, G. W. (1962). "Molecular Structure and the Properties of Liquid Crystals." Academic Press, New York.
KRUYT, H. R. (1952). "Colloid Science." Elsevier, New York.
McBAIN, J. W. (1950). "Colloid Science." Heath, Indianapolis, Indiana.
MYSELS, K. J. (1959). "Introduction to Colloid Chemistry." Wiley (Interscience), New York.
VAN WAZER, J. R., LYONS, J. W., KIM, K. Y., AND COLWELL, R. E. (1963). "Viscosity and Flow Measurement." Wiley (Interscience), New York.
VERWEY, E. J. W., AND OVERBEEK, J. TH. G. (1948). "Theory of the Stability of Lyophobic Colloids." Elsevier, New York.
WHITE, A., HANDLER, P., AND SMITH, E. L. (1968). "Principles of Biochemistry," 4th ed. McGraw-Hill, New York.

CITED REFERENCE

ADAMSON, A. W. (1967). "The Physical Chemistry of Surfaces," 2nd ed. Wiley (Interscience), New York.

Exercises

20-1 Calculate the attractive potential due to dispersion forces between two platelets (say, of a colloidal suspension of a mica, vermiculite) for which $H = 3.0 \times 10^{-13}$ erg and the surface-to-surface distance is 250 Å. Express your result in units of kT (at 25°C).

Ans. 3.1×10^{10} cm^{-2}.

20 Colloids and Macromolecules

20-2 For what value of ψ is $e\psi/kT = 1$ at 25°C?

> *Ans.* 25.6 mV.

20-3 A surface of potential 51.2 mV is in contact with a 0.1 M solution of NaCl at 25°C. Calculate the concentrations of Na^+ and of Cl^- ions at the surface.

> *Ans.* $(Na^+) = 0.0136\ M$, $(Cl^-) = 0.734\ M$.

20-4 Referring to Exercise 20-3, calculate ψ and (Na^+), (Cl^-), and the charge density ρ at a distance of 15 Å from the surface.

> *Ans.* 10.8 mV, 0.0656 M, 0.152 M,
> 0.0864 mole of charge liter^{-1} or 2.50×10^{10} esu cm^{-3}.

20-5 Still referring to Exercise 20-3 (and 20-4), calculate the repulsion energy per square centimeter between two charged surfaces for $\psi_0 = 51.2$ mV when in 0.1 M NaCl and 15 Å apart (at 25°C).

> *Ans.* 0.144 erg cm^{-2}.

20-6 Calculate the attractive potential between two slabs of area 10^{-9} cm^2 each when separated by 15 Å. Using the result of Exercise 20-5, obtain the net interaction energy for these slabs (or colloidal platelets) when immersed in 0.1 M NaCl at 25°C. Assume H to be 3.0×10^{-13} erg.

> *Ans.* Attractive potential energy is 3.54×10^{-10} erg;
> net potential energy is -2.09×10^{-10} erg (attractive).

20-7 A rheological study of a certain fluid gives $y = 0.1\,x + 2x^2$, where y is the rate of shear in second^{-1} and x is the shear stress in dynes per square centimeter. Calculate the viscosity at a shear stress of 10 dyn cm^{-2}. What type of rheological behavior is being exhibited?

> *Ans.* 0.0497 P.

20-8 Suppose that the polymerization kinetics of Eqs. (20-14) and (20-15) is followed, but that the initiation step is photochemical, with radicals produced by the process $R \xrightarrow{h\nu} 2M$. Show that Eq. (20-18) becomes $-d(M)/dt = k_P(2\phi I/k_t)^{1/2}(M)$, where ϕ is the quantum yield and I the rate of absorption of light quanta.

20-9 The relative viscosity of a solution of polystyrene has the following values:

C (g per 100 cm³)	0.08	0.12	0.16	0.20
n_r	1.213	1.330	1.452	1.582

Find $[\eta]$ and estimate v_2 for the polymer. Calculate K of Eq. (20-21) if the molecular weight of the polymer is 250,000 g mole^{-1}, and calculate the relative viscosity of a 0.10 g per 100 cm³ of solution of polymer of molecular weight 500,000. (The slope of the plot of $\eta_{sp}/100C$ should vary as $[\eta]^2$.)

> *Ans.* $[\eta] = 2.49$, $v_2 = 100$ cm³ g^{-1}, $K = 4.98 \times 10^{-3}$, $\eta_r = 1.394$.

Special Topics Problems

Problems

20-1 Derive Eq. (20-2) from Eq. (20-1) by carrying out the required triple integration.

20-2 Calculate the interaction energy in calories per mole for an argon atom adsorbed on a hypothetical argon surface; assume the atom–surface distance to be 3.5 Å. (Note Table 8-8.)

20-3 The value of x for which ψ/ψ_0 is $1/e$ is called the double layer "thickness" τ. Calculate τ as a function of concentration of NaCl at 25°C up to 0.5 M and plot the result.

20-4 Show that Eq. (20-9) can be phrased as $\sigma = -(D/4\pi)(d\psi/dx)_{x=0}$ and further show that an approximate value for σ is $D\kappa\psi_0/4\pi$.

20-5 (Calculator problem)   Calculate, using Eqs. (20-3) and (20-10), the net interaction energy in units of kT for two colloidal platelets as a function of their distance of separation and for $\kappa = 10^5$ cm^{-1}, 10^6 cm^{-1}, and 10^7 cm^{-1}. Assume that $H = 3 \times 10^{-13}$ erg, $\psi_0 = 25.6$ mV, $T = 25°C$, and assume an aqueous NaCl medium. For each κ value, plot your results as ϵ/kT versus x in angstroms up to about 200 Å. The area of each platelet is 10^{-9} cm^2.

20-6 The following data were obtained for the viscosity of nitrocellulose in butyl acetate:

C (g per 100 cm³)	0.032	0.075	0.135	0.180
n_r	1.540	2.323	3.964	8.025

Calculate the intrinsic viscosity of this polymer and its specific volume.

20-7 The following relative viscosities were measured for a polyisobutylene in cyclohexane.

C (g per 100 cm³)	0.050	0.152	0.271	0.441
n_r	1.2895	2.067	3.312	6.579

Calculate the molecular weight of the polymer if the constants in Eq. (20-22) are $a = 0.73$ and $K = 5.1 \times 10^{-4}$.

20-8 The viscosity of a globular protein is investigated at 5°C using an Ubbelohde viscometer (based on the Poiseuille equation, Section 8-10; note that $P_1 - P_2$ is proportional to the density of the liquid). The following data are obtained:

C (g per 100 cm³)	0	2.10	4.20	6.30	8.36	10.45
Density (g cm⁻³)	—	1.0052	1.0106	1.0160	1.0213	1.0268
Flow time (sec)	42.1	44.0	46.3	49.2	53.7	60.3

The true density of the protein is 1.310 g cm⁻³. Making appropriate calculations, decide whether this protein is hydrated or not and if it is, about what volume of solvent is bound to (moves with) a gram of protein.

Special Topics Problems

20-1 While the result should not have very exact physical meaning, as an exercise, calculate the zeta potential of sodium ion, knowing that its equivalent conductivity is 50 cm² equiv^{-1} ohm^{-1} in water at 25°C.

20-2 Calculate the expected streaming potential E for pure water at 25°C when flowing through a quartz tube under 10 atm pressure. Take ζ to be 150 mV.

20-3 A quartz particle of 1.5×10^{-4} cm in diameter moves through water at a velocity of 2.50×10^{-3} cm sec^{-1} at 25°C under a potential gradient of 10.0 V cm^{-1}. Calculate the zeta potential of the particle in this medium. Assuming Stokes's law to hold, what total charge does the particle appear to carry? What is the equivalent conductivity of the particle?

20-4 A 15 cm length of rubber of cross section 0.1 cm^2 contains polymer of molar volume 3×10^4 cm^3 mole^{-1}. Calculate force as a function of length of the extended rubber up to 30 cm and plot the result. If the heat capacity of the rubber is 0.8 cal °K cm^{-3}, what temperature change should occur on stretching to 25 cm? Assume 25°C.

21 NUCLEAR CHEMISTRY AND RADIOCHEMISTRY

21-1 Introduction

The subjects of nuclear chemistry and radiochemistry are marked by many major, far-reaching discoveries. Three early lines of development are those relating to the electrical nature of matter, to radioactivity, and to the nuclear model for the atom. The modern subject has branched into the separate fields of radiochemistry and nuclear chemistry, radiation chemistry, and the physics of fundamental particles. The historical outline that follows will serve as a foundation for the more detailed and modern aspects taken up in subsequent sections.

A. Electrical Nature of Matter

Various studies on the emission of electrified particles into the evacuated space around a hot electrode were made in the 19th century; the device was called a Crookes tube. It was not until about 1898, however, that J. Thomson carried out a series of experiments which allowed the determination of the ratio of charge to mass of these particles (now known as electrons). As illustrated in Fig. 21-1, a collimated beam from a hot cathode (called a *cathode ray beam*) is deflected by an electric field $\mathbf{E}$ or by a magnetic field $\mathbf{H}$. Application of the latter alone produces a force on the electrons in the beam given by $\mathbf{H}ev$, where e is the charge on the electron and v is its velocity; the particle follows a curved path such that this force is just balanced by the centrifugal force mv^2/r, r being the radius of the path, determined from the deflection of the beam. If an electrical field is also applied, just sufficient to annul the deflection, then $\mathbf{E}e = \mathbf{H}ev$. Elimination of v between

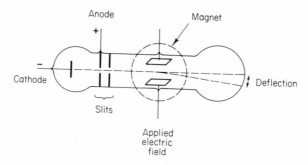

Fig. 21-1.   *Cathode ray tube for determining e/m of electrons.*

these two relationships gives $e/m = \mathbf{E}/\mathbf{H}^2r$. The modern value of e/m for the electron is 5.273×10^{17} esu g^{-1}.

Thomson also obtained an approximate value for e. Later, in 1909, R. Millikan obtained a precise value by measuring the rate of fall of individual oil droplets in air and the electrical field needed to just prevent their falling. The limiting velocity of fall v is such that the frictional force $6\pi\eta rv$ [as given by Stokes's law, Eq. (10-33)] is just equal to that due to gravity, where η is the viscosity of air. If an electrical field is now applied which is just sufficient to keep the drop from falling, it follows that $\mathbf{E}q = 6\pi\eta rv$, where q is the charge carried by the drop. Millikan determined the drop radius by microscopic examination and measured v and $\mathbf{E}$ to obtain q. The measured q values for various drops were integral multiples of a unit charge, that of the electron. Millikan's value for e of 4.77×10^{-10} esu differs from the modern one of 4.803×10^{-10} esu mainly due to an error in the then available value for the viscosity of air.

The procedure for determining e/m for the electron may be applied to positive ions. That is, positive ions generated by a hot filament or by collisions with a beam of electrons may be accelerated electrostatically, the accelerated ions collimated into a beam by means of slits, and the bending of the beam by a magnetic field then determined. The procedure was first applied by J. Aston in 1919, with the arrangement of Fig. 21-2. The figure shows, in exaggerated fashion, how the

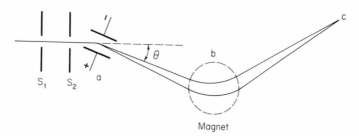

Fig. 21-2.   *One of Aston's early mass spectrographs. The beam of positive ions is collimated by slits S_1 and S_2, then bent by an angle θ by the electric field of the charged plates at* a. *A magnetic field at* b *bends the beam back, the geometry working out so that the ions come to a focus at* c.

positive ion beam is first deflected by a small angle θ and then focused by a magnetic field. Aston's work led to the discovery of stable isotopes and then to the precise measurement of isotopic atomic weights.

Modern mass spectrometry is a highly instrumented science, now largely used in the analysis of the isotopic content of samples and in the study of the fragments produced in the electron bombardment of polyatomic molecules. Detailed, computer-assisted analysis of the distribution of the fragments from a sample consisting of a mixture of organic compounds allows its composition to be determined.

B. Radioactivity

We turn now to a second line of discovery, that of radioactivity. W. Roentgen reported in 1895 that cathode rays (that is, an electron beam) generated a penetrating radiation on hitting a solid target. X rays, as they were called, could penetrate matter and were not deflected by electrical or magnetic fields. The electromagnetic nature of x rays was later established, and in 1912 their wavelength was measured by crystal diffraction experiments (see Section 19-5).

It was at first thought that x rays were a kind of fluorescence and it was for this reason that H. Becquerel looked for x radiation from naturally fluorescing minerals. Among others he tried potassium uranyl sulfate, $K_2UO_2(SO_4)_2 \cdot 2H_2O$. His great discovery, in 1896, was that this mineral emitted penetrating radiation without any prior exposure to light. He called the phenomenon *radioactivity*.

Chemical fractionation of UO_2^{2+} solutions led Marie Curie (working with her husband, Pierre Curie) to the discovery first of *polonium*, and then, in 1898, of *radium*. By 1902, pure radium had been isolated and its atomic weight determined.

Three types of radiation were characterized in due course. These are known as α, β, and γ radiation, in order of their penetrating power. We now know that they consist, respectively, of high-speed He^{2+} ions, electrons, and short-wavelength electromagnetic radiation. It was recognized very early that these radiations are emitted from individual atoms. The early radiochemists also appreciated that in the process the atom disintegrates or is converted to some other kind of atom. The development of the nuclear model for the atom led to the realization that α, β, and γ radiation came from the nucleus itself, and permitted a precise formulation of the radioactive decay process. For example, the first two steps of the uranium decay series are written

$$^{238}_{92}U \rightarrow {}^{4}_{2}He \ (\alpha \text{ particle}) + {}^{234}_{90}Th, \tag{21-1}$$

$$^{234}_{90}Th \rightarrow {}^{0}_{-1}\beta \ (\beta^- \text{ particle}) + {}^{234}_{91}Pa. \tag{21-2}$$

It is conventional to write the atomic number (or nuclear charge) Z as a lower left subscript and the *mass number* A (atomic weight to the nearest whole number) as a left superscript. Nuclear processes are balanced with respect to mass number and with respect to atomic number.

The energy of nuclear radiations is usually expressed in electron volts (eV): 1 eV is the energy gained by a particle of unit charge falling through a potential difference of 1 V; nuclear radiations may have energies as high as several million electron volts (MeV). It is not surprising that they ionize air or other matter in their path. A very useful application of this behavior is the *cloud chamber* which was developed by E. Wilson in 1912. The principle is that if a vapor is super-saturated, then the ionization caused by high-speed particles induces condensation to occur along the track of each particle. A spray of α particle tracks is illustrated in Fig. 21-3; notice that each particle travels a definite length before stopping.

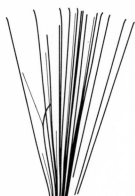

Fig. 21-3. *Spray of α particle tracks in a cloud chamber. Each particle travels an essentially straight line path until it has lost nearly all of its energy; the bending that then occurs is known as straggling. Note that one particle has undergone a large angular deflection as a result of a nuclear collision.*

The cloud chamber helped E. Rutherford to make the discovery of nuclear transmutation; he observed tracks in a cloud chamber which terminated abruptly with the appearance of a new track which could only be that of a proton. Such an event is shown in Fig. 21-3. The reaction is

$$^{14}_{7}\text{N} + {}^{4}_{2}\text{He} \rightarrow {}^{1}_{1}\text{H} + {}^{17}_{8}\text{O}. \qquad (21\text{-}3)$$

A number of such transmutations were studied during the period 1919–1930 and eventually a new type of penetrating radiation was noticed. This was identified in 1932 by J. Chadwick as a neutral particle, which he named the *neutron*. A typical neutron-producing reaction is

$$^{10}_{5}\text{B} + {}^{4}_{2}\text{He} \rightarrow {}^{1}_{0}\text{n} + {}^{13}_{7}\text{N}. \qquad (21\text{-}4)$$

The actual atomic weight of the neutron is 1.0086654 (see Table 21-1). About the same time C. Anderson discovered another new particle, the *positron*, a particle identical to the electron except for having the opposite charge. A further major discovery made in this very active period was that of artificial radioactivity. Irene Curie (daughter of M. and P. Curie) and her husband F. Joliot (both known as Joliot-Curie) observed reactions such as the following:

$$^{24}_{12}\text{Mg} + {}^{4}_{2}\text{He} \rightarrow {}^{27}_{14}\text{Si} + {}^{1}_{0}\text{n}. \qquad (21\text{-}5)$$

The isotope produced, $^{27}_{14}$Si, is radioactive, emitting positrons,

$$^{27}_{14}\text{Si} \rightarrow {}^{27}_{13}\text{Al} + {}^{0}_{1}\beta. \tag{21-6}$$

Up to this point the study of transmutation reactions was limited to the use of natural α particle emitters. Various electrostatic accelerating devices were developed but the major advance came in 1932 with the invention of the *cyclotron* by E. Lawrence. The very clever principle involved was the following. If a charged particle is injected into the region of a magnetic field, it will follow a circular orbit of radius $r = mv/\textbf{H}e$. The circumference of the orbit is $2\pi r$, so that the frequency of revolution of the particle is $\omega = v/2\pi r$, or $\omega = \textbf{H}e/2\pi m$. The important point is that this frequency is independent of the velocity and hence of the energy of the particle. As illustrated in Fig. 21-4, the particles move inside hollow electrodes

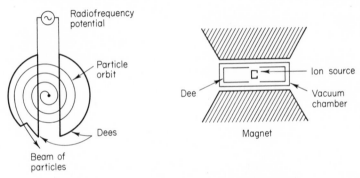

Fig. 21-4. *Schematic arrangement of a cyclotron.*

called "dees" (after their shape), crossing the gap between them twice on each revolution. Since the frequency of crossing is constant, one may impose an alternating potential on the dees such that the particle is accelerated each time it crosses the gap. Its actual path is therefore the spiral one shown in the figure, and the particle eventually emerges through a window (such as one of thin mica) with very high energy. By using alternating voltages of 50,000–100,000 V, early cyclotrons quickly achieved the production of 20-MeV particles (protons and deuterons). Later models reached energies of several hundred MeV. Today we have very large doughnut-shaped cyclotron-type accelerators as well as linear accelerators in which the particle is accelerated through successive high-voltage gaps. Attainable energies are now in the GeV (giga-electron volt = 10^9 eV) range.

With the advent of artificially produced high-energy particles it became practical to generate high-intensity beams of neutrons and to study neutron-induced transmutations. Such studies culminated in 1939 with the discovery of uranium fission. Interestingly, it was a pair of chemists, O. Hahn and F. Strassmann, who made the discovery. The first nuclear chain reaction was demonstrated at the University of Chicago in 1942 and the first fission or "atomic" bomb in 1945. In 1952, an

Table 21-1. *Selected Isotopic Masses*[a]

Species	Abundance (%)	Isotopic mass	Spin	Half-life	Decay mode[b]
e	—	0.0005486	$\frac{1}{2}$	—	—
$^1_0$n	—	1.0086654	$\frac{1}{2}$	12.8 min	β^- 0.782
$^1_1$H	99.985	1.0078252	$\frac{1}{2}$	—	—
^{2}H	0.015	2.0141022	1	—	—
^{3}H	—	3.0160494	$\frac{1}{2}$	12.26 yr	β^- 0.0186
$^3_2$He	$\sim 1 \times 10^{-4}$	3.0160299	$\frac{1}{2}$	—	—
^{4}He	100	4.0026036	0	—	—
^{6}He	—	6.01890	0	0.82 sec	β^- 3.51
$^6_3$Li	7.42	6.015126	1	—	—
^{7}Li	92.58	7.016005	$\frac{3}{2}$	—	—
^{8}Li	—	8.022488	—	0.84 sec	β^- 13
$^7_4$Be	—	7.016931	—	53.6 day	EC; γ 0.477
^{8}Be	—	8.005308	—	10^{-16} sec	2 α's
^{9}Be	100	9.01218	$\frac{3}{2}$	—	—
^{10}Be	—	10.013535	—	2.5×10^6 yr	β^- 0.555
$^{10}_5$B	18	10.012939	3	—	—
^{11}B	80.39	11.0093051	$\frac{3}{2}$	—	—
^{12}B	—	12.0143535	—	0.020 sec	β^- 13.37
$^{11}_6$C	—	11.011433	$\frac{3}{2}$	20.4 min	β^+ 2.1, γ 0.72
^{12}C	98.893	12.0000000	0	—	—
^{13}C	1.107	13.003354	$\frac{1}{2}$	—	—
^{14}C	—	14.0032419	0	5720 yr	β^- 0.155
$^{13}_7$N	—	13.005739	$\frac{1}{2}$	10.0 min	β^+ 1.19
^{14}N	99.634	14.0030744	1	—	—
^{15}N	0.366	15.000108	$\frac{1}{2}$	—	—
^{16}N	—	16.00609	—	7.38 sec	β^- 4.26, 10.4, 3.3; γ 6.13 (others)
$^{15}_8$O	—	15.003072	$\frac{1}{2}$	2.0 min	β^+ 1.72
^{16}O	99.759	15.9949149	0	—	—
^{17}O	0.0374	16.999133	$\frac{5}{2}$	—	—
^{18}O	0.2039	17.9991598	0	—	—
^{19}O	—	19.003577	—	29.4 sec	β^- 3.25, 4.60; γ 0.20 (m)
$^{20}_{10}$Ne	90.92	19.9923304	0	—	—
^{21}Ne	0.257	20.993849	$\frac{3}{2}$	—	—
^{22}Ne	8.82	21.991385	0	—	—
$^{22}_{11}$Na	—	21.994435	3	2.58 yr	β^+ 0.544; EC; γ 1.274
^{23}Na	100	22.989773	$\frac{3}{2}$	—	—
^{24}Na	—	23.990967	4	15.0 hr	β^- 1.39; γ 1.368, 2.753
$^{23}_{12}$Mg	—	23.99414	0	—	—
^{24}Mg	78.79	23.985045	0	—	—
^{25}Mg	10.13	24.985840	$\frac{5}{2}$	—	—
^{26}Mg	11.17	25.982591	0	—	—
^{27}Mg	—	26.984354	—	9.5 min	β^- 1.75, 1.59; γ 0.834, 1.015 (others)
$^{27}_{13}$Al	100	26.981535	$\frac{5}{2}$	—	—
^{28}Al	—	27.981908	—	2.3 min	β^- 2.87; γ 1.78

Table 21-1 *(cont.).*

Species	Abundance (%)	Isotopic mass	Spin	Half-life	Decay mode[b]
$^{27}_{14}\text{Si}$	—	26.98670	—	4.2 sec	β^+ 3.85; (γ)
^{28}Si	92.21	27.976927	0	—	—
^{29}Si	4.70	28.976491	$\frac{1}{2}$	—	—
^{30}Si	3.09	29.973761	0	—	—
$^{34}_{17}\text{Cl}$	—	33.97376	—	1.6 sec	β^+ 4.4
^{35}Cl	75.53	34.968854	$\frac{3}{2}$	—	—
^{36}Cl	—	35.96831	2	3.0×10^5 yr	β^- 0.714; (EC); (β^+)
^{37}Cl	24.47	36.965896	$\frac{3}{2}$	—	—
^{38}Cl	—	37.96800	—	37.3 min	β^- 4.81, 1.11, 2.77; γ 2.15, 1.60
$^{39}_{19}\text{K}$	93.10	38.963714	$\frac{3}{2}$	—	—
^{40}K	0.0118	39.964008	4	1.27×10^9 yr	β^- 1.32; EC; γ 1.46; (β^+)
^{41}K	6.88	40.961835	$\frac{3}{2}$	—	—
^{42}K	—	41.96242	2	12.36 hr	β^- 3.55, 1.98; γ 1.52
$^{56}_{26}\text{Fe}$	91.66	55.93493	—	—	—
$^{57}_{27}\text{Co}$	—	56.93629	$\frac{7}{2}$	270 days	EC; γ (e$^-$) 0.122, e$^-$ (γ) 0.0144 (m), $(\gamma$ 0.136)
^{59}Co	100	58.933189	$\frac{7}{2}$	—	—
^{60}Co	—	59.93381	5	5.26 yr	β^- 0.32; γ 1.173, 1.333
$^{88}_{38}\text{Sr}$	82.56	87.9056	0	—	—
$^{111}_{48}\text{Cd}$	12.75	109.90300	—	—	—
$^{113}\text{Cd}^{m}$	—	—	—	14 yr	β^- 0.57
$^{140}_{56}\text{Ba}$	—	—	—	12.8 days	β^- 1.02, 0.48; γ's
$^{140}_{57}\text{La}$	—	—	3	40.2 hr	1.34; γ's
$^{140}_{88}\text{Pr}$	—	139.90878	—	3.5 min	EC; β^+ 2.4; γ 1.2
$^{197}_{79}\text{Au}$	100	196.96655	$\frac{3}{2}$	—	—
$^{232}_{90}\text{Th}$	100	232.03821	—	1.39×10^{10} yr	γ 4.01, 3.95; e$^-$ (γ) 0.059
$^{238}_{92}\text{U}$	99.274	238.0508	—	4.51×10^9 yr	α 4.19 (others); $(\gamma$ 0.045): (SF)

[a] From G. Friedlander, J. W. Kennedy, and J. M. Miller, "Nuclear and Radiochemistry," 2nd ed. Wiley, New York, 1964. Beyond oxygen only selected stable isotope masses are given.

[b] Energies of the indicated radiations are given in MeV; SF denotes spontaneous fission; the designation m stands for metastable; EC is electron capture.

inventive contribution of E. Teller led to the first fusion or "hydrogen" bomb; the energy release comes from a reaction of the type

$$^2_1\text{H} + ^2_1\text{H} \rightarrow ^3_2\text{He} + ^1_0\text{n}. \tag{21-7}$$

The period from 1950 to date has been marked more by a steady exploitation of past discoveries than by major new ones. Nuclear weaponry and nuclear power have become rather exact technologies. Many new transuranic elements have been discovered; accelerating devices have become incredibly powerful machines capable of generating a host of transient new particles of the meson type.

21-2   Nuclear Energetics and Existence Rules

We consider nuclei to be made up of protons and neutrons moving in a mutual potential field. The number of protons must be just the nuclear charge Z and since the proton and neutron both have a mass number of unity, the total number of *nucleons* must be A, the mass number of the nucleus. The number of neutrons N is then $A - Z$. Nuclei of the same Z but differing N are called *isotopes*; those of the same N but differing Z are called *isotones*.

A.   Existence Rules for Nuclei

Figure 21-5 shows a plot of Z versus N for the stable isotopes. It is evident that the existence of stable nuclei is not random but is confined to a rather narrow zone. An important corollary is that one can predict the type of radioactivity an unstable nucleus should show. Figure 2-6 shows a portion of the isotope chart; the shaded

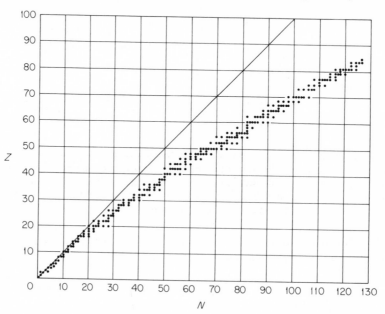

Fig. 21-5.   *A plot of Z versus N for stable nuclei. (From G. Friedlander, J. W. Kennedy, and J. M. Miller, "Nuclear and Radiochemistry," 2nd ed. Copyright 1964, Wiley, New York. Used with permission of John Wiley & Sons, Inc.)*

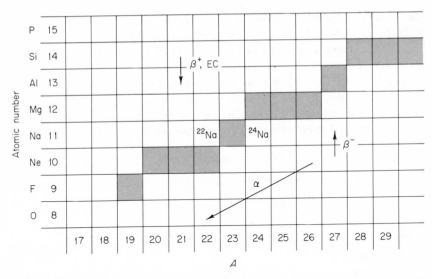

Fig. 21-6. *Illustration of how the atomic and mass numbers change for various types of disintegration process.*

squares mark stable isotopes. Consider the nucleus ^{24}Na. Possible modes of disintegration are β^- emission, β^+ emission, *electron capture* (EC), α emission, and spontaneous fission. The last two modes are important only for heavy elements. The first three processes may be written for a general isotope ^A_ZI:

$$^A_Z\text{I} \rightarrow {}^A_{Z+1}\text{I}' + \beta^-, \tag{21-8}$$

$$^A_Z\text{I} \rightarrow {}^A_{Z-1}\text{I}' + \beta^+, \tag{21-9}$$

$$^A_Z\text{I} \rightarrow {}^A_{Z-1}\text{I}' \ (\text{EC}). \tag{21-10}$$

Electron capture is a process whereby a K- or an L-orbital electron is acquired by the nucleus. As in positron emission, Z decreases by one unit.

It is evident that $^{24}_{11}$Na is most unlikely to decay by either β^+ emission or EC since the consequence would be to produce $^{24}_{10}$Ne, or an isotope yet further removed from the line of stability. We conclude (correctly) that the most likely process is that of β^- emission to give stable $^{24}_{12}$Mg. Similar reasoning leads to the conclusion that $^{22}_{11}$Na should decay by either positron emission or EC; the former is the observed process.

B. Nuclear Energetics

The energy change in a nuclear reaction is large enough to be measured as a gain or loss of mass using the Einstein relativity relationship $E = mc^2$, where c

is the velocity of light.[†] Accordingly, the table of isotopic masses (or "weights") (see Table 21-1) may be used to calculate energy changes in a transmutation process. One mass unit corresponds to $(1)(2.9979 \times 10^{10})^2/(6.0225 \times 10^{23}) = 1.499 \times 10^{-3}$ erg. This may be related to the electron volt unit of energy: 1 eV corresponds to 1.602×10^{-19} J; hence 1 MeV corresponds to 1.602×10^{-6} erg and the energy equivalent of one mass unit corresponds to 931 MeV.

Consider reaction (21-4). We calculate the energy release Q by adding the masses of the reactants and subtracting from the masses of the products:

$$^{10}_{5}B \quad + \quad ^{4}_{2}He \quad \rightarrow \quad ^{1}_{0}n \quad + \quad ^{13}_{7}N \qquad [\text{Eq. (21.4)}]$$

$$10.012939 \quad 4.002604 \quad 1.008665 \quad 13.005739$$
$$14.015543 \qquad\qquad 14.014404$$

so that $Q = 14.015543 - 14.014404 = 0.001139$ mass units or $(1.139)(0.931) = 1.06$ MeV. Thus about 1 MeV of energy is released, in the form of kinetic energy of the products.

A similar calculation may be made for a disintegration process. Consider

$$^{14}_{6}C \rightarrow ^{14}_{7}N + \beta^-. \tag{21-11}$$

From Table 21-1, $Q = 14.0032419 - 14.0030774 = 0.0001645$ mass units or 0.153 MeV. Most of this energy appears as kinetic energy of the β^- particle, although there is a small recoil energy of the $^{14}_{7}N$. Notice that the mass of the β^- particle is not used. This is because isotopic masses are given for the *neutral atoms*; the value for $^{14}_{6}C$ thus includes the mass of the six outer electrons, and that for $^{14}_{7}N$ includes the mass of its seven outer electrons. The extra electron in Eq. (21-11) is automatically taken care of. In the case of the positron emission, however, the mass of *two* electrons must be included in the products in order for the bookkeeping to be correct.

A useful quantity is the *mass defect* Δ, defined as $W - A$, where W is the atomic weight of the isotope. The demonstration that $Q = \Sigma \Delta_{\text{reactants}} - \Sigma \Delta_{\text{products}}$ is left as an exercise. It may be noticed from Table 21-1 that the mass defects are initially positive, decrease to a minimum of about -0.07 near iron, and then increase to about 0.05 near uranium. The initial decrease can be explained as reflecting the mutual attraction between protons and neutrons. The minimum and subsequent rise is due to the increasing mutual electrostatic repulsion of the protons. Also, as Z increases it becomes energetically favorable for nuclei to take on additional neutrons over the otherwise preferred 1:1 ratio, thus increasing the N/Z ratio and "diluting" the charge.

The energetics of nuclei can be treated in terms of the *nuclear binding energy* Q_B. This is defined as the energy released when a given isotope is assembled from

[†] A related consequence is that the mass of a particle increases with its velocity v and approaches infinity as $v \rightarrow c$. The equation obtained by Einstein is $m = m_0/[1 - (v/c)^2]^{1/2}$, where m_0 is the mass at $v = 0$, called the *rest mass*.

the requisite number of protons and neutrons (actually, the neutral atom is assembled from hydrogen atoms and neutrons). Thus we write

$$3 \, {}_{1}^{1}\text{H} + 4 \, {}_{0}^{1}\text{n} \rightarrow {}_{3}^{7}\text{Li}. \tag{21-12}$$

$Q_{\text{B}} = (3)(1.007852) + (4)(1.0086654) - 7.016005 = 0.04221$ mass units or 39.3 MeV. This last corresponds to about 6 MeV per nucleon, a figure which is roughly constant for the light elements. We may also speak of the binding energy for the addition or the removal of one neutron or one proton. A general observation is that the binding energy for an additional neutron is again 6–7 MeV.

21-3 Nuclear Reactions

A. Types of Reactions

Observable nuclear transmutation reactions were at first confined to the Rutherford type, illustrated by Eq. (21-3). A given element was bombarded with α particles, or, with the advent of accelerators, with protons or deuterons. The products typically consist of another light particle and a new element. Such reactions can be written ${}_{Z}^{A}\text{I}(x, y)_{Z'}^{A'}\text{I}'$, where x might be α, p (proton), or d (deuteron) and y might be α, p, or n. With the development of neutron sources, such as from (α, n) reactions, x could be n and y could be α, p, or γ. In this last case the neutron simply adds to the initial isotope and the binding energy appears as a γ photon, usually of 6–7 MeV energy. A further possibility for neutrons is the $(\text{n}, 2\text{n})$ reaction, for which Q is usually -6 to -7 MeV.

The energy of the bombarding particle x must of course be at least equal to the Q of the reaction if Q is negative. However, if x is a charged particle, its energy must be at least several MeV even though Q is positive. The reason is that the particle x must have sufficient energy to surmount the Coulomb repulsion between it and the nucleus. An empirical formula gives

$$E_{\text{barrier}} = \frac{0.9zZ}{A_{x}^{1/3} + A_{\text{I}}^{1/3}}, \tag{21-13}$$

where z is the charge number of x and E is in MeV. Thus the Coulomb barrier for Eq. (21-3) is 3.15 MeV. The Q for the reaction is -1.22 MeV, so that in this case the barrier determines the minimum or *threshold* energy of the α particles.

With the development of the cyclotron and of other high-energy accelerators it became possible to make bombardments with particles of much higher energy than the 5–10 MeV needed for simple (x, y) reactions. Roughly speaking, each additional 7–10 MeV allows the escape of one additional small particle. With 30-MeV α's, for example, reactions of the type $(\alpha, 3\text{n})$ and/or $(\alpha, 2\text{p})$ become possible. If yet higher energies are used, the number of multiple small product nuclei increases. The process is now called a *spallation*. The mechanism is thought to be one in which the x particle passes through the nucleus knocking out bits and pieces on the way.

B. Fission

Nuclei of very large atomic number show a new type of process: fission. The mutual Coulomb repulsion of the protons in such nuclei is so large that a spontaneous breakup into two approximately equal fragments occurs. For example, an isotope of californium $^{254}_{98}$Cf has a half-life for spontaneous fission of about 60 days.

It turns out that $^{235}_{92}$U is close to the point of being able to undergo spontaneous fission. The binding energy of about 7 MeV gained by the addition of a neutron is sufficient to make the product nucleus, $^{236}_{92}$U, unstable. A typical fission process is

$$^{235}_{92}\text{U} + ^{1}_{0}\text{n} \rightarrow [^{236}_{92}\text{U}] \rightarrow ^{140}_{56}\text{Ba} + ^{93}_{36}\text{Kr} + 3\,^{1}_{0}\text{n}. \tag{21-14}$$

The Q for the process is about 200 MeV; uranium has a large positive $\varDelta$ while the two fission products have negative $\varDelta$'s. Equation (21-14) is merely typical; the fission may occur in various ways, and the observed distribution of fission products is shown in Fig. 21-7. Since fission products tend to be neutron-rich, they lie

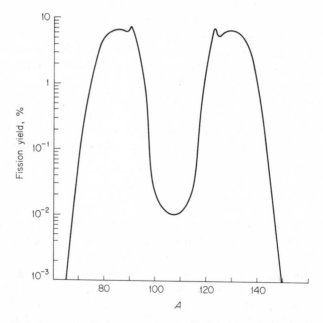

Fig. 21-7.   *Mass distribution of the fission products of* ^{235}U. *Note the two small peaks at "magic number" values of A (Section 21-ST-3). (From G. Friedlander, J. W. Kennedy, and J. M. Miller, "Nuclear and Radiochemistry," 2nd ed. Copyright 1964, Wiley, New York. Used with permission of John Wiley & Sons, Inc.)*

below the line of stable isotopes and hence are β^- emitters. The fission product ^{140}Xe undergoes a succession of β^- decays, for example, until stable ^{140}Ce is finally reached.

Equation (21-14) makes clear the stoichiometric basis for a fission chain reaction. Each neutron that induces fission leads to the production of two or three new neutrons, or to one or two extra ones. A brief discussion of nuclear reactors is given in the Commentary and Notes section.

C. Reaction Probabilities

There are two distinct situations involved in the treatment of the probability of a nuclear transmutation reaction. The first is that dealing with charged particles. As discussed in Section 21-4, such particles steadily lose energy through Coulomb interactions with the orbital electrons of the atoms of the absorbing medium. As a consequence, charged particles such as α particles possess a definite range or path length. If a target thicker than this range is used, one observes that a certain fraction of the particles produce a transmutation. This fraction, called the *yield*, is typically around 10^{-6}.

In the case of neutrons, however, there is no Coulomb interaction with orbital electrons of the absorber, and neutrons disappear only by nuclear collisions (their natural decay time is long enough not to compete appreciably with transmutation processes). We write for each layer dx of absorbing medium

$$-dI = \mathbf{I}n\sigma \, dx, \tag{21-15}$$

where I is the number of neutrons incident per square centimeter per second, $\mathbf{n}$ is the number of target nuclei per cubic centimeter, and σ is the probability of a neutron capture process. The quantity σ is called a *cross section* and is usually expressed in units of 10^{-24} cm^2, called a *barn* (b).[†] Cross sections for transmutation reactions are often around 1 b so that σ corresponds roughly to the physical target area of a nucleus. However, σ for some (n, γ) reactions is hundreds to thousands of barns. Integration of Eq. (21-15) gives

$$k = I_0 - I = I_0(1 - e^{\mathbf{n}\sigma x}), \tag{21-16}$$

where k is the rate of reaction per square centimeter of target bombarded.

Suppose that a neutron beam of 10^8 neutrons cm^{-2} sec^{-1} strikes a gold sheet 0.2 mm thick and 2 cm^2 in area. The capture cross section for the reaction $^{197}_{79}$Au(n, γ)$^{198}_{79}$Au is 100 b. The density of Au is 19.3 g cm^{-3} and its atomic weight is 197.2. Thus $\mathbf{n} = (19.3)(6.02 \times 10^{23})/197.2 = 5.89 \times 10^{22}$ cm^{-3} and application of Eq. (21-16) gives $(10^8)(2)\{1 - \exp[-(5.89 \times 10^{22})(100)(10^{-24})(0.02)]\} = 2.22 \times 10^7$ ^{198}Au nuclei formed per second.

[†] The story, probably not apocryphal, is that in the early days of the atomic energy project, boron was a serious impurity because of its large capture cross section for neutrons. E. Fermi is said to have exclaimed at one point that boron had a cross section as big as a barn—and the term became the unit of cross section.

Neutrons may lose their kinetic energy by collisions with nuclei, and if this occurs in a medium for which the capture cross section is small (as in graphite or heavy water), the neutrons may reach thermal energy, that is, an average energy corresponding to the ambient temperature. Nuclear reactors, for example, are often constructed so that most of the fission product neutrons are reduced to thermal energy before they undergo any capture process. A sample inserted in a reactor is therefore immersed in some concentration **n** of thermal neutrons. The number hitting a target of 1 cm² cross section of sample is then **n**v per second, where v is the average neutron velocity. The quantity **n**v is called the *neutron flux*; a typical value for an experimental nuclear reactor is 10^{12}–10^{14} neutrons cm^{-2} sec^{-1}. This quantity then replaces I in Eq. (21-15).

Suppose 2 g of NaCl is placed in a nuclear reactor whose slow neutron flux is 10^{13} neutrons cm^{-2} sec^{-1}. The cross section of ^{23}Na for the reaction ^{23}Na(n, γ)^{24}Na is 0.536 b. The rate of production of ^{24}Na is then $k = [2(6.02 \times 10^{23})/58.5]10^{13}(0.536 \times 10^{-24}) = 1.10 \times 10^{11}$ atoms sec^{-1}.

21-4 Absorption of Radiation

Radiation, such as α particles, β particles, and γ rays, is absorbed by matter due to interactions with orbital electrons. All such particles dissipate their energy to form ions, that is, positive and negative ion pairs, in the absorbing medium. On the average, 35 eV is expended per ion pair; a 1-MeV particle produces about 30,000 ion pairs before its energy is lost. However, while the overall process is the same, the rate and the mechanism vary considerably.

A. Charged Particles

Charged particles lose energy continuously as they pass through matter, as a result of Coulomb interactions with the orbital electrons of atoms. As a consequence, a charged particle exhibits a definite range or distance it can traverse before coming to rest. In the case of heavy particles, such as high-speed α particles, protons, deuterons, and so on, the path is nearly straight, as illustrated in Fig. 21-3. Heavy charged particles are not very penetrating. The range of a 5-MeV α particle is only about 3 cm in air, for example; such particles cannot penetrate skin and would not be dangerous externally.

Beta particles also have a definite range. An empirical equation by N. Feather gives

$$R = 0.543E - 0.160, \qquad (21\text{-}17)$$

where R is the range in aluminum in grams per square centimeter and E is in million electron volts. Note that R is about 100 times that for an α particle of the same energy. The range of β particles is hard to measure, however, since, being very light, they are easily deflected by the atoms of the absorber and therefore pursue a tortuous path. If the radiation from a β^- emitter is measured through successive increases in thickness of absorber, the intensity is found to diminish approximately exponentially with distance for two or perhaps three half-thicknesses before beginning its rapid drop to zero as the range is approached.

There is a second reason for the approximately exponential absorption curve for beta emitters. It turns out that the energy of a β^- particle emitted from a given nucleus may have a value ranging from near zero up to a maximum, as illustrated in Fig. 21-8. It is this maximum energy that appears in Eq. (21-17). The reason

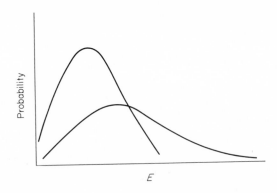

Fig. 21-8.   *Shapes of β-particle energy distributions.*

for the energy distribution is that the total decay energy is shared with a *neutrino* which is also emitted. The neutrino is a neutral particle of zero or near zero rest mass and spin $\frac{1}{2}$; its interaction with matter, although very weak, has been detected.

The situation with positrons is very similar to that with β^- particles; similar absorption curves are found and a similar range–energy relationship. The positron, however, being "antimatter" in nature, eventually fuses with an electron, and the combined mass energy is converted into two γ quanta. The atomic weight of an electron or of a positron is 0.00055 mass units, corresponding to 0.5 MeV. Thus positron emission is always accompanied by 0.5-MeV γ radiation, known as *annihilation* radiation.

B.   Electromagnetic Radiation

Gamma and x rays, being electromagnetic in nature, obey the same Beer–Lambert absorption law as does ordinary light (Section 3-2). The equation

$$I = I_0 e^{-\mu x} \tag{21-18}$$

applies, where μ is the linear absorption coefficient. The corresponding half-thickness is $0.693/\mu$. Figure 21-9 shows the variation of half-thickness with energy for various absorbers. For example, 1-MeV γ radiation has a half-thickness of about 10 g cm^{-2} in aluminum.

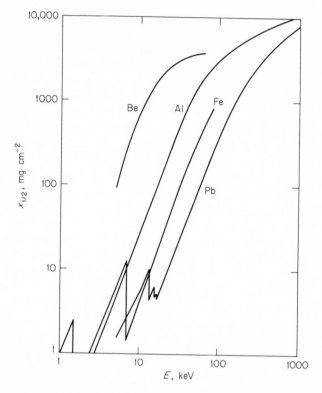

Fig. 21-9. *Half-thickness for the absorption of γ or x radiation in various substances. [Data from "Handbook of Chemistry and Physics" (C.D. Hodgman, ed.), 44th ed. Chem. Rubber Publ., Cleveland, Ohio, 1963.]*

The absorption process is primarily one of ionizing orbital electrons of the atoms in the absorbing material. The gamma quantum may impart all of its energy to the electron, in the *photoelectric* effect, or it may make an elastic collision with it, resulting in an accelerated electron and a gamma quantum of reduced energy, in the *Compton effect*. Gamma quanta of above 1.1 MeV energy may also, by interaction with the field of a nucleus, create an electron–positron pair; the effect is known as *pair formation*.

If we consider gamma quanta of successively lower energy, we reach the x-ray region. The energy becomes comparable to that required to ionize a K or an L electron of the absorbing medium. As Fig. 21-9 shows, the half-thickness suddenly rises when the energy falls to just *below* that necessary to ionize a particular type of electron. This happens first at the ionization energy of the K electrons of the absorber, then at that of the L electrons, and so on. The effect is known as *critical absorption*; it allows one to select combinations of absorbers that will preferentially pass a particular energy range of x rays.

X-ray emission occurs, of course, when an L electron falls into a K vacancy, or an M electron into an L vacancy. An alternative to such emission is the ejection of an outer electron in an intra-atomic photoelectric process known as the *Auger* effect.

C. Dosage

Radiation *dosimetry* is the measurement of the amount of energy expended in absorbing material; 1 *rad* is that radiation dose which deposits 100 erg in 1 g of material. An earlier, more complicated unit, is the *roentgen* (R), defined as the quantity of γ or x radiation which produces ions carrying 1 esu of electrical charge per cubic centimeter of dry air at STP; 1 R corresponds to the absorption of about 84 erg of energy. The roentgen and the rad are thus roughly equivalent; 1 g of radium gives a dose of about 3 rad hr^{-1} at a point 1 m away.

The biological hazard of radiation varies with the type. Neutrons cause more damage per rad than does γ radiation, for example. The dosage in rads is therefore scaled accordingly to give dosage in *rems* (roentgen equivalent man). One rad of γ or of β^- radiation is equivalent to about 1 rem, but 1 rad of neutron radiation corresponds to 10 rem.

The allowed industrial radiation level is about 3 mrem hr^{-1} (mrem = millirem) for whole body exposure and about 30 mrem hr^{-1} for hands or feet only. The total *accumulated* dose should not exceed, in rem, about five times the number of working years or the person's age minus 20. Acute and chronic exposure have different effects. A person might receive 150 rem over a working career with no harm, but 150 rem received all at once would cause some radiation sickness, The median lethal *acute* dose is about 500 rem (whole body exposure).

The dosage from cosmic radiation, natural radioactivity in the earth and in bricks, and so on amounts to about 0.1 rem yr^{-1} or about 0.003 of the maximum industrial exposure. Radiation due to fallout from nuclear testing is even less than this. The matter has been much debated, of course, but it is questionable whether such low levels of radiation have even a statistical effect on human longevity or health [see, for example, Holcomb (1970)].

Radiation chemistry is the study of chemical change induced by high-energy radiation. It is customary to measure efficiencies in terms of the number of molecules destroyed or reacted per 100 eV of energy absorbed; this is called the *G* value. For example, irradiation of aqueous solutions leads primarily to ionization and dissociation of water as the primary processes. A typical sequence of events is that assumed for dilute, air-saturated, and acidic ferrous sulfate:

$$H_2O \rightarrow H + OH, \qquad OH + Fe^{2+} \rightarrow Fe^{3+} + OH^-, \qquad H + O_2 \rightarrow HO_2,$$
$$H^+ + HO_2 + Fe^{2+} \rightarrow H_2O_2 + Fe^{3+}, \qquad H_2O_2 + Fe^{2+} \rightarrow OH + Fe(OH)^{2+} \qquad \text{(and so on)}.$$

Thus for every H_2O molecule decomposed in the primary reaction, four Fe^{2+} ions are oxidized.

21-5   Kinetics of Radioactive Decay

Nuclear disintegration or decay is a statistical event. With a large enough sample, however, the observed decay rate approximates the most probable one and we can therefore treat it as a simple first-order rate process. Thus

$$D = -\frac{dN}{dt} = \lambda N, \tag{21-19}$$

where D is the disintegration rate, N is the number of atoms present, and λ is the decay constant. This is the same as Eq. (14-4), and the integrated forms, Eqs. (14-6) and (14-7), also apply. Equation (14-9) gives the half-life as $t_{1/2} = 0.6931/\lambda$.

One ordinarily measures a radioactive material by its disintegration rate rather than by the number of atoms present. The *curie* (Ci) is defined as 3.700×10^{10} disintegrations sec^{-1}. As an example, the disintegration rate of 1 g of ^{14}C may be calculated by means of Eq. (21-19). The number of atoms present is $(1)(6.02 \times 10^{23})/14 = 4.30 \times 10^{22}$; $t_{1/2} = 5720$ yr, so that

$$\lambda = 0.6931/(5720)(365.3)(24)(60)(60) = 3.8 \times 10^{-12} \quad sec^{-1}.$$

Then $D = (4.30 \times 10^{22})(3.8 \times 10^{-12}) = 1.65 \times 10^{11}$ dis sec $^{-1}$ g^{-1} or 4.46 Ci g^{-1}.

An important special case is that in which a radioactive species is produced at some constant rate k. The differential equation is

$$\frac{dN}{dt} = k - \lambda N, \tag{21-20}$$

which integrates to give

$$D = k(1 - e^{-\lambda t}). \tag{21-21}$$

In the example of Section 21-3C, the rate of production of ^{24}Na is 1.10×10^{11} sec^{-1}. The half-life of ^{24}Na is 15.0 hr, and, for example, a 15 hr irradiation would yield $D = k/2$ or 5.5×10^{10} dis sec^{-1}. With a sufficiently prolonged irradiation, D approaches k. The *saturation* activity is then 1.10×10^{11} dis sec^{-1}.

A second common situation is that in which a mixture of radioactive species is present. The case of two species, 1 and 2, is illustrated in Fig. 21-10. Each decays independently, and $D_{tot} = D_1 + D_2$. If species 1 is the longer-lived, then $D_{tot} \rightarrow D_1$ at large times. As illustrated in the figure, subtraction of the D_1 line from D_{tot} gives D_2; we thus find $D_1{}^0 = 2000$ dis sec^{-1}, $t_{1/2}(1) = 3$ hr, and $D_2{}^0 = 4000$ dis sec^{-1}, $t_{1/2}(2) = 0.5$ hr.

The third case to be considered is that in which a parent radioactive species 1 decays to a daughter 2 which is also radioactive,

$$\text{species 1} \xrightarrow{\lambda_1} \text{species 2} \xrightarrow{\lambda_2} \text{stable product.}$$

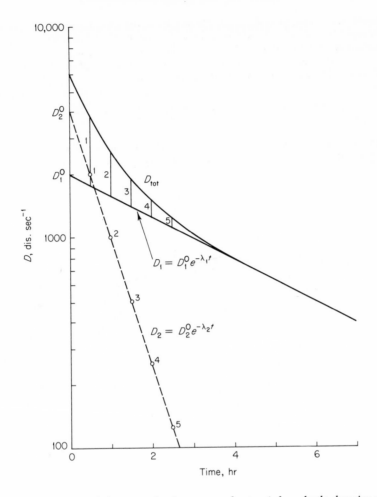

Fig. 21-10. *Analysis of the composite decay curve for two independently decaying species.*

This situation is discussed in Section 15-ST-1B; Eq. (15-17) may be written

$$D_2 = \frac{\lambda_2 D_1^0}{\lambda_2 - \lambda_1} (e^{-\lambda_1 t} - e^{-\lambda_2 t}). \tag{21-22}$$

If $\lambda_2 > \lambda_1$, then at large times Eq. (21-22) reduces to that for *transient equilibrium*

$$D_2 = \frac{\lambda_2}{\lambda_2 - \lambda_1} D_1. \tag{21-23}$$

If $\lambda_2 \gg \lambda_1$, then at times large compared to $1/\lambda_2$, species 1 has still not appreciably decayed and $D_2 = D_1^0$. This situation is known as one of *secular equilibrium*.

The experimental application of Eq. (21-22) may be illustrated as follows. We suppose that a sample of pure ^{140}Ba has been isolated. It decays with a half-life of 12.8 days into daughter ^{140}La, whose half-life is 40.2 hr; both emit β^- particles. The plot of D_{tot} versus time is shown in Fig. 21-11; D_{tot} goes through a maximum due to the growth of the daughter ^{140}La but eventually becomes linear with time in the semilogarithmic plot. That is,

$$D_{tot}(t \text{ large}) \rightarrow D_1{}^0\, e^{-\lambda_1 t} \left(1 + \frac{\lambda_2}{\lambda_2 - \lambda_1}\right). \tag{21-24}$$

The slope of the limiting line thus gives λ_1, corresponding in this case to $t_{1/2} = 12.8$ days. Subtraction of the limiting line from D_{tot} yields a difference line whose slope gives λ_2, corresponding to $t_{1/2} = 40.2$ hr.

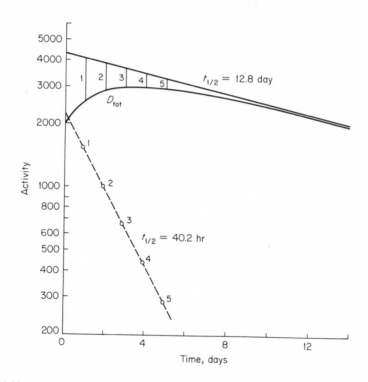

Fig. 21-11. *Analysis of the composite decay curve for the parent–daughter sequence* ^{140}Ba $\xrightarrow{12.8\,\text{day}}$ ^{140}La $\xrightarrow{40.2\,\text{hr}}$ ^{140}Ce.

COMMENTARY AND NOTES

21-CN-1 Theories of Radioactive Decay

The theoretical treatment of radioactive decay is in some ways similar to that of emission from a molecular excited state. Thus the emission of a gamma quantum from a nucleus is essentially a nuclear fluorescence or phosphorescence (see Section 18-4), although it is usually called an *isomeric transition* (IT). The emission is subject to selection rules; its probability depends on the change in nuclear angular momentum Δl that occurs, and on whether or not a change occurs in the electric charge distribution in the nucleus. An allowed transition occurs in about 10^{-13} sec, but if Δl is large, the half-life can be quite large. Thus, referring to Table 21-1, $^{113}Cd^m$ decays to ground-state ^{113}Cd with a half-life of 14 yr.

A complication is that an alternative to actual gamma emission is the ejection of an orbital electron which carries off the energy of the isomeric transition. The effect is called *internal conversion* (IC), and the probability that the decay will take this route increases with increasing Δl. Thus in the case of $^{113}Cd^m$ the actual emission is by IC, with monoenergetic 0.58-MeV electrons produced.

Beta decay is also treated as an emission process, but with the complication that there is a simultaneous emission of two particles from the nucleus: an electron and a neutrino. The theoretical treatment of the lifetime of beta decay is somewhat complicated, but again the half-life increases with increasing Δl for the transition.

The treatment of α emission is quite different from the preceding two cases since the particle emitted is essentially a piece of the nucleus itself. The situation is sketched in Fig. 21-12. If we consider the process $_{Z}^{A}I \rightarrow {}_{Z-2}^{A-4}I' + {}_{2}^{4}He$, the reverse reaction has a $Q_{barrier}$ as given by Eq. (21-13). In the case of $_{90}^{234}Th$ this barrier

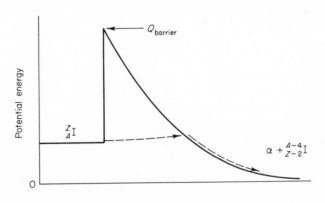

Fig. 21-12. *Quantum mechanical model for α emission.*

amounts to about 20 MeV, so that it would require a 20-MeV α particle to enter the $^{234}_{90}$Th nucleus to give $^{238}_{92}$U. Yet the reverse process is spontaneous and the emitted α particle has *only* 4 MeV energy. Clearly the emitted particles are never at the potential energy of the top of the Coulomb barrier.

The explanation of this energy paradox constituted one of the first great triumphs of wave mechanics. The theory is that of a particle in a box with a finite barrier. It turns out that the wave function for the particle (the α particle in this case) has a finite value outside of the box (the Coulomb barrier), and the square of this value gives the probability of the particle being outside and hence of its being emitted. The process is known as "tunneling."

21-CN-2   Nuclear Reactors and "Atomic" Bombs

A nuclear reactor is a device which allows a nuclear fission reaction to be self-sustaining. We consider first the problem of arranging this situation in the case of natural uranium, which contains 99.27% ^{238}U and 0.72% ^{235}U. According to Eq. (21-14), the slow neutron fission of ^{235}U produces additional neutrons which could, in turn, lead to further fissions. The problem is that ^{238}U also captures neutrons:

$$^{238}_{92}U + {}^{1}_{0}n \rightarrow {}^{239}_{92}U \xrightarrow[23.5\,min]{\beta^-} {}^{239}_{94}Np \xrightarrow[2.35\,day]{\beta^-} {}^{229}_{94}Pu. \qquad (21\text{-}25)$$

The result is the production of plutonium (half-life 2.44×10^4 yr). The capture cross section of ^{238}U for neutrons goes through a peak or *resonance* absorption region as the neutrons lose their energy, and the consequence is that a sample of natural uranium is unable to sustain a chain reaction; too many neutrons go into reaction (21-25).

The solution to this problem that was found during World War II was to place the uranium in a lattice of highly purified graphite. Carbon does not absorb neutrons strongly, and the neutrons produced by the fission of ^{235}U wander through the graphite until they are slowed down by collisions to thermal energies before again encountering uranium atoms. Thus the dangerous resonance absorption region is spent in graphite and away from ^{238}U. A sufficient fraction of the neutrons produced by each act of ^{235}U fission now survives to carry the chain reaction. This fraction is called the *reproduction constant k*.

If k is greater than unity, a chain reaction should occur. In any actual reactor, however, there is a loss of neutrons from the surface into surrounding space, so that the finite reactor has a practical reproduction constant $k' < k$. The importance of the surface effect diminishes with increasing size of the reactor, so that if a particular infinite reactor has $k > 1$, then there will be some critical size of an actual structure such that k' is just equal to unity.

The lifetime of a neutron is about 10^{-5} sec; this is the time from its formation in a fission event to its eventual capture by another ^{235}U nucleus. Since the concentration of neutrons in a reactor should increase by the factor k' with each generation, this means that the neutron concentration and hence the power output of the reactor should increase by $(k')^{10^5}$ per second. If this were actually the case, the situation would be extremely dangerous. As soon as construction of the reactor exceeded its critical size, the power would rise catastrophically in a fraction of a second. No actual explosion would occur in ordinary reactors; the reactor would be ruined, however.

There is a most fortunate natural situation which prevents this catastrophe from happening. It so happens that about 1% of the neutrons produced in fission are tied up in isotopes called delayed neutron emitters. These are energetic β^- emitters decaying to excited nuclear states that then promptly emit a neutron. The half-lives of the β^- emitters range from milliseconds to seconds. Thus if k' is less than about 1.01, the effective generation time is not 10^{-5} sec but about 1 sec. A reactor that is just critical in size thus increases its power only slowly and may easily be controlled by moving neutron-absorbing control rods inward so as to bring k' back to unity whenever the power level is to be stabilized.

The original reactors of World War II were intended not to produce power, but to produce ^{239}Pu by reaction (21-25). The reason was that ^{239}Pu was expected to fission easily, like ^{235}U, and being chemically different from uranium, could be concentrated into the pure element. The alternative approach used was to fractionate natural uranium into relatively pure ^{235}U by isotopic fractionation procedures.

Atomic bombs (strictly speaking, nuclear bombs) consist of relatively pure ^{239}Pu or ^{235}U. One modern arrangement is to have a sphere of the material which has *just* too much surface area for k' to exceed unity. The sphere is surrounded by a conventional high explosive and when this is detonated it compresses the sphere, thereby reducing its area and making k' greater than unity. The ensuing chain reaction is very rapid in this case since the neutrons need not be slowed down; the generation time is much less than 10^{-5} sec and the result is the incredible nuclear explosion.

Contemporary power-producing nuclear reactors may use plutonium or ^{235}U enriched uranium. Uranium- or plutonium-containing ceramic rods may, for example, be spaced in a bath of heavy water, or, if sufficiently enriched, in ordinary water. The fission energy appears ultimately as heat, of course, and heat exchangers transfer this heat to a working fluid which is then used for power generation.

21-CN-3 Nuclear Chemistry

The term nuclear chemistry applies to the study of the properties of nuclei and of "fundamental" particles. It is possible, for example, to draw inferences about the size, shape, and ease of deformation of nuclei from a study of how they scatter high-energy particles such as protons or neutrons. It appears that most nuclei are not spherical but are prolate ellipsoids. Scattering experiments also allow a mapping of nuclear energy states. These states are quantized and charts of them look much like those from atomic spectroscopy.

We have considered nuclei to be made up of neutrons and protons, with the implication that these last are fundamental particles. Actually, the experiments of high-energy physics have disclosed some 80 "fundamental" particles. These may be classified as *baryons*, which are heavy particles and include the proton and the neutron, *mesons*, whose rest masses range down to about 0.1 mass units, and *leptons*, which comprise the electron, the *mu* particle, and the neutrino. The study of the properties of these particles has led to the formulation of several quantities which are conserved in nuclear processes. In addition to charge, mass number, spin angular momentum, and parity, quantities called hypercharge, isotopic spin, and strangeness have been defined [see Chew *et al.* (1964)].

It also appears that for every elementary particle there is an antiparticle; the two annihilate each other in a collision. Thus the positron is the antimatter equivalent of the electron. Antiprotons and antineutrons as well as various other antibaryons have been discovered. It is possible, then, to imagine a hydrogen atom consisting of an antiproton nucleus and an orbital positron—or, indeed, an antimatter universe. The detection of astronomical antimatter seems impossible at present. Stellar spectra cannot be used, for example, since these should be invariant with respect to the type of matter involved.

21-CN-4   Quantum Statistics

The usual Boltzmann expression is actually a limiting case of more general expressions. Particles whose wave function is antisymmetric, such as the electron or proton, obey the Pauli exclusion principle in that no two can have the same wave function. In an assemblage of such particles, detailed analysis gives the probable number N_i of particles having energy ϵ_i as

$$N_i = \frac{g_i}{\alpha e^{\epsilon_i/kT} + 1},\tag{21-26}$$

where g_i is the degeneracy of the state and α is the normalization factor required to make $\sum N_i = 1$. Equation (21-26) reduces to the Boltzmann expression if $\alpha e^{\epsilon_i/kT} \gg 1$. It turns out that α can be identified with the reciprocal of the absolute or rational activity (Section 9-CN-3), and the condition for Eq. (21-26) to reduce to the Boltzmann law is therefore that either $\epsilon_i \gg kT$ or the system is very dilute so that α is large. The analysis giving Eq. (21-26) is known as *Fermi–Dirac* statistics. Particles to which it applies are called *fermions*.

If a particle contains an even number of fermions, such as deuterium or a helium nucleus, then its wave function is symmetric and the Pauli exclusion principle does not apply; any number of such particles may be in a given state. The change puts -1 instead of $+1$ in the denominator of Eq. (21-26). The analysis is known as *Bose–Einstein* statistics and the particles obeying these statistics are called *bosons*. Interestingly, it is found that photons obey Bose–Einstein statistics, which suggests that they are not simple particles but are somehow composite.

21-CN-5 Experimental Detection Methods

Most detection devices are based on the ability of high-energy radiation to ionize matter. A quartz fiber may be electrostatically charged, for example, so as to be repelled from its support. Radiation ionizes the air, rendering it somewhat conducting so that the charge leaks away and the fiber slowly returns to its rest position. The rate of such return is a measure of the intensity of the radiation. Such *electroscopes* are widely used for personal dosimeters; they can be constructed in the size and shape of a fountain pen.

Photographic film is exposed by high-energy radiation and is much used, of course, in medical x-ray examinations. Film has the two advantages of providing a cumulative measure of radiation and of mapping its intensity distribution. However, the photographic method is inconvenient to use for accurate measurements or where discrimination among different kinds of radiation is desired.

The ionization produced by radiation may be measured electronically. A potential of several hundred volts is applied through a high resistance to a pair of electrodes separated by an air gap. The ions produced by the radiation collect on the electrodes to generate a small current, which drops the voltage, and this voltage change can be amplified by a dc amplifier. Since each high-speed particle produces a burst of ions, the current actually occurs in pulses, and each pulse can be amplified by means of an ac amplifier. Discrimination between different kinds of particles is now possible since the pulse sizes will be different. It is thus possible to "count" α particle pulses in the presence of a heavy background of β^- or of γ radiation.

If the potential between the electrodes is raised to about 1000 V, the ions produced by the radiation are so strongly accelerated as to produce further ionization. The result is a cascade of ions and a very large pulse—one that can be detected with little amplification. The device is known as a *Geiger* counter. It does not, of course, discriminate among kinds of particles since all pulses are now the same.

Perhaps the most common modern detection device is the *scintillation counter*. Materials such as crystalline anthracene and sodium iodide [with a trace of Tl(I)] emit light under irradiation; each high-speed particle produces a quick burst of photons and the light pulse is detected by means of a photomultiplier. The use of

NaI(Tl) is particularly advantageous for the detection of γ rays since the heavy I atoms absorb electromagnetic radiation strongly. Moreover, each photoelectron has the energy of the γ quantum, and the light pulse resulting from such electrons is proportional to their energy. It is thus possible to measure the energy spectrum of incident γ radiation. Semiconductors have also been used. Each ionizing particle produces a current pulse very nearly proportional to its energy.

21-CN-6 The Mössbauer Effect

Gamma rays emitted in an isomeric transition ordinarily have less than the true energy difference between the two nuclear states involved. Conservation of momentum demands that some energy go into a recoil of the emitting nucleus. The discovery by R. Mössbauer in 1958 was that if the emitting isotope is embedded in a fairly stiff crystal lattice, then part of the time the emission is recoilless. In effect, the recoil momentum is absorbed by the crystal as a whole, and the recoil *energy* loss of the emitted γ ray becomes negligible.

The energy of such γ quanta is now exactly that between the two nuclear states, and such gammas show a strong resonance absorption by ground-state nuclei. The wavelength spread of the recoilless radiation is so narrow that if the source is moving even a few centimeters per second, the Doppler effect is enough to destroy the resonance absorption by a stationary absorber.

Much as with nmr, the Mössbauer effect, although remarkable, would have a limited application except that gamma energies are measurably affected by the density of orbital electrons in the vicinity of the nucleus, and hence by the chemical environment of the atom. There is thus a chemical shift in the energy of the recoilless γ emission. If the source and the absorber atoms are in different chemical states, resonance is destroyed.

A typical experimental procedure is as follows. Some ^{57}Co (270 day half-life) is deposited on the surface of some cobalt metal. This isotope decays to an excited state of iron ^{57}Fe^m which then emits a 14.4-keV γ quantum. The absorber consists of iron in the chemical state to be studied, and one looks for resonance absorption by stable ^{57}Fe. With source and absorber stationary there will in general be no resonance because their chemical states are different, and one therefore puts the source through a periodic velocity cycle (it may be driven by a loudspeaker cone, for example). At those velocities at which the Doppler shift restores resonance, absorption is strong, and the intensity of radiation passing through the absorber decreases. A Mössbauer spectrum is shown typically as a plot of radiation intensity through the absorber versus source velocity. The general flavor of Mössbauer spectrometry is similar to that of nmr, and the derived information is somewhat analogous.

SPECIAL TOPICS

21-ST-1   The Natural Decay Series. Age Dating

An early triumph of radiochemistry was the working out of the rather complex sequences of successive decays that occur with the heavy elements. The best known of these series is that beginning with ^{238}U. It may be summarized by the equation

$$^{238}_{92}\text{U} \rightarrow \,^{206}_{82}\text{Pb} + 8\,^4_2\text{He} + 6\beta^-. \tag{21-27}$$

Isotopes of Th, Pa, Ra, Rn, Po, Bi, and Tl constitute intermediate members of the series, but the important point is that ^{238}U is the longest-lived of all, with a half-life of 4.49×10^{10} yr. The series therefore comes to secular equilibrium; for each uranium atom that disintegrates, on the average eight α particles (ending up as He) and six β^- particles are released by daughter nuclei.

The time elapsed since a uranium-containing mineral first crystallized may be determined from the amount of the entrapped helium. Thus $N_\text{U} + \frac{1}{8}N_\text{He}$ gives the original number of uranium atoms present, or $N_\text{U} = (N_\text{U} + \frac{1}{8}N_\text{He})\, e^{-\lambda_\text{U} t}$. A determination of the ratio N_He/N_U in a rock sample thus allows a calculation of t. Alternatively, the ratio $^{206}\text{Pb}/^{238}\text{U}$ may be used. Very old minerals have shown ages up to about 10^9 yr by this method.

Since change in mass numbers occurs only by α emission, the members of the uranium series have mass numbers which may be written as $4n + 2$, where n is an integer. The thorium series belongs to the $4n$ family, and is, in summary,

$$^{282}_{90}\text{Th} \rightarrow \,^{208}_{82}\text{Pb} + 6\,^4_2\text{He} + 4\beta^-. \tag{21-28}$$

The actinium series begins with ^{235}U and thus belongs to the $4n + 3$ family. A fourth series, the $4n + 1$ series, has been pieced together only relatively recently.

Age dating on a more modest time scale is possible from measurement of the ^{14}C content of organic matter. Cosmic radiation is constantly generating ^{14}C, probably through the reaction $^{14}_7\text{N} + ^1_0\text{n} \rightarrow \,^{14}_6\text{C} + ^1_1\text{H}$, so that a low level of this isotope is always present. W. Libby realized that this circumstance permitted a determination of the age of wood or of other biological material. The living organism continuously incorporates ^{14}C in its structure, but, once killed, biological activity ceases and the radiocarbon begins to decay away. The half-life is 5720 yr, so that quite ancient objects can be dated. It is assumed that cosmic ray intensity has remained constant, so that a piece of, say, early Egyptian wood with half the proportion of ^{14}C to ^{12}C as in present-day wood must be 5720 yr old.

Tritium is also produced in the atmosphere at a low concentration, probably by the reaction $^{14}_{7}N + ^{1}_{0}n \rightarrow ^{12}_{6}C + ^{3}_{1}H$. The time scale is now a very contemporary one since the half-life of tritium is only 12.26 yr. However, ground waters have been dated by means of their tritium content (and also some good wines!).

It must be emphasized that these cosmic-ray-produced radioactivities are at a minute and entirely nonhazardous level of concentration. Quite sophisticated instrumentation is needed even to detect their presence.

21-ST-2 Statistical Fluctuations in Radioactive Decay

Consider N atoms of a radioactive substance. The probability that any arbitrarily selected set of exactly m nuclei will decay during an interval t is

$$(1 - e^{-\lambda t})^m (e^{-\lambda t})^{N-m} = p^m q^{N-m}, \tag{21-29}$$

where p^m is the probability that the m nuclei will decay and q^{N-m} is the probability that the other $N - m$ nuclei will not. The probability given by (21-29) must be multiplied by the number of ways of picking m nuclei out of N total ones. This is $N!/(N - m)!$. However, since the order of picking the m nuclei is immaterial, we must divide by the ways of permuting m objects, $m!$. The final equation for the probability $W(m)$ is

$$W(m) = \frac{N!}{(N - m)!\, m!}\, p^m q^{N-m} \tag{21-30}$$

We can relate this result to the standard deviation of a measurement of m. In general, the standard deviation σ of a series of n measurements of a quantity x is given by

$$\sigma^2 = \frac{1}{n} \sum_{i=1}^{n} (x_i - \bar{x})^2. \tag{21-31}$$

Expansion of the sums leads to the alternative form

$$\sigma^2 = \overline{x^2} - \bar{x}^2. \tag{21-32}$$

That is, σ^2 is given by the difference between the average value of x^2 and the square of the average value of x.

The quantities $\bar{m}$ and $\overline{m^2}$ may be evaluated from Eq. (21-30). It turns out that $\bar{m} = N(1 - e^{-\lambda t})$, which reduces to Eq. (21-19) if t is small. Also, $(N - 1)\, Np^2 = \overline{m^2} - \bar{m}$, and insertion of these results into Eq. (21-32) gives $\sigma^2 = \bar{m}q$. If $\bar{m}$ is small compared to N, then q is essentially unity, and $\sigma = \bar{m}^{1/2}$. Thus the standard deviation of a measurement of the disintegrations occurring in time t is just the square root of the average value.

If a particular sample of radioactive material registers 1000 disintegrations in 10 min, we assume that the figure of 1000 is close to the true $\bar{m}$, and estimate σ to be $(1000)^{1/2}$ or 31.6. The activity is then reported as 100 ± 3.2 dis min^{-1}, or $\pm 3.2\%$. Were 10,000 disintegrations observed over 100 min, σ would be 100 and we would now report 100 ± 1 dis min^{-1}, or an uncertainty of 1%. Thus the more total disintegrations or emitted particles counted, the smaller is the percentage of error in the measurement.

21-ST-3   Nuclear Shell Model

Empirical observation indicates that nuclei having 2, 8, 20, 28, 50, 82, or 126 protons or neutrons are especially stable. These numbers have been called "magic" or closed-shell numbers. Their natural isotopic abundance of stable closed-shell nuclei is unusually high, as, for example, $^{4}_{2}$He, $^{16}_{8}$O, and $^{40}_{20}$Ca, for which both proton and neutron numbers correspond to closed-shell values, and $^{88}_{38}$Sr and $^{208}_{82}$Pb, for which the neutron number is magic. Tin, with $Z = 50$, has no less than ten stable isotopes, which is. taken as an indication of the stabilizing effect of the presence of a closed shell of protons. The two pips on the fission yield plot of Fig. 21-7 correspond to neutron numbers of 50 and 82—again closed-shell numbers.

The presence of magic numbers has been explained in terms of a relatively simple wave mechanical model of the nucleus which assumes that protons and neutrons move in a spherically symmetric potential. The energy states are given by quantum numbers n and ℓ, defined similarly to those for the hydrogen atom, although n does not now limit the possible ℓ values. One can have 1s, 1p, 1d, 1f, ... states. In this scheme protons and neutrons have separate sets of energy levels, and the magic numbers are found to correspond to certain groupings of filled n and ℓ shells. More elaborate theories permit the nucleus to be deformed from a spherical shape and allow yet more detailed calculations of nuclear properties.

GENERAL REFERENCES

Friedlander, G., Kennedy, J. W., and Miller, J. M. (1964). "Nuclear and Radiochemistry," 2nd ed. Wiley, New York.

Siegbahn, K., Ed. (1965). "Alpha-, Beta-, and Gamma-Ray Spectroscopy." North-Holland Publ., Amsterdam.

CITED REFERENCES

CHEW, G. F., GELL-MANN, M., AND ROSENFELD, A. H. (1964). *Sci. Amer.* (February), p. 74.
HOLCOMB, R. (1970). *Science* **168**, 853.

Exercises

21-1 What is the field **H** required to cause electrons to follow a path of radius 2 cm if the compensating electric field to prevent such curvature is 10^4 V cm^{-1}?

Ans. 170 G.

21-2 Calculate **E** in volts per centimeter required to maintain from falling a water droplet which, in the absence of the field, falls at the rate of 10^{-4} cm sec^{-1}. Assume the drop carries three units of electronic charge and the viscosity of air to be 1.85×10^{-4} P.

Ans. 0.67 V cm^{-1}.

21-3 Calculate the specific activity of ^{238}U in disintegrations per second per gram.

Ans. 1230 dis sec^{-1} g^{-1}.

21-4 A sample of ^{38}Cl (as NaCl) shows 1 Ci of activity initially. What should be the activity in disintegrations per second 3 hr later?

Ans. 1.3×10^9 dis sec^{-1}.

21-5 Calculate the high-voltage frequency for the cyclotron acceleration of deuteron in a field of 10,000 G and the maximum radius achieved by the spiraling deuterons if the final energy is to be 10 MeV (neglect relativistic effects).

Ans. 7.6 MHz, 55 cm.

21-6 What is the relativistic increase in mass of a 10-MeV deuteron, of a 10-MeV electron? What is the velocity of a 1-MeV electron?

Ans. 0.537%, 19.6-fold, 0.94 c.

21-7 Explain how it is possible that ^{36}Cl may decay by either β^- or β^+ emission. How should $^{30}_{16}$S decay?

21-8 Calculate Q for Eq. (21-7).

Ans. 3.27 MeV.

21-9 Calculate Q for Eq. (21-6).

Ans. 3.8 MeV.

21-10 Calculate the binding energy of the last neutron added to (a) ^{16}O, (b) ^{17}O. Comment on the difference between the two values.

Ans. (a) 15.7 MeV, (b) 4.13 MeV.

Problems

21-11 Calculate the Coulomb barrier in the bombardment of ^{209}Bi with α particles.

Ans. 22.9 MeV.

21-12 The cross section for the reaction ^{59}Co$(n, \gamma)^{60}$Co is 20 b. Calculate the number of ^{60}Co atoms formed if 2 g of metal foil is exposed to a neutron flux of 1.5×10^{13} neutrons cm^{-2} sec^{-1} for 10 min, and the resulting radioactivity in millicuries.

Ans. 0.415 mCi.

21-13 Calculate the dosage in roentgens per hour 1 m away from a 1-Ci source of 1-MeV γ radiation. [*Note*: Estimate the absorption coefficient per centimeter of air from Fig. 21-9 to determine the fraction of the γ radiation absorbed per centimeter and hence the energy dissipated; this gives the number of ions produced. The number of ions per cubic centimeter 1 m away can then be calculated, and thence the dosage.]

Ans. 1.26 R hr^{-1}.

21-14 ^{31}Si is formed at the rate of 2×10^8 atoms per second by the neutron irradiation of silica. How many millicuries will be present (a) immediately after a 5-hr irradiation, and (b) 10 hr after the irradiation is over? What is the saturation activity?

Ans. (a) 1.45 mCi; (b) 0.103 mCi; 5.4 mCi.

21-15 The total activity is followed as a function of time for a sample suspected of consisting of two or more independently decaying radioisotopes. Find the half-life of each component and the number of disintegrations per minute of each component present at zero time.

t (hr)	0	0.5	1.0	1.5	2.0	2.5
Dis min^{-1}	7300	4500	2900	1950	1350	990
t (hr)	3.0	3.5	4.0	5.0	6.0	7.0
Dis min^{-1}	740	580	480	370	310	280
t (hr)	8	10	12	14		
Dis min^{-1}	255	210	180	155		

Ans. (a) $t_{1/2} = 0.7$ hr, $D^0 = 6800$;
(b) $t_{1/2} = 9$ hr, $D^0 = 470$.

21-16 ^{146}Ce decays by beta emission to ^{146}Pr, with $t_{1/2} = 14$ min; the ^{146}Pr decays in turn to stable ^{146}Nd with $t_{1/2} = 25$ min. A sample consists initially of 0.5 mCi of pure ^{146}Ce. Calculate the activity of ^{146}Ce and of ^{146}Pr present 30 min later. Is this a case of secular equilibrium?

Ans. $D_1 = 0.11$ mCi, $D_2 = 0.44$ mCi.

Problems

21-1 The specific activity of a sample of pure ^{99}Tc is 10^5 dis sec^{-1} mg^{-1}. Calculate the half-life of ^{99}Tc.

21-2 Calculate the isotopic mass of $^{200}_{80}\mathrm{Hg}$ from Eq. (21-33) and also the Q for adding one neutron to obtain $^{201}_{80}\mathrm{Hg}$.

21-3 What is the average binding energy of a proton in $^{23}\mathrm{Na}$?

21-4 Calculate the Q for the reaction $^{9}\mathrm{Be}(\alpha, \mathrm{n})^{12}\mathrm{C}$.

21-5 Derive the equation for the total binding energy of an isotope in terms of its mass number for isotopes of optimum charge. Use the equation

$$E\,(\mathrm{MeV}) = 11.6A - \frac{20}{A}(A - 2Z)^2 - 0.06Z^2 \qquad (21\text{-}33)$$

to find $Z_A = f(A)$ such that $(\partial E/\partial Z)_A = 0$. By means of this result make a plot of the mass defect against A; also compare your result with the plot for stable isotopes as actually found (compare with Fig. 21-5).

21-6 By means of the equations developed in Problem 21-5, calculate the energy of α emissions for

$$^{A}_{Z_A}\mathrm{I} = \,^{A-4}_{Z_A-2}\mathrm{I} + \,^{4}_{2}\mathrm{He}$$

when $A = 200$. Estimate the average number of betas per alpha for a decay series around $A = 200$.

21-7 When a magnetic field of 5000 G is imposed in a cloud chamber, the electrons and positrons formed by pair production from incident γ radiation are found to follow a path of 2 cm radius of curvature. What is the energy in MeV of the γ ray?

21-8 How many centimeters of lead absorber are needed to reduce the intensity of a source of 5-MeV γ radiation 100-fold (absorption coefficient, $\mu = 0.30\ \mathrm{cm}^{-1}$)?

21-9 What is the dosage in roentgens per hour 1 m away from a 100-Ci point source of 1-MeV gamma rays of absorption coefficient $\mu = 7 \times 10^{-5}\ \mathrm{cm}^{-1}$ in air? Assume that only singly charged ions are formed and that 30 eV are required to produce each ion pair.

21-10 The high voltage across the dees of a cyclotron has a frequency of 12 MHz. What must the magnetic field be if deuterons are to be accelerated?

21-11 What is the most energetic decay process for $^{10}\mathrm{C}$, and how much energy is liberated?

21-12 A radioelement of half-life T_1 yields a daughter of half-life T_2. Assuming that at zero time no daughter is present, derive the expression for the time of maximum combined activity (that is, disintegrations per unit time) of parent plus daughter.

21-13 What is the cross section for the formation of $^{14}\mathrm{C}$ by (n, p) reaction if, on irradiation of 100 liter of 0.1 M ammonium nitrate for 1 wk at an average pile power of 3000 kW, 0.1 mCi of $^{14}\mathrm{C}$ is obtained? (Assume 10^5 neutrons $\mathrm{cm}^{-2}\ \mathrm{sec}^{-1}\ \mathrm{W}^{-1}$.)

21-14 If the cross section for the reaction $^{31}\mathrm{P}(\mathrm{n}, \gamma)^{32}\mathrm{P}$ is 0.32 b, what will be the saturation activity for 1.0 g of P irradiated in a neutron flux of 1.2×10^{12} neutrons $\mathrm{cm}^{-2}\ \mathrm{sec}^{-1}$.

Special Topics Problems

21-15 The following decay data are obtained on a sample suspected of containing several radioelements:

t (hr)	0.0	0.5	1.0	1.5	2.0	3.0	4.0	5.0	6.0	8.0
Dis min^{-1}	8000	1875	850	543	410	288	211	168	139	108
t (hr)	10	12	14							
Dis min^{-1}	90	80	73							

Analyze the data graphically to obtain the half-lives of all the radioelements present, and the percentage of the initial total activity due to each.

21-16 A sample of radioactive zirconium is obtained in pure form by an appropriate processing of a fission product mixture. The activity of the sample increased with time, as shown by the tabulated activity (total disintegrations per minute), due to the growth of a niobium daughter. Analyze the data to determine the half-lives of the parent and the daughter.

t (days)	0	20	40	60	100	150	200	300	400	500
D_{tot} (dis min^{-1})	2000	2250	2200	2050	1600	1050	666	240	82	28

21-17 A sample of ^{140}Ba is allowed to come to transient equilibrium with its daughter ^{140}La:

$$^{140}\text{Ba} \rightarrow {}^{140}\text{La} + \beta^- \qquad \text{half-life 12.5 days,}$$
$$^{140}\text{La} \rightarrow {}^{140}\text{Ba (assume to be stable)} + \beta^- \qquad \text{half-life 40 hr.}$$

A chemical separation is then made, giving two fractions containing the following weight percentages of the total Ba and La: (a) 90% of the barium, 10% of the lanthanum; (b) 10% of the barium, 90% of the lanthanum. At the time of the chemical separation the sample contained 3×10^6 dis min^{-1} due to the combined Ba and La activities. Calculate the *total* number of disintegrations per minute for each fraction 2 days and 25 days after the separation.

Special Topics Problems

21-1 A meteorite contains 1.5×10^{-3}% U. Calculate its minimum age in years if 0.066 cm^3 of He (STP) can be extracted from 10 g of the meteorite.

21-2 A counter has a background of about 35 counts min^{-1}. How long should a sample of approximately 1000 counts min^{-1} be counted and how long a background count should be taken in order that the net count can be determined in a minimum total counting time with a probable standard deviation of less than 1%?

21-3 The age of some pitchblende U_3O_8 is estimated by weighing out a small sample of the crushed mineral and determining the alpha activity. The measurement is made one week after crushing and gives 21 dis sec^{-1} mg^{-1}. It is to be assumed that no gases or other materials escape from the mineral during its geological existence, but that on crushing, the radon and helium present escape freely, but nothing else. Neglecting any complications due to ^{235}U or ^{234}U present, calculate the age of the mineral. [*Note*: The ore is assumed to have been pure U_3O_8 originally, although in the course of time its composition may well have changed appreciably.]

21-4   The standard deviation of a counts per minute determination on a sample is 10 %. Neglecting background, what was the activity in counts per minute after the sample had been counted for 5 min?

21-5   A counter has a measured background rate of 600 counts in 25 min. With a sample in place the total measured rate is 1050 counts in 20 min. Give the net counting rate per minute for the sample and its standard deviation.

21-6   Estimate the age of a rock which is found to contain 4×10^{-5} cm^3 of helium at STP and 3.5×10^{-7} g of uranium per gram.

SUBJECT INDEX

Many subjects are listed both under their name(s) and under the general category to which they belong. Thus, all material relating to crystals is collected under *Crystalline state*; and all types of potential are listed under *Potential*. The Index therefore provides summaries of related subjects as well as the locations of specific items by name. Tables are indicated by page numbers followed by (T).

A

Absolute rate theory, *see* Theory
Absolute temperature, 3
Absolute zero, 5
  attainment of, 235
Absorbance, 87
Absorption
  of charged particles, 1042
  coefficient, *see* Coefficient(s)
  critical, 1045
  of electromagnetic radiation, 86, 911, 1042–1043
  resonance, 1050
Absorptivity, 87
Acceptor (in photosensitization), 891
Acetic acid
  dimer, 298
  dissociation, 519(T)
Acid(s), 542
  Brønsted, 543
  conjugate, 544
  dissociation constants, 529(T)

hard (soft), 545
Lewis, 545, 1009
weak, 532, 554
Acid–base reactions, *see* Reaction(s)
Actinium series, 1055
Activated complex, 649, 717, *see also* Theory
Activation energy, 638, 642
Activation parameters, 648(T), 661
Activity, 360
  absolute, 379
  calculation, 361
  conventions, 409, 425
  of electrolytes, 513
  mean, 515
  rational, 272, 379
  of solutions, 358
Activity coefficient, 360
  calculation, 361
  chemical equilibrium and, 276
  conventions, 409, 425
  determination, 518, 575

of electrolytes, 513, 521(T), 539
  mean, 515
  reaction rate and, 708
  from solubility, 516
  of solutions, 358
Additive property, 85, 99
  kinetic studies and, 625
Adiabatic calorimeter, 169
Adiabatic demagnetization, 235
Adiabatic process, 127
Adsorption, 666
  chemical, *see* Chemisorption
  Gibbs equation, 234, 387
  Langmuir equation, 666
  negative, 378
  physical, 666
Aerosol, 339
Affine transformation, 1024
Age dating, 1055
Alkali metal halides, *see* Crystalline state
Alpha helix, 1013
Alpha particle emission, 1049
Amagat's law, 10

Subject Index

4
5
C 6
D 7
E 8
F 9
G 0
H 1
I 2
J 3